> *Il più accurato ed economico*
> *dizionario tascabile*
> **ITALIANO—INGLESE**
> **INGLESE—ITALIANO**
> *finora pubblicato*

È un' opera concepita espressamente come strumento pratico per tutte le categorie di pubblico: dagli studenti agli insegnanti, dai turisti agli uomini di affari, ai corrispondenti, ai tecnici. Oltre 25.000 voci disposte in ordine alfabetico. Concise ma esaurienti note di grammatica italiana e inglese. Tavole dei verbi irregolari delle due lingue. Pronuncia figurata inglese. Neologismi tecnici, idiomatici e di gergo. Tavole dei numerali, dei pesi, delle misure e delle monete.

Compilato con criteri modernissimi da esperti filologi, è un volume essenziale, una guida pratica, indispensabile e di sommo valore.

The above text appears in English on the back cover.

DIZIONARIO
TASCABILE
MONDADORI
Italiano-Inglese
Inglese-Italiano

DUE VOLUMI IN UNO

Di

Alberto Tedeschi e Carlo Rossi Fantonetti
Con la Collaborazione di SEYMOUR A. COPSTEIN

A KANGAROO BOOK
PUBLISHED BY POCKET BOOKS NEW YORK

MONDADORI'S
POCKET
Italian-English
English-Italian
DICTIONARY

TWO VOLUMES IN ONE

By

Alberto Tedeschi & Carlo Rossi Fantonetti
With the Assistance of SEYMOUR A. COPSTEIN

A KANGAROO BOOK
PUBLISHED BY POCKET BOOKS NEW YORK

MONDADORI'S ITALIAN-ENGLISH
ENGLISH-ITALIAN DICTIONARY

POCKET BOOK edition published October, 1959
22nd printing.........................May, 1977

The system of indicating pronunciation is used by permission. From THE MERRIAM-WEBSTER POCKET DICTIONARY. Copyright, ©, 1961, by G. & C. Merriam Company, publishers of Merriam-Webster dictionaries.

Mondadori's Italian-English English-Italian Dictionary was formerly published under the imprint of WASHINGTON SQUARE PRESS, a division of Simon & Schuster, Inc.

This original POCKET BOOK edition is printed from brand-new plates made from newly set, clear, easy-to-read type.
POCKET BOOK editions are published by
POCKET BOOKS,
a Simon & Schuster Division of
GULF & WESTERN CORPORATION
1230 Avenue of the Americas,
New York, N.Y. 10020.
Trademarks registered in the United States
and other countries.

ISBN: 0-671-81693-4.
Copyright, ©, 1959, by Arnoldo Mondadori, Editore. All rights reserved.

Printed in the U.S.A.

CONTENTS

PART ONE: ITALIAN-ENGLISH

PARTE SECONDA: INGLESE-ITALIANO

MONDADORI'S
POCKET
Italian-English
English-Italian
DICTIONARY

Part One

ITALIAN - ENGLISH

LIST OF ABBREVIATIONS

abbr.	abbreviation	mech.	mechanics
account.	accounting	med.	medicine
adj.	adjective	mil.	military
adv.	adverb	min.	mining
aeron.	aeronautics	mus.	music
agr.	agriculture	myth.	mythology
anat.	anatomy	naut.	nautical
arch.	architecture	nw.	new word
artil.	artillery	obs.	obsolete
astr.	astronomy	onom.	onomatopoeia
auto.	automobile	opt.	optic
bank.	banking	ornith.	ornithology
biol.	biology	paint.	painting
bot.	botany	part.	participle
chem.	chemistry	pass.	passive
coll.	colloquial	pathol.	pathology
comm.	commerce	pers.	personal
comp.	comparative	pharm.	pharmacy
conj.	conjunction	philos.	philosophy
cook.	cooking	photo.	photography
demonstr.	demonstrative	phys.	physics
derog.	derogatory	physiol.	physiology
dial.	dialect	pol.	politics
eccl.	ecclesiastic	pp.	past participle
elec.	electric	pr.	proper name
entom.	entomology	prep.	preposition
exch.	exchange	pron.	pronoun
f.	feminine	rail.	railroad
fam.	familiar	recipr.	reciprocal
fig.	figurative	refl.	reflexive
fin.	finance	rhet.	rhetoric
fort.	fortification	sci.	science
geog.	geography	sup.	superlative
geol.	geology	surg.	surgery
geom.	geometry	t.	transitive
gramm.	grammar	teleph.	telephone
hist.	history	telev.	television
ichthyol.	ichthyology	text.	textile
impers.	impersonal	theat.	theater
indef.	indefinite	typog.	typography
interj.	interjection	univ.	university
interr.	interrogative	U.S.	United States
It.	Italian	v.	verb
journ.	journalism	vi.	intransitive verb
L.	Latin	vr.	reflexive verb
liter.	literary	vt.	transitive verb
m.	masculine	vulg.	vulgar
mach.	machinery	zool.	zoology
math.	mathematics		

ITALIAN PRONUNCIATION

The Italian alphabet consists of 21 letters: *a, b, c, d, e, f, g, h, i, l, m, n, o, p, q, r, s, t, u, v, z* (*j, k, w, x, y* are found only in words of foreign origin).

I. VOWELS

Each Italian vowel has one fundamental sound, which is maintained in diphthongs and triphthongs.

1. a as in *star, are* — examples: amore, casa.
2. e has two distinct sounds: a broad sound similar to *e* in *where* — examples: festa, messa; and another almost like *e* in *bet* — examples: pera, tela.
3. o is sometimes open as *o* in *orb* — examples: cosa, porta, and sometimes closed as *o* in *foe* — examples: dono, sole.
4. i as in *police* — examples: asilo, riso.
5. u like *u* in *rude*, or *oo* in *food* — examples: muro, tubo.

II. CONSONANTS

1. b has the same sound as in English.
2. c before *a, o, u*, and before consonants has a hard sound similar to the English *k* — examples: calore, corpo, cura; crosta, clava, acme; chilo, perchè. Before *e* and *i* c is pronounced like English *ch* in *church*.
   When an *i* appears between *c* and *a*, *c* and *o*, or *c* and *u*, for the purpose of indicating this *ch* sound, the *i* is inaudible — examples: pancia, ciondolo, ciuffo. However, when the *i* is stressed it is pronounced — examples: farmacia, vocìo.
3. d and f are sounded as in English.
4. g before *a, o, u* and before consonants sounds like *g* in *good* — examples: gallo, gola, gusto; globo, grande; laghetto, ghiro. Before *e* and *i* g is pronounced as in English *general* — examples: gente, giro. When *i* is inserted between *g* and *a*, *g* and *o*, or *g* and *u*, for the purpose of indicating this sound, the *i* is inaudible — examples: giacca, giostra, giusto.
   The combination gn sounds like the combination *n* and *y* in *can you* — examples: sognare, dignità, bagno, ignudo.
   The combination gl sounds like the *l* and *y* in *will you*, pronounced rapidly — examples: foglia, figlie, gigli, consiglio. In some exceptional cases *g* before *l* sounds hard — examples: negligenza, glicerina.
5. h has no sound. It is found only in the present indicative of avere (*to have*) — io ho, tu hai, egli ha, essi hanno — and in certain interjections, such as: ah!, oh!, ahi! Otherwise h is used only to indicate hard *c* and *g* before *e* and *i*.
6. l, m, n, p are sounded as in English.
7. q is always followed by *u* and another vowel. It sounds like *qu* in *square* — examples: quaderno, questo, liquido, quota.
8. r is pronounced as in English, but is more strongly trilled.
9. s when it begins a word and is followed by a vowel or an unvoiced consonant sounds hard as in *essence* — examples: sapere, senno, sicuro, sonno, subito; scopo, sforzo, spazio, rosso, stima. Between vowels or before a voiced consonant it sounds soft like *s* in *rose* and *z* in *gàze* — examples: casa, mese, risi, viso; sbaglio, sdegno, sgranare, sleale, smania, snello, sradicare, sviare.

sce and sci are pronounced like *she* in *shelter* and *shi* in *ship* — examples: scelta, scivolare.

scia and scio are pronounced like *sha* and *sho* in *shah* and *show* — examples: scialle and sciocco.

sciu is pronounced like *chu* in *chute* — example: asciutto.

sche and schi sound like *ske* in *sketch* and *ski* in *skit* — examples: scherzo, schizzo.

10. t is similar to English *t* in *stun*, *astonish* — examples: talpa, telo, tiro, tono, tutto, treno.
11. v is sounded as in English.
12. z is regularly like English *ts* — examples: scorza, grazia, scherzo, pazzo. Very often, however, it sounds like English *dz* — examples: zanzara, zero, zio, zona, zufolo, mezzo, azzurro.

Note. Every Italian consonant can be doubled, and is then strongly pronounced — examples: abbaino, accadere, addetto, affare, agguato, allarme, ammettere, annullare, appena, arresto, assenso, attacco, avvilito, azzurro.

III. STRESS AND ACCENT

Italian words may be accented on the last, or next to the last, or third from the last syllable. Usually, the accent mark (grave accent) is used only when the stress is to be put on the final vowel — examples: civiltà, caffè, così, perciò, virtù. Certain monosyllabic words are written with an accent mark to distinguish between pairs — examples: dà (*gives*) — da (*from*); dì (*day*) — di (*of*); là (*there*) — la (*the*); lì (*there*) — li (*them*); sè (*himself, oneself*) — se (*if*).

IV. APOSTROPHE

In Italian, the apostrophe indicates the omission of the last vowel of a word when this is followed by another word beginning with a vowel — examples: *la aria* — l'aria; *lo emblema* — l'emblema; *lo indice* — l'indice; *lo orologio* — l'orologio; *lo uccello* — l'uccello; *gli inglesi* — gl'inglesi; *questo uomo* — quest'uomo; *un bello albero* — un bell'albero.

V. SYLLABIC DIVISION

Italian words are divided according to the syllables forming them. Except at the beginning of a word, each syllable normally starts with a consonant — examples: a-ni-ma-le; car-ta; pen-sa-re; la-scia-re. The vowels of a diphthong generally are not separated — examples: fià-to, piè-no, suò-no; fiù-me; àu-ra, lài-co, fèu-do. When, however, the vowels are pronounced separately they are treated as separate syllables — examples: pa-ù-ra, vì-a, flù-i-do, a-è-re-o, pa-è-se, o-cè-ano.

Double consonants are always divided — examples: eb-be, tac-co, ad-di-o, zuf-fa, rag-gio, pal-la, stem-ma, pan-no, tap-po, ac-qua, car-ro, sas-so, pat-to, bev-ve, maz-zo.

When s is followed by one or more consonants, it belongs to the subsequent syllable — examples: po-sta, ri-schio, a-spet-to.

THE NOUN

I. GENDER

Italian nouns are either masculine or feminine. There is no neuter gender. Names of things and abstractions are either masculine or feminine.

Masculine gender:

1. Names of male beings are masculine by nature — examples: uomo *man*, ragazzo *boy*, fratello *brother*; cane *dog*, gallo *cock*, leone *lion*.

2. Nouns ending in o are usually masculine — examples: **libro** *book*, **martello** *hammer*, **telefono** *telephone*; **dubbio** *doubt*, **coraggio** *courage*, **odio** *hatred*.

Feminine gender:

1. Names of female beings are feminine by nature — examples: **donna** *woman*, **fanciulla** *girl*, **sorella** *sister*; **cagna** *bitch*, **mucca** *cow*, **gallina** *hen*.
2. Nouns ending in a are usually feminine — examples: **penna** *pen*, **lampada** *lamp*, **finestra** *window*; **speranza** *hope*, **umiltà** *humbleness*, **fermezza** *firmness*.

Exceptions:

1. Some nouns ending in o are feminine — examples: **mano** *hand*, **eco** *echo*.
2. Some nouns ending in a are masculine — examples: **poeta** *poet*, **problema** *problem*, **tema** *theme*.
3. Some nouns are feminine but relate to male beings — examples: **spia** *spy*, **recluta** *recruit*, **sentinella** *sentry*.
4. Some nouns are masculine but relate to female beings — examples: **il soprano** *the soprano*, **il contralto** *the contralto*, **un donnone** *a big woman*.
5. Some nouns ending in a may be either masculine or feminine — examples: **il ginnasta** *the man-gymnast*, **la ginnasta** *the woman-gymnast*.
6. Nouns ending in e may be either masculine or feminine — examples: **leone** *lion* (m.), **fiore** *flower* (m.), **pane** *bread* (m.); **arte** *art* (f.), **luce** *light* (f.), **salute** *health* (f.).

Formation of the feminine:

1. Masculine nouns ending in o or e change o or e to a to form the feminine — examples: **zio** *uncle* = **zia** *aunt*, **signore** *gentleman* = **signora** *lady*, **Carlo** *Charles* = **Carla** *Caroline*.
2. Certain nouns have a special form for the feminine — examples: **attore** *actor* = **attrice** *actress*; **principe** *prince* = **principessa** *princess*; **eroe** *hero* = **eroina** *heroine*.
3. The corresponding feminine word for certain nouns is an entirely different word — examples: **uomo** *man* = **donna** *woman*, **marito** *husband* = **moglie** *wife*, **maiale** *pig* = **scrofa** *sow*.

II. PLURAL OF NOUNS

1. Masculine nouns ending in o form the plural by changing the o to i — examples: **palo** = **pali**, **albero** = **alberi**, **sarto** = **sarti**.
2. Feminine nouns ending in a form the plural by changing the a to e — examples: **scarpa** = **scarpe**, **palla** = **palle**, **donna** = **donne**.
3. Nouns ending in e, whether masculine or feminine, change the e to i — examples: **luce** = **luci**, **serpente** = **serpenti**, **eroe** = **eroi**.
4. Nouns ending in cia and gia have two forms of plural: cie and gie, and ce and ge.

   They end in cie and gie when:
   (a) the stressed i of the singular is also stressed in the plural — examples: **farmacia** = **farmacie**, **bugia** = **bugie**.
   (b) although the i is not stressed, cia and gia are preceded by a vowel — examples: **camicia** = **camicie**, **audàcia** = **audàcie**, **valigia** = **valigie**.

   They end in ce and ge when:
   (a) the i is not stressed and cia and gia are preceded by a consonant — examples: **lància** = **lance**, **bòlgia** = **bolge**.

   Note. There are quite a few exceptions to this rule (**ciliègia** = **ciliege**, **provincia** = **province** and **provincie**), and only by consulting a dictionary can any particular case be settled.
5. The ending io becomes ii if the i is stressed; otherwise it becomes just i — examples: **mormorio** = **mormorii**, **zio** = **zii**; **stùdio** = **stùdi**, **òzio** = **òzi**.
6. The endings co and go change to chi and ghi if preceded by a consonant — examples: **parco** = **parchi**, **solco** = **solchi**, **fungo** = **funghi**, **gorgo** = **gorghi**. If preceded by a vowel, however, they sometimes change to

chi and ghi and sometimes to ci and gi — examples: parroco = parroci, carico = carichi; asparago = asparagi, dialogo = dialoghi.

7. Masculine nouns ending in ca and ga change to chi and ghi — examples: monarca = monarchi, collega = colleghi.
8. Nouns ending in i, in a consonant, in an accented vowel, as well as monosyllabic nouns, do not change — examples: la crisi = le crisi, l'autobus = gli autobus, la città = le città, il re = i re.
9. Certain nouns form the plural irregularly — examples: uomo = uomini, dio = dei, bue = buoi.
10. There are some masculine nouns that change their gender in the plural and take the ending a — examples: l'uovo (m.) = le uova (f.), il lenzuolo (m.) = le lenzuola (f.), un paio (m.) = due paia (f.).

COMMON ITALIAN SUFFIXES

I. DIMINUTIVES

The following convey an idea of lesser size, niceness and affection:

-ino,	-ina	letto = lettino (a small bed), casa = casina (a tiny house), maestra = maestrina (young teacher)
-etto,	-etta	scarpa = scarpetta (small, light shoe), bimbo = bimbetto (small, lovely child)
-ello,	-ella	birbone = birboncello (naughty boy), finestra = finestrella (small window)
-olo,	-ola	figlio = figliolo (dear son), carezza = carezzuola (light caress)
-uccio,	-uccia	caldo = calduccio (comfortable warmth), bocca = boccuccia (small, nice mouth)

II. AUGMENTATIVES

The following convey an idea of greater size:

-one, -ona   libro = librone (big book), finestra = finestrona *or* finestrone (large window), porta = portone (huge door)
Note. The feminine form ona is not always used. Feminine nouns very often take the suffix one, which causes them to change their gender — example: donna (f.) = donnone (m.)

III. DEPRECIATIVES

The following convey an idea of something bad, ugly or despicable. Note, however, that a depreciative or ironic connotation is often conveyed by the augmentatives and by many of the diminutive endings.

-accio, -accia	vento = ventaccio (harsh wind), libro = libraccio (bad, mean book), donna = donnaccia (woman of loose morals)
-astro, -astra	poeta = poetastro (poetaster), medico = medicastro (quack doctor)
-ucolo, -ucola	paese = paesucolo (small town, small village)
-onzolo, onzola	medico = mediconzolo (inexperienced doctor, inept doctor)

IV. OTHER SUFFIXES

-aggine	(a) is sometimes equal to English *ness*: stupidaggine = foolishness; (b) expresses also a particular act: stupidaggine = foolish act, piece of foolishness
-aio	indicates a person who makes, sells, or is in charge of: fornaio = baker, libraio = bookseller, lampionaio = lamplighter
-anza	is used to make abstract nouns: vedovanza = widowhood, arroganza = arrogance

-ata	(a) is sometimes equal to the English suffix *ful*: **cucchiaiata** = spoonful
	(b) often indicates a blow: **testata** = blow with one's head, **pugnalata** = dagger stab
	(c) often indicates an action: **sfaticata** = spell of hard work, **cabrata** = zoom of an airplane
-enza	is used to make abstract nouns: **magnificenza** = magnificence, **prepotenza** = overbearance
-ere	indicates a person who makes, sells, or is engaged in a certain profession: **panettiere** = baker, **banchiere** = banker
-eria	(a) denotes a place where something is made or sold: **panetteria** = bakery, **libreria** = bookstore
	(b) indicates a profession, business, or occupation: **ingegneria** = engineering, **editoria** = publishing
	(c) is sometimes equal to the English suffixes *ry* and *ness*: **cretineria** = foolery, foolishness
-ero	is an adjective-forming suffix: **ciarliero** = talkative, **guerriero** = warlike, fighting
-eto, -eta	denote a grove or plantation: **agrumeto** = citrus grove, **pineta** = pine forest
-ezza	is used to make abstract nouns: **giovinezza** = youth, **grandezza** = greatness
-ia	(a) is the ending of the names of many arts and sciences: **geologia** = geology
	(b) is the ending of many abstract nouns: **maestria** = master, **fantasia** = imagination
-iccio	is a suffix meaning *tending to* or *somewhat*: **rossiccio** = reddish, **sudaticcio** = rather wet with perspiration
-issimo	is the ending of the absolute superlative: **bellissimo** = extremely beautiful
-mente	is the adverbial ending attached to the feminine form of the adjective: **estremamente** = extremely, **improvvisamente** = suddenly
-one	(a) is an augmentative suffix
	(b) is also a suffix to add impressiveness to a word: **giocherellone** = playful person, **piagnucolone** = tearful person, crybaby, **strattone** = strong jerk
-ore	(a) is equal to the English suffixes *or* and *er*: **conquistatore** = conqueror, **rilegatore** = bookbinder
	(b) may also be used to form adjectives: **regolatore** = regulator *and* regulating, **trasmettitore** = broadcaster *and* broadcasting
-oso	is an adjective-forming suffix which usually means: *having*, *full of*, *characterized by*: **roccioso** = rocky, **piovoso** = rainy, **famoso** = famous
-tà	is a suffix forming abstract nouns and is equivalent to the English suffix *ty*: **fraternità** = fraternity, **beltà** = beauty, **eternità** = eternity
-ura	is a suffix forming abstract and also concrete nouns: **bravura** = skill, **calura** = heat, **altura** = highland
-uto	is an adjective-forming suffix meaning *having* or *characterized by*: **barbuto** = bearded, **panciuto** = bigbellied.

THE ARTICLE

Italian articles are either definite or indefinite.

I. DEFINITE ARTICLES

These are **il, lo, la** in the singular forms, and **i, gli, le** in the plural forms.

Il and i	are used before masculine nouns beginning with a consonant: **il libro — i libri, il serpente — i serpenti, il maestro — i maestri**

lo and gli   are used:

(a) before masculine nouns beginning with "s impura" (that is an s followed by a consonant: *st, sp, sc, sb*): lo stato — gli stati, lo sparo — gli spari, lo scolaro — gli scolari, lo sciocco — gli sciocchi, lo sbaglio — gli sbagli

(b) before masculine nouns beginning with z: lo zoppo — gli zoppi, lo zero — gli zeri

(c) before a masculine noun beginning with a vowel: l'asino — gli asini, l'esempio — gli esempi, l'italiano — gl'italiani l'osso — gli ossi, l'urlo — gli urli

Note. The *o* of lo is dropped before masculine nouns beginning with a vowel, and an apostrophe takes its place; gli may be changed to gl' only before plural masculine nouns beginning with *i.*

la and le   are used before feminine nouns: la mamma — le mamme, la bambola — le bambole, l'anima — le anime

Note. la is changed into l' before feminine nouns beginning with a vowel. The elision of le is very rarely made before feminine plural nouns.

II. INDEFINITE ARTICLES

These are un, uno, una.

un   is used before masculine nouns beginning either with a vowel or with a consonant: un albero, un uomo, un contadino, un gatto, un dubbio

uno   is used before masculine nouns beginning with "s impura" and z: uno scoiattolo, uno specchio, uno straccio, uno zingaro, uno zuccone

una and un'   are used before feminine nouns; una before nouns beginning with a consonant: una dama, una sposa, una farfalla; un' before nouns beginning with a vowel: un'automobile, un'eroina, un'opera.

THE PREPOSITION

The commonest Italian prepositions are: di = of, a = to, da = from, by, in = in, con = with, by, su = on, tra, fra = between, among, per = for, to, by.

The prepositions *di, a, da, in, con, su* blend with the definite articles *il, lo, la, i, gli, le* into the following forms:

del, dello, della, dei, degli, delle,	of the
al, allo, alla, ai, agli, alle,	to the
dal, dallo, dalla, dai, dagli, dalle,	from the, by the
nel, nello, nella, nei, negli, nelle,	in the
col, collo (*con lo*),* colla, coi, cogli, colle,	with the, by the
sul, sullo, sulla, sui, sugli, sulle,	on the

Note. The preposition con is more frequently found separated from the definite article because collo also means *neck*, colla also means *glue*, and colle also means *hill*.

The preposition di expresses the possessive case of the English noun. The name of the possessor follows the name of the thing possessed — example: Mary's book = il libro di Maria. The prepositions del, dello, della, dei, degli, delle also precede nouns taken in the partitive sense — examples: I bought some books = ho comprato dei libri, give me some more bread = dammi dell'altro pane.

THE ADJECTIVE AND ADVERB

I. THE ADJECTIVE

Agreement:

The adjective in Italian agrees in gender and number with the noun it modifies: scolaro studioso (*m.*, *sing.*) — scolari studiosi (*m.*, *pl.*) — scolara studiosa (*f.*, *sing.*) — scolare studiose (*f.*, *pl.*).

Formation of the plural:

Adjectives ending in o (masculine) form their plural by changing into i: buono — buoni; adjectives ending in e (both masculine and feminine) change to i: mite — miti; adjectives ending in a change to e: buona — buone.

Formation of the feminine:

1. Adjectives ending in o form their feminine by changing to a: amaro — amara
2. Adjectives ending in e do not alter: prepotente (*m.*) — prepotente (*f.*)

II. THE ADVERB

Many adverbs are formed by adding -mente to the feminine form of the adjective: certo — certamente; when the adjective ends in e and has its stress on the antepenult, the final e is dropped: facile — facilmente.

III. COMPARISON OF ADJECTIVES AND ADVERBS

Comparative of inequality:

The comparative of inequality is obtained by placing più (more) or meno (less) before the positive form of the adjective or the adverb, and di or che (than) before the second member of the comparison — examples: You are happier than I = tu sei più felice di me; as a man he is more lucky than intelligent = è un uomo più fortunato che intelligente; it is less nice *or* not so nice = è meno bello; you must speak faster = devi parlare più velocemente.

Comparative of equality:

The comparative of equality is formed in two ways:

1. come — examples: my book is as interesting as yours = il mio libro è interessante come il tuo; he spoke as convincingly as his brother = ha parlato convincentemente come il fratello.
2. tanto ... quanto — examples: my book is as interesting as yours = il mio libro è tanto interessante quanto il tuo. This form, however, is now regarded as rather stilted.

Superlative of adjectives and adverbs:

1. *Relative superlative of adjectives* is formed by placing the definite article before the unequal comparative form of the adjective — examples: the largest town in the world = la più grande città del mondo; the least kind of my friends = il meno gentile dei miei amici.
2. *Absolute superlative of adjectives* is obtained in three ways:
   (a) by adding the suffix -issimo: forte (strong) = fortissimo;
   (b) by placing the adverb molto or assai before the positive form of the adjective: forte = molto forte, assai forte;
   (c) by repeating the adjective: forte = forte forte.

The following adjectives have in addition irregular forms of comparison:

buono (good) migliore (better) ottimo (very good), il migliore (the best)
cattivo (bad) peggiore (worse) pessimo (very bad), il peggiore (the worst)
grande (large) maggiore (larger) massimo (very large), il maggiore (the largest)

piccolo (little)	minore (lesser)	minimo, il minore (the least)
alto (high)	superiore (higher)	supremo, sommo (the highest)
basso (low)	inferiore (lower)	infimo (the lowest)
interno (inside)	interiore (inner)	intimo (innermost)

3. *Absolute superlative of adverbs* is obtained by adding the invariable suffix -issimo to the positive form of the adverb: bene = benissimo, tardi = tardissimo, molto = moltissimo.
   Note that the last vowel of the adverb is dropped before the suffix.
   — Adverbs ending in -mente form the absolute superlative by adding the suffix -issimo to the superlative feminine form of the corresponding adjective: lentissimo = lentissimamente.

Note. The English *than* is translated with di when the second member of comparison is a noun or a pronoun — examples: gold is more expensive than silver = l'oro è più caro dell'argento; he is richer than I = egli è più ricco di me. It is translated with che when the comparison is between two different adjectives or two nouns — examples: he is more handsome than intelligent = egli è più bello che intelligente; there is more bread than meat = c'è più pane che carne.

ITALIAN IRREGULAR VERBS

The superior number after a verb entry indicates that it is conjugated like the model verb in this section bearing the corresponding number. Only the tenses that have irregular forms or spelling changes are given. The irregular forms and spelling changes are shown in bold-face type.

1. ACCENDERE

past	accesi, accendesti, accese, accendemmo, accendeste, accesero
past part.	acceso

2. ACCLUDERE

past	acclusi, accludesti, accluse, accludemmo, accludeste, acclusero
past part.	accluso

3. ADDURRE

past	addussi, adducesti, addusse, adducemmo, adduceste, addussero
fut.	addurrò, addurrai, addurrà, addurremo, addurrete, addurranno
cond.	addurrei, addurresti, addurrebbe, addurremmo, addurreste, addurrebbero
past part.	addotto
	Note. All regular forms derive from the infinitive form adducere.

4. ADEMPIERE

pres. ind.	adempio, adempi, adempie, adempiamo, adempite, adempiono
pres. sub.	adempia, adempia, adempia, adempiamo, adempiate, adempiano
imper.	adempi, adempia, adempite, adempiano.
past	adempii, adempisti, adempì, adempimmo, adempiste, adempirono
past part.	adempito *or* adempiuto
	Note. See also empiere, 52 *and* empire, 53.

5. AFFLIGGERE

past	afflissi, affligesti, afflisse, affliggemmo, affliggeste, afflissero
past part.	afflitto

6. ALLUDERE

past	allusi, alludesti, alluse, alludemmo, alludeste, allusero
past part.	alluso

7. ANDARE

pres. ind.	vado, vai, va, andiamo, andate, vanno
pres. sub.	vada, vada, vada, andiamo, andiate, vadano
imp.	vai or va', vada, andiamo, andate, vàdano
fut.	andrò, andrai, andrà, andremo, andrete, andranno
cond.	andrei, andresti, andrebbe, andremmo, andreste, andrebbero

8. ANNETTERE

past	annettei or annessi, annettesti, annettè or annesse, annettemmo, annetteste, annetterono or annessero
past part.	annesso

9. APPARIRE

pres. ind.	apparisco or appaio, apparisci or appari, apparisce or appare, appariamo, apparite, appariscono or appàiono
past	apparvi or apparii, apparisti, apparve or apparì or apparse, apparimmo, appariste, apparvero or apparirono or apparsero
pres. sub.	apparisca or appaia, apparisca or appaia, apparisca or appaia, appariamo, appariate, appariscano or appaiano
imper.	apparisci or appari, apparisca or appaia, apparite, appariscano or appaiano
past part.	apparso

10. APPENDERE

past	appesi, appendesti, appese, appendemmo, appendeste, appesero
past part.	appeso

11. APRIRE

pres. ind.	apro, apri, apre, apriamo, aprite, àprono
past	aprii or apersi, apristi, aprì or aperse, aprimmo, apriste, aprirono or apersero
past part.	aperto

12. ARDERE

past	arsi, ardesti, arse, ardemmo, ardeste, arsero
past part.	arso

13. ASPERGERE

past	aspersi, aspergesti, asperse, aspergemmo, aspergeste, aspersero
past part.	asperso

14. ASSALIRE

pres. ind.	assalgo or assalisco, assali or assalisci, assale or assalisce, assaliamo, assalite, assalgono or assaliscono
past	assalii or assalsi, assalisti, assalì or assalse, assalimmo, assaliste, assalirono or assalsero
pres. sub.	assalga or assalisca, assalga or assalisca, assalga or assalisca, assaliamo, assaliate, assalgano or assaliscano

15. ASSIDERSI

past	mi assisi, ti assidesti, si assise, ci assidemmo, vi assideste, si assisero
past part.	assiso

16. ASSISTERE

past	assistei *or* assistetti, assistesti, assistè *or* assistette, assistemmo, assisteste, assisterono *or* assistettero
past part.	assistito

17. ASSOLVERE

past	assolsi *or* assolvei *or* assolvetti, assolvesti, assolse *or* assolvette, assolvemmo, assolveste, assolsero *or* assolvettero
past part.	assolto *or* assoluto

18. ASSORBIRE

pres.	assorbo *or* assorbisco, assorbi *or* assorbisci, assorbe *or* assorbisce, assorbiamo, assorbite, assorbono *or* assorbiscono
past part.	assorbito *or* assorto

19. ASSUMERE

past	assunsi, assumesti, assunse, assumemmo, assumeste, assunsero
past part.	assunto

20. ASSURGERE

past	assursi, assurgesti, assurse, assurgemmo, assurgeste, assursero
past part.	assurto

21. BERE

pres. ind.	bevo, bevi, beve, beviamo, bevete, bevono
imp. ind.	bevevo, bevevi, beveva, bevevamo, bevevate, bevevano
past	bevvi *or* bevei, bevesti, bevve *or* bevè *or* bevette, bevemmo, beveste, bevvero *or* beverono *or* bevettero
fut.	berrò, berrai, berrà, berremo, berrete, berranno
cond.	berrei, berresti, berrebbe, berremmo, berreste, berrebbero
pres. sub.	beva, beva, beva, beviamo, beviate, bevano
imp. sub.	bevessi, bevessi, bevesse, bevessimo, beveste, bevessero
imper.	bevi, beva, bevete, bevano
past part.	bevuto
	Note. All regular forms derive from the infinitive form bevere.

22. CADERE

past	caddi, cadesti, cadde, cademmo, cadeste, caddero
fut.	cadrò, cadrai, cadrà, cadremo, cadrete, cadranno
cond.	cadrei, cadresti, cadrebbe, cadremmo, cadreste, cadrebbero

23. CEDERE

past	cedei *or* cedetti, cedesti, cedè *or* cedette, cedemmo, cedeste, cederono *or* cedettero

24. CHIEDERE

past	chiesi, chiedesti, chiese, chiedemmo, chiedeste, chiesero
past part.	chiesto

25. CHIUDERE

past	chiusi, chiudesti, chiuse, chiudemmo, chiudeste, chiusero
past. part.	chiuso

26. CINGERE

past	cinsi, cingesti, cinse, cingemmo, cingeste, cinsero
past part.	cinto

27. COGLIERE

pres. ind.	colgo, cogli, coglie, cogliamo, cogliete, colgono
past	colsi, cogliesti, colse, cogliemmo, coglieste, colsero
pres. sub.	colga, colga, colga, cogliamo, cogliate, colgano
past part.	colto

28. COMPIERE

pres. ind.	compio, compi, compie, compiamo, compite, compiono
past	compii, compisti, compi, compimmo, compiste, compirono
pres. sub.	compia, compia, compia, compiamo, compiate, compiano
imper.	compi, compia, compite, compiano
past part.	compito *or* compiùto

Note. See also empiere, 52 *and* empire, 53.

29. COMPRIMERE

past	compressi, comprimesti, compresse, comprimemmo, comprimeste, compressero
past part.	compresso

30. CONOSCERE

past	conobbi, conoscesti, conobbe, conoscemmo, conosceste, conobbero

31. CONQUIDERE

past	conquisi, conquidesti, conquise, conquidemmo, conquideste, conquisero
past part.	conquiso

32. CONTUNDERE

past	contusi, contundesti, contuse, contundemmo, contundeste, contusero
past part.	contuso

33. CONVERGERE

past	conversi *or* convergei, convergesti, converse *or* convergè, convergemmo, convergeste, conversero *or* convergerono
past part.	converso

34. CONVERTIRE

past	convertii, convertisti, converti, convertimmo, convertiste, convertirono
past part.	convertito

35. COPRIRE

pres. ind.	copro, copri, copre, copriamo, coprite, coprono
past	coprii *or* copersi, copristi, copri *or* coperse, coprimmo, copriste, coprirono *or* copersero
past part.	coperto

36. CORRERE

past	corsi, corresti, corse, corremmo, correste, corsero
past part.	corso

37. COSTRUIRE

past	costruii *or* costrussi, costruisti, costrui *or* costrusse, costruimmo, costruiste, costruirono *or* costrussero
past part.	costruito *or* costrutto

38. CRESCERE

past	crebbi, crescesti, crebbe, crescemmo, cresceste, crebbero

39. CUOCERE

pres. ind.	cuocio, cuoci, cuoce, cociamo, cocete, cuociono
imp. ind.	cocevo, cocevi, coceva, cocevamo, cocevate, cocevano
past	cossi, cocesti, cosse, cocemmo, coceste, cossero
fut.	cocerò, cocerai, cocerà, coceremo, cocerete, coceranno
pres. sub.	cuòcia, cuòcia, cuòcia, cociamo, cociate, cuòciano
imp. sub.	cocessi, cocessi, cocesse, cocessimo, coceste, cocessero
cond.	cocerei, coceresti, cocerebbe, coceremmo, cocereste, cocerebbero
imper.	cuoci, cuocia, cocete, cuociano
pres. part.	cocente
past part.	cotto *or* cociuto

40. DARE

pres. ind.	do, dai, da, diamo, date, danno
imp. ind.	davo, davi, dava, davamo, davate, davano
past	diedi, desti, diede, demmo, deste, diedero
fut.	darò, darai, darà, daremo, darete, daranno
pres. sub.	dia, dia, dia, diamo, diate, diano
imp. sub.	dessi, dessi, desse, dessimo, deste, dessero
cond.	darei, daresti, darebbe, daremmo, dareste, darebbero
imper.	da, dia, date, diano
pres. part.	dando
past part.	dato

41. DECIDERE

past	decisi, decidesti, decise, decidemmo, decideste, decisero
past part.	deciso

42. DEVOLVERE

past	devolvei *or* devolvetti, devolvesti, devolvè *or* devolvette, devolvemmo, devolveste, devolverono *or* devolvettero
past part.	devoluto

43. DIFENDERE

past	difesi, difendesti, difese, difendemmo, difendeste, difesero
past part.	difeso

44. DIRE

pres. ind.	dico, dici, dice, diciamo, dite, dicono
imp. ind.	dicevo, dicevi, diceva, dicevamo, dicevate, dicevano
past	dissi, dicesti, disse, dicemmo, diceste, dissero
fut.	dirò, dirai, dirà, diremo, direte, diranno
pres. sub.	dica, dica, dica, diciamo, diciate, dicano
imp. sub.	dicessi, dicessi, dicesse, dicessimo, diceste, dicessero
cond.	direi, diresti, direbbe, diremmo, direste, direbbero
imper.	di, dica, dite, dicano
pres. part.	dicendo
past part.	detto

Note. All regular forms derive from the infinitive form dicere.

45. DIRIGERE

past	diressi, dirigesti, diresse, dirigemmo, dirigeste, diressero
past part.	diretto

46. DISCUTERE

past	discussi *or* discutei, discutesti, discusse *or* discutè, discutemmo, discuteste, discussero *or* discuterono
past part.	discusso

47. DISTINGUERE

past	distinsi, distinguesti, distinse, distinguemmo, distingueste, distinsero
past part.	distinto

48. DIVIDERE

past	divisi, dividesti, divise, dividemmo, divideste, divisero
past part.	diviso

49. DOLERSI

pres. ind.	mi dolgo, ti duoli, si duole, ci doliamo or dogliamo, vi dolete, si dolgono
past	mi dolsi, ti dolesti, si dolse, ci dolemmo, vi doleste, si dolsero
fut.	mi dorrò, ti dorrai, si dorrà, ci dorremo, vi dorrete, si dorranno
pres. sub.	mi dolga, ti dolga, si dolga, ci doliamo, vi doliate, si dolgano
imp. sub.	mi dolessi, ti dolessi, si dolesse, ci dolessimo, vi doleste, si dolessero
cond.	mi dorrei, ti dorresti, si dorrebbe, ci dorremmo, vi dorreste, si dorrebbero
imper.	duoliti, si dolga, doletevi, si dolgano
pres. part.	dolente
past part.	dolutosi

50. DOVERE

pres. ind.	devo or debbo, devi, deve, dobbiamo, dovete, devono or debbono
past	dovei or dovetti, dovesti, dovè or dovette, dovemmo, doveste, doverono or dovettero
fut.	dovrò, dovrai, dovrà, dovremo, dovrete, dovranno
pres. sub.	deva or debba, deva or debba, deva or debba, dobbiamo, dobbiate, devano or debbano
imper.	devi, deve, dovete, devono
past part.	dovuto

51. EMERGERE

past	emersi, emergesti, emerse, emergemmo, emergeste, emersero
past part.	emerso

52. EMPIERE

> *another infinitive form for* empire, 53, *which see for conjugation.*

53. EMPIRE

pres. ind.	empio, empi, empie, empiamo, empite, empiono
imp. ind.	empivo, empivi, empiva, empivamo, empivate, empivano
past	empii, empisti, empì, empimmo, empiste, empirono
fut.	empirò, empirai, empirà, empiremo, empirete, empiranno
pres. sub.	empia, empia, empia, empiamo, empiate, empiano
imp. sub.	empissi, empissi, empisse, empissimo, empiste, empissero
cond.	empirei, empiresti, empirebbe, empiremmo, empireste, empirebbero
imper.	empi, empia, empite, empiano
pres. part.	empiente
past part.	empito

54. ERGERE
past   ersi, ergesti, erse, ergemmo, ergeste, ersero
past part.   erto

55. ESAURIRE
past part.   esaurito *or* esausto

56. ESIGERE
past   esigei *or* esigetti, esigesti, esigè *or* esigette, esigemmo,
                esigeste, esigerono *or* esigettero
past part.   esatto

57. ESIMERE
past   esimei *or* esimetti, esimesti, esimè *or* esimette, esimemmo,
                esimeste, esimerono *or* esimettero
past part.   *lacking; it is replaced by the forms* esente *and* esentato.

58. ESPELLERE
past   espulsi, espellesti, espulse, espellemmo, espelleste, espul-
                sero
past part.   espulso

59. ESPLODERE
past   esplosi, esplodesti, esplose, esplodemmo, esplodeste,
                esplosero
past part.   esploso

60. EVADERE
past   evasi, evadesti, evase, evademmo, evadeste, evasero
past part.   evaso

61. FARE
pres. ind.   faccio *or* fo, fai, fa, facciamo, fate, fanno
imp. ind.   facevo, facevi, faceva, facevamo, facevate, facevano
past   feci, facesti, fece, facemmo, faceste, fecero
fut.   farò, farai, farà, faremo, farete, faranno
cond.   farei, faresti, farebbe, faremmo, fareste, farebbero
pres. sub.   faccia, faccia, faccia, facciamo, facciate, facciano
imp. sub.   facessi, facessi, facesse, facessimo, faceste, facessero
imper.   fai *or* fa', faccia, fate, facciano
pres. part.   facente
past part.   fatto
                Note. All regular forms derive from the infinitive form
                facere.

62. FENDERE
past   fendei *or* fendetti, fendesti, fendè *or* fendette, fendemmo,
                fendeste, fenderono *or* fendettero
past part.   fesso *or* fenduto

63. FIGGERE
past   fissi, figgesti, fisse, figgemmo, figgeste, fissero
past part.   fitto

64. FLETTERE
past   flettei *or* flessi, flettesti, flettè *or* flesse, flettemmo, flet-
                teste, fletterono *or* flessero
past part.   flesso

65. FONDERE

   past   **fusi, fondesti, fuse, fondemmo, fondeste, fusero**
   past part.   **fuso**

66. FRANGERE

   past   **fransi, frangesti, franse, frangemmo, frangeste, fransero**
   past part.   **franto**

67. FRIGGERE

   past   **frissi, friggesti, frisse, friggemmo, friggeste, frissero**
   past part.   **fritto**

68. GIACERE

   pres. ind.   **giaccio, giaci, giace, giacciamo** *or* **giaciamo, giacete, giacciono**
   past   **giacqui, giacesti, giacque, giacemmo, giaceste, giacquero**
   pres. sub.   **giaccia, giaccia, giaccia, giacciamo, giacciate, giacciano**
   past part.   **giaciuto**

69. INDULGERE

   past   **indulsi, indulgesti, indulse, indulgemmo, indulgeste, indulsero**
   past part.   **indulto**

70. INFERIRE

   past   **inferii** *or* **infersi, inferisti, inferì** *or* **inferse, inferimmo, inferiste, inferirono** *or* **infersero**
   past part.   **inferito** *or* **inferto**

71. INSERIRE

   past part.   **inserito** *or* (*rare*) **inserto**

72. INTRUDERE

   past   **intrusi, indrudesti, intruse, intrudemmo, intrudeste, intrusero**
   past part.   **intruso**

73. LEDERE

   past   **lesi, ledesti, lese, ledemmo, ledeste, lesero**
   past part.   **leso**

74. LEGGERE

   past   **lessi, leggesti, lesse, leggemmo, leggeste, lessero**
   past part.   **letto**

75. MESCERE

   pres. ind.   **mesco, mesci, mesce, mesciamo, mescete, mescono**
   past   **mescei, mescesti, mescè, mescemmo, mesceste, mescerono**
   pres. sub.   **mesca, mesca, mesca, mesciamo, mesciate, mescano**
   past part.   **mesciuto** *or* **misto**

76. METTERE

   past   **misi, mettesti, mise, mettemmo, metteste, misero**
   past part.   **messo**

77. MORDERE

   past   **morsi, mordesti, morse, mordemmo, mordeste, morsero**
   past part.   **morso**

78. MORIRE

pres. ind.	muoio, muori, muore, moriamo, morite, muolono
fut.	morirò or morrò, morirai or morrai, morirà or morrà, moriremo or morremo, morirete or morrete, moriranno or morranno
cond.	morirei or morrei, moriresti or morresti, morirebbe or morrebbe, moriremmo or morremmo, morireste or morreste, morirebbero or morrebbero
pres. sub.	muoia, muoia, muoia, moriamo, moriate, muoiano
imper.	muori, muoia, morite, muoiano
past part.	morto

79. MUNGERE

past	munsi, mungesti, munse, mungemmo, mungeste, munsero
past part.	munto

80. MUOVERE

past	mossi, movesti, mosse, movemmo, moveste, mossero
past part.	mosso

81. NASCERE

past	nacqui, nascesti, nacque, nascemmo, nasceste, nacquero
past part.	nato

82. NASCONDERE

past	nascosi, nascondesti, nascose, nascondemmo, nascondeste, nascosero
past part.	nascosto

83. NUOCERE

pres. ind.	nuoccio or noccio, nuoci, nuoce, nociamo, nocete, nuocciono or nocciono
past	nocqui, nocesti, nocque, nocemmo, noceste, nocquero
pres. ind.	noccia, noccia, noccia, nociamo, nociate, nocciano
imper.	nuoci, noccia, nocete, nocciano
past part.	nociuto

84. OFFRIRE

past	offrii or offersi, offristi, offrì or offerse, offrimmo, offriste, offrirono or offersero
past part.	offerto

85. PARERE

pres. ind.	paio, pari, pare, paiamo, parete, paiono
past	parvi, paresti, parve, paremmo, pareste, parvero
fut.	parrò, parrai, parrà, parremo, parrete, parranno
pres. sub.	paia, paia, paia, pariamo, pariate or paiate, paiano
cond.	parrei, parresti, parrebbe, parremmo, parreste, parrebbero
imper.	*lacking*
pres. part.	parvente
past part.	parso

86. PARTIRE

pres. ind.	parto, parti, parte, partiamo, partirte, partono

87. PERDERE

past	persi or perdetti, perdesti, perse or perdette, perdemmo, perdeste, persero or perdettero
past part.	perso or perduto

88. PERSUADERE

past	persuasi, persuadesti, persuase, persuademmo, persuadeste, persuasero
past part.	persuaso

89. PIACERE

pres. ind.	piaccio, piaci, piace, piacciamo, piacete, piacciono
past	piacqui, piacesti, piacque, piacemmo, piaceste, piacquero
pres. sub.	piaccia, piaccia, piaccia, piacciamo, piacciate, piacciano
past part.	piaciuto

90. PIANGERE

past	piansi, piangesti, pianse, piangemmo, piangeste, piansero
past part.	pianto

91. PIOVERE

past	piovvi, piovesti, piovve, piovemmo, pioveste, piovvero

92. PORGERE

past	porsi, porgesti, porse, porgemmo, porgeste, porsero
past part.	porto

93. PORRE

pres. ind.	pongo, poni, pone, poniamo, ponete, pongono
imp. ind.	ponevo, ponevi, poneva, ponevamo, ponevate, ponevano
past	posi, ponesti, pose, ponemmo, poneste, posero
fut.	porrò, porrai, porrà, porremo, porrete, porranno
cond.	porrei, porresti, porrebbe, porremmo, porreste, porrebbero
pres. sub.	ponga, ponga, ponga, poniamo, poniate, pongano
imp. sub.	ponessi, ponessi, ponesse, ponessimo, poneste, ponessero
imper.	poni, ponga, ponete, pongano
pres. part.	ponente
past part.	posto
	Note. All regular forms derive from the infinitive form ponere.

94. POTERE

pres. ind.	posso, puoi, può, possiamo, potete, possono
fut.	potrò, potrai, potrà, potremo, potrete, potranno
cond.	potrei, potresti, potrebbe, potremmo, potreste, potrebbero
pres. sub.	possa, possa, possa, possiamo, possiate, possano
past part.	potuto

95. PREDILIGERE

past	predilessi, prediligesti, predilesse, prediligemmo, prediligeste, predilessero
past part.	prediletto

96. PRENDERE

past	presi, prendesti, prese, prendemmo, prendeste, presero
past part.	preso

97. PRESCINDERE

past	prescindei *or* prescissi, prescindesti, prescindè *or* prescisse, prescindemmo, prescindeste, prescinderono *or* prescissero
past part.	prescisso
	Note. See also scindere, 121.

98. PREVEDERE
see **vedere, 151**

99. PROFERIRE
past   proferii, proferisti, proferì, proferimmo, proferiste, proferirono
past part.   proferito
            Note. See **profferire, 100.**

100. PROFFERIRE
past   proffersi, profferisti, profferse, profferimmo, profferiste, proffersero
past part.   profferto

101. PROTEGGERE
past   protessi, proteggesti, protesse, proteggemmo, proteggeste, protessero
past part.   protetto

102. RADERE
past   rasi, radesti, rase, rademmo, radeste, rasero
past part.   raso

103. REDIGERE
past   redassi, redigesti, redasse, redigemmo, redigeste, redassero
past part.   redatto

104. REDIMERE
past   redensi, redimesti, redense, redimemmo, redimeste, redensero
past part.   redento

105. REGGERE
past   ressi, reggesti, resse, reggemmo, reggeste, ressero
past part.   retto

106. RENDERE
past   resi, rendesti, rese, rendemmo, rendeste, resero
past part.   reso

107. RESTRINGERE
past part.   ristretto

108. RIDERE
past   risi, ridesti, rise, ridemmo, rideste, risero
past part.   riso

109. RIFLETTERE
past   riflettei *or* riflessi, riflettesti, riflettè *or* riflesse, riflettemmo, rifletteste, rifletterono *or* riflessero
past part.   riflettuto *or* riflesso

110. RIFULGERE
past   rifulsi, rifulgesti, rifulse, rifulgemmo, rifulgeste, rifulsero
past part.   rifulso

111. RILUCERE
past   rilucei, rilucesti, rilucè, rilucemmo, riluceste, rilucerono,
past part.   lacking

112. RIMANERE

pres. ind.	rimango, rimani, rimane, rimaniamo, rimanete, rimangono
past	rimasi, rimanesti, rimase, rimanemmo, rimaneste, rimasero
fut.	rimarrò, rimarrai, rimarrà, rimarremo, rimarrete, rimarranno
cond.	rimarrei, rimarresti, rimarrebbe, rimarremmo, rimarreste, rimarrebbero
pres. sub.	rimanga, rimanga, rimanga, rimaniamo, rimaniate, rimangano
imper.	rimani, rimanga, rimanete, rimangano
past part.	rimasto

113. RISPONDERE

past	risposi, rispondesti, rispose, rispondemmo, rispondeste, risposero
past part.	risposto

114. RODERE

past	rosi, rodesti, rose, rodemmo, rodeste, rosero
past part.	roso

115. ROMPERE

past	ruppi, rompesti, ruppe, rompemmo, rompeste, ruppero
past part.	rotto

116. SALIRE

pres. ind.	salgo, sali, sale, saliamo, salite, salgono
pres. sub.	salga, salga, salga, saliamo, saliate, salgano
imper.	sali, salga, salite, salgano

117. SAPERE

pres. ind.	so, sai, sa, sappiamo, sapete, sanno
past	seppi, sapesti, seppe, sapemmo, sapeste, seppero
fut.	saprò, saprai, saprà, sapremo, saprete, sapranno
cond.	saprei, sapresti, saprebbe, sapremmo, sapreste, saprebbero
pres. sub.	sappia, sappia, sappia, sappiamo, sappiate, sappiano
imper.	sappi, sappia, sappiate, sappiano
pres. part.	sapiente

118. SCEGLIERE

pres. ind.	scelgo, scegli, sceglie, scegliamo, scegliete, scelgono
past	scelsi, scegliesti, scelse, scegliemmo, sceglieste, scelsero
pres. sub.	scelga, scelga, scelga, scegliamo, scegliate, scelgano
imper.	scegli, scelga, scegliete, scelgano
past part.	scelto

119. SCENDERE

past	scesi, scendesti, scese, scendemmo, scendeste, scesero
past part.	sceso

120. SCERNERE

past	scernei *or* scernetti, scernesti, scernè *or* scernette, scernemmo, scerneste, scernerono *or* scernettero
past part.	*lacking*

121. SCINDERE

past	scissi, scindesti, scisse, scindemmo, scindeste, scissero
past part.	scisso

122. SCOLPIRE

past	scolpii, scolpisti, scolpi, scolpimmo, scolpiste, scolpirono; *poet.* sculsi, scolpisti, sculse, scolpimmo, scolpiste, sculsero
past part.	scolpito; *poet.* sculto

123. SCORGERE

past	scorsi, scorgesti, scorse, scorgemmo, scorgeste, scorsero
past part.	scorto

124. SCRIVERE

past	scrissi, scrivesti, scrisse, scrivemmo, scriveste, scrissero
past part.	scritto

125. SCUOTERE

past	scossi, scotesti, scosse, scotemmo, scoteste, scossero
past part.	scosso

126. SEDERE

pres. ind.	siedo *or* seggo, siedi, siede, sediamo, sedete, siedono *or* seggono
past	sedei *or* sedetti, sedesti, sedè *or* sedette, sedemmo, sedeste, sederono *or* sedettero
pres. sub.	sieda *or* segga, sieda *or* segga, sieda *or* segga, sediamo, sediate, siedano *or* seggano
imper.	siedi, sieda *or* segga, sedete, siedano *or* seggano

127. SEPPELLIRE

past part.	seppellito *or* sepolto

128. SODDISFARE

pres. ind.	soddisfo *or* soddisfaccio, soddisfi *or* soddisfai, soddisfa *or* soddisfa, soddisfiamo *or* soddisfacciamo, soddisfate, soddisfano *or* soddisfanno
pres. sub.	soddisfi *or* soddisfaccia, soddisfi *or* soddisfaccia, soddisfi *or* soddisfaccia, soddisfacciamo, soddisfacciate, soddisfino *or* soddisfacciano
imper.	soddisfa, soddisfi *or* soddisfaccia, soddisfate, soddisfino *or* soddisfacciano

129. SOLERE

pres. ind.	soglio, suoli, suole, sogliamo, solete, sogliono; *or* sono solito, sei solito, è solito, siamo soliti, siete soliti, sono soliti
imp. ind.	solevo, solevi, soleva, solevamo, solevate, solevano
fut.	*lacking*
cond.	*lacking*
pres. sub.	soglia, soglia, soglia, sogliamo, sogliate, sogliano
imp. sub.	solessi, solessi, solesse, solessimo, soleste, solessero
past	solei, solesti, solè, solemmo, soleste, solerono (*rare*); *now most commonly:* fui solito, fosti solito, fu solito, fummo soliti, foste soliti, furono soliti
imper.	*lacking*
pres. part.	*lacking*
past part.	solito

130. SORGERE

past	sorsi, sorgesti, sorse, sorgemmo, sorgeste, sorsero
past part.	sorto

131. SPANDERE

past	spandei *or* spansi, spandesti, spandè *or* spanse, spandemmo, spandeste, spanderono *or* spansero
past part.	spanto *or* spanduto *or* spanso (*all rare*); *now most commonly:* sparso

132. SPARGERE

past	sparsi, spargesti, sparse, spargemmo, spargeste, sparsero
past part.	sparso

133. SPARIRE

past	sparii *or* sparvi, sparisti, sparì *or* sparve, sparimmo, spariste, sparirono *or* sparvero

134. SPEGNERE *or* SPENGERE

pres. ind.	spengo, spegni *or* spengi, spegne *or* spenge, spegniamo *or* spengiamo, spegnete *or* spengete, spengono
past	spensi, spegnesti *or* spengesti, spense, spegnemmo *or* spengemmo, spegneste *or* spengeste, spensero
pres. sub.	spenga, spenga, spenga, spegniamo *or* spengiamo, spegniate, *or* spengiate, spengano
imper.	spegni *or* spengi, spenga, spegnete *or* spengete, spengano
past part.	spento

135. STARE

pres. ind.	sto, stai, sta, stiamo, state, stanno
past	stetti, stesti, stette, stemmo, steste, stettero
fut.	starò, starai, starà, staremo, starete, staranno
cond.	starei, staresti, starebbe, staremmo, stareste, starebbero
pres. sub.	stia, stia, stia, stiamo, stiate, stiano
imp. sub.	stessi, stessi, stesse, stessimo, steste, stessero
imper.	stai *or* sta', stia, state, stiano
past part.	stato

136. STRINGERE

past	strinsi, stringesti, strinse, stringemmo, stringeste, strinsero
past part.	stretto

137. STRUGGERE

past	strussi, struggesti, strusse, struggemmo, struggeste, strussero
past part.	strutto

138. SVELLERE

pres. ind.	svelgo *or* svello, svelli, svelle, svelliamo, svellete, svelgono *or* svellono
past	svelsi, svellesti, svelse, svellemmo, svelleste, svelsero
past part.	svelto

139. TACERE

pres. ind.	taccio, taci, tace, taciamo, tacete, tacciono
past	tacqui, tacesti, tacque, tacemmo, taceste, tacquero
pres. sub.	taccia, taccia, taccia, taciamo, tacciate, tacciano
imper.	taci, taccia, tacete, tacciano

140. TENDERE

past	tesi, tendesti, tese, tendemmo, tendeste, tesero
past part.	teso

141. TENERE

pres. ind.	tengo, tieni, tiene, teniamo, tenete, tengono
past	tenni, tenesti, tenne, tenemmo, teneste, tennero
fut.	terrò, terrai, terrà, terremo, terrete, terranno
cond.	terrei, terresti, terrebbe, terremmo, terreste, terrebbero
pres. sub.	tenga, tenga, tenga, teniamo, teniate, tengano
imper.	tieni, tenga, tenete, tengano

142. TERGERE

past	tersi, tergesti, terse, tergemmo, tergeste, tersero
past part.	terso

143. TINGERE

past	tinsi, tingesti, tinse, tingemmo, tingeste, tinsero
past part.	tinto

144. TOGLIERE

pres. ind.	tolgo, togli, toglie, togliamo, togliete, tolgono
past	tolsi, togliesti, tolse, togliemmo, toglieste, tolsero
pres. sub.	tolga, tolga, tolga, togliamo, togliate, tolgano
imper.	togli, tolga, togliete, tolgano
cond.	toglierei *or* torrei, toglieresti *or* torresti, toglierebbe *or* torrebbe, toglieremmo *or* torremmo, togliereste *or* torreste, toglierebbero *or* torrebbero
fut.	toglierò *or* torrò, toglierai *or* torrai, toglierà *or* torrà, toglieremo *or* torremo, toglierete *or* torrete, toglieranno *or* torranno
past part.	tolto

145. TORCERE

past	torsi, torcesti, torse, torcemmo, torceste, torsero
past part.	torto

146. TRARRE

pres. ind.	traggo, trai, trae, traiamo, traete, traggono
imp. ind.	traevo, traevi, traeva, traevamo, traevate, traevano
fut.	trarrò, trarrai, trarrà, trarremo, trarrete, trarranno
past	trassi, traesti, trasse, traemmo, traeste, trassero
cond.	trarrei, trarresti, trarrebbe, trarremmo, trarreste, trarrebbero
pres. sub.	tragga, tragga, tragga, traiamo, traiate, traggano
imp. sub.	traessi, traessi, traesse, traessimo, traeste, traessero
imper.	trai, tragga, traete, traggano
pres. part.	traente
past part.	tratto.
	Note. All regular forms derive from the infinitive form traere.

147. TRASPARIRE

see apparire, 9

148. UDIRE

pres. ind.	odo, odi, ode, udiamo, udite, odono
fut.	udirò *or* udrò, udirai *or* udrai, udirà *or* udrà, udiremo *o* udremo, udirete *or* udrete, udiranno *or* udranno
pres. sub.	oda, oda, oda, udiamo, udiate, odano
imper.	odi, oda, udite, odano
pres. part.	udente *or* udiente

149. USCIRE

pres. ind.	esco, esci, esce, usciamo, uscite, escono
pres. sub.	esca, esca, esca, usciamo, usciate, escano
imper.	esci, esca, uscite, escano

150. VALERE

pres. ind.	valgo, vali, vale, valiamo, valete, valgono
past	valsi, valesti, valse, valemmo, valeste, valsero
fut.	varrò, varrai, varrà, varremo, varrete, varranno
cond.	varrei, varresti, varrebbe, varremmo, varreste, varrebbero
pres. sub.	valga, valga, valga, valiamo, valiate, valgano
imper.	vali, valga, valete, valgano
past part.	valso or valuto

151. VEDERE

past	vidi, vedesti, vide, vedemmo, vedeste, videro
fut.	vedrò, vedrai, vedrà, vedremo, vedrete, vedranno
cond.	vedrei, vedresti, vedrebbe, vedremmo, vedreste, vedrebbero
pres. part.	vedente or veggente
past part.	visto or veduto

152. VENIRE

pres. ind.	vengo, vieni, viene, veniamo, venite, vengono
past	venni, venisti, venne, venimmo, veniste, vennero
fut.	verrò, verrai, verrà, verremo, verrete, verranno
cond.	verrei, verresti, verrebbe, verremmo, verreste, verrebbero
pres. sub.	venga, venga, venga, veniamo, veniate, vengano
imper.	vieni, venga, venite, vengano
pres. part.	veniente
past part.	venuto

153. VINCERE

past	vinsi, vincesti, vinse, vincemmo, vinceste, vinsero
past part.	vinto

154. VIVERE

past	vissi, vivesti, visse, vivemmo, viveste, vissero
fut.	vivrò, vivrai, vivrà, vivremo, vivrete, vivranno
cond.	vivrei, vivresti, vivrebbe, vivremmo, vivreste, vivrebbero
past part.	vissuto

155. VOLERE

pres. ind.	voglio, vuoi, vuole, vogliamo, volete, vogliono
past	volli, volesti, volle, volemmo, voleste, vollero
fut.	vorrò, vorrai, vorrà, vorremo, vorrete, vorranno
cond.	vorrei, vorresti, vorrebbe, vorremmo, vorreste, vorrebbero
pres. sub.	voglia, voglia, voglia, vogliamo, vogliate, vogliano
past part.	voluto

156. VOLGERE

past	volsi, volgesti, volse, volgemmo, volgeste, volsero
past part.	volto

NUMERALS

	Cardinal numbers	Numeri cardinali	Ordinal numbers	Numeri ordinali
1	one	uno	first	primo
2	two	due	second	secondo
3	three	tre	third	terzo
4	four	quattro	fourth	quarto
5	five	cinque	fifth	quinto
6	six	sei	sixth	sesto
7	seven	sette	seventh	settimo
8	eight	otto	eighth	ottavo
9	nine	nove	ninth	nono
10	ten	dieci	tenth	decimo
11	eleven	undici	eleventh	undicesimo
12	twelve	dodici	twelfth	dodicesimo
13	thirteen	tredici	thirteenth	tredicesimo
14	fourteen	quattordici	fourteenth	quattordicesimo
15	fifteen	quindici	fifteenth	quindicesimo
16	sixteen	sedici	sixteenth	sedicesimo
17	seventeen	diciassette	seventeenth	diciassettesimo
18	eighteen	diciotto	eighteenth	diciottesimo
19	nineteen	diciannove	nineteenth	diciannovesimo
20	twenty	venti	twentieth	ventesimo
21	twenty-one	ventuno	twenty-first	ventunesimo
22	twenty-two	ventidue	twenty-second	ventiduesimo
23	twenty-three	ventitrè	twenty-third	ventitreesimo
26	twenty-six	ventisei	twenty-sixth	ventiseesimo
30	thirty	trenta	thirtieth	trentesimo
40	forty	quaranta	fortieth	quarantesimo
50	fifty	cinquanta	fiftieth	cinquantesimo
60	sixty	sessanta	sixtieth	sessantesimo
70	seventy	settanta	seventieth	settantesimo
80	eighty	ottanta	eightieth	ottantesimo
90	ninety	novanta	ninetieth	novantesimo
100	one hundred	cento	hundredth	centesimo
1000	one thousand	mille	(one) thousandth	millesimo
10000	ten thousand	diecimila	ten thousandth	decimillesimo
100000	one hundred thousand	centomila	(one) hundred thousandth	cento-millesimo
1000000	one million	un milione	(one) millionth	millonesimo

Note. Venti drops the i in ventuno and in ventotto.

Trenta, quaranta, etc., drop the last a in trentuno, trentotto, quarantuno, quarantotto, etc.

Cento and mille are not preceded by the indefinite article or by the number uno.

Cento is invariable.

Mille has the plural form mila.

Eleven hundred, twelve hundred, etc., are expressed in Italian as mille e cento, mille e duecento, etc.

Ordinal numbers are declined like any other adjective.

A

a, ad *prep.* to, at, in, by, for, on.
a'baco *m.* abacus (*pl.* abaci).
abate *m.* abbot, priest.
abbacchiarsi *vr.* to lose courage.
abbacchiato *adj.* dejected.
abbac'chio *m.* lamb (*killed*).
abbacinare *vt.* to dazzle.
abbadessa *f.* abbess.
abbagliante *adj.* dazzling.
abbagliare *vt.* to dazzle, blind; to charm.
abba'glio *m.* mistake, dazzling (*fig.*).
abbaiamento *m.* bark.
abbaiare *vi.* to bark.
abbai'no *m.* dormer, dormer window.
abbandonare *vt.* to abandon, forsake; **abbandonarsi** *vr.* to abandon oneself, trust (*to*); to relax.
abbandonato *adj.* abandoned.
abbandono *m.* abandonment.
abbarbicarsi *vr.* to cling, stick.
abbassamento *m.* lowering.
abbassare *vt.* to lower: — **gli occhi**, to cast down one's eyes; **abbassarsi** *vr.* to lower oneself, stoop.
abbasso *adv., prep.* down, below. *interj.* down with!
abbastanza *adv.* enough.
abbat'tere *vt.* to pull down; to shoot down; to slaughter; **abbat'tersi** *vr.* to fall; to lose courage.
abbattimento *m.* dejection; demolition.
abbazi'a *f.* abbey; abbacy.
abbeceda'rio *m.* spelling book.
abbellimento *m.* embellishment, decoration.
abbellire *vt.* to embellish, adorn; **abbellirsi** *vr.* to adorn oneself.
abbeverare *vt.*, **abbeverarsi** *vr.* to water; to drink.
abbeveratoio *m.* watering place.
abbiadare *vt.* to accustom a horse to oats.
abbicci *m.* alphabet; spelling book.
abbiente *adj.* wealthy.
abbigliamento *m.* attire.
abbigliare *vt.*, **abbigliarsi** *vr.* to dress.
abbinamento *m.* coupling.
abbinare *vt.* to couple.
abbindolare *vt.* to deceive.
abbisognare *vi.* to need, want.
abboccamento *m.* interview.
abboccare *vt.* to bite; **abboccarsi** *vr.* to confer (*with*).
abbonamento *m.* subscription: **bi-glietto d'—,** season ticket.
abbonare *vt.* to grant a discount (*to*); **abbonarsi** *vr.* to subscribe.

abbonato *m.* subscriber.
abbondante *adj.* abundant.
abbondantemente *adv.* abundantly.
abbondanza *f.* plentifulness, plenty.
abbondare *vi.* to abound (*in*).
abborda'bile *adj.* accessible, approachable; cheap.
abbordag'gio *m.* boarding (*a boat*).
abbordare *vt.* to board; to accost, approach: — **un argomento**, to broach a subject.
abborracciare *vt.* to bungle, mess.
abborracciatura *f.* bungle.
abbottonare *vt.* to button.
abbottonatura *f.* fastening.
abbozzare *vt.* to sketch.
abbozzo *m.* sketch.
abbracciare *vt.* to embrace: — **una causa**, to espouse a cause; — **una professione**, to enter a profession.
abbrac'cio *m.* embrace, hug.
abbrancare *vt.* to grab; **abbrancarsi** *vr.* to cling (*to*).
abbreviare *vt.* to shorten, abridge, curtail.
abbreviatura *f.* abridgment.
abbreviazione *f.* abbreviation.
abbrivo *m.* (*naut.*) headway.
abbronzare *vt.*, **abbronzarsi** *vr.* to bask, tan.
abbronzatura *f.* tan.
abbrunare *vt.* to brown; to drape with black: — **le bandiere**, to fly at half-mast (*as flags*).
abbrustolire *vt.* to broil, toast, roast.
abbrutimento *m.* stupor.
abbrutire *vt., vi.* **abbrutirsi** *vr.* to brutalize.
abbuiarsi *vr.* to darken, dim.
abbuono *m.* allowance, discount.
abburattamento *m.* sifting.
abburattare *vt.* to sift.
abburattatura *f.* sifting; bran.
abdicare *vt., vi.* to abdicate.
abdicazione *f.* abdication.
aberrazione *f.* aberration.
abete *m.* fir tree.
abia'tico *m.* grandchild.
abiettezza *f.* baseness.
abietto *adj.* base, abject, despicable.
abiezione *f.* despicableness; misery.
abigeato *m.* cattle rustling.
a'bile *adj.* able, capable; fit, apt.
abilità *f.* ability, skill.
abilitare *vt.*, **abilitarsi** *vr.* to qualify.
abilitazione *f.* qualification.
abilmente *adv.* skillfully.
abisso *m.* abyss, chasm, gulf.

abita'bile *adj.* habitable.

abita'colo *m.* (*aeron.*) cockpit.

abitante *m.* inhabitant, dweller.

abitare *vt.* to inhabit, occupy. *vi.* to dwell, live (*in*).

abitato *m.* inhabited area. *adj.* inhabited, occupied, lived-in.

abitatore *m.* dweller.

abitazione *f.* abode, residence.

a'bito *m.* suit; dress; (*pl.*) clothes: — **mentale**, habit of mind.

abituale *adj.* usual, habitual.

abitualmente *adv.* usually.

abituare *vt.* to accustom; **abituarsi** *vr.* to become accustomed.

abitudina'rio *adj.* methodical, regular.

abitu'dine *f.* habit, custom.

abituro *m.* hut, shanty.

abiura *f.* abjuration.

abiurare *vt.* to abjure.

ablativo *m.*, *adj.* ablative.

ablazione *f.* ablation.

abluzione *f.* ablution.

abnegazione *f.* self-denial.

abolire *vt.* to abolish.

abolizione *f.* abolition, repeal.

abolizionismo *m.* abolitionism.

abolizionista *m.* abolitionist.

abominare *vt.* to abominate, loathe.

abominazione *f.* abomination.

abomine'vole *adj.* abominable.

abori'geno *m.* aborigine. *adj.* aboriginal.

aborrire *vt.*, *vi.* to abhor, loathe.

abortire *vi.* to miscarry; to fail.

aborto *m.* abortion, miscarriage.

abrasione *f.* abrasion, scraping off.

abrasivo *m.*, *adj.* abrasive.

abrogare *vt.* to abrogate.

abrogazione *f.* abrogation.

ab'side *f.* apse; apsis (*pl.* apsides).

abuli'a *f.* abulia, aboulia.

abu'lico *adj.* abulic.

abusare *vi.* to abuse, misuse; to take advantage (*of*); overdo: — **nel bere**, to drink to excess.

abusivamente *adv.* improperly.

abusivo *adj.* unwarranted.

abuso *m.* abuse, excess.

aca'cia *f.* (*bot.*) acacia.

acanto *m.* acanthus.

a'caro *m.* mite, acarus.

acca *f.* the letter "h": **non ci capisco un'—**, I cannot make head or tail of it; **non valere un'—**, to be worthless.

accade'mia *f.* academy.

accademicamente *adv.* academically.

accade'mico *m.* academician. *adj.* academic.

accadere *vi.* to happen, occur.

accaduto *m.* case, event: **raccontami l'—**, tell me what happened.

accagliare *vt.*, **accagliarsi** *vr.* to curdle, coagulate.

accalappiacani *m.* dogcatcher.

accalappiamento *m.* snare.

accalappiare *vt.* to ensnare.

accalappiatore *m.* snarer.

accalcare *vt.*, **accalcarsi** *vr.* to crowd, throng, swarm.

accaldarsi *vr.* to get hot.

accaldato *adj.* hot.

accalorarsi *vr.* to get excited.

accampamento *m.* camp, camping, encampment.

accampare *vt.*, *vi.* to camp, encamp: — **diritti su**, to lay claim to; **accamparsi** *vr.* (*mil.*) to encamp.

accanimento *m.* fury, stubbornness.

accanirsi *vr.* to persist; (*foll. by* **su**, **contro**) to badger.

accanito *adj.* furious; relentless; stubborn; tenacious; bitter.

accanto *prep.*, *adv.* beside, by, near.

accantonamento *m.* billeting.

accantonare *vt.* to billet; to set aside; **accantonarsi** *vr.* to camp.

accaparramento *m.* cornering.

accaparrare *vt.* to hoard, corner; **accaparrarsi** *vr.* to grab.

accaparratore *m.* hoarder.

accapigliarsi *vr.* to scuffle, come to blows, quarrel.

accappato'io *m.* bathrobe.

accapponare *vt.* to caponize; **accapponarsi** *vr.* to creep: **far accapponare la pelle**, to make one's flesh creep.

accarezzare *vt.* to caress; to cherish.

accartocciare *vt.* to wrap up; **accartocciarsi** *vr.* to curl up.

accasare *vt.*, **accasarsi** *vr.* to marry.

accasciamento *m.* dejection.

accasciare *vt.* to enfeeble; to dishearten, discourage; **accasciarsi** *vr.* to weaken; to lose courage.

accasermare *vt.*, **accasermarsi** *vr.* to quarter, billet.

accatastare *vt.* to heap up.

accattabrighe *m.* brawler.

accattare *vt.* to beg.

accattonag'gio *m.* begging.

accattone *m.* beggar.

accavallamento *m.* overlapping, twist.

accavallare *vt.* to overlap, cross; **accavallarsi** *vr.* to overlap, twist.

accecamento *m.* blinding.

accecante *adj.* blinding.

accecare *vt.* to blind; to dazzle. *vi.* to become blind; **accecarsi** *vr.* to blind oneself.

acce'dere *vi.* to accede; to approach; to enter.

accelerare *vt.*, *vi.* to accelerate, hasten, to speed up.

accelerato *m.* local train. *adj.*, *pp of* **accelerare**, accelerated: **corso —**, intensive course.

acceleratore *m.* accelerator; throttle.
accelerazione *f.* acceleration; pickup.
accen'dere *vt.*[1] to light; to ignite; accendersi *vr.* to light, take fire; to get excited.
accendisi'garo *m.* lighter.
accenditore *m.* lighter.
accennare *vt., vi.* to point at; to outline; to beckon; to hint (*at*).
accenno *m.* hint, allusion.
accensione *f.* firing, ignition.
accentare *vt.* to accent.
accentatura *f.* accentuation.
accento *m.* accent, stress.
accentramento *m.* centralization.
accentrare *vt.* to centralize.
accentratore *m.* centralizer.
accentuare *vt.* to accentuate; to emphasize; accentuarsi *vr.* to increase.
accentuazione *f.* accentuation.
accerchiamento *m.* encirclement.
accerchiare *vt.* to encircle, encompass; to surround.
accerta'bile *adj.* verifiable.
accertamento *m.* verification, ascertainment, estimate.
accertare *vt.* to assure; to ascertain; accertarsi *vr.* to make sure.
acceso *adj.* alight; hot. *pp.* of accendere, lighted, lit.
accessi'bile *adj.* accessible; reasonable.
accesso *m.* fit, burst; entrance.
accesso'rio *adj.* complementary; accessori *m. pl.* fittings.
accetta f. ax, hatchet.
accetta'bile *adj.* acceptable.
accettante *m.* acceptor.
accettare *vt.* to accept.   [bill.
accettazione *f.* acceptance; accepted
accetto *adj.* agreeable: bene —, welcome; male —, unwelcome.
accezione *f.* meaning, case, acceptance.
acchiappare *vt.* (*It. slang*) to catch.
acchito *m.* lead: di primo —, at first, at once.
acciaccare *vt.* to crush; to bruise.
acciaccatura *f.* bruise; grace note.
acciacco *m.* infirmity.
acciaieri'a *f.* steelworks.
accia'io *m.* steel.
acciarino *m.* steel; tinderbox.
accidentale *adj.* accidental.
accidentalmente *adv.* accidentally.
accidentato *adj.* paralyzed; uneven.
accidente *m.* accident, mishap; stroke (of apoplexy).
accidenti! *interj.* the deuce!, damn!
acci'dia *f.* laziness, sloth.
accidioso *adj.* lazy, slothful.
accigliarsi *vr.* to frown.
accigliato *adj.* frowning.

accin'gersi *vr.* to gird oneself; to set about.
acciocchè *conj.* so that.
acciottolare *vt.* to cobble.
acciottolato *m.* (*cobbled*) paving.
acciottoli'o *m.* clatter.
acciuffare *vt.* to catch, seize; acciuffarsi *vr.* to quarrel.
acciuga *f.* anchovy.
acclamare *vt., vi.* to acclaim.
acclamatore *m.* acclaimer.
acclamazione *f.* acclamation.
acclimatare *vt.* to acclimatize; acclimatarsi *vr.* to become acclimatized.
acclimatazione *f.*, acclimatization.
acclive *adj.* steep.
acclu'dere *vt.*[2] to enclose.
accluso *adj.* enclosed: qui —, herein enclosed. *pp.* of accludere.
accoccare *vt.* to notch, fit.
accoccolarsi *vr.* to cuddle, squat.
accodarsi *vr.* to follow, line up in file.
accogliente *adj.* cozy, hospitable.
accoglienza *f.* reception, welcome.
acco'gliere *vt.*[2] to receive, welcome;
acco'lito *m.* acolyte.   [to grant.
accollare *vt.* to lay on; accollarsi *vr.* to take upon oneself.
accollato *adj.* high-necked (*as a gown*); high-cut (*as shoes*).
accolta *f.* assembly, gathering.
accoltellare *vt.* to knife.
accolto *adj.* received; granted. *pp.* of accogliere.
accomandante *m.* limited partner, depositor.
accomandata'rio *m.* general partner, unlimited partner.
accoman'dita *f.* limited partnership: società in —, joint-stock company.
accomiatare *vt.* to dismiss; accomiatarsi *vr.* to take one's leave.
accomodamento *m.* arrangement.
accomodante *adj.* obliging.
accomodare *vt.* to mend; to tidy; to settle; to adapt. *vi.* to suit; accomodarsi *vr.* to adapt oneself; to come to an agreement; to sit down; to make oneself comfortable.
accomodatura *f.* mending.
accompagnamento *m.* attendance, escort; accompaniment.
accompagnare *vt.* to accompany, escort; to match: Dio li fa, poi li accompagna, birds of a feather flock together; accompagnarsi *vr.* to go (*with*); to match.
accompagnatore *m.* escort, companion; accompanist.
accomunare *vt.* to join, associate; to mingle; accomunarsi *vr.* to join (*with*).
acconciamente *adv.* properly.

acconciare vt. to prepare for use; to adorn; to attire; to dress the hair of; **acconciarsi** vr. to adorn oneself; to adapt oneself; to dress one's hair.

acconciatura f. attire; hairdo.

acconcio adj. fit, proper.

accondiscen´dere see **condiscendere**.

acconsentire vt. to admit, approve. vi. to acquiesce, agree.

accontentare vt. to please, satisfy; to humor; **accontentarsi** vr. to be content (with).

acconto m. account; retainer; advance.

accoppare vt. to kill; to club.

accoppia´bile adj. matchable.

accoppiamento m. coupling; copulation.

accoppiare vt. to couple, pair; to cross; to yoke; **accoppiarsi** vr. to couple; to mate; to copulate.

accoramento m. grief, sorrow.

accorarsi vr. to grieve (over).

accorato adj. grieved, sorrowful.

accorciamento m. shortening; shrinkage.

accorciare vt., **accorciarsi** vr. to shorten; to shrink.

accordamento m. concordance; tuning.

accordare vt. to tune; to match; to put in agreement; to reconcile; to grant; **accordarsi** vr. to agree (upon); to match.

accordatore m. (mus.) tuner.

accordatura f. (mus.) tuning.

accordo m. agreement, harmony; concordance.

accor´gersi vr.[6] to perceive, become aware (of), realize.

accorgimento m. device, trick, stratagem.

accor´rere vi. to run, rush.

accortamente adv. shrewdly.

accortezza f. shrewdness.

accorto adj. shrewd, sly, clever.

accosciarsi vr. to squat.

accosta´bile adj. approachable.

accostamento m. approach, comparison.

accostare vt. to approach; to set ajar; to bring near. vi. to stand close; **accostarsi** vr. to approach; to look like.

accosto adj. near. adv., prep. by, close to, near.

accovacciarsi vr. to crouch.

accovonare vt. to sheaf.

accozza´glia f. medley, mixed crowd.

accozzare vt., **accozzarsi** vr. to huddle, assemble.

accozzo m. jumble, medley.

accredita´bile adj. that may be credited.

accreditamento m. crediting.

accreditare vt. to credit; to confirm; to accredit.

accre´scere vt. **accre´scersi** vr. to increase.

accrescimento m. increase.

accucciarsi vr. to crouch.

accudire vi. to attend (to), take care (of).

accumulare vt., **accumularsi** vr. to accumulate.

accumulatore m. storage battery.

accumulazione f. accumulation.

accuratamente adv. accurately.

accuratezza f. accuracy.

accurato adj. accurate, careful.

accusa f. charge; prosecution.

accusare vt. to charge (with); to feel, show: — ricevuta, to acknowledge receipt.

accusativo m., adj. accusative.

accusato m. accused; defendant.

accusatore m. accuser: — pubblico, prosecutor.

acerbamente adv. prematurely; bitterly, mercilessly, sharply.

acerbo adj. unripe; sour; merciless; inexperienced; sharp.

a´cero m. maple.

acer´rimo adj. (superl. of **acre**) cruel, fierce, relentless.

acetato m. (chem.) acetate.

ace´tico adj. acetic.

acetilene f. acetylene.

aceto m. vinegar.

acetone m. acetone.

acetosa f. (bot.) sorrel.

acetosella f. (bot.) wood sorrel.

acidificare vt. to acidify.

acidità f. acidity, sourness.

a´cido m., adj. acid.

aci´dulo adj. acidulous.

a´cino m. (bot.) acinus (pl. **acini**); grapestone; grape.

acme f. climax.

acne f. acne.

aco´nito m. aconite, wolfsbane.

acqua f. water: — cheta, dissembler; — dolce, soft water; — ossigenata, hydrogen peroxide; fare —, to leak; fare un buco nell'—, to fail.

acquaforte f. aqua fortis; etching.

acquafortista m. etcher.

acqua´io m. sink.

acqualuolo m. water carrier.

acquamarina f. aquamarine.

acquaplano m. aquaplane.

acquaragia f. turpentine oil.

acqua´rio see **aqua´rio**.

acquartierare vt., **acquartierarsi** vr. to quarter.

acqua´tico adj. aquatic.

acquatinta f. aquatint.

acquattare vt. to hide, shelter; **acquattarsi** vr. to crouch; to hide.

acquavite f. brandy.

acquazzone m. shower.

acquedotto m. aqueduct.

ac'queo adj. watery.

acquerellare vt. to paint with water colors.

acquerellista m. aquarellist.

acquerello m. water color.

acqueru'giola f. drizzle.

acquetare see acquietare.

acquiescente adj. acquiescent.

acquiescenza f. acquiescence.

acquietare vt. to appease; **acquietarsi** vr. to calm down.

acquirente m. purchaser.

acquisire vt. to acquire.

acquistare vt. to acquire; to buy; to obtain.

acquisto m. purchase; acquisition: potere d'—, buying power.

acquitrino m. marsh, swamp.

acquitrinoso adj. marshy.

acquolina f. drizzle: far venire l'— in bocca, to make one's mouth water.

acquoso adj. watery.

acre adj. acrid; sour; sharp.

acre'dine f. sourness; acrimony.

acrimo'nia f. acrimony.

acro m. acre.

acro'bata m. acrobat.

acroba'tico adj. acrobatic.

acrobatismo m. acrobatism.

acrobazi'a f. acrobatics, stunt.

acro'coro m. plateau.

acuire vt. to sharpen, whet.

acu'leo m. prickle; sting; quill; thorn; goad, spur.

acume m. acumen, keenness.

acuminare vt. to sharpen.

acuminato adj. pointed, sharp.

acu'stica f. acoustics.

acu'stico adj. acoustic: cornetto —, ear trumpet.

acutamente adv. acutely, sharply.

acutezza f. acuteness, sharpness.

acutizzare vt., **acutizzarsi** vr. to sharpen.

acuto adj. high note. adj. acute, sharp; shrill; high-pitched.

ad see a.

adagiare vt. to lay, lower (to); **adagiarsi** vr. to lie down.

adagino adv. slowly, gently.

ada'gio m. adage. adv. slowly; softly.

adamantino adj. adamantine.

adami'tico adj. adamitic: in costume —, naked.

Adamo m. pr. Adam.

adatta'bile adj. adaptable.

adattabilità f. adaptableness.

adattamento m. adaptation: spirito d'—, compliance, adaptability.

adattare vt. to adapt, adjust; **adattarsi** vr. to fit, suit; to resign oneself.

adatto adj. fit, suitable, proper, expedient.

addebitare vt. to debit with, charge with.

adde'bito m. debit, charge.

addensamento m. thickening.

addensare vt. to thicken; **addensarsi** vr. to thicken; to crowd, surge.

addentare vt. to bite; (mach.) to mesh, to throw into gear.

addentellare vt. to indent.

addentrarsi vr. to penetrate, make one's way into.

addentro adv. inside.

addestramento m. training.

addestrare vt. to train.

addestratore m. trainer.

addetto m. attaché. adj. assigned, appointed.

addì adv. on: — 30 Novembre, on the 30th of November.

addiac'cio m. bivouac; sheepfold.

addietro adv. ago, before; behind.

addi'o m. farewell. interj. good-bye.

addirittura adv. straightway, directly; absolutely, quite.

addirsi vr. to become, suit.

additare vt. to point at.

addivenire vi. to come to.

addizionale adj. additional.

addizionare vt. to add up.

addizione f. addition.

addobbamento m. decoration.

addobbare vt. to adorn, decorate, attire.

addobbatore m. decorator.

addobbo m. decoration; hanging.

addolcimento m. sweetening.

addolcire vt., **addolcirsi** vr. to sweeten; to calm down; to soften.

addolorare vt., **addolorarsi** vr. to grieve.

addolorato adj. grieved: l'Addolorata, Our Lady of Sorrows.

addome m. abdomen.

addomestica'bile adj. tamable.

addomesticamento m. taming.

addomesticare vt. to tame; to refine; to accustom.

addomesticato adj. tame; domesticated.

addominale adj. abdominal.

addormentare vt. to put to sleep; to benumb; to assuage; **addormentarsi** vr. to fall asleep, go to sleep.

addormentato adj. asleep; benumbed; stupid.

addossare vt. to lay (on), load with; to entrust; to impute; **addossarsi** vr. to take upon oneself; to lean (against).

addosso adv., prep. on, upon, against, near; about (oneself).

addotto adj. alleged; brought. pp. of addurre.

addottorare vt., **addottorarsi** vr. to graduate.
addurre vt.⁴ to allege; to bring.
adduttore m. (anat.) adductor.
adeguamento m. proportionment.
adeguare vt. to proportion; **adeguarsi** vr. to become adequate, adapt oneself.
adeguatamente adv. adequately.
adeguato adj. adequate, fit, fair.
adem'piere⁵⁵ see adempire.⁴⁴
adempimento m. fulfillment; discharge.
adempire vt.⁵⁵ to accomplish; to fulfill; **adempirsi** vr. to come true.
adempiuto adj. fulfilled, pp. of adempire.
adeno'idi f. pl. (med.) adenoids.
adepto m. initiate; affiliate.
aderente m. supporter. adj. adherent; close-fitting.
aderenza f. adherence; (med.) adhesion; (pl.) connections, "pull."
aderire vi. to adhere; to accede (to).
adescamento m. enticement.
adescare vt. to bait, decoy, entice.
adesione f. adhesion.
adesivo adj. adhesive.
adesso adv. now, at present; nowadays: per —, for the moment.
adiacente adj. adjacent, adjoining.
adiacenze f. pl. neighborhood.
adianto m. (bot.) maidenhair.
adibire vt. to adhibit; to set apart; to appropriate; to use (as, for).
a'dipe m. fat.
adiposità f. fatness.
adiposo adj. adipose, fat.
adirarsi vr. to get angry.
adirato adj. angry, mad.
adire vt. to apply to (court): — le vie legali, to take legal steps, to sue.
a'dito m. entrance; cause.
adocchiare vt. to spot; to eye; to glimpse.
adolescente m., f., adj. adolescent.
adolescenza f. adolescence.
adombrare vt. to shadow; to conceal; to outline; **adombrarsi** vr. to bridle; to take umbrage.
Adone m. pr. Adonis.
adontarsi vr. to take offense.
adoperare, adoprare vt. to use, employ; **adoperarsi** vr. to endeavor (to), strive (to).
adora'bile adj. adorable, charming.
adorare vt. to worship, adore.
adorato adj. adored, beloved.
adoratore m. worshipper.
adorazione f. adoration, worship.
adornare vt. to adorn; **adornarsi** vr. to adorn oneself.
adorno adj. adorned, fine, lovely.
adóttante m. adopter.

adottare vt. to adopt.
adottivo adj. adoptive; adopted.
adozione f. adoption.
Adria'tico m., adj. Adriatic.
adulare vt. to flatter, cajole.
adulatore m. flatterer.
adulatrice f. flatteress.
adula'rio adj. flattering.
adulazione f. flattery.
adul'tera f. adulteress.
adulterare vt. to adulterate.
adulterazione f. adulteration.
adulterino adj. adulterine.
adulte'rio m. adultery.
adul'tero m. adulterer. adj. adulterous.
adulto m. adult. adj. grown up.
adunanza f. meeting.
adunare vt. to assemble; **adunarsi** vr. to gather, meet.
adunata f. meeting, rally; (mil.) muster: segnale d' —, bugle call.
adunco adj. hooked, crooked.
adunghiare vt. to claw.
adusto adj. adust, tanned.
aerare vt. to air, ventilate.
aerato adj. aired, ventilated.
aerazione f. aeration, airing.
ae'reo m. aircraft; aerial. adj. aerial.
aerodina'mico adj. aerodynamic; streamlined.
aero'dromo m. airfield.
aero'grafo m. airbrush.
aerolito m. aerolite, aerolith.
aerologi'a f. aerology.
aerometri'a f. aerometry.
aero'metro m. aerometer.
aeromezzo m., **aeromo'bile.** m. aircraft.
aeromodello m. model plane.
aerona'uta m. aeronaut.
aerona'utica f. aeronautics, aviation.
aerona'utico adj. aeronautic, flying.
aeronave f. airship.
aeroplano m. airplane.
aeroporto, aeroscalo m. airport.
aerorazzo m. rocket ship.
aerosilurante m. torpedo plane.
aerosta'tico adj. aerostatic.
aero'stato m. aerostat.
aerotaxi m. taxiplane.
aeroterapi'a f. aerotherapeutics.
afa f. sultriness.
affa'bile adj. affable, friendly.
affabilità f. affability, friendliness.
affaccendarsi vr. to bustle about; to busy oneself (with); to fuss.
affaccendato adj. busy.
affacciare vt. to present at a window; to allege: — un dubbio, to raise a doubt; **affacciarsi** vr. to show oneself at (the window, etc.); to lean out of; to look out (of); to look (over).
affamare vt. to starve.
affamato m. starveling. adj. starved; greedy, eager (for).

affamatore *m*. starver.

affannare *vt*. to worry, pester; affannarsi *vr*. to bustle; to fuss; to worry.

affannato *adj*. panting; uneasy.

affanno *m*. breathlessness; uneasiness; sorrow.

affannosamente *adv*. anxiously; pantingly; hurriedly.

affannoso *adj*. anxious; hurried; difficult.

affrac'cio *m*. mess.

affare *m*. business, bargain; affair; matter.

affarismo *m*. mercantilism.

affarista *m*. speculator.

affarone *m*. excellent bargain.

affascinante *adj*. charming.

affascinare *vt*. to charm.

affascinatore *m*., affascinatrice *f*. bewitcher.

affastellare *vt*. to bundle; to heap up.

affaticare *vt*., affaticarsi *vr*. to weary.

affaticato *adj*. weary, exhausted.

affatto *adv*. entirely, quite: niente —, by no means, not at all.

affatturare *vt*. to bewitch.

affermare *vt*. to assert; to affirm; affermarsi *vr*. to make a reputation; to prove oneself.

affermativa *f*. affirmative.

affermativamente *adv*. affirmatively.

affermativo *adj*. affirmative.

affermazione *f*. assertion, statement; success.

afferrare *vt*. to grasp; afferrarsi *vr*. to cling (to).

affettare *vt*. to slice; to affect.

affettatamente *adv*. affectedly.

affettato *adj*. sliced; affected.

affettazione *f*. affectation.

affettivo *adj*. affective.

affetto *m*. affection, love.

affetto *adj*. affected; afflicted (with), suffering (from).

affettuosamente *adv*. affectionately.

affettuosità *f*. affectionateness.

affettuoso *adj*. affectionate, loving: affettuosi saluti da, love from.

affezionarsi *vr*. to grow fond (of).

affezionato *adj*. fond (of), devoted.

affezione *f*. affection, love; devotion; disease.

affiancare *vt*. affiancarsi *vr*. to flank.

afflatamento *m*. harmony.

affiatarsi *vr*. to hit it off, get together.

affiatato *adj*. well-integrated.

affibbiare *vt*. to buckle, fasten; to shift (on); to deal.

affidamento *m*. confidence, trust; assurance; guaranty: dare —, to be reliable; fare — su, to trust; to rely upon.

affidare *vt*. to commit, entrust (with);

affidarsi *vr*. to trust (to), depend (on).

affievolire *vt*., affievolirsi *vr*. to weaken.

affig'gere *vt*.[48] to affix, post up: — lo sguardo su, to stare at.

affilare *vt*. to whet, sharpen, strop; affilarsi *vr*. to thin.

affilata *f*. sharpening, whetting.

affilatura *f*. stropping,

affiliare *vt*., affiliarsi *vr*. to affiliate.

affiliato *m*. affiliate.

affiliazione *f*. affiliation.

affinare *vt*., affinarsi *vr*. to thin; to sharpen; to refine; to improve.

affinchè *conj*. that, so that, in order that: — non, lest.

affine *m*. relative.

affinità *f*. kinship; affinity.

affiochire *vt*., *vi*.; affiochirsi *vr*. to weaken, dim.

affioramento *m*. outcrop; emergence.

affiorare *vi*. to surface; to outcrop.

affissare *vt*. to fix; to affix.

affissione *f*. posting.

affisso *m*. poster, bill; frame (of a door); sash (of a window); (gramm.) affix; *adj*. fastened, affixed. *pp*. of affiggere.

affitta'bile *adj*. rentable.

affittaca'mere *m*., *f*. landlord (*m*.), landlady (*f*.).

affittanza *f*. rent; lease.

affittare *vt*. (dare in affitto) to let; (prendere in affitto) to rent; to hire.

affitto *m*. lease; rent: dare in —, to let, hire out; prendere in —, to rent; to hire.

affittua'rio *m*. tenant, renter.

affiato *m*. breath; afflatus.

affliggente *adj*. grievous.

afflig'gere *vt*.[48] to afflict; affliggersi *vr*. to grieve (over, for).

afflitto *adj*. afflicted (with); grieved *pp*. of affliggere.

afflizione *f*. affliction, distress.

afflosciarsi *vr*. to sag; to slouch.

affloscire *vt*., afflosicirsi *vr*. to soften.

affluente *m*. affluent.

affluenza *f*. concourse, affluence.

affluire *vi*. to flock (to), flow (to); to pour (in o).

afflusso *m*. afflux; concourse.

affogamento *m*.drowning, smothering.

affogare *vt*. to drown, smother; to poach (eggs); *vi*. to drown.

affollamento *m*. crowding; crowd.

affollare *vt*., affollarsi *vr*. to crowd, throng.

affondamento *m*. sinking.

affondare *vt*., *vi*. to sink, submerge; (naut.) to drop anchor; affondarsi *vr*. to sink.

affondatore *m*. sinker.

afforcare *vi.*, afforcarsi *vr.* to moor with two anchors.

affossamento *m.* ditching.

affossare *vt.* to ditch, dig; affossarsi *vr.* to sink.

affrancare *vt.* to free, affranchise; to stamp; affrancarsi *vr.* to free oneself; to take heart.

affrancatura *f.* postage stamp.

affranto *adj.* weary, broken.

affratellamento *m.* fraternization.

affratellare *vt.*, affratellarsi *vr.* to fraternize; to unite, join.

affrescare *vt.* to paint a fresco.

affresco *m.* fresco (*pl.* frescoes).

affrettare *vt.*, affrettarsi *vr.* to hasten, hurry, speed.

affrettatamente *adv.* hastily.

affrettato *adj.* hasty, hurried.

affrontare *vt.* to face; affrontarsi *vr.* to meet; to come to blows.

affronto *m.* affront, insult.

affumicamento *m.* smoking; curing.

affumicare *vt.* to smoke, soot; to fumigate; to cure (*as meat, etc.*).

affusolare *vt.* to taper.

affusolato *adj.* tapering, slender.

affusto *m.* (*artill.*) carriage.

a'fono *adj.* aphonic; voiceless.

aforisma *m.* aphorism.

afoso *adj.* sultry.

africano *m.*, *adj.* African.

afrodis'iaco *adj.*, *m.* aphrodisiac.

afta *f.* aphta (*pl.* aphtae).

a'gape *f.* agape (*pl.* agapae).

a'gata *f.* agate.

agenda *f.* memorandum book.

agente *m.* agent, broker; detective, policeman.

agenzi'a *f.* agency, branch.

agevolare *vt.* to facilitate.

agevolazione *f.* facility.

age'vole *adj.* facile, easy.

agevolezza *f.* facileness.

agevolmente *adv.* easily.

agganciare *vt.* to hook, clasp; to fasten; (*rail.*) to couple.

agget'gio *m.* trifle; gadget; device.

aggettivo *adj.* adjective.

agghiacciare *vt.* to freeze, chill; (*fig.*) to horrify; agghiacciarsi *vr.* to freeze, be horrified.

agghindare *vt.* to array; agghindarsi *vr.* to array oneself, dress up.

ag'gio *m.* agio, premium.

aggiogare *vt.* to yoke.

aggiornamento *m.* adjournment; bringing up-to-date.

aggiornare *vt.* to adjourn; to bring up-to-date; aggiornarsi *vr.* to keep oneself posted, modernize.

aggiotag'gio *m.* dealings in exchange.

aggiramento *m.* cheat; (*mil.*) out-flanking.

aggirare *vt.* to cheat, swindle; (*mil.*) to outflank; aggirarsi *vr.* to rove, wander; to deal (*with*): il prezzo si aggira sulle mille lire, the price is about a thousand lire.

aggiudicare *vt.* to adjudge, award; aggiudicarsi *vr.* to win.

aggiun'gere *vt.* to add; aggiungersi *vr.* to join, be added.

aggiunta *f.* addition; eking piece.

aggiuntare *vt.* to join.

aggiuntivo *adj.* additional.

aggiunto *m.* assistant; (*gramm.*) epithet, adjective. *adj.* added. *pp.* of aggiungere.

aggiustare *vt.* to adjust, fit; to settle; to mend; aggiustarsi *vr.* to make oneself comfortable; to adapt oneself; to adorn oneself.

aggiustatore *m.* mender.

aggiustatura *f.* mending.

agglomerare *vt.*, agglomerarsi *vr.* to agglomerate.

agglomerato *m.* agglomerate. *adj.* agglomerated; thick.

agglomerazione *f.* agglomeration.

agglutinare *vt.*, agglutinarsi *vr.*, to agglutinate.

aggobbire *vt.* to become hunchbacked.

aggomitolare *vt.*, aggomitolarsi *vr.* to coil; to cuddle.

aggradare *vi.* to like: non mi aggrada, I don't like it.

aggraffare *vt.* to grab.

aggranchire *vt.* to benumb.

aggrapparsi *vr.* to cling (to).

aggravamento *m.* aggravation.

aggravante *f.* aggravating circumstance. *adj.* aggravating.

aggravare *vt.* to make worse; aggravarsi *vr.* to grow worse.

aggra'vio *m.* burden.

aggraziare *vt.* to embellish; aggraziarsi *vr.* to grow pretty; to ingratiate oneself (*with*).

aggraziato *adj.* graceful.

aggredire *vt.* to attack, assault.

aggregare *vt.* to aggregate; aggregarsi *vr.* to join.

aggressione *f.* aggression, assault.

aggressività *f.* aggressiveness.

aggressivo *adj.* aggressive.

aggressore *m.* aggressor, assaulter.

aggricciare *vt.*, aggricciarsi *vr.* to freeze; to stiffen.

aggrinzare *vt.*, aggrinzarsi *vr.* to wrinkle.

aggrottare *vt.* to contract, pucker; (*agr.*) to embank: — le sopracciglia, to frown.

aggrovigliare *vt.* to entangle; aggrovigliarsi *vr.* to get entangled.

aggrumare *vi.*, aggrumarsi *vr.* to clot, curdle.

aggruppare vt., **aggrupparsi** vr. to group, assemble.

agguagliare vt. to level, equalize; to compare.

agguantare vt. to catch.

agguato m. ambush.

agguerrire vt. to train, inure to war; **agguerrirsi** vr. to get trained; to set up defenses.

agiatamente adv. comfortably.

agiatezza f. prosperity, wealth: nell'—, on easy street.

agiato adj. well-off, well-to-do.

a'gile adj. agile, nimble.

agilità f. agility, nimbleness.

agilmente adv. agilely, nimbly.

a'gio m. ease, comfort; time: non trovarsi a proprio —, to be ill at ease.

agire vi. to act; to behave; to work.

agitare vt. to toss, agitate; to stir; to wave; **agitarsi** vr. to toss; to get excited; to agitate (for).

agitato adj. agitated, restless.

agitatore m. agitator.

agitazione f. agitation; disturbance; restlessness.

agli comp. prep. to the, see a prep.

aglia'ceo adj. garlicky.

a'glio m. garlic: spicchio d'—, clove of garlic.

agnellino m. lambkin.

agnello m. lamb.

agnizione f. recognition.

agno'stico adj. agnostic.

ago m. needle; (rail.) point.

agognare vt. to covet.

agonali m. pl. agones.

agone m. agon; combat, fight.

agoni'a f. death struggle; agony, anguish: in —, at the point of death.

agoni'stico adj. agonistical.

agonizzante adj. dying.

agonizzare vi. to be dying.

agorafobi'a f. agoraphobia.

agora'io m. needlecase.

agosto m. August.

agra'ria f. agronomics.

agra'rio m. landowner. adj. agrarian.

agreste adj. agrestic, rural.

agretto adj. sourish.

agrezza f. sourness.

agri'colo adj. agricultural.

agricoltore m. farmer.

agricoltura f. agriculture.

agrifo'glio m. holly.

agrimensore m. land surveyor.

agrimensura f. land surveying.

agro (1) m. land, field.

agro (2) m. sourness. adj. sour.

agrodolce adj. bittersweet.

agronomi'a f. agronomy.

agro'nomo m. agronomist.

agrume m. citrus fruit.

agucchiare vi. to stitch.

agu'glia f. spire; magnetic needle.

aguzzare vt. to sharpen.

aguzzino m. jailer; slave driver; torturer.

aguzzo adj. sharp, acuminate.

ah! interj. ah!, aha!

ahi! interj. ouch!, oh!

ahimè! interj. alas!

ai comp. prep. to the, see a prep.

a'ia (1) f. yard; threshing floor: menare il can per l'—, to beat about the bush.

a'ia (2) f. governess.

Aia (L') f. The Hague.

a'io m. tutor, preceptor.

ai're m. swing, start; course.

airone m. heron.

aitante adj. sturdy, stalwart.

aiuola f. flower bed.

aiutante m. assistant: — di campo, aide-de-camp.

aiutare vt. to help; **aiutarsi** vr. to make shift; to help one another.

aiuto m. help, aid, assistance.

aizzare vt. to goad.

al comp. prep. to the, see a prep.

ala f. wing: abbassare le ali, to come down a peg.

alabarda f. halberd.

alabardiere m. halberdier.

alabastro m. alabaster.

a'lacre adj. alacritous; active.

alacrità f. alacrity.

alag'gio m. haulage, towage: scalo d'—, slip.

alamaro m. loop; gimp.

alambicco m. alembic.

alano m. boarhound, mastiff.

alare (1) m. andiron.

alare (2) vt. to haul, tow. [span.

alare (3) adj. wing: apertura —, wing

alato adj. winged; lofty.

alba f. dawn, daybreak.

albagi'a f. haughtiness, pride.

albanese m., adj. Albanian.

al'batro m. (bot.) arbutus; (ornith.) albatross.

albeggiamento m. dawning.

albeggiare vi. to dawn.

alberare vt. to plant trees; (naut.) to mast.

alberato adj. treed, tree-bordered.

alberatura f. trees; (naut.) masting.

albergare vt., vi. to lodge; to shelter.

albergatore m. hotelkeeper.

alberghiero adj. hotel: industria alberghiera, hotel trade.

albergo m. hotel.

al'bero m. tree; (mach.) shaft; (naut.) mast: — genealogico, family tree.

albicocca f. apricot.

albicocco m. apricot tree.

albina f. albiness.

albino m. albino. adj. whitish.

albo m. album.

albore m. dawn; whiteness; (pl.) beginning.

albume m. albumen.

albumina f. albumin.

al'cali m. alkali (pl. alkalies).

alcalino adj. alkaline.

alcalo'ide m. alkaloid.

alce f. (zool.) moose, elk.

alchimi'a f. alchemy.

alchimista m. alchemist.

alcione m. halcyon.

al'cole, alcool m. alcohol: — denaturato, methylated spirit.

alcoo'lico adj. alcoholic.

alcoolismo m. alcoholism.

alcoolizzato m. dipsomaniac.

alcova f. alcove.

alcunchè pron. anything.

alcuno adj. any, some, no. pron. anyone, someone, none, nobody, anything, a few, something, nothing.

a'lea f. chance, hazard, risk.

Aleardi, Aleardo, Italian poet and patriot (1812–1878).

aleato'rio adj. aleatory, precarious

aleggiare vi. to flutter; to linger; to hover.

alerone m. (aeron.) aileron.

alesag'gio m. reaming.

alesare vt. to bore, ream.

alesatrice f. reamer.

Alessan'dria d'Egitto f. Alexandria (Egypt).

aletta f. fin; lug.

alettone m. (aeron.) aileron.

alfa (1) f. alpha: dall'— all'omega, from A to Z.

alfa (2) f. (bot.) esparto grass.

alfabeticamente adv. alphabetically.

alfabe'tico adj. alphabetical.

alfabeto m. alphabet.

alfiere m. ensign, standard-bearer; bishop (at chess).

Alfieri, Vittorio, Italian dramatist (1749–1803).

alfine adv. in the end, finally, at last; after all.

alga f. (bot.) seaweed.

al'gebra f. algebra.

alge'brico adj. algebraical.

Algeri f. Algiers.

Algeri'a f. Algeria.

Algerino m., adj. Algerian.

aliante m. (aeron.) glider.

a'libi m. alibi.

alice f. anchovy.

aliena'bile adj. alienable.

alienabilità f. alienability.

alienare vt., **alienarsi** vr. to alienate.

alienato m. madman.

alienazione f. alienation, madness.

alienista m. alienist.

alieno adj. alien; loath, averse (to).

alimentare (1) adj. alimentary.

alimentare (2) vt. to feed; to fuel; to aliment; to keep up; **alimentarsi** vr. to feed (on).

alimentari m. pl. foodstuff.

alimenta'rio adj. alimentary: assegno —, alimony.

alimentatore m. feeder.

alimentazione f. feeding; diet.

alimento m. aliment, food; (pl.) alimony.

ali'nea m. section, paragraph.

ali'quota f. quota, share.

aliscafo m hydrofoil boat.

aliseo m. trade wind.

alitare vi. to breathe; to blow.

a'lito m. breath.

alla comp. prep. to the, see a prep.

allacciamento m. linking.

allacciare vt. to lace; to connect; to tie; to link.

allacciatura f. lacing, noose.

allagamento m. flood.

allagare vt. to flood.

allampanare vi. to thin.

allampanato adj. scraggy, thin.

allargamento m. broadening.

allargare vt. to broaden; to spread out; to open; **allargarsi** vr. to widen, spread.

allarmante adj. alarming, startling.

allarmare vt. to alarm; to startle; **allarmarsi** vr. to be alarmed; to worry.

allarme m. alarm, warning: cessato—, all clear.

allarmista m. alarmist.

allascare vt., vi. (naut.) to ease.

allato, a lato adv. beside; near.

allattamento m. nursing.

allattare vt. to nurse.

alle comp. prep. to the, see a prep.

alleanza f. alliance.

allearsi vr. to ally (oneself); to join forces.

alleato m. ally. adj. allied.

allegare (1) vt. to allege; to enclose.

allegare (2) vt. to set (teeth) on edge.

allegato m. enclosure.

alleggerimento m. lightening.

alleggerire vt. to lighten; to relieve, mitigate; **alleggerirsi** vr. to relieve oneself; to put on lighter clothes.

allegori'a f. allegory.

allego'rico adj. allegorical.

allegramente adv. cheerfully.

allegri'a f. merrymaking; cheerfulness, mirth.

allegro adj. cheerful, merry, gay.

allelu'ia m. halleluiah.

allenamento m. training.

allenare vt., **allenarsi** vr. to train, coach.

allenatore *m.* trainer, coach.

allentare *vt.*, **allentarsi** *vr.* to slacken, loosen.

allergi'a *f.* allergy.

aller'gico *adj.* allergic.

allessare *vt.* to boil.

allesso *m.* boiled meat. *adj.* boiled.

allestimento *m.* preparation; (*naut.*) fitting out; (*theat.*) production.

allestire *vt.* to set, prepare, get up; (*naut.*) to fit out; (*theat.*) to produce.

allettamento *m.* allurement.

allettante *adj.* alluring.

allettare *vt.*, *vi.* to allure; to attract.

allevamento *m.* breeding; rearing.

allevare *vt.* to rear; to breed; to nurse; to bring up.

allevatore *m.* breeder.

alleviamento *m.* alleviation.

alleviare *vt.* to alleviate.

allibire *vi.* to startle, be astonished.

allietare *vt.* to cheer; **allietarsi** *vr.* to cheer up, rejoice.

allievo *m.* pupil, disciple: — **ufficiale**, cadet.

alligatore *m.* alligator.

allignare *vi.* to live; to flourish.

allineamento *m.* alignment.

allineare *vt.*, **allinearsi** *vr.* to align, range, dress.

allitterazione *f.* alliteration.

allo *comp. prep.* to the, *see* a *prep.*

allocco *m.* owl; simpleton, fool.

allocuzione *f.* address.

allo'dio *m.* allodium.

allo'dola *f.* skylark.

allogare *vt.* to settle; to rent; to marry.

allo'geno *m.*, *adj.* alien.

alloggiamento *m.* lodging, quarters.

alloggiare *vt.* to put up; *vi.* to lodge, stay, live.

allog'gio *m.* lodging, quarters.

allontanamento *m.* removal; dismissal; swerving.

allontanare *vt.* to remove; to send away, dismiss; to estrange; **allontanarsi** *vr.* to get away, leave; to swerve.

allora *adv.* then, at that time, in that case: — —, just then; **di qui** —, by that time; **fino** —, up to then; **e** —? well?, what then?

allorchè *adv.* when.

alloro *m.* (*bot.*) laurel.

allorquando *adv.* when.

al'luce *m.* hallux, great toe.

allucinare *vt.* to hallucinate; to dazzle.

allucinazione *f.* hallucination.

allu'dere *vi.°* to hint (*at*), allude (*to*).

allume *m.* alum.

allumina *f.* alumina.

allumi'nio *m.* aluminum.

allungamento *m.* lengthening.

allungare *vt.* to lengthen; to hand; to dilute: — **la mano**, to reach; — **le braccia**, to stretch one's arms; **allungarsi** *vr.* to lengthen, stretch oneself out; to grow tall.

allungatura *f.* lengthening; eking piece.

allusione *f.* allusion, hint.

allusivo *adj.* allusive.

alluso *pp. of* **alludere**.

alluvionale *adj.* alluvial.

alluvione *f.* alluvion, flood.

almanaccare *vi.* to fancy, muse.

almanacco *m.* almanac.

almeno *conj.* at least.

alno *m.* (*bot.*) alder.

a'loe *m.* aloe.

alone *m.* halo.

al'paca *f.* alpaca.

alpacca *f.* Britannia metal.

alpe *f.* alp; (*pl.*) **le Alpi**, the Alps mountains.

alpestre *adj.* alpine.

alpigiano *m.* mountaineer.

alpinismo *m.* alpinism, mountaineering.

alpinista *m.* alpinist, mountaineer.

alpino *adj.* alpine.

alquanto *adj.* some; (*pl.*) several. *adv.* somewhat, to some extent; rather; a little. *pron.* some; (*pl.*) a good many.

alsaziano *m.*, *adj.* Alsatian.

alt *interj.* halt.

altalena *f.* swing; seesaw; alternation.

altalenare *vi.* to seesaw, swing.

altamente *adv.* highly; greatly.

altana *f.* belvedere.

altare *m.* altar.

altarini *m. pl. in the phrase:* **scoprire gli** —, to let the cat out of the bag.

altea *f.* (*bot.*) althea.

altera'bile *adj.* alterable.

alterabilità *f.* alterableness.

alteramente *adv.* haughtily.

alterare *vt.* to alter; to forge; to distort, misrepresent; **alterarsi** *vr.* to alter, get angry.

alterato *adj.* altered; forged; drunk.

alterazione *f.* alteration; anger.

altercare *vi.* to quarrel.

alterco *m.* quarrel, fight.

alteri'gia *f.* haughtiness.

alternamente *adv.* alternately.

alternare *vt.*, **alternarsi** *vr.* to alternate.

alternativa *f.* alternation; alternative.

alternato *adj.* alternate: **corrente alternata**, alternating current.

alternatore *m.* alternator.

alternazione *f.* alternation.

alterno *adj.* alternate, reciprocal.

altero *adj.* proud, dignified.

altezza *f.* height; width; depth; highness; loftiness.

altezzoso adj. haughty.

altic'cio adj. tipsy.

altimetri'a f. altimetry.

alti'metro m. altimeter.

altipiano m. plateau.

altisonante adj. high-sounding.

altis'simo adj. sup. very high: **l'Altissimo**, the Most High.

altitu'dine f. altitude.

alto m. height, top: **gli alti e bassi della vita**, the ups and downs of life; **guardare qualcuno dall'—**, to look down on someone. adj. high, tall; loud, deep: **la Camera Alta**, the Upper House; **l'Alta Italia**, Northern Italy. adv. high; aloud.

altolocato adj. lofty: **un uomo —**, a bigwig.

altoparlante m. loudspeaker.

altresì adv. also, too; further.

altrettanto adj., pron. as much; (pl.) as many; so much; (pl.) so many. adv. as much, so much; equally, the same.

altri pron. sing. another person, somebody else.

altrieri (l') m., adv. the day before yesterday.

altrimenti adv. otherwise, else.

altro adj. other, another, else, more; next; further; previous: **dell'—vino**, some more wine; **quest'altra settimana**, next week. pron. indef. other, another, else, more: **un giorno o l'—**, some day or other; **non te ne posso dare dell'—**, I can't give you any more; **l'uno e l'—**, both; **nè l'uno nè l'—**, neither; **l'uno o l'—**, either; **l'un l'—**, each other; **fra l'—**, among other things, by the way; **senz'altro!**, certainly!; **tutt'altro!**, on the contrary!

altronde, see **d'altronde**.

altrove adv. elsewhere.

altrui pron. indef. sing. another's (pl.) other people's.

altruismo m. unselfishness, altruism.

altruista adj. unselfish.

altruistico adj. altruistic.

altura f. mound, height.

alunno m., **alunna** f. pupil.

alveare m. hive, beehive.

al'veo m. bed, river bed.

alve'olo m. alveolus (pl. alveoli).

alza'ia f. hawser; towpath.

alzare vt. to raise, lift; to heave, hoist: **— le spalle**, to shrug; **— il gomito**, to drink too much; **— le carte**, to cut cards; **alzarsi** vr. to rise, get up; to lift.

alzata f. raising, lifting: **— di terra**, embankment; **— d'ingegno**, brainstorm.

alzato adj. risen; raised; up.

ama'bile adj. amiable; sweetish.

amabilità f. amiability.

amabilmente adv. amiably.

amaca f. hammock.

amal'gama m. amalgam; mixture, blend.

amalgamare vt. to amalgamate, blend.

amalgamazione f. amalgamation.

amante m. lover; f. mistress; adj. fond.

amanuense m. clerk.

amaramente adv. bitterly.

amaranto m. amaranth.

amarasca f. morello.

amare vt., vi. to love; to be in love (with); to like, be fond of: **amarsi reciprocamente**, to love each other.

amareggiare vt. to embitter, grieve; **amareggiarsi** vr. to fret, worry, grieve.

amarena f. amarelle.

amarezza f. bitterness.

amarilli f. (bot.) amaryllis.

amaro m. bitter; bitters. adj. bitter.

amaro'gnolo adj. bitterish.

amarra f. (naut.) hawser.

amarrare vi. to moor.

amato m. **amata** f. sweetheart. adj. beloved.

amatore m. lover; amateur.

amaz'zone f. horsewoman; (myth.) Amazon.

amba'scia f. pant; sorrow.

ambasciata f. embassy; errand, message.

ambasciatore m. ambassador.

ambasciatrice f. ambassadress.

ambedue adj., pron. both.

ambidestro m., adj. ambidexter.

ambientare vt. to accustom; **ambientarsi** vr. to get accustomed.

ambiente m. ambient air; sphere; surroundings, environment; room.

ambiguità f. ambiguity.

ambiguo adj. ambiguous.

am'bio m. amble.

ambire vt. to covet; vi. to aspire (to, after).

am'bito m. sphere; bounds.

ambizione f. ambition.

ambizioso adj. ambitious.

ambo adj., pron. both.

ambra f. amber.

ambrare vt. to amber.

ambrato adj. amber.

ambulacro m. lobby.

ambulante adj. itinerant: **venditore —**, peddler.

ambulanza f. ambulance; first-aid station; (mil.) field hospital.

ambulare vi. to ambulate.

ambulato'rio m. ambulatory; dispensary.

ameba f. amoeba.

amenità *f.* amenity, pleasantness; pleasantry.

ameno *adj.* pleasant; jocular.

americano *m.*, *adj.* American.

americanismo *m.* Americanism.

americanizzare *vt.* to Americanize.

ametista *f.* amethyst.

amianto *m.* asbestos.

amica *f.* friend, lady friend, girl friend.

amichevole *adj.* friendly.

Amicis, Edmondo de, Italian traveler and writer, *Cuore* (1846–1908).

amici'zia *f.* friendship: stringere —, to make friends.

amico *m.* friend. *adj.* friendly.

amicone *m.* chum, pal, crony.

amida'ceo *adj.* starchy.

a'mido *m.* starch.

ammaccare *vt.* to bruise, contuse; to batter.

ammaccatura *f.* bruise.

ammaestramento *m.* instruction, teaching, training; lesson.

ammaestrare *vt.* to instruct, teach, train, coach.

ammainare *vt.* to lower.

ammalarsi *vr.* to fall ill.

ammalato *m.* patient, invalid. *adj.* ill, sick.

ammaliare *vt.* to bewitch.

ammaliatore *m.* enchanter. ammaliatrice, *f.* enchantress.

ammanco *m.* leakage, deficit.

ammanettare *vt.* to handcuff.

ammannire *vt.* to dish up.

ammansire *vt.* to tame; to appease; to mollify; ammansirsi *vr.* to become tamed; to sober.

ammantare *vt.* to cloak; ammantarsi *vr.* to mantle oneself, wrap oneself up (*in*).

ammarare *vi.* to alight.

ammassare *vt.* to amass, pile up; ammassarsi *vr.* to gather, pile up.

ammasso *m.* heap, pile, stack.

ammattimento *m.* nuisance.

ammattire *vi.* to go mad: far —, to drive mad.

ammattonato *m.* tile floor.

ammazzare *vt.* to kill; to murder; ammazzarsi *vr.* to commit suicide; to be killed.

ammazzasette *m.* swashbuckler.

ammazzato'io *m.* shambles.

ammenda *f.* amends (*pl.*); fine.

ammenni'colo *m.* adminicle; artifice; quibble; gewgaw.

ammesso *pp. of* ammettere admitted; allowed: — che, supposing that.

ammet'tere *vt.*[16] to admit; to let in; to allow; to acknowledge.

ammezzato *m.* mezzanine.

ammiccare *vi.* to wink.

amministrare *vt.* to handle, manage, administer.

amministrativo *adj.* administrative.

amministratore *m.* manager, administrator; director: — delegato, managing director.

amministrazione *f.* management, administration: cattiva —, mismanagement; consiglio d'—, board of directors.

ammiragliato *m.* admiralty.

ammira'glio *m.* admiral.

ammirare *vt.* to admire.

ammiratore *m.*, ammiratrice *f.* admirer; suitor, wooer; fan.

ammirazione *f.* admiration.

ammissi'bile *adj.* permissible.

ammissione *f.* admission.

ammobiliare *vt.* to furnish.

ammodo *adj.* mannerly, respectable, nice. *adv.* properly.

ammogliarsi *vr.* to get married (*of a man*).

ammogliato *adj.* married (*of a man*).

ammollire *vt.*, ammollirsi *vr.* to soften; to weaken.

ammoni'aca *f.* ammonia.

ammoniacale *adj.* ammoniacal.

ammonimento *m.* warning.

ammo'nio *m.* ammonium.

ammonire *vt.* to warn, admonish.

ammonizione *f.* warning.

ammontare *m.* amount, sum. *vi.* to amount.

ammonticchiare *vt.* to heap.

ammorbare *vt.* to taint.   [soften.

ammorbidire *vt.*, ammorbidirsi *vr.* to

ammortamento *m.* amortization: fondo d'—, sinking fund.

ammortizzare *vt.* to amortize.

ammortizzatore *m.* shock absorber.

ammosciare *vi.*, ammosciarsi *vr.* to sag; to get flabby.

ammucchiare *vt.*, ammucchiarsi *vr.* to heap up.

ammuffire *vi.* to mold.

ammutinamento *m.* mutiny.

ammutinare *vt.* to stir up; ammutinarsi *vr.* to mutiny.

ammutinato *m.* mutineer.

ammutolire *vt.* to strike dumb. *vi.* to become dumb; to be dumbfounded.

amnesi'a *f.* amnesia.

amnisti'a *f.* amnesty.

amnistiare *vt.* to grant amnesty to.

amo *m.* hook: abboccare l'—, to take the bait.

amorale *adj.* amoral, unmoral.

amoralità *f.* amorality.

amore *m.* love, fondness, sake: un — di bambino, a charming baby; per — o per forza, by hook or by crook.

amoreggiare *vi.* to flirt.

amore'vole *adj.* loving, affectionate.

amorfo adj. amorphous.

amorosa f. sweetheart; actress playing lover's part.

amoroso m. sweetheart; actor playing lover's part. adj. loving.

amperag'gio m. amperage.

ampero'metro m. ammeter.

ampiamente adv. widely.

ampiezza f. wideness, width, ampleness.

am'pio adj. wide, ample; roomy.

amplesso m. embrace, hug.

ampliamento m. amplification.

ampliare vt., **ampliarsi** vr. to widen; to increase.

amplificare vt. to amplify, extend; to exaggerate.

amplificatore m. amplifier; exaggerator.

amplificazione f. amplification.

ampolla f. cruet; ampulla.

ampolliera f. cruet stand.

ampollosamente adv. pompously.

ampollosità f. pompousness.

ampolloso adj. turgid; pompous.

amputare vt. to amputate.

amputazione f. amputation.

amuleto m. amulet.

a'nace m. anise; aniseed.

anacoreta m. anchorite, hermit.

anacronismo m. anachronism.

ana'grafe f. register of births, deaths and marriages, Hall of Records.

anagramma m. anagram.

analco'lico adj. nonalcoholic: bevande analcoliche, soft drinks.

anale adj. anal.

analfabeta m., adj. illiterate.

analfabetismo m. illiteracy.

analge'sico m., adj. analgesic.

ana'lisi f. test; analysis (pl. analyses): — grammaticale, parsing; — del sangue, blood test.

anali'tico adj. analytical.

analizzare vt. to analyze, test.

analogi'a f. analogy.

ana'logo adj. analogous.

ananasso m. pineapple.

anarchi'a f. anarchy; anarchism.

anar'chico m. anarchist. adj. anarchical.

anastigma'tico adj. anastigmatic.

anasto'mosi f. anastomosis.

anatema m. anathema, curse.

anatomi'a f. anatomy.

anato'mico adj. anatomical.

a'natra f. duck; drake.

anatroc'colo m. duckling.

anca f. hip, haunch.

ancella f. maid, maidservant.

anche adv., conj. also, too, even.

anchilosato adj. ankylosed.

anchilosi f. ankylosis.

an'cora f. anchor.

ancóra adv. again; still; more; longer; even: — meglio, still better; — no, non —, not yet; ne vuoi —?, do you wish any more?.

ancorag'gio m. anchorage.

ancorare vt., **ancorarsi** vr. to anchor.

ancorchè conj. though.

ancorotto m. grapnel, kedge.

andamento m. course, bent, trend.

andante m. (mus.) andante. adj. cheap.

andare m. going; gait: a lungo —, in the long run.

andare vi. to go; to run, work; to sell; to like; to have to: ciò andava fatto, it had to be done; questo mi va, I like this; ne va del nostro onore, our honor is at stake; — a male, to deteriorate; andarsene, to go away.

andata f. going; departure: biglietto d'—, single ticket; biglietto d'— e ritorno, return ticket.

andato adj., pp. gone: il tempo —, the past. pp. of andare.

andatura f. gait; pace, speed.

andazzo m. practice, trend (of things).

andirivieni m. coming and going; bustle.

an'dito m. passage; hall.

androne m. lobby.

aned'doto m. anecdote.

anelare vt., vi. to pant; to yearn (for).

ane'lito m. breath; panting; yearning.

anellino m. ringlet.

anello m. ring; curl; link; bow (of a key); loop (of rope, etc.).

anemi'a f. anemia.

ane'mico adj. anemic.

anemo'metro m. anemometer.

ane'mone m. anemone.

anestesi'a f. anesthesia.

aneste'tico m., adj. anesthetic.

anestetizzare vt. to anesthetize.

aneurisma m. aneurysm.

anfi'bio m., adj. amphibious, amphibian.

anfiteatro m. amphitheater.

an'fora f. amphora.

anfratto m. anfractuosity.

angariare vt. to vex.

ange'lico adj. angelical.

Angelico, Fra (Giovanni da Fiesole), Italian painter (1387-1455).

an'gelo m. angel: — custode, guardian angel.

angheri'a f. vexation.

angina f. angina.

angioino m., adj. Angevin.

angiporto m. blind alley.

anglicano m., adj. Anglican.

anglicismo m. Anglicism.

anglicizzare vt. to Anglicize.

anglosas'sone m., adj. Anglo-Saxon.

angolare adj. angular, corner.

an'golo *m.* corner; angle; nook.

angoloso *adj.* angular.

an'gora *f.* mohair (*wool*).

ango'scia *f.* anguish, distress.

angosciare *vt.* to distress.

angoscioso *adj.* painful, distressing: sogno —, nightmare.

anguilla *f.* eel.

angui'naia *f.* (*anat.*) groin.

angu'ria *f.* watermelon.

angu'stia *f.* narrowness; distress, misery: angustie pecuniarie, financial straits.

angustiare *vt.*, angustiarsi *vr.* to worry.

angusto *adj.* narrow.

a'nice *m.* anise; aniseed.

anidride *f.* anhydride: — carbonica, carbon dioxide.

anilina *f.* aniline.

a'nima *f.* soul, spirit, mind, being, essence; core, pith; mold (*of a button*); stock (*of a gun*); shaft (*of a column*); sounding board (*of a violin*): con tutta l'—, wholeheartedly; un paese di mille anime, a village with one thousand inhabitants.

animale *m.*, *adj.* animal.

animalesco *adj.* bestial.

animare *vt.* to animate, enliven; animarsi *vr.* to become lively; to take courage; to warm up.

animato *adj.* lively, spirited; animated.

animatore *m.* animator. *adj.* animating.

animazione *f.* animation, excitement, liveliness.

animella *f.* sweetbread.

a'nimo *m.* mind; heart; courage; grandezza d'—, magnanimity; stato d'—, frame of mind, mood; avere in — di, to have a mind to; perdersi d'—, to lose courage.

animosamente *adv.* boldly; hostilely.

animosità *f.* animosity; hatred.

animoso *adj* bold, brave.

anisetta *f.* anisette.

anna *f.* (*coin*) anna.

annacquare *vt.* to water; to dilute.

annaffiare *vt.* to water, sprinkle.

annaffiato'io *m.* sprinkler.

annali *m. pl.* annals.

annaspare *vi.* to reel. *vi.* to grope; to flounder.

annata *f.* a year's time; crop; vintage.

annebbiare *vt.* to befog; to dim; annebbiarsi *vr.* to grow foggy; to dim; to blur.

annegamento *m.* drowning.

annegare *vt.* to drown. *vi.* to be drowned; annegarsi, *vr.* to drown oneself.

annerimento *m.* blackening.

annerire *vt.*, annerirsi *vr.* to blacken; to tarnish.

annessione *f.* annexation.

annesso *m.* annex. *adj.* annexed. *pp.* of annettere.

annet'tere *vt.*[8] to annex: — importanza, to attach significance.

annichilire *vt.* to annihilate.

annidarsi *vr.* to nestle; to hide, burrow.

annientamento *m.* annihilation.

annientare *vt.* to annihilate.

anniversario *m.*, *adj.* anniversary.

anno *m.* year: — bisestile, leap year.

annodare *vt.*, annodarsi *vr.* to knot.

annoiare *vt.* to bore, weary; annoiarsi *vr.* to become bored, weary.

annona *f.* provisions.

annona'rio *adj.* relating to provisions: carta annonaria, ration card.

annoso *adj.* old.

annotare *vt.* to annotate; to note, jot down, scribble.

annotazione *f.* annotation, note.

annoverare *vt.* to count, number, comprise.

annuale *m.* anniversary. *adj.* yearly.

annualità *f.* annuity.

annualmente *adv.* yearly.

annua'rio *m.* yearbook; directory.

annuire *vi.* to nod, assent.

annullamento *m.* annulment.

annullare *vt.* to cancel, annul; to void.

annunciare, annunziare *vt.* to announce; to advertise; to foretell.

annunziatore *m.*, annunziatrice *f.* announcer; speaker.

annunziazione *f.* Annunciation.

annun'zio *m.* announcement; omen; advertisement.

Annunzio, Gabriele d' (1864–1938), Italian novelist, dramatist, and poet. Leader of Fiume expedition of 1919–20.

an'nuo *adj.* yearly.

annusare *vt.* to smell, sniff.

annuvolamento *m.* cloudiness.

annuvolare *vt.*, annuvolarsi *vr.* cloud, overcast.

ano *m.* anus.

anodino *m.*, *adj.* anodyne; inane.

a'nodo *m.* anode.

anomali'a *f.* anomaly.

ano'malo *adj.* anomalous.

ano'nimo *m.* anonym. *adj.* anonymous: società anonima, joint-stock company, corporation.

anormale *adj.* abnormal.

anormalità *f.* abnormality.

ansante *adj.* panting.

ansare *vi.* to pant.

ansia, ansietà *f.* anxiety.

ansimare *vi*. to pant.
ansiosamente *adv*. anxiously.
ansioso *adj*. anxious; uneasy; eager.
antagonismo *m*. antagonism.
antagonista *m*. antagonist, opponent.
antar'tico *m*., *adj*. antarctic.
antecedente *adj*. antecedent.
antecedenza *f*. antecedence.
antece'dere *vi*. to precede.
antefatto *m*. background, antecedents.
anteguerra *m*. prewar time.
antelucano *adj*. antelucan, before the dawn.
antenato *m*. ancestor.
antenna *f*. (*naut*.) sailyard; (*zool*.) antenna (*pl*. antennae); (*radio*) aerial.
anteporre *vt*. to put before.
anteprima *f*. preview.
anteriore *adj*. earlier; fore, front.
antesignano *m*. forerunner.
antiabbaglianti *m*. *pl*. (*auto*.) dimmers.
antia'cido *m*., *adj*. antacid.
antiae'reo *adj*. antiaircraft.
antica'glia *f*. trash, junk.
anticamente *adv*. anciently.
antica'mera *f*. hall, waiting room.
antichità *f*. antiquity; ancient times; antique.
anticiclone *m*. anticyclone.
anticipare *vt*. to anticipate; to advance; to forestall; to hasten.
anticipatamente *adv*. in advance.
anticipazione *f*. advance.
anti'cipo *m*. advance.
antico *adj*. ancient, old; obsolete.
anticristiano *adj*. antichristian.
anticristo *m*. antichrist.
antidiluviano *adj*. antediluvian.
anti'doto *m*. antidote.
anti'fona *f*. antiphon; reprimand: capire l'—, to take the hint.
anti'lope *f*. antelope.
antimeridiano *adj*. antemeridian, A.M.
antimilitarismo *m*. antimilitarism.
antimo'nio *m*. antimony.
antinazionale *adj*. antinational.
antincendi *adj*. firefighting: servizio —, fire department.
antipasto *m*. hors d'oeuvre.
antipati'a *f*. dislike, antipathy.
antipa'tico *adj*. disagreeable: egli mi è —, I don't like him.
antipatriot'tico *adj*. antipatriotic.
anti'podi *m*. *pl*. antipodes.
antiqua'rio *m*., *adj*. antique dealer.
antiquato *adj*. old-fashioned, outantirab'bico *adj*. antirabic. [moded.
antireligioso *adj*. irreligious.
antisala *f*. anteroom.
antisemita *m*. anti-Semite.
antisemitismo *m*. anti-Semitism.
antiset'tico *adj*. antiseptic.
antisociale *adj*. antisocial.

anti'tesi *f*. antithesis (*pl*. antitheses).
antite'tico *adj*. antithetical.
antitossina *f*. antitoxin.
antivigi'lia *f*. the day before the eve.
antologi'a *f*. anthology.
antonoma'sia *f*. antonomasia: per —, par excellence.
antracite *f*. anthracite.
antro *m*. den; (*anat*.) antrum.
antropofagi'a *f*. cannibalism.
antropo'fago *m*. cannibal.
antropo'ide *m*., *adj*. anthropoid.
antropologi'a *f*. anthropology.
antropo'logo *m*. anthropologist.
anulare *m*. ring finger. *adj*. annular.
anzi *adv*., *conj*. on the contrary; nay; actually; even: — che, rather than; — che no, rather. *prep*. before.
anzianità *f*. seniority.
anziano *adj*. senior; old, aged.
anzianotto *adj*. elderly.
anzichè *conj*. rather than; instead of.
anzidetto *adj*. afore-mentioned.
anzitutto *adv*. first of all.
aorta *f*. aorta.
apati'a *f*. apathy, indifference.
apa'tico *adj*. apathetic.
ape *f*. bee: — operaia, worker.
aperitivo *m*. aperitif.
apertamente *adv*. openly.
aperto *adj*. open; unlocked; broad. *pp*. of aprire.
apertura *f*. opening; hole; (*arch*.) span: — d'ali, wingspread.
a'pice *m*. apex, vertex; summit; climax; height.
apicoltore *m*. apiarist.
apicultura *f*. apiculture.
Apocalisse *f*. Apocalypse.
apocalit'tico *adj*. Apocalyptical.
apo'crifo *adj*. apochryphal.
apo'fisi *f*. apophysis.
apoge'o *m*. apogee; top.
apoli'tico *adj*. non-party.
apolli'neo *adj*. apollonian.
apologe'tico *adj*. eulogistic.
apologi'a *f*. eulogy, apology.
apo'logo *m*. apologue.
apoplessi'a *f*. apoplexy.
apoplet'tico *adj*. apoplectic.
apostasi'a *f*. apostasy.
apo'stata *m*. apostate.
apostolato *m*. apostolate.
aposto'lico *adj*. apostolical.
apo'stolo *m*. apostle.
apostrofare *vt*., *vi*. to apostrophize; to address.
apo'strofe *f*. apostrophe.
apo'strofo *m*. apostrophe.
apotema *m*. (*geom*.) apothegm.
apoteosi *f*. apotheosis.
appagare *vt*. to satisfy, gratify; to please; appagarsi *vr*. to be content (*with*).

appaiare vt., **appaiarsi** vr. to couple, match.

appallottolare vt. to make a ball, pellet; **appallottolarsi** vr. to clot, ball; to roll oneself up.

appaltare vt. to contract.

appaltatore m. contractor.

appalto m. bid, contract.

appannag'gio m. appanage.

appannamento m. tarnishing; blurring.

appannare vt., **appannarsi** vr. to blur; to steam up.

apparato m. decoration, display; (mach.) apparatus: — scenico, scenery.

apparecchiare vt. to prepare, dress: — la tavola, to lay the table.

apparecchiatura f. apparatus.

apparec'chio m. apparatus, instrument, set; (aeron.) airplane.

apparente adj. apparent, seeming.

apparentemente adv. seemingly; outwardly.

apparenza f. appearance; aspect.

apparire vi.[8] to appear; to seem, look.

appariscente adj. showy, flashy.

appariscenza f. showiness.

apparizione f. apparition.

apparso pp. of apparire.

appartamento m. apartment, suite.

appartarsi vr. to seclude oneself; to withdraw.

appartato adj. secluded, lonely.

appartenenza f. belonging; membership.

appartenere vi.[141] to belong; to be a member of.

appartenuto pp. of appartenere.

appassionare vt. to impassion; to grip; **appassionarsi** vr. to be, grow fond (of), take a warm interest (in).

appassionatamente adv. passionately.

appassionato m. amateur; fan. adj. passionate; fond (of).

appassire vt., vi. to dry; **appassirsi** vr. to wither, fade.

appassito adj. withered, faded.

appellante m. appellant.

appellare vt., vi. to name; **appellarsi** vr. to appeal.

appellativo m., adj. appellative.

appello m. appeal; roll call; call: ricorrere in —, to appeal; fare l'—, to call the roll; fare — a, to appeal to.

appena adv., conj. hardly, scarcely; as soon as; just; just ... when, no sooner ... than: non — sarò arrivato, as soon as I arrive; avevo — finito, I had just finished; lo aveva — visto che sparò, he had just seen him when he fired.

appen'dere vt.[10] to hang (up).

appendice f. appendix (pl. also appendices): romanzo d'—, serial.

appendicite f. appendicitis.

appesantire vt. to weigh, burden, overload; **appesantirsi** vr. to grow heavy; to don warmer clothing.

appeso pp. of appendere; hung (up).

appestare vt., vi. to infect, taint; to stink.

appeti'bile adj. appetible; desirable.

appetibilità f. desirableness.

appetire vt. to crave for; vi. to be appetizing.

appetito m. appetite.

appetitoso adj. appetizing.

appetto prep. in front (of).

appezzamento m. plot, lot.

appianare vt. to smooth, level; to settle.

appianato'io m. roller.

appiattare vt., **appiattarsi** vr. to hide.

appiattire vt., **appiattirsi** vr. to flatten.

appiccare vt. to hang up; to hang: — fuoco a, to set on fire; **appiccarsi** vr. to hang oneself; to spread.

appiccatic'cio adj. sticky.

appiccicare vt. to stick; (fig.) to saddle (with). vi. to be sticky; **appiccicarsi** vr. to stick (to).

appiccicatic'cio adj. sticky.

appicco m. pretext, quibble.

appiè, a piè (di), prep. at the foot of: — nota — di pagina, footnote.

appiedare vt. to dismount.

appieno adv. fully.

appigionare vt. to let.

appigliarsi vr. to cling (to).

appi'glio m. pretext; opportunity.

appiombo m., adv. plumb.

appioppare vt. to strike, deal; to palm (off on).

appisolarsi vr. to doze off.

applaudire vt., vi. to applaud.

applauso m. applause; cheer.

applica'bile adj. appliable.

applicabilità f. appliableness.

applicare vt. to apply; **applicarsi** vr. to apply oneself, devote oneself.

applicato m. clerk.

applicazione f. application.

appoggiare vt. to lay, lean, rest; to support; **appoggiarsi** vr. to lean; (fig.) to rely upon.

appoggiato'io m. rest, support.

appog'gio m. support, prop.

appollaiarsi vr. to perch.

apporre vt.[91] to affix, put.

apportare vt. to bring.

apportatore m. **apportatrice** f. bearer.

apporto m. contribution.

appositamente see apposta.

appo'sito adj. apposite, proper.

apposizione f. apposition.

apposta adv. expressly; on purpose; deliberately.

appostamento *m.* ambush.
appostarsi *vr.* to lie in ambush.
appren'dere *vt.*⁹⁶ to learn.
apprendista *m.* apprentice.
apprensione *f.* uneasiness; dread.
apprensivo *adj.* apprehensive.
appreso *pp.* of apprendere; learnt.
appressamento *m.* approach.
appressare *vt.* appressarsi *vr.* to approach, draw near.
appresso *prep.* near. *adv.* soon after. *adj.* next.
apprestamento *m.* preparation.
apprestare *vt.*, apprestarsi *vr.* to prepare, set, get ready.
apprettare *vt.* to size.
appretto *m.* size.
apprezza'bile *adj.* appreciable.
apprezzamento *m.* appreciation; judgment.
apprezzare *vt.* to appreciate.
approc'cio *m.* approach, feeler.
approdare *vi.* to land.
approdo *m.* landing.
approfittare *vi.* to profit by; to avail oneself (*of*); to take advantage (*of*); approfittarsi *vr.* to take advantage (*of*); to impose (*upon*).
approfondire *vt.* to deepen; to investigate; approfondirsi *vr.* to deepen; to become conversant (*with*).
approntare *vt.* to prepare, set.
appropriarsi *vr.* to appropriate.
appropriato *adj.* fit, proper.
appropriazione *f.* appropriation: — indebita, embezzlement, graft.
approssimare *vt.*, approssimarsi *vr.* to approximate.
approssimativamente *adv.* approximately.
approssimativo *adj.* approximate.
approssimazione *f.* approximation.
approvare *vt.* to approve (*of*).
approvazione *f.* approval.
approvvigionamento *m.* supply; provisions.
approvvigionare *vt.* to supply (*with*), provision.
appuntamento *m.* appointment, engagement; date.
appuntare *vt.* to sharpen; to fasten, stick, pin.
appuntato *m.* private first class; corporal.
appuntino *adv.* punctiliously.
appuntito *adj.* pointed.
appunto *m.* note; charge; blame; remark. per l'— just, exactly, quite so.
appurare *vt.* to ascertain.
apribottiglia *m.* bottle opener.
aprico *adj.* sunny, open.
aprile *m.* April: primo d'—, All Fools' Day.

apripista *m.* bulldozer.
aprire *vt.*,¹¹ aprirsi *vr.*¹¹ to open; to unlock.
aprisca'tola *m.* can opener.
aquario *m.* aquarium; (*astr.*) Aquarius.
aqua'tico *adj.* aquatic.
a'quila *f.* eagle.
aquilino *adj.* aquiline.
aquilone *m.* north wind; kite.
aquilotto *m.* eaglet; air cadet.
ara (*1*) *f.* are (*surface measure*).
ara (*2*) *f.* altar.
arabesco *m.* arabesque.
ara'bico *adj.* Arabic, Arabian.
a'rabo *m.* Arab. *adj.* Arabian.
ara'chide *f.* peanut.
arac'nide *m.* (*zool.*) arachnid.
aragosta *f.* lobster.
aral'dica *f.* heraldry.
aral'dico *adj.* heraldic.
araldo *m.* herald.
aranceto *m.* orange grove.
aran'cia *f.* orange.
aranciata *f.* orangeade.
aran'cio *m.* orange tree.
arancione *m.*, *adj.* orange.
arare *vt.* to plow.
aratro *m.* plow.
aratura *f.* plowing.
arazzo *m.* tapestry, arras.
arbitrag'gio *m.* arbitrage.
arbitrale *adj.* arbitral.
arbitrare *vt.*, *vi.* to arbitrate; to referee; arbitrarsi *vr.* to presume.
arbitrariamente *adv.* arbitrarily.
arbitra'rio *adj.* arbitrary.
arbitrato *m.* arbitration.
arbi'trio *m.* discretion; license: libero —, free will.
ar'bitro *m.* arbitrator; referee.
arboscello *m.* small tree, shrub.
arbusto *m.* shrub.
arca *f.* ark: un'— di scienza, a very learned person.
arca'ico *adj.* archaic.
arcaismo *m.* archaism.
arcan'gelo *m.* archangel.
arcano *m.* mystery. *adj.* mysterious.
arcata *f.* arch.
archeologi'a *f.* archeology.
archeolo'gico *adj.* archeological.
archeo'logo *m.* archeologist.
archetipo *m.* archetype.
archetto *m.* (*mus.*) fiddle bow.
archibu'gio *m.* harquebus.
Archimede *m.* *pr.* Archimedes.
architettare *vt.* to devise; to plan.
architetto *m.* architect.
architetto'nico *adj.* architectural.
architettura *f.* architecture.
architrave *f.* architrave; lintel.
archiviare *vt.* to file.
archi'vio *m.* archives; (*comm.*) files (*journ.*) "morgue."

archivista *m.* archivist.
arcicontento *adj.* most glad.
arcidia'cono *m.* archdeacon.
arciduca *m.* archduke.
arciduchessa *f.* archduchess.
arciere *m.* archer, bowman.
arcigno *adj.* sulky, sullen.
arcimiliona'rio *m.,* *adj.* multimillionaire.
arcione *m.* saddlebow.
arcipe'lago *m.* archipelago.
arciprete *m.* archpriest.
arcivescovado *m.* archbishopric.
arcivescovile *adj.* archiepiscopal.
arcive'scovo *m.* archbishop.
arco *m.* (*geom.*) arc; (*hist.*) arch; (*mus.*, *weapon*) bow: **strumenti ad —,** strings.
arcobaleno *m.* rainbow.
arcola'io *m.* reel.
arcuare *vt.* to bend, curve.
arcuato *adj.* bent, curved.
ardente *adj.* ardent; burning.
ardentemente *adv.* ardently.
ar'dere *vt.*, *vi.*[11] to burn; to shine.
arde'sia *f.* slate.
ardimento *m.* boldness, daring.
ardimentoso *adj.* bold, daring.
ardire *m.* courage; impudence. *vi.* to dare: **come ardite?**, how dare you?
arditamente *adv.* boldly.
ardito *adj.* bold.
ardore *m.* ardor.
ar'duo *adj.* arduous, hard.
a'rea *f.* area; surface; lot.
a'rem *m.* harem.
arena *f.* arena; (*sabbia*) sand.
arena'ria *f.* (*min.*) sandstone.
arengo *m.* assembly, forum.
arenile *m.* sandpit.
arenoso *adj.* arenaceous, sandy.
Aretino, Pietro, Italian satirist (1492–1557).
Arezzo, Guido d', Italian reformer of music (ca. 990–1050).
ar'gano *m.* capstan.
argentare *vt.* to silver.
argentato *adj.* silver-plated: **volpe argentata,** silver fox.
argentatura *f.* silvering.
argen'teo *adj.* silver, silvery.
argenteri'a *f.* silverware.
argentiere *m.* silversmith.
argentina *f.* T-shirt.
argentino (1) *m.,* *adj.* Argentine.
argentino (2) *adj.* argentine, silver, silvery.
argento *m.* silver: **— vivo,** quicksilver.
argentone *m.* German silver.
argilla *f.* clay.
argilloso *adj.* clayey.
arginare *vt.* to stem, dam.
ar'gine *m.* embankment, dam.

argomentare *vt.*, *vi.* to argue.
argomentazione *f.* argumentation.
argomento *m.* argument; subject, topic.
argona'uta *m.* argonaut.
arguire *vt.* to infer, surmise.
argutamente *adv.* wittily.
arguto *adj.* witty; shrewd.
argu'zia *f.* witticism; wit; shrewdness.
a'ria *f.* air; tune: **camera d'—,** pneumatic tube; **castelli in —,** castles in Spain.
aridità *f.* aridness, dryness.
a'rido *adj.* arid, dry; barren; lifeless; parched; unfeeling.
arieggiare *vt.* to air. *vi.* (*foll. by* a) to look like; to sound like.
ariete *m.* (*zool.*) ram; (*mil.*) battering ram; (*astr.*) Aries.
aringa *f.* herring.
arioso *adj.* airy.
Ariosto, Ludovico, Italian poet *Orlando Furioso* (1474–1533).
a'rista *f.* pork chine; (*bot.*) arista.
aristocra'tico *m.* aristocrat. *adj.* aristocratic.
aristocrazi'a *f.* aristocracy.
aristote'lico *adj.* Aristotelian.
aritme'tica *f.* arithmetic.
aritme'tico *m.* arithmetician. *adj.* arithmetic.
aritmi'a *f.* (*med.*) arrhythmia.
arlecchinata *f.* harlequinade.
Arlecchino *m.* pr. Harlequin.
arma *f.* corps, force, service; weapon, arm. *see* arme.
arma'dio *m.* wardrobe, cupboard: **— a muro,** closet.
armaiuolo *m.* gunsmith.
armamenta'rio *m.* outfit.
armamento *m.* armament; equipment.
armare *vt.* to arm; (*obs.*) to prop; (*naut.*) to equip; **armarsi** *vr.* to arm oneself.
armata *f.* army; fleet.
armatore *m.* shipowner.
armatura *f.* armor; framework; scaffolding.
arme *f.* arm, weapon; firearm, gun: **essere sotto le armi,** to be in the army; **essere alle prime armi,** to be a beginner.
armeggiare *vt.* to fumble; to scheme.
armeno *m.,* *adj.* Armenian.
armento *m.* herd.
armeri'a *f.* armory.
armi'gero *m.* armiger.
armisti'zio *m.* armistice.
armoni'a *f.* harmony.
armo'nica *f.* harmonica.
armo'nico *adj.* harmonical.
armo'nio *m.* harmonium.
armonioso *adj.* harmonious.

armonizzare *vt.*, *vi.* to harmonize.

arnese *m.* implement, tool: **in cattivo —**, down at heel.

ar'nia *f.* beehive.

aroma *m.* flavor; (*pl.*) spices.

aroma'tico *adj.* aromatic.

aromatizzare *vt.* to flavor, spice.

arpa *f.* harp.

arpeg'gio *m.* arpeggio.

arpi'a *f.* harpy.

arpione *m.* hinge; spike.

arpista *m.* harper, harpist.

arrabattarsi *vr.* to endeavor.

arrabbiare *vi.*, **arrabbiarsi** *vr.* to get angry: **fare arrabbiare,** to make angry.

arrabbiato *adj.* angry.

arrabbiatura *f.* rage: **prendersi un'—,** to fly into a passion, lose one's temper.

arraffare *vt.* to snatch.

arrampicarsi *vr.* to climb (*up*).

arrancare *vi.* to limp; to trudge; to row away; to labor.

arrangiare *vt.* to arrange; **arrangiarsi** *vr.* to make shift; to manage.

arrecare *vt.* to bring; to cause.

arredamento *m.* interior decoration; furnishings.

arredare *vt.* to furnish, fit up.

arredatore *m.* interior decorator.

arredo *m.* furniture; fittings; decoration.

arrembag'gio *m.* boarding (*by force*): **andare all'—,** to board.

arrenarsi *vr.* to strand.

arrenato *adj.* stranded; in a deadlock.

arren'dersi *vr.*[108] to surrender.

arrende'vole *adj.* amenable, pliant.

arrendevolezza *f.* compliance.

arreso *pp.* of **arrendersi.**

arrestare *vt.* to stop; to arrest; **arrestarsi** *vr.* to stop, halt.

arresto *m.* arrest; stop, halt.

arretrare *vt.*, *vi.* to w thdraw.

arretrato *m.* arrears, arrearage; back number; *adj.* behindhand; late.

arricchimento *m.* enrichment.

arricchire *vt.* to enrich. *vi.* **arricchirsi** *vr.* to get rich.

arricchito *m.* upstart, parvenu.

arricciare *vt.*, **arricciarsi** *vr.* to curl (*up*); to wrinkle.

arricciatura *f.* curling.

arri'dere *vi.*[111] to smile (*on*); to favor.

arringa *f.* harangue; plea.

arringare *vt.*, *vi.* to harangue.

arrischiare *vt.* to risk; **arrischiarsi** *vr.* to risk, dare.

arrischiato *adj.* risky; rash.

arriso *pp.* of **arridere.**

arrivare *vt.* to reach, arrive, get to; (*fig.*) to go so far (*as*).

arrivato *adj.* arrived, come; successful; **ben —!,** welcome!

arrivismo *m.* scrambling.

arrivista *m.* go-getter, scrambler.

arrivo *m.* arrival, coming.

arroccamento *m.* (*chess*) castling.

arroccare *vt.* to fill the distaff; to castle (*at chess*).

arrochire *vt.* to make hoarse; **arrochirsi** *vr.* to grow hoarse.

arrogante *adj.* arrogant.

arroganza *f.* arrogance.

arrogarsi *vr.* to arrogate to oneself.

arrolamento *m.* enlistment.

arrolare *vt.*, **arrolarsi** *vr.* to enlist.

arrossamento *m.* reddening; rash.

arrossare *vt.*, **arrossarsi** *vr.* to redden.

arrossire *vi.* to blush, flush.

arrostire *vt.*, **arrostirsi** *vr.* to roast; to bask.

arrostitura *f.* roasting.

arrosto *m.*, *adj.* roast: **non c'è fumo senz' —,** there is no smoke without a fire; **molto fumo e poco —,** great cry and little wool.

arrotare *vt.* to whet, sharpen: **— i denti,** to grind one's teeth.

arrotino *m.* grinder.

arrotolare *vt.* to roll up.

arrotondare *vt.* to round.

arrovellarsi *vr.* to fret.

arroventare *vt.* to make red hot; **arroventarsi** *vr.* to become red hot.

arruffapo'poli *m.* ringleader.

arruffare *vt.*, **arruffarsi** *vr.* to tangle, ruffle.

arruffi'o *m.* tangle, jumble.

arruffone *m.* jumbler.

arrugginire *vt.*, *vi.*, **arrugginirsi** *vr.* to rust.

arrugginito *adj.* rusty.

arsella *f.* mussel, clam.

arsenale *m.* arsenal, navy yard.

arse'nico *m.* arsenic.

arsenobenzolo *m.* arsphenamine.

arso *adj.* burnt; dry. *pp.* of **ardere.**

arsura *f.* sultriness; thirst.

artatamente *adv.* artfully.

arte *f.* art; skill; wile.

artefatto *adj.* adulterated; artificial; sophisticated.

arte'fice *m.* artificer, craftsman.

arte'ria *f.* artery; thoroughfare.

arteriosclerosi *f.* arteriosclerosis.

arterioso *adj.* arterial.

artesiano (pozzo) *m.* Artesian well.

ar'tico *adj.* arctic.

articolare *vt.*, **articolarsi** *vr.* to articulate.

articolato *adj.* articulate.

articolazione *f.* articulation.

articolista *m.* columnist; free-lancer.

arti'colo *m.* article, item.

artificiale *adj.* artificial, fictitious; **fuochi artificiali,** fireworks.

artificialmente *adv.* artificially.

artificiere m. (mil.) artificer.

artifi'cio m. artifice; wile; guile.

artificioso adj. artful, fictitious.

artigiano m. artisan, craftsman.

artigliare vt. to claw.

artigliere m. artilleryman.

artiglieri'a f. artillery: pezzo d' — piece of ordnance.

arti'glio m. claw; clutch.

artista m. artist; player, actor.

arti'stico adj. artistic, artistical.

arto m. limb.

artrite f. arthritis.

artri'tico adj. arthritic.

arzigogolare vi. to muse; to dream, fancy.

arzigo'golo m. cavil, subtlety.

arzillo adj. sprightly; hale.

asbesto m. asbestos.

a'scaro m. askari (pl. askaris).

ascella f. armpit; (bot.) axil.

ascendente m. ancestor; ascendancy; (astr.) ascendant. adj. upward.

ascendenza f. ancestry.

ascen'dere vt., vi.[119] to ascend, mount; to amount: — al trono, to ascend the throne.

ascensione f. ascension, ascent.

ascensore m. elevator.

ascesa f. ascent.

asceso pp. of ascendere.

ascesso m. abscess.

asceta m. ascetic.

asce'tico adj. ascetical.

ascetismo m. asceticism.

a'scia f. ax.

asciugamano m. towel.

asciugante adj. drying: carta —, blotting paper.

asciugare vt. to dry; to wipe. vi., asciugarsi vr. to dry (up); to become dry: — gli occhi, to dry one's eyes; — la bocca, to wipe one's mouth.

asciugato'io m. towel.

asciugatura f. drying.

asciutto adj. dry; lean. adv. dryly: essere all'—, to be penniless.

ascoltare vt., vi. to listen (to).

ascoltatore m. listener.

ascoltazione f. listening; auscultation.

ascolto m. listening: prestare —, to listen (to).

ascritto adj. ascribed. pp. of ascrivere.

ascri'vere vt.[114] to ascribe; to impute: ascriversi vr. to claim.

asepsi f. asepsis.

aset'tico adj. aseptic.

asfaltare vt. to asphalt.

asfalto m. asphalt.

asfissi'a f. asphyxia.

asfissiante adj. asphyxiating.

asfissiare vt., vi., asfissiarsi vr. to asphyxiate.

asfodelo m. asphodel.

asia'tico adj. Asiatic.

asilo m. refuge, shelter: — infantile, preschool; kindergarten.

asimmetri'a f. asymmetry.

asimme'trico adj. asymmetrical.

asinag'gine f. foolishness.

asina'io m. donkey driver.

asin'crono adj. asynchronous.

asineri'a f. foolishness, asininity.

asinino adj. asinine: tosse asinina, whooping cough.

a'sino m. ass, donkey; f. asina she-ass.

asma f. asthma.

asma'tico m., adj. asthmatic.

a'sola f. buttonhole.

aspa'rago m. asparagus.

asper'gere vt.[11] to sprinkle (with).

asperità f. asperity.

aspersione f. aspersion; spraying.

asperso adj. sprinkled. pp. of aspergere.

asperso'rio m. aspergillum.

aspettare vt., vi. to wait (for), await; to look forward to: far —, to keep waiting; aspettarsi vr. to expect; to anticipate.

aspettativa f. expectation; leave of absence.

aspetto (1) m. appearance, look, aspect.

aspetto (2) m. waiting: sala d'—, waiting room; battuta d'— (mus.), bar rest.

a'spide f. asp.

aspirante (1) m. candidate; (naut.) midshipman.

aspirante (2) adj. suction, sucking.

aspirapol'vere m. vacuum cleaner.

aspirare vt. to inhale; to aspirate; to suck. vi. (foll. by a) to aspire (to, after), aim (at).

aspiratore m. aspirator; vacuum cleaner.

aspirazione f. aspiration; intake, suction.

aspo m. reel.

asporta'bile adj. removable.

asportare vt. to remove, take away; (surg.) to extirpate.

asportazione f. removal; extirpation.

aspramente adv. harshly.

asprezza f. harshness; sourness.

aspro adj. sour; harsh.

assaggiare vt. to taste; to assay.

assag'gio m. tasting; sample; test; assay.

assai adv. very, much: — meno, much less; — più, much more.

assale m. axle.

assalire vt.[14] to attack, assail; (fig.) to seize.

assalitore m. assailant.

assaltare vt. to assault.

assalto *m.* attack, assault: **prender d'—**, to take by storm.

assaporare *vt.* to relish.

assassinare *vt.* to murder.

assassi'nio *m.* murder.

assassino *m.* murderer, killer.

asse (*1*) *f.* plank.

asse (*2*) *m.* (*sci.*) axis (*pl.* axes): **— patrimoniale,** estate.

assecondare *vt.* to second.

assediante *m.* besieger.

assediare *vt.* to besiege; to beset.

asse'dio *m.* siege.

assegnamento *m.* allotment; reliance: **fare — su,** to rely upon.

assegnare *vt.* to assign, allow, award.

assegnato, (in porto) freight charges to be paid.

assegnazione *f.* assignation, allotment, appointment, award.

assegno *m.* allowance; check: **contro —,** cash on delivery (*abbr.* c.o.d.).

assemblea *f.* assembly; meeting.

assembramento *m.* gathering.

assennato *adj.* wise, sensible.

assenso *m.* assent, agreement.

assentarsi *vr.* to absent oneself.

assente *adj.* absent; missing; absent-minded: **— dalla città,** out of town.

assenteismo *m.* absenteeism.

assentire *vi.* to assent (*to*).

assenza *f.* absence; lack, want.

assen'zio *m.* absinthe.

asserire *vt.* to assert, state.

asserragliarsi *vr.* to barricade oneself.

asserto *m.* assertion, statement.

assertore *m.* advocate.

asservire *vt.* to subjugate; **asservirsi** *vr.* to submit (*to*).

asserzione *f.* statement.

assessore *m.* assessor, alderman.

assestamento *m.* settlement.

assestare *vt.* to settle; to tidy.

assetare *vt.* to make thirsty.

assetato *adj.* thirsty; eager.

assettare *vt.* to settle; to trim.

assettato *adj.* tidy, trim.

assetto *m.* order, shape; (*naut.*) trimming.

asseverare *vt.* to asseverate.

assicurare *vt.* to make safe; to fasten; to secure; to affirm, assure; (*comm.*) to insure; **assicurarsi** *vr.* to make sure, ascertain; (*comm.*) to insure oneself; to fasten oneself (*to*), hold on (*to*); to secure: **— sulla vita,** to take out life insurance.

assicurato *m., adj.* (*comm.*) insured; **assicurata** *f.* insured letter.

assicuratore *m.* insurer.

assicurazione *f.* assurance; (*comm.*) insurance.

assideramento *m.* frostbite: **morire per —,** to freeze to death.

assiderare *vt.*, **assiderarsi** *vr.* to freeze.

assiderato *adj.* frostbitten.

assi'dersi *vr.*[16] to take one's seat.

assiduamente *adv.* assiduously.

assiduità *f.* assidulty.

assi'duo *adj.* assiduous.

assieme *adv.* together. *prep.* with, together with.

assieparsi *vr.* to crowd.

assillare *vt.* to spur; to worry, badger.

assillo *m.* gadfly; spur, goad; worry.

assimilare *vt.*, **assimilarsi** *vr.* to assimilate.

assimilazione *f.* assimilation.

assioma *m.* axiom.

assioma'tico *adj.* axiomatical.

Assiro *m., adj.* Assyrian.

assisa *f.* uniform; livery.

assise *f.pl.* assizes.

assiso *adj.* seated.

assistente *m., adj.* assistant: **— sociale,** social worker.

assistenza *f.* assistance, aid.

assistenziale *adj.* assistance: **comitato —,** aid committee; **opere assistenziali,** charities; **ente —,** welfare organization.

assis'tere *vt.*[16] to assist, help; to tend, nurse. *vi.* to attend; to be a witness (*to*).

assito *m.* planking.

asso *m.* ace: **piantare in —,** to leave in the lurch.

associare *vt.* to associate; to consolidate; to make a member (*of*); **associarsi** *vr.* to associate; to share; to join; to subscribe.

associato *m.* partner; subscriber.

associazione *f.* association; partnership; subscription; membership: **— a delinquere,** conspiracy.

assodare *vt.* to solidify, harden; to ascertain; **assodarsi** *vr.* to harden.

assoggettare *vt.* to subdue; **assoggettarsi** *vr.* to submit.

assolato *adj.* sunny.

assoldare *vt.* to hire; to enlist; **assoldarsi** *vr.* to enlist.

assolo, a solo *m.* solo.

assolto *adj.* absolved; acquitted. *pp.* of **assolvere.**

assolutamente *adv.* absolutely.

assolutismo *m.* absolutism.

assolutista *m.* absolutist.

assoluto *adj.* absolute, dire.

assoluzione *f.* acquittal; (*rel.*) absolution.

assol'vere *vt.*[17] to acquit; to absolve; to forgive.

assomigliante *adj.* resembling.

assomiglianza *f.* resemblance.

assomigliare *vi.* to be like; to look like; to taste like; to sound like; to smell like; **assomigliarsi** *vr.* to resemble each other, be alike.

assommare *vt.* to add. *vi.* to amount (to).

assonanza *f.* assonance.

assonnato *adj.* sleepy.

assopimento *m.* drowsiness.

assopirsi *vr.* to doze off.

assorbente *m.* absorbent. *adj.* absorbing: carta —, blotting paper.

assorbimento *m.* absorption.

assorbire *vt.*[18] to absorb; to engross; to take up.

assordante *adj.* deafening.

assordare *vt.* to deafen, stun.

assortimento *m.* assortment.

assortire *vt.* to assort.

assorto *pp.* absorbed, engrossed. *pp. of* assorbire.

assottigliare *vt.* to thin; to sharpen; to reduce; assottigliarsi *vr.* to thin down; to decrease.

assuefare *vt.* to inure, accustom; assuefarsi *vr.* to get accustomed.

assuefazione *f.* habit.

assu'mere *vt.*[19] to assume, take; to hire, engage: — informazioni, to make inquiries; assumersi *vr.* to take upon oneself, undertake.

Assunta *f.* Assumption Day.

assunto *m.* theory. *pp. of* assumere hired; assumed.

assuntore *m.* contractor.

Assunzione (1) *f.* Assumption Day.

assunzione (2) *f.* hiring.

assurdità *f.* absurdity.

assurdo *adj.* absurd, preposterous.

assur'gere *vi.*[20] to rise.

asta *f.* staff; rod; (*naut.*) boom; spear; auction; straight stroke.

astante *m.* bystander.

aste'mio *m.* teetotaler. *adj.* abstemious, abstaining.

astenersi *vr.*[141] to abstain (*from*); to refrain (*from*); to forbear.

astensione *f.* abstention.

asterisco *m.* asterisk.

asticciuola *f.* small rod; penholder; rib (*of an umbrella*).

astigmatismo *m.* astigmatism.

astinenza *f.* abstinence.

a'stio *m.* grudge, hate.

astioso *adj.* spiteful.

astrale *adj.* astral.

astrarre *vt.*[154] to abstract; to divert. *vi.* to prescind; astrarsi *vr.* to wander.

astratto *m.* abstract. *adj.* abstract; abstracted. *pp. of* astrarre.

astrazione *f.* abstraction; abstractedness.

astringente *m.*, *adj.* astringent.

astro *m.* star; (*bot.*) aster.

astrola'bio *m.* astrolabe.

astrologi'a *f.* astrology.

astro'logo *m.* astrologer.

astrona'utica *f.* space navigation.

astronave *f.* space ship.

astronomi'a *f.* astronomy.

astrono'mico *adj.* astronomical.

astro'nomo *m.* astronomer.

astrusità *f.* abstruseness.

astruso *adj.* abstruse.

astuc'cio *m.* case, box, container.

astutamente *adv.* cunningly.

astuto *adj.* astute, cunning, smart.

astu'zia *f.* cunning; trick, wile.

ata'vico *adj.* atavistic.

atavismo *m.* atavism.

ateismo *m.* atheism.

ateneo *m.* athenaeum, university.

ateniese *m.*, *adj.* Athenian.

a'teo *m.* atheist.

atlante *m.* atlas.

atlan'tico *m.*, *adj.* Atlantic.

atleta *m.* athlete.

atle'tica *f.* athletics.

atle'tico *adj.* athletic.

atmosfera *f.* atmosphere.

atmosfe'rico *adj.* atmospheric.

atollo *m.* atoll.

atomicità *f.* atomicity.

ato'mico *adj.* atomic: bomba atomica, atom bomb; energia atomica, atomic power.

a'tomo *m.* atom: disintegrazione dell'—, atomic fission.

a'tono *adj.* atonic.

atrio *m.* entrance hall, hall.

atroce *adj.* atrocious, awful.

atrocità *f.* atrocity.

atrofi'a *f.* atrophy.

atro'fico *adj.* atrophic.

atrofizzare *vt.*, atrofizzarsi *vr.* to atrophy.

attaccabottoni *m.* buttonholer.

attaccabrighe *m.* quarreler, spitfire.

attaccapanni *m.* rack.

attaccare *vt.* to attach, connect; to stick; to seam up; to pin; to hang; to communicate; to hitch; to attack. *vi.* to stick; to take root; to take; to start: — lite, to quarrel; attaccarsi *vr.* to stick (*to*); to be contagious.

attaccatic'cio *adj.* sticky; tiresome; contagious.

attaccatura *f.* junction; armhole.

attacchino *m.* bill poster.

attacco *m.* attack; joint; (*radio*) jack; (*med.*) fit.

attagliarsi *vr.* to fit, suit.

attanagliare *vt.* to grip.

attardarsi *vr.* to linger.

attecchire *vi.* to take root, stick.

atteggiamento *m.* attitude.

atteggiarsi *vr.* to attitudinize; to pose as.

attempato *adj.* elderly.

attendamento *m.* camping.

attendarsi *vr.* to camp.

attendente *m.* (*mil.*) orderly.

atten'dere *vt.*, *vi.* [40] to wait (*for*); to await; to attend (*to*); **attendersi** *vr.* to expect, anticipate.

attendi'bile *adj.* reliable.

attendibilità *f.* reliability.

attenere *vi.* [41] to relate (*to*); **attenersi** *vr.* to conform (*to*); to stick (*to*): **— a**, to follow.

attentamente *adv.* attentively.

attentare *vi.* to attempt: **— alla vita di una persona**, to attempt to kill someone; **attentarsi** *vr.* to dare; to try.

attentato *m.* attempt (*upon*).

attentatore *m.* infringer; murderer; would-be murderer.

attenti! *interj.* attention!; watch out!: **stare sull'—**, to stand at attention.

attento *adj.* attentive: **stare —**, to pay attention; to be careful.

attenuante *f.* (*law*) extenuation.

attenuare *vt.* to attenuate, mitigate.

attenzione *f.* attention, heed: **con —**, carefully.

atterrag'gio *m.* landing.

atterrare *vt.* to knock down; to fell. *vi.* (*aeron.*) to land.

atterrire *vt.* to frighten; **atterrirsi** *vr.* to take fright.

attesa *f.* waiting; delay.

atteso *adj.* awaited; expected. *pp. of* **attendere**.

attesochè *conj.* in consideration of, considering.

attestare *vt.* to certify, state.

attestato *m.* certificate.

attestazione *f.* attestation.

atticciato *adj.* stout.

at'tico *m.* attic, garret.

attiguo *adj.* adjacent, contiguous.

attillato *adj.* tight, fitting.

at'timo *m.* moment, minute.

attinente *adj.* relating, regarding.

attinenza *f.* relation, connection.

attin'gere *vt.* [48] to draw; to get.

attinto *pp. of* **attingere**.

attirare *vt.* to draw, attract, lure; **attirarsi** *vr.* to draw upon oneself; to win.

attitu'dine *f.* aptitude, bent.

attivamente *adv.* actively.

attivare *vt.* to activate.

attività *f.* activity; liveliness; (*comm. pl.*) assets.

attivo *m.* (*comm.*) assets. *adj.* active; lively.

attizzare *vt.* to poke, stir (*a fire*).

attizzato'io *m.* poker.

atto (**1**) *adj.* inclined; fit (*for*).

atto (**2**) *m.* act; gesture; action; deed: **all'— pratico**, practically; **tradurre in —**, to carry out; **far — di**

presenza, to put in an appearance; **dar —**, to acknowledge; **prender —**, to take note.

atti *m.pl.* proceedings: **fare gli —**, to prosecute; **passare agli —**, to file.

atto'nito *adj.* amazed, astonished.

attorcigliare *vt.*, **attorcigliarsi** *vr.* to twist; to wind.

attore *m.* actor, player; (*law*) plaintiff.

attorniare *vt.* to surround.

attorno *prep.*, *adv.* about, around, round: **darsi d'—**, to busy oneself; **levati d'—!**, get out of here!; **levarsi uno d'—**, to get rid of one.

attracco *m.* moorage, moorings.

attraccare *vt.*, *vi.* to moor.

attraente *adj.* attractive, alluring.

attrarre [44] *see* **attirare**.

attrattiva *f.* attraction, appeal.

attratto *pp. of* **attrarre**.

attraversare *vt.* to move across, cross; to go through; to thwart.

attraverso *prep.* through, across. *adv.* wrong; across.

attrazione *f.* attraction, appeal.

attrezzare *vt.* to outfit.

attrezzatura *f.* equipment.

attrezzista *m.* (*theat.*) property man.

attrezzo *m.* implement, tool: **— sce-nico** (*theat.*) property, prop.

attribuire *vt.* to ascribe; to allot; **— importanza a**, to attach importance to; **attribuirsi** *vr.* to claim.

attributo *m.* attribute.

attribuzione *f.* attribution.

attrice *f.* actress.

attrito *m.* friction; variance.

attrupparsi *vr.* to troop.

attua'bile *adj.* feasible.

attuabilità *f.* feasibility.

attuale *adj.* actual; present, current.

attualità *f.* actuality; current events: **essere d'—**, to be of topical interest; **— cinematografiche**, newsreel.

attualmente *adv.* at present; actually.

attuare *vt.* to accomplish, carry out.

attua'rio *m.* actuary.

attuazione *f.* fulfillment, carrying out.

attutire *vt.*, **attutirsi** *vr.* to deaden, mitigate.

audace *adj.* bold, daring.

audacemente *adv.* boldly, daringly.

auda'cia *f.* boldness, daring.

auditore *m.* listener, auditor; judge.

audito'rio *m.* auditorium; (*radio*) studio.

audizione *f.*, audition, hearing.

auge *m.* summit, apex; (*astr.*) apogee: **in —**, on top; popular.

augello *m.* bird.

augurale *adj.* auspicious.

augurare *vt.* to wish, bid; to foretell; **augurarsi** *vr.* to wish, hope.

a'ugure m. augur.

augu'rio m. wish; omen.

augusteo adj. Augustan.

augusto adj. august, majestic.

a'ula f. hall; room; schoolroom.

a'ulico adj. aulic.

aumentare vt., vi. to increase, augment; to rise.

aumento m. increase; raise; rise.

a'ura f. breeze; aura.

a'ureo adj. gold, golden.

aure'ola f. halo, aureole, glory.

auri'fero adj. auriferous: giacimento —, gold field.

aurora f. dawn, daybreak: — boreale, aurora borealis.

auscultare vt., vi. to auscultate.

auscultazione f. auscultation.

ausiliare, ausilia'rio adj. auxiliary.

ausilia'ria f. Wac (in the Army); Wave (in the Navy); Wasp (in the Air Force).

ausi'lio m. help, aid.

auspicare vt. to wish, hope for.

auspi'cio m. auspice, omen.

austerità f. austerity.

austero adj. austere.

australe adj. austral, southern.

australiano m., adj. Australian.

austri'aco m., adj. Austrian.

autarchi'a f. autarchy.

autenticare vt. to authenticate.

autenticazione f. authentication.

autenticità f. authenticity.

auten'tico adj. genuine.

autiere m. military driver.

autista m. driver.

auto m. motorcar, car, automobile.

autoambulanza f. ambulance.

autobiografi'a f. autobiography.

autoblindata f. armored car.

au'tobus m. autobus, motorbus, bus.

autocarro m. motor truck.

autoclave f. autoclave.

autocombustione f. self-ignition.

autocrazi'a f. autocracy.

autoc'tono m. autochthon. adj. autochthonous, autochthonal.

autodafè m. auto da fè (pl. autos da fè).

autodecisione f. free will.

autodidatta m. self-taught person.

auto'dromo m. motordrome.

auto'geno adj. autogenous.

autogiro m. autogyro.

auto'grafo m. autograph. adj. autographic.

autolesionista m. self-wounder.

autolettiga f. (motor) ambulance.

automa m. automaton, robot.

automaticamente adv. automatically.

automa'tico m. snap fastener. adj. automatic.

automatismo m. automatism.

automezzo m. motor vehicle.

automo'bile m. motorcar, car, automobile: viaggiare in —, to motor. adj. automobile.

automobilismo m. motoring.

automobilista m. (car) driver.

automotrice f. Diesel, railroad car.

autonomi'a f. autonomy, self-government; (mach.) range: — di volo, flight range.

auto'nomo adj. autonomous.

autopompa f. fire engine.

autopsi'a f. autopsy, post-mortem examination.

autopub'blica f. taxicab, taxi.

autore m. author: diritti d'—, copyright.

autore'vole adj. authoritative.

autorimessa f. garage.

autoristoro m. drive-in, roadhouse.

autorità f. authority.

autorita'rio adj. authoritative, peremptory, domineering.

autoritratto m. self-portrait.

autorizzare vt. to authorize.

autorizzazione f. authorization.

autoscatto m. (photo.) automatic releaser.

autoservizi m.pl. bus lines.

autostello m. motel.

autostop m. hitchhike: fare l'—, to hitchhike.

autostrada f. motor road, highway, toll road.

autosuggestione f. autosuggestion, self-deception.

autotreno m. trailer truck.

autovei'colo m. motor vehicle.

autrice f. authoress.

autunnale adj. autumnal.

autunno m. autumn, fall.

ava f. ancestress.

avallante m. guarantor.

avallare vt. to guarantee.

avallo m. guaranty, endorsement.

avambrac'cio m. forearm.

avamposto m. outpost.

avanguar'dia f. van, vanguard.

avannotto m. small fry.

avanti prep., adv. forward; before; in front of, ahead: andare —, to go on; avanti!, come on!, go ahead!, come in!; il mio orologio va —, my watch is fast; da ora in —, from now on; più —, farther on; later on.

avantieri adv. the day before yesterday.

avanzamento m. advancement; promotion.

avanzare vt. to advance, put forth; to be creditor of. vi. to advance, move forward; to superabound; to be left; avanzarsi vr. to move forward; to draw near.

avanzata f. advance.

avanzato adj. advanced; progressive; left over.

avanzo m. remnant, residue; (*math.*) remainder: — di galera, jailbird; d'—, more than enough.

avari'a f. damage; breakdown; (*comm.*) average.

avariare vt. to damage.

avari'zia f. avarice, stinginess.

avaro m. miser. adj. stingy.

avello m. tomb.

avena f. oats: farina d'—, oatmeal.

avere (1) m. credit, credit side; (*pl.*) possessions.

avere (2) vt., vi. to have; to get; to own: aver da dare, to owe; aver caldo, freddo, fame, sete, to be hot, cold, hungry, thirsty; aver ragione, to be right; — 30 anni, to be thirty (years old).

aviatore m. pilot, airman; **aviatrice** f. aviatrix, airwoman.

aviazione f. aviation; Air Force.

avicoltura f. aviculture.

avidamente adv. greedily.

avidità f. greed; eagerness.

a'vido adj. greedy; eager.

aviere m. (*mil.*) airman.

avioli'nea f. air line.

aviotrasportato adj. airborne.

avitaminosi f. avitaminosis.

avito adj. ancestral.

avo m. ancestor.

avo'rio m. ivory.

avvalersi vr. to avail oneself.

avvallamento m. sinking.

avvallare vt. to hollow; **avvallarsi** vr. to sink.

avvalorare vt. to confirm, strengthen.

avvantaggiare vt. to benefit; to increase; to improve; **avvantaggiarsi** vr. to benefit (by).

avvedersi vr.[181] to perceive, become aware (of); to realize.

avvedutezza f. shrewdness.

avveduto adj. shrewd, sagacious. pp. of avvedersi.

avvelenamento m. poisoning.

avvelenare vt. to poison; **avvelenarsi** vr. to poison oneself.

avvenimento m. event.

avvenire (1) m. future; prospects.

avvenire (2) vi.[181] to happen, take place; to chance: avvenga che può, come what may.

avventarsi vr. to dash; to pounce.

avventatezza f. rashness.

avventato adj. rash, reckless.

avventi'zio m., adj. supernumerary.

avvento m. advent, accession.

avventore m. customer.

avventura f. adventure.

avventurarsi vr. to venture.

avventuriera f. adventuress.

avventuriere m. adventurer.

avventuroso adj. adventurous.

avverare vt. to verify; **avverarsi** vr. to come true; to happen.

avver'bio m. adverb.

avversare vt. to antagonize.

avversa'rio m. foe; opponent.

avversione f. aversion, dislike, disinclination.

avversità f. adversity, misfortune.

avverso adj. adverse, averse, hostile.

avvertenza f. caution, thoughtfulness; note, foreword; direction; warning.

avvertimento m. caution, warning.

avvertire vt. to caution; to warn; to notice, feel, sense.

avvezzare vt. to accustom; **avvezzarsi** vr. to get accustomed.

avvezzo adj. accustomed, used.

avviamento m. starting, start, outset; introduction, beginning.

avviare vt. to start, set going; to introduce, initiate; **avviarsi** vr. to start; to set out.

avvicendamento m. alternation; rotation.

avvicendare vt., **avvicendarsi** vr. to alternate; to rotate.

avvicinare vt., **avvicinarsi** vr. to approach, draw near, accost.

avvilimento m. humiliation, dejection.

avvilire vt. to humiliate; to degrade; to dishearten, deject; to lower; **avvilirsi** vr. to humble oneself; to degrade oneself; to lose courage.

avviluppare vt. to wrap up; to entangle; **avvilupparsi** vr. to wrap oneself up; to tangle.

avvinazzato m. tippler.

avvincente adj. fascinating.

avvin'cere vt.[144] to bind, tie; to hug; to fascinate.

avvinghiare vt. to catch, clutch; **avvinghiarsi** vr. to cling.

avvinto adj. bound; fascinated. pp. of avvincere.

avvi'o m. start, beginning.

avvisa'glia f. skirmish; hint, symptom.

avvisare vt. to inform; to warn.

avvisatore m. warner, alarm: — d'incendio, fire alarm.

avviso m. notice; warning; opinion; caution; poster; advertisement; aviso (ship).

avvistare vt. to sight, espy.

avvitamento m. (*aeron.*) barrel roll; tailspin.

avvitare vt. to screw; **avvitarsi** vr. to screw; (*aeron.*) to spin in.

avviticchiare vt., **avviticchiarsi** vr. to twine (around).

avvizzire vt., vi. to wither.

avvocatessa *f.* female lawyer.
avvocato *m.* lawyer; barrister; solicitor; counsel.
avvocatura *f.* bar: esercitare l'—, to practice law.
avvol'gere *vt.*[146] to wrap up; to wind up; avvolgersi *vr.* to wrap oneself up; to wind.
avvolgi'bile *f.* roller blind.
avvolgimento *m.* winding.
avvolto *adj.* wound; twisted. *pp. of* avvolgere.
avvolto'io *m.* vulture.
avvoltolare *vt.* to roll up; avvoltolarsi *vr.* to roll, wallow.
Azeglio, Massimo d', Italian statesman and author (1798–1866).
azienda *f.* concern, firm, business.
azionare *vt.* to operate.
aziona'rio *adj. (comm.)* stock.
azione *f.* action; *(comm.)* share; lawsuit.
azionista *m.* shareholder.

azotare *vt.* to nitrogenize.
azoto *m.* nitrogen, azote.
azzannare *vt.* to tusk, gore.
azzardare *vt.* to stake; to risk. *vi.* to dare; azzardarsi *vr.* to venture; to dare.
azzardato *adj.* risky; rash.
azzardo *m.* hazard, risk: gioco d'—, gamble, gambling.
azzardoso *adj.* hazardous, risky.
azzeccagarbugli *m.* pettifogger.
azzeccare *vt.* to hit: azzeccarla, to hit the mark.
azzimato *adj.* dressed up.
az'zimo *adj.* unleavened, azymous.
azzittire *vt.* to silence; azzittirsi *vr.* to be quiet.
azzoppare *vt.* to lame. *vi.* to become lame.
azzoppato *adj.* lame.
azzuffarsi *vr.* to come to blows.
azzurro *m., adj.* blue, azure.
azzurrognolo *adj.* bluish.

B

babau *m.* bugbear, bogy.
babbeo *m.* fool, dupe.
babbo *m.* father, dad, daddy.
babbuc'cia *f.* slipper.
babbuino *m.* baboon.
babele *f.* babel.
babe'lico *adj.* uproarious.
babilonese *m., adj.* Babylonian.
babilo'nia *f.* hubbub, babel, confusion.
babordo *m.* port side.
bacarsi *vr.* to rot.
bacato *adj.* rotten; wormeaten.
bacca *f.* berry.
baccalà *m.* cod, codfish.
baccanale *m.* bacchanal, orgy.
baccano *m.* noise, din, hubbub.
Baccante *f.* Bacchante.
baccarà *m.* baccarat.
baccello *m. (bot.)* pod.
Bacchelli, Riccardo, Italian novelist (1891–   ).
bacchetta *f.* rod, wand.
bacchettone *m.* sanctimonious person, pietist.
Bacco *m.* Bacchus: per —!, by Jove!
bacheca *f.* showcase.
bachelite *f.* bakelite.
bacherozzo *m.* earthworm.
bachicoltura *f.* sericulture.
bachicultore *m.* sericulturist.
baciamano *m.* hand-kissing.
baciapile *m., f.* sanctimonious person.
baciare *vt.* to kiss; baciarsi *vr.* to kiss *(one another).*
bacillare *adj.* bacillary.
bacillo *m.* bacillus *(pl.* bacilli).
bacinella *f.* basin; *(photo.)* tray.
bacino *m.* basin; dock; reservoir; *(anat.)* pelvis.

ba'cio *m.* kiss.
baco *m.* worm; *(da seta)* silkworm.
bacologi'a *f.* sericiculture.
bacte'rio *see* batte'rio.
bada *f. in the phrase:* tenere a —, to stave off, to check.
badare *vi.* to mind; to look *(after),* tend; to listen: badate! watch out!
badessa *f.* abbess.
badi'a *f.* abbey.
badilante *m.* shoveler, digger.
badile *m.* shovel.
baffetti *m pl.* clipped mustache.
baffo *m.* mustache; whisker: baffi all'amer cana, clipped mustache.
bagaglia'io *m.* baggage car.
baga'glio *m.* baggage; luggage.
bagarinag'gio *m. (theat.)* scalping.
bagarino *m. (theat.)* scalper.
baga'scia *f.* harlot, whore.
bagattella *f.* trifle.
bagglanata *f.* nonsense; foolery.
baggiano *m.* fool, blockhead.
ba'glio *m. (naut.)* beam.
bagliore *m.* gleam, glimmer; dazzle.
bagnante *m., f.* bather.
bagnare *vt.* to bathe; to wash; to water; to wet; to soak; bagnarsi *vr.* to get wet; to bathe.
bagnarola *f.* bathtub.
bagnasciuga *m. (naut.)* waterline.
bagnino *m.* lifeguard.
bagno *m.* bath; bathroom; prison: andare ai bagni, to go to the seaside.
bagnomari'a *m.* bain-marie, double boiler.
bagordo *m.* revelry.
ba'ia *f.* bay; jest; hooting.

baiadera *f.* bayadere.

ba'io *m.*, *adj.* bay (*horse*).

baionetta *f.* bayonet.

ba'ita *f.* mountain hut.

balaustrata *f.* balustrade.

balbettamento *m.* stammering; baby talk.

balbettare *vt.*, *vi.* to stammer.

Balbo, Cesare, Italian writer and statesman (1789–1853).

Balbo, Italo, Italian aviator and politician (1896–1940).

balbu'zie *f.* stammer.

balbuziente *m.*, *f.* stammerer. *adj.* stammering.

balca'nico *adj.* Balkan.

balconata *f.* balcony.

balcone *m.* balcony.

baldacchino *m.* canopy.

baldanza *f.* boldness, arrogance.

baldanzosamente *adv.* boldly.

baldanzoso *adj.* bold, arrogant.

baldo *adj.* bold, fearless.

baldo'ria *f.* revelry.

baldracca *f.* harlot, strumpet.

balena *f.* whale.

balenare *vi.* to flash.

baleniera *f.* whaler, whaleship.

baleno *m.* flash, lightning.

balenot'tera *f.* (*zool.*) rorqual.

balenotto *m.* whale calf.

balestra *f.* crossbow; (*mach.*) leaf spring: foglia di —, spring leaf.

ba'lia *f.* nurse.

bali'a *f.* mercy: in — di, at the mercy of.

ba'lio *m.* foster-father.

bali'stica *f.* ballistics.

bali'stico *adj.* ballistic.

balistite *f.* ballistite.

balla *f.* bale; heap.

balla'bile *m.* dance tune.

ballare *vt.*, *vi.* to dance. *vi.* to shake, be loose.

ballata *f.* ballad.

ballato'io *m.* gallery; perch.

ballerino *m.* dancer, partner; ballerina *f.* dancer; ballerina; ballet girl, partner.

balletto *m.* ballet.

ballo *m.* dance; ball: corpo di —, ballet; tirare in —, to call in question.

ballonzolare *vi.* to hop.

ballottag'gio *m.* second ballot.

balneare *adj.* bathing: stazione —, seaside resort.

baloccarsi *vr.* to toy; to trifle.

balocco *m.* toy, plaything.

balordag'gine *f.* silliness; foolery.

balordo *m.* fool; *adj.* foolish, giddy; phony.

balsa'mico *adj.* balmy, balsamic.

bal'samo *m.* balm, balsam.

bal'tico *adj.* Baltic.

baluardo *m.* bulwark.

baluginare *vi.* to flash.

balza *f.* cliff; flounce.

balzano *adj.* white-footed (*horse*); queer, odd, unpredictable.

balzare *vi.* to jump, leap.

balzello *m.* tax; stalk.

balzo *m.* leap: coglier la palla al —, to seize the opportunity.

bamba'gia *f.* cottonwool.

bambina *f.* child, little girl.

bambina'ia *f.* nursemaid.

bambino *m.* child, little boy, "kid."

bamboc'cio *m.* baby; doll; puppet.

bam'bola *f.* doll.

bambù *m.* bamboo.

banale *adj.* banal, trivial, commonplace.

banalità *f.* banality, triviality, platitude.

banano *m.*, banana *f.* banana.

banca *f.* bank: biglietti di —, banknotes.

bancarella *f.* stall.

banca'rio *m.* bank clerk. *adj.* bank, banking: assegno —, check.

bancarotta *f.* bankruptcy: far —, to go bankrupt.

banchettare *vi.* to banquet.

banchetto *m.* banquet, feast.

banchiere *m.* banker.

banchina *f.* dock; platform.

banchisa *f.* ice pack, floe.

banco *m.* counter, desk, bench; bank; form, school desk: — degli accusati, dock; — dei testimoni, witness stand; — di prova (*mach.*), test stand; — di coralli, coral reef.

bancogiro *m.* clearing.

banconota *f.* banknote, note.

banda *f.* side; band; stripe; gang.

Bandello, Matteo, Italian writer of novelle (1480–1562).

banderuola *f.* banderole; weathercock.

bandiera *f.* flag, colors (*pl.*), banner: mutar —, to change sides.

bandire *vt.* to announce; to banish, dismiss; to outlaw.

bandista *m.* bandsman.

bandito *m.* bandit, outlaw, gangster. *pp. of* bandire banished, outlawed: corte bandita, open house.

banditore *m.* crier, hawker; auctioneer.

bando *m.* announcement; ban; exile: mettere al —, to banish.

bandoliera *f.* bandoleer.

ban'dolo *m.* skeining thread.

bar *m.* saloon, barroom, bar.

bara *f.* bier.

barabba *adj.* rogue, scoundrel.

baracca *f.* hut.

baraccamento *m.* hutment.
baraccone *m.* tent (*of a circus*).
baraonda *f.* hurly-burly, mess.
barare *vi.* to cheat.
ba'ratro *m.* abyss, gulf, chasm.
barattare *vt.* to barter, trade, bargain.
baratto *m.* barter.
barat'tolo *m.* pot; can, canister.
barba *f.* beard; hair; (*bot.*) barb: farsi la —, to shave; far venire la —, to bore to death.
barbabie'tola *f.* beet; beetroot.
barbagianni *m.* owl.
barba'glio,*m.* dazzle.
barbaramente *adv.* barbarously.
barba'rico *adj.* barbaric.
barba'rie *f.* barbarity.
barbarismo *m.* barbarism.
bar'baro *m.* barbarian. *adj.* barbarous.
barbazzale *m.* curb.
Barberini, Francesco, Italian cardinal; founder of Barberini Library (1597–1679).
barbetta *f.* goatee; fetlock; (*fort., naut.*) barbette.
barbiere *m.* barber.
barberi'a *f.* barber shop.
barbino *adj.* poor.
bar'bio *m.* barbel.
barbo'gio *adj.* doting.
barbone *m.* poodle; (*dial.*) vagabond, bum.
barbuto *adj.* bearded; (*bot.*) barbate.
barca *f.* boat; rowboat; sailboat.
barcac'cia *f.* (*theat.*) box.
barcaiuolo *m.* boatman.
barcamenarsi *vr.* to get along, manage.
barcarizzo *m.* gangway.
barcarola *f.* (*mus.*) barcarole.
barcollante *adj.* reeling, staggering.
barcollare *vi.* to reel, stagger, sway.
bardare *vt.* to harness.
bardatura *f.* harness.
bardo *m.* bard.
bardosso, (a) *adv.* bareback.
barella *f.* stretcher.
bargello *m.* (*hist.*) constable.
bargi'glio *m.* wattle.
baricentro *m.* barycenter.
barile *m.* barrel, cask, keg.
barilozzo *m.* keg; bull's-eye.
ba'rio *m.* barium.
barista *m.* bartender. *f.* barmaid.
bari'tono *m.* baritone.
barlume *m.* gleam, glimmer.
baro *m.* cheat, sharper.
baroccia'io *m.* carter.
baroccino *m.* tilbury; pushcart.
baroc'cio *m.* cart.
barocco *m., adj.* baroque.
baro'grafo *m.* barograph.
baro'metro *m.* barometer.
baronale *adj.* baronial.
baroncino *m.* young baron.

barone *m.* baron.
baronessa *f.* baroness.
baronetto *m.* baronet; Sir.
barosco'pio *m.* baroscope.
barra *f.* bar; rod; (*naut.*) tiller.
barricare *vt.* to barricade; barricarsi *vr.* to barricade oneself.
barricata *f.* barricade.
barriera *f.* barrier; (*fig.*) obstacle.
barrire *vi.* to trumpet.
barrito *m.* trumpeting, trumpet.
barroc'cio *see* baroccio.
baruffa *f.* scuffle, fight.
baruffare *vi.* to quarrel.
barzelletta *f.* joke, gag, story.
basalto *m.* basalt.
basamento *m.* base.
basare *vt.* to base, found; basarsi *vr.* to base oneself, rest.
basco *m., adj.* Basque: berretto —, beret.
basculla *f.* balance.
base *f.* base; basis, ground.
basetta *f.* whisker.
ba'sico *adj.* (*chem.*) basic.
basilare *adj.* basal, basilar.
basi'lica *f.* basilica.
basi'lico *m.* basil.
basilisco *m.* basilisk.
bassezza *f.* shortness; baseness; meanness; base action.
basso *m.* low, down; bass: alti e bassi, ups and downs. *adj.* low; short; common; shallow.
bassofondo *m.* shoal, shallow: i bassifondi, the underworld.
bassopiano *m.* lowland.
bassorilievo *m.* bas-relief.
bassotto *m.* basset; dachshund.
basta (1) *f.* tuck.
basta (2) *interj.* stop it!
bastante *adj.* sufficient, enough.
bastardo *m., adj.* bastard; mongrel.
bastare *vi.* to suffice, do, be enough; to last: così basta, that will do.
baste'vole *adj.* sufficient.
bastimento *m.* ship, vessel.
bastione *m.* bulwark, rampart.
basto *m.* pack saddle.
bastonare *vt.* to cudgel.
bastonata *f.* buffet, blow.
bastonatura *f.* thrashing.
bastone *m.* cane, stick, staff; club; bat; baton; (*pl., in playing cards*) clubs: mettere i bastoni fra le ruote a qualcuno, to put a spoke in someone's wheel.
batac'chio *m.* clapper, tongue.
batiscafo *m.* bathyscaphe.
batisfera *f.* bathysphere.
batista *f.* batiste, cambric.
batosta *f.* blow; damage; defeat.
batrace *m.* batrachian.
batta'glia *f.* battle, fight.

battagliare *vi.* to fight.
battagliero *adj.* bellicose, warlike.
batta'glio *m.* clapper, tongue.
battaglione *m.* battalion.
battelliere *m.* boatman.
battello *m.* boat.
battente *m.* shutter; knocker. *adj. in the phrase:* a tamburo —, right away, pronto.
bat'tere *vt., vi.* to beat, hit; to knock: — le mani, to clap; — i piedi, to stamp one's feet; battersi *vr.* to strike oneself; to fight: battersela, to take to one's heels.
batterì'a *f.* battery; (*mus.*) drums; (*sport*) heat.
batte'rico *adj.* bacterial.
batte'rio *m.* bacterium (*pl.* bacteria).
batteriologi'a *f.* bacteriology.
batterio'logo *m.* bacteriologist.
battesimale *adj.* baptismal.
batte'simo *m.* baptism, christening, consecration: nome di —, Christian name.
battezzare *vt.* to baptize, christen; to name; to water, add water.
battibecco *m.* squabble, tiff.
batticuore *m.* palpitation.
battimano *m.* applause.
battipanni *m.* clothes beater.
battistero *m.* baptistery.
battistrada *m.* harbinger; (*auto.*) tread.
bat'tito *m.* beat, throb; tick.
battitore *m.* beater; scout.
battuta *f.* beat; witticism, joke; cue; battue; (*mus.*) bar: — d'arresto, halt.
battuto *adj.* beaten; wrought: a spron —, full speed.
batuf'folo *m.* flock, tuft.
bau'le *m.* trunk: fare, disfare i bauli, to pack up, to unpack.
bava *f.* drivel, slaver, slobber.
bavaglino *m.* bib.
bava'glio *m.* gag.
bavarese *m., adj.* Bavarian.
ba'vero *m.* collar.
bavoso *adj.* driveling, slobbery.
bazar *m.* bazaar.
bazza *f.* protruding chin; capital bargain, windfall.
bazze'cola *f.* trifle, fiddlestick.
bazzicare *vt., vi.* to frequent; to consort (*with*).
bazzotto *adj.* soft-boiled.
beare *vt.* to delight; bearsi *vr.* to delight (*in*).
beatamente *adv.* blissfully.
beatificare *vt.* to beatify.
beatificazione *f.* beatification.
beatitu'dine *f.* beatitude, bliss.
beato *adj.* blessed, blissful: — te! you lucky man!

beccac'cia *f.* woodcock.
beccaccino *m.* snipe.
becca'io *m.* butcher.
beccamorti *m.* gravedigger.
beccare *vt.* to peck; to earn; to catch; beccarsi *vr.* to peck each other; to tiff; to get; to catch.
Beccaria, Cesare, Italian economist (1735–1794).
beccheggiare *vi.* to pitch.
beccheg'gio *m.* pitching.
becchime *m.* birdseed.
becchino *m.* gravedigger.
becco (*1*) *m.* beak, bill; burner: non avere il — di un quattrino, to be penniless.
becco (*2*) *m.* he-goat; cuckold.
beccuc'cio *m.* spout.
beduino *m., adj.* Bedouin.
befana *f.* white witch; hag; Epiphany.
beffa *f.* mockery; jest.
beffardo *m.* mocker. *adj.* mocking.
beffare *vt.* to mock; beffarsi *vr.* to mock (*at*).
beffeggiare *vt.* to ridicule.
bega *f.* trouble; quarrel; litigation.
beghina *f.* sanctimonious woman.
bego'nia *f.* begonia.
belare *vi.* to bleat.
belato *m.* bleat, bleating.
belga *m., f., adj.* Belgian.
bella *f.* sweetheart; final game.
belletto *m.* rouge, cosmetic, makeup.
bellezza *f.* beauty; comeliness: che —!, how wonderful!
bel'lico *adj.* war.
bellicoso *adj.* bellicose, belligerent, warlike.
belligerante *m., adj.* belligerent.
belligeranza *f.* belligerency.
bellimbusto *m.* dandy, fop.
Bellini, Vincenzo, Italian composer of operas (1802–1835).
bello *m.* beauty; beau. *adj.* fine, beautiful, handsome, good-looking: il bel mondo, the high life; a bella posta, on purpose.
belluino *adj.* beastly, ferocious.
belva *f.* wild beast.
belvedere *m.* belvedere; (*naut.*) mizzen-topgallant sail; carrozza —, observation car.
Belzebù *m.* Beelzebub.
bemolle *m.* (*mus.*) flat.
benaccetto *adj.* welcome.
benchè *conj.* though, although.
benda *f.* band; bandage.
benda'ggio *m.* bandage.
bendare *vt.* to bandage: — gli occhi a, to blindfold.
bene *m.* good; love; gift, blessing; possession; welfare: beni mobili, chattels; beni immobili, real estate; voler —, to love. *adv.* well; very:

star —, to be well; star — a uno, to become, suit, one; di — in meglio, better and better.

benedetto adj. blessed, holy.

benedire vt.[44] to bless.

benedizione f. blessing; bliss.

beneducato adj. well-bred; polite.

benefattore m. benefactor.

benefattrice f. benefactress.

beneficare vt. to benefit.

beneficenza f. charity.

beneficiare vt., vi. to benefit.

beneficia'rio m. beneficiary; payee. adj. beneficial.

beneficiata f. benefit performance.

benefi'cio m. benefit; profit.

bene'fico adj. beneficent.

benemerenza f. merit, desert.

beneme'rito m. benefactor, supporter. adj. well-deserving.

benepla'cito m. consent.

benes'sere m. welfare; prosperity; well-being, comfort.

benestante m. well-to-do person. adj. well-to-do, well-off.

benestare m. assent; O.K.: dare il —, to approve, to O.K.

benevolenza f. benevolence.

bene'volo adj. benevolent, kindly.

benfatto adj. well-made; shapely.

bengala m. Bengal-light, firework.

beniamino m. favorite.

benignità f. benignity, mildness.

benigno adj. benign, favorable; mild.

beninteso adv. of course.

benis'simo adv. very well, O.K.

bennato adj. well-born; well-bred.

benone adv. very well.

benpensante m. sensible person.

benservito m. testimonial, character; dismissal, brushoff.

bensì conj. indeed; but; on the contrary: è — venuto, ma non l'ho visto, indeed he came but I did not see him.

benvenuto m., adj. welcome: dare il —, to welcome.

benvisto adj. liked, popular.

benvoluto adj. loved, popular.

benzina f. gasoline (abbr.: gas).

beone m. drunkard, sot, toper.

beota m., adj. Boeotian.

bequadro m. (mus.) natural.

berciare vi. to scream.

bere vt.[31] to drink; to swallow: darla a — a qualcuno, to take somebody in.

bergamotto m., **bergamotta** f. bergamot.

berlina f. pillory; berlin; limousine, sedan.

bernoc'colo m. swelling, bump; (fig.) knack: avere il — della pittura, to have a knack for painting.

berretto m., **berretta** f. cap; biretta.

bersagliare vt. to bombard; to harass; to badger.

bersa'glio m. target, butt: tiro al —, rifle practice.

berta f. (mach.) pile driver.

bertuc'cia f. macaque, pithecus.

bestem'mia f. oath, blasphemy.

bestemmiare vt., vi. to curse, swear.

be'stia f. beast, animal: montare in —, to fly into a passion; — nera, pet aversion.

bestiale adj. bestial, beastly, brutish.

bestialità f. beastliness; nonsense, bosh.

bestiame m. cattle; livestock.

betatrone m. betatron.

Betlemme f. Bethlehem.

bet'tola f. tavern.

betto'nica f. betony.

betulla f. birch.

bevanda f. drink, beverage.

bevatrone m. bevatron.

beverag'gio m. beverage, drink.

bevi'bile adj. potable.

bevitore m. drinker.

bevuto pp. of **bere**.

biacca f. white lead.

biada f. feed; oats; crops.

biancastro adj. whitish.

biancheri'a f. linen; underwear.

bianchezza f. whiteness.

bianco m. white; blank; linen; whitewash: di punto in —, all of a sudden. adj. white; blank: dare carta bianca, to give carte blanche; notte bianca, sleepless night; carbone —, electricity.

biancore m. whiteness.

biancospino m. hawthorn.

biascicare vt., vi. to mumble.

biasimare vt. to blame.

biasime'vole adj. reprehensible.

bia'simo m. blame, censure.

Bibbia f. Bible.

biberon' m. feeding bottle, nursing bottle.

bi'bita f. drink, beverage.

bi'blico adj. Biblical.

biblio'filo m. bibliophile.

bibliografi'a f. bibliography.

bibliogra'fico adj. bibliographic.

biblio'grafo m. bibliographer.

biblioteca f. library: — circolante, lending library.

biblioteca'rio m. librarian.

bicarbonato m. bicarbonate.

bicchiere m. glass, cup.

bicicletta f. bicycle; bike.

biciclo m. ordinary, bicycle.

bici'pite m. biceps.

bicocca f. shanty.

bicolore adj. two-colored.

bicon'cavo adj. biconcave.

biconvesso adj. biconvex.
bidè m. bidet.
bidello m. school janitor.
bidente m. pitchfork.
bidone m. can, canister; (slang) cheat.
bieco adj. oblique; sullen; sinister; wicked, dark.
biella f. (mach.) connecting rod.
biennale f. biennial show. adj. biennial.
biennio m. two-year period.
bie'tola f. beet.
bietta f. wedge.
bifase adj. diphase, two-phase.
bifocale adj. bifocal.
bifolco m. farmer; boor.
bi'fora f. mullioned window.
biforcarsi vr. to bifurcate.
biforcazione f. bifurcation.
biforcuto adj. bifurcated.
biga f. chariot.
bigami'a f. bigamy.
bi'gamo m. bigamist. adj. bigamous.
bighellonare vi. to saunter, stroll; to idle.
bighellone m. stroller; idler.
bi'gio m., adj. gray.
biglietteri'a f. ticket bureau; booking office; (theat.) box office.
biglietto m. ticket; card; note: — d'andata, one-way ticket; — d'andata e ritorno, round-trip ticket.
bigotta f. sanctimonious woman, pietist; (naut.) dead-eye.
bigotteri'a f. sanctimony.
bigotto m. sanctimonious man, pietist.
bilancella f. (naut.) trawler.
bilan'cia f. scales (pl.), balance; trawl net; whiffletree.
bilanciare vt., · **bilanciarsi** vr. to balance.
bilanciere m. balance; balance wheel; cross-beam.
bilan'cio m. balance; budget; estimate: — fallimentare, financial statement; fare il —, to balance (books).
bilaterale adj. bilateral; reciprocal.
bile f. bile; rage.
bi'lia f. pocket; billiard ball: far —, to pocket a ball.
biliardo m. billiards.
biliare adj. biliary.
bi'lico m. balance, equipoise, equilibrium; fulcrum: in —, poised.
bilingue adj. bilingual.
bilione m. (U.S.) billion; (Engl.) milliard.
bilioso adj. bilious.
bimba f. child; infant; little girl.
bimbo m. child; infant; little boy, "kid."

bimensile adj. semimonthly.
bimestrale adj. bimestrial.
bimestre m. two months.
bimotore m. twin-engined plane.
bina'rio m. track, rails: — morto, siding.
binda f. jack, screwjack.
binoc'colo m. binoculars (pl.)
bino'mio m. binomial.
bioc'colo m. flake; flock, tuft.
biochi'mica f. biochemistry.
bioge'nesi f. biogenesis.
biografi'a f. biography.
bio'grafo m. biographer.
biologi'a f. biology.
biolo'gico adj. biological.
bio'logo m. biologist.
bionda f. blonde.
biondo m. fawn, yellow; blond man. adj. blond, fair; fawn-colored, yellow.
bios'sido m. dioxide.
bipartito adj. bipartite.
bi'pede m. biped. adj. bipedal.
biplano m. biplane.
birba f., **birbante** m. scoundrel.
birbanteri'a f. knavery; trick.
birbonata f. knavery.
birbone m. rogue.
birichinata f. prank, escapade.
birichino m. urchin.
birillo m. skittle: i birilli, ninepins.
birmano m., adj. Burmese.
biroc'cio m. cart.
birra f. beer, ale.
birra'io m. brewer.
birreri'a f. alehouse.
bis adv. encore; bis: chiedere il —, to request an encore.
bisac'cia f. wallet, haversack.
bisa'vola f. great-grandmother.
bisa'volo m. great-grandfather.
bisbe'tica f. shrew.
bisbe'tico adj. irritable, peevish.
bisbigliare vt., vi. to whisper.
bisbi'glio m. whisper.
bisboc'cia f. merrymaking; food spree.
bisca f. gamblinghouse, hell.
biscaglina f. Jacob's ladder.
biscazziere m. gamblinghouse operator; marker.
bi'scia f. watersnake, snake.
biscottare vt. to bake.
biscotto m. biscuit.
bisestile adj. bissextile: anno —, leap year.
bisettrice f. bisector.
bisil'labo m. disyllable.
bislacco adj. queer, wayward.
bislungo adj. oblong.
bismuto m. bismuth.
bisnonna f. great-grandmother.
bisnonno m. great-grandfather.

bisogna f. task, business.

bisognare vi. to be necessary; must, shall; to need, to want, to be in need of; to be compelled to, to have to.

bisogno m. need, want, necessity.

bisognoso adj. needy, poor.

bisolfuro m. disulphide.

bisonte m. bison.

bissare vt. to call for an encore.

bistecca f. beefsteak.

bisticciare vi., **bisticciarsi** vr. to quarrel, squabble.

bistic'cio m. squabble; pun.

bistrattare vt. to maltreat.

bistro m. bister, bistre.

bi'sturi m. bistoury.

bisunto adj. greasy.

bitor'zolo m. bump; pimple.

bitume m. bitumen.

bituminare vt. to bituminize.

bivaccare vi. to bivouac (ppr. bivouacking; pass., pp. bivouacked).

bivacco m. bivouac.

bivalente adj. bivalent.

bi'vio m. crossroad; quandary.

bizantino adj. Byzantine.

bizza f. flare, freak, whim.

bizzarri'a f. oddity, queerness.

bizzarro adj. bizarre, queer.

bizzeffe, (a) adv. in plenty, galore.

bizzoso adj. peevish, whimsical.

blandire vt. to blandish, soothe, cajole.

blandi'zia f. blandishment.

blando adj. bland, subdued.

blasfemo adj. blasphemous.

blasonato adj. noble.

blasone m. coat of arms; blazon.

blaterare vi. to babble.

blatta f. cockroach, black beetle.

blenorragi'a f. blenorrhoea.

bleso adj. lisping.

blindare vt. to armor.

blindato adj. armored, plated.

bloccare vt. to block; to blockade.

blocco m. blocking; blockade; block, lump; pad: in —, in bulk.

blu m., adj. blue.

bluastro adj. bluish.

blusa f. blouse.

boa (1) m. (zool.) boa.

boa (2) f. (naut.) buoy.

boato m. bellow, boom, roar.

bobina f. coil, reel, spool.

bocca f. mouth; muzzle; opening, hole: — da fuoco, ordnance piece; — da incendio, fire hydrant; in — al lupo! good luck!; acqua in —! mum's the word; a — aperta, agape.

boccac'cia f. grimace.

Boccaccio, Giovanni, Italian author and writer of novelle, Decamerone (1313–1375).

boccale m. cup, jug, tankard.

boccaporto m. hatch, hatchway.

boccascena f. apron stage.

boccata f. mouthful; puff.

boccheggiare vi. to gasp, fight for breath; to be dying.

Boccherini, Luigi, Italian composer (1743–1805).

bocchetta f. hole, spout; keyhole.

bocchino m. cigarette holder; (mus.) mouthpiece.

boc'cia f. pot; bowling ball.

bocciare vt. to reject; to bowl.

boccino m. jack.

boc'cio, bocciuolo m. bud.

boc'cola f. earring; (mach.) bush.

bocconcino m. morsel.

boccone m. mouthful; bit, scrap: a pezzi e bocconi, by fits and starts.

bocconi adv. flat on one's face.

bodino m. pudding.

boemo m., adj. Bohemian.

boero m., adj. Boer.

bo'ia m. executioner, hangman.

Boiardo, Matteo Maria, Italian poet (1434?–1494).

boiata f. infamy; trash.

boicottag'gio m. boycottage.

boicottare vt. to boycott.

Boito, Arrigo, Italian composer, Mefistofele (1842–1918).

bol'gia f. hellpit; chaos.

bo'lide m. bolide; racer.

bolina f. (naut.) bowline.

bolla f. bubble; blister; bull (as papal).

bollare vt. to stamp; to brand (with, as).

bollatura f. stamping, branding.

bollente adj. boiling, hot.

bolletta f. bill; receipt; certificate: essere in —, to be stone-broke.

bolletta'rio m. counterfoil-book.

bollettino m. bulletin; report: — meteorologico, weather forecast.

bollire vt., vi. to boil; to simmer.

bollitore m. boiler.

bollo m. stamp: carta da —, stamped paper; marca da —, revenue stamp.

bollore m. boil; boiling point; bubbling; turmoil; ardor.

bolscevico m., adj. Bolshevist.

bolscevismo m. Bolshevism.

bolso adj. broken-winded.

boma f. (naut.) boom.

bomba f. bomb: tornare a —, to return to the point; a prova di —, bombproof; — atomica, atom bomb.

bombardamento m. bombing: aereo da —, bomber.

bombardare vt. to bomb; to bombard.

bombardiere m. gunner; bombardier; bomber.

bombetta f. derby hat.

bom'bola *f.* bottle, cylinder: — di ossigeno, oxygen tank.
bomboniera *f.* candy box.
bompresso *m.* (*naut.*) bowsprit.
bonac'cia *f.* calm.
bonaccione *m.* good fellow.
bonariamente *adv.* good-naturedly.
bonarietà *f.* good nature, kindliness.
bona'rio *adj.* good-natured, kindly.
boni'fica *f.* reclamation.
bonificare *vt.* to reclaim; to grant a discount of.
bonomi'a *f.* good nature.
bonsenso *m.* sense, good sense.
bontà *f.* goodness; kindness.
bontempone *m.* free liver; jolly good fellow.
bonzo *m.* bonze.
bora *f.* bora.
borace *m.* borax.
borato *m.* borate.
borbottare *vt.*, *vi.* to grumble.
borbotti'o *m.* grumble.
borchia *f.* boss.
bordare *vt.* to hem.
bordata *f.* (*naut.*) broadside.
bordatura *f.* hem, border.
bordeggiare *vi.* to tack.
bordello *m.* brothel; noise.
borderò *m.* account, list.
bordo *m.* border; board; hem, edge: a —, on board; virare di —, to veer around; — del marciapiede, curb.
bordura *f.* hem, edge.
bo'rea *m.* north wind.
boreale *adj.* boreal, northern.
borgata *f.* hamlet.
borghese *m.*, *adj.* bourgeois; civilian: in —, in civvies; poliziotto in —, plain-clothesman.
borghesi'a *f.* bourgeoisie, middle class.
Borgia, Cesare, Italian cardinal and military leader (1476–1507).
Borgia, Lucrezia, sister and political Contemporary of Cesare (1480–1591).
borgo *m.* hamlet.
borgomastro *m.* burgomaster.
bo'ria *f.* conceit, haughtiness.
bo'rico *adj.* boric.
borioso *adj.* haughty.
boro *m.* (*chem.*) boron.
borra *f.* flocks; stuffing; hair.
borrac'cia *f.* canteen.
Borromeo, Carlo, Italian cardinal and saint (1538–1584).
borsa *f.* purse, pouch, bag, sack: Borsa Valori, Stock Exchange; — di studio, scholarship.
borsaiuolo *m.* pickpocket.
borseggiare *vt.* to rob, pick (*some-body's*) pocket.
borseg'gio *m.* pocket-picking.

borsellino *m.* purse, pouch.
borsetta *f.* handbag.
borsista *m.* stock-broker.
bosca'glia *f.* brushwood, bush.
boscaiuolo *m.* woodcutter.
bosco *m.* wood, woods, forest: — ceduo, coppice.
boscoso *adj.* woody.
bosso *m.* box tree; boxwood.
bos'solo *m.* box; boxwood; cartridge case.
bota'nica *f.* botany.
bota'nico *m.* botanist. *adj.* botanic.
bo'tola *f.* trap door.
botta *f.* blow, thump; thrust.
botta'io *m.* cooper.
bottata *f.* thrust, hint.
botte *f.* barrel, cask.
bottega *f.* shop; workshop.
bottega'io *m.* shopkeeper.
botteghino *m.* box office.
Botticelli, Sandro, Italian painter (1447?–1510).
botti'glia *f.* bottle.
bottiglieri'a *f.* wineshop.
bottino *m.* booty, loot.
botto *m.* stroke; toll.
botto, (di) *adv.* suddenly.
bottoncino *m.* small button; stud; bud.
bottone *m.* button; knob; bud: bottoni gemelli, links; attaccare un — a, to buttonhole.
bovaro *m.* cowherd, cowboy.
bove *see* bue.
bovino *adj.* bovine.
bozza *f.* sketch; proof; bump; (*naut.*) stopper.
bozzello *m.* (*naut.*) block.
bozzetto *m.* sketch, drawing.
boz'zolo *m.* cocoon; lump.
braccare *vt.* to hunt, stalk; to bay.
braccetto, (a) arm in arm: prendere uno a —, to take one's arm.
bracciale *m.* armlet.
braccialetto *m.* bracelet: orologio a —, wrist watch.
bracciante *m.* day laborer.
bracciata *f.* armful; stroke.
braccio *m.* arm; limb; wing; branch; bracket; fathom.
bracciuolo *m.* arm (*of a chair*).
bracco *m.* hound; setter; pointer.
bracconiere *m.* poacher.
brace *f.* live coal, ember.
braciere *m.* firepan, brazier.
braciuola *f.* chop.
brado *adj.* wild.
bragozzo *m.* (*naut.*) lugger.
brama *f.* greed; longing.
Bramante, Donato d'Agnolo, Italian architect and painter (1444–1514).
bramare *vt.* to covet.
bramino *m.* Brahmin.

bramire *vi.* to bellow, bell.
bramito *m.* bellow, roar; bell.
bramosi'a *f.* greed.
bramoso *adj.* greedy, covetous.
branca *f.* claw; tentacle; flight; branch.
bran'chia *f.* gill.
brancicare *vt.* to handle.
branco *m.* flock, pack, herd; (*ichthyol.*) shoal, school.
brancolare *vi.* to grope.
branda *f.* cot, folding bed.
brandello *m.* shred, tatter.
brandire *vt.* to brandish.
brando *m.* sword.
brano *m.* shred, tatter; passage.
branzino *m.* bass (fish).
brasile *m.* brazilwood.
brat'tea *f.* bract.
bravac'cio *m.* bully, braggart.
bravata *f.* bluster, brag.
bravo (*1*) *m.* bravo.
bravo (*2*) *adj.* brave; clever, skillful: un — **ragazzo**, a good, nice boy.
bravura *f.* courage; skill.
brec'cia *f.* breach, gap; breccia; metal.
brefotro'fio *m.* foundling hospital.
bretelle *f.pl.* suspenders.
breve (*1*) *m.* (papal) brief.
breve (*2*) *adj.* short, brief; concise.
brevemente *adv.* briefly.
brevettare *vt.* to patent.
brevettato *adj.* patented.
brevetto *m.* patent; brevet
brevia'rio *m.* breviary. license.
brevità *f.* shortness, brevity.
brezza *f.* breeze.
bricco *m.* kettle, pot, urn.
bricconata *f.* knavery, roguery.
briccone *m.* rascal, scamp.
bricconeri'a *f.* roguery.
bri'ciola *f.* crumb, bit.
briga *f.* trouble; care; quarrel: attaccar —, to pick a quarrel.
brigadiere *m.* brigadier.
brigantag'gio *m.* brigandage.
brigante *m.* brigand, bandit.
brigantino *m.* (*naut.*) brig.
brigare *vi.* to intrigue.
brigata *f.* party; brigade.
brighella *m.* clown.
bri'glia *f.* bridle; (*pl.*) reins: a — **sciolta**, full speed.
brigoso *adj.* hard, difficult.
brillamento *m.* firing; husking; glare.
brillante *m.* brilliant, diamond; comic (actor). *adj.* brilliant; shining.
brillantemente *adv.* brilliantly.
brillantina *f.* brilliantine, pomade.
brillare *vt.* to fire, blow up; to husk. *vi.* to shine, sparkle.
brillo *adj.* tipsy, woozy.
brina *f.* hoarfrost, rime.
brinare *vi.* to frost.

brindare *vi.* to toast.
brin'disi *m.* toast.
bri'o *m.* sprightliness, liveliness.
briosamente *adv.* lively, briskly.
brioso *adj.* brisk, lively.
bri'scola *f.* trump.
britan'nico *adj.* British.
bri'vido *m.* shiver, shudder; thrill.
brizzolato *adj.* grizzled.
brizzolatura *f.* grizzling.
brocca *f.* jug, pitcher; (*bot.*) shoot.
broccatello *m.* brocatel.
broccato *m.* brocade.
brocco *m.* twig; iron-sting; jade.
broc'colo *m.* broccoli.
broda *f.* slops; rigmarole.
broda'glia *f.* slops.
brodetto *m.* fish soup.
brodo *m.* broth, soup.
brodoso *adj.* thin, juicy.
brogliazzo *m.* waste book.
bro'glio *m.* intrigue, cabal.
brolo *m.* kitchen garden.
bromo *m.* bromine.
bromuro *m.* bromide.
bronchi *m.pl.* bronchi.
bronchiale *adj.* bronchial.
bronchite *f.* bronchitis.
bron'cio *m.* pout; **mettere il —**, to pout.
broncopolmonite *f.* bronchopneumonia.
brontolamento *see* brontolio.
brontolare *vi.* to grumble.
brontoli'o *m.* grumbling; rumbling.
brontolone *m.* grumbler.
bronzare *vt.* to bronze.
bronzatura *f.* bronzing.
bron'zeo *adj.* bronzy; tanned.
bronzina *f.* bushing; bearing.
bronzo *m.* bronze: **faccia di —**, brazen face.
brossura *f.* brochure; unbound book.
brucare *vt.* to graze.
bruciacchiare *vt.* to scorch.
bruciacchiatura *f.* scorching.
bruciante *adj.* burning.
bruciapelo, (a) *adv.* point-blank.
bruciare *vt., vi.* to burn; to sear; to cauterize; **bruciarsi** *vr.* to burn oneself.
bruciatic'cio *m.* smell of burning.
bruciatura *f.* burning; burn, sear.
bruciore *m.* burning sensation.
bruco *m.* caterpillar, worm.
brughiera *f.* heath.
brulicare *vi.* to swarm.
brulichi'o *m.* swarm, swarming.
brullo *adj.* barren, bare.
bruma *f.* cold weather; mist; (*zool.*) shipworm.
bruna, brunetta *f.* brunette.
Brunelleschi, Filippo, Florentine architect (1377–1446).

brunire vt. to burnish, polish; to blue.
brunitura f. burnish; blueing.
bruno m. brown; brunet. adj. brown, dark; swarthy.
Bruno, Giordano, Italian philosopher, burned at the stake (1548–1600).
brusca f. horse brush.
bruscamente adv. sharply; roughly, curtly, gruffly; abruptly.
brusco adj. sharp; sour; rough; curt; gruff; abrupt.
bru'scolo m. mote, speck.
brusi'o m. hubbub, buzzing.
brutale adj. brutal, beastly.
brutalità f. brutality.
brutalmente adv. brutally.
bruto m., adj. brute.
bruttare vt. to soil, foul.
bruttezza f. ugliness.
brutto adj. ugly; bad.
bruttura f. ugliness; turpitude.
bubbone m. bubo.
bubbo'nico adj. bubonic.
buca f. hole; pocket: — **delle lettere**, letterbox.
bucaneve m. (bot.) snowdrop.
bucaniere m. buccaneer.
bucare vt. to bore, pierce; to puncture: to prick; **bucarsi** vr. to prick oneself, be punctured.
bucato m. wash, washing.
bucatura f. boring; puncture.
buc'cia f. peel, rind, skin.
bucherellare vt. to riddle.
buco m. hole.
buco'lico adj. bucolic, pastoral.
Budda m. Buddha.
buddismo m. Buddhism.
buddista m., adj. Buddhist.
budello m. bowel, gut, catgut; casing (for sausages).
budino m. pudding.
bue m. ox (pl. oxen).
bu'falo m. buffalo.
bufera f. storm.
buffare vt. to huff (at draughts).
buffetto m. flip of the finger, a puff of wind.
buffo (1) m. gust.
buffo (2) adj. funny, droll; comic.
buffonata f. buffoonery, jest.
buffone m. buffoon, clown.
buffoneri'a f. clownery.
bugi'a f. lie; taper.
buglardo m. liar. adj. false.
bugigat'tolo m. cubbyhole.
bugliuolo m. bucket, bail.
bugna f. boss; (naut.) clew.
bu'io m. darkness.
bulbo m. bulb.
bulboso adj. bulbous.
bul'garo m. Russia leather. adj., m. Bulgarian.
bulinare vt. to engrave.

bulino m. burin.
bulletta f. tack.
bullone m. bolt.
buona, (alla) adv. plainly; informally. adj. plain; informal.
buonamano f. tip, gratuity.
Buonarroti, Michelangelo, see **Michelangelo**.
buongusta'io m. gourmet; connoisseur.
buono m. good; bond; coupon: — **postale internazionale**, international reply coupon. adj. good; kind, kindly; fit; fine: **alla buona**, plain, plainly; **con le buone o con le cattive**, willy-nilly.
buonsenso m. common sense.
buonuscita f. good will.
burattare vt. to bolt, to sift.
burattina'io m. puppet showman.
burattinata f. mummery.
burattino m. puppet.
buratto m. bolter, sifter.
burbanza f. arrogance.
burbanzoso adj. arrogant.
bur'bero adj. churlish, surly; gruff.
burchiello m. (naut.) lighter.
buricco m. donkey.
burla f. joke, jest, trick, prank.
burlare vt., vi., **burlarsi** vr. to make fun of; to jeer, poke fun at.
burlesco adj. burlesque, comic.
burletta f. farce.
burlone m. jester, joker, prankster.
buro'crate m. bureaucrat.
burocra'tico adj. bureaucratic.
burocrazi'a f. bureaucracy, red tape.
burrasca f. storm.
burrascoso adj. stormy.
burrifi'cio m. dairy.
burro m. butter.
burrone m. ravine.
burroso adj. buttery.
buscare vt., **buscarsi** vr. to get; to catch.
busec'chia f. casing (for sausages); tripe.
busillis m. problem, question.
Busoni, Ferruccio Benvenuto, Italian pianist and composer (1866–1924).
bussa f. blow; (pl.) beating.
bussare vi. to knock.
bus'sola (1) f. compass: **perdere la —** to lose one's head.
bus'sola (2) f. screen door.
bussolotto m. juggler's box: **giuoco del bussolotti**, hocus-pocus.
busta f. envelope; portfolio; case.
busta'ia f. corsetmaker.
bustina f. small envelope; (mil.) cap.
busto m. trunk, torso; bust; corset.
butano m. butane.
butirroso adj. buttery.
buttafuori m. (theat.) callboy; (naut.) outrigger.

buttare *vt.* to throw, fling, hurl; to squander; to throw away; to secrete; **buttarsi** *vr.* to throw oneself.

butterato *adj.* pockmarked.

but'tero (*1*) *m.* pockmark; (*2*) *m.* herder, cowboy.

buzzo *m.* belly.

C

ca'bala *f.* cabbala; swindle; cabal, plot.

cabali'stico *adj.* cabbalistic.

cabina *f.* cabin, cab; booth; bath-house; cockpit (*of an airplane*); car (*of an elevator*): — **di lusso** (*naut.*), stateroom.

cablogramma *m.* cable.

cabotag'gio *m.* cabotage; foreign trade.

cabrare *vi.* (*aeron.*) to zoom.

cabrata *f.* (*aeron.*) zoom, chandelle.

cacao *m.* cocoa.

cacare *vi.* to defecate.

cacasenno *m.* wiseacre.

cacatoa *m.* parakeet.

cacca *f.* ordure; (*fig.*) dirt.

cac'cia (*1*) *f.* hunting; fowling; chase; game.

cac'cia (*2*) *m.* (*aeron.*) fighter; (*naut.*) destroyer.

cacciagione *f.* game, venison.

cacciare *vt.*, *vi.* to go hunting; to chase; to rout; to send away; to thrust, drive in; to throw; **cacciarsi** *vr.* to thrust oneself, hide oneself: **cacciare un urlo**, to utter a cry, scream.

cacciasommergi'bili *m.* submarine chaser.

cacciata *f.* routing.

cacciatora *f.* hunting jacket.

cacciatore *m.* hunter, huntsman: — **di frodo**, poacher.

cacciatorpediniere *m.* destroyer.

cacciatrice *f.* huntress.

cacciavite *m.* screw driver.

cac'cola *f.* rheum; mucus; grease.

cachi *m.* khaki, Japanese persimmon. *adj.* khaki-colored.

cachinno *m.* cachinnation.

ca'cio *m.* cheese.

cacofoni'a *f.* cacophony.

cacofo'nico *adj.* cacophonous.

cadauno *adj.* each.

cada'vere *m.* corpse, body.

cadave'rico *adj.* cadaverous.

cadente *adj.* falling decrepit.

cadenza *f.* cadence rhythm.

cadere *vi.*" to fall; to drop; to set.

cadetto *m.* cadet.

cad'mio *m.* cadmium.

Cadorna, Luigi, Italian general (1850–1928).

caducità *f.* transiency, perishableness.

caduco *adj.* deciduous; transient: **mal** —, falling sickness.

caduta *f.* fall, crash; downfall.

caduto *m.* dead. *pp. of* **cadere,** fallen.

caffè *m.* coffee; café: — **concerto**, music-hall.

caffeina *f.* caffeine.

caffettiera *f.* coffeepot.

cafone *m.* boor.

cagionare *vt.* to cause.

cagione *f.* cause: **a** — **di**, on account of, because of.

cagione'vole *adj.* sickly.

cagliare *vi.* to curdle.

ca'glio *m.* rennet.

cagna *f.* bitch.

cagnara *f.* barking; uproar; brawl.

cagnesco *adj.* doggish: **guardare in** —, to look askance at.

Caienna, (**pepe di**) *m.* cayenne (pepper).

caimano *m.* caiman.

caino *m.* (Cain); traitor.

Cairoli, Benedetto, Italian statesman (1826–1889).

cala *f.* creek; hold.

calabrone *m.* hornet, bumblebee.

calafatare *vt.* to calk.

calama'io *m.* inkpot, inkstand.

calamaro *m.* cuttlefish.

calamita *f.* loadstone; magnet.

calamità *f.* calamity.

calamitare *vt.* to magnetize.

calamitoso *adj.* calamitous.

ca'lamo *m.* (*bot.*) calamus.

calandra *f.* (*mach.*) calender.

calandrare *vt.* to calender.

calante *adj.* declining; setting.

calap'pio *m.* noose; snare.

calare *vt.* to lower; to strike. *vi.* to descend (*upon*); to decline; to set; to drop; to decrease: **il** — **della notte**, nightfall; **calarsi** *vr.* to let oneself down; to dive.

calata *f.* dropping; lowering; descent; wharf.

calca *f.* throng, crowd.

calcagno *m.* heel.

calcara *f.* limekiln.

calcare *vt.* to tread (*upon*); to trample; to press; to force; to stress.

cal'care *m.* limestone.

calca'reo *adj.* calcareous.

calce (*1*) *f.* lime.

calce (*2*) *f.* bottom, foot: **in** —, at (the) foot.

calcedo'nio *m.* chalcedony.

calcese *m.* (*naut.*) masthead.

calcestruzzo *m.* concrete.
calciare *vi.* to kick.
calciatore *m.* kicker; soccer player.
calcificare *vt.* to calcify.
calcificazione *f.* calcification.
calcina *f.* lime, mortar.
calcinac'cio *m.* plaster rubbish; (*pl.*) ruins, debris, rubble.
calcina'io *m.* lime pit.
calcinare *vt.* to calcine; to lime.
cal'cio (*1*) *m.* kick; butt, stock; (*sport*) soccer.
cal'cio (*2*) *m.* (*chem.*) calcium.
calcioclanamide *f.* calcium cyanamide.
calco *m.* cast; trace.
calcografia *f.* chalcography.
calcola'bile *adj.* calculable.
calcolare *vt.*, *vi.* to calculate; to reckon; to value; to plan; to rely (on).
calcolatore *m.* reckoner; schemer. *adj.* calculating.
calcolatrice *f.* reckoner: macchina —, calculator, calculating machine.
cal'colo *m.* calculation; estimate; guess; plan; calculus (*pl.* calculi).
calcolosi *f.* (*pathol.*) stone.
calcomani'a *f.* decalcomania.
calcopirite *f.* chalcopyrite.
calcotipi'a *f.* copperplate.
calda'ia *f.* boiler.
calda'io *m.* caldron.
caldallessa *f.* boiled chestnut.
caldamente *adv.* warmly.
caldana *f.* flush; infatuation.
caldarrosto *f.* roast chestnut.
caldeggiare *vt.* to favor, support.
caldera'io *m.* coppersmith.
calderone *m.* caldron.
caldo *m.* warmth, heat: aver —, to be hot; fa —, it is warm; tener —, to keep warm. *adj.* warm; hot.
calefazione *f.* calefaction.
caleidosco'pio *m.* kaleidoscope.
calenda'rio *m.* almanac, calendar.
calende *f.pl.* kalends: rimandare alle — greche, to put off till doomsday.
calendimag'gio *m.* May Day.
calesse *m.* calèche, buggy.
calettare *vt.* to mortise.
calibrare *vt.* to calibrate.
ca'libro *m.* caliber; gauge (*fig.*) size.
ca'lice *m.* cup; chalice.
califfo *m.* caliph.
cali'gine *f.* fog, mist, smog.
caliginoso *adj.* foggy, misty.
calla'ia *f.* gap; path.
calle *f.* lane.
calli'fugo *m.* corn plaster.
calligrafi'a *f.* calligraphy, penmanship; handwriting.
calli'grafo *m.* calligrapher.
callista *m.* podiatrist, chiropodist.
callo *m.* corn: fare il — a, to become inured to.

callosità *f.* callosity, callus.
calloso *adj.* corny, horny.
calma *f.* calm; composure.
calmante *m.*, *adj.* sedative.
calmare *vt.* to calm, soothe; calmarsi *vr.* to calm down; to abate.
calmiere *m.* compulsory price ceiling.
calmo *adj.* quiet, still; cool.
calo *m.* decrease; shrinkage.
calomelano *m.* calomel.
calore *m.* heat; warmth; inflammation.
calori'a *f.* calorie, calory.
calori'fero *m.* heater.
calori'fico *adj.* calorific.
caloroso *adj.* warm; calorific.
calo'scia *f.* galosh, overshoe.
calotta *f.* skull cap; cap: — cranica, brainpan, skull.
calpestare *vt.* to trample.
calun'nia *f.* slander, calumny.
calunniare *vt.* to slander.
calunniatore *m.* slanderer.
calunnioso *adj.* slanderous.
calura *f.* heat.
Calva'rio *m.* Calvary.
calvi'zie *f.* baldness.
calvo *adj.* bald.
calza *f.* stocking; sock; hose; wick; fare la —, to knit.
calzare (*1*) *vt.* to boot; to put on; to wear. *vi.* to fit, suit.
calzare (*2*) *m.* boot.
calzato'io *m.* shoe horn.
calzatura *f.* footwear (*pl.*).
calzaturifi'cio *m.* shoe factory.
calzerotto *m.* sock.
calzetta'io *m.* hosier.
calzettone *m.* woolen sock.
calzola'io *m.* shoemaker.
calzoleri'a *f.* shoemaker shop.
calzoncini *m.pl.* shorts.
calzoni *m.pl.* trousers; pants; slacks; breeches.
camaleonte *m.* chameleon.
camarilla *f.* camarilla, cabal.
cambiale *f.* bill (*of exchange*), IOU; draft; promissory note; — di favore, accommodation bill.
cambiamento *m.* change.
cambiare *vt.*, *vi.* to change, alter: — vita, to turn over a new leaf; cambiarsi *vr.* to change; to turn into.
cambiavalute *m.* moneychanger.
cam'bio *m.* change, shift; exchange; (*mach.*) gear box, transmission; (*mil.*) relief.
cambri *m.* cambric.
cambusa *f.* galley, caboose.
cambusiere *m.* steward.
came'lia *f.* camellia.
ca'mera *f.* room, chamber; parliament: — di combustione, firebox; —

d'aria, inner tube; — ardente, chapelle ardente.

camerata (1) f. dormitory.

camerata (2) m. friend; comrade.

cameratismo m. comradeship.

cameriera f. maid; waitress.

cameriere m. valet, servant; waiter.

camerino m. cubbyhole; dressing room; lavatory.

ca'mice m. alb; gown.

camiceri'a f. shirt shop.

camicetta f. blouse.

cami'cia f. shirt; chemise; wrapper; (mach.) jacket: — di forza, strait jacket.

camicia'io m., camicia'ia f. shirt maker.

camiciola f. sports shirt; T-shirt.

camiciotto m. blouse, shirt.

caminetto, m. fireplace.

camino m. chimney.

ca'mion m. truck; lorry.

camiona'bile, camionale f. highway.

camionetta f. pickup truck, jeep.

camionista m. truckdriver.

cami'tico adj. Hamitic.

camma f. (mach.) cam.

cammelliere m. cameldriver.

cammello m. camel.

camme'o m. cameo.

camminamento m. communication trench.

camminare vi. to walk; to stroll.

camminata f. walk; gait.

camminatore m. walker, stroller.

cammino m. way; road; path.

camomilla f. camomile.

camorra f. Camorra; graft.

camorrista m. Camorrist; grafter.

camosciare vt. to shammy.

camo'scio m. chamois, shammy; suède.

campagna f. country, countryside; campaign: artiglieria da —, field artillery.

campagnuola f. countrywoman.

campagnuolo m. countryman. adj. country, rural.

campale adj. decisive; pitched.

campana f. bell: — di vetro, bell jar.

campanac'cio m. cattle bell.

campanaro m. bellringer.

campanella f. small bell; (bot.) bellflower.

Campanella, Tommaso, Italian philosopher, City of the Sun (1568–1639).

campanello m. bell.

campanile m. steeple, belfry.

campanilismo m. localism.

campa'nula f. campanula.

campare vi. to live.

campata f. span.

compato adj.: — in aria, farfetched, improbable.

campeggiare vi. to stand out; to camp.

campeggiatore m., campeggiatrice f. camper.

campeg'gio m. camping; logwood.

campestre adj. rural, country: corsa —, cross-country race.

Campido'glio m. capitol.

campionare vt. to sample.

campiona'rio m. sample book, sample set; pattern book.

campionato m. championship; competition.

campione m. champion; ace; sample; pattern; specimen: — senza valore, sample of no commercial value.

campionessa f. championess.

campo m. field; camp; ground; trade, industry: — visivo, range of vision; — d'onda (radio), wave band; — di tennis, tennis court; aiutante di —, adjutant; —lungo (moving pictures), long shot.

camposanto m. churchyard.

camuffamento m. disguise.

camuffare vt. to disguise; camuffarsi vr. to disguise oneself.

camuso adj. snub-nosed.

canadese m., adj. Canadian.

cana'glia f. rabble; scoundrel.

canagliata f. knavery.

canale m. channel; canal; gutter; drain; (anat.) duct.

canaletto m. gutter; groove.

canalizzare vt. to canalize.

canalizzazione f. canalization.

canalone m. ravine.

ca'napa f. hemp.

canapè m. settee, sofa.

canapifi'cio m. hemp mill.

ca'napo m. rope, cable.

cana'pulo m. stalk of hemp.

canarino m. canary.

cancan m. can-can; racket; gossip.

cancella'bile adj. erasable.

cancellare vt. to cross out; to erase; to wipe out; to cancel; to efface.

cancellata f. railing.

cancellatura f. erasure.

cancellazione f. cancellation.

cancelleri'a f. chancellery; stationery.

cancelliere m. chancellor; clerk.

cancello m. gate, gateway.

canceroso adj. cancerous.

cancrena f. gangrene.

cancrenoso adj. gangrenous.

cancro m. cancer; (astr.) Cancer.

candeggiare vt. to bleach.

candeg'gio m. bleaching.

candela f. candle; chandelle; spark plug; (aeron.) nose dive.

candelabro m. chandelier.

candeliere m. candlestick.

Candelora f. Candlemas.

candelotto m. icicle.
candidato m. candidate.
candidatura f. candidature.
can'dido adj. white. candid; naive.
candire vt. to candy.
candito m. candy. adj. candied.
candore m. whiteness. candor.
cane m. dog, hound. cock (of a gun); unskilled person s; bad actor, "flop": menare il can per l'aia, to beat about the bush.
canea f. rabble, hubbub.
canestro m., **canestra** f. basket.
can'fora f. camphor.
canforare vt. to camphorate.
cangiante adj. changeable; shot: seta —, shot silk.
canguro m. kangaroo.
cani'cola f. dog days. (astr.) Dog Star.
canile m. kennel doghouse.
canino (1) m. canine tooth.
canino (2) adj. canine. tosse canina, whooping cough
cani'zie f. frostiness old age.
canna f. cane, reed pipe pole; barrel (of a gun): — da pesca, fishing rod; — del camino, flue.
cannella f. cinnamon.
cannello m. pipe; stick, rod: — della pipa, pipestem.
canni'bale m., adj. cannibal.
cannicciata f. reed fence.
cannic'cio m. wattle
cannocchiale m. spyglass, binoculars (pl.); field glass. opera glass.
cannonata f. gunshot. (it. slang) hit (something excellent).
cannoncino m. small gun, howitzer; pleat; sweet roll.
cannone m. gun, cannon; pipe; tube; box pleat (of a skirt); (it. slang) "smart apple," "corker."
cannoneggiare vt. to cannonade.
cannoniera f. gunboat.
cannoniere m. gunner.
cannuc'cia f. tubule; penholder; pipestem.
can'nula f. (med.) cannula.
canoa f. canoe.
ca'none m. rule, tenet, canon; rent.
cano'nica f. parsonage, presbytery.
canonicato m. canonicate.
cano'nico m. canon. adj. canonical: diritto —, canon law.
canonizzare vt. to canonize.
canoro adj. canorous, singing.
Canossa f. Canossa: andare a —, to eat humble pie, to get off one's high horse.
canottag'gio m. boating, rowing.
canottiera f. undershirt; straw hat.
canottiere m. oarsman, rower.
canotto m. boat: — di gomma, rubber raft.

Canova, Antonio, Italian sculptor (1757–1822).
canovac'cio m. canvas; dishcloth; plot (of a story).
cantante m., f. singer.
cantare vt., vi. to sing; (fig.) to squeal.
canta'ride f. (entom.) cantharis, Spanish fly; (chem.) cantharides.
cantasto'rie m. folk singer.
cantatore m., **cantatrice** f. singer.
canterano m. chest of drawers.
canterellare vt. to hum, croon.
canterino m., **canterina** f. songster.
can'tero m. chamber pot.
canticchiare vt. to hum, croon.
can'tico m. canticle, hymn, song.
cantiere m. yard; (naut.) shipyard; (mil.) navy yard.
cantilena f. dirge; singsong.
cantina f. cellar; coal cellar; wine shop.
cantiniere m. cellarman.
canto (1) m. song; singing; canto.
canto (2) m. corner; side: d'altro —, on the other hand; dal — mio, for my part; da —, aside.
cantonata f. corner, street corner; blunder.
cantone m. corner; (geog.) canton.
cantoniera, (casa) f. roadkeeper's house.
cantoniere m. roadkeeper; road mender; (rail.) trackwalker.
cantore m. chorister; singer.
cantori'a f. choir.
Cantù, Cesare, Italian historian (1807–1895).
cantuc'cio m. corner; nook.
canuto adj. hoary, white-haired.
canzonare vt. to mock.
canzonato'rio adj. mocking.
canzonatura f. mockery, gibe.
canzone f. song: — in voga, hit song.
canzonetta f. song; canzonet.
canzonettista m. songster. f. songstress.
canzoniere m. songbook.
caolino m. kaolin.
caos m. chaos.
capace adj. capacious, roomy; able, clever, capable.
capacità f. capaciousness; capacity; cleverness; faculty.
capacitare vt. to persuade; capacitarsi vr. to be persuaded.
capanna f. hut, cabin; shanty.
capannello m. shanty; group.
capanno m. bower; cabana; booth.
capannone m. barn; hangar, shed.
caparbietà f. stubbornness.
capar'bio adj. stubborn, opinionated.
caparra f. down payment, deposit; retainer.
capatina f. call: dare una — da, to drop in on.

capeggiare *vt.* to lead.

capello *m.* hair: tre capelli, three hairs; pettinarsi (i capelli), to comb one's hair.

capelluto *adj.* hairy, long-haired: cuoio —, scalp.

capelve'nere *m.* maidenhair.

capestro *m.* halter.

capezzale *m.* bolster; bedside.

capez'zolo *m.* nipple; udder.

capido'glio *m.* sperm whale.

capienza *f.* capacity.

capigliatura *f.* hair.

capillare *adj.* capillary.

capillarità *f.* capillarity.

capinera *f.* blackcap.

capire *vt.* to understand, comprehend; to perceive; to realize. *vi.* to enter (into).

capitale *m., f., adj.* capital: peccato —, mortal sin.

capitalismo *m.* capitalism.

capitalista *m.* capitalist.

capitalizzare *vt.* to capitalize. *vi.* to save.

capitana *f.* flagship.

capitanare *vt.* to lead.

capitaneri'a *f.* harbor office, harbor authority.

capitano *m.* captain; (*naut.*) skipper: — di lungo corso, shipmaster; — di porto, harbormaster; — di ventura, condottiere.

capitare *vi.* to happen, occur: mi è capitato d'incontrarla, I happened to meet her.

capitello *m.* capital; headband.

capitolare *vi.* to capitulate.

capitolato *m.* capitulation.

capitolazione *f.* capitulation.

capi'tolo *m.* chapter; article.

capitombolare *vi.* to tumble.

capitom'bolo *m.* tumble.

capitone *m.* big eel.

capo *m.* head; top; end; (*geog.*) cape; chief, boss; item: da — a fondo, from top to toe; da —, over again; andare da —, to make a paragraph; — di vestiario, garment; — di un partito, party leader; — d'accusa, charge.

capobanda *m.* bandmaster; ringleader.

capocac'cia *m.* master of the hounds.

capoc'chia *f.* head: a —, foolishly.

capoc'cia *m.* head, chief, boss.

capoco'mico *m.* actor-manager.

capocronista *m.* city editor (U.S.).

capocuoco *m.* chef, head cook.

Capodanno *m.* New Year's Day.

capofab'brica *m.* foreman.

capofami'glia *m.* head of the family.

capofitto, (a) *adv.* headlong.

capogiro *m.* dizziness, vertigo.

capolavoro *m.* masterpiece.

capoli'nea *m.* terminus.

capolino *m.*: far —, to peep (in, out).

capoluogo *m.* county town, county seat, capital.

capomastro *m.* builder.

capopezzo *m.* gunner.

capopo'polo *m.* demagogue.

caporale *m.* corporal.

caporeparto *m.* head of a department; floorwalker.

caporione *m.* ringleader, chief.

caposaldo *m.* datum point; stronghold; basis; datum.

caposca'rico *m.* merry andrew.

caposezione *m.* head of a department.

caposquadra *m.* squad chief; foreman.

capostazione *m.* station master.

caposti'pite *m.* founder (*of a family*).

capotare *vi.* to capsize.

capota'vola *m.* head of the table.

capotreno *m.* (*rail.*) conductor.

capoverso *m.* paragraph.

capovol'gere *vt.* to overturn, reverse; capovolgersi *vr.* to overturn, capsize.

capovolgimento *m.* overturn.

capovolta *f.* somersault.

cappa (1) *f.* vault; mantle; frock; cowl.

cappa (2) *f.* (*naut.*) trysail.

cappa (3) *f.* the letter "k."

cappeggiare *vi.* (*naut.*) to lie to.

cappella *f.* chapel.

cappella'io *m.* hatter.

cappellano *m.* chaplain, padre.

cappellata *f.* hatful.

cappelleri'a *f.* hat store.

cappelliera *f.* hatbox.

cappello *m.* hat; cover, cap; pileus (*of a mushroom*); heading, caption: — a cilindro, tophat; prender —, to take offense.

cappellotto *m.* percussion cap.

cap'peril *interj.* by Jove!

cap'pero *m.* (*bot.*) caper.

cap'pio *m.* bow; noose.

cappona'la *f.* coop.

capponare *vt.* to caponize.

cappone *m.* capon.

cappotta *f.* cape; coif; hood.

cappotto *m.* overcoat; slam.

cappuccino *m.* Capuchin; coffee with cream.

capra *f.* goat.

capra'io *m.* goatherd.

capretto *m.* kid.

capriata *f.* truss.

capric'cio *m.* whim; fancy; flirtation.

capriccioso *adj.* whimsical, bizarre; moody; peevish; refractory (*of a child*).

Capricorno *m.* Capricorn.

caprifo'glio *m.* honeysuckle.

caprino *adj.* caprine, goatish.

capriuola *f.* caper.

capriuolo *m.* roebuck.

capro, caprone *m.* he-goat: **capro espiatorio,** scapegoat.

cap'sula *f.* capsule; percussion cap.

captare *vt.* to intercept.

captazione *f.* detecting.

Capuana, Luigi, Italian novelist, poet, and critic (1839-1915).

capzioso *adj.* captious.

carabat'tola *f.* trifle, gimcrack.

carabina *f.* carbine.

carabiniere *m.* carabineer.

Caracciolo, Francesco, gallant Neapolitan admiral; sentenced to be hanged by Nelson (1752–1799).

carachiri *m.* hara-kiri.

caracollare *vi.* to caracole.

caraffa *f.* decanter.

caram'bola *f.* carom.

carambolare *vi.* to carom.

caramella *f.* candy, drop; monocle.

caramellare *vt.* to candy.

caramente *adv.* dearly.

carato *m.* carat; share; *(naut.)* part-ownership.

carat'tere *m.* character; disposition, nature; handwriting; type; feature; temper: — **corsivo,** italics.

caratterista *m.* character actor; *f.* character actress.

caratteri'stica *f.* characteristic, feature, trait, peculiarity, hallmark.

caratteri'stico *adj.* characteristic.

caratterizzare *vt.* to characterize.

caratura *f. (comm.)* share.

Caravaggio, da, Michelangelo Amerighi, Italian painter (1569-1609).

caravella *f.* caravel, carvel.

carbona'io *m.* coalman, coal vendor.

carbonato *m.* carbonate.

carbon'chio *m.* carbuncle; smut *(in wheat).*

carboncino *m.* charcoal (pencil).

carbone *m.* coal; carbon: carbon fossile, mineral coal; — **di legna,** charcoal.

carbonella *f.* slack, small coal.

carbo'nico *adj.* carbonic.

carboniera *f. (naut.)* collier.

carboni'fero *adj.* carboniferous.

carbonile *m.* coal bunker.

carbo'nio *m.* carbon.

carbonizzare *vt.,* **carbonizzarsi** *vr.* to carbonize.

carburante *m.* fuel. [char.

carburare *vt.* to carburize.

carburatore *m.* carburetor.

carburazione *f.* carburization.

carburo *m.* carbide.

carcassa *f.* carcass; framework; ribbing *(of a ship);* wreck; decrepit person, "fossil"; jalopy.

carcera'rio *adj.* prison: **guardia carceraria,** prison guard, jailor.

carcerato *m.* prisoner.

car'cere *m., f.* prison, jail.

carceriere *m.* jailer, jailor.

carciofo *m.* artichoke.

carda *f.* carding machine.

carda'nico *adj.* universal: **sospensione cardanica,** gimbals; **giunto** —, universal joint.

cardare *vt.* to card.

cardatore *m.* carder.

cardatrice *f.* carding machine.

cardatura *f.* carding.

cardellino *m.* goldfinch.

cardi'aco *adj.* cardiac: **attacco** —, heart attack.

cardinale *m., adj.* cardinal.

cardinali'zio *adj.* cardinalesque.

car'dine *m.* hinge, pivot.

cardiologi'a *f.* cardiology.

cardio'logo *m.* heart specialist.

cardiopalmo *m.* heart disease.

cardo *m.* cardoon; teasel.

Carducci, Giosuè, Italian poet and man of letters. Nobel prize in literature, 1906 (1836-1907).

carena *f. (naut.)* bottom.

carenag'gio *m.* careen: **bacino di** —, dry dock.

carenare *vt.* to careen; to fair.

carenatura *f. (aeron.)* fairing.

carenza *f.* lack, want.

caresti'a *f.* famine; dearth.

carezza *f.* caress; expensiveness.

carezzare *vt.* to caress, fondle.

carezze'vole *adj.* fondling, sweet.

cariare *vt.,* **cariarsi** *vr.* to decay, rot.

caria'tide *f.* caryatid.

ca'rica *f.* office, appointment; charge: **tornare alla** —, to try again.

caricamento *m.* loading; lading.

caricare *vt.* to lade, burden; to charge; to load; to wind up; to exaggerate; **caricarsi** *vr.* to burden oneself; to take upon oneself.

caricatore *m.* loader; magazine *(of a pistol);* *(photog.)* cartridge, spool.

caricatura *f.* caricature; cartoon.

caricaturista *m.* caricaturist, cartoonist.

ca'rico *m.* load, burden; charge; lot; trump; cargo. *adj.* loaded *(with);* wound up; deep.

ca'rie *f.* decay, caries.

carino *adj.* nice, cute, fine; funny.

carità *f.* charity, love; mercy; alms: **chiedere la** —, to beg.

carite'vole *adj.* charitable.

carlinga *f. (aeron.)* fuselage.

carlona, (alla) *adv.* carelessly.

carme *m.* poem.

carmi'nio *m.* carmine.

carnagione *f.* complexion.

carnale *adj.* carnal, lustful.

carname *m.* carrion, carnage.

carne *f.* meat; flesh.
carne'fice *m.* executioner.
carneficina *f.* slaughter.
carnevale *m.* carnival.
carniere *m.* game bag.
carni'voro *adj.* carnivorous.
carnoso *adj.* fleshy.
caro *adj.* dear; expensive.
Caro, Annibal, Italian poet and translator (1507–1566).
carogna *f.* carrion; *(fig.)* "heel," cad.
carosello *m.* carousel.
carota *f.* carrot.
caro'tide *f.* carotid.
carovana *f.* caravan.
carovaniera *f.* desert trail.
carovaniere *m.* caravaneer.
carovi'veri *m.* high cost of living: indennità per —, high-cost-of-living bonus.
carpa *f.* carp.
Carpaccio, Vittore, Italian painter (1450–1522).
carpentiere *m.* carpenter.
carpire *vt.* to extort; to wheedle.
carponi *adv.* on all fours.
carradore *m.* carter.
carra'ia, carrarec'cia *f.* cartway.
carreggiata *f.* rut; cartway; gauge.
carrelata *f.* *(moving pictures)* dolly shot; boom shot.
carrello *m.* trolley; truck; *(aeron.)* landing gear; *(moving pictures)* dolly.
carretta *f.* cart.
carrettiere *m.* carter.
carretto *m.* pushcart.
carriera *f.* career.
carriola *f.* wheelbarrow.
carrista *m.* tank corpsman.
carro *m.* cart; truck, lorry; *(astr.)* the Great Bear; Wain: — armato, armored car; — funebre, hearse.
carrozza *f.* carriage, coach; cab: — ristorante, dining car; — letto, sleeper.
carrozza'bile *adj.* practicable.
carrozzeri'a *f.* carriage factory; body; — fuori serie, custom-built body.
carrozzina *f.* perambulator.
carrozzino *m.* tilbury; sidecar.
carrozzone *m.* wagon; caravan.
carrubo *m.*, carruba *f.* carob.
carru'cola *f.* pulley.
carta *f.* paper; map; card; — assorbente, blotting paper; — da parati, wallpaper; — moneta, paper money; dare — bianca, to give a free hand.
cartac'cia *f.* waste paper.
carta'io *m.* papermaker.
cartape'cora *f.* parchment.
cartapesta *f.* papier-mâché.
cartastrac'cia *f.* wastepaper.

carteg'gio *m.* correspondence, letters.
cartella *f.* file, folder; form; certificate, policy; ticket; portfolio; satchel; brief case; sheet: — clinica, chart *(med.).*
cartellino *m.* ticket; label.
cartello *m.* poster; cartel.
cartellone *m.* placard, poster; playbill.
cartiera *f.* papermill.
cartila'gine *f.* cartilage.
cartina *f.* *(pharm.)* dose; leaf.
cartoc'cio *m.* cornet; cornetful.
carto'grafo *m.* cartographer.
cartola'io *m.* stationer.
cartoleri'a *f.* stationery store; stationery.
cartolina *f.* card; post card: — illustrata, picture post card; — vaglia, postal order.
cartomante *m.*, *f.* fortuneteller.
cartoncino *m.* card, cardboard.
cartone *m.* cardboard; pasteboard; cartoon.
cartuc'cia *f.* cartridge.
cartucciera *f.* cartridge box.
Caruso, Enrico, Italian operatic tenor (1873–1921).
casa *f.* house, building; home: — editrice, publishing house; — madre, head office; — di pena, prison; — da gioco, gambling house; fatto in —, homemade.
Casa, della, Giovanni, Italian prelate and poet (1503–1556).
casacca *f.* coat, jacket.
casac cio, (a) *adv.* at random, rashly.
casalingo *adj.* homey; homemade; plain: articoli casalinghi, kitchenware.
casamatta *f.* casemate; bunker.
casamento *m.* building; tenement.
casata *f.* house, lineage.
casato *m.* family name.
cascame *m.* waste.
cascante *adj.* falling, limp.
cascare *vi.* to fall, drop.
cascata *f.* fall, waterfall.
cascina *f.* farm.
casco *m.* helmet; topee.
caseggiato *m.* block; building.
caseifi'cio *m.* cheese dairy.
caseina *f.* casein.
casella *f.* pigeonhole; box, case; cell *(of a beehive):* — postale, Post Office Box *(abb.* P.O.B.).
Casella, Alfredo, Italian composer (1883–1947).
casellante *m.* trackwalker.
casella'rio *m.* filing cabinet.
casello *m.* trackwalker's lodge.
caserma *f.* barracks *(pl.).*
casino *m.* clubhouse; bungalow.
caso *m.* case; chance; event; instance: in — affermativo, in the affirmative;

in — contrario, otherwise; fare al
— di, to suit; non fateci —, never
mind; — mal, in case; if at all.
casolare *m.* hovel.
casotto *m.* booth, box.
ca'spital, *interj.* bless me! you don't
say! why!
cassa *f.* case, box; cash; coffin: —
toracica, chest; — del violino,
belly; — di risparmio, savings bank;
a pronta —, cash down.
cassaforte *f.* safe.
cassapanca *f.* wooden chest; settle.
cassare *vt.* to quash, cancel.
cassazione *f.* cassation.
cas'sero *m.* quarterdeck.
casseruola *f.* stew pan, casserole.
cassetta *f.* box, case; coachman's
seat: — di sicurezza, safe deposit
box; — per lettere, mailbox.
cassetto *m.* drawer.
cassettone *m.* chest of drawers.
cassiera *f.* cashier.
cassiere *m.* cashier; teller.
cassone *m.* coffer; cofferdam.
casta *f.* caste.
castagna *f.* chestnut.
castagno *m.* chestnut tree; chestnut
wood. *adj.* chestnut, chestnut-
colored.
castano *adj.* chestnut-colored.
castellana *f.* lady of the manor.
castellano *m.* squire.
castello *m.* castle, manor; scaffold:
— di poppa, quarterdeck; — di
prua, forecastle; castell' in aria,
castles in Spain.
castigare *vt.* to punish.
castigato *adj.* severely correct.
Castiglione, Baldassarre, Italian
statesman and author (1478–1529).
castigo *m.* punishment.
castità *f.* chastity.
casto *adj.* chaste, pure.
castone *m.* bezel, setting.
castoro *m.* beaver.
castrare *vt.* to castrate.
castrato *m.* mutton. *pp. of* castrare
castrated.
castrone *m.* gelding (*horse*); wether
(*sheep*).
castroneri'a *f.* blunder; nonsense.
casuale *adj.* fortuitous.
casualmente *adv.* fortuitously, by
chance.
casu'pola *f.* hovel, hut.
cataclisma *m.* cataclysm.
catacomba *f.* catacomb.
catafalco *m.* catafalque.
catafa'scio, (a) *adv.* topsy-turvy.
Catalani, Alfredo, Italian composer,
Loreley, Wally (1854–1893).
catalessi *f.* catalepsy.
cata'lisi *m.* catalysis.

catalizzatore *m.* catalyzer.
catalogare *vt.* to catalogue.
cata'logo *m.* catalogue, list.
catapec'chia *f.* tumble-down house,
hovel.
cataplasma *m.* poultice.
catapulta *f.* catapult.
catapultare *vt.* to launch, catapult.
cataratta *see* cateratta.
catarro *m.* catarrh.
catarsi *f.* catharsis.
catasta *f.* heap, pile, stack.
catastale *adj.* cadastral.
catasto *m.* cadastre.
cata'strofe *f.* catastrophe.
catastro'fico *adj.* catastrophic.
catechismo *m.* catechism.
catechizzare *vt.* to catechize.
categori'a *f.* category, class.
categoricamente *adv.* categorically.
catego'rico *adj.* categorical, direct.
catena *f.* chain; bondage; range (*of
mountains*): — di montaggio, assembly line; reazione a —, chain
reaction.
catenac'cio *m.* bolt.
catena'ria *f.* catenary.
catenella *f.* chainlet: punto —, chain
stitch.
cateratta' *f.* sluice gate; cataract,
waterfall; (*med.*) cataract.
caterva *f.* crowd; heap, pile.
cateto *m.* cathetus (*pl.* catheti).
catinella *f.* water basin.
catino *m.* basin.
ca'todo *m.* cathode.
catramare *vt.* to tar.
catrame *m.* tar.
cat'tedra *f.* desk; cathedra; chair;
professorship.
cattedrale *f.* cathedral.
cattedra'tico *adj.* professorial: parlare
con tono —, to pontificate.
cattivarsi *vr.* to gain, win.
cattive'ria *f.* wickedness; spite.
cattività *f.* captivity.
cattivo *adj.* bad, ill; wicked; evil;
naughty; wrong; captive.
cattolice'simo *m.* Catholicism.
catto'lico *m., adj.* Catholic.
cattura *f.* capture, arrest.
catturare *vt.* to capture, seize.
caucciù *m.* caoutchouc, rubber.
ca'usa *f.* cause, motive; (*law*) suit: a
— di, on account of, because of.
causale *f.* cause. *adj.* causal.
causare *vt.* to cause.
causi'dico *m.* pettifogger.
ca'ustico *adj.* caustic.
cautamente *adv.* cautiously, warily.
cautela *f.* caution, care.
cautelare *vt.* to protect; cautelarsi
vr. to take precautions, provide
(*against*).

cauterizzare vt. to cauterize.
cauterizzazione f. cauterization.
ca'uto adj. cautious, wary.
cauzione f. security; bail.
cava f. quarry; mine.
cavadenti m. tooth puller.
cavagno m. basket.
Cavalcanti, Guido, Italian poet, friend of Dante (?-1300).
cavalcare vt. to ride (a horse). vi. to ride (on a horse).
cavalcata f. ride, cavalcade.
cavalcatura f. mount, horse.
cavalcavi'a f. overpass.
cavalcioni adv. astraddle.
cavalierato m. knighthood.
cavaliere m. rider, horseman; cavalryman; knight; escort; partner: **cavalier servente**, gallant, escort.
cavalla f. mare.
cavalleresco adj. chivalrous; knightly: **ordine —**, Order of Knighthood.
cavalleri'a f. cavalry; chivalry; chivalrousness.
cavallerizza f. horsewoman.
cavallerizzo m. horseman, rider; horsebreaker.
cavalletta f. grasshopper.
cavalletto m. trestle; easel.
cavallino m. colt. adj. equine: **mosca cavallina**, horse fly.
cavallo m. horse, knight (at chess); horsepower: **— a dondolo**, hobbyhorse; **— di battaglia**, fad, pièce de résistance; **cavalli di Frisia**, chevaux-de-frise.
cavallone m. big horse; billow.
Cavallotti, Felice, Italian poet, dramatist and politician (1842-1898).
cavare vt. to pull out, draw out; to get; to dig, hollow out: **cavar sangue**, to bleed; **cavarsi la voglia di**, to gratify one's desire for; **cavarsi d'impiccio**, to pull through; **cavarsi dai piedi**, to get out of the way; **cavarsi (uno) d'attorno**, to get rid of (one).
cavastivali m. bootjack.
cavatappi, **cavaturac'cioli** m. corkscrew.
caverna f. cavern, cave.
cavernoso adj. cavernous, hollow.
cavezza f. halter.
ca'via f. guinea pig.
caviale m. caviar.
cavic'chio m. wooden peg.
cavi'glia f. ankle; peg; spoke.
cavillare vi. to cavil, quibble.
cavillo m. cavil, quibble.
cavilloso adj. captious.
cavità f. cavity, hollow.
cavo (1) m. rope, cable, hawser.
cavo (2) m., adj. hollow.
cavolfiore m. cauliflower.
ca'volo m. cabbage.

Cavour, **di**, Emilio Benso, Italian statesman (1810-1861).
cazzeruola f. stew pan.
cazzottare vt. to punch; **cazzottarsi** vr. to fight.
cazzotto m. punch, "sock."
cazzuola f. trowel.
ce (1) adv. there: **non — n'è**, there is none.
ce (2) pron. us, to us: **egli — lo diede**, he gave it to us; **— lo dissero**, they told us so.
cecamente adv. blindly.
Cecchi, Emilio, Italian writer and essayist. Bitter America, English and American Authors (1884-   ).
cece m. chickpea.
cecità f. blindness.
ceco m., adj. Czech.
ceco-slovacco m., adj. Czechoslovak.
ce'dere vt., vi.[38] to cede, yield; to surrender; to transfer; to give in; to sink.
cede'vole adj. yielding; soft.
cedi'bile adj. transferable: **non —**, non-transferable.
cedimento m. yielding; sinking.
ce'dola f. coupon.
cedrata f. citron syrup.
cedrina f. balm mint, melissa.
cedrino adj. citrine.
cedro m. citron.
cedrone m. wood grouse.
ce'duo (bosco) m. coppice.
ceduto pp. of cedere.
cefalea f. headache.
ce'falo m. mullet.
ceffo m. snout; ugly face.
ceffone m. slap in the face.
celare vt., **celarsi** vr. to hide.
celeber'rimo adj. famous, renowned.
celebrare vt. to celebrate.
celebrazione f. celebration.
ce'lebre adj. famous, renowned.
celebrità f. fame, renown.
ce'lere adj. quick, swift: **la "Celere,"** the flying squad.
celerità f. swiftness, speed.
celermente adv. quickly, swiftly.
celeste adj. heavenly, celestial; skyblue.
celestiale adj. heavenly.
ce'lia f. jest, joke; fun.
celiare vi. to jest, joke.
celibato m. celibacy, bachelorhood.
ce'libe m. bachelor. adj. single.
cella f. cell; closet, storeroom.
Cellini, Benvenuto, Italian goldsmith, sculptor and author (1500-1571).
cellofane f. cellophane.
cel'lula f. cell.
cellulare m. jail; police wagon. adj. cellular: **segregazione —**, close confinement.

cellulo'ide f. celluloid.
cellulosa f. cellulose.
cel'tico adj. Celtic, Keltic.
cementare vt. to cement.
cemento m. cement; concrete: —arma-to, ferroconcrete, reinforced con-crete.
cena f. supper.
cena'colo m. supper room; the Lord's Supper; society.
cenare vi. to have supper.
cenciaiuolo m. ragpicker.
cen'cio m. rag, tatter; duster.
cencioso adj. ragged, tattered.
ce'nere f. ash; ashes.
Ceneren'tola f. Cinderella.
cenno m. sign; nod; wave, beck; gesture; hint; intimation.
ceno'bio m. convent, monastery.
cenobita m. cenobite.
censimento m. census.
censire vt. to take the census of.
censo m. census; income; wealth.
censore m. censor.
censura f. censure; censorship.
censurare vt. to censure.
centa'uro m. centaur; (astr.) Centau-rus; motorcycle racer.
centellinare vt. to sip.
centena'rio m., adj. centennial; cente-narian.
cente'simo m. hundredth (part); cent. adj. hundredth.
centi'grado adj. centigrade.
centigramma m. centigram.
centi'litro m. centiliter.
centi'metro m. centimeter.
cen'tina f. centering; (aeron.) rib.
centina'io m. hundred: a centinaia, by hundreds.
cento m., adj. a hundred, one hundred: — volte, a hundred times; uno per —, one per cent; al — per —, hundred per cent.
centomila adj. a hundred thousand.
centrale f. main house, head office; headquarters: — elettrica, power station; — telefonica, telephone exchange.
centrale adj. central; middle; head; main.
centralinista m., f. (teleph.) operator.
centralino m. telephone exchange.
centralità f. centrality.
centralizzare vt. to centralize.
centrare vt. to center; to hit the mark.
centrifugare vt. to centrifuge.
centri'fugo adj. centrifugal.
centri'peto adj. centripetal.
centro m. center; heart, core; bull's-eye: — attacco, center forward; andare in — to go downtown.
centuplicare vt. to centuple.
cen'tuplo m. centuplicate. adj. cen-tuple, hundredfold.

centu'ria f. century.
centurione m. centurion.
ceppo m. stump; log; chopping block; anchor stock; brakeshoe; stock; (pl.) bonds, chains.
cera f. wax; polish; look, mien: — da pavimenti, floor wax; — da scarpe, shoe polish.
ceralacca f. sealing wax.
cera'mica f. ceramics; (pl.) pottery.
ceramista m. ceramist.
cerare vt. to wax.
cerata f. oilcloth.
Cer'bero m. Cerberus; disciplinarian, martinet.
cerbiatta f. young hind.
cerbiatto m. fawn.
cerbottana f. blow gun.
cerca f. search, quest.
cercare vt. to look for, seek; to ask; to want. vi. to try, endeavor.
cercatore m. seeker, searcher: — d'oro, gold prospector.
cer'chia f. circle; circuit; sphere.
cerchiare vt. to rim, hoop.
cerchiatura f. rimming, hooping.
cer'chio m. circle; hoop, ring: — della morte (aeron.), loop.
cerchione m. felly, wheel rim.
cereale m., adj. cereal.
cerebrale adj. cerebral.
ce'reo adj. waxen; waxy; wan.
cerfo'glio f. chervil.
cerimo'nia f. ceremony, rite.
cerimoniale m., adj. ceremonial.
cerimoniere m. Master of Ceremonies.
cerimonioso adj. ceremonious.
cerino m. wax match; taper.
cernec'chio m. lock, tuft.
cer'nere vt.[110] to choose, sort.
cerniera f. hinge; clasp: — lampo, zipper.
cer'nita f. choice, selection.
cero m. church candle.
cerone m. grease paint, make-up.
cerotto m. plaster.
certamente adv. certainly.
certezza f. certainty.
certificare vt. to certify.
certificato m. certificate.
certo m., adj. certain. adv. certainly.
certi pron.pl. some.
certosa f. charterhouse.
certosino m., adj. Carthusian.
certuno pron.indef. somebody.
ceru'leo adj. cerulean, sky-blue.
cerume m. cerumen, ear wax.
cerussa f. ceruse, white lead.
cerva f. (zool.) hind.
cervelletto m. cerebellum.
cervello m. brain; brains; sense; mind.
cervello'tico adj. absurd, preposterous, fantastic.
cervicale adj. cervical.

cervice *f.* nape; cervix; head.

Cervino, (Monte) *m.* Matterhorn.

cervo *m.* stag, hart: — **volante,** stag-beetle.

cesa'reo *adj.* Caesarean: **taglio —,** Caesarean section.

cesellare *vt.* to chase, (en) grave.

cesellatore *m.* chaser, (en) graver.

cesellatura *f.* chasing, graving.

cesello *m.* burin, graver, chisel.

ceso'ia *f.* shears, scissors; (*mach.*) shearing machine.

ce'spite *m.* tuft; source.

cespo *m.* tuft.

cespu'glio *m.* bush, thicket.

cessare *vt., vi.* to cease, stop, discontinue, quit.

cessazione *f.* cessation.

cessiona'rio *m.* assignee.

cessione *f.* assignment, cession.

cesso *m.* privy, water closet.

cesta *f.* basket, hamper.

cestinare *vt.* to throw into the wastebasket; to reject.

cestino *m.* wastebasket.

cestista *m., f.* basketball player.

cesto *m.* basket, hamper.

ceta'ceo *m., adj.* cetacean.

ceto *m.* class, rank: **il basso —,** the lower classes; **il — medio,** the middle classes; **il — superiore,** the upper classes.

cetra *f.* cithara.

cetriolino *m.* gherkin.

cetriuolo *m.* cucumber.

che *conj.* that, as to, to; for; when, at; like; than; whether; tanto —, so much that; **è tempo — tu parta,** it is time for you to leave; **più (meno) —,** more (less) than; **lo stesso —,** the same as; **a meno —,** unless; **non importa — egli venga o no,** it doesn't matter whether he comes or not. *pron.rel.* who; whom; that; which; when, where; something: **colui —,** he who; **il —,** which; **col —,** wherewith; **al —,** dopo di —, whereupon; **il giorno —,** the day when; **paese — vai,** any place you go; **non c'è di —,** don't mention it; **avere di — andare avanti,** to have enough to get along; **non c'è nessuno — non sappia,** everyone knows. *adj., pron.interr.excl.* what, how: **— ora è?,** what time is it?; **— peccato!,** what a pity!; **— bello!** how beautiful!

chè *conj.* because, for, since.

checchè *pron.indef.* whatever.

checchessi'a *pron.indef.* anything, everything.

chemioterapi'a *f.* chemotherapy.

Cherubini, Maria Luigi, Italian composer (1760-1842).

cherubino *m.* cherub.

chetare *vt.* to quiet, appease; **chetarsi** *vr.* to quiet down, subside.

chetichella, (alla) *adv.* surreptitiously; stealthily; noiselessly.

cheto *adj.* quiet.

chi *pron.rel., demonstr.* who; whom; whose; he who (that), him who, he whom; she who, her who, she whom; they who, those who, those whom; whoever, whomever; one who; some: **— è?,** who is he?; **di — parli?,** of whom are you speaking?; **di — è questo libro,** whose book is this?; **— vuol mangiare deve lavorare,** he who (that) wants to eat has got to work; **— sarà mai?,** who (ever) can it be?; **chiedilo a — ti pare,** ask whomever you like; **— lo dice e — no,** some say it some don't; **— di loro?,** which of them?

chiac'chiera *f.* chatter, hoax; gossip; glibness: **fare quattro chiacchiere con,** to have a chat with.

chiacchierare *vi.* to chatter; to talk.

chiacchierata *f.* chat, talk.

chiacchieri'o *m.* chatter, prattle.

chiacchierone *m.* chatterbox.

chiama *f.* roll call.

chiamare *vt.* to call (*for*); to send for; to draft; to name; to summon; to ring up: **— in causa,** to bring into court; **chiamarsi** *vr.* to be called, be named: **come ti chiami?,** what is your name?

chiamata *f.* call, summons.

chiappa *f.* buttock.

chiappamosche *m.* fly trap.

chiappare *vt.* to catch.

chiara *f.* glair.

chiaramente *adv.* clearly; frankly.

chiaretto *m.* claret.

chiarezza *f.* clearness.

chiarificare *vt.* to clarify.

chiarificazione *f.* clarification.

chiarimento *m.* explanation.

chiarire *vt.* to clarify, make clear, clear up; to explain; **chiarirsi** *vr.* to clear up, become clear.

chiaro *m.* light; brightness: **— di luna,** moonlight. *adj.* clear; bright; light; illustrious; fair. *adv.* clearly; frankly: **— e tondo,** bluntly.

chiarore *m.* light; glimmer.

chiaroscuro *m.* light and shade; mezzotint.

chiaroveggente *m.* wizard. *adj.* clairvoyant, farsighted.

chiaroveggenza *f.* clairvoyance, farsightedness.

chiassata *f.* hubbub, uproar.

chiasso *m.* noise; uproar.

chiassoso *adj.* noisy; gaudy.

chiatta *f.* punt, barge.
chiavarda *f.* bolt.
chiave *f.* key; wrench, spanner: — inglese, monkey wrench.
chiavetta *f.* small key; tap.
chia'vica *f.* sewer.
chiavistello *m.* bolt, latch.
chiazza *f.* mottle; spot, stain.
chiazzare *vt.* to mottle; to stain, speck.
chiazzato *adj.* mottled; stained.
chicca *f.* sweet, candy.
chic'chera *f.* cup, barge.
chicchessi'a *pron.indef.* anyone, anybody.
chicchirichi *m.* cock-a-doodle-doo.
chicco *m.* grain; seed, pip: — d'uva, grape; — di caffè, coffee bean; — di grandine, hailstone; — di riso, rice grain.
chiedere *vt.*, *vi.*⁵⁴ to ask (*for*), inquire (*about*); to question; to beg (*for*): — scusa, to beg pardon; chiedersi *vr.* to wonder.
chie'rica *f.* tonsure.
chie'rico *m.* minor clerk; clergyman.
chiesa *f.* church.
chiesto *pp.* of chiedere.
chiesuola *f.* (*naut.*) binnacle.
chi'glia *f.* keel.
chilo (1) *m.* (*med., biol.*) chyle: fare il —, to take one's siesta.
chilo (2) *m.* (*weight*) kilogram.
chilociclo *m.* (*radio*) kilocycle.
chilogramma *m.* kilogram.
chilometrag'gio *m.* kilometrage.
chilome'trico *adj.* kilometrical.
chilo'metro *m.* kilometer.
chilowatt *m.* kilowatt.
chimera *f.* chimera; daydream.
chime'rico *adj.* chimerical.
chi'mica *f.* chemistry.
chi'mico *m.* chemist. *adj.* chemical.
chimono *m.* kimono.
china (1) *f.* slope, descent.
china (2) *f.* (*bot.*) cinchona.
chinare *vt.* to bend; chinarsi *vr.* to bend, stoop.
chincagliere *m.* knickknack dealer.
chincaglieri'a *f.* knickknacks; curio shop.
chinino *m.* quinine.
chino *adj.* bent, stooping.
chioc'cia *f.* brood hen: fare la —, to brood.
chiocciare *vi.* to cluck.
chiocciata *f.* hatch.
chioc'cio *adj.* hoarse.
chioc'ciola *f.* snail: scala a —, spiral staircase.
chiodare *vt.* to nail.
chiodo *m.* nail; debt; craze: — di garofano, clove.
chioma *f.* hair; mane; coma (*of a comet*); foliage (*of a tree*).

chiomato *adj.* haired; leafy.
chiosa *f.* gloss, note.
chiosare *vt.* to gloss, annotate.
chiosatore *m.* annotator.
chiosco *m.* kiosk; booth; newsstand.
chiostra *f.* enclosure, fence; set (*of teeth*).
chiostro *m.* cloister.
chiotto *adj.* quiet, still.
Chirico, Giorgio di, Italian painter, founder of "metaphysical" painting (1888–   ).
chirografa'rio *adj.* chirographer.
chiro'grafo *m.* chirograph.
chiromante *m.* chiromancer, palmist, crystal gazer.
chiromanzi'a *f.* chiromancy, crystal gazing.
chirurgi'a *f.* surgery.
chirur'gico *adj.* surgical.
chirurgo *m.* surgeon.
chitarra *f.* guitar.
chitarrista *m.* guitarrist.
chiù *m.* horned owl.
chiu'dere *vt.*, *vi.*³⁹ to close, shut (*up*), lock; to fasten; to enclose; to bar; to seal; to conclude; to stop; to clench (*one's fist*): — un occhio (*fig.*), to wink (at); non — occhio, not to sleep a wink; chiudersi *vr.* to shut, close; to shut oneself up.
chiunque *pron.indef.* whoever, whosoever; whomsoever; anyone, anybody.
chiurlo *m.* curlew.
chiusa *f.* lock, sluice; dam, weir; close, end.
chiusino *m.* lid; manhole.
chiuso *m.* enclosure; fold, pen: al —, indoors. *adj.* shut (*in*), closed; ended, stopped. *pp.* of chiudere.
chiusura *f.* close; closing, shutting; lock; fastening: — ermetica, hermetical sealing; — lampo, zipper.
ci *pron.pers.* us, to us. *pron.refl.* ourselves; each other, one another. *pron.demonstr.* that, it, about it, of it: non — credo, I don't believe it. *adv.* here; there; of it: c'è un po' di pane, there is some bread.
ciabattare *vi.* to shuffle.
ciabattino *m.* cobbler.
ciak *m.* (*moving pictures*) clapper, slate.
cialda *f.* wafer.
cialdone *m.* cone (*as for ice cream*).
cialtrone *m.* draggletail; rascal, "heel."
ciambella *f.* ring-cake; wase.
ciambellano *m.* chamberlain.
ciampicare *vi.* to stumble.
cianamide *m.* cyanamide.
cian'cia *f.* idle talk; gossip.
cianciafru'scola *f.* trifle.

cianciare *vi.* to chatter.

cianfrusa'glia *f.* trifle, (*pl.*) trinkets.

ciani'drico *adj.* hydrocyanic.

ciano'geno *m.* cyanogen.

ciano'tico *adj.* cyanotic.

cianuro *m.* cyanide.

ciao (*lt. slang*) hello, hi; bye-bye, so long.

ciarla *see* chiac'chera.

ciarlare *vi.* to chatter.

ciarlatanata, ciarlataneri'a *f.* quackery.

ciarlatanesco *adj.* quackish.

ciarlatano *m.* charlatan, quack.

ciarliero *adj.* talkative.

ciarpame *m.* litter, rubbish.

ciascheduno, ciascuno *adj.* each. *pron. indef.* each, each one; everyone, everybody.

cibare *vt.* to feed; **cibarsi** *vr.* to feed on; to live on.

ciba'ria *f.* food, foodstuff.

cibo *m.* food; meal.

cibo'rio *m.* ciborium, pyx.

cicala *f.* cicada; (*fig.*) chatterbox; (*naut.*) anchor ring.

cicalare *vi.* to babble, prattle.

cicalec'cio *m.* babbling, prattle.

cicatrice *f.* scar, cicatrice.

cicatrizzare *vt.*, *vi.*, **cicatrizzarsi** *vr.* to cicatrize, heal.

cicatrizzazione *f.* cicatrization.

cicca *f.* stump, butt; quid.

ciccare *vi.* to chew tobacco.

cicchetto *m.* dram, nip, "shot"; lecture, dressing.

cic'cia *f.* meat; fat.

ciccione *m.* fatty.

cicciuto *adj.* fleshy, plump.

cicer'chia *f.* chickpea.

cicerone *m.* guide, cicerone.

ciclamino *m.* cyclamen.

ciclismo *m.* cycling.

ciclista *m.* cyclist.

ciclo *m.* cycle.

ciclone *m.* cyclone, tornado.

ciclo'nico *adj.* cyclonic.

ciclo'pico *adj.* Cyclopean.

ciclostilare *vt.* to mimeograph.

ciclostile *m.* mimeograph, cyclostyle.

ciclotrone *m.* cyclotron.

cicogna *f.* stork.

cico'ria *f.* chicory.

cicuta *f.* hemlock.

cieco *m.* blind man; **i ciechi,** the blind. *adj.* blind: **lanterna cieca,** dark lantern; **intestino —,** caecum; **mosca cieca,** blindman's buff; **alla cieca,** blindly.

cielo *m.* sky; heaven: **un fulmine a ciel sereno,** a bolt out of the blue; **portare ai sette cieli,** to praise to the skies.

cifra *f.* figure; sum, amount; cipher; monogram.

cifrare *vt.* to code; to mark.

cifra'rio *m.* cipher, code.

cifrato *adj.* ciphered, coded.

ci'glio *m.* eyelash, lash; border, edge; shoulder (*of a road*).

ciglione *m.* embankment, bank.

cignale *m.* wild boar.

cigno *m.* swan.

cigolare *vi.* to creak, squeak; to hiss.

cigoli'o *m.* squeaking, hissing.

cilecca *f.* misfire.

cilestrino *m.* sky-blue.

cili'cio *m.* sackcloth.

cilie'gia *f.* cherry; bigarreau.

cilie'gio *m.* cherry tree.

cilindrare *vt.* to calender; to roll.

cilindrata *f.* cylinder displacement.

cilin'drico *adj.* cylindrical.

cilindro *m.* cylinder; top hat; calenderer, roller.

cima *f.* top, summit; apex; vertex; (*naut.*) rope; (*bot.*) cyme; (*fig.*) genius.

Cimabue, Giovanni, early Florentine painter (1240?–1302?).

Cimarosa, Domenico, Neapolitan composer (1749–1801).

cimasa *f.* cyma, coping.

cime'lio *m.* relic, antique.

cimentare *vt.* to provoke, vex; to put to test; **cimentarsi** *vr.* to hazard, engage; to venture.

cimento *m.* ordeal.

ci'mice *f.* bedbug.

cimiero *m.* crest.

ciminiera *f.* smokestack; funnel.

cimitero *m.* churchyard, cemetery.

cimosa *f.* selvage; eraser.

cimurro *m.* distemper, glanders.

cinabro *m.* cinnabar.

cincilla *f.* chinchilla.

cincischiare *vt.*, *vi.* to shred; to babble; to dawdle.

cineasta *m.* moving picture maker; moving picture fan.

cinegiornale *m.* newsreel.

cinege'tica *f.* hounding.

cinema'tica *f.* cinematics.

cinematografare *vt.* to film, shoot.

cinematografi'a *f.* cinematography; moving picture show; film.

cinematogra'fico *adj.* moving picture.

cinemato'grafo *m.* cinema, moving picture theater, moving pictures (*pl.*).

cine'reo *adj.* cinereous, ashen.

cinese *m.*, *adj.* Chinese.

cineteca *f.* film library.

cine'tica *f.* kinetics.

cingallegra *f.* tomtit.

cin'gere *vt.*[46] to gird, girdle (*with*); to crown; to surround; to fold: **— d'assedio,** to besiege.

cin'ghia *f.* belt, strap; driving belt.

cinghiale *m.* wild boar.
cinghiata *f.* lash.
cin'golo *m.* belt; girdle; (*mach.*) track.
cinguettare *vi.* to chirp, twitter.
cinguetti'o *m.* chirping, twittering.
ci'nico *m.* cynic. *adj.* cynical.
cini'glia *f.* chenille.
cinismo *m.* cynicism.
cino'filo *m.* dog fancier.
cinquanta *m.*, *adj.num.* fifty.
cinquantena'rio *m.* fiftieth anniversary. *adj.* quinquagenarian.
cinquantenne *m.*, *adj.* quinquagenarian.
cinquanten'nio *m.* half century.
cinquante'simo *adj.num.* fiftieth.
cinquantina *f.* some fifty: essere sulla —, to be on the verge of fifty; aver passato la —, to be past fifty.
cinque *m.*, *num. adj.* five.
cinquecento *m.*, *num. adj.* five-hundred: il Cinquecento, the Cinquecento, the 16th century.
cinquina *f.* five, five numbers; (*mil.*) soldier's pay.
cinta *f.* enclosure, fence; girdle; fencing wall.
cinto *m.* belt: — erniario, truss. *pp. of* cingere.
cin'tola *f.* waist; belt.
cintura *f.* belt, girdle; waist: — di salvataggio, lifebelt.
cinturino *m.* belt, strap.
cinturone *m.* belt; Sam Browne belt.
ciò *pron.demonstr.* this, that, it: — che, what; tutto — che, all that; — non di meno, nevertheless; oltre a —, besides, moreover.
ciocca *f.* lock; cluster.
ciocco *m.* log.
cioccolata *f.*, *adj.* chocolate.
cioccolatino *m.* chocolate.
ciociaro *m.* a peasant of the Roman country.
cioè *conj.* that is, that is to say, namely, viz.
ciondolare *vt.* to dangle. *vi.* to dangle; to idle, to hang about.
cion'dolo *m.* trinket, pendant.
ciondoloni *adv.* dangling, droopingly, loosely.
cio'tola *f.* bowl, cup.
ciottolato *m.* cobblestone paving.
ciot'tolo *m.* pebble, cobblestone.
ciottoloso *adj.* pebbly, pebbled.
cipi'glio *m.* frown, scowl.
cipolla *f.* onion; bulb.
cipresso *m.* cypress.
ci'pria *f.* powder, face powder.
cipriota *m.*, *adj.* Cypriote.
circa *adv.*, *prep.* about, approximately, some; concerning, as to.
c'rcense *adj.* circensial.

circe'o *adj.* Circean.
circo *m.* circus.
circolante *m.* currency. *adj.* circulating.
circolare *vi.* to circulate.
circolare *f.*, *adj.* circular.
circolarmente *adv.* circularly.
circolato'rio *adj.* circulatory.
circolazione *f.* circulation; traffic.
cir'colo *m.* circle; circumference; club, society; sphere.
circonci'dere *vt.*[41] to circumcise.
circoncisione *f.* circumcision.
circonciso *adj.* circumcised. *pp. of* circoncidere.
circondare *vt.* to surround, encircle.
circonda'rio *m.* district.
circonferenza *f.* circumference.
circonflesso *adj.* circumflex.
circonlocuzione *f.* circumlocution.
circonvallazione *f.* belt line; circular road.
circonvenire *vt.* to circumvent.
circonvenzione *f.* circumvention.
circonvicino *adj.* neighboring.
circonvoluzione *f.* circumvolution.
circoscritto *adj.* circumscribed.
circoscrivere *vt.*[134] to circumscribe.
circoscrizione *f.* circumscription; district.
circospetto *adj.* cautious, wary.
circospezione *f.* circumspection.
circostante *adj.* surrounding.
circostanza *f.* circumstance.
circostanziare *vt.* to detail.
circostanziato *adj.* detailed.
circuire *vt.* to circumvent.
circu'ito *m.* circuit.
circumnavigazione *f.* circumnavigation.
cirene'o *m.* drudge; scapegoat.
ciril'lico *adj.* Cyrillic.
cirro *m.* cirrus (*pl.* cirri); curl.
cirrosi *f.* cirrhosis.
cispa *f.* eye rheum.
cisposità *f.* rheuminess.
cisposo *adj.* rheumy.
cistercense *adj.* Cistercian.
cisterna *f.* cistern, tank.
cisti *f.* cyst.
cistifel'lea *f.* gall bladder.
cistite *f.* cystitis.
citante *m.*, *f.* plaintiff.
citare *vt.* to quote, cite; to sue; to serve a summons.
citazione *f.* quotation; summons; subpoena.
cito'fono *m.* intercom, interphone.
citrato *m.* citrate.
ci'trico *adj.* citric.
citrullo *m.* dumbbell.
città *f.* city; town.
cittadella *f.* citadel.
cittadina *f.* small town.

cittadinanza *f.* citizenship; towns-people.

cittadino *m.* citizen; townsman. *f.* townswoman. *adj.* civic.

cluco *m.* donkey, ass.

ciuffo *m.* lock, tuft; forelock.

ciuffolotto *m.* bullfinch.

ciurlare *vi.* to waver: — nel manico, to go back on one's word.

ciurma *f.* crew.

ciurmadore *m.* swindler.

ciurma'glia *f.* mob, rabble.

civetta *f.* owl; coquette, flirt.

civettare *vi.* to flirt.

civetteri'a *f.* coquetry.

civettuolo *adj.* pretty.

ci'vico *adj.* civic, municipal.

civile *adj.* civil; civilized: parte —, plaintiff.

civilista *m.* solicitor.

civilizzare *vt.* to civilize.

civilizzatore *m.* civilizer. *adj.* civilizing.

civilizzazione *f.* civilizing; civilization.

civilmente *adv.* civilly: sposarsi —, to contract civil marriage.

civiltà *f.* civilization; politeness.

civismo *m.* civism.

cla'mide *f.* chlamys (*pl.* chlamydes).

clamore *m.* clamor, noise.

clamorosamente *adv.* clamorously.

clamoroso *adj.* clamorous.

clandestinamente *adv.* clandestinely; surreptitiously.

clandestino *adj.* clandestine: passeggiero —, stowaway.

clangore *m.* clangor.

clarinetto *m.* clarinet.

clarino *m.* clarion.

classe *f.* class, order, rank; grade: la — media, the middle classes.

clas'sico *m.* classic. *adj.* classical.

classi'fica *f.* score, rating.

classifica'bile *adj.* classifiable.

classificare *vt.* to classify.

classificatore *m.* classifier.

classificazione *f.* classification.

claudicante *adj.* limping, lame.

clau'sola *f.* clause, proviso.

claustrofobi'a *f.* claustrophobia.

clausura *f.* seclusion.

clava *f.* club.

clavicem'balo *m.* harpsichord.

clavi'cola *f.* clavicle.

clemente *adj.* clement, merciful.

clemenza *f.* clemency, mercy.

clepto'mane *m.* kleptomaniac.

cleptomani'a *f.* kleptomania.

clericale *m.* clericalist. *adj.* clerical.

clericalismo *m.* clericalism.

clero *m.* clergy.

clessidra *f.* clepsydra.

cliente *m.* customer, patron; client.

clientela *f.* custom; practice, clientele.

clima *m.* climate.

climaterio *m.* menopause, climacteric.

clima'tico *adj.* climatic.

cli'nica *f.* clinic; hospital.

cli'nico *m.* clinician. *adj.* clinical.

cli'peo *m.* carapace; shield.

clistere *m.* enema, clyster.

cloaca *f.* sewer.

clora'lio *m.* chloral.

clorato *m.* chlorate.

clori'drico *adj.* hydrochloric.

cloro *m.* chlorine.

clorofilla *f.* chlorophyll.

cloroformio *m.* chloroform.

cloroformizzare *vt.* to chloroform.

cloromicetina *f.* chloromycetin.

cloruro *m.* chloride.

coabitante *m.*, *f.* fellow tenant.

coabitare *vi.* to share lodgings.

coadiutore *m.* coadjutor.

coadiuvare *vt.* to assist.

coagulare *vt.*, **coagularsi** *vr.* to coagulate, curdle, clot.

coagulazione *f.* coagulation.

coa'gulo *m.* clot, coagulum.

coalizione *f.* coalition.

coalizzare *vt.* to rally.

coartare *vt.* to coerce.

coartazione *f.* coercion.

coatto *adj.* coercive.

cobra *m.* cobra.

cocaina *f.* cocaine.

cocca *f.* notch; bowstring; corner.

coccarda *f.* cockade.

cocchiere *m.* coachman; cabman.

coc'chio *m.* chariot, coach.

coc'cia *f.* rind; pod; hilt; shell; pate.

coc'cige *m.* coccyx.

coccinella *f.* ladybird.

coccini'glia *f.* cochineal.

coc'cio *m.* earthen pot; potsherd.

cocciutag'gine *f.* stubbornness.

cocciuto *adj.* stubborn.

cocco *m.* coco; coconut; coccus; darling.

coccodè *m.* cackle.

coccodrillo *m.* crocodile.

coccolare *vt.* to fondle, nestle.

cocente *adj.* burning.

coco'mero *m.* watermelon.

cocorita *f.* parakeet, lovebird.

cocuz'zolo *m.* crown; peak.

coda *f.* tail; pigtail; queue; train: — di ratto (*naut.*), ratline.

codardi'a *f.* cowardice.

codardo *m.*, *adj.* coward.

codazzo *m.* train, retinue.

codeina *f.* codeine.

codesto *see* cotesto.

co'dice *m.* code; codex (*pl.* codices).

codicillo *m.* codicil.

codificare *vt.* to codify.

codino *m.* short tail; pigtail; (*fig.*) conformist.

coefficiente *m.* coefficient.
coercitivo *m.* coercive, compulsory.
coercizione *f.* compulsion.
coerede *m.* coheir. *f.* coheiress.
coerente *adj.* consistent, logical.
coerenza *f.* consistency.
coesione *f.* cohesion.
coesistenza *f.* coexistence.
coesi'stere *vi.* to coexist.
coeta'neo *m.*, *adj.* coeval, contemporary.
co'fano *m.* coffer, chest; bonnet.
coffa *f.* (*naut.*) top.
cogitabondo *adj.* cogitative.
cogitare *vi.* to cogitate.
cogli *comp.prep.* with, by the. *see* con.
co'gliere *vi.*[17] to catch; to seize; to gather; to pluck.
cognac *m.* brandy, cognac.
cognata *f.* sister-in-law.
cognato *m.* brother-in-law.
cognizione *f.* knowledge.
cognome *m.* surname.
coi *comp.prep.* with, by the. *see* con.
coibente *adj.* nonconducting, insulating.
coimputato *m.* co-defendant.
coincidenza *f.* coincidence; (*rail.*) connection.
coinci'dere *vi.*[41] to coincide.
coinciso *pp. of* coincidere.
cointeressare *vt.* to make a sharer of.
cointeressenza *f.* share, percentage.
coinvol'gere *vt.*[144] to involve.
col *comp.prep.* with, by the. *see* con.
cola *f.* (*bot.*) kola.
colà *adv.* there.
colabrodo *m.* colander.
colare *vt.* to strain, drain; (*metal.*) to melt. *vi.* to drip; to flow, leak; to gutter: — a picco, to sink.
colata *f.* cast; stream.
colato'io *m.* colander; strainer.
colazione *f.* breakfast; lunch.
cole'i *pron.f.* she; her.
coleot'tero *m.* coleopteron, beetle.
colera *m.* cholera.
colibrì *m.* hummingbird.
co'lica *f.* colic.
co'lico *adj.* colic.
colino *m.* strainer.
colite *f.* (*pathol.*) colitis.
colla (*1*) *f.* glue, paste: — di pesce, isinglass.
colla (*2*) *comp.prep.* with, by the. *see* con.
collaborare *vi.* to collaborate, co-operate; to contribute (*to*).
collaboratore *m.* co-operator; assistant, contributor.
collaborazione *f.* collaboration, co-operation; contribution.

collaborazionismo *m.*collaborationism.
collaborazionista *m.* collaborationist, quisling.
collana *f.* necklace; series.
collare *m.* collar; hoop.
collasso *m.* breakdown, collapse.
collaterale *m.*, *adj.* collateral.
collaudare *vt.* to test, try.
collaudatore *m.* tester; test pilot.
colla'udo *m.* test.
colle (*1*) *m.* hill, hillock.
colle (*2*) *comp.prep.* with, by the. *see* con.
collega *m.*, *f.* colleague.
collegamento *m.* connection; linkage: ufficiale di —, liaison officer.
colleganza *f.* colleagueship.
collegare *vt.*, collegarsi *vr.* to connect, join.
collegiale *m.* schoolboy. *f.* schoolgirl.
colle'gio *m.* college, body, board; boarding school: — elettorale, constituency.
Colleoni, Bartolomeo, Venetian condottiere (1400-1475).
col'lera *f.* anger, rage, wrath: in —, angry.
colle'rico *adj.* irascible, hot-tempered.
colletta *f.* collection; collect.
collettivamente *adv.* collectively.
collettivismo *m.* collectivism.
colettivista *m.* collectivist.
collettività *f.* community.
collettivo *adj.* collective.
colletto *m.* collar.
collettore *m.* collector; manifold.
collezionare *vt.* to collect.
collezione *f.* collection.
collezionista *m.* collector.
colli'dere *vi.* to collide.
collimare *vi.* to tally.
collina *f.* hill, hillock.
collinoso *adj.* hilled, hilly.
colli'rio *m.* collyrium, eyewash.
collisione *f.* collision, crash.
collo (*1*) *m.* neck; parcel.
collo (*2*) *comp.prep.* with, by the. *see* con.
collocamento *m.* placement; investment; employment.
collocare *vt.* to place; to station; to employ; to invest; to arrange; to sell; to settle; collocarsi *vr.* to place oneself; to get a situation; to get married.
collo'dio *m.* collodion.
collo'quio *m.* interview, talk.
collosità *f.* glueyness.
colloso *adj.* sticky, gluey.
collot'tola *f.* nape.
collusione *f.* collusion.
colluttazione *f.* fight, scuffle.
colmare *vt.* to fill (*up*); to load (*with*), overwhelm (*with*).

colmo m. top. adj. full, bulging; full to the brim.

colofo'nia f. colophony, rosin.

colomba f. dove.

colomba'ia f. dovecote.

colombo m. pigeon.

Colombo, Cristoforo. Genoese navigator, discoverer of America (1446?-1506).

colo'nia f. settlement colony; cologne.

coloniale adj. colonial generi coloniali, spices; casco — , topee.

colo'nico adj. farm.

colonizzare vt. to colonize.

colonizzatore m. colonizer.

colonizzazione f. colonization.

colonna f. column pillar, post.

colonnato m. colonnade.

colonnello m. colonel.

colono m. settler farmer.

coloramento m. dyeing.

colorante m. dye. adj. dyeing.

colorare vt. to dye, color; **colorarsi** vr. to color up; to blush.

colorato adj. colored dyed.

colorazione f. coloring.

colore m. color, hue paint, dye: uomo di —, colored man. Negro.

colorifi'cio m. dye factory.

colorire see **colorare**.

colorito m. complexion. adj. colored; painted; ruddy.

coloritura f. coloring.

coloro pron. pl. they them, those.

colossale adj. colossal. huge.

Colosseo m. Coliseum.

colosso m. colossus, giant.

colpa f. fault; guilt.

colpe'vole m. culprit. adj. guilty.

colpevolezza f. guilt.

colpire vt. to strike, hit; to impress; to smite; to injure. hurt.

colpo m. stroke, blow, knock; shot; coup; hit: — di mano, coup de main; — di scena, c up de théâtre; — di stato, coup c'etat — di grazia, coup de grâce, finishing stroke; di —, sharply; far —, to impress, be impressive.

colposo adj. guilty (but without malicious intent): omicidio —, manslaughter.

coltellac'cio m. chopper, cleaver; (naut.) studding sail.

coltellata f. cut, stab; knife wound.

coltellina'io m. cutler.

coltello m. knife; clasp knife: avere il — per il manico, to have the upper hand.

coltivare vt. to cultivate.

coltivatore m. farmer.

coltivazione f. cultivation.

colto (1) caught; gathered. pp. of **cogliere**.

colto (2) adj. cultivated, learned.

coltre f. coverlet, quilt.

coltro m. colter.

coltura f. culture.

colubrina f. culverin.

colu'i pron. he, him.

coma m. (med.) coma.

comandamento m. commandment.

comandante m. commander.

comandare vt., vi. to command; to order; to be in charge (of).

comando m. command; order; (mach.) control.

comare f. housewife; godmother.

comatoso adj. comatose.

combaciare vt. to tally.

combattente m. combatant, fighter. adj. fighting: ex —, veteran.

combat'tere vt., vi. to fight; to struggle (against).

combattimento m. fight; battle.

combattivo adj. pugnacious.

combinare vt. to combine; to settle; **combinarsi** vr. to combine.

combinazione f. combination; agreement; chance; arrangement; woman's underdress, slip.

cambric'cola f. cabal; gang.

comburente m., adj. comburent.

combusti'bile m. fuel. adj. combustible.

combustione f. combustion.

combutta f. cabal, gang.

come m., adv. how; as; like, as good as; as soon as. conj. that, how, why; as ... as: — avete detto?, what did you say?; — mai?, how come?

cometa f. comet.

comicità f. comicalness; ludicrousness.

co'mico m. comic, comedian. adj. comic, funny.

comi'gnolo m. chimneypot; coping.

cominciare vt., vi. to begin, start.

comitato m. committee.

comitiva f. party, company.

comi'zio m. meeting.

comme'dia f. comedy, play.

commediante m. player, actor; shammer. f. actress; shammer.

commedio'grafo m. playwright.

commemorare vt. to commemorate.

commemorativo adj. commemorative, memorial.

commemorazione f. commemoration.

commenda f. Knight-Commandership; (eccl.) commendam.

commendare vt. to commend.

commendati'zia f. credentials (pl.).

commendatore m. Knight-Commander.

commendevole adj. commendable.

commensale m. commensal.

commentare vt. to comment.

commenta'rio *m.* commentary.
commentatore *m.* commentator.
commento *m.* comment; remark.
commerciale *adj.* commercial.
commerciante *m.* merchant, dealer.
commerciare *vt.* to deal in, negotiate. *vi.* to trade.
commer'cio *m.* commerce, trade; business: — all'ingrosso, wholesale trade; — al minuto, retail trade.
commesso (1) *m.* clerk; shopman: — viaggiatore, traveling salesman. *f.* shopgirl.
commesso (2) *pp. of* commettere.
commesti'bile *m., adj.* eatable, edible.
commettere *vt.*[76] to join; to fit in; to order; to intrust; to commit, perform.
commettitura *f.* joint; joining.
commiato *m.* leave, departure.
commilitone *m.* comrade.
comminare *vt.* to comminate.
comminato'ria *f.* commination, threat.
commiserare *vt.* to pity.
commiserazione *f.* commiseration, pity; contempt.
commissariato *m.* commissaryship; commissariat; police station.
commissa'rio *m.* commissary; inspector; commissar: — di bordo, purser.
commissionare *vt.* to order.
commissiona'rio *m.* commission agent, selling agent.
commissione *f.* commission; errand; committee; order.
commisurare *vt.* to proportion; to compare; to measure.
committente *m.* buyer; customer.
commodoro *m.* commodore.
commosso *adj.* moved; excited; upset. *pp. of* commuovere.
commovente *vt.* touching.
commozione *f.* emotion; agitation.
commuo'vere *vt.*[80]to touch, move;commuoversi *vr.* to be moved, touched.
commutare *vt.* to commute.
commutatore *m.* commutator, switch.
comò *m.* chest of drawers, bureau.
comodamente *adv.* comfortably; at ease; snugly; easily.
comodino *m.* night table.
comodità *f.* comfort; convenience; opportunity.
co'modo *m.* convenience; ease, comfort; opportunity. *adj.* comfortable, convenient; commodious; easy.
compaesano *m.* fellow countryman.
compa'gine *f.* assemblage; body.
compagno *m., compagna *f.* companion, fellow, mate; comrade; pal, partner: — di scuola, schoolfellow; — d'armi, comrade-in-arms. *adj.* alike, similar.

compagni'a *f.* company; troop; set, gang: dama di —, (lady) companion.
compana'tico *m.* viand.
comparare *vt.* to compare.
comparativo *m., adj.* comparative.
comparazione *f.* comparison.
compare *m.* companion, chum; godfather; confederate.
comparire *vi.*[9] to appear.
comparizione *f.* appearance in court: mandato di —, subpoena.
comparsa *f.* appearance; supernumerary, extra; (law) appearance before the court; record.
comparso *pp. of* comparire.
compartecipazione *f.* sharing.
comparte'cipe *adj.* sharing (in).
compartimento *m.* compartment.
compassato *adj.* formal, poised, stiff.
compassionare *vt.* to pity.
compassione *f.* pity, compassion.
compassione'vole *adj.* compassionate; piteous; pitiful.
compasso *m.* compasses (pl.).
compati'bile *adj.* consistent; excusable.
compatibilità *f.* compatibility.
compatibilmente *adv.* compatibly.
compatimento *m.* pity; forbearance.
compatire *vt.*[65] to pity; to forbear.
compatriota *m.* compatriot.
compattezza *f.* compactness.
compatto *adj.* compact.
compendiare *vt.* to epitomize, summarize, condense.
compen'dio *m.* epitome, summary, condensation, digest.
compendioso *adj.* compendious.
compenetra'bile *adj.* penetrable.
compenetrabilità *f.* penetrability.
compenetrare *vt.* to penetrate; compenetrarsi *vr.* to impress on one's mind.
compensa'bile *adj.* rewardable; balanceable; indemnifiable.
compensare *vt.* to compensate; to reward; to counterbalance; to indemnify.
compensato *m.* plywood.
compensazione *f.* compensation: stanza di —, clearing.
compenso *m.* compensation; reward.
comperare *see* comprare.
competente *m., adj.* expert.
competenza *f.* competence.
competenze *f.pl.* fees.
compe'tere *vi.* to compete; to belong.
competitore *m.* competitor.
competizione *f.* competition, contest, [game.
compiacente *adj.* obliging.
compiacenza *f.* obligingness.
compiacere *vt.* to please; compiacersi *vr.* to be pleased; to enjoy; to be so

kind as; to be fond of; to congratulate.

compiacimento *m.* complacence; pleasure.

compiaciuto *adj.* pleased.

compian'gere *vt.* to pity; to lament.

compianto *m.* complaint; regret. *adj.* pitied; lamented. *pp.* of **compiangere.**

compiegare *vt.* to enclose.

com'piere *vt.* to accomplish, fulfill; to perform; to complete: *domani compio gli anni*, tomorrow is my birthday; *ho compiuto 20 anni*, I am 20 years old.

compilare *vt.* to compile, fill.

compilatore *m.* compiler.

compilazione *f.* compilation.

compimento *m.* accomplishment; fulfillment; completion.

compire *see* **compiere.**

compitare *vt.* to spell.

compitezza *f.* politeness.

com'pito *m.* task; mission.

compi'to *adj.* polite; *also, pp.* of **compiere.**

compiutamente *adv.* completely.

compiuto *adj.* accomplished. *pp.* of **compiere.**

compleanno *m.* birthday.

complementare *adj.* additional, complemental.

complemento *m.* complement: *ufficiale di —,* reserve officer.

complessione *f.* build, constitution.

complessità *f.* complexity.

complessivamente *adv.* on the whole.

complessivo *adj.* total, aggregate.

complesso *m.* complex, whole. *adj.* complex; compound; complicated.

completamente *adv.* completely.

completamento *m.* completion.

completare *vt.* to complete.

completo *m.* suit. *adj.* complete.

complicare *vt.* to complicate; **complicarsi,** *vr.* to become complicated, entangled.

complicazione *f.* complication.

com'plice *m., f.* accomplice.

complicità *f.* complicity.

complimentare *vt.* to compliment, congratulate.

complimento *m.* compliment.

complimentoso *adj.* ceremonious.

complottare *vi.* to plot.

complotto *m.* plot, conspiracy.

componente *adj.* component; *m.* component; member.

componimento *m.* composition.

comporre *vt.* to compose; to compound; to arrange, settle; *(print.)* to set (type); **comporsi** *vr.* to consist (*of*).

comportamento *m.* behavior.

comportare *vt.* to bear, tolerate; to allow; to entail; **comportarsi** *vr.* to behave.

comporto *m.* allowance; delay.

composito'io *m.* composing stick.

compositore *m.* composer; typesetter.

composizione *f.* composition; settlement.

composta *f.* compote.

compostamente *adv.* composedly.

compostezza *f.* composure.

composto *m.* compound. *adj.* composed; compound. *pp.* of **comporre.**

compra *f.* purchase: *andare a fare le compre,* to go shopping.

comprare *vt.* to purchase, buy.

compratore *m.* buyer.

compraven'dita *f.* buying and selling.

compren'dere *vt.* to understand; to realize; to include; to imply.

comprendo'nio *m.* understanding.

comprensi'bile *adj.* understandable, intelligible.

comprensione *f.* understanding, grasp; sympathy.

comprensiva *f.* perception.

comprensivo *adj.* understanding; sympathetic; inclusive.

compreso'rio *m.* reclamation area.

compreso *adj.* understood; included; aware. *pp.* of **comprendere.**

compressa *f.* compress, pad; tablet.

compressibilità *f.* compressibility.

compressione *f.* pressure.

compresso *adj.* compressed. *pp.* of **comprimere.**

compressore *m.* compressor; supercharger; roller; steamroller.

comprima'rio *m.* second leading man.

compri'mere *vt.* to compress, press; to squeeze; to restrain.

compromesso *m.* compromise. *adj.* compromised; involved; endangered; committed.

compromettente *adj.* compromising; dangerous.

compromet'tere *vt.* to compromise; to involve; to endanger; **compromettersi** *vr.* to commit oneself; to get involved (*in*).

compropietà *f.* joint ownership.

compropieta'rio *m.* joint owner.

comprova'bile *adj.* provable.

comprovare *vt.* to prove.

compulsare *vt.* to consult.

compunto *adj.* demure, contrite.

compunzione *f.* compunction, demureness.

computa'bile *adj.* computable.

computare *vt.* to compute.

computista *m.* bookkeeper.

computisteri'a *f.* bookkeeping.

com'puto *m.* computation.

comunale *adj.* municipal: *palazzo —,* town hall.

comunanza *f.* community.
comunardo *m.* Communard.
comune *m.* community; municipality; borough; town hall; main exit; Commune: la Camera dei Comuni, the House of Commons. *adj.* common; usual; vulgar; trite; mutual; joint.
comunella *f.* cabal, gang.
comunemente *adv.* generally.
comunicando *m.* communicant.
comunicante *m.* communicator. *adj.* communicating (*with*).
comunicare *vt., vi.* to communicate; comunicarsi *vr.* to communicate; to spread.
comunicativa *f.* communicativeness.
comunicativo *adj.* communicative.
comunicato *m.* communiqué.
comunicazione *f.* communication; connection; message: mettere in —, to connect; to put in touch; togliere la —, to disconnect.
comunione *f.* communion.
comunismo *m.* communism.
comunista *m., f., adj.* communist.
comunità *f.* community.
comunque *adv.* no matter how; however; anyhow.
con *prep.* with; by, through; in: — tutto che, although; — tutto ciò, nevertheless.
conato *m.* effort; conatus; qualm.
conca *f.* basin, depression; dell; lock; (*anat.*) concha.
concatenamento *m.* linking.
concatenare *vt.* to link.
concatenazione *f.* linking.
conca'usa *f.* joint cause.
concavità *f.* concavity.
con'cavo *m., adj.* hollow.
conce'dere *vt.*[11] to grant.
concentramento *m.* concentration.
concentrare *vt.*, concentrarsi *vr.* to concentrate; to gather.
concentrato *m.* concentrate. *adj.* concentrated.
concentrazione *f.* concentration; condensation.
concen'trico *adj.* concentric.
concepi'bile *adj.* conceivable.
concepimento *m.* conception.
concepire *vt.* to conceive.
conceri'a *f.* tannery.
concer'nere *vt.* to concern.
concertare *vt.* to orchestrate; to arrange, plan; concertarsi *vr.* to agree (*on*).
concertatore *m.* conductor.
concertista *m.* concert performer.
concerto *m.* concert; agreement.
concessiona'rio *m.* agent.
concessione *f.* concession; agency.
concesso *adj.* granted. *pp. of* concedere.

concetto *m.* conception; idea; reputation; meaning.
concettoso *m.* meaningful.
concezione *f.* conception; idea.
conchi'glia *f.* shell, conch.
conchiu'dere[25] *see* concludere.
con'cia *f.* tanning; processing; seasoning.
conciare *vt.* to tan; to process; to season; to reduce: — per le feste, to beat to a pulp; conciarsi *vr.* to make of oneself.
conciatore *m.* tanner.
concilia'bolo *m.* conventicle.
conciliante *adj.* conciliatory.
conciliare *vt.* to conciliate; to win: — il sonno, to induce sleep; conciliarsi *vr.* to win.
conciliativo *adj.* conciliatory.
conciliatore *m.* peacemaker: giudice —, justice of the peace.
conciliazione *f.* conciliation.
conci'lio *m.* council.
concima'ia *f.* dunghill.
concimare *vt.* to manure.
concime *m.* manure.
concionare *vi.* to harangue.
concione *f.* harangue, speech.
conciossiachè *conj.* inasmuch as.
concisamente *adv.* concisely.
concisione *f.* concision.
conciso *adj.* concise.
concistoro *m.* consistory.
concitare *vt.* to excite, stir.
concitato *adj.* excited; breathless; frantic.
concitazione *f.* excitement.
concittadino *m.* fellow citizen.
conclamare *vt.* to proclaim.
conclave *m.* conclave.
conclu'dere *vt., vi.*[3] to conclude.
conclusionale *f.* record.
conclusione *f.* conclusion.
conclusivo *adj.* conclusive.
concluso *adj.* concluded. *pp. of* concludere.
concomitante *adj.* concomitant.
concomitanza *f.* concomitance.
concordanza *f.* concordance.
concordare *vt.* to arrange; to agree upon. *vi.* to agree; to tally; (*gramm.*) to agree.
concordato *m.* concordat; agreement.
concorde *adj.* concordant.
concordemente *adv.* concordantly, unanimously.
concor'dia *f.* concord, agreement.
concorrente *m.* competitor; entrant; candidate; bidder.
concorrenza *f.* concurrence, attendance; competition; extent.
concor'rere *vi.*[16] to concur; to flock (*to*); to co-operate; to compete; to contribute; to bid.

concorso *m.* attendance; co-operation; competition, contest; contribution; concurrence: partecipare a un —, to enter a contest.

concozione *f.* concoction.

concretare *vt.* to actualize; to concretize; to conclude; to accomplish, bring about.

concretezza *f.* concreteness.

concreto *m., adj.* concrete, real.

concubina *f.* concubine.

concubinato *m.* concubinage.

conculcare *vt.* to trample on.

concupiscente *adj.* covetous.

concupiscenza *f.* covetousness.

concussiona'rio *m.* extortioner.

concussione *f.* extortion.

condanna *f.* conviction, sentence.

condanna'bile *adj.* condemnable.

condannare *vt.* to condemn, sentence; to find guilty; to blame.

condannato *m.* convict. *adj., pp.* condemned, sentenced.

condebitore *m.* joint debtor.

condensa'bile *adj.* condensable.

condensare *vt., condensarsi vr.* to condense; to thicken.

condensato *m.* condensation. *adj., pp.* condensed.

condensatore *m.* condenser.

condensazione *f.* condensation.

condimento *m.* condiment.

condire *vt.* to season, flavor; to dress.

condirettore *m.* joint manager.

condiscendente *adj.* condescending; complying.

condiscendenza *f.* condescension.

condiscen'dere *vi.* to condescend; to yield (*to*); to consent.

condisce'polo *m.* schoolfellow.

condivi'dere *vt.*[48] to share.

condizionale *m., adj.* conditional; (*gramm.*) conditional mood. *f.* (*law*) suspended sentence.

condizionare *vt.* to condition (*upon*); to trim.

condizionato *adj.* conditioned.

condizione *f.* condition; term: a — che, provided; essere in — di, to be in a position to; mettere in — to enable.

condoglianza *f.* condolence.

condolersi *vr.* to condole.

condomi'nio *m.* joint (house) ownership.

condo'mino *m.* joint (house) owner.

condonare *vt.* to forgive, remit.

condono *m.* remission, pardon.

condotta *f.* conduct, behavior.

condottiero *m.* leader; condottiere.

condotto (1) *m.* duct; flue; pipeline.

condotto (2) *pp. of* condurre.

conducente *m.* driver.

condurre *vt., vi.*[3] to conduct, lead;

to drive; to take; to give rise (*to*); to manage; condursi *vr.* to behave.

conduttore *m.* conductor; driver; manager.

conduttura *f.* pipeline.

conduzione *f.* management; conduction; tenancy.

confabulare *vi.* to confabulate.

confacente *adj.* becoming, proper.

confarsi *vr.*[61] to suit, agree (*with*).

confederare *vt., confederarsi vr.* to confederate.

confederato *m., adj.* confederate.

confederazione *f.* confederation, confederacy.

conferenza *f.* lecture; conference.

conferenziere *m.* lecturer.

conferimento *m.* conferment; bestowal; grant.

conferire *vt.* to confer, bestow (*on, upon*). *vi.* to consult (*with*); to agree (*with*).

conferma *f.* confirmation.

confermare *vt.* to confirm.

confessa'bile *adj.* avowable.

confessare *vt., confessarsi vr.* to confess.

confessionale *m., adj.* confessional.

confessione *f.* confession.

confesso *adj.* self-convicted.

confessore *m.* confessor.

confettare *vt.* to candy.

confettiere *m.* confectioner.

confetto *m.* comfit.

confettura *f.* jam.

confezione *f.* manufacture.

confezionare *vt.* to manufacture, make.

conficcare *vt.* to drive in; conficcarsi *vr.* to get embedded; to bury oneself.

confidare *vt.* to confide; to entrust. *vi.* to rely (*on*), trust; confidarsi *vr.* to unbosom oneself.

confidente *m.* confidant. *f.* confidante. *adj.* confident.

confidenza *f.* confidence, trust; familiarity; secret.

confidenziale *adj.* confidential.

configurazione *f.* configuration.

confinante *adj.* bordering, neighboring.

confinare *vt.* to confine. *vi.* to border (*upon*).

confina'rio *adj.* border.

confinato *m.* confined prisoner. *adj.* confined.

confine *m.* border, frontier; (*pl.*) boundaries.

confino *m.* confinement.

confisca *f.* confiscation.

confiscare *vt.* to confiscate.

confitto *adj.* driven in; embedded

conflagrazione f. outbreak.
conflitto m. conflict, struggle.
confluente m., adj. confluent.
confluenza f. confluence.
confluire vi. to converge.
confon'dere vt.[68] to confuse; to mix up; to mistake; to bewilder; **confondersi** vr. to get confused; to mingle (with); to flounder.
confondi'bile adj. mistakable.
conformare vt., **conformarsi** vr. to conform (to).
conformazione f. conformation.
conforme adj. conformable; true.
conforme a adv. in conformity with, in compliance with.
conformemente adv. conformably, in conformity (with).
conformista m. conformist.
conformità f. conformity.
confortante adj. comforting.
confortare vt. to comfort.
confortatore m. comforter. adj. comforting.
conforte'vole adj. comfortable.
conforto m. comfort, solace; assistance.
confratello m. brother (archaic and Biblical pl. brethren).
confraternità f. brotherhood.
confricare vt. to rub.
confrontare vt. to compare (with, to).
confronto m. comparison.
confusamente adv. confusedly.
confusiona'rio m. jumbler. adj. meddlesome; blundering.
confusione f. confusion.
confuso adj. confused; mixed up.
confuta'bile adj. confutable.
confutare vt. to confute.
confutazione f. confutation.
congedare vt. to dismiss; (mil.) to discharge; **congedarsi** vr. to take one's leave (of).
congedo m. leave; discharge.
congegnare vt. to contrive.
congegno m. contrivance.
congelamento m. congealment.
congelare vt., vi.; **congelarsi** vr. to freeze, congeal.
congelazione f. freezing.
conge'nito adj. congenital, inborn.
conge'rie f. congeries; jumble.
congestionare vt. to congest.
congestione f. congestion.
congettura f. conjecture, guess.
congetturare vt. to conjecture, guess, suppose.
congiun'gere vt.,[79] **congiungersi** vr. to join; to weld: — **in matrimonio**, to get married.
congiuntamente adv. jointly.
congiuntiva f. conjunctiva.
congiuntivite f. conjunctivitis.

congiuntivo m., adj. subjunctive.
congiunto m. relative. adj. joined, connected; related. pp. of congiungere.
congiuntura f. conjuncture; predicament; emergency.
congiunzione f. junction; conjunction.
congiura f. conspiracy, plot.
congiurare vi. to plot.
congiurato m. conspirator.
conglobare vt. to conglobate.
conglomerare vt. to conglomerate.
conglomerato m., adj. conglomerate.
congratularsi vr. to congratulate.
congratulazione f. congratulation.
congrega f. gang, set, coterie.
congregare vt., **congregarsi** vr. to congregate, assemble.
congregazione f. congregation.
congressista m. congressman.
congresso m. congress.
congruamente adv. congruously.
congruità f. congruity.
con'gruo adj. congruous, adequate.
congua'glio m. balance.
coniare vt. to coin, strike.
coniatore m. coiner, minter.
coniatura f. coinage, minting.
co'nico adj. conical.
coni'fera f. conifer.
conigliera f. warren.
coni'glio m. rabbit.
co'nio m. coinage: **di nuovo —**, newly-coined.
coniugale adj. conjugal.
coniugare vt. to conjugate.
coniugato adj. conjugate; married.
coniugazione f. conjugation.
co'niuge m. mate, spouse: **una coppia di coniugi**, a married couple; **i coniugi Smith**, the Smith couple.
connaturale adj. inborn.
connazionale m. fellow countryman. f. fellow countrywoman.
connessione f. connection.
connesso adj. connected. pp. of connettere.
connessura f. joint.
connet'tere vt.[8] to connect; to link. vi. to reason.
connettivo adj. connective.
connivente adj. conniving.
connivenza f. connivance.
connotato m. feature.
connu'bio m. union, match, wedding.
cono m. cone.
conoc'chia f. distaff.
conoscente m. acquaintance.
conoscenza f. knowledge; acquaintance; consciousness.
cono'scere vt.[90] to know, be acquainted with; **conoscersi** vr. to know oneself; to know each other.
conoscitore m. connoisseur.

conosciuto *adj.* known. *pp. of* conoscere.

conqui'dere *vt.*[21] to win, conquer.

conquiso *adj.* conquered, won. *pp. of* conquidere.

conquista *f.* conquest.

conquistare *vt.* to conquer, win.

conquistatore *m.* conqueror.

consacrare *vt.* to consecrate.

consacrazione *f.* consecration.

consanguineità *f.* consanguinity.

consangui'neo *m.* kinsman. *f.* kinswoman. *adj.* consanguineous.

consape'vole *adj.* aware.

consapevolezza *f.* consciousness, awareness.

consapevolmente *adv.* consciously.

con'scio *adj.* conscious, aware.

consecutivo *adj.* consecutive.

consegna *f.* delivery; order; watchword; confinement; safekeeping: dare in —, to entrust; ricevere in —, to be entrusted with.

consegnare *vt.* to deliver.

consegnata'rio *m.* consignee.

conseguente *adj.*, consequent, consistent. *ppr. of* conseguire.

conseguenza *f.* consequence; result: in — di, as a result of.

conseguimento *m.* attainment.

conseguire *vt.* to attain; to acquire. *vi.* to ensue, result.

consenso *m.* consent.

consensuale *adj.* consensual.

consentire *vt.* to allow. *vi.* to agree; to yield.

consenziente *adj.* consentient.

conserto *adj.* folded: a braccia conserte, with folded arms.

conserva *f.* preserve, sauce.

conservare *vt.* to preserve, keep; conservarsi *vr.* to keep.

conservativo *adj.* conservative.

conservatore *m.* conservator; conservative.

conservato'rio *m.* conservatory.

conservazione *f.* preservation: stato di —, state of repair; istinto di —, instinct of self-preservation.

consesso *m.* assembly.

considerare *vt.* to consider.

consideratezza *f.* considerateness.

considerato *adj.* considerate; considered: tutto —, all in all.

considerazione *f.* consideration.

conside're'vole *adj.* considerable.

consiglia'bile *adj.* advisable.

consigliare *vt.* to advise; consigliarsi *vr.* to consult (*with*).

consigliere *m.* adviser; counselor; director.

consi'glio *m.* advice; counsel; council: — d'amministrazione, board of directors.

consi'mile *adj.* similar.

consistente *adj.* substantial, solid.

consistenza *f.* consistence; solidity; worth.

consi'stere *vi.*[16] to consist (*of, in*); to amount (*to*).

consociare *vt.* to syndicate.

consociazione *f.* association, syndicate.

conso'cio *m.* associate; copartner.

consolante *adj.* comforting.

consolare (1) *vt.* to console; consolarsi *vr.* to take comfort; to cheer up.

consolare (2) *adj.* consular.

consolato *m.* consulate; consulship.

consolatore *m.* consoler.

consolazione *f.* consolation, solace.

con'sole *m.* consul.

consolidamento *m.* consolidation.

consolidare *vt.* to consolidate.

consolidato *m.* funded debt.

consonante *f.*, *adj.* consonant.

consonanza *f.* consonance.

con'sono *adj.* consonant, consistent (*with*).

consore la *f.* sister.

consorte *m.*, *f.* mate, consort.

consorteri'a *f.* clique, clan.

consor'zio *m.* syndicate.

constare *vi.* to consist; to be known (*to*): mi consta che, I understand that; a quanto mi consta, as far as I know.

constatare, constatazione *see* costatare, costatazione.

consueto *adj.* usual, customary.

consuetudina'rio *adj.* customary.

consuetu'dine *f.* custom, habit.

consulente *m.* adviser; consulting physician.

consulta *f.* council: — araldica, Heralds' College.

consultare *vt.* to consult; to peruse; consultarsi *vr.* to take counsel (*with*).

consultazione *f.* consultation.

consultivo *adj.* advisory.

consulto *m.* consultation.

consulto'rio *m.* dispensary.

consumare *vt.* to consume, waste; to use up; to perpetrate; to consummate; consumarsi *vr.* to waste away.

consumato *adj.* consummate.

consumatore *m.* consumer.

consumazione *f.* consummation; refreshment; consumption: fino alla — dei secoli, till doomsday.

consumo *m.* consumption.

consuntivo *m.* balance sheet.

consunto *adj.* worn; consumptive.

consunzione *f.* consumption.

conta'bile *m.* accountant.

contabilità *f.* bookkeeping.

contachilo'metri m. speedometer.
contadinesco adj. rustic.
contadino m., f. peasant; farmer.
contado m. country.
contagiare vt. to infect (with).
conta'gio m. contagion.
contagioso adj. contagious, catching.
contagiri m. tachometer.
contagocce m. dropper (as for medicine).
contaminare vt. to contaminate, taint.
contaminazione f. contamination.
contante m. cash, ready money. adj. ready: a contanti, cash down.
contare vt. to count, reckon. vi. to rely (on); to intend; to count, matter.
contatore m. reckoner; meter.
contatto m. contact, touch.
conte m. count; earl.
conte'a f. county; earldom.
conteggiare vt. to compute.
conteg'gio m. reckoning.
contegno m. behavior.
contegnoso adj. grave, dignified.
contemplare vt. to contemplate.
contemplativo adj. contemplative.
contemplazione f. contemplation.
contempo (nel) adv. meanwhile.
contemporaneamente adv. contemporaneously.
contemporaneità f. contemporaneousness.
contempora'neo m., adj. contemporary, contemporaneous.
contendente m. contender; competitor
conten'dere vi.[140] to contest. vi. to contend, fight; contendersi vr. to fight (for).
contenere vt.[141] to contain; contenersi vr. to restrain oneself; to behave.
contentare vt. to please, satisfy; contentarsi vr. to content oneself (with).
contentezza f. joy, gladness.
contentino m. makeweight.
contento adj. glad, pleased.
contenuto m. contents (pl.). adj. contained; repressed.
conteri'a f. glassware; beads (pl.).
conterra'nea f. fellow countrywoman.
conterra'neo m. fellow countryman.
contesa f. contest, strife.
conteso pp. of contendere.
contessa f. countess.
contesta'bile adj. contestable.
contestare vt. to dispute; to deny; to notify.
contestazione f. dispute.
contesto m. context.
contiguità f. contiguity.
conti'guo adj. contiguous.
continentale adj. continental.
continente m. continent.
continenza f. continence.
contingentamento m. quota; rationing,

contingentare vt. to allot; to assign a quota; to ration.
contingente m., contingent; quota. adj. contingent.
contingenza f. contingency.
continuamente adv. unceasingly; always.
continuare vt. to continue; vi. to go on.
continuativo adj. continuative.
continuatore m. continuer.
continuazione f. continuation.
continuità f. continuity.
conti'nuo adj. continuous: di —, continuously, often; corrente continua, direct current.
conto m. reckoning; account; bill: per — di, on behalf of; a buon —, anyway; in fin dei conti, after all; rendersi — di, to realize; estratto —, statement of account.
contor'cere vt.[148] to twist; contor'cersi vr. to twist; to writhe.
contorcimento m. twisting.
contornare vt. to surround (with).
contorno m. contour, outline.
contorsione f. writhing.
contorto adj. twisted.
contrabbandiere m. smuggler.
contrabbando m. contraband.
contrabbasso m. contrabass.
contraccambiare vt. to reciprocate.
contraccambio m. requital.
contraccolpo m. rebound; recoil.
contrada f. road; country.
contraddire vt., vi. to contradict; contraddirsi vr. to contradict oneself; to be inconsistent.
contraddistin'guere vt. to earmark; to characterize.
contraddittore m. contradictor.
contraddittо'rio m. debate. adj. contradictory; inconsistent.
contraddizione f. contradiction; inconsistency, discrepancy.
contraente m. party (to a contract).
contrae'rea f. antiaircraft artillery.
contrae'reo adj. antiaircraft.
contraffare vt. to counterfeit; to imitate; to mimic; to simulate.
contraffatto adj. counterfeit; adulterated; distorted.
contraffazione f. forgery; fake.
contrafforte m. buttress; range.
contrammira'glio m. rear admiral.
contrappeso m. counterweight.
contrapporre vt. to oppose; to compare.
contrapposto m. opposite, opposed, compared. pp. of contrapporre.
contrappunto m. counterpoint.
contrariamente adv. contrarily.
contrariare vt. to vex; to thwart.
contrarietà f. contrariety.

contra'rio *m.* contrary, opposite. *adj.* contrary; unfavorable; averse; aver qualcosa in —, to object (*to*); in senso —, contrariwise.

contrarre *vt.*[146] to contract; contrarsi *vr.* to contract, shrink.

contrassegnare *vt.* to earmark.

contrassegno *m.* earmark; badge. *adv.* cash on delivery (*abbr.* c.o.d.)

contrastante *adj.* conflicting.

contrastare *vt.* to oppose. *vi.* to contrast (*with*); to quarrel.

contrastato *adj.* (*photog.*) contrasty.

contrasto *m.* contrast; conflict; quarrel.

contrattaccare *vt.*, *vi.* to counterattack.

contrattacco *m.* counterattack.

contrattare *vt.*, *vi.* to bargain.

contrattazione *f.* negotiation.

contrattempo *m.* contretemps, "hitch"; (*mus.*) syncopation.

contratto (*1*) *m.* contract.

contratto (*2*) *adj.* contracted. *pp.* of contrarre.

contrattuale *adj.* contractual.

contravveleno *m.* antidote.

contravvenire *vi.* to infringe (*upon*).

contravvenzione *f.* violation; fine.

contrazione *f.* contraction.

contribuente *m.* taxpayer: — moroso tax delinquent.

contribuire *vi.* to contribute.

contributo *m.* contribution.

contribuzione *f.* contribution.

contristare *vt.* to afflict.

contrito *adj.* contrite.

contrizione *f.* contrition.

contro *m.* con: il pro e il —, the pros and cons. *prep.*, *adv.* against; counter: — assegno, cash on delivery.

controbat'tere *vt.*, *vi.* to contest, argue (*against*); to answer.

controbilanciare *vt.* to counterbalance

controcampo *m.* (*moving pictures*) reverse shot.

controcassa *f.* outer case.

controchi'glia *f.* keelson.

controcorrente *f.* countercurrent. *adv.* upstream.

controffensiva *f.* counteroffensive.

controfigura *f.* (*moving pictures*) double, stand-in: — acrobatica, stunt man.

controfiocco *m.* flying jib.

controfirmare *vt.* to countersign.

controindicazione *f.* contraindication.

controllare *vt.* to control, verify, check; controllarsi *vr.* to control oneself.

controllo *m.* control, check.

controllore *m.* controller; conductor.

controluce *adv.* against the light.

contromarca *f.* countermark; check.

contromar'cia *f.* countermarch; reverse.

contromezzana *f.* mizzen topsail.

controparte *f.* opponent.

controproposta *f.* counterproposition.

contror'dine *m.* countermand.

controsenso *m.* nonsense, absurdity.

controspionag'gio *m.* counterespionage.

controvelaccino *m.* foreroyal.

controvelac'cio *m.* mainroyal.

controvento *adv.* windward.

controver'sia *f.* controversy.

controverso *adj.* controversial, moot.

contumace *adj.* defaulting.

contuma'cia *f.* default; quarantine: giudizio in —, judgment by default.

contume'lia *f.* contumely, insult.

contundente *adj.* blunt.

conturbante *adj.* disturbing.

conturbare *vt.* to disturb, upset.

contusione *f.* contusion, bruise.

contuso *adj.* bruised.

contuttoché *conj.* although.

contuttociò *adv.* yet, still.

convalescente *m.*, *f.*, *adj.* convalescent.

convalescenza *f.* convalescence.

convalescenzia'rio *m.* nursing home.

conva'lida *f.* validation; sanction.

convalidare *vt.* to validate; to confirm; to sanction.

convegno *m.* meeting; convention; rendezvous.

convene'vole *m.* propriety; (*pl.*) manners, proprieties. *adj.* fit, proper.

convenevolmente *adv.* properly.

conveniente *adj.* convenient; appropriate; cheap; profitable.

convenienza *f.* advantage; suitability; propriety.

convenire *vt.*[152] to convene. *vi.* to assemble; to agree; to admit; to suit; to be convenient: conviene che tu te ne vada, you had better go.

conventi'cola *f.* conventicle.

convento *m.* convent.

convenuto *m.* defendant; attendant. *adj.* agreed (*upon*); convened. *pp. of* convenire.

convenzionale *adj.* conventional.

convenzione *f.* convention.

convergente *adj.* convergent.

conver'gere *vi.*[11] to converge.

conversa *f.* lay sister.

conversare *vt.* to converse.

conversazione *f.* conversation.

conversione *f.* conversion.

converso *m.* lay brother.

converso (per) *adv.* conversely.

converti'bile *adj.* convertible.

convertibilità *f.* convertibility.

convertire *vt.*[44] to convert (*to*, *into*); to turn (*into*); convertirsi *vr.* to be convert ed (*to*); to turn (*into*).

convertito *m.* convert. *adj.* converted.

convertitore *m.* converter.
convessità *f.* convexity.
convesso *adj.* convex.
convincente *adj.* convincing.
convin'cere *vt.*[111] to convince, persuade; to convict; **convin'cersi** *vr.* to be (become) convinced.
convincimento *m.* firm belief.
convinto *adj.* persuaded; convicted. *pp. of* convincere.
convinzione *f.* firm belief; conviction.
convitato *m.* guest.
convito *m.* feast, banquet.
convitto *m.* boarding school.
convittore *m.* boarding pupil.
convivente *m.* cohabitant. *adj.* cohabiting.
convivenza *f.* cohabitation, life in common.
convi'vere *vi.*[111] to cohabit, live together.
conviviale *adj.* convivial.
convi'vio *see* convito.
convocare *vt.* to summon.
convocazione *f.* convocation.
convogliare *vt.* to convoy; to channel.
convo'glio *m.* convoy; (*rail.*) train.
convulsamente *adv.* convulsively.
convulsione *f.* convulsion.
convulsivo *adj.* convulsive.
convulso *m.* convulsion. *adj.* convulsive, spasmodic.
cooperare *vi.* to co-operate.
cooperativa *f.* co-operative.
cooperativo *adj.* co-operative.
cooperazione *f.* co-operation.
coordinamento *m.* co-ordination.
coordinare *vt.* to co-ordinate.
coordinatore *m.* co-ordinator.
coordinazione *f.* co-ordination.
coorte *f.* cohort.
copale *see* coppale.
coper'chio *m.* lid, cover.
coperta *f.* cover; coverlet; blanket; rug; bedspread; (*naut.*) deck.
copertina *f.* cover.
coperto *m.* shelter; safety; cover: **al —**, sheltered. *adj.* covered; coated; clothed; hidden. *pp. of* coprire.
copertone *m.* tarpaulin; (*auto.*) tire, shoe.
copertura *f.* covering; cover; coverage; screen.
co'pia *f.* copy; plenty.
copialet'tere *m.* copybook; copying press.
copiare *vt.* to copy.
copiativo *adj.* copying.
copiatore *m.* copyist; plagiarist.
copiatura *f.* copying; plagiarism.
copione *m.* script.
copiosamente *adv.* plentifully.
copioso *adj.* copious, plentiful.
copista *m.* copyist.

copisteri'a *f.* copying office.
coppa *f.* cup, bowl; heart (*in playing cards*); trophy; nap; saveloy.
coppale *m.* copal; patent leather.
coppella *f.* cupel: **oro di —**, pure gold.
coppetta *f.* cupping glass.
cop'pia *f.* couple, pair, brace.
coppiere *m.* cupbearer.
coppo *m.* tile; jar, pitcher.
copribusto *m.* bodice.
copricapo *m.* headgear.
coprifuoco *m.* curfew; blackout.
copripiedi *m.* coverlet, blanket.
coprire *vt.*[22] to cover; to hide; to fill (*an office*); to coat; to clothe: **— di ingiurie**, to revile; **coprirsi** *vr.* to cover oneself (*with*); to put on one's **coprivivande** *m.* dish cover.   [hat.
copto *m.* Copt; Coptic. *adj.* Coptic.
co'pula *f.* sexual intercourse; (*sci.*) copulation; (*gramm.*) copula.
corag'gio *m.* courage: **farsi —**, to take courage; **fare — a**, to hearten.
coraggiosamente *adv.* bravely.
coraggioso *adj.* courageous, brave.
corale *m., adj.* choral.
coralli'fero *adj.* coralliferous.
corallo *m.* coral.
corame *m.* leather.
Corano *m.* Koran.
corata *f.* lights (*pl.*).
corazza *f.* armor plate; breastplate; (*zool.*) carapace, shell.
corazzare *vt.* to armor; to steel; **corazzarsi** *vr.* to steel oneself.
corazzata *f.* battleship.
corazziere *m.* cuirassier.
corba *f.* basket.
corbelleri'a *f.* nonsense, blunder.
corbez'zolo *m.* arbute.
corbez'zoli *interj.* by Jove!
corda *f.* rope, cable; halter; chord; (*mus.*) string; (*anat.*) cord: **— di rame**, copper plait; **— di pianoforte**, piano wire; **mostrare la —**, to be threadbare; **dare la — a un orologio**, to wind up a clock.
cordame *m.* rope; cordage.
cordata *f.* (*mountaineering*) roped team.
cordiale *m.* cordial. *adj.* hearty.
cordialità *f.* cordiality.
cordialmente *adv.* cordially.
cordigliera *f.* cordillera.
cordo'glio *m.* grief, sorrow.
cordonata *f.* ramp, gradient.
cordone *m.* cordon; cord; girdle; (*archit.*) stringcourse; curb, curbstone.
core'a *f.* (*med.*) St. Vitus's dance.
Corea *f.* (*geog.*) Korea.
coreg'gia *f.* strap.
Corelli, Arcangelo, Italian violinist (1653–1713).

coreografi'a f. choreography.
coreogra'fico adj. choreographic.
coreo'grafo m. choreographer.
coria'ceo adj. coriaceous, tough.
corian'dolo m. confetto (pl. confetti); (bot.) coriander.
coricare vt. to lay down; coricarsi vr. to lie down; to go to bed; to set.
corindone m. corundum.
corin'zio m., adj. Corinthian.
corista m. chorus singer; chorister; diapason. f. chorus girl.
co'rizza f. coryza.
cormorano m. cormorant.
cornac'chia f. crow, rook.
cornamusa f. bagpipe.
cornata f. butt.
cor'nea f. cornea.
cornetta f. cornet.
cornetto m. little horn; amulet; (bread) croissant: — acustico, ear trumpet; — telefonico, receiver.
cornice f. frame; cornice.
cornicione m. entablature.
cornificare vt. to be unfaithful to; to cuckold.
cor'niola f. (bot.) dogberry; (min.) carnelian.
cor'niolo m. cornel, dogwood.
corno m. horn: corna ramificate, antlers; fare le corna al marito, to cuckold one's husband; portare le corna, to be a cuckold.
cornuto m. cuckold. adj. horned.
coro m. chorus; choir.
corografi'a f. chorography.
coro'grafo m. chorographer.
coro'ide f. choroid.
corolla f. corolla.
corolla'rio m. corollary.
corona f. crown; coronet; corona; rim; wreath; rosary, beads (pl.).
coronamento m. crowning; fulfillment.
coronare vt. to crown; to fulfill.
corona'rio adj. coronary.
coronato adj. crowned; coronate.
corpetto m. waistcoat, vest.
corpo m. body; staff; corpus; (typog.) size, type; (mil.) corps: — di ballo, corps de ballet; — del reato, corpus delicti; spirito di —, esprit de corps; a — morto, rashly.
corporale adj. corporal, bodily; physical.
corporativismo m. corporative system.
corporativo adj. corporative.
corporatura f. size, build.
corporazione f. corporation.
corpo'reo adj. corporeal, bodily.
corpulento adj. corpulent, portly.
corpulenza f. corpulence.
corpu'scolo m. corpuscle.
Corpusdo'mini m. Corpus Christi.

corredare vt. to equip, provide (with); to accompany (with); to supplement (with).
corredo m. outfit; kit; trousseau.
correg'gere vt.[105] to correct, amend; to rebuke: — le bozze, to read proofs; correg'gersi vr. to correct oneself; to improve.
correg'gia f. strap.
Correggio, da, Azzo (Antonio Allegri), Italian painter (1494-1534).
correggi'bile adj. corrigible.
corregionale m. fellow countryman.
correità f. complicity.
correlativo adj. correlative.
correlazione f. correlation.
correligiona'rio m. coreligionist.
corrente f. current; draft; school; tendency: — del Golfo, Gulf Stream; contro —, upstream; essere al — di, to be acquainted with; mettere uno al — di, to acquaint one with. adj. current, running, flowing; instant; middling; circulating; common, prevailing.
correntemente adv. currently, fluently.
correntista m. depositor.
corre'o m. codefendant; corespondent.
cor'rere vt., vi.[36] to run; to hurry; to flow; to be current; to circulate: coi tempi che corrono, as times go; corre voce che, there is a rumor that; lasciar —, to bear with it; — i mari, to sail the seas; far — un cavallo, to race a horse.
corresponsa'bile adj. jointly responsible; corespondent.
corresponsione f. payment.
correttamente adv. correctly.
correttezza f. correctness.
correttivo m., adj. corrective.
corretto adj. correct; corrected; right; upright; laced, "spiked" (as of coffee). pp. of correggere. adv. correctly.
correttore m. corrector: — di bozze, proofreader.
correzione f. correction: — delle bozze, proofreading; casa di —, reformatory.
corrido'io m. passage; aisle; corridor.
corridore m. racer, competitor.
corriera f. stagecoach; motor bus.
corriere m. messenger, courier; carrier, forwarder; mail: a volta di —, by return mail.
corrigendo m. reformatory boy.
corrimano m. handrail.
corrispettivo m. return, requital, reward; consideration.
corrispondente m. correspondent. adj. correspondent, corresponding.

corrispondenza *f.* correspondence; relation; agreement; reciprocity; mail.

corrispon'dere *vt.*[118] to allow. *vi.* to correspond (*to, with*); to match; to fit; to reciprocate; to answer, fulfill; to comply (*with*).

corrisposto *adj.* reciprocated, returned; allowed. *pp.* of **corrispondere**.

corrivo *adj.* rash; accommodating; lenient.

corroborante *m.*, *adj.* corroborative.

corroborare *vt.* to corroborate, strengthen; to invigorate.

corroborazione *f.* corroboration.

corro'dere *vt.*[114] to corrode, to eat (*into*); **corrodersi** *vr.* to corrode, to be eaten (*into*).

corrom'pere *vt.*[118] to corrupt; to taint; to bribe, **corrom'persi** *vr.* to corrupt, decay, rot.

corrosione *f.* corrosion.

corrosivo *m.*, *adj.* corrosive.

corroso *adj.* corroded. *pp.* of **corrodere**.

corrotto *adj.* corrupt, rotten; corrupted, tainted; bribed. *pp.* of **corrompere**.

corrucciarsi *vr.* to get angry; to worry.

corrucciato *adj.* angry; worried.

corruc'cio *m.* anger; worry.

corrugare *vt.*, **corrugarsi** *vr.* to wrinkle, knit: — **la fronte**, to frown.

corruttela *f.* corruption; bribing.

corrutti'bile *adj.* corruptible; bribable.

corruttibilità *f.* corruptibility; bribability.

corruttore *m.* corrupter; briber.

corruzione *f.* corruption; seducement; bribing: **prezzo della —**, bribe.

corsa *f.* run; race; trip; (*aeron.*) taxiing; (*mach.*) stroke: — **di andata e ritorno**, round trip; **prezzo della —**, fare; **di —**, in a hurry; **perdere la —**, to miss (one's train, one's bus, etc.); **di gran —**, full speed; **sala delle corse**, horse (betting) room.

corsaletto *m.* corselet.

corsaro *m.* privateer; pirate.

corsi'a *f.* aisle, passageway; ward; alley; (*aeron.*) catwalk.

corsiere *m.* race horse, courser.

corsivo *m.* (*typog.*) italics (*pl.*).

corso (1) *m.* course; avenue: — **d'acqua**, watercourse; — **del cambio**, rate of exchange; **capitano di lungo —**, shipmaster; **avere — legale**, to be legal tender; **fuori —**, withdrawn from circulation; **nel — della settimana**, during the week; **in —**, under way; **in — di stampa**, in the press.

corso (2) *pp.* of **correre**.

corso (3) *m.*, *adj.* Corsican.

corso'io *adj.* running, sliding: **nodo —**, running knot.

corte *f.* courtyard; court; retinue; addresses (*pl.*), courtship: **Corte Marziale**, court martial; **dama di —**, lady-in-waiting; **fare la — a**, to court **tenere — bandita**, to keep open house.

cortec'cia *f.* bark; cortex.

corteggiamento *m.* courtship.

corteggiare *vt.* to court, woo.

corteg'gio *m.* retinue.

corteo *m.* procession, train; parade: — **funebre**, funeral train.

corteggiatore *m.* beau (*pl.* beaux), wooer.

cortese *adj.* kind, polite, obliging.

cortesemente *adv.* kindly, politely; obligingly.

cortesi'a *f.* politeness; kindness; obligingness: **per —**, please, if you please.

cortezza *f.* shortness; lack, want: — **di mente**, dullness.

cor'tice *m.* cortex (*pl.* cortices).

cortigiana *f.* courtesan.

cortigiano *m.* courtier.

cortile *m.* courtyard, court, yard.

cortina *f.* curtain, screen: — **di ferro**, Iron Curtain.

cortinag'gio *m.* canopy.

corto *adj.* short, brief; wanting; short-witted: — **di vista**, short-sighted; **essere a — di**, to be short of; **venire alle corte**, to get down to brass tacks.

cortometrag'gio *m.* short; documentary.

corvetta *f.* corvette.

corvino *adj.* corvine; raven.

corvo *m.* crow, raven; (*naut.*) grappling iron; (*mach.*) tongs (*pl.*).

cosa *f.* thing; matter; work; gadget: **che —?** what? **qualche —**, something; **nessuna —**, nothing; **alcuna —**, anything, **ogni —**, everything; **per la qual —**, therefore.

Cosacco *m.* Cossack.

coscetto *m.* leg (*of mutton, etc.*).

co'scia *f.* thigh; leg; (*arch.*) abutment; (*mach.*) jaw.

josciale *m.* cuisse, cuish.

cosciente *adj.* conscious, aware.

coscienza *f.* conscience; awareness; uprightness: **libertà di —**, freedom of conscience. religion.

coscienziosità *f.* conscientiousness.

cescienzioso *adj.* conscientious.

coscritto *m.* recruit. *adj.* conscript.

coscrizione *f.* conscription.

così *adv.*, *adj.* so, thus, this way, like this, like that, such.

osicchè *conj.* so that.

cosiddetto *adj.* so-called.

cosiffatto *adj.* such, of that kind.

cosmesi *f.* cosmesis.

cosme'tico *m.*, *adj.* cosmetic.

co'smico *adj.* cosmic.

cosmo *m.* cosmos.

cosmografi'a *f.* cosmography.

cosmologi'a *f.* cosmology.

cosmopolita *m.* cosmopolite. *adj.* cosmopolitan.

coso *m.* thing, thingumbob, thingummy.

cospar'gere *vt.*[188] to spread; to sprinkle; to smear.

cosparso *adj.* besprinkled, sprinkled, besmeared. *pp. of* cospargere.

cospetto *m.* presence; view.

cospetto! *interj.* bless me!

cospi'cuo *adj.* conspicuous, outstanding; substantial; prominent.

cospirare *vi.* to conspire, plot.

cospiratore *m.* conspirator.

cospiratrice *f.* conspiratress.

cospirazione *f.* conspiracy.

costa *m.* rib; slope; coast; back (*of a knife*); middle nerve (*of a leaf*).

costà *adv.* there.

costaggiù *adv.* down there.

costante *adj.* constant; loyal; lasting; uniform; steady.

costantemente *adv.* steadily.

costanza *f.* constancy; steadiness; loyalty.

costare *vi.* to cost.

costassù *adv.* up there.

costata *f.* chop, cutlet.

costatare *vt.* to ascertain; to perceive.

costatazione *f.* ascertainment, verification; discovery.

costato *m.* chest, ribs (*pl.*).

costeggiare *vt.* to coast; to flank, border. *vi.* to coast (*along*).

coste'i *pron.f.* this woman, she.

costellare *vt.* to spangle.

costellazione *f.* constellation.

costernare *vt.* to cause consternation (*in*), dismay, grieve.

costernazione *f.* consternation.

costì *adv.* there.

costiera *f.* coast, shore.

costiere *m.* pilot.

costiero *adj.* coastal: nave costiera, coaster.

costipare *vt.* to constipate; to give (*one*) a cold; costiparsi *vr.* to become constipated; to catch a cold.

costipazione *f.* constipation; cold.

costituente *adj.* constituent.

costituire *vt.* to constitute, to form; to amount to; to appoint; to assign; costituirsi *vr.* to form, be constituted; to appoint oneself; to give oneself up: costituirsi parte civile, to sue.

costitutivo *adj.* constitutive.

costituzionale *adj.* constitutional.

costituzione *f.* constitution, formation; make-up; establishment; appointment.

costo *m.* cost: — di produzione, prime cost; a nessun —, by no means.

co'stola *f.* rib; back.

costoletta *f.* chop, cutlet.

costoro *pron.pl.* these people; they; these men; these women.

costoso *adj.* costly, expensive.

costretto *adj.* compelled, forced, obliged; pressed. *pp. of* costringere.

costrin'gere *vt.*[188] to compel, force; to press, cramp.

costrittore *m.* constrictor.

costrizione *f.* compulsion.

costruire *vt.*[97] to build, construct; (*gramm.*) to construe.

costruito *adj.*, *pp.* built; construed.

costrutto *m.* (*gramm.*) construction; sense, meaning; point; use.

costruttore *m.* builder.

costruzione *f.* construction, manufacture; arrangement; make; building.

costu'i *pron.m.* this man, he.

costumanza *f.* custom, habit.

costumare *vi.* to be usual, customary.

costumatezza *f.* good manners.

costumato *adj.* well-behaved; polite.

costume *m.* custom, habit; costume; fancy dress: — da bagno, bathing suit; buoni costumi, good morals; cattivi costumi, loose morals.

costumista *m.*, *f.*, (*theat.*) costumer.

costura *f.* seam.

cotale *adj.*, *pron.* such.

cotanto *see* tanto.

cote *f.* hone.

cotechino *m.* (a certain) sausage.

cotenna *f.* pigskin; rind; scalp.

cotesto *adj.* that (*pl.* those); such. *pron.* that one.

co'tica *f.* pigskin; rind.

cotile'done *m.* cotyledon.

cotogna *f.* quince.

cotognata *f.* quince jam.

cotogno *m.* quince tree.

cotoletta *see* costoletta.

cotonato *m.* cotton cloth.

cotone *m.* cotton; cottonwool.

cotoneri'e *f.pl.* cotton goods.

cotoniere *m.* cotton manufacturer; cotton spinner.

cotoniero *adj.* cotton.

cotonifi'cio *m.* cotton mill.

cotonina *f.* calico.

cotta (1) *f.* cooking; baking; ovenful; kilnful; infatuation: prendere una — per, to fall hard for; un furfante di tre cotte, an unmitigated scoundrel.

cotta (2) f. (eccl.) surplice.
cottimista m. pieceworker.
cot'timo m. piecework.
cotto m. earthenware. adj. done;
cooked: poco —, underdone, rare;
troppo —, overdone; innamorato
—, head over heels in love. pp. of
cuocere.
cottura f. boiling; roasting; baking;
grilling; cooking; ovenful.
coturno m. cothurnus (pl. cothurni),
buskin.
cova f. brooding; brood.
covare vt., vi. to brood, sit (on); to
harbor, cherish; to smolder (as
embers).
covata f. brood; hatch.
covile m. den, lair; couch.
covo m. den, lair; burrow.
covone m. sheaf (pl. sheaves).
cozza f. cockle.
cozzare vt., vi. to butt (at, against);
to hit (against); to clash.
cozzo m. butt; clash.
crac m. crack; failure; slump.
crampo m. cramp.
cra'nico adj. cranial: scatola cranica,
skull.
cra'nio m. skull.
cra'pula f. crapulence; debauchery.
crapulone m. debauchee.
crasso adj. crass, gross: intestino —,
large intestine.
cratere m. crater.
cra'uti m.pl. sauerkraut.
cravatta f. tie, necktie; four-in-hand:
— a farfalla, bow tie.
creanza f. politeness: mala —, bad
manners, rudeness.
creare vt. to create; to appoint.
creativo adj. creative.
creato m. creation, universe. adj., pp
created, formed.
creatore m. creator.
creatrice f. creatrix.
creatura f. creature: povera —! the
poor thing!
creazione f. creation.
credente m., f. believer.
credenza (1) f. belief; faith.
credenza (2) f. sideboard.
credenziale f., adj. credential.
cre'dere vt., vi. to believe; to trust; to
think: fa come credi, do as you like;
cre'dersi vr. to think oneself.
credi'bile adj. credible.
credito m. credit; trust; reputation:
a —, on credit; istituto di —, bank.
creditore m. creditor.
credo m. credo, creed; faith.
credulità f. credulity.
cre'dulo adj. credulous, gullible.
crema f. cream; custard: — da scarpe,
shoe polish.

cremagliera f. (mach.) rack: ferrovia
a —, cog railway.
cremare vt. to cremate.
cremato'io m. crematory.
cremato'rio adj. crematory.
cremazione f. cremation.
cre'misi m., adj. crimson.
Cremlino m. Kremlin.
cremore m. cream of tartar.
creolina f. creolin.
cre'olo m., adj. Creole.
creosoto m. creosote.
crepa f. crack, crevice, chink.
crepac'cio m. cleft; crevasse.
crepacuore m. heartbreak.
crepapelle (a) adv. excessively: ridere
a —, to burst with laughter.
crepare vi. to crack, split; to burst;
"to croak," die; creparsi vr. to
crack, burst.
crepitare vi. to crackle.
crepiti'o m. crepitation, crackling.
crepu'scolo m. twilight.
crescendo m. crescendo.
crescente adj. growing; increasing;
rising.
crescenza f. growth.
cre'scere vt.[16] to increase, raise; to
bring up, breed: farsi — la barba,
to grow a beard. vi. to increase, rise;
to grow; to be left.
crescione m. water cress.
cre'scita, cresciuta f. growth.
cresciuto adj. grown (up); increased;
bred; developed. pp. of crescere.
cre'sima f. Confirmation.
cresimare vt. to confirm.
crespa f. wrinkle; ripple.
crespo m. crepe. adj. crispy, crinkled.
cresta f. crest; comb; tuft; bonnet;
top; peak.
cresta'ia f. (ladies') milliner.
creta f. clay.
cretese m., f., adj. Cretan.
cretineri'a f. idiocy; nonsense.
cretino m. cretin; idiot, fool.
cribrare vt. to sift.
cribro m. sieve.
cricca f. clique, gang, coterie.
cricco m. jack.
criminale m., adj. criminal.
criminalità f. criminality.
cri'mine m. crime.
criminologi'a f. criminology.
crimino'logo m. criminologist.
criminoso adj. criminal.
crinale m. ridge; hairpin.
crine m. hair.
criniera f. mane; crest.
crino m. hair.
crinolina f. crinoline.
cripta f. crypt.
criptocomunista m. fellow traveler.
crisa'lide f. chrysalis.

crisantemo *m.* chrysanthemum.
crisi *f.* crisis (*pl.* crises); attack; burst; climax.
crisma *f.* chrism.
Crispi, Francesco, Italian statesman (1819-1901).
cristalleri'a *f.* crystal works; crystalware.
cristalliera *f.* glass case.
cristallino *m.* (*anat.*) crystalline lens. *adj.* crystalline, crystal.
cristallizzare *vt.* to crystallize.
cristallizzazione *f.* crystallization.
cristallo *m.* crystal, glass.
cristiane'simo *m.* Christianity.
cristia'nia *m.* (*sport*) christiania turn, christy.
cristianità *f.* Christendom.
cristiano *m.*, *adj.* Christian.
Cristo *m.pr.* Christ: un povero —, a poor fellow.
crite'rio *m.* criterion; standard; idea; sense; principle; rule.
cri'tica *f.* criticism; critique.
criticare *vt.* to criticize; to review.
cri'tico *m.* critic. *adj.* critical.
criticone *m.* faultfinder.
critto'gama *f.* cryptogam.
crittografi'a *f.* cryptography.
crittogramma *m.* cryptogram.
crivellare *vt.* to sift; to riddle (*with*).
crivello *m.* sieve, riddle.
croato *m.* Croat. *adj.* Croatian.
croccante *adj.* crisp, crackling.
crocchetta *f.* croquette.
croc'chia *f.* chignon, bun.
crocchiare *vi.* to crackle; to cluck.
croc'chio *m.* crackle; cluck; group.
croce *f.* cross; cross-mark: a —, crosswise; a occhio e —, at a rough guess; testa e —, head or tail.
Croce, Benedetto, Italian philosopher and historian (1866- 1952).
crocerossina *f.* Red Cross Sister.
crocetta *f.* crosslet.
crocevi'a *f.* crossroads (*pl.*), intersection.
crociata *f.* crusade.
crociato *m.* crusader. *adj.* crossed.
crocic'chio *m.* crossroads (*pl.*), intersection.
crociera *f.* intersection; cruise: volta a —, cross vault.
croci'fera *f.* crucifer.
crocifig'gere *vt.*[st] to crucify.
crocifissione *f.* crucifixion.
crocifisso *m.* crucifix. *adj.* crucified. *pp. of* crocifiggere.
croco *m.* crocus, saffron.
crogiolarsi *vr.* to cuddle, bask.
crogiuolo *m.* crucible.
crollare *vt.* to shake; to shrug. *vi.* to fall; to collapse; to break down.
crollo *m.* fall, collapse, breakdown.

croma *f.* (*mus.*) quaver.
cromare *vt.* to plate with chromium.
cromato *m.* chromate. *adj.* chromium-plated.
cromatura *f.* chromium plating.
cromo *m.* chrome, chromium.
cromolitografi'a *f.* chromolithography.
cro'naca *f.* chronicle; report, news.
cro'nico *m.*, *adj.* chronic.
cronista *m.* chronicler; reporter: capo —, city editor.
cronisto'ria *f.* chronicle.
cronologi'a *f.* chronology.
cronolo'gico *adj.* chronological.
cronometrare *vt.* to time.
cronome'trico *adj.* chronometrical.
cronometrista *m.* timekeeper.
crono'metro *m.* stop watch, chronometer.
crosciare *vt.* to shower; to rustle.
crosta *f.* crust; scab, eschar.
crosta'ceo *m.*, *adj.* crustacean.
crostata *f.* pie.
crostino *m.* toast.
croupier *m.* dealer.
cro'talo *m.* rattle; rattlesnake.
crucciare *vt.* to torment; to worry; **crucciarsi** *vr.* to worry; to get angry; to fret.
cruc'cio *m.* sorrow; worry.
cruciale *adj.* crucial.
cruciverba *m.* crossword puzzle.
crudamente *adv.* crudely, rudely.
crudele *adj.* cruel, ruthless.
crudeltà *f.* cruelty.
crudezza *f.* crudeness, roughness.
crudo *adj.* raw; cruel; b unt; hard; unripe.
cruento *adj.* bloody.
crumiro *m.* scab, strikebreaker.
cruna *f.* needle's eye, eye.
crusca *f.* bran; freckles (*pl.*).
cruschello *m.* middlings (*pl.*).
cruscotto *m.* dashboard; (*aeron.*) control panel.
cubatura *f.* cubature.
cu'bico *adj.* cubic; radice cubica, cube root.
cubi'colo *m.* cubicle.
cubismo *m.* cubism.
cubista *m.*, *adj.* cubist.
cubitale *adj.* cubital; (*anat.*) ulnar: caratteri cubitali, large type.
cu'bito *m.* cubit; (*anat.*) ulna.
cubo *m.* cube. *adj.* cubic.
cuccagna *f.* Cockaigne; windfall: albero della —, greased pole.
cuccetta *f.* berth.
cucchiaiata *f.* spoonful.
cucchiaino *m.* teaspoon.
cucchia'io *m.* spoon.
cucchiaione *m.* ladle.
cuc'cia *f.* couch; doghouse.
cuc'ciolo *m.* puppy, whelp.

cuccù *m.* cuckoo.

cuc'cuma *f.* kettle; coffeepot.

cucina *f.* kitchen; cookery, cuisine; cooking: — **economica**, kitchen range.

cucinare *vt.*, *vi.* to cook; to dress.

cuciniere *m.* cook.

cucinino *m.* kitchenette.

cucire *vt.* to sew, stitch: **macchina per** —, sewing machine.

cucirini *m.pl.* sewing threads.

cucitrice *f.* seamstress.

cucitura *f.* seam; sewing.

cu'culo *m.* cuckoo.

cucur'bita *f.* gourd; alembic.

cucurbita'ceo *adj.* cucurbitaceous.

cuf'fia *f.* cap; hood; headset.

cugino *m.*, cugina *f.* cousin.

cui a, di, *etc. rel. pron.* whom, whose, to whom, which, of which, to which.

culatta *f.* breech.

culina'ria *f.* cookery.

culina'rio *adj.* culinary.

culla *f.* cradle.

cullare *vt.* to rock; lull, to fondle.

culminante *adj.* highest, culminating.

culminare *vi.* to culminate.

cul'mine *m.* top, summit.

culo *m.* buttocks; bottom.

culto *m.* worship, cult.

cultore *m.* dilettante, devotee.

cultura *f.* culture; learning.

cumulativo *adj.* cumulative, joint.

cu'mulo *m.* pile, heap; lot; pool; cumulus (*pl.* cumuli).

cuna *f.* cradle.

cu'neo *m.* wedge.

cunetta *f.* ditch; gutter.

cuni'colo *m.* tunnel; adit.

cuo'cere *vt.*, *vi.*," cuo'cersi *vr.* to cook; to bake; to stew; to boil; to roast; (*fig.*) to sting.

cuoco *m.*, cuoca *f.* cook.

cuo'io *m.* leather.

cuore *m.* heart; soul: **amico del** —, bosom friend; **senza**—, heartless; **nel** — **della notte**, in the dead of night.

cupezza *f.* gloominess.

cupidi'gia *f.* greed, cupidity.

cu'pido *adj.* greedy, covetous.

Cupido *m.* (*myth.*) Cupid.

cupo *adj.* gloomy; sullen; deep; dark.

cu'pola *f.* dome, cupola.

cura *f.* care; cure, treatment, nursing; remedy; editorship; **a** — **di**, edited by.

cura'bile *adj.* curable.

curare *vt.* to take care of, manage; to edit; to treat, nurse; to cure; curarsi *vr.* to subject oneself to medical treatment; to take care of oneself; to care; to take care (*of*).

curaro *m.* curare, curari.

curatela *f.* guardianship; trusteeship.

curativo *adj.* curative, healing.

curato *m.* curate.

curatore *m.* curator; trustee; custodian.

curdo *m.*, *adj.* Kurd.

cu'ria *f.* curia; court of justice.

curialesco *adj.* jurisprudential.

curiosare *vi.* to pry (*into*).

curiosità *f.* curiosity; inquisitiveness; quaintness, oddness; curio.

curioso *m.* onlooker. *adj.* curious; inquisitive; quaint, odd, funny.

curro *m.* roller; (*mach.*) dolly.

cursore *m.* process server; (*mach.*) slider.

curva *f.* curve, bend; camber.

curvare *vt.* to curve, to bend; to camber; curvarsi *vr.* to bend, bow, stoop.

curvatura *f.* curving, bending.

curvo *adj.* curved, bent; stooping.

cuscinetto *m.* small cushion; (*mach.*) bearing; (*fig.*) buffer: — **per timbri**, pad; — **a sfere**, ball bearing.

cuscino *m.* cushion; pillow.

cu'spide *f.* cusp.

custode *m.* custodian; guardian; keeper; janitor; watchman; warder.

custo'dia *f.* custody, keeping; guardianship; care; case: **agente di** —, custodian.

custodire *vt.* to keep, preserve; to watch over; to take care of; to cherish.

cuta'neo *adj.* cutaneous, skin.

cute *f.* skin.

cuticagna *f.* nape; scalp.

cutret tola *f.* wagtail.

D

da *prep.* from; by; to; at; since; as, like; for: — **principio**, at first; **dal principio alla fine**, from first to last; **un contegno** — **gentiluomo**, a gentlemanlike behavior; — **vendere**, for sale; — **affittare**, to let; — **parte**, aside; — **basso**, downstairs; **auto** — **turismo**, touring car.

dabbasso *adv.* downstairs.

dabbenag'gine *f.* candor; credulity.

dabbene *adj.* upright, honest.

daccanto *prep.* beside, by, close to. *adv.* near, near by.

daccapo *adv.* again, over again; paragraph; (*mus.*) da capo.

dacchè *conj.* since.

dadaismo *m.* dadaism.

dadaista m. dadaist.

dado m. die (pl. dice); cube; (mach.) nut; (obs.) die (pl. dies).

daffare m. occupation bustle: avere un gran —, to be ve y busy; darsi un gran —, to bustle about.

daga f. dagger, dirk.

dagherro'tipo m. daguerreotype.

dagli, dai comp.prep. from, by the. see da.

dàil interj. come on now!; hurry up!; go on!

da'ina f. doe.

da'ino m. deer (pl. deer); buck.

dal, dalla comp.prep. from, by the. see da.

da'lia f. dahlia.

dallato adv. beside; aside.

dalle, dallo comp.prep. from, by the. see da.

dal'mata m., adj. Dalmatian.

dalto'nico adj. color-blind.

daltonismo m. daltonism.

d'altronde adv. on the other hand; besides, moreover.

dama (1) f. lady; (dancing) partner.

dama (2) f. checkers: king: fare —, to become a king.

damascare vt. to damask.

damasco m. brocade, damask.

Damasco f. (geog.) Damascus.

damerino m. dandy fop.

damigella f. damsel maid.

damigiana f. demijohn.

danaro see denaro.

danaroso adj. wealthy.

Dan'dolo, Enrico admiral and blind doge of Venice (1108? 1205).

danese m. Dane; Great Dane. adj. Danish.

dannare vt. to damn; dannarsi vr. to damn oneself; to rack oneself; to fret.

dannato m., adj. damned.

dannazione f. damnation; curse.

danneggiare vt. to damage, injure; to impair, harm; to damnify.

danneggiato m. victim loser. adj. damaged, harmed; damnified.

danno m. damage, injure harm; loss.

dannoso adj. hurtful, harmful.

D'Annunzio, Gabriele, ee Annunzio.

dante (pelle di) m. buckskin.

Dante see Alighieri.

dantesco adj. Dantean, Dantesque.

dantista m. Dentist.

danza f. dance, dancing.

danzante adj. dancing.

danzare vt., vi. to dance.

danzatore m., danzatrice f. dancer.

dappertutto adv. everywhere.

dappiè adv. at the foot.

dappoco adj. worthless, inept.

dappoi adv. afterwards.

dappresso adv. closely, close by.

dapprima adv. at first; first of all.

dapprinci'pio adv. in the beginning, at first.

dardeggiare vt., vi. to dart (at).

dardo m. dart.

dare vt.** to give; to hand over (to); to confer, bestow (on), award; to grant; to afford; to produce; to utter; to deal: — torto a, to disagree with; — ragione a, to agree with; — alla luce, to give birth to; — da mangiare a, to feed; — uno schiaffo a, to slap; — una commedia, to produce a play — la buona notte, to wish good night; — l'addio a, to bid good-bye to; — in affitto, to rent; — in prestito, to lend; — a qualcuno 20 anni di età, to take someone to be twenty; gli diedero 10 anni (di prigione), he was sentenced to ten years' imprisonment. vi. to hit; to lead; to look (upon): — alla testa, to go to one's head; — allo stomaco, to turn one's stomach; — ai nervi, to irk; — nell'occhio, to strike the eye; darsi vr. to give oneself; to surrender oneself; to devote oneself (to); to pass oneself off (as); to take (to): — per vinto, to give up; — pensiero, to take pains, to worry; — il caso, to happen; può —, maybe; darsela a gambe, to take to one's heels.

dare m. (comm.) debit: il — e l'avere, debit and credit.

dar'sena f. dock; boathouse.

data f. date: in — d'oggi, under today's date; di — recente, recent; alla — stabilita, on the appointed day; a 30 giorni —, 30 days after date; sino alla — d'oggi, down to date.

datare vt., vi. to date: a — da oggi, (starting) from today.

dativo m., adj. dative.

dato m. datum (pl. data). adj. given: — che, since, supposing that, provided. pp.of dare.

datore m. giver: — di lavoro, employer.

dat'tero m. date; date palm: — di mare, lithodomus.

dattilografare vt., vi. to typewrite, to type.

dattilografi'a f. typewriting.

dattilo'grafo m., dattilo'grafa f. typist.

dattiloscritto m. typescript.

d'attorno adv., prep. about, round, around: levarsi —, to get out of the way; togliersi qualcuno —, to get rid of someone; darsi —, to busy oneself.

davanti *m.*, *adj.* fore, front. *adv.* in front (*of*), before.

davanzale *m.* sill, window sill.

davanzo *adv.* enough and to spare.

davvero *adv.* really, indeed: dire —, to be in earnest.

dazia'rio *adj.* toll.

daziere *m.* exciseman.

da'zio *m.* excise; custom duty; toll-house: esente da —, duty free.

dea *f.* goddess.

debellare *vt.* to conquer; to overcome.

debilitante *adj.* debilitative.

debilitare *vt.* to debilitate.

debilitazione *f.* debilitation.

debitamente *adv.* duly, properly.

de'bito *m.* debt; obligation. *adj.* proper, due.

debitore *m.* debtor.

de'bole *m.* weakness. *adj.* weak, feeble.

debolezza *f.* weakness; feebleness.

debolmente *adv.* weakly; faintly.

debosciato *m.* debauchee. *adj.* debauched.

debuttante *m.* debutant. *f.* debutante. *m.*, *f.* beginner.

debuttare *vi.* to open; to make one's debut.

debutto *m.* opening; debut.

de'cade *f.* ten days; decade.

decadente *m.*, *adj.* decadent.

decadenza *f.* decadence; decline: — da un diritto, forfeiture.

decadere *vi.*[11] to decline; to fall: — da un diritto, to forfeit a right.

decadimento *m.* decay.

decalcificazione *f.* decalcification.

decalcomani'a *f.* decalcomania.

deca'logo *m.* decalogue.

decampare *vi.* to decamp; to recede.

decano *m.* dean.

decantare *vt.* to praise; to decant.

decapitare *vt.* to behead.

decapitazione *f.* beheading.

dece'dere *vi.*[11] to decease.

deceduto *m.*, *adj.* deceased.

decennale *m.*, *adj.* decennial.

decenne *adj.* decennial; ten years old.

decen'nio *m.* decade.

decente *adj.* decent; fair.

decentramento *m.* decentralization.

decentrare *vt.* to decentralize.

decenza *f.* decency.

decesso *m.* decease, death.

deci'dere *vt.*, *vi.*[41] to decide; decidersi *vr.* to make up one's mind, resolve.

deci'duo *adj.* deciduous.

decifrare *vt.* to decipher, decode.

decifrazione *f.* decipherment.

decigrammo *m.* decigram.

deci'litro *m.* deciliter.

de'cima *f.* tithe.

decimale *m.*, *adj.* decimal.

decimare *vt.* to decimate.

decimazione *f.* decimation.

deci'metro *m.* decimeter: doppio —, ruler.

de'cimo *m.*, *adj.* tenth.

decimoterzo *adj.* thirteenth.

decina *f.* half a score, ten or so.

decisamente *adv.* decidedly; resolutely; unhesitatingly.

decisione *f.* decision, resolution; resoluteness.

decisivo *adj.* decisive.

deciso *adj.* determined; settled, decided. *pp.of* decidere.

declamare *vt.*, *vi.* to declaim, mouth.

declamato'rio *adj.* declamatory, mouthy.

declamazione *f.* declamation.

declinare *vt.* to decline; to declare. *vi.* to decline, sink; to slope; to set.

declinazione *f.* (*gramm.*) declension; (*astr.*) declination.

declino *m.* decline, wane.

decli'vio *m.* declivity, slope.

decollare *vt.* to behead. *vi.* (*aeron.*) to take off.

decollo *m.* (*aeron.*) take-off.

decolorare *vt.* to decolor.

decomporre *vt.*,[71] decomporsi *vr.* to decompose.

decomposizione *f.* decomposition.

decomposto *adj.* putrid; decomposed.

decorare *vt.* to decorate.

decorativo *adj.* decorative.

decoratore *m.* decorator.

decorazione *f.* decoration.

decoro *m.* decorum, propriety.

decoroso *adj.* decorous; dignified.

decorrenza *f.* beginning.

decor'rere *vi.*[16] to elapse; to date (*from*).

decorso *m.* lapse; development; course. *adj.* past.

decotto *m.* decoction.

decrepitezza *f.* decrepitude.

decre'pito *adj.* decrepit.

decrescente *adj.* decreasing.

decre'scere *vi.*[38] to decrease.

decretare *vt.* to decree; to award.

decreto *m.* decree.

decu'bito *m.* decubitus: piaga da —, bedsore.

decuplicare *vt.* to decuple.

de'cuplo *m.*, *adj.* decuple.

decurtare *vt.* to decurtate; to diminish, curtail; to cut (*down*).

decurtazione *f.* diminution, curtailment.

de'dalo *m.* labyrinth, maze.

De'dalo *m.pr.* (*myth.*) Daedalus.

de'dica *f.* dedication.

dedicare *vt.* to dedicate; to devote; dedicarsi *vr.* to devote oneself.

de'dito *adj.* devoted; addicted.

dedizione f. submission; devotion.
dedotto adj. deduced; deducted. pp.of
  dedurre.
dedurre vt.¹ to deduce; to deduct.
deduttivo adj. deductive.
deduzione f. deduction.
defalcare vt. to deduct.
defalco m. deduction.
defecare vt., vi. to defecate.
defenestrare vt. to throw (one) out of
  the window; to oust; to dismiss.
defenestrazione f. defenestration.
deferente adj. deferential.
deferenza f. deference.
deferire vt. to commit, submit; to
  report. vi. to defer (to): — il giuramento, to put (one) on oath.
defezione f. defection, apostasy.
deficiente m. idiot. adj. deficient.
deficienza f. deficiency; shortage.
defini'bile adj. definable.
definire vt. to define; to settle.
definitivamente adv. definitively.
definitivo adj. definitive, final.
definito adj. definite.
definizione f. definition; settlement.
deflagrare vi. to deflagrate.
deflagrazione f. deflagration.
deflazionare vi. to deflate.
deflazione f. deflation.
deflet'tere vi.⁶⁴ to swerve; to yield; to
  recede.
deflorare vt. to deflower.
defluire vi. to flow, run down.
deflusso m. flow; reflux.
deformante adj. deforming.
deformare vt. to deform, disfigure;
  to twist; **deformarsi** vr. to become
  deformed; to get out of shape.
deformazione f. deformation.
deforme adj. misshapen, deformed.
deformità f. deformity.
defraudare vt. to defraud, cheat.
defunta f., **defunto** m., adj. deceased,
  late, dead.
De Gasperi, Alcide, Italian statesman
  and postwar premier; leader of the
  Christian Democratic Party from
  1943 (1881–1954).
degenerare vi. to degenerate.
degenerato m., adj. degenerate.
degenerazione f. degeneration.
dege'nere adj. degenerate; unworthy.
degente m., f. patient. adj. bedridden.
degenza f. stay in hospital; confinement to bed.
degli comp.prep. of the. part. some,
  any. see di.
deglutire vt. to swallow.
deglutizione f. deglutition.
degnamente adv. worthily; deserving-
  ly; adequately.
degnare vt., vi., **degnarsi** vr. to deign,
  condescend; to stoop.

degnazione f. condescension: **con —**,
  patronizingly.
degno adj. deserving, worth; worth-
  while; adequate; worthy.
degradante adj. degrading.
degradare vt. to degrade; to debase; to
  cashier; **degradarsi** vr. to degrade
  oneself.
degradazione f. degradation.
degustare vt. to taste.
degustazione f. tasting.
deh! interj. alas!; oh please!
dei m.pl. gods.
dei comp.prep. of the. part. some, any.
  see di.
deificare vt. to deify.
deità f. deity.
del comp.prep. of the. part. some, any.
  see di.
delatore m. informer.
delazione f. delation.
Deledda, Grazia, Italian novelist,
  Nobel prize in literature, 1926
  (1875–1936).
de'lega f.de legation; power of attorney.
delegare vt. to delegate; to entrust.
delegato m. delegate: — **apostolico**,
  nuncio.
delegazione f. delegation, precinct
  house.
delete'rio adj. deleterious.
del'fico adj. Delphic, Delphian.
delfino m. (ichthyol.) dolphin.
Delfino m. (hist.) Dauphin.
delibazione f. scrutiny of a foreign
  sentence.
deli'bera f. adjudication.
deliberare vt. to rule; to resolve
  (upon); to adjudge. vi. to deliberate.
deliberato adj. deliberate; resolved.
deliberazione f. resolution; determination deliberation.
delicatamente adv. delicately, softly.
delicatezza f. delicacy; tactfulness.
delicato adj. delicate; soft; tactful.
delimitare vt. to delimit.
delimitazione f. delimitation.
delineare vt. to delineate, outline.
delinquente m., f., adj. criminal.
delinquenza f. criminality.
delin'quere vi. to offend, sin.
deli'quio m. swoon: **cadere in —, to**
  swoon, to faint.
delirante adj. delirious, raving.
delirare vi to rave, to be delirious.
deli'rio m. delirium; wild excitement:
  andare in —, to become delirious.
delitto m. crime; offense; murder.
delittuoso adj. criminal.
deli'zia f. delight.
deliziare vt. to delight, charm; **deli-**
  ziarsi vr. to delight (in).

delizioso adj. delicious, delightful.
della, delle, dello comp.prep. of the. part. some, any. see di.
del pari adv. likewise.
del resto conj. as to the rest; besides; anyway.
delucidare vt. to trace.
delucidazione f. elucidation.
deludente adj. disappointing.
delu'dere vt.[4] to disappoint.
delusione f. disappointment.
deluso adj. disappointed. pp.of deludere.
deluso'rio adj. disappointing.
demagogi'a f. demagogy.
demago'gico adj. demagogic.
demagogo m. demagogue.
demandare vt. to commit.
dema'nio m. demesne.
demarcazione f. demarcation.
demarrare vi. (aeron.) to alight.
demente m., adj. lunatic, insane.
demenza f. insanity, madness.
deme'rito m. demerit.
demiurgo m. demiurge.
democra'tico m. democrat. adj. democratic.
democrazi'a f. democracy.
democristiano adj. Christian Democratic.
demografi'a f. demography.
demolire vt. to demolish, tear down.
demolitore m. demolisher.
demolizione f. demolition.
de'mone m. demon.
demoni'aco adj. demoniacal, fiendish.
demo'nio m. devil, demon; fiend.
demoralizzare vt. to dispirit, deject; **demoralizzarsi** vr. to lose heart.
demoralizzazione f. dejection.
denaro m. money (pl. in playing cards) diamonds; penny: — contante, cash; — spicciolo, change.
denaturato adj. methylated.
denicotinizzare vt. to denicotinize.
denigrare vt. to denigrate, defame; to traduce; to criticize.
denigratore m. denigrator.
denigrazione f. denigration.
denominare vt. to denominate, name.
denominatore m. denominator. adj. denominative.
denominazione f. denomination.
denotare vt. to denote.
densità f. density, thickness.
denso adj. dense, thick.
dentale f., adj. dental.
dentato adj. toothed; dentate: ruota dentata, cogwheel.
dentatura f. set of teeth.
dente m. tooth (pl. teeth); tusk; cog; notch: — di forchetta, prong; — dell'ancora, fluke; mal di denti, toothache; mettere i denti, to cut

teeth; mi battono i denti, my teeth are chattering; parlare fuori dei denti, to speak out.
dentellare vt. to indent, notch.
dentello m. notch; dentil; scallop.
den'tice m. dentex.
dentiera f. denture; rack.
dentifri'cio m. toothpaste.
dentista m. dentist.
dentizione f. dentition.
dentro adv. in, within; inside: essere —, to be in prison; mettere —, to pull in; in —, inward. prep. within; inside: — di sè, inwardly.
denudare vt. to denude, strip; **denudarsi** vr. to strip.
denun'cia f. denunciation; complaint; charge, statement.
denunciante m., f. complainant.
denunciare vt. to denounce; to state; to bring a charge against; to lodge a complaint against.
denunciatore see denunciante.
denutrito adj. undernourished.
denutrizione f. undernourishment.
deodorante m., adj. deodorant.
deodorare vt. to deodorize.
depauperare vt. to impoverish.
dep nnare vt. to expunge.
deperi'bile adj. perishable.
deperimento m. decay; wasting.
deperire vi. to decline, waste (away); to deteriorate.
depilare vt. to depilate.
depilato'rio m., adj. depilatory.
depilazione f. depilation.
deplorare vt. to deplore, regret; to blame; to complain of.
deplorevole adj. deplorable.
deporre vt.[53] to lay (down); to place; to dismiss, dethrone; to depose; to deposit. vi. to testify, depose; (chem.) to settle: — la speranza, to give up hope.
deportare vt. to deport, exile.
deportato m. deportee, exile.
deportazione f. deportation.
deporto m. (bank.) backwardation (British).
depositare vt. to deposit.
deposita'rio m. depositary.
depo'sito m. deposit; sediment; storage; warehouse; (mil.) depot; pledge; keeping: — bagagli (rail.), cloakroom.
deposizione f. deposition.
deposto adj. deposed; laid down. pp.of deporre.
depravare vt. to deprave, pervert.
depravato adj. depraved, degenerate.
depravazione f. depravation.
deprecare vt. to deprecate.
depredare vt. to depredate.
depressione f. depression.

depresso *adj.* depressed; lowered; weak. *pp.of* deprimere.

deprezzamento *m.* depreciation.

deprezzare *vt.* to depreciate.

deprimente *adj.* depressing; gloomy.

depri'mere *vt.*²⁵ to depress.

depurare *vt.* to depurate, purify.

depurativo *m., adj.* depurative.

depuratore *m.* depurator; cleaner.

deputare *vt.* to depute, delegate, appoint.

deputato *m.* deputy; representative.

deputazione *f.* deputation; delegation.

deragliamento *m.* derailment.

deragliare *vi.* to derail.

derelitto *m., adj.* derelict.

deretano *m.* buttocks, rump.

deri'dere *vt.* to ridicule, mock.

derisione *f.* derision, mockery.

deriso *adj.* ridiculed, mocked. *pp.of* deridere.

deriso'rio *adj.* derisive, mocking.

deriva *f.* drift, leeway: andare alla —, to drift, go adrift.

derivare *vt.* to derive; to deviate. *vi.* to derive, come (*from*); to ensue; to make leeway.

derivato *m., adj.* derivative.

derivazione *f.* derivation, shunt: — telefonica, telephone extension.

dermatologi'a *f.* dermatology.

dermato'logo *m.* dermatologist.

dermo'ide *f.* leatheroid.

de'roga *f.* infringement; exception.

derogare *vi.* to derogate, depart (*from*); to transgress.

derrate *f.pl.* foodstuff.

derubare *vt.* to rob.

De Sanctis, Francesco, Italian essayist, man of letters and patriot (1817–1883).

desco *m.* table; mess.

descrittivo *adj.* descriptive.

descri'vere *vt.*¹³⁴ to describe.

descrizione *f.* description.

deser'tico *adj.* desert.

deserto *m.* desert, wilderness. *adj.* desert, lonely, empty, vacant.

desiderare *vt.* to desire, wish (*for*); to long (*for*); to want; to recommend: farsi —, to make oneself wanted.

deside'rio *m.* wish, desire; longing, lust.

desideroso *adj.* eager, desirous.

designare *vt.* to designate.

designazione *f.* designation.

desinare *n.* dinner.

desinare *vi.* to dine.

desinenza *f.* desinence.

desi'stere *vi.* to desist (*from*), cease, stop; to give up.

desolante *adj.* disheartening, distressing.

desolare *vt.* to desolate; to grieve, distress.

desolato *adj.* desolate; sorrowful, distressed.

desolazione *f.* desolation, grief.

de'spota *m.* despot.

destare *vt.* destarsi *vr.* to wake (*up*), awaken, stir.

destinare *vt.* to destine; to assign, allot; to appoint; to address; to intend (*for*).

destina'rio *m.* addressee.

destinazione *f.* destination.

destino *m.* destiny, fate; lot; destination.

destituire *vt.* to dismiss, remove.

destituito *adj.* destitute; devoid; dismissed, removed.

destituzione *f.* dismissal, removal.

desto *m.* awake; quick; shrewd.

destra *f.* right right side; right hand.

destreggiarsi *vr.* to maneuver, manage, make shift.

destrezza *f.* dexterity.

destriero *m.* steed; charger.

destrina *f.* dextrin.

destro *adj.* right; skiliful, clever. *m.* opportunity; right-handed blow, right.

destrorso *adj.* clockwise; dextrorse.

destro'sio *m.* (*chem.*) dextrose.

desu'mere *vt.*¹⁹ to draw, take (*from*); to deduce.

desunto *pp.of* desumere.

detenere *vt.*¹⁴¹ to hold; to detain.

detentore *m.* holder.

detenuto *m.* prisoner. *pp.of* detenere, held, detained.

detenzione *f.* keeping; imprisonment.

detergente *m., adj.* detergent.

deter'gere *vt.*¹⁴⁸ to cleanse, deterge.

deteriorare *vt., vi.*; deteriorarsi *vr.* to deteriorate.

determinante *adj.* determining.

determinare *vt.* to determine; to cause; determinarsi *vr.* to resolve (*upon*); to arise.

determinatezza *f.* determinedness.

determinativo *adj.* (*gramm.*) definite.

determinatore *m.* determinant.

determinazione *f.* determination.

detersivo *m., adj.* detersive.

detesta'bile *adj.* detestable, hateful.

detestare *vt.* to detest, hate.

detonare *vi.* to detonate.

detonatore *m.* detonator.

detonazione *f.* detonation, report (*of a gun*), pop.

detrarre *vt.*¹⁴⁸ to detract, subtract.

detratto *adj.* detracted, subtracted.

detrattore *m.* decrier.

detrazione *f.* deduction.

detrimento *m.* detriment.

detrito *m.* fragment, debris.

detronizzare *vt.* to dethrone.
detta *f.*: **a — di**, according to.
dettagliante *m.* retailer.
dettagliare *vt.* to detail; to retail.
detta'glio *m.* detail; retail
dettame *m.* dictate, precept, tenet.
dettare *vt.* to dictate; to suggest: **— legge**, to lay down the law.
dettato *m.* dictation.
dettatura *f.* dictation: **scrivere sotto —**, to write from dictation.
detto *m.* word; saying. *adj.* said, named; above-mentioned, aforesaid: **— fatto!** immediately! *pp.of* **dire.**
deturpare *vt.* to disfigure; to mar.
deturpazione *f.* disfigurement.
devastare *vt.* to devastate, ravage.
devastatore *m.* ravager. *adj.* ravaging
devastazione *f.* devastation, ravage.
deviare *vt.* to deviate, turn aside. *vi.* to deviate, swerve, depart (*from*), derail.
deviatore *m.* switchman.
deviazione *f.* deviation; shift, detour; (*naut.*) deflection.
devoluto *pp.of* **devolvere.**
devol'vere *vt.*¹³ to devolve; to appropriate.
devoto *adj.* devout, pious; devoted, faithful, loyal.
devozione *f.* devotion.
di *prep.* of, 's; by; with; than; from, out, out of; to, on, about; at, after; in: **è più alto — te — due dita,** he is taller than you by two inches; **lavorare — cervello,** to work with one's brains; **essere — Milano,** to be from Milan; **un poco —** some, any; **qualcosa — buono,** something good; **niente — buono,** nothing good; **un poco — buono,** a shady character; **soffrir —,** to suffer from; **piangere — gioia,** to cry with joy; **— mattina,** in the morning; **— notte,** by night; **riempire —,** to fill with; **nutrirsi — to** feed on; **— sopra,** upstairs, on top; **— sotto,** downstairs, below. **di** *after verbs,* that, to, at. **di** *adv form*: **— passo,** at a pace; **— gran lunga,** by far; **— punto in bianco,** all of a sudden; **— tanto in tanto,** now and then. **di** *partitive art.* some, any, no.
dì *m.* day.
diabete *m.* diabetes.
diabe'tico *m., adj.* diabetic.
diabo'lico *adj.* diabolic.
diac'cio *adj.* ice-cold.
dia'cono *m.* deacon.
diadema *m.* diadem, tiara.
dia'fano *adj.* diaphanous.
diaframma *m.* diaphragm.

dia'gnosi *f.* diagnosis.
diagnosticare *vt.* to diagnose.
diagno'stico *m.* diagnostician.
diagonale *f., adj.* diagonal.
diagramma *m.* diagram.
dialettale *adj.* dialectal.
dialet'tica *f.* dialectic; dialectics.
dialet'tico *adj.* dialectic.
dialetto *m.* dialect.
dialogare *vt.* to express in dialogue.
dia'logo *m.* dialogue.
diamante *m.* diamond.
diamanti'fero *adj.* diamantiferous.
diametralmente *adv.* diametrically.
dia'metro *m.* diameter.
dia'mine! *interj.* the deuce!
diana *f.* reveille; tocsin.
dianzi *adv.* a short time ago.
diapositiva *f.* transparency, slide.
dia'ria *f.* expenses (*pl.*).
dia'rio *m.* diary, journal.
diarrea *f.* diarrhea.
diaspro *m.* jasper.
dia'stole *f.* diastole.
diatermi'a *f.* diathermy.
diatriba *f.* diatribe; debate.
diavolac'cio *m.* devil; chap.
diavoleri'a *f.* deviltry.
diavole'rio *m.* uproar, hubbub.
diavoletto *m.* devilkin, imp.
dia'volo *m.* devil, fiend. *interj.* the devil!: **un buon —,** a good chap; **fare il —'a quattro,** to try hard, to put oneself out.
Diaz, Armando, Duca della Vittoria, Italian general, commander in chief of the Italian Army from 1917 to 1919 (1861-1928).
dibat'tere *vt.* to debate, discuss; **dibat'tersi** *vr.* to struggle; to writhe.
dibattimento *m.* trial; debate.
dibat'tito *m.* debate, dispute.
diboscare *vt.* to deforest.
di botto *adv.* suddenly.
dicastero *m.* department, office.
dicembre *m.* December.
diceri'a *f.* rumor, hearsay.
dichiarare *vt.* to declare, state; to appoint; **dichiararsi** *vr.* to declare, proclaim oneself.
dichiarato *adj.* professed.
dichiarazione *f.* declaration, statement.
diciannove *m., adj.* nineteen.
diciannove'simo *m., adj.*, nineteenth.
diciassette *m., adj.* seventeen.
diciassette'simo *m., adj.* seventeenth.
diciotte'simo *m. adj.* eighteenth.
diciotto *m., adj.* eighteen.
dicitura *f.* wording; inscription.
didascali'a *f.* caption; subtitle.
didat'tica *f.* didactics.
didat'tico *adj.* didactic; educational, instructional.

didentro m., adv. inside.
dieci m., adj. ten.
diecimila m., adj. ten thousand.
diecina see decina.
die'resi f. dieresis (pl. diereses).
diesis m. (mus.) sharp.
dieta f. diet: a —, on a diet.
diete'tica f. dietetics.
dietro prep., adv. behind; after, along; andare — a, to follow; portarsi —, to bring along.
difen'dere vt.⁶⁴ to defend, guard; difen'dersi vr. to defend oneself; to protect oneself (against); to get along.
difensiva f. defensive.
difensivo adj. defensive.
difensore m. defender, pleader; avvocato —, counsel for the defense.
difesa f. defense; plea; pleading: legittima—, self-defense (as a legal plea).
difeso pp. of difendere.
difettare vi. to lack, be wanting (in); to be short (of).
difettivo adj. defective.
difetto m. defect, fault, flaw, blemish; lack; shortcoming: far —, see difettare.
difettoso adj. defective, faulty.
diffalcare vt. to deduct.
diffalco m. deduction.
diffamare vt. to slander.
diffamatore m. slanderer.
diffamato'rio adj. slanderous.
diffamazione f. slander.
differente adj. different.
differenza f. difference: a — di, unlike.
differenziale m., adj. differential.
differenziare vt. to differentiate.
differire (1) vt. to defer, postpone.
differire (2) vi. to differ (from).
difficile adj. difficult, hard; unlikely.
difficilmente adv. hardly.
difficoltà f. difficulty; trouble.
difficoltoso adj. difficult, hard.
diffida f. notice; warning.
diffidare vt. to give notice to, warn: — a comparire, to summon. vi. to mistrust.
diffidente adj. mistrustful, suspicious.
diffidenza f. mistrust.
diffon'dere vt.⁹⁶ to diffuse, spread; to broadcast; diffon'dersi vr. to spread; to enlarge (upon).
difforme adj. unlike.
diffrazione f. diffraction.
diffusamente adv. diffusely.
diffusione f. diffusion; spreading; circulation (of papers, books, etc.); (radio) broadcast.
diffusivo adj. diffusive.
diffuso adj. diffused; widespread. pp. of diffondere.

diffusore m. spreader; (elec.) light globe; (mach.) choke tube.
difilato adv. straight, straightaway.
difte'rico adj. diphtheritic.
difterite f. diphtheria.
diga f. dam, dike.
digerente adj. digestive.
digeri'bile adj. digestible.
digerire vt. to digest; (fig.) to stand.
digestione f. digestion.
digestivo m., adj. digestive.
digitale f. (bot.) digitalis. adj. (anat.) digital: impronte digitali, fingerprints.
digiunare vi. to fast.
digiunatore m. faster.
digiuno m fast: a —, on an empty stomach. adj. empty; (fig.) unacquainted: essere — di, to be totally ignorant of, unacquainted with.
dignità f. dignity.
dignita'rio m. dignitary.
dignitoso adj. dignified
digradare vi. to slope; to fade.
digressione f. digression.
digrignare vt. to gnash.
digrossare vt. to trim; to rough-cast.
diguazzare vt. to beat, whip; vi. to dabble, splash.
dilagare vi. to spread.
dilaniare vt. to tear to pieces (as flesh)
dilapidare vt to squander.
dilatabilità f dilatability.
dilatare vt., dilatarsi vr. to dilate, expand.
dilatazione f. dilatation.
dilato'rio adj. dilatory.
dilavare vt. to wash away.
dilazionare vt. to put off, delay; (comm) to extend.
dilazione f respite; extension.
dileggiare vt to scoff at.
dileg'gio m. scoff.
dileguarsi vr. to vanish.
dilemma m. dilemma; quandary.
dilettante m. amateur.
dilettantesco adj. amateurish.
dilettare vt. to entertain; dilettarsi vr. to delight (in); to dabble (in).
dilette'vole adj. entertaining.
diletto (1) m. pleasure, delight.
diletto (2) m., adj. beloved, darling.
diligente adj. diligent.
diligenza (1) f. diligence.
diligenza (2) f. stagecoach.
diluire vt. to dilute.
dilungare vt. to lengthen, delay; dilungarsi vr. to linger.
diluviare vi. to shower, pour.
dilu'vio m. flood, downpour, deluge: il Diluvio Universale, the Flood.
dimagrare, dimagrire vt. to thin. vt. to grow thin.

dimane f. dawn; the next day.

dimani see **domani**.

dimenare vt. to toss; to whip; to wag; **dimenarsi** vr. to toss, fidget.

dimensione f. dimension, size.

dimenticanza f. oversight; negligence; omission.

dimenticare vt., vi., **dimenticarsi** vr. to forget; to neglect, omit.

dimenticato'io m. oblivion.

dimen'tico adj. forgetful, oblivious.

dimesso adj. modest, humble; shabby. pp.of **dimettere**.

dimestichezza f. familiarity.

dimet'tere vt.⁷⁶ to dismiss; **dimet'tersi** vr. to resign (from).

dimezzare vt. to halve.

diminuire vt., vi. to diminish, reduce; to abate, decrease; to shorten; to subside; to ebb.

diminutivo m., adj. diminutive.

diminuzione f. diminution, decrease.

dimissiona'rio adj. resigning.

dimissioni f.pl. resignation: dare le —, to resign.

dimora f. abode, home, residence.

dimorante adj., ppr. dwelling, residing.

dimorare vi. to live, reside, stay.

dimostrante m., f. rioter.

dimostrare vt., vi. to show; to demonstrate: — 20 anni, to look twenty; **dimostrarsi** vr. to prove, show oneself.

dimostrativo adj. demonstrative.

dimostrazione f. demonstration.

dina'mica f. dynamics.

dina'mico adj. dynamic; energetic.

dinamismo m. dynamism; energy.

dinamitardo m. dynamiter.

dinamite f. dynamite.

di'namo f. dynamo; generator.

dinamo'metro m. dynamometer.

dinanzi prep. before; in front (of); in the presence (of). adv. on the front.

dinasti'a f. dynasty.

dina'stico adj. dynastic.

dindo m. turkey cock.

diniego m. denial; refusal.

dinoccolato adj. disjointed; gangling; listless.

dinosa'uro m. dinosaur.

dintorni m.pl. surroundings; neighborhood.

dintorno adv., prep. around, about, round.

Dio m. God; Lord: come — vuole, anyhow; — volesse! would to God! — non voglia, God forbid! grazia di —, plenty, abundance; quando — volle! arrivammo eventually we arrived.

dio'cesi f. diocese.

diodo m. (radio) diode.

diottri'a f. diopter.

dipanare vt. to wind off (into skeins); to reel; to unravel.

dipartimento m. department.

dipartirsi vr. to depart (from); to swerve (from).

dipartita f. departure; demise.

dipendente m. subordinate. adj. dependent, subservient.

dipendenza f. subservience; annex: essere alle dipendenze di uno, to be in one's employ.

dipen'dere vi.¹⁰ to depend (on, upon); to rest (with); to derive; to be subject (to); to be up (to).

dipeso pp.of **dipendere**.

dipin'gere vt.¹⁸ to paint: — a olio, to paint in oil; **dipin'gersi** vr. to paint oneself.

dipinto m. painting, picture. adj. painted. pp.of **dipingere**.

diploma m. diploma, degree.

diplomare vt., **diplomarsi** vr. to graduate (in).

diploma'tico m. diplomat. adj. diplomatic.

diplomato m. graduate.

diplomazi'a f. diplomacy.

dipoi adj. following.

diporto m. pastime; pleasure; sport.

dipresso (a un) adv. about, more or less.

diradare vt., **diradarsi** vr. to rarefy, thin, disperse; to make, become, less frequent.

diramare vt. to circulate, issue; **diramarsi** vr. to branch off.

diramazione f. branching out; ramification; (rail.) siding; branch.

dire vt., vi.⁴⁴ to tell, say; to speak; to call; to celebrate (Mass): dite davvero? are you in earnest? voler —, to mean; un si dice, a mere rumor; per sentito —, by hearsay; vale a —, that is to say; dirsela con uno, to get along with one; o per meglio —, or rather.

direttamente adv. directly.

direttis'simo m. express (train).

direttiva f. direction, guidance.

direttivo adj. directive, leading.

diretto m. (rail.) fast train; (boxing) straight blow. adj. direct; straight; managed; directed; aiming; addressed; bound; meant; fast; through. pp.of **dirigere**.

direttore m. manager; director; conductor; managing editor (of a paper); principal (of a school).

diretto'rio m. (hist.) Directory; (pol.) executive.

direttrice f. directress, manageress; headmistress (of a school); (geom.) directrix. adj. leading, guiding:

ruote direttrici, guiding wheels (of a car).

direzione f. direction, way; management, managing board; lead; steering.

dirigente m. executive. adj. managerial.

diri'gere vt.[45] to direct; to manage; to address; to aim; (mus.) to conduct; to guide, lead; to turn; diri'gersi vr. to make, head (for); to be bound to; to address oneself (to).

dirigi'bile m. airship.

dirimpetto adv., prep. opposite, in front (of).

diritta f. right, right hand, right side.

diritto (1) m. right, title, claim; tax, duty, fee; law: — penale, criminal law; — d'autore, copyright.

diritto (2) m. right side, face. adj. straight; right; canny; upright; erect. adv. directly, straight: rigar —, to behave. see dritto.

dirittura f. straightness, uprightness: — d'arrivo (horse racing) home stretch.

dirizzone m. whim; blunder: prendere un —, to fly off at a tangent.

diroccato adj. crumbled, dilapidated.

dirottamente adv. copiously, heavily: piangere —, to weep one's eyes out.

dirotto (a) see dirottamente.

dirozzare vt. to rough-hew, improve; to civilize.

dirupato adj. steep; craggy.

dirupo m. cliff, crag.

disabbigliare vt., disabbigliarsi vr. to undress.

disabitato adj. uninhabited; empty.

disabituare vt. to disaccustom.

disaccordo m. disagreement, variance.

disadatto adj. unfit (for).

disadornare vt.-to disadorn.

disadorno adj. unadorned; bare; plain.

disaffezionare vt. to disaffect; disaffezionarsi vr. to become disaffected.

disaffezione f. disaffection.

disage'vole adj. uncomfortable; hard.

disagiare vt. to inconvenience, trouble.

disagiato adj. uncomfortable; straitened.

disa'gio m. discomfort; uneasiness.

disalberare vt. (naut.) to dismast.

disamare vt. to stop loving.

disameno adj. unpleasant.

disa'mina f. scrutiny; criticism.

disaminare vt. to sift, weigh.

disamorare vt. to estrange; to deter (from); disamorarsi vr. to become disaffected; to tire (of).

disamorato adj. disaffected.

disancorare vt. to up anchor. vi. to weigh anchor.

disanimare vt. to dishearten.

disappetenza f. lack of appetite.

disapprovare vt. to disapprove (of).

disapprovazione f. disapproval.

disappunto m. disappointment.

disarcionare vt. to unseat.

disarmare vt. to disarm; (naut.) to unrig.

disarmo m. disarmament.

disarmoni'a f. discord; dissonance.

disarmo'nico adj. inharmonious.

disarticolare vt. to disarticulate.

disastro m. disaster: — ferroviario, railroad accident.

disastroso adj. disastrous.

disattento adj. inattentive; careless.

disattenzione f. inattention; carelessness.

disavanzo m. deficit.

disavveduto adj. inadvertent, heedless.

disavventura f. misadventure.

disavvezzare vt. to wean, cure.

disavvezzo adj. unused.

disborso m. disbursement.

disboscare vt. to disforest.

disbrigare vt. to settle, dispatch; disbrigarsi vr. to get rid of.

disbrigo m. dispatch; settlement.

discacciare see scacciare.

disca'pito see scapito.

disca'rico m. exculpation; extenuation: testimone a —, witness for the defense.

discaro adj. unwelcome, unpleasant.

discendente m. descendant, offspring. adj. descending, sloping.

discendenza f. descent; offspring.

discen'dere vt.,[119] vi. to descend, go down, come down; to slope (down); to slant; to fall, drop; to land; to alight (from a train, etc.): — a un albergo, to put up at a hotel; — da cavallo, to dismount.

disce'polo m. disciple, pupil.

discer'nere vt.[120] to discern.

discerni'bile adj. discernible.

discernimento m. discernment; discrimination.

discesa f. descent; slope, grade; fall; dropping; landing; decline: strada in —, sloping road; prezzi in —, falling prices.

dischiodare vt. to unnail.

dischiu'dere see schiu'dere.

dischiuso see schiuso.

discinto adj. scantily dressed; slovenly.

disclo'gliere see scio'gliere.

disciolto see sciolto.

disciplina f. discipline.

disciplinare (1) vt. to discipline.

disciplinare (2) adj. disciplinary.

disciplinatamente adv. orderly; obediently.

disciplinato adj. orderly; obedient.

disco m. disk, disc; discus; record; (rail.) signal: — microsolco, micro-groove record.

disco'bolo m. discus thrower.

di'scolo m. rogue; imp.

discolpa f. vindication, defense.

discolpare vt. to exculpate, vindicate; **discolparsi** vr. to exculpate oneself; to apologize (for).

discono'scere vt.[40] to deny, gainsay.

discontinuità f. discontinuity.

disconti'nuo adj. discontinuous.

discordante adj. discordant, dissonant.

discordanza f. disagreement; dissonance.

discordare vt. to discord, disagree; to differ (from).

discorde adj. discordant, conflicting.

discor'dia f. discord, dissension: pomo della —, bone of contention.

discor'rere vi.[38] to talk, speak: e via discorrendo, and so forth.

discorsivo adj. discursive.

discorso m. speech; talk; conversation; address: cambiare —, to switch to another subject.

discostare see scostare.

discosto adj. detached. adv., prep. far, away: poco — da, not far from.

discoteca f. record library, collection.

discre'dito m. discredit.

discrepanza f. discrepancy.

discretamente adv. discreetly; fairly; rather; moderately.

discretezza f. discreetness.

discreto adj. discreet; fair; good enough.

discrezionale adj. discretional.

discrezione f. discretion: arrendersi a —, to surrender at discretion.

discriminare vt. to discriminate.

discriminazione f. discrimination.

discussione f. argument, discussion; debate.

discusso adj. debated; controversial pp.of discutere.

discu'tere vt., vi.[46] to discuss, debate; to argue.

discuti'bile adj. debatable, questionable.

disdegnare vt., vi. to disdain, scorn.

disdegno m. disdain, scorn.

disdegnoso adj. scornful.

disdetta (1) f. misfortune, ill luck.

disdetta (2) f. notice.

disdice'vole adj. unseemly.

disdire vt.[44] to cancel; to countermand; to give notice of. vi. to contradict oneself; to be unbecoming (to); **disdirsi** vr. to contradict oneself, be inconsistent.

disdoro m. shame; detriment.

disegnare vt., vi. to draw, outline; to plan.

disegnatore m. draftsman; designer; cartoonist.

disegno m. drawing; outline; plan; scheme: — di legge, bill.

diseguale etc. see disuguale.

disellare vt. to unsaddle.

diseredare vt. to disinherit.

diseredato m. beggar. adj. poor, wretched. pp. disinherited.

disertare vt., vi. to desert.

disertore m. deserter.

diserzione f. desertion.

disfacimento m. disintegration; ruin.

disfare vt.[61] to undo; to defeat; to pull down; to ruin, destroy; to untie (a knot); to melt; **disfarsi** vr. to melt; to decay, go to pieces; to get rid (of); to come undone, untied.

disfatta f. defeat.

disfattismo m. defeatism.

disfattista m. defeatist.

disfatto adj. broken; defeated; melted; decayed; untied.

disfavore m. disfavor; detriment.

disfida f. challenge.

disfunzione f. dysfunction.

disgelare vt., vi., **disgelarsi** vr. to thaw.

disgelo m. thaw, thawing.

disgiun'gere vt.,[75] **disgiun'gersi** vr. to disjoin, separate.

disgiunto adj. separate, disjoined. pp.of disgiungere.

disgra'zia f. misfortune, ill luck; accident; blow; disaster; disfavor: — volle che, as ill luck would have it; portar —, to bring bad luck.

disgraziatamente adv. unfortunately.

disgraziato m. wretch. adj. unfortunate; unlucky.

disgregamento m. disintegration.

disgregare vt., **disgregarsi** vr. to disintegrate, dissolve; to crumble.

disguido m. miscarriage (failure to arrive).

disgustare vt. to disgust, displease; **disgustarsi** vr. to sicken; to fall off.

disgusto m. disgust, dislike, distaste.

disgustoso adj. disgusting.

disidratare vt. to dehydrate.

disillu'dere vt. to disillusion.

disillusione f. disappointment.

disilluso adj. disillusioned; disappointed.

disimparare vt. to unlearn, forget.

disimpegnare vt. to extricate; to redeem; to dispatch, perform.

disimpegno m. disengagement; redemption; performance.

disincagliare vt. (naut.) to set afloat; to free, disentangle.

disincantare vt. to disenchant.

disincantato adj. disenchanted.

disincantamento m. disenchantment

disinfestare vt. to fumigate.

disinfestazione f. fumigation.

disinfettante m., adj. disinfectant.

disinfettare vt. to disinfect.

disinfezione f. disinfection.

disinfiammare vt. to soothe, salve, relieve.

disingannare vt. to undeceive.

disinganno m. disillusion; disappointment.

disinnestare vt. (mach.) to declutch; (elec.) to disconnect.

disintegrare vt. to disintegrate; to split (an atom).

disintegrazione f. disintegration; fission (of an atom).

disinteressarsi vr. to take no interest (in).

disinteressatamente adv. disinterestedly, unselfishly.

disinteressato m. disinterested, unbiased; unselfish.

disinteresse m. disinterestedness; unselfishness; indifference.

disinvolto adj. unconstrained, easy.

disinvoltura f. unconstraint; ease; unconcern.

disistima f. disesteem.

disistimare vt. to disesteem.

dislivello m. drop; unevenness.

dislocamento m. (naut.) displacement; (mil.) posting.

dislocare vt. (naut.) to displace; (mil.) to post.

dislocazione f. (naut., geol.) displacement; removal; transportation; posting.

dismisura (a) f. measurelessly.

disobbediente adj. disobedient.

disobbedienza f. disobedience.

disobbedire vt., vi. to disobey.

disobbligarsi vr. to repay an obligation.

disoccupato m., adj. unemployed.

disoccupazione f. unemployment.

disonestà f. dishonesty; fraud.

disonestamente adv. dishonestly.

disonesto adj. dishonest, immoral.

disonorante adj. dishonorable.

disonorare vt. to dishonor, disgrace; **disonorarsi** vr. to dishonor oneself, disgrace oneself.

disonore m. dishonor, disgrace, shame, ignominy: **essere il — di**, to be the shame of; **essere un — per**, to be a shame to.

disonorevole adj. dishonorable, disgraceful.

disopra m. top, upper side; upper (of a shoe); upper hand. adj. upper. adv. on, upon, over; above; upstairs: **al — delle proprie possibilità**, beyond one's possibilities.

disordinare (1) vt. to mess up, disarrange.

disordinare (2) vi. to indulge oneself.

disordinatamente adv. untidily; confusedly, haphazardly.

disordinato adj. disorderly, untidy, messy; unruly.

disor'dine m. disorder; confusion, mess; **not: in —**, in a mess.

disorganizzare vt. to disorganize.

disorganizzazione f. disorganization.

disorientamento m. bewilderment.

disorientare vt. to mislead, lead astray; to bewilder; to mix up; **disorientarsi** vr. to get mixed up; to lose one's bearings.

disorientato adj. confused, bewildered.

disormeggiare vt. to unmoor.

disossare vt. to ossify.

disotto m. bottom, lower part. adj. lower. adv. below; downstairs: **al — di**, underneath.

dispac'cio m. dispatch.

disparato adj. disparate, heterogeneous.

disparere m. variance.

di'spari adj. odd; uneven.

disparità f. disparity; difference; discrepancy; dissimilarity; unevenness.

disparte (in) adv. apart, aside.

dispen'dio m. expense; waste.

dispendioso adj. expensive; wasteful.

dispensa f. distribution; dispensation; pantry; installment.

dispensare vt. to dispense, distribute; to exempt, exonerate (from); **dispensarsi** vr. to excuse oneself (from); to beg off.

dispensa'rio m. dispensary.

dispensatore m. dispenser.

dispensiere m. steward.

dispepsi'a f. dyspepsia.

dispep'tico m., adj. dyspeptic.

disperare vt., vi. to despair (of), give up all hope (of); **far —**, to drive to despair; **disperarsi** vr. to be in despair.

disperatamente adv. desperately.

disperato adj. desperate; hopeless.

disperazione f. despair: **per —**, in despair.

disper'dere vt., **disper'dersi** vr. to scatter.

dispersione f. dispersion.

dispe sivo adj. dispersive.

disperso adj. lost, missing; scattered. pp.of disperdere.

dispetto m. vexation, spite.

dispettosamente adv. spitefully.

dispettoso adj. spiteful.

dispiacente adj. sorry.

dispiacere (1) m. sorrow, grief; regret.

dispiacere (2) vi. to dislike; to displease; to mind, regret, be sorry (for): **mi dispiace per voi**, I am sorry for you; se **non vi dispiace**, if you do not mind; **quel quadro non mi dispiace**, I rather like that picture.

displu'vio m. watershed; slope.

disponente m. testator. f. testatrix.

disponi'bile adj. available; free; vacant.

disponibilità f. availability; assets.

disporre vt.[88] to arrange; to settle. vi. to dispose, order: — **di**, to command, have at one's disposal; **disporsi** vr. to place oneself; to get ready, be about (to).

dispositivo m. purview; device.

disposizione f. disposition; disposal; arrangement; leaning, bent; order, direction; provision.

disposto adj. disposed; arranged; willing. pp.of **disporre**.

dispo'tico adj. despotic.

dispotismo m. despotism.

dispregiativo adj. derogatory.

dispre'gio m. contempt, defiance.

disprezza'bile adj. contemptible; negligible.

disprezzare vt. to despise, scorn.

disprezzo m. contempt, scorn.

di'sputa f. dispute, debate; quarrel.

disputare vt. to contend (for). vi. to fight for; to fight, quarrel.

disquisizione f. dissertation.

dissaldare vt. to unsolder.

dissanguare vt., **dissanguarsi** vr. to bleed.

dissanguato m. bloodless: **morire —**, to bleed to death.

dissapore m. disagreement, grudge.

disseccare vt., **disseccarsi** vr. to desiccate, dry (up); to wither.

dissellare vt. to unsaddle.

disseminare vt. to disseminate, scatter.

dissennato adj. mad, insane.

dissenso m. disagreement; dissension.

dissenteri'a f. dysentery.

dissentire vi. to disagree (with).

dissenziente m., adj. dissentient.

disseppellire vt.[137] to exhume, disinter.

dissertare vi. to dissertate.

dissertazione f. dissertation.

disservi'zio m. disorganization; disservice.

dissestare vt. to get (one) into trouble; to unsettle; **dissestarsi** vr. to get into trouble; to unsettle; to run into debt; to go bankrupt.

dissestato adj. in debt; bankrupt.

dissesto m. financial crisis: **subire un — finanziario**, to go bankrupt.

dissetante m. quencher. adj. quenching.

dissetare vt., **dissetarsi** vr. to quench, slake (one's) thirst.

dissezione f. dissection.

dissidente m. adj. dissident.

dissidenza f. dissidence.

dissi'dio n. disagreement, conflict.

dissigillare vt to unseal.

dissi'mile adj unlike.

dissimulare vt to dissimulate, dissemble **dissimularsi** vr. to conceal oneself, hide

dissimulatore m. dissembler.

dissimulazione f. dissimulation.

dissipare vt to dissipate, to disperse, scatter, to dispel, to squander.

dissipatezza f. dissipation.

dissipato adj dissipated, dissolute; dispelled.

dissipatore m. dissipator, squanderer.

dissociare vt., **dissociarsi** vr. to dissociate.

dissociazione f. dissociation.

dissodare vt to harrow.

dissolto pp.of **dissolvere**.

dissolutezza f dissoluteness.

dissoluto adj dissolute.

dissoluzione f. dissolution; dissoluteness.

dissolvente m. adj. dissolvent.

dissolvenza f (motion pictures) dissolve: — **in apertura**, fade-in; — **in chiusura** fade-out.

dissol'vere vt., **dissol'versi** vr.[17] to dissolve melt.

dissonanza f dissonance.

dissotterrare vt to disinter, exhume.

dissuadere vt to dissuade, deter.

dissuaso pp.of **dissuadere**.

dissuggellare vt to unseal.

distaccamento m. detachment.

distaccare vt to detach; to unfasten; to remove to separate; (mach.) to disconnect to distance; to outstrip, **distaccarsi** vr. to fall off, sever to part (from); to differ.

distacco m. detachment separation; departure difference, advantage.

distante adj distant, far; remote; aloof. adv. far, away.

distanza f. distance; interval; — **focale**, focal length **tenere a —**, to keep at a distance, **a — di un mese**, with an interval of a month; **in —**, in the distance; **controllo a —**, remote control.

distanziare vt. to distance, outstrip.

distare vi. to be distant: **quanto dista la casa dalla strada?**, how far is it from the house to the road?; **la casa dista un miglio dal confine**, the house is a mile from the border.

disten'dere vt.[140] to spread, lay out, stretch; to lay down; to stretch out; to relax; **disten'dersi** vr. to spread, stretch; to lie (down); to open; to relax.

distensione f. relaxation, pacification.

distesa f. expanse; spread; (aeron.) wingspread: **suonare a —** to ring a full peal.

disteso adj. spread out, stretched out; relaxed: **cadere lungo —,** to fall flat.

distillare vt., vi. to distill.

distillato m. distillate.

distillato'io m. distiller.

distillatore m. distiller.

distillazione f. distillation.

distilleri'a f. distillery.

di'stilo adj. (archit.) distyle.

distin'guere vt.[67] to distinguish; to discern; to mark; **distin'guersi** vr. to distinguish oneself; to stand out; to excel.

distinta f. note, slip, list, detail.

distintamente adv. distinctly, clearly: **— vi salutiamo,** we are respectfully yours.

distintivo m. badge. adj. distinctive, distinguishing.

distinto adj. distinguished; different; separate; clear; **un uomo —,** a man of distinction. pp.of distinguere.

distinzione f. distinction.

disto'gliere vt.[144] to distract, divert; to dissuade, deter; **distogliersi** vr. to distract oneself; to be diverted.

distolto pp.of distogliere.

distor'cere vt.[145] to distort.

distorsione f. distortion; dislocation.

distrarre vt.[146] to distract; to divert (one's attention, a sum); to amuse; **distrarsi** vr. to distract, divert oneself; to wander, be inattentive; to amuse oneself.

distrattamente adv. casually; absent-mindedly; inattentively.

distratto adj. absent, absent-minded; inattentive.

distrazione f. heedlessness, absent-mindedness; oversight; inattention; entertainment; misappropriation.

distretto m. district.

distrettuale adj. district: **procuratore —,** district attorney.

distribuire vt. to distribute; to deal out; to spread; to deliver (mail); to circulate (papers).

distributivo adj. distributive.

distributore m. distributor; slot machine: **— di benzina,** gasoline pump.

distribuzione f. distribution; allotment; sharing; delivery.

districare vt. to disentangle, extricate; to free; **districarsi** vr. to disentangle oneself.

distrug'gere vt.[137] to destroy; to waste.

distruttivo adj. destructive.

distrutto adj. destroyed. pp.of distruggere.

distruttore m. destroyer.

distruzione f. destruction.

disturbare vt. to disturb, trouble; to annoy; to interfere with; **disturbarsi** vr. to trouble (oneself).

disturbato adj. troubled; unwell.

disturbatore m. disturber; nuisance.

disturbo m. trouble; annoyance; (radio) static.

disubbidiente adj. disobedient.

disubbidienza f. disobedience.

disubbidire see disobbedire

disuguaglianza f. inequality; unevenness; unlikeness; disagreement.

disuguale adj. different; uneven.

disumano adj. brutish, inhuman.

disunione f. disunion.

disunire vt., **disunirsi** vr. to disunite, disjoin.

disunito adj. disunited, disjointed.

disusato adj. unused; obsolete.

disuso m. disuse; desuetude: **in —,** obsolete.

disu'tile adj. useless; harmful.

ditale m. thimble; fingerstall.

ditata f. fingermark.

ditirambo m. dithyramb.

dito m. finger; toe (of foot); finger breadth, digit: **mostrare a —,** to point at; **legarsela al —,** to have it in for.

ditta f. concern, firm, house.

dittatore m. dictator.

dittato'riale adj. dictatorial.

dittatura f. dictatorship.

dittongo m. diphthong.

diure'tico m., adj. diuretic.

diurno adj. diurnal, daytime.

diuturno adj. diuturnal; unrelenting.

diva f. goddess; diva; star.

divagare vt. to divert; to amuse. vi. to wander (from the subject); **divagarsi** vr. to amuse oneself; to relax.

divagazione f. digression, rambling.

divampare vi.to flare up, blaze; to rage.

divano m. divan, couch, sofa.

divaricare vt. to divaricate, spread apart.

diva'rio m. difference, discrepancy.

divedere vi.: **dare a —,** to pretend; to give to understand.

divel'lere vt.[138] to uproot, tear off.

divelto adj. uprooted, torn off. pp.of divellere.

divenire, diventare vi.[101] to become, get; to grow; to turn (into): **diventare pazzo,** to go insane; **far diventare pazzo,** to drive (one) crazy.

diver'bio m. quarrel, argument.

divergente adj. divergent.

divergenza f. divergence; disagreement.

diver'gere vi.** to diverge; to swerve.
diversamente adv. differently; otherwise.
diversificare vt. to diversify.
diversione f. diversion.
diversità f. difference; unlikeness; variety.
diversivo m. diversion; pastime.
diverso adj. different; various; distinct. adv. differently. **diversi** adj. pl. several, various.
divertente adj. amusing.
divertimento m. amusement, fun.
divertire vt. to amuse, entertain; **divertirsi** vr. to amuse oneself, have fun: divertirsi alle spalle di, to make fun of.
divezzare vt. to wean.
dividendo m. dividend.
divi'dere.⁴⁸ to divide; to part, separate; to share; to split; **divi'dersi** vr. to separate; to part company (with).
divieto m. prohibition: — di transito, no thoroughfare; — di sosta, no parking.
divinamente adv. divinely.
divinare vt. to divine; to foresee; to foretell.
divinatore m. diviner, prophet. adj. prophetic.
divinato'rio adj. divinatory, prophetic.
divinazione f. divination.
divincolamento m. struggling; writhing, wriggling.
divincolare vt. to twist, writhe; **divincolarsi** vr. to struggle; to writhe; to wriggle.
divinità f. divinity; deity.
divinizzare vt. to deify.
divino adj. divine; heavenly; wonderful.
divisa f. dress; uniform; motto, device; coat of arms; parting; currency.
divisamento m. design.
divisare vt., vi. to plan; to intend, mean; to determine.
divisi'bile adj. divisible.
divisionale adj. divisional.
divisione f. division; separation; partition; department.
divisionismo m. pointillism.
divisionista m. pointillist.
divismo m. (moving pictures) star system; idolizing of stars.
diviso adj. divided; separated. pp.of dividere.
divisore m. divisor.
diviso'rio m. partition. adj. dividing, separating.
divo m. star, lead. adj. divine.
divorare vt. to devour, gobble up; to squander.

divoratore m. devourer. adj. devouring.
divorziare vi. to divorce: — dalla moglie (dal marito), to divorce one's wife (one's husband).
divorziata f. divorcée.
divorziato m. divorcé. adj. divorced.
divulgare vt. to divulge; **divulgarsi** vr. to spread.
divulgatore m. divulger.
divulgazione f. divulgation.
divulsione f. divulsion.
diziona'rio m. dictionary: — geografico, gazetteer.
dizione f. diction; wording; pronunciation.
do m. (mus.) do, C.
doc'cia f. showerbath, douche: fare la —, to take a shower.
docente m. docent, teacher.
docenza f. docentship.
do'cile adj. docile; tame.
docilità f. docility, tameness.
documentare vt. to document.
documenta'rio m. documentary film: — di viaggi, travelogue. adj. documental.
documentazione f. documentation.
documento m. document, paper.
dodecafoni'a f. mus. twelve-tone system.
dodecasil'labo m. dodecasyllable.
dodicenne adj. twelve years old.
dodice'simo m., num. adj. twelfth.
do'dici m., adj. twelve.
dodicimila m., num. adj. twelve thousand.
doga f. stave.
dogana f. customs; duty; custom house, custom office: esente da —, duty free.
doganale adj. customs: bolla —, bill of entry; unione —, customs union.
doganiere m. customs agent.
doge m. doge.
do'glia f. pain, ache, pang, throe.
dogma m. dogma.
dogma'tico adj. dogmatic.
dogmatismo m. dogmatism.
dogmatizzare vi. to dogmatize.
dolce m. sweet. adj. sweet; mild: clima —, mild climate; ferro —, soft iron; acqua —, fresh water; — pendio, gentle slope; consonante —, soft consonant.
dolcemente adv. sweetly; gently; softly.
dolcezza f. sweetness; mildness; kindness: — mia! my darling!
dolciastro adj. sweetish.
dolcificare vt. to sweeten.
dolciume m. sweetmeat, candy.
dolente adj. grieved; aching; sad; sorry; mournful: i dolenti, the mourners.

dolere vi. to ache, hurt, cause pain: mi duole per voi, I am sorry for you; **dolersi** vr. to be sorry, regret; to complain; to lament.

dolicoce'falo adj. dolichocephalic.

dol'laro m. dollar.

dolo m. fraud; malice.

dolomite f. dolomite.

dolomi'tico adj. dolomitic.

dolorante adj. aching.

dolorare vi. to ache; to suffer.

dolore m. pain, ache; sorrow, grief.

dolorosamente adv. painfully.

doloroso adj. painful; deplorable.

doloso adj. fraudulent; malicious: incendio —, arson; omicidio —, murder.

doma'bile adj. tamable.

domanda f. question; request; application; (comm.) demand: fare una —, to ask a question.

domandare vt. to ask (for). vi. to ask (about), inquire (about); **domandarsi** vr. to ask oneself, wonder.

domani m. morrow; (fig.) future. adv. tomorrow: — l'altro, the day after tomorrow; — a otto, a week from tomorrow; a —, till tomorrow.

domare vt. to tame; to break; to subdue, suppress.

domatore m. tamer; horsebreaker.

domatrice (1) f. tamer.

domatrice (2) f. break, brake (carriage frame for breaking in horses).

domattina adv. tomorrow morning.

dome'nica f. Sunday.

domenicale adj. Sunday.

domenicano m., adj. Dominican.

dome'stica f. maid, servant.

dome'stico m. servant, valet. adj. domestic, household; tame: utensili domestici, kitchenware; lavori domestici, housework, chores.

domiciliare (1) adj. domiciliary.

domiciliare (2) vt. to domicile; **domiciliarsi** vr. to settle (at, in).

domici'lio m. domicile; residence: consegna a —, home delivery.

dominante adj. dominant; prevailing, predominant.

dominare vt. to dominate, rule over; to overlook; to master. vi. to rule (over); to prevail (over, against); **dominarsi** vr. to restrain, control oneself.

dominatore m. ruler, master; winner, conqueror (in games). adj. ruling, domineering.

dominazione f. rule, domination.

Dominedd'io m. the Lord, God.

domi'nio m. possession, dominion; rule, power: — pubblico, public property; — di sè, self-control.

domo adj. tamed; beaten.

donare (1) vt. to donate; to bestow (upon), present (one with).

donare (2) vi. to suit, become.

donata'rio m. donee.

Donatello, Italian sculptor, David in Florence (1386-1466).

donatore m. donor.

donazione f. donation; transfer.

Don Chisciotte m.pr. Don Quixote.

donchisciottesco adj. quixotic.

donde adv. where from, from where, from which.

dondolare vt., vi. to swing, sway, rock, shake, oscillate; **dondolarsi** vr. to swing, sway, rock; to idle.

dondoli'o m. swinging, swaying.

don'dolo m. swing, pendulum: cavallo a —, rocking horse.

Donizetti, Gaetano, Italian operatic composer, Lucia di Lammermoor, Elisir d'amore (1797-1848).

donna f. woman (pl. women); wife (pl. wives); (as a title, before Christian names of women) Lady; queen (in playing cards): — di servizio, maid.

donnac'cia f. woman of the town.

donnaiuolo m. lady-killer.

donnesco m. womanly, womanlike.

donnina f. little woman; flirt.

don'nola f. weasel.

dono m. gift, present.

donzella f. damsel.

donzello m. page.

dopo prep. after: — di che..., whereupon; — tutto, after all. adv. after, afterwards; then; later, later on; next.

dopodomani adv. the day after tomorrow.

dopoguerra m. postwar period.

doppiag'gio m. (motion pictures) dubbing.

doppiamente adv. doubly; deceitfully.

doppiare vt. to double; (naut.) to double, go round; (motion pictures) to dub.

doppiato m. (motion pictures) dubbing. adj. dubbed.

doppiere m. candelabrum, (pl. candelabra), candelabra.

doppietta f. double-barreled gun.

doppiezza f. duplicity.

dop'pio m. double; peal (of bells); ti darò il —, I will give you twice as much. adj. double; twice as great; paired: giacca a — petto, double-breasted coat; — senso, double entendre; colonne doppie, paired pillars. adv. double, twofold.

doppione m. double, duplicate, replica.

dorare vt. to gild.

dorato *adj.* gilt. *pp.* gilded.

doratore *m.* gilder.

doratura *f.* gilding.

Doria, Andrea, Genoese statesman and admiral (1468–1560).

dormicchiare *vi.* to doze.

dormiente *m.* sleeper. *adj.* sleeping.

dormiglione *m.* slugabed, sleepyhead.

dormire *vi.* to sleep: andare a —, to go to bed; dormirci sopra, to sleep on it.

dormito'rio *m.* dormitory.

dormive'glia *m.* doze.

dorsale *f.* ridgeline. *adj.* back, dorsal: spina —, backbone.

dorso *m.* back.

dosag'gio *m.* dosage.

dosare *vt.* to dose.

dosatura *f.* dosage.

dose *f.* dose, quantity.

dosso *m.* back: mettersi in —, to put on; togliersi di —, to take off; (*fig.*) to get rid of.

dotare *vt.* to provide with a dowry; to endow (*with*); to furnish, equip (*with*).

dotato *adj.* endowed; equipped (*with*); complete (*with*); gifted.

dotazione *f.* endowment; outfit; (*mil.*) equipment: dare in —, to equip (*with*).

dote *f.* dowry; endowment; gift; talent.

dotto (1) *m.* scholar. *adj.* learned.

dotto (2) *m.* duct.

dottore *m.* doctor; physician.

dottoressa *f.* doctor, lady doctor.

dottrina *f.* doctrine; catechism.

dove *adv.* where; wherever; while: di (da) —, where ... from, wherefrom, whence; dove? where? di —, where ... from.

dovere (1) *m.* duty; task; obligation: sentire il — di, to feel bound to; farsi un — di, to make a point of; i miei doveri a, my regards to.

dovere (a) (2) *adv.* properly

dovere (3) *vt.*[50] to owe (*to*). *vi.* must, to be compelled (bound, forced, obliged), to have to; to be to; shall; should, ought to; si deve sperare che, it is to be hoped that; non avreste dovuto partire, you should not have left; dovreste vergognarvi, you ought to be ashamed; il treno deve arrivare alle quattro, the train is due (to arrive) at four.

doveroso *adj.* dutiful, fair.

dovi'zia *f.* plenty, abundance.

dovizioso *adj.* plentiful, rich.

dovunque *adv.* wherever, anywhere; everywhere.

dovuto *m.* due *adj.* due; fair; proper. *pp.* of dovere.

dozzina (1) *f.* dozen: alla —, by the dozen; di (da) —, cheap.

dozzina (2) *f.* board: stare a —, to board (*at, with*); tenere a —, to board.

dozzinale *adj.* cheap.

dozzinante *m.* boarder.

draconiano *adj.* draconian, drastic.

draga *f.* dredge.

dragag'gio *m.* dredging.

dragamine *m.* minesweeper.

dragare *vt.* to dredge.

dra'glia *f.* (*naut.*) stay.

drago *m.* dragon.

dragona *f.* sword knot.

dragone *m.* dragon; dragoon.

dramma (1) *m.* drama; play; tragedy.

dramma (2) *f.* (¹/₈ ounce) dram; (*coin*) drachma.

drammaticità *f.* tragicalness.

dramma'tico *adj.* dramatic, tragic: attore, autore —, tragedian; attrice drammatica, tragedienne.

drammatizzare *vt.* to dramatize.

drammaturgo *m.* playwright.

drappeggiare *vt.* to drape.

drappeg'gio *m.* drape, fold.

drappella *f.* pennon.

drappello *m.* platoon.

drapperi'a *f.* drapery.

drappo *m.* silk cloth; drape.

dra'stico *adj.* drastic.

drenag'gio *m.* drainage.

drenare *vt.* to drain.

dribblare *vi.* (*sport*) to dribble.

dritta *f.* right, right hand; (*naut.*) starboard.

dritto *m.* right side, face: (*It. slang*) clever person; "old fox": — di poppa, sternpost. *see* diritto *for other meanings*, *adj.*, *adv.*

drizza *f.* (*naut.*) hoisting rope.

drizzare *vt.* to straighten; to erect: — le orecchie, to prick up one's ears; drizzarsi *vr.* to straighten (*up*).

droga *f.* drug; spice, spices.

drogare *vt.* to drug; to spice.

drogheri'a *f.* grocery.

droghiere *m.* grocer.

dromeda'rio *m.* dromedary.

drupa *f.* drupe.

dualismo *m.* dualism; antagonism.

dub'bio *m.* doubt; misgiving: mettere in —, to doubt, question. *adj.* dubious; doubtful, uncertain; unreliable.

dubbioso *adj.* doubtful; dubious; uncertain; irresolute.

dubitare *vi.* to doubt: — di, to mistrust; to suspect; non —, to have no doubt (*about*).

dubitativo *adj.* dubitative.

duca *m.* duke.

ducato *m.* duchy; (*coin*) ducat.

duce *m.* leader.
duchessa *f.* duchess.
duchessina *f.* young duchess.
duchino *m.* young duke.
due *m.*, *num.adj.* two: — **volte**, twice; **tutt'e** —, both; — **volte tanto**, twice as much.
duecente'simo *m.*, *num.adj.* two hundredth.
duecento *m.*, *num.adj.* two hundred: **il Duecento**, the 13th century.
duellante *m.* duellist.
duellare *vi.* to duel. [lenge.
duello *m.* duel: **sfidare a** —, to challenge.
duemila *m.*, *num.adj.* two thousand.
duetto *m.* duet.
duna *f.* down, dune.
dunque *conj.* then; well.
duode'cimo *num.adj.* twelfth.
duodeno *m.* duodenum.
duolo *m.* sorrow, grief.
duomo *m.* cathedral; dome.
duplicare *vt.* to duplicate.
duplicato *m.*, *adj.* duplicate.
duplicatore *m.* duplicator; (*radio*) doubler.
du'plice *adj.* twofold, double: **in — copia**, in duplicate.
duplicità *f.* duplicity.
duplo *m.*, *adj.* double.
dura *f.* (*bot.*) durra, sorghum.

dura'cino *adj.* clingstone.
durallumi'nio *m.* duralumin.
duramente *adv.* hard; harshly, sharply; bitterly.
durante *prep.* during; in the course of; for; in the process of: — **tutto l'anno**, throughout the year. *ppr.of* **durare** lasting, during: **vita natural** —, during one's lifetime; forever, for good.
durare *vt.* to endure, bear. *vi.* to last; to continue, go on; to wear well: — **fatica a**, to find it hard to.
durata *f.* duration: **per tutta la — di**, throughout (the).
duraturo *adj.* lasting, durable: **essere** —, to last long.
dure'vole *see* duraturo.
durezza *f.* hardness, toughness; harshness, roughness.
duro *adj.* hard, tough; firm, solid; strong; rigid, stiff; harsh, callous: — **di comprendonio**, slow-witted; — **d'orecchio**, hard of hearing; **tener** —, to stick to it, hold out; **a muso** —, boldly.
durone *m.* callosity.
Duse, Eleonora, famous Italian tragedienne (1859–1924).
dut'tile *adj.* ductile.
duttilità *f.* ductility.

E

e, ed *conj.* and: **tutti e due**, both (of them); **tutti e tre**, the three of them.
ebanista *m.* cabinetmaker.
ebanite *f.* ebonite, vulcanite.
e'bano *m.* ebony.
ebbene *conj.* well, well then.
ebbrezza *f.* intoxication.
ebbro *adj.* inebriated, drunk, intoxicated.
ebdomada'rio *m.*, *adj.* weekly.
e'bete *adj.* dull, stupid.
ebetu'dine *f.* hebetude; dullness.
ebollizione *f.* boiling, ebullition.
ebra'ico *m.* Hebrew. *adj.* Hebraic, Hebrew. [Jewish.
ebrea *f.* Jewess.
ebreo *m.* Hebrew, Jew. *adj.* Jewish, Hebrew.
ebro, *etc. see* ebbro.
ebur'neo *adj.* eburnine, ivory.
ecatombe *f.* massacre, hecatomb.
eccedente *adj.* exceeding, extra.
eccedenza *f.* excess, surplus.
ecce'dere *vt.*, *vi.* to exceed, go beyond; to surpass, be beyond; to exaggerate, go too far.
eccellente *adj.* excellent.
eccellenza *f.* excellence; Excellency: **per** —, par excellence.

eccel'lere *vi.* to excel.
eccelso *adj.* surpassing; highest; sublime; exalted.
eccentricità *f.* eccentricity.
eccen'trico *m.*, *adj.* eccentric.
eccepi'bile *adj.* exceptionable.
eccepire *vt.* to object (*to*), except.
eccessivamente *adv.* excessively, exceedingly, to excess.
eccessivo *adj.* excessive.
eccesso *m.* excess: — **di bagaglio**, excess baggage; **all'**—, to excess, excessively.
ecce'tera *adv.* and so on, and so forth; etcetera (*abb.*: etc.).
eccetto *prep.* except, but: **tutti — uno**, all but one.
eccetto che *conj.* except that; provided (*that*); unless.
eccettuare *vt.* to except, exclude.
eccettuato *adj.* excepted.
eccezionale *adj.* exceptional; unusual; unwonted: **in via** —, as an exception.
eccezionalmente *adv.* exceptionally.
eccezione *f.* exception: **ad — di**, with the exception of, excepting; **uno scrittore di** —, an outstanding writer.

ecchi'mosi f. ecchymosis, bruise.

ecci'dio m. slaughter, massacre.

eccita'bile adj. excitable.

eccitabilità f. excitability.

eccitamento m. excitement.

eccitante adj. stimulating; exciting, thrilling.

eccitare vt. to excite, stir up, arouse, stimulate; to thrill; **eccitarsi** vr. to get excited; to be thrilled.

eccitazione f. excitement, thrill.

ecclesia'stico m. clergyman. adj. ecclesiastical.

ecco adv. here, there, that's; well: **eccomi,** here I am; **eccoli qua (là),** here (there) they are; — **fattol,** that's done!

eccome adv. "and how!", indeed!

echeggiare vi. to echo; to resound; to reverberate.

eclet'tico adj. eclectic; versatile.

eclissare vt. to eclipse; to outshine; **eclissarsi** vr. to be eclipsed; to steal away; to disappear.

eclissi f. eclipse.

ec'loga f. eclogue.

eco m., f. (pl. always m.) echo: **far —,** to echo.

economato m. stewardship.

economi'a f. economy; saving; thrift; (pl.) savings: — **domestica,** housewifery; **fare —,** to economize; **per — di tempo,** to save time.

economicamente adv. economically.

econo'mico adj. economic; thrifty; cheap: **bilancia economica,** monetary standard.

economista m. economist.

economizzare vt., vi. to economize, save.

eco'nomo m. steward. adj. thrifty.

eczema m. eczema.

ed conj. see e.

E'den m. Eden.

e'dera f. ivy.

edi'cola f. shrine; newsstand.

edificante adj. edificatory, edifying.

edificare vt. to build; (fig.) to edify.

edificatore m. builder; (fig.) edifier. adj. building; (fig.) edificatory.

edificazione f. building; (fig.) edification.

edifi'cio, edifi'zio m. building; edifice.

edile m. mason. adj. building: **perito —,** masterbuilder.

edili'zia f. building.

edili'zio adj. building.

e'dito adj. published, issued.

editore m. publisher. adj. publishing.

editori'a f. publishing trade.

editoriale m. editorial. f. publishing firm. adj. publishing; editorial.

editrice f. publishing house. adj., f. publishing.

editto m. edict.

edizione f. edition; publication: — **straordinaria,** extra (edition).

edonismo m. hedonism.

edonista m. hedonist.

edoni'stico adj. hedonistic.

edotto adj. acquainted (with); aware.

educanda f. schoolgirl, inmate (of a boarding school).

educandato m. boarding school for girls.

educare vt. to educate; to polish; to teach; to train; to raise, bring up; **educarsi** vr. to train, educate oneself.

educativo adj. educative.

educato adj. well-bred; polite; educated; trained.

educatore m. educator; teacher; tutor. adj. educatory.

educazione f. education, training; instruction, schooling; politeness, breeding, manners.

edulcorare vt. to edulcorate.

efebo m. ephebe.

efe'lide f. freckle.

efeme'ride, effeme'ride f. ephemeris (pl. ephemerides).

effeminatezza f. effeminacy.

effeminato adj. effeminate, womanish.

efferatezza f. cruelty, savageness.

efferato adj. ferocious, savage.

effervescente adj. effervescent.

effervescenza f. effervescence.

effettivamente adv. actually; really, in fact, as a matter of fact.

effettivo m. cash, amount; (mil.) effective. adj. actual, real; effective, effectual: **socio —,** active member.

effetto m. effect; result, outcome, consequence; impression; promissory note; article (of clothing); (mach.) action; (pl.) effects, property: **mandare ad —,** to carry out; **fare l'— di,** to give the impression of; **di grande —,** impressive; **fare —,** to make a sensation, to be impressive; to work; **a doppio —,** double-acting; **in —,** in fact, actually.

effettua'bile adj. effectible, feasible.

effettuare vt. to effect, bring about, accomplish, carry out; to perform; to make; **effettuarsi** vr. to be effected, accomplished; to come true; to take place.

efficace adj. efficacious, effectual.

efficacemente adv. efficaciously.

effica'cia f. efficacy, effectiveness, efficiency.

efficiente adj. efficient.

efficienza f. efficiency.

effigiare vt. to portray, represent.

effi'gie f. effigy, image, portrait.

effi'mero *adj.* ephemeral, short-lived, fleeting.

efflu'vio *m.* effluvium; fragrance.

effrazione *f.* breaking, housebreaking.

effusione *f.* effusion; effusiveness.

effusivo *adj.* (*geol.*) effusive.

egemoni'a *f.* hegemony.

egemo'nico *adj.* hegemonic.

e'gida *f.* aegis; sponsorship.

egiziano, egi'zio *m.*, *adj.* Egyptian.

egli *pron.pers.* he.

e'gloga *f.* eclogue.

egocen'trico *m.*, *adj.* egocentric.

egocentrismo *m.* egocentricity.

egoismo *m.* selfishness; egoism.

egoista *m.*, *f.* selfish person.

egoisticamente *adv.* selfishly, egoistically.

egoi'stico *adj.* selfish, egoistical.

egotismo *m.* egotism.

egotista *m.* egotist.

egregiamente *adv.* excellently.

egre'gio *adj.* excellent; (*derog.*) egregious: **— signore**, (*beginning of letter*) Dear sir; **all'— signor X.Y.** (*addressing a letter*), Mr. X.Y.

eguale, *etc. see* **uguale**.

ehi! *interj.* hey!

ehm! *interj.* hem!

ei *pron.pers.* he; they.

Einaudi, Luigi, Italian economist and statesman (1874–   ).

elaborare *vt.* to elaborate, work out.

elaboratezza *f.* elaborateness.

elaborato *adj.* elaborate; labored.

elaborazione *f.* elaboration.

elargire *vt.* to lavish (on).

elargizione *f.* bestowal; gift.

elasticità *f.* elasticity, resiliency; nimbleness.

ela'stico *m.* elastic, rubber band. *adj.* elastic, resilient; nimble.

elce *m.*, *f.* holm oak, ilex.

elefante *m.* elephant.

elegante *adj.* elegant, graceful; stylish, smart (*as a garment*); well-dressed; fashionable.

elegantemente *adv.* elegantly.

elegantone *m.* dandy.

eleganza *f.* elegance; stylishness, smartness.

eleg'gere *vt.*[14] to elect, choose, appoint.

elegi'a *f.* elegy.

elementare *adj.* elementary, primary; (*phys.*) elemental.

elemento *m.* element; factor.

elemo'sina *f.* alms: **chiedere l'—**, to beg.

elemosinare *vi.* to beg (*for alms*).

elencare *vt.* to list; to enumerate.

elenco *m.* list, roll; directory.

elettivo *adj.* elective.

eletto *m.* nominee; elect: **gli eletti di**

Dio, the elect. *adj.* elected; elect; chosen; choice. *pp.of* **eleggere**.

elettorale *adj.* electoral: **operazioni elettorali**, polls.

elettore *m.* elector, voter.

elettricamente *adv.* electrically.

elettricista *m.* electrician.

elettricità *f.* electricity.

elet'trico *adj.* electric, electrical.

elettrificare *vt.* to electrify.

elettrificazione *f.* electrification.

elettrizzare *vt.* to electrify; to thrill.

elettrocalamita *f.* electromagnet.

elettrocardio'grafo *m.* electrocardiograph.

elettrocardiogramma *m.* electrocardiogram.

elet'trodo *m.* electrode.

elettro'lisi *f.* electrolysis.

elettroli'tico *adj.* electrolytic.

elettrone *m.* electron.

elettro'nico *adj.* electronic: **microscopio —**, electron microscope; **valvola elettronica**, electron tube.

elettrotec'nica *f.* electrical technology.

elettrotec'nico *m.* electrician. *adj.* electrical.

elettroterapi'a *f.* electrotherapy.

elettrotreno *m.* electric train.

elevamento *m.* lifting; elevation.

elevare *vt.* to elevate, lift; to exalt; to erect, raise; **elevarsi** *vr.* to rise; to improve, elevate oneself.

elevatezza *f.* highness; loftiness.

elevato *adj.* elevated, lofty, high; exalted.

elevatore *m.* elevator, hoist.

elevazione *f.* elevation: **— a potenza** (*math.*), involution.

elezione *f.* election, choice, appointment; poll.

e'lica *f.* (*geom.*) helix (*pl.* helices, helixes); (*naut.*) screw; (*aeron.*) propeller: **— a passo variabile**, variable-pitch propeller.

elicoidale *adj.* helicoidal.

elicoplano *m.* cyclogiro.

elicot'tero *m.* helicopter.

eli'dere *vt.*[68] to elide.

eliminare *vt.* to eliminate; **eliminarsi** *vr.* to be eliminated; to eliminate one another.

eliminato'ria *f.* (*sport*) trial heat.

eliminazione *f.* elimination.

e'lio *m.* helium.

eliografi'a *f.* heliography.

elio'grafo *m.* heliograph.

elioterapia *f.* insolation, treatment by sunbaths.

eliotro'pio *m.* heliotrope.

elisabettiano *m.*, *adj.* Elizabethan.

elisione *f.* elision.

elisir *m.* elixir: **— di lunga vita**, elixir vitae.

eliso pp.of elidere.

e'litra f. elytron (pl. elytra).

ella pron.pers. she.

elle f. l: fatto a —, L-shaped.

ellisse f. (geom.) ellipse.

ellissi f. (gramm.) ellipsis (pl. ellipses).

ellit'tico adj. elliptical.

elmetto m. helmet.

elmo m. helmet, helm.

elogiare vt. to praise, commend.

elo'gio m. eulogy; praise: ti faccio i miei elogi, I congratulate you.

eloquente adj. eloquent.

eloquenza f. eloquence.

elo'quio m. enunciation, delivery.

elsa f. hilt.

elucubrazione f. lucubration; musing.

elu'dere vt.⁶ to elude, evade, dodge.

elusivo adj. elusive.

eluso pp.of eludere.

elve'tico m., adj. Helvetian.

elzeviro m. leading literary article; (typog.) Elzevir.

emaciato adj. emaciated, gaunt.

emanare vt. to issue; to diffuse. vi. to emanate, issue (from); to spring.

emanazione f. emanation.

emancipare vt. to emancipate; emanciparsi vr. to emancipate oneself.

emancipazione f. emancipation.

emarginare vt. to caption.

ematoma m. hematoma.

embargo m. embargo: mettere l'— su, to embargo.

emblema m. emblem, symbol.

emboli'a f. embolism.

em'bolo m. embolus.

em'brice m. roof tile.

embrionale adj. embryonic; rudimentary, undeveloped.

embrione m. embryo.

emendamento m. amendment; improvement.

emendare vt. to amend; to improve; emendarsi vr. to amend, reform.

emergenza f. emergence; emergency.

emer'gere vi.³¹ to emerge; to surface; to issue, come out.

eme'rito adj. emeritus; (derog.)ĝegregious.

emersione f. emersion: in —, afloat.

emerso adj. emersed. pp.of emergere.

eme'tico m., adj. emetic.

emet'tere vt.¹⁶ to emit, send forth, issue; to utter.

emiciclo m. hemicycle.

emicra'nia f. migraine, headache.

emigrante m., f., adj. emigrant.

emigrare vi. to emigrate; to migrate.

emigrato m. emigrant: — politico, refugee.

emigrazione f. emigration; migration.

eminente adj. eminent, outstanding.

eminentemente adv. eminently.

eminenza f. eminence.

emisfero m. hemisphere.

emissa'rio m. emissary; drain; effluent.

emissione f. emission (of bonds, etc.); radio broadcast.

emittente m. issuer; broadcasting station, broadcaster. adj. emissive; broadcasting.

emofili'a f. hemophilia.

emolliente m., adj. emollient.

emolumento m. emolument, fee.

emorragi'a f. hemorrhage.

emorro'idi f.pl. hemorrhoids.

emosta'tico adj. hemostatic: laccio —, tourniquet.

emoteca f. blood bank.

emotività f. emotivity.

emotivo adj. emotional.

emottisi f. hemoptysis.

emozionante adj. thrilling.

emozione f. thrill; emotion; turmoil; suspense.

em'piere⁸⁸ see empire.

empietà f. impiety, meanness.

em'pio m., adj. impious, unholy; cruel.

empire⁸⁸ vt., empirsi vr. to fill.

empi'rico m., adj. empiric.

empirismo m. empiricism.

e'mpito (1) m. fit, spell, drive.

empito (2) pp.of empire.

empo'rio m. emporium, department store.

emulare vt. to emulate.

emulatore m. emulator.

emulatrice f. emulatress.

emulazione f. emulation.

e'mulo m. emulator; rival.

emulsionare vt. to emulsify.

emulsione f. emulsion.

encefalite f. encephalitis.

enci'clica f. encyclical.

enciclopedi'a f. encyclopedia.

enciclope'dico a. encyclopedic.

enciclopedista m. encyclopedist.

encomia'bile adj. praiseworthy.

encomiare vt. to commend, praise.

enco'mio m. encomium, eulogy.

endecasil'labo m. hendecasyllable.

ende'mico adj. endemic.

endocardite f. endocarditis.

endo'crino adj. endocrine.

endovenoso adj. intravenous.

energe'tico adj. (med.) tonic.

energi'a f. energy; (elec.) power.

energicamente adv. energetically.

ener'gico adj. energetic.

energu'meno m. energumen.

en'fasi f. emphasis; pomposity.

enfaticamente adv. emphatically; pompously.

enfa'tico adj. pompous, declamatory.

enfiagione f. swelling.

enfiare *vt.*, *vi.*, enfiarsi *vr.* to swell, inflate.

enfiato *adj.*, *pp.* swollen.

enfisema *m.* emphysema.

enfite'usi *f.* emphyteusis.

enigma, enimma *m.* enigma, riddle.

enimmatico *adj.* enigmatical.

enimmista *m.* riddler; puzzler.

enne'simo *adj.* nth.

eno'logo *m.* oenologist.

enorme *adj.* enormous, huge.

enormità *f.* enormity.

ente *m.* being, entity; institution; office, agency: — statale, government agency.

enterite *f.* enteritis.

enteroclisma *m.* enema.

entità *f.* entity; consequence.

entrambi *pron.pl.* both: potete andare —, you can go, both of you; mi piacciono —, I like them both.

entrante *adj.* next.

entrare *vi.* to enter, get in, go in, come in: — in una casa, to enter a house; — nell'esercito, to enter the army; — in carica, to take office; — in possesso, to take possession (of); il 3 nel 9 entra 3 volte, 3 goes into 9,3 times; voi non c'entrate! it is no business of yours! questo non c'entra, that is beside the point.

entrata *f.* entrance; admittance; income: — in vigore, enforcement; imposta sull'—, income tax.

entratura *f.* entrance; entree.

entro *prep.*, *adv.* in, within, inside: — la casa, indoors.

entroterra *m.* hinterland.

entusiasmare *vt.* to fill with enthusiasm, enthuse; entusiasmarsi *vr.* to become enthusiastic, enthuse.

entusiasmo *m.* enthusiasm.

entusiasta *m.*, *f.* enthusiast.

entusia'stico *adj.* enthusiastic.

enumerare *vt.* to enumerate.

enumerazione *f.* enumeration.

enunciare *vt.* to enunciate.

enunciazione *f.* enunciation.

epa *f.* belly.

epa'tico *adj.* hepatic.

epatite *f.* hepatitis.

e'pica *f.* epic; epic poetry.

e'pico *adj.* epic, epical.

epicentro *m.* epicenter.

e'pico *adj.* epic, epical.

epicureo *m.*, *adj.* epicurean.

epidemi'a *f.* epidemic.

epide'mico *adj.* epidemic.

epider'mico *adj.* epidermal; (*fig.*) skin deep.

epider'mide *f.* epidermis.

epifani'a *f.* Epiphany.

epi'grafe *f.* epigraph.

epigramma *m.* epigram.

epilessi'a *f.* epilepsy.

epilet'tico *m.*, *adj.* epileptic.

epi'logo *m.* epilogue.

episcopato *m.* episcopate.

episo'dico *adj.* episodical.

episo'dio *m.* episode.

epi'stola *f.* epistle.

epistolare *adj.* epistolary.

epistola'rio *m.* letters.

epitaf'fio *m.* epitaph.

epite'lio *m.* epithelium.

epi'teto *m.* epithet.

epi'tome *f.* epitome.

epizoo'tico *adj.* epizoötic.

e'poca *f.* epoch, era, age, period, time: una scoperta che ha fatto —, an epoch-making discovery.

epopea *f.* epopée.

eppure *adv.* still; nevertheless; yet, however.

epurare *vt.* to purify; to purge.

epurazione *f.* purge, purging.

equamente *adv.* equitably.

equa'nime *adj.* equanimous.

equanimità *f.* equanimity.

equatore *m.* equator, the Line.

equazione *f.* equation.

equestre *adj.* equestrian: circo —, circus.

equidistante *adj.* equidistant.

equilibrare *vt.* to balance, poise.

equilibrato *adj.* level-headed.

equili'brio *m.* equilibrium, balance, equipoise.

equilibrismo *m.* acrobatics.

equilibrista *m.* equilibrist.

equino *adj.* equine.

equino'zio *m.* equinox.

equipaggiamento *m.* equipment, outfit.

equipaggiare *vt.* to equip, fit out; (*naut.*) to man; to rig.

equipag'gio *m.* equipage; (*naut.*) crew.

equiparare *vt.* to compare (*with*); to equalize, equate.

equipollente *adj.* equipollent.

equità *f.* equitableness, fairness.

equitazione *f.* riding.

equivalente *m.*, *adj.* equivalent.

equivalenza *f.* equivalence.

equivalere *vi.* to be equivalent (*to*), amount (*to*).

equivoca'bile *adj.* equivocal.

equivocare *vi.* to misunderstand; to equivocate.

equi'voco *m.* misunderstanding; ambiguous term. *adj.* equivocal; ambiguous, shady.

equo *adj.* equitable, fair.

era *f.* era.

era'rio *m.* Treasury, Revenue.

erba *f.* grass; herb: — benedetta, herb bennet; — .medica, lucerne; — mala, weed; scrittore in —, writer in embryo.

erbac'cia *f.* weed.
erbaggi *m.pl.* vegetables.
erbiven'dolo *m.* greengrocer.
erbi'voro *adj.* herbivorous.
erborista *m.* herbalist.
erboso *adj.* grassy, turfy.
Er'cole *m.* Hercules.
ercu'leo *adj.* Herculean.
erede *m.* heir. *f.* heiress.
eredità *f.* inheritance; heredity.
ereditare *vt.*, *vi.* to inherit (*from*).
ereditarietà *f.* hereditariness.
eredita'rio *adj.* hereditary.
ereditiera *f.* heiress.
eremita *m.* hermit.
e'remo *m.* hermitage.
eresi'a *f.* heresy.
ere'tico *m.*, *adj.* heretic.
eretto *adj.* erect; upright; erected, built. *pp.of* erigere.
erezione *f.* erection.
ergastolano *m.* life convict.
erga'stolo *m.* life sentence; life imprisonment.
er'gere *vt.*[44] to raise; er'gersi *vr.* to raise oneself, rise; to straighten.
ergo *adv.* (*Latin*) therefore.
ergon *m.* erg.
e'rica *f.* heather.
eri'gere *vt.*[44] to erect, build, raise; eri'gersi *vr.* to set up (*for*).
eritema *m.* erythema.
eritreo *m.*, *adj.* Eritrean.
erma *f.* herma (*pl.* hermae).
ermafrodito *m.*, hermaphrodite. *adj.* hermaphroditic.
ermellino *m.* ermine.
ermeticamente *adv.* hermetically.
erme'tico *adj.* hermetic; airtight.
ermetismo *m.* (*philos.*) hermetics; obscureness.
er'nia *f.* hernia, rupture.
ernia'rio *adj.* hernial: cinto —, truss.
eroe *m.* hero
erogare *vt.* to distribute; to deliver.
erogazione *f.* distribution; output.
ero'ico *adj.* heroic.
eroico'mico *adj.* heroicomic.
eroina *f.* heroine.
eroismo *m.* heroism.
erom'pere *vi.*[116] to flow forth.
erosione *f.* erosion.
ero'tico *adj.* erotic.
erotismo *m.* eroticism.
er'pete *m.* herpes.
erpicare *vt.* to harrow.
er'pice *m.* harrow.
errabondo *adj.* nomadic, vagrant.
errante *adj.* wandering, errant: cavaliere errante, knight-errant.
errare *vi.* to wander, ramble; to sin; to err, be mistaken; to be wrong.
erratacor'rige *f.* (*typog.*) errata.
errato *adj.* wrong, fallacious.

erroneamente *adv.* erroneously; by mistake; wrongly.
erro'neo *adj.* erroneous; wrong.
errore *m.* error, fault, mistake; oversight, slip: — di stampa, misprint; — di calcolo, misreckoning; — di traduzione, mistranslation; — giudiziario, miscarriage of justice; essere in —, to be mistaken; indurre in —, to mislead; salvo —, errors excepted.
erta *f.* ascent, slope.
ertal, (all') *interj.* beware!: stare —, to be on the look out.
erto *adj.* steep, sloping; *pp.of* ergere.
erudire *vt.* to educate; erudirsi *vr.* to learn.
erudizione *f.* learning.
eruttare *vt.*, *vi.* to erupt.
eruttazione *f.* eructation, belch.
eruttivo *adj.* eruptive.
eruzione *f.* eruption.
esacerbare *vt.* to exacerbate, embitter; to exasperate.
esagerare *vt.*, *vi.* to exaggerate.
esagerato *adj.* exaggerated; excessive.
esagerazione *f.* exaggeration.
esagitare *vt.* to frenzy.
esa'gono *m.* hexagon.
esalare *vt.*, *vi.* to exhale: — l'ultimo respiro, to breathe one's last.
esalazione *f.* exhalation; fume.
esaltare *vt.* to extol; to extol; esaltarsi *vr.* to get excited.
esaltato *m.* crank; fanatic; *adj.* exalted; fanatic; crazy.
esaltazione *f.* exaltation; excitement.
esame *m.* examination; inspection; scrutiny; perusal; test: — di coscienza, self-examination; — di collaudo, test: — di riparazione, make-up; — della vista, sight-test; prendere in —, to take into consideration.
esa'metro *m.* hexameter.
esaminare *vt.* to examine; to inspect; to scrutinize; to peruse; to test; to weigh, consider.
esaminatore *m.* examiner.
esangue *adj.* bloodless.
esa'nime *adj.* inanimate, lifeless.
esasperante *adj.* maddening.
esasperare *vt.* to exasperate, drive (*one*) crazy.
esasperazione *f.* exasperation.
esattamente *adv.* exactly; quite so!
esattezza *f.* exactitude; accuracy.
esatto *adj.* exact; accurate; punctual; *pp.of* esigere.
esattore *m.* collector.
esattori'a *f.* collector's bureau.
esaudire *vt.* to grant; to comply with; to satisfy.
esauriente *adj.* exhaustive.

esaurimento *m.* exhaustion: — nervoso, nervous breakdown.

esaurire *vt.*[66] to exhaust; to use up; to enervate; **esaurirsi** *vr.* to be exhausted, used up, sold out; to wear off.

esaurito *adj.* exhausted; used up; sold out; out of print; *pp. of* esaurire.

esausto *adj.* exhausted.

esautorare *vt.* to deprive of authority; to discredit.

esazione *f.* collection, exaction.

esborso *m.* disbursement.

esca *f.* bait; enticement; tinder, touchwood: **dare — a**, to foment; to invite.

escandescenze *f.pl.* fit of temper, burst of rage: **dare in —**, to fly off the handle.

escavatore *m.*, **escavatrice** *f.* excavator, digger.

eschimese *m.* Eskimo.

escire *see* uscire.

esclamare *vi.* to exclaim, cry out.

esclamativo *adj.* exclamatory: **punto —**, exclamation mark.

esclamazione *f.* exclamation.

esclu'dere *vt.*[2] to exclude.

esclusione *f.* exclusion; exception: **a — di**, with the exception of.

esclusiva *f.* exclusive; privilege; sole right.

esclusivamente *adv.* exclusively, solely.

esclusivista *m.* sole agent.

esclusivo *adj.* exclusive: **agente —**, sole agent.

escluso *adj.* excluded; excepted; *pp. of* escludere.

escogitare *vt.* to devise, think out.

escoriare *vt.* to excoriate.

escoriazione *f.* excoriation.

escremento *m.* excrement.

escrescenza *f.* excrescence.

escursione *f.* excursion, tour.

escursionista *m.* excursionist.

escussione *f.* examination (*of a witness*).

esecrare *vt.* to execrate.

esecrazione *f.* execration.

esecutivo *m.*, *adj.* executive.

esecutore *m.* executor; executioner; (*mus.*) performer.

esecuzione *f.* execution; performance; make; actuation: **mettere in —**, to carry out.

eseguire *vt.* to execute, effect, carry out; to fulfill, discharge; to perform, make.

esem'pio *m.* example, instance; pattern, specimen, model: **per —**, for instance.

esemplare *m.* exemplar; sample; pattern; specimen; copy; *adj.* exemplary.

esemplificare *vt.* to exemplify, illustrate.

esentare *vt.* to exempt.

esente *adj.* exempt, free.

esenzione *f.* exemption.

ese'quie *f.pl.* obsequies.

esercente *m.* merchant, dealer: — **cinematografico**, film exhibitor. *adj.* practicing.

esercire *vt.* to keep, run.

esercitare *vt.* to exercise, train; to practice, discharge, perform; to carry on; **esercitarsi** *vr.* to train (*oneself*), practice.

esercitazione *f.* exercise, practice; training; (*mil.*) drill.

eser'cito *m.* army.

eserci'zio *m.* exercise, training; drill; practice, discharge, performance; shop; management; — **finanziario**, financial year; — **provvisorio**, interim management.

esibire *vt.* to exhibit, display; to offer; to produce; **esibirsi** *vr.* to exhibit, show (*oneself*); to show off.

esibizione *f.* show, exhibition.

esigente *adj.* exacting; demanding.

esigenza *f.* exigency; need, demand; pretension.

esi'gere *vt.*[66] to collect; to exact; to ask; to require; to call for; to demand; to want.

esigi'bile *adj.* collectible; exigible.

esiguità *f.* exiguity.

esiguo *adj.* scanty, meager; thin.

esilarante *adj.* exhilarating.

esilarare *vt.* to exhilarate.

e'sile *adj.* thin, lean; weak.

esiliare *vt.* to exile.

esiliato *m.* exile; *adj.* exiled.

esi'lio *m.* exile.

esi'mere *vt.*[37] to exempt, dispense (*from*); **esimersi** *vr.* to exempt oneself (*from*): **esimersi da**, to avoid, shun.

esi'mio *adj.* eminent, prominent.

esistente *adj.* existent; extant.

esistenza *f.* existence; life.

esistenze *f.pl.* stock on hand.

esistenzialismo *m.* existentialism.

esistenzialista *m.* existentialist.

esi'stere *vi.* to exist; to live; to be.

esita'bile *adj.* salable.

esitante *adj.* hesitant.

esitare (1) *vi.* to hesitate, waver; to pause.

esitare (2) *vt.* to dispose of, sell.

esitazione *f.* hesitation.

e'sito *m.* result, outcome; sale.

esiziale *adj.* fatal, deadly.

e'sodo *m.* exodus.

eso'fago *m.* esophagus.

esonerare *vt.* to exonerate; to exempt; to dismiss.

eso'nero *m.* exoneration, exemption; dispensation; dismissal.

Esopo *m.pr.* Aesop.

esorbitante *adj.* exorbitant.

esorbitare *vi.* to exceed.

esorcismo *m.* exorcism.

esordiente *m.*, beginner; debutant. *f.* beginner; debutante.

esor'dio *m.* debut.

esordire *vi.* to begin, start; to make one's debut; to open.

esortare *vt.* to exhort, urge.

esortazione *f.* exhortation.

esoso *adj.* stingy; greedy.

eso'tico *adj.* exotic.

espan'dere *vt.*, espan'dersi *vr.* to expand, spread.

espansione *f.* expansion; effusion.

espansionismo *m.* expansionism.

espansionista *m.* expansionist.

espansività *f.* effusiveness.

espansivo *adj.* effusive; expansive.

espatriare *vi.* to expatriate oneself; to emigrate.

espa'trio *m.* expatriation.

espediente *m.* expedient; shift; stratagem; device; vivere di espedienti, to live by one's wits.

espel'lere *vt.*[58] to expel, eject; to oust, dismiss.

esperienza *f.* experience; experiment.

esperimento *m.* experiment, trial.

esperto *m.* expert; connoisseur. *adj.* experienced; expert, skilful.

espettorare *vi.* to expectorate.

espiare *vt.* to explate, atone for; to serve.

espiato'rio *adj.* explatory: capro —, scapegoat.

espiazione *f.* explation.

espletare *vt.* to dispatch, carry out.

esplicare *vt.* to explicate; to explain; to practice.

esplicativo *adj.* explanatory.

esplicitamente *adv.* explicitly.

espli'cito *adj.* explicit.

esplo'dere *vi.*, *vi.*[58] to explode, burst; to fire (*at*); to burst out.

esplorare *vt.* to explore; (*telev.*) to scan.

esplorativo *adj.* exploratory.

esploratore *m.* explorer; scout.

esplorazione *f.* exploration; (*telev.*) scanning.

esplosione *f.* explosion: — a catena, chain detonation.

esplosivo *m.*, *adj.* explosive.

esploso *pp.of* esplodere.

esponente *m.* exponent.

esporre *vt.*[58] to expose; to display, exhibit; to subject; to expound, set forth, explain; esporsi *vr.* to expose oneself (*to*); to run the risk (*of*).

esportare *vt.* to export.

esportatore *m.* exporter.

esportazione *f.* exportation, export.

esposi'metro *m.* (*photo.*) exposure meter.

espositore *m.* exhibitor.

esposizione *f.* exhibition; display; exposition, explanation; exposure.

esposto *m.* complaint; statement; *adj.* exposed, exhibited; *pp.of* esporre.

espressamente *adv.* expressly.

espressione *f.* expression.

espressionismo *m.* expressionism.

espressivo *adj.* expressive.

espresso *m.* express; *adj.* explicit; expressed; *pp.of* esprimere.

espri'mere *vt.*[58] to express; to utter; espri'mersi *vr.* to express oneself.

espropriare *vt.* to expropriate; to dispossess; to condemn (*as real property*).

espro'prio *m.* expropriation.

espugnare *vt.* to conquer.

espulsione *f.* expulsion; ejection; dismissal; banishment.

espulso *adj.* expelled, ejected; *pp.of* espellere.

espulsore *m.* ejector.

espurgare *vt.* to expurgate.

esquimese *see* eschimese.

essa *demonstr.pron. f.* it; (*pl.*) they; *pers.pron.* (*fam.*) she; (*pl.*) they; her; (*pl.*) them.

essenza *f.* essence.

essenziale *m.*, *adj.* essential.

es'sere (1) *m.* being, creature; condition; existence.

es'sere (2) *vi.*, *va.* to be; (*foll. by pass., refl., recipr. verbs*) to have; to belong (*to*): sia questo sia quello, both this and that; sia che ... sia che, whether ... or; sia come sia, be it as it may; comunque sia, however it may be; così sia, so be it; c'è, there is; siete voi? is it you? siamo noi, it is we; se io fossi in voi, if I were you; chi c'è? who is there? che c'è di nuovo? what is new? chi è stato? who was it? che cosa sarà di noi? what will become of us? due anni or sono, two years ago.

essiccare *vt.* to desiccate, dry; essiccarsi *vr.* to dry up.

essiccazione *f.* desiccation.

esso *demonstr.pron. m.* it; (*pl.*) they; *pers.pron.* (*fam.*) he; (*pl.*) they; him; (*pl.*) them.

est *m.* east: dell'—, eastern; verso l'—, eastward.

e'stasi *f.* ecstasy, rapture.

estasiare *vt.* to enrapture, delight; estasiarsi *vr.* to delight, be enraptured.

estate *f.* summer.
esta'tico *adj.* ecstatic.
estempora'neo *adj.* extemporaneous, impromptu, offhand.
esten'dere *vt.*[140] to extend; to lengthen; to expand, spread; to increase; esten'dersi *vr.* to extend, stretch out; to spread.
estensione *f.* extension, extent; range; surface, area; expanse; development; lengthening.
estensivo *adj.* extensive.
estenso (per) *adv.* in full.
estensore *m.* recorder; (*pl.*) stretchers.
estenuante *adj.* enervating; oppressive.
estenuare *vt.* to enervate.
estenuazione *f.* exhaustion.
e'steri *m.pl.* (*chem.*) esters.
esteriore *adj.* exterior, outer.
esteriorità *f.* exteriority.
esteriormente *adv.* outside, outwardly.
esternamente *adv.* externally, outwardly, outside.
esternare *vt.* to manifest.
esterno *m.* outside; day pupil; (*motion pictures*) exterior; *adj.* external, exterior, outer, outside.
e'stero *m.* foreign countries; (*pl.*) foreign affairs: all'—, abroad; dall'—, from abroad; *adj.* foreign.
esterrefatto *adj.* dumfounded.
estesamente *adv.* extensively.
esteso *adj.* wide; widespread: per —, in full.
esteta *m.* aesthete.
este'tica *f.* aesthetics.
esteticamente *adv.* aesthetically.
este'tico *adj.* aesthetical.
e'stimo *m.* survey.
estin'guere *vt.*[67] to extinguish, put out; to slake; estin'guersi *vr.* to go out; to become extinct; to die, pass away.
estingui'bile *adj.* extinguishable.
estinto *m.* deceased; *adj.* extinguished; extinct; deceased; *pp.* of estinguere.
estintore *m.* extinguisher.
estirpare *vt.* to extirpate; to uproot, eradicate; to extract.
estirpatore *m.* (*agr.*) weeder.
estivo *adj.* summer.
estol'lere *vt.* to extol.
estor'cere *vt.*[146] to extort.
estorsione *f.* extortion.
estorto *adj.* extorted; *pp.* of estorcere.
estradare *vt.* to extradite.
estradizione *f.* extradition.
estra'neo *m.* stranger; *adj.* extraneous; strange; alien; unrelated.
estrarre *vt.*[148] to extract; to pull out; to draw (*out*); to dig out.

estrattivo *adj.* extractive.
estratto *m.* extract; estreat; abstract; excerpt; offprint: — di conto, statement of account; *adj.* extracted; abstracted; *pp.of* estrarre.
estrazione *f.* extraction; extirpation; digging, drawing (*by lot*): — di radice, (*math.*) evolution.
estremamente *adv.* extremely.
estremità *f.* extremity; end; verge.
estremo *m.* extreme, highest degree *or* point; end, extremity; *adj.* extreme, last; farthest; excessive; utmost: all'—, extremely; sino al limite —, to the limit.
estro *m.* whim; inspiration; fancy, imagination; impulse.
estromet'tere *vt.*[78] to oust; to exclude.
estroso *adj.* freakish; fantastic.
estua'rio *m.* estuary.
esuberante *adj.* exuberant.
esuberanza *f.* exuberance.
esulare *vi.* to emigrate; to be alien (*to*): — da, to exceed.
esulcerare *vt.* to exasperate.
e'sule *m.*, *f.* exile; refugee, displaced person.
esultante *adj.* exultant.
esultanza *f.* exultation.
esultare *vi.* to exult.
esumare *vt.* to exhume.
esumazione *f.* exhumation.
età *f.* age: l'— dell'oro, the Golden Age; nel fiore dell'—, in the prime of life; in — minore, underage; in — maggiore, of age; raggiungere l'— maggiore, to come of age; un uomo in —, an elderly man.
e'tere *m.* ether.
ete'reo *adj.* ethereal.
eternamente *adv.* eternally, forever.
eternare *vt.* to make eternal.
eternità *f.* eternity.
eterno *adj.* eternal, everlasting: in —, forever.
eteroge'neo *adj.* heterogeneous.
e'tica *f.* ethics.
etichetta (1) *f.* tag, label, sticker: mettere l'— a, to label.
etichetta (2) *f.* etiquette.
e'tico (1) *adj.* consumptive.
e'tico (2) *adj.* ethical.
etile *m.* ethyl.
eti'lico *adj.* ethylic.
etilismo *m.* alcoholism.
etimologi'a *f.* etymology.
etisi'a *f.* phthisis.
et'nico *adj.* ethnic, ethnical.
etrusco *m.*, *adj.* Etruscan.
etta'gono *m.* heptagon.
ette *m.* nothing; anything: mancò un —, it was touch and go.
etto, ettogrammo *m.* hectogram.
etto'litro *m.* hectoliter.

etto'metro *m.* hectometer.
ettowatt *m.* one hundred watts.
eucalipto *m.* eucalyptus.
eufemismo *m.* euphemism.
eufori'a *f.* euphoria, elation.
eufo'rico *adj.* elated.
eunuco *m.* eunuch.
europeo *m.*, *adj.* European.
eutanasia *f.* euthanasia.
evacuare *vt.*, *vi.* to evacuate; to vacate.
evacuazione *f.* evacuation.
eva'dere *vt.*⁴⁶ to evade; to deal with, settle: — una lettera, to reply to a letter; *vi.* to evade, escape.
evange'lico *adj.* evangelical.
evangelista *m.* evangelist.
Evangelo *m.* Gospel, Evangel.
evaporare *vt.*, *vi.* to evaporate.
evaporazione *f.* evaporation.
evasione *f.* evasion; escape: dare —, to reply (to).
evasivamente *adv.* evasively.
evasivo *adj.* evasive, elusive; noncommittal.
evaso *m.* runaway, fugitive; *adj.* evaded, escaped; *pp. of* evadere.
evasore *m.* dodger.
evenienza *f.* occurrence, contingency: per ogni —, just in case.

evento *m.* event, occurrence; development.
eventuale *adj.* eventual; possible.
eventualità *f.* eventuality; event, occurrence: nell'— che, in the event of.
eventualmente *adv.* in case; anyway.
evidente *adj.* evident, obvious.
evidentemente *adv.* evidently.
evidenza *f.* evidence, obviousness: mettere in —, to point out; mettersi in —, to make oneself conspicuous.
evirare *vt.* to emasculate.
evita'bile *adj.* avoidable.
evitare *vt.* to avoid; to shun, dodge; to spare; to prevent (*from*); to refrain (*from*).
evo *m.* age, time, era: Evo Antico, ancient times; Evo Moderno, modern era.
evocare *vt.* to evoke, conjure.
evoluto *adj.* developed; civilized; broad-minded; *pp.* evolved.
evoluzione *f.* evolution.
evol'versi *vr.* to evolve, develop.
evviva *m.* cheer; *interj.* long live!; hooray!: gridare —, to cheer.
ex *pref.* ex, former, past.
eziandi'o *adv.* also; moreover.

F

fa (*1*) *adj.* ago.
fa (*2*) *m.* (*mus.*) fa, F: — diesis, F sharp.
fabbisogno *m.* necessities (*pl.*), requirement; demand.
fab'brica *m.* building; factory, mill, plant, works; manufacture: prezzo di —, cost price.
fabbricante *m.* manufacturer, maker.
fabbricare *vt.* to build; to manufacture; to make; to fabricate.
fabbricato *m.* building; *pp.* built, manufactured, made.
fabbricazione *f.* manufacture; manufacturing; make.
fabbro *m.* smith, blacksmith.
faccenda *f.* business, matter, thing: faccende domestiche, household chores.
faccetta *f.* facet; side.
faccettare *vt.* to facet, to cut in facets.
facchino *m.* porter; drudge; boor.
fac'cia *f.* face; look; page; side: in — a, in front of, opposite, in the presence of; visto di —, as seen from the front; — tosta, effrontery, brass.
facciale *adj.* (*anat.*) facial.
facciata *f.* front, façade.
face *f.* torch; light.

faceto *adj.* facetious.
face'zia *f.* joke, witticism.
fachiro *m.* fakir.
fa'cile *adj.* easy; facile; likely; prone, ready; liable: aver la parola —, to have a glib tongue; facili costumi, loose morals.
facilità *f.* facility, ease.
facilitare *vt.* to facilitate; to aid.
facilitazione *f.* facility.
facilmente *adv.* easily; likely.
facinoroso *m.* rioter; *adj.* riotous.
facoltà *f.* faculty; ability, aptitude; power; right; authority; permission; capability: — di scelta, option, election.
facoltativo *adj.* optional; elective.
facoltoso *adj.* wealthy, affluent.
facon'dia *f.* eloquence.
facondo *adj.* eloquent, voluble.
fag'gio *m.* beech.
fagiano *m.* pheasant.
fagiolino *m.* string bean.
fagiuolo *m.* bean: andare a —, to suit, to please.
fagotto *m.* bundle; (*mus.*) bassoon: far —, to pack off.
faina *f.* stone marten.
falange *f.* phalanx.

falce *f.* scythe, sickle; crescent (*of moon*).

falciare *vt.* to scythe, mow.

falciatrice *f.* mowing machine.

falcidiare *vt.* to cut down.

falco *m.* hawk.

falcone *m.* falcon.

falconiere *m.* falconer.

falda *f.* brim (*of a hat*); flap (*of a garment*); tail (*of a coat*); snowflake; slope; slice; layer.

falegname *m.* carpenter.

falena *f.* moth.

Faliero, Marino, Doge of Venice (1274-1355).

falla *f.* leak.

fallace *adj.* fallacious, misleading.

fallare *vi.* to err, make a mistake.

fallimentare *adj.* bankrupt; (*fig.*) disastrous.

fallimento *m.* bankruptcy; (*fig.*) failure.

fallire *vt.* to miss; *vi.* to fail, be unsuccessful; to go bankrupt.

fallito *m.* bankrupt; failure; *adj.* bankrupt; unsuccessful.

fallo (*1*) *m.* fault, mistake, flaw; sin: **senza —,** without fail; **cogliere in —,** to catch red-handed; **mettere un piede in —,** to take a wrong step.

fallo (*2*) *m.* phallus (*pl.* phalli).

falò *m.* bonfire.

falsare *vt.* to alter; to distort; to misconstrue.

falsariga *f.* ruling; pattern.

falsario *m.* forger, counterfeiter.

falsificare *vt.* to forge, counterfeit.

falsificazione *f.* falsification, forgery, counterfeiting, adulteration; misrepresentation.

falsità *f.* falseness; untruth, falsehood; duplicity.

falso *m.* untruth; forgery; *adj.* false; forged, counterfeit; wrong, mistaken; sham: **essere nel —,** to be mistaken; **giurare il —,** to perjure oneself.

fama *f.* fame, notoriety, renown; reputation; rumor, report.

fame *f.* hunger; famine; longing: **avere —,** to be hungry; **patire la —,** far **morire di —,** to starve; **sciopero della —,** hunger strike; **lungo come la —,** slow as molasses in January.

fame'lico *adj.* hungry, famished.

famigerato *adj.* notorious.

fami'glia *f.* family: **sentirsi in —,** to feel at home.

familiare *m.* familiar; relative; *adj.* familiar; friendly; domestic, homelike: **un ambiente —,** a homelike atmosphere.

familiarità *f.* familiarity.

familiarizzare *vt.* to familiarize; **familiarizzarsi** *vr.* to become familiar (*with*); to get used (*to*).

famoso *adj.* famous, renowned.

fanale *m.* lamp; light, headlight; beacon; lamppost.

fana'tico *m.*, *adj.* fanatic.

fanatismo *m.* fanaticism.

fanatizzare *vt.*, *vi.* to make, or become fanatic.

fanciulla *f.* little girl; girl.

fanciullesco *adj.* childish.

fanciullezza *f.* childhood.

fanciullo *m.* boy; *adj.* as a boy.

fando'nia *f.* humbug; fib.

fanfara *f.* brass band; fanfare.

fanfaronata *f.* fanfaronade, brag.

fanfarone *m.* braggart.

fanghi'glia *f.* mire.

fango *m.* mire, mud.

fangosità *f.* muddiness.

fangoso *adj.* muddy, miry.

fannullone *m.* loafer, idler.

fanone *m.* whalebone.

fantaccino *m.* foot soldier.

fantascienza *f.* science fiction.

fantasi'a *f.* fantasy, imagination; whim, fancy; mind.

fantasioso *adj.* fanciful.

fantasma *m.* ghost, phantom.

fantasmago'rico *adj.* phantasmagoric.

fantasticare *vi.* to daydream; to dream; to wander.

fantasticheri'a *f.* reverie, daydream.

fanta'stico *adj.* fantastic; imaginary; (*fam.*) wonderful, great.

fante *m.* infantryman; jack (*in playing cards*).

fanteri'a *f.* foot, infantry.

fantesca *f.* housemaid.

fantino *m.* jockey.

fantoc'cio *m.* puppet; figurehead.

fantoma'tico *adj.* ghostly.

farabutto *m.* cad, "heel."

faraglione *m.* cliff.

faraona *f.* guinea hen.

Faraone *m.* Pharaoh.

faraone *m.* faro.

farcire *vt.* to stuff.

fardello *m.* bundle; burden.

fare (*1*) *vt.*,[s1] *vi.* to do; to make; to act; to work; to manufacture; to gather; to form; to play; to be: to practice; to get; to cause; to order; to say: **— del male a,** to harm, hurt; **— debiti,** to run into debt; **— il callo,** to get accustomed (*to*); **— la parte di Macbeth,** to play Macbeth; **— da mangiare,** to cook; **che mestiere fai?** what is your trade? **faccio il falegname,** I am a carpenter; **— benzina,** to fuel; **— compassione,** to stir pity; **— paura,**

to frighten; — le carte, to deal cards; non fa nulla, it doesn't matter; — al caso di, to suit; — da testimone, to act as a witness; — il nome di, to mention the name of; a far tempo da, dating from; — lo stupido, to behave as a fool; non — lo sciocco! don't be a fool!; — un bagno, to take a bath; — una domanda, to ask a question; — domanda di, to file for; —fuoco contro, to fire at; — uno scherzo a, to play a trick upon; — silenzio, to keep silent; — visita, to pay a visit (to); — coraggio a, to enhearten; — attenzione, to pay attention; — la calza, to knit; — caso a, to notice; non farci caso! never mind!; — la coda, to queue up; fa caldo (freddo), it is hot (cold); — finta di, to pretend; far venire il medico, to call the doctor; far fare qualcosa, to have something done; far fare qualcosa a uno, to have one do something; far aspettare, to keep waiting; far vedere, to show; far sapere, to let (one) know; — tardi, to be late; — presto, to hurry; — fronte ai propri impegni, to meet one's obligations; — a pugni, to fight; to clash; — a meno di, to do without, dispense with; non potei — a meno di dirglielo, I couldn't help telling him; — in modo che, to see that, manage; lascia — a me, leave it to me; faresti meglio ad andare, you had better go; che tempo fa? how is the weather?; come si fa a dirglielo? how can we tell him? cammin facendo, while walking; — fagotto, to pack up; — fiasco, to fail, be unsuccessful; — l'indiano, to act the fool; far pari e patta, to get even (*with*); farla in barba a, to outwit; farsi *vr.* to be done; to be made; to become; to get, grow, turn; to move; farsi vecchio, to grow old; si fa tardi, it is getting late; si fa notte, night is falling; farsi avanti, to step forward; farsi incontro, to meet; farsi male, to hurt oneself; farsi il nodo alla cravatta, to tie one's necktie; farsi il segno della croce, to make the sign of the cross; farsi la barba, to shave (*oneself*); farsi fare la barba, to have a shave; farsi capire, to make oneself understood; farsi pregare, to want to be coaxed; farsi coraggio, to take courage, to be brave.
fare (2) *m.* manners (*pl.*), behavior; style; beginning: una casa sul — della nostra, a house like ours; sul — del giorno, at daybreak; sul — della notte, at nightfall; tra il dire e il — c'è di mezzo il mare, easier said than done, "there's many a slip."

farfalla *f.* butterfly.
farfugliare *vi.* to mumble.
farina *f.* meal, flour.
faringe *f.* pharynx.
faringite *f.* pharyngitis.
fariseo *m.* Pharisee.
farmaci'a *f.* pharmacy; drugstore.
farmacista *m.* chemist.
far'maco *m.* remedy.
farneticare *vi.* to rave.
faro *m.* beacon, light; lighthouse.
farra'gine *f.* farrago; medley.
farraginoso *adj.* motley, medley.
farsa *f.* farce.
farsesco *adj.* farcical.
farsetto *m.* doublet; jersey, sweater.
fascetta *f.* band; girdle.
fa'scia *f.* band; belt; bandage; (*pl.*) swaddling bands (*for infants*); (*pl. mil.*) puttees.
fasciame *m.* (*naut.*) timbers.
fasciare *vt.* to wrap; to swaddle (*as an infant*); to bandage, dress.
fasciatura *f.* bandaging; dressing.
fasci'colo *m.* dossier; number, issue; pamphlet; (*anat.*) fascicle.
fascina *f.* fagot, fascine.
fascinatore *m.* fascinator.
fa'scino *m.* charm, glamour.
fa'scio *m.* bundle, beam (*of light*); (*hist.*) fasces (*pl.*).
fascismo *m.* fascism.
fascista *m.*, *adj.* fascist.
fase *f.* phase; stage.
fastello *m.* fagot.
fasti *m.pl.* rise: —e nefasti, rise and fall.
fasti'dio *m.* trouble, worry; dislike, distaste; nuisance; dare — a, to irk; to annoy.
fastidioso *adj.* irksome, annoying.
fasto *m.* pomp; display.
fastoso *adj.* sumptuous, gorgeous.
fata *f.* fairy.
fatale *adj.* fatal; inevitable.
fatalismo *m.* fatalism.
fatalista *m.* fatalist.
fatalità *f.* fatality, fate.
fatato *adj.* fairy, fairylike.
fatica *f.* exertion, effort, toil; fatigue, exhaustion; difficulty: a —, scarcely, hardly; with difficulty; uomo di —, hand laborer, odd-job man; animale da —, beast of burden.
faticare *vi.* to toil, drudge.
faticoso *adj.* hard, tiring, wearisome; toilsome.
fati'dico *adj.* fatidic; fateful, prophetic.

fato m. fate, destiny, lot.

fatta f. sort, kind.

fattac'cio m. crime.

fattezze f.pl. features.

fatti'bile adj. feasible; possible.

fattivo adj. active, practical.

fatto (1) m. fact, deed; business, affair, thing; point; matter, feat; act: badare ai fatti propri, to mind one's own business; venire al —, to come to the point; passare alle vie di —, to resort to violence; cogliere sul —, to catch red-handed; dire a uno il — suo, to give one a piece of one's mind; sapere il — proprio, to know what's what.

fatto (2) adj. done, made; accomplished; fit; grown-up, ripe; shaped: giorno —, broad daylight; a notte fatta, in the dead of night; a conti fatti, when all is said and done. pp.of fare.

fattore m. maker; factor; steward; farmer.

fattori'a f. farm.

fattorino m. messenger; runner.

fattrice f. (zool.) dam.

fattucchiera f. sorceress, witch.

fattura f. invoice, itemized bill; make; workmanship, form.

fatturare vt. to adulterate; to invoice; to charge.

fa'tuo adj. vain; fatuous: fuoco —, will-o'-the-wisp.

fa'uci f.pl. jaws.

fauna f. fauna.

fauno m. faun, satyr.

fausto adj. auspicious.

fautore m. supporter, advocate.

fava f. bean.

favella f. speech; idiom; language.

favilla f. spark.

favo m. honeycomb; (med.) favus.

fa'vola f. fable; tale; fairy tale; humbug: la — della città, the talk of the town.

favolosità f. fabulousness.

favoloso adj. fabulous.

favore m. favor; kindness; aid, help: prezzo di —, reduced price; entrata di —, complimentary admission; a — di, in favor of; col — della notte, under cover of night; per —, please; cambiale di —, accommodation bill.

favoreggiamento m. abetting.

favoreggiare vt. to aid; to abet.

favoreggiatore m. abettor.

favore'vole adj. favorable.

favorevolmente adv. favorably.

favorire vt. to favor; to second; to encourage, further; to oblige (with); to help, assist, aid; to be conducive to; to protect: favorite da questa

parte! this way, please!; favorite uscire! out you go!; volete favorirmi quel libro? would you mind handing me that book?; volete — ? won't you partake?; mi dispiace di non poter favorirti, I am sorry to disoblige you.

favoritismo m. favoritism.

favorito m., adj. favorite.

fazione f. faction; watch.

fazioso adj. factious, riotous.

fazzoletto m. kerchief; handkerchief.

febbra'io m. February.

febbre f. fever; temperature.

febbricitante adj. feverish.

febbrile adj. feverish.

fec'cia f. dregs (pl.); rabble: fino alla —, to the bitter end.

feci f.pl. feces, excrement.

fe'cola f. starch, fecula.

fecondare vt. to fecundate.

fecondazione f. fecundation: — artificiale, artificial insemination.

fecondità f. fecundity.

fecondo adj. fecund, prolific.

fede, f. faith; confidence, trust; belief; wedding ring: prestar — a, to give credit to; — di nascita, birth certificate.

fedele m. believer; follower, adherent. adj. faithful, loyal, true: i fedeli, believers, churchgoers; the fold.

fedelmente adv. faithfully.

fedeltà f. faithfulness, loyalty.

fe'dera f. pillowcase.

federalismo m. federalism.

federalista m. federalist.

federazione f. federation.

fedi'frago m. traitor.

fedina (1) f. whisker.

fedina (2) f. certificate, record.

fe'gato m. liver; (fig.) courage.

felce f. fern.

felceta f. fernery.

feldspato m. feldspar.

felice adj. happy, glad; lucky; felicitous.

felicemente adv. happily.

felicità f. happiness, bliss.

felicitarsi vr. to congratulate: — con uno per, to congratulate one on.

felicitazione f. congratulation.

felino m., adj. feline.

felpa f. plush.

felpato adj. plushy.

feltrare vt. to felt.

feltro m. felt.

feluca f. cocked hat.

fem'mina f. female.

femminile m., adj. feminine.

femminilità f. femininity.

femminismo m. feminism.

femminista m., f., adj. feminist.

fe'more m. femur.

fendente m. slash.

fen'dere vt.[63] to split, cleave; to plow (waters): — la folla, to elbow one's way through the crowd; **fen'dersi** vr. to cleave, split.

fenditura f. cleft, split.

fenduto pp. of fendere.

fenice f. (myth.) phoenix.

fe'nico (acido) m. phenol.

fenicot'tero m. flamingo.

fenolo m. phenol.

fenomenale adj. phenomenal; (fig.) grand, great, wonderful.

feno'meno m. phenomenon (pl. phenomena): sei un —! you are just great!

ferale adj. ominous, tragic.

fe'retro m. coffin.

fe'ria f. holiday, vacation; (eccl.) weekday.

feriale adj. working: giorno —, working day, weekday.

ferimento m. wounding.

ferire vt. to wound; to hurt: — l'orecchio, to grate on the ear; **ferirsi** vr. to wound oneself; to get wounded.

ferita f. wound, injury.

ferito adj. wounded.

ferito'ia f. loophole.

feritore m. wounder.

ferma f. enlistment.

fermacarte m. paperweight.

ferma'glio m. clasp; buckle; clip.

fermamente adv. steadfastly.

fermare vt. to stop, arrest, check; to fasten, fix, halt; to interrupt, discontinue; to stop up, block; **fermarsi** vr. to stop, halt; to cease; to pause; to stay.

fermata f. stop; station; halt; pause.

fermentare vi. to ferment.

fermentazione f. fermentation.

fermento m. ferment; excitement.

fermezza f. firmness.

Fermi, Enrico, Italian physicist, Nobel Prize in physics 1938 (1901–1954).

fermo m. stop, catch, stop-switch; arrest; distress, distraint. adj. firm, steady; still, motionless: terra ferma, firm land; punto —, full stop, period; — in posta, general delivery; tener —, to hold fast; tener per —, to take for granted.

feroce adj. ferocious, wild, savage; ruthless.

fero'cia f. ferociousness.

ferragosto m. mid-August holiday.

ferra'io (fabbro) m. blacksmith.

ferramenta f. pl. hardware.

ferrato adj. shod; iron-fitted; conversant (with): strada ferrata, railroad; essere — in, to be well versed in.

fer'reo adj. iron (also fig.).

ferriera f. ironworks; iron mine.

ferro m. iron; tool, implement; sword: — grezzo, pig iron; — chirurgico, surgical instrument; — da calza, knitting needle; — da cavallo, horseshoe; venire ai ferri corti, to come to close quarters.

ferrovi'a f. railroad: — sotterranea, subway.

ferrovia'rio adj. railroad.

ferroviere m. railroadman.

fer'tile adj. fertile, productive.

fertilità f. fertility.

fertilizzante m. fertilizer.

fertilizzare vt. to fertilize.

fervente adj. hot, fervent.

fer'vere vi. to be intense; to rage.

fer'vido see fervente.

fervore m. heat, fervor.

fervorino m. lecture.

fesseria f. (vulgar It. slang) nonsense; blunder, boner.

fesso m. crack; (vulgar It. slang.) dolt, sucker. adj. cracked; stupid: far —, to play for a sucker. pp. of fendere.

fessura f. crack.

festa f. feast; holiday; saint's day; birthday; party; festival: far la — a, to make away with; far — a, to welcome; guastare la —, to spoil sport; augurare le buone feste, to give the compliments of the season; conciare uno per le feste, to beat one black and blue.

festante adj. merry; cheering.

festeggiamento m. celebration.

festeggiare vt. to celebrate; to welcome; to applaud.

festino m. party, banquet.

festività f. festivity, festival.

festivo adj. festive: giorno —, holiday.

festone m. festoon.

festosamente adv. merrily; heartily.

festosità f. gaiety; heartiness.

festoso adj. hearty, warm; merry.

festuca f. straw, blade.

fetente adj. stinking.

feti'cio m. fetish.

feticismo m. fetishism.

fe'tido adj. fetid, stinking.

feto m. foetus.

fetore m. fetor, stench.

fetta f. slice: a fette, sliced.

fettuc'cia f. tape; ribbon.

fettuccine f. pl. noodles.

feudale adj. feudal.

feudata'rio m., adj. feudatory.

fe'udo m. feud; fief.

fiaba f. fairy tale.

fiacca f. sluggishness; weakness: batter —, to idle.

fiaccare vt. to break, crush, smash; to weary, weaken.

flacchera'io m. cabdriver.

flacchezza f. sluggishness; weariness; weakness.

flacco adj. sluggish, lazy; weak.

flac'cola f. torch.

fiala f. phial, vial.

fiamma f. flame, blaze, flare; (naut.) pennant; badge: ritorno di —, backfire; — ossidrica, welding blowpipe.

fiammante adj. blazing; scarlet; gaudy: nuovo —, brand-new.

fiammata f. blaze; bonfire.

fiammeggiante adj. blazing.

fiammeggiare vi. to flame, blaze; to sparkle.

fiammi'fero m. match.

fiammingo m. Fleming; Flemish; (zool.) flamingo. adj. Flemish.

fiancata f. flank, side.

fiancheggiare vt. to border; to flank; to aid, support.

fiancheggiatore m. supporter.

fianco m. side, flank; hip: prestare il — alle critiche, to invite criticism; a — di, beside; di —, sideways.

fiasca f. flask.

fiaschetteri'a f. wineshop.

fiasco m. flask; fiasco, failure.

fiata f. (archaic) time.

fiatare vi. to breathe; to speak.

fiato m. breath: tirare il —, to take breath; avere il — grosso, to pant, to breathe hard; bere d'un —, to drink in a gulp; senza —, breathless, out of breath; strumenti a —, wind instruments.

fib'bia f. buckle.

fibra f. fiber.

fibroso adj. fibrous.

ficcanaso m. busybody.

ficcare vt. to thrust, drive (in, into); to throw: — il naso in, to poke one's nose into; ficcarsi vr. to thrust oneself; to intrude (upon); to hide.

fico m. fig; fig tree: un — secco! "nuts!"

ficodin'dia m. prickly pear.

fidanzamento m. engagement.

fidanzarsi vr. to become engaged.

fidanzata f. fiancée, sweetheart.

fidanzato m. fiancé, sweetheart. adj. engaged (to be married).

fidare vi. to trust (in), rely (on, upon); fidarsi vr. to rely (upon): fidarsi a, to risk, venture, dare; fidarsi di, to trust, rely upon.

fidato adj. trustworthy, faithful, reliable.

fidente adj. confident.

fido m. trusty; (comm.) credit. adj. faithful, trusty.

fidu'cia f. confidence, trust, reliance; belief, faith; hope.

fiducia'rio m., adj. fiduciary.

fiducioso adj. confident, trustful.

fiele m. bile, gall.

fienile m. hayloft.

fieno m. hay.

fiera (1) f. wild beast.

fiera (2) f. fair; trade exhibition; market.

fierezza f. pride.

fiero adj. proud; cruel; sharp.

Fie'sole, da, Giovanni, see Angelico.

fie'vole adj. feeble.

fifa f. (It. slang) scare; cowardice.

fifone m. coward, softy.

fi'garo m. barber; bolero.

fig'gere vt. to drive in; to fix: figgersi in capo, to take into one's head.

fi'glia f. daughter.

figliare vt., vi. to bring forth.

figliastra f. stepdaughter.

figliastro m. stepson.

fi'glio m. son: aver figli, to have sons, children.

figlioc'cia f. goddaughter.

figlioc'cio m. godson.

figliolanza f. brood, children.

figliuola f. daughter; girl.

figliuolo m. son; boy.

figura f. figure; face; features; character; court card.

figurac'cia f. bad figure; blunder.

figurante m., f. supernumerary; figurant (m.), figurante (f.).

figurare vt. to figure; to represent; to symbolize. vi. to pretend; to figure; to appear; to be present; figurarsi vr. to imagine.

figurato adj. figurative; illustrated.

figurazione f. figuration.

figurina f. figurine.

figurinista m., f. costume designer.

figurino m. fashion plate: rivista di figurini, fashion magazine.

figuro m. scoundrel: un losco —, a shady character.

figurone m. success, hit.

fila f. line, row; (theat.) tier; queue; list: fuoco di —, enfilading fire; far la —, to queue up; tre notti di —, three nights running.

filaccioso adj. thready, fibrous.

filamento m. filament.

filanda f. spinnery.

filantropi'a f. philanthropy.

filan'tropo m. philanthropist.

filare (1) vt., vi. to spin; to run; to run away; (naut.) to sail; to flirt; to shadow: fila! scat!

filare (2) m. row, line.

filastrocca f. rigmarole.

filateli'a f. philately.

filate'lico m. philatelist. adj. philatelic.

filato m. yarn. adj. spun; consistent.

filato'io m. spinning machine; spinnery.

filatura f. spinning; spinnery.

filettare vt. to fillet; (mach.) to thread.

filettatura f. filleting; thread.

filetto m. fillet; (mil.) stripe; snaffle; thread (of a screw).

filiale f. branch. adj. filial.

filiazione f. filiation.

filibustiere m. filibuster; swindler.

filiera f. (mach.) wiredrawer.

filiforme adj. threadlike.

filigrana f. filigree; thread mark.

fillos'sera f. phylloxera.

film m. film, moving picture show: — in bianco e nero, black and white film; — a colori, color film.

filmare vt. to film.

filo m. thread, wire; string; edge: — d'erba, blade of grass; — a piombo, plumbline; telegrafo senza fili, wireless telegraph; passare a fil di spada, to sword; con un — di voce, in a thin voice; dar — da torcere, to be a hard nut to crack; per — e per segno, in full detail.

filobus m. trolley bus.

filodramma'tico m. amateur actor.

filo'logo m. philologist.

filone m. lode, vein; loaf (of bread).

filosofi'a f. philosophy.

filoso'fico adj. philosophical.

filo'sofo m. philosopher.

filovi'a f. trolley bus line.

filtrare vt. to filter, strain. vi. to leak, filter.

filtro m. filter; philtre.

filugello m. silkworm.

filza f. string; dossier.

finale m. finale; (typog.) tailpiece. f. (sport) final trial. adj. final.

finalista f. (sport) finalist.

finalità f. finality; end.

finalmente adv. finally; at last.

finanche adv. even.

finanza f. finance; **finanze** f. pl. treasury; (fam.) money.

finanziamento m. backing.

finanziare vt. to finance; to back.

finanziariamente adv. financially.

finanzia'rio adj. financial; fiscal.

finanziatore m. backer.

finanziere m. financier.

finché conj. till, until, as long as, as far as, while.

fine (1) f. end, close; limit, verge; conclusion, outcome: fare una brutta —, to go to the dogs; senza —, endless; alla —, at last; eventually; alla fin —, after all.

fine (2) m. end, object, purpose, aim: andare a buon —, to come off; (of an IOU) to be honored.

fine (3) adj. choice, fine; nice; refined; delicate; thin; cunning.

finestra f. window.

finestrino m. window; peephole.

finezza f. nicety; delicacy; refinement; shrewdness; kindness.

fin'gere vt.,[18] vi. to feign, pretend, simulate; fingersi vr. to feign (oneself), simulate, pretend to be.

finimenti m.pl. harness.

finimondo m. the end of the world; hurly-burly.

finire vt. to finish, end; to get over. vi. to finish, end, come to an end; to be over; to die; to turn into; to wind up: dove andremo a —? where shall we wind up?; dove è andato a — il mio libro? wherever is my book?; finirla, to stop it.

finito adj. finished; over; complete; broken; (gramm.) finite: farla finita, to cut it off; fatto e —, downright.

finitura f. finish.

finlandese m. Finlander, Finn. adj. Finnish.

fino adj. thin; subtle; fine, pure; delicate; keen, quick.

fino (a) prep. until, till; as far as, so far as; up to, down to; as much as; even.

finoc'chio m. fennel.

finora adv. till now, up to this time; hitherto, yet, so far.

finta f. pretense, fake; feint: far — di, to feign, pretend to; far — che, to make as if.

fintantoché see finché.

finto adj. feigned, simulated; sham, mock; false, artificial.

finzione m. pretense, make-believe; fiction; hypocrisy; sham.

fi'o, m. penalty.

fioccare vi. to snow; to fall; to pour in: fiocca, it is snowing.

fiocco m. bow; tassel; flock; flake (of snow); (naut.) jib: roba coi fiocchi, first-rate stuff.

fio'cina f. harpoon.

fioco adj. feeble; dim.

fionda f. sling, slingshot.

fiora'ia f. flower girl.

fiora'io m. florist, horticulturist.

fiordaliso m. (bot.) iris.

fiore m. flower, blossom, bloom; (pl., in playing cards) clubs; fior di farina, patent flour; il fior —, the pick, the cream, the chosen few; un fior di birbante, a downright rascal; un fior di galantuomo, a man of honor; fior di quattrini, big money; nel fior degli anni, in the prime of life; a fior di pelle, skin-deep.

fiorente adj. blooming; flourishing.

fiorentino *m.*, *adj.* Florentine.
fioretto *m.* foil; (*rel.*) vow.
fiorino *m.* florin.
fiorire *vi.* to flower; to embellish. *vi.* to bloom, blossom, flower; to flourish; to effloresce.
fiorista *m.* florist.
fiorito *adj.* flowery.
fioritura *f.* flowering.
fiorone *m.* early fig; rosette.
fiotto *m.* gush, rush.
firma *f.* signature; name.
firmamento *m.* firmament, sky.
firmare *vt.* to sign.
firmata'rio *m.* signer.
fisarmo'nica *f.* accordion.
fiscale *adj.* fiscal: avvocato — (*official*) prosecutor.
fischiare *vt.*, *vi.* to whistle, hiss; to buzz; to hoot.
fischiettare *vt.*, *vi.* to whistle.
fischietto *m.* whistle.
fi'schio *m.* whistle; hiss; hoot.
fisco *m.* treasury.
fi'sica *f.* physics.
fi'sico *m.* physicist; constitution; build, physique. *adj.* physical.
fi'sima *f.* whim; nonsense.
fisiologi'a *f.* physiology.
fisiolo'gico *adj.* physiological.
fisionomi'a, fisonomi'a *f.* countenance, appearance; physiognomy.
fisionomista *m.* physiognomist: poco —, (*fam.*) not good at remembering faces.
fiso *adj.* fixed. *adv.* fixedly.
fissag'gio *m.* (*photo.*) fixing.
fissamente *adv.* fixedly.
fissare *vt.* to fix; to fasten; to stick; to gaze (*at*), stare (*at*); to agree; to secure, book; **fissarsi** *vr.* to stick; to settle down; to set one's mind (*on*).
fissato *adj.* fixed; deranged. *m.* (*fam.*) "crank."
fissatore *m.* fixer, fixative.
fissazione *f.* fixation; delusion.
fis'sile *adj.* fissionable.
fissità *f.* fixity, steadiness.
fisso *adj.* fixed, steady; firm; regular.
fi'stola *f.* fistula.
fitta *f.* stitch, sharp pain.
fitti'zio *adj.* fictitious.
fitto (*1*) *m.* lease; rent.
fitto (*2*) *m.*, *adj.* thick: a capo —, headlong.
fitto (*3*) *adj.* driven in. *pp.* of figgere.
fiumana *f.* stream, flow.
fiume *m.* river; (*fig.*) flow.
fiutare *vt.* to smell, sniff; to scent.
fiuto *m.* smell, scent.
flac'cido *adj.* flabby, flaccid.
flacone *m.* vial, bottle.
flagello *m.* scourge; plague.

flagrante *adj.* flagrant: in —, red-handed.
flanella *f.* flannel.
flan'gia *f.* flange.
fla'uto *m.* flute.
fle'bile *adj.* feeble, weak; thin.
flemma *f.* phlegm, coolness.
flemma'tico *adj.* phlegmatic, cool, self-possessed.
flessi'bile *adj.* flexible.
flesso *pp.* of flettere.
flessuoso *adj.* flexuous.
flet'tere *vt.* [64] to flex.
flora *f.* flora.
Flora, Francesco, Italian author and essayist (1891–).
floreale *adj.* floral.
flo'rido *adj.* florid; flourishing.
flo'scio *adj.* flabby; soft.
flotta *f.* fleet; navy.
flotti'glia *f.* flotilla.
fluente *adj.* flowing.
fluido *m.*, *adj.* fluid.
fluire *vi.* to flow.
fluorescente *adj.* fluorescent.
fluori'drico *adj.* hydrofluoric.
fluoro *m.* fluorine.
fluoruro *m.* fluoride.
flussione *f.* fluxion.
flusso *m.* flux, flow.
flutto *m.* wave.
fluttuante *adj.* fluctuating; floating.
fluttuare *vi.* to fluctuate.
fluttuazione *f.* fluctuation; flutter.
fluviale *adj.* fluvial, river.
fobi'a *f.* phobia.
foca *f.* seal; sealskin.
focac'cia *f.* cake, bun; rendere pan per —, to pay in one's own coin.
foca'ia (pietra) *f.* flint.
focale *adj.* focal.
foce *f.* mouth.
fochista *m.* stocker.
focola'io *m.* (*pathol.*) focus; (*fig.*) hot-bed.
focolare *m.* hearth, fireside; home; furnace.
focoso *adj.* fiery; high-spirited.
fo'dera *f.* lining; case.
foderare *vt.* to line; to cover (*with*); to upholster.
foderato *adj.* lined.
fo'dero *m.* scabbard, sheath.
foga *f.* dash, heat; vehemence.
Fogazzaro, Antonio, Italian novelist, *Piccolo Mondo Antico* (1842–1911).
fog'gia *f.* shape; manner; pattern, fashion.
foggiare *vt.* to shape, fashion.
fo'glia *f.* leaf (*pl.* leaves); petal, foil; oro in foglie, gold leaf; mangiare la —, to get wise.
fogliame *m.* foliage.
fo'glio *m.* sheet; newspaper.

fogna f. drain, sewer.
fognatura f. sewerage.
fo'laga f. coot.
folata f. blast, gust.
folgorare vt. to strike down; (fig.) to paralyze. vi. to flash.
fol'gore f. thunderbolt.
folla f. crowd, throng; host.
folle m., f. lunatic; (mach.) neutral. adj. insane: in — (mach.) in neutral.
follemente adv. madly.
folletto m. goblin.
folli'a f. madness, lunacy; folly.
folto m., adj. thick.
fomentare vt. to foment.
fonda, (alla) f. at anchor.
fon'daco m. store; warehouse.
fondale m. bottom; (theat.) back cloth.
fondamenta f.pl. foundation.
fondamentale adj. fundamental.
fondamentalmente adv. fundamentally, basically.
fondamento m. foundation; ground; (pl.) elements.
fondare vt. to found; to build (up); to establish; to base, ground; **fondarsi** vr. to ground, rest (upon); to rely (on).
fondatezza f. groundedness.
fondato adj. well-founded; legitimate.
fondatore m. founder.
fondazione f. foundation.
fon'dere vt.,“ **fon'dersi** vr. to melt; to blend.
fonderi'a f. foundry, smeltery.
fondina f. holster; soup plate.
fonditore m. melter, smelter.
fondo m. bottom; fund; end; ground, background; property, land; (pl.) grounds, dregs; funds, money: — **dei calzoni**, seat; — **di cassa**, cash on hand; **fondi di magazzino**, unsold stocks; **bassi fondi**, shallows; slums; **dar** — **a**, to exhaust; **in —**, after all. adj. deep.
fone'tica f. phonetics.
fone'tico adj. phonetic.
fono'grafo m. phonograph.
fonogramma m. phonogram.
fontana f. fountain.
fontaniere m. water gauger.
fonte f. spring; fountain; source: **sapere da — accreditata**, to know from a reliable source.
fonte battesimale m. (baptismal) font.
forag'gio m. fodder, forage.
fora'neo adj. rural; outer.
forare vt. to hole, bore; to punch (a ticket); to puncture (a tire).
foratura f. boring; puncture.
for'bici f.pl. scissors; (zool.) pincers.
forbire vt. to furbish, polish; **forbirsi** vr. to wipe oneself.
forbito adj. polished; lofty.

forca f. fork, pitchfork; gallows: **mandare sulla —**, to send to the devil; **fare — a**, to cross, thwart.
forcella f. fork; hairpin.
forchetta f. fork.
forchettata f. forkful.
forchettone m. carving fork.
forcina f. hairpin.
for'cipe m. forceps (pl.).
forcone m. pitchfork.
forcuto adj. forked.
forense adj. forensic.
foresta f. forest.
forestale adj. forestal: **guardia —**, forester.
foresteri'a f. guest chambers.
forestiero m. stranger; foreigner; guest. adj. foreign.
for'fora f. dandruff.
for'gia f. forge, smithy.
forgiare vt. to forge.
foriero adj. forerunning.
forma f. form, shape; outline; mold; way, manner; last (for shoes); hat block; cheesecake.
formag'gio m. cheese.
formale adj. formal.
formalità f. formality.
formalizzarsi vr. to take exception (to), be shocked (at).
formalmente adv. formally.
formare vt. to form; to shape, mold; to train; **formarsi** vr. to form; to grow.
formato m. shape; size; format. adj. formed, shaped, molded; made; grown; developed.
formazione f. formation; (aeron.) flight.
formica f. ant.
formica'io m. anthill; swarm.
formichiere m. anteater.
formicolare vi. to swarm (with); to creep.
formicoli'o m. creeping sensation; swarming.
formida'bile adj. formidable.
formoso adj. stalwart; (f.) buxom.
for'mula f. formula.
formulare vt. to formulate.
formula'rio m. formulary.
fornace f. furnace; kiln.
forna'io m. baker.
fornello m. stove, kitchen range; pipe bowl; chamber (of a mine).
fornire vt. to furnish, supply (with); to cater to; to equip (with); to endow (with).
fornitore m. purveyor; tradesman; dealer; caterer; chandler.
fornitura f. supply.
forno m. furnace; kiln; oven; bakery; (theat.) empty house, poor attendance, absent treatment: **al —**, baked.

foro (*1*) *m.* hole.

foro (*2*) *m.* forum; bar; jurisdiction.

forse *m.* doubt: mettere in —, to doubt, question. *adv.* perhaps, maybe; probably.

forsennato *m.* maniac.

forte *m.* fort; strong point, forte; sourness. *adj.* strong; sturdy; proficient; firm, steady; brave; loud; sour; heavy: prestar man —, to help; è più — di me, I can't stand it; I can't help it. *adv.* hard, strongly; loudly; fast.

fortemente *adv.* strongly; deeply; highly; loudly; hard.

fortezza *f.* strength; fortress.

fortificare *vt.* to fortify.

fortificazione *f.* fortification.

fortino *m.* blockhouse, outpost.

fortis'simo *adj.sup.* most powerful; extremely loud.

fortu'ito *adj.* fortuitous.

fortuna *f.* luck; chance, lot; success; fortune, property; **campo di —,** emergency landing field; **atterraggio di —,** forced landing; **per —,** luckily.

fortunale *m.* storm, tempest.

fortunatamente *adv.* fortunately, luckily.

fortunato *adj.* lucky; happy; successful.

fortunoso *adj.* eventful; stormy.

forun'colo *m.* furuncle, boil.

foruncolosi *f.* furunculosis.

forza *f.* strength, power, might; force; violence: **— pubblica,** police; **a —,** by force, agire per —, to act in spite of oneself; **a — di,** by dint of; **per forza!** of course!; **per amore o per —,** by hook or by crook; **di prima —,** first-rate.

forzare *vt.* to force; to compel; to break open; to strain: **— un blocco,** to run a blockade.

forzatamente *adv.* by compulsion, perforce; unwillingly.

forzato *m.* convict. *adj.* forced; broken open; compulsory: **lavori forzati,** penal servitude.

forziere *m.* safe.

forzoso *adj.* forced, compulsory.

forzuto *adj.* strong, sinewy.

Foscari, Francesco, Doge of Venice (1373–1457).

foschi'a *f.* mist, fog.

fosco *adj.* dark, gloomy, dim.

Foscolo, Ugo, Italian poet and patriot, *I Sepolcri* (1778–1827).

fosforescente *adj.* phosphorescent.

fosfo'rico *adj.* phosphoric.

fo'sforo *m.* phosphorus.

fosfuro *m.* phosphide.

fossa *f.* pit, hole; grave: del senno di poi son piene le fosse, hindsight is easier than foresight.

fossato *m.* ditch.

fossetta *f.* dimple.

fos'sile *m.,* *adj.* fossil: **carbon —,** mineral coal.

fossilizzare *vt.,* **fossilizzarsi** *vr.* to fossilize.

fosso *m.* ditch.

fotoelettrico *adj.* photoelectric.

fotoge'nico *adj.* photogenic.

fotografare *vt.* to photograph.

fotografi'a *f.* photograph, photo; photography; snapshot.

fotogra'fico *adj.* photographic.

foto'grafo *m.* photographer.

fotogramma *m.* still; frame.

fotoincisione *f.* photogravure.

fotolitografi'a *f.* photolithography.

fotometri'a *f* photometry.

fotome'trico *adj.* photometric.

foto'metro *m.* photometer, exposure meter.

fra (*1*) *prep.* in, within; between; among; amid: **— l'altro,** by the way; **— sè,** to oneself.

fra (*2*) *see* **frate.**

frac *m.* tails.

fracassare *vt.,* **fracassarsi** *vr.* to smash, shatter, crash.

fracasso *m.* crash; racket.

fra'dicio *adj.* rotten; sodden: **ubriaco —,** blind drunk.

fra'gile *adj.* fragile, brittle; frail.

fragilità *f.* brittleness, frailty.

fra'gola *f.* strawberry.

fragore *m.* din, rattle.

fragoroso *adj.* noisy.

fragorosamente *adv.* noisily.

fragrante *adj.* fragrant.

fragranza *f.* fragrance.

frainten'dere *vt.* to misunderstand, get wrong.

frammassone *m.* freemason.

frammassoneri'a *f.* freemasonry.

frammenta'rio *adj.* fragmentary.

frammento *m.* fragment, scrap.

frana *f.* landslide, landslip.

franare *vt.* to slide, crumble.

francamente *adv.* frankly.

Francesca, della, Piero, Umbrian painter (1406?–1492).

francese *m.* Frenchman; French (*language*). *f.* Frenchwoman. *adj.* French.

francesismo *m.* gallicism.

franchezza *f.* frankness.

franchi'gia *f* franchise; leave: **in — duty-free; post-free.**

franco (*1*) *adj.* frank, open; outspoken; firm: **porto —,** free port; **— di porto,** free delivery.

franco (*2*) *m.* (*coin*) franc.

francobollo *m.* postage stamp, stamp.

frangente *m.* breaker; emergency, difficulty.

frangere *vt.*[44] **fran'gersi** *vr.* to break.

fran'gia *f.* fringe.

frangiflutti *m.* breakwater.

franto *pp.of* frangere.

franto'io *m.* oilpress; oil mill.

frantumare *vt.*, **frantumarsi** *vr.* to shatter, smash, crush.

frantumi *m.pl.* fragments, smithereens: andare in —, to shatter.

frapporre *vt.* to interpose, insert; **frapporsi** *vr.* to interfere, intrude.

frasa'rio *m.* language, jargon.

frasca *f.* branch: saltare di palo in —, to ramble, speak desultorily.

frase *f.* phrase, sentence: —fatta, commonplace.

fraseologi'a *f.* phraseology.

fras'sino *m.* ash, ash tree.

frastagliare *vt.* to slit; to make jagged.

frastagliato *adj.* slit, split, indented, jagged; uneven.

frastornare *vt.* to disturb.

frastuono *m.* din, racket.

frate *m.* friar, monk, brother.

fratellanza *f.* brotherhood; brotherliness.

fratellastro *m.* half-brother.

fratello *m.* brother; **fratelli** *pl.* brothers; (*friars*) brethren: fratelli di latte, foster brothers; fratelli gemelli, twins; fratelli siamesi, Siamese twins.

fraternità *f.* fraternity.

fraternizzare *vi.* to fraternize.

fraterno *adj.* fraternal, brotherly.

fratricida *m.* fratricide. *adj.* fratricidal.

fratrici'dio *m.* fratricide.

fratta *f.* bush; hedge.

fratta'glie *f.pl.* pluck.

frattanto *adv.* meanwhile.

frattempo, (nel) *adv.* meanwhile.

frattura *f.* fracture; breach.

fratturare *vt.*, **fratturarsi** *vr.* to fracture, break.

fraudolento *adj.* fraudulent.

fraudolenza *f.* fraudulence.

frazionamento *m.* fractionization.

frazionare *vt.* to fractionize.

faziona'rio *adj.* fractional.

frazione *f.* fraction; hamlet.

frec'cia *f.* arrow, dart; hand (*of a watch*); pointer; needle (*of a compass*).

frecciata *f.* thrust; gibe.

freddamente *adv.* coldly.

freddare *vt.* to kill.

freddezza *f.* coldness.

freddo *m.* cold; cold weather. *adj.* cold, chilly; unemotional; avere, fare —, to be cold; a —, deliberately; sangue —, courage; a sangue —, cold-bloodedly.

freddoloso *adj.* chilly, sensitive to cold, cold-blooded.

freddura *f.* funny story; pun.

freddurista *m.* punster.

fregagione *m.* rubbing, massage.

fregare *vt.* to rub; (*lt. slang*) to cheat, lick; to outwit, outdo; (*school jargon*) to pluck; **fregarsene** (*lt. slang*), not to care a rap.

fregata *f.* frigate; (*ornith.*) frigatebird; (*lt. slang*) cheat, plant, crooked deal.

fregiare *vt.* to decorate.

fre'gio *m.* frieze, decoration.

frego *m.* line, stroke.

fre'gola *f.* rut; breeding time; (*fig.*) lust.

fremente *adj.* quivering, throbbing; thrilled.

fre'mere *vi.* to quiver; to shudder, shake; to thrill, be thrilled; to fume, fret: — dal desiderio di, to long for.

fre'mito *m.* thrill; shudder.

frenare *vt.* to brake; to control; to check, curb, restrain; **frenarsi** *vr.* to control oneself, check oneself.

frenata *f.* check, braking.

frenatore *m.* brakeman.

frenatura *f.* braking.

frenello *m.* (*naut.*) tiller line.

frenesi'a *f.* frenzy; craze.

freneticamente *adv.* frenziedly, wildly.

frene'tico *adj.* frenzied.

fre'nico *adj.* (*anat.*) phrenic.

freno *m.* brake; control, check, restraint: tenere a —, to keep in check; stringere i freni (*fig.*), to rein in; mordere il —, to champ at the bit.

frequentare *vt.* to frequent; to patronize; to attend; to associate with.

frequentatore *m.* patron, customer; constant visitor.

frequente *adj.* frequent; di —, frequently: polso —, throbbing pulse.

frequenza *f.* frequency; attendance.

fresa *f.* fraise, countersink.

fresare *vt.* to fraise, to countersink.

fresatrice *f.* milling machine.

fresatura *f.* fraising.

freschezza *f.* freshness.

fresco *m.* cool, coolness. *adj.* fresh; cool: far —, to be cool; stai —! now you are in for it!; forget it!

Frescobaldi, Girolamo, Italian organist and composer (1583–1644).

frescura *f.* coolness.

fretta *f.* haste, hurry: aver —, to be in a hurry; fate in —! hurry up!

frettolosamente *adv.* hastily.

frettoloso *adj.* hasty; rash.

fria'bile *adj.* friable.

friabilità *f.* friability.
frig'gere *vt.*[67] to fry. *vi.* to fry; to hiss; to sizzle; to fret; to fume.
frigidezza, frigidità *f.* frigidity.
fri'gido *adj.* frigid.
fri'gio *m.*, *adj.* Phrygian.
frignare *vi.* to whimper.
frigori'fero *m.* refrigerator.
fringuello *m.* chaffinch.
frinire *vi.* to chirp.
frittata *f.* omelet: far la) — (*fig.*), to make a mess of it.
frittella *f.* fritter.
fritto *adj.* fried. *pp. of* friggere.
frittura *f.* fry.
frivolezza *f.* frivolity.
fri'volo *adj.* frivolous, trifling.
frizione *f.* rubbing, massage; (*mach.*) clutch; friction.
frizzante *adj.* sparkling, racy.
frizzare *vt.* to sparkle.
frizzo *m.* witticism.
frodare *vt.* to cheat, swindle.
frode *f.* swindle, cheat.
frodo *m.* smuggling: cacciar di —, to poach; cacciatore di —, poacher.
fro'gia *f.* nostril (*of a horse*).
frollo *adj.* high; tender: pasta frolla, puff paste.
fronde *f.pl.* foliage.
frondoso *adj.* leafy.
frontale *adj.* frontal.
fronte (1) *f.* forehead; front, façade: far — a, to face; to meet; corrugare la —, to frown; di — a, facing; opposite.
fronte (2) *m.* front: dietro front! about face!; — a destra! right face!
fronteggiare *vt.* to face; to meet; to cope (*with*).
frontespi'zio *m.* title page.
frontiera *f.* frontier, border.
fron'zolo *m.* bauble, gewgaw.
frotta *f.* crowd, swarm; flock.
frot'tola *f.* fib, humbug.
frugale *adj.* spare, meager; frugal.
frugalità *f.* frugality.
frugare *vt.*, *vi.* to search, rummage.
fru'golo *m.* imp.
fruire *vt.* to enjoy.
frullare *vt.* to beat, whip. *vi.* to flutter; to whirl.
frullino *m.* whisk: — elettrico, blender, mixer.
frumento *m.* wheat.
frumentone *m.* maize.
frusciare *vi.* to rustle.
frusci'o *m.* rustle, rustling.
frusta *f.* whip; scourge; lash.
frustare *vt.* to whip, lash; to wear; frustarsi *vr.* to wear.
frustata *f.* lash.
frustino *m.* riding whip.
frusto *adj.* worn; threadbare.

frustrare *vt.* to frustrate.
frutta *f.* (*sing.*, *coll.*, *pl.*) fruit, fruits.
fruttare *vt.* to yield, produce, bring. *vi.* to bring profit, pay.
frutteto *m.* orchard
frutticultore *m.* fruit grower.
fruttiera *f.* fruit dish.
frutti'fero *adj.* fructiferous; interest-bearing; profitable.
fruttificare *vi.* to fructify; to yield profit.
fruttiven'dolo *m.* fruiterer.
frutto *m.* fruit; result; profit.
fruttuoso *adj.* fruitful, profitable; successful.
fu *adj.* late (*deceased*).
fucilare *vt.* to shoot.
fucilata *f.* rifle shot; rifle report.
fucilazione *f.* execution (*by shooting*).
fucile *m.* gun; rifle.
fuciliere *m.* rifleman.
fucina *f.* forge, smithy.
fuc'sia *f.* fuchsia.
fuga *f.* flight, escape; leak; leakage; (*mus.*) fugue.
fugace *adj* fleeting; passing.
fugare *vt.* to put to flight, rout; to dispel.
fugge'vole *adj.* fleeting.
fuggevolmente *adv.* fleetingly.
fuggiasco *m.*, *adj.* fugitive, runaway.
fuggifuggi *m.* stampede.
fuggire *vt.* to avoid; to escape. *vi.* to flee, run away, take flight; to fly, speed (*away, along*).
fulcro *m.* fulcrum (*pl.* fulcra); (*fig.*) pivot.
fulgente *adj.* fulgent, shining.
ful'gido *adj.* refulgent, shining.
fulgore *m.* refulgence, sparkle.
fulig'gine *f.* soot.
fuligginoso *adj.* sooty.
fulmicotone *m.* guncotton.
fulminante *adj.* fulminant.
fulminare *vt.* to strike (*by lightning*); to fulminate; to flash. *vi.* to thunder; fulminarsi *vr.* to burn out.
ful'mine *m* thunderbolt, lightning, flash: un — a ciel sereno, a bolt out of the blue.
fulmi'neo *adj.* lightning-swift; sudden; flashing.
fulvo *adj.* tawny.
fumaiuolo *m.* funnel, smokestack.
fumante *adj.* smoking; steaming.
fumare *vt.*, *vi.* to smoke; to steam; to fume.
fumata *f.* smoke; smoke signal.
fumatore *m.* smoker.
fumetti *m.pl.* strips, comics.
fumigare *vt.* to smoke; to steam.
fumista *m.* stove repairer; (*liter.*) mystificator.
fumisteri'a *f.* (*liter.*) mystification.

fumo *m.* smoke; vapor, steam; smoking. **fumi** *pl.* fumes.

fumoso *adj.* smoky.

funambolismo *m.* rope dancing.

funam'bolo *m.* rope dancer; aerialist.

fune *f.* rope; cable.

fu'nebre *adj.* funeral.

funerale *m.* funeral.

funera'rio *adj.* funeral.

fune'reo *adj.* funereal, dismal.

funestare *vt.* to sadden; to ruin.

funesto *adj.* ominous, fatal, tragic; baneful.

funga'ia *f.* mushroom bed; swarm.

fun'gere *vi.* to act, serve (*as*).

fungo *m.* fungus; mushroom.

fungosità *f.* fungosity.

fungoso *adj.* fungous.

funicolare *f.* funicular railway.

funivi'a *f.* telpher.

funzionamento *m.* working.

funzionare *vi.* to work, run, operate; to act (*as*).

funziona'rio *m.* official, executive.

funzione *f.* function; office, duty; (*eccles.*) service.

fuoco *m.* fire; fireplace; heat; focus: **fuochiartificiali,** fire works; **— fatuo,** will-o'-the-wisp; **far — (contro),** to fire (*at*); **mettere a —,** to [focus.

fuorchè *prep.* except.   [focus.

fuori *prep.* out, beyond, off. *adv.* out, outside, off; abroad; **— servizio,** off duty; **out** of commission; **— gioco,** offside; **— di sè,** beside oneself; **il di —,** the outside; **all'infuori di,** except.

fuoribordo *m.* outboard-motor boat. *adv.* outboard.

fuoruscito *m.* refugee.

furbacchione *m.* slyboots.

furberi'a *f.* cunning; subtlety.

furbi'zia *f.* cunning, cleverness.

furbo *adj.* sly, cunning.

furente *adj.* furious.

fureri'a *f.* company headquarters.

furetto *m.* (*zool.*) ferret.

furfante *m.* knave; racketeer.

furfanteri'a *f.* knavery, racketeering.

furgoncino *m.* van.

furgone *m.* wagon.

fu'ria *f.* fury, wrath; vehemence; hurry: **andare su tutte le furie,** to fly off the handle; **aver —,** to be in a hurry; **in fretta e —,** hurry-scurry; **a — di,** by dint of.

furibondo *adj.* furious, wild.

furiere *m.* quartermaster.

furiosamente *adv.* furiously.

furioso *adj.* furious, wild: **pazzo —,** raving lunatic.

furore *m.* fury, wrath; vehemence; frenzy: **far —,** to make a hit; to be the rage.

furoreggiare *vi.* to be the rage.

furtivamente *adv.* stealthily.

furtivo *adj.* stealthy, surreptitious.

furto *m.* theft, larceny: **— con scasso,** housebreaking.

fuscello *m.* twig; (*fig.*) slip.

fusciacca *f.* sash.

fusello *m.* bobbin; axle spindle.

fusi'bile *m.* fuse. *adj.* fusible.

fusione *f.* fusion, melting; casting; blending; (*comm.*) amalgamation.

fuso (*1*) *m.* spindle; distaff; shaft; shank: **— orario,** time zone; **far le fusa,** to purr.

fuso (*2*) *adj.* fused; melted; blended, cast. *pp. of* **fondere.**

fusoliera *f.* (*aeron.*) fuselage.

fustagno *m.* fustian.

fustella *f.* hollow punch.

fustigare *vt.* to flog; to scourge.

fustigazione *f.* scourging.

fusto *m.* trunk, stalk; shaft; bar; frame; barrel, cask; (*it. slang*) burly young fellow, "husky"; boy friend.

fu'tile *adj.* futile, trifling.

futilità *f.* futility; trifle.

futurismo *m.* futurism.

futurista *m., adj.* futurist.

futuro *m.* future. *adj.* future, coming, to come: **il — presidente,** the president to be.

G

gabbamondo *m.* swindler.

gabbano *m.* gaberdine, frock.

gabbare *vt.* to cheat, impose upon.

gab'bia *f.* cage; (*naut.*) top: **vela di —,** main topsail.

gabbiano *m.* gull.

gabbiere *m.* (*naut.*) topman.

gabbo *m.* fun: **pigliare a —,** to make fun of; to make light of.

gabella *f.* (*fiscal*) duty.

gabellare *vt.* to palm off (*on*).

gabelliere *m.* exciseman.

gabinetto *m.* cabinet; laboratory; consulting room; study, den; closet; water closet: **— di lettura,** reading room; **— da bagno,** bathroom.

gaffa *f.* (*naut.*) gaff, hook.

gagà *m.* (*it. slang*) fop, dandy, dude.

gaggi'a *f.* (*bot.*) acacia, mimosa.

gagliardetto *m.* pennon.

gagliardi'a *f.* stalwartness.

gagliardo *adj.* powerful; stalwart.

gaglioffo *m.* knave, rascal.

gaiamente *adv.* gaily.

gaiezza *f.* gaiety.

gaio *adj.* gay, merry; gaudy.

gala *f.* gala; frill.

galalite *f.* casein plastic.

galante *adj.* courtly, flattering: donna —, wanton.

galanteri'a *f.* courtliness; flattery; beauty; daintiness.

galantina *f.* galantine.

galantuomo *m.* honest man, gentleman; (*fig.*) fellow.

galas'sia *f.* galaxy.

galateo *m.* politeness, manners; treatise on good manners.

galena *f.* (*min.*) galena; (*radio*) crystal.

galenista *m.* (*med.*) Galenist.

galeone *m.* galleon.

galeotto *m.* convict; galley slave.

galera *f.* (*naut.*) galley; jail; (*fig.*) hell: pezzo di —, jailbird.

Galilei, Galileo, great Italian astronomer and philosopher, *Dialogo sopra i due massimi sistemi* (1564-1642).

galla *f.* (*bot.*) gall.

galla, (a) *adv.* afloat: venire a galla, to come to the surface.

galleggiamento *m.* floating.

galleggiante *m.* float; *adj.* buoyant, floating.

galleggiare *vi.* to float.

galleri'a *f.* gallery; tunnel; (*theat.*) balcony: prima —, dress circle; seconda —, balcony.

gallese *m.* Welshman. *f.* Welshwoman; Welsh (*language*). *adj.* Welsh.

galletta *f.* hardtack.

galletto *m.* cockerel; (*mach.*) wing bolt: fare il —, to swagger.

gallina *f.* hen: zampe di — (*fig.*), scrawls.

gallo (1) *m.* cock, rooster: fare il —, to strut.

gallo (2) *m.* Gaul.

gallone (1) *m.* chevron, stripe.

gallone (2) *m.* gallon.

galoppare *vi.* to gallop.

galoppata *f.* gallop.

galoppato'io *m.* riding (*ground*).

galoppatore *m.* galloper.

galoppino *m.* runner; errandboy; canvasser.

galoppo *m.* gallop.

galo'scia *f.* galosh, overshoe.

Galvani, Luigi, Italian discoverer of galvanism (1737-1798).

galva'nico *adj.* galvanic.

galvanizzare *vt.* to galvanize.

galvano *m.* (*typ.*) electrotype.

galvanopla'stica, *f.* galvanoplasty, electrotyping.

galvanopla'stico *adj.* galvanoplastic.

gamba *f.* leg: darsela a gambe, to show a clean pair of heels; andare a gambe levate, to fall head over heels; prendere sotto —, to make light of; essere in —, to be all right, to be a "corker."

gambale *m.* legging; puttee.

gamberetto *m.* shrimp.

gam'bero *m.* crawfish: fare come i gamberi, to go backwards.

gambo *m.* stem, stalk; shaft.

gamella *f.* (*mil.*) messtin.

gamma *f.* gamut; gamma.

gana'scia *f.* jaw.

gan'cio *m.* hook; clasp; grapple.

ganga *f.* gangue.

gan'ghero *m.* hinge: uscire dai gangheri, to fly off the handle.

gan'glio *m.* ganglion (*pl.* ganglia).

ganzo *m.* paramour, lover, beau.

gara *f.* competition, contest; match, race; fare a —, to vie.

garante *m.* guarantor, guarantee.

garantire *vt.* to guarantee; to assure; to promise.

garanzi'a *f.* guaranty; security.

garbare *vi.* to suit, please: non mi garba, I don't like.

garbatamente *adv.* politely.

garbatezza *f.* politeness.

garbato *m.* polite; graceful.

garbo *m.* politeness; grace; shape, fashion.

garbu'glio *m.* tangle; mess.

gareggiare *vi.* to vie, compete.

garetta *f.* sentrybox.

garetto *m.* hock; ankle.

garganella *f.* gullet: bere a —, to gulp down.

gargarismo *m.* gargling; gargle.

gargarizzare *vt.*, gargarizzarsi *vr.* to gargle.

gargarozzo *m.* throat.

Garibaldi, Giuseppe, Italian patriot and general; leader of the expedition of *The Thousand* (1807-1882).

garitta *f.* sentrybox.

garo'fano *m.* pink, carnation: chiodi di —, cloves.

garrese *m.* withers (*pl.*).

garretto *see* garetto.

garrire *vi.* to warble; to wave (*as flags*).

garrito *m.* warble.

gar'rulo *adj.* garrulous.

garza *f.* gauze.

garzare *vt.* to teasel.

garzo *m.* teasel.

garzone *m.* shopboy; stableboy.

gas *m.* gas, vapor; firedamp.

gasificare *vt.* to gasify.

gasista *m.* gasfitter, gasman.

gas(s)o'geno *m.* gazogene.

gas(s)o'metro *m.* gasometer, gas holder.

gas(s)oso *adj.* gassy.

ga'strico *adj.* gastric.

gastronomi'a *f.* gastronomy.

gatta f. she-cat, tabby; puss; — ci cova, something is brewing.

gattamorta f. unfeeling woman.

gatto m. cat, tomcat.

gatton gattoni adv. on all fours; stealthily.

gattopardo m. serval.

gaudente m., adj. epicurean.

gau'dio m. joy, happiness.

gavetta f. messtin: venire dalla —, to rise from the ranks, to be a self-made man.

gazza f. magpie.

gazzarra f. uproar; riot.

gazzella f. gazelle.

gazzetta f. gazette.

gazzettino m. bulletin; newsmonger.

gelare vt., vi. to freeze: mi si gela il sangue, my blood runs cold.

gelata f. frost.

gelateri'a f. ice-cream parlor.

gelatiera f. ice-cream freezer.

gelatiere m. ice-cream vendor.

gelatina f. jelly; aspic; (chem.) gelatine.

gelatinoso adj. gelatinous.

gelato m. ice cream. adj. frozen.

gelidamente adv. icily.

ge'lido adj. icy, ice-cold.

gelo m. frost; frostiness.

gelone m. chilblain.

gelosi'a (1) f. jealousy.

gelosi'a (2) f. blind, shutter (of a window).

geloso adj. jealous.

gelso m. mulberry.

gelsomino m. jasmine.

gemebondo adj. moaning, plaintive.

gemello m., adj. twin; gemelli pl. cuff links, studs; (astr.) Gemini, the Twins.

ge'mere vi. to groan, moan.

ge'mito m. moan; howl.

gemma f. gem; (bot.) bud.

gendarme m. gendarme.

genealogi'a f. pedigree, genealogy.

genealo'gico adj. genealogical.

generale m., adj. general: — di Brigata, brigadier general; — di Divisione, major general; — di Corpo d'Armata, lieutenant general; — d'Armata, general; in —, generally; as a rule.

generalità f. generality: le —, the personal data.

generalizzare vt., vi. to generalize.

generalmente adv. generally; as a rule.

generare vt. to generate.

generatore m. generator.

generazione f. generation.

ge'nere m. kind, sort; genus; gender: il — umano, mankind; generi diversi, assorted articles: generi ali-

mentari, foodstuff; in —, generally speaking; as a rule.

gene'rico m. (theat.) utility man. adj. generic; vague.

ge'nero m. son-in-law.

generosità f. generosity.

generoso adj. generous.

ge'nesi f. genesis.

gene'tica f. genetics.

genetli'aco m. birthday.

gengiva f. gum.

gengivale adj. gingival.

geni'a f. breed; covey.

geniale adj. ingenious; clever.

genialità f. ingeniousness, cleverness; race.

genialo'ide m. man of unfulfilled, undisciplined, genius.

geniere m. (mil.) engineer.

ge'nio (1) m. genius (pl. geniuses); genius (pl. genii); talent, gift: andare a —, to be to one's liking.

ge'nio (2) m. (mil.) corps of engineers; municipal engineering department.

genitivo m., adj. genitive.

genitore m., **genitrice** f. parent: i genitori, parents.

genna'io m. January.

genta'glia f. scum, rabble.

gente f. people, folk; folks; race.

gentildonna f. lady, gentlewoman.

gentile m. gentile, pagan. adj. kind, nice; soft; polite: il gentil sesso, the fair sex.

Gentile, Giovanni, Italian philosopher and politician (1875–1943).

gentilezza f. kindness; politeness; favor; gracefulness; obligingness: per —, if you please, if you don't mind.

gentili'zio adj. nobiliary; armorial.

gentilmente adv. kindly.

gentiluomo m. gentleman; nobleman.

genuflessione f. genuflection.

genuflesso adj. kneeling.

genuflet'tersi vr. to kneel down.

genuino adj. genuine, real.

genziana f. gentian.

geografi'a f. geography.

geogra'fico adj. geographical.

geo'grafo m. geographer.

geologi'a f. geology.

geolo'gico adj. geological.

geo'logo m. geologist.

geo'metra m. land surveyor.

geometri'a f. geometry.

geome'trico adj. geometric.

gera'nio m. geranium.

gerarca m. hierarch; leader.

gerarchi'a f. hierarchy.

gerar'chico adj. hierarchical.

gerente m. manager, operator; editor.

gerenza f. management; editorship.

gergo m. jargon, slang.

gerla *f.* basket.
germano (*1*) *m.* brother-german. *adj.* german.
germano (*2*) *m.* (*ornith.*) mallard.
germe *m.* germ; seed; embryo.
germinare *vt.*, *vi.* to germinate.
germogliare *vt.*, *vi.* to shoot, sprout; (*fig.*) to issue.
germo'glio *m.* sprout, bud.
gerogli'fico *m.* hieroglyph.
gerun'dio *m.* gerund.
gessare *vt.* to plaster; to chalk.
gesso *m.* chalk; (*chem.*) gypsum; plaster; plaster cast.
gessoso *adj.* chalky, plastery.
gesta *f. pl.*, *sing.* exploit, deed, a- chievement.
gestante *f.* woman in childbirth.
gestazione *f.* gestation.
gesticolare *vi.* to gesticulate.
gestione *f.* management.
gestire *vi.* to operate, manage, run. *vi.* to gesticulate, gesture.
gesto *m.* gesture; attitude.
gestore *m.* operator; (*rail.*) traffic manager.
Gesù *m.* Jesus.
gesuita *m.* Jesuit.
gettare *vt.* to throw, cast, fling; to toss; to shoot; to send forth; get- tarsi *vr.* to throw, fling oneself; to rush; to flow (*out*, *into*): gettarsi in ginocchio, to fall on one's knees.
gettata *f.* jetty; cast; layer.
gettato *adj.* thrown; wasted.
get'tito *m.* flow; revenue, income.
getto *m.* throw, throwing; spurt, gush; jet; shoot; cast, casting; ejecta (*pl.*); discharge: di —, at a stretch; a — continuo, uninter- ruptedly.
gettone *m.* counter, chip; check; tag.
ghepardo *m.* cheetah.
gheri'glio *m.* kernel.
gherlino *m.* (*naut.*) warp.
gherminella *f.* stratagem, trick; mis- chief.
ghermire *vt.* to clutch; to seize.
gherone *m.* gusset.
ghetta *f.* spat, gaiter; (*mil.*) legging.
ghiaccia'ia *f.* icebox.
ghiaccia'io *m.* glacier.
ghiacciare *vt.*, *vi.* ghiacciarsi *vr.* to freeze; sentirsi ghiacciare il sangue, to feel one's blood run cold.
ghiacciata *f.* iced drink.
ghiacciato *adj.* frozen; icy; iced.
ghiac'cio *m.* ice; frost: farsi di —, to freeze. *adj.* icy.
ghiacciuolo *m.* icicle; flaw (*in a gem*).
ghia'ia *f.* gravel.
ghianda *f.* (*bot.*) acorn.
ghianda'ia *f.* (*ornith.*) jay.
ghiera *f.* ferrule.

ghigliottina *f.* guillotine; sash.
ghigliottinare *vt.* to guillotine.
ghigna *f.* (*evil*) face.
ghignare *vi.* to grin, sneer.
ghigno *m.* grin, smirk.
ghinea *f.* guinea.
ghin'gheri, (in) *adv.* in gorgeous attire, dressed up.
ghiotto *adj.* gluttonous; eager (*for*); appetizing.
ghiottone *m.* glutton.
ghiottoneri'a *f.* gluttony; dainty, deli- cacy.
ghiozzo *m.* miller's thump.
ghirba *f.* skin.
ghiribizzo *m.* whim, freak.
ghirigoro *m.* flourish, curlicue.
ghirlanda *f.* garland, wreath.
Ghirlandaio, il (*Domenico di Tommaso Bigordi*) Florentine painter (1449- 1494).
ghiro *m.* dormouse (*pl.* dormice).
ghisa *f.* cast iron.
già *adv.* already; once, formerly, pre- viously: il caso — citato, the above (*mentioned*) case; eh, già! of course!
giacca *f.* jacket, coat.
giacchè *conj.* since, as; for.
giacchetta *f.* jacket.
giacente *adj.* in abeyance; unclaimed.
giacenza *f.* abeyance; unsold stock; demurrage.
giacere *vi.*[48] to lie; to be situated; to find oneself.
giaci'glio *m.* bed, cot.
giacimento *m.* layer, bed.
giacinto *m.* hyacinth.
giaciuto *pp.of* giacere.
Giacosa, Giuseppe, Italian dramatist and poet, *Come le foglie*, *Partita a scacchi* (1847 1906).
giaculato'ria *f.* prayer.
giada *f* (*min.*) jade.
giaguaro *m.* jaguar.
gialappa *f.* jalap.
giallastro *adj.* yellowish.
giallo *m.*, *adj.* yellow: libro —, thriller, "whodunit."
giammai *adv.* never.
gianniz'zero *m.* janizary; (*fig.*) par- tisan, follower; papal officer.
giapponese *m.*, *adj.* Japanese.
giara *f.* jar.
giardinag'gio *m.* gardening.
giardinetta *f.* station wagon.
giardiniera *f.* woman gardener; jar- diniere; wagonette; mixed salad.
giardiniere *m.* gardener.
giardino *m.* garden: — zoologico, zoo; — d'infanzia, kindergarten.
giarrettiera *f.* garter.
giavellotto *m.* javelin.
gibbosità *f.* gibbosity.
gibboso *adj.* gibbous, humped.

giberna f. cartridge box; (pl.) cartridge belt.

gigante m., adj. giant.

gigantesco adj. gigantic, giant.

gigione m. (theat.) "ham."

gi'glio m. lily; fleur-de-lis.

gilè m. waistcoat, vest.

ginecologi'a f. gynecology.

gineco'logo m. gynecologist.

ginepra'io m. (fig.) mess, scrape.

ginepro m. (bot.) juniper.

ginestra f. broom, genista.

ginevrino m.; adj. Genevan.

gingillare vi., **gingillarsi** vr. to trifle, idle, dawdle.

gingillo m. toy; trifle; trinket.

ginna'sio m. junior high school; grammar school; gymnasium.

ginnasta m. gymnast, athlete.

ginna'stica f. gymnastics.

gin'nico adj. gymnastic.

ginocchiera f. kneelet.

ginoc'chio m. knee: in —, on one's knees; sino alle ginocchia, knee-deep; knee-high.

ginocchioni adv. on one's knees.

Gioberti, Vincenzo, Italian philosopher and statesman, Del Primato morale e civile degl' Italiani (1801–1852).

giocare vt., vi. to play; to bet, stake; to gamble; to outwit; **giocarsi** vr. to wager, stake; to lose.

giocata f. stake, bet; game; play.

giocatore m. player; gambler.

giocat'tolo m. plaything, toy.

giocherellare vi. to play, trifle (with); to toy (with).

glochetto m. pastime; trick; walkover.

gioco see giuoco.

giocoliere m. juggler.

giocondo adj. merry, gay.

giocoso adj. jocose, jocular; comic.

gioga'ia f. dewlap; mountain range.

giogo m. yoke; crest, ridge.

gio'ia f. joy, delight; happiness; jewel; darling: che —! how wonderful!, I'm so happy!

gioielleri'a f. jewelry; jeweler's shop.

gioielliere m. jeweler; goldsmith.

gioiello m. jewel.

gioioso m. joyful.

gioire vi. to rejoice (at, in).

Giolitti, Giovanni, Italian statesman (1842–1928).

giorna'io m. newsdealer; newsboy.

giornale m. newspaper; journal; (comm.) daybook: — di bordo, log; — radio, newscast, news broadcast.

giornaletto m. tabloid.

giornaliero m. day laborer. adj. daily.

giornalismo m. journalism.

giornalista m. journalist, newspaper-man, columnist: — pubblicista, free lance.

giornali'stico adj. journalistic.

giornalmente adj. daily.

giornata f. day; day's work; day wages: vivere alla —, to live from hand to mouth; in —, before night; today.

giorno m. day: sul far del —, at daybreak; di —, by day; al — d'oggi, nowadays; un — sì e l'altro no, every other day.

giostra f. tournament; merry-go-round.

Giotto (Giotto di Bondone), great Florentine painter and architect (1276?–1337).

giovamento m. advantage, avail; solace; aid.

giovane m. young man, boy, youth. f. young woman, girl; youth: i giovani, young people. adj. young; junior.

giovanetta f. girl.

giovanetto m. boy, lad.

giovanile adj. youthful: opera —, early work.

giovanotto m. young man; bachelor; (naut.) sailor lad.

giovare vi. to help; to be useful, of use; to be good (for); **giovarsi** vr. to avail oneself (of); to profit (by).

giovedì m. Thursday.

giovenca f. heifer.

gioventù f. youth.

giove'vole adj. advantageous.

gioviale adj. jovial, hearty.

giovialità f. heartiness.

giovinastro m. scamp, wastrel.

giovincello m. lad, stripling.

gio'vine see giovane.

giovinezza f. youth.

giradischi m. record player.

giraffa f. giraffe.

giran'dola f. girandole; pinwheel.

girante m. (comm.) endorser.

girare vt. to turn; to travel over; to round; (comm.) to endorse; (moving pictures) to shoot. vi. to turn; to revolve, rotate; to whirl; to walk about; **girarsi** vr. to turn, turn around.

girarrosto m. spit.

girasole m. sunflower.

girata f. turn; (comm.) endorsement.

girata'rio m. (comm.) endorsee.

giravolta f. turning; pirouette.

girellare vi. to loaf; to walk around.

gire'vole adj. revolving.

girino m. tadpole.

giro m. turn, round; walk; drive; ride; tour; circle; circulation: mettere in — voci, to spread rumors; nel — di un anno, in a year's time;

prendere in — uno, to pull one's leg; a — di posta, by return (mail); — d'affari, (comm.) turnover.

gironzare, gironzolare vi. to loiter, loaf.

girosco'pio m. gyroscope.

girotondo m. ring-around-a-rosy.

girotta f. weathercock.

girovagare vi. to roam, wander.

giro'vago m., adj. vagrant· mercante —, peddler, hawker.

gita f. excursion; tour, trip.

gitano m., adj. gypsy

gitante m. excursionist.

giù adv. down; off: buttar — una persona (fig.), to blacken a person's character; mandar —, to swallow; — di lì, su per —, approximately; — le mani! hands off!; buttarsi —, to jump down; to lose heart.

giubba f. jacket, coat.

giubbetto m. jacket: — di salvataggio, life belt.

giubilante adj. jubilant.

giubilare vt. to superannuate, pension off. vi. to jubilate, exult.

giubileo m. jubilee.

giu'bilo m. jubilation, joy, glee.

giucco m. fool. adj. foolish.

Giuda m. Judas.

giuda'ico adj. Judaic.

giudeo m., Jew. adj. Jewish, Judean.

giudicare vt., vi. to judge; to consider, deem.

giu'dice m. judge; justice; referee: — conciliatore, justice of the peace; — istruttore, coroner.

giudizia'rio adj. judicial.

giudi'zio m. judgment; sentence, verdict; sense, wisdom; opinion: il giorno del —, doomsday; chiamare in —, to summon before court.

giudizioso adj. sensible, wise.

giugno m. June.

giulivo adj. gay, joyful.

giullare m. jester.

giumenta f. mare.

giunca f. (naut.) junk.

giunchi'glia f. jonquil.

giunco m. reed, rush.

giun'gere vt." to join. vi. to come (to); to arrive: — a, to reach; to go so far as; mi giunge nuovo, this is news to me.

giungla f. jungle.

giunta (1) f. addition; makeweight: per —, moreover; to boot.

giunta (2) f. junta; committee; council.

giuntare see aggiuntare.

giunto (1) m. coupling, joint; universal joint.

giunto (2) pp. of giungere.

giuntura f. juncture; joint.

giuoco m. play, game; joke, trick, jest; pleasure, fun; gambling: (mach.) clearance; — di prestigio, sleight of hand; — di parole, pun; — di Borsa, stockjobbing; pigliarsi — di, to make fun of; mettere in —, to stake; fare il doppio —, to play both ends against the middle.

giuramento m. oath, pledge.

giurare vt., vi. to swear, take an oath: giurarla a, to swear revenge upon.

giurato m. juryman. adj. sworn.

giuri'a f. jury; committee.

giuri'dico adj. juridical.

giurisdizione f. jurisdiction.

giurisprudenza f. jurisprudence.

giurista m. jurist.

giusta prep. in conformity with.

giustamente adv. rightly; exactly; fitly.

giustezza f. justness; fitness; accuracy.

giustifica'bile adj. justifiable.

giustificare vt. to justify; giustificarsi vr. to justify oneself, excuse oneself.

giustificativo m. (comm.) voucher. adj. justificatory.

giustificato adj. justified; just.

giustificazione f. justification; extenuation; excuse.

giusti'zia f. justice; law.

giustiziare vt. to execute, put to death.

giustiziere m. executioner; avenger.

giusto m. just man; just reward; right price; due. adj. just, right, fair; proper; exact; correct: il — mezzo, the golden mean. adv. just, right, exactly: giusto, giusto, just in time; giust'appunto! exactly!

glabro adj. smooth; shaved.

glaciale adj. icy, glacial.

gladiatore m. gladiator.

gla'dio m. sword.

glan'dola f. gland.

gli art.m.pl. the. pron.pers. him, to him; (fam.) (to) them.

glicerina f. glycerin.

gli'cine f. wistaria.

gliela compound pron. her (it) to him, her (it) to her, her (it) to them.

gliele, glieli them to him, them to her. glielo him (it) to him, him (it) to her.

gliene compound pron. (to) him some (or some to him), (to) her some (or some to her), of it to him (her): — diedi, I gave him (her) some, — parlai, I spoke of it to him (her).

globale adj. total, aggregate.

globalmente adv. altogether.

globo m. globe; eyeball.

glo'bulo m. globule, corpuscle.

glo'ria f. glory; fame.

gloriarsi *vr.* to pride oneself (*on*); to boast, glory (*in*).

glorificare *vt.* to glorify.

glorioso *adj.* glorious.

glossare *vt.* to gloss.

glossa'rio *m.* glossary.

glot'tide *f.* glottis.

gluco'sio *m.* glucose.

glu'teo *m.* buttock.

glu'tine *m.* gluten.

gnocco *m.* dumpling.

gnomo *m.* gnome.

gnorri: far lo —, to play possum.

gobba *f.* hunch, hump.

gobbo *m.* hump; humpback. *adj.* humpbacked: **naso** —, crooked nose.

goc'cia *f.* drop, bead; luster (*of a chandelier*): **somiglianti come due gocce d'acqua**, as like as two peas.

gocciolare *vi.* to drip, trickle.

gocciolato'io *m.* dripstone.

godere *vt.*, *vi.* to enjoy, take pleasure (*in*); to benefit (*by*); to rejoice; **godersi** *vr.* to enjoy: **godersela**, to revel; to have a good time.

godimento *m.* enjoyment, pleasure; fruition.

goffo *adj.* clumsy, awkward.

gogna *f.* pillory.

gola *f.* throat; gluttony; longing; gorge; flue; drain: **preso alla —**, hard-pressed.

Goldoni, Carlo, the greatest Italian dramatist and writer of comedies (in Venetian dialect) (1707–1793).

goletta *f.* schooner.

golfo *m.* gulf.

Golgi, Camillo, Italian physician, Nobel Prize 1906 (1844–1926).

goliardo *m.* university student.

golosità *f.* gluttony.

goloso *m.* glutton. *adj.* gluttonous, greedy; sweet-toothed.

go'mena *f.* cable, hawser.

gomitata *f.* nudge: **farsi largo a gomitate**, to elbow one's way.

go'mito *m.* elbow: **far di —**, to nudge; **a —**, elbow-shaped.

gomi'tolo *m.* ball (of thread).

gomma *f.* rubber; elastic; gum; eraser; tire: **— di ricambio**, spare tire.

gommato *adj.* gummed.

gommoso *adj.* gummy; sticky.

gonfalone *m.* gonfalon.

gonfaloniere *m.* gonfalonier.

gonfiare *vt.*, *vi.* to inflate; to pump; to exaggerate; **gonfiarsi** *vr.* to swell, puff.

gonfiatura *f.* inflation; swelling; exaggeration.

gon'fio *adj.* inflated, swollen.

gonfiore *m.* swelling.

gongolante *adj.* elated.

gongolare *vi.* to rejoice (*at*), be elated.

gonio'metro *m.* goniometer, protractor.

gonna *f.* skirt: **— scampanata**, flared skirt.

gonnella *f.* skirt; underskirt, petticoat.

gonnellino *m.* kilt.

gonzo *m.* fool, dolt.

gora *f.* millpond.

gorgheggiare *vi.* to warble.

gorgo *m.* whirlpool.

gorgogliare *vi.* to gurgle; to bubble.

gorgogli'o *m.* gurgling; bubbling.

gota *f.* cheek; chap.

go'tico *m.*, *adj.* Gothic.

gotta *f.* (*pathol.*) gout.

gottazza *f.* (*naut.*) scoop.

gottoso *adj.* gouty.

governante *m.* ruler, governor. *f.* nurse; governess; housekeeper.

governare *vt.* to govern, rule; to lead; to tend; (*naut.*) to steer.

governativo *adj.* governmental.

governatorato *m.* governorship.

governatore *m.* governor; mayor.

governo *m.* government; rule: **— della casa**, housekeeping.

Gozzi, Carlo, Italian dramatist and novelist, *L'amore delle tre melarance* (1720–1806).

gozzo *m.* goiter; crop (*of a bird*).

gozzovi'glia *f.* debauch, spree.

gozzovigliare *vi.* to debauch, go on a spree.

gracchiare *vi.* to croak.

gracidare *vi.* to croak; cluck.

gra'cile *adj.* thin; weak; ailing.

gradassata *f.* swagger, swashbuckling.

gradasso *m.* braggart, boaster, swashbuckler.

gradatamente *adv.* gradually.

gradazione *f.* gradation; proof.

grade'vole *adj.* agreeable.

gradimento *m.* satisfaction; liking; approval.

gradinata *f.* stoop, flight (*of stairs*); tiers (*of seats*), balcony.

gradino *m.* step.

gradire *vt.* to like; to accept, welcome; to appreciate.

gradito *adj.* agreeable, pleasant, welcome, congenial.

grado *m.* degree, stage; level, rank; position: **a gradi**, by degrees; **essere in — di**, to be able to; **mettere uno in — di**, to enable one to; **di buon —**, willingly.

graduale *adj.* gradual.

gradualmente *adv.* gradually.

graduare *vt.* to grade, graduate.

graduato *m.* noncommissioned officer. *adj.* graduated.

graduato'ria f. classification; score.

graffa see **grappa** (1).

graffetta f. (fam.) paper clip.

graffiare vi. to scratch.

graffiatura f. scratch; graze.

graf'fio m. scratch; grapnel.

grafi'a f. writing, spelling.

gra'fico m. chart; blueprint. adj. graphic.

gragnuola f. hail; shower.

grama'glie f.pl. weeds; mourning.

gramlgna f. weed.

gramma'tica f. grammar.

grammatura f. weight (in grams).

grammo m. gram.

grammo'fono m. gramophone.

gramo adj. wretched; bad; poor.

gran see **grande**.

grana (1) f. grain; texture.

grana (2) m. Parmesan cheese.

grana (3) f. (It. slang) trouble; money, "dough": **piantare grane**, to make trouble; **andare in cerca di grane**, to look for trouble.

grana'glie f.pl. cereals.

grana'io m. granary, barn.

granata (1) f. broom.

granata (2) f. (artil.) grenade.

granatiere m. grenadier.

granato m. pomegranate.

grancassa f. bass drum.

gran'chio m. crab; (fig.) blunder.

grandangolare adj. wide-angle: **obiettivo —**, wide-angle lens.

grande m. great man; adult; grandee. adj. great; big, large; tall, lofty, high; grown-up; long; wide; broad; **grand: fare il —**, to show off; **in —**, on a large scale.

grandemente adv. very, very much; greatly, highly; strongly.

grandezza f. greatness; bigness; surface, extent; capacity; width; size; loftiness: **mania di —**, delusion of grandeur.

grandinare vi. to hail.

grandinata f. hailstorm.

gran'dine f. hail.

grandiosità f. grandiosity, grandness.

grandioso adj. grandiose, grand.

granello m. grain; seed; speck.

granita f. sherbet.

granito m. granite.

grano m. grain, corn; wheat; bead; bit; grain (unit of measure): (It. slang) money, "dough": **— saraceno**, maize; **— d'orzo**, barleycorn; **un — d'uva**, a grape.

granoturco m. Indian corn, maize.

granulare adj. granular.

granulare vt. to granulate.

gra'nulo m. granule.

grappa (1) f. cramp; brace, bracket.

grappa (2) f. brandy.

grappetta f. staple (for binding books); (surg.) metal stitch.

grap'polo m. bunch, cluster.

grassatore m. highwayman.

grassazione f. robbery.

grassetto m. (typ.) boldface.

grassezza f. fatness; stoutness.

grasso m. fat; grease: **giorno di —**, meat day. adj. fat, stout; plentiful; greasy, fatty; lewd: **martedì —**, Shrove Tuesday.

grata f. grating.

gratella f. grill, gridiron.

gra'ticcio m. trellis.

grati'cola f. grill, gridiron; grate; graticule.

gratifica see **gratificazione**.

gratificare vt. to gratify; to reward.

gratificazione f. bonus, gratuity.

gratile m. (naut.) boltrope.

gratitu'dine f. gratitude.

grato adj. grateful, thankful; pleasant, agreeable.

grattacapo m. trouble, worry.

grattacielo m. skyscraper.

grattare vt. to scratch, scrape; to grate; (fam.) to steal. vi. to grate; **grattarsi** vr. to scratch (oneself).

grattu'gia f. grater.

grattugiare vt. to grate.

gratuitamente adv. free; gratuitously.

gratu'ito adj. free; gratuitous; unasked for.

gravame m. tax; duty; burden; complaint.

gravare vt. to load, burden (with); vi. to weigh (upon).

grave adj. heavy; grievous; stern; serious; weighty; grave, austere; dangerous; deep, low (in pitch).

gravemente adv. heavily; sternly; seriously; dangerously; deeply.

graveolente adj. stinking.

gra'vida f., adj. pregnant.

gravidanza f. pregnancy.

gra'vido m. pregnant, fraught.

gravità f. gravity; heaviness; seriousness; dignity; depth (of a sound).

gravitare vi. to revolve (about); to weigh; to gravitate.

gravitazione f. gravitation.

gravoso adj. burdensome; unpleasant.

gra'zia f. grace; charm; favor; privilege; permission; mercy, pardon: **senza garbo nè —**, shapeless; **troppa — Sant'Antonio**, it never rains but it pours!; **nell'anno di — ...**, in the year of our Lord ...

graziare vt. to pardon.

gra'zie! interj. thank you!, thanks!

grazioso adj. pretty, graceful; gracious; free.

greca f. fret, Greek fret; tunic.

greco m. Greek. adj. Greek, Grecian.
grega'rio m. follower; serviceman.
gregge m. herd, flock.
greg'gio see grezzo.
grembiale, grembiule m. apron; (auto.) drip pan.
grembo m. lap: in — alla famiglia, in one's family's bosom; — materno, womb.
gremire vt. to overcrowd, fill.
gremito adj. overcrowded (with).
grep'pia f. crib, manger.
gres m. sandstone; stoneware.
greto m. gravel bank.
grettezza f. narrow-mindedness; stinginess.
gretto adj. narrow-minded; stingy.
greve adj. heavy.
grezzo adj. raw, coarse; unrefined.
gridare vt., vi. to cry, cry out, shout; to yell; to bellow; to scream; to scold.
grido m. cry, shout, yell, squeal, scream: di —, famous; l'ultimo — della moda, the height of fashion.
grifagno adj. predatory; fierce.
grifo m. snout; gryphon.
grifone m. gryphon; griffon.
grigiastro adj. grayish.
gri'gio adj. gray.
gri'glia f. grate; gridiron; grid.
grilletto m. trigger.
grillo m. cricket; (fig.) whim, fancy.
grimaldello m. picklock.
grin'fia f. claw, clutch.
grinta f. grim countenance.
grinza f. wrinkle; crease.
grinzoso adj. wrinkly; creasy.
grippag'gio m. (mach.) seizing.
grippare vi. (mach.) to seize.
griselle f.pl. (naut.) ratlines.
grissino m. bread stick.
grisù m. firedamp.
gromma f. tartar.
gronda f. eaves (pl.).
gronda'ia f. gutter.
grondante adj. pouring, dripping.
grondare vt., vi. to shed, pour (out), drip; to be drenched: — sangue, to bleed.
groppa f. back; horseback.
groppata f. curvet, buck.
groppo m. knot; lump.
groppone m. back, shoulders.
grossa f. (12 dozen) gross (pl. gross).
grossezza f. thickness; bulk, size; coarseness.
grossista m. wholesaler.
grosso m. gross, main, bulk. adj. big, bulky; thick; swollen; large; coarse; hard: mare —, rough sea; il dito —, the big toe; un pezzo — (fig.) a bigwig; caccia grossa, big-game hunting; fare la voce grossa,

to raise one's voice; to storm; sbagliare di —, to be grossly mistaken.
grossolanità f. coarseness; boorishness.
grossolano adj. coarse; boorish.
grotta f. grotto, cave.
grottesco adj. grotesque.
groviera m. gruyère.
grovi'glio m. tangle, snarl.
gru f. crane.
gruc'cia f. crutch; perch; hanger.
gruera m. gruyère.
grufolare vi. to grub, snout.
grugnire vi. to grunt.
grugnito m. grunt.
grugno m. snout.
grulleri'a f. foolishness.
grullo m. fool. adj. foolish.
grumo m. clot.
gruppetto m. cluster; small group.
gruppo m. group, set.
gruz'zolo m. hoard, savings.
guadagnare vt., guadagnarsi vr. to earn, gain; to get; to win; to reach; to look better.
guadagnato adj. earned, gained; de-servéd: tanto di —, so much the better.
guadagno m. earning; earnings; gain, advantage; profit; winnings.
guadare vt. to ford.
guado m. ford.
gua'ina f. case; scabbard, sheath.
gua'io m. trouble, scrape; accident, mishap; inconvenience; damage: il tuo — è che..., the trouble with you is that...
guaire vi. to yelp; to whine.
gualto m. yelp; whine.
gualcire vt. to crumple.
gualdrappa f. saddlecloth.
guan'cia f. cheek.
guanciale m. pillow.
guanta'io m. glover.
guantiera f. tray.
guanto m. glove: gettare (raccogliere) il —, to fling down (to take up) the gauntlet; calzare come un —, to suit to a turn.
guantone m. mitten, boxing glove.
guardaboschi m. forester.
guardacac'cia m. gamekeeper.
guardacoste m. coast guard.
guardafili m. lineman.
guardali'nee m. (sport) linesman.
guardaportone m. doorkeeper.
guardare vt., vi. to eye; to look (at, on, upon, up, etc.); to look after; to guard; to look out, mind; to see to it (that): — la realtà, to face facts; non — in faccia a nessuno, to make no distinctions; guarda, guarda! well, well!; guardarsi vr.

to look at each other; to abstain, forbear (*from*); to avoid; to beware.

guardaroba *f.* wardrobe; closet; cloakroom.

guardarobiera *f.* seamstress; check girl.

guardarobiere *m.* cloakroom attendant.

guardasala *m.* warden.

guardasigilli *m.* attorney general.

guar'dia *f.* watch, lookout; watchman; guard, policeman; flyleaf: **turno di —,** watch; **cambio della —,** relief; **— medica,** emergency hospital, first-aid station.

guardiamarina *m.* ensign: **allievo —,** midshipman.

guardiano *m.* watchman; keeper.

guardina *f.* guardroom.

guardingo *adj.* wary, cautious.

guarigione *f.* recovery.

guarire *vt.* to heal, cure; to rid;|*vi.* to recover (*from*); to get rid (*of*).

Guarneri, Giuseppe Antonio, Italian violinmaker (1683–1745).

guarnigione *f.* garrison.

guarnire *vt.* to trim; to adorn; to equip; to garnish; (*naut.*) to rig.

guarnizione *f.* trimming; garnish; (*mach.*) packing.

guascone *m.* Gascon.

guastafeste *m.* kill-joy, spoilsport.

guastare *vt.* to spoil; to destroy, wreck; to mar; to taint, infect; (*mach.*) to put out of gear; **guastarsi** *vr.* to spoil, get spoiled; to rot, decay; (*mach.*) to get out of gear; to quarrel; to become overcast.

guastatore *m.* (*mil.*) commando.

guasto *m.* damage; breakdown. *adj.* spoiled; wrecked; rotten, decayed; (*mach.*) out of gear.

guatare *vt.* to watch; to look askance at.

guazza *f.* dew.

guazzabu'glio *m.* medley; mess.

guazzare *vi., vi.* to wallow.

guazzetto *m.* stew.

guer'cio *m.* squint-eyed.

guernire *see* guarnire.

guerra *f.* war; warfare.

guerrafonda'io *m.* warmonger.

Guerrazzi, Francesco Domenico, Italian author and patriot, *Beatrice Cenci* (1804–1873).

guerreggiare *vi.* to fight.

guerresco *adj.* warlike.

guerriero *m.* warrior. *adj.* warlike; martial; bellicose.

guerri'glia *f.* irregular war, skirmish.

guerrigliero *m.* guerrilla.

gufo *m.* owl.

gu'glia *f.* spire, pinnacle.

gugliata *f.* needleful.

Guicciardini, Francesco, Italian historian (1483–1540).

guida *f.* guide; guidance; leadership; guidebook; directory; driving; (*mach.*) slide: **— interna, sedan; — a destra, (a sinistra),** right- (left-) hand drive.

guidare *vt., vi.* to guide; to lead; to drive; (*naut.*) to steer.

guidatore *m.,* **guidatrice** *f.* driver.

guiderdone *m.* reward.

Guido d'Arezzo, Italian reformer of music (990–1050).

guidoslitta *f.* bobsleigh.

guinza'glio *m.* leash.

guisa *f.* way, guise: **a — di,** as; **in — che,** so that.

guitto *m.* (*theat.*) stroller, "barnstormer."

guizzare *vi.* to dart; to swim; to flash.

guizzo *m.* dart; flash.

gu'scio *m.* case; pod; shell.

gustare *vt., vi.* to taste, try; to enjoy; to relish.

gusto *m.* taste; enjoyment; pleasure, relish.

gustoso *adj.* tasty, palatable; amusing, funny.

guttaperca *f.* gutta-percha.

gutturale *f., adj.* guttural, rasping.

H

han'gar *m.* hangar, shed.

ha'rem *m.* harem.

havaiano *m., adj.* Hawaiian.

hennè *m.* henna.

hertziano *m.* Hertzian: **onda hertziana, hertzian** wave.

hòi! *interj.* ah! (*to express surprise*); alas! (*to express sorrow*).

honorem, (ad) (*L.*) honorary, *honoris causa.*

hurrà *interj.* hurrah: **lanciare degli —,** to hurrah.

I

iato *m.* (*gramm.*) hiatus.

iattanza *f.* braggadocio.

iattura *f.* calamity.

ibe'rico *adj.* Iberian.

i'brido *m., adj.* hybrid.

ica'stico *adj.* truthlike, lifelike.

iconoclasta *m.* iconoclast.

iconografi'a *f.* iconography.

idalgo *m.* hidalgo.

Iddio *see* Dio.

idea *f.* idea, notion; opinion: neanche per —! not in the least!

ideale *m.*, *adj.* ideal.

idealismo *m.* idealism.

idealista *m.* idealist.

idealizzare *vt.* to idealize.

ideare *vt.* to conceive, imagine; to devise; to plan.

ideatore *m.* inventor, deviser.

iden'tico *adj.* identical.

identificare *vt.* to identify; identificarsi *vr.* to identify oneself.

identificazione *f.* identification.

identità *f.* identity.

ideogramma *m.* ideograph.

ideologi'a *f.* ideology.

idi *m.*, *f.pl.* ides.

idilli'aco *adj.* idyllic.

idil'lio *m.* idyl; romance.

idioma *m.* idiom, language.

idiosincrasi'a *f.* allergy.

idiota *m.* idiot; *adj.* idiotic.

idiotismo *m.* idiom; idiocy.

idiozi'a *f.* idiocy.

idolatrare *vt.* to idolize, worship.

i'dolo *m.* idol.

idoneità *f.* fitness; aptitude.

ido'neo *adj.* qualified; suitable, fit (for).

idrante *m.* hydrant.

idra'ulica *f.* hydraulics.

idrau'lico *m.* plumber; *adj.* hydraulic.

i'drico *adj.* hydric.

idrocarburo *m.* hydrocarbon.

idro'filo *adj.* hydrophilous: cotone —, absorbent cotton.

idrofobi'a *f.* hydrophobia.

idro'fobo *adj.* hydrophobic; (*fig.*) rabid.

idrogenare *vt.* to hydrogenate.

idrogenazione *f.* hydrogenation.

idro'geno *m.* hydrogen.

idro'pico *adj.* dropsical.

idroplano *m.* hydroplane, seaplane.

idroscalo *m.* seaplane airport.

idroscivolante *m.* hydroplane.

idrovolante *m.* seaplane.

idro'vora *f.* water pump.

iella *f.* bad luck.

iena *f.* hyena.

iera'tico *adj.* hieratic.

ieri *adv.* yesterday: l'altro —, the day before yesterday; — sera, last night.

iettatore *m.* bird of ill omen; (*fam.*) hoodoo.

iettatura *f.* evil eye; (*fam.*) hoodoo.

igiene *f.* hygiene; sanitation.

igie'nico *adj.* hygienic; sanitary.

ignaro *adj.* unaware, ignorant.

igna'via *f.* sluggishness.

ignavo *adj.* sluggish.

igno'bile *adj.* ignoble.

ignomi'nia *f.* ignominy.

ignominioso *adj.* ignominous.

ignorante *m.* ignoramus, philistine; *adj.* ignorant; illiterate.

ignoranza *f.* ignorance.

ignorare *vt.* not to know; to be unaware of; to ignore.

ignoto *adj.* unknown.

ignudo *adj.* bare, naked.

il *def. art m.sing.* the.

i'lare *adj.* cheerful, hilarious.

ilarità *f.* hilarity; laughter.

i'lice *f.* ilex, holm oak.

i'lio *m.* ilium (*pl.* ilia).

illanguidire *vt.* to enfeeble; *vt.*, *vi.* to weaken.

illazione *f.* illation; inference, surmise.

ille'cito *adj.* illicit, unlawful.

illegale *adj.* illegal, unlawful.

illegalità *f.* unlawfulness.

illegi'bile *adj.* illegible.

illegit'timo *adj.* illegitimate.

illeso *adj.* unhurt, unharmed, uninjured, safe and sound.

illetterato *m.*, *adj.* illiterate.

illibato *adj.* irreproachable, pure.

illimitato *adj.* unlimited, boundless.

illogicità *f.* illogicalness.

illo'gico *adj.* illogical, absurd.

illu'dere *vt.* to delude, beguile, "kid"; illu'dersi *vr.* to delude, "kid" oneself.

illuminare *vt.* to light up; (*fig.*) to enlighten; illuminarsi *vr.* to light up.

illuminato *adj.* lit; (*fig.*) enlightened.

illuminazione *f.* light, lighting; illumination; (*fig.*) enlightenment.

illusione *f.* delusion; illusion: farsi illusioni, to delude oneself.

illusionismo *m.* legerdemain; (*philos.*) illusionism.

illusionista *m.* conjurer, juggler; (*philos.*) illusionist.

illuso *m.* optimist; dreamer; *adj.* deluded; deceived. *pp.* of illudere.

illuso'rio *adj.* illusory; illusive; deceptive.

illustrare *vt.* to illustrate.

illustrato *adj.* illustrated: cartolina illustrata, picture post card.

illustratore *m.* illustrator; cartoonist.

illustrazione *f.* illustration, picture; drawing; cartoon.

illustre *adj.* illustrious, distinguished.

imbacuccare *vt.*, imbacuccarsi *vr.* to wrap (up).

imbaldanzire *vi.* to embolden; imbaldanzirsi *vr.* to grow bold.

imballag'gio *m.* packing; wrapping paper.

imballare *vt.* to pack (up); imballarsi *vr.* (of motors) to race.

imballatore *m.* packer.
imballo *m.* packing.
imbalsamare *vt.* to embalm; to stuff (*animals*).
imbalsamatore *m.* embalmer; stuffer, taxidermist.
imbambolato *adj.* hazy; dull; drowsy; stunned.
imbandierare *vt.* to flag.
imbandire *vt.* to decorate (*the table*).
imbarazzante *adj.* embarrassing, uncomfortable; bewildering.
imbarazzare *vt.* to obstruct, encumber; to embarrass, hinder.
imbarazzato *adj.* obstructed; embarrassed, uneasy; constipated.
imbarazzo *m.* encumbrance; uneasiness; difficulty; embarrassment; constipation.
imbarcadero *m.* landing stage.
imbarcare *vt.* to embark; imbarcarsi *vr.* to embark, sail; to board a ship; to engage (*in*).
imbarcazione *f.* embarkation; boat, craft.
imbarco *m.* embarkation; shipping; loading.
imbardare *vi.* (*aeron.*) to yaw.
imbardata *f.* (*aeron.*) yaw.
imbastardire *vt.* to adulterate; *vi.*, imbastardirsi *vr.* to degenerate.
imbastire *vt.* to baste; to sketch; to start, set up, organize.
imbastitura *f.* basting.
imbat'tersi *vr.* to stumble (*upon*), come (*across*).
imbatti'bile *adj.* undefeatable; unsurpassable.
imbattuto *adj.* undefeated; unsurpassed.
imbavagliare *vt.* to gag.
imbeccare *vt.* to feed; to prompt; to coach.
imbeccata *f.* beakful; (*fig.*) prompting, cue.
imbecillag'gine *f.* foolishness.
imbecille *m.*, *adj.* imbecile.
imbecillità *f.* imbecility.
imbelle *adj.* pusillanimous.
imbellettare *vt.*, imbellettarsi *vr.* to rouge (*oneself*).
imberbe *adj.* beardless.
imbestialire *vt.* to madden; imbestialirsi *vr.* to go berserk.
imbe'vere *vt.* to steep (*in*); (*fig.*) to imbue (*with*); imbe'versi *vr.* to soak (*with*); (*fig.*) to become imbued (*with*).
imbevuto *adj.* soaked; (*fig.*) imbued.
imbiancare *vt.* to whiten; to whitewash; to bleach; *vi.* to whiten.
imbianchino *m.* whitewasher, house painter.
imbianchire *vi.* to whiten.

imbizzarrirsi *vr.* to bolt.
imboccare *vt.* to put into the mouth; to prompt; to enter (*as a road*).
imboccatura *f.* inlet, mouth, entrance; mouthpiece; bit (*of a horse*).
imbocco *see* imboccatura.
imbonimento *m.* claptrap.
imbonire *vt.* to allure; to soothe.
imbonitore *m.* crier, showman.
imboscare *vt.* to corner; imboscarsi *vr.* (*mil.*) to shirk (*conscription*).
imboscata *f.* ambush.
imboscato *m.* (*mil.*) slacker, shirker.
imboschire *vi.* to plant or grow woods.
imbottigliare *vt.* to bottle (*up*).
imbottire *vt.* to pad; to stuff.
imbottita *f.* quilt.
imbottitura *f.* padding.
imbracciare *vt.* to level (*a gun*).
imbrancare *vt.* to herd; imbrancarsi *vr.* to consort (*with*).
imbrattare *vt.*, imbrattarsi *vr.* to sully, soil.
imbrattatele *m.* dauber.
imbrigliare *vt.* to bridle.
imbroccare *vt.* to hit; imbroccarla, to hit the mark; to succeed.
imbrodare *vt.*, imbrodarsi *vr.* to sully: chi si loda s'imbroda, self-praise is no recommendation.
imbrogliare *vt.* to tangle; to cheat, swindle; imbrogliarsi *vr.* to get mixed up; to get involved.
imbro'glio *m.* mess, tangle; fraud.
imbroglione *m.* swindler.
imbronciarsi *vr.* to pout; to sulk.
imbronciato *adj.* sulky.
imbrunire *vi.* to grow dark: all'—, at nightfall.
imbruttire *vt.* to uglify; *vi.* to grow ugly (*or* uglier).
imbucare *vt.* to mail (*a letter*).
imburrare *vt.* to butter.
imbuto *m.* funnel.
imitare *vt.* to imitate; to mimic.
imitatore *m.* imitator.
imitazione *f.* imitation.
immacolato *adj.* immaculate.
immagazzinare *vt.* to store.
immaginare *vt.* to imagine; to conceive (*of*); to guess, figure; immaginarsi *vr.* to imagine, figure.
immagina'rio *adj.* imaginary.
immaginativa *f.* imagination.
immaginazione *f.* imagination.
imma'gine *f.* image.
immaginoso *adj.* imaginative.
immalinconire *vt.* to sadden.
immanca'bile *adj.* unfailing; certain; usual.
immancabilmente *adv.* without fail.
immane *adj.* huge, gigantic, great.
immangia'bile *adj.* inedible.

immarcesci'bile *adj*. undecayable.

immatricolare *vt*., immatricolarsi *vr*. to matriculate.

immatricolazione *f*. matriculation; (*univ*.) initiation.

immaturità *f*. immaturity.

immaturo *adj*. immature, unripe; untimely.

immedesimare *vt*. to identify (*with*); immedesimarsi *vr*. to identify oneself (*with*).

immediatamente *adv*. immediately.

immediatezza *f*. immediateness.

immediato *adj*. immediate.

immemora'bile *adj*. immemorial.

imme'more *adj*. forgetful.

immensità *f*. immensity; (*fig*.) lot.

immenso *adj*. immense; huge.

immer'gere *vt*.[51] to dip, immerse; immergersi *vr*. to immerge, plunge.

immeritato *adj*. undeserved.

immersione *f*. immersion: linea d'—, waterline.

immet'tere *vt*.[76] to let in.

immigrante *m*., *adj*. immigrant.

immigrare *vi*. to immigrate.

immigrazione *f*. immigration.

imminente *adj*. impending; forthcoming.

imminenza *f*. imminence.

immischiare *vt*. to involve; immischiarsi *vr*. to meddle (*with*).

immiserire *vt*. to impoverish.

immissa'rio *m*. affluent.

immissione *f*. immission, introduction

immo'bile *m*. house; (*pl*.) real estate; *adj*. motionless, still; immovable.

immobiliare *adj*. real, landed: agente —, realtor.

immobilità *f*. immobility.

immobilizzare *vt*. to immobilize; immobilizzarsi *vr*. to become motionless.

immolare *vt*. to immolate.

immondezza'io *m*. dump.

immondi'zia *f*. filth; garbage.

immondo *adj*. filthy.

immorale *adj*. immoral.

immoralità *f*. immorality.

immortalare *vt*. to immortalize, make eternal.

immortale *m*., *adj*. immortal.

immortalità *f*. immortality.

immoto *adj*. motionless.

immune *adj*. immune; uninjured; exempt (*from*).

immunità *f*. immunity.

immunizzare *vt*. to immunize (*against*).

immuta'bile *adj*. immutable.

immutato *adj*. unchanged.

imo *m*. bottom; *adj*. lowermost.

impacchettare *vt*. to parcel.

impacciare *vt*., *vi*. to hinder, hamper; to trouble.

impacciato *adj*. awkward, clumsy; uneasy, uncomfortable.

impac'cio *m*. hindrance; trouble: essere d'—, to be in the way.

impacco *m*. compress.

impadronirsi *vr*. to grasp, seize, take possession (*of*).

impaga'bile *adj*. priceless.

impaginare *vt*. (*typog*.) to set up as (*or* make up into) pages.

impaginatore *m*. pager.

impaginazione *f*. (*typog*.) make-up.

impagliare *vt*. to wicker; to straw; to stuff (*as animals*).

impalato *adj*. (*fig*.) stiff.

impalcatura *f*. scaffolding; frame.

impallidire *vi*. to pale, turn pale.

impalpa'bile *adj*. impalpable.

impanare *vt*. (*cook*.) to bread; (*mach*.) to thread.

impantanare *vt*., impantanarsi *vr*. to swamp.

impaperarsi *vr*. to blunder, flounder.

impappinarsi *vr*. to blunder, stammer.

imparare *vt*. to learn: — a memoria, to learn by heart.

impareggia'bile *adj*. imcomparable.

imparentarsi *vr*. to become related; to marry.

im'pari *adj*. odd; unequal; unfit (*for*).

impartire *vt*. to impart.

imparziale *adj*. impartial, unbiased.

imparzialità *f*. impartiality.

impassi'bile *adj*. impassive; unmoved.

impassibilità *f*. impassiveness.

impastare *vt*. to knead; to impaste; to paste.

impastatrice *f*. kneading machine.

impasto *m*. dough; mixture.

impastolare *vt*. to fetter.

impataccare *vt*. to besmear.

impaurire *vt*. to scare; impaurirsi *vr*. to get scared.

impaurito *adj*. scared, afraid.

impa'vido *adj*. fearless.

impaziente *adj*. impatient; eager.

impazientirsi *vr*. to lose one's patience; to get angry.

impazienza *f*. impatience; eagerness.

impazzare *vi*. to go mad; to run riot.

impazzata *f*. folly: all'—, madly.

impazzire *vi*. to go mad, become insane; to run riot: fare —, to drive mad.

impazzito *adj*. crazed, mad.

impecca'bile *adj*. faultless.

impeciare *vt*. to tar.

impedimento *m*. hindrance; obstacle; illness; trouble.

impedire *vt*. to prevent; to avoid; to hinder; to obstruct; to stop.

impegnare *vt*. to pawn, pledge; to bind; to engage; to retain; impegnarsi *vr.* to promise, undertake (*to*); to bind oneself.

impegnativo *adj.* binding; challenging.

impegno *m.* engagement; pledge, promise; care; obligation.

impegolarsi *vr.* (*fig.*) to get involved.

impelagarsi *vr.* to involve oneself, get in trouble.

impellente *adj.* impellent, urging.

impellicciare *vt.* to fur; to veneer.

impellicciatura *f.* veneering.

impenetra'bile *adj.* impenetrable.

impenetrabilità *f.* impenetrableness; (*phys.*) impenetrability

impenitente *adj.* unrepenting; confirmed.

impennaggi *m.pl.* (*aeron.*) tall vanes.

impennare *vt.* (*aeron.*) to zoom; impennarsi *vr.* to rear; (*fig.*) to rear up; (*aeron.*) to zoom nose up.

impennata *f.* rearing; (*aeron.*) zoom.

impensato *adj.* unexpected; unforeseen.

impensierire *vt.* impensierirsi *vr.* to worry

imperante *adj.* ruling; (*fig.*) prevailing.

imperare *vi.* to rule (*over*); (*fig.*) to prevail.

imperativo *m., adj.* imperative.

imperatore *m.* emperor.

imperatrice *f.* empress.

impercetti'bile *adj.* imperceptible.

imperdona'bile *adj.* unpardonable.

imperfetto *m.* imperfect (*tense*); *adj.* imperfect, faulty.

imperfezione *f.* imperfection, fault, flaw.

imperiale *m.* imperial; upper deck (*of a bus, etc.*); *adj.* imperial.

imperialismo *m.* imperialism.

impe'rio *m.* rule, authority.

imperiosità *f.* imperiousness.

imperioso *adj.* imperious, domineering.

imperituro *adj.* immortal; eternal.

imperi'zia *f.* unskillfulness.

imperlare *vt.* to bead; to dew.

impermalire *vt.* to offend, hurt, vex; impermalirsi *vr.* to sulk: impermalirsi di, per, to resent.

imperme'abile *m., adj.* waterproof.

impermeabilità *f.* impermeability.

imperniare *vt.* to pivot; imperniarsi *vr.* to hinge.

impero *m.* empire.

imperscruta'bile *adj.* inscrutable.

imper onale *adj.* impersonal.

impersonare *vt.* to impersonate.

imperter'rito *adj.* undaunted.

impertinente *adj.* impertinent, pert.

impertinenza *f.* impertinence.

imperturba'bile *adj.* imperturbable.

imperturbabilità *f.* imperturbability, composure.

imperversare *vi.* to storm, rage; to run riot.

imper'vio *adj.* impervious.

im'peto *m.* rush; impact; impulse; vehemence; transport.

impetrare *vt.* to impetrate.

impettito *adj.* strutting; stiff.

impetuosità *f.* impetuosity.

impetuoso *adj.* impetuous; rash.

impiallacciare *vt.* to veneer.

impiallacciatura *f.* veneering.

impiantare *vt.* to found, establish; to set up.

impiantito *m.* floor.

impianto *m.* establishment; setting up; plant, outfit.

impiastrare, impiastricciare *vt.* to besmear; to daub.

impiastro *m.* plaster; poultice; (*fig.*) bore.

impiccagione *f.* hanging.

impiccare *vt.* to hang.

impiccato *adj.* hanged.

impicciare *vt.* to hinder; impicciarsi *vr.* to meddle (*with*).

impic'cio *m.* hindrance, nuisance; trouble.

impiccione *m.* busybody.

impiccolire *vt.* to reduce, lessen.

impiegare *vt.* to employ; to use, apply; to invest; to spend: ci impiegherò tre giorni, it will take me three days; impiegarsi *vr.* to employ oneself, find a job.

impiegati'zio *adj.* clerical.

impiegato *m.* employee, clerk.

impiego *m.* employment, job; use, application.

impietosire *vt.* to stir pity, touch; impietosirsi *vr.* to relent, feel touched; to feel sorry (*for*).

impietrire *vt., vi.* to petrify.

impigliare *vt.* to entangle; impigliarsi *vr.* to get entangled.

impigrire *vt.* to enervate, make lazy; *vi.* to grow lazy.

impinguare *vt., vi., impinguarsi *vr.* to fatten.

impinzare *vt., impinzarsi *vr.* to cram, stuff (*oneself*).

impiombare *vt.* to lead; to plumb, seal; to stop (*teeth*).

impiombatura *f.* leading, lead seal; stopping.

implaca'bile *adj.* implacable.

implicare *vt.* to implicate, involve; to imply.

impli'cito *adj.* implicit.

implorare *vt.* to entreat.

implorazione *f.* entreaty.

implume *adj.* featherless.

impolverare *vt.* to make dusty; impolverarsi *vr.* to get dusty.

impolverato *adj.* dusty.

impomatare *vt.* to pomade.

impondera'bile *adj.* imponderable.

imponente *adj.* imposing, stately; powerful.

imponenza *f.* imposingness, stateliness; powerfulness.

impopolare *adj.* unpopular.

impopolarità *f.* unpopularity.

imporre *vt.*[90] to impose, force upon; to call for: — un nome, to give a name (to); — rispetto, to command respect; imporsi *vr.* to prevail (upon); to be imperative; to inspire awe; to win.

importante *m.* (the) essential, (main) point; *adj.* important.

importanza *f.* importance, consequence: darsi —, to look big.

importare (1) *vt.* to import (goods).

importare (2) *vt.* to imply, involve; to call for; *vt.impers.* to matter; to be necessary, essential; to care: non importa! it does not matter; non me ne importa, I don't care.

importatore *m.* importer.

importazione *f.* import, importation.

importo *m.* amount, cost.

importunare *vt.* to importune, nag, tease.

importuno *m.* bore; *adj.* importunate; irksome.

imposizione *f.* imposition.

impossessarsi *see* impadronirsi.

impossi'bile *adj.* impossible.

impossibilità *f.* impossibility.

imposta (1) *f.* shutter.

imposta (2) *f.* duty, tax.

impostare *vt.* to start, begin; to post, mail; to attune (one's voice); to lay (a ship).

impostazione *f.* starting; laying; mailing.

impostore *m.* impostor.

impostura *f.* imposture.

impotente *m.* impotent; *adj.* impotent; powerless; helpless.

impotenza *f.* impotence.

impoverimento *m.* impoverishment.

impoverire *vt.* to impoverish; impoverirsi *vr.* to grow poor, go to seed.

impratica'bile *adj.* impracticable.

impraticabilità *f.* impracticability.

impratichire *vt.* to train; to familiarize (with); impratichirsi *vr.* to get trained; to become conversant, familiar (with).

imprecare *vi.* to curse.

imprecazione *f.* imprecation, oath.

imprecisione *f.* vagueness; inaccuracy.

impreciso *adj.* vague; inaccurate.

impregiudicato *adj.* unprejudiced.

impregnare *vt.* to impregnate, saturate, imbue (with), soak, steep (in).

imprendi'bile *adj.* impregnable; elusive.

imprenditore *m.* contractor.

impreparato *adj.* unprepared; unaware.

impreparazione *f.* unpreparedness.

impresa *f.* enterprise; deed; company.

impresa'rio *m.* contractor; (theat.) impresario, manager: — di pompe funebri, undertaker.

imprescindi'bile *adj.* indispensable; unavoidable.

impressiona'bile *adj.* impressionable.

impressionante *adj.* striking; awesome; frightful.

impressionare *vt.* to impress; to disturb; to shock, strike; (photo.) to expose; impressionarsi *vr.* to be impressed or disturbed; to become afraid.

impressione *f.* impression.

impressionismo *m.* impressionism.

impresso *adj.* printed; engraved. *pp.* of imprimere.

imprevedi'bile *adj.* unforeseeable.

impreveduto *adj.* unforeseen; unexpected.

imprevidente *adj.* improvident.

imprevidenza *f.* improvidence.

imprevisto *adj.* unexpected, unforeseen.

imprigionare *vt.* to imprison.

impri'mere *vt.*,[90] imprimersi *vr.* to impress.

improba'bile *adj.* unlikely.

improbabilità *f.* unlikelihood.

improbità *f.* improbity.

im'probo *adj.* hard; dishonest.

improduttivo *adj.* unproductive; unprofitable.

impronta *f.* impression, print, mark; footprint: impronte digitali, fingerprints.

improntare *vt.* to characteriz ; impress.

improntitu'dine *f.* impudence.

imprope'rio *m.* insult.

impro'pzio *adj.* unfavorable.

impropriamente *adv.* improperly; loosely.

improprietà *f.* impropriety.

impro'prio *adj.* improper; unsuitable.

improroga'bile *adj.* undelayable.

improv'vido *adj.* improvident.

improvvisamente *adv.* suddenly, unexpectedly.

improvvisare *vt.* to improvise; to ad-lib; improvvisarsi *vr.* to turn (out).

improvvisata *f.* surprise.

improvvisato *adj.* ex tempore.

improvvisatore *m.* improviser.

improvvisazione *f.* extemporization, improvisation, ad lib.

improvviso m. (*mus.*) impromptu; *adj.* sudden: all'—, suddenly.
imprudente *adj.* imprudent; rash.
imprudenza f. imprudence, rashness.
impudente *adj.* impudent, pert.
impudenza f. impudence.
impudici'zia f. shamelessness.
impu'dico *adj.* shameless, brazen, immodest.
impugnare *vt.* to grip, wield; to impugn.
impugnatura f. grip, handle; hilt.
impulsività f. impulsiveness.
impulsivo *adj.* impulsive, rash.
impulso m. impulse, impact; urge; drive; motive; (*phys.*) impulsion: dare — a, to promote.
impunemente *adv.* safely.
impunità f. impunity.
impunito *adj.* unpunished.
impuntarsi *vr.* to insist (*on*), persist (*in*), set one's mind (*on*, *to*); to stop short; to stutter.
impuntigliarsi *vr.* to persist (*in*), set one's mind (*on*, *to*).
impuntura f. stitching, sewing.
impurità f. impurity.
impuro *adj.* impure; tainted.
imputare *vt.* to ascribe, impute; to charge (*with*).
imputato m. defendant; *adj.* accused.
imputazione f. imputation; charge.
imputridire *vi.* to rot.
in *prep.* in, at; to; within; into; with, by; inside; on, upon; against: eravamo — tre, we were three.
ina'bile *adj.* inept; unqualified.
inabilità f. inability, disability.
inabilitare *vt.* to disable; to disqualify.
inabilitazione f. disqualification.
inabissare *vt.*, **inabissarsi** *vr.* to sink.
inabita'bile *adj.* uninhabitable.
inabitabilità f. uninhabitability.
inabitato *adj.* uninhabited.
inaccessi'bile *adj.* inaccessible.
inaccetta'bile *adj.* inacceptable.
inacidire *vi.* to sour.
inacidito *adj.* sour.
inadatto *see* disadatto.
inadeguato *adj.* inadequate.
inadempiente *adj.* unfulfilling.
inafferra'bile *adj.* unseizable; elusive.
inalazione f. inhalation.
inalberare *vt.* to hoist; **inalberarsi** *vr.* to rear up.
inaltera'bile *adj.* inalterable.
inalterato *adj.* unaltered.
inamidare *vt.* to starch.
inammissi'bile *adj.* inadmissible; preposterous.
inamovi'bile *adj.* irremovable; steadfast.
inane *adj.* inane; futile.

inanellato *adj.* curly; ringleted; beringed.
inanimato *adj.* lifeless.
inappagato *adj.* ungratified.
inappella'bile *adj.* unappellable.
inappetenza f. inappetence.
inapprezza'bile *adj.* inappreciable.
inappunta'bile *adj.* faultless; dapper.
inarcare *vt.*, **inarcarsi** *vr.* to arch, camber: inarcare le sopracciglia, to raise one's eyebrows.
inargentare *vt.* to silver.
inaridire *vt.* to dry, parch; *vi.*, **inaridirsi** *vr.* to dry up.
inaridito *adj.* dry; hardened.
inarriva'bile *adj.* unattainable; superlative.
inaspettato *adj.* unexpected.
inasprimento m. exacerbation.
inasprire *vt.* to embitter; to aggravate; to exacerbate; to sharpen; **inasprirsi** *vr.* to grow bitter; to sharpen.
inastare *vt.* to hoist: — una baionetta, to fix a bayonet.
inattacca'bile *adj.* unassailable.
inatteso *adj.* unexpected.
inattivo *adj.* inactive, inert.
inaudito *adj.* unheard-of; incredible.
inaugurale *adj.* inaugural, opening: viaggio —, maiden voyage.
inaugurare *vt.* to inaugurate, open.
inaugurazione f. inauguration, opening.
inavveduto *adj.* rash. [ing.
inavvertenza f. inadvertence.
inavvertitamente *adv.* heedlessly; unintentionally; carelessly.
inavvertito *adj.* unnoticed.
incagliare *vt.* to hinder; to strand; to get stuck; (*mach.*) to jam; **incagliarsi** *vr.* to strand; to jam; to run aground; to become stuck.
inca'glio m. hindrance; jamming.
incalcola'bile *adj.* incalculable.
incallire *vt.*, **incallirsi** *vr.* to harden.
incallito *adj.* hardened, inveterate.
incalzante *adj.* pressing.
incalzare *vt.*, *vi.* to press, chase; to urge.
incamerare *vt.* to confiscate, sequester.
incamminare *vt.* to start; to set going; to direct; **incamminarsi** *vr.* to set out (*for*); to start walking.
incanalare *vt.* to canalize.
incancella'bile *adj.* ineffaceable.
incancrenire *vi.* to gangrene.
incandescente *adj.* incandescent.
incandescenza f. incandescence.
incannare *vt.* to wind, spool.
incantare *vt.* to charm, enchant; **incantarsi** *vr.* to become spellbound; to jam, get stuck.
incantato *adj.* spellbound; enchanted, magic; jammed, stuck.

incantatore m. enchanter.

incantatrice f. enchantress.

incante'simo m. spell, charm.

incante'vole adj. charming; delightful.

incanto (1) m. enchantment, magic: d'—, wonderfully.

incanto (2) m. auction: vendere all'—, to sell at auction.

incanutire vi. to hoar.

incanutito adj. hoary.

incapace m., adj. incapable.

incapacità f. inability, incapacity.

incaponirsi see ostinarsi.

incappare vi. to stumble (on, upon); to incur, run into.

incappucciare vt. to hood.

incapricciarsi vr. to take a fancy (to).

incarcerare vt. to imprison.

incaricare vt. to entrust (with), charge (with); **incaricarsi** vr. to charge oneself (with), see to it, attend (to).

incaricato m. deputy, messenger: — d'affari, chargé d'affaires.

inca'rico m. task, errand; office, duty; mission: per — di, in behalf of.

incarnare vt. to incarnate, embody.

incarnato m. complexion; adj. incarnate.

incarnazione f. incarnation.

incarnito adj. ingrown.

incartamento m. dossier, file.

incartapecorito adj. parchmentlike.

incartare vt. to wrap in paper.

incasellare vt. to pigeonhole.

incassare vt., vi. to box; to cash, collect, bring in; to fit (in); (boxing) to take it.

incasso m. collection; receipts.

incastellatura f. frame.

incastonare vt. to set.

incastrare vt. to infix; to insert; to fit (in, together); to mortise; to embed; **incastrarsi** vr. to get embedded, jam; to squeeze (into).

incastro m. fitting together; socket; groove; mortise; inlaid work.

incatenare vt. to chain.

incatramare vt. to tar.

incautamente adv. rashly.

incauto adj. rash, incautious.

incavallatura f. roof truss.

incavare vt., **incavarsi** vr. to hollow, cave in.

incavato adj. hollow.

incavatura f. hollow.

incavo m. hollow, cavity.

ince'dere vi. to stride.

incendiare vt. to set on fire; **incendiarsi** vr. to take fire.

incendia'rio m. arsonist; adj. incendiary.

incen'dio m. conflagration, fire: — doloso, arson; pompa da —, fire engine.

incenerire vt. to incinerate, burn to ashes.

incensamento m. (fig.) flattery.

incensare vt. to incense; (fig.) to flatter.

incensatore m. flatterer.

incenso m. incense.

incensurato adj. blameless; crimeless.

incentivo m. incentive.

inceppare vt., **incepparsi** vr. to jam.

incerata f. oilcloth.

incertezza f. uncertainty, doubt.

incerto adj. uncertain, dubious; doubtful; unsteady.

incespicare vi. to stumble.

incessante adj. steady, unceasing.

incesto m. incest.

incetta f. cornering.

incettare vt. to corner.

incettatore m. cornerer.

inchiesta f. inquiry, investigation.

inchinare vt. to bend; **inchinarsi** vr. to bow; to submit.

inchino m. bow; curtsy.

inchiodare vt. to nail; to rivet (as one's eyes); to hammer.

inchiostrare vt. to ink.

inchiostro m. ink.

inciampare vi. to stumble (over); to bump (into); to chance (upon).

inciampo m. hitch, hindrance.

incidentale adj. incidental.

incidentalmente adv. incidentally; by the way.

incidente m., adj. incident.

inci'dere vt.[41] to engrave; to etch; (surg.) to incise.

incinta adj. f. pregnant.

incipiente adj. incipient.

incipriare vt., **incipriarsi** vr. to powder (oneself).

incirca, (all') adv. about.

incisione f. incision; notch; engraving, etching.

incisivo m. incisor (tooth); adj. incisive.

incisore m. engraver, etcher.

incitamento m. incitement.

incitare vt. to urge, stimulate, incite.

incivile adj. uncivilized; boorish.

incivilire vt., **incivilirsi** vr. to civilize.

inclemente adj. merciless; inclement.

inclemenza f. mercilessness; inclemency.

inclinare vt., vi. to incline, bend, lean, tilt; **inclinarsi** vr. to lean, bend; to incline; to slant.

inclinazione f. inclination; slope; bent; talent; tendency.

incline adj. inclined, bent.

inclu'dere vt.[2] to include.

incluso adj. included.

incoerente adj. incoherent, inconsistent.

incoerenza *f.* incoherence, inconsistency.

inco'gliere *vi.*[27] to befall.

inco'gnita *f.* (*math.*) unknown quantity; (*fig.*) uncertainty.

inco'gnito *m.* incognito; *adj.* incognito; unknown: **viaggiare in —**, to travel incognito.

incollare *vt.* to paste, stick, glue; to gum; **incollarsi** *vr.* to stick (*to*).

incollatura *f.* sticking; (*turf*) neck.

incollerirsi *vr.* to get angry.

incollerito *adj.* angry.

incolore *adj.* colorless.

incolpa'bile *adj.* accusable.

incolpabilità *f.* innocence.

incolpare *vt.* to accuse (*of*), charge (*with*), blame (*for*).

incolto *adj.* uncultivated; unlearned.

inco'lume *adj.* unhurt, uninjured.

incolumità *f.* safety.

incombente *adj.* impending.

incombenza *f.* errand, task.

incom'bere *vi.* to impend; to be incumbent (*upon*); to be up to.

incominciare *vt.*, *vi.* to begin, start.

incommensura'bile *adj.* incommensurable.

incomodare *vt.* to inconvenience, disturb; **incomodarsi** *vr.* to bother.

inco'modo *m.* inconvenience; *adj.* inconvenient, bothersome; uncomfortable.

incompara'bile *adj.* incomparable, matchless.

incompati'bile *adj.* incompatible, inconsistent, incongruous.

incompatibilità *f.* incompatibility, inconsistency, incongruity.

incompetente *m.*, *adj.* incompetent.

incompetenza *f.* incompetence.

incompiuto *adj.* unfinished.

incompleto *adj.* incomplete.

incomposto *adj.* disorderly; unseemly, unbecoming, unmannerly.

incomprensi'bile *adj.* incomprehensible, unintelligible.

incomprensione *f.* incomprehension, lack of understanding.

incompreso *adj.* misunderstood.

inconcepi'bile *adj.* inconceivable.

inconcilia'bile *adj.* irreconcilable.

inconcludente *adj.* inconclusive.

inconcusso *adj.* unshaken, firm.

incondizionato *adj.* unconditional.

inconfessa'bile *adj.* unavowable.

inconfessato *adj.* unavowed.

inconfuta'bile *adj.* unconfutable.

incongruente *adj.* inconsistent.

incongruenza *f.* inconsistency.

incongruità *f.* incongruity.

incon'gruo *adj.* incongruous.

inconsape'vole *adj.* unconscious, unaware.

incon'scio *m.*, *adj.* unconscious.

inconsiderato *adj.* rash.

inconsistente *adj.* flimsy.

inconsistenza *f.* flimsiness.

inconsueto *adj.* unusual.

inconsulto *adj.* unadvised, rash.

incontaminato *adj.* unpolluted.

incontentabile *adj.* insatiable; hard to please.

incontesta'bile *adj.* incontestable.

incontrare *vt.* to meet, encounter; to meet with; to find; **incontrarsi** *vr.* to meet; to agree.

incontrastato *adj.* undisputed.

incontro (*1*) *m.* meeting, encounter; rendezvous; match, game, fight.

incontro (*2*) *prep.* towards, to; opposite: **andare — a metà strada**, to meet halfway; **andare — a guai**, to be in for trouble.

inconveniente *m.* inconvenience, contretemps, hitch; shortcoming.

incoraggiamento *m.* encouragement.

incoraggiante *adj.* encouraging.

incoraggiare *vt.* to encourage.

incorniciare *vt.* to frame.

incoronare *vt.* to crown.

incoronazione *f.* coronation.

incorporare *vt.*, **incorporarsi** *vr.* to incorporate; to annex.

incorpo'reo *adj.* incorporeal.

incorregi'bile *adj.* incorrigible.

incor'rere *vi.*[16] to incur, suffer.

incorrutti'bile *adj.* incorruptible.

incosciente *m.*, *adj.* irresponsible; unconscious; inanimate.

incoscienza *f.* irresponsibility; unconsciousness.

incostante *adj.* inconstant, changeable; unsteady; fickle.

incostanza *f.* inconstancy, changeableness; fickleness.

incredi'bile *adj.* incredible.

incredulità *f.* incredulity.

incre'dulo *m.* skeptic, unbeliever; *adj.* skeptical, unbelieving.

incrementare *vt.* to foster.

incremento *m.* increment.

increscioso *adj.* disagreeable; deplorable, regrettable.

increspare *vt.*, **incresparsi** *vr.* to ripple; to wrinkle; to crisp.

incriminare *vt.* to incriminate.

incriminato *adj.* incriminated; (*fig.*) offending.

incrinare *vt.*, **incrinarsi** *vr.* to crack, flaw.

incrinatura *f.* crack, flaw.

incrociare *vt.* to cross; to fold; *vi.* (*naut.*) to cruise; **incrociarsi** *vr.* to cross.

incrociato *adj.* crossed: **parole incrociate**, crossword puzzle; **punto —**, cross-stitch.

incrociatore *m.* cruiser.
incro'cio *m.* crossing; cross; cross-roads.
incrolla'bile *adj.* unshakable.
incrostare *vt.* to incrust; to inlay; **incrostarsi** *vr.* to become incrusted.
incrostazione *f.* incrustation.
incruento *adj.* bloodless.
incubatrice *f.* incubator.
incubazione *f.* incubation.
in'cubo *m.* nightmare, incubus.
incu'dine *f.* anvil.
inculcare *vt.* to inculcate (*on, upon*), to impress (*on, upon*).
incuneare *vt.* to wedge.
incura'bile *m., adj.* incurable.
incurante *adj.* heedless.
incu'ria *f.* neglect.
incuriosire *vt.* to make curious, intrigue; **incuriosirsi** *vr.* to become curious.
incuriosito *adj.* intrigued, curious.
incursione *f.* raid, incursion: — aerea, air raid.
incurvare *vt.*, **incurvarsi** *vr.* to bend, stoop; to curve.
incurvatura *f.* incurvation.
incustodito *adj.* unwatched, unguarded.
incu'tere *vt.*⁹⁹ to rouse, command: — terrore, to strike with terror.
in'daco *m.* indigo.
indaffarato *adj.* busy, bustling.
indagare *vt., vi.* to investigate.
indagatore *m.* investigator; *adj.* searching.
inda'gine *f.* investigation, inquiry.
indebitamente *adv.* unduly.
indebitare *vt.* to burden with debts; **indebitarsi** *vr.* to run into debt.
inde'bito *adj.* undue.
indebolimento *m.* enfeeblement.
indebolire *vt.* to weaken; **indebolirsi** *vr.* to weaken; (*fig.*) to fade.
indecente *adj.* indecent.
indecenza *f.* indecency, shame.
indecifra'bile *adj.* indecipherable.
indecisione *f.* indecision, hesitation.
indeciso *adj.* uncertain; irresolute.
indecoroso *adj.* indecorous, unseemly.
indefesso *adj.* unrelenting, indefatigable.
indefini'bile *adj.* indefinable; vague.
indegnità *f.* shamefulness; shame; disgrace; indignity.
indegno *adj.* unworthy; disgraceful.
indelicatezza *f.* indelicacy.
indelicato *adj.* indelicate.
indemoniato *adj.* possessed.
indenne *adj.* undamaged.
indennità *f.* indemnity.
indennizzare *vt.* to indemnify.
indennizzo *m.* indemnity, compensation.

indescrivi'bile *adj.* indescribable.
indeterminato *adj.* indeterminate.
indi *adv.* then; afterwards; hence.
indianista *m.* Indologist.
indiano *m., adj.* Indian.
indiavolato *adj.* frenzied; spirited; excessive.
indicare *vt.* to indicate; to show; to point out; to point at.
indicativo *m., adj.* indicative.
indicato *adj.* fit, suitable; advisable.
indicatore *m.* indicator; gauge; pointer; directory.
indicazione *f.* indication; direction; pointer.
in'dice *m.* index; catalogue; sign; pointer; forefinger: mettere all'—, to place on the (*prohibited*) index.
indici'bile *adj.* inexpressible.
indietreggiare *vi.* to back, fall back, draw back; to withdraw, give way; to shrink.
indietro *adv.* back; backward; backwards; behind; behindhand: il mio orologio è — di tre minuti, my watch is three minutes slow.
indifeso *adj.* defenseless, unprotected.
indifferente *m., adj.* indifferent: egli (ciò) mi è —, he (this) is nothing to me, I can take him (it) or leave him (it).
indifferenza *f.* indifference.
indi'geno *m., adj.* native.
indigente *adj.* poor.
indigenza *f.* poverty.
indigestione *f.* indigestion.
indigesto *adj.* indigestible; uncongenial; boresome.
indignare *vt.* to make indignant; to incense, shock; **indignarsi** *vr.* to become indignant, be outraged.
indignato *adj.* indignant, outraged.
indignazione *f.* indignation.
indimentica'bile *adj.* unforgettable.
indipendente *m., adj.* independent.
indipendentemente *adv.* independently (*of*).
indipendenza *f.* independence.
indire *vt.* to call; to fix.
indirettamente *adv.* indirectly.
indiretto *adj.* indirect.
indirizzare *vt.* to address; to direct.
indirizzo *m.* address; direction; turn; bent.
indisciplina *f.* indiscipline, lack of discipline.
indisciplinato *adj.* unruly.
indiscreto *adj.* indiscreet, inquisitive.
indiscrezione *f.* indiscretion; blunder.
indiscusso *adj.* undisputed.
indiscuti'bile *adj.* indisputable.
indiscutibilmente *adv.* indisputably, unquestionably.
indispensa'bile *adj., m.* indispensable.

indispettire vt. to peeve; **indispettirsi** vr. to get sore.

indisporre vt. to indispose; to disgust, annoy, vex.

indisposizione f. indisposition.

indisposto adj. indisposed, ill.

indissolu'bile adj. indissoluble.

indistinto adj. indistinct, dim, vague.

indistrutti'bile adj. indestructible.

indisturbato adj. unmolested.

indi'via f. endive.

individuale adj. individual.

individualmente adv. individually.

individuare vt. to individuate; to single out; to spot.

indivi'duo m. individual; fellow, "guy," man.

indivisi'bile adj. indivisible; (fig.) inseparable.

indiviso adj. undivided.

indizia'rio adj. circumstantial.

indiziato m., adj. suspect.

indi'zio m. clue, symptom.   ●

indo'cile adj. unruly, indocile.

in'dole f. disposition, temper; character, nature.

indolente adj. indolent, lazy.

indolenza f. indolence, laziness.

indolenzimento m. aching.

indolenzire vi. to ache; **indolenzirsi** vr. to become sore.

indolenzito adj. aching.

indoma'bile adj. untamable; indomitable.

indomani m. morrow: all'—, on the morrow, the following day.

indo'mito adj. indomitable.

indorare vt. to gild: — la pillola, to sugar-coat the pill.

indorato adj., pp. gilt.

indoratore m. gilder.

indoratura f. gilding.

indossare vt. to wear; to don, put on.

indossatrice f. model, mannequin.

indosso adv. on: avere, mettere —, to have (to put) on.

indotto m. (elec.) rotor; adj. induced. pp. of indurre.

indovinare vt. to guess; to foresee; to imagine: **indovinarla**, to guess right; to hit the mark.

indovinato adj. felicitous, effective.

indovinello m. riddle, puzzle.

indovino m. diviner; fortuneteller.

indubbiamente adv. certainly.

indub'bio adj. certain.

indugiare vi. to delay, linger; to hesitate; to dwell (upon).

indu'gio m. delay: rompere gli indugi, to stop being hesitant, to make up one's mind and take decisive action.

indulgente adj. indulgent, lenient.

indulgenza f. indulgence, leniency.

indul'gere vi.[*] to be indulgent (to); to allow; to indulge (in).

indulto m. pardon; indult.

indumento m. garment; (pl.) clothes.

indurimento m. hardening.

indurire vt., vi. to harden.

indurre vt.[*] to induce; to lead; to persuade; **indursi** vr. to bring oneself (to).

indu'stria f. industry; manufacture.

industriale m. manufacturer, industrialist; adj. industrial.

industrializzare vt. to industrialize.

industrializzazione f. industrialization.

industriarsi vr. to endeavor (to); to make shift.

industrioso adj. industrious; enterprising, energetic.

induttivo adj. inductive.

induttore m. inductor.

induzione f. induction.

inebetire vt., vi. to dull.

inebetito adj. dazed, stupefied.

inebriare vt. to inebriate, intoxicate.

ineccepi'bile adj. unexceptionable.

ine'dia f. starvation.

ine'dito adj. unpublished.

ineducato adj. ill-bred, rude.

ineffa'bile adj. ineffable.

inefficace adj. ineffectual.

inefficac'cia f. inefficacy.

ineguaglianza see disuguaglianza.

ineguagliato adj. unequaled.

ineguale see disuguale.

inelutta'bile adj. ineluctable, inevitable.

inenarra'bile adj. unspeakable, untellable.

inerente adj. inherent.

inerenza f. inherence.

inerme adj. unarmed, defenseless.

inerpicarsi vr. to clamber.

inerte adj. inert; idle.

iner'zia f. inertness; inertia; idleness.

inesattezza f. inaccuracy; mistake.

inesatto adj. inaccurate, inexact.

inesaudito adj. ungranted.

inesauri'bile adj. inexhaustible.

inescusa'bile adj. inexcusable.

inesigi'bile adj. uncollectible.

inesistente adj. inexistent.

inesistenza f. inexistence.

inesora'bile adj. inexorable.

inesperienza f. inexperience.

inesperto adj. inexperienced, unskilled.

inesplica'bile adj. inexplicable.

inesplorato adj. unexplored.

inesploso adj. unexploded.

inesprimi'bile adj. unexpressible.

inespugna'bile adj. impregnable.

inespugnato adj. unconquered.

inestima'bile adj. inestimable, priceless.

inestingui'bile *adj.* inextinguishable, unquenchable.

inestrica'bile *adj.* inextricable.

inettitu'dine *f.* ineptitude.

inetto *adj.* inept; worthless.

inevaso *adj.* unanswered.

inevita'bile *m., adj.* inevitable.

ine'zia *f.* trifle.

infagottare *vt.* to muffle up.

infalli'bile *adj.* infallible.

infallibilità *f.* infallibility.

infamante *adj.* disgraceful.

infamare *vt.* to disgrace; to slander.

infame *adj.* infamous; distasteful.

infa'mia *f.* infamy, disgrace.

infangare *vt.* to muddy; to bespatter; **infangarsi** *vr.* to become muddy; (*fig.*) to degrade oneself.

infante *m.* infant, baby; Infante (*royal prince of Spain*).

infantici'dio *m.* infanticide.

infantile *adj.* infantile; childish.

infan'zia *f.* infancy, childhood.

infarcire *vt.* to stuff (*with*), cram.

infarinare *vt.* to flour, dredge; **infarinarsi** *vr.* to get covered with flour; to powder (*oneself*).

infarinatura *f.* (*fig.*) smattering.

infarto *m.* infarction; (*popularly*) heart disease.

infastidire *vt.* to annoy, irk; to irritate; **infastidirsi** *vr.* to fret, feel annoyed.

infatica'bile *adj.* tireless.

infatti *adv.* in fact; indeed; that's it.

infatuare *vt.* to infatuate; **infatuarsi** *vr.* to become infatuated.

infatuazione *f.* infatuation.

infa'usto *adj.* unfortunate, inauspicious, ominous.

infecondo *adj.* infecund, barren.

infedele *m.* infidel; *adj.* unfaithful.

infedeltà *f.* unfaithfulness; infidelity.

infelice *m.* wretch; *adj.* unhappy, miserable; unlucky; unfortunate.

infelicità *f.* unhappiness, misery.

inferiore *m.* inferior, subordinate; *adj.* inferior; lower.

inferiorità *f.* inferiority.

inferire *vt.* to infer.

infermeri'a *f.* infirmary.

infermiera *f.* nurse.

infermiere *m.* (male) nurse.

infermità *f.* infirmity, disease.

infermo *m.* patient; *adj.* ill, sick.

infernale *adj.* infernal.

inferno *m.* hell, inferno: **mandare all'—**, to consign to the devil.

inferocire *vt.* to fiercen; to madden.

inferocito *adj.* infuriated.

inferriata *f.* grating.

infervorarsi *vr.* to warm up.

infervorato *adj.* excited, fervid.

infestare *vt.* to infest.

infettare *vt.* to infect; **infettarsi** *vr.* to become infected.

infettivo *adj.* infectious.

infetto *adj.* infected, tainted.

infezione *f.* infection.

inflacchire *vt., vi.,* **inflacchirsi** *vr.* to weaken.

infiamma'bile *adj.* inflammable.

infiammare *vt.* to inflame; **infiammarsi** *vr.* to become inflamed.

infiammato'rio *adj.* inflammatory.

infiammato *adj.* aflame; inflamed (*with*).

infiammazione *f.* inflammation.

infido *adj.* treacherous.

in fieri *adv.* (*L.*) pending; to come, to become.

infierire *vi.* to rage: **— su**, to harass.

infig'gere *vt.* to infix, drive (*into*).

infilare *vt.* to insert; to slip; to thread (*a needle*); to string (*beads*); **infilarsi** *vr.* to slip into: **infilarsi un vestito**, to slip one's dress on, to step into a dress.

infilata *f.* string; row.

infiltrarsi *vr.* to infiltrate; to leak (*into*).

infiltrazione *f.* infiltration.

infilzare *vt.* to string; to pierce through.

infilzata *f.* string.

in'fimo *adj.* lowest, basest.

infine *adv.* after all; at last; well.

infingardo *m.* sluggard; *adj.* sluggish.

infinità *f.* infinity; infinitude.

infinitamente *adv.* infinitely; (*fig.*) awfully.

infinite'simo *m.* infinitesimal.

infinito *m.* infinite; (*gramm.*) infinitive; *adj.* infinite.

infino (a) *see* **fino (a)**.

infinocchiare *vt.* to fool.

infioccare *vt.* to tassel.

infiorare *vt.* to flower; to embellish.

infirmare *vt.* to invalidate.

infischiarsi *vr.* not to care (*about*); to make light (*of*).

infisso *m.* fixture; *adj.* infixed.

infittire *vt., vi.* to thicken.

inflazione *f.* inflation.

inflessi'bile *adj.* inflexible, unbending.

inflessibilità *f.* inflexibility.

inflessione *f.* inflection.

inflig'gere *vt.* to inflict.

influente *adj.* influential.

influenza *f.* influence; influenza, flu.

influenzare *vt.* to influence, sway.

influire *vi.* to act (*on*): **— su**, to affect.

influsso *m.* influence.

infocare *vt.* to make red-hot; to incandesce; **infocarsi** *vr.* to become red-hot.

infocato *adj.* incandescent, red-hot.

infognarsi *vr.* to plunge; to get involved.

infoltire *vi.* to thicken.

infondato *adj.* groundless.

infon'dere *vt.* to infuse, inspire, instill.

inforcare *vt.* to fork; to mount (*on*):
— **gli occhiali**, to put on one's glasses.

informare *vt.* to shape; to inspire; to inform, advise; to acquaint (*with*); **informarsi** *vr.* to inquire (*about*); to conform (*to*).

informativo *adj.* informative.

informatore *m.* informer.

informazione *f.* information; tip.

informe *adj.* shapeless.

infornare *vt.* to put into an oven.

infornata *f.* batch.

infortunato *adj.*, *m.* casualty.

infortu'nio *m.* accident.

infossare *vt.* to hollow, cave; to bury; **infossarsi** *vr.* to sink, hollow, cave in.

infossato *adj.* sunken; buried; caved-in.

infradiciare *vt.*, **infradiciarsi** *vr.* to make sodden; to rot.

inframmettente *m.* busybody; *adj.* meddlesome.

inframmettenza *f.* meddlesomeness.

infran'gere *vt.*,⁴⁴ **infran'gersi** *vr.* to break, shatter, crush.

infrangi'bile *adj.* infrangible; shatter-proof.

infranto *adj.* broken, shattered.

infrarosso *m.*, *adj.* infrared.

infrazione *f.* infringement.

infreddatura *f.* cold.

infreddolirsi *vr.* to chill.

infreddolito *adj.* chilly.

infrequenza *f.* infrequency.

infruttuoso *adj.* unprofitable, unfruitful; useless.

infuriare *vi.* to rage; **infuriarsi** *vr.* to flare up; to get angry.

infuriato *adj.* furious.

infusione *f.* infusion.

infuso *m.* infusion; *adj.* infused.

ingabbiare *vt.* to encage.

ingaggiare *vt.* to engage, enlist.

ingag'gio *m.* engagement; (*mil.*) enlistment.

ingagliardire *vt.*, *vi.*; **ingagliardirsi** *vr.* to strengthen.

ingannare *vt.* to deceive, mislead; to while away (*time*); to ward off (*hunger, sleep*); **ingannarsi** *vr.* to deceive oneself, fool oneself; to be mistaken.

ingannatore *m.* deceiver; *adj.* deceitful.

inganne'vole *adj.* deceitful, misleading.

inganno *m*; deception; fraud: **trarre in —**, to deceive.

ingarbugliare *vt.*, **ingarbugliarsi** *vr.* to tangle; to jumble.

ingegnarsi *vr.* to endeavor; to make shift.

ingegnere *m.* engineer.

ingegneri'a *f.* engineering.

ingegno *m.* genius, talent.

ingegnosità *f.* ingeniousness.

ingegnoso *adj.* ingenious.

ingelosire *vt.* to make jealous. *vi.*, **ingelosirsi** *vr.* to become jealous.

ingemmare *vt.* to gem; to bejewel; *vi.* (*bot.*) to bud.

ingenerare *vt.* to engender.

ingeneroso *adj.* ungenerous, illiberal.

ingente *adj.* very great; very heavy.

ingentilire *vt.*, *vi.*, **ingentilirsi** *vr.* to refine; to soften.

ingenuamente *adv.* naïvely.

ingenuità *f.* naïveness, artlessness.

inge'nuo *adj.* naïve, artless.

ingerenza *f.* connection; interference.

ingerire *vt.* to ingest; **ingerirsi** *vr.* to meddle (*with*).

ingessare *vt.* to plaster; to cast.

ingessatura *f.* plastering; cast.

Inghilterra *f.* England.

inghiottire *vt.* to swallow.

inghirlandare *vt.* to wreathe.

ingiallire *vt.*, *vi.* to yellow.

ingiallito *adj.* yellowed, faded.

ingigantire *vt.* to exaggerate, amplify. *vi.* to become enormous.

inginocchiarsi *vr.* to kneel (*down*).

inginocchiato'io *m.* kneeler.

ingioiellare *vt.* to bejewel.

ingiù *adv.* downwards, down.

ingiun'gere *vt.*⁷⁸ to enjoin, order.

ingiunzione *f.* injunction; order.

ingiu'ria *f.* insult, abuse, slight; injury.

ingiuriare *vt.* to abuse, revile.

ingiurioso *adj.* insulting, reviling.

ingiustamente *adv.* unfairly; wrongly.

ingiustificato *adj.* unjustified; unwarranted.

ingiusti'zia *f.* injustice; wrong.

ingiusto *adj.* unjust; unfair; wrong.

inglese *m.* Englishman; *f.* Englishwoman; English, (the) English language. *adj.* English, British: **andarsene all'—**, to take French leave.

inglorioso *adj.* inglorious.

ingoiare *see* **inghiottire**.

ingolatore *m.* swallower.

ingolfarsi *vr.* to plunge (*into*); to involve oneself.

ingollare *vt.* to gulp (*down*).

ingolosire *vt.* to make greedy, tempt. **ingolosirsi** *vr.* to become gluttonous; to be tempted.

ingombrante *adj.* cumbersome.

ingombrare *vt.* to encumber; to obstruct; to clutter.

ingombro *m.* encumbrance; *adj.* cluttered, encumbered (*with*).

ingommare *vt.* to gum; to stick.

ingordi'gia *f.* greed.

ingordo *m.* glutton. *adj.* greedy.

ingorgamento *m.* obstruction.

ingorgare *vt.*, **ingorgarsi** *vr.* to clog, choke up.

ingorgo *m.* obstruction: **— stradale**, traffic jam.

ingoverna'bile *adj.* ungovernable.

ingozzare *vt.* to gobble; to cram.

ingranag'gio *m.* gear; gearing.

ingranare *vt.* to throw into gear; *vi.* to engage; (*fam.*) to go, succeed.

ingrandimento *m.* enlargement; (*photo.*) blow-up: **lente d'—**, magnifying glass.

ingrandire *vt.*, *vi.* to enlarge; to grow; to increase; (*opt.*) to magnify; (*photo.*) to enlarge; **ingrandirsi** *vr.* to enlarge, increase; to expand.

ingrassare *vt.* to fatten; to grease. *vi.* to fatten, grow fat.

ingratitu'dine *f.* ingratitude.

ingrato *m.* ingrate; *adj.* ungrateful; unpleasant; thankless.

ingraziarsi *vr.* to ingratiate oneself (*with*).

ingrediente *m.* ingredient.

ingresso *m.* entrance; admittance; entry.

ingrossamento *m.* bulge; swelling; increase.

ingrossare *vt.* to enlarge, make bigger; to increase; to swell; *vi.*, **ingrossarsi** *vr.* to enlarge, grow bigger; to increase; to swell.

ingrosso, (all') *adv.* (by) wholesale.

inguainare *vt.* to sheathe.

inguari'bile *adj.* incurable.

in'guine *m.* groin.

ingurgitare *vt.* to ingurgitate.

inibire *vt.* to inhibit.

inibizione *f.* inhibition.

inido'neo *adj.* unfit, unqualified.

iniettare *vt.* to inject.

iniettato *adj.* injected: **— di sangue**, bloodshot.

iniettore *m.* injector.

iniezione *f.* injection, needle.

inimicare *vt.* to estrange (*from*); **inimicarsi** *vr.* to estrange from oneself; to fall off.

inimici'zia *f.* enmity; hatred.

inimita'bile *adj.* inimitable.

inimmagina'bile *adj.* unimaginable.

inintelligi'bile *adj.* unintelligible.

ininterrotto *adj.* uninterrupted.

iniquità *f.* iniquity.

iniquo *adj.* iniquitous; wicked; unfair.

iniziale *f.*, *adj.* initial.

iniziare *vt.* to begin, start; to initiate (*into*).

iniziativa *f.* initiative; enterprise: **mancare d'—**, to lack initiative.

iniziato *m.*, *adj.* initiate.

iniziatore *m.* initiator.

iniziazione *f.* initiation.

ini'zio *m.* beginning: **sin dall'—**, from the beginning.

innaffiare *vt.* to water; to sprinkle.

innaffiato'io *m.* watering pot, sprinkler.

innalzare *vt.* to raise, elevate, lift; to erect; to exalt; **innalzarsi** *vr.* to rise; to elevate oneself; to tower.

innamorare *vt.* to charm, fascinate; **innamorarsi** *vr.* to fall in love (*with*).

innamorato *m.*, **innamorata** *f.* sweetheart, lover. *adj.* in love (*with*); (*fig.*) fond (*of*).

innanzi *prep.*, *adv.* before; in front of; ahead; on, forward: **tirare —**, to get along; **d'ora —**, from now on; **— tutto**, first of all; **— tempo**, prematurely.

innato *adj.* inborn, native.

innega'bile *adj.* undeniable.

inneggiare *vt.*, *vi.* to exalt; to cheer.

innesco *m.* primer.

innestare *vt.* (*med.*) to inoculate (*with*); to insert; (*bot.*, *surg.*) to graft; (*mach.*) to engage.

innesto *m.* (*med.*) inoculation; (*bot.*, *surg.*) graft; (*mach.*) coupling, clutch.

inno *m.* hymn; anthem.

innocente *m.* innocent; *adj.* innocent, guiltless; harmless; candid.

innocenza *f.* innocence, candor.

inno'cuo *adj.* innocuous, harmless.

innominato *adj.* unnamed; nameless.

innovatore *m.* innovator; *adj.* innovating.

innovazione *f.* innovation, novelty.

innumere'vole *adj.* numberless.

inoculare *vt.* to inoculate.

inoculazione *f.* inoculation.

inodoro *adj.* odorless, inodorous.

inoffensivo *adj.* inoffensive, harmless.

inoltrare *vt.* to forward; **inoltrarsi** *vr.* to advance.

inoltre *adv.* besides, moreover.

inoltro *m.* forwarding.

inondare *vt.* to flood.

inondazione *f.* inundation, flood.

inoperosità *f.* idleness.

inoperoso *adj.* idle.

inopinatamente *adv.* unexpectedly.

inopinato *adj.* unexpected, sudden.

inopportunità *f.* inopportuneness; untimeliness.

inopportuno *adj.* inopportune, untimely.

inoppugna'bile *adj.* indisputable.

inorgoglire *vt.* to elate; *vi.*, **inorgo-**

glirsi vr. to become elated; to pride oneself (upon).

inorridire vt. to horrify; vi. to be horrified, shudder.

inorridito adj. horrified.

inospitale adj. inhospitable

inosservante adj. remiss; non observant.

inosservanza f. remissness, nonobservance.

inosservato adj. unnoticed.

inossida'bile adj. inoxidizable; stainless.

inquadrare vt. to frame; to arrange; (moving pictures) to frame; (mil.) to rank, marshal; **inquadrarsi** vr. to be framed; (fig.) to conform, adjust (to).

inqualifica'bile adj. despicable.

inquietante adj. disquieting.

inquietare vt. to worry; to irk; to trouble; **inquietarsi** vr. to get angry.

inquieto adj. worried, uneasy fretful; angry; impatient, restless.

inquietu'dine f. uneasiness, worry; restlessness; fretfulness.

inquilino m. lodger, tenant.

inquinare vt. to pollute.

inquirente adj. investigating.

inquisitore m. inquisitor.

inquisizione f. inquisition.

insabbiare vt. to sand; (fig.) to put aside, pigeonhole; **insabbiarsi** vr. to cover oneself with sand; (fig.) to go native.

insaccare vt. to sack; (fig.) to cram, stuff.

insalata f. salad.

insalubre adj. unhealthy, insalubrious.

insalutato adj. unsaluted: andarsene — ospite, to take French leave.

insana'bile adj. irremediable.

insanguinare vt. to stain with blood, make gory; **insanguinarsi** vr to stain oneself with blood.

insanguinato adj. gory, bloody.

insano adj. mad, insane.

insaponare vt. to soap; to lather.

insaporire vt. to flavor.

insaputa, (all') adv. unknown (to).

insazia'bile adj. insatiable.

inscenare vt. to stage.

inscindi'bile adj. unseverable.

inscri'vere etc. see iscrivere.

insecchire vt., vi. to dry up.

insediamento m. induction (into).

insediare vt. to install; **insediarsi** vr. to install oneself; to settle.

insegna f. insigne (pl. insignia); flag; sign, signboard; emblem; coat of arms.

insegnamento m. teaching; education; doctrine, tuition.

insegnante m., f. teacher; adj. teaching.

insegnare vt. to teach; to show.

inseguimento m. chase, pursuit.

inseguire vt. to pursue.

inseguitore m. pursuer.

insellare vt. to saddle.

insellatura f. saddle.

insenatura f. inlet, creek.

insensatag'gine f. nonsensicalness; nonsense, folly.

insensatezza see insensataggine.

insensato m. fool; adj. foolish; nonsensical; rash.

insensi'bile adj. insensible; unfeeling; imperceptible.

insensibilità f. insensibility.

insepara'bile adj. inseparable.

insepolto adj. unburied.

inserire vt.[1] to insert; to enclose; **inserirsi** vr. to enter (into).

inserto m. dossier.

inservi'bile adj. unserviceable, useless.

inserviente adj. attendant.

inserzione f. insertion; advertisement, "ad."

inserzionista m. advertiser.

insetticida m. insecticide; adj. insecticidal.

insetto m. insect.

insi'dia f. snare; ambush; danger.

insidiare vt. to endanger, undermine.

insidioso adj. insidious; tricky.

insieme m. (the) whole; ensemble: nell'—, on the whole; adv., prep. together (with); at the same time, simultaneously.

insigne adj. distinguished, eminent.

insignificante adj. insignificant.

insignire vt. to confer upon.

insincero adj. insincere.

insindaca'bile adj. undisputable.

insinuante adj. insinuating.

insinuare vt. to insinuate, hint; to insert; **insinuarsi** vr. to insinuate oneself, creep (in).

insinuazione f. insinuation, hint, innuendo.

insi'pido adj. insipid.

insipienza f. insipience.

insistente adj. insistent; steady.

insistenza f. insistence.

insi'stere vi. to insist (on); to dwell (upon).

in'sito adj. inborn, inherent.

insoddisfatto adj. dissatisfied.

insofferente adj. intolerant.

insofferenza f. intolerance.

insoffri'bile adj. unbearable.

insolazione f. sunstroke.

insolente m., f., adj. insolent.

insolentire vt. to insult, abuse.

insolenza f. insolence; insult.

inso'lito adj. unusual, uncommon.

insolu'bile adj. insoluble.

insoluto adj. unsolved; unpaid.

insolvenza *f.* insolvency.
insolvibilità *f.* insolvency.
insomma *adv.* finally; in short, in a word; after all.
insonda'bile *adj.* unfathomable.
insonne *adj.* sleepless.
inson'nia *f.* sleeplessness.
insonnolito *adj.* drowsy, sleepy.
insopporta'bile *adj.* unbearable.
insor'gere *vi.*[110] to rise, rebel; to arise: far —, to rouse.
insormonta'bile *adj.* insuperable.
insorto *m., adj.* insurgent, rebel.
insospetta'bile *adj.* above suspicion.
insospettire *vt.* to make suspicious; insospettirsi *vr.* to become suspicious.
insospettito *adj.* suspicious.
insosteni'bile *adj.* unsustainable.
insozzare *vt.* to sully.
isperato *adj.* unhoped for; unexpected.
inspessimento *m.* thickening.
inspessire *vt.,* inspessirsi *vr.* to thicken.
inspirare *vt.* to inhale.
inspirazione *f.* inhalation.
insta'bile *adj.* unstable, unsteady; fickle.
instabilità *f.* unsteadiness.
installare *vt.* to install; to establish, set up. installarsi *vr.* to settle.
installazione *f.* installation.
instancabile *adj.* untiring.
instaurare *vt.* to establish.
instaurazione *f.* establishment.
instillare *see* istillare.
instradare *vt.* to direct, guide; to coach.
insù *adv.* upwards, up.
insubordinato *m., adj.* insubordinate.
insubordinazione *f.* insubordination.
insuccesso *m.* failure, fiasco.
insudiciare *vt.* to dirty.
insufficiente *adj.* insufficient.
insufficienza *f.* insufficiency.
insulare *adj.* insular.
insulina *f.* insulin.
insulsag'gine *f.* silliness; nonsense.
insulso *adj.* insipid, vapid, insignificant.
insultante *adj.* insulting, abusive.
insultare *vt.* to insult, abuse.
insulto *m.* slight, insult; (*pl.*) abuse.
insupera'bile *adj.* insuperable; unsurpassable.
insuperato *adj.* unsurpassed.
insuperbire *vt., vi.,* insuperbirsi *vr.* to swell (*with pride*).
insurrezione *f.* insurrection.
insussistente *adj.* flimsy.
intabarrare *vt.* to wrap up (*in a cloak*).
intaccare *vt.* to notch; to injure; to gnaw: — un capitale, to draw upon a capital.

intaccatura *f.* notch.
intagliare *vt.* to intaglio; to engrave; to carve.
inta'glio *m.* intaglio; indentation.
intangi'bile *adj.* intangible.
intangibilità *f.* intangibility.
intanto *adv.* meanwhile; for the time being.
intarsiare *vt.* to inlay.
intarsiato *adj.* inlaid.
intar'sio *m.* inlaying.
intasare *vt., vi.,* intasarsi *vr.* to choke, clog.
intasatura *f.* obstruction.
intascare *vt.* to pocket.
intatto *adj.* intact, untouched.
intavolare *vt.* to board, plank: — una conversazione, to start a conversation; — trattative, to open up negotiations.
integer'rimo *adj.* blameless, righteous.
integrale *adj.* integral; unabridged.
integrante *adj.* integrant, integrating.
integrare *vt.* to complete, integrate.
integrazione *f.* integration.
integrità *f.* integrity.
in'tegro *adj.* whole, complete; honest, upright.
intelaiatura *f.* framing; frame.
intelletto *m.* intellect; understanding.
intellettuale *m., adj.* intellectual.
intellettualità *f.* intellectuality.
intelligente *adj.* intelligent; clever; smart.
intelligenza *f.* intelligence; cleverness; intellect.
intelligi'bile *adj.* intelligible.
intemerata *f.* reprimand.
intemerato *adj.* unblemished.
intemperante *adj.* intemperate.
intemperanza *f.* intemperance.
intempe'rie *f. pl.* inclement weather.
intempestività *f.* untimeliness.
intempestivo *adj.* untimely.
intendente *m.* manager; superintendent.
intendenza *f.* intendancy, superintendence.
inten'dere *vt.*[110] to intend (*to*), mean; to understand; to hear: far —, to give to understand; — a rovescio, to misunderstand; non — ragioni, not to listen to reason; inten'dersi *vr.* to understand each other; to be conversant (*with*), be well versed (*in*); to get along (*with*), agree: s'intende! of course!
intendimento *m.* understanding; purpose.
intenditore *m.* expert; connoisseur: a buon — poche parole, a word to the wise is sufficient.
intenerire *vt.,* intenerirsi *vr.* to soften.
intensamente *adv.* intensely.

intensificare vt., **intensificarsi** vr. to intensify, increase.

intensità f. intensity.

intenso adj. intense.

intentare vt. to institute, bring (action against).

intentato adj. unattempted.

intento (1) m. intent; aim; intention: **con l'— di,** with a view to.

intento (2) adj. intent.

intenzionale adj. intentional, deliberate.

intenzionato adj. determined; willing: **ben' (mal') —,** well- (ill-) intentioned.

intenzione f. intention; design, view, mind.

intepidire vt. to make tepid; to warm (anything cold); to cool (anything hot); **intepidirsi** vr. to get tepid; to warm up; to cool down.

interamente adv. wholly.

intercalare m. recurring word; refrain; adj. intercalary.

intercalare vt. to intercalate, interpolate.

intercape'dine f. air space, hollow space; gap; cavity.

interce'dere vi.²⁸ to intercede (with).

intercessione f. intercession.

intercettare vt. to intercept.

intercomunale adj., f. (teleph.) long-distance (call).

intercor'rere vi. to elapse; to intervene.

interdetto adj. disabled; nonplussed.

interdire vt. to interdict, forbid; to incapacitate.

interdizione f. interdiction.

interessamento m. interest, concern; co-operation.

interessante adj. interesting: **in stato —,** pregnant.

interessare vt. to interest; to concern, regard; vi. to be of interest (to); to matter; **interessarsi** vr. to take an interest (in); to concern oneself (with); to take care (of), attend (to).

interessato m. interested party. **a tutti gli interessati,** to all concerned; adj. interested; greedy; biased.

interesse m. interest; advantage; care, concern; importance.

interessenza f. percentage.

interferenza f. interference.

interferire vi. to interfere.

interfogliare vt. to interleave.

interiezione f. interjection.

interinale adj. interim.

interinato m. interim office.

interino m. substitute; adj. temporary.

interiora f.pl. entrails.

interiore m. inside, interior; adj. inside, inner, interior.

interli'nea f. interline; (typog.) lead.

interlineare vt. to interline; (typog.) to lead.

interlineatura f. (typog.) leading.

interlocutore m. interlocutor.

interloquire vi. to chime in.

interlu'dio m. interlude.

intermedia'rio m. intermediary, go-between; (comm.) middleman; adj. intermediate, intermediary.

interme'dio adj. middle, intermediate.

intermezzo m. intermission, interval.

intermina'bile adj. endless.

intermittente adj. intermittent.

intermittenza f. intermittence.

internamente adv. internally.

internamento m. internment.

internare vt. intern; **internarsi** vr. to penetrate (into).

internato m. internee; adj. interned.

internazionale adj. international.

internazionalizzare vt. to internationalize.

interno m. inside, interior; inland; intern; (moving pictures) set, interior; adj. inside, internal; interior, inner: **commercio —,** home trade; **alunno —,** boarder.

intero see **intiero.**

interpellanza f. interpellation.

interpellare vt. to consult; to interpellate; to question.

interpianeta'rio adj. interplanetary.

interpolare vt. to interpolate.

interpolazione f. interpolation.

interporre vt.,³¹ **interporsi** vr. to interpose.

interposto adj. interposed: **interposta persona,** go-between, intermediary.

interpretare vt. to interpret; (theat.) to play, act; (mus.) to perform.

interpretazione f. interpretation; (theat.) acting; (mus.) performance.

inter'prete m. interpreter; actor, player; performer.

interpunzione f. punctuation.

interrare vt. to inter.

interregno m. interregnum.

interrogare vt. to question.

interrogativo m. question; adj. interrogative: **punto —,** interrogation mark.

interroga'rio m. examination; questioning. adj. interrogatory.

interrogazione f. interrogation; question, query.

interrom'pere vt. to interrupt; **interrompersi** vr. to interrupt oneself; to cease, stop.

interruttore m. interrupter; (elec.) switch.

interruzione f. interruption.

intersecare vt., **intersecarsi** vr. to intersect.

intersezione f. intersection.

intersti'zio m. interstice.

interurbana, (chiamata) f. (teleph.) long-distance call.

intervallo m. interval; gap.

intervenire vi. to intervene; to interfere; to attend; (surg.) to operate.

intervento m. intervention; interference; attendance; (surg.) operation.

intervista f. interview.

intervistare vt. to interview.

intervistatore m. interviewer.

intesa f. agreement; entente.

inteso adj. agreed, understood: **non darsene per —,** to take no notice, not to take the hint.

intestare vt. to head, caption; to inscribe, register; **intestarsi** vr. to take into one's head.

intestato adj. headed, captioned, inscribed, entered (in the name of); determined, dogged; (law) intestate.

intestazione f. heading.

intestinale adj. intestinal.

intestino m., adj. intestine.

intiepidire see intepidire.

intiero m. whole; adj. whole, complete; entire: **per —,** wholly, completely, fully.

intimamente adv. intimately; inside; at heart.

intimare vt. to order; to enjoin: **— la resa a,** to summon to surrender.

intimazione f. order; injunction; notice.

intimidazione f. intimidation.

intimidire vt. to abash; **intimidirsi** vr. to feel abashed.

intimidito adj. bashful.

intimità f. intimacy.

in'timo m. soul, heart; adj. intimate, deep; inmost.

intimorire vt. to frighten; **intimorirsi** vr. to get frightened.

intin'gere vt.[144] to dip.

intin'golo m. gravy, sauce.

intinto pp. of intingere.

intirizzire vt. to benumb; to stiffen.

intirizzito adj. numb; stiff.

intisichire vi. to wither.

intitolare vt. to title; to dedicate; to name; **intitolarsi** vr. to be titled; to be named (after).

intollera'bile adj. intolerable.

intollerante adj. intolerant.

intolleranza f. intolerance.

intonacare vt. to plaster.

into'naco m. plaster.

intonare vt. to intone; to tone; to tune; **intonarsi** vr. to harmonize (with).

intonato adj. tuned; in tune (with).

intonazione f. intonation; tune.

intonso adj. uncut.

intontire vt. to stun, dull.

intoppare vt., vi. to stumble (on).

intoppo m. hindrance.

intorbidare, intorbidire vt., **intorbidarsi** vr. to muddy; to blur.

intorno prep., adv. around, about, round: **togliersi uno d'—,** to get rid of one.

intorpidimento m. numbness, torpor.

intorpidire vt. to benumb, make torpid; **intorpidirsi** vr. to get benumbed.

intossicare vt. to poison.

intossicazione f. poisoning.

intraduci'bile adj. untranslatable.

intralciare vt. to hinder.

intral'cio m. hindrance.

intramezzare vt. to intersperse, alternate.

intransigente m., adj. intransigent.

intransigenza f. intransigence.

intransitivo m., adj. intransitive.

intrappolare vt. to entrap.

intraprendente adj. enterprising.

intraprendenza f. enterprise, daring, initiative.

intrapren'dere vt. to start; to undertake; to engage in.

intratta'bile adj. unmanageable; peevish.

intrattenere vt. to entertain; **intrattenersi** vr. to linger; to dwell (upon).

intravedere vt.[181] to glimpse, catch a glimpse of.

intravisto pp. of intravedere.

intrecciare vt. to intertwine; to plait: **— rapporti,** to establish relations; **— le dita,** to lace one's fingers. **intrecciarsi** vr. to intertwine; to crisscross.

intrec'cio m. plaiting, interlacement; plot (as of a novel).

intre'pido adj. fearless, intrepid.

intricare vt., **intricarsi** vr. to tangle.

intricato adj. tangled, intricate, complicated.

intrico m. tangle, intricacy.

intri'dere vt.[45] to soak (with), steep (in).

intrigante m. intriguer; adj. crafty, meddlesome.

intrigare vi. to plot, intrigue; **intrigarsi** vr. to meddle (with).

intrigo m. plot, intrigue.

intrin'seco m. intrinsicality; core; heart, inside; intimate friend; adj. intrinsic, inherent; intimate.

intriso adj. steeped (in), soaked (with): **— di sangue,** imbrued with blood. pp. of intridere.

intristire vi. to degenerate, sour; to wither, droop, waste away.

introdotto pp. of introdurre.

introdurre vt.[.] to introduce, insert; to show in; to slip; to thrust (into); to

import; introdursi vr. to introduce oneself; to slip (*into*); to penetrate.
introduttivo adj. introductory.
introduzione f. introduction; preface; (*mus.*) overture.
introitare vt. to cash.
introito m. gains, returns.
intromet'tere vt. to intromit, insert, introduce; to interpose; **intromettersi** vr. to intrude, interpose, interfere, meddle (*with*).
intromissione f. intrusion.
intronare vt. to stun; to deafen.
introspezione f. introspection.
introva'bile adj. not to be found.
introverso m., adj. introvert.
intru'dere vt.[71] **intru'dersi** vr. to intrude.
intrufolarsi vr. to intrude (*in*), wriggle in.
intru'glio m. hodgepodge.
intrusione f. intrusion.
intruso m. intruder.
intuire vt. to guess; to perceive by intuition; to sense.
intuitivo adj. intuitive; instinctive.
intu'ito m. insight, intuition.
intui'to adj. sensed; intuitive. pp. of intuire.
intuizione f. intuition.
inturgidire vi. to swell.
inumano adj. inhuman.
inumare vt. to inhume.
inumazione f. inhumation.
inumidire vt., **inumidirsi** vr. to moisten, wet.
inurbano adj. inurbane, rude.
inusato adj. unwonted; obsolete.
inusitato adj. unusual.
inu'tile adj. useless; pointless; vain.
inutilità f. uselessness.
inutilizzato adj. unused; discarded.
inutilmente adv. uselessly, in vain.
invadente adj. meddlesome.
invadenza f. meddlesomeness.
inva'dere vt.[16] to invade.
invaghirsi vr. to fall in love (*with*); (*fig.*) to take a liking (*to*).
invalere vi.[110] to prevail; to spread.
invalica'bile adj. impassable.
invalida'bile adj. voidable.
invalidare vt. to void; to invalidate, nullify.
invalidazione f. invalidation.
invalidità f. invalidity; infirmity.
inva'lido m. invalid; disabled man: **piccolo —**, crippled child; adj. invalid; null, void; disabled, crippled.
invalso adj. prevailing.
invano adv. in vain, vainly.
invaria'bile adj. invariable.
invariato adj. unchanged; unvaried.
invasato adj. possessed.
invasione f. invasion.

invaso adj. invaded.
invasore m. invader; adj. invading.
invecchiamento m. aging.
invecchiare vt., vi. to age; to make (*one*) look older; to grow old.
invece adv. instead (*of*); on the contrary.
inveire vi. to rail (*at*).
invelenire vt. to envenom; (*fig.*) to embitter. **invelenirsi** vr. to grow venomous; (*fig.*) to sour, to get exacerbated.
invendi'bile adj. unsalable.
invendicato adj. unavenged.
invenduto adj. unsold.
inventare vt. to invent, devise; to create; to fabricate (*as lies*).
inventariare vt. to inventory.
inventa'rio m. inventory.
inventiva f. inventiveness.
inventivo adj. inventive.
inventore m. inventor.
invenzione f. invention; fabrication.
inverecon'dia f. immodesty.
inverecondo adj. immodest.
invernale adj. winter; wintry.
inverno m. winter: **a metà —**, in midwinter.
invero adv. indeed, truly.
inverosimiglianza f. unlikelihood, implausibility.
inverosi'mile adj. unlikely, improbable.
inversamente adv. inversely.
inversione f. inversion.
inverso adj. inverse, reverse; opposite.
invertire vt. to invert, reverse.
invertitore m. inverter.
investigare vt. to investigate.
investigativo adj. investigative.
investigatore m. investigator; detective.
investigazione f. investigation.
investimento m. collision; accident, running down; investment.
investire vt. to invest (*with*); to invest; to attack; to knock against; to run down; to assail (*with*); **investirsi** vr. to become conscious (*of*); to collide; to attack one another: **— della pro'pria parte**, to merge into one's role.
investitura f. investiture.
inveterato adj. inveterate, ingrained.
invetriata f. glass frame.
invettiva f. invective.
inviare vt. to send.
inviato m. messenger; envoy; correspondent (*of a newspaper*).
invi'dia f. envy: **fare —**, to stir envy.
invidia'bile adj. enviable.
invidiare vt. to envy.
invidioso adj. envious; m. envier, envious person.

invigorire *vt.*, *vi.*, **invigorirsi** *vr.* to strengthen, invigorate.

invinci'bile *adj.* invincible.

invi'o *m.* sending, forwarding; mailing (*of letters*); shipment (*of goods*); remittance (*of money*).

inviola'bile *adj.* inviolable.

inviolato *adj.* inviolate.

inviperire *vt.*, **inviperirsi** *vr.* to get sore.

inviperito *adj.* sore, enraged.

invischiare *vt.* to lime.

invisi'bile *adj.* invisible.

inviso *adj.* disliked.

invitante *adj.* inviting.

invitare *vt.* to invite, ask.

invitato *m.* guest; *adj.* invited.

invito *m.* invitation; request.

invitto *adj.* unvanquished.

invocare *vt.* to invoke; to entreat; to solicit.

invocazione *f.* invocation.

invogliare *vt.* to tempt, entice; to induce, move; **invogliarsi** *vr.* to bring oneself (*to*), be induced; to take a fancy (*for, to*).

involare *vt.* to abduct; **involarsi** *vr.* to flee, run away; to disappear; to elope.

invol'gere *vt.*[168] to wrap up, envelop.

involontariamente *adv.* unintentionally, unwittingly.

involonta'rio *adj.* unintentional.

involto (*1*) *m.* bundle.

involto (*2*) *pp.* of involgere.

invo'lucro *m.* case; shell; envelope.

involuto *adj.* involved; involute.

involuzione *f.* involution.

invulnera'bile *adj.* invulnerable.

inzaccherare *vt.*, **inzaccherarsi** *vr.* to muddy; to spatter.

inzeppare *vt.* to wedge; to fill.

inzuccherare *vt.* to sugar.

inzuccherato *adj.* sugared.

inzuppare *vt.* to soak.

io *pers.pron.* I: — **stesso**, I myself; *m.* I, self; (*sci.*) ego: **il mio —**, my own self.

Iodato *adj.* iodized.

Io'dio *m.* iodine.

Ioduro *m.* iodide.

Ione *m.* (*sci.*) ion.

Ionizzare *vt.* to ionize.

Iosa, (a) *adv.* in plenty, galore.

Iota *m.* iota; jot.

Iper'bole *f.* (*rhet.*) hyperbole; (*math.*) hyperbola.

Iperbo'lico *adj.* hyperbolical.

Ipercri'tico *adj.* hypercritical.

Ipernutrizione *f.* overnourishment.

Ipersensi'bile *adj.* hypersensitive.

Ipersensibilità *f.* hypersensitiveness.

Ipertensione *f.* hypertension.

Ipertrofi'a *f.* hypertrophy.

Ipertro'fico *adj.* hypertrophic.

Ipnosi *f.* hypnosis.

Ipno'tico *adj.* hypnotic.

Ipnotismo *m.* hypnotism.

Ipnotizzare *vt.* to hypnotize.

Ipnotizzatore *m.* hypnotizer.

Ipocloridri'a *f.* (*gastric*) hypoacidity.

Ipocondri'a *f.* hypochondria.

Ipocondri'aco *m.*, *adj.* hypochondriac.

Ipocrisi'a *f.* hypocrisy.

Ipo'crita *m.* hypocrite.

Ipo'crito *adj.* hypocritical.

Ipoder'mico *adj.* hypodermic.

Ipogeo *m.* hypogeum.

Iposolfito *m.* hyposulphite.

Ipoteca *f.* mortgage.

Ipotecare *vt.* to mortgage, hypothecate.

Ipoteca'rio *adj.* mortgage.

Ipotenusa *f.* hypotenuse.

Ipo'tesi *f.* hypothesis (*pl.* hypotheses); theory, conjecture, surmise: **nella migliore delle ipotesi,** at best; **nella peggiore delle ipotesi,** if the worst comes to the worst.

Ipote'tico *adj.* hypothetical.

Ip'pica *f.* horse racing, turf.

Ip'pico *adj.* turf.

Ippocampo *m.* sea horse.

Ippocastano *m.* horse chestnut.

Ippodromo *m.* race track.

Ippopo'tamo *m.* hippopotamus.

Iprite *f.* mustard gas.

Ipso facto *adv.* (*L.*) pronto, right away.

Ira *f.* wrath, fury, rage.

Iracon'dia *f.* wrathfulness.

Iracondo *adj.* wrathful.

Irasci'bile *adj.* irascible, irritable.

Irascibilità *f.* irascibleness, irritably.

Irato *adj.* angry.

Ire *vi.* to go.

I'reos *m.* (*bot.*) iris, German iris.

Iridato *adj.* iridescent.

I'ride *f.* rainbow; (*anat., bot.*) iris.

Iridescente *adj.* iridescent.

Iridescenza *f.* iridescence.

Iri'dio *m.* iridium.

Irlandese *m.*, *adj.* Irish.

Ironi'a *f.* irony.

Iro'nico *adj.* ironical.

Iroso *adj.* wrathful, angry.

Irradiare *vt.*, *vi.* to irradiate; **Irradiarsi** *vr.* to radiate.

Irradiazione *f.* irradiation.

Irraggiungi'bile *adj.* unattainable.

Irragione'vole *adj.* unreasonable.

Irragionevolezza *f.* unreasonableness.

Irrancidire *vi.* to (*grow*) rank.

Irrazionale *adj.* irrational.

Irrazionalità *f.* irrationality.

Irreale *adj.* unreal.

Irrealtà *f.* unreality.

Irreconcilia'bile *adj.* irreconcilable.

Irrecusa'bile *adj.* irrecusable.

irredento adj. unredeemed: una re-gione irredenta, an irredenta (It.).
irrefrena'bile adj. unrestrainable.
irrefuta'bile adj. irrefutable.
irreggimentare vt. to regiment.
irregolare m., adj. irregular.
irregolarità f. irregularity.
irreligioso adj. irreligious.
irremissi'bile adj. irremissible.
irremovi'bile adj. firm; adamant; stubborn.
irrepara'bile adj. irreparable.
irreperi'bile adj. not to be found, elusive.
irreprensi'bile adj. irreproachable.
irrequietezza f. restlessness.
irrequieto adj. restless.
irresisti'bile adj. irresistible.
irresoluto adj. irresolute.
irresponsa'bile adj. irresponsible.
irretire vt. to ensnare.
irrevoca'bile adj. irrevocable.
irriconosci'bile adj. unrecognizable.
irri'dere vt.[108] to scoff at.
irriduci'bile adj. irreducible; stubborn.
irriflessivo adj. rash, thoughtless.
irrigare vt. to irrigate.
irrigazione f. irrigation.
irrigidimento m. stiffening.
irrigidire vt., vi., **irrigidirsi** vr. to stiffen.
irri'guo adj. well-watered.
irrimedia'bile adj. irremediable.
irrisione f. mockery, scorn.
irriso pp. of irridere.
irriso'rio adj. derisive; paltry.
irrita'bile adj. irritable.
irritabilità f. irritability.
irritante adj. irritating.
irritare vt. to irritate; **irritarsi** vr. to chafe; to become irritated or in-flamed.
irritazione f. irritation.
irriverente adj. irreverent.
irriverenza f. irreverence.
irrobustire vt., **irrobustirsi** vr. to strengthen.
irrom'pere vi.[118] to burst (in).
irrorare vt. to sprinkle, spray.
irrotto pp. of irrompere.
irruente adj. rash, impetuous.
irruenza f. impetuosity.
irruzione f. irruption: fare —, to burst (in).
irsuto adj. hirsute, shaggy.
irto adj. bristling, bristly.
iscritto m. member; entrant (in a contest); adj. inscribed, entered, recorded. pp. of iscrivere.
iscri'vere vt.[144] to inscribe; to enter, record; to enroll; **iscri'versi** vr. to enter, join.
iscrizione f. inscription; entry; admis-sion.

islandese m. Icelander; adj. Icelandic.
i'sola f. island, isle.
isolamento m. isolation; (elec.) insu-lation.
isolano m. islander.
isolante adj. isolating; (elec.) insulat-ing.
isolare vt. to isolate; (elec.) to insulate; **isolarsi** vr. to seclude oneself.
isolato m. block; adj. isolated; (elec.) insulated.
isolatore m. insulator.
isolazionismo m. isolationism.
isolazionista m. isolationist.
isoletta f. islet.
isolotto m. islet.
iso'topo m. isotope; adj. isotopic.
ispettorato m. inspectorate; inspector-ship.
ispettore m. inspector.
ispettrice f. inspectress.
ispezionare vt. to inspect.
ispezione f. inspection.
i'spido adj. shaggy, hispid.
ispirare vt. to inspire (with); to in-fluence; **ispirarsi** vr. to draw inspi-ration (from); to conform oneself
ispirazione f. inspiration. [(to).
issare vt. to hoist.
istanta'nea f. (photo.) snapshot.
istanta'neo adj. instantaneous.
istante (1) m. instant, moment: sull'—, all'—, at once, instantly; da un — all'altro, any moment; in the twinkling of an eye.
istante (2) m. petitioner.
istante (3) adj. impending, imminent.
istanza f. instance; application; pe-tition.
iste'rico m., adj. hysteric.
isterilire vt. to sterilize; vi. to become sterile.
isterismo m. hysteria.
istigare vt. to instigate.
istigatore m. instigator.
istigazione f. instigation.
istillare vt. to instill.
istintivamente adv. instinctively.
istintivo adj. instinctive.
istinto m. instinct.
istituire vt. to institute.
istituto m. institute.
istitutore m. institutor; tutor.
istitutrice f. governess.
istituzione f. institution.
istmo m. isthmus.
istoriare vt. to adorn a story (with historical figures).
istoriato adj., pp. storied.
i'strice m., f. porcupine.
istrione m. ham (actor).
istruire vt.[87] to teach; to coach; to educate; to instruct; (mil.) to drill; (law) to institute; **istruirsi** vr. to learn; to study.

istruito *adj.* learned, educated; enlightened.
istrumento *m.* instrument.
istruttivo *adj.* instructive.
istruttore *m.* instructor, coach.
istrutto'ria *f.* inquest.
istrutto'rio *adj.* preliminary.
istruzione *f.* instruction; education;
   teaching; learning; direction.
istupidire *vt.* to dull.
italiano *m.*, *adj.* Italian.
iterare *vt.* to iterate.
itinera'rio *m.* itinerary.

ito *pp. of* ire, gone.
itteri'zia *f.* jaundice.
ittiolo *m.* ichthyol.
ittiologi'a *f.* ichthyology.
iu'gero *m.* juger, jugerum.
iugulare (*1*) *adj.* jugular.
iugulare (*2*) *vt.* to strangle; (*fig.*) to
   dupe.
iugulato'rio *adj.* (*fig.*) iniquitous.
iuniore *m.*, *adj.* junior.
iuta *f.* jute.
iutifi'cio *m.* jute factory.
ivi *adv.* there.

K

kaki *adj.* khaki.
kan *m.* khan.
kapoc *m.* kapok.
kedivè *m.* Khedive.

kimono *m.* kimono.
kola *f.* (*bot.*) kola.
kummel *m.* kummel.
kursaal *m.* kursaal.

L

la (*1*) *definite article sing.f.* her; *neuter* it.
la (*2*) *pron.sing.f.* her; *neuter* it.
la (*3*) *m.* (*mus.*) la, A: dare il "la," to
   give the pitch.
là *adv.* there: andare troppo in —, to
   go too far; l'al di —, the hereafter;
   farsi in —, to move aside; al di — di,
   beyond, across; più in —, further.
labbro *m.* lip.
la'bile *adj.* weak, changeable.
labirinto *m.* labyrinth, maze.
laborato'rio *m.* workshop; laboratory.
laboriosità *f.* laboriousness.
laborioso *adj.* laborious.
lacca *f.* lacquer.
laccare *vt.* to lacquer.
laccatura *f.* lacquering.
lacchè *m.* footman, lackey.
lac'cio *m.* noose; snare; shoelace.
lacerante *adj.* rending.
lacerare *vt.* to lacerate; to tear (*up*);
   to rend; **lacerarsi** *vr.* to tear.
lacerazione *f.* laceration.
la'cero *adj.* torn; tattered.
lacerto *m.* sinew.
laco'nico *adj.* laconic.
la'crima *f.* tear; drop.
lacrimale *adj.* lachrymal.
lacrimare *vi.* to shed tears, weep; to
   water.
lacrime'vole *adj.* lamentable.
lacrimo'geno *adj.* lachrymatory: gas
   —, tear gas.
lacrimoso *adj.* tearful.
lacuale *adj.* of *or* growing in lakes.
lacuna *f.* gap; blank.
lacustre *adj.* of *or* growing in lakes.
laddove *conj.* while; *adv.* (there)
   where.

ladresco *adj.* thievish.
ladro *m.* thief, burglar, robber.
ladrone *m.* highwayman.
ladrun'colo *m.* pilferer.
laggiù *adv.* down there, yonder.
lagnanza *f.* complaint.
lagnarsi *vr.* to complain (*of*).
lagno *see* lamento.
lago *m.* lake.
la'grima, *etc. see* lacrima, *etc.*
laguna *f.* lagoon.
lai *m.pl.* lamentations.
la'ico *m.* layman; *adj.* laic.
la'ido *adj.* ugly, foul.
lama (*1*) *f.* blade.
lama (*2*) *m.* (*zool.*) llama.
lambiccare *vt.* to distill: **lambiccarsi il**
   cervello, to rack one's brains.
lambicco *m.* alembic, still.
lambire *vt.* to lick; to lap.
lamella *f.* scale; lamella.
lamentanza *f.* complaint.
lamentare *vt.* to lament, regret;
   lamentarsi *vr.* to complain (*about*);
   to moan.
lamentazione *f.* lamentation.
lamente'vole *adj.* lamentable; whin-
   ing.
lamento *m.* moan; complaint.
lamentoso *adj.* doleful.
lametta *f.* (little) blade: — da rasoio,
   razor blade.
lamiera *f.* sheet metal; sheet iron: —
   ondulata, corrugated iron.
la'mina *f.* lamina; plate.
laminare *vt.* to laminate, roll.
laminato'io *m.* rolling mill.
lam'pada *f.* lamp.
lampada'rio *m.* chandelier, luster.

lampadina *f.* bulb: — **tascabile,** flashlight, torch.

lampante *adj.* glaring, evident.

lampeggiante *adj.* flashing.

lampeggiare *vi.* to lighten; (*fig.*) to flash; (*auto.*) to blink.

lampeggiatore *m.* (*auto.*) blinker.

lampioncino *m.* lantern; Chinese lantern.

lampione *m.* street lamp.

lampo *m.* lightning flash: **cerniera —,** zip fastener; **guerra —,** blitzkrieg.

lampone *m.* raspberry.

lana *f.* wool: **guanti di —,** woolen gloves.

lancetta *f.* (*surg.*) lancet; hand (*of a watch*); pointer (*of a gauge*).

lan'cia *f.* lance, spear; (*naut.*) launch.

lanciabombe *m.* howitzer.

lanciafiamme *m.* flame thrower.

lanciarazzi *m.* rocket launcher.

lanciare *vt.* to throw, fling, pitch, hurl; (*fig.*) to launch; to cast, set; to bring out; to advertise; **lanciarsi** *vr.* to throw, fling, hurl oneself; to launch: **lanciarsi col paracadute,** to bail out.

lanciasiluri *m.* torpedo tube.

lanciatore *m.* thrower; (*baseball*) pitcher.

lanciere *m.* lancer, lance.

lancinante *adj.* lancinating.

lan'cio *m.* throwing; leap, jump; (*baseball*) pitch: — **del peso,** shot-putting.

landa *f.* moor, heath.

languente *adj.* languishing.

languidezza *f.* languidness.

lan'guido *adj.* languid.

languire *vi.* to languish, pine (*away*); to flag; to pine (*for*).

languore *m.* languor; faintness.

lanifi'cio *m.* woolen mill.

lanoso *adj.* woolly.

lanterna *f.* lantern.

lanu'gine *f.* down.

lanuto *adj.* woolly.

lanzichenecco *m.* lansquenet.

laonde *adv.* therefore.

lapalissiano *adj.* obvious: **osservazione lapalissiana,** truism.

laparatomi'a *f.* laparatomy.

lapidare *vt.* to lapidate, stone.

lapida'rio *adj.* lapidary.

la'pide *f.* tablet: — **sepolcrale,** tombstone.

lapillo *m.* lapillus (*pl.* lapilli).

lapis *m.* pencil: — **per labbra,** lipstick.

lappone *m.*, *adj.* Lappic, Lapponian.

lapsus (**calami, linguae**) *m.* slip (*of the pen, of the tongue*).

lardellare *vt.* to lard.

lardo *m.* lard, bacon.

largheggiare *vi.* to give freely; to abound (*in, with*).

larghezza *f.* width, breadth; plenty; liberality: — **di vedute,** broad-mindedness.

largire *vt.* to bestow (*upon*).

largizione *f.* bestowal.

largo *m.* width, breadth; room; square, circus; (*naut.*) offing: **far —,** to make room; **farsi —,** to elbow one's way; **prendere il —,** (*naut.*) to sail out to sea; (*fig.*) to run away; **al — di,** off; **in lungo e in —,** far and wide; *adj.* broad, wide, extensive; open; liberal: **di manica larga,** lenient, generous.

la'rice *m.* larch.

laringe *f.* larynx.

larva *f.* larva (*pl.* larvae).

larvatamente *adv.* disguisedly.

larvato *adj.* disguised.

lasagna *f.* noodle.

lasciapassare *m.* pass, safe-conduct.

lasciare *vt.* to leave; to abandon, quit; to omit; to let, allow; to stop: — **in eredità,** to will, bequeath; — **cadere,** to drop; **lasciarsi** *vr.* to let oneself, allow oneself; (*reciprocal*) to part, to quit each other: — **andare,** to let oneself go; — **sfuggire una parola,** to let slip a word.

la'scito *m.* bequest, legacy.

lasci'via *f.* lust.

lasci'vo *adj.* lustful.

lassativo *m.*, *adj.* aperient, laxative.

lasso *m.* lapse (*of time*).

lassù *adv.* up there.

lastra *f.* plate; pane; slab.

lastricare *vt.* to pave.

lastricato *m.* pavement; *adj.* paved.

la'strico *m.* pavement: **ridursi sul —,** to come upon the parish; **essere sul —,** to be on one's uppers.

lastrone *m.* slab.

latente *adj.* latent.

laterale *adj.* lateral, side.

lateri'zio *m.*, *adj.* brick.

latifondista *m.* landowner.

latifondo *m.* large landed estate.

latino *m.*, *adj.* Latin: **vela latina,** lateen sail.

latitante *m.* absconder; *adj.* absconding.

latitanza *f.* hiding: **darsi alla —,** to abscond.

latitu'dine *f.* latitude.

lato (1) *m.* side; part; face; viewpoint: **a —,** aside; **a — di,** beside.

lato (2) *adj.* broad: **in senso —,** broadly speaking.

latore *m.* bearer.

latrare *vi.* to bark.

latrato *m.* bark.

latrina f. lavatory, privy.
latta f. tin.
latta'ia f. milkmaid.
latta'io m. milkman.
lattante m. suckling; adj. sucking.
latte m. milk.
lattemiele m. whipped cream.
lat'teo adj. milky: Via Lattea, Milky Way.
latteri'a f. dairy.
lat'tice m. (bot.) latex.
latticini m.pl. dairy products.
lattiginoso adj. milky, lacteous.
lattiven'dolo m. milkman.
lattoniere m. tinsmith.
lattuga f. lettuce.
la'urea f. degree, doctorate: prendere la —, to graduate, to take one's doctorate.
laurearsi vr. to graduate.
laureato m. graduate; adj. graduated.
la'uro m. laurel.
la'uto adj. sumptuous, large.
lava f. lava.
lavablancheri'a m. washing machine.
lava'bile adj. washable.
lavabo m. washstand.
lavacro m. washing.
lavag'gio m. washing: — a secco, dry cleaning.
lavagna f. slate; blackboard.
lavamano m. washstand.
lavanda (1) f. (bot.) lavender.
lavanda (2) f. (med.) lavage.
lavanda'ia f. laundress.
lavanda'io m. laundryman.
lavanderi'a f. laundry.
lavandino m. sink.
lavapiatti m. scullion.
lavare vt. to wash: — a secco, to dryclean; **lavarsi** vr. to wash (oneself).
lavata f. wash, washing: — di capo, wigging, scolding.
lavativo m. enema; (It. slang) bore; faultfinder, fusser; loafer, "bum."
lavato'io m. washtub, laundry.
lavatrice f. washwoman: washing machine.
lavatura f. washing: — a secco, dry cleaning; — di piatti, dishwater.
lavorante m. workman; f. workwoman.
lavorare vt., vi. to work: — la terra, to till land; — di fantasia, to fabricate.
lavorativo adj. working, work: giornata lavorativa, workday.
lavorato adj. worked; wrought; manufactured.
lavoratore m. worker, workman.
lavoratrice f. working woman.
lavorazione f. manufacturing, working; make: — della terra, tillage; — a catena, assembly line process.

lavori'o m. bustle; (fig.) plotting.
lavoro m. work, labor: — in legno, woodwork; **lavori forzati,** penal servitude.
lazzarone m. lazybones; "heel," cad.
lazzo m. jest, banter.
le (1) definite article pl.f. the.
le (2) pron.sing.f. her, to her.
le (3) deferential pron.m., f. (to) you: Le assicuro, signore, che è così, I assure you, sir, that it is so.
le (4) pron.pl.f. them: — vedemmo a Roma, we saw them in Rome.
leale adj. loyal; fair.
lealmente adv. loyally; fairly.
lealtà f. loyalty; fairness.
lebbra f. leprosy.
lebbrosa'rio m. leper house, leprosarium.
lebbroso m. leper; adj. leprous.
leccapiedi m. toady, bootlicker.
leccarda f. dripping pan.
leccare vt. to lick; (fig.) to flatter; — le scarpe (a), to bootlick; **leccarsi** vr. to lick (oneself); to polish oneself.
leccata f. lick, licking.
leccato adj. (fig.) affected; sophisticated; "corny"; sleek.
lec'cio m. holm oak, ilex.
leccorni'a f. dainty, delicacy.
le'cito m. right. adj. licit, permissible.
le'dere vt. [4] to damage, injure.
lega f. union, league.
legac'cio m. string.
legale m. lawyer; adj. legal, lawful, legitimate: medicina —, medical jurisprudence.
legalità f. legality.
legalita'rio adj. legalistic.
legalizzare vt. to legalize; to authenticate.
legalmente adv. legally, lawfully.
legame m. bond, tie, link; connection.
legamento m. binding, tying, linkage; ligature; (anat.) ligament.
legare vt. to bind, tie (up); to fasten; (surg.) to ligate; (law) to bequeath; **legarsi** vr. to bind, tie oneself; to unite, combine.
legata'rio m. legatee.
legato m. (eccl.) legate; (law) legacy; adj. tied (up), fastened; bound.
legatore m. bookbinder; (law) legator.
legatori'a f. bindery.
legatura f. binding; ligature.
legazione f. legation.
legge f. law; act: progetto di —, bill.
leggenda f. legend; caption.
leggenda'rio adj. legendary.
leg'gere vt. [4] to read.
leggerezza f. lightness; nimbleness; fickleness; levity, thoughtlessness.
leggermente adv. lightly; thoughtlessly; slightly.

leggero *see* leggiero.
leggiadri'a *f.* grace, loveliness.
legglladro *adj.* graceful, lovely.
leggi'bile *adj.* readable.
leggiero *adj.* light; nimble; fickle; lightheaded, thoughtless; slight: alla leggiera, superficially.
leggi'o *m.* bookstand; music stand.
legiona'rio *m.*, *adj.* legionary.
legione *f.* legion.
legislativo *adj.* legislative.
legislatore *m.* legislator.
legislatura *f.* term of office; legislature.
legislazione *f.* legislation.
legit'tima *f.* legitim.
legittimare *vt.* to legitimate.
legittimità *f.* legitimacy.
legit'timo *adj.* legitimate, legal, lawful: — proprietario, lawful owner.
legna *f.* firewood: fare —, to cut wood.
legna'ia *f.* woodshed.
legname *m.* timber, lumber.
legnata *f.* cudgel blow.
legno *m.* wood.
legnoso *adj.* ligneous, woody.
legule'io *m.* pettifogger.
legume *m.* legume.
lei *sing.pron.* she; her.
lei *deferential appellative pron.* you.
lembo *m.* edge, border; patch, strip.
lemme lemme *adv.* leisurely.
lena *f.* breath, wind; vigor, energy, zest.
len'dine *m.* nit.
lenire *vt.* to allay.
lenitivo *m.*, *adj.* lenitive.
lenoci'nio *m.* pandering; artifice.
lenone *m.* pander, pimp.
lentamente *adv.* slowly.
lente *f.* lens, glass: — d'ingrandimento, magnifying glass.
lentezza *f.* slowness; sluggishness.
lentic'chia *f.* lentil.
lentig'gine *f.* freckle.
lentigginoso *adj.* freckly.
lento *adj.* slow; loose; tardy.
lenza *f.* line: pescare con la —, to angle.
lenzuolo *m.* sheet.
Leonardo da Vinci *see* Vinci.
Leoncavallo, Ruggiero, Italian composer, *I Pagliacci* (1858–1919).
leone *m.* lion; (*astr.*) Leo.
leonessa *f.* lioness.
Leopardi, Giacomo, greatest Italian poet of the 19th century (1798–1837).
leopardo *m.* leopard.
lepidezza *f.* humor; witticism.
le'pido *adj.* witty.
leporino *adj.* leporine: labbro —, harelip.

lepre *f.* hare.
leprotto *m.* leveret.
ler'cio *adj.* filthy, dirty.
lerciume *m.* filth, dirt.
le'sina *f.* awl.
lesinare *vt.* to grudge; *vi.* to be stingy.
lesione *f.* injury, lesion.
lesivo *adj.* harmful (*to*).
leso *adj.* damaged: parte lesa (*law*), plaintiff; lesa maestà, lese majesty. *pp. of* ledere.
lessare *v .* to boil.
les'sico *m.* lexicon, dictionary.
lesso *m.* boiled meat; *adj.* boiled.
lesto *adj.*, *adv.* swift: — di mano, light-fingered.
lestofante *m.* swindler.
letale *adj.* lethal, deadly.
letama'io *m.* dunghill.
letame *m.* litter; manure.
letargi'a *f.* lethargy.
letar'gico *adj.* lethargic: encefalite letargica, sleeping sickness.
letargo *m.* lethargy.
leti'zia *f.* gladness, joy.
let'tera *f.* letter: belle lettere, belles lettres.
letterale *adj.* literal.
lettera'rio *adj.* literary.
letterata *f.* literary woman.
letterato *m.* litterateur.
letteratura *f.* literature.
lettiera *f.* bedstead; litter.
lettiga *f.* stretcher; sedan chair.
letto (*1*) *m.* bed: — a una piazza, single bed; — a due piazze, double bed.
letto (*2*) *pp. of* leggere.
lettore *m.* lettrice *f.* reader.
lettura *f.* reading.
leva *f.* (*mach.*) lever; (*mil.*) draft, levy; class: esser di —, to be due for drafting.
levante *m.* Levant; East.
levantino *m.*, *adj.* Levantine.
levare *vt.* to raise, lift (*up*); to take (*off, away*), remove; to pull (*out*); to take, subtract: da 9 levo 4, I take 4 from 9; — l'ancora, to weigh anchor; — le tende, to break camp; levarsi *vr.* to rise; to get out (*of*); to take off, remove: — uno d'attorno, to get rid of one.
levata *f.* rising; withdrawal; collection (*of mail*):— di scudi, hue and cry.
levatac'cia *f.* early rising.
levato'io (ponte) *m.* drawbridge.
levatrice *f.* midwife.
levatura *f.* understanding.
levigare *vt.* to smooth.
levigatezza *f.* smoothness.
levigato *adj.* smooth.

levità f. levity.

levriere m. greyhound.

lezione f. lesson; lecture; reading.

lezioso adj. lackadaisical, affected.

lezzo m. stink, stench.

li (1) pron.pl. them: — odio, I hate them; guardateli, look at them.

li (2) definite article m.pl. (archaic) the.

li (3) adv. there, over there: giù di —, thereabout; — per —, at first, at once; essere — — per, to be on the verge of.

liana f. liane, liana.

libbra f. pound.

libecciata f. southwester.

libec'cio m. southwest wind.

libello m. libel.

libel'lula f. dragonfly.

liberale m., adj. liberal.

liberalità f. liberality.

liberamente adv. freely.

liberare vt. to free, set free; to release; to rescue; to rid (of); liberarsi vr. to free oneself; to get rid (of).

liberatore m. liberator, deliverer; rescuer; adj. rescuing.

liberazione f. release, liberation, deliverance.

liberismo m. free trade.

liberista m. free trader.

li'bero adj. free; exempt; vacant.

libertà f. freedom, liberty: — provvisoria, parole; mettere in —, to set free; to dismiss; mettersi in —, to make oneself comfortable.

libertina'gio m. libertinism, license, licentiousness.

libertino m., adj. libertine, rake.

libi'dine f. lustfulness, lust.

libidinoso adj. lustful.

libra'io m. bookseller.

librarsi vr. to poise; to hover, soar.

libreri'a f. bookstore; bookcase, bookshelf.

libretto m. booklet; (mus.) libretto: — di banca, bankbook, passbook.

libro m. book: — mastro, ledger.

licenza f. license, licentiousness; license, permission; leave, furlough; degree, diploma: in —, on furlough.

licenziamento m. dismissal.

licenziare vt. to dismiss; to graduate; (typog.) to pass; licenziarsi vr. to resign; to take one's leave; to graduate.

licenziosità f. licentiousness.

licenzioso adj. licentious.

liceo m. high school.

licitazione f. auction sale.

lido m. shore; land.

lieto adj. glad; merry.

lieve adj. slight; light; mild.

lievemente adv. slightly; lightly.

lievitare vt. to leaven; vi. to yeast.

lie'vito m. leaven, yeast.

li'gio adj. true, abiding.

lignag'gio m. lineage.

lilla m., adj. lilac.

lima f. file.

limaccioso adj. muddy, miry.

limare vt. to file; to polish.

limatura f. filing; filings (pl.).

limbo m. limbo.

limitare (1) vt. to confine, limit; to restrict; to bound; limitarsi vr. to confine oneself; to check oneself.

limitare (2) m. threshold.

limitato adj. restricted, limited; narrow (minded); meager.

limitazione f. limitation.

li'mite m. limit, bound; boundary: passare i limiti (fig.), to go too far.

limi'trofo adj. limitrophe, adjacent.

limo m. slime, mud.

limonata f. lemonade.

limone m. lemon.

limpidezza, limpidità f. limpidness.

lim'pido adj. limpid.

lince f. lynx.

linciag'gio m. lynching.

linciare vt. to lynch.

lindezza f. neatness.

lindo adj. neat.

lindura f. neatness.

li'nea f. line: a grandi linee, in outline.

lineamento m. feature.

lineare adj. linear.

lineetta f. dash; hyphen.

linfa f. (anat.) lymph; (bot.) sap.

lingotto m. ingot.

lingua f. tongue; language; strip (of land): mala —, backbiter.

linguacciuto adj. gossipy; m. gossip.

linguag'gio m. language.

linguetta f. small tongue; clip.

linifi'cio m. flax spinnery.

linimento m. liniment.

lino m. flax.

linosa f. linseed.

linotipista m. linotypist.

liquefare vt., liquefarsi vr. to liquefy, melt.

liquefazione f. liquefaction.

liquidare vt. to liquidate; to settle (an account); to sell out.

liquidazione f. liquidation; settlement (of an account); clearance sale: prezzi di —, bargain prices.

li'quido m., adj. liquid: denaro —, cash.

liquiri'zia f. licorice.

liquore m. liquor; liqueur.

lira f. lira (Italian coin); (mus.) lyre: — sterlina, pound (sterling).

li'rica f. lyric; lyric poetry; (mus.) opera.

li'rico adj. lyrical; (mus.) operatic.

lirismo m. lyricism.

lisca f. shive; fishbone.

lisciare vt. to smoothe; to "soft-soap"; **lisciarsi** vr. to smoothen.

li'scio adj. smooth, sleek: **passarla liscia**, to go scot free.

lisci'via f. lye.

liso adj. threadbare; frayed.

lista f. stripe, band; list, note; bill; — **delle vivande**, bill of fare; — **elettorale**, slate.

listare vt. to stripe.

listello m. listel.

listino m. list; price list; market letter.

litani'a f. litany.

litantrace m. lithanthrax.

lite f. quarrel; lawsuit.

litigante m. quarreler; (law) litigant.

litigare vi. to quarrel.

liti'gio m. quarrel.

litigioso adj. quarrelsome.

litorale m., adj. littoral.

litro m. liter.

liturgi'a f. liturgy.

liuta'io m. lutemaker, lutist.

liuto m. lute.

livella f. level.

livellamento m. leveling.

livellare vt. to level.

livellatore m. leveler; adj. leveling.

livellazione f. leveling.

livello m. level; dumpy level: **passaggio a —**, level crossing, grade crossing.

li'vido m. bruise; adj. livid, lurid.

lividura f. bruise.

livore m. grudge, spite.

livrea f. livery.

lizza f. lists (pl.), competition, contest: **entrare in —**, to enter the lists.

lo (1) definite article m.sing. the.

lo (2) pers.pron.m.sing. it, him: **egli —è**, he is; — **so**, I know (it).

lob'bia f. fedora (hat).

lobo m. lobe.

locale m. room; resort; (pl.) premises; (rail.) local train: — **notturno**, night club; adj. local.

località f. locality, spot.

localizzare vt. to localize; to circumscribe.

locanda f. inn.

locandiera f., **locandiere** m., innkeeper.

locare vt. to rent.

locata'rio m. tenant.

locatore m. lessor.

locazione f. lease.

locomotiva f. locomotive, engine.

locomotore m. electric locomotive; adj. locomotor.

locomozione f. locomotion: **mezzi di —**, transportation.

lo'culo m. loculus; burial niche.

locusta f. locust.

locuzione f. locution.

loda'bile adj. praiseworthy.

lodare vt. to praise; to commend.

lode f. praise; commendation.

lode'vole adj. commendable.

lodo m. arbitrament.

logaritmo m. logarithm.

log'gia f. loggia: — **massonica**, masonic lodge.

loggiato m. loggia, gallery.

loggione m. (upper) gallery; the gallery gods.

lo'gica f. logic.

lo'gico adj. logical; natural.

logi'stico adj. logistic.

lo'glio m. darnel.

logoramento m. wear, wearing.

logorare vt. to wear (out, down, away); to fray; to spoil; **logorarsi** vr. to wear (oneself) out; to fray, become frayed.

logori'o m. wear and tear.

lo'goro adj. worn (out, down); frayed, threadbare.

lombag'gine f. lumbago.

lombo m. sirloin; (anat.) loin.

lombrico m. earthworm.

Lombroso, Cesare, Italian psychiatrist (1836-1909).

londinese m. Londoner; cockney; adj. Londonese.

longa'nime adj. forbearing.

longanimità f. forbearance.

longarone m. (aeron.) longeron, spar; (auto.) longitudinal member.

longevità f. longevity.

longevo adj. longevous; long-lived.

longitudinale adj. longitudinal, lengthwise.

longitu'dine f. longitude.

lontanamente adv. remotely, far.

lontananza f. farness, remoteness, distance; absence: **in —**, at a distance.

lontano adj. far, distant, remote, away; adv. far, afar: **venire di —**, to come from afar.

lontra f. otter.

lonza f. loin; (zool.) ounce.

loquace adj. talkative.

loquacità f. talkativeness.

loquela f. speech: — **facile**, glibness.

lordare vt. to dirty.

lordo adj. dirty; (comm.) gross.

lordume m. filth, dirt.

loro pron.pl.m., f. they; them, to them: **ero da — quando accadde**, I was at their house when it happened. deferential appellative pron. pl. you: — **desiderano il caffè?** would you like to have some coffee? poss.adj. their. poss.pron. theirs.

losanga f. diamond, lozenge, rhomb.
losco adj. short-sighted; one-eyed; sinister, shady.
loto m. mud; (bot.) lotus.
lotta f. struggle, fight; (sport) wrestling: — **libera**, catch-as-catch-can; **esser in** —, to be at war.
lottare vi. to fight, struggle; to strive; (sport) to wrestle.
lottatore m. fighter; wrestler.
lotteri'a f. lottery; sweepstakes.
lotto m. number lottery; area, lot.
lozione f. lotion.
lu'brico adj. lubricous; lubricious, slippery.
lubrificante m., adj. lubricant.
lubrificare vt. to lubricate.
lubrificazione f. lubrication.
lucchetto m. padlock.
luccicare vi. to glitter.
lucci'chi'o m. glitter, sparkle.
luc'cio m. pike.
luc'ciola f. firefly; glowworm: **mostrare lucciole per lanterne**, to pull the wool over one's eyes.
luce f. light; window; mirror; (arch.) span: **dare alla** —, to give birth to.
lucente adj. bright, shining.
lucentezza f. brightness, gloss.
lucerna f. lamp.
lucerna'rio m. skylight.
lucer'tola f. lizard.
lucidare vi. to polish, shine; to gloss; to trace (drawings).
lucidatore m. polisher.
lucidatrice f. polisher: — **per pavimenti**, floor polisher.
lucidatura f. polishing; shine.
lucidità f. lucidity.
lu'cido m. shine, gloss; polish; shoe polish; tracing; adj. shining, glossy; (fig.) lucid: **carta lucida** (photo.), glossy paper.
luci'gnolo m. wick.
lucrare vt. to gain.
lucro m. lucre.
lucroso adj. lucrative.
ludi'brio m. mockery; laughing stock.
lue f. lues, syphilis.
lue'tico adj. luetic.
lu'glio m. July.
lu'gubre adj. lugubrious, somber.
lui pron.m.sing. he; him.
lumaca f. snail.
lume m. light; lamp; candle: **perdere il — degli occhi**, to get blind with rage.
lumeggiare vt. to outline.
lumicino m. lamplet: **al** —, on one's last legs.
luminare m. luminary.
lumina'ria f. illumination.
lumino m. lamplet; night lamp.
luminosità f. luminosity.
luminoso adj. luminous, bright.

luna f. moon: — **di miele**, honeymoon; **al chiaro di** —, by moonlight; **avere la** —, to have the blues.
lunare adj. lunar.
luna'rio m. almanac: **sbarcare il** —, to make both ends meet.
luna'tico adj. moody.
lunedì m. Monday.
lunetta f. (archit.) lunette.
lungag'gine f. delay.
lungamente adv. long, lengthily.
lunghezza f. length; span.
lungi adv. far.
lungo m. length: **per il** —, lengthwise; **per** — **e per largo**, far and wide; **andare per le lunghe**, to drag; adj. long; lengthy; tall; slow; diluted, thin: **a** —, long, lengthily; **a** — **andare**, in the long run; **di gran lunga**, by far; prep. along: — **le rive**, along the banks.
luogo m. place, spot, site; room; way: — **comune**, commonplace; **aver** —, to take place; **dar** — **a**, to give rise to; **in** — **di**, in lieu of; **in qualche** —, somewhere; **in qualunque** —, anywhere, wherever; **in nessun** —, nowhere; **in primo** — ... **e in secondo** —, for one thing ... and secondly.
luogotenente m. lieutenant; deputy; vice regent.
lupa f. she-wolf.
lupanare m. brothel.
lupino m. (bot.), adj. lupine.
lupo m. wolf (pl. wolves): — **mannaro**, (pathol.) lycanthrope, werewolf; (fig.) **big bad wolf**; — **di mare**, seadog; **in bocca al lupo!** good luck!
lup'polo m. hops.
lu'rido adj. filthy, foul.
lusco adj. dim-sighted: **tra** — **e brusco**, in the twilight.
lusinga f. flattery; delusion.
lusingare vt. to flatter; to entice; to deceive.
lusinghiero adj. flattering; promising; satisfactory.
lussare vt. to dislocate.
lussazione f. dislocation.
lusso m. luxury; display: **di** —, luxurious, de luxe.
lussuoso adj. luxurious; expensive.
lussureggiante adj. luxuriant.
lussu'ria f. lustfulness, lust.
lussurioso adj. lustful.
lustrare vt. to polish; to shine.
lustrascarpe m. bootblack.
lustrino m. tinsel.
lustro (1) m. luster; polish, sheen; distinction; adj. glossy, shining.
lustro (2) m. lustrum (five years).
lutto m. mourning; sorrow, grief; loss.
luttuoso adj. mournful, sad.

M

ma *conj.* but; yet, still; why!; who knows?: — no! why, no!; dov'è? ma! where is he?, who knows?; — che! you don't say!; nonsense!

ma'cabro *adj.* macabre, grisly.

macaco *m.* macaque; (*fig.*) dolt.

maccherone *m.* macaroni.

mac'chia (1) *f.* stain, spot; speckle; blemish: — solare, sunspot; senza —, spotless, blameless.

mac'chia (2) *f.* woodland; bush: darsi alla —, to become an outlaw; stampare alla —, to print clandestinely.

macchiare *vt.* to stain; to speckle, spray; macchiarsi *vr.* to stain oneself, get stained (with): macchiarsi d'un reato, to commit a crime.

macchietta *f.* caricature; character; (*theat.*) comedian, mimicker.

macchiettare *vt.* to speckle.

macchiettista *m.* (*paint.*) cartoonist; (*theat.*) comedian, mimicker.

mac'china *f.* machine, engine; car, automobile: — per scrivere, typewriter; — da presa, — fotografica, camera; andare in — (*auto.*) to go by car; (*typog.*) to go to press.

macchinale *adj.* mechanical.

macchinalmente *adv.* mechanically.

macchinare *vt.*, *vi.* to plot.

macchina'rio *m.* machinery.

macchinazione *f.* machination, plot.

macchinista *m.* engineer; stagehand.

macchinoso *adj.* complicated, heavy.

macchiolina *f.* speck.

macedo'nia *f.* fruit cup.

macella'lo *m.* butcher.

macellare *vt.*, *vi.* to butcher.

macellazione *f.* butchering.

macelleri'a *f.* butcher shop.

macello *m.* shambles; massacre, slaughter.

macerare *vt.*, macerarsi *vr.* to macerate.

macerazione *f.* maceration.

mace'rie *f.pl.* ruins, debris.

ma'cero *m.* macerator.

Machiavelli, Niccolò, Italian political writer and statesman, *Il Principe* (1469-1527).

machiavel'lico *adj.* Machiavellian.

machiavellismo *m.* Machiavellism.

macigno *m.* boulder.

macilento *adj.* emaciated.

ma'cina *f.* millstone.

macinacaffè *m.* coffee mill.

macinapepe *m.* pepper mill.

macinare *vt.* to grind.

macinato *adj.* milled, ground.

macinatura, macinazione *f.* grinding.

macinino *m.* mill; (*fig.*) rattletrap, "jalopy."

maciullare *vt.* to crush.

madama *see* signora.

madamigella *see* signorina.

ma'dia *f.* kneading trough; bread bin.

ma'dido *adj.* wet, damp.

Madonna *f.* Madonna; lady.

madornale *adj.* huge, enormous; (*fig.*) preposterous, gross.

madre *f.* mother; (*anat.*) mater; counterfoil; stub: casa — (*comm.*), head office.

madreggiare *vi.* to take after one's mother.

madrepa'tria *f.* mother country.

madreperla *f.* mother-of-pearl.

madreperla'ceo *adj.* nacreous.

madreselva *f.* honeysuckle.

madrevite *f.* female screw.

madrigale *m.* madrigal.

madrigna *f.* stepmother.

madrina *f.* godmother.

maestà *f.* majesty.

maestosità *f.* stateliness, majesty.

maestoso *adj.* majestic, stately.

maestra (1) *f.* teacher, mistress.

maestra (2) *f.* (*naut.*) mainsail.

maestrale *m.* northwester.

maestranza *f.* workmen (*pl.*).

maestri'a *f.* skill, mastery.

maestro *m.* master; teacher, schoolmaster; conductor: colpo da —, master stroke; *adj.* master; main: strada maestra, main road.

ma'fia *f.* mafia; (*fig.*) swagger.

maga *f.* sorceress.

magagna *f.* fault, flaw; trouble.

magari! *interj.* would to God!; *adv.* perhaps, possibly: — ci fossi andato! I wish I had gone there!

magazzinag'gio *m.* storage.

magazziniere *m.* warehouseman.

magazzino *m.* warehouse; store; magazine.

magenta *m.* magenta.

maggese *m.*, *adj.* fallow.

mag'gio *m.* May.

maggiolino *m.* cockchafer.

maggioranza *f.* majority.

maggiorare *vt.* to majorate, augment, increase.

maggiorazione *f.* majoration.

maggiordomo *m.* butler; majordomo.

maggiore *m.* elder; ancestor; (*mil.*) major; *adj.* major; greater; greatest; larger; largest; main; bigger;

biggest; older, oldest; elder, eldest: **altar —**, high altar; **stato —**, staff; **per forza —**, perforce; **essere in età —**, to be of age; **andaré per la —**, to be "tops."

maggiorenne m. major; adj. of age.

maggiorente m. notable.

maggiormente adv. the more; more.

magi'a f. magic.

ma'gico adj. magic, magical.

magistero m. mastery; teaching; (pharm.) magistery.

magistrale adj. magisterial; masterly.

magistralmente adv. masterly.

magistrato m. magistrate.

magistratura f. magistracy.

ma'glia f. stitch; loop; link; vest; coat of mail: **lavorare a —**, to knit.

maglieri'a f. underwear; pull-overs and sweaters.

maglietta f. undervest.

maglifi'cio m. knitwear factory.

ma'glio m. hammer; drop hammer.

maglione m. jersey.

magna'nimo adj. magnanimous.

magnano m. locksmith.

magnate m. magnate, tycoon.

magne'sia f. magnesia.

magne'sio m. magnesium.

magnete m. magnet; magneto.

magne'tico adj. magnetic.

magnetizzare vt. to magnetize.

magneto'fono m. tape recorder.

magnificare vt. to exalt.

magnificenza f. magnificence; wonder.

magnifi'co adj. magnificent.

magno adj. great: **Magna Carta, Magna Charta; Carlo Magno**, Charlemagne; **aula —**, assembly hall, auditorium.

mago m. wizard, magician, sorcerer.

magone m. gizzard; (fig.) sorrow.

magra f. low water; dearth.

magrezza f. thinness; scantiness.

magro m. lean; meager fare: **giorno di —**, fast day; adj. lean; thin; gaunt; meager, scanty, poor; paltry.

mai adv. never; ever: **come —?** how come?

maiale m. pig, swine; pork.

maio'lica f. majolica.

maionese f. mayonnaise.

mais m. Indian corn, maize.

maiu'scolo adj. capital.

malaccorto adj. awkward; rash.

malacreanza f. boorishness.

malafede f. bad faith.

malaffare m. turpitude: **donna di —**, whore; **gente di —**, scum.

malage'vole adj. difficult.

malagra'zia f. ungraciousness.

malalin'gua f. backbiter.

malamente adv. badly; awkwardly.

malandato adj. in a bad way; in disrepair; battered.

malandrino m. ruffian, knave.

mala'nimo m. ill will, malice.

malanno m. calamity, mishap; disease, illness; ill luck.

malapena, (a) adv. hardly.

malatic'cio adj. sickly.

malato m. patient; adj. sick, ill: **esser — di cuore**, to have a bad heart.

malatti'a f. disease, illness, complaint.

malauguratamente adv. unfortunately, unluckily.

malaugurato adj. damned; unfortunate, unlucky.

malaugu'rio m. ill omen; ill luck.

malavita f. underworld.

malavo'glia f. unwillingness; slothfulness: **di —**, reluctantly.

malcaduco adj. epilepsy.

malcapitato m., adj. unfortunate.

malcon'cio adj. battered: **uscirne —**, to come out the worse for wear.

malcontento m. malcontent; dissatisfaction; disappointment; adj. dissatisfied; disappointed.

malcostume m. bad practice; immorality.

maldestro adj. clumsy.

maldicente m., f. slanderer; gossip; adj. slanderous, gossipy.

maldicenza f. slander; gossip.

male m. evil, ill; sin; illness, disease; swoon; harm, injury, damage; ache, pain; sorrow; misfortune, mishap: **mal di testa**, headache; **— di cuore**, heart disease; **— di mare**, seasickness; **farsi —**, to get hurt; **far — a**, to hurt; **andare a —**, to fall through; to rot; **voler — a**, to hate; **aversela a —**, to take offense (at); **che — c'è?** what's wrong with it?; **non c'è —** (it is) not bad; **meno —!** so much the better!; **thank heaven!** adv. bad, badly, ill, wrong: **dire — di**, to speak ill of; **restare —**, to be disappointed, to feel humiliated; **riuscir —**, to be a failure, fail, turn out wrong; **stare —**, to be in a bad way; **sentirsi —**, to feel sick; to feel faint; **il rosso vi sta—**, red does not become you; **capir —**, to misunderstand.

maledetto adj. damned; hellish: **sia —! curse him!**; pp. of **maledire**.

maledire vt. " to curse.

maledizione f. malediction, curse.

maleducato m. boor; adj. ill-bred, rude.

malefatta f. mischief, sin.

malefi'cio m. sorcery; curse.

male'fico adj. evil, maleficent.

malerba f. weed.

males'sere m. malaise; discomfort; uneasiness.

malevolenza *f.* malevolence.
male'volo *adj.* malevolent.
malfamato *adj.* ill-famed.
malfatto *m.* mischief; *adj.* ill-done; misshapen.
malfattore *m.* criminal.
malfermo *adj.* unsteady, faltering, tottering.
malfido *adj.* unreliable; tricky.
malgarbo *m.* ungraciousness.
malgoverno *m.* misrule.
malgrado *prep.*, *adv.* despite, in spite of: **mio —**, against my will; **— ciò**, nevertheless.
mali'a *f.* charm.
maliarda *f.* witch; enchantress, vamp.
malignare *vi.* to malign.
malignità *f.* malignity.
maligno *adj.* malignant; pernicious.
malinconi'a *f.* melancholy, sadness.
malinco'nico *adj.* melancholy, sad.
malincuore, (a) *adv.* unwillingly, reluctantly.
malintenzionato *m.* evildoer; *adj.* evil-minded.
malinteso *m.* misunderstanding; *adj.* misunderstood: **orgoglio —**, misplaced pride.
mali'zia *f.* malice; trick; cunning.
malizioso *adj.* malicious; mischievous, quizzical.
mallea'bile *adj.* malleable; (*fig.*) manageable.
malle'olo *m.* malleolus.
mallevadore *m.* surety: **farsi —**, to stand surety (*for*).
malleveri'a *f.* suretyship.
mallo *m.* husk.
malmenare *vt.* to manhandle.
malmesso *adj.* down at heel, seedy.
malnato *m.* wastrel; *adj.* loutish.
malo *adj.* bad, wicked, evil: **a mal partito**, on one's beam-ends; **prendere in mala parte**, to take amiss.
maloc'chio *m.* evil eye.
malora *f.* ruin.
malore *m.* swoon; disease.
malsano *adj.* unhealthy, unwholesome.
malsicuro *adj.* unsteady; unsafe.
malta *f.* mortar; mud.
maltempo *m.* bad weather.
malto *m.* malt.
maltolto *m.* ill-gotten property.
maltrattamento *m.* maltreatment.
maltrattare *vt.* to maltreat.
malumore *m.* ill-humor; spleen; discontent; discord: **essere di —**, to sulk, be sulky, be in a bad temper.
malva *f.* mallow.
malva'gio *adj.* wicked.
malvagità *f.* wickedness.
malvasi'a *f.* malmsey.
malversazione *f.* embezzlement.

malvisto *adj.* unpopular, hated.
malvivente *m.* criminal.
malvolentieri *adv.* unwillingly.
malvolere *m.* malice.
mamma *f.* mother; **ma: — mia!** dear me!
mammalucco *m.* Mameluke; (*fig.*) simpleton, dolt.
mammella *f.* breast, mamma (*pl.* mammae).
mammi'fero *m.*, *adj.* mammalian.
manata *f.* slap; handful.
manca *f.* left hand; left.
mancante *adj.* failing, lacking, missing, wanting.
mancanza *f.* lack, want; default, gap; shortcoming; fault; blunder: **sentir la — di**, to miss.
mancare *vt.* to miss; *vi.* to fail, miss, be lacking; to run short; to blunder, slip; to stay away (*from*); to be missing; to take; to want, be in need (*of*); to die: **— a un appuntamento**, to miss an appointment; **— alla promessa**, to break one's promise; **manca il tempo di**, there is no time to; **quanto ti manca per finire?**, how long will it take you to get through?; **mancano tre minuti alle quattro**, it is three minutes to four; **ci mancherai**, we shall miss you; **sentirsi — il respiro**, to stifle; **poco mancò che mi vedesse**, I just missed being seen by him.
mancato *adj.* unsuccessful; passed away (deceased); uneffected: **— omicidio**, attempted murder; **mancata esecuzione**, non-performance.
manche'vole *adj.* faulty, wanting.
manchevolezza *f.* shortcoming.
man'cia *f.* gratuity, tip; reward.
manciata *f.* handful.
mancina *f.* left hand.
mancino *adj.* left-handed; (*fig.*) treacherous, underhanded.
manco *adv.* not even: **— a dirlo**, of course.
mandamento *m.* jurisdiction.
mandante *m.* (law) principal.
mandare *vt.* to send; to dispatch; to forward: **— a chiamare**, to send for; **— a dire**, to send word; **— a monte**, to throw overboard; **— a picco**, to sink; **— a quel paese**, to send to Jericho.
mandarino *m.* mandarin; (*bot.*) tangerine.
mandata *f.* batch; turn (*of the key*): **chiudere a doppia —**, to double-lock.
mandata'rio *m.* mandatary.
mandato *m.* warrant; mandate; order; mission: **— di pagamento**, payment voucher.

mandi'bola *f.* mandible, jaw.

mandolino *m.* mandolin.

man'dorla *f.* almond.

mandorlato *m.* nougat, almond cake.

man'dorlo *m.* almond tree.

man'dria *f.* herd.

mandriano *m.* herdsman.

mandrino *m.* (*mach.*) mandrel.

manegge'vole, maneggia'bile *adj.* wieldy, manageable; kindly, docile.

maneggiare *vt.* to handle; to manage; to use.

maneg'gio *m.* handling, use; machination; manège.

maneggione *m.* factotum; meddler.

manesco *adj.* violent, brutal.

manetta *f.* hand lever; handcuff.

manette *f.pl.* handcuffs.

manforte *f.* aid.

manganello *m.* cudgel.

man'gano *m.* calender; mangonel.

mangerec'cio *adj.* edible.

mangeri'a *f.* graft, swindle.

mangiapane *m.* idler, wastrel.

mangiapreti *m.* anticlerical.

mangiare *vt., vi.* to eat (*up*); to have one's meals; to eat away; to graft: — pane a tradimento, to eat the bread of idleness; — con gli occhi, to devour with one's eyes.

mangiata *f.* gorge, meal.

mangiato'ia *f.* manger, crib.

mangiatore *m.* (*hearty*) eater.

mangime *m.* food; fodder; birdseed.

mangione *m.* glutton.

mangiucchiare *vt., vi.* to nibble (*at*).

mangusta *f.* mongoose.

mani'a *f.* mania; hobby; craze.

mani'aco *m.* eccentric; *adj.* crazy.

ma'nica *f.* sleeve; band, gang: — a vento, wind cone; di — larga, broad-minded; di — stretta, stingy, narrow-minded; è un altro paio di maniche, it is another matter.

Ma'nica, (La) *f.* The Channel.

manicaretto *m.* titbit, treat (*to eat*).

manichino *m.* manikin; model; cuff.

ma'nico *m.* handle; stick.

manico'mio *m.* mental hospital.

manicotto *m.* muff.

manicure *f.* manicure, manicurist.

maniera *f.* way, manner; politeness; kind, sort; behavior; style: un'opera di —, a manneristic work; in nessuna —, by no means.

manierato *adj.* affected, conventional.

manierismo *m.* mannerism.

maniero *m.* manor house.

manifattura *f.* manufacture; manufacturing; manufactory, plant.

manifestare *vt.* to manifest, show; to reveal; manifestarsi *vr.* to manifest oneself, prove.

manifestazione *f.* manifestation; demonstration.

manifestino *m.* little poster; throwaway.

manifesto *m.* poster, placard; manifesto; *adj.* manifest, clear, plain.

mani'glia *f.* handle.

manigoldo *m.* scoundrel, cad.

Manin, Daniele, Italian patriot and statesman (1804–1857).

manipolare *vt.* to manipulate, handle.

manipolazione *f.* manipulation.

mani'polo *m.* handful; maniple; band.

maniscalco *m.* blacksmith.

manna *f.* manna.

manna'ia *f.* ax; knife (*of the guillotine*).

mannaro, (lupo) *m.* werewolf; "big bad wolf."

mano *f.* hand; side, way; power, control; care, custody; workmanship; touch; handwriting; coat (*of paint*); lead (*at cards*); — d'opera, labor; stringere la — a, to shake hands with; chiedere la — a, to propose to; starsene con le mani in —, to idle; fare man bassa, to loot; avere le mani in pasta, to know the ropes; tenere — a, to abet; venire alle mani, to come to blows; essere di —, to have the lead (*in a game*); a —, by hand; con le mani nel sacco, red-handed; a portata di —, within one's reach, near at hand; a — a — che arrivano, as they arrive.

manodo'pera *f.* labor.

manomesso *adj.* tampered with.

mano'metro *m.* manometer, gauge.

manomet'tere *vt.* to tamper with.

manomissione *f.* tampering (*with*).

manomorta *f.* mortmain.

mano'pola *f.* gauntlet; handgrip; button; knob (*of a radio, etc.*).

manoscritto *m.* manuscript.

manovale *m.* laborer.

manovella *f.* crank, winch.

manovra *f.* maneuver; operation.

manovrare *vt.* to maneuver; to operate; to handle.

manovratore *m.* operator; driver.

manrove'scio *m.* backhander.

mansalva, (a) *adv.* unrestrainedly, immoderately.

mansione *f.* duty, function, capacity.

mansueto *adj.* tame, meek.

mansuetu'dine *f.* tameness, meekness.

Mantegazza, Paolo, Italian anthropologist (1831–1910).

Mantegna, Andrea, Italian painter, engraver (1431–1506).

mantella *f.* cloak.

mantellina *f.* mantlet, cape.

mantello *m.* cloak; (*zool.*) coat.

mantenere vt.[141] to keep, maintain; to support, provide for; to keep (to); **mantenersi** vr. to keep; to last: **mantenersi col proprio lavoro,** to earn one's living.

mantenimento m. preservation; maintenance, support; keeping.

mantenuta f. kept woman, "gold digger."

mantenuto m. gigolo, gagger. adj. supported; preserved.

man'tice m. bellows (pl.); hood (of a carriage).

manto m. mantle; (fig.) cloak.

manuale m. handbook; adj. manual.

manu'brio m. handle; handlebar; dumbbell.

manufatto m. ware; adj. handmade.

manuten'golo m. accomplice; (law) accessory, abettor.

manutenzione f. maintenance; upkeep; servicing.

Manuzio, Aldo (Teobaldo Mannucci), Italian printer, designer of the italic type (1450–1515).

manza f. heifer.

manzo m. steer; beef.

Manzoni, Alessandro, Italian novelist and poet, I Promessi Sposi (1785–1873).

maomettano m., adj. Mohammedan.

mappa f. map.

mappamondo m. terrestrial globe.

marachella f. mischief, fault.

maragià m. maharajah.

maramaldo m. traitor.

marasma m. marasmus; (fig.) chaos.

maratona f. marathon race.

maratoneta m. marathoner.

marca f. brand; mark; trademark: — da bollo, revenue stamp.

marcare vt. to mark; to score; to emphasize, stress.

marcato adj. marked; stressed.

marchesa f. marchioness.

marchese m. marquis, marquess.

marchiano adj. gross, glaring.

marchiare vt. to brand.

mar'chio m. brand; trademark; stamp.

mar'cia (1) f. march; (auto.) gear: — indietro, reverse gear; mettersi in —, to start, set out.

mar'cia (2) f. pus.

marciapiede m. sidewalk; platform (of a railroad station).

marciare vi. to march.

mar'cio m. rot, rotten matter; adj. rotten, decayed; corrupted: aver torto —, to be all in the wrong; a — dispetto di, in spite of.

marcire vi. to putrefy, rot, decay; to suppurate: — nell'ozio, to waste away in idleness.

marcita f. marsh.

marciume m. rot, rottenness.

marco m. mark.

Marconi, Guglielmo, Italian electronics pioneer and inventor of wireless telegraphy, Nobel Prize in physics, 1909 (1874–1937).

marconigramma m. radiogram.

marconista m. wireless operator.

mare m. sea; seaside: — grosso, rough sea; — interno, inland waters; — magno, watery waste, (fig.) jumble; **mal di** —, seasickness; **tenere il** —, to be seaworthy; **buttare a** —, to throw overboard; **un** — **di gente,** a lot of people.

marea f. tide: **alta (bassa)** —, high (ebb) tide.

mareggiata f. tidal wave.

maremoto m. seaquake.

marena f. amarelle.

marengo m. (coin) napoleon.

maresciallo m. marshal; warrant officer.

maretta f. choppy sea.

margarina f. margarine.

margherita f. daisy.

marginare vt. to marginate.

marginatura f. margination.

mar'gine m. margin; border, edge.

marina f. navy; sea; shore, beach; (paint.) marine, seascape: — mercantile, merchant marine.

marina'io m. sailor, mariner.

marinare vt. to marinate, pickle: — la scuola, to play truant.

marinaresco adj. sailorly.

marinaro m. sailor; adj. maritime.

marinato adj. pickled.

Marinetti, Filippo Tommaso, Italian writer and poet, founder of futurism (1876–1944).

marino adj. marine, sea.

marioleri'a f. knavery.

marionetta f. puppet.

maritale adj. marital.

maritalmente adv. maritally: **vivere** —, to cohabit.

maritare vt. to marry; **maritarsi** vr. to get married.

maritata f. married woman.

marito m. husband: **ragazza da** —, eligible girl.

marit'timo m. seafarer; adj. maritime, marine, sea.

mariuolo m. scoundrel, rascal.

marma'glia f. riffraff, rabble.

marmellata f. jam: — di arance, marmalade.

marmista m. marbler.

marmitta f. kettle: — di scappamento, exhaust box, muffler.

marmo m. marble.

marmoc'chio m. brat, bantling.

marmo'reo adj. marmoreal.

marmorizzare *vt.* to marble.

marmotta *f.* marmot; sluggard.

marna *f.* marl.

marocca *f.* trash.

marocchino *m.*, *adj.* Moroccan; *m.* morocco (leather).

maroso *m.* billow, sea.

marra *f.* hoe; fluke (*of an anchor*).

marrano *m.* marrano; (*fig.*) cad.

marrone *m.* chestnut; *adj.* maroon, brown.

marsigliese *m.*, *adj.* Marseillais; *f.* Marseillaise.

marsina *f.* dress coat, "tails."

martedì *m.* Tuesday.

martellare *vt.*, *vi.* to hammer; to throb.

martellata *f.* hammer blow.

martello *m.* hammer.

martinello, martinetto *m.* jack.

martingala *f.* martingale.

Martini, Ferdinando, Italian statesman and author (1841–1928).

Martini, Simone, Italian painter (1283?–1344).

martinicca *f.* brake.

mar'tire *m.* martyr.

marti'rio *m.* martyrdom; torment.

martirizzare *vt.* to martyrize.

mar'tora *f.* marten.

martoriare *vt.* to torture.

marzapane *m.* marzipan.

marziale *adj.* martial, warlike.

marziano *m.*, *adj.* Martian.

marzo *m.* March.

mas *m.* torpedo boat.

Masaccio (*Tommaso Guidi*), Italian painter (1401–1428).

Masaniello (*Tommaso Aniello*), Neapolitan insurgent (1620–1647).

Mascagni, Pietro, Italian composer, *Cavalleria Rusticana* (1863–1945).

mascalzonata *f.* knavery.

mascalzone *m.* scoundrel, cad.

mascella *f.* jaw.

mascellare *m.*, *adj.* maxillary.

ma'schera *f.* mask; usher (*m.*), usherette (*f.*): — antigas, gas mask; ballo in —, fancy-dress ball, masquerade party.

mascheramento *m.* camouflage.

mascherare *vt.*, **mascherarsi** *vr.* to mask; (*mil.*) to camouflage.

mascherata *f.* masquerade.

mascherina *f.* little mask; masker; toecap; (*theat.*) usherette.

maschiac'cio *m.* romp.

maschietta *f.* tomboy; "bobby soxer."

maschile *m.* masculine; *adj.* male, masculine, manly.

ma'schio *m.* male; son, boy; (*mech.*) shaft (*as of a key*, *etc.*); *adj.* male, manly.

mascolino *adj.* masculine.

masnada *f.* gang, mob.

masnadiere *m.* highwayman.

massa *f.* mass; bunch; (*elec.*) ground: in —, en masse.

massacrante *adj.* (*fig.*) toilsome.

massacrare *vt.* to massacre, butcher.

massacro *m.* massacre.

massaggiare *vt.* to massage.

massaggiatore *m.* masseur.

massaggiatrice *f.* masseuse.

massag'gio *m.* massage.

massa'ia *f.* housewife.

massello *m.* ingot, block.

masseri'a *f.* farm.

masseri'zie *f.pl.* household goods.

massicciata *f.* road ballast.

massic'ciom. (*geog.*) massif; *adj.* massive; compact; stocky.

mas'sima *f.* maxim, rule; proverb.

mas'simo *m.* maximum, most, top: al —, at most; al — della velocità, at top speed. *adj.* maximum; greatest; best; highest; extreme, top: peso — (*boxing*), heavyweight fighter.

masso *m.* boulder.

massone *m.* freemason.

massoneri'a *f.* freemasonry.

masso'nico *adj.* masonic.

mastello *m.* (wooden) tub; bucket.

masticare *vt.* to chew, masticate; to mumble: — veleno, to feel sore.

masticazione *f.* mastication.

ma'stice *m.* mastic.

mastino *m.* mastiff.

ma'stio *m.* keep.

mastodonte *m.* mastodon.

mastodon'tico *adj.* mammoth, huge.

mastro *m.* master; ledger.

matassa *f.* skein.

matema'tica *f.* mathematics.

matema'tico *m.* mathematician; *adj.* mathematical: **avere la certezza matematica che,** to be dead sure that.

materassa'io *m.* mattress maker.

materasso *m.* mattress.

mate'ria *f.* matter; substance; subject; ground; pus; material: — prima, raw material.

materiale *m.* materiel, material; *adj.* material; bulky; rough.

materialmente *adv.* materially; absolutely.

maternità *f.* maternity, motherhood; maternity hospital.

materno *adj.* motherly, maternal: lingua materna, mother tongue.

matita *f.* pencil: — a sfera, ball point pen.

matriarcato *m.* matriarchy.

matrice *f.* matrix; counterfoil; stub.

matricida *m.*, *f.* matricide.

matrici dio *m.* matricide.

matri'cola f. freshman; register; roll: numero di —, serial number.

matricolato adj. matriculated; arrant: furbo —, old fox.

matrigna f. stepmother.

matrimoniale adj. matrimonial: letto —, double bed.

matrimo'nio m. marriage; wedding.

matrina f. godmother.

matrizzare see madreggiare.

matrona f. matron.

matta f. madwoman; joker (playing card).

mattacchione m. joker; jester.

mattana f. madness: farsi prender dalla —, to lose one's temper.

mattato'io m. shambles.

Matteotti, Giacomo, Italian socialist, murdered by fascists (1885–1924).

matterello m. rolling pin.

mattina f. morning.

mattinata f. morning; (theat.) matinée.

mattiniero adj. early-rising: essere —, to be an early riser.

mattino m. morning: di buon —, early in the morning.

matto m. madman: un mezzo —, a madcap; adj. mad, insane: farsi matte risate, to roar with laughter; andare — per, to be crazy about; — da legare, mad as a hatter.

matto'ide m. madcap.

mattonato m. tile floor.

mattone m. brick; bore: — cavo, air brick.

mattonella f. tile.

mattutino adj. matutinal, morning.

maturare vt., vi. to ripen.

maturazione f. ripening.

maturità f. maturity, ripeness.

maturo adj. ripe, mature: — esame, due consideration.

mausoleo m. mausoleum.

mazurca f. mazurka.

mazza f. cane; cudgel; mace; sledge (hammer).

mazzata f. cudgel blow; blow.

mazziere m. macer.

Mazzini, Giuseppe, Italian patriot and revolutionist (1805–1872).

mazzo m. bunch, cluster; bundle; pack (of cards); bouquet.

mazzolino m. posy.

mazzuolo m. mallet.

me pers.pron. I; me, myself: è più giovane di —, he is younger than I; tra — e —, within myself; in quanto a —, as to me; secondo —, in my opinion.

meandro m. meander, labyrinth.

mecca'nica f. mechanics.

meccanicamente adv. mechanically.

mecca'nico m. mechanician, mechanic; adj. mechanical.

meccanismo m. mechanism; gear: aver il — guasto, to be out of gear.

meccanizzare vt. to mechanize.

mecenate m. patron (of the arts).

mecenatismo m. patronage (of the arts).

meco compound pron. with me; to me.

meda'glia f. medal.

medaglione m. medallion.

mede'simo m., adj. same; self: io —, I myself; egli —, he himself.

me'dia f. average: fare (avere, sostenere) la — di, to average.

media'nico adj. mediumistic.

mediano m. (sport) halfback; adj. mean, middle.

mediante prep. by means of, through.

mediatore m. mediator; (comm.) middleman, broker.

mediazione f. mediation; (comm.) brokerage.

me'dica, (erba) f. lucerne.

medicamento m. remedy.

medicamentoso adj. medicinal.

medicare vt. to dress, medicate.

medicastro m. quack (doctor).

medicazione f. medication; treatment; dressing.

medichessa see dottoressa.

Me'dici, de, Alessandro, first duke of Florence, assassinated (1510–1537).

Me'dici, de, Cosimo, Il Vecchio, chief of the Florentine Republic (1389–1464).

Me'dici, de, Cosimo I, Il Grande, first grand duke of Tuscany (1519–1574).

Me'dici, de, Giulio, Clement VII, Pope 1523–34 (1478–1534).

Me'dici, de, Lorenzo, Il Magnifico, Florentine ruler and patron of the arts (1449–1492).

Me'dici, de, Caterina, queen of Henry II of France (1519–1589).

medicina f. medicine; remedy.

medicinale m. medicament, remedy; adj. healing, medicinal.

me'dico m. physician, doctor; general practitioner: — chirurgo, surgeon; — condotto, parish doctor.

medievale adj. medieval.

me'dio m. middle finger; adj. middle; mean; average; medium.

mediocre adj. mediocre, ordinary.

mediocrità f. mediocrity.

medioevale adj. medieval.

Medioevo m. Middle Ages.

meditabondo adj. thoughtful.

meditare vt., vi. to meditate; to muse (upon), ponder (over); to plan.

meditato adj. deliberate.

meditazione f. meditation.

Mediterra'neo m., adj. Mediterranean.

medusa *f.* jellyfish; (*myth.*) Medusa.

mefi'tico *adj.* mephitic.

mega'fono *m.* megaphone.

megalo'mane *m.* megalomaniac.

megalomani'a *f.* delusion of grandeur, megalomania.

megera *f.* Mégaera; (*old*) hag.

me'glio *m.*, *f.* best: alla —, anyhow; avere la —, to win, have the best of it; *adj.* better, best; *adv.* better; rather: faresti — ad andare, you had better go; di bene in —, better and better; tanto —! so much the better!

mela *f.* apple; quince.

melagrana *f.* pomegranate.

melanconi'a *see* malinconi'a.

melanzana *f.* eggplant, aubergine.

melaran'cia *f.* orange.

melassa *f.* molasses, treacle.

melato *adj.* honeyed.

melenso *adj.* silly.

melitense *adj.* Maltese: febbre —, Malta fever.

melli'fluo *adj.* mellifluous.

melma *f.* mud, mire.

melmoso *adj.* muddy, miry.

melo *m.* apple tree.

melodi'a *f.* melody.

melo'dico *adj.* melodic.

melodioso *adj.* melodious.

melodramma *m.* melodrama.

melodramma'tico *adj.* melodramatic.

melograno *m.* pomegranate (tree).

melone *m.* melon.

membrana *f.* membrane.

membratura *f.* frame.

membro *m.* limb; member.

memora'bile *adj.* memorable.

memorando *adj.* memorable.

memorandum *m.* memorandum; notebook.

me'more *adj.* mindful, unforgetful; grateful.

memo'ria *f.* memory; recollection; souvenir; note; memoir; memoir: imparare a —, to memorize, learn by heart.

memoriale *m.* memorial.

mena *f.* intrigue, machination.

menabò *m.* (*typog.*) dummy copy.

menadito, (a) *adv.* perfectly; inch by inch.

menare *vt.* to lead; to take; to deal; to bring: menar le mani, to resort to violence, to come to blows; — calci, to kick; — il can per l'aia, to beat about the bush.

menda *f.* blemish, flaw.

mendace *adj.* mendacious.

menda'cio *m.* falsehood.

mendicante *m.* beggar.

mendicare *vt.*, *vi.* to beg.

mendicità *f.* beggary: ricovero di —, poorhouse.

mendico *m.* pauper, beggar.

menestrello *m.* minstrel.

menimpipo *m.* devil-may-care.

meninge *f.* meninx.

meningite *f.* meningitis.

menisco *m.* meniscus.

meno *m.* less, least; (*math.*) minus (sign): parlare del più e del —, to talk about the weather; per lo —, at least; *adj.* lesser; lower, inferior; fewer; *adv.* less, least; except, but; (*math.*) minus: le tre — un quarto, a quarter to three; venir —, to faint; to break one's word; to fail; fare a — di, to dispense with; to abstain from; non potei fare a — di dirlo, I couldn't help saying it; a — che non, unless; in men che non si dica, before you can say Jack Robinson.

menomamente *adv.* by no means, by any means.

menomare *vt.* to lessen; to impair.

menomazione *f.* diminution; impairment.

me'nomo *adj.* least.

Menotti, Ciro, Italian patriot (1798–1831).

Menotti, Gian Carlo, Italian composer in U.S. Il medium, Il console (1911–).

mensa *f.* table; (*mil.*) mess; Eucharist: — aziendale, company cafeteria; — universitaria, faculty cafeteria.

mensile *m.* (*monthly*) salary; monthly allowance; *adj.* monthly.

mensilità *f.* monthly payment; installment.

mensilmente *adv.* monthly.

men'sola *f.* bracket, console.

menta *f.* mint.

mentale *adj.* mental: alienazione —, insanity.

mentalità *f.* mentality.

mente *f.* mind; intellect; understanding; memory: imparare a —, to learn by heart; a — fredda, in cold blood; malato di —, lunatic.

mentecatto *m.*, *adj.* lunatic.

mentire *vi.* to lie, tell lies.

mentito *adj.* false: sotto mentite spoglie, in disguise.

mentitore *m.* liar.

mento *m.* chin.

mentolo *m.* menthol.

men'tore *m.* mentor, counselor.

mentre *conj.*, *adv.* while: in quel —, just then.

menù *m.* menu, bill of fare.

menzionare *vt.* to mention.

menzione *f.* mention: degno di —, worth mentioning.

menzogna *f.* falsehood, lie.

menzognero *adj.* false; deceitful.

meravi'glia *f.* wonder; surprise; amazement: far —, to surprise; far meraviglie, to work wonders; fare le meraviglie, to feign surprise; a —, wonderfully.

meravigliare *vt.* to surprise, astonish; meravigliarsi *vr.* to be surprised (*at, to*); to wonder (*at*).

meraviglioso *adj.* wonderful.

Mercadante, Saverio, Italian composer (1795-1870).

mercante *m.* merchant, trader, dealer: fare orecchio da —, to turn a deaf ear.

mercanteggiare *vi.* to trade, barter, deal; to bargain.

mercantile *adj.* mercantile.

mercanzi'a *f.* merchandise, goods (*pl.*); commodities (*pl.*).

mercato *m.* market, store: a buon —, cheap, cheaply: far — di, to barter away.

merce *f.* goods (*pl.*); commodities (*pl.*).

mercè *f.* mercy, thanks: — sua, thanks to him; alla — di, at the mercy of.

mercena'rio *m.*, *adj.* mercenary.

merceologi'a *f.* commodity research.

merceri'a *f.* notions (*tapes, pins, buttons, etc.*); notions store; haberdashery.

mercerizzare *vt.* to mercerize.

mercia'io *m.* haberdasher.

mercimo'nio *m.* illicit barter.

mercoledì *m.* Wednesday.

mercu'rio *m.* quicksilver; mercury.

merenda *f.* snack, bite: questo c'entra come i cavoli a —, that is beside the point.

meretrice *f.* prostitute.

meridiana *f.* sundial.

meridiano *m.*, *adj.* meridian.

meridionale *m.* Southerner; *adj.* southern, south.

meridione, (il) *m.* the South, Southern

merig'gio *m.* noon, midday. [Italy.

meringa *f.* meringue.

meritare *vt.*, meritarsi *vr.* to be worth, deserve; to win.

meritato *adj.*, *pp.* deserved.

merite'vole *adj.* deserving, worthy, worth: — di fiducia, trustworthy; — di essere letto, worth reading.

me'rito *m.* merit, desert; worth; credit; subject; proficiency: render —, to reward; to give credit (*to*); per — di, thanks to.

merito'rio *adj.* meritorious.

merlatura *f.* battlements.

merletto *m.* lace (*pl.* lace).

merlo *m.* blackbird; (*fig.*) dolt; (*fort.*) battlement.

merluzzo *m.* codfish, cod.

mero *adj.* mere.

mesata *f.* month; month's wages.

me'scere *vt.*[7b] to pour out.

meschineri'a, meschinità *f.* meanness; stinginess.

meschino *adj.* poor; weak; mean, cheap; stingy.

me'scita *f.* pouring; bar, saloon.

mescolanza *f.* mixture, blend.

mescolare *vt.* to mix (*up*), mingle; to blend; to stir; to shuffle (*playing cards*); mescolarsi *vr.* to mix, mingle, blend.

mese *m.* month; monthly salary: mi pagarono tre mesi, they paid me three months' wages.

messa (1) *f.* (*eccl.*) mass: — cantata, high mass; requiem.

messa (2) *f.* putting, placing, laying; stake, bet; — a punto, setup; (*mach.*) truing, tuning; — in opera, installation; — in marcia (*auto.*), starter; — in piega, finger wave; — in scena, staging; — a fuoco (*photo.*), focus, focusing.

messaggeri'a *f.* forwarding agency; shipping office.

messaggiero *m.* messenger.

messag'gio *m.* message, dispatch.

messale *m.* missal.

messe *f.* crop, harvest.

messere *m.* gentleman, sir; mister.

Messi'a *m.* Messiah.

messo *m.* messenger; ambassador. *adj.* put; placed; dressed: mal —, down at heel. *pp.* of mettere.

mestare *vt.* to stir.

mestatore *m.* intriguer, meddler; (*pol.*) ringleader.

mestierante *m.* craftsman; potboiler.

mestiere *m.* occupation, trade; metier; housework.

mesti'zia *f.* sadness.

mesto *adj.* sad.

me'stola *f.* ladle.

me'stolo *m.* wooden ladle.

mestruazione *f.* menstruation.

me'struo *m.* menses (*pl.*).

meta *f.* aim, object, end, goal.

metà *f.* half (*pl.* halves); middle; wife, "better half": fare a —, to go fifty-fifty, to go shares.

metafi'sica *f.* metaphysics.

metafi'sico *m.* metaphysician; *adj.* metaphysical.

meta'fora *f.* metaphor.

metal'lico *adj.* metallic.

metalli'fero *adj.* metalliferous.

metallizzare *vt.* to metallize.

metallo *m.* metal.

metallurgi'a *f.* metallurgy.

metallur'gico *m.* metallurgist; steelworker; *adj.* metallurgical.

metamor'fosi *f.* metamorphosis (*pl.* metamorphoses).

metano *m.* (*chem.*) methane.

metanodotto *m.* natural gas pipeline.

metapsi'chica *f.* metapsychics.

Metastasio (*Pietro Antonio Domenico Bonaventura Trapassi*), Italian poet and dramatist (1698–1782).

mete'ora *f.* meteor.

meteorismo *m.* tympanites, meteorism.

meteorite *f.* meteoroid; meteorite.

meteografi'a *f.* meteorography.

meteorologi'a *f.* meteorology.

meteorolo'gico *adj.* meteorologic: bollettino —, weather forecast.

metic'cio *m.* mestizo, half-breed; *adj.* half-breed.

meticoloso *adj.* meticulous, painstaking, finicky.

metile *m.* methyl.

meti'lico (alcool) *m.* methyl alcohol, methanol.

meto'dico *adj.* methodical.

me'todo *m.* method.

metrag'gio *m.*, **metratura** *f.* length in meters.

me'trica *f.* metrics.

me'trico *adj.* metrical, metric.

metro *m.* meter; measure; (*fig.*) yardstick.

metro'poli *f.* metropolis.

metropolitana *f.* subway.

metropolitano *m.* policeman; *adj.* metropolitan.

met'tere *vt.*[8] to put, place; to lay; to charge; to use, employ; to compare; to suppose: ci ho messo tre ore, it took me three hours; — un freno a, to check; — la luce elettrica, to install electricity; — radici, to take root; — i denti, to cut one's teeth; — giudizio, to reform; — a tacere, to hush up; — a disagio, to make uneasy; — a parte di un segreto, to let a secret; — fuori combattimento, to knock out; — in rilievo, to emphasize, stress; — in scena, to stage, produce.

met'tersi *vr.* to put, place oneself; to begin, start; to put on: — a letto, to go, take, to bed; — a sedere, to sit down; — in cammino, to set out, start walking; — in vista, to make oneself conspicuous; — in urto con, to fall out with.

Meucci, Antonio, Italian physicist (1809–1889).

mezzadro *m.* metayer, sharecropper.

mezzalúna *f.* crescent; chopping knife; (*fort.*) lunette.

mezzana *f.* procuress; (*naut.*) mizzen.

mezzanino *m.* mezzanine.

mezzano *m.* pimp. *adj.* middle, mean.

mezzanotte *f.* midnight.

mezzo (1) *m.* way; means: mezzi di trasporto, means of transportation.

mezzo (2) *m.* middle; half. nel (bel) —, in the (very) middle; togliersi di —, to get out of the way; andarci di —, to get involved; *adj.* half; middle; *adv.* half; almost: le tre e —, half past three.

mezzodi, mezzogiorno *m.* midday, noon; south.

mezzuc'cio *m.* expedient, ruse.

mi (1) *pers.pron.* me, to me, at me; (*refl.*) myself, to (at) myself: ec'comi, here I am.

mi (2) *m.* (*mus.*) mi, E.

miagolare *vi.* to mew, miaow.

miagoli'o *m.* mewing.

mica (1) *f.* (*min.*) mica.

mica (2) *f.* crumb.

mica (3) *adv.* (*not*) at all, ever; never.

mic'cia *f.* fuse.

Michelac'cio *m.* loafer.

Michela'ngelo (*Buonarroti Michelangelo*), Italian painter, sculptor, architect, poet; chief works as a painter: *Sacra Famiglia, Giudizio Universale*; as a sculptor: *Pietà, Davide, Mosè, Tombe Medicee*; as an architect: *Dome of San Pietro* (1475–1564).

mi'cia *f.* she-cat, pussy.

micidiale *adj.* deadly.

mi'cio *m.* tomcat.

micro'bio, mi'crobo *m.* microbe.

microce'falo *m.* microcephalus; *adj.* microcephalous.

micro'fono *m.* microphone.

microfotografi'a *f.* photomicrography.

microsco'pico *adj.* microscopic.

microsco'pio *m.* microscope.

microsolco *adj.* microgroove.

midolla *f.* crumb.

midollo *m.* marrow; medulla; pith; spinal cord: bagnato fino al —, drenched, soaked.

miele *m.* honey.

mie'tere *vt.* to mow; (*fig.*) to reap.

mietitore *m.* harvester.

mietitrice *f.* harvester; (*mach.*) reaping machine.

mietitura *f.* harvesting; harvest.

miglia'io *m.* thousand.

mi'glio (1) *m.* mile.

mi'glio (2) *m.* (*bot.*) millet.

miglioramento *m.* improvement.

migliorare *vt.* to improve, better: — un primato, to break a record; *vi.* to improve, get better.

migliore *m.*, *adj.* better; best: — di, better than; il —, the best.

migliori'a *f.* improvement.

Migliorini, Bruno, Italian lexicographer, *Lingua contemporanea, La lingua nazionale, Conversazioni sulla lingua italiana, Appendice al Dizionario moderno* di A. Panzini (1896-   ).

mignatta *f.* leech.

mi'gnolo *m.* little finger; little toe.

migrare *vi.* to migrate.

migratore *m., adj.* migrant.

migrazione *f.* migration.

miliarda'rio *m.* millionaire; owner of milliards.

miliardo *m.* milliard.

miliare, (pietra) *f.* milestone.

miliona'rio *m.* millionaire.

milione *m.* million.

milione'simo *adj.* millionth.

militante *adj.* militant.

militare (*1*) *m.* soldier; *adj.* military.

militare (*2*) *vi.* to serve (*in the army*); (*fig.*) to militate.

militaresco *adj.* soldierly.

militarismo *m.* militarism.

militarizzare *vt.* to militarize.

mi'lite *m.* militiaman: **Milite Ignoto,** Unknown Soldier.

mili'zia *f.* militia; (*pl.*) army.

millanta *adj.* a thousand; (*fig.*) a great many.

millantare *vt.* to vaunt, boast.

millantatore *m.* boaster.

millanteri'a *f.* brag, boast.

mille *m., adj.* a (*or* one) thousand: -cento, -duecento, ecc., eleven hundred, twelve hundred, etc.

millena'rio *m., adj.* millenary.

millen'nio *m.* millennium.

millepiedi *m.* millipede.

mille'simo *adj.* thousandth.

milligramma *m.* milligram.

milli'metro *m.* millimeter.

milza *f.* spleen.

mime'tico *adj.* mimetic.

mimetismo *m.* (*zool.*) mimicry.

mimetizzare *vt.* to camouflage.

mimetizzazione *f.* camouflage.

mi'mica *f.* mimicry.

mimo *m.* mime.

mina *f.* mine; lead (*of a pencil*).

minac'cia *f.* threat, menace.

minacciare *vt., vi.* to threaten (*with*).

minaccioso *adj.* threatening.

minare *vt.* to mine; to undermine.

minatore *m.* miner; coal miner.

minato'rio *adj.* threatening.

minchionare *vt.* to ridicule; to take in.

minchionatura *f.* banter; deception.

minchione *m.* simpleton, "goof."

minchioneri'a *f.* nonsense; "goofiness."

minerale *m.* mineral; ore; *adj.* mineral.

minera'rio *adj.* mining.

minestra *f.* soup.

mingherlino *adj.* spare, thin.

Minghetti, Marco, Italian statesman and author (1818–1886).

miniatura *f.* miniature.

miniera *f.* mine.

minimamente *adv.* at all, by any (no) means, in the least.

minimizzare *vt.* to belittle.

mi'nimo *m., adj.* least, minimum; (*the*) smallest; (*the*) lowest; (*the*) shortest.

mi'nio *m.* minium, red lead.

ministeriale *adj.* ministerial, cabinet.

ministero *m.* ministry, office, department; cabinet: **Ministero degli Esteri,** Department of State; **Pubblico Ministero,** Public Prosecutor.

ministro *m.* minister, secretary (*of state*); ambassador; (*eccl.*) minister.

minoranza *f.* minority.

minorare *vt.* to disable.

minorato *adj.* disabled.

minorazione *f.* disablement; diminution.

minore *m.* minor; youngest (*son*), junior; *adj.* less, lesser, minor; minimum, least; smaller; smallest; lower; lowest; shorter; shortest; younger; youngest: di — età, under age.

minorenne *m.* minor; *adj.* under-age.

minorità *f.* minority.

minuetto *m.* minuet.

minu'scola *f.* small letter.

minu'scolo *adj.* small; (*typog.*) lower case; (*fig.*) diminutive.

minuta *f.* rough copy.

minuta'glia *f.* trifles; "small fry."

minuteri'e *f.pl.* smallware.

minuto (*1*) *m.* minute: — primo, minute; — secondo, second; spaccare il —, to keep time to the minute.

minuto (*2*) *m.* (*comm.*) retail.

minuto (*3*) *adj.* minute, small.

minu'zia *f.* trifle.

minuzioso *adj.* minute, finical.

mio *poss.adj.* my; *poss.pron.* mine; *m.* my own (*money*): i miei, my parents, my family, my folks.

mi'ope *m.* short-sighted person. *adj.* myopic, short-sighted.

miopi'a *f.* myopia, myopy.

mira *f.* sight; aim, target; design, plan: prendere di —, to aim at; (*fig.*) to make a target of.

mirabile *adj.* admirable.

mirabi'lia *f.pl.* wonders: dir —, to speak highly (*of*).

miracolato *m.* one miraculously restored to health.

mira'colo *m.* miracle; wonder.

miracoloso *adj.* miraculous.

mirag'gio *m.* mirage.

mirare *vt.* to look at; *vi.* to sight (*at*), take aim; to aim (*at*).

miri'ade *f.* myriad.

mirino *m.* sight; (*photo.*) finder.

mirra *f.* myrrh.

mirtillo *m.* whortleberry.

mirto *m.* myrtle.

misantropi'a *f.* misanthropy.

misan'tropo *m.* misanthropist.

miscela *f.* mixture; blend.

miscelare *vt.* to mix.

miscella'nea *f.* miscellany.

mi'schia *f.* tussle, fray; (*sport*) scrimmage.

mischiare *see* mescolare.

misconos'cere *vt.*[10] to gainsay; to disregard.

misconosciuto *adj.* unappreciated; disregarded; misunderstood.

miscredente *m.* unbeliever.

miscu'glio *m.* medley; mixture; concoction.

misera'bile *m.* wretch; *adj.* unhappy, wretched; despicable.

miseramente *adv.* poorly; piteously.

miserando, misere'vole *adj.* pitiable.

mise'ria *f.* poverty, destitution; woe; trifle; meanness; want, dearth.

misericor'dia *f.* mercy.

misericordioso *adj.* merciful.

mi'sero *adj.* miserable; meager; stingy; mean; pinched; piteous.

miser'rimo *superl.adj.* extremely miserable (meager, *etc.*).

misfatto *m.* misdeed, crime.

miso'gino *m.* misogynist.

mis'sile *m.*, *adj.* missile: — telecomandato, guided missile.

missiona'rio *m.* missionary.

missione *f.* mission.

missiva *f.*, *adj.* missive.

misterioso *adj.* mysterious.

mistero *m.* mystery.

misticismo *m.* mysticism.

mi'stico *m.*, *adj.* mystic.

mistificare *vt.* to mystify, hoodwink.

mistificatore *m.* mystifier, cheat.

mistificazione *f.* mystification, trick.

misto *m.* mixture. *adj.* mixed: scuola mista, coeducational school.

mistura *f.* mixture.

misura *f.* measure; size; tape measure; moderation, composure; step, action: oltrepassare la —, to go too far.

misurare *vt.* to measure; to try on; to gauge; to weigh; to deal; to judge; to estimate; misurarsi *vr.* to measure oneself; to contend.

misurato *adj.* measured; scanty; moderate; cautious.

misuratore *m.* gauger, measurer; meter.

misurazione *f.* measurement.

mite *adj.* mild; kindly; meek.

mitezza *f.* mildness, meekness.

mi'tico *adj.* mythical.

mitigare *vt.* to allay, mitigate; mitigarsi, *vr.* to abate.

mito *m.* myth.

mitologi'a *f.* mythology.

mitolo'gico *adj.* mythological.

mitra *f.* mitre; submachine gun.

mitra'glia *f.* grapeshot.

mitragliare *vt.* to machine-gun.

mitragliatore *m.* machine gunner: fucile —, submachine gun.

mitragliatrice *f.* machine gun.

mitragliere *m.* machine gunner.

mittente *m.* sender.

mo' *m.* (*abbr. of* modo) way: a — di, by way of; as; a — d'esempio, for instance.

mo'bile (1) *m.* piece of furniture; (*pl.*) furniture.

mo'bile (2) *adj.* movable; portable; variable; fickle, inconstant.

mobi'lia *f.* furniture.

mobiliere *m.* furniture maker.

mobilità *f.* mobility; changeableness.

mobilitare *vt.* to mobilize.

mobilitazione *f.* mobilization.

moca *m.* mocha.

moc'cio *m.* snivel, snot.

moccioso *m.* sniveler, brat.

moc'colo *m.* candle stump; curse.

moda *f.* fashion: di —, fashionable.

modalità *f.* modality; (*pl.*) procedure.

modanatura *f.* molding.

modella *f.* model.

modellare *vt.* to model, mold; to pattern (*after*).

modello *m.* model; pattern, specimen.

moderare *vt.* to moderate, temper; to restrain; moderarsi *vr.* to moderate, restrain oneself.

moderatezza *f.* soberness; restraint.

moderato *m.*, *adj.* moderate.

moderazione *f.* moderation.

modernità *f.* modernity.

modernizzare *vt.* to modernize.

moderno *m.*, *adj.* modern.

mode'stia *f.* modesty.

modesto *adj.* modest; moderate.

mo'dico *adj.* cheap, reasonable.

modi'fica *f.* alteration.

modificare *vt.* to modify, alter.

modificazione *f.* modification.

Modigliani, Amedeo, Italian painter (1884–1920).

modista *f.* milliner.

modisteri'a *f.* millinery.

modo *m.* way, manner; means; behavior, ways (*pl.*); (*gramm.*) mood: essere a —, to be well-mannered; di — che, so that; in — da, so as; oltre —, beyond measure; in certo qual —, somehow; per — di dire, so to speak.

modulare *vt.* to modulate.

modulatore *m.* modulator: — di frequenza, (*radio*) modulator tube.

modulazione *f.* modulation.

mo'dulo *m.* model, standard; form, blank; (*arch.*) module.

mo'gano *m.* mahogany.

mog'gio *m.* bushel.

mo'gio *adj.* crestfallen; downhearted.

mo'glie *f.* wife; bride.

moina *f.* blandishment, guile.

mola *f.* grindstone; millstone.

molare (1) *m.*, *adj.* molar.

molare (2) *vt.* to grind; to bevel.

molato *adj.* ground; beveled.

mole *f.* mass, bulk; pile; size.

mole'cola *f.* molecule.

molecolare *adj.* molecular.

molestare *vt.* to irk, annoy, tease.

mole'stia *f.* trouble; uneasiness.

molesto *adj.* irksome, troublesome.

molla *f.* (*mach.*) spring.

mollare *vt.* to loosen; to let go; to drop. *vi.* to give in, yield: — gli ormeggi, to cast off.

molle (1) *f.pl.* tongs.

molle (2) *adj.* soft; flabby; wet; weak.

molleggiamento *see* molleggio.

molleggiare *vi.* to spring, be resilient.

molleg'gio *m.* suspension.

mollettone *m.* Canton flannel.

mollezza *f.* softness; weakness.

mollica *f.* crumb.

mollificare *vt.* to soften.

mollo *adj.* damp: mettere a—, to steep.

mollusco *m.* mollusk.

molo *m.* wharf, pier.

molte'plice *adj.* manifold.

molti'plica *f.* multiplication; chain gearing.

moltiplicando *m.* multiplicand.

moltiplicare *vt.*, **moltiplicarsi** *vr.* to multiply.

moltiplicatore *m.* multiplier.

moltiplicazione *f.* multiplication.

moltitu'dine *f.* multitude.

molto (1) *m.* much, a great deal; **molti** *pl.* many.

molto (2) *adj.* much; great; long: per — tempo, for a long time; — tempo fa, long ago; **molti** *pl.* many.

molto (3) *adv.* greatly, very; a great deal; (*followed by adj., adv., ppr.*) very; (*followed by pp., comp.*) much.

moltis'simo *adv.* very much; *m.*, a great deal; *adj.* very much; very great; very long; **moltissimi** *pl.* very many.

momentaneamente *adv.* temporarily; just now.

momenta'neo *adj.* momentary; fleeting.

momento *m.* moment; opportunity; importance: dal — che, since; a momenti, almost; shortly, any moment.

mo'naca *f.* nun.

monacale *adj.* monachal.

mo'naco *m.* monk.

monarca *m.* monarch.

monarchi'a *f.* monarchy.

monastero *m.* monastery.

mona'stico *adj.* monastic.

moncherino *m.* stump.

monco *adj.* maimed; incomplete, unfinished; one-armed.

moncone *m.* stump.

Mondadori, Arnoldo, leading Italian publisher (1889-).

mondana *f.* fancy woman.

mondanità *f.* worldliness.

mondano *adj.* worldly; earthly.

mondare *vt.* to clean; to cleanse; to hull; to weed.

mondariso *m.* rice weeder.

mondiale *adj.* world-wide, world.

mondina *see* mondariso.

mondo (1) *m.* world; earth: l'altro —, the world beyond; caschi il —! come what may!; mettere al —, to bring forth.

mondo (2) *adj.* clean; pure; free (*from*).

monella *f.* romp; "bobby-soxer."

monelleri'a *f.* prank, mischief.

monello *m.* urchin, imp.

moneta *f.* coin, piece; money; change.

monetare *vt.* to coin.

moneta'rio *adj.* monetary.

monile *m.* necklace.

mo'nito *m.* warning.

monitore *m.* monitor.

monna *f.* lady; (*zool.*) pithecus.

mono'colo *m.* one-eyed man; monocle.

monofase *adj.* single-phase.

monogami'a *f.* monogamy.

monografi'a *f.* monograph.

monogramma *m.* monogram.

monolito *m.* monolith.

mono'logo *m.* monologue.

monopat'tino *m.* scooter.

monopo'lio *m.* monopoly.

monoplano *m.* monoplane.

monopolizzare *vt.* to monopolize.

monosil'labo *m.* monosyllable.

monotipi'a *f.* monotype.

monotipista *m.* monotyper.

monotoni'a *f.* monotony.

mono'tono *adj.* monotonous.

monsignore *m.* (*eccl.*) Monsignor; (*archaic*) Your (His) Lordship.

monsone *m.* monsoon.

monta *f.* covering; stud; jockey.

montaca'richi *m.* freight elevator.

montag'gio *m.* (*mach.*) assemblage; (*moving pictures*) editing, montage.

montagna f. mountain; pile, heap: montagne russe, roller coaster.

montagnola f. mound.

montagnoso adj. mountainous.

Montale, Eugenio, Italian poet (1896-   ).

montanaro m. mountaineer.

montano adj. mountain.

montante m. amount; step; post; (boxing) uppercut; (aeron.) strut; adj. rising, mounting.

montare vt. to mount, climb; to set; (mach.) to assemble; to fit up; to frame; (zool.) to cover; to whip (cream); to stage (a show); to edit (a moving-picture film); vi. to mount; to rise; to swell: — su un treno, to board a train; — in bestia, to fly off the handle; montarsi vr. to swell; to work oneself up.

montatore m. assembler.

montatura f. assembling; setting; (fig.) hocus-pocus;"hokum". "ballyhoo."

montavivande m. lift, dumbwaiter.

monte m. mount, mountain, heap, pile: — di pietà, pawnbroking establishment; andare a —, to end in smoke; mandare a —, to throw overboard; to call off.

Montessori, Maria, Italian educator (1870-1952).

Monteverdi, Claudio, Italian composer (1567-1643).

montone m. ram; mutton.

montuoso adj. mountainous.

montura f. uniform.

monumentale adj. monumental.

monumento m. monument;immemorial.

mora (1) f. (law) arrearage.

mora (2) f. blackberry; mulberry; brambleberry.

mora (3) f. Negro woman; brunette.

morale (1) f. moral; morality, morals.

morale (2) m. morale: il — delle truppe, the morale of the troops; giù di —, downhearted; su di —, in high spirits.

morale (3) adj. moral.

moralista m. moralist.

moralità f. morality; character.

moralizzare vt., vi. to moralize.

moralmente adv. morally.

morato'ria f. moratorium.

Moravia, Alberto (Alberto Pincherle), Italian novelist (1907-   ).

morbidezza f. softness.

mor'bido adj. soft; delicate.

morbillo m. measles.

morbo m. illness, disease; plague.

morboso adj. morbid.

mor'chia f. oil dregs.

mordace adj. mordant, mordacious.

mordente m. mordant; (fig.) bite; vim, "zing."

mor'dere vt.," vi. to bite; to sting: — il freno, to champ at the bit.

mordicchiare vt. to nibble (at).

morena f. moraine.

morente adj. dying; (fig.) fading.

moresco adj. Moorish, Moresque.

moretta f. brunette; Negro girl.

moretto m. brunet; Negro boy.

morfina f. morphine, morphia.

morfologi'a f. morphology.

morgana'tico adj. morganatic.

mori'a f. high mortality.

moribondo m., adj. moribund.

morigerato adj. temperate, moderate, sober, subdued.

morire vi." to die; to die away: — di noia, to be bored to death.

morituro adj. dying, doomed.

mormorare vt., vi. to murmur; to grumble; to rustle; to gossip.

mormori'o m. murmur; grumble; whisper; rustle.

moro (1) m. mulberry tree.

moro (2) m. Moor; Negro; brunet. adj. dark, swarthy.

morosità f. insolvency.

moroso (1) adj. insolvent: contribuente —, tax delinquent.

moroso (2) m., morosa f. (colloq.) sweetheart, lover.

morsa f. vise; (naut.) davit.

morsetto m. clamp.

morsicare vt. to bite.

morsicatura f. bite; sting.

morso (1) m. bite; sting; morsel; bit, snaffle.

morso (2) pp. of mordere.

morta'io m. mortar; trench gun.

mortale m. mortal. adj. mortal, deadly, fatal: salto —, somersault.

mortalità f. mortality.

mortalmente adv. mortally; deadly.

mortaretto m. firecracker.

morte f. death.

mortella f. myrtle.

mortificante adj. mortifying.

mortificare vt. to mortify, snub.

mortificato adj. abashed, crestfallen.

mortificazione f. mortification, shame.

morto m. dead (man); deceased; corpse; dummy (at bridge and other games); adj. dead, deceased: a corpo —, headlong; natura morta, still life. pp. of morire.

morto'rio m. funeral; gloom.

mosa'ico m. mosaic; adj. Mosaic.

mosca f. fly; gadfly; imperial: una — bianca, one in a million; — cieca, blindman's buff.

moscatello m. muscatel.

moscato m. muscat: noce moscata, nutmeg.

moscerino m. gnat.

moschea f. mosque.

moschettiere *m.* musketeer.

moschetto *m.* musket, rifle.

moschettone *m.* clasp, slip hook.

moschicida *adj.* fly-killing: carta —, flypaper.

mo'scio *adj.* flabby.

moscone *m.* bluebottle fly.

mossa *f.* move, movement; gesture: essere sulle mosse, to be about (*to*).

mossiere *m.* starter (*in a race*).

mosso *adj.* moved; stirred; lively: mare —, rough sea. *pp. of* muovere.

mostarda *f.* mustard.

mosto *m.* must.

mostra *f.* exhibition; show; display; show window; pretense: mettersi in —, to show off; far — di, to pretend to.

mostrare *vt.* to show, exhibit; to point out; to disclose; to pretend: — la corda, to be threadbare; mostrarsi *vr.* to show; to reveal oneself; to prove; to feign.

mostriciat'tolo *m.* little monster; freak.

mostrine *f.pl.* collar insignia.

mostro *m.* monster.

mostruoso *adj.* monstrous.

mota *f.* mud, mire.

motivare *vt.* to explain; to motivate; to justify; to cause, occasion.

motivato *adj.* grounded (*on*); justified.

motivazione *f.* allegation, motivation.

motivo *m.* motive, reason, cause; ground; motif; tune: — per cui, therefore; a — di, owing to.

moto *m.* motion, movement; exercise; riot; urge, impulse; *f.* motorcycle.

motocarrozzetta *f.* sidecar.

motobarca *f.* motorboat.

motocicletta *f.* motorcycle.

motociclismo *m.* motorcycling.

motociclista *m.* motorcyclist.

motociclo *m.* motorcycle.

motofurgone *m.* motorcycle truck.

motona'uta *m.* motorboatman.

motonau'tica *f.* boat racing.

motonave *f.* motor ship.

motopescherec'cio *m.* motor fishing boat.

motore *m.* motor, engine: — a reazione, jet engine.

motoretta *f.* motor scooter.

motorista *m.* motorist; mechanician.

motorizzare *vt.* to motorize.

motoscafo *m.* motor launch, motorboat.

motrice *f.* driving car; *adj.* motive.

motteggiare *vt.* to mock; *vi.* to banter.

motteg'gio *m.* jest, mockery.

motto *m.* motto; slogan; saying; witticism.

movente *m.* motive, reason.

movenza *f.* movement.

movi'bile *adj.* movable.

movimentato *adj.* lively, animated; eventful; checkered.

movimento *m.* movement; motion; traffic; bustle.

mozione *f.* motion.

mozzare *vt.* to lop (*off*), sever; to cut.

mozzicone *m.* stump; butt.

mozzo (1) *m.* stableboy; (*naut.*) sailor boy.

mozzo (2) *m.* hub (*of a wheel*); boss (*of a screw propeller*).

mozzo (3) *adj.* severed: butt. mozzo (3) *adj.* severed: fiato —, panting breath; coda mozza, dock.

mucca *f.* cow.

muc'chio *m.* heap, pile, mass; crowd; stack.

mucillag'gine *f.* mucilage.

muco *adj.* mucus.

mucosa *f.* mucous membrane.

muffa *f.* must, mold.

muffire *vi.* to grow musty.

muffito *adj.* musty, moldy.

muffoso *adj.* musty, moldy; (*fig.*) fusty.

muflone *m.* mouflon.

mugghiare *vi.* to bellow, low; to howl; to roar.

mug'gine *m.* mullet.

muggire *see* mugghiare.

muggito *m.* low, bellow.

mughetto *m.* lily of the valley.

mugna'io *m.* miller.

mugolare *vi.* to yelp; to moan.

mugoli'o *m.* yelping, moan.

mugo'lio *m.* pine tar.

mulattiera *f.* mule track, pack road.

mulattiere *m.* muleteer.

mulatto *m.*, *adj.* mulatto.

muliebre *adj.* womanly, feminine.

mulinello 'm. whirligig; whirlwind; whirlpool.

mulino *m.* mill; watermill: — a vento, windmill.

mulo *m.* mule.

multa *f.* fine.

multare *vt.* to fine.

multicolore *adj.* multicolored, motley.

mul'tiplo *m.*, *adj.* multiple.

mum'mia *f.* mummy.

mummificare *vt.*, mummificarsi *vr.* to mummify.

mun'gere *vt.* to milk; (*fig.*) to sponge.

municipale *adj.* municipal.

munici'pio *m.* municipality; town hall.

munificenza *f.* munificence.

muni'fico *adj.* munificent.

munire *vt.* to provide, equip, furnish, supply (*with*); munirsi *vr.* to provide oneself (*with*).

munizione *f.* ammunition.

munto *pp. of* mungere.

muo'vere *vt.* to move; to displace; to stir (*up*); to drive, lead; to prompt, urge; to raise; *vi.* to go; to come; to move; to advance: — incontro a qualcuno, to go to meet someone; muoversi *vr.* to move; to stir; to act; to leave.

mura *f.pl.* walls (*of a city*).

mura'glia *f.* wall, rampart.

murale *adj.* mural.

murare *vt.* to wall; to immure.

murata *f.* (*naut.*) bulwark.

muratore *m.* bricklayer.

muratura *f.* bricklaying: lavoro in —, brickwork.

murena *f.* moray.

muro *m.* wall: mettere con le spalle al —, to corner; — del suono, sound barrier.

musa *f.* Muse, inspiration.

mu'schio *m.* musk; moss.

muscolare *adj.* muscular.

mu'scolo *m.* muscle, sinew.

muscoloso *adj.* muscular, brawny.

museo *m.* museum.

museruola *f.* muzzle.

mu'sica *f.* music; score; band.

musicale *adj.* musical.

musicalità *f.* musicalness.

musicante *m.* musician.

musicare *vt.* to (*set to*) music.

musicista *m.* musician.

muso *m.* muzzle; snout, face; nose: mettere il —, to pout; avere il —, to sulk.

musone *m.* sulker.

musoneri'a *f.* sullenness, sulkiness.

mus'sola *f.* (*muslin*) delaine.

mussolina *f.* muslin.

Mussolini, Benito (*il Duce*), Italian fascist premier and dictator (1883-1945).

mussulmano *see* musulmano.

mustacchi *m.pl.* mustache.

mustela *f.* stone marten.

musulmano *m.,* *adj.* Moslem.

muta *f.* change; shift; outfit; pack (*of hounds*); relay (*of horses*); set of sails.

mutamento *see* cambiamento.

mutande *f.pl.* drawers (*clothing*).

mutandine *f.pl.* trunks, shorts.

mutare, mutarsi *see* cambiare, cambiarsi.

mute'vole *adj.* changeable; variable; fickle.

mutilare *vt.* to mutilate, maim.

mutilato *m.* cripple; *adj.* mutilated, maimed.

mutilazione *f.* mutilation, maiming, mayhem.

mutismo *m.* muteness, dumbness; silence.

muto *m.* mute; *adj.* dumb, mute; silent; speechless; voiceless: scena muta, dumbshow.

mu'tria *f.* sulk; "crust," "nerve."

mu'tua *f.* medical aid center.

mutuare *vt.* to borrow; to lend.

mu'tuo *m.* loan; *adj.* mutual.

N

nababbo *m.* nabob.

nac'chera *f.* castanet.

nafta *f.* naphtha; diesel oil.

naftalina *f.* naphthalene.

na'ia *f.* cobra; (*It. slang*) military life, service.

na'iade *f.* naiad, waternymph.

nailon *m.* nylon.

nanerot'tolo *m.* dwarf.

nanna *f.* sleep: fare la —, to sleep.

nano *m.,* *adj.* dwarf.

napoletano *m.,* *adj.* Neapolitan.

nappa *f.* tassel.

narciso *m.* daffodil, narcissus.

narcosi *f.* narcosis; anesthesia.

narco'tico *m.,* *adj.* narcotic.

narcotizzare *vt.* to narcotize; to anesthetize.

nare, narice *f.* nostril.

narrare *vt.* to recount, narrate, relate.

narrativa *f.* fiction.

narrativo *adj.* narrative, fiction.

narratore *m.* narrator; storyteller.

narrazione *f.* narration; story.

nasale *adj.* nasal.

nascente *adj.* rising, springing; arising; sprouting.

na'scere *vi.*[31] to be born; to spring, sprout; to derive; to originate, proceed; to rise: far —, to give birth to; — con la camicia, to be born with a silver spoon in one's mouth.

na'scita *f.* birth; extraction, descent.

nascituro *m.* child to be born; *adj.* to be born.

nascon'dere *vt.*[39] to conceal, hide; to mask; to screen; to disguise; nascon'dersi *vr.* to hide.

nascondi'glio *m.* hideout; lair.

nascostamente *adv.* hiddenly; stealthily; secretly.

nascosto *adj.* concealed, hidden; underhand; secret: di —, secretly; stealthily. *pp. of* nascondere.

nasello *m.* whiting.

naso *m.* nose: con un palmo di —, like a duck in thunder.

nastrino *m.* badge, ribbon.

nastro *m.* ribbon, band, strip, tape: metro a —, tapeline; sega a —, bandsaw.

natale (*1*) *m.* birth; birthday: avere i natali a, to be born in; dare i natali a, to be the birthplace of.

Natale (*2*) *m.* Christmas.

natale (*3*) *adj.* native.

natalità *f.* natality; birth rate.

natal'zio *adj.* natal; Christmas; *m.* birthday.

natante *m.* craft; *adj.* floating.

natato'ia *f.* flipper.

natato'rio *adj.* natatorial, swimming.

na'tica *f.* buttock.

nati'o *adj.* native.

natività *f.* nativity, birth.

nativo *m.*, *adj.* native.

nato *adj.* born; arisen, risen. *pp.* of **natta** *f.* wen.　　　　　[nascere.

natura *f.* nature: pagare in —, to pay in kind.

naturale *adj.* natural; pure; genuine: di grandezza —, life-size; al —, true to nature.

naturalezza *f.* naturalness; spontaneity.

naturalizzare *vt.*, **naturalizzarsi** *vr.* to naturalize.

naturalizzazione *f.* naturalization.

naturalmente *adv.* naturally; by nature; of course.

naufragare *vi.* to shipwreck; to sink; to fall, wreck.

naufra'gio *m.* shipwreck.

nau'frago *m.* shipwreck survivor; (*fig.*) outcast.

nau'sea *f.* nausea: aver la —, to feel sick.

nauseabondo, nauseante *adj.* sickening, disgusting.

nauseare *vt.* to sicken, nauseate, disgust.

nauseato *adj.* disgusted (*with*), sick.

nau'tica *f.* nautics.

nau'tico *adj.* nautical.

nau'tilo *m.* nautilus.

navale *adj.* naval, navy.

navata *f.* nave; aisle.

nave *f.* ship, boat, vessel: — cisterna, tanker; — traghetto, ferryboat; — portaerei, aircraft carrier.

navetta *f.* shuttle.

navicella *f.* (*naut.*) bark; (*aeron.*) nacelle.

naviga'bile *adj.* navigable.

navigante *m.*, *f.* navigator, seafarer; *adj.* sailing.

navigare *vi.* to navigate, sail, voyage.

navigato *adj.* experienced.

navigatore *m.* navigator.

navigazione *f.* navigation: — aerea, aviation, flying.

navi'glio *m.* craft; canal; fleet; merchant marine.

nazionale *f.* national team; *adj.* national.

nazionalità *f.* nationality.

nazionalizzare *vt.* to nationalize.

nazionalizzazione *f.* nationalization.

nazione *f.* nation.

Nazzareno *m.*, *adj.* Nazarene.

ne (*1*) *adv.* from there, therefrom; from here.

ne (*2*) *pron. particle* his, of (*about*) him; her, of (*about*) her; its, of (*about*) it; their, of (*about*) them.

ne (*3*) *partitive pron.* any, some, none.

ne (*4*) (*pleonastic, not to be translated*): me — vado, I am going away; — va del mio onore, my honor is at stake.

nè *neg.conj.* neither, nor: non poteva — leggere — scrivere, he could neither read nor write; non lo vidi più, — mi dispiacque, I never saw him again, nor did I regret it; — l'uno — l'altro, neither.

neanche *see* **nemmeno**.

neb'bia *f.* fog; mist; haze.

nebbione *m.* thick fog, sop.

nebbioso *adj.* foggy.

nebulizzare *vt.* to atomize.

nebulizzatore *m.* atomizer.

nebulosa *f.* (*astr.*) nebula.

nebuloso *adj.* nebulous, hazy.

necessa'rio *m.* necessary, necessity, necessaries (*pl.*); *adj.* necessary; essential, requisite; due.

necessità *f.* necessity, need, want.

necessitare *vt.* to necessitate, need; *vi.* to be necessary; to call (*for*).

necro'foro *m.* gravedigger.

necrologi'a *f.* obituary.

necrolo'gio *m.* necrology, obituary.

necrosi *f.* necrosis.

necrotizzare *vt.* to necrose.

nefandezza *f.* nefariousness.

nefando *adj.* nefarious, unspeakable.

nefasto *adj.* ominous; unfortunate.

nefrite *f.* (*pathol.*) nephritis; (*min.*) nephrite.

negare *vt.* to deny.

negativa *f.* negative, denial; (*photo.*) negative.

negativamente *adv.* negatively.

negativo *adj.* negative.

negato *adj.* denied; unfit; untalented: essere — alla musica, to have no bent for music.

negazione *f.* denial, negation; (*gramm.*) negative: essere la — di (*fig.*), to have no talent for; to be the opposite of.

neghittoso *adj.* slothful.

negletto *adj.* neglected.

negli *comp.prep.* in the. *see* **in**.

negligente *adj.* negligent, careless.

negligenza *f.* negligence, neglect, remissness.

negoziante *m.* shopkeeper; dealer.

negoziare vt. to negotiate, transact; vi. to trade (in); to deal (in).
negoziato m. negotiation.
negoziatore m. negotiator.
nego'zio m. shop; bargain, transaction.
negra f. Negro woman; Negro.
negriero m. slave trader, slaver; (fig.). slavedriver.
negro m. Negro; (fig.) ghost writer; adj. Negro, black.
nei, nel, nella, nelle, nello comp.prep. in the. see in.
nembo m. (rain) cloud; storm.
ne'mesi f. nemesis.
nemico m. enemy, foe; adj. enemy, hostile (to), averse (to).
nemmanco, nemmeno conj. not even, not either, neither: — per sogno! by no means!
ne'nia f. dirge.
neo m. mole; flaw, blemish.
neologismo m. neologism.
neomicina f. neomycin.
ne'on m. neon: scritta, insegna al —, neon sign.
neonato m., **neonata** f. newborn child; adj. newborn.
nepote see nipote.
neppure see nemmanco.
nequi'zia f. iniquity.
nerastro adj. blackish.
nerbata f. scourging.
nerbo m. sinew; lash, scourge; strength, vigor.
nerboruto adj. sinewy, brawny.
neretto m. (typog.) boldface.
nerezza f. blackness.
nero m. black; blackness; adj. black, dark: pane —, brown bread.
nerofumo m. lampblack.
Nerone m. (hist.) Nero.
nervatura f. nervation.
nervo m. nerve; tendon, sinew: avere i nervi, to be peevish, irritable.
nervosamente adv. nervously, irritably.
nervosismo m. nervousness, irritableness.
nervoso m. ill humor; adj. nervous; irritable; peevish.
nesci m. know-nothing: fare il —, to pretend to know nothing.
ne'spola f. medlar; (colloq.) blow.
ne'spolo m. medlar tree.
nesso m. link, connection.
nessuno adj. no; pron. nobody, no one, none; any, anybody, anyone: nessuna cosa, nothing; in nessun luogo, nowhere; a nessun patto, by no means.
nettamente adv. cleanly; markedly; utterly; clearly.
nettapenne m. penwiper.

nettapipe m. pipe cleaner.
nettare vt. to clean, cleanse.
net'tare m. nectar.
nettezza f. cleanliness; neatness: — urbana, garbage collection service.
netto adj. clean; net; clear; marked.
neutrale m., adj. neutral.
neutralità f. neutrality.
neutralizzare vt. to neutralize.
ne'utro m., adj. neuter; neutral.
neutrone m. neutron.
neva'io m. snowfield.
neve f. snow.
nevicare vi. to snow.
nevicata f. snowfall.
nevischio m. sleet.
nevoso adj. snowy.
nevralgi'a f. neuralgia.
nevrasteni'a f. neurasthenia.
nevraste'nico m., adj. neurasthenic.
nevvero? isn't it (so)?
nib'bio m. (ornith.) kite.
nic'chia f. niche, recess.
nicchiare vi. to hesitate, be reluctant.
nichel, niche'lio m. nickel.
nichelare vt. to nickel, nickelplate.
nichelato adj. nickel-plated.
nicotina f. nicotine.
nicta'lope m. hemeralope.
nidiata f. nestful; brood.
nidificare vi. to build a nest.
nido m. nest: — d'infanzia, nursery school.
niente m. nothing, naught; trifle: far finta di —, to feign indifference; non fa —, it does not matter; adj. no: una ferita da —, a slight wound; un uomo da —, a good-for-nothing; indef.pron. nothing; anything; adv. nothing, not at all.
nientemeno adv. nothing less (than); no less (than); fancy!
Nievo, Ippolito Italian novelist, poet and patriot. Le confessioni di un ottuagenario (1831-1861).
Nilo m. (geog.) Nile.
ninfa f. nymph.
ninfea f. (bot.) waterlily.
ninnananna f. lullaby.
nin'nolo m. trinket, trifle.
nipote m., f. nephew (m.), niece (f.); grandchild (m., f.), grandson (m.), granddaughter (f.).
nipotino m. little nephew; grandchild.
nippo'nico adj. Japanese.
nitidezza f. clearness.
ni'tido adj. clear; distinct; nitid.
nitore m. brightness, polish.
nitrato m. nitrate.
nitrire vi. to neigh.
nitrito (1) m. neigh, whinny.
nitrito (2) m. (chem.) nitrite.

nitro *m.* (*chem.*) saltpeter.

nitrocellulosa *f.* nitrocellulose.

nitro'geno *m.* nitrogen.

Nitti, Francesco Saverio, Italian statesman and economist (1868–1953).

niuno *see* nessuno.

nl've *adj.* snow-white; niveous.

no *adv.* no, not: dir di —, to say no; sé —, otherwise.

no'bile *m.* nobleman; *f.* noblewoman; *adj.* noble: piano —, second story.

nobiliare *adj.* nobiliary.

nobilitare *vt.* to ennoble; to exalt.

nobiltà *f.* nobility; nobleness.

nocca *f.* knuckle.

nocchiero *m.* pilot, steersman.

nocciola *see* nocciuola.

noc'ciolo *m.* (*fruit*) stone: il — della questione, the heart of the matter.

nocciuola *f.* hazelnut; *adj.* hazel.

nocciuolo *m.* hazel.

noce *f.* walnut; walnut tree: — moscata, nutmeg.

nociuto *pp. of* nuocere.

nocivo *adj.* harmful, detrimental.

nocumento *m.* damage, harm.

nodo *m.* knot: un — in gola, a lump in one's throat; — scorsoio, noose.

nodoso *adj.* knotty, gnarly.

noi *pers.pron.* we; us.

no'ia *f.* boredom; weariness; trouble: prendere a —, to get tired of; dar — a, to molest, badger, irk.

noioso *adj.* boresome, tedious; irksome; *m.* bore.

noleggiare *vt.* to hire; to rent; to charter (*as a ship*).

noleggiatore *m.* hirer; charterer; freighter.

noleg'gio *m.* hire; rent; chartering: contratto di —, charter party.

nolente *adj.* unwilling: volente o —, willy-nilly.

nolo *m.* hire; (*naut.*) freight: contratto di —, charter party.

no'made *m.* nomad; *adj.* nomadic.

nome *m.* name; (*gramm.*) noun; fame, repute: — di battesimo, Christian name; senza —, nameless; a — di, in behalf of.

nomea *f.* reputation.

nomi'gnolo *m.* nickname.

no'mina *f.* appointment; reputation.

nominale *adj.* nominal.

nominalmente *adv.* nominally.

nominare *vt.* to name, call; to mention; to elect; to appoint.

nominativo *m.* (*gramm.*) nominative (*case*); name; *adj.* nominative.

non *adv.* not, no; *pref.* non: un — so che, something (*indefinable*).

nonagena'rio *m.* nonagenarian.

nonage'simo *adj.* ninetieth.

noncurante *adj.* heedless, careless.

noncuranza *f.* carelessness, unconcern.

nondimeno *adv.* nevertheless, still, yet.

nonna *f.* grandmother.

nonno *m.* grandfather.

nonni *m.pl.* grandparents.

nonnulla *m.* nothing, trifle.

nono *adj.* ninth.

nonostante *prep.* in spite of, despite, notwithstanding: ciò —, nevertheless, yet, still, however; — che, although.

nonpertanto *prep.* still, yet.

nonplusultra *m.* the ultimate, ne plus ultra.

nonsenso *m.* nonsense.

nontiscordardimè *m.* forget-me-not.

nord *m.* North.

nor'dico *m.* Northerner; *adj.* north, northern.

norma *f.* rule, regulation: di —, as a rule; a — di, in compliance with; per vostra —, for your guidance.

normale *f.* perpendicular line; *adj.* normal; ordinary.

normalità *f.* normality.

normalizzare *vt.* to normalize.

normalmente *adv.* normally.

normo'grafo *m.* lettering guide.

norvegese *m.*, *adj.* Norwegian.

nosoco'mio *m.* hospital.

nossignora *adv.* no, madam.

nossignore *adv.* no, sir.

nostalgi'a *f.* homesickness; nostalgia; longing.

nostal'gico *adj.* homesick; nostalgic.

nostrano *adj.* home; national; regional.

nostro *adj.* our; *poss.pron.* ours.

nostromo *m.* boatswain.

nota *f.* note; mark; memorandum; list; bill, invoice: note caratteristiche, fitness report; degno di —, noteworthy; prima — (*comm.*), waste book.

nota'bile *m.*, *adj.* notable.

nota'io *m.* notary (*public*); lawyer.

notare *vt.* to note; to jot down, scribble; to notice; to remark: farsi —, to make oneself conspicuous.

notarile *adj.* notarial.

notaro *see* notaio.

note'vole *adj.* remarkable, considerable, notable, noteworthy.

notevolmente *adv.* remarkably; considerably.

noti'fica *see* notificazione.

notificare *vt.* to notify; to serve (*as a summons*).

notificazione *f.* notification; service (*of a writ*).

noti'zia *f.* (*piece of*) news; (*pl.*) news, report; notice; knowledge; reference.

notizia'rio *m.* news report; (*radio*) newscast; (*cinema*) newsreel.

noto *m.* the known; *adj.* known; famous; notorious.

notoriamente *adv.* notoriously.

notorietà *f.* renown, notoriety.

noto'rio *adj.* well known; notorious.

nottam'bulo *m.* night wanderer, noctambulist.

nottata *f.* night: fare —, to burn the midnight oil.

notte *f.* night; night time; darkness: — bianca, sleepless night; sul far della — at nightfall; di —, by (*at*) night.

nottetempo *adv.* by night.

not'tola *f.* (*zool.*) bat; (*mach.*) latch.

notturno *m.* (*mus.*) nocturne; *adj.* nightly, nocturnal.

novanta *m.*, *adj.* ninety.

novantenne *m.*, *f.*, *adj.* nonagenarian.

novante'simo *m.*, *adj.* ninetieth.

novantina *f.* some ninety: sulla —, about ninety.

nove *m.*, *adj.* nine: fare la prova del —, to cast out nines.

novecentista *m.* modernist.

novecento *m.*, *adj.* nine hundred; *m.* twentieth century.

novella *f.* short story; (*archaic*) news.

novelliere *m.* storyteller, short-story writer.

novellino *m.* beginner, tyro; *adj.* inexperienced, green.

novelli'stica *f.* story-telling; fiction.

novello *adj.* new; tender: sposi novelli, newlyweds.

novembre *m.* November.

novena'rio *adj.* nine-syllabled.

no'vero *m.* number, class.

novis'simo *adj.* quite new.

novità *f.* novelty; innovation; news: — librarie, teatrali, new books, plays.

noviziato *m.* novitiate, apprenticeship.

novi'zio *m.* novice; apprentice; beginner, tyro.

nozione *f.* notion; knowledge; cognition; rudiment.

nozze *f.pl.* wedding; marriage.

nube *f.* cloud.

nubifra'gio *m.* rainstorm; downpour.

nu'bile *f.* maiden; *adj.* unmarried.

nuca *f.* nape, scruff.

nucleare *adj.* nuclear.

nu'cleo *m.* nucleus (*pl.* nuclei); group; squad, force.

nudismo *m.* nudism.

nudista *m.* nudist.

nudità *f.* nudity, nakedness.

nudo *m.* nude; *adj.* naked, bare; stripped (*of*).

nu'golo *m.* cloud; swarm.

nulla *m.* nothingness. see niente.

nullaosta *m.* visa, "okay": dare il — per, to visa, "okay."

nullatenente *m.* unpropertied person.

nullità *f.* worthlessness; nullity; voidness, nonentity, (a) nobody.

nullo *adj.* worthless; null, void; no; *pron.* none, no one.

nume *m.* deity, god.

numerale *m.*, *adj.* numeral.

numerare *vt.* to number.

numerato *adj.*, *pp.* numbered.

numerazione *f.* numeration.

numericamente *adv.* numerically.

nume'rico *adj.* numerical.

nu'mero *m.* number, numeral, figure; (*theat.*) act, scene; number, issue (*of a newspaper, etc.*): — legale, quorum; due di —, two and no more.

numeroso *adj.* numerous; (*pl.*) several.

numisma'tica *f.* numismatics.

numisma'tico *m.* numismatist; *adj.* numismatic.

nunziatura *f.* nunciature.

nun'zio *m.* nuncio, papal envoy.

nuo'cere *vi.*[81] to be detrimental (*to*): — a, to damage, injure, harm; non tutto il male vien per —, every cloud has its silver lining.

nuociuto *pp.* of nuocere.

nuora *f.* daughter-in-law.

nuotare *vi.* to swim.

nuotatore *m.* swimmer.

nuoto *m.* swimming.

nuova *f.* news.

nuovamente *adv.* once more; again, afresh.

nuovo *adj.* new; novel; unusual; unused; fresh: di —, again, anew, afresh; rimettere a —, to renovate; — di zecca, brand-new.

nutrice *f.* nurse; wet nurse.

nutriente *adj.* nourishing, rich.

nutrimento *m.* nourishment, food.

nutrire *vt.* to nourish, nurture; to feed; (*fig.*) to harbor, cherish; nutrirsi *vr.* to feed (*on*).

nutritivo *adj.* nutritious.

nutrito *adj.* well-fed; (*fig.*) sustained.

nutrizione *f.* nutrition; nourishment.

nu'vola *f.* cloud.

nu'volo *m.* storm cloud; swarm.

nuvolosità *f.* cloudiness.

nuvoloso *adj.* cloudy, overcast.

nuziale *adj.* wedding, bridal, nuptial: cerimonia —, wedding.

O

o, od *conj.* or, either; else, otherwise.
o'asi *f.* oasis (*pl.* oases).
obbedire *see* ubbidire.
obbiettare *see* obiettare.
obbligare *vt.* to compel, force; obbligarsi *vr.* to undertake; to bind oneself; to guarantee (*for*).
obbligatis'simo *adj.* deeply indebted.
obbligato *adj.* forced, bound; obliged.
obbligato'rio *adj.* mandatory, compulsory.
obbligazione *f.* obligation; (*comm.*) debenture, bond.
ob'bligo *m.* obligation; duty; compulsion; condition: avere l'— di, to be under the obligation to, to have to.
obbro'brio *m.* opprobrium, shame, infamy; (*fig.*) eyesore.
obbrobrioso *adj.* opprobrious.
obelisco *m.* obelisk.
oberato *adj.* burdened (*with*).
obesità *f.* obesity.
obeso *adj.* obese.
o'bice *m.* howitzer.
obiettare *vt.* to argue (*against*).
obiettività *f.* objectivity, impartiality.
obiettivo *m.* lens, objective; aim, object. *adj.* objective, unbiased.
obiezione *f.* objection.
obito'rio *m.* mortuary, morgue.
oblazione *f.* donation.
obliare *vt.* to forget.
obli'o *m.* oblivion.
obli'quo *adj.* oblique, slanting.
obliterare *vt.* to obliterate.
oblò *m.* porthole.
oblungo *adj.* oblong.
o'bolo *m.* mite, contribution; alms.
oca *f.* goose (*pl.* geese); (*male*) gander: pelle d'—, gooseflesh; far venire la pelle d'—, to give the creeps.
occasionale *adj.* occasional; chance.
occasione *f.* occasion; circumstance; opportunity, chance; pretext: in — di, in the occurrence of.
occhia'ia *f.* eyesocket; dark ring: aver le occhiaie, to have dark rings under one's eyes.
occhiaia'io *m.* optician.
occhialetto *m.* lorgnette.
occhiali *m.pl.* spectacles, glasses: — da sole, sunglasses.
occhialoni *m.pl.* goggles.
occhialuto *adj.* bespectacled.
occhiata *f.* glance.
occhiatac'cia *f.* glare.
occhieggiare *vi.* to glance.
occhiello *m.* eyelet, eye; buttonhole; (*typog.*) flyleaf.

occhietto *m.* small eye: far l'— a, to wink at.
oc'chio *m.* eye; sight; look, glance; shrewdness; bud: averne fin sopra gli occhi, to be fed up (*with*); perdere d'—, to lose sight of; tenere d'—, to keep an eye on; a — e croce, at a rough guess; a colpo d'—, at a glance; a perdita d'—, as far as the eye can reach; a quattr'occhi, in private; con la coda dell'—, out of the corner of one's eye; a vista d'—, visibly.
occhiolino *see* occhietto.
occidentale *adj.* western, occidental, west.
occidente *m.* west, occident.
occi'pite *m.* occiput.
occlusione *f.* occlusion.
occorrente *m.* necessities (*pl.*); materials (*pl.*); *adj.* necessary.
occorrenza *f.* need; event, occurrence: all'—, if need be, in case.
occor'rere (1) *vi.*,*se impers.* to be necessary; must, shall, ought to; to want, be in need of: occorre che io, I must; occorrerebbe che noi, we should; mi occorre, I want, need.
occor'rere (2) *see* accadere.
occorso *pp.* of occorrere.
occultamento *m.* concealment; suppression.
occultare *vt.* to conceal; to suppress.
occultismo *m.* occultism.
occulto *adj.* occult, hidden.
occupante *m.*, *f.* occupier, occupant.
occupare *vt.* to occupy; to take possession of; to employ: — una carica, to hold an office; — il proprio tempo, to spend one's time; occuparsi *vr.* to occupy oneself (*with*, *in*); to mind; to find an occupation; to take care (*that*, *of*); to be interested (*in*).
occupato *adj.* engaged, occupied, busy (*with*); taken, occupied (*as a seat*).
occupazione *f.* occupation; trade; employment, situation.
ocea'nico *adj.* oceanic.
oce'ano *m.* ocean.
ocra *f.* ocher.
oculare *m.*, *adj.* ocular: testimone —, eyewitness.
oculatezza *f.* shrewdness.
oculato *adj.* wise; careful; wary.
oculista *m.* oculist.
od *see* o.
odalisca *f.* odalisque.
ode *f.* ode.
odiare *vt.* to hate.
odierno *adj.* today's; present, current.

o'dio *m.* hatred.

odioso *adj.* hateful; loathsome.

Odissea *f.* Odyssey; (*fig.*) vicissitudes (*pl.*); ordeal.

odontoiatra *m.* odontologist.

odontoiatri'a *f.* odontology.

odontoia'trico *adj.* odontological.

odorac'cio *m.* stink.

odorare *vt., vi.* to smell; to scent: — di, to smell like, to smack of.

odorato *m.* smell; scent.

odore *m.* smell, odor; scent; (*pl.*) seasoning herbs, spice.

odoroso *adj.* fragrant, sweet-smelling, odorous.

offen'dere *vt.*⁴⁸ to offend; to abuse; to hurt; offen'dersi *vr.* to take offense (*at*); to be hurt.

offensiva *f.* offensive, attack.

offensivo *adj.* offensive, rude.

offerente *m.* offerer, bidder: il miglior —, the highest bidder.

offerta *f.* offer; proposal; bid; offering; gift; (*comm.*) tender.

offerto *pp.* of offrire.

offesa *f.* offense; resentment; wrong.

offeso *adj.* offended; hurt. *pp.* of offendere.

officiare *vi.* to officiate.

officina *f.* workshop, works.

offrire *vt.*⁸⁴ to offer, tender; to afford. offrirsi *vr.* to offer (*oneself*); to volunteer.

offuscamento *m.* obfuscation.

offuscare *vt.* to obfuscate; to blur, dim; to outshine; offuscarsi *vr.* to darken, dim.

oftalmi'a *f.* ophthalmia.

oftal'mico *adj.* ophthalmic.

oggettività *f.* objectivity; impartiality.

oggettivo *adj.* objective; unbiased.

oggetto *m.* object; thing; article; subject: complemento —, direct object.

oggi *m., adv.* today; nowadays: dall'— al domani, overnight; — come —, at present; — a otto, today week; da — in poi (in avanti), from now on, henceforth.

oggidì, oggigiorno *adv.* nowadays.

ogiva *f.* ogive.

ogivale *adj.* ogival.

ogni *indef.adj.* any; each; every: — tanto, (every) now and then; — due giorni, every other day; per — dove everywhere.

ogniqualvolta *conj.* whenever.

Ognissanti *m.* All-Saints Day.

ognora *adv.* always.

ognuno *pron.* everyone, everybody, each, each one.

ohimè! *interj.* alas!

oibò! *interj.* ah!, fie!

olà! *interj.* hallo!

olandese *m.* Dutch; Dutchman; *f.* Dutchwoman; *adj.* Dutch.

oleandro *m.* oleander.

olea'rio *adj.* oil.

oleifi'cio *m.* oil mill.

oleografi'a *f.* oleography.

oleosità *f.* oiliness.

oleoso *adj.* oily.

olezzare *vi.* to smell sweet.

olezzo *m.* perfume, fragrance.

olfatto *m.* (*sense of*) smell; scent.

oliare *vt.* to oil.

oliera *f.* cruet.

oligarchi'a *f.* oligarchy.

olimpi'ade *f.* Olympiad.

olim'pico *adj.* Olympian, Olympic: calma olimpica, imperturbable composure.

olimpio'nico *m.* (*sport*) Olympian; *adj.* Olympic.

Olimpo *m.* Olympus.

o'lio *m.* oil: — di ricino, castor oil; sott'—, in oil; liscio come l'—, smooth; — di fegato di merluzzo, cod-liver oil.

oliva *f.* olive.

olivastro *adj.* olivaceous; swarthy.

oliveto *m.* olive grove.

olivo *m.* olive (*tree*).

olla *f.* olla, earthen pot.

olmo *m.* elm tree, elm.

oloca'usto *m.* holocaust.

olo'grafo *adj.* holograph.

oltraggiare *vt.* to outrage; to insult.

oltrag'gio *m.* outrage; offense; abuse; ravage.

oltraggioso *adj.* outrageous; insulting.

oltranza *f.* uttermost: lotta ad —, fight to the finish.

oltre *prep.* beyond, past; more than: — che, besides; *adv.* on, ahead; far; farther, further, longer: troppo —, too far; non posso andare più —, I can't go any further.

oltremare *m.* ultramarine; *adv.* overseas: terre d'—, overseas lands.

oltremodo *adv.* exceedingly.

oltrepassare *vt.* to go beyond (*past*); to exceed; to surpass; to overstep.

oltretomba *m.* (*the*) beyond.

omaccione *m.* burly man.

omag'gio *m.* homage; present; (*pl.*) compliments: copia in —, complimentary copy.

ombelico *m.* navel, umbilicus.

ombra *f.* shadow; shade; umbrage.

ombreggiare *vt.* to shade.

ombreggiatura *f.* shading.

ombrella *f.* (*bot.*) umbel. *see* ombrello.

ombrella'io *m.* umbrella maker.

ombrellino *m.* parasol.

ombrello *m.* umbrella.

ombrellone *m.* beach umbrella.

ombrosità f. shadiness; umbrageous- ness; skittishness.
ombroso adj. shady; umbrageous; skittish.
omelí'a f. homily.
omeopa'tico m. homeopathist; adj. homeopathic.
ome'rico adj. Homeric.
o'mero m. (anat.) humerus.
omertà f. code of silence.
omesso adj. left out, omitted. pp. of omettere.
omet'tere vt.⁷ᵇ to leave out, omit; to forget; to skip.
ometto m. little man.
omicida m. homicide, murderer; adj. homicidal, murderous.
omici'dio m. homicide, murder.
omino m. little man.
omissione f. omission.
om'nibus m. omnibus, bus.
omoge'neo adj. homogeneous.
omologare vt. to homologate; to pro- bate.
omologazione f. homologation; pro- bation.
omonimí'a f. homonymy.
omo'nimo m. namesake; adj. homon- ymous.
omosessuale m., adj. homosexual.
onagro m. onager.
on'cia f. (weight) ounce.
onda f. wave; billow, breaker; lunghezza d'—, wave length; andare in —, to go on the air.
ondata f. wave.
onde adv. whence; pron. of which; for which; by which, whereby; conj. in order to, so that; where- fore.
ondeggiamento m. waving; swaying; wavering.
ondeggiante adj. waving; swaying; wavering.
ondeggiare vi. to undulate; to wave; to sway, swing; to waver.
ondina f. (myth.) undine.
ondoso adj. wavy; undulatory.
ondulare vt. to wave; vi. to undulate.
ondulato adj. wavy; scalloped: cartone —, corrugated paper.
ondulato'rio adj. undulatory.
ondulazione f. waving, undulation: — permanente, permanent wave.
o'nere m. onus, burden.
oneroso adj. onerous, heavy.
onestà f. honesty; fairness.
onesto adj. honest; fair; moderate; decent, respectable.
o'nice f. onyx.
onnipossente, onnipotente adj. om- nipotent, almighty.
onnipotenza f. almightiness.
onnipresente adj. omnipresent.

onnisciente adj. omniscient.
onni'voro adj. omnivorous.
onoma'stico m. name day.
onomatopea f. onomatopoeia.
onomatope'ico adj. onomatopoeic.
onora'bile adj. honorable.
onorabilità f. honorableness.
onoranza f. honor; celebration.
onorare vt. to honor; to be an honor to; onorarsi vr. to take pride (in); to be proud (of, to).
onora'rio m. fee; adj. honorary.
onorato adj. honored; honorable; decent.
onore m. honor; (pl. in card games) honors: l'— del mento, the beard; partita d'—, duel; serata d'—, gala night; fare — a un impegno, to meet an obligation; a — del vero, to tell the truth.
onore'vole adj. honorable.
onorificenza f. honor; decoration.
onori'fico adj. honorific.
onta f. disgrace, shame: ad — di, in spite of.
ontano m. (bot.) alder.
onusto adj. laden (with).
opacità f. opacity.
opaco adj. opaque, dim, dull.
opale m. opal.
o'pera f. work; act, deed; (mus.) opera: Opera Pia, charitable in- stitution; mano d'—, labor; messa in —, installation; per — di, through.
opera'ia f. workwoman: ape —, worker (bee).
opera'io m. workman, worker, labor- er; machinist: — specializzato, skilled workman; capo —, foreman; adj. working.
operare vt., vi. to act; to work; to perform; (surg.) to operate (upon); farsi —, to undergo an operation.
operato m. action; behavior; adj. operated; fancy (of a cloth or pattern).
operatore m. operator; (moving pic- tures) cameraman.
operato'rio adj. operative; (surg.) surgical: sala operatoria, surgery.
operazione f. operation; (comm.) transaction.
operetta f. operetta.
operista m. opera composer.
operoso adj. operose, hard-working.
opifi'cio m. works, factory.
opimo adj. fat, rich.
opinare vi. to deem, judge.
opinione f. opinion, view.
oppia'ceo, oppiato m., adj. opiate.
op'pio m. opium.
oppio'mane m., f. opium addict.
opponente m., adj. opponent.

opporre *vt.*¹¹ to oppose; **opporsi** *vr.* to oppose; to object.

opportunista *m.* opportunist.

opportunità *f.* fitness; advisability; expediency; opportunity.

opportuno *adj.* fit, suitable, advisable; timely: **a tempo —**, in due time.

oppositore *m.* opponent.

opposizione *f.* opposition; argument: **fare — a,** to object to.

opposto *m.*, *adj.* opposite, contrary; opposed. *pp. of* **opporre.**

oppressione *f.* oppression; choking sensation.

oppresso *adj.* oppressed, overwhelmed; depressed. *pp. of* **opprimere.**

oppressore *m.* oppressor.

opprimente *adj.* oppressive.

oppri'mere *vt.*¹¹ to oppress; to overwhelm; to choke; to press; to depress.

oppugnare *vt.* to oppugn.

oppugnazione *f.* confutation.

oppure *conj.* or; else.

optare *vi.* to opt, make one's choice: **— per,** to choose.

opulento *adj.* opulent.

opulenza *f.* opulence.

opu'scolo *m.* pamphlet; booklet.

opzione *f.* option.

ora (1) *f.* hour; time; **è — di,** it is time to; **che — è?** what time is it?; **non vedere l'— di,** to look forward to, to be eager to; **ore piccole,** late hours; **a quest'—,** at this time; by now; **di — in —,** hourly; any time; **di buon'—,** early; **a tarda —,** late; **alla buon'—!** at last!

ora (2) *adv. see* **adesso.**

ora'colo *m.* oracle.

o'rafo *m.* goldsmith.

orale *adj.* oral; verbal.

oramai *adv.* now; by this time; already.

orango, orangutan' *m.* orangutan.

ora'rio *m.* hours (*pl.*), time; timetable, schedule: **— d'ufficio,** office hours; **in —,** on schedule, punctual; *adj.* hourly, per hour; **fuso —,** time zone.

oratore *m.* speaker, orator.

orato'ria *f.* oratory; eloquence.

orato'rio *m.* oratory; (*mus.*) oratorio. *adj.* oratorical.

orazione *f.* oration; prayer.

orbare *vt.* to bereave.

orbe *f.* orb, sphere, globe.

orbene *adv.* well now, well.

or'bita *f.* orbit; eye socket; sphere, range: **con gli occhi fuori dall'—,** popeyed.

orbo *adj.* blind; bereft: **botte da orbi,** thrashing blows.

orche'stra *f.* orchestra; band: **direttore d'—,** conductor, bandleader.

orchestrale *m.*, *f.* musician, performer. *adj.* orchestral.

orchestrare *vt.* to orchestrate.

orchestrazione *f.* orchestration.

orchidea *f.* orchid.

or'cio *m.* jar.

orco *m.* ogre.

orda *f.* horde.

ordigno *m.* contrivance.

ordinale *m.*, *adj.* ordinal.

ordinamento *m.* regulation.

ordinanza *f.* ordinance; (*mil.*) orderly: **uniforme d'—,** regimentals.

ordinare *vt.* to order; to arrange, straighten up; to ordain; to prescribe; **ordinarsi** *vr.* (*mil.*) to draw up; (*eccl.*) to become ordained.

ordinariamente *adv.* usually.

ordina'rio *m.* ordinary; professor; *adj.* ordinary; cheap.

ordinato *adj.* trim; orderly; (*eccl.*) ordained.

ordinazione *f.* (*comm.*) order; (*med.*) prescription; (*eccl.*) ordination: **su —,** to order.

or'dine *m.* order; class, rank; warrant: **— d'idee,** train of ideas; **parola d'—,** password; **di prim'—,** first class.

ordire *vt.* to weave: **— un complotto,** to plot, devise a plot.

ordito (1) *m.* (*text.*) warp.

ordito (2) *pp. of* **ordire.**

orec'chia *see* **orecchio.**

orecchietta *f.* auricle (*of the heart*).

orecchino *m.* earring.

orec'chio *m.* ear; hearing; dog-ear (*of a page*) **fare — da mercante,** to turn a deaf ear (*to*); **mettere una pulce nell'— a,** to put a doubt in (*someone's*) mind.

orecchioni *m.pl.* (*med.*) mumps.

ore'fice *m.* goldsmith.

oreficeri'a *f.* goldsmithery; goldsmith's shop.

or'fano *m.*, **or'fana** *f.* orphan; *adj.* orphaned: **— di padre,** fatherless; **— di madre,** motherless.

orfanotro'fio *m.* orphanage.

organetto *m.* barrel organ.

orga'nico *m.* list, roll; staff (*as of an office*) *adj.* organic.

organino *m.* barrel organ.

organismo *m.* organism; system.

organista *m.* organist.

organizzare *vt.* to organize; to set up; to form.

organizzatore *m.* organizer.

organizzazione *f.* organization.

or'gano *m.* organ.

orgasmo *m.* excitement; anxiety; frenzy; (*physiol.*) orgasm, climax.

or'gia *f.* orgy.

orgia'stico *adj.* orgiastic.

orgo'glio *m.* pride; dignity.

orgoglioso *adj.* proud; dignified.

orientale *m.* oriental; *adj.* eastern, east, oriental.

orientamento *m.* orientation; bearing; bent, attitude.

orientare *vt.* to orient; **orientarsi** *vr.* to orient oneself, find one's bearings; to turn (*towards*).

oriente *m.* East: **estremo, medio, vicino —**, Far, Middle, Near East.

orifi'zio *m.* orifice, hole.

ori'gano *m.* origan.

originale *m.* original; manuscript; queer fish; *adj.* original; eccentric, queer.

originalità *f.* originality; eccentricity.

originare *vt.* to originate; to cause; *vi.* to originate, arise.

originariamente *adv.* originally; formerly.

origina'rio *adj.* original; native (*of*).

ori'gine *f.* origin; source; beginning; birth; extraction: **dare — a**, to occasion, give rise (to).

origliare *vi.* to eavesdrop.

origliere *m.* pillow.

orina *f.* urine.

orinale *m.* chamber pot.

orinare *vi.* to urinate.

orinato'io *m.* urinal.

oriundo *adj.* native (*of*): **— francese**, of French origin.

orizzontale *adj.* horizontal.

orizzontare *see* **orientare.**

orizzonte *m.* horizon; (*fig.*) prospect: **giro d'—**, survey.

Orlando *m.* (*hist.*) Roland: **montare sul cavallo d'—**, to mount one's high horse.

Orlando, Vittorio Emanuele, Italian statesman and premier (1860–1952).

orlare *vt.* to hem, edge; to rim.

orlatore *m.*, **orlatrice** *f.* hemmer.

orlatura *f.* rimming, hemming.

orlo *m.* edge, margin, verge; rim; brim; brink; hem: **— a giorno**, hemstitch.

orma *f.* footprint; trace, track; mark: **ritornare sulle proprie orme**, to retrace one's steps.

ormai *adv.* now, by now; such being the situation; already.

ormeggiare *vt.*, *vi.*; **ormeggiarsi** *vr.* to moor.

ormeg'gio *m.* moorings.

ormone *m.* hormone.

ormo'nico *adj.* hormonic.

ornamentale *adj.* ornamental.

ornamento *m.* ornament.

ornare *vt.* to adorn, deck.

ornato *m.* ornamental design; ornament; *adj.* ornate, decked, adorned.

ornito'logo *m.* ornithologist.

ornitorinco *m.* ornithorhynchus, duckbill.

oro *m.* gold; money; (*pl.*) gold works: **— zecchino**, fine gold; **febbre dell'—**, gold rush; **d'—**, golden; **libro d'—**, roll of honor.

orologeri'a *f.* watchmaking; watchmaker's shop.

orologia'io *m.* watchmaker.

orolo'gio *m.* clock; watch: **— da polso**, wrist watch: **il mio — è avanti (indietro) di 3 minuti**, my watch is 3 minutes fast (slow).

oro'scopo *m.* horoscope.

orpello *m.* tinsel.

orrendo *adj.* horrible, hideous, ghastly.

orri'bile *adj.* horrible, awful, dreadful.

or'rido *m.* gorge, ravine; *adj.* horrid, dreadful, hideous, ghastly.

orripilante *adj.* terrifying; loathsome.

orrore *m.* horror: **fare —**, to strike with horror, to be hideous.

orsacchiotto *m.* bear cub; Teddy bear.

Orsini, Felice, Italian patriot, who attempted to assassinate Napoleon III (1819–1858).

orso *m.* bear.

orsù *interj.* come on!

ortag'gio *m.* vegetable.

orta'glia *f.* truck garden.

orten'sia *f.* hydrangea.

ortica *f.* nettle.

ortica'ria *f.* nettle rash.

orti'colo *adj.* horticultural.

orticultore *m.* truck gardener.

orto *m.* truck garden: **— botanico**, botanic garden; **non è la via dell'—**, it is no bed of roses.

ortodosso *adj.* orthodox.

ortografi'a *f.* orthography.

ortogra'fico *adj.* orthographic.

ortolano *m.* gardener; greengrocer.

ortope'dico *m.* orthopedist; *adj.* orthopedic.

orza *f.* (*naut.*) bowline.

orzaiuolo *m.* stye, sty.

orzare *vi.* (*naut.*) to luff.

orzata (1) *f.* (*naut.*) luff.

orzata (2) *f.* orgeat.

orzo *m.* barley.

osannare *vt.* to hosanna.

osare *vt.*, *vi.* to dare, venture.

oscenità *f.* obscenity.

osceno *adj.* obscene.

oscillante *adj.* oscillating, swinging.

oscillare *vi.* to swing, oscillate; to waver; to fluctuate.

oscillazione *f.* oscillation, sway, fluctuation.

oscuramento *m.* darkening: **— antiaereo**, blackout.

oscurare *vt.* to darken; to dim; to outshine; **oscurarsi** *vr.* to darken; to dim; to grow cloudy.

oscurità *f.* darkness, obscurity; dimness.

oscuro *adj.* dark; dim, gloomy; obscure.

ospedale *m.* hospital.

ospedaletto *m.* hospital station.

ospitale *adj.* hospitable.

ospitalità *f.* hospitality.

ospitare *vt.* to entertain; to house, shelter, accommodate.

o'spite *m.* guest, visitor.

ospi'zio *m.* hospice: — **di mendicità**, poorhouse; — **di trovatelli**, foundling hospital.

ossatura *f.* frame.

os'seo *adj.* osseous, bony.

ossequente *adj.* observant (*of*); respectful: — **alle leggi**, law-abiding.

ossequiare *vt.* to pay one's respects to; to honor.

osse'quio *m.* homage, respect; obedience, compliance; (*pl.*) regards.

ossequioso *adj.* deferential; respectful; obsequious.

osservante *adj.* observant (*of*).

osservanza *f.* observance; deference; compliance.

osservare *vt.* to observe; to notice; to watch; to point out, remark; to obey; to comply (*with*); **far — una legge**, to enforce a law.

osservatore *m.* observer; *adj.* observant, alert.

osservato'rio *m.* observatory.

osservazione *f.* observation; remark; comment.

ossessionante *adj.* obsessive, haunting.

ossessionare *vt.* to obsess, haunt; to harass.

ossessione *f.* obsession; nightmare.

ossesso *m.* demoniac; *adj.* possessed.

ossi'a *conj.* or; that is.

ossida'bile *adj.* oxidizable.

ossidante *adj.* oxidizing.

ossidare *vt.*, **ossidarsi** *vr.* to oxidize.

ossidazione *f.* oxidization.

os'sido *m.* oxide.

ossi'drico *adj.* oxyhydrogen: **cannello —**, oxyhydrogen blowpipe.

ossigenare *vt.* to oxygenate; to peroxide (*hair*).

ossigenato *adj.* oxygenated: **bionda ossigenata**, a peroxide blonde; **acqua ossigenata**, (*hydrogen*) peroxide.

ossi'geno *m.* oxygen.

osso *m.* bone; stone (*of a fruit*): — **di seppia**, cuttlebone; — **sacro**, sacrum; **un — duro**, a hard nut to crack; **avere le ossa rotte** (*fig.*), to be bone-tired; **bagnato sino alle ossa**, wet through; **in carne e ossa**, in flesh and blood.

ossuto *adj.* bony.

ostacolare *vt.* to hinder; to interfere with; to obstruct.

osta'colo *m.* obstacle, hindrance; (*sport*) hurdle.

ostag'gio *m.* hostage.

ostare *vi.* to be in opposition (*to*); to prevent (*from*): **nulla osta a**, no objection to. *see* **nullaosta**.

oste *m.* innkeeper: **fare i conti senza l'—**, to reckon without one's host.

osteggiare *vt.* to antagonize, oppose, be averse to.

ostello *m.* mansion; inn; hostel.

ostensi'bile *adj.* ostensible.

ostenso'rio *m.* ostensory.

ostentare *vt.* to affect, to show off, display; to feign.

ostentato *adj.* affected; ostentatious.

ostentazione *f.* ostentation; show, display.

osteri'a *f.* public house; (*fam.*) "joint."

ostessa *f.* landlady.

oste'trica *f.* midwife.

ostetri'cia *f.* obstetrics.

oste'trico *m.* obstetrician; *adj.* obstetrical.

o'stia *f.* wafer: — **consacrata**, host.

o'stico *adj.* distasteful; hard.

ostile *adj.* hostile; averse.

ostilità *f.* hostility; aversion: **le —** (*mil.*) hostilities.

ostinarsi *vr.* to insist, persist (*in*); to be stubborn (*about*).

ostinato *adj.* obstinate, stubborn; steady.

ostinazione *f.* obstinacy, stubbornness.

ostracismo *m.* ostracism: **dar l'— a**, to ostracize.

o'strica *f.* oyster.

ostrica'io *m.* oysterer.

ostruire *vt.* to obstruct, stop; **ostruirsi** *vr.* to become obstructed, to clog.

ostruzione *f.* obstruction.

ostruzionismo *m.* obstructionism.

otite *f.* otitis.

otorinolaringoiatra *m.* otolaryngologist.

otre *m.* skin (*bag*).

ottaedro *m.* octahedron.

otta'gono *m.* octagon.

ottanta *m.*, *adj.* eighty.

ottantenne *m.*, *f.*, *adj.* octogenarian.

ottante'simo *m.*, *adj.* eightieth.

ottantina *f.* fourscore, some eighty: **essere sull'—**, to be about eighty.

ottava *f.* octave.

ottavo *m.*, *adj.* eighth; octavo.

ottemperare *vi.* to submit (*to*): — **a**, to obey; to fulfill; to abide (*by*).

ottenebrare *vt.* to befog.

ottenere *vt.*[141] to obtain, get; to attain, reach; to extract.

ottenuto *pp. of* **ottenere**.

ot'tica *f.* optics.

ot'tico *m.* optician; *adj.* optic.

ottimismo *m.* optimism.

ottimista *m.* optimist.

ot'timo *m.*, *adj.* excellent; optimum.

otto *m.*, *adj.* eight: oggi a —, within a week; in quattro e quattr'—, in the twinkle of an eye; — volante, roller coaster.

ottobre *m.* October.

ottomana *f.* ottoman.

Ottomano *m.*, *adj.* Ottoman.

ottoname *m.* brassware.

ottone *m.* brass.

ottuagena'rio *m.*, *adj.* octogenarian.

ottun'dere *vt.*[11] to blunt.

otturamento *see* otturazione.

otturare *vt.* to obturate, stop, fill; otturarsi *vr.* to clog.

otturatore *m.* (*photo.*) shutter; (*artil.*) breechblock.

otturazione *f.* stopping; obstruction.

ottusità *f.* obtuseness.

ottuso *adj.* obtuse; blunt. *pp.* of ottun'dere.

ova'ia *f.* ovary.

ovale *m.*, *adj.* oval.

ovatta *f.* wadding.

ovattare *vt.* to wad; to muffle.

ovazione *f.* ovation.

ove- *adv.* where; when. *conj.* if; in case.

o'vest *m.* west.

ovile *m.* fold, sheepfold.

ovino *adj.* ovine: gli ovini, sheep.

ovi'paro *adj.* oviparous.

ovo *m.* egg.

o'volo *m.* egg-shaped mushroom.

o'vulo *m.* ovule.

ovunque *see* dovunque.

ovvero *conj.* or.

ovviamente *adv.* obviously; of course.

ovviare *vi.* to obviate.

ov'vio *adj.* obvious; evident.

oxfordiano *m.*, *adj.* Oxonian.

oziare *vi.* to idle, loiter.

o'zio *m.* idleness, laziness; leisure.

oziosità *f.* slothfulness; idle talk.

ozioso *m.* idler, dawdler; *adj.* idle.

ozono *m.* ozone.

P

pacare *vt.* to appease.

pacatezza *f.* collectedness, quietness.

pacato *adj.* collected, quiet.

pacca *f.* slap.

pacchetto *m.* package, small parcel.

pac'chia *f.* gorge; (*fig.*) windfall.

pacchiano *adj.* boorish; garish.

pacco *m.* package; bundle; parcel.

paccotti'glia *f.* cheap stuff, trinketry.

pace *f.* peace; quiet, stillness; rest: lasciare in —, to leave alone.

pachiderma *m.* pachyderm.

paciere *m.* peacemaker.

pacificamente *adv.* peacefully.

pacificare *vt.* to pacify; to reconcile; pacificarsi *vr.* to quiet; to make one's peace.

pacificatore *m.* peacemaker.

pacificazione *f.* pacification.

paci'fico *adj.* peaceful, peaceable, peaceloving; out of question.

Pacinotti, Antonio, Italian physicist, discoverer of principle of dynamo (1841 1912).

pacioccone *m.*, pacioccona *f.* chubby-faced person; easygoing person.

padella *f.* pan, frying pan; bedpan: dalla — nella brage, out of the frying pan into the fire.

padiglione *m.* pavilion; stand; lodge.

padre *m.* father; (*pl.*) forefathers.

padreggiare *vi.* to take after one's father.

padrino *m.* godfather; second (*in a duel*).

padrona *f.* mistress; owner; landlady.

padronale *adj.* proprietorial; private.

padronanza *f.* mastery, command, possession; proprietorship; masterfulness: — di una lingua, command of a language; — di se stesso, self-possession, self-control.

padrone *m.* master, boss, owner, proprietor: — di casa, landlord.

padroneggiare *vt.* to master, dominate; padroneggiarsi *vr.* to keep one's self-control.

padule *m.* marsh.

paesag'gio *m.* landscape.

paesana *f.* countrywoman.

paesano *m.* villager; peasant; fellow countryman; *adj.* rural, country; local.

paese *m.* country; village; hamlet; country, land: mandare a quel —, to send to Jericho.

paf!, paf'fete! *interj.* bang!, wham!

paffuto *adj.* chubby.

paga *f.* pay, reward, wages.

paga'bile *adj.* payable.

paga'ia *f.* paddle.

pagamento *m.* payment; cover.

pagane'simo *m.* heathenism, paganism.

Paganini, Nicolò, Italian violinist, composer (1782–1840).

pagano *m.*, *adj.* heathen; pagan.

pagante *m.* payer; *adj.* paying.

pagare *vt.* to pay; to pay for; to reward: far —, to make (*one*) pay; to charge; farsi —, to get paid.

pagato *adj.* paid.

pagatore m. payer.

pagella f. school report, report card.

pag'gio m. page.

paghèrò m. promissory note, IOU.

pa'gina f. page; leaf: prima —, front page.

pa'glia f. straw: coda di —, uneasy conscience; fuoco di —, short-lived passion.

pagliacciata f. clownery, farce.

pagliac'cio m. clown.

paglia'io m. strawstack; straw barn.

paglieric'cio m. paillasse.

paglierino adj. pale yellow.

paglietta f. straw hat, boater.

pagliuzza f. straw.

pagnotta f. loaf (pl. loaves).

pago adj. satisfied, content (with).

pa'io m. pair; couple.

Paisiello, Giovanni, Italian composer (1741–1816).

paiuolo m. cauldron.

pala f. shovel; paddle (of a water wheel); blade (of a propeller, of an oar); vane, sail (of a windmill): — d'altare, altarpiece.

paladino m. paladin; champion.

palafitta f. pile, palafitte.

palafreniere m. groom.

palanca f. copper coin; (naut.) gangplank.

palanco m. (naut.) tackle.

palandrana f. gaberdine.

palata f. shovelful: a palate, in plenty.

palatino m., adj. palatine.

palato m. palate.

Palazzeschi, Aldo, Italian novelist and poet (1885–   ).

Palazzi, Fernando, Italian lexicographer and novelist, *Novissimo dizionario della lingua italiana* (1884–   ).

palazzina f. villa.

palazzo m. mansion; palace: — municipale, town hall.

palchetto m. shelf; (theat.) box.

palco m. scaffold; planking, flooring; (theat.) box; stand; bandstand.

palcosce'nico m. stage.

palesare vt. to manifest; to disclose; to show; **palesarsi** vr. to reveal oneself, prove (to be).

palese adj. evident; known.

palesemente adv. openly; obviously.

palestra f. gymnasium.

Palestrina, da, Giovanni Pierluigi, Italian composer (1526–1594).

paletta f. shovel; pallet; paddle (of a paddle wheel); blade (of a ventilating fan, etc.).

paletto m. picket; peg; bolt.

pa'lio m. cloak; race: essere in —, to be at stake.

palissandro m. rosewood.

palizzata f. fence, palisade.

palla f. ball; bullet; sphere: — a nuoto, water polo; cogliere la — al balzo, to jump at the opportunity.

pallacanestro f. basketball.

Palla'dio, Andrea, Italian architect (1518–1580).

palleggiare vt., vi. to dribble (in soccer); to toss: **palleggiarsi le responsabilità**, to shift responsibilities on one another, to "pass the buck."

palleg'gio m. dribbling (in soccer); tossing (in tennis).

palliativo m., adj. palliative.

pal'lido adj. pale, wan; faint.

pallina f. small ball; marble.

pallino m. red ball (in billiards); jack (in bowls); shot (for a shotgun); polka dot; (coll.) hobby, craze, bee in the bonnet: avere il — di, to be "nuts" about.

pallone m. balloon; ball, soccer: un — gonfiato, a "stuffed shirt."

pallore m. pallor.

pallot'tola f. pellet; bullet.

pallottoliere m. abacus.

palma f. palm.

palmare adj. clear, evident.

palmi'zio m. palm.

palmo m. palm; span: restare con un — di naso, to be baffled; a — a —, inch by inch.

palo m. pole, post, stake; pile.

palombaro m. diver.

palombo m. (ornith.) wood pigeon; (ichthyol.) dogfish.

paipa'bile adj. palpable; evident.

palpare vt. to handle, finger; (med.) to palpate.

pal'pebra f. eyelid: batter le palpebre, to blink.

palpeggiare see palpare.

palpitante adj. throbbing; aflutter: di — attualità, topical, newsmaking.

palpitare vi. to throb; to pine.

palpitazione f. palpitation; throb, throbbing.

pal'pito m. throb; beat; anxiety.

paltò m. greatcoat.

palude f. marsh.

paludoso adj. marshy.

palustre adj. paludal.

pam'pino m. vine tendril; vine leaf.

panacea f. panacea.

pa'nama m. panama hat.

panca f. bench, settee.

pancetta f. potbelly; bacon.

panchetto m. footstool.

panchina f. bench.

pan'cia f. belly, paunch.

panciera f. bellypiece; girdle.

panciolle, (stare in) to idle away time in comfort.

panciotto m. waistcoat, vest.

panciuto *adj.* potbellied; bulging.
pane *m.* bread; loaf; cake; ingot; worm (*of a screw*): dire — al —, to call a spade a spade; **pan per focaccia**, tit for tat.
panegi'rico *m.* panegyric.
panetteri'a *f.* bakery.
panettiere *m.* baker.
panetto *m.* cake.
panfi'lio, pan'filo *m.* yacht.
pa'nia *f.* lime; (*fig.*) snare.
pa'nico *m.*, *adj.* panic.
paniere *m.* pannier: **rompere le uova nel —**, to queer (*one's*) pitch.
panificazione *f.* breadmaking.
panifi'cio *m.* bakery.
panino *m.* roll (*of bread*): — **imbottito**, sandwich.
panna *f.* cream; breakdown, car trouble: **rimanere in —**, to have a breakdown.
pannello *m.* panel.
panni'colo *m.* membrane, tissue.
panno *m.* cloth; **panni** *pl.* clothes.
pannoc'chia *f.* corncob.
pannolino *m.* diaper.
panorama *m.* panorama, view.
panora'mico *adj.* panoramic.
pantaloni *see* calzoni.
pantano *m.* bog, quagmire.
pantera *f.* panther.
panto'fola *f.* slipper.
pantomima *f.* pantomime; sham.
panzana *f.* fib, hoax.
Panzini, Alfredo, Italian novelist and lexicographer, *Dizionario Moderno delle parole che non si trovano nei dizionari comuni* (1863-1939).
paonazzo *m.*, *adj.* purple.
papà *m.* papa, pa, dad, daddy.
Papa *m.* pope.
papale *adj.* papal.
papalina *f.* skullcap.
papalino *adj.* papal.
papato *m.* papacy.
papa'vero *m.* poppy, papaver: **alto —**, "big shot."
pa'pera *f.* goose; (*theat.*) "fluff"; blunder.
pa'pero *m.* gander; gosling.
Papini, Giovanni, Italian novelist and essayist (1881-1956).
pappa *f.* pap; soup; food.
pappafico *m.* (*naut.*) topgallant.
pappagallo *m.* parrot.
pappagor'gia *f.* double chin.
pappare *vt.* to gorge, gobble, wolf.
pappataci *m.* gnat.
pappina *f.* pap; poultice.
para *f.* crepe rubber.
para'bola *f.* parable; (*geom.*) parabola.
parabordo *m.* (*naut.*) buffer, bumper.
parabrezza *m.* windshield.
paracadutare *vt.* to parachute.

paracadute *m.* parachute: **lanciarsi col —**, to bail out.
paracadutista *m.* parachutist.
paracarro *m.* curbstone.
parac'qua *m.* umbrella.
paradisi'aco *adj.* heavenly.
paradiso *m.* heaven, paradise: — **terrestre**, garden of Eden.
paradossale *adj.* paradoxical.
paradossa *m.* paradox.
parafa *f.* paraph.
parafango *m.* mudguard.
parafare *vt.* to paraph, to initial.
paraffina *f.* paraffin.
para'frasi *f.* paraphrase.
paraful'mine *m.* lightning rod.
parafuoco *m.* firescreen.
paraggi *m.pl.* neighborhood.
paragonare *vt.* to compare (*with*).
paragone *m.* comparison: **pietra di —**, touchstone.
para'grafo *m.* paragraph.
para'lisi *f.* paralysis, palsy.
parali'tico *m.*, *adj.* paralytic.
paralizzare *vt.* to paralyze.
parallela *f.* parallel.
parallelo *m.*, *adj.* parallel.
paralume *m.* lampshade.
paramano *m.* wristband.
paramento *m.* vestment; hanging.
paranco *m.* (*naut.*) tackle.
paraninfo *m.* pander.
parano'ico *m.*, *adj.* paranoiac.
paraocchi *m.pl.* blinkers.
parapetto *m.* parapet; bulwark; railing.
parapi'glia *m.* hurly-burly, melee.
parapiog'gia *m.* umbrella.
parare *vt.*, *vi.* to adorn, drape, hang; to stop, parry; to catch; to shield, protect; to keep off; **pararsi** *vr.* to deck oneself: **pararsi dinanzi a uno**, to loom before one, to confront one.
parasole *m.* parasol, sunshade.
parassita *m.* parasite.
parastatale *adj.* government-controlled.
parata *f.* catch; parry; (*mil.*) parade.
parati'a *f.* (*naut.*) bulkhead.
parato *m.* drape; (*pl.*) drapery; wallpaper.
paraurti *m.* bumper.
paravento *m.* screen.
Parca *f.* (*myth.*) Parca; Death: **le Parche**, the Fates, the Parcae.
parcare *vt.* to park.
parcella *f.* bill.
parcheg'gio *m.* parking lot; parking.
parco (1) *m.* park.
parco (2) *adj.* sparing, frugal.
parec'chio *adj.* a good deal (*of*); a long time; **parecchi** *pl.* several, a good many; **parecchio** *pron.* a good deal of it; (*pl.*) several; **parecchio** *adv.* a good deal, enough.

pareggiare *vt.* to equalize; to equal; to level, even; to balance; to square; — **un conto,** to square an account; — **il bilancio,** to balance the budget; *vi. (in games)* to tie, break even.

pareg'gio *m.* equalization; balance; *(sport)* tie: **raggiungere il —,** *(comm.)* to balance the budget, *(sport)* to end in a tie.

parentado *m.* kinsfolk; relatives.

parente *m., f.* relative, relation, kin.

parentela *f.* relationship; kinsfolk.

paren'tesi *f.* parenthesis (*pl.* parentheses); bracket: **fra — (***fig.***),** by the way, incidentally.

parere (1) *vi.*[38] to seem; to look (*like*); to sound (*like*); to feel (*like*); to taste (*like*); to smell (*like*); to like; to appear; to deem, think: **che te ne pare?** what do you think of it?; **mi pare di sì,** I think so.

parere (2) *m.* opinion, mind; judgment; advice.

parete *f.* wall.

par'golo *m.* baby.

pari *m.* peer, like, equal, match: **i propri pari,** one's likes; **senza —,** matchless; **da — a —,** on a level footing; *adj.* equal, even, level; like; same; equivalent; tantamount; up to, fit; smooth; balanced: **essere — e patta,** to be quits; **saltare a piè — (***fig.***),** to skip altogether; **al — di,** as, like, as much as; **alla — con,** on a par with; **del —,** likewise; **titoli alla —,** bonds

pa'ria *m.* pariah, outcast.   [at par.

parificare *see* pareggiare.

parigino *m., adj.* Parisian.

pari'glia *f.* pair; couple; team (*of horses*): **rendere la —,** to give tit for

parimenti *adv.* likewise.   [tat.

Parini, Giuseppe, Italian poet, *Il giorno* (1729–1799).

parità *f.* parity, equality.

parlamentare (1) *m.* parliamentarian; *(mil.)* parleyer; *adj.* parliamentary; civil.

parlamentare (2) *vi.* to parley.

parlamento *m.* parliament; congress.

parlante *adj.* talking; lifelike.

parlantina *f.* glibness.

parlare *vt., vi.* to speak; to talk: — **fra sé e sé,** to speak to oneself; — **del più e del meno,** to talk about the weather; — **a quattr'occhi,** to talk in private; **far — di sé,** to make oneself talked about; **se ne è fatto un gran —,** there has been a lot of talk about it.

parlata *f.* speech, way of speaking; pronunciation.

parlatore *m.* speaker, talker, orator.

parlato'rio *m.* parlatory.

parlottare *vi.* to confabulate.

parmigiano *m., adj.* Parmesan.

parodi'a *f.* parody.

parodiare *vi.* to parody; to mimic.

parola *f.* word; speech; promise, pledge: — **d'ordine,** password; **parole incrociate,** crossword puzzle, puzzles; **giuoco di parole,** pun; **essere di —,** to be as good as one's word; **venire a parole,** to have words (*with*); **a buon intenditor poche parole,** a word to the wise is enough; **è una —!** no sooner said than done!

parolac'cia *f.* nasty word; abuse.

parola'io *m.* wordmonger.

parossismo *m.* paroxysm; climax.

parricida *m.* parricide; *adj.* parricidal.

parrici'dio *m.* parricide.

parrocchetto *m.* fore-topsail; fore-topmast.

parroc'chia *f.* parish.

parrocchiano *m.* parishioner.

par'roco *m.* parson, vicar.

parrucca *f.* wig, periwig.

parrucchiere *m.* wigmaker; hairdresser; barber.

parrucchino *m.* partial wig; scratch (*wig*).

parsimo'nia *f.* parsimony.

parso *pp. of* parere.

partac'cia *f.* scene.

parte *f.* part; portion; share; member; place; side, hand; direction; role; party: — **civile,** plaintiff; **da un po' di tempo a questa —,** for some time past; **in —,** partly; **in ogni —,** everywhere, on all sides; **da —,** aside; **da qualche (altra)—,** somewhere (*else*); **da queste parti,** hereabouts; **da una — all'altra,** through, from side to side; **d'altra —,** on the other hand; **prendere in mala —,** to take amiss; **far le due parti in commedia,** to play both ends against the middle; **mettere a — d'un segreto,** to let into a secret; **da ambe le parti,** on both sides.

partecipante *m., adj.* participant: **i partecipanti a una gara,** the contestants.

partecipare *vt.* to notify, announce; *vi.* to participate, share (*in*); to take part (*in*); to partake (*of*): — **a una riunione,** to attend a meeting.

partecipazione *f.* participation, sharing; announcement, card.

parte'cipe *adj.* partaking, sharing.

parteggiare *vi.* to side (*with*); to take sides (*with*).

partente *m.* leaver, departer.

partenza *f.* departure, leaving; (*naut.*) sailing; (*aeron.*) take-off; (*sport*) start: **punto di —,** starting point.

particella f. particle.
partici'pio m. participle.
parti'cola f. (eccl.) Host.
particolare m. detail, particular; adj. particular; peculiar; private: **segni particolari**, distinguishing features; **in —**, especially.
particolareggiato adj. detailed.
particolarità f. peculiarity; partiality.
particolarmente adv. particularly.
partigiana f. partisan.
partigianeri'a f. partisanship; partiality.
partigiano m., adj. partisan; member of underground resistance.
partire vi., **partirsi** vr. to leave, start, set out, depart; to sail; to go away, quit; to move; to begin: **a — da oggi, (as)** from today; **far — un colpo,** to fire a shot.
partita f. (sport) match; (account.) entry: **— a carte,** card game; **— di merce,** stock, lot; **— doppia,** double entry; **— di caccia,** hunting party.
partitivo m., adj. partitive.
partito m. alternative, choice; resolution; advantage; catch; (pol.) party: **prendere un —,** to make up one's mind; **ridursi a mal —,** to go to the dogs; **mettere il cervello a —,** to reform; **prendere — per,** to take one's stand for; **trarre — da,** to make the best of.
partitura f. (mus.) score.
partizione f. partition.
parto m. parturition, delivery, childbirth: **doglie l —,** throes.
partoriente adj. parturient.
partorire vt., vi. to bring forth; to give birth to; to produce.
parvenza f. appearance, semblance; shadow.
parziale adj. partial; unfair; biased.
parzialità f. partiality.
parzialmente adv. partially.
pa'scere vt., vi. to graze; to pasture; to feed; **pa'scersi** vr. to feed (on).
pascià m. pasha.
pasciuto adj. fed: **ben —,** well-fed.
Pascoli, Giovanni, Italian poet and critic (1855-1912).
pascolare see pascere.
pa'scolo m. pasture, grassland; pasturage; food.
Pasqua f. Easter: **contento come una —,** happy.
pasquale adj. Easter; paschal.
passa'bile adj. passable.
passag'gio m. passage; passageway; way; crossing; traffic; lapse; interchange: **— a livello,** grade crossing; **vietato il —,** no thoroughfare; **ospite di —,** transient (guest).
passamaneri'a f. ribandry.

passamano m. riband.
passamontagna m. woollen helmet.
passante m. passerby (pl. passers-by); strap.
passaporto m. passport.
passare vt. to pass; to go beyond, through; to cross; to run through; to exceed, surpass; to pierce; to spend (one's time); to hand (over); to experience, undergo. vi. to move on, proceed; to pass; to fade; to elapse; to stop, cease; to enter, get in; to pass muster; to pass (for), go (for); to call (on, upon, at): **— per le armi,** to put to death; **— a miglior vita,** to pass away; **— sopra a,** to overlook, wink at; **passarsela bene** (male), to be well (badly) off; **passarsela liscia,** to go scot free.
passatempo m. pastime.
passati'sta m. misoneist, old fogy.
passato m. past: **— prossimo,** present perfect; **— remoto,** past indefinite; adj. past, previous, former; withered, faded; overripe; gone by: **l'anno —,** last year.
passato'ia f. carpet strip, runner.
passeggiare vi. to walk; to stroll.
passeggiata f. stroll, walk; excursion; drive.
passeggiero m. passenger; adj. passing.
passeg'gio m. promenade: **andare a —,** to take a walk, stroll.
passerella f. footbridge; (naut.) gangplank.
pas'sero, passerotto m. sparrow.
passi'bile adj. liable (to), subject (to).
passiflora f. passionflower.
passionale m., adj. passional, temperamental.
passione f. passion; suffering; craze.
passività f. passivity; (comm.) liabilities (pl.).
passivo m. (gramm.) passive; (comm.) liabilities, debts; debit, debit sides (in bookkeeping); adj. passive.
passo (1) m. step, pace, gait, tread; passage; pass; (moving pictures) width, pitch: **fare due passi,** to take a walk; **fare il — secondo la gamba,** to cut the coat according to the cloth; **— —,** leisurely.
passo (2) adj. dried; faded, withered: **uva passa,** raisins.
pasta f. paste; dough; pastry, cake, cookie: **di buona —,** good-natured; **aver le mani in —,** to know the ropes.
pasteggiare vi. to feed (on): **— a birra,** to drink beer at one's meals.
pastello m. pastel.
pastetta f. batter; (coll.) shady business, hocus-pocus.

pasticca *f.* tablet.
pasticceri'a *f.* confectionery; pastry.
pasticciere *m.* confectioner; pastry cook.
pasticcino *m.* cake, bun.
pastic'cio *m.* pie; pudding; (*fig.*) jumble, mess, fix, scrape; pastiche.
pasticcione *m.* bungler. muddler.
pastifi'cio *m.* macaroni factory.
pasti'glia *f.* tablet, tabloid.
pasto *m.* meal: vino da —, table wine.
pasto'la *f.* hobble, fetter; pastern.
pastone *m.* mash.
pastorale *m.*, *adj.* pastoral.
pastore *m.* shepherd; pastor.
pastorella *f.* shepherdess.
pastori'zia *f.* sheep raising.
pastorizzare *vt.* to pasteurize.
pastoso *adj.* mellow.
pastrano *m.* greatcoat.
pastura *f.* pasture.
patacca *f.* coin; badge; stain.
patata *f.* potato: — americana, sweet potato.
patatrac! *m.* (*onomatopoeic*) bang! crash!
patella *f.* limpet.
patema *f.* anxiety, distress.
patentato *adj.* licensed; (*fig.*) downright, regular.
patente *f.* patent; license; *adj.* patent, plain, glaring.
paterec'cio *m.* whitlow.
paternale *f.* reprimand; *adj.* paternal.
paternità *f.* paternity.
paterno *adj.* paternal, fatherly.
pate'tico *adj.* pathetic.
patibolare *adj.* criminal, forbidding.
pati'bolo *m.* gallows, scaffold.
patimento *m.* torment; suffering.
pa'tina *f.* patina; film; gloss; furring (*of the tongue*).
patinare *vt.* to patinate; to gloss.
patinato *adj.* patinated: carta —, plate paper.
patire *vi.*, *vi.*³⁴ to suffer (*from*); to endure, bear; to undergo: — la fame, to starve; — di, to suffer from; — il freddo (il caldo), to be sensitive to cold (to heat).
patito *adj.* sickly, gaunt.
patologi'a *f.* pathology.
patolo'gico *adj.* pathological.
patos *m.* pathos.
pa'tria *f.* country, fatherland.
patriarca *m.* patriarch.
patriarcale *adj.* patriarchal.
patricida *see* parricida.
patrigno *m.* stepfather.
patrimo'nio *m.* fortune; estate, patrimony; property.
pa'trio *adj.* patrial; paternal; patria potestà, parental right.
patriota *m.* patriot.

patriot'tico *adj.* patriotic.
patriottismo *m.* patriotism.
patri'zio *m.*, *adj.* patrician.
patrizzare *see* padreggiare.
patrocinare *vt.* to sponsor, favor, support; to plead.
patrocinatore *m.* sponsor; pleader.
patroci'nio *m.* sponsorship; legal assistance.
patronato *m.* patronage; foundation (*for charitable purposes, etc.*).
patronessa *f.* patroness.
patroni'mico *m.*, *adj.* patronymic.
patrono *m.* patron saint; counsel.
patta *f.* flap: essere pari e —, to be quits.
patteggiare *vt.*, *vi.* to negotiate; to bargain, come to terms.
pattinag'gio *m.* skating.
pattinare *vi.* to skate.
pattinatore *m.* skater.
pat'tino *m.* skate; (*aeron.*) skid; (*mach.*) block; shoe, skid (*of a brake*).
patto *m.* agreement; pact, compact; condition, term: a — che, provided.
pattu'glia *f.* patrol.
pattugliare *vi.* to patrol.
pattuire *see* patteggiare.
pattuito *adj.* agreed (*upon*).
pattume *m.* garbage.
pattumiera *f.* dustbin.
patur'nie *f.pl.* sulks.
paura *f.* fear, dread; fright, scare: aver — di, to be afraid of; far —, to frighten; da far —, fearful.
pauroso *adj.* fearful; coward; shy.
pa'usa *f.* pause; (*mus.*) rest.
paventare *vt.*, *vi.* to fear; to be afraid (*of*).
pavesare *vt.* to array, dress.
pavese *f.* shield; (*naut.*) hoist.
pa'vido *m.*, *adj.* coward.
pavimentare *vt.* to pave; to floor.
pavimentazione *f.* paving; flooring.
pavimento *m.* floor.
pavone *m.* peacock.
pavoneggiarsi *vr.* to strut, swagger.
pazientare *vi.* to be patient; to bear (*with*).
paziente *m.*, *adj.* patient.
pazienza *f.* patience: far scappare la —, to drive mad; pazienza! all right!, never mind!
pazzesco *adj.* crazy, preposterous.
pazzi'a *f.* madness, lunacy; folly: far pazzie per, to go crazy for.
pazzo *see* matto.
pecca *f.* flaw; shortcoming.
peccaminoso *adj.* sinful.
peccare *vi.* to sin (*against*); to err.
peccato *m.* sin: che —! what a pity!, too bad!
peccatore *m.* sinner.
peccatuc'cio *m.* peccadillo.

pec'chia *f.* bee.
pecchione *m.* drone.
pece *f.* pitch: — greca, rosin.
pechinese *m.*, *adj.* pekingese.
pe'cora *f.* sheep; (*fig.*) yes man.
pecora'io *m.* shepherd.
pecorella *f.* sheep; cielo a pecorelle, fleecy sky.
pecorino *m.* Roman cheese; *adj.* sheep.
peculato *m.* peculation; embezzlement.
peculiare *adj.* peculiar.
peculiarità *f.* peculiarity.
pecu'lio *m.* savings.
pecu'nia *f.* money.
pecunia'rio *adj.* pecuniary.
pedag'gio *m.*, toll.
pedagogi'a *f.* pedagogics.
pedago'gico *adj.* pedagogic.
pedago'go *m.* pedagogue.
pedalare *vi.* to pedal.
pedale *m.* pedal; treadle.
pedaliera *f.* pedals; (*mus.*) pedal keyboard; (*aeron.*) rudder bar.
pedalina *f.* treadle printing press.
pedana *f.* platform; carpet.
pedante *m.* pedant; *adj.* pedantic.
pedanteri'a *f.* pedantry.
pedantesco *adj.* pedantic.
pedata *f.* kick; footprint.
pedestre *adj.* pedestrian; commonplace.
pediatra *m.*, *f.* pediatrician.
pediatri'a *f.* pediatrics.
pedicure *m.*, *f.* chiropodist.
pedilu'vio *m.* footbath.
pedina *f.* man (*at checkers*); pawn (*at chess*).
pedinare *vi.* to follow, shadow, tail.
pedis'sequo *adj.* literal; servile.
pedivella *f.* pedal crank.
pedone *m.* pedestrian.
pedun'colo *m.* peduncle.
pegamo'ide *f.* pegamoid.
peg'gio *m.*, *f.* worst; *adv.* worse: tanto —, so much the worse; di male in —, from bad to worse; — che, di, worse than.
peggioramento *m.* worsening.
peggiorare *vt.*, *vi.* to worsen; to change for the worse; to get worse.
peggiore *adj.* worse; worst: — di, worse than.
pegno *m.* pledge; pawn; token; forfeit.
pel *comp. prep.* for the. *see* per.
pe'lago *m.* open sea; (*fig.*) tangle.
pelame *m.* hair, coat.
pelare *vt.* to peel, pare; to pluck; to fleece; pelarsi *vr.* to peel off; to grow bald.
pelata *f.* bald spot; baldness.
pelato *adj.* peeled; hairless, bald.
pellame *m.* skins, hides.

pelle *f.* skin; hide; peel, rind: — d'uovo, mull; amici per la —, fast friends; non stare più nella —, to jump out of one's skin; far la — a uno, "to bump someone off."
pellegrinag'gio *m.* pilgrimage.
pellegrinare *vi.* to make a pilgrimage; to wander.
pellegrino *m.* pilgrim.
pelletteri'a *f.* leatherware.
pellicano *m.* pelican.
pelliceri'a *f.* furriery.
pellic'cia *f.* fur; coat; fur coat.
pelliccia'io *m.* furrier.
pellicciotto *m.* fur jacket.
Pellico, Silvio, Italian patriot and writer, *Le mie prigioni* (1789–1854).
pelli'cola *f.* film.
pellirossa *m.* redskin, Indian.
pelo *m.* hair; pile (*of a carpet, etc.*); fur; hairbreadth: di primo —, green; — dell'acqua, water surface; avere il — sullo stomaco, to be unscrupulous; cercare il — nell' uovo, to split hairs; per un —, almost, by a hairbreadth; non aver peli sulla lingua, to be outspoken.
peloso *adj.* hairy: carità pelosa, charity with strings attached.
peltro *m.* pewter.
pelu'ria *f.* fuzz, down.
pena *f.* punishment, penalty; pain, ache; distress; pity; trouble, pains: a mala —, barely, hardly; scontare una —, to serve a sentence; (non) valere la pena, (not) to be worth (*while*).
penale *f.* penalty; *adj.* penal, criminal.
penalista *m.* criminal lawyer.
penalità *f.* penalty.
penalizzare *vt.* to penalize.
penare *vi.* to suffer; to find it difficult.
pencolare *vi.* to totter; to waver.
penda'glio *m.* pendant.
pendente *m.* pendant, eardrop; *adj.* hanging (*down*); leaning; pending.
pendenza *f.* inclination, slope, slant; controversy; liability: la questione è ancora in —, the matter is still pending.
pen'dere *vi.*[18] to hang; to lean; to slope, slant; to be pending; to incline.
pendice *f.* slope, declivity, slant.
pen'dola *f.* clock.
pen'dolo *m.* pendulum.
pen'dulo *adj.* dangling.
penetrante *adj.* penetrating.
penetrare *vt.*, *vi.* to pierce; to penetrate; to enter; to fathom.
penetrazione *f.* penetration.
penicillina *f.* penicillin.

peni'sola f. peninsula.

penitente m., f., adj. penitent.

penitenza f. penance; penitence; penalty.

penitenzia'rio m. penitentiary.

penna f. feather; pen: — d'oca, quill; — stilografica, fountain pen; — a sfera, ball point pen.

pennac'chio m. plume, tuft; panache.

pennaiuolo m. hack writer.

pennellare vt. to touch; to brush.

pennellata f. stroke of the brush.

pennello m. brush: fare (stare) a —, to do (to suit) to a turn.

pennino m. nib, steel pen.

pennone m. pennant; yard.

pennuto m. bird; adj. feathered.

penombra f. dimness, half light.

penoso adj. painful, distressing.

pensante adj. thinking: i ben pensanti, right-minded people.

pensare vt., vi. to think; to conceive; to intend; to mean; to believe, suppose; to devise, think up; to take care (of), see (that); to mind: pensa agli affari tuoi! mind your own business!; dar da —, to worry, perplex.

pensata f. thought; brainstorm.

pensato adj. deliberate; weighed.

pensatore m. thinker.

pensiero m. thought; mind; idea, conception; intention, mind; opinion; worry, care: stare in —, to be worried; sopra —, lost in thought; absentminded; darsi — per, to worry about.

pensieroso adj. thoughtful; worried.

pen'sile adj. hanging: giardino —, roof garden.

pensilina f. shelter, shed; marquee.

pensionante m., f. boarder, lodger, paying guest.

pensionare vt. to pension (off).

pensionato m. pensioner; boarding school; adj. pensioned.

pensione f. pension; boarding house: stare a —, to board (at); tenere a —, to board; — completa, room and board.

pensoso adj. thoughtful, pensive.

penta'gono m. pentagon.

pentagramma m. (mus.) staff; (geom.) pentagram.

Pentecoste f. Whitsunday.

pentimento m. repentance; qualm.

pentirsi vr. to repent (of); to change one's mind (about); to be sorry (for): — di, to regret.

pentito adj. repenting; reformed.

pen'tola f. pot: qualcosa bolle in —, something is brewing.

pentolino m. small pot; pannikin; kettle.

penul'timo m., adj. last but one, penultimate.

penu'ria f. dearth, penury.

penzolare vi. to dangle, hang.

penzoloni adv. danglingly, adangle.

peo'nia f. peony.

pepato adj. peppery; stinging.

pepe m. pepper.

peperone m. (bot.) pepper.

pepita f. (min.) nugget.

pepsina f. pepsin.

per prep. for, by; to; on; from; out of, on account of; through; during, along; towards; in, into; in favor of; as; about to; per: — natura, by nature; — modo di dire, so to speak; — tutta la città, throughout the town; stavo — parlare, I was about to speak; — lo più, mostly; — lo meno, at least; — di più, moreover.

pera f. pear; (fig.) pate.

perbene adj. nice; decent; adv. nicely.

percalle m. percale.

percentuale f. percentage, percent; commission; rate.

percepi'bile adj. perceptible.

percepire vt. to perceive; to get; to earn; to feel; to catch.

percetti'bile adj. perceptible.

percettibilità f. perceptibility.

percettiva f. perceptivity.

percettivo adj. perceptive.

percezione f. perception.

perchè conj. why?; because; so that; for, as, since; m. why, reason.

perciò conj. therefore, so; that's why.

percome m. wherefore: il perchè e il —, the whys and wherefores.

percorrenza f. distance; way; range.

percor'rere[4] vt. to run along, cover; to run through, across; to travel over.

percorso (1) pp. of percorrere.

percorso (2) m. route, course, way; distance.

percossa f. blow, stroke.

percosso pp. of percuo'tere.

percuo'tere vt.[15] to strike, hit; to beat.

percussione f. percussion.

percussore m. firing pin.

perdente m. loser; adj. losing.

per'dere vt., vi.[87] to lose; to miss; to leak; to waste; to ruin: — di vista, to lose sight of; perdersi vr. to get lost: — d'animo, to lose heart.

perdifiato, (a) adv. breathlessly; madly.

perdigiorno m. idler.

perdincı! interj. good Lord!; by Jove!; "gee!"

per'dita f. loss; waste; discharge; leakage; damage: a — d'occhio, as far as the eye can reach.

perditempo m. waste of time.

perdizione f. perdition.

perdonare vt., vi. to forgive; to excuse; pardon.

perdono m. forgiveness, pardon.

perdurare vi. to last; to persist.

perdutamente adv. desperately; madly.

perduto adj. lost; done for.

peregrinare vi. to wander, ramble.

peregrinazione f. wandering.

peregrino adj. unusual, far-fetched; peculiar; peregrine.

perenne adj. perennial; everlasting; continuous, steady.

perento'rio adj. peremptory.

perequazione f. equalization.

perfetto adj. perfect; utter; downright.

perfezionamento m. perfecting; improvement.

perfezionare vt. to perfect; to complete; to improve; **perfezionarsi** vr. to become perfect; to improve; to become proficient.

perfezione f. perfection: alla —, perfectly.

perfi'dia f. perfidy; wickedness.

per'fido adj. perfidious; wicked; nasty, foul.

perfino adv. even.

perforante adj. perforating.

perforare vt. to perforate, pierce.

perforatore m. perforator.

perforatrice f. punch, perforator; (mach.) boring machine; drilling machine; rock drill.

perforazione f. perforation.

pergamena f. parchment.

per'gamo m. pulpit.

pergolato m. pergola, arbor.

Pergolesi, Giovanni Battista, Italian composer (1710–1736).

pericolante adj. unsafe; tottering.

peri'colo m. danger, peril, jeopardy; threat; risk; (fig.) chance.

pericoloso adj. dangerous.

periferi'a f. outskirts (pl.).

peri'frasi f. periphrasis.

perimetrale adj. surrounding.

peri'metro m. perimeter.

periodicità f. periodicity.

perio'dico m. periodical; adj. periodic.

peri'odo m. period; time; cycle; sentence.

peripezi'a f. vicissitude.

pe'riplo m. periplus.

perire vi. to perish, die.

perisco'pio m. periscope.

peristi'lio m. peristyle.

peritarsi vr. to hesitate.

perito (1) m. expert: — agrimensore, land surveyor; — settore, medical examiner.

perito (2) adj. dead.

peritoneo m. peritoneum.

peritonite f. peritonitis.

peri'zia f. skill; expertness; expert's report, estimate, survey; examination.

periziare vt. to appraise, estimate; to survey.

perla f. pearl.

perla'ceo adj. pearly.

perli'fero adj. pearl-bearing.

perlina f. seed pearl; bead.

perlustrare vt. to reconnoiter; to scout; to patrol.

perlustrazione f. reconnaissance, patrolling.

permaloso adj. touchy.

permanente f. permanent wave; adj. permanent.

permanenza f. permanence; stay.

permanere vi. to remain, linger; to go on.

permanganato m. permanganate.

permeare vt. to permeate.

permesso m. permission; permit; leave, license; leave of absence; furlough. adj. permitted, allowed: è permesso? may I (come in)?

permet'tere vt. to permit, allow; to suffer; **permettersi** vr. to take the liberty of; to allow oneself to; permettersi il usso di, to afford.

per'muta f. permutation; barter.

permutare vt. to barter.

pernac'chia f. (vulg.) "raspberry."

pernice f. partridge.

perniciosa f. (med.) pernicious malaria.

pernicioso adj. pernicious.

pernio, perno m. pivot, pin.

pernottamento m. overnight stop.

pernottare vi. to stay overnight.

pero m. pear tree.

però conj. but; yet. still; therefore.

perorare vt., vi. to plead.

perorazione f. peroration.

perpendicolare f., adj. perpendicular.

perpendi'colo m. plummet: a —, perpendiculary.

perpetrare vt. to perpetrate.

perpe'tua f. parson's housekeeper.

perpetuare vt. to perpetuate.

perpetuità f. perpetuity.

perpe'tuo adj. perpetual; everlasting: moto —, perpetual motion.

perplessità f. perplexity.

perplesso adj. perplexed.

perquisire vt. to search.

perquisizione f. search.

persecutore m. persecutor.

persecuzione f. persecution.

perseguire vt. to pursue; to follow; to prosecute.

perseguitare vt. to persecute, harass; to pester.

perseverante *adj.* persevering.

perseveranza *f.* perseverance.

perseverare *vi.* to persevere.

persiana *f.* shutter.

per'sico *m.* (*ichthyol.*) perch.

persino *adv.* even.

persistente *adj.* persistent.

persistenza *f.* persistence.

persi'stere *vi.* to persist.

perso *adj.* lost; wasted: **a tempo —,** in one's spare time. *pp. of* **perdere.**

persona *f.* person; fellow; body; size: **— fisica,** natural person; **— giuridica,** artificial person; **di —,** in person, personally.

personag'gio *m.* personage; character.

personale *m.* body, figure; personnel, staff; *adj.* personal.

personalità *f.* personality; (*pl.*) authorities.

personalmente *adv.* personally; in person.

personificare *vt.* to personify.

personificazione *f.* personification, embodiment.

perspicace *adj.* perspicacious, keen.

perspica'cia *f.* perspicacity, keenness.

persuadere *vt.* [88] to persuade.

persuasione *f.* persuasion.

persuasiva *f.* persuasiveness.

persuasivo *adj.* persuasive.

persuaso *adj.* persuaded; satisfied. *pp. of* **persuadere.**

pertanto *conj.* therefore: **non —,** nevertheless.

per'tica *f.* perch; pole.

pertinace *adj.* pertinacious.

pertina'cia *f.* pertinacity.

pertinente *adj.* pertinent; belonging.

pertinenza *f.* pertinence.

pertosse *f.* whooping cough.

pertu'gio *m.* hole, opening.

perturbare *vt.* to perturb.

perturbatore *m.* perturber.

perturbazione *f.* disturbance.

Perugino, il (*Pietro Vannucci*), Italian painter (1446–1523).

perva'dere *vt.* to pervade.

pervenire *vi.* to arrive (*at*).

perversione *f.* perversion.

perversità *f.* perversity, wickedness.

perverso *adj.* perverse, wicked.

pervertimento *m.* perversion.

pervertire *vt.* to pervert; **pervertirsi** *vr.* to go astray.

pervicace *adj.* obstinate; perverse.

pervica'cia *f.* obstinacy; perverseness.

pervinca *f.* (*bot.*) periwinkle.

pesa *f.* weighbridge; weighing.

pesalet'tere *f.* letter scales.

pesante *adj.* heavy; tiresome.

pesantezza *f.* heaviness; weight.

pesare *vt., vi.* to weigh.

pesatrice *f.* weighing device.

pesatura *f.* weighing.

pesca (*1*) *f.* peach.

pesca (*2*) *f.* fishing; catch; fishery: **— alla lenza,** angling.

pescag'gio *m.* (*naut.*) draught.

pesca'ia *f.* dam.

pescare *vt.* to fish; to find, fish (*up, out*); *vi.* (*naut.*) to draw: **— alla lenza,** to angle; **— nel torbido,** to fish in troubled waters.

pescatore *m.* fisher, angler.

pesce *m.* fish: **non saper che pesci pigliare,** to be in a quandary, not to know which way to turn; **— d'aprile,** April-fool joke.

pescecane *m.* shark; profiteer, parvenu.

pescherec'cio *m.* fishing boat.

pescheri'a *f.* fish market.

peschiera *f.* fishpond.

pesciven'dolo *m.* fishmonger.

pesco *m.* peach tree.

peso *m.* weight; load, burden; (*turf*) paddock: **— massimo** (*boxing*), heavyweight; **sollevare di —,** to lift bodily; **lancio del —,** shot-put.

pessimismo *m.* pessimism.

pessimista *m.* pessimist.

pes'simo *superl.adj.* worst; very bad.

pesta *f.* footprint; track.

pestare *vt.* to pound; to trample; to stamp; to batter.

peste *f.* plague; pest.

pestello *m.* pestle.

pesti'fero *adj.* pestiferous.

pestilenza *f.* pestilence; stench.

pestilenziale *adj.* pestilential, stinking.

pesto *m.* Genoese sauce; *adj.* crushed, battered: **buio —,** pitch dark; **occhi pesti,** black-ringed eyes; **ossa peste,** aching bones; **carta pesta,** papier-mâché.

pe'talo *m.* petal.

petardo *m.* petard; hand grenade.

petente *m.* petitioner.

petizione *f.* petition.

peto *m.* breaking of wind.

petonciano *m.* aubergine, egg plant.

Petrocchi, Policarpo, Italian lexicographer, *Novo dizionario universale della lingua italiana* (1852–1902).

petroliera *f.* (*naut.*) tanker.

petroli'fero *adj.* petroliferous: **zona petrolifera,** oil field.

Petrolini, Ettore, Italian comedian and playwright (1886–1936).

petro'lio *m.* petroleum; oil; kerosene: **pozzi di —,** oil wells.

pettegolare *vi.* to gossip.

pettegolezzo *m.* rumor, gossip.

pette'golo *m.* gossip; *adj.* gossipy.

pettinare *vt.* to comb; **pettinarsi** *vr.* to comb one's hair.

pettinatrice f. hairdresser.
pettinatura f. coiffure, hairdo.
pet'tine m. comb.
pettiniera f. comb case; dressing table.
pettirosso m. robin.
petto m. breast; chest: a doppio —, double-breasted; — di camicia, shirt front; prendere di —, to face up to.
pettorale m. breast strap; adj. pectoral.
pettorina f. stomacher.
pettorute adj. strutting.
petulante adj. petulant, testy.
petulanza f. petulance.
pezza f. patch; piece; bolt (of goods): — da piedi, foot wrapper; — giustificativa, voucher; da lunga —, for a long while.
pezzato adj. spotted; dapple.
pezzatura f. length (of goods); dapple.
pezzente m. beggar.
pezzo m. piece; chunk; part, portion; fragment; tract: un — grosso, a bigwig; un — fa, long ago; a pezzi e bocconi, by fits and starts; pezzi di ricambio, spare parts.
pezzuola f. diaper; handkerchief.
piacente adj. attracting.
piacere (1) m. pleasure; joy; amusement; will, liking; favor: per — please; mi fa —, I am glad (of it).
piacere (2) vi.⁹⁹ to like; to love; to win; to be admired: mi piace il mare, I like the sea.
piace'vole adj. pleasant; agreeable; nice.
piacevolezza f. pleasantness; agreeableness; witticism.
piacimento m. pleasure, liking.
piaga f. fester, sore; evil, plague; bore.
piagare vt. to fester.
piaggeri'a f. flattery.
piaggiare vt. to flatter, blandish.
piaggiatore m. flatterer, "yes man."
piagnisteo m. wailing, whine.
piagnone m. weeper.
piagnucolare vi. to whimper.
piagnucolone m. whimperer, crybaby.
piagnucoloso adj. tearful, whimpering.
pialla f. plane.
piallac'cio m. veneer.
piallare vt. to plane.
piallatrice f. (mach.) planer.
piallatura f. planing.
piana f. plain.
pianeggiante adj. level.
pianella f. slipper; tile.
pianerot'tolo m. landing.
pianeta m. (astr.) planet; (eccl.) chasuble.
pian'gere vt., vi. ⁹⁹ to weep, cry, shed tears: — miseria, to pretend poverty.

pianino m. barrel organ.
pianissimo adv. very slowly; very softly.
pianista m. pianist.
piano (1) m. plain; plan, project; level; footing; surface, plane; story, floor; layer; (mus.) piano; (geom.) plane; (moving pictures) shot; (aeron.) stabilizer, vane: primissimo, primo, mezzo — (moving pictures), close up, full shot, medium shot; — inclinato, cant; piani di coda (aeron.), tail vanes.
piano (2) adj. plane, level; flat; plain, clear.
piano (3) adv. slowly; softly.
pianoforte m. piano: — a coda, grand piano.
pianola f. pianola.
pianoro m. plateau.
pianta f. plant; tree; map; payroll (of employees); sole (of a foot, shoe, etc.): di sana —, wholly, all over again.
piantagione f. plantation.
piantare vt. to plant; to drive in; to fix; to place, put; (fam.) to abandon, jilt: — chiodi (fig.), to make debts; — grane, to make trouble; — in asso, to give the slip to; to leave in the lurch; piantarsi vr. to plant oneself; (recipr.) to part.
piantato adj. planted: ben —, well-knit, brawny, sturdy.
piantatore m. planter.
pianterreno m. ground floor.
pianticella f. plantlet.
pianto m. weeping; adj. lamented. pp. of piangere.
piantonare vt. to watch.
piantone m. (bot.) shoot; (mil.) orderly; sentry.
pianura f. plain.
piastra f. plate; plaster (coin).
piastrella f. tile.
piatire vi. to litigate.
piattaforma f. platform: — girevole, turntable; — di lancio, springboard.
piattino m. small plate; saucer; dainty.
piatto m. dish. plate; scale; (mus.) cymbal: — forte, pièce de résistance; adj. flat.
piat'tola f. crab-louse; bore.
piazza f. square; place; clearing; (comm.) market: — d'armi, drill ground; fare — pulita, to make a clean sweep.
piazzaforte f. stronghold.
piazzale m. esplanade.
piazzare see collocare, piazzarsi vr. (turf, etc.) to place: il favorito si è piazzato, the favorite was placed.

piazzata f. scene; row, brawl.

piazzato adj. (turf, etc.) placed, to place.

piazzista m. (comm.) salesman.

piazzuola f. emplacement.

picca f. spike; spite; spade (in playing cards): per —, out of spite.

piccante adj. piquant; risqué.

piccare vi. to sparkle; **piccarsi** vr. to insist; to plume oneself (on).

piccato adj. piqued.

picchè m. (textiles) piqué.

picchetto m. stake; (mil.) picket; piquet: di —, on guard duty.

picchiare vt. to hit, beat, knock, strike. vi. to knock; to tap; (aeron.) to dive; **picchiarsi** vr. to strike oneself; (recipr.) to come to blows.

picchiata f. blow; (aeron.) dive.

picchiatore m. dive bomber; (boxing) puncher.

picchiettare vt. to drum; to speckle, spot.

picchiettato adj. spotted.

pichietti'o m. drumming.

pic'chio m. knock; woodpecker.

piccina f. child, little girl.

piccineri'a f. meanness.

piccino m. child, baby; adj. tiny; mean.

picciona'ia m. dovecot; (theat.) upper gallery; gallery gods.

piccione m. pigeon.

picciuolo m. stem, stalk.

picco m. peak: a —, perpendicularly; andare (mandare) a —, to sink.

pic'cola f. little girl, baby.

piccolezza f. smallness; trifle.

pic'colo m. boy, kid; adj. little, small, short; trivial; narrow; mean: in —, on a small scale.

piccone m. pick, pickax.

piccozza f. hatchet.

Pico della Mirandola, Italian humanist (1463–1494).

pidocchieri'a f. stinginess; meanness.

pidoc'chio m. louse; miser.

pidocchioso adj. lousy; stingy.

piede m. foot (pl. feet); bottom: sui due piedi, right away, offhand; in punta di piedi, on tiptoe; saltare a piè pari, to skip altogether; tenere i piedi in due staffe, to play both ends against the middle.

piedestallo m. pedestal.

piega f. fold; crease; pleat: prendere una buona (cattiva) —, to take a good (bad) turn.

piegamento m. folding; flexion.

piegare vt. to fold (up); to bend, bow; to tame; vi. to lean; to yield; **piegarsi** vr. to fold, bend; to yield.

piegatura f. folding; fold; crook.

pieghettare vt. to plait.

pieghe'vole m. folder; adj. folding; pliable, pliant; yielding.

piego see plico.

piena f. swell; flood; crowd; fullness: in —, swollen.

pienamente adv. fully.

pienezza f. fullness, plenitude.

pieno m. top, height; bloom; fill: fare il —, to fuel; in —, full; squarely; smack; adj. full; crammed; crowded: a pieni voti, by absolute majority; with flying colors.

pietà f. pity, mercy; piety: far —, to stir pity.

pietanza f. viand, main course.

pietismo m. pietism.

pietista m. pietist.

pietoso adj. merciful; wretched; pitiful.

pietra f. stone: — da affilare, whetstone, hone; — dello scandalo, shame.

pietrificare vt. to petrify.

pietrina f. flint (for lighters).

pietrisco m. rubble, metal.

pievano m. parson, curate.

pieve f. parish.

piffera'io m. fifer.

pif'fero m. fife.

pigiama m. pajamas.

pi'gia pi'gia m. crowd, press.

pigiare vt. to press, crush; **pigiarsi** vr. to crowd; to squeeze.

pigiatrice f. (mach.) presser, press.

pigiatura f. pressing.

pigionante m., f. tenant.

pigione f. rent: prendere a —, to rent; dare a —, to let.

pigliare see pren'dere.

pi'glio (1) m. mien, countenance.

pi'glio (2) m. hold: dar di — a, to lay hold of.

pigmentazione f. pigmentation.

pigmento m. pigment.

pigmeo m., adj. Pygmy, pygmy.

pigna f. pine cone; (obs.) dome.

pignatta f. pot.

pignoleri'a f. fastidiousness, fussiness, meticulousness.

pignolo m. (bot.) pine nut; (fig.) fussy man.

pignone m. embankment; (mach.) pinion.

pignoramento m. distraint.

pignorare vt. to distrain.

pigolare vi. to peep.

pigoli'o m. peeping, chirping.

pigri'zia f. laziness; sluggishness.

pigro adj. lazy; sluggish.

pila f. heap; pile; baptismal font; battery; basin: — atomica, atomic pile; — a secco, dry battery.

pilastro m. pillar.

Pilato *m.* (*hist.*) Pilate: da Erode a —, from pillar to post.
piliac'chera *f.* splash.
pil'lola *f.* pill, pillule.
pilone *m.* pylon: — d'ormeggio, mooring tower.
piloro *m.* pylorus.
pilota *m.* pilot; driver.
pilotag'gio *m.* pilotage.
pilotare *vt.* to pilot; to drive; to steer.
piluccare *vt.* to pluck.
pinacoteca *f.* picture gallery.
pineta *f.* pine wood, pinery.
pin'gue *adj.* fat; substantial, rich; big.
pingue'dine *f.* fatness.
pinguino *m.* penguin.
pinna *f.* fin; rubber flipper (*for skin divers*).
pinna'colo *m.* pinnacle.
pino *m.* pine.
pinoc'chio, pinolo *m.* pine nut.
pinta *f.* pint.
Pinturicchio, il (*Bernardino Betti*), Italian painter (1454 1513).
pinza *f.*, **pinze** *f.pl.* pincers, pliers.
pinzetta *f.* tweezers (*pl.*).
pinzimo'nio *m.* (oil, salt, and pepper) dressing.
pio *adj.* pious; merciful; charitable.
pioggerella *f.* drizzle.
piog'gia *f.* rain; shower.
piolo *see* **piuolo**.
piombare *vi.* to lead; to plumb, seal; *vi.* to fall, drop; to pounce (*on*); to dive (*upon*).
piombatura *f.* lead coating; sealing.
piombino *m.* plummet, plumb bob.
piombo *m.* lead; bullets: a —, perpendicularly; filo a —, plumb line; col piedi di —, cautiously.
pioniere *m.* pioneer.
pioppo *m.* poplar.
piorrea *f.* pyorrhea.
piovana, (acqua) *f.* rain water.
piovasco *m.* squall.
piovente *m.* slope (*of a roof*).
pio'vere *vi.*[81] to rain; to pour: — a catinelle, to rain cats and dogs.
piovigginare *vi.* to drizzle.
piovigginoso *adj.* drizzling.
piovoso *adj.* rainy.
piovra *f.* octopus.
pipa *f.* pipe.
pipare *vi.* to smoke a pipe.
pipata, pipatina *f.* pipe; pipeful.
pipistrello *m.* bat.
pipita *f.* hangnail; (*veterinary*) pip.
pira *f.* pyre, funeral pipe.
pira'mide *f.* pyramid.
Pirandello, Luigi, Italian novelist and dramatist, *Sei personaggi in cerca d'autore, Il fu Mattia Pascal*, Nobel Prize, 1934 (1867–1936).

Piranesi, Giambattista, Italian engraver (1720–1778).
pirata *m.* pirate.
pirateggiare *vt.*, *vi.* to pirate.
pirateri'a *f.* piracy.
pi'rica, (pol'vere) *f.* gunpowder.
pirite *f.* pyrites.
piroetta *f.* pirouette.
piroettare *vi.* to pirouette.
piroga *f.* pirogue, piragua.
piro'scafo *m.* steamer, ship.
pirotec'nico *adj.* pyrotechnic.
Pisano, Andrea (*Andrea da Pontedera*), Italian sculptor (1270?–1348).
Pisano, Giovanni, Italian sculptor (1245–1314).
pi'scia *f.* (*vulg.*) urine.
pisciare *vi.* (*vulg.*) to urinate.
pisciato'io *m.* (*vulg.*) urinal.
piscina *f.* swimming pool.
pisello *m.* pea.
pisolare *vi.* to doze, nap.
pisolino, pi'solo *m.* nap.
pista *f.* track; race course; (*aeron.*) runway.
pistac'chio *m.* pistachio.
pistillo *m.* pistil.
pistola *f.* pistol, gun.
pistolettata *f.* pistol shot.
pistolotto *m.* lecture; peroration.
pistone *m.* piston.
pitago'rico *adj.* Pythagorean: tavola pitagorica, multiplication table.
pitale *m.* chamberpot.
pitoccare *vi.* to beg, to be miserly.
pitoccheri'a *f.* beggary; stinginess.
pitocco *m.* beggar; miser.
pitone *m.* python.
pit'tima *f.* plaster; bore.
pittore *m.* painter.
pittoresco *adj.* picturesque.
pittrice *f.* painter (*female*).
pittura *f.* painting; paint.
pitturare *vt.*, *vi.* to paint.
più *m.* most: i —, most people; il — delle volte, more often than not; dal — al meno, more or less; *adj.* more; several; *adv.* more (*than*); most; longer; plus: non —, no more, any more; mai —, never again, by no means; non ho — che un vestito, I have but one suit left; credersi da — di, to think oneself superior to; sempre —, more and more; sempre — in alto, higher and higher; tutt'al —, at most; per lo —, mainly, mostly; — in là, further on, later on; per di —, in addition; tanto — che, the more so as.
piuma *f.* feather.
piumac'cio *m.* feather pillow.
piumag'gio *m.* plumage.

piumino *m.* down quilt; powder puff; feather duster; "slug."

piumoso *adj.* feathery.

piuolo *m.* peg: **scala a piuoli,** ladder.

piuttosto *adv.* rather (*than*); instead.

piva *f.* bagpipe: **con le pive nel sacco,** disappointed.

pizzardone *m.* policeman, "flatfoot," "cop."

pizzica'gnolo *m.* pork butcher.

pizzicare *vt., vi.* to pinch, nip; to sting, prick; to itch; (*mus.*) to pluck.

piz'zico *m.* pinch.

pizzicore *m.* itch.

pizzicotto *m.* pinch, nip.

pizzo *m.* lace; Vandyke beard; peak.

placare *vt.* to appease, pacify; to allay, soothe; **placarsi** *vr.* to calm down; to subside.

placca *f.* plaque; spot.

placcare *vt.* to plate: — **in oro,** to gold-plate.

pla'cido *adj.* placid.

plafone *m.* ceiling, plafond.

plaga *f.* region.

plagiare *vt., vi.* to plagiarize.

plagia'rio *m.* plagiarist.

pla'gio *m.* plagiarism.

planare *vi.* to volplane, glide; to level off.

plan'cia *f.* planchet; (*naut.*) bridge.

planimetri'a *f.* planimetry; (*arch.*) layout, blueprint.

plasma *m.* plasma.

plasmare *vt.* to mold, shape.

pla'stica *f.* plastic, plastic art; (*surg.*) skin grafting.

plasticità *f.* plasticity.

pla'stico *m.* modeler; model; *adj.* plastic.

pla'tano *m.* plane tree.

platea *f.* pit, orchestra, parquet; audience.

plateale *adj.* vulgar, plebeian, common.

platinare *vt.* to platinize; to bleach (*hair*).

platinato *adj.* platinized; bleached: **bionda platinata,** platinum blonde.

pla'tino *m.* platinum.

plaudire *vi.* to applaud.

plausi'bile *adj.* plausible.

pla'uso *m.* applause; praise.

pleba'glia *f.* mob, rabble.

plebe *f.* common people, populace.

plebeo *m., adj.* plebeian.

plebiscito *m.* plebiscite.

plena'rio *adj.* plenary.

plenilu'nio *m.* full moon.

plenipotenzia'rio *m., adj.* plenipotentiary.

ple'tora *f.* plethora.

pleto'rico *adj.* plethoric.

plettro *m.* plectrum.

pleurite *f.* pleurisy.

plico *m.* folder, cover; letter.

plotone *m.* platoon: — **d'esecuzione,** firing squad.

plum'beo *adj.* leaden.

plurale *m., adj.* plural.

plu'rimo *adj.* plural.

plusvalore *m.* excess value.

pluto'crate *m.* plutocrat.

pneuma'tico *m.* (*pneumatic*) tire; tube; *adj.* pneumatic: **posta pneumatica,** pneumatic dispatch.

po' *see* **poco.**

pochezza *f.* littleness, smallness.

pochis'simo *adj., adv.* very little; very seldom; very cheap; **pochissimi** *pl.* very few.

poco *m.* little; **pochi** *m.pl.* few (people): **con quel po' po' di patrimonio,** with such a fortune; *adj.* little; some, any; small; scarce; short; *adv.* little; a little (while); slightly; some, any; cheap, cheaply: — **fa,** a few moments ago; **fra** —, soon, in a short time; **per** —, almost, nearly; — **più** — **meno,** more or less; **né punto né** —, not at all; **a** — **a** —, little by little; **un bel po' di,** a good deal of; **un altro** —, some more, a little longer; **da** —, cheap; **da** — **tempo,** not long ago; — **prima, dopo,** shortly before, after.

podere *m.* farm.

poderoso *adj.* powerful, mighty.

podestà *m.* mayor.

podismo *m.* foot racing.

podista *m.* foot racer.

poema *m.* (*long*) poem.

Poerio, Carlo, Italian statesman (1803–1867).

poesi'a *f.* poetry; poem.

poeta *m.* poet.

poetessa *f.* poetess.

poe'tico *adj.* poetic, poetical.

poggiare *vt.* to lay, rest; *vi.* to rest (*upon*); to move; (*naut.*) to move leeward.

pog'gio *m.* knoll.

poggiuolo *m.* balcony.

poi *adv.* after, afterwards; then; later (*on*); next: **d'ora in** —, from now on; **d'allora in** —, since then; **prima o** —, sooner or later.

poiana *f.* (*ornith.*) buzzard.

poichè *conj.* since; for, as; when; after; as soon as.

polacco *m.* Polish (*language*); Pole; *adj.* Polish.

polare *adj.* polar: **stella** —, polestar.

polarizzare *vt.* to polarize; to focus.

polarizzatore *m.* polarizer.

polca *f.* polka.

pole'mica *f.* polemic; controversy.

polemista *m.* polemicist.

polemizzare *vi.* to argue, polemize.

polentina *f.* poultice.

poliambulanza *f.* dispensary.

poli'cromo *adj.* polychrome.

polifase *adj.* (*elec.*) multiphase.

poligami'a *f.* polygamy.

poli'gamo *m.* polygamist; *adj.* polygamous.

poligiotta *m.*, *adj.* polyglot.

poli'gono *m.* polygon: — di tiro, shooting range.

poliomielite *f.* poliomyelitis, infantile paralysis.

po'lipo *m.* polyp.

politeama *m.* theater.

politec'nico *m.* polytechnic; (*univ.*) engineering institute; *adj.* polytechnic.

poli'tica *f.* politics; policy.

politicante *m.* politician.

poli'tico *adj.* political; politic: uomo —, politician.

polizi'a *f.* police: agente di —, policeman, officer.

Poliziano, Angelo, Italian humanist (1454-1494).

poliziesco *adj.* police: romanzo —, detective story.

poliziotto *m.* policeman; detective.

po'lizza *f.* policy; draft; certificate: — di carico, bill of lading; — di pegno, pawn ticket.

polla *f.* spring.

polla'io *m.* poultry yard.

pollame *m.* poultry.

pollanca, pollastra, pollastrella, *f.* pullet, hen.

pollastro *m.* cockerel; (*fam.*) chicken.

polleri'a *f.* poultry shop.

pol'lice *m.* thumb (*of the hand*); big toe (*of the foot*); inch.

pol'line *m.* (*bot.*) pollen.

polliven'dolo *m.* poulterer.

pollo *m.* chicken, fowl; dupe: conoscere i propri polli, to be nobody's fool.

polmone *m.* lung: — d'acciaio, pulmotor.

polmonite *f.* pneumonia.

polo *m.* pole (*of the earth, of a magnet, etc.*); (*sport*) polo.

Polo, Marco, Italian traveler in Asia, author of *Il Milione* (1254?-1324).

polpa *f.* pulp.

polpac'cio *m.* (*anat.*) calf.

polpastrello *m.* finger tip.

polpetta *f.* croquette.

polpettone *m.* hash.

polpo *m.* (*zool.*) octopus.

polposo *adj.* pulpy, fleshy, meaty.

polsino *m.* cuff.

polso *m.* wrist; pulse; wristband; nerve, will.

polti'glia *f.* pulp; mud.

poltrire *vi.* to idle.

poltrona *f.* armchair, easy chair; (*theat.*) orchestra seat, pit stall.

poltroncina *f.* (*theat.*) orchestra seat (*in the last rows*).

poltrone *m.* lazybones.

poltroneri'a *f.* laziness.

pol'vere *f.* dust; (*chem.*) powder: da sparo, gunpowder; orologio a —, sand glass.

polveriera *f.* powder magazine.

polverina *f.* powder.

polverino *m.* sand; sandbox; (*min.*) slack.

polverizzare *vt.*, polverizzarsi *vr.* to pulverize.

polverizzatore *m.* pulverizer; sprayer.

polverizzazione *f.* pulverization.

polverone *m.* dust cloud.

polveroso *adj.* dusty.

pomata *f.* pomade; ointment.

pomellato *adj.* dappled.

pomello *m.* cheekbone.

pomeridiano *adj.* (*in the*) afternoon, P. M.

pomerig'gio *m.* afternoon.

po'mice *f.* pumice (stone).

pomidoro *see* pomodoro.

pomo *m.* apple; knob; pommel: pomo della discordia, bone of contention.

pomodoro *m.* tomato.

pompa (1) *f.* pomp; display: impresario di pompe funebri, undertaker.

pompa (2) *f.* (*mach.*) pump.

pompare *vt.* to pump.

pompelmo *m.* grapefruit.

pompiere *m.* fireman.

pomposo *adj.* pompous, solemn.

Ponchielli, Amilcare, Italian composer (1834-1886).

ponderare *vt.* to weigh, ponder.

ponderatezza *f.* caution.

ponderato *adj.* careful, cautious.

ponderoso *adj.* ponderous; weighty.

pondo *m.* weight, burden.

ponente *m.* west.

Pontano, Giovanni, Italian statesman, historian and poet (1426-1503).

ponte *m.* bridge; scaffold; (*naut.*) deck: — aereo, air lift.

ponte'fice *m.* pontiff, pope.

ponticello *m.* footbridge; bridge (*of a fiddle, etc.*).

pontiere *m.* pontonier.

pontifi'cio *adj.* papal.

pontile *m.* landing stage; pier.

pontone *m.* pontoon.

ponzare *vi.* to labor; to cogitate.

popolano *m.*, *adj.* plebeian.

popolare (1) adj. popular: posti popolari, "bleachers."

popolare (2) vt. to people; popolarsi vr. to become populated.

popolarità f. popularity.

popolazione f. population.

po'polo m. people.

popoloso adj. populous.

popone m. melon.

poppa f. (anat.) breast; (naut.) stern, poop: col vento in —, before the wind.

poppante m. suckling.

poppare vi. to suckle.

poppato'io m. nursing bottle.

porca f. (agr.) ridge; (zool.) sow.

porca'io m. swineherd; pigsty.

porcellana f. porcelain, china.

porcellino m. piggy: — d'India, guinea pig.

porcello m. pig.

porcheri'a f. dirt; trash; dirty trick; obscenity.

porchetta f. roast pig.

porcile m. sty, pigsty.

porco m. pig, swine; pork.

porcospino m. porcupine.

por'fido m. porphyry.

por'gere vt.** to hand; to hold out; to offer.

poro m. pore.

porosità f. porosity.

poroso adj. porous.

por'pora f. purple; (med.) purpura.

Por'pora, Niccolò, Italian composer (1686–1766).

porporato m. cardinal.

porporina f. purpurin.

porporino adj. purple.

porre vt.** to put, place; to suppose; to pay (attention).

porro m. (bot.) leek; (path.) wart.

porta f. door; doorway; gate; (sport) goal.

Porta, Carlo, Italian poet in Milanese dialect (1776–1821).

Porta, della, Giambattista, Italian physicist (1538–1615).

portabagagli m. porter; rack.

portabandiera m. standard-bearer, ensign.

porta'bile adj. portable.

portacatino m. basin stand.

portace'nere m. ash tray.

portaceste m. (theat.) property man.

portaci'pria m. vanity case, compact.

portae'rei f. aircraft carrier.

portaferiti m. stretcher-bearer.

portafiori m. flower stand; flowerpot.

portafo'glio m. pocketbook; wallet; (fin., pol.) portfolio.

portafortuna m. talisman.

portagioielli m. jewel case.

portale m. portal.

portalet'tere m. postman.

portamento m. carriage, bearing; behavior.

portamonete m. purse.

portante adj. carrying: piano —, supporting surface.

portantina f. sedan-chair.

portaor'dini m. messenger, courier.

portapenne m. penholder.

portare vt. to bring; to fetch; to take (away); to carry; to wear; to move; to drive; to lead; portarsi vr. to bring, take along; to behave.

portaritratti m. frame.

portasciugamani m. towel horse, towel rack.

portasigarette m. cigarette case.

portasi'gari m. cigar case.

portaspilli m. pincushion.

portata f. reach; power, strength; capacity; range; (naut.) tonnage; lifting power (of a crane); carrying capacity (of a truck); purport; scope; course, dish: a — di mano, within one's reach.

porta'tile adj. portable.

portato m. result; adj. worn; inclined.

portatore m. bearer.

portavasi m. (naut.) cradle-bar.

portavoce m. speaking tube; megaphone; spokesman, mouthpiece.

portello m. wicket; porthole.

portento m. wonder, marvel.

portentoso adj. wonderful.

porticato m. porch, gallery, piazza.

por'tico m. portico; porch.

portiera f. portiere; portress; door (of an automobile).

portiere m. doorkeeper, doorman; janitor; (sport) goalkeeper.

portina'ia f. portress.

portina'io see portiere.

Portinari, Beatrice, Florentine lady, immortalized by Dante, who made her the central figure of his Divina Commedia (? –1290).

portineri'a f. janitor's lodge.

porto (1) m. carriage; postage: franco di —, carriage free; — d'arme, license to carry arms.

porto (2) m. harbor, port, haven: — franco, free port; condurre a buon —, to bring off.

porto (3) m. port (wine).

porto (4) pp.of porgere.

portoghese m., adj. Portuguese; "gate crasher."

portone m. gate, portal.

porzione f. portion, share.

posa f. posture; attitude, pose; pause; rest; (photo.) time exposure: senza —, endlessly.

posace'nere m. ash tray.

posamine m. minelayer.

posapiano m. slow coach.

posapiedi m. footrest.

posare vt. to lay (down); to rest; vi. to rest; to lie; to pose; **posarsi** vr. to place oneself; to (come to) rest; to alight.

posata f. knife fork and spoon.

posato adj. sedate; placed, laid.

posato'io m. rest; perch, roost.

posatore m. poseur.

po'scia adv. then, afterwards.

poscritto m. postscript.

posdatare vt. to postdate.

posdomani adv. the day after tomorrow.

positiva f. (photo.) positive.

positivo m. positive; adj. positive, practical, matter-of-fact: **di —**, for sure.

posizione f. position; posture, attitude; condition; location: **prendere — per (contro)**, to take one's stand for (against).

posporre vt. to postpone, put off; to subordinate.

posposto pp. of posporre.

possa, possanza f. strength, power, vigor.

possedere vt. to own, possess; to have; to master.

possedimento m. possession; estate.

possente adj. powerful, mighty.

possessivo m., adj. possessive.

possesso m. possession.

possessore m. possessor, owner; holder.

possi'bile adj. possible: **fare il —**, to do one's level best.

possibilità f. possibility; opportunity; chance; power; means.

possibilmente adv. possibly; if possible.

possidente m. man of property; m., f. landowner.

posta f. mail, post; post office; stake; size: — **aerea**, air mail; **fermo in —**, general delivery; **spese di —**, postage; **stare alla —**, to lie in ambush; **a — per**, expressly for; **a (bella) —**, on purpose.

postale m. mail boat; adj. postal, mail, post.

postare vt. to establish, post.

postazione f. emplacement.

postbel'lico adj. postwar.

posteggiare vt. to park.

posteg'gio m. stand; parking lot.

po'steri m.pl. posterity.

posteri'a f. general store.

posteriore adj. posterior, hind, back.

posteriormente adv. posteriorly; later.

posterità f. posterity.

postic'cio adj. provisional; artificial; false.

posticipare vt. to postpone.

posticipato adj. postponed; deferred; on delivery.

postiglione m. postillion.

postilla f. note, apostil.

postillare vt. to annotate.

postino m. postman.

posto (1) m. place; spot; room; seat; job, situation: — **di medicazione**, first-aid station; — **di polizia**, police station; **automobile a due posti**, two-seater; **tenere la lingua a —**, to hold one's tongue; **mettere a —**, to tidy up, to straighten up.

posto (2) pp. of porre.

postochè conj. supposing that; provided; since.

postremo adj. last.

postri'bolo m. brothel.

postulante m. petitioner.

postulato m. postulate.

po'stumo m. aftermath; sequel; adj. posthumous.

pota'bile adj. drinkable.

potare vt. to prune, lop.

potassa f. potash.

potas'sio m. potassium.

potatura f. pruning, lopping.

potentato m. potentate.

potente adj. powerful, mighty; influential.

potenza f. power, might; strength; **in —**, potentially.

potenziale m., adj. potential.

potenzialmente adv. potentially.

potere (1) m. power: **il quarto —**, the fourth estate; **cadere in — di**, to fall into the hands of.

potere (2) vi.[44] can, may; to be able; to be allowed: **non posso**, I cannot; **posso andare?** may I go?; **avrebbe potuto scrivere**, he could have written; **può darsi che**, it may be that; **non posso far altro che andare**, I cannot but go; **non posso fare a meno di pensare**, I can't help thinking; **non poterne più**, to be fed up; **to be exhausted**; **a più non posso**, with might and main.

potestà f. power, authority: **patria —**, patria potestas.

po'vero m. pauper; beggar; adj. poor; needy; scanty, meager; late (dead): — **me!** woe is me!

povertà f. poverty; poorness, scantiness.

pozione f. potion, draft.

pozza f. puddle, pool.

pozzan'ghera f. puddle.

pozzo m. well; pit; (min.) shaft: — **petrolifero**, oil well; — **nero**, cesspool.

pramma'tica f. custom: **di —**, customary; obligatory, de rigueur.

pranzare *vi.* to dine.

pranzo *m.* dinner; banquet: sala da —, dining room.

prassi *f.* praxis, procedure.

prateri'a *f.* prairie.

pra'tica *f.* practice; experience; skill; habit; matter, business; dossier, file; apprenticeship; training; (*naut.*) pratique: far le pratiche per, to take steps to.

pratica'bile *adj.* practicable; (*theat.*) practical.

praticamente *adv.* practically.

praticante *m.* apprentice; practitioner; *adj.* practicing.

praticare *vt.* to practice; to perform; to frequent; to associate with: — buoni prezzi, to charge low prices; — un'apertura, to open a gap.

praticità *f.* practicalness.

pra'tico *adj.* practical; experienced, practiced: all'atto —, in practice.

praticone *m.* empiric.

prato *m.* meadow.

pravo *adj.* wicked.

pream'bolo *m.* preamble.

preannunziare *vt.* to announce; to forebode.

preannun'zio *m.* warning; foreboding.

preavvertire, preavvisare, *vt.* to forewarn.

preavviso *m.* notice; warning.

prebenda *f.* prebend.

preca'rio *adj.* precarious.

precauzione *f.* precaution; caution.

prece *f.* prayer.

precedente *m.* precedent: senza —, unprecedented; *adj.* previous, preceding, former.

precedentemente *adv.* previously.

precedenza *f.* priority, precedence: in —, previously.

prece'dere *vt.*, *vi.* to precede: farsi — da, to send ahead.

precetto *m.* precept; rule; principle; writ, warrant.

precettore *m.* tutor, teacher.

precipitare *vt.*, *vi.* to precipitate; to drop, fall down, crash; precipitarsi *vr.* to precipitate oneself; to rush, dash; (*aeron.*) to fall, crash.

precipitato *m.* precipitate; *adj.* precipitate, hasty; rash.

precipitazione *f.* rashness; haste, hurry; precipitation.

precipitoso *adj.* precipitate; precipitous; rash.

precipi'zio *m.* precipice; ruin: a —, precipitously, precipitately.

preci'puo *adj.* chief, main.

precisa'mente *adv.* precisely.

precisare *vt.* to determine; to specify; to stress.

precisione *f.* precision, accuracy.

preciso *adj.* precise, accurate; exact; like, alike: alle dieci precise, at ten (*o'clock*) sharp.

preclu'dere *vt.*[2] to preclude.

precluso *pp.* of precludere.

precoce *adj.* precocious; premature, untimely.

preconcetto *m.* preconception; bias, prejudice; *adj.* preconceived.

preconizzare *vt.* to preconize, predict.

precor'rere *vt.* to forerun.

precursore *m.* precursor, forerunner.

preda *f.* prey; booty.

predare *vt.* to plunder.

predecessore *m.* predecessor.

predella *f.* dais; footboard.

predellino *m.* footboard.

predestinare *vt.* to predestine; to doom.

predestinato *adj.* predestinate; fated.

predetto *adj.* aforesaid. *pp.* of predire.

pre'dica *f.* sermon; lecture.

predicare *vt.*, *vi.* to preach.

predicato *m.* predicate.

predicatore *m.* preacher.

predicazione *f.* preaching.

predicozzo *m.* lecture.

prediletto *m.*, *adj.* favorite. *pp. of* prediligere.

predilezione *f.* predilection.

predili'gere *vt.*[4] to prefer, like best.

predire *vt.*[44] to foretell.

predisporre *vt.*[31] to predispose; to bias; to prearrange.

predisposizione *f.* predisposition; prearrangement.

predisposto *pp.* of predisporre.

predizione *f.* prediction.

predominante *adj.* predominant; prevailing.

predominare *vt.*, *vi.* to predominate (*over*); to prevail.

predomi'nio *m.* predominance; supremacy.

predone *m.* marauder.

prefazione *f.* preface, introduction.

preferenza *f.* preference: a — di, rather than; di —, preferably.

preferi'bile *adj.* preferable.

preferire *vt.* to prefer, like better; to choose.

preferito *m.*, *adj.* favorite.

prefetto *m.* prefect.

prefettura *f.* prefecture.

prefig'gere *vt.*[22] to prefix, fix in advance; prefiggersi *vr.* to set one's mind (*on*)

prefisso (1) *m.* prefix.

prefisso (2) *pp.* of prefiggere.

pregare *vt.* to pray; to beg; to entreat: farsi —, to deny oneself; vi prego! please!

prege'vole *adj.* valuable; good.

preghiera *f.* prayer; request; entreaty.

pregiarsi vr. to have the honor to.

pregiatis'simo superl.adj. priceless: — Signore, Dear Sir.

pregiato adj. valued, valuable: la vostra pregiata lettera del, your favor of.

pre'gio m. esteem; virtue; quality; merit; value, worth: tenere in —, to value.

pregiudicare vt. to prejudice; to be prejudicial to; to jeopardize.

pregiudicato m. man with a police record.

pregiudiziale f. exception; adj. prejudicial.

pregiudi'zio m. prejudice; bias; detriment: essere di —, to be detrimental (to).

pregno adj. filled (with); pregnant.

prego, please; not at all.

pregustare vt. to foretaste; to anticipate.

preisto'rico adj. prehistoric.

prelato m. prelate.

prelazione f. pre-emption.

prelevamento m. draft: — in scoperto (bank.), overdraft.

prelevare vt. to draw, take away; to withdraw; to pick up.

prelibato adj. delicious, dainty.

prelievo see prelevamento.

preliminare m., adj. preliminary.

prelu'dere vi.⁶ to prelude.

prelu'dio m. prelude.

preluso pp. of preludere.

prematuro adj. premature, untimely.

premeditare vt. to premeditate, to design.

premeditato adj. premeditated.

pre'mere vt., vi. to press; to push; to squeeze; to weigh (upon); to urge; to insist (on); to be important; to mean a lot.

premessa f. preliminary; foreword; premise.

premet'tere vt. to premise.

premiare vt. to award a prize to; to reward.

premiato m. prize winner; adj. prize-winning, rewarded.

premiazione f. prize awarding.

pre'mio m. prize; trophy; reward; premium; bonus: monte premi, win-pool.

pre'mito m. contraction.

premolare m., adj. premolar.

premonizione f. premonition.

premunire vt. to safeguard: premunirsi vr. to take precautions.

premura f. care; solicitude; urgency; haste: aver —, to be in a hurry; di —, hastily, in a hurry.

premurosamente adv. solicitously; readily.

premuroso adj. solicitous, considerate.

pren'dere vt., vi.⁸⁶ to take; to catch; to steal; to get; to begin; to hold; to turn: — alle proprie dipendenze, to engage; — le mosse (da), to start (from); — sonno, to go off to sleep; — quota, to climb; — terra, to land; pren'dersi vr. to take, catch, seize, get; to secure: — a pugni, to come to blows, to fight; prendersela a male (calda), to take amiss (to heart); prendersela con uno, to lay the blame on one, to take it out on one.

prenome m. Christian name, given name.

prenotare vt. to book, engage, reserve.

prenotazione f. booking, reservation.

pren'sile adj. prehensile.

preoccupare vt., preoccuparsi vr. to worry.

preoccupato adj. preoccupied; worried, anxious.

preoccupazione f. preoccupation; worry, anxiety.

preparare vt. to prepare; to organize; to arrange: — la tavola, to lay the table; — il terreno, to pave the way; prepararsi vr. to prepare (for); to get ready.

preparativo m. preparation.

preparato m. preparation, compound; adj. prepared; ready.

preparato'rio adj. preparatory.

preparazione f. preparation.

preponderante adj. preponderant; prevailing.

preponderanza f. preponderance.

preporre vt.⁸¹ to put, place before; to put in charge (of).

preposizione f. preposition.

preposto m. parson, vicar; adj. in charge of. pp. of preporre.

prepotente m. bully; adj. overbearing; overwhelming.

prepotenza f. outrage; arrogance.

prerogativa f. prerogative.

presa f. taking, seizing, hold, grasp; (elec.) plug-jack: — d'aria, air shaft; — di tabacco, pinch; essere alle prese con, to be struggling with; far —, to take; macchina da — (moving pictures), camera.

presa'gio m. presage, premonition.

presagire vt. to presage.

pre'sbite m. presbyope; adj. presbyopic, long-sighted, far-sighted.

presbite'rio m. presbytery.

prescelto adj. chosen, preferred.

prescienza f. prescience.

prescin'dere vi.⁹⁷ to prescind: — da, to disregard, leave aside.

prescritto m. prescript. adj. prescribed; prescript. pp. of prescrivere.

prescri'vere vt.[314] to prescribe.
prescrizione f. prescription.
presenta'bile adj. presentable.
presentare vt. to present; to show, exhibit; to offer; to introduce; to propose: — la propria candidatura a, to run for; presentarsi vr. to present, introduce oneself; to report; to show oneself, appear; to arise; to look; to promise: — a un esame, to appear for an examination; si presentò il destro per, an opportunity offered itself to.
presentatore m. introducer; (theat.) host, showman.
presentazione f. presentation; introduction.
presente (1) m. present (time); (gramm.) present (tense); bystander; present: i presenti, those present; the on-lookers; esclusi i presenti, present company excepted.
presente (2) adj. present: tener —, to bear in mind; essere — a se stesso, to have all one's wits about one; presente! here!
presentemente adv. at present.
presentimento m. foreboding.
presentire vt., vi. to presage, foresee, feel.
presenza f. presence: — di spirito, presence of mind; far atto di —, to put in an appearance.
presenziare vt., vi. to attend; to be present (at).
presepe, prese'pio m. manger; crèche.
preservare vt. to preserve.
preservativo m. preservative; contraceptive sheath; adj. preservative.
pre'side m. president; principal (of a school).
presidente m. president; chairman: Presidente del Consiglio (dei Ministri), premier.
presidenza f. presidency; chairmanship.
presidenziale adj. presidential.
presidiare vt. to garrison.
presi'dio m. garrison.
presie'dere vi., vi. to preside (over); to be in charge (of).
preso adj. taken, seized; busy. pp. of prendere.
pressa f. press.
pressante adj. pressing.
pressappoco adv. about, thereabout; more or less; approximately.
pressare vt. to press; to urge.
pressi m.pl. neighborhood, vicinity.
pressione f. pressure.
presso prep. near, by; beside; at, in; with; care of (abb.: c/o): — un amico, at a friend's; godere di

popolarità — i propri allievi, to enjoy popularity with one's pupils; essere impiegato —, to work with; adv. near, nearby; about.
pressoché adv. almost, nearly.
prestabilire vt. to pre-establish, fix in advance.
prestabilito adj. pre-established, appointed.
prestanome m. figurehead.
prestante adj. personable.
prestanza f. personableness.
prestare vt. to lend: — aiuto, to give help; — attenzione, to pay attention; — fede, to believe, trust; — giuramento, to swear an oath; — servizio, to work (with, in, for); farsi —, to borrow; prestarsi vr. to lend oneself (itself); to volunteer; prestato adj. lent. [to help.
prestatore m. lender: — d'opera, worker.
prestazione f. service; (sport) performance.
prestidigitatore m. juggler.
presti'gio m. prestige; influence: giuoco di —, legerdemain.
pres'tito m. loan: dare a —, to lend; prendere a —, to borrow.
presto adj. quick, ready; adv. early, soon; quickly: far —, to make haste; è — detto, it is sooner said than done; — o tardi, sooner or later; al più —, as soon as possible; ben —, very soon.
pre'sule m. archbishop.
presu'mere vt., vi.[19] to presume, suppose.
presumi'bile adj. presumable.
presumibilmente adv. presumably.
presuntivo m. (comm.) budget; adj. presumptive.
presunto adj. presumptive; supposed, alleged. pp. of presumere.
presuntuoso adj. conceited.
presunzione f. presumption; conceit.
presupporre vt. to presuppose.
presupposto m. assumption.
prete m. priest; clergyman; (fam.) bedwarmer.
pretendente m. pretender, claimant; suitor.
preten'dere vt., vi.[140] to exact, demand; to charge; to claim; to pretend; to maintain; to ask; to be hard to please.
pretenzioso adj. pretentious.
preterintenzionale adj. unintentional.
prete'rito m. (the) past; m., adj. (gramm.) preterit.
pretesa f. pretension; claim; pretense.
preteso adj. claimed; alleged. pp. of pretendere.

pretesto *m.* pretext, excuse, pretense.

pretore *m.* judge.

prettamente *adv.* genuinely.

pretto *adj.* genuine, pure; undiluted.

pretura *f.* court of first instance.

prevalente *adj.* prevailing.

prevalenza *f.* predominance; supremacy.

prevalere *vi.*[110] to prevail (over, against), to win.

prevalso *pp.* of prevalere.

prevaricatore *m.* grafter, embezzler.

prevaricazione *f.* graft.

prevedere *vt.*[41] to foresee; to anticipate.

prevedi'bile *adj.* foreseeable.

prevenire *vt.* to forestall; to anticipate; to warn, forewarn; to prevent, avoid.

preventivare *vt.* to estimate; to appropriate.

preventivo *m.* estimate; tender; budget; *adj.* preventive.

prevenuto *m.* (law) defendant; *adj.* forewarned; prevented; biased, prejudiced.

prevenzione *f.* prevention; prejudice, [bias.

previdente *adj.* provident.

previdenza *f.* foresight: — sociale, social security; fondo di —, reserve fund.

pre'vio *adj.* previous: — accordo, subject to an agreement.

previsione *f.* prevision, anticipation; forecast; expectation.

previsto *adj.* expected: più del —, more than was expected. *pp.* of prevedere.

prevosto *m.* parson, vicar.

prezioso *adj.* precious; valuable: fare il —, to deny oneself.

prezze'molo *m.* parsley.

prezzo *m.* price; cost.

prezzolare *vt.* to hire.

prezzolato *adj.* hired, bribed.

prigione *f.* jail, prison.

prigioni'a *f.* imprisonment.

prigioniero *m.* prisoner, captive.

prillare *vi.* to whirl, spin.

prima (1) *prep.* before; rather (than). *adv.* before; earlier; beforehand; first; once, formerly: sulle prime, at first; quanto —, shortly, soon; non è più quello di —, he is no longer what he used to be.

prima (2) *f.* (rail.) first class; first grade (in a school); (theat.) opening, première; (auto.) first speed.

prima'rio *m.* chief physician; *adj.* primary; initial.

primatista *m.* champion, record holder.

primato *m.* supremacy; (sport) record, championship.

primavera *f.* spring, springtime.

primaverile *adj.* spring.

primeggiare *vi.* to excel.

primitivo *m.*, *adj.* primitive.

primi'zia *f.* first fruit; novelty; (journ.) advance copy, beat, "scoop."

primo *adj.* first, initial, early; next: minuto —, minute; materia prima, raw material; per prima cosa, first of all; sulle prime, at first; a tutta prima, at first blush; pron. (the) first (one); (the) former.

primoge'nito *m.*, *adj.* first-born; eldest.

primogenitura *f.* primogeniture.

primordiale *adj.* primeval.

primordi *m. pl.* beginning, origins.

pri'mula *f.* primrose.

principale *m.* employer, boss; *adj.* principal, main, chief: sede —, head office.

principalmente *adv.* chiefly.

principato *m.* principality.

prin'cipe *m.* prince.

principesco *adj.* princely.

principessa *f.* princess.

principiante *m.*, *f.* beginner.

principiare *see* cominciare.

princi'pio *m.* beginning, start; principle: in —, sul —, da —, at first; per —, on principle.

priorato *m.* priorate.

priore *m.* prior.

priorità *f.* priority.

prisma *m.* prism.

privare *vt.* to deprive; privarsi *vr.* to deprive oneself; privarsi di, to give up.

privatamente *adv.* privately.

privatista *m.* private-school student.

privativa *f.* monopoly; patent (right); sole (right); tobacco shop.

privato *m.* private citizen; *adj.* private; *pp.* of privare, deprived, bereft.

privazione *f.* privation; loss; deprivation.

privilegiare *vt.* to privilege; to grant.

privilegiato *m.* favorite; *adj.* privileged.

privile'gio *m.* privilege; advantage.

privo *adj.* destitute; lacking (in); wanting (in).

pro (1) *m.* advantage, avail; good; benefit; profit: a che —? what is the use?; il — e il contro, the pros and cons.

pro (2) *prep.* in favor of, for.

proba'bile *adj.* probable, likely.

probabilità *f.* probability, likelihood; chance.

probabilmente *adv.* probably.

probato'rio *adj.* probative, probatory.

problema *m.* problem.

probo *adj.* upright, honest.
probo'scide *f.* proboscis; trunk (*of an elephant*).
procac'cia *m.* rural postman.
procace *adj.* forward, bold; buxom.
proce'dere *vi.* to proceed; to go, move on; to behave; to derive, originate: non luogo a —, no cause of action; modo di —, conduct, behavior.
procedimento *m.* proceeding; proceedings; process.
procedura *f.* procedure.
procella *f.* storm, tempest.
processare *vt.* to try.
processione *f.* procession, parade.
processo *m.* process; trial; lawsuit.
processuale *adj.* trial.
procinto *m.*: essere in — di, to be about to.
proclama *m.* proclamation; manifesto.
proclamare *vt.* to proclaim.
proclamazione *f.* proclamation.
proclive *adj.* prone, liable.
procrastinare *vt.*, *vi.* to procrastinate.
procreare *vt.*, *vi.* to procreate, generate.
procura *f.* proxy; power of attorney; prosecutor's office: per —, by proxy.
procurare *vt.* to procure, get; to try to; to manage, see to it that; to cause; to give; procura che il lavoro sia fatto bene, see to it that the work is done well; procurarsi *vr.* to obtain, acquire, get, secure; to catch.
procuratore *m.* attorney.
proda *f.* bank; edge.
prode *m.*, *adj.* gallant.
prodezza *f.* feat, exploit; gallantry, daring.
prodigalità *f.* prodigality.
prodigare *vt.* to dispense, lavish; to bestow (*upon*); to give; prodigarsi *vr.* to try; to go out of one's way.
prodi'gio *m.* prodigy, wonder.
prodigioso *adj.* prodigious, miraculous; wonderful.
pro'digo *m.* spendthrift; *adj.* prodigal, extravagant.
prodito'rio *adj.* traitorous.
prodotto *m.* product; produce; result. *adj.* produced. *pp. of* produrre.
pro'dromo *m.* portent, symptom.
produrre *vt.* to produce; to yield, bear; to generate; to create; to engender, cause; to exhibit; prodursi *vr.* to happen; to form; to perform: prodursi una ferita, to wound oneself.
produttivo *adj.* productive; fruitful.
produttore *m.* producer; (*comm.*) canvasser.

produzione *f.* production, output; creation; (*comm.*) canvassing.
proe'mio *m.* proem, preface.
profanare *vt.* to profane, desecrate.
profanazione *f.* profanation.
profano *m.* layman; *adj.* lay, uninformed; profane, ignorant, not sacred.
proferire *vt.*[98] to utter.
proferto *pp. of* proferire.
professare *vt.* to profess; professarsi *vr.* to profess oneself.
professionale *adj.* professional; occupational.
professione *f.* profession; calling: attore di —, professional actor.
professionista *m.* professional.
professore *m.* professor.
profeta *m.* prophet.
profe'tico *adj.* prophetic.
profetizzare *vt.*, *vi.* to prophesy.
profezi'a *f.* prophecy.
profferire *vt.*[100] to offer.
profferta *f.* offer.
profferto *pp. of* profferire.
profi'cuo *adj.* profitable.
profilare *vt.* to delineate; to hem; profilarsi *vr.* to loom.
profilassi *f.* prophylaxis.
profilato *m.* (*metal.*) section iron.
profilo *m.* profile; outlook; angle.
profittare *vi.* to benefit (*by*).
profitte'vole *adj.* profitable.
profitto *m.* profit; profits, returns; benefit; advantage.
proflu'vio *m.* flow, overflow; plenty.
profondamente *adv.* deeply: dormire —, to sleep soundly.
profon'dere *vt.* to squander; to lavish (*on*); profon'dersi *vr.* to be profuse (*in*, *of*).
profondità *f.* depth, deep.
profondo *adj.* deep, profound: poco —, shallow.
pro'fugo *m.* refugee, displaced person; *adj.* fugitive.
profumare *vt.* to perfume, scent; profumarsi *vr.* to put on perfume.
profumatamente *adv.* handsomely; dearly.
profumato *adj.* sweet-smelling, scented.
profumeri'a *f.* perfumery. [ed.
profumo *m.* perfume, scent; fragrance: avere — di, to smell of.
profusione *f.* profusion: a —, profusely, in plenty.
proge'nie *f.* progeny, breed.
progenitore *m.* ancestor.
progettare *vt.* to plan.
progettista *m.* draftsman, planner, blueprinter.
progetto *m.* plan, project, schema; layout, blueprint: — di legge, bill (*proposed law*).

programma m. program; prospectus; plan; schedule: — politico, platform.

progredire vi. to advance, progress; to improve.

progredito see evoluto.

progressione f. progression.

progressista m., adj. progressive.

progressivo adj. progressive.

progresso m. progress; improvement; development.

proibire vt. to forbid, prohibit.

proibitivo adj. prohibitive.

proibito adj. forbidden: — fumare, no smoking; — l'ingresso, no admittance.

proibizione f. prohibition.

proiettare vt., vi. to project; to cast; to show; proiettarsi vr. to be projected; to fall.

proiet'tile m. missile; bullet, slug.

proiettore m. searchlight; projector.

proiezione f. projection; moving picture show.

prole f. offspring, issue.

proletariato m. proletariat.

proleta'rio m., adj. proletarian.

proli'fico adj. prolific.

prolisso adj. prolix, long-winded.

pro'logo m. prologue.

prolungamento m. prolongation, extension; lengthening.

prolungare vt. to prolong, lengthen; to postpone; prolungarsi vr. to extend, continue; to speak at length.

promemoria m. memorandum.

promessa f. promise.

promesso adj. promised: i promessi sposi, the betrothed. pp. of promettere.

promettente adj. promising.

promet'tere vt.¹⁸ to promise.

prominente adj. prominent.

promi'scuo adj. promiscuous: scuola promiscua, coeducational school.

promonto'rio m. promontory.

promotore m. promoter; adj. promotive, supporting.

promozione f. promotion.

promulgare vt. to promulgate.

promulgazione f. promulgation.

promuo'vere vt. to promote; to further; to organize.

pronipote m., f. great-grandchild; grandnephew (m.), grandniece (f.).

prono adj. prone, prostrate.

pronome m. pronoun.

pronosticare vt. to prognosticate; to forebode; to predict.

prono'stico m. forecast; prediction; omen: formulare un —, to make a prediction.

prontamente adv. promptly, readily.

prontezza f. promptness, readiness; quickness.

pronti, (a) adv. (comm.) cash.

pronto adj. ready, prompt, quick; interj. pronto! (teleph.), hello!; a pronta cassa, cash.

prontua'rio m. handbook: — dei conti fatti, (ready) reckoner.

pronun'cia, pronun'zia f. pronunciation, accent, speech.

pronunziare vt. to pronounce; to utter; to deliver; pronunziarsi vr. to pronounce, pass judgment.

pronunziato adj. pronounced.

propaganda f. propaganda; advertising; canvassing.

propagandista m. propagandist; canvasser.

propagare vt., propagarsi vr. to propagate, spread.

propag'gine f. ramification.

propalare vt. to spread, divulge.

propen'dere vi. to incline (to), be inclined (to); to tend (to).

propensione f. inclination, bent.

propenso adj. inclined, prone.

propinare vt. to administer (to); to palm off (on).

propin'quo adj. near, related.

propiziare vt., propiziarsi vr. to propitiate,

propi'zio adj. propitious; favorable.

proponente m., adj. proponent.

proponi'bile adj. proposable.

proponimento m. plan; resolution.

proporre vt.⁴⁵ to propose; to suggest; to propound; proporsi vr. to intend, mean; to resolve.

proporzionare vt. to proportion.

proporzione f. proportion; ratio; dimension, size.

propo'sito m. purpose, design; resolution; plan; object; subject: in —, on the subject; a —, by the way; opportunely; a — di, in regard to, about: di —, deliberately; fuor di —, out of place, out of turn; rispondere a —, to answer to the point.

proposizione f. clause; sentence.

proposta f. proposal; offer.

proposto pp. of proporre.

propriamente adv. exactly: — detto, proper.

proprietà f. property; possession; ownership; peculiarity; propriety: — letteraria, copyright; — immobiliare, real estate.

proprieta'rio m. owner; proprietor; man of property; landowner; landlord.

pro'prio m. one's own (property, etc.): lavorare in —, to be on one's own; adj. own, one's own; his; her; very;

of one's own; proper, appropriate, suitable; peculiar: vero e —, regular; adv. just, exactly; really: — bello, really fine; proprio? really?; — io (lui, noi), I myself (he himself, we ourselves).

propugnare vt. to advocate.

propugnatore m. advocate.

propulsione f. propulsion.

propulsore m. propeller; adj. propelling.

prora f. prow, bow.

pro'roga f. delay, respite; (comm.) extension.

prorogare vt. to put off, postpone; to extend.

prorom'pere vi. to burst (out); to break forth: — in lagrime, to burst into tears; — in una risata, to burst out laughing.

prosa f. prose; (theat.) drama; compagnia (stagione) di —, theatrical company (season).

prosa'ico adj. prosaic.

prosce'nio m. proscenium: palco di —, stage box.

proscio'gliere vt. to acquit (of); to clear (from, of).

prosciugare vt. to dry; to drain; prosciugarsi vr. to dry (up.)

prosciutto m. ham.

proscritto m. exile; adj. banished, exiled.

proscrivere vt. to proscribe, banish.

prosecuzione f., **proseguimento** m. continuation.

proseguire vt., vi. to go on, continue.

prose'lito m. proselyte.

prosopopea f. self-importance.

prosperare vi. to prosper, thrive.

prosperità f. prosperity.

pro'spero adj. prosperous.

prosperoso adj. prosperous; healthy.

prospettare vt. to expound; to outline.

prospettiva f. perspective; prospect; view.

prospetto m. prospect; front view; table; diagram.

prossimamente adv. shortly, soon.

prossimità f. proximity, nearness.

pros'simo m. neighbor; fellow creatures. adj. next; near (at hand); coming: passato (trapassato) —, present (past) perfect.

prostituire vt. to prostitute; prostituirsi vr. to prostitute oneself.

prostituta f. prostitute.

prostituzione f. prostitution.

prostrare vt. to prostrate.

prostrazione f. prostration.

protagonista m. protagonist; hero (m.), heroine (f.): la parte del (della) —, the leading role.

proteg'gere vt.[101] to protect; to shelter; to preserve; to defend, guard.

proteina f. (chem.) protein.

proten'dere vt., **proten'dersi** vr. to stretch out; to lean (out).

proteso adj. outstretched.

protesta f. complaint; protestation.

protestare vt., vi. to protest; to complain; to assert, aver.

protesto m. protest; notice of dishonor.

protettivo adj. protective.

protetto m. favorite, protégé; adj. protected. pp. of proteggere.

protettorato m. protectorate.

protettore m. protector; patron.

protezione f. protection.

protezionismo m. protectionism.

protezionista m. protectionist.

proto m. foreman; printer.

protocollo m. protocol.

protoplasma m. protoplasm.

proto'tipo m. prototype; personification.

protrarre vt.[146] to protract; to delay; to defer, postpone.

protratto pp. of protrarre.

protuberante adj. protuberant, bulging.

protuberanza f. protuberance, bulge.

prova f. proof; evidence; attempt; trial, test; fitting; essay; examination; ordeal; token; (theat., mus.) rehearsal: — generale, dress rehearsal; periodo di —, tryout; in —, on trial; sapere per —, to know by experience; a — di bomba, bombproof.

provare vt. to try; to test; to attempt; to experience; to taste; to feel; to prove; to show; to try on; (theat., mus.) to rehearse; provarsi vr. to try, attempt; to endeavor; to dare; to try on (as a garment).

provato adj. tried.

proveniente adj. coming (from).

provenienza f. provenience, origin, source.

provenire vi. to come (from); to derive (from).

provento m. proceeds, profit; income.

proverbiale adj. proverbial: essere —, to be a byword.

prover'bio m. proverb.

provetta f. test tube.

provetto adj. masterly.

provin'cia f. province.

provinciale m., adj. provincial.

provino m. (chem.) test tube; (moving pictures) screen test.

provocante adj. provoking; enticing.

provocare vt. to provoke; to excite; to cause, arouse; to entice.

provocatore m. provoker; adj. provoking: **agente** —, agent provocateur.
provocato'rio adj. provocative.
provocazione f. provocation; defiance.
provvedere vt.[151] to provide (with), supply (with); to store up; vi. to provide (for); to attend (to); **provvedersi** vr. to provide onself (with).
provvedimento m. provision; measure, step.
provvidenza f. providence; windfall.
provvidenziale adj. providential.
prov'vido adj. provident.
provvigione f. provision; (comm.) commission.
provviso'rio adj. temporary, provisional.
provvista f. provision; supply.
provvisto pp. of **provvedere**.
prozi'a f. great-aunt.
prozi'o m. great-uncle.
prua f. prow, bow.
prudente adj. prudent; cautious; wise; advisable.
prudenza f. prudence, caution.
pru'dere vi. to itch.
prugna f. plum.
prugno m. plum tree.
pruno m. thorn, bramble.
prurito m. itch, itching.
pseudo'nimo m. pseudonym; pen name.
psicana'lisi f. psychoanalysis.
psicanalista m. psychoanalyst.
psichiatra m. psychiatrist.
psichiatri'a f. psychiatry.
psicologi'a f. psychology.
psicolo'gico adj. psychologic.
psico'logo m. psychologist.
psicopa'tico adj. psychopathic.
psicosi f. psychosis, scare: — **di guerra**, war scare.
pubblicamente adv. publicly.
pubblicare vt. to publish, issue; to spread.
pubblicazione f. publication: **pubblicazioni matrimoniali**, marriage banns.
pubblicista m. free lance.
pubblicità f. publicity; advertising; advertisement.
pubblicita'rio adj. advertising: **annuncio** —, advertisement, ad.
pub'blico m. public; audience; adj. public: **forza pubblica**, police; **debito** —, national debt.
Puccini, Giacomo, Italian composer, *La Bohème, Tosca, Madame Butterfly* (1858–1924).
pudici'zia f. modesty; bashfulness.
pudico adj. modest; bashful.
pudore m. decency, modesty; restraint; shame.
puerile adj. childish.

puerilità f. childishness.
pugilato m. boxing.
pugilatore, **pu'gile** m. boxer, prizefighter.
pu'glia f. counter; stake.
pugnace adj. pugnacious.
pugnalare vt. to stab.
pugnalata f. stab.
pugnale m. dagger.
pugno m. fist; punch, blow; fistful: **di proprio** —, with one's own hand; **fare a pugni**, to fight; to clash; **avere in** —, to have in one's grasp.
pula f. chaff.
pulce f. flea.
Pulci, Luigi, Italian poet (1432–1484).
pulcino m. chick.
puledra f. filly.
puledro m. colt, foal.
puleg'gia f. (mach.) pulley.
pulire vt. to clean, cleanse; to wipe; to polish: — **a secco**, to dry-clean; **pulirsi** vr. to clean oneself.
pulito adj. clean; cleaned: **farla pulita**, to go scot-free; — **a secco**, dry-cleaned.
pulitura f. cleaning.
pulizi'a f. cleanliness; cleaning.
pullulare vi. to swarm; (bot.) to pullulate; to spring.
pul'pito m. pulpit.
pulsante m. (push) button.
pulsare vi. to pulsate, beat; to throb.
pulvi'scolo m. haze.
pulzella f. maid.
puma m. cougar.
pungente adj. pungent, stinging; sharp.
pun'gere vt.[79] to prick, sting.
pungiglione m. sting.
pungolare vt. to goad, prod, spur.
pun'golo m. goad; prod; spur.
punire vt. to punish.
punizione f. punishment; penalty.
punta f. point; top, summit, peak; end, tip; bit, tinge; top chuck (of veal, etc.): **cane da** —, pointer; **a** —, pointed; **in** — **di piedi**, on tiptoe; **sulla** — **delle dita**, at one's fingertips; **fare la** — **a**, to sharpen.
puntale m. ferrule.
puntare vt. to point; to direct; to aim (at); to level (at), train (on); to wager, stake: — **i piedi**, to make a stand; vi. to make (for); to push (toward); to wager.
puntata f. thrust; part, installment; stake: **pubblicare a puntate**, to serialize.
punteggiare vt., vi. to dot; (gramm.) to punctuate.
punteggiatura f. dotting; (gramm.) punctuation.
punteggio m. score.

puntellare *vt.* to prop.

puntello *m.* prop.

punteruolo *m.* punch; awl.

puntiglio *m.* punctilio; pique; obstinacy.

puntiglioso *adj.* punctilious; stubborn.

puntina *f.* tackle: — da disegno, thumbtack; — per grammofono, phonograph needle.

puntino *m.* dot: a —, properly, nicely.

punto (*1*) *m.* point; period; dot; stitch; place, spot; stage; detail: — fermo, full stop; due punti, colon: — e virgola, semicolon; — esclamativo (interrogativo), exclamation (question) mark; di tutto —, completely; di — in bianco, suddenly; riportare buoni punti, to get good marks; dare dei punti a uno, to outdo one; far —, to stop; fare il — (*naut.*), to shoot the sun; fare il — di, to sum up; vincere ai punti, to win by a decision.

punto (*2*) *adj.* at all: non ho — voglia di, I have no wish at all to; *adv.* by no means, not at all.

punto (*3*) *pp.* of pungere.

puntuale *adj.* punctual.

puntualità *f.* punctuality.

puntura *f.* puncture, prick; sting; stitch; injection.

puntuto *adj.* pointed.

punzecchiare *vt.* to prick; to goad; to tease.

punzecchiatura *f.* sting; bite; jest.

punzonare *vt.* to punch.

punzonatrice *f.* punch press.

punzone *m.* punch.

pupat'tola *f.* doll.

pupazzo *m.* puppet.

pupilla *f.* pupil (*of the eye*).

pupillo *m.*, pupilla *f.* ward; pupil.

puramente *adv.* purely; merely.

purchè *conj.* provided (*that*).

purchessi'a *adv.* any, any ... whatever.

pure *adv.*, *conj.* also, too; even; yet, still; only; likewise, as well (as); by all means: pur di vederti, just to see you; fate pure!, dite pure! go ahead!

purè *m.* purée.

purezza *f.* pureness, purity.

purga *f.*, purgante *m.* purge.

purgare *vt.* to purge; to expurgate; purgarsi *vr.* to purge oneself.

purgato'rio *m.* purgatory.

purificare *vt.* to purify, cleanse.

purità *m.* purity, pureness.

puritano *m.*, *adj.* Puritan.

puro *adj.* pure; clear, clean; mere, sheer; chaste, innocent.

purosangue *m.* thoroughbred.

purpu'reo *adj.* purple (red).

purtroppo *adv.* unfortunately.

purulento *adj.* purulent.

pus *m.* pus, purulent matter.

pusilla'nime *m.* coward; *adj.* cowardly.

pu'stola *f.* pustule, pimple.

putativo *adj.* putative.

putife'rio *m.* hullabaloo: scoppierà un —, there will be the devil to pay; costare un —, to be expensive *or* "sky high."

putrefare *vi.*, putrefarsi *vr.* to putrefy, rot.

putrefazione *f.* putrefaction.

putrella *f.* I-girder, I-beam.

pu'trido *adj.* putrid, rotten.

puzza *see* puzzo.

puzzare *vi.* to stink; to smell (*of*).

puzzo *m.* stink, stench, smell.

puz'zola *f.* (*zool.*) skunk.

puzzolente *adj.* stinking.

puzzone *m.* (*it. slang*) "skunk."

puzzonata *f.* (*it. slang*) trash; underhand trick, bad joke.

Q

qua *adv.* here: di — e di là, on both sides; per di —, this way; ecco qua! here!; da due giorni in —, for the past two days; da quando in —? since when?

quaderno *m.* copybook; booklet.

quadra *f.* (*naut.*) square sail.

quadragena'rio *m.*, *adj.* quadragenarian.

quadrage'simo *adj.* fortieth.

quadran'golo *m.* quadrangle.

quadrante *m.* quadrant; face (*of a watch*).

quadrare *vt.*, *vi.* to square (*with*); to satisfy, please.

quadrato *m.* square; (*naut.*) wardroom; (*boxing*) ring: elevare al — (*math.*), to square; *adj.* square; solid, strong-minded.

quadratura *f.* squaring; quadrature.

quadrello *m.* square tile.

quadreri'a *f.* picture gallery.

quadrettato *adj.* checkered.

quadretto *m.* small picture; checker.

quadricromi'a *f.* process printing; color type.

quadrifo'glio *m.* four-leaf clover.

quadrimestre *m.* four months.

quadrimotore *m.* four-engine plane.

quadri'vio *m.* quadrivium; crossroads.

quadro *m.* painting, picture; sight, view; square; table; (*mil.*) cadre, list; (*mach.*) board; (*theat.*) scene; (*moving pictures*) frame: — plastico, tableau vivant; — murale, bulletin board; *adj.* square; quadri *m. pl.* diamonds (*in playing cards*).

quadruplicare *vt.*, **quadruplicarsi** *vr.* to quadruple.

qua'druplo *m.*, *adj.* quadruple.

quaggiù *adv.* down here.

qua'glia *f.* quail.

quagliare *vi.* to curdle.

qualche *adj.* some, any; a few.

qualcheduno *see* qualcuno.

qualcosa *f.* something, anything.

qualcuno, qualcuna *pron.* someone, somebody, some, anyone, anybody any.

quale *adj.* which, what; as, same; just as; il quale, i quali (*pl.*) *rel. pron.* who, whom; which; del quale, dei quali, whose; of whom; of which; al quale, ai quali, to whom: il quadro al quale sto lavorando, the picture I am working at.

quale?, quali? *interr.pron.* what ?; which ?, which one ?

quali'fica *f.* qualification; grade, mark, score (*in a game*).

qualificare *vt.* to qualify.

qualità *f.* quality; gift, good point; kind, sort: di prima —, first-rate.

qualora *adv.* in case, if; provided.

qualsiasi, qualunque *indef.adj.* any, whatever; ordinary, indifferent: qualsiasi cosa, whatever.

quando *conj.* when; while; if; whenever: da —, (ever) since; da —? since when ?; di — in —, from time to time, now and then.

quantità *f.* quantity.

quantitativo *m.* quantity; *adj.* quantitative.

quanto *adj.*, *pron.*, *adv.* how; how much; as, what; all (*that*); quanti, *pl.* how many; as many: tanto —, as much as; tanti quanti, as many as; tutti quanti, all of them; (all) those who, whom, which; — tempo, how long; quanta distanza, how far; quante volte? how often ?; — a, as to; — prima, very soon; per — possibile, as far as possible; — più posso, as much as I can; — più . . . tanto più, the more . . . the more; — meno . . . tanto meno, the less . . . the less; per — egli facesse, try as he might.

quantunque *conj.* though, although.

quaranta *m.*, *adj.* forty.

quarantena *f.* quarantine.

quarantenne *m.*, *adj.* quadragenarian; *adj.* forty years old.

quarantesimo *m.*, *adj.* fortieth.

quarantina *f.* some forty: esser sulla —, to be about forty.

quarantotto *m.*, *adj.* forty-eight; (*fig.*) mess.

quare'sima *f.* Lent.

quartetto *m.* quartet.

quartiere *m.* quarter; district; flat, apartment; barracks: lotta senza —, war to the knife.

quarto *m.* fourth; quarter: le tre meno un —, a quarter to three; le tre e un —, a quarter past three; le tre e tre quarti, a quarter to four; *adj.* fourth.

quarzo *m.* quartz.

quasi *adv.* almost, nearly; about; as if; close to: — —, almost; — parto, I have half a mind to leave; — direi —, I dare say.

Quasimodo, Salvatore, Italian poet (1901-   ).

quassù *adv.* up here.

quatto *adj.* cowering, crouching: — —, quietly; stealthily.

quattordicenne *adj.* fourteen years old.

quattordice'simo *m.*, *adj.* fourteenth.

quattor'dici *m.*, *adj.* fourteen.

quattrino *m.* farthing; quattrini *pl.* money, "dough": non aver il becco d'un —, to be penniless.

quattro *m.*, *adj.* four: fare — passi, to take a stroll; fare — salti, to do some dancing; dirne — a uno, to give one a piece of one's mind; farsi in —, to spare no effort; in — e quattr'otto, in the twinkling of an eye; a quattr'occhi, in private.

quattrocento *num.adj.* four hundred: il —, the fifteenth century.

quattromila *adj.* four thousand.

quegli *pron.m.sing.* that man.

quegli, quei *pron.*, *adj.m.pl.* those, *see* quel.

quel, quello *adj.m.*, quella *adj.f.* that; *pron.m.*, *f.* that one; the former; quelli *pron.*, *adj.m.pl.*, quelle *pron.*, *adj.f.pl.* those; the ones: — che, the one (ones) who; the one (ones) whom, the one (ones) that; what; è per quello che, that is why; non è più quello, he is not the same any more.

quer'cia *f.* oak: di —, oak, oaken.

querela *f.* complaint.

querelante *m.* plaintiff.

querelare *vt.* to sue.

que'rulo *adj.* querulous.

quesito *m.* problem, question; quiz.

questi *see* questo.

questionare *vi.* to quarrel.

questiona'rio *m.* questionnaire; form.

questione f. question, matter; problem; quarrel.

questo adj.m., **questa** adj.f. this; pron.m., f. this one; the latter; **questi** pron.m.sing. this, this fellow; he; pron.m.pl. these; these people; **questi** adj.m.pl., **queste** adj.f.pl. these: è per questo che, that is why; e con questo? so what?; quest'ultima (ultimo), the latter.

questore m. superintendent of police.

que'stua f. alms collection.

questura f. police headquarters.

questurino m. plain-clothes man, "flatfoot," "cop."

queto see quieto.

qui adv. here: — vicino, close by, hereabout; di —, this way; hence; from here; fin —, so far; di — a tre anni, in three years.

quiescenza f. quiescence; superannuation.

quietanza f. receipt.

quietanzare vt. to give a receipt.

quietare vt. to quiet; quietarsi vr. to quiet down.

quiete f. quiet, stillness.

quieto adj. quiet, still, peaceful.

quindi adv. therefore; then; hence.

quindicenne adj. fifteen years old.

quindice'simo m., adj. fifteenth.

quin'dici m., adj. fifteen: — giorni, a fortnight.

quindicina f. some fifteen; fortnight; semimonthly pay.

quindicinale m., adj. fortnightly.

quinquennale adj. quinquennial: piano —, five-year plan.

quinta f. (theat.) wing, tormentor; (mus.) quint; (fencing) quinte; (educ.) fifth grade: dietro le quinte, behind the scenes.

quintale m. quintal.

quinterno m. quinternion.

quintessenza f. quintessence.

quinto m., adj. fifth.

Quirinale m. Quirinal.

quirquilia f. trifle.

quitanza see quietanza.

quivi adv. there; here.

quota f. share; quota; installment; elevation; (aeron.) height: prender —, to climb; volare ad alta (bassa) —, to fly high (low).

quotare vt. to quote; quotarsi vr. to subscribe.

quotato adj. (exch.) quoted; valued, esteemed.

quotazione f. quotation.

quotidiano m. daily (paper); adj. daily.

quoto, quoziente m. quotient.

R

rabar'baro m. rhubarb.

rabberciare vt. to patch (up).

rab'bia f. rabies; anger: far —, to make angry.

rabbino m. rabbi.

rabbioso adj. rabid, mad; angry.

rabbonire vt. to pacify; rabbonirsi vr. to quiet down.

rabbrividire vi. to shudder.

rabbuffo m. rebuke.

rabbuiarsi vr. to cloud, darken.

rabdomante m. diviner.

rabdomanzi'a f. divination.

raccapezzare vt. to gather; raccapezzarsi vr. to find one's bearings.

raccapricciante adj. horrific, blood-curdling, lurid.

raccapric'cio m. horror.

raccattare vt. to pick up.

racchetta f. racket (as in tennis): — da neve, snowshoe.

rac'chio adj. (It. slang) ugly, ratty; poor, atrocious, crummy: piuttosto —, no great shakes.

racchiona f. (It. slang) clock-stopper, "bust."

racchiu'dere vt. to contain.

racco'gliere vt." to gather (up); to collect; to assemble; to pick up;

to reap: — la sfida, to take up the gauntlet; racco'gliersi vr. to gather, assemble; to concentrate.

raccoglimento m. concentration, meditation.

raccoglitore m. collector; folder.

raccolta f. gathering; collection; harvest; chiamare a —, to rally.

raccolto m. crop, harvest; adj. gathered, collected; engrossed. pp. of racco'gliere.

raccomanda'bile adj. recommendable: poco —, shady.

raccomandare vt. to recommend; raccomandarsi vr. to recommend oneself; to entreat.

raccomandata f. registered letter.

raccomandato m. protégé; adj. recommended; registered.

raccomandazione f. recommendation; entreaty; registration; connection, "in."

raccontare vt. to tell; to relate.

racconto m. story; tale; narration; report, recital.

raccorciare see accorciare.

raccordare vt. to connect, joint.

raccordo m. link, connection; (rail.) siding.

rachi'tico *adj.* rachitic, rickety.
racimolare *vt.* to glean, gather; to scrape together.
rada *f.* roadstead.
radar *m.* radar.
radazza *f.* (*naut.*) swab.
raddobbare *vt.* (*naut.*) to repair.
raddolcire *vt.*, **raddolcirsi** *vr.* to sweeten; to soften, mollify.
raddoppiare *vt.*, **raddoppiarsi** *vr.* to double, redouble.
raddrizzare *vt.* to straighten; **raddrizzarsi** *vr.* to straighten (*up*).
radente *adj.* grazing.
ra'dere *vt.*[103] to graze, shave: — al suolo, to level with the ground; **radersi** *vr.*, to shave.
radiare *vt.* to expel; to disbar.
radiatore *m.* radiator.
radiazione *f.* radiation; expulsion.
ra'dica *f.* brierwood. brier.
radicale *m.*, *f.*, *adj.* radical.
radicalmente *adv.* radically.
radicare *vt.*, **radicarsi** *vr.* to root.
radice *f.* root.
ra'dio *f.* radius; radium; radio, wireless: **stazione** —, broadcasting station; **giornale** —, news broadcast.
radioamatore *m.* radio amateur, "ham."
radioascoltatore, **radioauditore** *m.* radio listener.
radioattivo *adj.* radioactive.
radiocomandato *adj.* remote-controlled.
radiocomando *m.* remote control.
radiodiffondere *vt.* to broadcast.
radiodiffusione *f.* broadcasting.
radiofaro *m.* radio beacon.
radiofoni'a *f.* radiophony.
radiofo'nico *adj.* wireless: **trasmissione radiofonica**, broadcast, radio program.
radiografi'a *f.* radiography.
radiologi'a *f.* radiology.
radio'logo *m.* radiologist.
radioonda *f.* radio wave.
radioscopi'a *f.* radioscopy.
radioso *adj.* radiant.
radiotelecomando *m.* remote control.
radiotelefoni'a *f.* radiotelephony, radio.
radiotelefo'fono *m.* radiotelephone: — portatile, walkie-talkie.
radiotelegrafi'a *f.* radiotelegraphy, wireless.
radiotelegra'fico *adj.* wireless.
radiotelegrafista *m.* wireless operator.
radiotelegramma *m.* radiotelegram.
radioterapi'a *f.* radiotherapy.
radiotrasmissione *f.* broadcast.
radiotrasmittente *f.* broadcasting station; *adj.* broadcasting.

rado *adj.* rare; scattered; thin; sparse: **di** —, rarely, seldom; **non di** —, often, frequently.
radunare *vt.*, **radunarsi** *vr.* to assemble, gather, collect; to rally.
raduno *m.* meeting, gathering, rally.
radura *f.* glade.
Raffaello Sanzio, Italian painter, sculptor and architect; one of the greatest of artists, his works, numerous and varied, included frescoes, cartoons, madonnas, portraits, easel pictures, drawings, besides sculpture and architectural designs (1483-1520).
raffazzonare *vt.* to botch; to patch up.
rafferma *f.* (*mil.*) re-enlistment.
raffermo *adj.* stale.
raf'fica *f.* squall; gust; volley.
raffigurare *vt.* to recognize; to represent.
raffinare *vt.* to refine.
raffinatezza *f.* refinement.
raffineri'a *f.* refinery.
raf'fio *m.* hook.
rafforzare *vt.* to strengthen.
raffreddamento *m.* cooling.
raffreddare *vt.* to cool; **raffreddarsi** *vr.* to grow cold; to catch a cold.
raffreddore *m.* cold.
raffrontare *vt.* to compare.
raffronto *m.* comparison.
raganella *f.* tree-frog; rattle.
ragazza *f.* girl; maid.
ragazzata *f.* escapade.
ragazzo *m.* boy; lad.
raggiante *adj.* radiant; beaming.
raggiera *f.* halo of rays; corona.
rag'gio *m.* ray; beam; (*geom.*) radius; spoke (*of a wheel*): — d'azione, range; — di sole, sunbeam.
raggirare *vt.* to swindle, cheat.
raggiro *m.* trick.
raggiun'gere *vt.*[79] to overtake; to reach; to attain; to rejoin; to strike.
raggiunto *pp. of.* **raggiungere**.
raggomitolare *vt.* to coil, roll up; **raggomitolarsi** *vr.* to coil up; to roll oneself up, curl up.
raggranellare *vt.* to collect, scrape together.
raggrinzare, **raggrinzire** *vt.*, *vi.*, **raggrinzarsi**, **raggrinzirsi** *vr.* to wrinkle.
raggrumare *vt.*, **raggrumarsi** *vr.* to clot.
raggruppamento *m.* grouping.
raggruppare *vt.* to collect, group; **raggrupparsi** *vr.* to rally.
ragguagliare *vt.* to compare; to inform.
raggua'glio *m.* comparison; information; report.
ragguarde'vole *adj.* considerable.
ragionamento *m.* reasoning.

ragionare *vi.* to reason; to discuss; to talk (*over*).

ragionato *adj.* logical.

ragione *f.* reason; right; ratio; motive: — sociale, style; — per cui, therefore; aver —, to be right; aver — di qualcuno, to get the better of somebody; dar — a qualcuno, to admit that somebody is right; to side with somebody; farsi una —, to resign oneself; rendersi — di, to satisfy oneself about; render di pubblica —, to make known.

ragioneri'a *f.* accountancy.

ragione'vole *adj.* reasonable; sensible.

ragioniere *m.* certified public accountant; bookkeeper.

ragliare *vi.* to bray.

ragliata *f.*, **ra'glio** *m.* bray.

ragnatela *f.* spiderweb, web.

ragno *m.* spider.

rallegramento *m.* congratulation.

rallegrare *vt.* to cheer, gladden; **rallegrarsi** *vr.* to cheer up; to congratulate.

rallentare *vt.*, *vi.* to slacken; to loosen; to lessen; to slow down.

rallentatore *m.* (*moving pictures*) slow motion.

ramanzina *f.* reprimand, lecture.

ramare *vt.* to coat with copper.

ramarro *m.* green lizard.

ramazza *f.* broom.

rame *m.* copper.

ramerino *m.* (*bot.*) rosemary.

ramificare *vi.*, **ramificarsi** *vr.* to branch off; to branch out.

ramificazione *f.* branching.

ramingo *adj.* wandering, roving.

rammaricarsi *vr.* to regret, be sorry; to complain.

ramma'rico *m.* regret, sorrow.

rammendare *vt.* to darn.

rammendatrice *f.* darner.

rammendo *m.* darn, darning.

rammentare *vt.* to remind; to remember; **rammentarsi** *vr.* to remember; to recall.

rammodernare *vt.* to modernize; to refashion.

rammollimento *m.* softening.

rammollire *vt.*, **rammollirsi** *vr.* to soften.

rammollito *m.* softy, weakling.

ramo *m.* branch; trade: un — di pazzia, a streak of madness.

ramoscello *m.* twig.

rampa *f.* ramp; flight (*of stairs*).

rampicante *m.* creeper; *adj.* creeping.

rampino *m.* hook; prong; quibble.

rampogna *f.* reprimand.

rampollo *m.* scion; child.

rampone *m.* harpoon, grapple.

rana *f.* frog.

ran'cido *m.* rankness; *adj.* rancid, rank.

ran'cio *m.* (*mil.*) mess.

rancore *m.* rancor, grudge.

randa *f.* (*naut.*) gaff.

randa'gio *adj.* wandering; stray.

randello *m.* cudgel.

ranella *f.* (*mach.*) washer.

rango *m.* rank, standing.

rannicchiarsi *vr.* to crouch.

ranno *m.* lye.

rannuvolarsi *vr.* to cloud, darken.

ranoc'chio *m.*, **ranoc'chia** *f.* frog.

rantolare *vi.* to sound the death rattle; to rattle; to groan.

ran'tolo *m.* death rattle; groan.

rapa *f.* (*bot.*) turnip.

rapace *m.* bird of prey; *adj.* rapacious, greedy.

rapacità *f.* rapacity, greed.

rapare *vt.* to shave (*one's*) hair.

rapato *adj.* shaven-headed.

rapè *m.* rappee.

ra'pida *f.* rapid.

rapidamente *adv.* swiftly.

rapidità *f.* swiftness.

ra'pido *m.* express (*train*); *adj.* rapid, swift.

rapimento *m.* rapture; abduction, kidnapping.

rapina *f.* robbery, plunder: uccello di —, bird of prey; — a mano armata, armed robbery, holdup.

rapinare *vt.*, *vi.* to plunder, rob.

rapinatore *m.* robber; holdup man.

rapire *vt.* to take away; to abduct, kidnap; to enrapture.

rapitore *m.* kidnapper.

rappacificare *vt.* to reconcile; **rappacificarsi** *vr.* to make up, become reconciled.

rappezzare *vt.* to patch (*up*).

rappezzo *m.* patch.

rapporto *m.* report; statement; relation, connection; intercourse; proportion; (*math.*, *mach.*) ratio: chiamare a —, to summon; andare a —, to report (*to*); mettersi a —, to ask for a hearing; in rapporti d'amicizia, on friendly terms.

rappren'dere, **rappren'dersi** *vr.* to coagulate; to curdle.

rappresa'glia *f.* retaliation.

rappresentante *m.* representative; agent; delegate.

rappresentanza *f.* agency; delegation.

rappresentare *vt.* to represent; to play, act, perform; to exhibit.

rappresentativo *adj.* representative.

rappresentazione *f.* representation; performance; exhibition; description.

rappreso *pp.* of **rapprendere**.

rapsodi'a *f.* rhapsody.

raramente *adv.* seldom.

rarefare *vt.*, rarefarsi *vr.* to rarefy.

rarefatto *adj.* rarefied.

rarità *f.* rarity; curio.

raro *adj.* rare; unusual: **rare volte**, seldom, rarely.

rasare *vt.* to smooth; to shave; to mow; **rasarsi** *vr.* to shave (*oneself*).

raschiare *vt.* to scrape; to erase; to scratch.

raschietto *m.* eraser.

ra'schio *m.* irritation; scratching.

rasentare *vt.* to graze; to brush, scrape; to border upon: — **il codice**, to sail close to the wind.

rasente *prep.* close to.

raso (*1*) *m.* satin.

raso (*2*) *adj.* shaven; short; even, level; brimful: **fare tabula rasa**, to make a clean sweep (*of*). *pp. of* radere.

raso'io *m.* razor; safety razor.

raspa *f.* rasp; scraper; (*It. slang*) a popular dance.

raspare *vt.* to rasp; to pinch; to scratch about.

rassegna *f.* review.

rassegnare *vt.* to resign: — **le dimissioni**, to resign; **rassegnarsi** *vr.* to resign oneself; to submit; to surrender.

rassegnazione *f.* resignation, patience.

rasserenare *vt.*, **rasserenarsi** *vr.* to clear up, brighten (*up*).

rassettare *vt.* to tidy up.

rassicurare *vt.* to reassure.

rassodare *vt.*, **rassodarsi** *vr.* to harden.

rassomigliare *see* assomigliare.

rastrellamento *m.* roundup.

rastrellare *vt.* to rake; to round up; to dredge.

rastrelliera *f.* rack, crib.

rastrello *m.* rake.

rastremare *vt.* to taper.

rata *f.* installment.

rateale *adj.*, **ratealmente** *adv.* by installments.

rati'fica *f.* ratification.

ratificare *vt.* to ratify.

ratto (*1*) *m.* abduction, kidnapping.

ratto (*2*) *m.* rat.

ratto (*3*) *adj.* quick; *adv.* quickly.

rattoppare *see* rappezzare.

rattrappire *vt.*, *vi.*, **rattrappirsi** *vr.* to contract, shrink.

rattristante *adj.* saddening.

rattristare *vt.*, **rattristarsi** *vr.* to sadden.

rauce'dine *f.* hoarseness.

rauco *m.* hoarse.

ravanello *m.* radish.

ravizzone *m.* rape.

ravvedersi *vr.*[141] to repent; to reform.

ravveduto *adj.* penitent, reformed. *pp. of* ravvedersi.

ravviare *vt.*, **ravviarsi** *vr.* to tidy up: — **i capelli**, to comb (*one's*) hair.

ravvicinamento *m.* reapproachment; reconciliation.

ravvicinare *vt.* to reapproach; to reconcile; **ravvicinarsi** *vr.* to become reconciled.

ravvisare *vt.* to recognize.

ravvivare *vt.* to revivify, reanimate; to enliven; to stir (*up*); **ravvivarsi** *vr.* to revive, brighten up.

ravvol'gere *see* avvolgere.

ra'yon *m.* rayon.

razioci'nio *m.* ratiocination; reason; sense.

razionale *adj.* rational.

razionamento *m.* rationing.

razionare *vt.* to ration.

razione *f.* ration; portion.

razza *f.* race; breed; kind: **di** — **pura**, thoroughbred; **che** — **di**, what a.

razzi'a *f.* raid; insect powder.

razziale *adj.* racial.

razziare *vt.*, *vi.* to raid.

razziatore *m.* raider.

razzismo *m.* racism, racialism.

razzista *m.* racist, racialist.

razzo *m.* rocket; spoke: — **interplanetario**, space ship.

razzolare *vi.* to scratch about.

re *m.* king.

reagire *vi.* to react.

reale *adj.* real; royal.

realismo *m.* realism.

realista *m.* realist; royalist.

reali'stico *adj.* realistic.

realizzare *vt.*, *vi.* to realize, accomplish, carry through; to convert into money, sell, cash, gain, to produce, make; **realizzarsi** *vr.* to come true.

realizzazione *f.* realization; accomplishment; production.

realizzo *m.* conversion into money, sale.

realmente *adv.* really, indeed.

realtà *f.* reality.

reame *m.* realm, kingdom.

reato *m.* crime.

reattore *m.* reactor; (*aeron.*) jet plane.

reazionario *m.*, *adj.* reactionary.

reazione *f.* reaction; jet propulsion: **a** —, jet-propelled.

reb'bio *m.* prong.

recalcitrante *adj.* recalcitrant.

recapitare *vt.* to deliver, hand.

reca'pito *m.* office; delivery; address.

recare *vt.* to bring, carry; to bear; to convey, take; **recarsi** *vr.* to go, betake oneself.

rece'dere *vi.*[a] to recede.

recensione *f.* review.

recensire *vt.* to review.

recensore *m.* reviewer.
recente *adj.* recent, new.
recentemente *adv.* recently.
recesso *m.* recess.
recettività *f.* receptivity.
recettivo *adj.* receptive.
reci'dere *vt.*⁴³ to cut off; to excise.
recidiva *f.* relapse.
recidivo *m.* relapser, repeater; *adj.* relapsing, tending to fall back into old habits.
recin'gere *vt.*³⁶ to enclose, fence in.
recinto *m.* enclosure; play pen; corral; *adj.* enclosed, fenced in. *pp. of* recingere.
recipiente *m.* container.
reciprocità *f.* reciprocity.
reci'proco *adj.* reciprocal, mutual.
reciso *adj.* cut off; determined, resolute. *pp. of* recidere.
re'cita *f.* recital, performance.
recitare *vt.* to recite; to play, act; to perform.
recitazione *f.* recitation; acting.
reclamante *m.* complainant.
reclamare *vt.* to claim demand, ask for; *vi.* to complain, protest.
re'clame *f.* advertising, ballyhoo.
reclami'stico *adj.* advertising.
reclamo *m.* complaint.
reclinare *vt.*, **reclinarsi** *vr.* to recline; to bend.
reclusione *f.* reclusion; imprisonment.
recluso *m.* recluse; prisoner, convict; *adj.* recluse.
recluso'rio *m.* prison, penitentiary.
re'cluta *f.* recruit.
reclutamento *m.* recruiting; levy, draft.
reclutare *vt.* to recruit, enlist.
recon'dito *adj.* hidden.
recriminare *vt.* to recriminate.
recriminazione *f.* recrimination.
recrudescenza *f.* recrudescence.
recuperare *vt.* to recover.
redarguire *vt.* to scold, reproach.
redatto *adj.* drawn up, written. *pp.of* redigere.
redattore *m.* editor.
redazione *f.* compilation; editorial department; editorial staff; newspaper offices.
redditi'zio *adj.* profitable, paying.
red'dito *m.* income, revenues.
redento *pp.of* redimere.
redentore *m.* redeemer: il Redentore, the Saviour.
redenzione *f.* redemption.
redi'gere *vt.*¹⁰⁸ to draw up, compile, compose.
redi'mere *vt.*¹⁰⁴ to redeem; to ransom; to free; **redi'mersi** *vr.* to redeem oneself; to reform.
redimi'bile *adj.* redeemable.

re'dine *f.* rein.
redivivo *adj.* returned to life, raised from the dead; *m.* revenant.
re'duce *m.*, *adj.* veteran: — da un viaggio, back from a journey.
refe *m.* thread.
referen'dum *m.* poll.
referenza *f.* reference, information; (*pl.*) testimonials, characters.
referto *m.* (medical) report.
refetto'rio *m.* refectory.
refezione *f.* refection.
refratta'rio *adj.* refractory; impervious; unruly; fireproof.
refrigerante *m.* refrigerator, freezer; *adj.* refrigerating.
refrigerazione *f.* refrigeration.
refrige'rio *m.* relief, comfort.
refurtiva *f.* stolen goods, booty.
refuso *m.* (typog.) misprint.
refutare *vt.* to refute.
rega'glie *see* rigaglie.
regalare *vt.* to present (one, with); to make a present of.
regale *adj.* regal; kingly; queenly.
regali'a *f.* gratuity.
regalità *f.* royalty.
regalmente *adv.* regally.
regalo *m.* present, gift.
regata *f.* regatta, boat race.
reggente *m.* regent.
reggenza *f.* regency.
reg'gere *vt.*¹⁰⁶ to support, bear, carry; to hold up; to manage; to govern, rule; (*gramm.*) to require; *vi.* to stand, resist; to last; to endure: — al confronto, to bear comparison (with), — alla prova, to stand the test; **reg'gersi** *vr.* to hold; to stand, hold up.
reg'gia *f.* royal palace.
reggicalze *m.* girdle.
reggimento *m.* regiment.
reggipetto *m.* brassière.
regi'a *f.* régie; (*moving pictures*) direction; (*theat.*) production.
regime *m.* regime; diet; regimen.
regina *f.* queen.
re'gio *adj.* royal.
regione *m.* region, district.
regista *m.* (*theat.*) producer; (*moving pictures*) director.
registrare *vt.* to record, register; to enter.
registratore *m.* recorder: — di cassa, cash register.
registrazione *f.* registration; (*comm.*) entry.
registro *m.* register; ledger; organ stop; watch regulator.
regnante *adj.* reigning, dominant.
regnare *vi.* to reign; to rule; to prevail.
regno *m.* kingdom; reign.

re'gola f. rule; example; moderation; guidance; order; diet: di —, as a rule; in —, in order.

regolamentare adj. prescribed, regulation.

regolamento m. settlement; regulations, rules.

regolare (1) adj. regular.

regolare (2) vt. to regulate; to adjust; to settle; to rule; regolarsi vr. to conduct oneself, behave; to proceed.

regolarità f. regularity.

regolarizzare vt. to regularize.

regolarmente adv. regularly.

regolatezza f. regulation, moderation.

regolato adj. regular, moderate.

regolatore m. regulator; adj. regulating.

regoli'zia f. licorice.

re'golo m. ruler.

regredire vi. to relapse, regress.

regresso m. relapse, regression.

reietto m., adj. outcast; castaway.

reintegrare vt. to reinstate, restore; to compensate.

reità f. guilt, guiltiness.

reiterare vt. to reiterate, repeat.

relativamente adv. relatively, comparatively: — a, with regard to.

relativo adj. relative; comparative: — a, concerning, pertaining.

relatore m. reporter; speaker.

relazione f. relation, connection; report, account.

relegare vt. to relegate.

religione f. religion.

religioso m. clergyman; adj. religious.

reli'quia f. relic; vestige.

reliquia'rio m. reliquary.

relitto m. wreck.

remare vi. to row.

rematore m. rower, oarsman.

reminiscenza f. reminiscence.

remissione f. remission; forgiveness: senza —, unremittingly.

remissivo adj. submissive.

remo m. oar: — sensile, sweep.

re'mora f. delay; hindrance.

remoto adj. remote, distant.

rena f. sand.

ren'dere vt.[106] to render; to make, do; to give back; to reciprocate; to bring, yield; to convey; vi. to pay, bring profit: — merito, to reward, give credit: — grazie, to thank; — lode, to praise; — conto di, to answer for; — pan per focaccia, to give tit for tat; ren'dersi vr. to make oneself; to become: rendersi conto di, to realize.

rendiconto m. report.

rendimento m. efficiency; yield; profit.

ren'dita f. income.

rene m. kidney.

reni f.pl. loins.

Reni, Guido, Italian painter (1575–1642).

renitente adj. reluctant, renitent: — alla leva, draft delinquent.

renitenza f. reluctance.

renna f. reindeer.

reo m. culprit; adj. guilty.

reparto m. department; (mil.) unit.

repellente adj. repellent, repulsive.

repel'lere vt. to repel.

repenta'glio m. jeopardy: a —, in jeopardy.

repente adj. sudden: di —, suddenly.

repentino adj. sudden.

reperi'bile adj. to be found.

reperire vt. to find (out).

reperto m. (law) exhibit.

reperto'rio m. repertory; (theat.) repertoire, stock.

re'plica f. reply; repetition; replica; (theat.) performance.

replicare vt. to reply, answer back; to repeat.

repressione f. repression.

represso adj. repressed; suppressed; stifled. pp.of reprimere.

reprimenda f. reprimand.

repri'mere vt.[30] to repress, suppress; to stifle.

re'probo m., adj. reprobate.

repub'blica f. republic.

repubblicano m., adj. republican.

repulisti m. clean sweep.

repulsione f. repulsion.

repulsivo adj. repulsive.

reputare vt., vi. to deem, consider; to think.

reputazione f. reputation.

re'quie f. rest; peace.

requisire vt. to requisition.

requisito m. requisite, qualification; adj. requisitioned.

requisito'ria f. denunciation; (law) summing-up.

requisizione f. requisition.

resa f. surrender; yield; return.

rescin'dere vt.[131] to rescind.

rescisso pp. of rescindere.

resezione f. resection.

residente m., adj. resident.

residenza f. residence; residency.

residuati m.pl. surplus.

resi'duo m. residue.

re'sina f. resin.

resipiscenza f. resipiscence.

resistente adj. resisting, strong, fast.

resistenza f. resistance; endurance; opposition; (pol.) underground.

resi'stere vi.[14] to resist: — a, to endure, stand; to oppose.

reso pp. of rendere.

resoconto *m.* report, relation.
Respighi, Ottorino, Italian composer (1879-1936).
respingente *m.* buffer.
respin'gere *vt.* to repel; to reject; to pluck: — al mittente, return to sender.
respirare *vt., vi.* to breathe.
respirazione *f.* breathing.
respiro *m.* breath; delay; respite.
responsa'bile *adj.* responsible: direttore —, managing editor.
responsabilità *f.* responsibility.
responso *m.* response; diagnosis.
ressa *f.* press, crowd.
resta *f.* awn, beard; fishbone; string.
restante *m.* residue; *adj.* remaining.
restare *see* rimanere.
restaurare *vt.* to restore, repair.
restaurazione *f.* restoration.
restauro *m.* restoration, repair.
resti'o *adj.* reluctant.
restituire *vt.* to return, give back; to restore.
restituzione *f.* restitution, return; restoration.
resto *m.* remainder, residue, rest; change; remains: del —, besides, after all.
restrin'gere *vt.,*[107] **restrin'gersi** *vr.* to narrow; to lessen; to shrink; to condense.
restrittivo *adj.* restrictive.
restrizione *f.* restriction.
resurrezione *f.* resurrection.
retag'gio *m.* heritage.
retata *f.* netful; roundup.
rete *f.* net; snare; reticule; (*sport*) goal: — metallica, wire mesh; — ferroviaria, railroad system.
reticella *f.* small net; reticule; hair net; (*rail.*) rack.
reticente *adj.* reticent.
reticenza *f.* reticence.
reticolato *m.* network; (*mil.*) barbed-wire fence.
re'tina *f.* (*anat.*) retina.
retino *m.* (*typog.*) screen.
reto'rica *f.* rhetoric.
reto'rico *adj.* rhetorical.
retribuzione *f.* pay, reward.
retro *adv.* behind: vedi —, turn over, please; *m.* verso, back.
retroattivo *adj.* retroactive.
retrobottega *f.* back room (*of a shop*).
retroca'rica *f.* breech-loading.
retroce'dere *vt.*[38] to demote; *vi.* to draw back; to retreat.
retrocesso *pp. of* retrocedere.
retrodatare *vt.* to antedate.
retro'grado *m.* old fogy, "back number"; *adj.* fogyish; backward.
retroguar'dia *f.* rearguard.
retromar'cia *f.* reverse (*gear*); backing.

retrospettiva *f.* retrospective show; revival.
retrospettivo *adj.* retrospective.
retrovi'e *f.pl.* (*mil.*) districts behind the lines.
retta (1) *f.* (*geom.*) straight line.
retta (2) *f.* tariff; terms.
retta (3) *f.* heed: dare —, to heed; to listen.
rettamente *adv.* straightforwardly.
rettangolare *adj.* rectangular.
rettan'golo *m.* rectangle.
retti'fica *f.* alteration, amendment; (*mach.*) honing; honing machine, grinder.
rettifica'bile *adj.* rectifiable.
rettificare *vt.* to rectify, alter, amend
rettifilo *m.* straight.
ret'tile *m.* reptile.
rettili'neo *m., adj.* straight.
rettitu'dine *f.* uprightness.
retto (1) *adj.* right; upright.
retto (2) *m.* (*anat.*) rectum.
retto (3) *pp. of* reggere.
rettore *m.* rector; principal.
re'uma, reumatismo *m.* rheumatism.
reverendo *adj.* reverend; *m.* padre.
reverente *adj.* reverent, respectful.
reverenza *see* riverenza.
revisione *f.* revision; (*mach.*) overhaul.
revisionare *vt.* (*mach.*) to overhaul.
revisore *m.* reviser; proofreader.
re'voca *f.* revocation, repeal.
revocare *vt.* to revoke.
revolver *m.* revolver, gun.
revolverata *f.* gunshot.
riabilitare *vt.* to rehabilitate.
riabilitazione *f.* rehabilitation.
riaccen'dere *vt.*, **riaccen'dersi** *vr.* to relight, rekindle.
riaccompagnare *vt.* to escort back. *see* accompagnare.
riaccostarsi *vr.* to draw near again; to make up.
riacquistare *vt.* to recover.
riaddormentarsi *vr.* to go back to sleep.
riaffermare *vt.* to reaffirm.
rialzare *vt.* to heighten; to lift up, raise; **rialzarsi** *vr.* to get up again; to pick oneself up.
rialzista *m.* (*exch.*) bull.
rialzo *m.* rise, rising: giocare al —, to bull the market.
riammogliarsi *vr.* to remarry.
riandare *vt.*[7] to recall, reminisce; *vi.* to go back.
rianimare *vt.* to reanimate.
riapertura *f.* reopening.
riapparire *vi.*[9] to reappear.
riaprire *vt.*[11] **riaprirsi** *vr.* to reopen.
riarmare *vt., vi.* to rearm.
riarmo *m.* rearmament.
riarso *adj.* dry; thirsty.

riascoltare *vt.* to relisten.
riassettare *vt.* to rearrange.
riassetto *m.* rearrangement.
riassicurare *vt.* to reinsure.
riassicurazione *f.* reinsurance.
riassorbire *vt.*[18] to reabsorb.
riassumere *vt.*[19] to summarize; to re-engage.
riassunto *m.* synopsis; summing up.
riassunzione *f.* re-engagement.
riattaccare *vt.* to refasten; to start afresh; (*mil.*) to attack again; riattaccarsi *vr.* to readhere; to go back (*to*).
riattare *vt.* to repair.
riattivare *vt.* to reactivate.
riattraversare *vt.* to recross.
riavere *vt.* to get back, recover; riaversi *vr.* to come to oneself.
riavvicinamento *see* ravvicinamento.
riavvicinare *vt.* to reapproach; to compare; to reconcile; riavvicinarsi *vr.* to reapproach; to become reconciled.
ribadire *vt.* to clinch; (*mach.*) to rivet.
ribalderi'a *f.* knavery. [rivet.
ribaldo *m.* knave, rascal.
ribalta *f.* lid; (*theat.*) apron stage: luci della —, footlights.
ribaltamento *m.* capsizing.
ribaltare *vt.*, ribaltarsi *vr.* to capsize.
ribaltone *m.* lurch.
ribassare *vt.* to lower, reduce; *vi.* to go down.
ribassista *m.* (*exch.*) bear.
ribasso *m.* fall, decline; discount, reduction: giocare al —, to bear the market; in —, in decline.
ribat'tere *vt.* to rivet; to smooth; to refute; to drive back; *vi.* to retort; to answer back.
ribattezzare *vt.* to rebaptize.
ribattino *m.* rivet.
ribellarsi *vr.* to rebel.
ribelle *m.*, *adj.* rebel.
ribellione *f.* rebellion.
ribes *m.* gooseberry.
riboccare *vt.* to overflow.
ribollire *vt.* to reboil; *vi.* to reboil; (*fig.*) to seethe (*with*).
ribrezzo *m.* disgust, horror.
ributtante *adj.* revolting, repulsive.
ributtare *vt.*, *vi.* to repel; to throw back again; to revolt.
ricacciare *vt.* to drive back.
ricadere *vi.*[21] to fall down; to fall again; to relapse.
ricaduta *f.* relapse.
ricalcare *vt.* to tread upon; to transfer (*as drawings*).
ricamare *vt.* to embroider.
ricamatrice *f.* embroiderer.
ricambiare *vt.* to return, reciprocate; to repay.

ricam'bio *m.* return, exchange: pezzo (ruota) di —, spare part (wheel); malattie del —, metabolic diseases.
ricamo *m.* embroidery.
ricapitolare *vt.* to sum up, recapitulate.
ricaricare *vt.* to reload (*as a gun*); to wind up again (*as a watch*).
ricattare *vt.* to blackmail.
ricattatore *m.* blackmailer.
ricatto *m.* blackmail.
ricavare *vt.* to draw, extract; to obtain.
ricavato, ricavo *m.* proceeds.
riccamente *adv.* richly.
richezza *f.* wealth, riches; richness; fortune.
riccio (1) *m.* (*zool.*) hedgehog: — di mare, sea urchin.
riccio (2) *m.* curl; *adj.* curly.
ric'ciolo *m.* curl.
ricciuto *adj.* curly.
ricco *adj.* rich; wealthy: nuovo —, nouveau riche.
ricerca *f.* research, investigation, inquiry; (*comm.*) demand: alla — di, in search of.
ricercare *vt.* to search for; to seek; to investigate; to hunt.
ricercatezza *f.* affectation; sophistication.
ricercato *adj.* affected; sophisticated; (*comm.*) in demand; popular.
ricercatore *m.* searcher; researcher.
ricetta *f.* recipe; prescription.
ricetta'colo *m.* receptacle.
ricettare *vt.* to receive (stolen goods), "fence."
ricetta'rio *m.* book of prescriptions; cook book.
ricettatore *m.* fence, receiver.
ricettazione *f.* fencing, receiving.
ricettivo *adj.* receptive.
ricetto *m.* refuge: dar —, to shelter.
rice'vere *vt.* to receive; to get; to greet: — cordialmente, to welcome.
ricevimento *m.* reception, party.
ricevitore *m.* receiver: — del registro, registrar; — postale, postmaster.
ricevitori'a *f.* post office.
ricevuta *f.* receipt.
ricezione *f.* (*radio*) reception.
richiamare *vt.* to recall; to call again; to draw; to reprove: — l'attenzione, to draw attention; — alla memoria, to remind; — in vita, to restore to life; — all'ordine, to take to task; — alle armi, to call to the colors, draft.
richiamato *m.* redrafted soldier.
richiamo *m.* call; admonition; cross-reference mark; (*mil.*) redraft.
richiedente *m.* applicant.
richie'dere *vt.*[24] to apply for; to require; to ask; to ask again.

richiesta *f.* request; application; (*comm.*) demand.

richiesto *pp. of* richiedere: essere molto —, to be in great demand.

richiu'dere *vt.*²⁴ to shut again.

ri'cino, (olio di) *m.* castor oil.

ricognitore *m.* (*aeron.*) scout plane.

ricognizione *f.* recognition; (*mil.*) reconnaissance; identification.

ricollegare *vt.* to connect; ricollegarsi *vr.* to be connected.

ricolmo *adj.* full; brimful.

ricominciare *vt.,* *vi.* to recommence, start afresh.

ricomparire *vi.*³ to reappear.

ricomparsa *f.* reappearance.

ricompensa *f.* reward.

ricompensare *vt.* to reward.

ricomperare *see* ricomprare.

ricomporre *vt.*⁹⁵ to recompose; to reassemble; ricomporsi *vr.* to recover oneself.

ricomposto *pp. of* ricomporre.

ricomprare *vt.* to buy again; to buy back.

riconciliare *vt.* to reconcile; riconciliarsi *vr.* to be (*or* become) reconciled.

riconciliazione *f.* reconciliation.

ricondurre *vt.*⁵ to bring back; to take back.

riconferma *f.* reconfirmation.

riconfermare *vt.* to reconfirm.

riconfortare *vt.* to comfort; give solace.

ricongiun'gere *vt.*⁷⁹ ricongiun'gersi *vr.* to reunite.

riconoscente *adj.* grateful.

riconoscenza *f.* gratitude.

ricono'scere *vt.*¹⁰ to recognize; to acknowledge; to identify; to admit: farsi —, to make oneself known; ricono'scersi *vr.* to recognize oneself; to declare oneself; to recognize each other; — colpevole, to plead guilty.

riconosci'bile *adj.* recognizable.

riconoscimento *m.* recognition; acknowledgment; identification; [avowal.

riconquista *f.* reconquest.

riconquistare *vt.* to reconquer.

riconsegnare *vt.* to redeliver, give back, return.

ricoperto *adj.* covered (*with*); coated (*with*).

ricopertura *f.* covering; coating.

ricopiare *vt.* to copy (*again*); to copy fair.

ricopiatura *f.* copying; copy.

ricoprire *vt.*⁵¹ to cover; to coat.

ricordare *vt.,* *vi.*; ricordarsi *vr.* to remember; to recollect; to remind; to mention.

ricordo *m.* memory; recollection.

ricorreg'gere *vt.*¹⁰⁶ to recorrect.

ricorrente *adj.* recurrent.

ricorrenza *f.* recurrence; anniversary; festivity.

rico'rrere *vi.*¹⁸ to resort; to have recourse; to turn; to appeal; to recur.

ricorso (*1*) *m.* recourse; appeal.

ricorso (*2*) *pp. of* ricorrere.

ricostituente *m.,* *adj.* tonic.

ricostituire *vt.* to reconstitute; to re-establish; ricostituirsi *vr.* to be reconstituted; to recover.

ricostruire *vt.*⁹⁷ to rebuild; to reconstruct.

ricostruzione *f.* rebuilding; reconstruction; rehabilitation.

ricotta *f.* fresh curd cheese resembling cottage cheese.

ricoverare *vt.* to shelter; ricoverarsi *vr.* to take shelter.

rico'vero *m.* shelter, refuge: — di mendicità, poorhouse.

ricreare *vt.* to recreate; to relieve; to entertain; ricrearsi *vr.* to recreate oneself; to amuse oneself.

ricreazione *f.* recreation.

ricre'dersi *vr.* to change one's mind, think better of it.

ricre'scere *vi.*⁶⁸ to grow again.

ricucire *vt.* to sew again; to sew up.

ricuperare *vt.* to recover.

ricu'pero *m.* recovery.

ricurvo *adj.* bent; crooked.

ricusare *vt.* to refuse; to reject.

ridacchiare *vi.* to giggle.

ridare *vt.*⁴⁰ to give back.

ridda *f.* roundelay; (*fig.*) confusion.

ridente *adj.* laughing; bright, pleasant.

ri'dere *vi.*¹⁰⁸ to laugh (*at*); — sotto i baffi, to laugh up one's sleeve; farsi — dietro, to make a fool of oneself; per —, for fun; ridersela di, to scorn; not to care (*about*).

ridestare *vt.,* ridestarsi *vr.* to wake, wake up.

ridetto *pp. of* ridire.

ridicolag'gine *f.* nonsense; trifle; ridiculousness.

ridi'colo *m.* ridicule; *adj.* ridiculous, paltry: mettere in —, to ridicule.

ridipin'gere *vt.*³⁶ to repaint.

ridire *vt.*⁴⁴ to repeat: trovare da — su, to find fault with; non ho nulla da —, I have no objection

ridiscen'dere *vt.,* *vi.*¹¹³ to redescend.

ridivenire, ridiventare *vi.*¹⁴³ to become again.

ridonare *vt.* to give back again.

ridondante *adj.* redundant.

ridorare *vt.* to regild.

ridosso: a — di, against.

ridotta *f.* (*mil.*) redoubt.

ridotto *m.* (*theat.*) foyer; *adj.* reduced; *pp. of* ridurre: mal —, in a bad way.

riduci'bile *adj.* reducible.

ridurre *vt.*[3] to reduce; to drive, bring; to adapt; **ridursi** *vr.* to reduce oneself; to shrink.

riduttore *m.* reducer.

riduzione *f.* reduction; adaptation; arrangement; rebate, discount.

riec'co *adv.* here he, she, it, is (*they are*) again: **riec'comil** here I am again!

riecheggiare *vt.*, *vi.* to reverberate; to remind.

riedificare *vt.* to rebuild.

rieducare *vt.* to re-educate.

riemer'gere *vi.*[51] to re-emerge.

riempire *vt.*[51] to fill (*in*); to stuff; to cram; **riempirsi** *vr.* to fill up; to cram oneself: **riempirsi di,** to get filled, covered, spattered with.

riempimento *m.* filling.

riempitivo *m.*, *adj.* expletive; fill-in.

rientrante *adj.* receding.

rientranza *f.* recess.

rientrare *vi.* to re-enter; to return; to sink; to shrink; to recede; to be included: — **in sè,** to come to one's senses.

riepilogare *vt.*, *vi.* to recapitulate.

riepi'logo *m.* recapitulation.

riesaminare *vt.* to re-examine.

rievocare *vt.* to reminisce; to commemorate.

rievocazione *f.* reminiscence; commemoration.

rifacimento *m.* remaking; manipulation; adaptation; treatment.

rifare *vt.*[51] to remake, do again; to retrace; to imitate; to indemnify, make good for; **rifarsi** *vr.* to start, move (*from*); to recoup.

rifatto *pp.of* rifare: **villano —,** upstart.

riferimento *m.* reference.

riferire *vt.* to relate, report; to refer; **riferirsi** *vr.* to refer; to concern.

rifermentare *vi.* to ferment again.

riffa *f.* lottery: **di — o di raffa,** by hook or by crook.

rifilare *vt.* to palm off (*on, upon*); to report; to deal.

rifinire *vt.* to finish, trim.

rifinitura *f.* finish.

rifiorire *vi.* to reflourish.

rifischiare *vt.* to report.

rifiutare *vt.*, *vi.* to refuse; to decline; to deny; to reject; **rifiutarsi** *vr.* to refuse, decline.

rifiuto *m.* refusal; refuse, rubbish; garbage.

riflessione *f.* reflection; consideration; meditation.

riflessivo *adj.* thoughtful; (*gramm.*) reflexive.

riflesso *m.* reflection, reflex; *adj.* reflected; reflex.

riflet'tere *vt.*[109] to reflect, cast back; to show, reveal; *vi.* to ponder, think (*over*): **senza —,** rashly; **riflet'tersi** *vr.* to reflect, be reflected.

riflettore *m.* searchlight, flood light; reflector.

rifluire *vi.* to ebb.

riflusso *m.* reflux; ebb.

rifocillare *vt.*, **rifocillarsi** *vr.* to refresh.

rifon'dere *vt.*[48] to melt again; to repay.

riforma *f.* reform; reformation; (*mil.*) discharge for military ineptitude.

riformare *vt.* to reform; to amend; (*mil.*) to discharge for military ineptitude.

riformato *adj.* reformed, amended; (*mil.*) discharged for military ineptitude.

riformatore *m.* reformer.

riformato'rio *m.* reformatory.

riformista *m.* reformist.

rifornimento *m.* supply, refill.

rifornire *vt.* to supply (*with*); to replenish; **rifornirsi** *vr.* to supply oneself (*with*): **rifornirsi di carburante,** to refuel.

rifran'gere *vt.*[64] to refract; **rifran'gersi** *vr.* to be refracted.

rifratto *pp.of* rifrangere.

rifrazione *f.* refraction.

rifrig'gere *vt.*[67] to fry again; to hackney.

rifritto *adj.* hackneyed.

rifuggire *vi.*: — **da,** to abhor, shun.

rifugiarsi *vr.* to take refuge; to take shelter.

rifu'gio *m.* shelter, refuge; haunt, den: — **alpino,** mountain hut.

riful'gere *vi.*[110] to shine.

rifusione *f.* remelting; repayment.

rifuso *pp.of* rifon'dere.

riga *f.* line; row; stripe; ruler: **a righe,** striped.

riga'glie *f.pl.* giblets.

riga'gnolo *m.* gutter.

rigare *vt* to rule; to streak: — **diritto,** to behave.

rigato *adj* ruled; striped; streaked.

rigattiere *m.* second-hand dealer.

rigatura *f.* ruling; striping.

rigenerare *vt.*, **rigenerarsi** *vr.* to regenerate.

rigettare (*1*) *vt.*, *vi.* to vomit.

rigettare (*2*) *vt.* to reject; to repel.

righello *m.* ruler.

righina *f* thin stripe; pin stripe.

rigidezza, rigidità *f.* stiffness; rigor; strictness; austerity.

ri'gido *adj.* rigid, stiff; unbending; strict, severe; rigorous.

rigirare *vt.*, *vi.* to turn again, over; to surround, gird; to turn; **rigirarsi** *vr.* to turn around.

rigo'glio m. bloom.

rigonfio m. swelling. *adj.* swollen.

rigore m. rigor; strictness: di —, obligatory; a — di termini, strictly speaking.

rigoroso *adj.* rigorous, strict.

rigovernare *vt.*, *vi.* to tidy up; to curry; to do the dishes.

riguadagnare *vt.* to earn again; to recover, recoup.

riguardare *vt.* to look again; to check; to revise; to regard, concern: per quanto mi riguarda, as far as I am concerned; riguardarsi *vr.* to take care of oneself.

riguardo m. regard, respect; consideration; care: — a, with regard to; mancare di — a, to be disrespectful to.

riguardoso *adj.* considerate, respectful.

rigurgitare *vi.* to regurgitate; to overflow.

rigur'gito m. regurgitation; backwash.

Rigutini, Giuseppe Italian lexicographer, author together with P. Fanfani of *Il vocabolario della lingua parlata* (1830 1903).

rilanciare *vt.* to fling again; to fling back; (*poker*) to raise.

rilan'cio m. return (*poker*) raise.

rilasciare *vt.* to free, release; to grant; rilasciarsi *vr.* to relax; to slacken.

rila'scio m. release; granting.

rilassamento m. slackening; relaxation.

rilassare *vt.*, rilassarsi *vr.* to relax; to slacken; to weaken.

rilassatezza *f.* laxity.

rilassato *adj.* lax; relaxed.

rilegare *vt.* to rebind.

rilegato *adj.* bound; rebound.

rilegatore m. bookbinder.

rilegatura *f.* binding.

rileg'gere *vt.*[4] to reread.

rilento, (a) *adv.* slowly.

rilevante *adj.* relevant; substantial.

rilevare *vt.* to notice; to point out; to emphasize; to relieve; to take over; to buy; to survey: — il calco di, to cast.

rilevata'rio m. purchaser, buyer.

rilevato *adj.* in relief.

rilievo m. relief; remark; survey: di —, prominent, outstanding; mettere in —, to emphasize.

rilucente *adj.* shining.

rilu'cere *vi.*[111] to shine, glitter.

riluttante *adj.* reluctant.

riluttanza *f.* reluctance.

rima *f.* rhyme.

rimandare *vt.* to send back; to reject; to defer, postpone, put off; to refer.

rimando m. postponement; (*sport*) return; (*mach.*) intermediate control: di —, in one's turn.

rimaneggiamento m. rearrangement.

rimaneggiare *vt.* to rearrange; to alter.

rimanente m. remainder; *adj.* remaining.

rimanenza *f.* remainder.

rimanere *vi.*[118] to remain, stay; to stop; to be left: — della propria opinione, to stick to one's opinion; mi rimangono due dollari, I have two dollari left; — di stucco, to be dumfounded; — male, to be crestfallen, to be abashed, to be disappointed; — d'accordo, to agree; — a letto, to keep to one's bed; — alzato, to stay up.

rimangiare *vt.* to eat again: rimangiarsi la parola, to go back on one's word.

rimarcare *vt.* to remark, notice.

rimarche'vole *adj.* remarkable.

rimare *vt.*, *vi.* to rhyme.

rimarginare *vi.* to heal.

rima'rio m. rhyming dictionary.

rimaritarsi *vr.* to get married again.

rimasto *pp.of* rimanere.

rimasu'glio m. remains.

rimatore m. rhymer.

rimbalzare *vi.* to rebound, bounce.

rimbalzo m. rebound, bouncing.

rimbambimento m. dotage.

rimbambinire, rimbambire *vi.* to become a dotard.

rimbambito m. dotard.

rimbeccare *vt.* to retort.

rimbecillimento m. dotage.

rimboccare *vt.* to tuck up.

rimbombare *vi.* to thunder, resound, boom.

rimbombo m. boom, loud noise.

rimborsare *vt.* to reimburse, repay.

rimborso m. repayment, reimbursement.

rimboschire *vt.* to reforest.

rimbrottare *vt.* to scold, reprove.

rimbrotto m. reprimand.

rimediare *vi.* to remedy; to repair.

rime'dio m. remedy; cure; help: non c'è —, it can't be helped.

rimembranza *f.* remembrance.

rimenare *vt.* to stir.

rimeritare *vt.* to reward.

rimescolare *vt.* to stir.

rimessa (1) *f.* carriage house; garage.

rimessa (2) *f.* remittance.

rimesso *pp.of* rimettere.

rimestare *vt.* to stir.

rimet'tere *vt.*[76] to put (lay, set) again, or back; to give back; to send back; to postpone, defer; to send; to remit, forgive; to entrust; to vomit: **rimetterci**, to lose, to be the loser; — **a nuovo**, to renovate: **rimet'tersi** vr. to put, place oneself again or back; to start afresh or again; to resume; to put on again; to recover, get better; to trust (to), rely (upon); — **in viaggio**, to resume one's journey; — **a sedere**, to resume one's seat; — **in piedi**, to stand up again; to pick oneself up.

rimirare vt. to contemplate, watch.

rimminchionire vt., vi. to grow dull, stupid.

rimodernare vt. to renovate.

rimonta f. vamping (of shoes).

rimontare vt., vi. to remount, go up; to go back (to); (mach., etc.) to reassemble; to vamp: — **la corrente**, to go upstream.

rimorchiare vt. to tow.

rimorchiatore m. tug, tugboat.

rimor'chio m. trailer: **a —**, in tow; **autocarro con —**, trailer truck.

rimor'dere vt.[71] (fig.) to prick, give remorse. [morse.

rimorso m. remorse.

rimosso pp.of **rimuovere**.

rimostranza f. expostulation.

rimozione f. removal.

rimpannucciare vt. to fit out again; **rimpannucciarsi** vr. to rig oneself up again.

rimpastare vt. (fig.) to re-form.

rimpasto m. re-forming: — **ministeriale**, reconstitution of the ministry.

rimpatriare vt., vi. to repatriate.

rimpa'trio m. repatriation.

rimpian'gere vt.[60] to regret, be sorry.

rimpianto (1) m. regret.

rimpianto (2) pp.of **rimpiangere**.

rimpiattare vt. to hide, conceal; **rimpiattarsi** vr. to hide oneself.

rimpiattino m. hide and seek.

rimpiazzare vt. to replace.

rimpicciolire vt. to lessen, make smaller; vi. to lessen; to become smaller.

rimpinzare vt. to stuff (with), cram; **rimpinzarsi** vr. to cram oneself.

rimproverare vt. to reproach, blame; to scold; **rimproverarsi** vr. to blame oneself, repent.

rimpro'vero m. reproach, reproof; reprimand.

rimuginare vt. to muse, ruminate.

rimunerare vt. to reward.

rimunerativo adj. remunerative.

rimunerazione f. reward.

rimuo'vere vt.[56] to remove.

rina'scere vi.[51] to be reborn; to grow up again; to revive: **sentirsi —**, to feel greatly relieved; **far —**, to revive.

rinascimento m. revival; Renaissance.

rina'scita f. revival, rebirth.

rincagnato adj. snub.

rincalzare vt. to tuck (in, up).

rincalzo m. reinforcement, support.

rincantucciarsi vr. to withdraw (into a corner).

rincarare vt., vi. to increase in price: — **la dose**, (fig.) to add a nail to one's coffin.

rincaro m. rise in prices.

rincasare vi. to return home.

rinchiu'dere vt.[35] to shut up; to inclose.

rinchiuso adj. shut up; hidden: pp. of **rinchiudere**.

rincitrullire vt., vi. to dull.

rincominciare see **ricominciare**.

rincorare vt. to encourage, cheer; **rincorarsi** vr. to take courage; to cheer up.

rincor'rere vt.[28] to pursue, run after.

rincorsa f. run.

rincre'scere vi.[28] to be painful: **mi rincresce per**, I am sorry for; **se non vi rincresce**, if you do not mind.

rincrescimento m. regret.

rincrudire vt. to aggravate; to embitter; vi. to grow (to get, to become) worse.

rinculare vi. to recoil; to fall back; to withdraw.

rinculo m. recoil.

rinfacciare vt. to reproach, throw in one's face.

rinfocolare vt. to inflame, rekindle.

rinfoderare vt. to sheathe.

rinforzare vt., **rinforzarsi** vr. to strengthen.

rinforzo m. reinforcement.

rinfrancare vt. to reanimate, strengthen; **rinfrancarsi** vr. to buck up.

rinfrescare vt. to cool, freshen; to restore. vi., **rinfrescarsi** vr. to freshen, refresh; to grow cool.

rinfresco m. refreshments; party.

rinfusa, (alla) adv. pell-mell.

ringalluzzire vt. to elate; **ringalluzzirsi** vr. to become elated.

ringhiare vi. to snarl, growl.

ringhiera f. balustrade, railing; banisters.

rin'ghio m. snarl, growl.

ringhioso adj. snarly.

ringhiottire vt. to swallow up again.

ringiovanire vt. to rejuvenate, make younger; to make (one) look younger; vi. to become younger; to become young again.

ringolare see **ringhiottire**.

ringraziamento m. thanks; thanksgiving.

ringraziare vt. to thank (for).

rinnegare vt. to disown; to forswear.

rinnegato *m.*, *adj.* renegade.

rinnovamento *m.* renewal; renovation; revival; reawakening.

rinnovare *vt.* to renew; to renovate; **rinnovarsi** *vr.* to renew; to recur, be repeated.

rinnovo *m.* renewal.

rinoceronte *m.* rhinoceros.

rinomanza *f.* renown, fame.

rinomato *adj.* renowned, famous.

rinsaldare *vt.* to strengthen; to starch.

rinsavire *vi.* to return to reason; to sober down.

rintanarsi *vr.* to burrow; to hide, hide oneself; to retire.

rintocco *m.* toll, knell.

rintracciare *vt.* to trace, find.

rintronare *vt.* to stun, deafen.

rintuzzare *vt.* to repel; to repress, suppress.

rinun'cia, rinun'zia *f.* renunciation.

rinunciare, rinunziare *vt.*, *vi.* to renounce; to relinquish; to give up; to resign.

rinvangare *vt.* to rake up.

rinvenire *vt.* to find; to find out; *vi.* to come to oneself.

rinviare *vt.* to send back; to defer; to adjourn.

rinvigorire *vt.* to strengthen, reinvigorate.

rinvi'o *m.* postponement, adjournment. [ment.

rio (1) *m.* brook, creek.

rio (2) *adj.* guilty; wicked.

rioccupare *vt.* to reoccupy.

rione *m.* district, quarter, section; neighborhood.

riordinare *vt.* to rearrange; to trim, put in order; to reorganize.

riorganizzare *vt.* to reorganize.

riorganizzazione *f.* reorganization.

riottoso *adj.* refractory, riotous, quarrelsome.

ripa *f.* bank, quay.

ripagare *vt.* to pay again; to repay, reward.

riparare *vt.* to protect; to shelter; to repair, mend; to redress, make good for; to repeat (*an examination*); *vi.* to remedy; to take refuge, repair; **ripararsi** *vr.* to take shelter.

riparazione *f.* repair; fixing; reparation: esame di —, make-up examination.

riparo *m.* remedy; shelter; protection, cover.

ripartire (1) *vi.* to leave again, start again; to resume one's journey.

ripartire (2) *vt.* to divide, subdivide; to distribute; to split.

ripartizione *f.* division; allotment; distribution.

ripassare *vt. vi.* to repass, pass again; to call again; to brush up; to

finish, polish; (*mach.*) to overhaul: — la parte (*theat.*), to go over one's lines.

ripasso *m.* review; (*mach.*) overhaul.

ripensare *vi.* to think again (*of*); to think over: ci ripenserò, I will think it over; ora che ci ripenso, now that I think of it.

ripercosso *pp. of* ripercuotere.

ripercuo'tere, ripercuo'tersi *vr.*[118] to rebound; to reverberate: — su, to affect.

ripercussione *f.* repercussion.

ripescare *vt.* to fish out; to catch, find again.

ripetente *m.* repeater (*pupil*).

ripe'tere *vt.* to repeat; to report; **ripe'tersi** *vr.* to repeat oneself; to happen again; to recur.

ripetitore *m.* repeater; coach.

ripetizione *f.* repetition; coaching: orologio, arma a —, repeater; dare — a, to coach; prendere — da, to coach with, to take lessons with.

ripetutamente *adv.* repeatedly.

ripiano *m.* shelf; ledge; landing.

ripicco *m.* pique.

ri'pido *adj.* steep, precipitous.

ripiegamento *m.* refolding; retreat.

ripiegare *vt.* to refold; to fold; to bend (*again*). *vi.* to retreat, withdraw; **ripiegarsi** *vr.* to fold; to bend, stoop.

ripiego *m.* expedient, remedy.

ripienezza *f.* repletion; surfeit.

ripieno *m.* stuffing; *adj.* full.

ripigliare *vt.* to take again.

ripiombare *vi.* to fall again; to fall back.

ripopolare *vt.* to repopulate.

riporre *vt.*[11] to put back; to put away; to hide; to place: — la propria fiducia in, to trust.

riportare *vt.* to bring again; to bring back; to take back; to report; to get.

riporto *m.* amount carried forward; (*exch.*) contango.

riposante *adj.* restful.

riposare *vt.* to lay again *or* back; to put down again: far —, to rest; *vi.* to rest; to sleep; **riposarsi** *vr.* to rest.

riposato *adj.* relaxed; quiet; rested.

riposo *m.* rest, repose; calm; relaxation: — festivo, holyday; buon — I sleep well; questa sera — (*theat.*), no performance tonight; riposo! (*mil.*), stand at ease!; collocare a —, to superannuate.

riposti'glio *m.* closet; hiding place.

riposto *adj.* hidden, secret. *pp. of* riporre: mal —, misplaced.

ripren'dere vt.[14] to take again; to get back; to recover; to resume; to reprove; (*moving pictures*) to shoot: — fiato, to pause for breath; vi. to start again; to go on; ripren'dersi vr. to recover; to catch oneself up.

ripresa f. resumption; recovery; revival; (*sport*) round: pickup (*of a motor*); (*moving pictures*) shooting.

ripresentare vt. to present again; ripresentarsi vr. to present oneself

ripreso pp.of riprendere. [again.

ripristinare vt. to restore.

ripri'stino m. restoration.

riprodotto pp.of riprodurre.

riprodurre vt.[5] to reproduce; riprodursi vr. to reproduce: to recur.

riproduzione f. reproduction.

ripromet'tersi vr.[14] to anticipate; to intend, mean, propose (to).

riproporre vt.[52] to propose again; riproporsi vr. to mean, intend, propose (to); to arise again.

riprova f. new proof, confirmation.

riprovare vt., vi. to try again; to experience again; to censure; riprovarsi vr. to try again.

riprovazione f. reprobation.

riprove'vole adj. blamable.

ripubblicare vt. to republish.

ripudiare vt. to repudiate: to disown.

ripugnante adj. loathsome repugnant.

ripugnanza f. loathing, repugnance; aversion: aver — a, to be loath to.

ripugnare vt., vi. to disgust, be repugnant, to make or feel sick.

ripulire vt. to clean again; to clean up; to polish; ripulirsi vr. to tidy (oneself) up.

ripulitura f. cleaning.

ripulsa f. repulse.

ripulsivo adj. repulsive.

riputazione f. reputation.

risacca f. surf.

risa'ia f. rice field.

risaiuolo m., risaiuola f. rice reaper.

risalire vi.[111] to go up again, ascend again: — la corrente, to go upstream; vi. to go up again, go back; to date from.

risaltare vi. to stand out; to project: far —, to set forth, to emphasize.

risalto m. relief; prominence; emphasis.

risanare vt. to heal, cure; to reclaim; to reform; vi. to recover.

risapere vt.[111] to know, come to know.

risaputo adj. known, well-known.

risarcimento m. compensation, indemnification.

risarcire vt. to compensate, indemnify (for).

risata f. (*burst of*) laughter.

riscaldamento m. heating.

riscaldare vt. to heat, warm (up); riscaldarsi vr. to warm up, warm oneself; to get excited.

riscattare vt. to ransom; to redeem.

riscatto m. ransom; redemption.

rischiarare vt. to clarify, make clear; to enlighten, light up; rischiararsi vr. to clear up, get clear; to brighten: rischiararsi la voce, to clear one's throat.

rischiare vt., vi. to run the risk of; to risk.

ri'schio m. risk; danger; daring.

rischioso adj. risky, dangerous.

risciacquare vt. to rinse.

risciacquatura f. rinsing; rinsing water.

riscontrare vt. to collate; to check; to find; to notice.

riscontro m. collation; checking; test; reply: — d'aria, current (*of air*).

riscossa f. insurrection; redress.

riscossione f. collection.

riscosso pp.of riscuotere.

riscri'vere vt.[114] to rewrite; to write again.

riscuo'tere vt.[114] to collect; to shake; to rouse; to win. riscuo'tersi vr. to start; to catch oneself up.

risentimento m. resentment.

risentire vt. to hear again; to listen to again; to feel (*again*); to experience; to show the effects, signs, traces of.

risentirsi vr. to suffer (*from*): risentirsi di, to resent; si risentì della sfaticata, the hard work told on him.

risentito adj. angry, resentful.

riserbare, *see* riservare.

riserbo m. discretion, reservedness.

riserva f. reservation; reserve: uomini di —, reserves (*mil.*).

riservare vt. to reserve; to set aside; riservarsi vr. to reserve oneself; to reserve to oneself, secure; to purpose.

riservatezza f. reservedness.

riservato adj. reserved; unobtrusive; private, confidential.

risguardo m. (*typog.*) flyleaf.

risie'dere vi. to reside.

risi'pola f. erysipelas.

risma f. ream; quality, kind.

riso (1) m. rice.

riso (2) m. laughing, laugh, laughter.

riso (3) pp.of ridere.

risolare vt. to resole.

risolatura f. resoling.

risolino m. little laugh, giggle.

risollevare vt. to raise again; to lift up again.

risolto pp.of risolvere.

risolutezza f. resolution.

risoluto *adj.* resolute; determined.

risoluzione *f.* resolution; solution; rescission: **prendere una —**, to make up one's mind.

risol'vere *vt.*[17] to resolve upon, decide; to solve; to rescind; **risol'versi** *vr.* to dissolve; to resolve (upon), decide; to end (in).

risonante *adj.* resonant.

risonanza *f.* resonance.

risonare *vi.* to resound, echo, reverberate, ring; to resonate.

risor'gere *vi.*[16] to rise again.

risorgimento *m.* revival, renaissance; (cap.) the movement for political unity in Italy in the 19th century.

risorsa *f.* resource.

risorto *adj.* reborn, resuscitated.

risparmiare *vt.* to save, spare; **risparmiarsi** *vr.* to spare oneself; to refrain from.

risparmiatore *m.* saver.

rispar'mio *m.* saving.

rispecchiare *vt.* to reflect.

rispedire *vt.* to send again or back; to forward.

rispetta'bile *adj.* respectable, decent; considerable.

rispettabilità *f.* respectability, decency.

rispettare *vt.* to respect: **farsi —**, to make oneself respected; **un uomo che si rispetti**, a self-respecting man.

rispettivamente *adv.* respectively.

rispettivo *adj.* respective; one's own.

rispetto *m.* respect; regard: **con — parlando**, excuse the word; **mancare di — a**, to be disrespectful to.

rispettoso *adj.* respectful.

risplendente *adj.* shining.

risplen'dere *vi.* to shine; to glitter, sparkle.

rispon'dere *vt., vi.*[118] to answer, reply; to correspond; to meet, come up (to); to answer (for): **— picche**, to say no, to turn down.

risposarsi *vr.* to marry again.

risposta *f.* answer, reply: **con — pagata**, with reply prepaid.

risposto *pp.of* rispondere.

rissa *f.* fray, fight.

rissare *vi.* to fight.

rissoso *adj.* quarrelsome, troublesome.

ristabilire *vt.* to re-establish; to restore; **ristabilirsi** *vr.* to recover.

ristagnare *vi.* to stagnate.

ristampa *f.* reprint.

ristampare *vt.* to reprint.

ristare *vi.* to pause.

ristorante *m.* restaurant.

ristorare *vt.* to refresh.

ristoratore *m.* restaurant.

ristoro *m.* refreshment; relief; rest.

ristrettezza *f.* narrowness; narrow-mindedness; straits.

ristretto *adj.* narrow; restricted, limited; reduced; *pp.of* restringere: **— di mente**, narrow-minded; **brodo —**, consommé.

risuc'chio *m.* swirl.

risultanza *f.* result, issue.

risultare *vi.* to result; to follow, ensue; to arise; to appear; to come out; to turn out: **da quel che mi risulta**, as far as I know; **mi risulta che**, I understand that.

risultato *m.* result; outcome.

risurrezione *f.* resurrection.

risuscitare *vt.* to resuscitate, revive; *vi.* to resuscitate, return to life.

risvegliare *vt.* to wake (up); to rouse, arouse; **risvegliarsi** *vr.* to wake up.

risve'glio *m.* awakening; revival.

risvolto *m.* lapel (of a coat); cuff (of sleeves); pleat (of trousers).

ritagliare *vt.* to clip (off), cut (out, off).

rita'glio *m.* snip; (newspaper) clipping: **— di tempo**, odd moment, spare time.

ritardare *vt.* to delay; to put off; to retard; *vi.* to be late; to be slow (as a watch).

ritarda'rio *m.* laggard; defaulter; latecomer.

ritardato *adj.* delayed; overdue.

ritardo *m.* delay; slowness: **essere in —**, to be late.

ritegno *m.* discretion; restraint; qualm.

ritemprare *vt.* to strengthen; (metal.) to retemper; **ritemprarsi** *vr.* to strengthen, harden.

ritenere (1) *vt.*[141] to check, detain; withhold: **— a memoria**, to commit to memory.

ritenere (2) *vt., vi.*[141] to deem; to think; to believe; to consider; **ritenersi** *vr.* to consider oneself.

ritentare *vi.* to try again.

ritirare *vt.* to withdraw; to take back; to collect; **ritirarsi** *vr.* to withdraw; to retreat; to retire; to go home; to shrink; to give up.

ritirata *f.* retreat; watercloset; (mil.) taps.

ritirato *adj.* retired; secluded.

ritiro *m.* withdrawal; collection; retreat: **in —**, retired.

ritmato *adj.* measured; rhythmical.

rit'mico *adj.* rhythmical.

ritmo *m.* rhythm, measure; dance music, "swing."

rito *m.* rite; ceremony; **essere di —**, to be the (very) thing, to be de rigueur.

ritoccare *vt.* to retouch.

ritoccatura, *f.* **ritocco** *m.* retouch; finishing touch; change; improvement.

ritor'cere *vt.* to twist, twine; to retort; **ritor'cersi** *vr.* to twist; to recoil (*on*).

ritornare *vt.* to return, give back; *vi.* to return; to go back; to come back; to recur: — **in sè,** to come to oneself.

ritornello *m.* refrain.

ritorno *m.* return; recurrence: **far —,** to go back; **esser di —,** to be back; **— di flamma,** backfire.

ritorsione *f.* retaliation.

ritorto *adj.* twisted.

ritradurre *vt.* to retranslate.

ritrarre *vt.*[146] to withdraw; to portray, represent; to draw, gain; **ritrarsi** *vr.* to withdraw, retreat.

ritrattare *vt.* to retract; to withdraw; to portray; **ritrattarsi** *vr.* to recant.

ritrattazione *f.* retraction.

ritrattista *m.* portrait painter.

ritratto (1) *m.* portrait, picture, image.

ritratto (2) *pp.of* ritrarre.

ritrito *adj.* stale, hackneyed.

ritrosi'a *f.* demureness; reluctance.

ritroso *adj.* demure, coy; reluctant: **a —,** backward.

ritrovamento *m.* finding, discovery.

ritrovare *vt.* to find (*again*); to meet again; to discover; **ritrovarsi** *vr.* to find oneself; to meet again; to get one's bearings.

ritrovato *m.* discovery; device; *adj.* found again; rediscovered.

ritrovo *m.* meeting; haunt: **— notturno,** night club.

ritto *see* diritto.

rituffare *vt.,* **rituffarsi** *vr.* to replunge.

riunione *f.* meeting, gathering.

riunire *vt.* to reassemble; to gather; to rejoin; to bring together; **riunirsi** *vr.* to reunite; to gather; to come together; to unite.

riuscire *vi.*[149] to get out again; to get to; to succeed (*in*); to turn out; to be proficient; to be; to prove: **non — a nulla,** to get nowhere; **non —,** to fail.

riuscita *f.* result, outcome: **buona —,** success; **cattiva —,** failure.

riuscito *adj.:* **— bene,** successful; satisfactory; **— male,** unsuccessful; unsatisfactory.

riva *f.* shore; bank; waterfront.

rivale *m., adj.* rival.

rivaleggiare *vi.* to rival.

rivalersi *vr.*[146] to take it out (*on*): **— di,** to retaliate upon.

rivalità *f.* rivalry.

rivalsa *f.* retaliation; (*fin.*) redraft.

rivalso *pp.of* rivalere.

rivalutare *vt.* to revalorize.

rivalutazione *f.* revalorization.

rivangare *vt.* to rake up.

rivedere *vt.*[181] to see again; to examine; to correct, revise; to go over; (*mach.*) to overhaul: **— le bozze,** to read proofs; **— le bucce a,** to pick to pieces.

riveduto *adj.* revised.

rivelare *vt.* to reveal, disclose; **rivelarsi** *vr.* to reveal oneself; to prove.

rivelatore *m.* revealer; (*radio, etc.*) detector; *adj.* revealing; telltale.

rivelazione *f.* revelation; disclosure.

riven'dere *vt.* to resell: **— al minuto,** to retail.

rivendicare *vt.* to vindicate; to claim.

rivendicazione *f.* vindication; claim.

riven'dita *f.* resale; shop.

rivenditore *m.* retailer; reseller.

rivendu'gliolo *m.* huckster.

river'bero *m.* reverberation; reflection.

riverente *adj.* reverent; respectful.

riverenza *f.* reverence; curtsy, bow.

riverire *vt.* to revere, venerate; to pay one's respects to.

riverniciare *vt.* to repaint.

riversare *vt.* to pour again or back; to pour down; to lay (*on*); **riversarsi** *vr.* to flow (*into*), pour (*into*); to invade.

riversi'bile *adj.* reversible.

riverso *adj.* on one's back.

rivestimento *m.* covering, lining, coating.

rivestire *vt.* to dress again; to cover (*with*); to line (*with*); to upholster; to hold (*as an office*).

riviera *f.* coast; Riviera.

rivin'cere *vi.* to win again; to win back.

rivin'cita *f.* revenge; return game or match.

rivista *f.* review; magazine; (*mil.*) parade; (*theat.*) musical comedy, revue.

rivisto *pp.of* rivedere.

rivi'vere *vt., vi.* to live again; to resurrect; to revive.

rivo *m.* stream; brook.

rivolere *vt.* to want back.

rivol'gere *vt.* to turn; to direct; to address; **rivol'gersi** *vr.* to turn (back); to address oneself; to turn (*to*), apply (*to*).

rivolgimento *m.* change; disturbance; upheaval.

rivolta *f.* insurrection; revolt.

rivoltante *adj.* disgusting, revolting.

rivoltare *vt.* to turn (*over*) again, turn back; to turn inside; to reverse, turn inside out; to upset, disgust: **— un indumento,** to turn a gar-

ment; **rivoltarsi** *vr.* to turn back;
to toss; to revolt; to feel sick.
rivoltato *adj.* turned (*out*); turned inside out: **colletto —,** turndown
collar.
rivoltella *f.* revolver.
rivoltellata *f.* revolver shot.
rivoltoso *m.* rioter; *adj.* rebellious.
rivoluzionare *vt.* to revolutionize.
rivoluziona'rio *m.*, *adj.* revolutionary.
rivoluzione *f.* revolution.
rivulsivo *adj.* revulsive.
rizzare, rizzarsi *see* **drizzare, drizzarsi.**
roano *m.*, *adj.* roan.
roba *f.* stuff; belongings: **— da poco,**
cheap stuff; trifles; **— da chiodi!**
things beyond description!, how
preposterous!, incredible!
robi'nia *f.* (*bot.*) locust tree.
robustezza *f.* robustness.
robusto *adj.* robust, sturdy.
rocca *f.* rock; fortress; distaff.
roccaforte *f.* stronghold.
rocchetto *m.* reel, spool.
roc'cia *f.* rock; cliff.
roccioso *adj.* rocky.
roco *adj.* hoarse.
rodag'gio *m.* running in: **mettere un**
automobile in **—,** to run a car in.
ro'dere *vt.*¹¹⁴ to gnaw; to corrode:
— il freno, to champ at the bit;
un osso duro da —, a hard nut to
crack; **ro'dersi** *vr.* to be gnawed or
eaten; to fret: **— le unghie,** to bite
one's nails.
rodimento *m.* gnawing; worry.
ro'dio *m.* (*metal.*) rhodium.
roditore *m.* rodent.
rododendro *m.* rhododendron.
rodomonte *m.* swashbuckler.
rogato'ria *f.* rogatory commission.
rog'gia *f.* gutter.
ro'gito *m.* instrument, deed.
rogna *f.* scab, mange.
rognone *m.* kidney (*as food*).
rognoso *adj.* mangy.
rogo *m.* pyre, stake.
romanesco *m.* Roman dialect.
romano *m.*, *adj.* Roman: **fare alla**
romana, to go Dutch treat.
romanticismo *m.* romanticism.
romantico *adj.* romantic, sentimental.
romanza *f.* song; romance, ballad.
romanzare *vt.* to novelize.
romanzesco *adj.* romantic, adventurous; extraordinary.
romanziere *m.* novelist.
romanzo *m.* novel.
rombante *adj.* roaring.
rombare *vi.* to roar.
rombo *m.* thunder, roar; (*geom.*)
rhomb, diamond.
romeno *m.*, *adj.* Rumanian.
romito *adj.* secluded, lonely.

rom'pere *vt.*¹¹⁵ to break; to shatter:
— le scatole a, to pester; **rom'persi**
vr. to break (*up*); to shatter.
rompicapo *m.* puzzle.
rompicollo *m.* madcap: **a —,** rashly.
rompighiaccio *m.* icebreaker.
rompisca'tole *m.* nuisance, pest.
ron'cola *f.* pruning knife.
ronda *f.* rounds, watch; patrol.
ron'dine, rondinella *f.* swallow.
rondone *m.* swift.
ronfare *vi.* to snore.
ronzare *vi.* to hum, buzz.
ronzino *m.* jade.
ronzi'o *m.* humming, buzzing.
rosa *f.* rose. *m.* pink; *adj.* pink, rose-
colored.
Rosa, Salvator, Italian painter and
poet (1615–1673).
ro'saio *m.* rosebush.
rosario *m.* beads, rosary.
rosato *adj.* rosy.
ro'seo *adj.* rose-colored, rosy.
roseto *m.* rose garden, rosary.
rosicante *m.*, *adj.* rodent.
rosicchiare *vt.* to nibble, gnaw.
rosmarino *m.* rosemary.
Rosmini, Antonio, Italian philosopher
(1797–1855).
roso *adj.* gnawed; eaten. *pp.of* **rodere.**
rosolare *vt.* to brown, broil; **rosolarsi**
vr. to get brown.
rosoli'a *f.* German measles.
rospo *m.* toad.
rossetto *m.* rouge; lipstick.
Rossi, Pellegrino, Italian statesman
(1787–1848).
rossic'cio *adj.* reddish.
Rossini, Gioacchino Antonio, Italian
composer, *Il Barbiere di Siviglia*
(1792–1868).
rosso *m.* red: **— d'uovo,** yolk; *adj.*
red: **diventar —,** to redden, blush.
rossore *m.* redness; blush, flush;
erythema, rash.
rosticceri'a *f.* cookshop, grill.
rostro *m.* rostrum (*pl.* rostra).
rota'bile *f.* highroad: **materiale —,**
(*rail.*) rolling stock.
rota'ia *f.* rail.
rotare *vi.* to rotate, revolve.
rotativa *f.* (*typog.*) rotary press.
rotato'rio *adj.* rotatory.
rotazione *f.* rotation; **movimento di**
—, rotatory motion.
roteare *vi.* to circle: **far — la spada,**
to flourish one's sword.
rotella *f.* small wheel; roller; caster;
(*anat.*) kneecap.
rotocalco *m.* rotogravure.
rotolare *vt.*, *vi.* to roll; **rotolarsi** *vr.*
to roll; to welter.
ro'tolo *m.* roll: **andare (mandare) a**
rotoli, to go (to send) to ruin.

rotolone m. tumble.

rotonda f. terrace.

rotondità f. roundness.

rotondo adj. round.

rotta f. rout; (*naut.*, *aeron.*) course, route: **essere in —** con, to be at odds with; **a — di collo**, at breakneck speed; **from bad to worse**; **far — per**, to sail for; **ufficiale di —**, navigator.

rottame m. fragment; wreckage; wreck: **rottami di ferro**, scrap iron.

rotto adj. broken; out of gear; inured. pp.of **rompere**.

rottura f. break; breakage; crack; breaking off; cessation; breach.

ro'tula f. kneecap.

rovello m. anger, rage.

rovente adj. red-hot; poignant.

ro'vere m. oak.

rovesciamento m. overturn.

rovesciare vt. to overturn, overthrow, upset; to turn inside out; to pour; to spill; **rovesciarsi** vr. to overturn; to capsize; to fall; to flow, discharge (*into*); to spill.

rove'scio m. reverse; wrong side; back; opposite, contrary; downpour; downfall, overthrow, lap, lapel; adj. reverse, inverse; wrong side out; upside down: **a —**, wrong; **alla rovescia**, upside down.

roveto m. bramble bush.

rovina f. ruin.

rovinare vt. to ruin; to spoil, wreck; vi. to ruin; to crumble (*down*); **rovinarsi** vr. to ruin oneself; to get rovini'o m. clatter.   [spoiled.

rovini'o m. clatter.

rovinoso adj. ruinous.

rovistare vt., vi. to rummage.

rovo m. bramble.

rozzo adj. rough, clumsy.

ruba f.: **andare a —**, to sell like hotcakes.

rubacchiare vt., vi. to pilfer.

rubacuori m. ladykiller.

rubare vt. to steal; to rob: **— sul peso**, to give short measure; **— a man salva**, to loot.

ruberi'a f. theft, robbery, graft, fraud.

rubicondo adj. ruddy, rubicund.

rubinetto m. tap.

rubino m. ruby.

ru'brica f. directory; column (*in a newspaper*, *etc.*)

rude adj. rough, rude, tough.

ru'dere m. ruin.

rudimentale adj. rudimentary.

rudimento m. rudiment.

ruffiana f. procuress, go-between.

ruffiano m. pander, pimp, go-between.

ruga f. wrinkle.

rug'gine f. rust: **aver della — con**, to harbor a grudge against.

rugginoso adj. rusty.

ruggire vi. to roar.

ruggito m. roar, roaring.

rugiada f. dew.

rugoso adj. wrinkled; ridged; rugose.

rullare vi. to roll; (*aeron.*) to taxi.

rulli'o m. roll; rub-a-dub.

rullag'gio m. (*aeron.*) taxiing: **pista di —**, runway.

rullo m. roll.

rumeno m., adj. Rumanian.

ruminante m., adj. ruminant.

ruminare vi. to ruminate.

rumore m. noise; rumor.

rumoreggiare vi. to rumble; to riot.

rumorosamente adv. noisily.

rumoroso adj. noisy.

ruolo m. roll, list; number, class; roster: **insegnante di —**, regular teacher.

ruota f. wheel; spread (*of a peacock's tail*): **seguire a —**, to follow closely.

rupe f. rock, cliff.

rurale adj. rural, farm.

ruscello m. brook.

russare vi. to snore.

russo m., adj. Russian.

rusticano adj. rustic.

ru'stico m. farmhouse; adj. rustic.

rutilante adj. shining, rutilant.

ruttare vi. to belch.

rutto m. belch.

ruvidezza, ruvidità f. roughness; harshness.

ru'vido adj. rough, harsh; coarse.

ruzzolare vi. to roll; to tumble down.

ruzzolone m. tumble, fall.

ruzzoloni adv. tumblingly.

S

sa'bato m. Saturday.

sab'bia f. sand.

sabbioso adj. sandy.

sabotag'gio m. sabotage.

sabotare vt. to sabotage.

sabotatore m. saboteur.

sacca f. bag, satchel; pocket.

saccarina f. saccharine.

saccaro'sio m. saccharose.

saccente m. sciolist, wiseacre; adj. presumptuous.

saccheggiare vt. to sack, plunder.

saccheg'gio m. sack, plunder.

sacchetto m. small bag.

sacco m. sack, bag; plunder; heap, lot: **con le mani nel —**, redhanded; **con la testa nel —**, harum-scarum; **colazione al —**, picnic; **mettere nel — (**fig.**)**, to outwit.

saccoc'cia *f.* pocket.

sacerdote *m.* priest.

sacerdotessa *f.* priestess.

sacerdo'zio *m.* priesthood.

sacramento *m.* sacrament.

sacra'rio *m.* sacrarium; sanctuary.

sacresti'a *f.* sacristy, vestry.

sacrificare *vt.*, *vi.* to sacrifice; sacrificarsi, *vr.* to sacrifice oneself.

sacrifi'zio *m.* sacrifice; privation.

sacrile'gio *m.* sacrilege.

sacri'lego *adj.* sacrilegious, impious.

sacrista *f.* sexton.

sacro *adj.* sacred, holy: osso — (*anat.*), sacrum.

sacrosanto *adj.* sacrosanct, sacred.

sa'dico *m.*, sadist; *adj.* sadistic.

sadismo *m.* sadism.

saetta *f.* dart; thunderbolt.

saettare *vt.*, *vi.* to shoot, dart.

sagace *adj.* sagacious, shrewd.

saga'cia, sagacità *f.* sagacity.

saggezza *f.* wisdom.

saggiamente *adv.* wisely.

saggiare *vt.* to try, test.

saggiatore *m.* assayer.

sag'gio (1) *m.* sage, wise man; *adj.* sage, wise, judicious.

sag'gio (2) *m.* essay; trial, test; specimen, sample; (*fin.*) rate.

sa'gola *f.* (*naut.*) halyard.

sa'goma *f.* mold; shape; outline.

sagomare *vt.* to mold, shape.

sagrato *m.* churchyard.

sagrestano *m.* sexton.

sagresti'a *f.* sacristy, vestry.

sa'io *m.* sackcloth; (*eccl.*) frock.

sala (1) *f.* hall, room; — operatoria, operating room.

sala (2) *f.* (*mach.*) axletree.

salace *adj.* spicy; salacious.

salamandra *f.* salamander.

salame *m.* sausage, salami.

salamelecco *m.* salaam; (*pop.*) |toadying greeting.

salamo'ia *f.* pickle.

salare *vt.* to salt.

salariato *m.* wage earner.

sala'rio *m.* wages, pay.

salassare *vt.* to bleed.

salasso *m.* bloodletting; extortion.

salato *m.* salami; *adj.* salted.

salatura *f.* salting.

saldamente *adv.* firmly.

saldare *vt.* to solder; to weld; to settle, pay up; to receipt.

saldatura *f.* soldering.

saldezza *f.* firmness.

saldo (1) *adj.* firm; resolute.

saldo (2) *m.* (*comm.*) balance; receipt.

sale *m.* salt; wit.

salgemma *f.* rock salt.

sa'lice *m.* willow tree.

saliente *m.*, *adj.* salient.

saliera *f.* saltcellar.

salina *f.* saltern, salt pond.

salino *adj.* salty, saline.

salire *vt.*, *vi.*[16] to rise; to mount; to ascend, climb; to go up.

saliscendi *m.* latch.

salita *f.* ascent; slope; rise, increase.

saliva *f.* saliva.

salma *f.* corpse.

salmastro *adj.* brinish.

salmeri'a *f.* (*mil.*) pack train; pack transport group *or* unit.

salmo *m.* psalm.

salmodiare *vi.* to psalmodize.

salmone *m.* salmon.

salnitro *m.* saltpeter.

salone *m.* hall.

salottino, salotto *m.* parlor, drawing room, sitting room.

salpare *vi.* to weigh anchor, sail.

salsa *f.* sauce.

salsamenta'rio *m.* pork butcher.

salse'dine *f.* saltiness, brininess.

salsic'cia *f.* sausage.

salsiera *f.* sauceboat.

salso *adj.* briny, salt, salty.

saltare *vt.* to jump, jump over; to skip. *vi.* to spring, leap; to vault; to explode, pop: far —, to blast; far — la mosca al naso, to put one's back up; gli è saltato il ticchio, he got a notion to; — all'occhio, to be evident, apparent, patent.

saltatore *m.* hurdle racer; hurdler.

saltellare, salterellare *vi.* to hop, skip.

saltimbanco *m.* tumbler, acrobat; mountebank.

salto *m.* jump, leap, bound: fare un — mortale, to perform a somersault.

saltua'rio *adj.* desultory, fitful.

salubre *adj.* salubr ous, wholesome.

saluma'io, salumiere *m.* pork butcher.

salume *m.* salt meat; salami.

salumeri'a *f.* pork-butcher's shop.

salutare (1) *vt.* to salute; to greet; to say good-bye (hello) to.

salutare (2) *adj.* healthy.

salute *f.* health; welfare; safety; salvation: bere alla — di uno, to drink one's health.

saluto *m.* salute; greeting.

salva *f.* salvo (*pl.* salvoes).

salvacondotto *m.* safe-conduct.

salvadana'io *m.* moneybox.

salvagente *m.* life preserver; platform, (*traffic*) island.

salvaguardare *vt.* to safeguard, protect.

salvaguar'dia *f.* safeguard. [tect.]

salvamento *m.* rescue; safety.

salvare *vt.* to save, rescue; salvarsi *vr.* to save oneself: — da, to avoid.

salvatag'gio *m.* rescue: barca di —, lifeboat; cintura di —, life belt.

salvatore m. rescuer, savior.

salvazione f. salvation.

salve! interj. hail!, hello!

Salve'mini, Gaetano, Italian historian (1873–1957).

salvezza f. safety; salvation; escape.

sal'via f. (bot.) sage.

salvietta f. napkin; towel.

salvo adj. safe, secure: in —, in safety; rubare a man salva, to plunder; prep., adv. except, excepted, barring, but.

sambuco m. elder tree.

San adj. (contr. of Santo) Saint.

sanare vt. to cure, heal; to reclaim; to remedy; to settle.

sanato'rio m. sanatorium, sanitarium.

sancire vt. to ratify, sanction.

Sanctis, de, Francesco, Italian critic (1817–1883).

san'dalo m. sandal; sandalwood.

sandolino m. kayak, flatboat.

sangue m. blood: — freddo, self-possession; a — freddo, in cold blood; spargimento di —, bloodshed; farsi cattivo —, to fret.

sanguigno adj. sanguine, bloody; red.

sanguinante adj. bleeding.

sanguinare vi. to bleed.

sanguina'rio adj. murderous; bloodthirsty.

sanguinolento adj. sanguinolent.

sanguinoso adj. bloody; mortal.

sanguisuga f. leech; bloodsucker.

sanità f. soundness; sanity; medical department; (mil.) medical corps.

sanita'rio m. doctor; adj. sanitary.

Sannazzaro, Jacopo, Italian poet (1458–1530).

sano adj. sound; healthy; wholesome; whole.

Sansovino, Andrea (Andrea Contucci), Italian sculptor (1460–1529).

Sansovino, Jacopo (Jacopo Tatti), Italian architect and sculptor (1486–1570).

santabar'bara f. (naut.) powder room.

santarellina f. plaster saint.

santificare vt. to sanctify.

santis'simo m. the Holy Host; adj. most sacred.

santità f. holiness, sanctity.

santo m. saint: non sapere più a che — votarsi, not to know which way to turn; non essere uno stinco di —, not to be much of a saint; adj. sainted; holy, sacred; blessed: tutto il — giorno, all day long; tutti i santi giorni, day in, day out.

santua'rio m. sanctuary, shrine.

sanzionare vt. to sanction.

sanzione f. sanction.

sapere (1) vt., vi.[117] to know; to be able; to be acquainted with; to be aware of, realize; to taste (of); to smell (of); venire a —, to get to know, to learn; — a menadito, to have at one's finger tips; saperla lunga, to know a thing or two; — nuotare (scrivere) bene, to be good at swimming (writing); non volerne più — di, to be through with, to want no part of.

sapere (2) m. knowledge; learning.

sa'pido adj. sapid, savory.

sapiente m. sage, scholar; adj. learned, wise.

sapientone m. wiseacre, know-it-all.

sapienza f. learning; wisdom.

sapona'ria f. soapwort.

saponata f. soapsuds, soaping.

sapone m. soap.

saponetta f. soap cake.

sapore m. savor, taste, relish.

saporitamente adv. relishingly: ridere —, to laugh heartily; dormire —, to sleep soundly.

saporito adj. savory; witty, salty.

saracinesca f. sluice, floodgate; rolling shutter (of a shop, etc.).

sarcasmo m. sarcasm.

sarca'stico adj. sarcastic.

sarchiare vt. to weed.

sarchiatrice f. weeder.

sarco'fago m. sarcophagus.

sardella f. pilchard.

sardina f. sardine.

sardo m., adj. Sardinian.

sardo'nico adj. sardonic, jeering.

Sarpi, Paolo, Italian philosopher and historian (1552–1623).

sarta f. dressmaker, tailoress.

sar'tia f. (naut.) shroud.

sartiame m. shrouds (pl.).

sarto m. tailor.

Sarto, del, Andrea, Florentine painter (1486–1531).

sartori'a f. tailor's shop; dressmaker's shop.

sassaiuola f. shower of stones; stone fight.

sassata f. stoneshot: prendere a sassate, to stone.

sasso m. stone; cobble; rock: restar di —, to stand aghast.

sasso'fono m. saxophone.

sassolino m. pebble.

sata'nico adj. satanic.

satel'lite m. satellite.

sa'tira f. satire.

sati'rico adj. satiric, satirical.

sa'tiro m. satyr.

saturare vt. to saturate; to imbue, soak (with); (chem.) to charge: — il mercato, to glut the market; saturarsi vr. to become saturated.

saturazione f. saturation.

saturnismo m. lead poisoning.

sa'turo *adj.* saturated; soaked.

sa'uro *adj.* chestnut, sorrel.

sa'vio *m.* sage; *adj.* wise.

Savonarola, Girolamo, Italian religious reformer (1452-1498).

saziare *vt.* to sate; to satisfy; to cloy; **saziarsi** *vr.* to sate oneself.

sazietà *f.* satiety.

sa'zio *adj.* sated, full.

sbadatag'gine *f.* inattention; oversight; carelessness; heedlessness.

sbadato *adj.* inattentive; careless.

sbadigliare *vi.* to yawn.

sbadi'glio *m.* yawn.

sbagliare *vt.*, *vi.* to make mistakes in; to miss: — **strada,** to take the wrong way; **sbagliarsi** *vr.* to be wrong, be mistaken, make a mistake.

sbagliato *adj.* wrong; mistaken.

sba'glio *m.* mistake; blunder; fault.

sbalestrare *vt.* to fling; to pack off.

sballare *vt.* to unpack, unbale: **sballarle grosse** (*fig.*), to talk big.

sballato *adj.* (*fig.*) foolish, wild.

sballottare *vt.* to toss.

sbalordimento *m.* astonishment.

sbalordire *vt.* to amaze, startle, astound; to bewilder; *vi.* to be astonished, bewildered.

sbalorditivo *adj.* amazing.

sbalzare *vt.* to overthrow, cast out; to dismiss: — **di sella,** to unhorse.

sbalzo *m.* leap, spring: — **di temperatura,** sudden change of temperature; **lavoro a —,** relief work.

sbancare *vt.* to clean out.

sbandamento *m.* disbandment, dispersion; (*naut.*) list, heel; (*auto.*) swerve, skid.

sbandare *vt.* to disband; *vi.* (*naut.*) to heel, list; (*auto.*) to swerve; **sbandarsi** *vr.* to disband, scatter.

sbandata *f.* swerve, skid; (*naut.*) list.

sbandato *m.* straggler.

sbaragliare *vt.* to rout.

sbara'glio *m.* rout; (*fig.*) jeopardy: **mettere allo —,** to jeopardize.

sbarazzare *vt.* to rid; to clear away; **sbarazzarsi** *vr.* to get rid.

sbarazzino *m.* wag.

sbarbare *vt.*, **sbarbarsi** *vr.* to shave: **farsi —,** to get shaved.

sbarbatello *m.* youngster, lad.

sbarcare *vt.*, *vi.* to disembark; to unload; to land: — **il lunario,** to make both ends meet.

sbarcatoio *m.* landing place, pier.

sbarco *m.* landing; unloading: **truppe da —,** landing troops.

sbarra *f.* bar; tiller (*of a rudder*).

sbarramento *m.* barrage; blockade.

sbarrare *vt.* to bar, obstruct; to hinder; to block up; to open wide (*as*

one's eyes): — **un assegno,** to stop a check.

sbarrato *adj.* blocked; wide open: **con occhi sbarrati,** with eyes wide open.

sbatacchiare *vt.* to strike; to slam, bang.

sbat'tere *vt.* to shake; to fling, toss; to slam (*as a door*); *vi.* to bang: — **uova,** to whip eggs; — **le ali,** to flap the wings.

sbattuto *adj.* shaken, tossed; haggard, emaciated; whipped.

sbavare *vt.*, *vi.* to drivel, slaver; (*metal.*) to trim.

sbavatura *f.* drivel; (*metal.*) burr.

sbellicarsi *vr.*: — **dalle risa,** to split one's sides with laughter.

sbendare *vt.* to unbandage.

sberleffo *m.* wry face, mocking grimace.

sbiadire *vi.* to fade, lose color.

sbiadito *adj.* faded, drab.

sbiancare *vt.* to whitewash; to bleach; *vi.* to whiten; to grow pale.

sbieco *adj.* slanting.

sbigottimento *m.* dismay.

sbigottire *vt.* to dismay; *vi.* to be dismayed.

sbigottito *adj.* dismayed.

sbilanciare *vt.* to unbalance; (*fig.*) to unsettle; to upset; **sbilanciarsi** *vr.* to lose one's balance; (*fig.*) to commit oneself.

sbilan'cio *m.* (*comm.*) deficit.

sbilenco *adj.* crooked, twisted.

sbirciare *vt.* to glance at; to peer in.

sbizzarrirsi *vr.* to satisfy one's fancy.

sbloccare *vt.* to free; to loosen, unjam.

sbobba *f.* slop.

sboccare *vi.* to flow (*into*); to open (*into*).

sboccato *adj.* foul; foul-tongued.

sbocciare *vi.* to blossom, bloom.

sbocco *m.* outlet; way out.

sbocconcellare *vt.* to nibble; to nick.

sbollire *vi.* (*fig.*) to calm down.

sbor'nia *f.* intoxication: **prendere la —,** to get drunk.

sborsare *vt.* to disburse, pay.

sborso *m.* disbursement; payment.

sbottare *vi.* to blurt out, burst out.

sbottonare *vt.* to unbutton; **sbottonarsi** *vr.* to unbutton one's clothes; (*fig.*) to break one's reserve, open up.

sbozzare *vt.* to rough-hew.

sbracciarsi *vr.* to tuck up one's sleeves; to strive; to flail one's arms.

sbracciato *adj.* bare-armed.

sbraitare *vi.* to shout, bawl.

sbranare *vt.* to tear to pieces.

sbreccare *vt.* to nick.

sbrecciare vt. to gap.

sbren'dolo m. rag, tatter.

sbriciolare vt., **sbriciolarsi** vr. to crumble.

sbrigare vt. to dispatch; **sbrigarsi** vr. to hurry up, make haste.

sbrigativo adj. cavalier, offhand; hasty, summary; businesslike.

sbrigliare vt. to unbridle.

sbrigliato adj. unbridled; lively.

sbrindellato adj. in rags.

sbrodolare vt., vi. to slobber.

sbrogliare vt., **sbrogliarsi** vr. to disentangle.

sbruffare vt. to squirt.

sbruffo m. sprinkle; bribe.

sbruffone m. braggart.

sbucare vi. to come out, issue, emerge.

sbucciare vt. to peel; to shell; **sbucciarsi**, vr. to skin oneself.

sbudellare vt. to disembowel.

sbuffare vi. to puff; to pant, gasp.

sbuffo m. puff: **maniche a —,** puffed sleeves.

scab'bia f. scabies, itch.

scabro adj. rough; rugged.

scabroso adj. scabrous; delicate; risqué.

scacchiera f. chessboard; draughtsboard.

scacchiere m. chessboard; (mil.) sector: **Cancelliere dello Scacchiere,** Chancellor of the Exchequer.

scacciamosche m. flyflap.

scacciapensieri m. (mus.) jew's harp.

scacciare vt. to drive away, oust; to expel; to dispel.

scaccino m. sexton, sacristan.

scacco m. chessman; square; **scacchi** pl. (game) chess: **giocare a scacchi,** to play chess; **— matto,** checkmate; **tessuto a scacchi,** checkered cloth; **subire uno —,** to suffer a defeat; **tenere in —,** to hold at bay; **vedere il sole a scacchi,** to be in prison.

scadente adj. inferior, cheap, poor.

scadenza f. maturity: **cambiale a breve (a lunga) —,** short- (long-) dated bill; **a breve —,** on short notice.

scadere vi.[11] to come due; to fall due; to expire; to decline, fall off.

scaduto adj. due, overdue; expired; outmoded. pp.of **scadere.**

scafandro m. diving suit.

scaffale m. shelf, bookcase.

scafo m. hull.

scagionare vt. to exculpate, excuse; **scagionarsi** vr. to exculpate oneself.

sca'glia f. scale; chip; spangle; fragment.

scagliare vt. to throw, fling, hurl; **scagliarsi** vr. to fling oneself; to dash.

scaglionare vt. to echelon.

scaglione m. echelon; unit.

scala f. staircase; (mus.) scale: **— a piuoli, portatile, ladder; — a chiocciola,** spiral staircase.

Scala, della, Can Grande, Prince of Verona, patron of Dante (1291–1329).

scalandrone m. gangway.

scalare vt. to scale, escalade, climb; to deduct.

scalata f. escalade.

scalatore m. climber, cragsman.

scalcagnato adj. down at heel, seedy.

scalciare vi. to kick.

scalcinato adj. (fig.) shabby.

scaldabagno m. water heater, geyser.

scaldare vt. to heat, warm; **scaldarsi** vr. to get warm; (fig.) to warm up; to get excited.

scalea f. flight of steps, stairway.

scaletta f. narrow stairway; ladder; (moving pictures) treatment.

scalfire vt. to scratch, graze.

scalfittura f. graze, scratch.

scalinata f. stairway, stoop.

scalino m. step.

scalmana f. cold: **prendere una — per,** to take a fancy to.

scalmanarsi vr. to bustle; to make a fuss, to warm up.

scalmo m. thole, tholepin.

scalo m. landing place, pier: **— merci,** freight station; **fare — a,** to touch at; **volo senza —,** nonstop flight.

scalogna f. (bot.) scallion; (fam.) bad luck.

scaloppina f. collop.

scalpellare vt. to chisel.

scalpellino m. stonecutter.

scalpello m. chisel.

scalpicci'o m. patter; shuffling of feet.

scalpitare vi. to paw.

scalpiti'o m. pawing.

scalpore m. bustle, fuss; sensation.

scaltrezza f. shrewdness, cunning.

scaltrire vt., **scaltrirsi** vr. to smarten.

scaltro adj. cunning, shrewd, sly.

scalzare vt. to hoe; to dislodge; to demolish; to undermine; to oust.

scalzo adj. barefoot.

scambiare vt. to exchange; to mistake.

scambie'vole adj. mutual.

scam'bio m. exchange; (rail.) switch, points: **libero —,** free trade.

scamiciato m. ragamuffin; firebrand; adj. shirtless, in one's shirt sleeves.

scamosciato adj. chamois-dressed.

scampagnata f. excursion.

scampanare vi. to peal, chime.

scampanato adj. flaring.

scampanellare vi. to ring the bell.

scampanellata *f.* loud ring, prolonged ring.

scampani'o *m.* toll.

scampare *vt.* to rescue, save; *vi.* to escape, avoid: **scamparla bella**, to escape by the skin of one's teeth; **Dio ci scampi!** God forbid!

scampo *m.* safety; escape.

scam'polo *m.* remnant.

scanalare *vt.* to groove.

scanalatura *f.* groove.

scancellare *see* cancellare.

scandagliare *vt.* to sound.

scanda'glio *m.* sounding lead.

scandalizzare *vt.* to scandalize, shock; **scandalizzarsi** *vr.* to be shocked.

scan'dalo *m.* scandal.

scandaloso *adj.* scandalous.

scandire *vt.* to scan; to spell.

scannare *vt.* to slaughter, butcher.

scannato'io *m.* shambles.

scanno *m.* bench.

scansafatiche *vt.* loafer.

scansare *vt.* to avoid, shun; **scansarsi** *vr.* to get out of the way, step aside; to duck.

scansi'a *f.* shelf; bookcase.

scansione *f.* (*telev.*) scanning.

scanso *m.* avoiding, avoidance: a — **di malintesi**, to avoid any misunderstanding.

scantinare *vi.* to go astray.

scantinato *m.* basement.

scantonamento *m.* turning (*of the corner*).

scantonare *vt.* to round off; *vi.* to turn the corner.

scanzonato *adj.* flippant; jaunty.

scapaccione *m.* slap.

scapestrato *m.* libertine, rake.

scapigliare *vt.* to dishevel.

scapigliato *adj.* disheveled; (*fig.*) giddy.

scapitare *vi.* to lose.

sca'pito *m.* damage; detriment.

sca'pola *f.* shoulder blade.

scapolare *vt.*, *vi.* to escape, avoid.

sca'polo *m.* bachelor.

scappamento *m.* escapement (*of a spring*); exhaust (*of a motor*): **marmitta di** —, muffler.

scappare *vi.* to fly away, run away, escape: **lasciarsi** — **un'occasione**, to miss an opportunity; **mi scappò la pazienza**, I lost my patience.

scappata *f.* escape; close call; slip.

scappato'ia *f.* expedient, shift.

scappellata *f.* unhatting.

scappellotto *m.* slap in the head.

scapricciarsi *see* sbizzarrirsi.

scarabat'tole *f.pl.* odds-and-ends.

scarabeo *m.* beetle.

scarabocchiare *vt.*, *vi.* to blot, smudge; to scribble.

scaraboc'chio *m.* scrawl; blot.

scarac'chio *m.* spit.

scarafag'gio *m.* cockroach.

scaramanzi'a *f.* exorcism.

scaramuc'cia *f.* skirmish.

scaraventare *vt.* to hurl, fling; **scaraventarsi** *vr.* to dash.

scarcerazione *f.* release (*from prison*).

scarcerare *vt.* to release from prison; to set free.

scardinare *vt.* to unhinge.

Scarfoglio, Eduardo, Italian writer and journalist (1860–1917).

sca'rica *f.* discharge; volley; shower (*of blows*).

scaricabarili *m.*: **fare a** —, to lay the blame upon one another, to shift responsibilities.

scaricare *vt.* to unload, discharge; **scaricarsi** *vr.* to discharge oneself; to relieve oneself; to run down (*as a watch*); to flow into (*as a river*).

scaricatore *m.* unloader; dockman; longshoreman.

sca'rico *m.* discharge; unloading; (*comm.*) transfer: **tubo di** —, wastepipe; *adj.* discharged, unloaded (*as a gun*); down, run-down (*as a watch*): **un capo** —, a scatterbrain.

Scarlatti, Domenico, Italian composer (1683–1757).

scarlattina *f.* scarlet fever.

scarlatto *adj.* scarlet.

scarmigliato *adj.* disheveled.

scarnificare *vt.* to scarify.

scarnire *vt.* to thin, make lean.

scarno *adj.* meager; thin.

scarpa *f.* shoe.

Scarpa, Antonio, Italian anatomist and surgeon (1747–1832).

scarpata *f.* bluff, cliff; scarp.

scarrozzare *vt.* to cart about; to take for a ride.

scarrozzata *f.* drive, ride.

scarseggiare *vi.* to lack, be scarce.

scarsella *f.* pocket; purse.

scarsità *f.* shortness; dearth.

scarso *adj.* scanty, short (*of*).

scartabellare *vt.* to ruffle.

scartafac'cio *m.* scratch pad; (*pl.*) papers.

scartamento *m.* discarding, rejecting; (*rail.*) gauge.

scartare *vt.* to discard; to reject; to unwrap; *vi.* to swerve.

scartata *f.* swerve.

scarto *m.* discarding, rejecting; discard; litter, rubbish; swerve: **merce di** —, cheap stuff.

scartocciare *vt.* to unpack, unwrap.

scartof'fie *f.pl.* papers.

scassare *vt.* to break; to grub up; plow up; to uncase.

scassatura *f.* breaking.

scassinare vt. to pick the lock of, break open, crack.

scassinatore m. picklock; burglar: — di casseforti, safecracker.

scassinatura f. lockpicking, cracking.

scasso m. lockpicking; (agr.) grubbing: furto con —, burglary.

scatenamento m. unchaining.

scatenare vt. to unchain; to foment; to provoke, kindle: — una guerra, to kindle a war; scatenarsi vr. to burst out; to fling oneself (against).

scantenato adj. wild, unruly.

sca'tola f. box; tin, can: carne in —, canned meat; caratteri di —, large types; rottura di scatole, nuisance; rompere le scatole a, to pester.

scatolame m. canned food.

scattare vi. to spring; to go off; to burst (with anger): — in piedi (sull'attenti), to spring to one's feet (to attention); far —, to release; to click.

scatto m. spring, start; dash; (fig.) outburst, spurt; click: di —, abruptly; a scatti, jerkily.

scaturi'gine f. source, spring.

scaturire vi. to spring, gush; to derive.

scavalcare vt. to unhorse; to climb over; to outrun, outstrip; (fig.) to steal a march (upon).

scavallare vi. to frolic.

scavamento m. excavation.

scavare vt. to excavate, dig.

scavatore m. digger; miner.

scavatrice f. digger; power shovel, excavator.

scavezzacollo m. scamp; playboy.

scavezzare vt. to break; to lop; scavezzarsi vr. to break.

scavo m. excavation.

scazzottare see cazzottare.

sce'gliere vt.[118] to choose, select, sort out.

scelleratag'gine, scelleratezza f. wickedness; crime.

scellerato m. villain; adj. wicked.

scellino m. shilling.

scelta f. choice; selection; option: di prima —, choice.

scelto adj. choice; chosen; selected. pp.of scegliere.

scemare vi. to diminish, drop.

scemenza f. silliness; foolery.

scemo m. fool, idiot; adj. foolish.

scempiag'gine f. foolishness.

scem'pio (1) m. fool; adj. silly; single.

scem'pio (2) m. slaughter; havoc.

scena f. scene: colpo di —, coup de théâtre; messa in —, stage setting, production; mettere in —, to set up, to produce, to stage.

scena'rio m. scenery; scenario, screenplay.

scenarista m. scenarist; script writer.

scenata f. row, scene.

scen'dere vt., vi.[118] to get down, descend; to slope down; to flow down, run down; to fall; to drop; to dismount: — a patti, to come to terms, to bargain.

scendiletto m. bedside carpet.

sceneggiare vt. to write a scenario.

sceneggiatura f. screenplay, script.

scenografia f. scene painting.

sceno'grafo m. scene designer, scene painter.

sceriffo m. sheriff.

scer'nere vt.[110] to discern; to select.

scervellarsi vr. to rack one's brains.

scervellato m. scatterbrain.

scesa see discesa.

sceso pp.of scendere.

scespiriano adj. Shakespearean.

scetticismo m. skepticism.

scet'tico m., adj. skeptic.

scettro m. scepter.

scevro adj. free, exempt.

scheda f. card; form.

sche'dario m. card index; file.

scheg'gia f. splinter.

scheggiare vt., scheggiarsi vr. to splinter.

sche'letrico adj. skeletal.

sche'letro m. skeleton; frame.

schema m. schema (pl. schemata), summary, outline; plan, blueprint.

schema'tico adj. schematic.

scherma f. fencing.

scherma'glia f. skirmish.

schermare vt. to screen.

schermirsi vr. to defend oneself; to dodge; to make shift.

schermitore m. fencer.

schermo m. screen: — panoramico, wide screen.

schernire vt. to mock, deride.

scherno m. sneer, mockery.

scherzare vi. to play; to joke, jest; to trifle (with).

scherzo m. joke, jest; trick; practical joke: — di natura, freak of nature; fare uno — a, to play a trick on.

scherzoso adj. playful.

schettinare see pattinare.

schiacciamento m. crushing.

schiaccianoci m. nutcrackers.

schiacciante adj. overwhelming.

schiacciapatate m. ricer.

schiacciare vt. to crush; to overwhelm.

schiaffeggiare vt. to slap.

schiaffo m. slap, smack; insult.

schiamazzare vi. to squawk; to clamor.

schiamazzo m. noise, hubbub; squawking.

schiantare vt. to break, fell; schiantarsi vr. to break; to burst: schiantarsi dalle risa, to split one's sides with laughter.

schianto m. crash, clap; pang: **di —,** suddenly; crash.

Schiaparelli, Giovanni Virginio, Italian astronomer (1835–1910).

schiappa f. splinter; (fig.) bungler.

schiarimento m. elucidation.

schiarire vt. to make clear; to lighten (as a shade); **schiarirsi** vr. to clear; to brighten; to fade, become lighter: **schiarirsi la voce,** to clear one's throat.

schiatta f. race, breed, issue.

schiattare vi. to burst (with).

schiavista m. slave trader: **Stati schiavisti,** slave states.

schiavitù f. slavery; bondage.

schiavo m., **schiava** f. slave.

schidionata f. spitful; spadeful.

schidione m. spit, broach.

schiena f. back.

schienale m. back.

schiera f. line, group; crowd; (mil.) rank.

schieramento m. drawing up; ranks; cordon.

schierare vt., **schierarsi** vr. to draw up; to side (with).

schietto adj. frank, straightforward; genuine; undiluted; adv. frankly.

schifare vt. to despise; to loathe; **schifarsi** vr. to be averse (to).

schifato adj. disgusted.

schifezza f. horror; shame.

schifiltoso adj. fastidious.

schifo (1) m. disgust; shame: **fare —,** to be disgusting; to make sick.

schifo (2) m. (naut.) skiff.

schifosità f. loathsomeness; horror.

schifoso adj. disgusting; filthy.

schioccare vt. to snap (one's fingers); to crack (a whip); to smack (one's lips).

schiocco m. snap; crack; smack. see schioccare.

schiodare vt. to unnail.

schioppettata f. shot, gunshot.

schioppo m. gun, shotgun.

Schipa, Tito, Italian tenor (1890–).

schiu'dere vt.[25] to open; **schiudersi** vr. to open; to part; (bot.) to expand.

schiuma f. froth, foam; (metal.) dross; scum; (min.) meerschaum: **pipa di —,** meerschaum; **aver la — alla bocca,** to foam at the mouth.

schiumare vt. to scum; vi. to foam, froth.

schiuso adj. open. pp. of schiudere.

schivare vt., vi. to avoid, shun.

schivo m. bashful, shy.

schizzare vt. to splash; to bespatter; to sketch; vi. to gush, squirt: **— via,** to dart away; **— faville,** to spark; **— veleno,** to vent one's spite.

schizzetto m. syringe; squirt.

schizzinoso adj. squeamish; fastidious.

schizzo m. splash; squirt, jet; sketch.

sci m. ski.

sci'a f. wake; track.

scia'bola f. saber.

sciacallo m. jackal.

sciacquare vt. to rinse; **sciacquarsi** vi. to rinse oneself: **— la bocca,** to rinse one's mouth, (fig.) to get (it) off one's chest.

sciacquatura f. rinsing.

sciacqui'o m. splash.

sciagura f. disaster; misfortune.

sciagurato m. wretch; adj. unlucky; unfortunate; wretched.

scialacquare vt. to squander.

scialare vi. to squander.

scialbo adj. pale, wan; dim.

scialle m. shawl.

scialo m. show; waste; lavishness.

scialuppa f. launch.

sciamannato adj. slovenly.

sciamare vi. to swarm.

sciame m. swarm; host.

sciampagna m. champagne.

sciancato m., adj. crippled, lame.

sciarada f. charade.

sciare vi. to ski.

sciarpa f. scarf; (mil.) sash.

sciatore m., **sciatrice** f. skier.

sciatteri'a f. slovenliness; inelegance.

sciatto adj. slovenly; unpolished.

sci'bile m. knowledge.

scientemente adv. knowingly.

scienti'fico adj. scientific.

scienza f. science; knowledge.

scienziato m. scientist.

scilingua'gnolo m. (anat.) frenum of the tongue: **aver lo — sciolto,** to have a glib tongue; **perdere lo —,** to dry up.

scim'mia f. ape, monkey.

scimmiesco adj. monkeyish, apish.

scimmiottare vt. to mimic, ape.

scimpanzè m. chimpanzee.

scimunito m. dolt.

scin'dere vt.[111] to separate.

scintilla f. sparkle, spark.

scintillante adj. sparkling.

scintillare vi. to sparkle.

scintilli'o m. sparkling.

sciocchezza f. silliness, foolishness, nonsense; mistake, folly.

sciocco m. fool, dolt; adj. silly.

scio'gliere vt.[144] to dissolve; to untie; to undo; to loosen; to free, release; to resolve, solve; to melt; to dilute; to disband; to break up: **— un voto,** to fulfill a vow; **— le vele,** to unfurl the sails; **sciogliersi** vr. to dissolve; to untie oneself; to get loose; to release oneself; to melt; to be disbanded; to break up.

scioglilin'gua *m.* tongue twister.

scioglimento *m.* dissolution; end, issue.

sci'oli'na *f.* ski wax.

sciolta *f.* diarrhea.

scioltezza *f.* nimbleness; ease; fluency.

sciolto *adj.* untied; loose; free; easy. *pp.of* **sciogliere**.

scioperante *m.* striker.

scioperare *vi.* to strike, be on strike.

scioperato *m.* loafer; *adj.* lazy.

scio'pero *m.* strike: fare —, to strike; in —, on strike.

sciorinare *vt.* to display.

sciovinismo *m.* chauvinism.

sciovinista *m.* chauvinist.

scipito *adj.* dull, insipid.

scirocco *m.* southeast wind, sirocco.

sciroppo *m.* syrup, sirup.

scisma *m.* schism.

scisma'tico *adj.* schismatic.

scissione *f.* scission; split.

scisso *adj.* parted, split; separated. *pp.of* **scindere**.

sciupare *vt.* to spoil; to damage; to squander; to waste.

sciupato *adj.* spoiled; run down.

sciupi'o *m.* waste, wastage.

sciupone *m.* waster; squanderer.

scivolare *vi.* to slip; to slide, glide: — d'ala, to sideslip; — di coda, to skid.

scivolata *f.* slide.

scivolone *m.* slip.

scoccare *vt., vi.* to shoot, dart; to strike *(as hours)*: — un bacio, to throw a kiss.

scocciante *adj. (fam.)* boring.

scocciare *vi.* to break; *(fam.)* to bore, bother.

scocciatore *m. (fam.)* bore.

scocciatura *f. (fam.)* nuisance.

scodella *f.* porringer, bowl.

scodellare *vt.* to dish up.

scodinzolare *vi.* to wag the tail.

scogliera *f.* cliffs; reef.

sco'glio *m.* rock; *(fig.)* facer, stumbling block.

scoiat'tolo *m.* squirrel.

scolara *f.* schoolgirl, pupil.

scolare *vt., vi.* to drain, drip.

scolaresca *f.* schoolchildren.

scolaro *m.* schoolboy, pupil.

scola'stico *adj.* scholastic; educational.

scolato'io *m.* drain; drainer.

scolatura *f.* draining; dripping; dregs.

scollacciato *adj. (fig.)* licentious; risqué.

scollare (1) *vt.* to unglue; scollarsi *vr.* to come off.

scollare (2) *vt.* to trim off at the neck.

scollato *adj.* décolleté; unglued.

scollatura *f.* neckhole.

scollo *see* **scollatura**.

scolo *m.* drainage; drip, dripping; *(pathol.)* gonorrhea.

scolopendra *f.* centipede.

scolorare *vt.* to discolor.

scolorire *vi.*, scolorirsi *vr.* to lose color; to grow pale.

scolpare *vt.* to exculpate; scolparsi *vr.* to exculpate oneself; to apologize.

scolpire *vt.*[ss] to sculpture; to engrave; *(fig.)* to impress.

scolpito *pp.of* **scolpire**.

scolta *f.* sentry, watch.

scombussolare *vt.* to upset.

scommessa *f.* wager, bet; stake.

scommesso *pp.of* **scommettere**.

scommet'tere (1) *vt.*[s] to wager, bet.

scommet'tere (2) *vt.*[s] to disconnect, disjoin.

scommettitore *m.* bettor.

scomodare *vt.* to disturb, trouble, inconvenience; scomodarsi *vr.* to trouble *(oneself)*; to take (the) trouble.

scomodità *f.* uncomfortableness, inconvenience.

sco'modo *adj.* uncomfortable, inconvenient.

scompaginare *vt.* to upset, disarrange; *(typog.)* to break up.

scompagnato *adj.* odd.

scomparire *vi.*[s] to disappear.

scomparsa *f.* disappearance; death.

scomparso *adj.* disappeared, vanished; missing; deceased. *pp.of* **scomparire**.

scompigliare *vt.* to upset; to tangle; to tousle.

scompi'glio *m.* confusion; disorder; bustle, fuss; hurly-burly.

scompisciarsi *vr.*: — dalle risa, to split one's sides with laughter.

scomporre *vt.*[s] to decompose, disintegrate; *(fig.)* to discompose, ruffle; *(math.)* to resolve; scomporsi *vr.* to be discomposed.

scomposto *adj.* uncomely, unseemly. *pp.of* **scomporre**.

scomu'nica *f.* excommunication.

scomunicare *vt.* to excommunicate.

scomunicato *m.*, *adj.* excommunicate.

sconcertante *adj.* disconcerting.

sconcertare *vt.* to disconcert, upset, trouble, baffle.

sconcerto *m.* disconcertion.

sconcezza *f.* obscenity.

scon'cio *m.* shame; *adj.* obscene, indecent; filthy, nasty.

sconclusionato *adj.* rambling.

sconcordanza *f.* disagreement.

scondito *adj.* unflavored.

sconfessare *vt.* to disavow.

sconfig'gere *vt.*[ss] to defeat.

sconfinamento *m.* trespass.

sconfinare vi. to trespass (on).
sconfinato adj. unlimited.
sconfitta f. defeat.
sconfitto adj. beaten, defeated. pp.of **sconfiggere**.
sconfortante adj. distressing.
sconfortare vt. to distress.
sconforto m. dejection, distress.
scongiurare vt. to implore; to avoid.
scongiuro m. exorcism: **fare gli scongiuri**, to touch wood.
sconnesso adj. disconnected. pp.of **sconnettere**.
sconnet'tere vt.⁸ to disconnect.
sconosciuto m. stranger; adj. unknown; obscure.
sconquassare vt. to shatter, smash.
sconquasso m. smash.
sconsacrare vt. to desecrate.
sconsideratezza f. inconsiderateness; thoughtlessness; rashness.
sconsiderato adj. inconsiderate; thoughtless; rash.
sconsiglia'bile adj. inadvisable.
sconsigliare vt. to discourage (from), dissuade (from).
sconsigliato adj. unadvised, rash.
sconsolato adj. disconsolate, sad.
scontare vt. (comm.) to discount; to atone (for); to serve (as a term of imprisonment).
scontato adj. atoned for; served; foregone; (fin.) discounted.
scontentare vt. to discontent.
scontento m., adj. discontent.
scontista m. discounter.
sconto m. discount; reduction; allowance.
scontrarsi vr. to meet (with); to come to blows; to collide.
scontrino m. check, ticket; receipt.
scontro m. collision; (mil.) engagement.
scontroso adj. morose, pouty.
sconveniente adj. unbecoming, unseemly; indecent.
sconvenienza f. unbecomingness, unseemliness; indecency.
sconvol'gere vt.¹⁸⁸ to upset.
sconvolgimento m. upsetting.
sconvolto adj. upset. pp.of **sconvolgere**.
scopa f. broom.
scopare vt. to sweep.
scoperchiare vt. to uncover.
scoperta f. discovery.
scoperto adj. uncovered; open; bare; unsheltered; (account.) overdrawn, unpaid: **allo —**, in the open; a **carte scoperte**, openly. pp. of **scoprire**.
scopo m. aim, purpose, object; use.
scoppiare vi. to burst, explode; to break out: **— in lagrime**, to burst

into tears; **— in riso**, to burst out laughing.
scoppiettare vi. to crackle.
scoppiettì'o m. crackling.
scop'pio m. burst, bursting, explosion; outbreak.
scop'pola f. blow.
scoprimento m. uncovering; detecting, finding out.
scoprire vt.¹⁸ to uncover; to strip; to unlid, lay open; to unveil; to reveal; to discover, find out: **— gli altarini**, to let the cat out of the bag; **scoprirsi** vr. to uncover; to denude oneself; to take off one's hat; to reveal oneself; to discover oneself.
scopritore m. discoverer.
scoraggiamento m. depression.
scoraggiante adj. discouraging.
scoraggiare vt. to discourage; **scoraggiarsi** vr. to be (to get) discouraged.
scoramento m. discouragement.
scorbu'tico m., adj. scorbutic.
scorbuto m. scurvy.
scorciatola f. short cut.
scorcio m. foreshortening, perspective; close.
scordare (1) vt., **scordarsi** vr. to forget.
scordare (2) vt. (mus.) to put out of tune, untune.
scordato adj. out of tune, untuned.
scoreggia f. (vulg.) breaking of wind.
scoreggiare vi. (vulg.) to break wind.
scor'gere vt.¹³⁸ to perceive; to descry; to discern.
sco'ria f. slag, scum, dross.
scornato adj. crestfallen.
scorno m. shame, disgrace.
scorpacciata f. bellyful.
scorpione m. scorpion.
scorrazzare vi. to ramble; to ride about.
scor'rere vt.¹⁸ to scour; to run over; vi. to run; to flow; to go by; to glide; to run smoothly.
scorreria f. incursion, raid.
scorrettezza f. incorrectness; impropriety; (sport) foul play.
scorretto adj. incorrect; improper.
scorrevole adj. smooth-running; fluent; sliding.
scorrevolezza f. smoothness; fluency.
scorribanda f. incursion, raid.
scorsa f. glance.
scorso adj. last, past.
scorso'lo, (nodo) m. running knot.
scorta f. convoy; provision; escort; chaperon.
scortare vt. to convoy; to escort; to chaperon.
scortecciare vt. to strip off bark.
scortese adj. impolite, unkind, rude.
scortesi'a f. impoliteness; rudeness.

scorticare vt. to skin; to fleece.

scorticatura f. excoriation, scratch.

scorto pp.of scorgere.

scorza f. bark; rind; outside.

scosceso adj. steep; sloping.

scossa f. shake; shock; jerk: — tellurica, tremor; — elettrica, electric shock.

scosso pp.of scuotere.

scossone m. jolt.

scostare vt. to thrust aside, remove; scostarsi vr. to step aside; to get off the way; to draw away.

scostumato adj. licentious.

scotennare vt. to scalp.

scotta f. (naut.) sheet.

scottante adj. scalding, burning; sore.

scottare vt., vi. to burn, scald; to sting; scottarsi vr. to burn oneself.

scottata, scottatura f. scald, burn.

scotto (1) m. bill, score.

scotto (2) adj. overdone, overcooked.

scovare vt. to run to earth; to find, fish out, unearth.

sco'volo m. (artil.) swab.

scozzese m. Scotsman, Scotswoman; adj. Scots, Scottish.

scozzonare vt. to break in.

scranna f. chair, seat.

screanzato m. boor; adj. unmannerly.

screditare vt. to discredit.

scre'dito m. discredit, disgrace.

scremare vt. to skim.

screpolare vi., screpolarsi vr. to crack, chap.

screpolatura f. crack, chap.

screziare vt. to variegate, marble.

screziato adj. variegated, marbled.

scre'zio m. tiff.

scribacchiare vt. to scribble, scrawl.

scribacchino m. scribbler.

scricchiolare vi. to creak.

scricchioli'o m. creaking.

scrigno m. jewel case.

scriminatura f. parting (of the hair).

scritta f. inscription; notice.

scritto m. writing; adj. written. pp.of scrivere.

scritto'lo m. writing desk.

scrittore m. writer, author.

scrittura f. writing; handwriting; deed; entry; (theat.) engagement, contract.

scritturale m. clerk, copyist.

scritturare vt. (theat.) to engage.

scrivani'a f. desk, table.

scrivano m. clerk.

scrivente m. writer.

scri'vere vt.[124] to write, write down.

scroccare vt. to sponge.

scrocco m. sponging.

scroccone m. sponger.

scrofa f. sow.

scrollare vt. to shake.

scrollata f. shake: — di spalle, shrug.

scrosciante adj. pelting; thunderous (as applause).

scrosciare vi. to shower, pelt; to thunder (as applause).

scro'scio m. shower; burst; clap.

scrostare vt. to scratch, rub off, peel; scrostarsi vr. to peel.

scroto m. scrotum.

scru'polo m. scruple; painstaking.

scrupoloso adj. scrupulous.

scrutare vt. to scan, search (into).

scrutatore m. investigator; scrutineer; adj. inquisitive.

scruti'nio m. scrutiny.

scucire vt. to seamrend, unseam; scucirsi vr. to rip.

scucitura f. seam-rent.

scuderi'a f. stable.

scudetto m. badge.

scudiere, scudiero m. esquire; groom.

scudisciare vt. to lash.

scudisciata f. lash.

scudi'scio m. lash, whip.

scudo m. shield; escutcheon; far da — a, to shield.

scugnizzo m. Neapolitan urchin.

sculacciare vt. to spank.

sculacciata f., sculaccione m. spank.

scultore m. sculptor.

scultrice f. sculptress.

scultura f. sculpture.

scuolare vt. to skin.

scuola f. school: i problemi della —, educational problems.

scuo'tere vt.[138] to shake; to rouse; to toss, jerk about; scuo'tersi vr. to rouse.

scure f. ax, hatchet.

scuriosare see curiosare.

scurire vt. to darken.; scurirsi vr. to grow dark, darken.

scuro m. dark; shutter; adj. dark, dim; obscure; swarthy.

scurrile adj. scurrilous.

scusa f. excuse; apology; pretext: chiedere —, to apologize.

scusante f. excuse; extenuation.

scusare vt. to excuse; to forgive, pardon; to justify; scusarsi vr. to apologize (for); to justify oneself (for).

sdaziare vt. to clear.

sdebitarsi see disobbligarsi.

sdegnare vt. to disdain, scorn; to abhor; sdegnarsi vr. to be outraged.

sdegnato adj. outraged.

sdegno m. indignation; disdain.

sdegnoso adj. disdainful, scornful; haughty.

sdentato adj. toothless.

sdilinquire vt. to weaken, enervate; sdilinquirsi vr. to soften; to go mawkish.

sdoganàre vt. to clear (at customs).

sdolcinato adj. mawkish; affected.

sdoppiare vt. to undouble; to split.

sdraiare vt., **sdraiarsi** vr. to stretch out.

sdra'io, (sedia a) f. chaise longue, deck chair.

sdrucciolare vi. to slip, slide.

sdrucciole'vole adj. slippery.

sdruc'ciolo m. slide; adj. (gramm.) proparoxytonal.

sdrucciolone m. slipping.

sdrucire vt. to seamrend, rip; **sdrucirsi** vr. to rip.

sdrucito adj. ripped; threadbare.

sdrucitura f. rent, rip.

se m. if; conj. if; whether; provided; in case, providing: — pure, anche —, even if, even though; — non altro, at least; — non che, but (it so happens that); — mai, if at all; in case; if by any chance.

sè pron.refl. oneself; himself, herself, itself; themselves: fare da —, to do by oneself; fuori di —, beyond oneself; ritornare in —, to come to one's senses; fra — e —, within oneself; — stesso, — medesimo, oneself.

sebbene conj. though, although.

sebo m. sebum, tallow, grease.

secca f. sandbank.

seccamente adv. dryly.

seccante adj. boring; annoying.

seccare vt., vi. to dry (up); to bore, annoy; to bother; **seccarsi** vr. to dry (up); to be annoyed.

seccatore m. bore, nuisance.

seccatura f. nuisance, trouble.

secchia f. pail, bucket.

secco adj. dry; lean; hard; sharp; adv. dryly, curtly.

secer'nere vt. to secrete.

seco pron. with him; with her; with them; with oneself.

secolare adj. secular; centuried.

se'colo m. century; age.

seconda, (a) adv. favorably: — di, according to

secondare vt. to second.

seconda'rio adj. secondary.

secondino m. warder.

secondo m. second; (naut.) second mate; adj. second; prep., adv. according to, in accordance with, in compliance with; after: — me, in my opinion; verrai? Secondo! are you coming? It depends!

secondoge'nito m., adj. second-born.

secrezione f. secretion.

se'dano m. celery.

sedare vt. to calm, appease.

sedativo m., adj. sedative.

sede f. residence; (eccl.) see.

sedentario adj. sedentary.

sedere (1) vt.[116] **sedersi** vr. to sit (down); to take one's seat; to be situated; to be sitting.

sedere (2) m. backside, rump.

se'dia f. chair.

sedicenne adj. sixteen years old.

sedicente adj. pretended, alleged, self-proclaimed.

sedice'simo m., adj. sixteenth.

se'dici m., adj. sixteen.

sedile m. seat, bench.

sedimento m. sediment; dregs.

sedizione f. sedition.

sedizioso adj. seditious, turbulent.

sedotto pp.of sedurre, alluring.

seducente adj. seducing, alluring.

sedurre vt.[2] to seduce; to charm.

seduta f. sitting, session; meeting: — stante, right away, on the spot.

seduto adj. sitting. pp.of sedere

seduttore m., **seduttrice** f. seducer.

seduzione f. seduction, charm.

sega f. saw.

se'gala, se'gale f. rye.

segaligno adj. (fig.) wiry.

Segantini, Giovanni, Italian painter (1858–1899).

segare vt. to saw; to mow.

segatura f. sawing; sawdust.

seg'gio m. seat; chair; see.

seg'giola see sedia.

seggiovi'a f. chair lift.

segheri'a f. sawmill.

seghettato adj. serrate; toothed.

segmento m. segment.

segna'colo m. mark, sign.

segnalare vt. to signal; to indicate; to point out; **segnalarsi** vr. to distinguish oneself.

segnalato adj. distinguished; great.

segnalazione f. s gna'ing; indication: — stradale, traffic signal.

segnale m. signal; sign; call: — d'allarme, alert, warning signal.

segnale'tico adj. anthropometric.

segnalibro m. bookmark.

segnali'nee m. (sport) linesman.

segnare vt. to mark; to note, jot down; to record; to sign; to indicate; to point out; to score.

segnatasse m. postage-due stamp.

segno m. sign, mark; token; trace; track; vestige; symptom; limit, boundary; target; aim; per filo e per —, in detail.

sego m. tallow.

segregare vt. to segregate.

segregazione f. segregation; seclusion.

segretamente adv. secretly.

segreta'rio m., **segreta'ria** f. secretary.

segreteri'a f. secretary's office.

segretezza f. secrecy.

segreto m. secret; secrecy; adj. secret; hidden; reticent.
seguace m. follower; disciple.
seguente adj. following, next.
segu'gio m. bloodhound; private detective.
seguire vt., vi. to follow; to continue, go on; to shadow; to comply with.
seguitare see **continuare.**
se'guito m. continuation; sequel; following; succession; retinue: di —, without interruption; in —, afterwards, later on; in — a, following, as a result of.
sei m., adj. six.
selce f. flint stone.
selciato m. pavement.
selettivo adj. selective.
selettività f. selectivity.
selezionare vt. to select, sort out.
selezione f. selection, choice; digest.
sella f. saddle.
sella'io m. saddler.
sellare vt. to saddle.
seltz m. seltzer.
selva f. forest, wood.
selvaggina f. game.
selvag'gio m., adj. savage.
selva'tico adj. wild; untamed.
sema'foro m. semaphore; traffic lights.
sembiante m., **sembianza** f. look, aspect.
sembrare see **parere** (I).
seme m. germ, seed; source.
semente f. seed.
semenza f. seed, seeds; origin.
semenza'io m. seedbed; hotbed.
semestrale adj. half-yearly, semi-annual.
semestre m. half year; semester.
semiaperto adj. half-open.
semi'as'se m. (mach.) axle shaft.
semicer'chio m. semicircle.
semichiuso adj. half-closed.
semicu'pio m. sitz bath.
semidi'o m. demigod.
se'mina, seminagione f. sowing.
seminare vt. to sow; to scatter.
semina'rio m. seminary.
seminarista m. seminarist.
seminato m.: uscire dal —, to digress.
seminatore m. sower.
seminatrice f. sower; seeding machine.
seminterrato m. basement.
seminudo adj. half-naked.
semioscurità f. half-darkness.
semiri'gido adj. semiflexible; semirigid.
semise'rio adj. serio-comic.
semisfera f. hemisphere.
semivivo adj. half-dead.
se'mola f. bran; freckles.
semovente adj. self-propelled.

sempiterno adj. everlasting.
sem'plice adj. simple; easy; plain; unsophisticated; mere; single: soldato —, private, serviceman.
semplicemente adv. simply, merely.
sempliciotto m. halfwit.
semplicità f. simplicity.
semplificare vt. to simplify.
sempre adv. always; at all times: per —, forever; — più, more and more; — meno, less and less.
semprechè conj. provided (that).
sempreverde m., adj. evergreen.
se'napa, se'nape f. mustard.
senapismo m. mustard poultice, mustard plaster.
senato m. senate; senate house.
senatore m. senator.
senile adj. senile.
senilità f. senility.
seniore m., adj. senior, elder.
senno m. wisdom: perdere il —, to go mad; fuor di —, insane; del — di poi son piene le fosse, hindsight is easier than foresight.
sennonchè conj. but, except that.
seno m. bosom; breast; cove.
sensale m. broker, middleman.
sensato adj. sensible, reasonable.
sensazionale adj. sensational; lurid.
sensazione f. feeling; sensation.
sensi'bile adj. sensitive; considerable; substantial; sensible.
sensibilità f. sensibility; sensitiveness; sensitivity.
sensibilmente adv. considerably.
sensitivo adj. sensitive.
senso m. sense; feeling; meaning; way, direction: — pratico, practicalness; buon —, common sense; doppio —, double-entendre; strada a — unico, one-way street; — vietato, no thoroughfare; privo di —, meaningless; privo di sensi, unconscious; perdere i sensi, to swoon; riprendere i sensi, to come to.
sensuale adj. sensual.
sensualità f. sensuality.
sentenza f. maxim; sentence; judgment; verdict: sputar sentenze, to dogmatize, pontificate.
sentenziare vt., vi. to lay down the law; to rule; to pontificate.
sentenzioso adj. sententious.
sentiero m. path.
sentimentale adj. sentimental; mawkish; "corny."
sentimentalismo m. sentimentalism.
sentimento m. feeling; sentiment; sense.
sentina f. (naut.) bilge.
sentinella f. sentinel, sentry.
sentire vt., vi. to feel; to hear; to learn; to smell of: — parlare di,

to hear about; **per sentito dire,** by hearsay; **stare a —,** to listen to; **sentirsi** *vr.* to feel: **sentirsela,** to feel like it.

sentitamente *adv.* heartily, sincerely.

sentito *adj.* heartfelt; hearty, sincere: **per — dire,** by hearsay. *pp.of* **sentire.**

sentore *m.* feeling; inkling; scent, smell.

senza *prep.* without: **senz'altro,** immediately; *(fig.)* say no more.

senzapa'tria *m.* renegade.

senzatetto *m.* homeless person.

separare *vt.,* **separarsi** *vr.* to separate; to part.

separato *adj.* separate; disjoined.

separazione *f.* separation; parting.

sepolcrale *adj.* sepulchral.

sepolcreto *m.* cemetery.

sepolcro *m.* sepulcher, grave.

sepolto *adj.* buried. *pp.of* **seppellire.**

sepoltura *f.* burial; grave.

seppellire *vt.*[137] 'to bury; to hide; **seppellirsi** *vr.* to hide, bury (oneself).

sep'pia *f. (ichthyol.)* cuttlefish; *(paint.)* sepia: **osso di —,** cuttlebone.

seppure *conj.* even if; supposing that.

sequela *f.* sequence, series.

sequenza *f.* sequence.

sequestrare *vt.* to seize, distrain; to suppress; to seclude.

sequestrata'rio *m.* sequestrator.

sequestro *m.* distraint; suppression: **— di persona,** unlawful detention.

sera *f.* evening; night.

sera'fico *adj.* seraphic.

serafino *m.* seraph.

serale *adj.* evening, nightly.

Serao, Matilde, Italian novelist (1856-1927).

serata *f.* evening; evening performance; evening party, soirée.

serbare *vt.* to preserve, keep: **— rancore a,** to bear a grudge against.

serbato'io *m.* reservoir, tank.

serbo *m.*: in serbo, in store.

serenata *f.* serenade.

serenità *f.* serenity.

sereno *m.* serene; *adj.* serene, clear, cloudless.

sergente *m.* sergeant.

seriamente *adv.* earnestly, seriously.

se'rie *f.* series, set, succession; line, row: **di —,** current, standard; **fuori —,** custom built.

serietà *f.* earnestness, seriousness; trustworthiness.

se'rio *adj.* serious, earnest; trustworthy, reliable; grave: **sul —,** in earnest; really.

sermone *m.* sermon; lecture.

serpa *f.* coach box.

serpe *m., f.* serpent, snake.

serpeggiare *vi.* to wind; to creep.

serpente *m.* snake, serpent.

serpentina *f.* coil; serpentine.

serpentino *m.* worm; serpentine.

ser'qua *f.* dozen; lot, lots.

serra *f.* greenhouse, hothouse.

serrafilo *m. (elec.)* contact plug screw.

serra'glio *m.* menagerie; seraglio.

serrama'nico, (coltello a) *m.* claspknife.

serramenti *m.pl.* window *or* door frames.

serranda *see* **saracinesca.**

serrare *vt.* to shut, close; to lock (up); to tighten; to press: **— i pugni,** to clench one's fists; **— le file,** to close ranks.

serrato *adj.* close; compact; concise.

serratura *f.* lock.

serva *f.* woman servant, maid.

servente *m., f.* servant; *(mil.)* gunner.

servi'bile *adj.* serviceable, useful.

servi'gio *m.* favor, service.

servile *adj.* servile, obsequious.

servilismo *m.* servility, servileness.

servire *vt.* to serve; to help; *vi.* to serve; to be of use, help: **non serve,** it is no use; **servirsi** *vr.* to help oneself: **— da,** to patronize; **servirsi di,** to use; to avail oneself of; to help oneself *(to food, etc.).*

servitore *m.* servant.

servitù *f.* servants; servitude, bondage, slavery.

serviziale *m.* clyster, enema.

servizie'vole *adj.* obliging, helpful.

servi'zio *m.* service; favor; outfit, set: **mezzo —,** part-time service; **donna a mezzo —,** part-timer; **in —,** on duty; **fuori —,** off duty.

servo *m.* manservant, valet; slave.

servofreno *m.* brake booster.

servomotore *m.* servomotor.

sessanta *m., adj.* sixty.

sessante'simo *m., adj.* sixtieth.

sessantina *f.* some sixty.

sessione *f.* session.

sesso *m.* sex: **il — debole, il gentil —,** the fair sex.

sessuale *adj.* sexual.

sestante *m.* sextant.

sesto *m., adj.* sixth.

se'stuplo *m., adj.* sextuple.

seta *f.* silk.

setacciare *see* **stacciare.**

setac'cio *m.* sieve, crib.

setaiuolo *m.* silk merchant.

sete *f.* thirst; craving; longing: **aver —,** to be thirsty; **aver — di,** to thirst for.

seter'a *f.* silk goods; silk factory.

setifi'cio *m.* silk factory, silk mill.

se'tola *f.* hair; bristle.

setta f. sect; faction.
settanta m., adj. seventy.
settante'simo m., adj. seventieth.
settantina f. some seventy.
setta'rio m., adj. sectarian.
sette m., adj. seven.
settembre m. September.
settentrionale m. northerner; adj. north, northern.
settentrione m. north.
setticemi'a f. septicemia.
settice'mico adj. septicemic.
set'tico m., adj. septic.
settimana f. week; weekly wages.
settimanale m., adj. weekly.
settimino m. seven month's child.
set'timo m., adj. seventh.
settore m. sector; branch; department.
severamente adv. sternly, harshly.
severità f. sternness, strictness.
severo adj. strict, stern.
sevi'zia f. cruelty.
seviziare vt. to torture.
seviziatore m., **seviziatrice** f. torturer.
sezionare vt. to cut up, dissect.
sezione f. section; department.
sfaccendato m. idler, loafer.
sfaccettatura f. faceting.
sfacchinare vi. to drudge.
sfacchinata f. tour de force; grind.
sfacciatag'gine f. impudence, "brass."
sfacciato adj. impudent; shameless.
sfacelo m. breakdown, collapse, ruin.
sfacimento m. ruin, decay.
sfaldare vt. to scale, flake off; **sfaldarsi** vr. to foliate; to scale off, flake off.
sfamare vt. to satiate; **sfamarsi** vr. to appease one's hunger.
sfare vt. to undo; to melt; **sfarsi** vr. to become undone; to melt; to decay.
sfarzo m. display; pomp; luxury.
sfarzosità f. gorgeousness.
sfarzoso adj. gorgeous; dazzling.
sfasare vt., vi. to throw; to go out of phase.
sfasciamento m. collapse, smashing.
sfasciare (1) vt. to unswathe; to unbandage.
sfasciare (2) vt. to smash; **sfasciarsi** vr. to smash, collapse.
sfatare vt. to explode, discredit.
sfaticato m. idler; bum; adj. lazy.
sfavillante adj. sparkling, glittering.
sfavillare vi. to glitter, sparkle.
sfavore m. disfavor.
sfavore'vole adj. unfavorable; averse.
sfebbrato adj. recovered from a fever.
sfegatato adj. passionate.
sfera f. sphere; hand (of a clock, etc.); globe; (mach.) ball.
sferico adj. spherical.

sferrare vt. to unshoe (as a horse); to deliver (as a blow).
sferruzzare vi. to knit away.
sferza f. scourge, lash, whip.
sferzare vt. to scourge, whip, lash.
sferzata f. lash.
sfiancare vt. to wear out, overwork; **sfiancarsi** vr. to tire, overwork oneself.
sfiatarsi vr. to talk oneself hoarse.
sfiatato adj. out of breath; worn out.
sfiatato'io m. vent.
sfibbiare vt. to unfasten.
sfibrare vt. to unfiber; to enervate.
sfida f. challenge.
sfidante m. challenger; adj. challenging.
sfidare vt. to challenge, dare; to brave.
sfidu'cia f. mistrust; pessimism: voto di —, vote of no confidence.
sfiduciato adj. disheartened.
sfigurare vt. to disfigure; vi. to cut a poor figure.
sfigurato adj. disfigured.
sfilacciare vt. to ravel; **sfilacciarsi** vr. to fray.
sfilacciato adj. frayed.
sfilacciatura f. fray; fraying.
sfilare vt. to unthread; to unstring (as pearls); vi. to defile, file off; **sfilarsi** vr. to get unthreaded, unstrung; to take off (as a garment).
sfilata f. parade, defiling: — di modelli, fashion parade.
sfinge f. sphinx.
sfinimento m. exhaustion.
sfinire vt. to wear out, exhaust.
sfinito adj. exhausted, worn out.
sfintere m. sphincter.
sfiorare vt. to graze; to touch lightly on; to skim.
sfiorire vi. to fade; to wither.
sfitto adj. untenanted.
sfocare vt. (photo.) to soft-focus.
sfocato adj. blurred.
sfociare vi. to debouch (into).
sfoderare vt. to unline; to unsheathe; to draw; to display.
sfogare vt. to vent, give vent to: — la collera su, to take it out on; **sfogarsi** vr. to vent oneself; to unbosom oneself.
sfogato'io m. vent, outlet.
sfoggiare vt. to flaunt, display.
sfog'gio m. display, show, parade.
sfo'glia f. foil; puff paste; paste; sole.
sfogliare vt. to unleaf, pluck; to leaf through (a book); to exfoliate; **sfogliarsi** vr. to shed leaves, petals; to exfoliate.
sfogliata f. puff paste.
sfogo m. vent; outburst; outlet; (med.) eruption, rash.
sfolgorante adj. blazing.

sfolgorare *vi.* to blaze.

sfolgori'o *m.* blazing.

sfollagente *m.* truncheon, club.

sfollamento *m.* evacuation.

sfollare *vt.*, *vi.* to evacuate.

sfondamento *m.* unbottoming; breaking through.

sfondare *vt.* to unbottom, stave in; to break, smash; to break through.

sfondato *adj.* bottomless; smashed: ricco —, rolling in riches.

sfondo *m.* background.

sfondone *m.* blunder.

sforacchiare *vt.* to riddle.

sforbiciare *vt.* to scissor.

sformare *vt.* to deform, pull out of shape; sformarsi *vr.* to lose one's shape.

sformato *adj.* shapeless.

sfornare *vt.* to take out of the oven.

sfornire *vt.* to deprive.

sfornito *adj.* destitute; unprovided, out of; lacking.

sfortuna *f.* ill *or* bad luck; misfortune.

sfortunatamente *adv.* unluckily; unfortunately.

sfortunato *adj.* unfortunate; unlucky; unhappy.

Sforza, Carlo, Italian statesman (1872-1952).

Sforza, Francesco, Duke of Milan, Italian warrior (1401-1466).

Sforza, Muzio Attendolo, Italian condottiere (1369-1424).

Sforza, Ludovico (*Ludovico il Moro*), Duke of Milan (1451-1508).

sforzare *vt.* to strain, urge, force; sforzarsi *vr.* to endeavor, strive.

sforzato *adj.* forced.

sforzo *m.* effort; exertion.

sfracassare *see* fracassare.

sfracellare *vt.* to smash, shatter; sfracellarsi *vr.* to get smashed.

sfrangiare *vt.* to ravel.

sfrangiatura *f.* raveling.

sfrattare *vt.* to evict; to give notice to.

sfratto *m.* notice to quit, eviction.

sfrecciare *vi.* to speed, dart, whizz.

sfregamento *m.* rubbing.

sfregare *vt.* to rub.

sfregiare *vt.* to disfigure; to slash.

sfregiato *m.* scarface; *adj.* scarfaced; disfigured.

sfre'gio *m.* gash; scar; slash; (*fig.*) disgrace, affront.

sfrenato *adj.* unrestrained.

sfrondare *vt.* to trim (*off*); to lop.

sfrontatezza *f.* effrontery; cheek.

sfrontato *adj.* impudent, brazen.

sfruttamento *m.* exploitation.

sfruttare *vt.* to exploit; to sponge on; to take advantage of.

sfruttatore *m.* exploiter; sponge, parasite: — di donne, gigolo.

sfuggire *vt.* to avoid; to shun; *vi.* to escape; to slip away (*from*); to elude; to evade: mi sfugge il suo nome, I can't recall his name; lasciarsi — un'occasione, to miss an opportunity.

sfuggita, (di, alla) *loc.adv.* in passing, cursorily; hastily; stealthily: vedere di —, to catch a glimpse of.

sfumare *vi.* to vanish, evaporate.

sfumato *adj.* lost, evaporated; shaded.

sfumatura *f.* shade, nuance.

sfumino *m.* stump.

sfuriata *f.* outburst; scolding.

sgabello *m.* stool.

sgabuzzino *m.* closet.

Sgambati, Giovanni, Italian composer (1841-1914).

sgambettare *vi.* to toddle; to kick; to frisk about.

sgambetto *m.* trip; jump; caper.

sganasciarsi *vr.*: — dalle risa, to laugh oneself silly.

sganciare *vt.* to unhook.

sgangherare *vt.* to unhinge.

sgangheratamente *adv.* immoderately, rudely.

sgangherato *adj.* unhinged; (*fig.*) immoderate, rude.

sgarbato *adj.* unmannerly, rude.

sgarbo *m.*, sgarberi'a *f.* rudeness, affront.

sgargiante *adj.* gaudy, flashy, showy.

sgarrare *vi.* to go wrong.

sgattaiolare *vi.* to slip away.

sgavazzare *vi.* to debauch.

sgelare *vt.*, *vi.* to thaw, melt.

sgelo *m.* thaw.

sghembo *m.* slant; *adj.* slanting, aslant.

sgherro *m.* bravo.

sghignazzare *vi.* to guffaw.

sghignazzata *f.* guffaw.

sghimbe'scio : di —, awry, askew.

sghiribizzo *m.* freak, whim.

sgobbare *vi.* to work hard, drudge.

sgobbone *m.* fag.

sgocciolare *vi.* to drip, trickle.

sgocciolatura *f.* drip.

sgoc'ciolo *m.* dripping: essere agli sgoccioli, to be at an end.

sgolarsi *vr.* to shout oneself hoarse.

sgomberare, sgombrare *vt.* to clear out *or* up; to quit; *vi.* to clear out; to move.

sgom'bero, sgombro *m.* clearance; moving; *adj.* clear (*from*), free (*from*); empty.

sgombro *m.* mackerel.

sgomentare *vt.* to dismay; sgomentarsi *vr.* to become dismayed; to lose courage.

sgomento *m.* dismay; *adj.* dismayed.

sgominare *vt.* to rout, overthrow.

sgonfiare vt. to deflate; **sgonfiarsi** vr. to get, become deflated.

sgon'fio adj. deflated, flat.

sgor'bia f. gouge.

sgor'bio m. scrawl, stain, daub.

sgorgare vi. to gush, spurt.

sgozzare vt. to slaughter; to cut the throat of.

sgrade'vole adj. disagreeable, unpleasant.

sgradire vt. to dislike.

sgradito adj. unwelcome.

sgraffignare vt. to steal, pilfer.

sgrammaticato adj. ungrammatical.

sgranare vt. to shell; to husk, hull: — il rosario, to tell one's beads; — gli occhi, to stare, open one's eyes.

sgranchire vt., **sgranchirsi** vr. to stretch (one's limbs).

sgranocchiare vt. to crunch.

sgrassare vt. to degrease.

sgravare vt. to lighten, relieve; **sgravarsi** vr. to relieve oneself; to give birth (to).

sgra'vio m. lightening; relief.

sgraziato adj. gawky, awkward.

sgretolamento m. crumbling.

sgretolare vt., **sgretolarsi** vr. to crumble.

sgridare vt. to scold, reprove.

sgridata f. scolding, reprimand.

sgroppata f. buck.

sgualatag'gine f. coarseness, vulgarity.

sgualato adj. coarse, loose, vulgar.

sguainare vt. to unsheathe, draw.

sgualcire vt. to wrinkle, crumple.

sgualdrina f. strumpet.

sguardo m. look, glance.

sguarnire vt. to untrim; to dismantle.

sguat'tera f. scullery maid.

sguat'tero m. scullery boy.

sguazzare vi. to splash, wallow.

sguinzagliare vt. to unleash, let loose.

sgusciare vt. to husk, hull; vi. to slip (away, in, out).

si refl.pron. oneself; himself; herself; itself; themselves. indef.pron. one; people, they: non — sa mai, one never knows; — capisce! of course!; — vede che, it is evident that. recipr. pron. each other, one another.

sì (1) adv. yes: un giorno — e l altro no, every other day.

sì (2) adv. see così.

sia ... **sia** conj. whether ... or; both ... and.

sibilante adj. sibilant, hissing.

sibilare vt. to sibilate; to whizz, hiss.

sibilla f. sibyl.

sibillino adj. sibylline.

si'bilo m. hiss, hissing.

sica'rio m. hired assassin.

sicchè conj. so that; so.

siccità f. dryness, drought.

siccome adv., conj. as, since.

sicumera f. self-assurance.

sicura f. safety bolt; safety stop.

sicuramente adv. certainly; safely.

sicurezza f. safety; certainty: pubblica —, police; uscita di —, emergency exit; spillo di —, safety pin.

sicuro (1) m. safety: al —, on the safe side, in safety; andare sul —, to play safe, to take no chances.

sicuro (2) adj. safe, secure; sure, certain; reliable; bold; firm, steady: a colpo —, with no risks; adv. (also di —) sure, certainly.

siderurgi'a f. siderurgy.

siderur'gico m. ironman; steelworker; adj. siderurgical.

sidro m. cider.

siepe f. hedge.

siero m. serum; whey.

siesta f. siesta, afternoon nap.

siffatto adj. such.

sifi'lide f. syphilis.

sifone m. siphon.

sigara'ia f. cigar seller; cigarette girl.

sigara'io m. cigar seller; cigarmaker.

sigaretta f. cigarette.

si'garo m. cigar.

sigillare vt. to seal.

sigillo m. seal.

sigla f. monogram, cipher, abbreviation, initials; (radio and telev.) signature, theme.

siglare vt. to initial.

significare vt. to mean; to express, signify.

significativo adj. significant.

significato m. meaning.

signora f. lady; madam; Mrs.; wife.

signore m. gentleman; Sir; Mr.; master; owner; lord: Nostro Signore, Our Lord; fare il —, to be on Easy Street.

signori'a f. seigniory; domain; Lordship; Ladyship: la Signoria Vostra, Your Lordship or Ladyship.

signorile adj. (m.) gentlemanly; (f.) ladylike; lordly; refined; lavish; luxurious.

signorilità f. distinction.

signorina f. young lady; miss.

signorino m. young gentleman; master.

signorotto m. lordling; squire.

silenziatore m. silencer; muffler.

silen'zio m. silence, quiet; (mil.) taps.

silenzioso adj. silent, quiet; noiseless.

sil'fide f. sylph.

si'lice f. silex, flint.

sil'laba f. syllable.

sillaba'rio m. spelling book.

silo'fono m. (mus.) xylophone.

silograf'ia f. xylography.
siluramento m. torpedoing; dismissal, firing.
silurante f. destroyer, torpedo boat.
silurare vt. to torpedo; to cashier, dismiss, fire.
siluro m. torpedo.
silvestre adj. sylvan.
simboleggiare vt., vi. to symbolize.
simbo'lico adj. symbolical.
simbolis'mo m. symbolism.
sim'bolo m. symbol.
similare adj. similar.
similarità f. similarity.
si'mile m. like; fellow creature; adj. like, alike, similar; such.
similitu'dine f. similitude; simile.
similmente adv. likewise.
similoro m. pinchbeck.
simmetri'a f. symmetry.
simme'trico adj. symmetrical.
Simoni, Renato, Italian playwright and critic (1875–1954).
simpamina f. benzedrine.
simpati'a f. liking; favor; sympathy: attirarsi la — di, to make oneself liked by.
simpa'tico adj. nice, pleasant; congenial: inchiostro —, sympathetic ink.
simpatizzante m. sympathizer.
simpatizzare vi. to sympathize (with); to hit it off (with); to become friends.
simpo'sio m. banquet.
simulare vt. to feign, simulate.
simulatore m. simulator; fraud.
simulazione f. simulation.
simulta'neo adj. simultaneous.
sincerarsi vr. to make sure.
sincerità f. sincerity.
sincero adj. sincere; genuine; loyal.
sincronizzare vt., vi. to synchronize, time.
sin'crono adj. synchronous.
sindacale adj. syndical.
sindacalismo m. syndicalism.
sindacalista m., f. syndicalist.
sindacare vt. to criticize; to dispute.
sindacato m. syndicate; (pol.) trade union, labor union.
sin'daco m. mayor; (comm.) auditor.
sinecura f. sinecure, walkover.
sinfoni'a f. symphony.
sinfo'nico adj. symphonic.
singhiozzare vi. to sob.
singhiozzo m. sob; hiccup.
singolare adj. singular; odd, strange; striking; single.
singolarità f. singularity.
sin'golo adj. single.
singulto see singhiozzo.
sinistra f. left, left hand; left wing.
sinistramente adv. sinisterly.
sinistrato m. damage sufferer.

sinistro m. accident, disaster; (boxing) left; adj. left; sinister.
sinistrorso adj. counterclockwise.
sino see fino (a).
sino'nimo m. synonym.
sinora see finora.
sinovite f. synovitis.
sintassi f. syntax.
sin'tesi f. synthesis.
sinte'tico adj. synthetical; concise.
sintetizzare vt. to synthesize.
sin'tomo m. symptom, sign.
sintoni'a f. syntony.
sintonizzare vt. to tune in (on).
sinuoso adj. sinuous, winding.
sipa'rio m. curtain.
sirena f. mermaid; siren, hooter; foghorn; (fam.) vamp.
siringa f. syringe; syringa.
siringare vt. to syringe.
si'smico adj. seismic.
sistema m. system.
sistemare vt. to arrange; to settle; sistemarsi vr. to settle.
sistema'tico adj. systematic.
sistemazione f. arrangement, settlement; situation, employment.
sito m. place, spot; adj. situated.
situare vt. to place.
situazione f. situation; position.
slabbrare vt. to jag; slabbrarsi vr. to become jagged.
slacciare vt. to unlace, undo; to untie; to unfasten; to unbutton; slacciarsi vr. to get untied, loose; to untie; to unbutton.
sladinare vt. (mach.) to run in.
slanciare vt. to throw; to thin out, taper; to streamline; slanciarsi vr. to rush; to venture; to get (more) slender.
slanciato adj. slim, slender.
slan'cio m. rush, impetus; enthusiasm, warmth: prendere lo —, to take the start.
slargare see allargare.
slattare vt. to wean.
slavato adj. wan, colorless.
sleale adj. disloyal, unfair, treacherous.
slealtà f. disloyalty.
slegare vt. to untie, unbind; slegarsi vr. to become untied, to get free.
slegato adj. untied; (fig.) disconnected.
slitta f. sled, sledge, sleigh.
slittare vi. to skid, slip, slide.
slogamento m., slogatura f. dislocation.
slogare vt. to dislocate; slogarsi vr. to become dislocated: slogarsi un braccio, to dislocate one's arm.
sloggiare vt. to dislodge; to oust, eject, remove; vi. to quit, move.
smacchiare vt. to scour, clean.

smacco *m.* affront, shame.

smagliante *adj.* dazzling, bright.

smagliare *vt.* to ravel; **smagliarsi** *vr.* to run, ravel.

smagliatura *f.* run; ladder.

smagrire *see* dimagrire.

smaliziare *vt.*, **smaliziarsi** *vr.* to make wise.

smaliziato *adj.* worldlywise.

smaltare *vt.* to enamel, glaze.

smaltatura *f.* enameling.

smaltire *vt.* to digest; to recover from (*drunkenness*); (*comm.*) to sell out.

smaltito'io *m.* sewer, drain.

smalto *m.* enamel.

smanceri'a *f.* fuss.

smangiare *vt.* to eat away; **smangiarsi** *vr.* to corrode; to fret.

sma'nia *f.* frenzy; craze, passion.

smaniare *vi.* to rave.

smanioso *adj.* eager.

smantellare *vt.* to dismantle.

smargiasso *m.* bully, blusterer.

smarrimento *m.* bewilderment, dismay; miscarriage; loss.

smarrire *vt.* to lose; to mislay; **smarrirsi** *vr.* to get lost; to become dismayed; to go astray.

smascellarsi *vr.*: — dalle risa, to split one's sides with laughter.

smascherare *vt.*, **smascherarsi** *vr.* to unmask.

smembramento *m.* dismemberment.

smembrare *vt.* to dismember.

smemoratag'gine *f.* forgetfulness; lack of memory.

smemorato *adj.* forgetful; absent-minded.

smentire *vt.* to disprove; to deny; to refute; to give the lie to; to belie; **smentirsi** *vr.* to belie oneself.

smentita *f.* denial, refutation; dissmeraldo *m.* emerald. [proval.

smerciare *vt.* to sell; to sell out.

smer'cio *m.* sale.

smergo *m.* (*ornith.*) cormorant.

smerigliare *vt.* to emery; to grind.

smerigliato *adj.* emeried; ground or frosted (*as glass*).

smeri'glio *m.* emery.

smerlare *vt.* to scallop.

smerlo *m.* scallop.

smesso *adj.* cast-off. *pp.* of smettere.

smet'tere *vt.*, *vi.*[76] to cease, stop, give up: — un vestito, to cast off a suit; smettila! stop it!

smezzare *see* dimezzare.

smidollato *m.* softy; *adj.* weakly.

smilzo *adj.* slim, slender, thin.

sminuire *vt.* to belittle.

sminuzzare *vt.* to mince.

smistamento *m.* distribution; (*rail.*) shunting.

smistare *vt.* to distribute; (*rail.*) to shunt.

smisurato *adj.* immense, enormous.

smobilitare *vt.* to demobilize.

smobilitazione *f.* demobilization.

smoccolare *vt.* to snuff; *vi.* to swear.

smodato *adj.* immoderate.

smontare *vt.* to dismount; to unhorse; to disassemble; to damp; to flatten; *vi.* to demobilize, alight; to fade; **smontarsi** *vr.* to cool down.

smor'fia *f.* wry face, grimace.

smorfiosa *f.* coquette.

smorfioso *adj.* mawkish.

smorto *adj.* pale, wan.

smorzare *vt.* to abate; to appease; to extinguish; to quench; to tone down; **smorzarsi** *vr.* to abate; to go out.

smosso *adj.* loose. *pp.of* smuovere.

smozzicare *vt.* to break; to clip.

smozzicato *adj.* broken.

smunto *adj.* haggard; faded.

smuo'vere *vt.*[1] to move; to displace; (*agr.*) to till; to remove; to budge; to deter; **smuoversi** *vr.* to budge.

smussare *vt.* to blunt; to bevel.

snaturare *vt.* to distort; to misrepresent.

snaturato *adj.* vicious, unnatural.

snebbiare *vt.*, **snebbiarsi** *vr.* to clear(up).

snellezza *f.* slenderness; nimbleness.

snello *adj.* slender; nimble; lively.

snervante *adj.* enervating.

snervare *vt.* to enervate; **snervarsi** *vr.* to break down; to weaken.

snidare *vt.* to drive out; to unburrow.

snobismo *m.* snobbery.

snocciolare *vt.* to cough up.

snodare *vt.* to untie, loosen, undo; **snodarsi** *vr.* to get untied; to wind.

snodo *m.* (*mach.*) joint, knuckle.

snudare *vt.* to bare; to unsheathe.

soave *adj.* sweet; mild.

soavità *f.* sweetness, softness.

sobbalzare *vi.* to start; to jolt.

sobbalzo *m.* start; jolt.

sobbarcarsi *vr.* to take upon oneself; to shoulder.

sobborgo *m.* suburb, outskirt.

sobillare *vt.* to instigate, stir up.

sobillatore *m.* instigator.

sobrietà *f.* temperance.

so'brio *adj.* temperate, sober; quiet.

socchiu'dere *vt.* to half-shut; to set ajar.

socchiuso *adj.* ajar.

soccom'bere *vi.* to succumb.

soccor'rere *vt.*[44] to succor, help; *vi.* to occur.

soccorso (1) *pp.* of soccorrere.

soccorso (2) *m.* succor, help, assistance, aid: pronto —, first aid; uscita di —, emergency exit.

sociale *adj.* social: **capitale —,** permanent capital; **ragione —,** style.

socialismo *m.* socialism.

socialista *m.* socialist.

società *f.* society; company; partnership; association; club: **— in accomandita, — a responsabilità limitata,** limited liability company; **— anonima,** corporation, joint stock company.

socie'vole *adj.* companionable.

so'cio *m.* associate; member; partner.

sociologi'a *f.* sociology.

socio'logo *m.* sociologist.

soda *f.* soda.

sodali'zio *m.* society; guild; association; brotherhood.

soddisfacente *adj.* satisfactory.

soddisfare *vt.*[138] to satisfy; to gratify; to please; to grant; to discharge.

soddisfatto *adj.* satisfied; gratified; pleased; content. *pp.of* soddisfare.

soddisfazione *f.* satisfaction; gratification.

so'dio *m.* sodium.

sodisfare *see* soddisfare.

sodo *adj.* compact, firm; fast; hard; *adv.* hard; soundly.

sodomi'a *f.* sodomy.

sodomita *m.* sodomite.

sofà *m.* sofa, davenport.

sofferente *adj.* suffering; sickly.

sofferenza *f.* suffering, pain.

soffermarsi *vr.* to linger.

sofferto *pp.of* soffrire.

soffiare *vi., vt.* to blow: **soffiarsi il naso,** to blow one's nose.

sof'fice *adj.* soft.

soffietto *m.* bellows (*pl.*); hood (*of a carriage*); puff, write-up (*journ.*)

sof'fio *m.* blowing; puff; blast; breath: **— al cuore,** heart murmur.

soffione *m.* blowpipe; fumarole.

soffitta *f.* attic, garret.

soffitto *m.* ceiling.

soffocamento *m.* stifling, suffocation.

soffocante *adj.* suffocating.

soffocare *vt., vi.* to stifle, smother, suffocate, choke; to hush up.

soffocato *adj.* stifled; muffled.

soffocazione *f.* suffocation.

sof'foco *m.* sultriness, oppression.

soffon'dere *vt.*[65] to suffuse (*with*).

soffregare *vt.* to rub.

soffrig'gere *vt.* to fry slightly.

soffrire *vt., vi.*[94] to suffer (*from*); to undergo; to endure, bear.

soffuso *adj.* suffused (*with*). *pp.of* soffondere

sofista *m.* sophist.

sofi'stico *adj.* sophistical; fault-finding, fastidious.

soggettista *m.* script writer.

soggettivo *adj.* subjective.

soggetto *m.* subject; matter; topic; person; scenario, story: **cattivo —,** rascal, scamp; *adj.* subject: **andar — a,** to be subject or liable to.

soggezione *f.* subjection; respect, awe; uneasiness: **incutere —, to** command respect, to awe.

sogghignare *vi.* to sneer.

sogghigno *m.* sneer.

soggiacere *vi.*[68] to be liable (*to*); to succumb.

soggiogare *vt.* to subdue, subjugate; (*fig.*) to enthrall.

soggiornare *vi.* to stay, sojourn.

soggiorno *m.* stay, sojourn: **stanza di —,** living room.

soggiun'gere *vt.* to add; *vi.* to remark, reply.

soggiuntivo *adj.* subjunctive.

so'glia *f.* threshold.

so'gliola *f.* sole.

sognare *vt., vi.* to dream: **— a occhi aperti,** to daydream.

sognatore *m.* dreamer.

sogno *m.* dream; reverie: **nemmeno per —,** by no means.

so'ia *f.* soybean, soya.

sola'io *m.* lumber room; garret.

solamente *adv.* only; solely; merely.

solare *adj.* solar.

sola'rio *m.* solarium; sunroom.

solati'o *adj.* sunny.

solatura *f.* soling.

solcare *vt.* to furrow.

solco *m.* furrow.

soldatesco *adj.* soldierlike, soldierly.

soldato *m.* soldier: **— semplice,** private; **— scelto,** private first class; **andare —,** to join the army.

soldo *m.* farthing, penny; money; pay: **non avere un —,** to be penniless; **al — di,** in the pay of.

sole *m.* sun; sunshine: **levar del —,** sunrise; **tramonto del —,** sunset; **cura di —,** heliotherapy; **alla luce del —,** in the daylight, openly.

soleggiare *vt.* to sun.

soleggiato *adj.* sunny.

solenne *adj.* solemn.

solennità *f.* solemnity.

solennizzare *vt.* to solemnize.

solere *vi.*[139] to be accustomed (*to*), be wont (*to*); to use.

solerte *adj.* industrious, diligent.

sole'rzia *f.* diligence.

soletta *f.* inner sole; ceiling.

soletto *adj.* alone, lonely.

solfa *f.* gamut.

solfanello *m.* match.

solfara, solfatara *f.* sulphur mine.

solfato *m.* sulphate.

solfeggiare *vi.* (*mus.*) to sol-fa.

solferino *m.* purplish, solferino.

solfo *see* zolfo.

solfo'rico adj. sulphuric.
solfuro m. sulphide.
solidale adj. joint, solidary; loyal (to).
solidarietà f. solidarity; loyalty, sympathy.
solidificare vt. to solidify.
solidità f. solidity; fastness.
so'lido adj. solid, firm; fast (as colors): in —, jointly.
solilo'quio m. soliloquy, monologue.
solino m. collar.
solista m., f. soloist.
solitamente adv. usually; as a rule.
solita'rio m. solitary, hermit; solitaire or patience (card game); solitaire (a gem set by itself); adj. solitary, lonely, secluded: verme —, tapeworm.
so'lito adj. usual; used, accustomed: al —, as usual; di —, usually, as a rule; essere —, to use. pp.of solere.
solitu'dine f. loneliness, solitude.
sollazzare vt. to amuse; sollazzarsi vr. to enjoy oneself.
sollazzo m. amusement, sport.
sollecitare vt. to request, solicit; to hasten.
sollecitazione f. solicitation.
solle'cito m. pressure, solicitation; adj. quick; prompt; solicitous.
sollecitu'dine f. diligence; promptness; solicitude, concern.
solleone m. dog days.
solleticare vt. to tickle; to flatter.
solle'tico m. tickling; excitement: fare il — a, to tickle.
sollevamento m. lifting.
sollevare vt. to lift, raise; to heave, hoist; to cause; to stir up; to alleviate, relieve; sollevarsi vr. to rise, get up; to lift; (aeron.) to take off; to be or feel relieved.
sollevazione f. sedition, riot, revolt.
sollievo m. relief, comfort.
sollu'chero m.: andare in —, to be in seventh heaven.
solo m. (the) only one: da — a —, in private; adj. alone; lonely; only; single, one; sole: da sè —, by oneself; adv. only.
solsti'zio m. solstice.
soltanto see solamente.
solu'bile adj. soluble.
solutore m. solver.
soluzione f. solution.
solvente m., adj. solvent.
solvi'bile adj. reliable, solvent.
solvibilità f. reliability, solvency.
soma f. load, burden; weight.
somaro m. donkey, ass.
somigliante adj. resembling, like.
somiglianza f. resemblance.
somigliare vi. to resemble, be like.
somma f. amount, sum; addition.

sommare vt. to add (up), total; vi. to amount to.
somma'rio m., adj. summary.
sommato adj.: tutto —, on the whole.
sommer'gere vt.[81] to submerge; to flood; sommergersi vr. to sink; (naut.) to submerge.
sommergi'bile m. submarine; adj. submersible.
sommerso pp.of sommergere.
sommessamente adv. in a subdued voice; softly.
sommesso adj. soft, subdued.
somministrare vt. to administer.
somministrazione f. administration.
sommità f. summit; top.
sommo m. top, summit; master talent; adj. highest, extreme, top: per sommi capi, summarily.
sommossa f. riot, rising.
sommosso pp.of sommuovere.
sommovimento m. disturbance.
sommozzatore m. (naut.) diver, frogman.
sommuo'vere vt.[80] to excite, stir up.
sonagliera f. collar of bells.
sona'glio m. rattle, bell.
sonare vt., vi. to sound; to ring; to play; to strike (hours as a clock); aver 60 anni sonati, to be on the wrong side of sixty.
sonata f. ring, peal; (mus.) sonata.
sonatore m. player.
sonda f. probe, sound; sounding line: pallone —, pilot balloon.
sondag'gio m. sounding.
sondare vt. to sound; to probe.
soneri'a f. alarum, alarm.
sonetto m. sonnet.
sonnacchioso adj. drowsy, sleepy.
sonnambulismo m. sleepwalking.
sonnam'bulo m., sonnam'bula f. sleepwalker.
sonnecchiare vi. to doze.
sonnellino m. doze, nap.
sonni'fero m. soporific, narcotic.
sonno m. sleep: aver —, to be sleepy; prendere —, to drop off.
sonnolento adj. sleepy, drowsy.
sonnolenza f. drowsiness.
sonorità f. sonorousness.
sonorizzazione f. sound recording.
sonoro adj. sonorous, sounding: film —, sound film; colonna (onda) sonora, sound track (wave).
sontuoso adj. sumptuous.
soperchieri'a see sopruso.
sopire vt. to appease, calm.
sopore m. drowsiness.
sopori'fero m., adj. soporific.
sopperire vi. to provide (for).
soppesare vt. to weigh (in one's hand).
soppiantare vt. to oust, supplant.
soppiatto, (di) adv. stealthily.

sopporta'bile *adj.* bearable.

sopportare *vt.* to bear, support; to endure, stand; to tolerate.

sopportazione *f.* forbearance, endurance; tolerance.

soppressione *f.* suppression, abolition.

soppri'mere *vt.*[39] to suppress; to abolish; to omit; to kill.

soppresso *pp.of* sopprimere.

sopra *m.* upper side; *prep.* on, upon; over; above; beyond; about: **al di — di**, above; **— pensiero**, lost in thought; **passar — a**, to pass over; *adv.* above, over; upstairs; overhead: **il piano di —**, the upper floor; **andare di —**, to go upstairs; **dormirci —**, to sleep on it; **pensarci —**, to think it over.

sopra'bito *m.* overcoat.

sopracci'glio *m.* eyebrow, brow.

sopraccoperta *f.* coverlet; cover, wrapper (*of a book*).

sopraffare *vt.* to overpower, overwhelm; to overcome.

sopraffazione *f.* overpowering, oppression, tyranny.

sopraffino *adj.* first-rate, excellent.

sopraggitto *m.* overcast stitch.

sopraggiun'gere *vi.* to come up, arrive; to occur, happen.

sopraintendente, soprintendente *m.* superintendent.

soprainten'dere *vi.* to superintend.

sopraluogo *m.* survey, inspection.

sopralzo *m.* (*building*) addition.

soprammercato, (per) *adv.* moreover, to boot.

soprammo'bile *m.* knickknack.

soprannaturale *m., adj.* supernatural.

soprannome *m.* nickname.

soprannominare *vt.* to nickname.

soprannu'mero, (in) *adv.* in excess, extra.

soprappassag'gio *m.* overpass.

soprappensiero *adv.* absent-minded y

soprappiù *m.* extra.

soprapprezzo *m.* additional price.

soprascarpa *f.* overshoe.

soprascritta *f.* address.

soprassalto *m.* start: **di —**, with a start; suddenly.

soprassedere *vi.* to wait; to bide one's time: **— a**, to delay; to suspend.

soprassoldo *m.* extra pay.

soprastante *adj.* overhanging; overhead, above.

soprastare *see* sovrastare.

soprattassa *f.* additional tax.

soprattutto *adv.* above all; mainly.

sopravanzare *vt.* to surpass, excel; *vi.* to project, jut out; to be left.

sopravanzo *m.* surplus.

sopravvalutare *vt.* to overrate.

sopravvenire *see* sopraggiungere.

sopravvento *m.* upper hand, advantage; *adv.* (*naut.*) windward.

sopravvissuto *m.* survivor.

sopravvivenza *f.* survival, surviving.

sopravvi'vere *vi.* to survive: **— a**, to outlive.

soprosso *m.* (*surg.*) exostosis.

sopruso *m.* offense; outrage.

soqquadro, (a) *adv.* topsy-turvy.

sorba *f.* sorb, sorb apple.

sorbetto *m.* ice cream.

sorbire *vt.* to sip; **sorbirsi** *vr.* (*fam.*) to put up with, endure.

sorbo *m.* sorb, service tree.

sor'cio *m.* mouse (*pl.* mice).

sor'dido *adj.* sordid.

sordina *f.* (*mus.*) mute, sordino: **mettere la —**, to muffle; **in —**, softly; stealthily.

sordità *f.* deafness.

sordo *m.* deaf man; *adj.* deaf; dull; hollow, muffled: **fare il —**, to turn a deaf ear.

sordomuto *m.* deaf-mute; *adj.* deaf and dumb.

sorella *f.* sister.

sorellastra *f.* half-sister; stepsister.

sorgente *f.* source, spring.

sor'gere *vi.*[110] to rise, arise; to spring up: **far — un dubbio**, to raise a doubt.

sormontare *vt.* to surmount.

sornione *m.* slyboots; *adj.* sly.

sorpassare *vt.* to run past, pass; to surpass; to outdo, excel.

sorpassato *adj.* old-fashioned, obsolete.

sorpasso *m.* overtaking. [lete.

sorprendente *adj.* astonishing.

sorpren'dere *vt.*[99] to surprise, astonish; to catch: **— la buona fede di**, to steal a march on.

sorpresa *f.* surprise: **di —**, unawares; by surprise.

sorpreso *adj.* surprised. *pp.of* sorprendere.

sorreg'gere *vt.*[105] to support.

sorretto *pp.of* sorreggere.

sorridente *adj.* smiling.

sorri'dere *vi.*[108] to smile: **mi sorride l'idea di**, I look forward to; **questa idea non mi sorride**, this idea does not appeal to me.

sorriso (1) *m.* smile.

sorriso (2) *pp.of* sorridere.

sorsata *f.* gulp, draft.

sorseggiare *vt., vi.* to sip.

sorso *m.* draft; drop: **bere d'un —**, to gulp down; **bere a piccoli sorsi**, to sip.

sorta *f.* kind, sort.

sorte *f.* lot, destiny, fate; luck, fortune; chance: **tirare a —**, to cast lots; **toccare in — a**, to fall to one's lot.

sorteggiare vt. to draw (by lot): — **un premio**, to draw a prize.

sorteg'gio m. drawing of lots.

sortile'gio m. sortilege, sorcery.

sortire vt. to get, obtain; to give, yield; vi. to be drawn (by lot); to go out, get out.

sortita f. (mil.) sally.

sorto pp.of sorgere.

sorvegliante m. inspector; caretaker, keeper; watchman; overseer.

sorveglianza f. surveillance; supervision.

sorvegliare vt. to oversee; to watch, watch over; **sorvegliarsi** vr. to control oneself; to watch one another.

sorvolare vi. to fly over; to pass over.

so'sia m. double.

sospen'dere vt.[10] to suspend; to hang; to interrupt, discontinue, stop; to defer, put off, adjourn.

sospensione f. suspension; suspense: — **cardanica**, gimbals.

sospenso'rio adj. suspensory; m. athletic supporter.

sospeso adj. suspended, hanging; in abeyance; pending: **ponte —**, suspension bridge; **con l'animo in —**, in suspense pp.of sospendere.

sospettare vt., vi. to suspect.

sospetto m. suspicion; suspect; adj. suspect, suspicious.

sospettoso adj. suspicious.

sospin'gere vt.[36] to drive, push.

sospinto adj. pushed, driven: **ad ogni pie' —**, at every moment. pp.of sospingere.

sospirare vt. to long for; vi. to sigh.

sospirato adj. longed for.

sospiro m. sigh.

sossopra adv. upside down, topsyturvy.

sosta f. halt, stay; rest; truce; pause; warehousing.

sostantivo m., adj. substantive.

sostanza f. substance; matter; gist; fortune: **in —**, in short; altogether.

sostanzioso adj. substantial.

sostare vi. to pause; to stop; to cease.

sostegno m. prop, support.

sostenere vt.[141] to support, sustain; to suffer; to stand; to undergo; to maintain: — **una parte**, to play a role; **sostenersi** vr. to support oneself; to lean (on); to support each other.

sostenitore m. supporter.

sostenimento m. sustenance.

sostentare vt. to support; **sostentarsi** vr. to support oneself.

sostenuto adj. aloof; stiff; (comm.) steady; (mus.) sustained.

sostituire vt. to substitute.

sostituto m. substitute.

sostituzione f. substitution.

sottacere vt.[110] to withhold, hold back.

sottaceti m.pl. pickles.

sottana f. petticoat; skirt; cassock, soutane.

sottecchi adv. surreptitiously.

sotterfu'gio m. subterfuge.

sotterra adv. underground.

sotterra'nea f. subway.

sotterra'neo m. cave, vault; adj. underground, subterranean.

sotterrare vt. to bury.

sottigliezza f. thinness; subtlety.

sottile adj. thin, slender; subtle.

sottilizzare vt. to subtilize; to quibble.

sottinten'dere vt. to imply.

sottinteso m. matter of course, thing implied; adj. implied, understood, implicit.

sotto adv., prep. under, underneath; beneath, below: **al piano di —**, downstairs; **sott'olio**, in oil; — **mano**, handy; — **voce**, in a low voice; **prendere — gamba**, to make light of.

sottobicchiere m. coaster.

sottobosco m. underbrush.

sottoc'chio adv. under one's eyes.

sottochiave adv. under lock and key.

sottocoperta f., adv. (naut.) below.

sottocuta'neo adj. subcutaneous.

sottogola f. chin strap; throatlatch.

sottolineare vt. to underscore; to emphasize, lay stress on.

sottomano m. writing pad; adv. underhand.

sottomarino m., adj. submarine.

sottomesso adj. submissive. pp.of sottomettere.

sottomet'tere vt.[76] to subdue, subjugate, subject; to conquer; **sottomet'tersi** vr. to submit; to yield.

sottomissione f. submission.

sottopassag'gio m. underpass.

sottoporre vt.[91] to submit; to subject; to put; **sottoporsi** vr. to submit; to undergo.

sottoposto m. subordinate. pp.of sottoporre.

sottoprodotto m. by-product.

sottoscritto m., adj. undersigned. pp. of sottoscri'vere.

sottoscrittore m. subscriber.

sottoscri'vere vt., vi.[184] to subscribe (to), underwrite; to sign; **sottoscri'versi** vr. to sign.

sottoscrizione f. subscription.

sottosegreta'rio m. undersecretary.

sottosopra adv. upside down; topsyturvy.

sottostante adj. lying below, lower.

sottostare vi.[131] to lie below; to submit; to give in.

sottosuolo *m.* underground.

sottotenente *m.* second lieutenant; (*navy*) ensign.

sottoterra *adv.* underground.

sottoti'tolo *m.* subtitle; caption.

sottovalutare *vt.* to underrate.

sottovento *adv.* leeward.

sottoveste *f.* undergarment; waistcoat.

sottovoce *adv.* in a low voice, softly.

sottrarre *vt.*[144] to subtract; to steal; to deduct; to rescue, save; to snatch; **sottrarsi** *vr.*: **sottrarsi a**, to escape, evade; to shirk.

sottratto *pp.of* sottrarre.

sottrazione *f.* subtraction, deduction; theft.

sottufficiale *m.* noncommissioned officer.

sovente *adv.* frequently, often.

soverchiante *adj.* overwhelming.

soverchiare *vt.* to overflow; to surpass; to overwhelm.

sover'chio *m.* surplus, excess; *adj.* excessive.

sovra *see* sopra.

sovrabbondante *adj.* superabundant.

sovrabbondanza *f.* superabundance.

sovrabbondare *vi.* to superabound.

sovraccaricare *vt.* to overburden.

sovracca'rico *m.* overweight; *adj.* overburdened.

sovrana *f.* sovereign.

sovrano *m.* sovereign; *adj.* sovereign; paramount.

sovrappopolare *vt.* to overpopulate.

sovrapporre *vt.*[35] to superimpose (*on*, *upon*); to overlay; **sovrapporsi** *vr.* to be superimposed: **sovrapporsi a**, to overlap; to overwhelm, outdo.

sovrapposizione *f.* superimposition.

sovrapproduzione *f.* overproduction.

sovrastante *adj.* overhanging; impending; overhead, above.

sovrastare *vt.*, *vi.*[144] to overhang; to impend; to tower (*over*); to crown; to surpass, excel.

sovreccitare *vt.* to overexcite.

sovreccitazione *f.* overexcitement.

sovrimposta *f.* additional tax.

sovrumano *adj.* superhuman.

sovvenire *vt.* to help, assist; **sovvenirsi** *vr.*: **sovvenirsi di**, to recall, remember.

sovvenzionare *vt.* to subsidize.

sovvenzione *f.* subvention, subsidy.

sovversivo *m.* (*pol.*) extremist; *adj.* subversive.

sovvertimento *m.* subversion.

sovvertire *vt.* to subvert.

sozzo *adj.* filthy, foul.

sozzura *f.* filth.

spaccamontagne *m.* braggart.

spaccare *vt.*, **spaccarsi** *vr.* to cleave, split, crack.

spaccato *m.* section; *adj.* split, cleft.

spaccatura *f.* split, crack, crevice.

spacciare *vt.* to sell off; to palm off; to pass off (*as counterfeit notes*); to spread; to dispatch; **spacciarsi** *vr.* to set up as.

spacciato *adj.* past cure.

spacciatore *m.* seller: — **di monete false**, passer of counterfeit money, **spac'cio** *m.* sale; shop. [layer.

spacco *m.* split; crack.

spacconata *f.* brag.

spaccone *m.* braggart, boaster.

spada *f.* sword: **passare a fil di —**, to put to the sword; **difendere a — tratta**, to defend doggedly.

spadaccino *m.* swordsman.

spadroneggiare *vi.* to boss.

spaesato *adj.* out of one's element.

spaghetto *m.* (*coll.*) fear: **avere un bello —**, to be in a blue funk; (*pl.*) spaghetti.

spagnoletta *f.* cigarette; spool; peanut.

spagnolo *m.* Spaniard; *adj.* Spanish.

spago *m.* string, twine.

spaiare *vt.* to unpair, unspan.

spalancare *vt.*, **spalancarsi** *vr.* to open wide, to throw open.

spalancato *adj.* wide open.

spalare *vt.* to shovel.

spalatore *m.* shoveler.

spalla *f.* shoulder; (*mus.*) second violin; (*theat.*) "stooge." **spalle** *pl.* shoulders, back: **con le spalle al muro**, cornered; **voltare le spalle a**, to turn one's back upon; **cogliere alle spalle**, to attack from the rear; **stringersi nelle spalle**, to shrug.

Spallanzani, Lazzaro, Italian naturalist (1729–1799).

spallata *f.* shouldering.

spalleggiare *vt.* to back, support.

spalletta *f.* retaining wall; jamb.

spalliera *f.* back (*of a chair, etc.*); head (*of a bed*); trellis (*for plants*).

spallina *f.* epaulette; shoulder strap; shoulder loop.

spalluc'cia *f.*: **far spallucce**, to shrug.

spalmare *vt.* to smear; to spread.

spanare *vt.* to mar or strip out the thread (*of a screw*).

spanciata *see* scorpacciata.

span'dere *vt.*[141] to spread; to diffuse; to scatter; to send forth; to shed: **spendere e —**, to squander; **spandersi** *vr.* to spread.

spanna *f.* span.

spannare *vt.* to skim.

spappolare *vt.*, **spappolarsi** *vr.* to crush, squash, pulp.

sparadrappo *m.* plaster.

sparare *vt.*, *vi.* to shoot (*at*), fire (*at*); to discharge: **spararle grosse**, to draw the long bow, tell a tall tale.

sparato m. shirtfront.

sparatore m. shooter.

sparato'ria f. shooting.

sparecchiare vt. to clear away.

spareg'gio m. disparity, deficit.

spar'gere vt.[182] to spread; to diffuse; to scatter; to shed; **spargersi** vr. to spread.

spargimento m. spreading, scattering: — di sangue, bloodshed.

spargitore m. spreader.

sparigliare vt. to unmatch.

sparire vi.[188] to disappear; far —, to conceal; to steal.

sparizione f. disappearance.

sparlare vi: — di, to slander.

sparo m. shot; report.

sparpagliare vt., **sparpagliarsi** vr. to scatter.

sparso adj. scattered: ordine —, extended order. pp.of **spandere** and **spargere**.

spartiac'que m. watershed.

spartire vt. to share, divide; to part, split: non aver nulla da — con, to have nothing in common with.

spartito m. (mus.) score.

spartizione f. division, sharing.

sparto m. esparto.

sparuto adj. gaunt.

sparviere, sparviero m. hawk.

spasimante m. lover, wooer.

spasimare vi. to agonize, writhe (with); to long (for): — per, to be head over heels in love with.

spa'simo m. pang, spasm.

spasmo'dico adj. spasmodic.

spassionato adj. unbiased; dispassionate.

spasso m. toy, pastime; fun: per —, for fun; andare a —, to go for a walk; mandare a —, to send packing; trovarsi a —, to be out of a job.

spassoso adj. amusing, droll.

spato m. (min.) spar.

spa'tola f. spatula; slapstick.

spaurac'chio m. scarecrow; bugaboo.

spaurire vt. to frighten.

spavalderi'a f. boldness; defiance.

spavaldo adj. bold; impudent.

spaventare vt. to frighten, scare; **spaventarsi** vr. to take fright, be scared.

spaventevole adj. frightful, dreadful.

spavento m. fright, fear, terror.

spaventoso adj. dreadful.

spaziale adj. space.

spaziare (1) vi. to rove, wander about; to soar.

spaziare (2) vt. to space.

spaziatura f. spacing.

spazientirsi see **impazientirsi**.

spa'zio m. space; room; extent; area; surface; distance; interval.

spazioso adj. spacious, large, wide, roomy.

spazzacamino m. chimney sweeper.

spazzamine m. minesweeper.

spazzaneve m. snowplow.

spazzare vt. to sweep (away, off).

spazzatura f. sweeping; sweepings.

spazzatura'io, spazzino m. sweeper, scavenger, dustman, garbageman.

spazzettone m. floor brush.

spaz'zola f. brush.

spazzolare vt. to brush; **spazzolarsi** vr. to brush oneself.

spazzolino m. toothbrush; nailbrush.

spazzolone see **spazzettone**.

specchiarsi vr. to look at oneself (in the mirror, in a reflecting surface); to be reflected.

specchiera f. looking glass, mirror.

specchietto m. hand mirror; schedule.

spec'chio m. mirror; looking glass; pattern; form, schedule, prospectus: — d'acqua, water surface.

speciale adj. special, peculiar.

specialista m. specialist.

specialità f. speciality; peculiarity; specialty: — farmaceutiche, proprietary medicines.

specializzare vt., **specializzarsi** vr. to specialize.

specialmente adv. especially.

spe'cie f. kind, sort, species: sotto — di, under pretense of; (in) —, especially; far —, to surprise.

speci'fica f. detailed note.

specificare vt. to specify.

speci'fico m., adj. specific.

specillo m. (surg.) probe, sound.

specioso adj. specious.

spe'cola f. observatory.

speculare vt., vi. to speculate.

speculativo adj. speculative.

speculatore m. speculator: — al rialzo, bull; — al ribasso, bear.

speculazione f. speculation.

spedire vt. to dispatch; to send; to ship, forward.

speditamente adv. expeditiously.

speditezza f. expeditiousness.

spedito adj. prompt; quick; easy.

speditore m. forwarder, sender.

spedizione f. expedition; consignment; sending, forwarding; dispatch: corpo di —, expeditionary force.

spedizioniere m. carrier, forwarding agent; shipping agent.

spe'gnere vt.[184] to extinguish, put out; (elec.) to switch out; to quench; **spe'gnersi** vr. to go out; to fade, fail; to die; to die away.

spelacchiare vt. to strip (of hair); (fig.) to fleece; **spelacchiarsi** vr. to lose one's hair.

spelacchiato *adj.* mangy, hairless.
spelare *vt.* to make bald; **spelarsi** *vr.* to become bald.
spelato *adj.* bald.
spellare *vt.* to skin; **spellarsi** *vr.* to get skinned; to peel.
spellatura *f.* excoriation.
spelonca *f.* cave, den.
spendaccione *m.* spendthrift.
spen'dere *vt.*, *vi.*[10] to spend.
spenderec'cio *adj.* prodigal.
spen'gere *see* spegnere.
spennacchiare *vt.* to unfeather; to pluck; to fleece.
spennare *see* spennacchiare.
spennellare *vt.* to touch.
spensieratezza *f.* lightheartedness.
spensierato *adj.* carefree.
spento *adj.* extinguished, put out; dead; lifeless. *pp.of* spegnere.
spenzolare *see* penzolare.
speranza *f.* hope; expectation: **di belle speranze,** promising.
speranzoso *adj.* hopeful, confident.
sperare *vt.*, *vi.* to hope (*for*); to expect; to trust: — **in bene,** to hope for the best; **speriamo in Dio,** in God we trust.
sper'dere *vt.*[57] to scatter, disperse; **sper'dersi** *vr.* to disperse; to get lost, go astray.
sperduto, sperso *adj.* lost. *pp.of* sperdere.
sperequazione *f.* disproportion.
spergiurare *vt.* to perjure oneself.
spergiuro *m.* perjurer; perjury.
spericolato *m.* daredevil; *adj.* reckless.
sperimentale *adj.* experimental.
sperimentare *vt.* to experiment, test, try.
sperimentato *adj.* experienced.
speronare *vt.* to ram.
sperone *m.* spur; abutment; ram.
sperperare *vt.* to squander.
sperperatore *m.* squanderer.
sper'pero *m.* waste, squandering.
sperso *see* sperduto.
sperticato *adj.* exaggerated, excessive.
spesa *f.* expenditure; expense; cost, charge: **andare a far la —,** to go out marketing; **fare le spese di,** to be the victim of; **fare le spese di una conversazione,** to be the main subject of a conversation.
spesato *adj.* supported.
speso *adj.* spent. *pp.of* spendere.
spessire *vt.*, **spessirsi** *vr.* to thicken.
spesso *adj.* thick: **spesse volte,** often; *adv.* frequently, often.
spetta'bile *adj.* respectable: — **Ditta,** Gentlemen, Dear Sirs.
spetta'colo *m.* sight, spectacle; show, performance: **dare — di sè,** to make a fool of oneself.

spettacoloso *adj.* spectacular, sensational; gorgeous; grand.
spettanza *f.* due: **essere di — di,** to belong to; to concern.
spettare *vi.* to belong (*to*); to be up (*to*); to be one's turn.
spettatore *m.* spectator; bystander: **gli spettatori,** the audience.
spettegolare *vi.* to gossip.
spettinare *vt.* to tousle; **spettinarsi** *vr.* to ruffle one's hair.
spettinato *adj.* tousled.
spettrale *adj.* ghostly, spectral: **analisi —,** spectrum analysis.
spettro *m.* ghost; (*phys.*) spectrum.
speziale *m.* chemist; druggist.
spe'zie *f.pl.* spices, spicery.
spezieri'a *f.* grocery; drugstore.
spezzare *vt.*, **spezzarsi** *vr.* to break.
spezzatino *m.* stew.
spezzettare *vt.* to mince.
spezzone *m.* bomb stick.
spi'a *f.* spy; informer, "stool pigeon."
spiaccicare *vt.* to crush, pulp.
spiacente *adj.* sorry; unpleasant.
spiacere *see* dispiacere (*2*).
spiace'vole *adj.* unpleasant.
spiag'gia *f.* shore; beach.
spianare *vt.* to smooth; to level; to settle; to raze, demolish: — **un fucile contro,** to level a gun at; — **la pasta,** to roll out dough; — **la strada a,** to pave the way for.
spianata *f.* esplanade.
spianato'ia *f.* smoothing board.
spianato'io *m.* rolling pin.
spiano, (a tutto) *adv.* profusely, abundantly; with a will.
spiantato *m.* (*coll.*) destitute; lame duck, have-not; *adj.* penniless.
spiare *vt.* to spy.
spiattellare *vt.* to blurt out.
spiazzo *m.* plaza; clearing.
spiccare *vt.* to detach; to pick: — **un balzo,** to jump up; — **il volo,** to fly away; — **tratta,** to draw a bill; *vi.* to stand out; to excel.
spiccato *adj.* marked; conspicuous.
spic'chio *m.* clove; slice.
spicciare, spicciarsi *see* sbrigare.
spicciativo *see* sbrigativo.
spiccicare *vt.* to detach; to pronounce.
spic'cio *adj.* expeditious, quick.
spicciolata, (alla) *adv.* little by little, a few at a time: **entrare (uscire) alla —,** to straggle in (out).
spic'cioli *m.pl.* change, money.
spic'ciolo *adj.* small.
spicco *m.* relief; prominence: **fare —,** to stand out.
spiedo *m.* spit.
spiegamento *m.* spreading out; (*mil.*) deployment.

spiegare *vt.* to explain; to unfold, spread out, lay out; to display; to unfurl (*as sails*); (*mil.*) to deploy; **spiegarsi** *vr.* to explain oneself; to make oneself understood; to unfurl (*as a flag*).

spiegato *adj.* explained; spread out; open; unfurled; unfolded: a voce spiegata, in a full voice.

spiegazione *f.* explanation.

spiegazzare *vt.* to rumple; to batter.

spietato *adj.* pitiless, ruthless.

spifferare *vt.* to speak out; to report; to blow.

spif'fero *m.* draft (*of air*).

spiga *f.* ear (*of corn*).

spigato *adj.* herringbone.

spighetta *f.* braid.

spigliatezza *f.* ease, promptness.

spigliato *adj.* easy, prompt.

spigo *m.* (*bot.*) lavender.

spigolare *vt.* to glean.

spigolatura *f.* gleaning.

spi'golo *m.* corner, corner edge.

spilla *f.* pin, brooch.

spillare *vt.* to broach, tap; to pierce: — danaro a, to squeeze money out of.

spilla'tico *m.* pin money.

spillo *m.* pin: — di sicurezza, safety pin.

spillone *m.* hatpin.

spilluzzicare *vt.* to nibble.

spilorceri'a *f.* niggardliness.

spilor'cio *m.* miser; *adj.* stingy.

spilungone *m.* lanky fellow.

spina *f.* thorn; (*elec.*) plug: — dorsale, spine; — di pesce, fishbone; a — di pesce, herringbone.

spina'cio *m.* spinach.

spinato, (filo) *m.* barbed wire.

spin'gere *vt.*⁶⁸ to push, shove; to drive; to propel; **spin'gersi** *vr.* to push, make one's way; to advance.

spino *m.* thorn.

spinone *m.* griffon.

spinoso *adj.* thorny.

spinta *f.* push; thrust; impulsion.

spintero'geno *m.* (*mach.*) (ignition) distributor.

spinto *adj.* excessive; risqué. *pp. of* spingere.

spintone *m.* push, shove, thrust.

spionag'gio *m.* espionage.

spioncino *m.* peephole.

spione *m.* spy, "stool pigeon."

spiovente *m.* slope; *adj.* drooping.

spira *f.* spire, coil.

spira'glio *m.* crack, fissure, airhole; gleam.

spirale *f.*, *adj.* spiral.

spirare *vt.*, *vi.* to blow; to expire, die; to issue, send forth, exhale: allo — di un mese, by the end of a month.

spiritato *adj.* possessed, crazy; wild.

spiri'tico *adj.* spiritualistic: seduta spiritica, seance.

spiritismo *m.* spiritualism.

spi'rito *m.* spirit; soul; ghost; tendency; virtue; faculty; wit; inspiration, impulse; spirits: — di sacrificio, abnegation, self-denial; — di corpo, esprit de corps; lampada a —, vapor lamp; fare dello —, to crack jokes.

spiritosag'gine *f.* witticism, crack.

spiritoso *adj.* witty; alcoholic.

spirituale *adj.* spiritual.

spiritualità *f.* spirituality.

spiz'zico, (a) *adv.* little by little; by fits and starts.

splendente *adj.* bright, shining.

splen'dere *vi.* to shine, sparkle.

splen'dido *adj.* splendid, glorious.

splendore *m.* splendor; grandeur.

spoc'chia *f.* haughtiness.

spocchioso *adj.* haughty.

spodestare *vt.* to dispossess; to dethrone; to oust.

spoetizzare *vt.* to disgust.

spo'glia *f.* spoil: — di guerra, spoils of war.

spogliare *vt.* to undress; to strip; to despoil; to plunder; **spogliarsi** *vr.* to undress; to give up; to deprive oneself; to get rid (*of*).

spogliarello *m.* "strip tease."

spogliato'io *m.* dressing room.

spogliazione *f.* dispossession; pillaging.

spo'glio *m.* castoff; scrutiny; perusal. *adj.* stripped; bare.

spola *f.* shuttle.

spoletta *f.* shuttle; fuse.

spolmonarsi *vr.* to talk one's head off; to shout oneself hoarse.

spolpare *vt.* to unflesh; to despoil.

spolverare *vt.* to dust.

spolveratura *f.* dusting; brushing; smattering.

spolverina *f.* duster; overall.

spolverino *m.* duster; sandbox.

spol'vero *m.* pounce; dusting; smattering.

sponda *f.* bank; edge; side.

sponsali *see* sposalizio.

spontaneità *f.* spontaneity.

sponta'neo *adj.* spontaneous.

Spontini, Gaspare, Italian composer (1774-1851).

spopolare *vt.* to depopulate; *vi.* (*coll.*) to make a hit; **spopolarsi** *vr.* to become depopulated.

spopolato *adj.* depopulated.

spora'dico *adj.* sporadic.

sporcaccione *m.* filthy person.

sporcare *vt.* to dirty, soil; **sporcarsi** *vr.* to dirty oneself, get dirty.

sporci'zia f. dirt, filth; dirtiness.

sporco adj. dirty, foul.

sporgente adj. jutting, protuberant.

sporgenza f. jut, projection, protuberance.

spor'gere vt.[88] to thrust out; to lodge (a complaint); vi. to jut; to protrude; spor'gersi vr. to lean out.

sport m. sport; game: per —, for pleasure.

sporta f. shopping bag: un sacco e una —, a lot; dirne un sacco e una — a, to abuse profusely.

sportello m. wicket; door; window.

sportivo m. sportsman; adj. sporting, sportsmanlike.

sporto m. jut, projection; adj. outstretched. pp.of sporgere.

sposa f. bride; wife.

sposali'zio m. wedding.

sposare vt. to marry, wed; to embrace; vi., sposarsi vr. to marry, get married.

sposo m. bridegroom; husband.

spossàre vt. to exhaust, prostrate.

spossatezza f. exhaustion, weakness.

spossato adj. weary; worn-out.

spostamento m. displacement, shifting; change.

spostare vt. to shift, move; to displace; to change; to bring; spostarsi vr. to shift, move.

spranga f. bar, crossbar, bolt.

sprangare vt. to bar, bolt.

sprazzo m. flash; splash.

sprecare vt. to waste, squander.

spreco m. squandering, waste.

sprege'vole adj. despicable.

spregiare vt. to despise.

spregiativo adj. disparaging.

spre'gio m. contempt, scorn.

spregiudicatezza f. broadmindedness.

spregiudicato adj. broadminded; unprejudiced, unbiased.

spre'mere vt. to squeeze, press; to wring: spremersi il cervello, to rack one's brain.

spremuta f. squash.

sprezzante adj. contemptuous.

sprezzare see disprezzare.

sprigionare vt. to exhale; to emit; sprigionarsi vr. to burst out.

sprimacciare vt. to plump up.

sprizzare vt. to sprinkle; to radiate; vi. to spring out.

sprofondare vt., vi., sprofondarsi vr. to sink, cave in.

sprolo'quio m. rigmarole.

spronare vt. to spur, goad; to urge.

sprone m. spur; (naut.) ram; a — battuto, full speed.

sproporzionato adj. disproportionate.

sproporzione f. disproportion.

spropositare vi. to blunder.

spropositato adj. blundering; (fig.) enormous, disproportionate, huge.

spropo'sito m. blunder; mistake: a —, at random; out of turn; costare uno —, to cost a fortune.

sprovvista, (alla) adv. unawares, unexpectedly.

sprovvisto adj. unprovided; lacking (in).

spruzzare vt. to spray, sprinkle.

spruzzatore m. sprayer.

spruzzo m. sprinkle; splash.

spudorato adj. impudent, shameless.

spugna f. sponge; (coll.) drunkard.

spugnatura f. sponge bath.

spugnoso adj. spongy.

spulciare vt. to free from fleas; (fig.) to scrutinize.

spuma f. foam, froth.

spumante m. champagne; adj. foaming, sparkling.

spumare vi. to foam, froth.

spumeggiante see spumante.

spumeggiare see spumare.

spumoso adj. foamy, frothy.

spuntare vt. to blunt; to clip, trim; to unpin; (comm.) to check, tick (off); vi. to appear, turn up; to grow; to peep out; to rise; to dawn; to spring; to cut (as teeth): spuntarla, to win out; spuntarsi vr. to blunt, become blunt; to get unpinned; to unfasten.

spuntino m. snack.

spunto m. cue; start; opening.

spurgare vt. to purge; vi. to discharge.

spurgo m. discharge.

spu'rio adj. spurious.

sputacchiera f. spittoon.

sputac'chio m. spit, spittle.

sputare vt., vi. to spit.

sputo m. spit, spittle.

squadra f. (geom.) square; (aeron.) squadron; (mil.) squad; gang, crew; (sport) team.

squadrare vt. to square.

squadri'glia f. squadron.

squagliare vt., squagliarsi vr. to melt: squagliarsela (coll.), to beat it, to take a powder.

squali'fica f. disqualification.

squalificare vt. to disqualify.

squal'lido adj. dreary, squalid.

squallore m. dreariness, squalor.

squalo m. shark.

squama f. scale.

squamare vt. to scale.

squarciagola, (a) adv. at the top of one's voice.

squarciare vt. to rend, tear apart; squarciarsi vr. to rend, tear.

squar'cio m. rent, tear, gash; (liter.) passage; rift.

squartare vt. to quarter, chop.

squartatore *m.* chopper.

squassare *vt.* to shake.

squattrinato *m.* pauper; *adj.* penniless.

squilibrato *m.* lunatic; *adj.* unbalanced, mad.

squili'brio *m.* want of balance; disparity; — **mentale**, insanity.

squillante *adj.* ringing.

squillare *vi.* to blare, ring.

squillo *m.* blare, ring.

squisito *adj.* exquisite.

squittire *vi.* to yelp, squeak.

sradicare *vt.* to uproot.

sragionare *vi.* to ramble; to talk nonsense.

sregolatezza *f.* disorder, intemperance, debauchery.

sregolato *adj.* intemperate.

stabbiuolo *m.* sty, pigsty.

sta'bile *m.* building; *adj.* stable, steady; permanent.

stabilimento *m.* establishment; factory, works, mill.

stabilire *vt.* to establish; to rule; to state; to decide; to settle; **stabilirsi** *vr.* to settle (*down*).

stabilità *f.* steadiness.

stabilizzatore *m.* stabilizer.

stabilizzare *vt.* to stabilize.

staccare *vt.* to detach; to separate; to pull off, tear away; (*mach.*) to disconnect; to take down (*from*); *vi.* to contrast; **staccarsi** *vr.* to become detached; to fall off; to part (*from*).

stacciare *vt.* to sift, sieve.

stac'cio *m.* sieve.

staccionata *f.* fence.

stacco *see* **spicco**.

stadera *f.* steelyard.

sta'dio *m.* stadium; stage, phase.

staffa *f.* stirrup: **perder le staffe**, to fly off the handle; **tenere il piede in due staffe**, to run with the hare and hunt with the hounds.

staffetta *f.* estafette: **corsa a —,** relay race.

staffiere *m.* groom, lackey.

staffilare *vt.* to lash.

staffilata *f.* lash.

staffile *m.* stirrup leather; whip.

stagionale *adj.* seasonal.

stagionare *vt., vi.* to season, ripen.

stagionato *adj.* seasoned; ripe.

stagliarsi *vr.* to stand out.

stagione *f.* season.

stagnante *adj.* stagnant.

stagnare *vt.* to tin; to solder; to stanch. *vi.* to stagnate.

stagnino *m.* tinsmith.

stagno *m.* tin; pond, pool; *adj.* tight, watertight; airtight.

sta'io *m.* bushel.

stalattite *f.* stalactite.

stalla *f.* stable.

stalliere *m.* stableman, groom.

stallo *m.* stall, seat.

stallone *m.* stallion.

stamane, stamattina *adv.* this morning.

stambecco *m.* ibex.

stamberga *f.*, **stambugio** *m.* den, hole.

stamburare *vi.* to drum.

stame *m.* (*bot.*) stamen; thread.

stampa *f.* print; printing; press: **in corso di —,** on press; **errore di —,** misprint; **stampe raccomandate,** registered printed matter; **godere di una buona (cattiva) —,** to have a good (bad) reputation.

stampare *vt.* to print; to publish; to impress.

stampatello *m.* block letters.

stampato *m.* (*printed*) form; *adj.* printed.

stampatore *m.* printer.

stampatrice *f.* printing press; press.

stampella *f.* crutch.

stamperi'a *f.* printing house.

stampi'glia *f.* stamp.

stampigliare *vt.* to stamp.

stampigliatura *f.* stamping.

stampino *m.* stencil.

stampo *m.* stamp; (*fig.*) kind, sort; mold.

stanare *vt.* to unburrow; to find out.

stancare *vt.* to tire, fatigue, weary; to annoy; to bore; **stancarsi** *vr.* to grow tired; to weary.

stanchezza *f.* tiredness, weariness.

stanco *adj.* tired (*of*), weary (*of*).

standardizzato *adj.* standard.

stanga *f.* bar; shaft.

stangata *f.* blow with a bar.

stanghetta *f.* bow (*of spectacles*).

stanotte *adv.* tonight, this night; last night.

stante *ddj.* being: **seduta —,** on the spot; **a sè —,** apart; *prep.* on account of: **— che,** since, as.

stanti'o *adj.* stale.

stantuffo *m.* piston; plunger.

stanza *f.* room, chamber: **essere di —,** to be stationed; **— di compensazione,** clearinghouse.

stanziamento *m.* appropriation.

stanziare *vt.* to appropriate.

stanzino *m.* closet; lumber room.

stappare *vt.* to uncork.

stare *vi.*[118] to stand; to be; to stay; to lie; to sit; to go on, keep; to live; to last; to be up to; to be in proportion to: **— sdraiato,** to lie; **— seduto,** to be sitting; **— zitto,** to keep silent; **— in piedi,** to stand; **tutto sta nella sua decisione,** everything depends upon his decision; **— per,** to be about to; **— alzati sino a**

tardi, to sit up late; — dietro a, to keep an eye upon; to court; — bene (male), to be well (ill); to be well (badly) off; questo vestito ti sta bene, this dress becomes you; ti sta bene! it serves you right!; come stai? how are you?; starci, to agree; to go shares; lasciar —, to leave alone; non — in sè, to be beside oneself.

starna f. gray partridge.

starnazzare vi. to flutter.

starnutare, starnutire vi. to sneeze.

starnuto m. sneeze, sneezing.

stasera adv. tonight.

stasi f. stasis.

statale adj. governmental: impiegato —, government official.

sta′tico adj. static, statical.

statista m. statesman.

stati′stica f. statistics.

stativo m. base (of a microscope).

stato (1) m. state; condition; status: — civile, registrar's office; in — interessante, pregnant; colpo di —, coup d'état; uomo di —, statesman; — maggiore, army staff; — d'assedio, martial law.

stato (2) pp. of stare and of essere.

sta′tua f. statue.

statua′rio m., adj. statuary.

statura f. stature, height.

statuto m. statute, constitution; (comm.) articles of association.

stavolta adv. this time.

stazionare vi. to stay, station.

staziona′rio adj. stationary.

stazione f. depot, station; stop; resort: — balneare, seaside resort.

stazza f. displacement.

stazzare vt. to gauge; to have a displacement of.

stazzonare vt. to crumple.

stecca f. stick; rib (of an umbrella); cue (for billiards); (mus.) false note; carton (of cigarettes).

steccato m. paling, palisade; rails.

stecchetto m.: stare a —, to stint (oneself); tenere a —, to keep on a meager pittance.

stecchino m. toothpick.

stecchito adj. lank: morto —, stark dead.

stecco m. (dry) twig.

stecconata f. stockade; fence.

stella f. star: — di mare, starfish; chiaror di stelle, starlight; stelle filanti, shooting stars; confetti.

stellare vt. to stellar; radial.

stellato adj. starry, star-spangled.

stelletta f. starlet; asterisk: portare le stellette (It. Army), to be in the army.

stelloncino m. paragraph.

stelo m. stem, stalk.

stemma m. coat of arms.

stemperare vt. to dilute; to melt; stemperarsi vr. to melt.

stendardo m. standard.

sten′dere vt.[140] to spread; to relax; to draw up; to hang; to stretch out; sten′dersi vr. to spread; to lie down; to stretch; to relax.

stenodattilo′grafo m., **stenodattilo′grafa** f. stenographer.

stenografare vt. to take in shorthand.

stenografato adj. shorthand.

stenografi′a f. shorthand.

stenogra′fico adj. shorthand.

steno′grafo m. stenographer.

stentare vt., vi. to halt; to starve; to be hardly able (to); to find it hard (to); to demur, be unwilling (to).

stentato adj. stunted; halting.

stento m. privation; hardship; toil: vivere di stenti, to starve; a —, hardly; with difficulty; stuntedly.

stento′reo adj. stentorian.

steppa f. steppe.

sterco m. dung.

stereoscopi′a f. stereoscopy.

stereosco′pico adj. stereoscopic.

stereotipato adj. stereotyped; stilted.

stereotipi′a f. stereotype.

stereo′tipo adj. stereotypic.

ste′rile adj. sterile, barren.

sterilire see isterilire.

sterilità f. sterility.

sterilizzare vt. to sterilize.

sterlina f. pound (sterling).

sterminare vt. to exterminate.

sterminato adj. immense, boundless.

sterminatore m. exterminator.

stermi′nio m. extermination.

sternutare, sternutire vi. to sneeze.

sterpo m. offshoot, weed.

sterrare vt. to dig up.

sterratore m. navvy, digger.

sterro m. digging.

sterzare vt., vi. to swerve.

sterzata f. swerve.

sterzo m. steering gear; steering wheel; handle bar.

steso pp. of stendere.

stesso adj. same; self; very: io —, I myself; noi stessi, we ourselves; se —, oneself, one's self; il giorno —, that very day; fa lo —, it makes no difference.

stesura f. drawing up.

stetosco′pio m. stethoscope.

sti′a f. coop.

stigmatizzare vt. to stigmatize.

stilare vt. to draw up.

stile m. style; stylet; dagger.

stilizzare vt. to stylize.

stilla f. drop.

stillare vt., vi. to ooze, exude, drip.

stillici'dio *m.* dripping; stillicidium.

stilo *m.* style.

stilogra'fica, (penna) *f.* fountain pen.

stima *f.* estimate; esteem.

stimare *vt.* to estimate, appraise; to esteem; to consider, deem.

stimatore *m.* appraiser.

stimolante *m.*, *adj.* stimulant.

stimolare *vt.* to stimulate.

sti'molo *m.* stimulus.

stinco *m.* shinbone, shin.

stin'gere *vt.*, **stin'gersi** *vr.*[148] to fade.

stinto *adj.* faded. *pp.of* stingere.

stipare *vt.*, **stiparsi** *vr.* to crowd, throng; to jam.

stipendiare *vt.* to salary; to hire.

stipen'dio *m.* salary, stipend.

sti'pite *m.* jamb; stem.

stipo *m.* cabinet.

stipulare *vt.* to stipulate.

stiracchiare *vt.*, *vi.* to stretch; to strain; to bargain, haggle; **stiracchiarsi** *vr.* to stretch (*oneself*).

stiracchiato *adj.* farfetched.

stirare *vt.* to stretch; to iron, press; **stirarsi** *vr.* to stretch (*oneself*).

stiratrice *f.* ironer; laundress.

stiratura *f.* ironing.

stireri'a *f.* laundry shop.

stiro, (ferro da) *m.* (*pressing*) iron.

stirpe *f.* birth; race; issue.

stitichezza *f.* constipation.

sti'tico *adj.* constipated.

stiva *f.* hold.

stivale *m.* boot.

stivare *vt.* to stow.

stivatore *m.* stevedore, longshoreman.

stizza *f.* vexation, anger.

stizzire *vt.* to irk, annoy; to peeve; **stizzirsi** *vr.* to get angry, flare up.

stizzito *adj.* cross, angry.

stizzoso *adj.* testy, peevish.

stoccafisso *m.* stockfish.

stoccata *f.* thrust; touch.

stoffa *f.* cloth, stuff, material.

stoicismo *m.* stoicism.

sto'ico *m.* stoic; *adj.* stoical.

stola *f.* stole.

sto'lido *adj.* stolid.

stoltezza *f.* foolishness, silliness.

stolto *m.* fool; *adj.* foolish, silly.

stomacare *vt.* to disgust, sicken.

stomache'vole *adj.* loathsome, disgusting.

sto'maco *m.* stomach: **dar di —**, to vomit; **avere il pelo sullo —**, to be utterly unscrupulous.

stonare *vi.* to be out of tune; to jar; to "fluff."

stonato *adj.* out of tune; jarring.

stonatura *f.* dissonance; jarring note.

stoppa *f.* tow; (*naut.*) oakum.

stoppac'cio *m.* wadding, wad.

stop'pia *f.* stubble.

stoppino *m.* wick.

storcere *vt.*[145] **storcersi** *vr.* to twist; to twitch; to sprain.

stordimento *m.* daze, dizziness.

stordire *vt.* to stun, daze; **stordirsi** *vr.* to dull one's senses.

storditag'gine *f.* heedlessness; mistake, oversight.

stordito *m.* fool, numskull; *adj.* dull, scatterbrained; heedless.

sto'ria *f.* history; story, tale; pretext: **fare un sacco di storie,** to quibble a lot; to kick up a row.

sto'rico *adj.* historical.

storiella *f.* short story; lie, fib; joke.

storione *m.* sturgeon.

stormire *vi.* to rustle.

stormo *m.* flight; flock; swarm; (*aeron.*, *mil.*) wing: **comandante di —**, wing commander.

stornare *vt.* to ward off; to divert; to misapply; (*comm.*) to transfer, adjust; to cancel.

stornello *m.* refrain, ditty.

storno (*l*) *m.* (*ornith.*) starling.

storno (*2*) *m.* (*comm.*) transfer; cancellation.

storpiare *vt.* to maim; to mar.

stor'pio *m.* cripple; *adj.* crippled.

storta *f.* sprain; (*chem.*) retort.

storto *adj.* crooked; askew, awry; twisted; wrong; misshapen; *adv.* awry; the wrong way: **avere gli occhi storti,** to be squint-eyed. *pp. of* storcere.

stortura *f.* twist; incongruity.

stovi'glie *f.pl.* pottery, earthenware.

stra- *pref.* over: **stramaturo,** overripe; **straricco,** excessively rich.

stra'bico *adj.* squinting, squint-eyed.

strabiliante *adj.* astonishing.

strabiliare *vi.* to be amazed: **far —**, to amaze.

strabismo *m.* squint, strabismus.

straboccare *vi.* to overflow.

strabocche'vole *adj.* overflowing.

strabuzzare *see* stralunare.

stracaricare *vt.* to overload.

straca'rico *adj.* overladen.

stracca, (alla) *adv.* lazily; halfheartedly.

straccali *m.pl.* suspenders.

straccare *see* stancare.

stracciare *vt.* to rend, tear; **stracciarsi** *vr.* to tear.

stracciato *adj.* in rags, torn.

strac'cio *m.* rag, tatter.

straccione *m.* ragged man, scarecrow.

stracco *adj.* tired.

stracotto *m.* stew; *adj.* overdone.

stracuo'cere *vt.* to overdo (*as meat*).

strada *f.* road; street; way; course: **— maestra,** highroad; **mettersi su una brutta —,** to go astray; mettere fuori di —, to throw off the track.

stradale *m.* avenue. *adj.* road: **carta** —, road map; **fondo** —, roadbed; **illuminazione** —, street lighting; **incidente** —, traffic accident; **polizia** —, traffic police; **regolamento** —, traffic regulations; **targa** —, street marker.

Stradella, Alessandro, Italian composer (1645–1682).

Stradivari, Antonio (*Antonius Stradivarius*), Italian violinmaker (1644–1737).

strafalcione *m.* blunder.

strafare *vi.* to overdo.

straforo, (di) *adv.* surreptitiously, stealthily; underhandedly.

strafottente *adj.* cocky, unconcerned; bumptious.

strafottenza *f.* unconcern; bumptiousness.

strage *f.* massacre; (*fig.*) plenty.

stragrande *adj.* enormous.

stralciare *vt.* to lop off; to cancel; to pigeonhole.

stral'cio *m.* (*agr.*) lopping: **vendita a** —, bargain sale.

strale *m.* dart, arrow.

strallo *m.* (*naut.*) stay.

stralunare *vt.* to roll; to open (*one's eyes*) wide.

stralunato *adj.* wild-eyed.

stramazzare *vi.* to fall heavily, drop.

stramazzo *m.* paillasse.

stramberi'a *f.* oddity, quaintness.

strambo *adj.* odd, queer, quaint.

strame *m.* litter.

strampalato *adj.* preposterous, absurd.

stranezza *f.* queerness.

strangolamento *m.* strangling.

strangolare *vt.* to strangle, throttle; to suffocate.

strangolatore *m.* strangler.

straniare *vt.* to estrange; **straniarsi** *vr.* to estrange oneself.

straniero *m.* foreigner, alien. *adj.* foreign, alien.

strano *adj.* strange, queer, odd.

straordina'rio *adj.* extraordinary; wonderful; unusual; (*comm.*) overtime: **lavoro** —, overtime work; **fare gli straordinari**, to work overtime.

strapagare *vt.* to overpay.

strapazzare *vt.* to misuse; to upbraid; to crumple; to scramble (*as eggs*); **strapazzarsi** *vr.* to overtask one's strength; to wear oneself out.

strapazzata *f.* reproof, rebuke.

strapazzo *m.* fatigue, excess.

strapieno *adj.* full up, overfull.

strapiombare *vi.* to jut out.

strapiombo *m.* drop, sheer drop: **a** —, sheer, sheerly.

strapotente *adj.* overpowerful.

strapotenza *f.* overpower.

strappare *vt.* to tear; to snatch; to pluck; to wrench; to extort; to pull: — **le lacrime**, to stir pity; — **il cuore**, to wring one's heart; **strapparsi** *vr.* to tear; to tear oneself away (*from*): **strapparsi i capelli**, to tear one's hair.

strappo *m.* pull, wrench; rent, tear strain: — **muscolare**, muscular strain; **a strappi**, jerkily; **fare uno** — **alla regola**, to stretch a point.

strapuntino *m.* jump seat, bucket seat.

straricco *adj.* immensely rich, rolling in riches.

straripamento *m.* overflowing.

straripare *vi.* to overflow.

strascicare *vt.* to shuffle; to drag; to drawl.

stra'scico *m.* sequel; train; aftermath.

strascinare *vt.* to drag.

stra'scino *m.* dragnet, trawl.

stratagemma *m.* stratagem.

stratega *m.* strategist.

strategi'a *f.* strategy.

strate'gico *adj.* strategic: **posizione strategica**, vantage point.

strato *m.* layer; stratum; stratus; film: — **sensibile** (*photo.*), sensitive surface.

stratosfera *f.* stratosphere.

stratosfe'rico *adj.* stratospheric.

strattone *m.* jerk, pull.

stravagante *m.*, *adj.* eccentric; whimsical; moody.

stravaganza *f.* oddity, eccentricity; vagary.

stravec'chio *adj.* very old.

stravin'cere *vi.* to triumph, to vaunt.

straviziare *vi.* to debauch.

stravi'zio *m.* intemperance, debauch.

stravol'gere *vt.*[148] to roll, twist.

stravolto *adj.* twisted; troubled.

straziante *adj.* heart-rending.

straziare *vt.* to tear, torture; to grate on; to make a mess of; to rend, wring: — **una lingua**, to murder a language.

straziato *adj.* torn, stricken: **col cuore** —, heart-stricken.

stra'zio *m.* torture, torment.

strega *f.* sorceress, witch.

stregare *vt.* to bewitch.

stregone *m.* wizard, sorcerer.

stregoneri'a *f.* witchcraft.

stregua *f.* rate, proportion: **alla stessa** —, by the same token; **alla** — **di,** as, the same as.

stremare *vt.* to exhaust.

strenna *f.* present, gift.

stre'nuo *adj.* vigorous, strenuous.

strepitare *vi.* to roar, shout, thunder.

stre'pito *m.* uproar; din, roar; hit: **far —** (*fig.*), to make a hit.

strepitoso *adj.* uproarious; sensational.

streptomicina *f.* streptomycin.

stretta *f.* tightening; hold, grasp, grip; pang: **— di mano**, handshake; **una — al cuore**, a pang in one's heart; **mettere alle strette**, to drive into a corner.

strettamente *adv.* tightly; strictly.

stretto (1) *m.* (*geog.*) straits.

stretto (2) *adj.* narrow; tight, close; strict; stingy: **pugno —**, clenched fist. *pp.of* **stringere.**

stret'toia *f.* straits.

stria *f.* stria; stripe; furrow.

striare *vt.* to stripe, streak.

stricnina *f.* strychnine.

stridente *adj.* jarring, strident, sharp.

stri'dere *vi.* to screech, squeak; to shriek; to clash, jar.

stridore *m.* screeching.

stri'dulo *adj.* piercing, shrill.

strigare *vt.* to disentangle.

stri'glia *f.* currycomb.

strigliare *vt.* to curry; to rebuke.

strillare *vi.* to shriek, scream.

strillo *m.* scream, shriek, cry.

strillone *m.* newsboy, newsman.

striminzito *adj.* scrubby, stunted.

strimpellare *vt.* to thrum.

strinare *vt.* to singe.

stringa *f.* shoelace.

stringato *adj.* terse, concise.

stringente *adj.* urgent; severe; cogent.

string'ere *vt.*[188] to tighten; to press, clench; to grip; to shorten; to narrow; to squeeze; *vi.* to be tight: **— un patto**, to make an agreement; **— d'assedio**, to besiege; **il tempo stringe**, there is no time to be lost; **stringersi** *vr.* to draw near, get close; to tighten; to narrow; to shorten: **stringersi nelle spalle**, to shrug.

stri'scia *f.* strip, band: **a strisce**, striped.

strisciante *adj.* creeping; fawning, cringing: **un essere —**, a toady, a "softsoaper."

strisciare *vt.* to shuffle; to drag; to raze; to fawn upon, flatter; *vi.* to crawl, creep: **— coi piedi**, to shuffle one's feet.

strisciata *f.* rub; track; flattery.

stri'scio *m.* graze: **di —**, grazingly.

striscione *m.* festoon.

stritolare *vt.* to smash, crush.

strizzare *vt.* to wring, squeeze.

strizzata *f.* wring, squeeze; wink.

strofa, strofe *f.* strophe.

strofinac'cio *m.* floorcloth; duster; wiper.

strofinare *vt.* to rub; to wipe; **strofinarsi** *vr.* to rub.

strofini'o *m.* rubbing, friction.

strombazzare *vt.* to flaunt; to divulge; to "ballyhoo."

strombettare *vi.* to toot.

stroncare *vt.* to break; to pull to pieces; to censure, slash.

stroncatura *f.* slashing criticism, slash.

stropicciare *vt.* to rub; to scrub.

stropicci'o *m.* rubbing.

strozza *f.* throttle, throat.

strozzare *vt.* to throttle, strangle; to choke; (*fig.*) to fleece.

strozzatura *f.* narrowing.

Strozzi, Giambattista (*Filippo II*), Florentine statesman (1488–1538).

strozzinag'gio *m.* usury.

strozzino *m.* usurer, loan shark.

strug'gere *vt.*[187] to melt; to consume, eat up; to torment; **strug'gersi** *vr.* to melt; to pine (*for, with*); to languish, waste away: **struggersi in lacrime**, to melt into tears; **struggersi d'invidia**, to burst with envy.

struggimento *m.* melting; pining; anxiety; torment.

strumento *m.* instrument; tool: **strumenti a fiato** (*mus.*), winds; **strumenti ad arco**, strings.

strusciare *vt.* to wear out; to rub.

strutto (1) *m.* lard.

strutto (2) *pp.of* **struggere.**

struttura *f.* structure, frame.

struzzo *m.* ostrich.

stuccare *vt.* to stucco; to putty; to fill up; to surfeit; **stuccarsi** *vr.* to grow weary, grow sick.

stuccatura *f.* plastering; filling.

stucche'vole *adj.* sickening; boring.

stucco *m.* stucco, plaster; putty: **rimanere di —**, to be nonplussed.

studente *m.* student.

studentesco *adj.* student, student-like.

studentessa *f.* girl student.

studiare *vt.* to study; to examine; to scrutinize, observe; **— legge**, to read, study, for the bar; **studiarsi** *vr.* to endeavor, try.

studiato *adj.* accurate; studied; deliberate; forced.

stu'dio *m.* study; studio; office.

studioso *m.* scholar; *adj.* studious.

stufa *f.* stove; conservatory.

stufare (1) *vt.* to bore, tire; **stufarsi** *vr.* to get bored, tired.

stufare (2) *vt.* to stew.

stufato *m.* stew, stewed meat.

stufo *adj.* sick, tired; bored.

stuo'ia *f.* mat, matting.

stuoino *m.* doormat.

stuolo *m.* troop, multitude.

stupefacente *m.* drug, dope: **dedito agli stupefacenti,** drug-addicted; *adj.* stupefying; astonishing.

stupefare *vt.* to stupefy; to astonish.

stupefatto *adj.* astonished, surprised, amazed. *pp.of* **stupefare.**

stupefazione *f.* astonishment.

stupendo *adj.* stupendous, wonderful.

stupidag'gine *f.* foolishness, silliness; nonsense.

stupidamente *adv.* foolishly.

stupidità *f.* stupidity, silliness.

stu'pido *m.* fool: **fare lo —,** to make a fool of oneself; **non fare lo —!** don't be a fool!; *adj.* stupid, silly.

stupire *vt.* to astonish; **stupirsi** *vr.* to be astonished, wonder (*at*).

stupore *m.* astonishment, amazement; (*med.*) stupor.

stuprare *vt.* to rape.

stupro *m.* rape, violation.

stura *f.*: **dare la — a,** to uncork; to set off, start.

sturare *vt.* to uncork.

stuzzicadenti *m.* toothpick.

stuzzicante *adj.* stimulating.

stuzzicare *vt.* to stimulate, stir; to tease: **stuzzicarsi i denti,** to pick one's teeth.

su *prep.* on, upon; over; above; about; against; after: **sul mezzogiorno,** about noon; **sulla cinquantina,** about fifty; **sul serio,** in earnest; **sui due piedi,** right away, offhand; *adv.* up, over; upstairs; overhead: **tirar —,** to bring up, rear; **venir —,** to grow; **in —,** up; **all'insù,** upturned; **più —,** higher; **— per giù,** approximately, more or less.

sua *see* **suo.**

suadente *adj.* persuasive, coaxing.

subac'queo *adj.* subaqueous, underwater: **pescatore —, nuotatore —,** skin diver; **fucile —,** speargun.

subaffittare *vt.* to sublet.

subaffitto *m.* sublease.

subalterno *m., adj.* subaltern, subordinate.

subbu'glio *see* **scompiglio.**

subcosciente *m., adj.* subconscious.

sub'dolo *adj.* shifty, deceitful.

subentrare *vi.*: **— a,** to succeed.

subire *vt.* to undergo; to suffer; *vi.* to bear with it.

subissare *vt.* to ruin; to overcome: **— di fischi,** to boo; **— d'applausi,** to applaud enthusiastically.

subisso *m.* ruin: **un — di,** plenty of; **un — d'applausi,** a roar of applause.

subita'neo *adj.* sudden; unexpected.

su'bito *adj.* sudden; *adv.* at once, right away; soon: **— dopo,** soon after.

sublimato *m., adj.* sublimate.

sublime *adj.* sublime.

subodorare *vt.* to suspect; **to get an inkling of.**

subordinare *vt.* to subordinate.

subordinato *m., adj.* subordinate.

subornare *vt.* to bribe.

substrato *m.* substratum.

suburbano *adj.* suburban.

subur'bio *m.* suburbs.

succea'neo *m.* substitute, ersatz; *adj.* succedaneous.

succe'dere *vi.* to ensue, happen, occur: **— a,** to follow; to succeed.

successione *f.* succession: **tasse di —,** inheritance taxes.

successivo *adj.* following; next.

successo (*1*) *m.* success; hit; outcome.

successo (*2*) *pp.of* **succedere.**

successore *m.* successor.

succhiare *vt.* to suck (*up*); (*fig.*) to put up with.

succhiello *m.* gimlet.

succinto *adj.* succinct; concise.

succo *m.* juice; sap; (*fig.*) gist.

succosamente *adv.* pithily, substantially.

succoso *adj.* juicy; sappy.

suc'cubo *m.* succubus; *adj.* (*fig.*) slave (*to*).

succulento *adj.* succulent, juicy.

succursale *f.* branch (office), agency.

su'cido *see* **sudicio.**

sud *m.* south.

sudamericano *adj.* South American.

sudafricano *adj.* South African.

sudare *vt., vi.* to sweat, perspire; to exude; to toil: **— freddo,** to be in a cold sweat; **— sette camicie,** to be hard put to it; to strive hard.

suda'rio *m.* shroud.

sudata *f.* sweat, sweating.

sudato *adj.* sweating.

suddetto *adj.* above-mentioned.

sud'dito *m.* subject.

suddivi'dere *vt.* to subdivide, break up.

suddivisione *f.* subdivision.

suddiviso *pp.of* **suddividere.**

sud-est *m.* southeast.

sudiceri'a *f.* dirtiness; indecency.

su'dicio *adj.* dirty, filthy; obscene.

sudiciume *m.* dirt, filth.

sudore *m.* sweat, perspiration: **madido di —,** wet with perspiration.

sud-ovest *m.* southwest.

sufficiente *m.. adj.* enough; sufficient.

sufficienza *f.* sufficiency: **a —,** enough; **con aria di —,** patronizingly.

suffisso *m.* suffix.

suffragare *vt.* to support; to corroborate.

suffragetta *f.* suffragette.

suffra'gio *m.* suffrage; approval.
suffumi'gio *m.* fumigation.
suggellare *vt.* to seal; to seal up.
suggello *m.* seal.
suggerimento *m.* suggestion.
suggerire *vt.* to suggest; to prompt.
suggeritore *m.* (*theat.*) prompter.
suggestiona'bile *adj.* suggestible.
suggestionare *vt.* to hypnotize; to influence.
suggestione *f.* suggestion.
suggestivo *adj.* suggestive.
su'ghero *m.* cork; cork tree.
sugli *comp.prep.* on the. *see* su.
sugna *f.* lard; grease.
sugo *m.* juice; gravy: — di pomidoro, tomato sauce; senza — (*fig.*), idle, empty, pointless, dull.
sugoso *see* succoso.
sui *comp.prep.* on the. *see* su.
suicida *m.* suicide; *adj.* suicidal.
suicidarsi *vr.* to commit suicide.
suici'dio *m.* suicide.
suino *m.* swine; *adj.* swinish: carne suina, pork meat.
sul *comp. prep.* on the. *see* su.
sulfamide, sulfami'dico *m.* sulfanilamide: i sulfamidici, sulfa drugs.
sulla, sulle, sullo *prep.* on the. *see* su.
sullodato *adj.* above (*mentioned*).
sunteggiare *vt.* to epitomize, condense.
sunto *m.* epitome, summary, condensation.
suo *poss.adj.* his; her; its; *poss.pron.* his; hers; the one belonging to it: un amico —, a friend of his (hers).
suo'cera *f.* mother-in-law; (*fig.*) termagant.
suo'cero *m.* father-in-law.
suola *f.* sole.
suolo *m.* ground, soil; floor: precipitare a — (*aeron.*), to crash.
suonare, suonatore, *etc. see* sonare.
suono *m.* sound: muro del —, sound barrier.
suora *f.* nun, sister.
superallenamento *m.* over-training.
superamento *m.* overcoming.
superare *vt.* to surpass; to overcome, get over; to negotiate; to exceed; to get the better of; to pass; to outrun; to outspeed; to climb over; to leave behind: — se stesso, to excel oneself; — una curva (*auto.*), to negotiate a turn.
super'bia *f.* haughtiness; conceit: montare in —, to put on airs.
superbioso *adj.* haughty, conceited.
superbo *adj.* proud; haughty; conceited, contemptuous; superb.
supereterodina *f.* superheterodyne.
superficiale *adj.* superficial; slight; cursory.
superficialità *f.* superficiality.

superfi'cie *f.* surface; area: — portante, airfoil; salire alla —, to surface.
super'fluo *m.* surplus; *adj.* superfluous; unnecessary; needless.
superfortezza *f.* superfortress: — volante, flying superfortress.
superiora *f.* mother superior.
superiore *m.* superior; *adj.* superior; higher; above; upper; excellent: ufficiale —, ranking officer; scuola —, high school.
superiorità *f.* superiority.
superlativo *m.*, *adj.* superlative.
superlavoro *m.* overwork.
superso'nico *adj.* supersonic.
super'stite *m.* survivor; *adj.* surviving.
superstizione *f.* superstition.
superstizioso *adj.* superstitious.
superuomo *m.* superman.
supino *m.*, *adj.* supine, on one's back.
suppellet'tili *f.pl.* fittings; furniture.
suppergiù *adv.* nearly; just about; more or less.
supplementare *adj.* supplementary, additional, extra; auxiliary.
supplemento *m.* supplement, addition; extra.
supplente *m.*, *f.* deputy, substitute.
sup'plica *f.* petition; entreaty.
supplicante *m.* petitioner, suppliant; *adj.* suppliant.
supplicare *vt.* to implore, entreat, beg, beseech.
suppliche'vole *adj.* imploring, beseeching.
supplire *vt.* to substitute, take the place of; *vi.* to provide (*for*); to make up (*for*): — a, to substitute.
suppli'zio *m.* torture; torment; punishment, execution: — di Tantalo (*fig.*), tantalization.
supporre *vt.*, *vi.*" to suppose; to surmise.
supporto *m.* support, prop; bearing; bracket.
supposizione *f.* supposition, surmise.
supposta *f.* (*med.*) suppository.
supposto *m.* supposition; *adj.* supposed. *pp.of* supporre.
suppurare *vi.* to suppurate.
suppurazione *f.* suppuration.
supremazi'a *f.* supremacy.
supremo *adj.* supreme.
surclassare *vt.* to outclass.
surrealismo *m.* surrealism.
surrealista *m.*, *adj.* surrealist.
surrenale *adj.* suprarenal.
surriscaldare *vt.* to overheat.
surrogato *m.* substitute, ersatz.
suscetti'bile *adj.* susceptible; receptive; touchy.
suscettibilità *f.* susceptibility; receptivity; touchiness.

suscitare vt. to raise; to stir (up); to provoke; to inspire.

susina f. plum.

susseguente adj. subsequent.

susseguire vi. to succeed, follow.

sussi'dio m. subsidy; allowance: — militare, separation allowance.

sussiego m. primness; aloofness.

sussistenza f. validity; subsistence; livelihood; (mil.) Quartermaster Corps.

sussi'stere vi. to subsist; to exist; to hold good; to last.

sussultare vi. to start, jump, quake.

sussulto m. start, jump, quake.

sussulto'rio adj. sussultorial.

sussurrare, susurrare vt., vi. to whisper; to murmur.

sussurratore m. murmurer.

sussurri'o m. whispering.

susurro m. murmur, rustle; whisper.

sutura f. suture.

suturare vt. to suture.

svagare vt. to distract, divert (one's attention); to amuse, entertain; to relax; **svagarsi** vr. to distract oneself, divert oneself; to enjoy oneself; to relax, take some recreation.

svagatezza f. absent-mindedness.

svagato adj. absent-minded; inattentive.

svago m. recreation; entertainment.

svaligiamento m. robbery.

svaligiare vt. to rob; to clean out.

svaligiatore m. robber, burglar.

svalutare vt. to depreciate.

svalutato adj. depreciated.

svalutazione f. depreciation.

svanire vi. to vanish; to fade (away, out); to evaporate.

svanito adj. vanished; muddled, addled.

svantag'gio m. drawback; disadvantage.

svantaggioso adj. unfavorable; detrimental.

svaporare vi. to evaporate.

svariato adj. varied; **svariati** pl. various, several.

svarione m. blunder; (typog.) misprint.

svasare vt. to flare (as a skirt).

svasato adj. flaring.

sva'stica f. swastika.

svecchiare vt. to renew.

sve'glia f. waking up; alarm clock; (mil.) reveille.

svegliare vt., **svegliarsi** vr. to wake (up), awaken, stir.

svegliarino m. prompter.

sve'glio adj. awake; quick-witted; lively; shrewd.

svelare vt. to unveil; to reveal, disclose; **svelarsi** vr. to reveal oneself.

svel'lere see divellere.

sveltezza f. quickness.

sveltire vt. to quicken; to make more self-confident; **sveltirsi** vr. to quicken; to become self-confident.

svelto (1) adj. quick; nimble; slender, quick-witted, smart; adv. quickly, fast.

svelto (2) pp. of svellere.

svenare vt. to bleed; **svenarsi** vr. to open one's veins; to bleed.

sven'dere vt. to undersell; to dispose of.

svene'vole adj. mawkish, spoony.

svenevolezza f. mawkishness.

svenimento m. swoon, faint.

svenire vi.¹¹¹ to swoon, faint.

sventagliare vt. to fan.

sventagliata f. fanning; volley.

sventare vt. to avert; to thwart.

sventatag'gine, sventatezza f. heedlessness, carelessness.

sventato m. scatterbrain; adj. heedless.

sven'tola f. fire fan; slap; (boxing) swing.

sventolare vt. to flutter; to wave; to fan; vi. to fly, flutter; **sventolarsi** vr. to fan oneself.

sventoli'o m. fluttering.

sventramento m. disembowelment; demolition.

sventrare vt. to eviscerate; to disembowel; to demolish, dismantle.

sventura f. misfortune; mishap.

sventurato m. wretch; adj. unlucky, unfortunate.

svenuto adj. unconscious, in a swoon. pp. of svenire.

sverginare vt. to deflower.

svergognare vt. to put to shame.

svergognato adj. shameless, impudent; abashed.

svergolare vi. to twist; (aeron.) to warp.

svernare vi. to winter.

sverniciare vt. to unpaint.

svestire vt. to undress; **svestirsi** vr. to undress (oneself).

svettare vt. to pollard; vi. to waver, sway; to soar.

Svevo, Italo (Ettore Schmitz), Italian novelist of German father (1861–1928).

svezzare vt. to wean; to cure.

sviare vt. to deviate; to avert; to lead astray, mislead; **sviarsi** vr. to go astray.

svignar'sela vi. to slip away, steal away; to "beat it," decamp.

svilire vt. to depreciate; to lower.

svillaneggiare vt. to treat rudely, insult, snub, knock about.

sviluppare vt. to develop; to increase; vi., **svilupparsi** vr. to develop; to grow; to spread; to thrive; to branch out.

sviluppo *m.* development; growth; increase: età dello —, age of puberty.

svincolare *vt.* to free, disengage; to redeem; to clear; **svincolarsi** *vr.* to free oneself, disengage oneself.

svin'colo *m.* clearing.

svisare *vt.* to misrepresent; to alter.

sviscerare *vt.* to eviscerate; to exhaust, examine thoroughly.

sviscerato *adj.* ardent, passionate.

svista *f.* oversight.

svitare *vt.* to unscrew.

svogliatezza *f.* listlessness.

svogliato *adj.* listless, lazy.

svolazzante *adj.* flitting.

svolazzare *vi.* to flutter.

svolazzo *m.* flourish, curlicue.

svol'gere *vt.*¹⁴⁴ to unwind; to undo, unroll; to develop; to perform, carry out, be engaged (*in*), discharge; **svol'gersi** *vr.* to unroll, unfold; to happen, occur, take place.

svolgimento *m.* development; performance; discharge; treatment.

svolta *f.* turn; corner; turning-point.

svolto *pp.*of **svolgere**.

svoltare *vi.* to make a turn; to turn.

svotare *vt.*, **svotarsi** *vr.* to empty.

T

tabacca'io *m.* tobacconist.

tabaccare *vi.* to snuff.

tabaccheri'a *f.* tobacco store, cigar store.

tabacchiera *f.* snuffbox.

tabacco *m.* tobacco: — da fiuto, snuff.

tabarro *m.* tabard.

tabella *f.* table; schedule; list.

taberna'colo *m.* tabernacle.

tabù *m.* taboo.

ta'bula *f.*: far — rasa, to make a clean sweep (*of*).

tacca *f.* notch; nick: di mezza —, middle-sized; mediocre.

taccagneri'a *f.* stinginess.

taccagno *m.* miser; *adj.* stingy.

taccheggiatore *m.*, **taccheggiatrice** *f.* shoplifter.

taccheg'gio *m.* shoplifting.

tacchino *m.* turkey.

tac'cia *f.* blemish, fault; charge; fame.

tacciare *vt.* to accuse (*of*), charge (*with*).

tacco *m.* heel (*of a shoe*): alzare i tacchi, to take to one's heels.

taccone *m.* patch.

taccuino *m.* notebook.

tacere *vt.*¹³⁹ to withhold, omit; *vi.* to keep silent, be silent, hold one's tongue; to stop (*talking*); to say nothing: far —, to silence; **tacete!** shut up!

tachi'metro *m.* tachometer; speedometer.

tacitare *vt.* to silence; to indemnify; to pay (*off*).

ta'cito *adj.* tacit, silent; implied.

taciturno *adj.* taciturn; sullen.

taciuto *pp.*of **tacere**.

tafano *m.* gadfly; oxfly.

tafferu'glio *m.* fray, scuffle, fight.

taffettà *m.* taffeta; court plaster.

ta'glia (*1*) *f.* levy, tribute; ransom; reward.

ta'glia (*2*) *f.* stature; size.

tagliaborse *m.* pickpocket.

tagliaboschi, **taglialegna** *m.* woodman, woodcutter.

tagliacarte *m.* paper knife.

tagliamare *m.* (*naut.*) breakwater.

tagliando *m.* coupon.

tagliare *vt.* to cut; to clip; to sever; to split; to cross; *vi.* to cut: — la strada a uno, to stand in one's way; — i panni addosso a, to slander; — i viveri, to cut off supplies; — la corda, to "vamoose"; farsi — i capelli, to have one's hair cut; **tagliarsi** *vr.* to cut oneself.

tagliatelle *f.pl.* noodles.

tagliatore *m.* cutter.

taglieggiare *vt.* to ransom.

tagliente *adj.* cutting; sharp.

taglierina *f.* paper cutter.

ta'glio *m.* cut, cutting; clipping; rent, fissure; edge (*of a blade*); denomination (*of banknotes*); fit, style; harvest: — di stoffa, piece of cloth; arma da —, edged weapon; di —, edgeways.

taglione *m.*: legge del —, law of retaliation.

tagliuola *f.* trap, snare.

tagliuzzare *vt.* to mince.

ta'lamo *m.* nuptial bed.

talare, (abito) *m.* soutane.

talchè *adv.* so that.

talco *m.* talc; talcum powder.

tale *adj.*, *pron.* such; like, similar; same; certain: — il padre — il figlio, like father like son; è — quale il mio, it is just like mine; una tal qual paura, a certain fear; nella — città, in such and such town; il — dei tali, Mr. So and So; un —, a "guy"; quei tali che, those (*people*) who; è — quale era, it is just as it was; — quale lo vedi, such as you see it.

talento *m.* talent, ability: **a vostro —,** at your will.

talismano *m.* talisman, charm.

tallire *vi.* to sprout.

tallone *m.* heel.

talmente *adv.* so much, so, so very.

talora *adv.* sometimes.

talpa *f.* mole; (*fig.*) dullard.

taluno *adj.*, *pron.* someone.

talvolta *adv.* sometimes.

tamarindo *m.* tamarind.

tambureggiare *vi.* to drum.

tamburello *m.* tambourine.

tamburino *m.* tambourine; drummer.

tamburo *m.* drum; drummer; barrel (*of a watch*): **a — battente,** instantly.

tamerice *m.* tamarisk.

Tamigi *m.* Thames.

tampoco, (nè) *adv.* neither, not even.

tamponare *vt.* to stop, tampon, plug.

tampone *m.* stopper, tampon.

tana *f.* lair, hole, den.

tana'glia *f.* pincers, nippers, tongs (*all pl.*); tenaille.

tanfo *m.* stench.

tangente *f.* share; (*geom.*) tangent; *adj.* tangent.

tan'gere *vi.* to touch; to concern.

tan'ghero *m.* bumpkin, boor.

tangi'bile *adj.* tangible.

tantino *m.* bit, little bit.

tanto (1) *adj.*, *pron.* so much, as much; much; enough, sufficient; **tanti** *pl.* so (as) many; many; many people: **— denaro quanto ne vuoi,** as much money as you want; **cinquanta e tante lire,** fifty odd lire; **da — tempo,** for quite a while; **— vale restar a casa,** we might as well stay at home; **due volte tanti,** twice as many.

tanto (2) *adv.* so, such; so much; as; both ... and: **è — caro!** he is such a dear!; **è — bella quanto buona,** she is as beautiful as she is good; **— l'Italia quanto l'Inghilterra,** both Italy and England; **— più che,** (all) the more so as; **una volta —,** once in a while; **di — in —,** now and then; **— per fare qualcosa,** just to.

tanto (3) *m.* (a) given quantity, (a) given amount: **un — per cento,** a percentage.

tapino *m.* wretch; *adj.* wretched.

tappa *f.* stop, halting place; stage; leg.

tappabuchi *m.* (*fig.*) stopgap.

tappare *vt.* to cork, plug; to stop (*up*); to shut; **tapparsi** *vr.* to shut oneself (*up*); **tapparsi il naso,** to stop one's nose.

tappeto *m.* carpet, rug: **— verde,** green cloth; **mettere al —,** to knock out.

tappezzare *vt.* to tapestry; to paper; to upholster.

tappezzeri'a *f.* tapestry; wallpaper; upholstery.

tappezziere *m.* upholsterer; paperhanger; decorator.

tappo *m.* stopper; bung; cork; plug.

tara *f.* tare; disease; stigma, brand.

tarare *vt.* to tare; to adjust.

tarato *adj.* branded; stigmatic.

tarchiato *adj.* thickset, stocky.

tardare *vt.*, *vi.* to delay; to be late.

tardi *adv.* late: **sul —,** at a late hour; **più —,** later; **al più —,** at the latest; **far —,** to be late.

tardivo *adj.* tardy; late; slow.

tardo *adj.* tardy; slow; slow-witted; late.

targa *f.* shield; plate; number plate, license plate; trophy: **— stradale,** street marker.

targare *vt.* (*auto.*) to register.

targatura *f.* (*auto.*) registration.

tariffa *f.* rates, tariff.

tarlarsi *vr.* to get worm-eaten.

tarlato *adj.* worm-eaten.

tarlo *m.* woodworm; moth.

tarma *f.* moth.

tarmare *vi.*, **tarmarsi** *vr.* to get motheaten.

tarmato *adj.* moth-eaten.

tarocchi *m.pl.* tarot.

tarpare *vt.* to clip.

tartagliare *vi.* to stammer, stutter.

tartaruga *f.* tortoise; turtle.

tartassare *vt.* to badger; to mangle.

tartina *f.* sandwich.

Tartini, Giuseppe, Italian violinist and composer, *Il trillo del diavolo* (1692–1770).

tartufo *m.* truffle.

tasca *f.* pocket: **rompere le tasche a,** to bother; **averne piene le tasche di,** to be fed up with.

tasca'bile *adj.* pocket.

tascapane *m.* pouch, haversack.

tassa *f.* tax; duty; fee.

tassa'metro *m.* taximeter.

tassare *vt.* to assess; to tax.

tassativamente *adv.* positively.

tassativo *adj.* positive, absolute.

tassazione *f.* assessment, taxation.

tassello *m.* dowel.

tassì *m.* taxi.

tasso (1) *m.* (*zool.*) badger.

tasso (2) *m.* (*bot.*) yew tree.

tasso (3) *m.* rate (*of interest*).

Tasso, Torquato, Italian poet, *La Gerusalemme Liberata* (1544–1595).

Tassoni, Alessandro, Italian poet and critic, *La secchia rapita* (1565–1635).

tastare *vt.* to finger, feel; (*med.*) to palpate: **— il terreno,** to feel one's way.

tastiera f. keyboard.

tasto m. fingering; touch; (mus., mach.) key: — telegrafico, tapper; un — delicato, a sore subject.

tastoni, (a) adv. gropingly.

tat'tica f. tactic, tactics; policy.

tat'tico m. tactician; adj. tactical.

tatto m. touch, feeling; tact.

tatuag'gio m. tattoo.

tatuare vt. to tattoo.

taumaturgo m. thaumaturgist.

taurino adj. bull-like, taurine.

taverna f. tavern, public house.

taverniere m. publican.

ta'vola f. table; plank; plate; board: — pitagorica, multiplication table; — reale, backgammon; — calda, cafeteria.

tavolac'cio m. plank bed.

tavolata f. tableful.

tavolato m. planking; plank wall; (geog.) plateau.

tavoletta f. small board; tablet; bar (of chocolate, etc.).

tavoliere m. chessboard; cardtable; (geog.) tableland.

tavolino m. small table.

ta'volo m. table.

tavolozza f. palette.

tazza f. cup, mug.

te pers.pron. you (fam.sing.); particle, (to) you.

tè m. tea.

teatrale adj. theatrical, stage.

teatro m. theater; playhouse; stage; drama: — dell'opera, opera house; — lirico, opera; — di prosa, drama, — di posa (moving pictures), studio.

teca f. case; (bot., anat.) theca.

tec'nica f. technique; technics.

tec'nico m. expert; technician; adj. technical.

teco pers.pron. with you; (poet.) with thee.

tedesco m., adj. German.

tediare vt. to bore; tediarsi vr. to get bored.

te'dio m. tedium, weariness.

tedioso adj. tedious, boring.

tegame m. pan.

te'glia f. bakepan.

te'gola f. tile; (fig.) brickbat.

te'golo m. tile.

teiera f. teapot.

tela f. linen, cloth; canvas; painting; (theat.) curtain: — di luta, burlap; — greggia, canvas; — incerata, oilcloth; — di ragno, cobweb.

tela'io m. loom; frame, framework; (text.) loom; (auto.) chassis; sash (as of a window).

telearma f. guided missile.

teleca'mera f. telecamera.

telecomandato adj. remote-controlled.

telecomando m. remote control.

telecomunicazione f. telecommunication.

telecro'naca f. telecast.

telefe'rica f. telpherage; telpher; telpherway.

telefonare vt. to telephone, phone.

telefonata f. telephone call.

telefo'nico adj. telephonic; telephone.

telefonista m., f. telephone operator.

tele'fono m. telephone, phone: — interno, interphone; chiamare uno al —, to call one up.

telefoto f. telephotograph.

telege'nico adj. telegenic.

telegiornale m. telenewscast.

telegrafare vt. to telegraph, wire, cable.

telegrafi'a f. telegraphy.

telegra'fico adj. telegraphic: indirizzo —, cable address.

telegrafista m., f. telegraph operator.

tele'grafo m. telegraph; telegraph office: — senza fili, radiotelegraph.

telegramma m. telegram, wire; cable: — lettera, lettergram.

tele'metro m. telemeter; (photo.) rangefinder.

teleobbiettivo m. telephoto lens.

telepati'a f. telepathy.

telepa'tico adj. telepathic.

teleproietto m. robot bomb, rocket-propelled bomb.

telesco'pio m. telescope.

telescrivente f. teletypewriter, teleprinter.

telespettatore m. televiewer.

teletrasmet'tere vt. to telecast.

televisionare vt. to telecast; to televise.

televisione f. television, TV.

televisivo adj. television, TV.

televisore m. televisor.

tellu'rico adj. telluric.

telo m. piece of cloth, sheet: telo da tenda, shelter half.

telone m. (theat.) curtain; (moving pictures) screen.

tema (1) m. theme; subject.

tema (2) f. see timore.

temerarietà see temerità.

temera'rio m. daredevil; adj. reckless.

temere vt., vi. to fear, be afraid (of); to dread.

temerità f. rashness.

temi'bile adj. redoubtable.

tem'pera f. (metal.) temper.

temperamatite m. pencil sharpener.

temperamento m. mitigation; temperament, disposition.

temperante adj. temperate, moderate.

temperanza f. temperance, sobriety.

temperare vt. to temper; to moderate; to sharpen (as a pencil).

temperatura f. temperature.
temperino m. penknife.
tempesta f. storm; tempest.
tempestare vt. to storm (with blows); vi. to storm: — di domande, to pelt with questions.
tempestato adj. spangled, studded (with).
tempestivo adj. timely, seasonable.
tempestoso adj. tempestuous, stormy.
tem'pia f. temple.
tem'pio m. temple.
tempo m. time; weather; (gramm.) tense; (moving pictures) part: fare a — per, to be in good time to; aver fatto il proprio —, to have seen one's days; da (molto) —, for (quite) a while; col —, in time; — fa, some time ago; molto — prima, long before; a — perso, in one,s spare moments; a suo —, in due time; previously; in questi ultimi tempi, lately; per —, early; a far — da, dating from.
temporale m. storm; adj. secular.
tempora'neo adj. transitory, temporary.
temporeggiare vi. to temporize, procrastinate; to stall.
temporeggiatore m. temporizer.
tempra f. make, disposition; (metal.) temper.
temprare vt. to temper; to harden; to inure; **temprarsi** vr. to get inured; to harden.
tenace adj. tenacious, stubborn.
tena'cia f. tenacity.
tena'glia f. see tana'glia.
tenda f. curtain; tent; awning.
tendenza f. inclination, tendency.
tendenzioso adj. tendentious.
ten'der (rail.) tender.
ten'dere vt.[146] to stretch (out); to hold out, hand; to tighten; to prepare, set; vi. to tend; to aim, drive (at); to incline (to): — le orecchie, to strain one's ears; — un arco, to draw a bow.
tendina f. blind; window curtain.
ten'dine m. tendon.
te'nebre f.pl. obscurity, darkness.
tenebroso adj. obscure, dark, gloomy; shady.
tenente m. lieutenant.
tenere vt.[141] to hold; to keep; to sustain; to wear; to contain; to stand; to follow; to observe; to make; to consider, think; to be valid; to hold, resist: — posto, to take room; la via da —, the way to be followed; — un discorso, to make, deliver a speech; — per amico, to consider a friend; — a mente, to bear in mind; — d'occhio, to keep an

eye on; — a battesimo, to be (one's) godfather or godmother; — dietro a, to follow; — le parti di, to stand up for; — per una squadra (sport), to root for a team; — conto di, to consider; — duro, to hold on; **tenerci**, to be keen (on); **tenersi** vr. to keep (oneself); to refrain, keep (from); to stick to: **tenersi per mano**, to hold hands.
tenerezza f. tenderness, fondness; softness.
te'nero adj. tender; loving, fond; soft.
te'nia f. tapeworm, taenia.
tenore m. tenor; standard; purport.
tensione f. tension; stress, strain.
tenta'colo m. tentacle.
tentare vt., vi. to try, attempt; to tempt; to endeavor; to touch; to feel.
tentativo m. attempt.
tentatore m. tempter; adj. tempting.
tentazione f. temptation.
tentennare vt. to shake; vi. to vacillate; to waver; to totter, stagger.
tentoni, (a) adv. gropingly.
te'nue adj. thin, slender; tenuous: intestino —, small intestine.
tenuta f. uniform; capacity; estate, farm: in alta —, in full dress; a — d'acqua, watertight.
tenuta'rio m. operator.
tenuto adj. bound; obliged. pp.of **tenere**.
teologi'a f. theology.
teo'logo m. theologian.
teorema m. theorem.
teore'tico adj. theoretic.
teori'a f. theory; row, procession.
teoricamente adv. in theory.
teo'rico adj. theoretical.
te'pido adj. lukewarm, tepid.
tepore m. warmth.
teppa f. underworld.
teppista m. hoodlum, tough.
terape'utico adj. therapeutic.
terapi'a f. therapeutics.
ter'gere vt.[148] to wipe (off, away); to polish; to clean.
tergicristallo m. windshield wiper.
tergiversare vi. to stall; to quibble.
tergo m. back: a —, behind; overleaf.
termale adj. thermal.
terme f.pl. thermae; thermal springs; bathing establishment; spa.
ter'mico adj. thermic.
terminare see **finire**.
terminazione f. end, close; termination, ending.
ter'mine m. term, limit; boundary; end: avere —, to end; a rigor di —, strictly speaking; in altri termini, in other words.
terminologi'a f. terminology.

termo'foro m. thermophore.
termo'metro m. thermometer.
ter'mos m. Thermos (*trademark*), vacuum bottle.
termosifone m. heating plant; radiator.
termo'stato m. thermostat.
terna f. tern.
terno m. tern; adj. triple.
terra f. earth; land; ground, soil; floor: scendere a —, to land; essere a —, to be downcast; to be on one's uppers.
terracotta f. earthenware; terracotta.
terra'glia f., terra'glie f.pl. pottery, earthenware.
terrapieno m. embankment.
terraza f., terrazzo m. balcony; terrace.
terremotato m. earthquake victim or survivor.
terremoto m. earthquake.
terreno m. ground; soil; land: preparare il —, to pave the way; tastare il —, to throw out feelers; adj. earthly; worldly: piano —, ground floor, first floor (*U.S.*).
ter'reo adj. ghastly; pale; wan, ashen.
terrestre adj. terrestrial; land, earthly.
terri'bile adj. dreadful, terrible.
terribilmente adv. awfully, dreadfully.
terrificante adj. appalling, terrific.
terrificare vt. to appall, terrify.
terrina f. tureen.
territoriale m., adj. territorial.
territo'rio m. territory.
terrone m., adj. (*It.slang*) Southerner.
terrore m. dread, terror.
terrorismo m. terrorism.
terrorista m. terrorist.
terrorizzare vt. to terrorize.
terso adj. terse, polished; clear. pp.of tergere.
terzaruolo m. (*naut.*) reef.
terzetto m. triplet; trio.
terzo m., adj. third.
terzul'timo m., adj. last but two.
tesa f. brim (*of a hat*).
teschio m. skull.
tesi f. thesis (*pl.* theses).
teso adj. tight, taut, strained. pp.of tendere.
tesoreri'a f. treasure, treasury.
tesoriere m. treasurer.
tesoro m. treasure; treasury: far —di, to treasure; buono del —, bond.
tes'sera f. card, ticket.
tesseramento m. rationing.
tesserare vt. to ration; to give a membership card to.
tesserato m. ration card holder; (*polit.*) cardholder.
tes'sere vt. to weave.

tes'sile m., adj. textile.
tessitore m., tessitrice f. weaver.
tessitura f. weaving; weaving mill.
tessuto m. fabric, cloth; tissue.
testa f. head: essere in —, to have the lead; colpo di —, plunge; mettere la — a partito, to reform; battere in — (*of a motor*), to ping; non saper dove battere la —, to be at one's wit's end; rompersi la —, to rack one's brains; to have the worst of it.
testamento m. testament, will.
testardag'gine f. stubbornness.
testardo m. stubborn.
testata f. head, headpiece; top; heading; blow with the head.
teste m. witness.
testè adv. a short time ago; just now.
testificare vt., vi. to testify.
testimone m. witness; best man (*at a wedding*): — oculare, eyewitness.
testimonianza f. witness; evidence.
testimoniare vt., vi. to serve as a witness; to testify, depose.
testimo'nio m. witness; best man (*at a wedding*).
testo m. text; contents.
testuale adj. verbatim.
testug'gine f. turtle, tortoise.
te'tano m. tetanus.
tetra'gono adj. tetragonal; resistant, unshaken (*by*).
tetro adj. gloomy, dark, bleak.
tetto m. roof.
tetto'ia f. shed; marquee.
ti pers.pron. you, to you; yourself.
tibia f. (*anat.*) shinbone.
ticchetti'o m. ticking.
tic'chio m. whim, fancy.
tie'pido adj. tepid, lukewarm.
Tie'polo, Giambattista, great Venetian painter (1696–1770).
tifo m. typhus: fare il — per (*sport*), to root for.
tifoidea f. typhoid fever.
tifone m. typhoon.
tifoso m. fan; (*sport*) rooter; adj. typhous.
ti'glio m. lime tree, lime.
tiglioso adj. fibrous; sinewy; tough.
tignola, tignuola f. moth.
tigrato adj. streaked, striped; tabby.
tigre f. tiger.
timbrare vt. to stamp.
timbratura f. stamping; postmarking.
timbro m. stamp; timbre (*of sounds*).
timidezza f. shyness, timidity.
ti'mido adj. timid, bashful, shy.
timone m. rudder, helm: — di profondità (*aeron.*), elevator.
timoneggiare vt. to steer.
timoniere m. steersman, helmsman.
timorato adj. pious.

timore *m.* fear, dread; awe.
timoroso *adj.* timid, timorous.
tim'pano *m.* eardrum; kettledrum.
tinca *f.* (*ichthyol.*) tench.
tinello *m.* breakfast room.
tin'gere *vt.*[144] to dye; to paint; to stain: **tingersi i capelli,** to dye one's hair.
tino *m.* tub, vat.
tinozza *f.* tub; bathtub.
tinta *f.* dye; hue, color; tinge.
tinteggiare *vt.* to tinge.
tintinnare *vi.* to tinkle; to clink.
tintinni'o *m.* tinkling; clinking.
tinto *pp.of* tingere.
tintore *m.* dyer; dry cleaner.
Tintoretto, il (*Iacopo Robusti*), Italian painter (1518–1594).
tintori'a *f.* dyeing; dyehouse; dry cleaner's shop.
tintura *f.* tincture; dye; dyeing: — **di iodio,** iodine.
ti'pico *adj.* typical.
tipo *m.* type, model, standard; specimen; fellow, guy.
tipografi'a *f.* printing house; typography.
tipogra'fico *adj.* typographic, printing.
tipo'grafo *m.* typographer, printer.
tipo'metro *m.* (*typog.*) em scale, pica rule, line gauge.
tirag'gio *m.* draught, drawing.
tirali'nee *m.* ruling pen.
tiranni'a *f.* tyranny.
tiran'nico *adj.* tyrannical.
tiran'nide *f.* tyranny.
tiranno *m.* tyrant.
tirante *m.* brace; trace (*of a harness*); (*mach.*) stag rod, drag link.
tirapiedi *m.* underling, man Friday.
tirare *vt.* to draw, pull; to stretch; to take in; to move; to trace; to fling hurl; to shoot; (*typog.*) to print; *vi.* to pull; to tend; to blow; to shoot (*at*): — **su,** to bring up; — **una somma,** — **le somme,** to sum up; — **calci,** to kick; — **pugni,** to punch; — **su le maniche,** to roll up one's sleeves; — **le cuoia,** to kick the bucket; — **avanti,** to get along; — **di scherma,** to fence; **tirarsi** *vr.* to draw: — **indietro,** to draw back; — **su,** to get up, rise; — **un colpo di rivoltella,** to shoot oneself.
tirata *f.* pull, draw; stretch; tirade.
tirato *adj.* taut; drawn; stingy.
tiratore *m.* marksman, shot, shooter: **franco —,** sniper.
tiratura *f.* printing; circulation.
tirchieri'a *f.* stinginess.
tir'chio *m.* miser; *adj.* stingy.
tiretto *m.* drawer.
tiritera *f.* rigmarole.

tiro *m.* draft; pull; shooting; shot; fire; range; trick; team (*of horses*): — **a segno,** rifle range; shooting gallery; **a —,** within one's reach; — **alla fune,** tug of war; **cavallo da —,** draft horse.
tiroci'nio *m.* apprenticeship.
tisana *f.* ptisan.
tisi *f.* consumption, phthisis.
ti'sico *adj.* consumptive; stunted.
titillare *vt.* to titillate, tickle.
titino *m.*, *adj.* (*pol.*) Titoist.
titolare *m.* owner; holder; *adj.* regular.
ti'tolo *m.* title; heading, caption; qualification; claim, right; stock, bond; insult; (*text.*) count; (*chem.*) titer: — **di studio,** diploma, degree; scholastic titles; **a — di,** as a.
titubante *adj.* hesitating, irresolute.
titubanza *f.* perplexity, diffidence.
titubare *vi.* to waver, hesitate.
Tiziano (*Tiziano Vecellio*), one of the greatest Italian painters, head of the Venetian school (1477–1576).
tizio *m.* fellow, guy.
tizzo, tizzone *m.* firebrand.
to' (*interj.*) here! take this! well! why!
toccare *vt.* to touch; to concern; to call at; *vi.* to happen, befall; to be up (*to*); to have (*to*); to belong (*to*); to be awarded; to be one's turn: — **sul vivo,** to sting to the quick; — **con mano,** to make sure; **gli estremi si toccano,** extremes meet; **mi tocca obbedire,** I have to obey.
toccasana *m.* cure-all, panacea.
tocco (*1*) *m.* touch; stroke; one o'clock.
tocco (*2*) *adj.* crackbrained, touched.
tocco (*3*) *m.* chunk; toque, mortarboard.
toga *f.* gown; toga.
to'gliere *vt.*[144] to take away *or* off; to remove; to subtract: — **il saluto a,** to cut; — **dalla testa,** to get out of (one's) head; — **di mezzo,** to get rid of; **ciò non toglie che egli sia benvoluto,** this does not prevent his being popular; — **d'impaccio,** to help out of a scrape; **to'gliersi** *vr.* to get off; to take off; to deprive oneself: — **la vita,** to commit suicide; — **di mezzo,** to get out of the way.
toh *see* **to'**.
tolda *f.* deck.
toletta *f.* toilette; attire; watercloset; dressing room; dressing table.
tollera'bile *adj.* tolerable.
tollerante *adj.* tolerant.
tolleranza *f.* endurance, tolerance.
tollerare *vt.* to endure, tolerate.
tolto *pp. of* togliere.
toma'ia *f.* vamp, upper.

tomba f. tomb, grave.

tombino m. road manhole; drain well.

tom'bola f. tombola; fall, tumble.

tom'bolo m. lace pillow: **merletto a —,** pillow lace.

Tommaseo, Nicolò, Italian lexicographer, novelist and patriot, *Dizionario dei sinonimi, Dizionario della lingua italiana* (1802–1874).

tomo m. volume, tome.

to'naca f. frock; (*eccl.*) cassock.

tonalità f. tonality.

tonante adj. thundering.

tonare *see* **tuonare.**

tondeggiante adj. roundish.

tondino m. (*iron*) rod.

tondo m. round; plate; (*typog.*) roman; adj. round, circular: **chiaro e —,** straight, outspokenly.

tonfo m. thud; splash.

to'nico m., adj. tonic.

tonificare vt. to invigorate.

tonnara f. tunny snare.

tonnellag'gio m. tonnage.

tonnellata f. (*Kg.* 1016) long ton; (*Kg.* 907) short ton; (*Kg.* 1000) metric ton.

tonno m. tunny.

tono m. tone; hue; tune; pitch: **darsi —,** to give oneself airs.

tonsilla f. tonsil.

tonsura f. tonsure.

Tonti, Lorenzo, Italian banker in France (*living in* 1653).

tontina f. tontine.

tonto adj. silly, dull.

topa'ia f. rats' nest; hovel.

topa'zio m. topaz.

to'pica f. blunder, *faux pas.*

topo m. mouse; rat: **— di biblioteca,** bookworm.

topografi'a f. topography.

topo'grafo m. topographer.

Topolino m. Mickey Mouse.

toporagno m. shrewmouse.

toppa (*1*) f. lock.

toppa (*2*) f. patch.

torace m. thorax.

torba f. peat.

tor'bido adj. turbid, murky, muddy; troubled; shady; m. trouble, disorder: **pescare nel —,** to fish in troubled waters.

tor'cere vt.[144] to twist, wring: **— il naso (la bocca),** to make a wry face; **dar del filo da —,** to cause a great deal of trouble; **tor'cersi** vr. to writhe, twist; to squirm.

torchiare vt. to press.

torchietto m. (*photo.*) printing frame.

tor'chio m. press.

tor'cia f. torch.

torcicollo m. stiff neck.

tordo m. thrush.

torello m. young bull; (*naut.*) garboard.

torio *see* **tuorlo.**

torma f. crowd, swarm; herd.

tormenta f. blizzard, snowstorm.

tormentare vt. to torment; **tormentarsi** vr. to torment oneself; to worry.

tormento m. torment; agony, pain.

tornaconto m. profit, benefit.

tornare vi. to return; to go back; to come back; to start afresh; to recur: **— a bomba,** to return to the point; **— indietro,** to get back; **— a onore,** to do (one) credit; **— comodo,** to suit, to be of use; **— amici,** to be friends again.

tornasole m. (*chem.*) litmus.

torneo m. tournament.

tor'nio m. lathe, turning lathe.

tornire vt. to turn; to shape, polish.

tornitore m. turner.

torno (*1*) m. period, length (*of time*).

torno (*2*) *prep.*, adv. round, about: **torno torno,** all around; **togliersi uno di —,** to get rid of one.

toro m. bull; (*astr.*) Taurus.

torpe'dine f. torpedo.

torpediniera f. destroyer escort, torpedo-boat destroyer.

torpedo f. (*auto.*) torpedo.

torpedone m. motor coach, bus.

tor'pido adj. torpid; drowsy.

torpore m. torpor, drowsiness.

torre f. tower; steeple.

torreggiare vi. to tower.

torrente m. torrent, stream.

torretta f. turret; conning tower (*of a submarine*).

Torricelli, Evangelista, Italian physicist, inventor of barometer (1608–1647).

tor'rido adj. torrid.

torrione m. keep.

torrone m. nougat.

torsione f. torsion, twist.

torso m. (*anat.*) trunk, torso.

tor'solo m. stump, stalk; core.

torta f. cake, tart, pie.

torto (*1*) m. wrong; injury; injustice; fault: **aver —,** to be wrong; **a — o a ragione,** rightly or wrongly.

torto (*2*) adj. twisted. *pp.of* **torcere.**

tor'tora f. turtledove.

tortuoso adj. tortuous; crooked; winding.

tortura f. torture.

torturare vt. to torture; **torturarsi** vr. to torment oneself.

torvo adj. grim, surly, stern.

tosare vt. to shear.

Toscanini, Arturo, Italian conductor (1867–1957).

toscano m., adj. Tuscan.

tosse f. cough: — **asinina**, whooping cough.

tos'sico m. poison; adj. toxic.

tossina f. toxin.

tossire vi. to cough.

tostare vt. to roast; to toast.

Tosti, Francesco Paolo, Italian composer (1846–1916).

tosto (1) adv. soon, immediately.

tosto (2) adj. compact, firm; bold: **faccia tosta**, cheek, impudence.

totale m., adj. total.

totalità f. totality, entirety, whole.

totalita'rio adj. totalitarian.

totalizzare vt. to totalize.

totalizzatore m. pari mutuel, betting machine.

to'tano m. cuttlefish.

totocal'cio m. soccer pool.

tova'glia f. tablecloth.

tovagliolo m. napkin.

tozzo m. bit, morsel; adj. stocky, squat.

tra see **fra**.

trabac'colo m. (naut.) lugger; (fig.) "jalopy."

traballante adj. tottering, shaky.

traballare vi. to reel, stagger, totter; to jolt.

trabic'colo m. warming pan; (fig.) "jalopy."

traboccante adj. overflowing.

traboccare vi. to overflow.

trabocchetto m. pitfall, trap.

tracagnotto adj. stocky, squat.

tracannare vt. to gulp down, swill.

traccia f. trace, track, trail; mark, impression; footprint; sketch, outline.

tracciare vt. to trace, sketch; to draw, mark out; to outline.

tracciato m. tracing, outline; lay.

trachea f. windpipe, trachea.

tracolla f. baldric: **a** —, baldric-wise.

tracollo m. breakdown; (exch.) slump; fall.

tracotante adj. overbearing.

tracotanza f. arrogance.

tradimento m. treason; treachery: **a** —, treacherously; unawares; **mangiar pane a** —, to eat the bread of idleness.

tradire vt. to betray; to deceive; **tradirsi** vr. to give oneself away.

traditore m. traitor, betrayer.

traditrice f. traitress.

tradizionale adj. traditional.

tradizione f. tradition.

tradotta f. troop train.

tradotto pp.of **tradurre**.

tradurre vt.³ to translate; to convey; to take: — **alle carceri**, to take to jail; — **in pratica**, to put into practice; **tradursi** vr. to result (in), turn out.

traduttore m. translator.

traduzione f. translation.

traente m. (comm.) drawer.

trafelato adj. panting, breathless.

trafficante m. dealer, trader.

trafficare vi. to trade, traffic.

traf'fico m. traffic; trade.

trafig'gere vt.⁴⁴ to transfix, stab.

trafila f. drawplate; series; routine; red tape.

trafilare vt. to wiredraw.

trafiletto m. paragraph; (journ.) box.

trafitto pp.of **trafiggere**.

trafittura f. stitch.

traforare vt. to bore; to openwork.

traforo m. piercing; tunnel; openwork.

trafugare vt. to steal.

trage'dia f. tragedy.

traghettare vt. to ferry.

traghetto m. ferryboat.

tra'gico adj. tragic.

tragitto m. route, course; journey.

traguardo m. winning post, finish line; aim: **tagliare il** —, to break the tape.

traietto'ria f. trajectory.

trainare vt. to tow, drag.

tra'ino m. sledge; tow; train.

tralasciare vt., vi. to interrupt; to cease; to omit, fail; to give up; to abstain (from).

tral'cio m. vine shoot, shoot.

tralic'cio m. trellis; ticking.

tralice, (in) adv. askance.

tralignare vi. to degenerate.

tram m. streetcar.

trama f. weft, woof; plot.

trama'glio m. dragnet.

tramandare vt. to hand down.

tramare vt., vi. to plot.

trambusto m. bustle; fuss.

tramesti'o m. bustle.

tramezza f. partition.

tramezzino m. sandwich.

tramezzo m. partition.

tra'mite: **per il** — **di**, through.

tramog'gia f. hopper.

tramontana f. northwind; north: **perdere la** —, to lose one's bearings.

tramontare vi. to set, go down; to decline; to end.

tramontato adj. faded; vanished; outmoded; forgotten.

tramonto m. setting; sunset; end.

tramortire vt. to stun, knock on the head.

tramortito adj. stunned.

trampoliere m. (ornith.) stilt.

trampolino m. springboard.

tram'polo m. stilt.

tramutare vt. to transform; **tramutarsi** vr. to turn (into).

tramvi'a f. streetcar line.

trancia f. shears; slice.

tranello m. trap, snare.

trangugiare vt. to swallow up.

tranne prep. save, except.

tranquillare, tranquillizzare vt. to pacify, quiet (down); **tranquillarsi, tranquillizzarsi** vr. to calm down.

tranquillità f. tranquillity, calm.

tranquillo adj. tranquil, quiet, calm: sta' —, don't worry; lasciar —, to leave alone.

transatlan'tico m. liner; adj. transatlantic.

transatto pp.of transigere.

transazione f. arrangement; compromise.

tran'sfuga m. deserter.

transi'gere vi.[16] to compromise; to bargain; to stretch a point.

transitare vi. to pass or move (across, through, over).

tran'sito m. transit, traffic.

transito'rio adj. transitory.

transizione f. transition.

tran tran m. routine.

tranvai m. streetcar, tramcar.

tranvia f. streetcar line.

tranviere m. streetcar man.

trapanare vt. to drill; to trephine.

trapanazione f. drilling; trephination.

tra'pano m. drill; trephine.

trapassare vi. to pierce (through).

trapasso m. passage; transfer; death.

trapelare vi. to ooze; to leak out.

trape'zio m. trapezium; trapeze.

trapiantare vt. to transplant.

trapiantarsi vr. to emigrate.

trapianto m. transplantation.

trap'pola f. trap, snare; rattletrap.

trapunta f. quilt.

trapuntare vt. to quilt.

trapunto adj. quilted.

trarre vt.[146] to draw; to throw; to get: — in salvo, to rescue; — in inganno, to deceive; — un sospiro, to heave a sigh; — d'impaccio, to get (one) out of a scrape; **trarsi** vr. to draw (back, out, aside).

trasalire vi. to start.

trasandato adj. careless; slovenly.

trasbordare vt. to transship, transfer.

trasbordo m. transshipment, transfer.

trascendentale adj. transcendental.

trascen'dere vt.[11] to transcend, exceed; vi. to exaggerate; to fly off the handle.

trascinare vt. to drag; to stir up, carry away, enthuse; **trascinarsi** vr. to drag oneself.

trasco'rere vt.[16] to spend, pass; vi. to go by; to elapse.

trascorso m. peccadillo; slip of the pen; adj. elapsed, gone by. pp.of **trascorrere**.

trascrivere vt. to transcribe.

trascrizione f. transcription.

trascura'bile adj. negligible.

trascurare vt. to neglect; to disregard; to omit; **trascurarsi** vr. not to take care of oneself.

trascuratezza f. carelessness; negligence; slovenliness.

trascurato adj. careless, negligent; neglected; slovenly.

trasecolare vi. to marvel, wonder.

trasecolato adj. astonished, nonplussed.

trasferi'bile adj. transferable.

trasferimento m. removal; transfer; move.

trasferire vt. to move, remove; to transfer. **trasferirsi** vr. to move (to).

trasferta f. mission; expenses.

trasforma'bile adj. transformable; (auto.) convertible.

trasformare vt. to transform; **trasformarsi** vr. to transform oneself; to turn (into).

trasformatore m. transformer.

trasformazione f. transformation.

trasformista m. transformist.

trasfusione f. transfusion.

trasgredire vi. to transgress.

trasgressione f. transgression.

trasgressore m. transgressor.

traslazione f. removal; translation.

traslocare vt., vi. to move.

trasloco m. move; household removal.

trasmet'tere vt. to transmit; (radio) to broadcast.

trasmettitore m. transmitter.

trasmigrare vi. to transmigrate.

trasmigrazione f. transmigration.

trasmissione f. transmission; (radio) broadcasting; (mach.) drive, gear: — idrau'lica, fluid drive; — del pensiero, thought transference.

trasmittente f. broadcasting station; adj. transmitting; (radio) broadcasting.

trasognato adj. dazed, stupefied.

trasparente adj. transparent, clear.

trasparenza f. transparence.

trasparire vi.[147] to appear through; to be transparent; to beam; to reveal oneself.

trasparso pp.of **trasparire**.

traspirare vi. to perspire.

traspirazione f. perspiration.

trasporre vt.[98] to transpose.

trasportare vt. to transport, convey; to carry; to translate; to postpone; to transpose.

trasporto m. transport; transportation, conveyance; freighter; transfer.

trasposto pp.of **trasporre**.

trastullarsi *vr.* to amuse oneself; to toy; to idle.

trastullo *m.* plaything; fun.

trasudare *vi.* to transude, ooze.

trasversale *f.* transverse; cross street; *adj.* transversal.

trasverso *adj.* transverse.

trasvolare *vi.* to fly (*across*).

trasvolata *f.* flight.

trasvolatore *m.* flyer.

tratta *f.* pull, jerk; (*comm.*) draft; leg (*of a journey*); (*slave*) trade: — delle bianche, white slavery.

trattabile *adj.* tractable; open to offer.

trattamento *m.* treatment; refreshment; party; board; wages, salary.

trattare *vt.* to treat, deal with; to handle; to transact; trattarsi *vr.* to treat oneself; to be (*a question of*).

trattativa *f.* negotiation.

trattato *m.* treatise; treaty.

trattazione *f.* treatment.

tratteggiare *vt.* to hatch; to delineate, trace, outline; to sketch.

tratteg'gio *m.* hatching.

trattenere *vt.* to keep, hold; to restrain; to check; to withhold; to deduct; trattenersi *vr.* to stay, remain; to linger (*on*); to refrain (*from*).

trattenimento *m.* entertainment; party.

trattenuta *f.* deduction; checkoff.

trattino *m.* hyphen, dash.

tratto (*1*) *m.* stroke; pull, jerk; stretch, distance; way; while; part; passage; manner, bearing; gesture; feature: — di spirito, witticism; disegnare al —, to hatch; a un —, suddenly; di — in —, now and then.

tratto (*2*) *pp.of* trarre.

trattore (*1*) *m.* restaurateur, landlord.

trattore (*2*) *m.* tractor, caterpillar.

trattori'a *f.* restaurant.

trattrice *f.* tractor.

tra'uma *m.* trauma, shock.

travagliare *vt.* to trouble; to torment; *vi.* to toil.

trava'glio *m.* labor, toil; trouble, worry.

travasare *vt.* to pour off.

travaso *m.* (*pathol.*) effusion.

trave *f.* beam.

travedere *vt.* to glimpse; *vi.* to see wrongly; to dote (*on*).

traveg'gole *f.:* aver le —, to see things.

traversa *f.* transverse; crossway; (*rail.*) tie.

traversale *adj.* transversal.

traversare *vt.* to cross.

traversata *f.* passage, crossing.

traversi'a *f.* misfortune, trial.

traversina *f.* (*rail.*) tie; (*Brit.*) sleeper.

traverso *adj.* transverse, cross, oblique; awry: via traversa (*fig.*), artful dodge; di —, across; wrong; the wrong way; askance.

traversone *m.* (*fencing*) traverse; (*fort.*) traverse trench; (*sport*) cross.

travestimento *m.* disguise.

travestire *vt.* to disguise; travestirsi *vr.* to disguise oneself.

traviare *vt.* to mislead; to corrupt, lead astray.

travisare *vt.* to distort, alter.

travolgente *adj.* forcible, driving; (*fig.*) enormous, roaring.

travol'gere *vt.* to overturn, upturn; to overthrow; to sweep away; to take by storm.

trazione *f.* traction.

tre *m.*, *adj.* three.

treb'bia *f.* flail.

trebbiare *vt.* to thresh.

trebbiatrice *f.* thresher.

trebbiatura *f.* threshing.

trec'cia *f.* plait; pigtail.

trecento *card.num.* three hundred.

tredice'simo *m.*, *adj.* thirteenth.

tre'dici *m.*, *adj.* thirteen.

tre'gua *f.* truce; rest; respite.

tremante *adj.* trembling, shivering.

tremàre *vi.* to tremble, shake; to quiver, shiver.

tremebondo *adj.* trembling, quaking.

tremendo *adj.* tremendous, dreadful.

trementina *f.* turpentine.

tre'mito *m.* trembling, shaking.

tremolare *vi.* to tremble; to flicker.

treno (*1*) *m.* train: — di lusso, train de luxe; — accelerato, local train; — belvedere, observation train, astradome train.

treno (*2*) *m.* train, retinue: — di vita, way of life.

trenta *m.*, *adj.* thirty.

trente'simo *m.*, *adj.* thirtieth.

trentina *f.* some thirty: essere sulla —, to be about thirty.

trepidare *vi.* to be anxious, fret.

trepidazione *f.* trepidation.

treppiede *m.* trivet; tripod.

tresca *f.* intrigue; love affair.

tre'spolo *m.* trestle.

trian'golo *m.* triangle.

tribolare *vt.* to trouble, harass; *vi.* to labor; to have trouble.

tribolato *adj.* afflicted, distressed.

tribolazione *f.* tribulation, ordeal.

tri'bolo *m.* trouble, trial, ordeal.

tribù *f.* tribe.

tribuna *f.* tribune; rostrum; grandstand: — stampa, press gallery, press row.

tribunale *m.* tribunal, court (*of law*).

tributare *vt.* to bestow.

tributa'rio *m.*, *adj.* tributary.
tributo *m.* tribute; tax.
tricheco *m.* walrus.
triciclo *m.* tricycle.
tricolore *m.*, *adj.* tricolor.
tricorno *m.* tricorne, cocked hat.
tricromi'a *f.* colortype.
triennale *adj.* triennial; *f.* triennial exhibition.
trifase *adj.* three-phase.
trifo'glio *m.* clover, trefoil.
tri'fola *f.* truffle.
trige'mino *adj.* trigeminous; trigeminal.
tri'glia *f.* (*ichthyol.*) mullet: fare l'occhio di — a, to ogle.
trillare *vi.* to trill; to ring, peal.
trillo *m.* trill; ring, peal.
trilogi'a *f.* trilogy.
Trilussa (*Carlo Alberto Salusti*), Italian poet in Roman dialect (1873–1950).
trimestrale *adj.* quarterly.
trimestre *m.* quarter.
trimotore *m.* trimotored plane.
trina *f.* lace.
trinca *f.* (*naut.*) gammon: nuovo di —, brand new.
trincare *vt.* to gulp down, swill.
trincea *f.* trench.
trincerarsi *vr.* to entrench oneself.
trincetto *m.* shoemaker's knife.
trinchettina *f.* (*naut.*) fore-topmast staysail.
trinchetto *m.* (*naut.*) foremast.
trinciante *m.* carving knife, carver.
trinciare *vt.* to cut up; to carve: — giudizi, to pontificate.
trinciato *m.* smoking tobacco.
trinità *f.* trinity.
trionfale *adj.* triumphal.
trionfante *adj.* triumphant, exulting
trionfare *vi.* to triumph (*over*).
trionfatore *m.* triumpher; winner.
trionfo *m.* triumph; trump card.
triplicare *vt.* to triplicate, triple, treble.
tri'plice *adj.* threefold, triple: in —, copia, in triplicate.
triplo *adj.* triple.
trippa *f.* tripe; belly.
tripudiare *vi.* to exult.
tripu'dio *m.* exultancy.
trisa'vola *f.* great-great-grandmother.
trisa'volo *m.* great-great-grandfather.
triste *adj.* sad, sorrowful; gloomy.
tristezza *f.* sadness, sorrow.
tristo *adj.* wicked; base; mean.
tritacarne *m.* meat grinder, masticator.
tritare *vt.* to mince; to hash.
tritatutto *m.* triturator.
trito *adj.* minced, trite, stale.
tritolo *m.* (*chem.*) trinitrotoluene.
trit'tico *m.* triptych.

triturare *vt.* to triturate, hash, mince.
trivella *f.* drill, auger, wimble.
trivellare *vt.* to bore, wimble.
triviale *adj.* low, vulgar.
trivialità *f.* vulgarity.
tri'vio *m.* crossroad; trivium: da —, vulgar.
trofeo *m.* trophy.
troglodita *m.* troglodyte.
tro'ia *f.* sow; (*vulg.*) whore.
tromba *f.* trumpet; (*mil.*) bugle; (*auto.*) horn; (*anat.*) tube: — delle scale, stairwell; — marina, waterspout; — d'aria, whirlwind.
trombare *vt.* to beat; to reject.
trombetta *f.* trumpet.
trombettiere *m.* trumpeter.
trombone *m.* trombone.
troncare *vt.* to truncate; to cut off; to break off; to discontinue; to interrupt.
tronchesino *m.* nipper.
tronco *m.* trunk; log; (*rail.*) section, siding: — di cono, truncated cone; *adj.* truncate: licenziare in —, to "fire," "sack."
troncone *m.* stump.
troneggiare *vi.* to tower.
tron'fio *adj.* smug, self-conceited.
trono *m.* throne.
tropicale *adj.* tropical.
tro'pico *adj.* tropic.
troppo *adj.*, *adv.* too; too much; too long; excessively; quite; troppi *m. pl.* too many.
trota *f.* trout.
trottare *vi.* to trot.
trotterellare *vi.* to trot along; to toddle.
trotto *m.* trot: al —, at a trot; corsa al —, trotting race.
trot'tola *f.* top, whip top.
trovare *vt.* to find; to discover, find out; trovarsi *vr.* to find oneself; to lie; to be; to meet.
trovarobe *m.* property man.
trovata *f.* invention; trick; idea; "gimmick."
trovatello *m.* foundling.
truccare *vt.* to make up; to disguise; to prearrange, rig (*as a game*); truccarsi *vr.* to make up one's face.
truccato *adj.* made up; disguised: incontro —, prearranged match, setup.
truccatore *m.* dresser, make-up man.
trucco *m.* trick; deceit; make-up.
truce *adj.* fierce, grim; cruel.
trucidare *vt.* to slay, kill.
tru'ciolo *m.* shaving, chip.
truculento *adj.* truculent.
truculenza *f.* truculence.
truffa *f.* cheat, swindle: — all'americana, confidence trick.

truffare *vt.* to cheat, swindle.
truffatore *m.* cheat, cheater: — **all'americana**, confidence man.
truo'golo *m.* trough.
truppa *f.* troop; rank and file.
tu *pers.pron.* you (*sing.*); (*poet.*) thou.
tuba *f.* tophat; (*mus.*) tuba.
tubare *vi.* to coo.
tubatura, tubazione *f.* piping, pipes, pipeline.
tubercolosa'rio *see* sanatorio.
tubercolosi *f.* tuberculosis.
tubercoloso *adj.* tuberculous; *m.* consumptive.
tu'bero *m.* tuber.
tubo *m.* pipe, tube; duct.
tubolare *adj.* tubular.
tuffare *vt.*, **tuffarsi** *vr.* to plunge, dive.
tuffo *m.* plunge, dive: **sentire un — al cuore**, to feel one's heart jump.
tufo *m.* tufa.
tuga *f.* (*naut.*) shelter deck.
tugu'rio *m.* doghole, hovel.
tulipano *m.* tulip.
tumefarsi *vr.* to tumefy.
tumefazione *f.* tumefaction.
tu'mido *adj.* tumid.
tumore *m.* tumor.
tumulare *vt.* to bury.
tumulazione *f.* burial.
tu'mulo *m.* tumulus.
tumulto *m.* tumult; uproar, riot.
tumultuoso *adj.* tumultuous.
tu'nica *f.* tunic; gown, robe.
tuo *adj.poss.* your; (*poet.*) thy; *poss. pron.* yours; (*poet.*) thine: **i tuoi**, yours; your people.
tuonare *vi.* to thunder; to roar.
tuono *m.* thunder; roar.
tuorlo *m.* yolk.
turac'ciolo *m.* stopper; cork.
turare *see* tappare.
turba *f.* crowd; mob, rabble.
turbamento *m.* agitation; commotion; uneasiness.
turbante *m.* turban.
turbare *vt.* to trouble, disturb; to touch; to upset; to worry; **turbarsi** *vr.* to be disturbed; to become **turbina** *f.* turbine.   [uneasy.
turbinare *vi.* to whirl; to eddy.

tur'bine *m.* whirl, whirlwind, eddy; hurricane.
turbinoso *adj.* whirling; tumultuous.
turboe'lica *f.* jet-prop engine.
turbolento *adj.* turbulent.
turbolenza *f.* turbulence.
turbolocomotiva *f.* turbomotive.
turbonave *f.* turbo-electric liner.
turboreattore *m.* turbojet.
turchese *m.* turquoise.
turchino *m.*, *adj.* dark blue.
turco *m.* Turk; Turkish (language); *adj.* Turkish: **bestemmiare iome un —**, to swear like a trooper; **fumare come un —**, to smoke like a chimney.
tur'gido *adj.* turgid, swollen, full.
turismo *m.* tourism: **auto da —**, touring car.
turista *m.* tourist.
turi'stico *adj.* tourist, touristic.
turlupinare *vt.* to swindle, hoodwink.
turlupinatura *f.* swindle.
turno *m.* turn, shift; duty: **fare a —**, to take turns.
turpe *adj.* filthy, base, shameful.
turpilo'quio *m.* foul language.
tuta *f.* overall.
tutela *f.* guardianship; protection, defense.
tutelare *vt.* to protect, defend; *adj.* tutelary.
tutore *m.*, **tutrice** *f.* guardian.
tuttavia *adv.* still, yet, nevertheless, however.
tutto (*1*) *m.* everything; whole.
tutto (*2*) *adj.* all; whole; **tutti** *m. pl.* every.
tutto (*3*) *pron.* all, everything. **tutti** *m. pl.* all; everybody, everyone.
tutto (*4*) *adv.* quite, all, wholly; fully; deeply: **essere tutt'uno**, to be the same (thing); **in — e per —**, completely; **da per —**, everywhere; **a tutt'oggi**, so far; **tutt'a un tratto**, all of a sudden; **del —**, quite, at all; **tutt'altro**, on the contrary; **tutt'altro che**, far from; **tutt'al più**, at most.
tuttora *adv.* still.
tzigano *m.*, *adj.* gipsy.

U

ubbi'a *f.* delusion, whim.
ubbidiente *adj.* obedient, dutiful.
ubbidienza *f.* obedience.
ubbidire *vt.*, *vi.* to obey.
ubbriacare, ubbriaco *see* ubriacare, ubriaco.
ubertoso *adj.* fertile, fruitful.
ubicazione *f.* location, emplacement.
ubiquità *f.* ubiquity, omnipresence.

ubriacare *vt.* to make drunk, intoxicate; **ubriacarsi** *vr.* to get drunk.
ubriachezza *f.* drunkenness.
ubriaco *adj.* drunk, intoxicated.
ubriacone *m.* drunkard.
uccelliera *f.* aviary, birdcage.
uccello *m.* bird: — **di bosco**, fugitive.
Uccello, Paolo (*Paolo di Dono*), Italian painter (1397–1475).

ucci'dere *vt.*[41] to kill, slay; to shoot;
  uccidersi *vr.* to kill oneself; to
  commit suicide.
uccisione *f.* killing, slaughter.
ucciso *m.* victim; *adj.* killed, slain.
  pp.of uccidere.
uccisore *m.* killer, slayer.
udienza *f.* hearing, interview; session.
udire *vt., vi.*[148] to hear; to listen (to).
udito (1) *pp.of* udire.
udito (2) *m.* hearing.
udito'rio *m.* audience.
ufficiale *m.* officer; official: — giudiziario, process server, bailiff; —
  di rotta, navigator; — pagatore,
  paymaster; *adj.* official.
ufficiare *vt.* to officiate.
uffi'cio *m.* office; bureau; function,
  duty: d'—, ex officio; buoni uffici,
  services.
ufficioso *adj.* officious; semiofficial;
  overkind.
uffi'zio *m.* (*rel.*) office.
ufo, (a) *adv.* for a thank-you, free.
ug'gia *f.* aversion, dislike: prendere in
  —, to take a dislike to.
uggiolare *vi.* to whimper.
uggioso *adj.* depressing, gloomy.
u'gola *f.* uvula; throat.
uguaglianza *f.* equality.
uguagliare *vt.* to equal; to make even;
  to equalize.
uguale *adj.* equal; like; same.
ul'cera *f.* ulcer.
ulcerazione *f.* ulceration.
uliva *f.* olive.
ulivo *m.* olive tree.
ulteriore   *adj.*   ulterior,   further,
  later.
ultimamente *adv.* lately, of late.
ultimare *vt.* to finish, complete.
ul'timo *adj.* last; latest; final; utmost: da —, finally; in —, in the
  end; fino all '—, to the last.
ultra *adv.*: il non plus —, the acme;
  the ultimate.
ultrarosso *adj.* infrared.
ultrasuono *m.* supersonant.
ultraso'nico *adj.* supersonic.
ultravioletto *adj.* ultraviolet.
ululare *vi.* to howl.
ululato *m.* howl, howling.
umane'simo *m.* humanism.
umanista *m.* humanist.
umanità *f.* humanity; mankind.
umanita'rio *m.*, *adj.* humanitarian.
umano *adj.* human; humane.
umettare *vt.* to moisten.
umidità *f.* dampness, moisture.
umidic'cio *adj.* dampish.
u'mido (1) *m.*, *adj.* damp.
u'mido (2) *m.* stew, ragout.
u'mile *adj.* humble.
umiliante *adj.* humiliating.

umiliare *vt.* to humble; umiliarsi *vr.*
  to humble oneself.
umiliazione *f.* humiliation.
umiltà *f.* humility, humbleness.
umore *m.* humor; mood, temper.
umorismo *m.* humor.
umorista *m.* humorist.
umori'stico *adj.* humoristic, comic.
un *see* uno.
una'nime *adj.* unanimous.
unanimità *f.* unanimity.
uncinare *vt.* to hook, grapple.
uncinetto *m.* crotchet; crochet.
uncino *m.* hook; clasp.
undice'simo *adj.* eleventh.
un'dici *m.*, *adj.* eleven.
Ungaretti, Giuseppe, most prominent
  contemporary Italian poet (1888-).
un'gere *vt.*[26] to grease, oil.
un'ghia *f.* nail; claw, talon; hoof.
unguento *m.* ointment, pomade.
u'nico *adj.* unique, only, sole, single,
  one: l'—, the only one.
unificare *vt.* to unite; to unify.
uniformare *vt.* to make uniform;
  uniformarsi *vr.* to conform (to),
  comply (with).
uniforme *f.*, *adj.* uniform.
uniformità *f.* uniformity.
unilaterale *adj.* unilateral, one-sided.
unione *f.* union, conjunction; unity.
unire *vt.*, unirsi *vr.* to unite, join: —
  in matrimonio, to marry.
uni'sono *m.* unison: all'—, in unison;
  simultaneously.
unità *f.* unity; unit.
unita'rio *m.*, *adj.* unitarian.
unito *adj.* united, joined: a tinta unita,
  plain.
universale *adj.* universal: giudizio —,
  final judgment.
università *f.* university.
universita'rio *m.* university *or* college student; *adj.* university.
universo *m.* universe.
uni'voco *adj.* univocal.
un, uno, una *indef.art.* a, an; one;
  uno *m.* una *f.* *adj.* one: marciare
  per —, to march in single file;
  indef.pron. one: l'— l'altro, each
  other.
unto (1) *m.* grease; *adj.* greasy.
unto (2) *pp.of* ungere.
untuoso *adj.* unctuous; greasy.
unzione *f.* unction.
uomo *m.* man: — fatto, grown man;
  come un sol —, with one accord.
uopo *m.*: all'—, if necessary.
uovo *m.* egg.
uragano *m.* hurricane.
ura'nio *m.* uranium.
urbane'simo *m.* urbanism.
urbanistica *f.* town planning.
urbanità *f.* urbanity, politeness.

urbano *adj.* urban; urbane, polite.
urgente *adj.* pressing, urgent.
urgenza *f.* urgency; hurry.
ur'gere *vt.* to urge, press; *vi.* to be urgent.
urina, *etc. see* **orina** *etc.*
urlare *vi.* to shout, howl, yell.
urlo *m.* shout, cry, yell, howl.
urna *f.* urn; ballot box.
urrà *interj.* hurra, hooray.
urtare *vt.* to knock against, push; to irk, annoy; **urtarsi** *vr.* to quarrel, fall out; to collide, clash; to be vexed.
urto *m.* clash; shock, impact, collision; tiff.
usanza *f.* custom, habit, practice.
usare *vt.* to use, employ; to show; *vi.* to be accustomed to, be in the habit of; to be fashionable; to be the custom; to make use (*of*): **usarsi,** to be in use, be in vogue, be the fashion.
usato *adj.* used; usual; second-hand, worn out.
usciere *m.* usher, porter; bailiff, process server.
u'scio *m.* door; entrance.
uscire *vi.*[149] to get out (*of*), issue; to go out; to come out; to flow out; to be issued; to escape: — **di senno,** to go insane; — **di strada,** to go astray.
uscita *f.* exit, way out; outlet; getting out; witticism, crack; (*comm.*)

expenditure, disbursement; issue: **dazio di —,** export duty; **in libera —,** off duty.
uscito *pp.,of* uscire.
usignuolo *m.* nightingale.
uso *m.* use; custom, usage: **fuori —,** obsolete; out of commission; *adj.* accustomed, used.
ustionare *vt.* burn, scorch.
ustione *f.* burn.
usuale *adj.* usual; common.
usufruire *vi.* to benefit (*by*); to avail oneself: — **di,** to enjoy.
usufrutto *m.* usufruct.
usufruttua'rio *m.* usufruary.
usura *f.* usury; wear and tear: **a —,** with usury.
usura'io *m.* usurer, moneylender, loanshark.
usurpare *vt.* to usurp.
usurpatore *m.* usurper.
utensile *m.* implement, tool.
utente *m.* user.
u'tero *m.* uterus.
u'tile *m.* profit, gain; *adj.* useful.
utilità *f.* utility; use; usefulness.
utilita'ria *f.* baby car.
utilizzare *vt.* to utilize; to use.
utilizzazione *f.* utilization.
uva *f.* grape: — **passa,** raisin; — **spina,** gooseberry.
uxoricida *m.* uxoricide (*agent*).
uxorici'dio *m.* uxoricide (*act*).
uz'zolo *m.* caprice, whim, fancy.

V

vacante *adj.* vacant, empty.
vacanza *f.* holiday, vacation.
vacca *f.* cow.
vaccaro *m.* cowboy.
vacchetta *f.* cowhide.
vaccinare *vt.* to vaccinate.
vaccinazione *f.* vaccination.
vaccino *m.,* *adj.* vaccine.
vacillamento *m.* wavering.
vacillante *adj.* wavering; flickering.
vacillare *vi.* to waver, vacillate.
va'cuo *adj.* vacuous, empty.
vagabondag'gio *m.* vagrancy; wandering.
vagabondare *vi.* to wander, rove.
vagabondo *m.* wanderer, vagrant; tramp. *adj.* vagabond, wandering.
vagamente *adv.* vaguely.
vagare *vi.* to wander, ramble.
vagheggiare *vt.* to cherish.
vagire *vi.* to wail.
vagito *m.* wail.
va'glia (1) *m.* money order: — **bancario,** check; — **telegrafico,** telegraph money order.

va'glia (2) *f.* good standing, worth.
vagliare *vt.* to sift.
va'glio *m.* sieve: **passare al —,** to sift.
vago *adj.* vague; pretty.
vagone *m.* car, coach; truck: — **letto** (**ristorante**), sleeping (dining) car.
va'io *m.* miniver; *adj.* dark grey.
vaiuolo *m.* smallpox.
valanga *f.* avalanche.
valente *adj.* clever, skillfull.
valenti'a *f.* cleverness, skill, ability.
valenza *f.* (*chem.*) valence.
valere *vi.*[148] to be worth; to deserve; to be equal to; to be valid; to succeed; to be of avail; to be equivalent to: **vale a dire,** that is to say, namely; — **la pena,** to be worth while; **farsi —,** to push oneself forward, to assert oneself; **far —,** to enforce; **non valsero i suoi sforzi,** his efforts were of no avail; **tanto valeva che,** we might as well; **valersi** *vr.* to avail oneself.
vale'vole *adj.* valid; good.
valicare *vt.* to pass; to cross.
va'lico *m.* pass; ford.

validità *f.* validity, effectiveness.

va'lido *adj.* effective; good; valid; able-bodied.

valigetta *f.* small bag, satchel.

vali'gia *f.* suitcase, portmanteau.

vallata, valle, *f.* valley.

valletto *m.* page, valet; bellboy.

valore *m.* value, worth, price; braveness; gallantry: campione senza —, sample parcel, no commercial value sample.

valorizzare *vt.* to increase the value of; to enhance; to improve.

valoroso *adj.* brave; valiant.

valso *pp. of* valere.

valuta *f.* value; money.

valutare *vt.* to value; to appraise; to reckon; to estimate.

valutazione *f.* valuation, estimation.

val'vola *f.* valve; (*radio*) tube, valve;

val'zer *m.* waltz. [(*elec.*) fuse.

vampa *f.* flame, blaze.

vampata *f.* burst of flame.

vampiro *m.* vampire.

vanaglorioso *adj.* vainglorious.

vaneggiare *vi.* to rave, be delirious.

vane'sio *adj.* vain, foppish.

vanga *f.* spade.

vangare *vt.* to spade, dig.

vangelo *m.* gospel; gospel truth.

vani'glia *f.* vanilla.

vanilo'quio *m.* idle talk.

vanità *f.* vanity.

vanitoso *adj.* vain, conceited.

vano *m.* room; opening; *adj.* vain, useless.

vantag'gio *m.* advantage; (*sport*) odds: essere in —, to have the lead.

vantaggioso *adj.* advantageous, profitable; favorable.

vantare *vt.* to praise; to boast (*of*); vantarsi *vr.* to boast, brag; to pride oneself (*on*).

vanteri'a *f.* boast.

vanto *m.* boast; pride.

van'vera, (a) *adv.* at random.

Vanvitelli, Luigi, Neapolitan architect (1700–1773).

vapore *m.* vapor; steam; steamship: a tutto —, full speed; cavallo —, horsepower.

vaporiera *f.* steam engine.

vaporizzare *vt.* to vaporize.

vaporizzatore *m.* vaporizer.

vaporosità *f.* vaporosity.

vaporoso *adj.* vaporous, airy.

varare *vt.* to launch: — una legge, to have an act passed.

varcare *vt.* to cross, pass.

varco *m.* passage, gap, way: attendere al —, to lie in wait (*for*).

varechina *f.* varec, kelp.

varia'bile *adj.* variable, unsteady, fickle.

variante *f.* variant; *adj.* varying.

variare *vt.*, *vi.* to vary.

variato *adj.* varied; various; changed.

variazione *f.* variation; change.

variegato *adj.* variegated.

varietà *f.* variety.

vari *m.pl.*, varie *f.pl.* several.

va'rio *adj.* various; different.

variopinto *adj.* multicolored.

varo *m.* (*naut.*) launch.

Vasari, Giorgio, Italian painter, architect and historian: builder of *Palazzo degli Uffizi* in Florence; author of *Le Vite* (1511–1574).

vasca *f.* basin; tub; pond; pool.

vascello *m.* vessel; ship.

vaselina, vasellina *f.* vaseline.

vasellame *m.* pottery.

vaso *m.* pot, vessel; vase.

vassallo *m.* vassal.

vasso'io *m.* tray.

vastità *f.* roominess; vastness; wideness; expanse.

vasto *adj.* roomy; wide; large, vast.

vate *m.* prophet; poet.

vaticinare *vt.* to prophesy.

vatici'nio *m.* prophecy, prediction.

ve, vi *m.*, *f.*, *pron.* you, to you. *adv.* there; here.

vec'chia *f.* old woman, old lady.

vecchia'ia, vecchiezza *f.* old age, oldness.

vec'chio *m.* old man; *adj.* old; elder: più —, older; il più —, the oldest; i vecchi, old people.

vece *f.* stead, place: in sua —, in his stead, in his place; fare le veci di, to act as.

vedere *vt.*, *vi.*[141] to see: ci vedo poco, I can see little; — di, to try to; non — l'ora di, to be anxious to; non poter — uno, to hate the sight of one; a mio modo di —, in my opinion; vedersi *vr.* to see oneself; (*recipr.*) to see one another; to meet: vedersi costretto a, to be forced to.

vedetta *f.* lookout, place; sentry; (*theat.*) star.

ve'dova *f.* widow.

vedovanza *f.* widowhood.

ve'dovo *m.* widower.

veduta *f.* sight, view.

veduto *pp. of* vedere.

veemente *adj.* vehement.

veemenza *f.* vehemence.

vegetale *m.*, *adj.* vegetable.

vegetare *vi.* to vegetate.

vegetazione *f.* vegetation.

ve'geto *adj.* vigorous.

vegetominerale, (acqua) *f.* lead water.

veggente *m.*, *f.* seer.

ve'glia *f.* wake; sitting up; watch; night party, revels.

vegliardo m. old man.

vegliare vt., vi. to be awake; to wake; to sit up; to watch, watch over.

veglione m. masked ball, fancy-dress ball.

vei'colo m. vehicle.

vela f. sail: far —, to sail; **a gonfie vele**, full sail; (fig.) very well.

velac'cio m. main topgallant sail.

velare vt. to veil; to conceal, disguise; **velarsi** vr. to veil oneself; to become veiled.

vela'rio m. (theat.) curtain.

velato adj. veiled; sheer.

velatura f. (naut.) sails; dimness; veiling.

veleggiare vt., vi. to sail.

veleno m. poison; venom.

velenoso adj. poisonous, venomous.

ve'lico adj. sailing.

veliero m. sailing-ship.

velina f. filmsy: **carta —**, tissue páper; **copia in —**, carbon copy.

vell'volo m. aircraft, aeroplane.

velleità f. velleity.

vellicare vt. to tickle, titillate.

velloso adj. hairy, shaggy.

vellutato adj. velvety.

velluto m. velvet.

velo m. veil.

veloce adj. quick, fast, speedy, swift.

velocemente adv. swiftly, speedily.

veloci'pede m. velocipede.

velocista m. (sport) sprinter.

velocità f. speed; velocity: **eccesso di —**, speeding.

vena f. vein; lode; mood.

venale adj. venal.

venalità f. venality.

venato adj. veined, variegated.

venato'rio adj. venatorial, hunting.

venatura f. veining.

vendem'mia f. vintage.

vendemmiare vt. to gather grapes.

ven'dere vt. to sell; **ven'dersi** vr. to sell oneself; to be sold: **quel libro si vende bene**, that book sells well.

vendetta f. revenge, vengeance.

vendicare vt. to avenge; **vendicarsi** vr. to avenge oneself; to retaliate (against).

vendicativo adj. revengeful.

vendicatore m. avenger; adj. avenging.

ven'dita f. sale; shop.

venditore m., **venditrice** f. seller; dealer: **— ambulante**, hawker, peddler.

venefi'cio m. poisoning.

vene'fico adj. poisonous.

venera'bile, venerando adj. venerable.

venerare vt. to worship, venerate.

venerazione f. veneration.

venerdì m. Friday: **mancare di un —**, to have a screw loose.

Ve'nere f. Venus.

vene'reo adj. venereal.

venire vi.[¹¹] to come; to turn out; **— alle mani**, to come to blows; **— a parole**, to have words; **— su bene**, to grow up well; **far — il medico**, to send for the doctor; **— meno**, to faint; to fail; **— bene**, to succeed, turn out well; **— in mente**, to occur; **— a sapere**, **— a conoscenza di**, to learn, hear.

venoso adj. venous.

venta'glio m. fan: **a —**, fanlike.

ventata f. gust.

vente'simo adj. twentieth.

venti m., adj. twenty.

venticello m. breeze.

ventilare vt. to winnow; to ventilate; to air.

ventila'tore m. ventilator, fan.

ventilazione f. ventilation.

ventina f. some twenty.

vento m. wind.

ven'tola f. fire fan; lampshade.

ventosa f. sucking disk; (med.) cupping glass.

ventoso adj. windy.

ventre m. belly, abdomen, womb: **correre — a terra**, to run at full speed; **giacere — a terra**, to lie flat on one's face.

ventriera f. belt.

ventrilo'quio m. ventriloquism.

ventri'loquo m. ventriloquist; adj. ventriloquous.

ventura f. fortune, luck, chance: **alla —**, at random.

venturo adj. next; future, coming.

venuta f. coming, arrival.

venuto (1) m. comer: **il nuovo —**, the newcomer; adj. come: **— da**, from.

venuto (2) pp.of venire.

verace adj. truthful.

veracità f. truthfulness.

veramente adv. truly; really, indeed; as a matter of fact.

veranda f. veranda.

verbale m. minutes, official report; adj. verbal.

verbena f. verbena, vervain.

verbo m. verb; word.

verbosità f. verbosity, prolixity.

verboso adj. verbose, prolix.

verdastro adj. greenish.

verde adj. green: **al —**, penniless; **ridere —**, to laugh on the wrong side of one's mouth.

verdeggiante adj. verdant.

verderame m. verdigris.

verdetto m. verdict.

Verdi, Giuseppe, the greatest Italian operatic composer, *Nabucco, I Lombardi alla Prima Crociata, Rigoletto, Il Trovatore, La Tra-*

viata, I Vespri Siciliani, La Forza del Destino, Aida, Falstaff (1813–1901).

verdo'gnolo *adj.* greenish.

verdura *f.* vegetables.

verecon'dia *f.* pudency, modesty.

verecondo *adj.* modest, bashful.

verga *f.* rod; cane; bar.

Verga, Giovanni, Italian novelist, *I Malavoglia, Vita dei Campi, Novelle Rusticane* (1840–1922).

vergare *vt.* to write.

vergato *adj.* ruled: **carta vergata,** ruled paper.

verginale *adj.* virgin, maidenly.

ver'gine *f.* virgin, maid; *adj.* virgin; free (*from*).

verginità *f.* virginity.

vergogna *f.* shame; bashfulness.

vergognarsi *vr.* to be ashamed: **vergognatevi!** shame on you!

vergognoso *adj.* shameful, disgraceful; shy, bashful.

veridicità *f.* veracity, genuineness.

veri'dico *adj.* veracious, true, genuine.

veri'fica *f.* verification; inspection; examination; overhaul.

verificare *vt.* to verify; to check; to audit (*as an account*); **verificarsi** *vr.* to happen.

verismo *m.* realism.

verista *m.* realist; *adj.* realistic.

verità *f.* truth, verity, actuality: **in —,** really, actually, as a matter of fact.

veritiero *adj.* truthful, veracious.

verme *m.* worm: **— solitario,** tapeworm.

vermi'glio *m., adj.* vermilion.

vernice, *f.* varnish, paint; glaze; polish; patent leather; varnishing day.

verniciare *vt.* to varnish, paint.

vero *m.* truth, reality; *adj.* true, real, veritable, genuine: (non è) —? isn't it it?; **dal —,** from nature, from life.

verone *m.* balcony.

Veronese, Paolo (*Paolo Cagliari*), Italian painter (1528–1588).

verosimiglianza *f.* likelihood.

verosi'mile *adj.* likely, probable.

Verrazzano, Giovanni, Florentine navigator (1485 ?–1528).

verricello *m.* windlass.

verro *m.* boar.

Verrocchio, del, Andrea, Italian sculptor and painter (1435–1488).

verruca *f.* wart.

versamento *m.* pouring; payment; (*bank.*) deposit.

versante *m.* side, slope.

versare *vt.* to pour; to spill, shed; to pay; (*bank.*) to deposit: **— in gravi condizioni,** to be in serious condition; **versarsi** *vr.* to pour (*into*); to spill.

versa'tile *adj.* versatile.

versatilità *f.* versatility.

versato *adj.* spilled; versed, skilled, proficient (*in*).

versione *f.* translation; version.

verso (*1*) *m.* verse, line; note, song, cry, hoot; sense, direction; way, means; verso; reverse: **versi liberi, vers libre,** free verse.

verso (*2*) *prep.* towards, to; about.

ver'tebra *f.* vertebra.

vertebrale *adj.* vertebral: **colonna —,** spine.

vertenza *f.* quarrel, question.

ver'tere *vi.* to be about, regard.

verticale *f., adj.* vertical.

ver'tice *m.* vertex, apex, top.

verti'gine *f.* giddiness, dizziness, staggers, vertigo: **avere le vertigini,** to be giddy; **dare le vertigini,** to make dizzy.

vertiginoso *adj.* dizzy; mad; breathtaking.

verza *f.* cabbage.

verziere *m.* vegetable market.

vescica *f.* bladder.

vescicante *m.* vesicant.

vescovado *m.* bishopric.

ve'scovo *m.* bishop.

vespa *f.* wasp.

vespa'io *m.* hornets' nest; (*med.*) favus.

vespasiano *m.* public urinal.

vespertino *adj.* evening; vespertine.

ve'spero *m.* evening.

vespro *m.* vesper; evening.

Vespucci, Amerigo, Florentine navigator; from his two voyages, 1499 and 1501, the two Americas derive their name (1451–1512).

vessare *vt.* to harass, wrong.

vessazione *f.* injustice, oppression.

vessillo *m.* flag.

vesta'glia *f.* dressing gown.

veste *f.* dress, gown; capacity; appearance: **— da camera,** dressing gown; **in — di,** as; **vesti** *pl.* clothes.

vestia'rio *m.* clothes: **oggetti di —,** garments.

vesti'bolo *m.* lobby, vestibule.

vesti'gio *m.* sign, trace, vestige.

vestire *vt., vi.* to dress; to wear; to clothe: **— la penne del pavone,** to put on borrowed plumes; **vestirsi** *vr.* to dress (oneself) **— da,** to disguise oneself (*as*).

vestito *m.* dress; suit; clothes; *adj.* dressed: **— da festa,** in one's Sunday best.

veterano *m., adj.* veteran.

veterina'rio *m., adj.* veterinary.

veto *m*. veto: mettere il — a, to veto.

vetra'io *m*. glass manufacturer; glass-blower; glazier.

vetrata *f*. glass window; glass door; glass partition: — a colori, stained glass window.

vetrato *adj*.: carta vetrata, sandpaper.

vetreri'a *f*. glass works.

vetrificare *vt*., *vi*. to vitrify.

vetrina *f*. show window; shop window; glass case.

vetrinista *m*., *f*. window dresser.

vetriolo *m*. vitriol.

vetro *m*. glass; pane, windowpane: — colorato, stained glass; — smerigliato, ground glass.

vetroso *adj*. glassy, vitreous.

vetta *f*. summit, top.

vettova'glie *f.pl*. victuals, food.

vettura *f*. carriage; coach; cab: in —, signori! all aboard, please!; lettera di —, carriage note.

vetturetta *f*. baby carriage.

vetturino *m*. cabman, driver.

vetusto *adj*. ancient, old.

vezzeggiare *vt*. to fondle, cuddle.

vezzeggiativo *m*. endearing term; diminutive.

vezzo *m*. bad habit; habit; fondling; charm; necklace.

vezzoso *adj*. graceful, pretty.

vi (*1*) *pron*. you, to you.

vi (*2*) *adv*. here, there: eccovi infine! there you are at last!

via (*1*) *f*. street; road; way: — d'uscita, way out; per — diplomatica, through diplomatic channels; venire a vie di fatto, to come to blows; vie legali, legal steps; la Via Lattea, the Milky Way; dare il —, to start; per vie traverse, by roundabout means; la Via Crucis, the Way of the Cross.

via (*2*) *adv*. away, off: via! go away!, go!; ma via! now come!; e così —, and so on; — — che vengono, as they come; in — di favore, as a favor; per — di, on account of.

viadotto *m*. viaduct.

viaggiare *vi*. to travel.

viaggiatore *m*., **viaggiatrice** *f*. traveler; passenger: — di comercio, commesso —, salesman.

viag'gio *m*. trip, journey, voyage, travel: — di piacere, tour; — d'andata, outward journey; — d'andata e ritorno, round trip.

viale *m*. avenue.

viandante *m*. wayfarer, pedestrian, passer-by.

via'tico *m*. viaticum.

viavai *m*. coming and going; bustle; swarm.

vibrante *adj*. vibrant, quivering

vibrare *vt*. to hurl; *vi*. to vibrate, quiver: — un colpo, to deal (strike) a blow.

vibrato *adj*. concise; energetic.

vibrazione *f*. vibration.

vica'rio *m*. vicar.

vice- *pref*. vice, assistant, deputy.

vice-direttore *m*. assistant director; assistant editor; assistant manager.

vicenda *f*. alternation; vicissitude; case; event, occurrence: a —, reciprocally, one another; in turn.

vicende'vole *adj*. reciprocal, mutual.

vicepresidente *m*. vice president, vice chairman.

vicerè *m*. viceroy.

viceversa *adv*. vice versa, conversely; on the contrary.

vicinanza *f*. nearness, closeness, vicinity; imminence; **vicinanze** (*pl*.) neighborhood.

vicinato *m*. neighborhood; neighbors.

vicino *m*. neighbor; *adj*. near, adjoining; neighboring; like, resembling; *adv*. near, near by, near at hand, close by: da —, at close quarters.

vicino, (a) *prep*. near, by, beside, close to.

vicissitu'dine *f*. vicissitude; event.

Vico, Giambattista, Italian philosopher, author of *Scienza Nuova*, by which he became the father of the modern philosophy of history (1668–1744).

vi'colo *m*. lane, alley.

vidimare *vt*. to authenticate; to sign; to visa.

vidimazione *f*. authentication, signature, visa.

vieppiù *adv*. more and more.

vietare *vt*. to forbid.

vietato *adj*. forbidden: — il transito, no thoroughfare; sosta vietata, no parking.

vieto *adj*. stale; trite; obsolete.

vigente *adj*. operative, current.

vi'gere *vi*. to be in force.

vigilante *adj*. vigilant, watchful, alert.

vigilanza *f*. vigilance, watchfulness.

vigilare *vi*. to watch, guard; *vi*. to be on guard; to keep watch.

vi'gile *m*. policeman: — del fuoco, fireman; *adj*. vigilant, watchful; wary.

vigi'lia *f*. eve; watch; fast, vigil.

vigliaccheri'a *f*. cowardice.

vigliacco *m*., *adj*. coward; dastard; cad, "heel."

vigna *f*., **vigneto** *m*., vineyard.

vignetta *f*. vignette, cartoon.

vignettista *m*. vignettist, cartoonist.

vigogna *f*. vicuña.

vigore m. vigor, strength, force: in —, in force; entrare in —, to take effect.

vigori'a f. vigor, strength.

vigoroso adj. vigorous, strong.

vile m. coward; adj. cowardly; vile, mean; cheap, low.

vilipen'dere vt.[16] to despise; to insult.

vilipen'dio m. contempt; insult.

vilipeso adj. despised. pp. of vilipendere.

villa f. villa, country house, cottage.

villag'gio m. village.

villanata f. slight, snub, insult.

Villani, Giovanni, Italian historian (1280?–1348).

villani'a f. rudeness, uncivility; insult.

villano m. peasant, countryman; boor; adj. rude.

villanzone m. boor.

villeggiante m. vacationist, vacationer.

villeggiare vi. to vacation.

villeggiatura f. summer vacation: luogo di —, summer resort.

villino m. cottage.

villoso adj. hairy, shaggy.

viltà f. cowardice; meanness.

viluppo m. tangle.

vi'mine m. osier, withe, wicker.

vina'io m. wine merchant.

vincente m. winner; adj. winning.

vin'cere vt., vi.[168] to win, gain; to vanquish; to beat, defeat; to overcome, master; vincersi vr. to master oneself.

Vinci, da, Leonardo, celebrated painter, sculptor and architect of the Florentine school; extraordinarily versatile, he distinguished himself in engineering as well as art; his most important works as a painter, Il Cenacolo, La Gioconda ("Mona Lisa"), La Vergine delle Rocce, San Giovanni Battista. La Battaglia di Anghiari (cartoon); he also wrote a Trattato della pittura and Del moto e misura dell'acqua (1452–1519).

vin'cita f. winning; winnings.

vincitore m. winner; conqueror.

vincolare vt. to bind; to engage; to entail; vincolarsi vr. to bind oneself; to engage (for).

vin'colo m. bond, tie, link.

vino m. wine.

vinto adj. conquered; vanquished; won; overcome: darsi per —, to give in or up. pp. of vincere.

viola (1) f. : — mammola, violet; — del pensiero, pansy; adj. violet, purple.

viola (2) f. (mus.) viola.

violacciocca f. wallflower.

viola'ceo adj. violet=blue; cyanotic.

violare vt. to violate.

violazione f. violation, infringement: — di domicilio, housebreaking.

violentare vt. to force; to rape.

violento adj. violent.

violenza f. violence: — carnale, rape.

violetta f. violet.

violetto m., adj. violet.

violinista m., f. violinist; fiddler.

violino m. violin; fiddle.

viot'tolo m. path.

vi'pera f. viper.

virag'gio m. (naut.) tacking; (aeron.) yaw; (photo.) toning.

virare vi. (naut.) to tack; (aeron.) to yaw; (photo.) to tone.

virata f. (naut.) tacking; (aeron.) yaw, turn.

virginale adj. maidenly, virginal.

vir'gola f. comma.

virgolette f.pl. quotation marks, inverted commas.

virgulto m. shoot; shrub.

virile adj. virile, manly; manful.

virilità f. manliness, virility; manhood.

virtù f. virtue; property.

virtuale adj. virtual.

virtuosismo m. virtuosity, stunt.

virtuoso m. virtuoso; adj. virtuous.

virulento adj. virulent.

virulenza f. virulence.

vi'scere f.pl. viscera; bowels; heart of hearts; entrails, innermost recesses.

vischio m. mistletoe; birdlime.

vi'scido adj. viscid, clammy.

viscosa f. viscose.

viscoso adj. viscous, clammy; viscose.

visi'bile adj. visible; obvious.

visibi'lio m. lot, heap, great deal: mandare in —, to enrapture; andare in —, to become enraptured.

visibilità f. visibility.

visiera f. visor; eyeshade; peak.

visiona'rio m., adj. visionary.

visione f. vision: prender —, to examine; prima — first showing (of a moving picture).

visita f. visit, call; examination; inspection; caller: marcar — (mil.) to report sick.

visitare vt. to visit; to pay a visit; to call on.

visitatore m., visitatrice f. visitor.

visivo adj. visual: facoltà visiva, sight.

viso m. face; features (pl.) far buon — a cattiva sorte, to put a good face on it; a — aperto, boldly, frankly, directly.

visone m. mink.

vispo adj. brisk, lively.

vissuto adj. lived; worldly-wise. pp. of vivere.

vista f. sight; eyes; view; landscape: far — di, to feign, pretend; persone in —, prominent people; punto di —, standpoint, opinion; a — d'occhio, apace.

vistare vt. to visa, sign.

visto (1) m. visa; approval.

visto (2) adj. seen: ben —, popular; mal —, disliked; — che, since, as. pp.of vedere.

vistoso adj. showy; considerable, large.

visuale f. view; adj. visual.

vita f. life; living, livelihood; lifetime; (anat.) waist: condannato a —, sentenced for life; — natural durante during one's lifetime; for vitale adj. vital. [ever.

vitalità f. vitality.

vitali'zio m. life annuity; adj. for life: pensione vitalizia, life pension.

vitamina f. vitamin.

vite (1) f. vine.

vite (2) f. screw; (aeron.) barrel roll; tail spin.

vitello m. calf, veal: — marino, seacalf.

vitellone m. young bullock; (coll.) "drugstore cowboy."

vitic'cio m. tendril.

vit'reo adj. vitreous.

vit'tima f. victim; casualty.

vitto m. food; board.

vitto'ria f. victory, victoria (carriage): cantar —, to crow.

Vittorio Emanuele I, King of Sardinia, 1802–21 (1759–1824).

Vittorio Emanuele II, first king of Italy, 1861–78 (1820–1878).

Vittorio Emanuele III, son of Umberto I, King of Italy, 1900–46 (1869–1947).

vittorioso adj. victorious.

vituperare vt. to vituperate.

vitupe'rio m. ignominy, shame; insult.

viuzza f. narrow street, lane.

viva! see vivere.

vivacchiare vi. to get along somehow, to live from hand to mouth.

vivace adj. lively, brisk; quick; bright.

vivacità f. vivacity, liveliness; quickness; brightness.

vivaddio! interj. by God!, so help me God!

vivagno m. selvage, selvedge.

viva'io m. hatchery.

vivamente adv. deeply, keenly; strongly; warmly.

vivanda f. food.

vivente adj. living, alive.

vi'vere (1) vt., vi.[154] to live; to enjoy one's life; to last: viva! hurrah!, long live!; sul chi vive, on the alert.

vi'vere (2) m. existence, living.

vi'veri m.pl. victuals, food, provisions; supplies: tagliare i —, to cut off (one's) allowance.

vivezza f. liveliness; brightness.

vi'vido adj. vivid, lively.

vivificare vt. to vivify.

vivisezione f. vivisection.

vivo m. living man; core: pungere sul —, to sting to the quick; una descrizione al —, a lifelike description; adj. alive; living; lively; strong; sharp, keen; bright: a viva forza, by main force; a viva voce, by word of mouth; farsi —, to show up; to let hear about oneself; vivi auguri, best wishes.

viziare vt. to spoil; to corrupt.

vi'zio m. vice; fault; bad habit; flaw.

vizioso adj. vicious; corrupt; profligate.

vizzo adj. withered.

vocabolario m. dictionary; vocabulary.

voca'bolo m. term; word; entry.

vocale f. vowel; adj. vocal.

vocazione f. vocation, calling; aptness.

voce f. voice; term; word; entry, item; rumor: — bianca, soprano voice; a —, by word of mouth; a —'alta, aloud; ad una —, in unison; non aver — in capitolo, to cut no ice; dare sulla — a, to contradict; to rebuke.

vociare vi. to bawl.

vociferare vi. to vociferate, shout: si vocifera, it is being rumored.

voga f. vogue, fashion; (naut.) rowing.

vogare vi. to row.

vogata f. row, rowing.

vogatore m. rower, oarsman; rowing machine.

voglia f. wish, desire; will, willingness; intention; craving, longing; birthmark: ho — di, I feel like; non ne ho —, I don't feel like it; di buona —, willingly; di mala —, reluctantly.

voglioso adj. desirous. [ly.

voi pers.pron. you: — stesso, yourself; — stessi, yourselves.

volano m. shuttlecock; (mach.) flywheel.

volante m. (steering) wheel; adj. flying.

volantino m. throwaway, leaflet.

volare vi. to fly.

volata f. flight; run: — finale (sport), homestretch; final dash; di —, in a hurry; full speed; at once.

vola'tile adj. volatile; flying; m. winged animal.

volatilizzare vt., vi., **volatilizzarsi** vr. to volatilize.

volatore *m.* flyer; *adj.* flying.

volente *adj.* willing: — o nolente, willy-nilly.

volenteroso *adj.* zealous; dedicated; willing.

volentieri *adv.* willingly.

volere (1) *m. see* volontà.

volere (2) *vt.*, *vi.*[148] to want; to wish, like; to ask, require; to will, command; to intend (*to*): voglio che tu, I want you to; vorrei avere, I wish I had; vorrei essere, I wish I were; ci vuole coraggio per, it takes courage to; — bene a, to love; voler male a, to hate; — dire, to mean; parla vuoi l'italiano vuoi l'inglese, he speaks both Italian and English; — è potere, where there is a will there is a way.

volgare *adj.* vulgar, coarse, low.

volgarità *f.* vulgarity, coarseness.

volgarizzare *vt.* to vulgarize.

vol'gere (1) *m.* turning; course; space: il — degli avvenimenti, the course of events; nel — di pochi anni, within a few years.

vol'gere (2) *vt.*, *vi.*[148] to turn; to elapse; go by: — alla fine, to draw to an end; — in fuga, to put to flight; **vol'gersi** *vr.* to turn.

volgo *m.* common people.

voliera *f.* aviary.

volitivo *adj.* determined, strong-willed.

volo *m.* flight, flying: prendere il —, to take to flight; — a vela, gliding; — librato, volplane.

volontà *f.* will: forza di —, will power.

volonta'rio *m.* volunteer; *adj.* voluntary.

volonteroso *see* volenteroso.

volontieri *see* volentieri.

volpe *f.* fox; vixen; (*bot.*) mildew.

volpino *adj.* foxy.

volpone *m.* (*fig.*) old fox.

volta (1) *f.* time; turn; vault: una —, once; due volte, twice; tre volte, thrice, three times; rare volte, seldom; a mia —, in my turn; una — tanto, for once; una — ogni tanto, once in a while; di — in —, each time; il più delle volte, mostly; spesse volte, often; chiave di —, keystone; partire alla — di Roma, to set out for Rome; gli diede di — il cervello, he went mad; a — di corriere, by return of post.

volta (2) *f.* (*elec.*) volt.

Volta, Alessandro, Italian physicist, inventor of the voltaic pile (1745–1827).

voltafac'cia *m.* volte-face.

voltag'gio *m.* (*elec.*) voltage.

volta'ico *adj.* (*elec.*) voltaic.

voltare *vt.*, *vi.* to turn; to translate; **voltarsi** *vr.* to turn; to change; to rebel.

voltata *f.* turn, turning.

volteggiare *vi.* to turn; to hover; to vault, circle.

volteg'gio *m.* vaulting.

volto *m.* face.

volto *adj.* turned; looking (*on*, *towards*): devoted. *pp.of* volgere.

voltura *f.* transfer.

volu'bile *adj.* fickle, changeable.

volubilità *f.* fickleness.

volume *m.* volume; mass, bulk.

voluminoso *adj.* voluminous.

voluta *f.* volute, scroll, coil.

voluto *adj.* artificial; farfetched; intentional. *pp.of* volere.

voluttà *f.* delight; voluptuousness.

voluttua'rio *adj.* superfluous, luxury.

voluttuoso *adj.* voluptuous.

vo'mere *m.* plowshare.

vo'mico *adj.* emetic: noce vomica, vomit nut, nux vomica.

vomitare *vt.*, *vi.* to vomit: aver voglia di —, to feel sick; far venire la voglia di —, to make sick.

vomitivo *adj.* emetic, disgusting.

vo'mito *m.* vomit.

von'gola *f.* mussel.

vorace *adj.* voracious; greedy.

voracità *f.* voracity; greediness.

vora'gine *f.* gulf, chasm, abyss.

vor'tice *m.* vortex; whirl; whirlpool; whirlwind.

vorticoso *adj.* vortical, whirling.

vostro *poss. adj.* your, of yours; *poss. pron.* yours.

votag'gine *f.* emptiness.

votante *m.* voter; *adj.* voting.

votare *vt.*, *vi.* to devote; to approve, pass; to vote; **votarsi** *vr.* to devote oneself: non sapere a che santo votarsi, not to know which way to turn.

votato *adj.* approved, passed; devoted, doomed.

votazione *f.* voting, poll; marks (*pl.*).

votivo *adj.* votive.

voto *m.* vow; wish; prayer; mark; vote: far voti, to pray; scheda di —, ballot paper; a pieni voti, with full marks, with flying colors.

vulca'nico *adj.* volcanic.

vulcanizzare *vt.* to vulcanize.

vulcanizzazione *f.* vulcanization.

vulcano *m.* volcano.

vulnera'bile *adj.* vulnerable.

vulnerabilità *f.* vulnerability.

vuotare *vt.* to empty: — il sacco (*fig.*), to make a clean breast of it; **vuotarsi** *vr.* to empty.

vuoto *m.* empty space, gap; (*phys.*)

vacuum, void: **andare a —,** to fail, come to nothing; **a —,** to no purpose; **assegno a —,** un-covered check; **— di cassa,** deficit; **— d'aria** (*aeron.*), air pocket; *adj.* empty; vain, void.

X

X *L. and Gr. letter.* x: **raggi x,** X rays.
xenofobi'a *f.* xenophobia.
xeno'fobo *m.* xenophobe.
Xeres *m.* sherry (*wine*).
xilofonista *m.* xylophone player.

xilo'fono *m.* xylophone.
xilografi'a *f.* xylograph; xylography.
xilogra'fico *adj.* xylographic.
xilo'grafo *m.* xylographer.

Z

zabaione *m.* eggnog.
Zacconi, Ermete, famous Italian stage actor (1857–1948).
zaffare *vt.* to bung; to tampon.
zaffata *f.* whiff.
zaffatura *f.* bunging; tamponment.
zafferano *m.* saffron.
zaffiro *m.* sapphire.
zaffo *m.* bung; tampon.
zaga'glia *f.* assagai.
za'gara *f.* orange blossom.
za'ino *m.* knapsack.
zampa *f.* paw, leg: **zampe di gallina,** crow's feet; **zampe di mosca,** scrawls.
zampettare *vi.* to toddle.
zampillare *vi.* to gush, spring, spout.
zampillo *m.* spurt.
zampogna *f.* bagpipe.
zampognaro *m.* bagpiper.
zampone *m.* pig's trotter.
zan'gola *f.* churn.
zanna *f.* tusk, fang.
zannata *f.* snap.
zanzara *f.* mosquito.
zanzariera *f.* mosquito net.
zappa *f.* hoe: **darsi la — sui piedi,** to cut the ground from under one's own feet.
zappare *vt.*, *vi.* to hoe, dig.
zappatore *m.* hoer, digger.
zat'tera *f.* raft.
zavorra *f.* ballast; dregs, trash.
zavorrare *vt.* to ballast.
zaz'zera *f.* mane, long hair.
zebra *f.* zebra.
zebrato *adj.* zebra-striped.
zecca *f.* mint: **nuovo di —,** brand new.
zecchino *m.* sequin: **oro di —,** pure gold.
zef'firo *m.* breeze, light wind.
zelante *adj.* zealous, overhelpful.
zelatore *m.* zealot; supporter.
zelo *m.* zeal.
zenit *m.* zenith.
zen'zero *m.* ginger.
zeppa *f.* wedge.
zeppo *adj.* chock-full, crammed (*with*); overcrowded.

zerbino *m.* doormat.
zerbinotto *m.* dandy.
zero *m.* zero, cipher, nought; 0; nothing, naught: **— via —!** absolutely nothing.
zeta *f.* zee, zed.
zia *f.* aunt.
zibaldone *m.* commonplace-book.
zibellino *m.* sable.
zibetto *m.* zibet.
zibibbo *m.* raisin.
zigano *m.*, *adj.* gypsy.
zi'gomo *m.* cheekbone.
zigrinato *adj.* shagreened; knurled.
zigrino *m.* shagreen.
zimarra *f.* robe, cloak.
zimbello *m.* laughingstock.
zincare *vt.* to zinc.
zinco *m.* zinc.
zincografi'a *f.* zincography.
zinco'grafo *m.* zincographer.
Zingarelli, Nicola, Italian lexicographer and essayist, *Vocabolario della lingua italiana* (1860–1935).
zingaresco *adj.* gypsyish.
zin'garo *m.* gypsy.
zinzino *m.* little bit.
zio *m.* uncle.
zi'polo *m.* spigot.
zirlare *vi.* to warble.
zirlo *m.* warbling.
zitella *f.* maid, old maid.
zittire *vt.*, *vi.* to hiss.
zitto *adj.* silent: **star —,** to keep silent; **zitto!** shut up!; **zitti!** quiet!
zizza'nia *f.* darnel: **seminar —,** to sow the seeds of dissension.
zoc'colo *m.* clog; hoof; (*archit.*) socle; dado.
zodi'aco *m.* zodiac.
zolfanello *m.* sulphur match.
zolfara *f.* sulphur mine.
zolfo *m.* sulphur.
zolla *f.* clod; sod, turf; lump (*of sugar*).
zolletta *f.* lump (*of sugar*).
zona *f.* zone, area; stripe.
zonzo, (a) *adv.* strolling: **andare a —** to stroll.

zoo'filo *m.* zoöphilist; *adj.* zoöphilous.

zoolo'gico *adj.* zoölogical: **giardino —,** zoölogical garden, zoo.

zootec'nico *adj.* zoötechnic: **patrimonio —,** livestock.

zoppicante *adj.* limping, halting.

zoppicare *vi.* to limp, halt.

zoppo *m.* lame person; *adj.* lame, limping; wobbling.

zo'tico *m.* boor; *adj.* boorish.

zoticone *m.* boor, lout, rustic.

zucca *f.* gourd, pumpkin; pate: **non aver sale in —,** to be shallow-brained.

zuccata *f.* bump with the head.

zuccherare *vt.* to sugar.

zuccherlera *f.* sugar basin.

zuccherifi'cio *m.* sugarworks.

zuccherino *m.* sweet; *adj.* sugary.

zuc'chero *m.* sugar.

zuccheroso *adj.* sugary.

zucchino *m.* Italian vegetable marrow, cocozelle, zucchini.

zuccone *m.* dunce.

zuffa *m.* scuffle, fight.

zufolare *vt.*, *vi.* to whistle.

zu'folo *m.* whistle; pipe.

zuppa *f.* soup.

zuppiera *f.* tureen.

zuppo *adj.* wet, drenched.

zuzzurullone *m.* hobbledehoy.

Parte Seconda

INGLESE - ITALIANO

ABBREVIAZIONI

abbr.	abbreviazione	*med.*	medicina
aeron.	aeronautica	*metall.*	metallurgia
agg.	aggettivo	*meteor.*	meteorologia
agr.	agricoltura	*mil.*	militare
am.	americano	*min.*	mineralogia
anat.	anatomia	*mus.*	musica
arch.	architettura	*n.*	nome
art. indef.	articolo indefinito	*naut.*	nautica
artigl.	artiglieria	*ornit.*	ornitologia
auto.	automobile	*ott.*	ottica
avv.	avverbio	*part.*	participio
biol.	biologia	*pass.*	passato, passivo
bot.	botanica	*pat.*	patologia
chim.	chimica	*pers.*	personale
comm.	commercio	*pitt.*	pittura
comp.	comparativo	*pl.*	plurale
cong.	congiunzione	*pp.*	participio passato
dimonstr.	dimonstrativo	*ppr.*	participio presente
ecc.	et cetera	*pref.*	prefisso
eccl.	ecclesiastico	*prep.*	preposizione
edil.	edilizia	*pret.*	preterito
elett.	elettricità	*pron.*	pronome
f.	femminile	*recipr.*	reciproco
fam.	familiare	*rel.*	relativo
ferr.	ferrovia	*rif.*	riferito
fis.	fisica	*rifl.*	riflessivo
fot.	fotografia	*sch.*	scherma
fr.	francese	*scherz.*	scherzenole
gen. pl.	genitivo plurale	*seg.*	seguente
geog.	geografia	*spec.*	speciale
geom.	geometria	*sprezz.*	sprezzante
giorn.	giornale	*S.U.*	Stati Uniti
giur.	giurisprudenza	*sup.*	superlativo
gramm.	grammatica	*t.*	transitivo
impers.	impersonale	*teat.*	teatro
indef.	indefinito	*tec.*	tecnico
ing.	ingegneria	*telef.*	telefono
Ingh.	Inghilterra	*tip.*	tipografia
ingl.	inglese	*T.V.*	televisione
inter.	interiezione	*univ.*	universita
interrog.	interrogativo	*v.*	verbo
intr.	intransitivo	*vet.*	veterinario
ittiol.	ittiologia	*vi.*	verbo intransitivo
m.	maschile	*vr.*	verbo riflessivo
mat.	matematica	*vt.*	verbo transitivo
mecc.	meccanica	*zool.*	zoologia

PRONUNCIA INGLESE FIGURATA

I simboli fonetici usati per la pronuncia figurata di questo vocabolario sono quelli del MERRIAM-WEBSTER POCKET DICTIONARY, 14a edizione, aprile 1955.

Accentazione:

L'accento principale è indicato con un segno pesante (´), e l'accento secondario con un segno leggiero (ˈ).

Voci senza pronuncia figurata:

Per alcune voci derivate da altre mediante l'aggiunta dei suffissi -er, -est, -ing, -ish, -less, -like, -ness, -ship, e per altre composte di due voci reperibili separatamente, a volte è stata omessa la pronuncia figurata. Si tratta di casi in cui la pronuncia della voce derivata o composta è assolutamente regolare, e può essere appresa studiando la pronuncia figurata della voce base o delle singole voci componenti.

ā	corrisponde al dittongo *ei* di *sei*, con la *i* a volte più marcata, a volte meno.
â	è simile alla precedente, ma con una pronuncia molto rapida, tale da non far quasi sentire la *i*.
ä	ha un suono che sta tra il dittongo *ea* e il dittongo *ei*, con una pronuncia molto fusa delle due vocali. Non ha equivalente in italiano.
ă	ha un suono che sta tra la *a* e la *e*, con maggior tendenza verso la *e*. Non ha corrispondente in italiano.
á	corrisponde alla *a* italiana, ma con un suono molto meno marcato.
ā	corrisponde alla *a* italiana.
à	ha un suono tra la *a* e la *e*, con maggiore tendenza verso la *a*. Non ha equivalente in italiano.
á	corrisponde alla *a* italiana, ma è molto meno udibile.
b	si pronuncia come in italiano.
ch	si pronuncia come la *c* dolce italiana di *cena*.
d	si pronuncia come in italiano, ma con un suono più pastoso, puntando la lingua contro l'interno delle gengive; è quasi uguale alla *d* siciliana di *bedda* (bella).
dū	corrisponde approssimativamente alla sillaba *giu* di *giusto*.
e	corrisponde alla *i* italiana di *vita*.
ē̦	si pronuncia, più o meno, *ia* come in *stia*, ma la *a* è quasi impercettibile. Non ha equivalente italiano.
ê	corrisponde alla *i* di *vita*, ma con un suono molto più breve.
ê	corrisponde alla *e* stretta italiana di *dentro*.
ĕ	è simile alla precedente, ma molto meno udibile, sino a diventare quasi muta. Non ha equivalente italiano.
ẽ	è una *e* strettissima, in certo modo affine alla *eu* francese. Non ha corrispondente italiano.
f	si pronuncia come in italiano.
g	ha sempre il suono della *g* aspra italiana di *gomma*.
gz	suona come sonerebbe in italiano il gruppo di consonanti *ghs*, con la *s* dolce.
h	si pronuncia, in principio di parola, quasi sempre aspirata.
ī	si pronuncia *ai* come in *mai*.
ĭ	corrisponde a una *i* molto breve.
ĭ	corrisponde approssimativamente alla *i* italiana, ma anch'essa è molto breve.
j	corrisponde alla *g* dolce di *gente*.

iii

k   corrisponde alla *c* aspra italiana di *canto*.

ks   suona come in italiano, con la *s* aspra.

kw   corrisponde al *qu* italiano di *quanto*.

l   suona come in italiano

m   suona come in italiano.

n   suona come in italiano.

ng   corrisponde, più o meno, alla *ng* di *sangue*, ma la *g*, quando è in fine di parola, è molto meno udibile.

ō   si pronuncia *ou*, ma con la *u* piuttosto debole. Non ha equivalente in italiano.

ŏ   si pronuncia come la *o* italiana di *Napoli*.

ô   si pronuncia approssimativamente come la *o* italiana di *ciò*.

ŏ̀   è una *o* estremamente aperta, che sconfina quasi nella *a*. Non ha corrispondente italiano.

ŏ̆   assomiglia molto alla precedente, ma è più breve.

ŏ̊   sta a indicare che si può pronunziare o come ŏ, o come ō

oi   si pronuncia come in italiano, ma con la *i* molto più debole.

o͞o   si pronuncia come la *u* italiana di *frutto*.

oͤo   si pronuncia come la *u* italiana, ma molto più breve.

ou   si pronuncia come la *au* italiana di *paura*, ma con la *u* più breve.

p   si pronuncia come in italiano.

r   si pronuncia come la *r* italiana, piegando però la punta della lingua verso la cima del palato. Ne risulta un suono molto sordo, che non ha corrispondente italiano.

s   si pronuncia come la *s* aspra in italiano.

sh   si pronuncia come l' *sc* italiano di *scena*.

t   si pronuncia come in italiano, ma con un suono più pastoso, puntando la lingua contro l'interno delle gengive.

th   si pronuncia come la *s* aspra italiana, mettendo però la punta della lingua tra i denti.

t̸h   si pronuncia come la *s* dolce italiana, mettendo però la punta della lingua tra i denti.

tū   si pronuncia approssimativamente come *ciù* in *ciarla*. Non ha corrispondente italiano.

ū   si pronuncia approssimativamente come *iù* in *fiume*.

ŭ   assomiglia alla precedente, ma la *i* è molto meno udibile.

û   si pronuncia come la *eu* francese, o la *oeu* lombarda.

ü   assomiglia alla *a* italiana, ma è un suono che sta tra la *a* e la *o*. Non ha equivalente italiano.

ŭ̈   assomiglia alla precedente, ma è molto meno udibile.

ṻ   corrisponde alla *u* francese e lombarda.

v   si pronuncia come in italiano.

w   si pronuncia come la *u* italiana di *uomo*.

y   si pronuncia come la *i* italiana di *ieri*.

z   si pronuncia come la *s* dolce di *rosa*.

zh   si pronuncia come la *j* francese di *joli*. Non ha corrispondente italiano.

'   indica che la vocale non si pronuncia.

Pronuncia della s del plurale:

1. La **s** del plurale è aspra quando la parola termina per consonante sorda— *f, k, p, t, th*: **cliffs, books, caps, mats, lengths.**

2. La **s** del plurale è dolce quando la parola termina per vocale (ivi compresa la *y*, che diventa ies), o per consonante sonora — *b, d, g, l, m, n, ng, th, v, w,*: **cries, robes, beds, rags, girls, terms, tins, songs, breathes, dives, blows.**

3. La **s** che si aggiunge alle parole terminanti in *ce, dge, ge, se*, e la **es** che si aggiunge alle parole terminanti in *ch, sh, ss, si* leggono entrambe *is*, con la *s* dolce: **faces, judges, fringes, roses, churches, ashes, kisses.**

IL SOSTANTIVO

I. GENERE DEL SOSTANTIVO

In inglese sono maschili i nomi di persona o animale di sesso maschile, e femminili i nomi di persona o animale di sesso femminile. Femminili sono pure considerati le nazioni, le navi, gli aeroplani e le automobili. Ogni altro nome in genere è neutro. L'articolo definito the vale per tutti i generi, sia al singolare, sia al plurale.

Formazione del femminile:

Quando non esistano forme distinte per il maschile e il femminile — es: uncle, zio = aunt, zia — il femminile si forma come segue:
1. con l'aggiunta di alcuni suffissi:
   -ess   poet = poetess; prince = princess
   -trix   aviator = aviatrix; creator = creatrix
2. facendo precedere al nome talune definizioni:
   woman   writer = woman writer
   lady   doctor = lady doctor
   girl   friend = girl friend
3. per i nomi di animali, facendo precedere la definizione:
   she   bear = she bear

II. PLURALE DEL SOSTANTIVO

1. Generalmente, si forma aggiungendo una s al singolare: book = books.
2. I sostantivi terminanti in ch (pronunziata come c dolce), o, ss, sh, x, z, prendono al plurale il suffisso es: church = churches; hero = heroes; kiss = kisses; brush = brushes; box = boxes; buzz = buzzes.
3. I sostantivi terminanti in ch aspra (pronunziata come k) prendono al plurale la s semplice: monarch = monarchs.
4. I sostantivi terminanti in y preceduta da consonante hanno il plurale in ies: family = families. Se la y è preceduta da vocale, il plurale si forma normalmente: day = days.
5. I sostantivi terminanti in fe e certi sostantivi terminanti in f hanno il plurale in ves: life = lives; leaf = leaves.
6. Alcuni sostantivi terminanti in is hanno il plurale in es: crisis = crises; axis = axes. Altri, terminanti in um, lo hanno in a: medium = media; serum = sera o serums.
7. Un certo numero di sostantivi ha il plurale irregolare: man = men; woman = women; mouse = mice; louse = lice; tooth = teeth; foot = feet; ox = oxen.

L'AGGETTIVO

L'aggettivo è invariabile nel numero e nel genere. Normalmente, si colloca davanti al sostantivo: a rainy day = *una giornata piovosa*; a big cup of coffee = *una gran tazza di caffè*; a witty man = *un uomo spiritoso*; green pastures = *verdi pascoli*.

I. COMPARATIVO E SUPERLATIVO

Comparativo di maggioranza e superlativo:

1. Sebbene non vi sia una regola severa e assoluta, in genere gli aggettivi monosillabi, gli aggettivi accentati sull'ultima sillaba e alcuni bisillabi formano il comparativo di maggioranza con l'aggiunta del suffisso -er, e il superlativo con l'aggiunta del suffisso -est. Tuttavia, quando tali aggettivi terminano per e muta, si aggiunge solo, rispettivamente, -r e -st: es: tall (alto)   taller (più alto)   the tallest (il più alto)
       nice (grazioso)   nicer (più grazioso)   the nicest (il più grazioso)

  polite (educato) politer (più educato) the politest (il più educato)
  narrow (stretto) narrower (più stretto) the narrowest (il più stretto)

2. Gli aggettivi terminanti per consonante preceduta da vocale raddoppiano la consonante:
  fat (grasso) fatter (più grasso) the fattest (il più grasso)

3. Gli aggettivi terminanti in y cambiano la y in i:
  happy (felice) happier (più felice) the happiest (il più felice)

4. In tutti gli altri casi, l'aggettivo è preceduto da more e most:
  intelligent, in- more intelligent, più the most intelligent, il più
   telligente intelligente intelligente.

5. I seguenti aggettivi hanno una forma irregolare:

good, well	better	best
bad, ill	worse	worst
little	less, lesser	least
far	farther, further	farthest, furthest
much	more	most
old	older, elder	oldest, eldest

Superlativo assoluto:

Si forma anteponendo very e, a volte, most, all'aggettivo:
  happy (felice) very happy opp. most happy (felicissimo)

Comparativo e superlativo di minoranza:

Si formano anteponendo all'aggettivo less e least:
  happy (felice) less happy (meno the least happy (il meno
    felice)   felice)

Comparativo di eguaglianza:

Si forma con gli avverbi as ... as davanti agli aggettivi:
  he is as poor as you are = è povero come te,
e con as much ... as davanti ai nomi:
  as much money as you want = tanto denaro quanto ne vuoi.

L'AVVERBIO

La maggioranza degli avverbi inglesi si forma aggiungendo all'aggettivo il suffisso -ly: great = greatly; nice = nicely; eternal = eternally.

Irregolarità:

1. Gli aggettivi terminanti in -ble cambiano solo la e in y: possible = possibly.
2. Gli aggettivi terminanti in -ic prendono il suffisso -ally: specific = specifically.
3. Gli aggettivi terminanti in -ll prendono solo la y: full = fully.
4. Gli aggettivi terminanti in -ue perdono la e: true = truly.
5. Gli aggettivi terminanti in y cambiano la y in i: happy = happily.

Comparativo e superlativo:

Come gli aggettivi, anche gli avverbi formano il comparativo e il superlativo con gli avverbi more, most, very, e con i suffissi -er e -est:

boldly	more boldly	most boldly	very boldly
generously	more generously	most generously	very generously
soon	sooner	soonest	very soon

I seguenti hanno forme irregolari di comparativo e superlativo:

well	better	best	very well
badly, ill	worse	worst	very badly
little	less	least	very little
much	more	most	very much
far	farther, further	farthest, furthest	very far

PRINCIPALI SUFFISSI INGLESI

-dom
Indica dominio, giurisdizione, stato, condizione, ecc.: kingdom = regno, reame; martyrdom = martirio; boredom = noia; freedom = libertà.

-ed, -d
è il suffisso del passato e participio passato dei verbi regolari: I handed = io porsi; handed = posto; I loved, io amai; loved = amato.

-ee
indica la persona che riceve o subisce l'azione: addressee = destinatario; draftee = coscritto.

-eer
indica mestiere, occupazione o professione: engineer = macchinista, ingegnere; cannoneer = cannoniere; auctioneer = banditore d'asta.

-en
(a) terminazione del participio passato di numerosi verbi irregolari: fallen, broken, shaken.
(b) suffisso che indica *fatto di*: golden = dorato, d'oro; wooden, ligneo, di legno.
(c) terminazione dei verbi che indica l'azione di *rendere*: whiten = imbiancare, rendere bianco; darken = oscurare, rendere oscuro.

-er
(a) indica mestiere, occupazione o professione: baker = fornaio, panettiere; trainer = allenatore; lawyer = avvocato.
(b) indica la persona che compie una determinata azione: player = giocatore; talker = chi parla, parlatore.
(c) indica residenza, cittadinanza: islander = isolano; New Yorker = newyorchese.
(d) è il suffisso per la formazione del comparativo degli aggettivi e degli avverbi (*vedi più sopra*).

-ess
si usa per formare il femminile di certi sostantivi: poet = poetess; count = countess.

-est
è il suffisso per la formazione del superlativo (*vedi più sopra*).

-fold
suffisso che significa *volte*: twofold = due volte; manyfold = molte volte, più volte.

-ful
(a) suffisso che equivale a *pieno di*: hopeful = speranzoso; careful = attento, prudente, guardingo;
(b) indica abitudine, tendenza: forgetful = smemorato.
(c) indica la quantità che una cosa può contenere o di cui è piena: spoonful = cucchiaiata; cartful = carrettata.

-hood
indica stato, condizione, carattere, gruppo: motherhood = maternità; falsehood = falsità; brotherhood = confraternita.

-ician
indica professione o specialità in un determinato ramo: musician = musicista; electrician = elettricista; beautician = specialista in cure di bellezza.

-ie
suffisso per formare taluni diminutivi: dog = doggie; bird = birdie; Gerald = Gerrie.

-ing
(a) suffisso per la formazione del participio presente e del gerundio: love = loving, amare, amando.
(b) si usa per formare anche taluni aggettivi: drinking water = acqua potabile; washing machine = lavatrice meccanica.
(c) si usa per la sostantivazione del verbo: understanding = il comprendere, comprensione, l'intendere, intesa.

-ish
(a) si usa per formare taluni aggettivi di nazionalità: English = inglese; Spanish = spagnolo.
(b) indica caratteristica, tendenza, somiglianza: boyish = fanciullesco; childish = infantile, puerile; whitish = bianchiccio; bookish = libresco.

-less
indica assenza: childless = senza figli; penniless = senza soldi, spiantato; endless = senza fine, interminabile.

-like
indica somiglianza: childlike = simile a un bambino, fanciullesco, infantile; lifelike = al naturale.

-ly
(a) suffisso avverbiale: slow = slowly; happy = happily; possible = possibly.

(b) aggiunto a certi sostantivi, indica caratteristica: **mother** = **motherly**, materno; **friend** = **friendly**, da amico, amichevole, cordiale; **man** = **manly**, da uomo, virile, mascolino.

(c) aggiunto a sostantivi di tempo indica periodicità: **day** = **daily**, quotidiano, ogni giorno; **week** = **weekly**, settimanale, settimanalmente.

-ness serve a formare i sostantivi astratti: **good** = **goodness**, bontà; **red** = **redness**, rossore; **tall** = **tallness**, altezza.

-ship (a) serve a formare certi sostantivi astratti: **friend** = **friendship**, amicizia.

(b) indica abilità particolare, bravura: **horseman**, cavallerizzo= **horsemanship**, abilità equestre.

(c) indica titoli, cariche, uffici, ecc: **professor** = **professorship**, carica di professore, cattedra; **chairman** = **chairmanship**, presidenza, carica di presidente; **lord** = **lordship**, signoria.

-some si aggiunge a taluni sostantivi per indicare il grado notevole cui giunge la cosa, o la qualità espressa dal sostantivo: **burden**, peso = **burdensome**, pesante, gravoso; **fear**, paura = **fearsome**, pauroso, spaventoso; **life**, vita = **lifesome**, vivace, arzillo.

-th si usa per formare gli aggettivi ordinali: **five** = **fifth**, quinto; **ten** = **tenth**, decimo.

-ty è la terminazione di moltissimi sostantivi astratti: **continuity** = continuità; **liberty** = libertà; **beauty** = bellezza, beltà.

-ward(s) indica, negli aggettivi e avverbi, direzione: **homeward** = **verso casa**; **downward** = verso il basso, discendente.

-ways, -wise esprimono maniera, direzione, posizione, ecc.: **edgewise** = di lato; **sideways** = di lato, di traverso; **lengthwise** = per il lungo.

-y (a) corrisponde alla terminazione italiana *ia*: **biology** = biologia; **glory** = glòria; **victory** = vittoria.

(b) come suffisso è diminutivo: **dog** = **doggy**, cagnolino.

(c) in taluni casi indica presenza, abbondanza: **rock**, roccia = **rocky**, roccioso, duro come la roccia; **hair**, capelli = **hairy**, capelluto, irsuto.

(d) esprime anche tendenza, somiglianza: **rosy** = rosato, roseo, tendente al rosa.

VERBI IRREGOLARI INGLESI

I GRUPPO

Infinito		*Passato*	*Part. passato*
(to) beat	battere	beat	beat, beaten
» burst	scoppiare	burst	burst
» cast	gettare	cast	cast
» cost	costare	cost	cost
» cut	tagliare	cut	cut
» hit	colpire	hit	hit
» hurt	ferire	hurt	hurt
» knit	far la calza	knit	knit
» let	lasciare, locare	let	let
» put	mettere	put	put
» rid	liberare	rid	rid
» set	posare	set	set
» shed	versare	shed	shed
» shred	tagliuzzare	shred	shred
» shut	chiudere	shut	shut
» slit	fendere	slit	slit
» spit	sputare	spit	spit
» split	spaccare, dividere	split	split
» spread	spandere	spread	spread
» sweat	sudare	sweat (sweated)	sweat (sweated)
» thrust	spingere	thrust	thrust

II GRUPPO

(Nota: i verbi contrassegnati da una R si conlugano anche regolarmente)

Infinito		Passato	Part. passato
(to) abide	dimorare	abode	abode
bend	piegare	bent	bent
bereave	orbare	bereft	bereft
beseech	implorare	besought	besought
bind	legare	bound	bound
bleed	sanguinare	bled	bled
breed	generare, allevare	bred	bred
bring	portare	brought	brought
build	costruire	built	built
burn	bruciare	burnt (R)	burnt (R)
buy	comperare	bought	bought
catch	afferrare	caught	caught
cleave	fendere	cleft	cleft
cling	aggrapparsi	clung	clung
creep	strisciare	crept	crept
deal	trattare	dealt	dealt
dig	scavare	dug (R)	dug (R)
dream	sognare	dreamt (R)	dreamt (R)
dwell	abitare	dwelt (R)	dwelt (R)
feed	nutrire	fed	fed
feel	sentire	felt	felt
fight	combattere	fought	fought
find	trovare	found	found
flee	fuggire	fled	fled
fling	lanciare	flung	flung
get	acquisire	got	got (gotten)
gild	dorare	gilt	gilt
gird	cingere	girt	girt
grind	macinare	ground	ground
hang	impiccare	hung	hung (hanged)
hear	udire	heard	heard
hold	tenere	held	held
keep	conservare	kept	kept
kneel	inginocchiarsi	knelt (R)	knelt (R)
lay	deporre	laid	laid
lead	guidare	led	led
leave	lasciare	left	left
lend	prestare	lent	lent
light	accendere, illuminare	lit (R)	lit (R)
lose	perdere	lost	lost
make	fare	made	made
mean	significare	meant	meant
meet	incontrare	met	met
pay	pagare	paid	paid
read	leggere	read	read
rend	lacerare	rent	rent
say	dire	said	said
seek	cercare	sought	sought
seethe	bollire, fremere	sod (R)	sod (R) (sodden)
sell	vendere	sold	sold
send	mandare	sent	sent
shine	brillare	shone	shone
shoe	calzare, ferrare	shod	shod
shoot	sparare	shot	shot
shrink	ritrarsi	shrank (shrunk)	shrunk (shrunken)
sit	sedere	sat	sat

Infinito		Passato	Part. passato
(to) sleep	dormire	slept	slept
» slide	slittare	slid	slid (slidden)
» sling	lanciare, appendere	slung	slung
» slink	svignarsela	slunk	slunk
» smell	fiutare	smelt	smelt
» spend	spendere	spent	spent
» spill	versare	spilt (R)	spilt (R)
» spin	filare	spun (span)	spun
» stand	stare in piedi	stood	stood
» stick	attaccare, attaccarsi	stuck	stuck
» sting	pungere	stung	stung
» stink	puzzare	stank (stunk)	stunk
» strike	colpire	struck	struck (stricken)
» string	infilare	strung	strung
» sweep	scopare	swept	swept
» swing	pendere	swung	swung
» teach	insegnare	taught	taught
» tell	dire	told	told
» think	pensare	thought	thought
» weep	piangere	wept	wept
» win	vincere	won	won
» wind	attorcigliare	wound	wound
» work	lavorare	wrought (R)	wrought (R)
» wring	torcere	wrung	wrung

III GRUPPO

Infinito		Passato	Part. passato
(to) awake	svegliare, svegliarsi	awoke (R)	awaken (awoke)
» be		was	been
» bear	portare	bore	borne (born)
» begin	cominciare	began	begun
» bid	ordinare	bade (bid)	bidden (bid)
» bite	mordere	bit	bitten (bit)
» blow	soffiare	blew	blown
» break	rompere	broke	broken
» chide	sgridare	chid (R)	chidden (chid) (R)
» choose	scegliere	chose	chosen
» come	venire	came	come
» crow	cantare (del gallo)	crew	crowed
» dare	osare	durst (R)	dared
» do	fare	did	done
» draw	disegnare	drew	drawn
» drink	bere	drank	drunk
» drive	guidare	drove	driven
» eat	mangiare	ate	eaten
» fall	cadere	fell	fallen
» fly	volare	flew	flown
» forsake	abbandonare	forsook	forsaken
» freeze	gelare	froze	frozen
» give	dare	gave	given
» go	andare	went	gone
» grow	crescere	grew	grown
» hew	potare	hewed	hewn (R)
» hide	nascondere	hid	hidden (hid)
» know	sapere, conoscere	knew	known
» lade	caricare	laded	laden
» lie	giacere	lay	lain
» mow	mietere	mowed	mown (R)
» ride	cavalcare	rode	ridden (rode)
» ring	suonare	rang	rung
» rise	alzarsi, sorgere	rose	risen

Infinito		Passato	Part. passato
(to) rive	spaccare	rived	riven
» run	correre	ran	run
» see	vedere	saw	seen
» shake	scuotere	shook	shaken
» shear	tosare	shore (R)	shorn (R)
» show	mostrare	showed (shew)	shown (shewn)
» sing	cantare	sang	sung
» sink	affondare	sank (sunk)	sunk
» slay	uccidere	slew	slain
» smite	percuotere	smote	smitten
» sow	seminare	sowed	sown (R)
» speak	parlare	spoke	spoken
» spring	balzare, scaturire	sprang	sprung
» steal	rubare	stole	stolen
» stride	camminare a lunghi passi	strode	stridden
» strive	sforzarsi	strove	striven
» swear	giurare, imprecare	swore	sworn
» swell	gonfiarsi	swelled	swollen (R)
» swim	nuotare	swam	swum
» take	prendere	took	taken
» tear	stracciare	tore	torn
» thrive	prosperare	throve	thriven
» throw	gettare	threw	thrown
» tread	camminare, calpestare	trod	trodden (trod)
» wear	indossare	wore	worn
» weave	tessere	wove	woven
» write	scrivere	wrote	written

PRINCIPALI PESI E MISURE INGLESI

Pesi (avoirdupois):

Dram (dragma) 1/16 di libbra	=	gr.	1,17718
Ounce (oncia)	=	»	28,3495
Pound (libbra)	=	Kg.	0,4535926
Stone	=	»	6,350
Quarter (quarto)	=	»	12,6956
Hundredweight	=	»	50,8009
Long ton (tonnellata)	=	»	1016,018
Short ton	=	»	907,2

Pesi (troy-weight):

Grain (grano)	=	gr.	0,064798
Pennyweight (1/20 di oncia)	=	»	1,55517
Ounce (oncia t.)	=	»	31,1035
Pound (libbra t.)	=	Kg.	0,37324

Misure di lunghezza:

Inch (pollice)	=	cm.	2,539954
Foot (piede)	=	m.	0,3047944
Yard (jarda) = 3 piedi	=	»	0,914383
Fathom = 2 jarde	=	»	1,828766
Pole, rod (pertica) = jarde 5,1/4	=	»	5,—
Furlong = jarde 220	=	»	201,64
Mile (miglio) = jarde 1760	=	»	1609,347
Nautical mile (miglio marittimo)	=	»	1853,248

Misure di superficie:

Square inch (pollice quadrato)	=	cm.²	6,451366
» foot (piede quadrato)	=	m.²	0,0929
» yard (jarda quadrata)	=	m.²	0,836097
Rod (jarde 230,1/4)	=	m.²	25,291939
Rood (1.210 jarde quadrate)	=	are	10,116775
Acre (4.840 jarde quadrate)	=	ha.	0,404687
Square mile (miglio quadrato)	=	Km.²	2,588881

Monete, banconote e denominazioni monetarie degli Stati Uniti d'America:

(Nota: il Dollaro è indicato dal simbolo $; il cent [centesimo di $] da una c.)

Mill	=	1/10 di c.
Cent (anche Penny)	=	1/100 » $.
Nickel	=	5 c.
Dime	=	10 c.
Quarter	=	25 c.
Half dollar	=	50 c.
Dollar	=	100 c.

Banconote in corso:

$ 1, 2, 5, 10, 20, 50, 100, 500, 1000, 5.000, 10.000.

INGLESE-ITALIANO

A

a (ā) prima lettera dell'alfabeto; (*mus.*) là. A 1 di prima classe; di primo ordine.

a (ā) *art.indef.* uno, una: what a ..., che razza di ... ' che ...; such a ..., un simile ..; un tale....

aback (á·băk') *avv.* all'indietro: taken —, colto alla sprovvista.

abaft (á·băft') *avv* da poppa. *prep.* dietro a, a poppavia.

abandon (á·băn'dǔn) *n.* abbandono. *vt.* abbandonare, cedere, lasciare, rinunciare a, desistere. —ed *agg.* abbandonato; dissoluto. —ment *n.* umiliazione.

abash (á·băsh') *vt.* intimidire, umiliare. —ed *agg.* intimidito, umiliato.

abate (á·bāt') *vt.* mitigare, abbassare, diminuire, attenuare. *vi.* diminuire; calmarsi. —ment *n.* diminuzione, indebolimento; sconto.

abbey (ăb'ĭ) *n.* abbazia.

abbot (ăb'ǔt) *n.* abate.

abbreviate (ă·brē'vĭ·āt) *vt.* abbreviare, accorciare.

abbreviation *n.* abbreviazione.

abdicate (ăb'dĭ·kāt) *vt.* abdicare, rinunciare a.

abdomen (ăb·dō'měn) *n.* addome; basso ventre.

abduct (ăb·dŭkt') *vt.* rapire, asportare.

abduction *n.* ratto, rapimento.

aberration (ăb'ěr·ā'shǔn) *n.* aberrazione.

abet (á·bět') *vt.* favoreggiare. [zione.

abeyance (á·bā'ǎns) *n.* stasi: in —, in sospeso, pendente.

abhor (ăb·hôr') *vt.* aborrire. —rence *n.* orrore, avversione.

abide (á·bīd') *vi.* attenersi; soggiornare; tollerare; resistere; essere fedele.

ability (á·bĭl'ĭ·tĭ) *n.* abilità, estro.

abject (ăb'jěkt) *agg.* abietto, vile.

ablaze (á·blāz') *agg.* in fiamme, splendente.

able (ā'b'l) *agg.* capace, abile, in grado di: —-bodied, robusto.

ably (ā'blĭ) *avv.* abilmente.

abnormal (ăb·nôr'mǎl) *agg.* anormale.

aboard (á·bōrd') *avv.* a bordo: to go —, imbarcarsi; all —! signori in carrozza!

abode (á·bō'd) *n.* abitazione, dimora.

abolish (á·bŏl'ĭsh) *vt.* abolire, annullare.

abolition (ăb'ō·lĭsh'ǔn) *n.* abolizione.

abominable (á·bŏm'ĭ·nǎb'l) *agg.* abominevole, infame.

abortion (á·bôr'shǔn) *n.* aborto.

abound (á·bound') *vi.* abbondare.

abounding *agg.* abbondante.

about (á·bout') *prep.* intorno, circa, riguardo a, sul punto di. *avv.* quasi, più o meno: to bring —, provocare; to be — to, stare per, essere sul punto di; to face —, voltarsi; — one's person, indosso.

above (á·bǔv') *prep.*, *avv.* al disopra, sopra, in alto, in cima; a monte di: — all, soprattutto; —-mentioned, suddetto.

aboveboard (á·bǔv'bōrd') *avv.* lealmente, apertamente.

abrasion (ăb·rā'zhǔn) *n.* abrasione, logoramento.

abreast (á·brěst') *avv.* di fronte, a fianco a fianco, in linea.

abridge (á·brĭj') *vt.* abbreviare, compendiare.

abroad (á·brôd') *avv.* fuori; all'estero; all'esterno; in circolazione: to spread —, divulgare.

abrupt (ăb·rŭpt') *agg.* improvviso; brusco; precipitoso; ripido. —ly *avv.* bruscamente, improvvisamente.

abscess (ăb'sěs) *n.* ascesso.

absence (ăb'sěns) *n.* assenza; distrazione; mancanza.

absent (ăb'sěnt) *agg.* assente: —-minded, distratto. *vt.* (ăb·sěnt') to — oneself, assentarsi, allontanarsi.

absolute (ăb'sō·lūt) *agg.* assoluto. —ly, *avv.* assolutamente.

absolution (ăb'sō·lū'shǔn) *n.* assoluzione.

absolve (ăb·zŏlv') *vt.* assolvere; svincolare.

absorb (ăb·zôrb') *vt.* assorbire. —ent *n.*, *agg.* assorbente.

absorption (ăb·zôrp'shǔn) *n.* assorbimento, l'essere assorto.

abstain (ăb·stān') *vi.* astenersi.

abstemious (ăb·stē'mĭ·ǔs) *agg.* astemio, temperante.

abstinence (ăb'stĭ·něns) *n.* astinenza.

abstract (ăb·străkt') *vt.* sottrarre; separare, staccare; riassumere. *n.* (ăb'străkt) estratto, riassunto; (*comm.*) estratto conto. *agg.* (anche

1

ăb·străkt′) astratto. —ion n. astrazione. —ed agg. distratto. —ly avv. astrattamente, distrattamente.

abstruse (ăb·strōōs′) agg. astruso, oscuro.

absurd (ăb·sûrd′) agg. assurdo. —ity n. assurdità.

abundance (á·bŭn′dăns) n. abbondanza; prosperità.

abundant (á·bŭn′dănt) agg. abbondante.

abuse (á·būz′) vt. insultare, ingiuriare; maltrattare; abusare di. n. (á·būs′) abuso, insulto.

abusive (á·bū′sĭv) agg. ingiurioso, abusivo.

abut (á·bŭt′) vi. sfociare, sboccare.

abysmal (á·bĭs′măl) agg. abissale, insondabile.

abyss (á·bĭs′) n. abisso.

academic (ăk′á·dĕm′ĭk) agg. accademico, universitario.

academy (á·kăd′ĕ·mĭ) n. accademia.

accede (ăk·sēd′) vi. accedere, consentire, assentire.

accelerate (ăk·sĕl′ĕr·āt) vt. accelerare.

acceleration (-ā′shŭn) n. accelerazione.

accelerator (ăk·sĕl′ĕr·ā′tĕr) n. acceleratore.

accent (ăk′sĕnt) vt. accentare, accentuare. n. accento, tono.

accentuate (ăk·sĕn′tū̇·āt) vt. accentuare, intensificare.

accept (ăk·sĕpt′) vt. accettare, accogliere, gradire, approvare. —able agg. accettabile, ammissibile. —ance n. accettazione; approvazione; (comm.) cambiale. —or n. (comm.) accettante.

access (ăk′sĕs) n. accesso, entrata. —ible agg. accessibile; abbordabile.

accessory (ăk·sĕs′ō·rĭ) agg. accessorio. n. complice: — before the fact, complice; — after the fact, favoreggiatore.

accident (ăk′sĭ·dĕnt) n. incidente, sciagura; contrattempo: by —, per caso. —al agg. accidentale, fortuito. —ally avv. casualmente.

acclaim (á·klām′) vt. acclamare, applaudire.

acclamation (ăk′lá·mā′shŭn) n. acclamazione.

acclimatize (á·klī′má·tīz) vt. acclimare, acclimatare.

accommodate (á·kŏm′ō·dāt) vt. accomodare, aggiustare; ospitare, alloggiare; contenere; fornire; favorire: to — oneself, adattarsi.

accommodating agg. accomodante, conciliante.

accommodation (-dā′shŭn) n. accomodamento; agevolazione, aiuto; alloggio: — bill, cambiale di favore.

accompaniment (á·kŭm′pánĭ·mĕnt). n. accompagnamento.

accompanist (-ĭst) n. accompagnatore.

accompany (á·kŭm′pá·nĭ) vt. accompagnare.

accomplice (á·kŏm′plĭs) n. complice.

accomplish (á·kŏm′plĭsh) vt. compiere, realizzare, terminare, effettuare. —ed agg. compiuto; perfetto; compito. —ment n. compimento, impresa, prodezza, merito, qualità; (pl.) cognizioni, nozioni.

accord (á·kôrd′) vt. accordare, concedere, conciliare. n. accordo, accomodamento, consenso: of one's own —, spontaneamente; with one —, simultaneamente, di comune accordo. —ance n. accordo, conformità. —ing agg. conforme: — as, a seconda che; — to, a seconda di, secondo, a detta di, in conformità di. —ingly avv. pertanto, di conseguenza; conformemente, in conformità.

accordion (á·kôr′dĭ·ŭn) n. fisarmonica.

accost (á·kŏst′) vt. accostare, abbordare.

account (á·kount′) (1) n. conto, calcolo; versione, resoconto: on — of, a causa di; by all accounts, a detta di tutti; of no —, di nessun valore, di nessuna importanza; to turn to —, approfittare di, trarre profitto da; on no —, per nessun motivo.

account (á·kount′) (2) vt. contare, valutare, stimare: to — for, render conto di, giustificare, rispondere di. —able agg. responsabile, spiegabile. —ant n. contabile. —ing n. contabilità.

accredit (á·krĕd′ĭt) vt. accreditare.

accrue (á·krōō′) vi. accumularsi.

accumulate (á·kū′mū·lāt) vt. accumulare, ammucchiare. vi. accumularsi, ammucchiarsi.

accumulation n. accumulazione, ammasso.

accumulator n. accumulatore.

accuracy (ăk′ū·rá·sĭ) n. accuratezza, esattezza, precisione.

accurate (ăk′ū·rĭt) agg. accurato, giusto, esatto, sicuro, preciso.

accursed (á·kûr′sĕd; á·kûrst′) agg. maledetto, malaugurato.

accusation (ăk·ū·zā′shŭn) n. accusa.

accuse (á·kūz′) vt. accusare.

accuser n. accusatore.

accustom (á·kŭs′tŭm) vt. abituare: to — oneself, abituarsi, ambientarsi.

ace (ās) n. asso; campione (sportivo, ecc.): within an — of, a un pelo da.

ache (āk) n. male, dolore. vi. dolere, soffrire.

aching (āk'ĭng) *agg.* dolorante.

achieve (*ȧ*-chēv') *vt.* eseguire, conseguire, realizzare, ottenere: **to — fame,** farsi una fama. **—ment** *n.* successo, affermazione, realizzazione; prodezza.

acid (ăs'ĭd) *n.*, *agg.* acido. **—ity** *n.* acidità.

ack-ack (ăk'ăk) *n.* cannone antiaereo; artiglieria antiaerea.

acknowledge (ăk·nŏl'ĕj) *vt.* riconoscere, confessare: **to — receipt,** accusare ricevuta.

acknowledgment *n.* riconoscimento, ringraziamento, cenno di ricevuta.

acorn (ā'kôrn) *n.* ghianda.

acoustics (*ȧ*-kōōs'tĭks) *n.* acustica.

acquaint (*ȧ*-kwānt') *vt.* informare, mettere al corrente, far sapere: **to be acquainted with,** conoscere, sapere; **to get acquainted with, to — oneself with,** fare la conoscenza di, rendersi edotto di. **—ance** *n.* conoscenza; conoscente.

acquiesce (ăk'wĭ·ĕs') *vi.* acconsentire, assentire. **—nce** *n.* acquiescenza, arrendevolezza.

acquire (*ȧ*-kwīr') *vt.* acquistare, ottenere; imparare.

acquisition (ăk'wĭ·zĭsh'ŭn) *n.* acquisto.

acquit (*ȧ*-kwĭt') *vt.* assolvere, prosciogliere: **to — oneself well,** fare una buona figura.

acquittal *n.* assoluzione.

acre (ā'kĕr) *n.* acro.

acrobat (ăk'rŏ·băt) *n.* acrobata.

across (*ȧ*-krôs') *prep.* attraverso; dirimpetto a, di là di; *avv.* dirimpetto; trasversalmente: **to come —,** imbattersi in.

act (ăkt) *vt.*, *vi.* agire; comportarsi; recitare, rappresentare, sostenere una parte; funzionare: **to — as,** fungere da. **—ing** *n.* rappresentazione, recitazione. **—ion** *n.* azione, fatto; causa; funzionamento. **—ive** *adj.* attivo, svelto. **—ivity.** (-ĭv'ĭ·tĭ) *n.* attività.

actor (ăk'tĕr) *n.* attore.

actress (ăk'trĕs) *n.* attrice.

actual (ăk'tū̇·ăl) *agg.* attuale; reale, effettivo. **—ity** (ăk'tū̇·ăl'ĭ·tĭ) *n.* realtà, attualità. **—ly** *avv.* realmente, effettivamente, addirittura.

acumen (*ȧ*·kū'mĕn) *n.* acume.

acute (*ȧ*·kūt') *agg.* aguzzo; acuto; perspicace.

Adam's apple (ăd'ămz ăp''l) *n.* pomo d'Adamo.

adamant (ăd'*ȧ*·mănt) *agg.* duro, saldo, inflessibile.

adapt (*ȧ*·dăpt') *vt.* adattare. **—ation** *n.* adattamento.

add (ăd) *vt.* aggiungere, sommare, aumentare.

addict (*ȧ*·dĭkt') **—ed** *agg.* dedito a: **drug addict,** tossicomane.

addition (*ȧ*·dĭsh'ŭn) *n.* aggiunta, addizione: **in — to,** oltre a. **—al** *agg.* addizionale, supplementare.

addleheaded (ăd'l·hĕd'ĕd) *agg.* stolto.

address (*ȧ*·drĕs') *vt.*, *vi.* indirizzare; apostrofare, rivolgere la parola a; rivolgersi a. *n.* indirizzo; discorso; destrezza: **to pay one's addresses to,** corteggiare.

addressee (ăd'rĕs·ē') *n.* destinatario.

adept (ăd'ĕpt) *n.* esperto, specialista.

adequate (ăd'ē.kwĭt) *agg.* proporzionato, sufficiente, all'altezza di.

adhere (ăd·hēr') *vi.* aderire; attenersi a.

adherence (-hēr'ĕns) *n.* aderenza.

adhesion (ăd·hē'zhŭn) *n.* adesione.

adhesive (-sĭv) *agg.* adesivo, vischioso, gommato: **— tape,** cerotto.

adjacent (*ȧ*·jā'sĕnt) *agg.* adiacente.

adjective (ăj'ĕk·tĭv) *n.* aggettivo.

adjoin (*ȧ*·join') *vt.* confinare con, essere attiguo a. **—ing** *agg.* attiguo.

adjourn (*ȧ*·jûrn') *vt.* aggiornare, rinviare; sospendere. *vi.* tresferirsi. **—ment** *n.* aggiornamento, rinvio.

adjunct (ăj'ŭngkt) *agg.* aggiunto, accessorio. *n.* aggiunta, appendice.

adjust (*ȧ*·jŭst') *vt.* aggiustare, adattare, regolare: **to — oneself,** adattarsi, conformarsi. **—ment** *n.* accomodamento, regolamento.

ad-lib (ăd'lĭb) *vt.*, *vi.*, improvvisare (*un discorso, ecc.*); *n.* improvvisazione; *agg.* improvvisato.

administer (ăd·mĭn'ĭs·tĕr) *vt.* amministrare, gestire; governare; somministrare.

administration (ăd·mĭn'ĭs·trā'shŭn) *n.* amministrazione, governo.

administrative (ăd·mĭn'ĭs·trā'tĭv) *agg.* amministrativo.

administrator (ăd·mĭn'ĭs·trā'tĕr) *n.* amministratore.

admirable (ăd'mĭ·rȧ·b'l) *agg.* ammirevole.

admirably *avv.* mirabilmente.

admiral (ăd'mĭ·rȧl) *n.* ammiraglio.

admiration (ăd'mĭ·rā'shŭn) *n.* ammirazione.

admire (ăd·mīr') *vt.* ammirare.

admirer (ăd·mīr'·ẽr) *n.* ammiratore.

admission (ăd·mĭsh'ŭn) *n.* ammissione, confessione; ingresso; entrata; entratura.

admit (ăd·mĭt') *vt.* ammettere, far entrare; confessare. **—tance** *n.* accesso, entrata, ammissione: **no —,** vietato l'ingresso.

admonish (ăd·mŏn'ĭsh) vt. ammonire, esortare, redarguire.

admonition (ăd'mō·nĭsh'ŭn) n. ammonizione, reprimenda.

ado (á·dōō') n. azione, trambusto, difficoltà.

adolescence (ăd'ō·lĕs'ĕns) n. adolescenza.

adolescent n., agg. adolescente.

adopt (á·dŏpt') vt. adottare.

adoption (á·dŏp'shŭn) n. adozione.

adorable (á·dōr'á·b'l) agg. adorabile.

adoration (ăd'ō·rā'shŭn) n. adorazione.

adore (á·dōr') vt. adorare.

adorn (á·dōrn') vt. ornare, adornare.

adornment n. ornamento.

adrift (á·drĭft') avv. alla deriva.

adroit (á·droit') agg. destro, accorto.

adulation (ăd'ū·lā'shŭn) n. adulazione.

adult (á·dŭlt'; ăd'ŭlt) n., agg. adulto.

adulterate (á·dŭl'tēr·āt) vt. adulterare, contraffare, alterare.

adulterer (á·dŭl'tēr·ēr) n. adultero.

adulteress (á·dŭl'tēr·ĕs; -ĭs) n. adultera.

adultery (á·dŭl'tēr·ĭ) n. adulterio.

advance (ăd·văns') vt. avanzare, far avanzare, far progredire, migliorare, promuovere; accelerare; anticipare, pagare in anticipo; rincarare. vi. avanzarsi, progredire; anticipare; andare avanti.

advance n. progresso, avanzamento; anticipo: to make advances, fare approcci.

advanced agg. avanzato, progredito.

advancement n. avanzamento, progresso.

advantage (ăd·văn'tĭj) n. vantaggio, profitto, interesse: to take — of, approfittare di, trarre profitto da, abusare di. —ous (ăd'văn·tā'jŭs) agg. vantaggioso.

advent (ăd'vĕnt) n. avvento.

adventure (ăd·vĕn'tŭr) n. avventura; caso; impresa.

adventurer (ăd·vĕn'tŭr·ēr) n. avventuriero.

adventuress (ăd·vĕn'tŭr·ĕs) n. avventuriera.

adventurous (-tŭr·ŭs) agg. avventuroso.

adverb (ăd'vûrb) n. avverbio.

adversary (ăd'vēr·sĕr'ĭ) n. avversario.

adverse (ăd·vûrs'; ăd'vûrs) agg. avverso, contrario, sfavorevole.

adversity (ăd·vûr'sĭ·tĭ) n. contrarietà, ostilità, avversità.

advertise (ăd'vēr·tĭz) vt., vi. divulgare, reclamizzare; mettere inserzioni sul giornale. —ment n. annuncio, inserzione.

advertiser (ăd'vûr·tĭz'ēr) n. divulgatore; inserzionista.

advice (ăd·vĭs') n. avviso, consiglio.

advisable (ăd·vĭz'á·b'l) agg. consigliabile, conveniente, opportuno.

advise (ăd·vĭz') vt. consigliare, avvertire, annunciare. vi. consigliarsi.

adviser (ăd·vĭz'ēr) n. consigliere.

advocate (ăd'vō·kāt) n. propugnatore, sostenitore, difensore, avvocato. vt. sostenere, difendere, propugnare.

aerial (á·ĕr'ĭ·ăl; ar'ĭ·ăl) agg. aereo; n., antenna radiofonica.

aerodrome (ā'ĕr·ō·drōm'; ar'ō-) n. aerodromo.

aerodynamics (ā'ĕr·ō·dī·năm'ĭks) n. aerodinamica.

aeroplane (ā'ĕr·ō·plăn'; ar'ō-) n. aeroplano, velivolo.

aerosol (ā'ĕr·ō·sŏl) n. aerosol.

aesthete (ĕs'thēt) n. esteta.

aesthetics (ĕs·thĕt'ĭks) n. estetica.

afar (á·fär') avv. lontano, in lontananza: from —, da lontano; — off, in distanza.

affable (ăf'á·b'l) agg. affabile.

affair (á·fâr') n. affare; tresca: love —, relazione amorosa.

affect (á·fĕkt') vt. influenzare, commuovere; fingere, ostentare. —ation (ăf'ĕk·tā'shŭn) n. affettazione. —ed agg. influenzato; affettato, ostentato; pretenzioso; commosso. —ion (á·fĕk'shŭn) n. affezione; amore; attaccamento; propensione. —ionate (á·fĕk'shŭn·ĭt) agg. affettuoso, affezionato.

affiliate (á·fĭl'ĭ·āt) vt. affiliare, adottare. vi. affiliarsi, associarsi.

affinity (á·fĭn'ĭ·tĭ) n. affinità.

affirm (á·fûrm') vt. affermare. —ative (á·fûr'má·tĭv) agg. affermativo: in the —, affermativamente.

affix (á·fĭks') vt. affiggere; apporre.

afflict (á·flĭkt') vt. affliggere, tormentare. —ion n. afflizione, calamità.

affluence (ăf'lū·ĕns) n. ricchezza, abbondanza.

affluent n. affluente. agg. ricco.

afford (á·fōrd') vt. concedere, fornire, accordare, permettere: I cannot — this luxury, non posso permettermi questo lusso.

affront (á·frŭnt') vt. affrontare; offendere, insultare. n. affronto, insulto.

afield (á·fēld') avv. sul campo: far —, molto lontano.

afire (á·fīr') agg. in fuoco, in fiamme.

afloat (á·flōt') agg. a galla; in navigazione: a rumor is —, corre voce.

afoot (á·fŏŏt') avv. a piedi, in movimento; in ballo.

aforesaid (á·fōr'sĕd') agg. sudetto, predetto.

afraid (á·frād') agg. spaventato, timoroso: to be —, temere.

afresh (á·frĕsh') *avv.* nuovamente; da capo.

after (áf'tĕr) *prep.* dopo, in seguito a; secondo, alla maniera di. *avv.* dopo, secondo, in seguito. *agg.* successivo, ulteriore: **the day — tomorrow,** posdomani. **aftereffect** (áf'tĕr·ĕ·fĕkt') *n.* conseguenza, contraccolpo.

aftermath (áf'tĕr·máth) *n.* postumo, conseguenza.

afternoon (áf'tĕr·nōōn') *n.* pomeriggio.

afterthought (áf'tĕr·thôt') *n.* riflessione postuma *o* tardiva.

afterward (áf'tĕr·wĕrd) *avv.* dopo, successivamente.

again (á·gĕn) *avv.* ancora, nuovamente: **— and —,** ripetutamente, a più riprese; **now and —,** di tanto in tanto; **as large —,** due volte tanto; **never —,** mai più.

against (á·gĕnst') *prep.* contro, di contro, addosso, in previsione di.

agape (á·gāp') *agg.* a bocca aperta.

age (āj) *n.* età, èra, secolo: **of —,** maggiorenne; **old —,** vecchiaia; **under —,** minorenne. *vt.*, *vi.* invecchiare.

aged *agg.* vecchio; invecchiato; stagionato: **middle—,** di mezza età.

agency (ā'jĕn·sī) *n.* azione; mezzo; influsso; agenzia, ente.

agent (ā'jĕnt) *n.* agente, rappresentante.

aggrandize (ăg'rán·dīz) *vt.* ingrandire.

aggravate (ăg'rá·vāt) *vt.* aggravare; provocare, esasperare.

aggregate (ăg'rē·gát) *n.* aggregato; complesso. *agg.* complessivo.

aggression (á·grĕsh'ŭn) *n.* aggressione.

aggressive (á·grĕs'ĭv) *agg.* aggressivo.

aggressor (á·grĕs'ĕr) *n.* aggressore.

aghast (á·gást') *agg.* sgomento, costernato.

agile (ăj'ĭl) *agg.* svelto.

agility (á·jĭl'ĭ·tĭ) *n.* agilità.

agitate (ăj'ĭ·tāt) *vt.* agitare, eccitare, smuovere, turbare.

agitation (ăj'ĭ·tā'shŭn) *n.* agitazione.

agitator (ăj'ĭ·tā'tĕr) *n.* agitatore.

ago (á·gō') *avv.* passato: **long —,** molto tempo fa; **two days —,** due giorni or sono.

agog (á·gŏg') *agg.* ansioso, bramoso: **to be all —,** non stare più nella pelle.

agonizing *agg.* angoscioso,-lancinante.

agony (ăg'ŏ·nĭ) *n.* dolore, angoscia; agonia.

agree (á·grē') *vi.* approvare, convenire, acconsentire; concordare; giovare, confarsi a: **I — with you,** sono d'accordo con voi. **—able** *agg.* gradevole, conforme, d'accordo. **—ment** *n.* accordo; convenzione, contratto; armonia.

agricultural (ag'rĭ·kŭl'tū̇r·ăl) *agg.* agricolo.

agriculture (ăg'rĭ·kŭl'tū̇r) *n.* agricoltura.

agriculturist *n.* agricoltore, agronomo.

aground (á·ground') *avv.* in secca.

ahead (á·hĕd') *avv.* avanti, alla testa, in prima fila: **go —!** fate pure; **— of time,** in anticipo.

aid (ād) *vt.* aiutare, assistere, agevolare. *n.* aiuto, assistenza; collaboratore, aiutante.

ail (āl) *vt.* affliggere. *vi.* soffrire, patire: **what ails you?** che vi piglia? **—ment** *n.* acciacco; indisposizione.

aileron (ā'lĕr·ŏn) *n.* alerone.

aim (ām) *vt.* mirare, dirigere, lanciare, puntare (*un'arma*). *vi.* mirare a, aspirare a, avere per meta. *n.* bersaglio, scopo, mira, aspirazione: **to take —,** mirare. **—less** *agg.* futile. **—lessly** *avv.* futilmente, senza scopo. **—lessness** *n.* futilità, mancanza di scopo.

air (âr) *vt.* arieggiare, sciorinare. *n.* aria, atmosfera; (*fig.*) atteggiamento: **—borne** aviotrasportato; **— conditioning,** aria condizionata; **— cushion,** cuscino pneumatico; **— balloon,** pallone, palloncino; **— bladder,** vescica d'aria; (*ittiol.*) vescica natatoria; **—gun,** fucile ad aria compressa; **—line,** aviolinea; **—liner,** apparecchio di linea; **— mail,** posta aerea; **— pocket,** sacca d'aria, vuoto; **— pump,** pompa pneumatica; **— shaft,** tromba d'aerazione; **— raid,** incursione aerea; **— sleeve,** **— sock,** manica a vento; **—tight,** impermeabile all'aria. **—ily** *avv.* leggermente, allegramente, con disinvoltura. **—iness** *n.* leggerezza, disinvoltura. **—ing** *n.* ventilazione, passeggiata all'aperto: **to get some —,** prendere una boccata d'aria.

Air Corps *n.* aviazione.

aircraft (âr'kráft') *n.* velivolo.

airdrop (âr'drŏp') *n.* lancio aereo di rifornimenti; lancio aereo di manifestini.

airlift (âr'lĭft') *n.* ponte aereo; *vt.* mandare rifornimenti per aereo (*a una zona bloccata*).

airman (âr'mǎn) *n.* aviatore.

airplane (âr'plān) *n.* aeroplano.

airport (âr'pōrt') *n.* aeroporto.

airship (âr'shĭp') *n.* dirigibile.

airy (âr'ĭ) *agg.* arioso, aerato; leggero; disinvolto.

aisle (īl) *n.* navata (*di chiesa*).

ajar (á·jär') *agg.* socchiuso.

akimbo (á·kĭm'bō) *avv.* con le mani sui fianchi.

akin (å·kĭn') agg. affine, imparentato, analogo.

alarm (å·lärm') vt. allarmare. n. allarme; ansia: — clock, orologio a sveglia. —ing adj. allarmante.

alas! (å·lås') inter. ahimè!

albeit (ôl·bē'ĭt) avv. benchè.

alcohol (ăl'kō·hŏl) n. alcole. —ic agg. alcolico.

alcove (ăl'kōv) n. alcova, nicchia.

alder (ôl'dẽr) n. ontano.

alderman (ôl'dẽr·măn) n. assessore municipale.

ale (āl) n. birra.

alert (·å·lûrt') agg. svelto, sveglio, vigile. n. allarme; segnale di allarme.

algebra (ăl'jḗ·brà) n. algebra.

alias (ā'lǐ·ăs) n. pseudonimo. avv. detto, altrimenti detto.

alien (āl'yĕn) n., agg. straniero, estraneo.

alienate (āl'yĕn·āt) vt. alienare; estraniare, inimicare.

alienist (āl'yĕn·ĭst) n. alienista.

alight (å·līt') vi. scendere (da un veicolo, ecc.); atterrare, posarsi.

alike (å·līk') avv. ugualmente. agg. analogo, uguale, somigliante: to be —, assomigliarsi.

alive (å·līv') agg. vivo, vitale, conscio: — with, pieno di; — to; conscio di; while —, vita natural durante.

all (ôl) agg. tutto, tutti: — at once, tutt'a un tratto; — right, benissimo, perfettamente; — clear, (segnale di) cessato allarme aereo; not at —, nient'affatto, non c'è di che; — the worse, tanto peggio; to be — in, essere esausto o affranto; —out, totale, radicale, completo; to go — out for, in, to, buttarsi a corpo morto (in un'impresa).

allay (å·lā') vt. chetare, mitigare, ammansire.

allegation (ăl'ḗ·gā'shŭn) n. affermazione.

allege (å·lĕj') vt. affermare, addurre.

allegiance (å·lē'jăns) n. fedeltà, obbedienza.

allergic (å·lûr'jĭk) agg. allergico; intollerante.

allergy (ăl'ẽr·jĭ) n. allergia.

alleviate (å·lē'vĭ·āt) vt. alleviare, sollevare, lenire.

alley (ăl'ĭ) n. vicolo: blind —, vicolo cieco.

alliance (å·lī'ăns) n. alleanza.

allied (å·līd') agg. alleato, parente.

alligator (ăl'ĭ·gā'tẽr) n. alligatore; (gergo) jazzomane.

allocate (ăl'ō·kāt) vt. assegnare, destinare, distribuire.

allot (å·lŏt') vt. assegnare; spartire.

allow (å·lou') vt. permettere; autorizzare, accordare; riconoscere; abbonare; ammettere: to — for, tener conto di. —able agg. ammissibile, lecito.

allowance (å·lou'ăns) n. assegno fisso; permesso, concessione; pensione; ribasso, sconto: to make — for, tener conto di.

alloy (å·loi') vt. fondere. n. (ăl'oi) lega metallica.

allude (å·lūd') vi. alludere.

allure (å·lūr') vt. allettare, adescare, sedurre. —mènt n. fascino, attrattiva, seduzione.

alluring (å·lur'ĭng) agg. attraente, seducente.

allusion (å·lū'zhŭn) n. allusione.

ally (å·lī') n. alleato. vt. alleare. vi. allearsi.

almanac (ôl'må·năk) n. almanacco, calendario.

almighty (ôl·mīt'ĭ) agg. onnipossente.

almond (ä'mŭnd; ăm'ŭnd) n. mandorla. — tree n. mandorlo.

almost (ôl'mōst; ŏl·mōst') avv. quasi, pressochè.

alms (ämz) n. elemosina.

aloft (å·lŏft') avv. in alto, dall'alto.

alone (å·lōn') agg. solo, solitario, unico. avv. solo, soltanto: to let —, lasciare in pace, lasciar stare.

along (å·lŏng') avv., prep. lungo, accanto, avanti: — with, insieme con; all —, sempre, da un capo all'altro di; to get —, tirare avanti; to get — with, andar d'accordo con; to carry — with one, portare seco; to go — with, andare con.

alongside (å·lŏng'sīd') prep., avv. accosto (a); accanto (a).

aloof (å·lōōf') agg. riservato, sostenuto, arcigno. avv. a distanza, in disparte, in modo sostenuto. —ness n. isolamento, scontrosità.

aloud (å·loud') avv. ad alta voce.

alphabet (ăl'fá·bĕt) n. alfabeto.

already (ôl·rĕd'ĭ) avv. già.

also (ôl'sō) avv. anche, inoltre.

altar (ôl'tẽr) n. altare.

alter (ôl'tẽr) vt. alterare, modificare. vi. modificarsi. —ation n. modifica, cambiamento.

alternate (ôl'tẽr·nĭt; ăl'-) agg. alternato, alterno. vi. (ôl'tẽr·nāt) alternare: alternating current, corrente alternata. —ly avv. alternativamente.

alternative (ôl·tûr'ná·tĭv; ăl-) n. alternativa. agg. alternativo.

although (ôl·thō') cong. benchè.

altitude (ăl'tǐ·tūd)n. altitudine.

altogether (òl'tŏŏ·gĕth'ĕr) *avv.* complessivamente, completamente.

aluminum (á·lū'mĭ·nŭm) *n.* alluminio.

alumnus (á·lŭm'nŭs) *n.* laureato, diplomato; ex allievo.

always (òl'wāz; -wĭz) *avv.* sempre.

am (ăm) *la pers.sing.ind.pres.* di *to be.*

amalgamate (á·măl'gá·māt) *vt.* amalgamare. *vi.* amalgamarsi; ambientarsi.

amass (á·măs') *vt.* ammassare, ammucchiare.

amateur (ăm'á·tûr'; ăm'á·tûr; ăm'á·tūr) *n.* dilettante; principiante.

amaze (á·māz') *vt.* stupire, sbalordire. —ment, —dness *n.* meraviglia, sbalordimento.

amazing *agg.* straordinario, sbalorditivo.

ambassador (ăm·băs'á·dĕr) *n.* ambasciatore.

ambassadress (ăm·băs'á·drĕs) *n.* ambasciatrice.

amber (ăm'bĕr) *n.* ambra.

ambergris (ăm'bĕr·grēs; -grĭs) *n.* ambra grigia.

ambient (ăm'bĭ·ĕnt) *agg.* ambiente.

ambiguity (ăm'bĭ·gū'ĭ·tĭ) *n.* ambiguità.

ambiguous (ăm·bĭg'û·ŭs) *agg.* ambiguo, equivoco.

ambition (ăm·bĭsh'ŭn) *n.* ambizione.

ambitious (ăm·bĭsh'ŭs) *agg.* ambizioso.

amble (ăm'b'l) *n.* ambio.

ambulance (ăm'bû·lăns) *n.* ambulanza.

ambulatory (ăm'bû·lá·tō'rĭ) *n.*, *agg.* ambulatorio.

ambuscade (ăm'bŭs·kād'), **ambush** (ăm'bŏŏsh) *n.* imboscata.

ameliorate (á·mēl'yō·rāt) *vt.*, *vi.* migliorare.

amelioration *n.* miglioramento.

amenable (á·mē'ná·b'l) *agg.* malleabile, trattabile: — to reason, ragionevole.

amend (á·mĕnd') *vt.* emendare, migliorare. *vi.* emendarsi, correggersi. —ment *n.* emendamento, riforma, modifica.

amends *n.pl.* risarcimento, riparazione.

amenity (á·mĕn'ĭ·tĭ) *n.* amentià. (*pl.*) complimenti, cerimonie.

American (á·mĕr'ĭ·kǎn) *n.*, *agg.* americano. —ize *vt.* americanizzare.

amethyst (ăm'ĕ·thĭst) *n.* ametista.

amiability (ā'mĭ·á·bĭl'ĭ·tĭ), amiableness *n.* cortesia, amabilità.

amiable (ā'mĭ·á·b'l) *agg.* amabile.

amicable (ăm'ĭ·ká·b'l) *agg.* amichevole.

amid (á·mĭd'), **amidst** (á·mĭdst') *prep.* tra, nel mezzo.

amidships (á·mĭd'shĭps) *avv.* (*naut.*) a mezzanave.

amiss (á·mĭs') *agg.* errato, deplorevole. *avv.* a sproposito, erroneamente: to take —, offendersi per, prendere in malaparte.

amity (ăm'ĭ·tĭ) *n.* amicizia.

ammeter (ăm'mē'tĕr) *n.* amperometro.

ammonia (á·mō'nĭ·á;- mōn'yá) *n.* ammoniaca.

ammunition (ăm'û·nĭsh'ŭn) *n.* munizione. *vt.* fornire munizioni a. — pouch *n.* giberna.

amnesty (ăm'nĕs·tĭ) *n.* amnistia. *vt.* amnistiare.

among (á·mŭng'), **amongst** (á·mŭngst') *prep.* tra, in mezzo.

amorous (ăm'ō·rŭs) *agg.* amoroso.

amorphous (á·môr'fŭs) *agg.* amorfo.

amortize (á·môr'tĭz; -tĭz) *vt.* ammortizzare. —ment, **amortization** *n.* ammortamento.

amount (á·mount') *vi.* ammontare, assommare, salire; risolversi. *n.* ammontare, totale, somma, prezzo.

amour (á·mŏŏr') *n.* tresca.

amperage (ăm'pēr·ĭj) *n.* amperaggio.

amphibian (ăm·fĭb'ĭ·ǎn) *n.*, *agg.* anfibio.

amphibious (ăm·fĭb'ĭ·ŭs) *agg.* anfibio.

amphitheater (ăm'fĭ·thē'á·tĕr) *n.* anfiteatro.

ample (ăm'p'l) *agg.* ampio, spazioso, abbondante.

amplification (ăm'plĭ·fĭ·kā'shŭn) *n.* amplificazione.

amplifier (ăm'plĭ·fĭ'ĕr) *n.* amplificatore; altoparlante.

amplify (ăm'plĭ·fĭ) *vt.* ampliare, estendere; esagerare.

amplitude (ăm'plĭ·tūd) *n.* amplezza.

amputate (ăm'pū·tāt) *vt.* amputare.

amputation (ăm·pū·tā'shŭn) *n.* amputazione.

amuck (á·mŭk') *avv.* freneticamente: to run —, smaniare, imbestialirsi.

amulet (ăm'û·lĕt) *n.* amuleto.

amuse (á·mūz') *vt.* divertire. —ment, *n.* divertimento.

amusing (á·mūz'ĭng) *agg.* divertente.

an (ǎn) *art.indef.* un, uno, una.

anachronism (á·năk'rŏ·nĭz'm) *n.* anacronismo.

anal (ā'nǎl) *agg.* anale.

analgesia (ăn'ăl·jē'zĭ·á; -sĭ·á) *n.* analgesia.

analgesic (-jē'sĭk) *n.*, *agg.* analgesico.

analogous (á·năl'ō·gŭs) *agg.* analogo.

analysis (á·năl'ĭ·sĭs) *n.* analisi.

analytic (ăn'á·lĭt'ĭk), **analytical** *agg.* analitico.

analyze (ăn'á·lĭz) *vt.* analizzare.

anarchical (ăn·ăr kĭ·kăl) *agg.* anarchico.

anarchist (ăn′ăr·kĭst) *n.* anarchico.

anarchy (ăn′ăr·kĭ), *n.* anarchia.

anatomical (ăn′ă·tŏm′ĭ·kăl) *agg.* anatomico.

anatomy (ă·năt′ō·mĭ) *n.* anatomia.

ancestor (ăn′sĕs′tĕr) *n.* antenato.

ancestral (ăn·sĕs′trăl) *agg.* atavico, avito.

ancestry (ăn′sĕs′trĭ) *n.* lignaggio, ascendenza.

anchor (ăng′kĕr) *n.* àncora: sheet — (*fig.*), ancora di salvezza; to drop —, gettare l'ancora; to weigh —, levar l'ancora; to ride at —, essere all'ancora.

anchorite (ăng′kō·rīt) *n.* anacoreta, eremita.

anchovy (ăn·chō′vĭ; ăn′chō·vĭ) *n.* acciuga.

ancient (ăn′shĕnt) *agg.* antico, vecchio: the ancients, gli antichi.

and (ănd) *cong.* e, ed: — so forth, eccetera, e così via; let us try — do it, cerchiamo di farlo; go — see, andate a vedere.

andiron (ănd′ī′ĕrn) *n.* alare.

anecdote (ăn′ĕk.dŏt) *n.* aneddoto.

anesthesiologist (ăn′ĕs·thē′zĭ·ŏl′ō·jĭst) *n.* anestesista.

anesthetic (ăn′ĕs·thĕt′ĭk) *n.*, *agg.* anestetico.

anew (ă·nū′) *avv.* daccapo, di nuovo.

angel (ăn′jĕl) *n.* angelo: guardian —, angelo custode.

anger (ăng′ĕr) *n.* collera, stizza. *vt.* incollerire, far arrabbiare.

angle (ăng′g′l) (1) *n.* angolo; prospettiva, punto di vista.

angle (2) *vi.* pescare alla lenza; adescare; presentare (*un argomento, un fatto, ecc.*) sotto un aspetto particolare.

angler (ăng′glĕr) *n.* pescatore.

angling (ăng′glĭng) *n.* pesca alla lenza.

Anglo-Saxon (ăng′glŏ·săk′s′n) *n.*, *agg.* anglosassone.

angry (ăng′grĭ) *agg.* collerico, incollerito, irritato: to get —, arrabbiarsi.

anguish (ăng′gwĭsh) *n.* angoscia, dolore. *vt.* angosciare.

angular (ăng′gū·lĕr) *agg.* angolare.

animadversion (ăn′ĭ·măd·vûr′shŭn) *n.* malanimo, rimprovero, censura, critica.

animal (ăn′ĭ·măl) *n.*, *agg.* animale. —cule (ăn′ĭ·măl′kūl) *n.* microrganismo.

animate (ăn′ĭ·māt) *vt.* animare.

animation (ăn′ĭ·mā′shŭn) *n.* animazione.

animosity (ăn′ĭ·mŏs′ĭ·tĭ) *n.* animosità, accanimento.

animus (ăn′ĭ·mŭs) *n.* astio; propensione.

anise (ăn′ĭs) *n.* anice.

ankle (ăng′k′l) *n.* caviglia. —deep *avv.* fino alla caviglia.

annals (ăn′ălz) *n.pl.* annali.

anneal (ă·nēl′) *vi.* temprare (*acciaio, ecc.*).

annex (ă·nĕks′) *vt.* annettere, unire. *vi.* unirsi. *n.* annesso, fabbricato annesso. —ation *n.* annessione.

annihilate (ă·nī′ĭ·lāt) *vt.* annientare.

Annie Oakley (ăn′ĭ ōk′lĭ) *n.*, biglietto di favore, ingresso di favore.

annihilation (ă·nī′ĭ·lā′shŭn) *n.* annientamento.

anniversary (ăn′ĭ·vûr′sá·rĭ) *n.*, *agg.* anniversario.

annotate (ăn′ō·tāt) *vt.* annotare.

annotation *n.* annotazione.

announce (ă·nouns′) *vt.* annunciare, proclamare. —ment *n.* annuncio, partecipazione.

annoy (ă·noi′) *vt.* molestare, tormentare, irritare, seccare. —ance *n.* irritazione, molestia, seccatura. —ing *agg.* molesto, noioso.

annual (ăn′ū·ăl) *n.* annuario. *agg.* annuale.

annuity (ă·nū′ĭ·tĭ) *n.* annualità, pensione: life —, vitalizio.

annul (ă·nŭl′) *vt.* annullare.

annular (ăn′ū·lĕr) *agg.* anulare.

annunciation (ă·nŭn′sĭ·ā′shŭn) *n.* annuncio, annunciazione.

anoint (ă·noint′) *vt.* ungere, consacrare.

anomalous (ă·nŏm′ă·lŭs) *agg.* anomalo.

anomaly (ă·nŏm′ă·lĭ) *n.* anomalia.

anon (ă·nŏn′) *avv.* subito: ever and —, di quando in quando.

anonymity (ăn′ō·nĭm′ĭ·tĭ) *n.* anonimità, l'anonimo.

anonymous (ă·nŏn′ĭ·mŭs) *agg.* anonimo.

another (ă·nŭth′ĕr) *agg.*, *pron.* un altro: one after —, l'uno dopo l'altro; one—, l'un l'altro, avicenda.

answer (ăn′sĕr) *n.* risposta. *vt.*, *vi.* rispondere, evadere, corrispondere, servire (*allo scopo*). —able *agg.* responsabile.

ant (ănt) *n.* formica. —eater *n.* formichiere. —hill *n.* formicaio.

antagonism (ăn·tăg′ō·nĭz′m) *n.* antagonismo.

antagonist (—nĭst) *n.* antagonista.

antagonize (—nīz) *vt.* avversare.

ante (ăn′tē) *n.* (*al poker*) buio.

antecedent (ăn′tē·sēd′ĕnt) *n.*, *agg.* antecedente.

antedate (ăn′tē·dāt′; ăn′tē·dāt′) *vt.* antidatare.

antelope (ăn'tē·lōp) *n.* antilope.

anterior (ăn·tēr'ǐ·ẽr) *agg.* anteriore.

anteroom (ăn'tē·rōōm') *n.* anticamera.

anthem (ăn'thĕm) *n.* inno.

anthology (ăn·thŏl'ŏ·jǐ) *n.* antologia.

anthracite (ăn'thrá·sīt) *n.* antracite.

antiaircraft (ăn'tǐ·âr'kráft') *agg.* antiaereo, contraereo.

antibiotic (ăn'tǐ·bǐ·ŏt'ǐk) *n., agg.* antibiotico.

antic (ăn'tǐk) *n.* buffonata, farsa; smania.

anticipate (ăn·tǐs'ǐ·pāt) *vt.* anticipare, prevedere, prevenire.

anticipation *n.* anticipazione, previsione; ansia.

anticlimax (ăn'tǐ·klī'măks) *n.* crollo, discesa.

antidote (ăn'tǐ·dōt) *n.* antidoto.

antipathy (ăn·tǐp'á·thǐ) *n.* antipatia.

antipodes (ăn·tǐp'ŏdēz) *n.pl.* antipodi.

antiquarian (ăn'tǐ·kwâr'ǐ·ăn) *n.* antiquario.

antiquated (ăn'tǐ·kwāt'ĕd) *agg.* antiquato.

antique (ăn·tēk') *n.* oggetto antico, antichità. *agg.* antico, arcaico. —**ly** *avv.* anticamente.

antiquity (ăn·tǐk'wǐ·tǐ) *n.* antichità.

antiseptic (ăn'tǐ·sĕp'tǐk) *n., agg.* antisettico.

antihistamine (ăn'tǐ·hǐs'tá·mēn) *n.* antistamina.

antithesis (ăn·tǐth'ĕsǐs) *n.* antitesi.

antitoxin (ăn'tǐ·tŏk'sǐn) *n.* antitossina.

antler (ănt'lẽr) *n.* corno di cervo.

antonym (ăn'tō·nǐm) *n.,* contrario, opposto.

anvil (ăn'vǐl) *n.* incudine.

anxiety (ăng·zī'ĕ·tǐ) *n.* ansia, inquietudine, premura.

anxious (ăngk'shŭs; ăng'shŭs) *agg.* inquieto; sollecito; impaziente; desideroso.

any (ĕn'ǐ) *agg.* alcuno, alcuni, qualche, un poco di, dei, della, dei, delle, più: — better, meglio; — further, più oltre; — man, qualunque uomo; in — case, comunque; have you — bread? avete del pane?; you do not know — of my friends, non conoscete nessuno dei miei amici; I haven't —, non ne ho.

anybody (ĕn'ǐ·bŏd'ǐ; -bŭd·ǐ), **anyone** (ĕn'ǐ·wŭn) *n.* chiunque, qualcuno, chicchessia.

anyhow (ĕn'ǐ·hou) *avv.* comunque, in qualche modo, alla meglio. *cong.* però.

anything (ĕn'ǐ·thǐng) *n.* qualunque cosa, qualcosa: not ... —, non ... niente; — but, tutt'altro.

anyway (ĕn'ǐ·wā) *avv.* in ogni modo, in tutti i casi, comunque.

anywhere (ĕn'ǐ·hwâr) *avv.* dovunque, da qualche parte: not ... —, non ... da alcuna parte; — else, da qualunque altra parte.

apace (á·pās') *avv.* rapidamente; a vista d'occhio.

apart (á·pärt') *avv.* a parte, in disparte, separatamente: to come —, dividersi, sfasciarsi; to take —, smontare, smantellare; to tear —, disfare, fare a pezzi.

apartheid (á·pärt'hīt) *n.* segregazione razziale.

apartment (á·pärt'mĕnt) *n.* stanza, camera; appartamento.

apathetic (ăp'á·thĕt'ǐk) *agg.* apatico.

apathy (ăp'á·thǐ) *n.* apatia.

ape (āp) *n.* scimmia. *vt.* scimmiottare, imitare.

aperient (á·pēr'ǐ·ĕnt) *n., agg.* lassativo.

aperture (ăp'ẽr·tụr) *n.* apertura.

apex (ā'pĕks) *n.* apice, vertice.

apiece (á·pēs') *avv.* ciascuno, ognuno, a testa.

apocryphal (á·pŏk'rǐ·fál) *agg.* apocrifo, falso.

apologetic (á·pŏl'ŏ·jĕt'ǐk) *agg.* di scusa, di giustificazione.

apologize (á·pŏl'ŏ·jīz) *vi.* scusarsi, chiedere perdono.

apology (á·pŏl'ŏ·jǐ) *n.* scusa, giustificazione.

apoplexy (ăp'ŏ·plĕk'sǐ) *n.* apoplessia.

apostle (á·pŏs''l) *n.* apostolo.

apostolic (ăp'ŏs·tŏl'ǐk) *agg.* apostolico.

apostrophe (á·pŏs'trō·fē) *n.* apostrofo.

appal (á·pôl') *vt.* sgomentare, impaurire; scandalizzare. —**ling** *agg.* spaventoso, terrorizzante.

apparatus (ăp'á·rā'tŭs) *n.* apparato, apparecchio, impianto.

apparel (á·păr'ĕl) *n.* vestiario, indumenti.

apparent (á·păr'ĕnt; á·pâr'-) *agg.* visibile, apparente, manifesto: heir —, erede legittimo. —**ly** *avv.* visibilmente, evidentemente; presumibilmente, a quanto pare.

apparition (ăp'á·rǐsh'ŭn) *n.* apparizione.

appeal (á·pēl') *vi.* appellarsi, fare appello a; ricorrere in appello; attrarre. *n.* appello; attrattiva. —**ing** *agg.* supplichevole; attraente.

appear (á·pēr') *vi.* apparire, comparire; sembrare, aver l'aria di. —**ance** *n.* apparizione, apparenza; comparizione.

appease (á·pēz') *vt.* calmare, pacificare, ammansire, sedare. —**ment** *n.* pacificazione.

appendix (á·pĕn'dǐks) *n.* appendice.

appertain (ăp'ẽr·tān') *vi.* appartenere, riguardare.

appetite (ăp'ĕ·tĭt) n. appetito, desiderio.

appetizer (ăp'ĕ·tīz'ẽr) n. aperitivo.

appetizing agg. appetitoso.

applaud (ă·plôd') vt. applaudire, lodare.

applause (ă·plôz') n. plauso, applauso.

apple (ăp''l) n. mela: — of the eye, pupilla. — tree n. melo.

appliance (ă·plī'ăns) n. applicazione; apparecchio, meccanismo: house appliances, elettrodomestici.

applicant (ăp'lĭ·kănt) n. postulante; candidato.

application (ăp'lĭ·kā'shŭn) n. domanda; richiesta.

apply (ă·plī') vt. applicare. vi. rivolgersi, richiedere, presentare una domanda; applicarsi: to — to, rivolgersi a; to — for, chiedere, sollecitare; to — on account, accreditare in conto.

appoint (ă·point') vt. nominare; designare; stabilire; arredare, ammobiliare. —ment n. nomina; decreto; designazione; appuntamento; incarico; arredamento, mobilia.

apportion (ă·pôr'shŭn) vt. distribuire, spartire, assegnare. —ment n. ripartizione, assegnazione.

appraisal (ă·prāz'ăl) n. valutazione, stima.

appraise (ă·prāz') vt. stimare, valutare.

appreciable (ă·prē'shĭ·à·b'l) agg. apprezzabile.

appreciate (ă·prē'shĭ·āt) vt. capire, apprezzare; valutare; rendersi conto di; gradire.

appreciation (ă·prē'shĭ·ā'shŭn; -sĭ·ā'shŭn) n. apprezzamento; giusta valutazione; gradimento; aumento, rialzo (di prezzo).

apprehend (ăp'rĕ·hĕnd') vt. catturare, arrestare; temere; afferrare, capire.

apprehension (ăp'rĕ·hĕn'shŭn) n. apprensione; assimilazione (di un' idea); timore; cattura.

apprehensive (ăp'rĕ·hĕn'sĭv) agg. timoroso; pronto di mente.

apprentice (ă·prĕn'tĭs) n. apprendista. vt. collocare come apprendista. —ship n. apprendistato, tirocinio.

approach (ă·prōch') n. accostamento; accesso; impostazione; metodo. vi. avvicinarsi; fare approcci. vt. accostare, abbordare; raggiungere; somigliare a.

approbation (ăp'rŏ·bā'shŭn) n. approvazione.

appropriate (ă·prō'prĭ·āt') vt. assegnare, aggiudicare; stanziare; appropriarsi di. agg. (ă·prō'prĭ·ĭt) appropriato, acconcio, proprio.

appropriation (ă·prō'prĭ·ā'shŭn) n. appropriazione, assegnazione; stanziamento.

approval (ă·prōōv'ăl) n. approvazione: on —, in prova.

approve (ă·prōōv') vt. approvare: to — of, essere favorevole a.

approving agg. approvativo.

approximate (ă·prŏk'sĭ·mĭt) agg. approssimativo. vt. (-māt) approssimare, avvicinare. vi. aprossimarsi. —ly avv. approssimativamente.

approximation (ă·prŏk'sĭ·mā'shŭn) n. approssimazione.

apricot (ā'prĭ·kŏt; ăp'rĭ-) n. albicocca.

April (ā'prĭl) n. aprile: — Fools' Day, primo di aprile.

apron (ā'prŭn) n. grembiale.

apropos (ăp'rŏ·pō') agg. opportuno; tempestivo. avv. a proposito; opportunamente.

apt (ăpt) agg. adatto; atto; proclive. —itude, (ăp'tĭ·tūd), —ness n. attitudine, capacità, tendenza.

aquacade (ăk'wà·kād) n. spettacolo aquatico.

aquarium (à·kwâr'ĭ·ŭm) n. acquario.

aquatic (à·kwăt'ĭk; -kwŏt'ĭk) agg. acquatico.

aqueduct (ăk'wē·dŭkt) n. acquedotto.

aqueous (ā'kwē·ŭs) agg. acquoso.

Arab (ăr'ăb), Arabian (à·rā'bĭ·ăn) n., agg. arabo: street arab, monello.

arbiter (är'bĭ·tẽr) n. arbitro.

arbitrament (är·bĭt'rà·mĕnt) n. arbitraggio.

arbitrary (är'bĭ·trĕr'ĭ) agg. arbitrario.

arbitrate (är'bĭ·trāt) vt., vi. arbitrare.

arbitration n. arbitrato.

arbitrator n. arbitro; mediatore.

arbor (är'bẽr) n. pergola; (mecc.) trave, albero, asse.

arc (ärk) n. arco: — lamp, lampada ad arco.

arcade (är·kād') n. portico, porticato.

arch (ärch) n. arco, volta. vt. arcuare, curvare. vi. arcuarsi. agg. malizioso, astuto. pref. arci, super: —criminal, superdelinquente; —foe, nemico giurato; —priest, arciprete.

archaic (är·kā'ĭk) agg. arcaico.

archbishop (ärch'bĭsh'ŭp) n. arcivescovo. —ric n. arcivescovado.

archdeacon (ärch'dē'kŭn) n. arcidiacono.

archipelago (är'kĭ·pĕl'à·gō) n. arcipelago.

architect (är'kĭ·tĕkt) n. architetto. —ural agg. architettonico. —ure n. architettura.

archive (är'kĭv) n. archivio.

archly (ärch'lĭ) agg. maliziosamente.

archway (ärch'wā') n. volta, andito.

arctic (ärk'tĭk) agg. artico.

ardent (är'děnt) *agg.* ardente: — spirits, bevande alcooliche.

ardor (är'dĕr) *n.* ardore.

arduous (är'gū·ŭs) *agg.* arduo, difficile; impervio.

are (är) *2a pers.pl. di* to be, sei, siete; siamo; (*essi*) sono.

area (ā'rē·á; ār'ē·á) *n.* area, superficie, zona.

arena (á·rē'ná) *n.* arena: — theater, teatro circolare, teatro a scena centrale.

Argentine (är'jĕn·tĭn; -tēn) *n. agg.* argentino.

argue (är'gū) *vt., vi.* discutere, ragionare; denotare, indicare: to — one into, convincere uno a; to — one out of, dissuadere uno da.

argument (är'gū·mĕnt) *n.* argomento, discussione, disputa, tesi.

arid (ăr'ĭd) *agg.* arido.

arise (á·rīz') *vi.* (*pass.* arose, *pp.* arisen) alzarsi, innalzarsi; sorgere; provenire, derivare.

aristocracy (ăr'ĭs·tŏk'rá·sĭ) *n.* aristocrazia.

aristocrat (á·rĭs'tô·krăt; ăr'ĭs·tô·krăt) *n.* aristocràtico.

aristocratic *agg.* aristocratico.

arithmetic (á·rĭth'mĕ·tĭk) *n.* aritmetica.

ark (ärk) *n.* arca: Noah's —, l'arca di Noè.

arm (ärm) *n.* braccio; arma; manica; bracciuolo: — in —, a braccetto; coat of arms, stemma. *vt.* armare. *vi.* armarsi.

armament (är'má·mĕnt) *n.* armamento.

armature (är'má·tūr) *n.* armatura.

armchair (ärm'châr') *n.* poltrona.

armful (ärm'fŏŏl) *n.* bracciata.

armistice (är'mĭs·tĭs) *n.* armistizio.

armlet (ärm'lĕt) *n.* bracciale.

armor (är'mĕr) *n.* armatura, corazza; corazzatura; forze corazzate; *vt.* blindare, corazzare. —ial *agg.* araldico. *n.* almanacco araldico. —ed *agg.* corazzato, blindato: — car, autoblindo.

armory (är'mĕr·ĭ) *n.* armeria.

armpit (ärm'pĭt') *n.* ascella.

army (är'mĭ) *n.* esercito; turba.

aroma (á·rō'má) *n.* aroma. —tic *agg.* (ăr'ô·măt'ĭk) aromatico.

arose (á·rōz') *pass. di* arise.

around (á·round') *avv.* intorno, all'intorno. *prep.* intorno a, in giro, tutt'attorno.

arouse (á·rouz') *vt.* svegliare, provocare, irritare. *vi.* svegliarsi, scuotersi.

arraign (á·rān') *vt.* accusare, citare in giudizio.

arrange (á·rānj') *vt., vi.* disporre, combinare; adattare; comporre (*una controversia*). —ment *n.* disposizione, organizzazione, accordo: to make arrangements, prender misure, accordarsi.

arrant (är'ănt) *adj.* notorio, famigerato.

array (á·rā') *n.* spiegamento, schiera; esposizione; lista dei giurati: in great —, in pompa magna; in battle —, in ordine di battaglia. *vt.* allineare, schierare; vestire, parare.

arrears (á·rērz') *n.pl.* arretrati, residuo.

arrest (á·rĕst') *n.* arresto, cattura; sospensione. *vt.* arrestare, catturare; fermare, sospendere.

arrival (á·rīv'ăl) *n.* arrivo.

arrive (á·rīv') *vi.* arrivare, giungere.

arrogance (ăr'ô·gáns) *n.* arroganza.

arrogant (ăr'ô·gănt) *agg.* arrogante.

arrow (ăr'ō) *n.* freccia. —head *n.* punta di freccia.

arsenal (är'sě·nǎl) *n.* arsenale.

arsenic (är'sě·nĭk) *n.* arsenico.

arson (är's'n) *n.* incendio doloso.

art (ärt) *n.* arte, abilità; Master of Arts, laureato in lettere.

artery (är'tĕr·ĭ) *n.* arteria.

artful (ärt'fŏŏl; -f'l) *agg.* subdolo, astuto; artificioso.

artichoke (är'tĭ·chōk) *n.* carciofo.

article (är'tĭ·k'l) *n.* articolo; Articles of War, codice militare.

articulate (är·tĭk'ū·lát) *agg.* articolato; scandito. *vt., vi.* (-ăt) articolare, scandire.

articulation *n.* articolazione.

artifice (är'tĭ·fĭs) *n.* artificio, astuzia.

artificial (är'tĭ·fĭsh'ăl) *agg.* artificiale; artificioso, affettato: — insemination, fecondazione artificiale.

artillery (är·tĭl'ĕr·ĭ) *n.* artiglieria.

artisan (är'tĭ·zăn) *n.* artigiano, operaio.

artist (är'tĭst) *n.* artista. —ic *agg.* artistico.

artless (ärt'lĕs) *agg.* ingenuo, spontaneo.

as (ăz) *cong.* come, nello stesso modo; poichè, dal momento che: as ... as, tanto ... quanto; — far —, sin dove; sino a; — large —, grande come; — much, altrettanto; — much —, tanto quanto; — yet, sino ad ora; — long —, fintanto che; the same —, lo stesso che; — well, come pure, anche; you can come — well, potete venire anche voi; — if, — though, come se; — soon — possible, il più presto possibile; — it were, per così dire.

asbestos (ăs·bĕs'tŏs; ăz-) *n.* amianto.

ascend (á·sĕnd') *vt., vi.* scalare; elevarsi, salire; risalire (*a*).

ascension (ă·sĕn'shŭn) n. ascensione.

ascent (ă·sĕnt') n. ascensione, salita; erta.

ascertain (ăs'ĕr·tān') vt. appurare, sincerarsi di, verificare.

ascribe (ăs·krīb') vt. attribuire; imputare.

ash (ăsh) n. cenere. — **colored** agg. cinereo. — **tray** n. portacenere: **Ash Wednesday,** Mercoledì delle Ceneri.

ash, ash tree n. frassino.

ashamed (ă·shāmd') agg. vergognoso (che si vergogna): **to be — of,** vergognarsi di.

ashen (ăsh'ĕn) agg. cinereo.

ashore (ă·shōr') avv. a terra, a riva: **to run —,** arenarsi; **to go —,** sbarcare.

aside (ă·sīd') avv. a lato; in disparte, lateralmente; eccetto: — **from,** eccetto, a prescindere da.

ask (ăsk) vt. domandare, chiedere; invitare: **to — a question,** rivolgere una domanda; **to — for,** chiedere, esigere; **to — after, about,** chiedere, informarsi di; **to — to dinner,** invitare a pranzo.

askance (ă·skăns') avv. sospettosamente, con diffidenza, obliquamente: **to look —,** guardare in tralice, con sospetto; disapprovare.

askew (ă·skū') avv. di sghimbescio.

asleep (ă·slēp') agg., avv. dormiente, addormentato: **to fall —,** addormentarsi.

asparagus (ăs·păr'ă·gŭs) n. asparago.

aspect (ăs'pĕkt) n. aspetto.

aspersion (ăs·pûr'shŭn; -zhŭn) n. aspersione; calunnia.

asphalt (ăs'fôlt; -fălt) n. asfalto.

asphyxiate (ăs·fĭk'sĭ·āt) vt. asfissiare.

asphyxiation n. asfissia.

aspiration (ăs'pĭ·rā'shŭn) n. aspirazione.

aspire (ăs·pīr') vi. aspirare, anelare.

ass (ăs) n. asino: **to make an — of oneself,** fare una figura barbina.

assail (ă·sāl') vt. assalire, aggredire. —**ant** n. assalitore.

assassin (ă·săs'ĭn) n. assassino. —**ate** vt. assassinare.

assault (ă·sôlt') n. assalto, grassazione: — **and battery,** vie di fatto. vt. aggredire, assaltare.

assay (ă·sā'; ăs'ā) n. saggio, prova; verifica. vt. saggiare.

assemblage (ă·sĕm'blĭj) n. montaggio.

assemble (ă·sĕm'b'l) vt. riunire, radunare; montare.

assembly (ă·sĕm'blĭ) n. assemblea; montaggio.

assent (ă·sĕnt') n. assenso, sanzione. vi. assentire, acconsentire.

assert (ă·sûrt') vt. asserire, affermare, sostenere; rivendicare. —**ion** n. asserzione; rivendicazione.

assess (ă·sĕs') vt. assegnare; tassare, multare; calcolare (l'imponibile). —**ment** n. tassazione, assegnazione.

asset (ăs'ĕt) n. vantaggio, qualità: **he is an — to his family,** egli fa onore alla sua famiglia. **assets** pl. beni; (comm.) attività: **assets and liabilities,** attività e passività.

assiduous (ă·sĭd'ū·ŭs) agg. assiduo.

assign (ă·sīn') vt. assegnare.

assignation (ăs'ĭg·nā'shŭn) n. assegnazione, appuntamento.

assignment (ă·sīn'mĕnt) n. assegnazione; missione; designazione; compito.

assimilate (ă·sĭm'ĭ·lāt) vt. assimilare, assorbire. vi. assimilarsi.

assimilation n. assimilazione.

assist (ă·sĭst') vt. aiutare. —**ance** n. aiuto. —**ant** n. aiutante: —**manager,** vice-direttore.

associate (ă·sō'shĭ·āt; -sĭ·āt) vt. associare. vi. associarsi: **to — with,** frequentare. n. socio, compare, complice. agg. associato, consociato.

association n. associazione.

assort (ă·sòrt') vt. assortire. vi. far comunella. —**ed** agg. assortito. —**ment** n. assortimento; accolita.

assuage (ă·swāj) vt. ammansire; attenuare; soddisfare; placarsi.

assume (ă·sūm') vt. ritenere; supporre; presumere; assumere; assumersi; arrogarsi.

assuming agg. arrogante, presuntuoso.

assumption (ă·sŭmp'shŭn) n. presupposto, supposizione; assunzione.

assurance (ă·shoor'ăns) n. assicurazione; affermazione; sicurezza; sicumera.

assure (ă·shoor') vt. assicurare.

assuredly (ă·shoor'ĕd·lĭ) avv. sicuramente.

asterisk (ăs'tĕr·ĭsk) n. asterisco.

astern (ă·stûrn') avv. (naut.) a poppa.

asthma (ăz'mă; ăsth'mă) n. asma.

astir (ă·stûr') agg., avv. in movimento; alzato (dal letto).

astonish (ăs·tŏn'ĭsh) vt. stupire. —**ing** agg. stupefacente, straordinario. —**ment** n. stupore, meraviglia.

astound (ăs·tound') vt. sbalordire, stordire.

astray (ă·strā') agg., avv. fuor della retta via, fuorviato, sbandato: **to go —,** perdersi, smarrirsi; deviare, traviarsi; **to lead —,** sviare, fuorviare, traviare.

astride (ă·strīd') avv. a cavalcioni.

astronomer (ăs·trŏn′ō·mĕr) *n.* astronomo.

astronomy (ăs·trŏn′ō·mĭ) *n.* astronomia.

astute (ăs·tūt′) *agg.* astuto.

asunder (ȧ·sŭn′dĕr) *avv.* separatamente, a pezzi, lontano: to tear —, fare a pezzi, separare violentemente.

asylum (ȧ·sī′lŭm) *n.* asilo, rifugio, ospedale: lunatic —, manicomio.

at (ăt; ȧt) *prep.* a, al, alla, in: — first, da principio, sulle prime; — hand, a portata di mano; — home, a casa; — last, alla fine, finalmente; — once, subito; — work, all'opera.

ate (āt) *pass. di* to eat.

atheist (ā′thē·ĭst) *n.* ateo.

athlete (ăth′lēt) *n.* atleta.

athletic (ăth·lĕt′ĭk) *agg.* atletico.

athletics (ăth·lĕt′ĭks) *n.* atletica.

Atlantic (ȧt·lăn′tĭk) *n., agg.* Atlantico.

atlas (ăt′lȧs) *n.* atlante geografico.

atmosphere (ăt′mŏs·fẽr) *n.* atmosfera.

atmospheric (ăt′mŏs·fĕr′ĭk) *agg.* atmosferico.

atom (ăt′ŭm) *n.* atomo: — bomb, bomba atomica. —ic, —ical *agg.* atomica. —ize, *vt.* atomizzare, polverizzare. —izer, *n.* atomizzatore, spruzzatore.

atone (ȧ·tōn′) *vt., vi.* espiare, riparare; attenuare. —ment *n.* espiazione, riparazione.

atrocious (ȧ·trō′shŭs) *agg.* atroce.

atrocity (ȧ·trŏs′ĭ·tĭ) *n.* atrocità.

atrophic (ȧ·trŏf′ĭk) *agg.* atrofico.

attach (ȧ·tăch′) *vt., vi.* attaccare, assicurare; attribuire, annettere; aderire, attaccarsi; sequestrare, requisire. —ment *n.* sequestro; attaccamento; vincolo; affetto; accessorio, parte aggiunta.

attack (ȧ·tăk′) *n.* assalto, aggressione; attacco, accesso. *vt.* attaccare, assalire.

attain (ȧ·tān′) *vt.* raggiungere, ottenere. *vi.* pervenire, arrivare. —ment *n.* raggiungimento, realizzazione; dote, abilità; successo.

attempt (ȧ·tĕmpt′) *n.* tentativo, attentato: — on someone's life, attentato alla vita di qualcuno. *vt.* tentare, provare, attentare.

attend (ȧ·tĕnd′) *vt.* assistere, presenziare; servire, scortare. *vi.* prestare attenzione, provvedere (*a*); accudire. —ance *n.* assistenza; presenza; pubblico (*affluenza di spettatori*). —ant *n.* inserviente; accompagnatore, assistente; guardiano; (*teatro*) maschera. *agg.* relativo (*a*), connesso.

attention (ȧ·tĕn′shŭn) *n.* attenzione; premura, cura: to pay —, fare attenzione, badare.

attentive (ȧtĕn′tĭv) *agg.* attento, premuroso.

attest (ȧ·tĕst′) *vt.* attestare.

attic (ăt′ĭk) *n.* attico, solaio.

attire (ȧ·tīr′) *n.* vestiario. *vt.* vestire, agghindare. *vi.* vestirsi, agghindarsi.

attitude (ăt′ĭ·tūd) *n.* atteggiamento, posa; attitudine.

attorney (ȧ·tûr′nĭ) *n.* procuratore, avvocato: — General, procuratore generale; District —, procuratore distrettuale; power of —, procura.

attract (ȧ·trăkt′) *vt.* attrarre. —ion *n.* attrazione. —ive *agg.* attraente, seducente. —iveness *n.* attrattiva, fascino.

attribute *n.* (ăt′rĭ·būt) attributo, qualità. *vt.* (ȧ·trĭb′ût) attribuire, imputare.

attrition (ȧ·trĭsh′ŭn) *n.* logorio.

auburn (ȯ′bẽrn) *agg.* castano, rosso Tizianesco.

auction (ȯk′shŭn) *n.* asta (*vendita*): to sell by —, vendere all'asta. —eer *n.* banditore.

audacious (ȯ·dā′shŭs) *agg.* audace.

audacity (ȯ·dăs′ĭ·tĭ) *n.* audacia.

audible (ȯ′dĭ·b'l) *agg.* udibile, percettibile.

audience (ȯ′dĭ·ĕns; ȯd′yĕns) *n.* udienza; uditorio, pubblico.

audio (ȯ′dĭ·ō) *agg.* auditivo, audio.

audit (ȯ′dĭt) *n.* controllo, verifica (*dei conti*). *vt.* verificare (*i conti*). —or *n.* revisore, sindaco (*di società*).

audition (ȯ·dĭsh′ŭn) *n.* audizione; *vt.* ascoltare in audizione; *vi.* avere un'audizione, esibirsi in audizione.

auditorium (ȯ′dĭ·tō′rĭ·ŭm) *n.* sala di udienza o di audizione.

auger (ȯ′gẽr) *n.* succhiello, trivella.

aught (ȯt) *pron.* qualcosa: for — I know, per quanto ne so io.

augment (ȯg·mĕnt′) *vt., vi.* aumentare.

augur (ȯ′gẽr) *vt., vi.* presagire, vaticinare, predire.

august (ȯ·gŭst′) *agg.* augusto.

August (ȯ′gŭst) *n.* agosto.

aunt (änt; ȧnt) *n.* zia: great —, prozia.

aureomycin (ȯ′rē·ō·mī′sĭn) *n.* aureomicina.

auspice (ȯs′pĭs) *n.* auspicio.

auspicious (ȯs·pĭsh′ŭs) *agg.* propizio, favorevole.

austere (ȯs·tẽr′) *agg.* austero.

austerity (ȯs·tĕr′ĭ·tĭ) *n.* austerità; economia obbligatoria.

Austrian (ȯs′trĭ·ȧn) *n., agg.* austriaco.

autarchy (ô′tär·kǐ) *n.* autarchia.
authentic (ô·thĕn′tǐk) *adj.* autentico.
author (ô′thĕr) *n.* autore.
authoritative (ô·thôr′ĭ·tā′tǐv) *agg.* autoritario; autorevole.
authority (ô·thôr′ĭ·tǐ) *n.* autorità: on good —, da fonte auterevole.
authorization *n.* autorizzazione.
authorize (ô′thĕr·ĭz) *vt.* autorizzare.
automatic (ô′tŏ·măt′ĭk) *agg.* automatico. *n.* pistola automatica. **—ally** *avv.* automaticamente.
automation *n.* automazione.
automaton (ô·tŏm′á·tŏn) *n.* automa.
automobile (ô′tŏ·mŏ·bēl′; -mŏ′bil *or* -bĕl) *n.* automobile.
automotive (ô′tŏ·mŏ′tǐv) *agg.* automotore.
autonomy (ô·tŏn′ŏ·mi) *n.* autonomia.
autopilot (ô′tŏ·pī′lŭt) *n.* autopilota, pilota automatico.
autosled (ô′tŏ·slĕd) *n.* autoslitta.
autumn (ô′tŭm) *n.* autunno. **—al** (ô·tŭm′năl) *agg.* autunnale.
auxiliary (ôg·zǐl′yd·rǐ) *n.*, *agg.* ausiliario, ausiliare.
avail (d·vāl′) *n.* vantaggio, utilità: of no —, inutile; *vt.* valere, giovare: to — oneself of, valersi di. **—able** *adj.* disponibile.
avalanche (ăv′á·lånch) *n.* valanga.
avarice (ăv′á·rǐs) *n.* avarizia, rapacità.
avaricious (ăv′á·rǐsh″ŭs) *agg.* avaro, cúpido.
avenge (d·vĕnj′) *vt.* vendicare.
avenger (d·vĕn′jĕr) *n.* vendicatore.
avenue (ăv′ĕ·nū) *n.* viale, corso.
aver (d·vûr′) *vt.* asserire.
average (ăv′ĕr·ĭj) *n.* media; (*naut.*) avaria, rischio. *agg.* medio. *vt.* fare o sostenere la media di.
averse (d·vûrs′) *agg.* avverso; contrario; ostile.
aversion (d·vûr′zhŭn; -shŭn) *n.* contrarietà, avversione.
avert (d·vûrt′) *vt.* evitare, schivare; distogliere.
aviary (ā′vǐ·ĕr′ǐ) *n.* uccelliera.
aviation (ā′vǐ·ā′shŭn) *n.* aviazione.
aviator (ā′vǐ·ā′tĕr; ăv′ǐ-) *n.* aviatore.
avid (ăv′ǐd) *agg.* avido.

avocation (ăv′ŏ·kā′shŭn) *n.* passatempo preferito, occupazione, professione.
avoid (d·void′) *vt.* evitare, schivare.
avow (d·vou′) *vt.* confessare, ammettere. **—al** *n.* confessione.
await (d·wāt′) *vt.* aspettare.
awake (d·wāk′) *vt.* (*pass.* awoke, *pp.* awaked) svegliare. *vi.* svegliarsi. *agg.* sveglio; conscio.
awaken (d·wāk′ĕn) *vt.* svegliare. **—ing** *n.* risveglio.
award (d·wòrd′) *n.* decisione, sentenza, attribuzione; premio; conferimento. *vt.* assegnare, aggiudicare, conferire (*premi, ecc.*).
aware (d·wâr′) *agg.* conscio, consapevole.
away (d·wā′) *avv.* via, lontano: to do — with, sopprimere; right —, subito, seduta stante; to give oneself —, tradirsi, svelarsi.
awe (ô) *n.* rispetto; sacro timore: to stand in — of, temere. *vt.* imporre rispetto; intimorire; stupire.
awful (ô′fōōl; -f'l) *agg.* terribile; solenne, imponente. **—ly** *avv.* terribilmente; notevolmente, molto.
awhile [(d·hwīl′) *avv.* momentaneamente, brevemente; un poco; un momento.
awkward (ôk′wĕrd) *agg.* goffo, maldestro; imbarazzante; imbarazzato; scomodo.
awl (ôl) *n.* lesina, punteruolo.
awning (ôn′ǐng) *n.* tenda, riparo.
awoke (d·wōk′) *pass. di* awake.
AWOL, awol (ā′wòl) *agg.*, assente senza permesso, assente ingiustificato (*mil.*).
awry (d·rī′) *agg.*, *avv.* storto, di sghimbescio.
ax, axe (ăks) *n.* ascia, scure.
axis (ăk′sǐs) *n.* (*pl.* axes) asse (*di rotazione*).
axle (ăk′s′l) *n.* assale, asse, sala (*di ruota*); — box, mozzo di ruota.
axletree (ăk′s′l trē′) *n.* assale.
ay, aye (I) *avv.* sì, davvero. *n.* voto favorevole, assenso.
azote (ăz′ōt) *n.* azoto.
azure (ăzh′ĕr; ā′zhĕr) *agg.* azzurro. **—stone** *n.* lapislazzuli.

B

babble (băb′'l) *n.* balbettìo, chiacchierìo; ciarla. *vi.* balbettare; straparlare; ciarlare. *vt.* far pettegolezzi, divulgare.
babbler *n.* chiacchierone.
babe (bāb) *n.* neonato; (*fam.*) ragazza.
baboon (bă·bōōn′) *n.* babbuino.

baby (bā′bǐ) *n.* bimbo, creatura; ragazza: — sitter, bambinaia a ore. *vt.* ninnare; coccolare. **—ish** *agg.* infantile. **—hood** *n.* infanzia.
bachelor (băch′ĕ·lĕr) *n.* celibe, scapolo: — of arts, diplomato in lettere.

bacillus (bå·sĭl'ŭs) n. (pl. **bacilli**) bacillo.

back (băk) n. schiena, dorso, tergo, parte posteriore; schienale. agg. posteriore; arretrato. avv. addietro; indietro; di ritorno: years —, anni addietro; to come —, tornare indietro; to call —, richiamare; to give —, restituire; — and forth, avanti e indietro. vt. sostenere, spalleggiare; aiutare; avallare. vi. retrocedere, ritirarsi: to — out, to — down, ritirarsi.

backbite (băk'bīt) vt. denigrare, sparlare (di).

backbone (băk'bōn') n. colonna vertebrale; fermezza; sostegno.

backer (băk'ēr) n. finanziatore; sostenitore.

backfire (băk'fīr') n. ritorno di fiamma.

background (băk'ground') n. fondo; sfondo; fondale; precedenti (di una persona); retroscena; musica di fondo.

backhand (băk'hănd') n. dorso della mano; scrittura revesciata; colpo rovescio.

backhanded (băk'hăn'děd) agg. revescio, a rovescio; indiretto; ironico: — stroke, manrovescio.

backing (băk'ĭng) n. appoggio; garanzia; scommessa.

backward (băk'wěrd) agg. arretrato, retrogrado. avv. (also **backwards**) dietro; indietro; a ritroso. —ness n. lentezza; riluttanza; mentalità retrograda.

bacon (bā'kŭn; -k'n) n. pancetta affumicata.

bacterial (băk·tēr'ĭ.ǎl) agg. batterico.

bacteriology (băk·tēr'ĭ·ŏl'ō·jĭ) n. batteriologia.

bad (băd) agg. cattivo, malvagio; cagionevole (in salute); sfavorevole; dannoso: — coin, moneta falsa; from — to worse, di male in peggio. —ly avv. malamente, fortemente; gravemente. —ness n. cattiveria; cattiva qualità.

bade (băd) pass. di to bid.

badge (băj) n. distintivo, insegna, emblema; decorazione.

badger (băj'ēr) (1) n. (zool.) tasso.

badger (2) vt. tormentare; perseguitare.

baffle (băf'l) vt. frustrare; disorientare, sconcertare, confondere.

bag (băg) n. borsa, valigia, sacco. vt. insaccare, rubare. vi. insaccarsi, gonfiarsi.

baggage (băg'ĭj) n. bagaglio.

bagpipe (băg'pīp) n. cornamusa.

bail (bāl) n. libertà provvisoria dietro cauzione; cauzione. vt. versare cauzione per scarcerare; (naut.) aggottare: to — out, lanciarsi col paracadute.

bait (bāt) vt. adescare; aizzare. n. esca.

bake (băk) vt. cuocere al forno. vi. fare il pane; cuocersi, abbrustolirsi.

baker (băk'ēr) n. fornaio.

bakery (băk'ēr.ĭ) n. panetteria.

baking-powder n. lievito in polvere.

balance (băl'ǎns) n. bilancia, equilibrio; (comm.) saldo; residuo attivo. vt. bilanciare, pesare, equilibrare; soppesare; saldare, pareggiare (un conto). vi. bilanciarsi, barcamenarsi.

balcony (băl'kō·nĭ) n. balcone; (teat.) balconata, galleria.

bald (bōld) agg. calvo; brullo; nudo; squallido, disadorno. —ness n. calvizie; squallore.

bale (bāl) n. balla. vt. imballare. —ful agg. minaccioso, funesto.

balk (bōk) n. ostacolo; delusione. vt. frustrare, ostacolare; sconcertare. vi. esitare, recalcitrare.

ball (bōl) (1) n. palla, sfera; gomitolo: —bearing, cuscinetto a sfere.

ball (2) n. ballo: —room, sala da ballo; — point pen, penna a sfera.

ballad (băl'ǎd) n. ballata.

ballast (băl'ǎst) n. zavorra; pietrisco. vt. zavorrare.

balloon (bå·lōōn') n. aerostato.

ballot (băl'ŏt) n. ballotta, palla o scheda (per votazioni); voto; — box, urna. vt., vi. votare.

balm (bäm) n. balsamo.

balmy (bäm'ĭ) agg. balsamico; scriterlato.

balsam (bōl'sǎm) n. balsamo.

bamboo (băm·bōō') n. bambù.

ban (băn) n. bando, interdizione. vt. bandire; vietare; maledire.

banal (bā'nǎl) agg. banale.

band (bănd) (1) n. fascia; banda; benda, nastro. vt. legare, fasciare. vi. imbrancarsi; —saw, sega a nastro.

band (2) n. banda, orchestra: — leader, capobanda. —stand n. podio dell'orchestra.

bandage (băn'dĭj) n. bendaggio. vt. bendare, medicare.

bandanna (băn·dăn'å) n. fazzolettone colorato.

bandit (băn'dĭt) n. bandito, brigante.

bang (băng) n. colpo, schianto, tonfo. vt. tempestare di colpi; sbattere, percuotere.

bangle (băng'g'l) n. braccialetto.

banish (băn'ĭsh) vt. bandire, esiliare. —ment n. bando, esilio.

banister (băn'ĭs.tēr) n. ringhiera.

bank (băngk) (1) n. sponda, riva, argine, altura, margine o ciglio (di *strada*); banco (*di nubi*); (*aeron.*) inclinazione in virata. *vt.* ammucchiare, ammonticchiare; (*aeron.*) inclinare in virata. —**ing** *n.* arginatura; diga.

bank (2) *n.* banca, banco; panca, sedile, seggio: blood —, banca del sangue; **piggy** —, salvadanaio. *vt.* depositare in banca: to — upon, contare su. —**book** *n.* libretto bancario. —**er** *n.* banchiere. —**ing** *n.* operazioni bancarie, attività bancaria. *agg.* bancario. —**note** *n.* banconota.

bankrupt (băngk'rŭpt) *agg.* fallito; rovinato. *vt.* far fallire, rovinare.

bankruptcy (băngk'rŭpt.sĭ) *n.* fallimento, bancarotta.

banner (băn'ĕr) *n.* stendardo, bandiera.

banns (bănz) *n.* pubblicazioni matrimoniali.

banquet (băng'kwĕt) *n.* banchetto.

banter (băn'tĕr) *n.* scherzo. *vt.* scherzare.

baptism (băp'tĭz'm) *n.* battesimo.

baptize (băp.tīz') *vt.* battezzare.

bar (bär) *n.* sbarra; bar, mescita; barriera, ostacolo; tavoletta (*di cioccolata*); tribunale; foro; magistratura; (*legge*) banco (*degli accusati*): **called to the** —, ammesso a esercitare l'avvocatura; **to read for the** —, studiare legge. *vt.* sbarrare, impedire, vietare, bloccare.

barb (bärb) *n.* punta di ferro. —**ed** *agg.* irto di punte, seghettato, spinato: —**wire,** filo spinato.

barbarian (bär.bâr'ĭ.ăn) *n.* barbaro.

barbarous (bär'bá.rŭs) *agg.* barbaro.

barbecue (bär'bē.kū) *n.* animale arrostito intero; festino all'aperto: **to** —, mettere allo spiedo (*un animale intero*).

barber (bär'bĕr) *n.* barbiere.

bard (bärd) *n.* bardo, trovatore.

bare (bâr) *agg.* nudo, scoperto; solo, semplice; squallido, brullo; palese; smobiliato: **to lay** —, mettere a nudo. *vt.* scoprire; denudare; spogliare, rivelare. —**foot** *agg.* scalzo. —**ly** *avv.* a malapena, soltanto. —**ness** *n.* nudità, squallore.

barfly (bär'flĭ) *n.* frequentatore di bar.

bargain (bär'gĭn) *n.* baratto, affare, contrattazione: **into the** —, per soprammercato; — **sale,** liquidazione. *vt.* mercanteggiare, contrattare: **to** — **for,** prevedere.

barge (bärj) *n.* chiatta, barcone.

bark (bärk) *n.* corteccia, scorza; brigantino, veliero; latrato. *vt.* scortecciare, scorticare. *vi.* latrare, abbaiare.

barley (bär'lĭ) *n.* orzo.

barn (bärn) *n.* baracca, granaio. —**yard** *n.* cortile di fattoria.

barometer (bá.rŏm'ē.tĕr) *n.* barometro.

baron (băr'ŭn) *n.* barone; finanziere.

barracks (băr'ăks) *n.pl.* caserma.

barrel (băr'ĕl) *n.* barile, botte; canna (*di arma da fuoco*). *vt.* imbarilare. *vi.* correre a grande velocità, filare.

barren (băr'ĕn) *agg.* nudo, sterile, squallido. —**ness** *n.* sterilità, squallore.

barricade (băr'ĭ.kād') *n.* barricata. *vt.* barricare.

barrier (băr'ĭ.ĕr) *n.* barriera, ostacolo.

barring (bär'ĭng) *prep.* eccetto, eccettuato, tranne: — **mistakes,** salvo errori.

barrister (băr'ĭs.tĕr) *n.* avvocato.

barrow (băr'ō) *n.* barella; carretto.

barter (bär'tĕr) *n.* baratto. *vi.* barattare.

base (bās) (1) *agg.* basso, vile, spregevole. —**ness** *n.* bassezza.

base (2) *n.* base, fondamento. *vt.* basare. —**ment** *n.* seminterrato, sotterraneo.

bashful (băsh'fŏŏl; -f'l) *agg.* timido, modesto, pudico. —**ness** *n.* timidezza.

basic (bās'ĭk) *agg.* basilare, fondamentale; (*chim.*) basico.

basin (bā's'n) *n.* bacile, catinella; bacino.

basis (bā'sĭs) *n.* (*pl.* bases) base, fondamento.

bask (bȧsk) *vi.* riscaldarsi; crogiolarsi: **to** — **in the sun,** crogiolarsi al sole.

basket (bås'kĕt) *n.* cesto, paniere. —**ball** *n.* pallacanestro.

bass (bås) (1) *n.,* *agg.* (*mus.*) basso: **double** —, contrabbasso. — **viol** *n.* violone.

bass (bås) (2) *n.* pesce persico.

bassoon (bȧ.sōōn') *n.* (*mus.*) fagotto.

bastard (băs'tĕrd) *n.,* *agg.* bastardo; farabutto.

baste (bāst) *vt.* imbastire; bastonare, redarguire; ungere (*la carne durante la cottura*).

bat (băt) (1) *n.* mazza; colpo; baldoria. *vt.,* *vi.* battere; fare il battitore, battere (*al baseball*): **not to** — **an eye,** non batter ciglio.

bat (2) *n.* pipistrello; missile radiocomandato.

batch (băch) *n.* infornata; lotto, partita.

bath (bȧth) *n.* bagno, stanza da bagno: — **house,** stabilimento balneare, cabina balneare, bagni pubblici; —**robe,** accappatoio; —**tub,** vasca (da bagno).

bathe (bāᵗh) *vt.* bagnare, lavare. *vi.* bagnarsi, fare il bagno.

bather (bāᵗh'ĕr) *n.* bagnante.

battalion (bǎ.tǎl'yŭn) *n.* battaglione.

batter (bǎt'ĕr) *vt.* battere, tempestare di colpi; logorare; sfigurare: **to —down**, demolire.

battery (bǎt'ĕr.ĭ) *n.* batteria, accumulatore; percosse; assalto.

battle (bǎt'ʼl) *n.* battaglia, combattimento. **—field**, *n.* campo di battaglia. **—ship**, *n.* corazzata.

bauble (bô'b'l) *n.* gingillo.

bawdy (bôd'ĭ) *agg.* osceno: **—house**, postribolo.

bawl (bôl) *n.* urlo, schiamazzo. *vi.* urlare, schiamazzare.

bay (bā) (1) *n.* alloro: **— tree**, lauro.

bay (2) *n.* baia, golfo, insenatura; alcova, rientranza: **bomb —**, rastrelliera *o* compartimento delle bombe.

bay (3) *n.* latrato. *vi.* latrare: **at —**, ai ferri corti, con le spalle al muro, in scacco.

bay (4) *agg.* baio.

bayonet (bā'ŏnĕt; -nĭt) *n.* baionetta. *vt.* colpire con baionetta.

bazooka (bȧ.zŏŏ'kȧ) *n.* cannone portatile anticarro.

be (bē) *vi.* (*pass.* was, *pl.* were, *pp.* been) essere, esistere, vivere, stare, dovere: so — it, così sia; **— that as it may**, comunque sia; **to — well**, star bene; **to — cold** (warm, hungry, right, wrong), aver freddo, (caldo, fame, ragione, torto); **to — ten years old**, avere dieci anni.

beach (bēch) *n.* spiaggia, riva. *vt.* tirare in secca. **—head**, *n.* testa di ponte.

beacon (bē'kŭn; -k'n) *n.* faro, segnalazione luminosa.

bead (bēd) *n.* grano, perlina, goccia, bolla: **to tell one's beads**, sgranare il rosario.

beak (bēk) *n.* becco, beccuccio; sperone (*di nave*); prómontorio.

beam (bēm) *n.* trave; timone (*di aratro, ecc.*); raggio (*di luce*); fusto (*dell'ancora*); sorriso; asta (*di bilancia*). *vt.* irradiare. *vi.* sorridere radiosamente, risplendere. **—ing** *agg.* raggiante, sorridente.

beamy (bēm'ĭ) *agg.* luminoso, radioso.

bean (bēn) *n.* fava, fagiolo; chicco, grano: **string—**, fagiolino; **to be full of beans**, essere di ottimo umore.

bear (bâr) *n.* orso; (*borsa*) giocatore al ribasso. *vt.* (*pass.* bore, *pp.* borne) reggere, sostenere; sopportare, subire; generare. *vi.* reggere, resistere; svoltare; pesare; avere attinenza, riferirsi; pazientare: **to — oneself**, comportarsi; **to — out**, sostenere,

convalidare; **to — witness**, testimoniare; **to — a grudge**, serbare rancore; **to — in mind**, tenere a mente; **to — up**, tener duro; **to — upon**, aver attinenza con. **—able** *agg.* sopportabile.

beard (bērd) *n.* barba. *vt.* affrontare, sfidare. **—ed** *agg.* barbuto.

bearer (bâr'ĕr) *n.* portatore, latore.

bearing (bâr'ĭng) *n.* comportamento, portamento, atteggiamento; rapporto, attinenza; orientamento: **ball —**, cuscinetto a sfere; **to lose one's bearings**, disorientarsi; **to get one's bearings**, orientarsi.

beast (bēst) *n.* bestia, animale. **—ly** *agg.* bestiale, orrendo.

beat (bēt) *n.* battito, palpito; itinerario, ronda. *vt.* (*pass.* beat, *pp.* beaten) battere, colpire, martellare; sconfiggere; sferzare: **to — about the bush**, tergiversare, menare il can per l'aia; **to — down**, abbattere, diminuire, sfondare. **—en** *agg.* abbattuto; vinto, battuto; scoraggiato. **—er** *n.* battitore; frullino. **—ing** *n.* battito; percosse; busse; sconfitta.

beatitude (bē.ǎt'ĭ.tūd) *n.* beatitudine, felicità.

beau (bō) *n.* spasimante, corteggiatore.

beau idéal (bō'ĭ·dē'ǎl) *n.* (*fr.*) bellezza perfetta; ideale perfetto.

beauteous (bū'tē·ŭs) *n.* bello, incantevole.

beautician (bū·tĭsh'ǎn) *n.* estetista.

beautiful (bū'tĭ·fŏŏl; -f'l) *agg.* bello.

beautify (bū'tĭ·fĭ) *vt.* abbellire. *vi.* abbellirsi, truccarsi.

beauty (bū'tĭ) *n.* bellezza: **— spot**, neo.

beaver (bē'vĕr) *n.* castoro; lana di castoro; cappello di feltro castoro.

beaverboard *n.* cartone per tramezze.

became (bē.kām') *pass. di* become.

because (bē·kôz'; -kŏz') *cong.* perchè: **— of**, a causa di, per.

beck (bĕk) *n.* cenno: **at one's — and call**, a completa disposizione (agli ordini) di uno.

beckon (bĕk'ŭn) *vt., vi.* far cenno; chiamare.

become (bē·kŭm') *vi.* (*pass.* became, *pp.* become) divenire, cominciare a essere, succedere. *vt.* addirsi, attagliarsi, essere degno di.

becoming (bē·kŭm'ĭng) *agg.* acconcio, adatto; che sta bene *o* si addice (*di vestiario, ecc.*)

bed (bĕd) *n.* giaciglio; letto; alveo; fondo (*del mare*); aiuola; giacimento (*min.*): **— and board**, vitto e alloggio; **to take to one's —**, mettersi a letto (*malato*); **to make one's own —**, and have to lie in it, agire di propria testa e sopportarne le conseguenze.

bedbug (bĕd′bŭg′) *n*. cimice.

bedclothes (bĕd′klōthz) *n.pl.* coltri.

bedfellow (bĕd′fĕl′ō) *n*. compagno di stanza.

bedlam (bĕd′lăm) *n*. pandemonio.

bedraggle (bĕ-drăg′′l) *vt*. infangare, insozzare. **—d** *agg*. malconcio, infangato.

bedside (bĕd′sīd′) *n*. capezzale.

bedtime (bĕd′tīm′) *n*. ora di coricarsi.

bee (bē) *n*. ape: **to have a — in one's bonnet**, avere una fissazione.

beech (bēch) *n*. faggio.

beechnut (bēch′nŭt′) *n*. faggiuola.

beef (bēf) *n*. manzo (*carne*). **—steak** *n*. bistecca. **—tea** *n*. brodo ristretto.

beehive (bē′hīv′) *n*. alveare.

beeline (bē′līn′) *n*. linea diretta, linea d'aria.

been (bĭn; Ingh. bēn) *pp. di* to be.

beer (bēr) *n*. birra. **—house**, **—shop** *n*. birreria.

beet (bēt) *n*. barbabietola.

beetle (bē′t′l) *n*. scarafaggio.

befall (bĕ-fôl′) *vt*., *vi*. (*pass*. befell, *pp*. befallen) accadere, succedere.

befit (bĕ-fĭt′) *vt*. convenire, addirsi.

before (bĕ-fōr′) *avv*., *prep*. davanti a, prima di; precedentemente; più avanti di, al cospetto di: **long —**, molto tempo prima.

beforehand (bĕ-fōr′hănd′) *avv*. in anticipo, precedentemente.

befriend (bĕ-frĕnd′) *vt*. aiutare, sostenere, soccorrere.

beg (bĕg) *vt*. pregare, implorare; chiedere. *vi*. elemosinare: **to — leave**, chiedere il permesso, prendersi la libertà; **to — the question**, supporre come vero.

began (bĕgăn′) *pass. di* to begin.

beget (bĕ-gĕt′) *vt*. (*pass*. begot, *pp*. begot, begotten) generare, produrre, causare.

beggar (bĕg′ĕr) *n*. mendicante, furfante. *vt*. impoverire, rovinare.

begin (bĕ-gĭn′) *vt*., *vi*. (*pass*. began, *pp*. begun) cominciare, iniziare, esordire, accingersi: **to — with**, innanzi tutto, per cominciare. **—ner** *n*. principiante. **—ning** *n*. inizio, esordio, principio, origine.

begot (bĕ-gŏt′) *pass., pp. di* to beget.

beguile (bĕ-gīl′) *vt*. ingannare, adescare.

begun (bĕ-gŭn′) *pp. di* to begin.

behalf (bĕ-häf′) *n.*: **in — of**, in favore di; **on — of**, a nome (*per conto*) di.

behave (bĕ-hāv′) *vi*. comportarsi; **to — oneself**, omportaersi bene.

behavior (bĕ-hāv′yĕr) *n*. condotta, comportamento.

behead (bĕ-hĕd′) *vt*. decapitare.

beheld (bĕ-hĕld′) *pass., pp. di* to behold.

behind (bĕ-hīnd′) *prep*., *avv*. dietro; indietro; in arretrato; in ritardo: **— time**, in ritardo. **—hand** *agg*. arretrato, tardo. *avv*. indietro, in arretrato.

behold (bĕ-hōld′) *vt*. (*pass., pp.* beheld) contemplare, guardare.

behoove (bĕ-hōōv′) *vt*. convenire, essere acconcio: **it behooves me to go**, conviene che io vada.

being (bē′ĭng) *n*. essere, esistenza: **human —**, essere umano; **for the time —**, per il momento.

belated (bĕ-lāt′ĕd; -ĭd) *agg*. tardivo, fuori orario.

belch (bĕlch) *n*. rutto; eruzione. *vt*., *vi*. ruttare; eruttare: **to — forth**, vomitare.

belfry (bĕl′frĭ) *n*. campanile.

Belgian (bĕl′jĭ.ăn) *n.*, *agg*. belga.

belie (bĕ-lī′) *vt*. smentire.

belief (bĕ-lēf′) *n*. credenza, convinzione, fede.

believable (bĕ-lēv′ȧ-b′l) *agg*. attendibile, credibile.

believe (bĕ-lēv′) *vt*., *vi*. credere, ritenere, prestar fede, supporre. **believer** *n*. credente, fedele.

belittle (bĕ-lĭt′′l) *vt*. sminuire, svalutare, minimizzare.

bell (bĕl) *n*. campana, campanello; rintocco; calice (*di fiore*): **— buoy**, boa sonora. *vi*. bramire: **to — the cat**, assumersi una responsabilità.

bellboy (bĕl′boi′), **bellhop** (bĕl′hŏp′) *n*. inserviente d'albergo.

belle (bĕl) *n*. bella: **the — of the village**, la bella del paese.

bellflower (bĕl′flou′ĕr) *n*. campanula.

belligerency (bĕl·lij′ĕr.ĕn.sĭ) *n*. aggressività; belligeranza.

belligerent (bĕl·lij′ĕr.ĕnt) *n*. belligerante. *agg*. battagliero, bellicoso.

bellow (bĕl′ō) *n*. muggito. *vi*. muggire, mugghiare; gridare, tuonare.

bellows (bĕl′ōz; -ŭs) *n.pl.* mantice.

belly (bĕl′ĭ) *n*. ventre, pancia.

belong (bĕ-lŏng′) *vi*. appartenere, essere di proprietà (*di*); far parte (*di*). **—ings** *n.pl.* effetti personali; beni; bagaglio.

beloved (bĕ-lŭv′ĕd; bĕ-lŭvd′) *n.*, *agg*. amato, adorato, diletto.

below (bĕ-lō′) *prep*. sotto, al disotto di; a valle di. *avv*. inferiormente, da basso, in basso.

belt (bělt) *n.* cinghia, cintura, cinturone, fascia: **to hit below the —,** infliggere un colpo basso, colpire slealmente. *vt.* cingere; staffilare.

bemoan (bě·mōn′) *vt.* compiangere, deplorare. *vi.* gemere, addolorarsi.

bemuse (bě·mūz′) *vt.* confondere, disorientare.

bench (běnch) *n.* sedile, panca; seggio; banco di lavoro; tribunale.

bend (běnd) *n.* curva, curvatura; inclinazione; (*naut.*) nodo. *vt.* (*pass.* bent, *pp.* bent, bended) piegare, curvare, inclinare, torcere; téndere (*l'arco*); flettere (*le ginocchia*); (*fig.*) adattare, orientare; (*naut.*) ormeggiare, guarnire: **to — one's endeavors to,** dedicare i propri sforzi a. *vi.* piegarsi, curvarsi, chinarsi, inclinarsi, adattarsi, propendere.

beneath (bě·nēth′) *avv., prep.* sotto, al disotto, in basso.

benediction (běn′ě·dĭk′shŭn) *n.* benedizione.

benefactor (běn′ě·făk′tĕr) *n.* benefattore.

beneficence (bě·něf′ĭ·sěns) *n.* beneficenza.

beneficent (-sěnt) *agg.* caritatevole.

beneficial (běn′ě·fĭsh′ăl) *agg.* benefico, vantaggioso.

benefit (běn′ě·fĭt) *n.* beneficio, profitto, vantaggio: **— performance,** spettacolo di beneficenza; **— society,** società di mutuo soccorso; **— night,** serata in onore. *vt.* beneficare. *vi.* beneficiare (*di*), trarre vantaggio (*da*); approfittare.

benevolence (bě·něv′ō·lěns) *n.* benevolenza, carità.

benevolent *agg.* benevolo, caritatevole.

benign (bě·nĭn′) **—ant** (bě·nĭg′nănt) *agg.* benevolo, benigno, affabile.

bent (běnt) *agg.* curvato, piegato, propenso; deciso, risoluto. *n.* tendenza, propensione; attitudine; curva. *pass., pp. di* to bend.

benumb (bě·nŭm′) *vt.* intirizzire, paralizzare; intontire; intorpidire.

benzene (běn′zēn; běn·zēn′) *n.* benzolo.

bequeath (bě·kwēth′) *vt.* legare, assegnare in eredità.

bequest (bě·kwěst′) *n.* legato, lascito.

berate (bě·rāt′) *vt.* redarguire.

berry (běr′ĭ) *n.* bacca, chicco: **coffee in the —,** caffè in grani.

berserk (bûr′sûrk; bûr·sûrk′) *agg.* infuriato: **to go —,** perdere la testa, abbandonarsi a violenze.

berth (bûrth) *n.* cuccetta, letto; riparo, nicchia; impiego; ormeggio: **to give a wide — to,** girar largo da, schivare. *vt., vi.* ormeggiarsi, dare *o* prendere alloggio.

beseech (bě·sēch′) *vt.* (*pass., pp.* besought) supplicare, implorare.

beset (bě·sět′) *vt.* (*pass., pp.* beset) assediare, assillare; ingombrare.

beside (bě·sīd′) *prep.* accanto a; di fianco a; vicino a; in confronto a; oltre a; all'infuori di: **to be — oneself,** esser fuori di sè.

besides (bě·sīdz′) *avv.* d'altronde, per giunta. *prep.* oltre a.

besiege (bě·sēj′) *vt.* assediare.

besieger *n.* assediante.

besought (bě·sòt′) *pass., pp. di* to beseech.

best (běst) *agg.* (*superl. di* good) (il) migliore, ottimo: **at —,** tutt'al più; **— man,** testimone alle nozze; **for the —,** per il meglio; **to do one's —,** fare del proprio meglio; **to have the — of,** avere il sopravvento su; **to make the — of,** trarre il miglior partito da. *avv.* meglio.

bestow (bě·stō′) *vt.* elargire, concedere, conferire: **to — a favor on,** rendere un servigio a.

bet (bět) *n.* scommessa, puntata. *vt., vi.* scommettere, puntare, sfidare: **you bet!** ci puoi scommettere!, eccome!

betake (bě·tāk′) *vt.* (*pass.* betook, *pp.* betaken): **to — oneself,** andare, dirigersi.

betatron (bē′tá·trŏn) *n.* betatrone.

betray (bě·trā′) *vt.* tradire, ingannare; rivelare; trarre in inganno: **—al** *n.* tradimento. **—er** *n.* traditore.

betrothed (bě·trŏtht′; -trŏthd′) *agg. n.* fidanzato.

betrothal (bě·trŏth′ăl) *n.* fidanzamento.

better (bět′ĕr) *agg.* (*comp. di* good) migliore, meglio: **you had —,** fareste meglio, vi converrebbe; **to get the — of,** aver la meglio, *o* il sopravvento su. *avv.* meglio: **— and —,** di bene in meglio; **a change for the —,** un cambiamento in meglio; **so much the —,** tanto meglio; **to be —,** stare meglio; **to get —,** migliorare; **to think — of it,** ripensarci, mutare parere. *vt.* migliorare: **to — oneself,** migliorare la propria posizione. **—ment** *n.* miglioramento.

betting *n.* scommessa, puntata.

bettor (bět′ĕr) *n.* scommettitore.

between (bě·twēn′) *prep., avv.* tra, fra, nel mezzo, in mezzo: **far —,** distante, a lunghi intervalli.

beverage (běv′ĕr·ĭj) *n.* beveraggio, bibita.

bevy (běv′ĭ) *n.* stormo, combriccola.

bewail (bě·wāl′) *vt.* piangere. *vi.* lamentarsi. **—ing** *n.* lamentazione.

beware (bḗ·wâr') *vi.* guardarsi, diffidare.

bewilder (bḗ·wĭl'dẽr) *vt.* disorientare, confondere, stupire, sconcertare. **—ing** *agg.* sconcertante. **—ment** *n.* smarrimento, disorientamento.

bewitch (bḗ·wĭch') *vt.* stregare, incantare, affascinare. **—ing** *agg.* affascinante, seducente.

beyond (bḗ·yŏnd') *prep.*, *avv.* al di là, oltre, al disopra, più lontano: — my reach, fuori della mia portata.

bias (bī'ẟs) *n.* inclinazione, pendenza; diagonale; sbieco; propensione; preconcetto, prevenzione: on the —, di sbieco. *agg.* di sbieco. *vt.* far pendere, influire su, influenzare. **—ed,** *agg.* prevenuto.

bib (bĭb) *n.* bavaglino, pettorina (*di* grembiule).

Bible (bī'b'l) *n.* bibbia.

biblical (bĭb'lĭ·kǎl) *agg.* biblico.

biceps (bī'sĕps) *n.* bicipite.

bicker (bĭk'ẽr) *vi.* bisticciare, discutere.

bicycle (bī'sĭk·'l) *n.* bicicletta.

bid (bĭd) *vt.* (*pass.* bade, *pp.* bidden) ordinare, ingiungere, esortare, offrire: to — farewell, dire addio; it bids fair to, promette di, c'è speranza che. *n.* offerta (*a un'asta*); invito; tentativo; appello.

bidden (bĭd''n) *pp. di* to bid.

bidder *n.* offerente.

bide (bīd) *vt.* aspettare pazientemente: to — one's time, aspettare il momento opportuno.

bier (bēr) *n.* catafalco, bara.

big (bĭg) *agg.* grande, grosso; ampio, spazioso; importante: to grow bigger, crescere; to act —, darsi delle arie; to talk —, fare il gradasso; — Dipper, Orsa Maggiore; — sister (brother), sorella (fratello) maggiore; — game, caccia grossa; — with child, incinta; **—-bellied,** panciuto; **—-hearted,** magnanimo. **—ness** *n.* grossezza, grandezza, importanza.

bigamist (bĭg'ǎ·mĭst) *n.* bigamo.

bigamy (bĭg'ǎ·mĭ) *n.* bigamia.

bigot (bĭg'ŭt) *n.* fanatico. **—ry** fanatismo.

bike (bīk) *n.* (*gergo*) bicicletta, bici.

bile (bīl) *n.* bile.

bilge (bĭlj) *n.* sentina.

bill (bĭl) (1) *n.* becco (*d'uccello*).

bill (2) *n.* conto, fattura, nota; banconota; cambiale; progetto di legge; manifesto: — of exchange, tratta, cambiale; — of fare, lista delle vivande; — of lading, lettera di carico; to draw a —, spiccare tratta; to take up a —, onorare una cambiale; — of rights, dichiarazione dei diritti; — of sale, atto di vendita. *vt.* aggiudicare; mandare un conto a; annunciare; mettere in programma. **—case,** **—fold** *n.* portafoglio, portacarte.

billet (bĭl'ĕt) *vt.* alloggiare, acquartierare.

billiards (bĭl'yẽrdz) *n.* biliardo.

billion (bĭl'yŭn) *n.* bilione, miliardo: (*in U.S.*) un miliardo = mille milioni; (*in G.B.*) un milione di milioni.

billow (bĭl'ō) *n.* onda, cavallone, maroso. *vi.* gonfiarsi, ingrossarsi.

bin (bĭn) *n.* barattolo, bidone; deposito.

bind (bīnd) *vt.* (*pass.*, *pp.* bound) legare, impegnare, assicurare, cingere; rilegare (*libri*). **—er** *n.* legatore, rilegatore. **—ing** *n.* rilegatura; bordatura. *agg.* impegnativo, obbligatorio.

biochemistry (bī'ō·kĕm'ĭs·trĭ) *n.* biochimica.

biographer (bī·ŏg'rá·fẽr) *n.* biografo.

biography (bī·ŏg'rá·fĭ) *n.* biografia.

biologist (bī·ŏl'ō·jĭst) *n.* biologo.

biology (bī·ŏl'ō·jĭ) *n.* biologia.

birch (bûrch) *n.* betulla, verga.

bird (bûrd) *n.* uccello. **—seed,** *n.* becchime. **—shot,** *n.* pallini da caccia.

birth (bûrth) *n.* nascita, origine, discendenza: to give— to, mettere alla luce, provocare, dar luogo a. **—day** *n.* compleanno. **—mark** *n.* voglia, segno caratteristico (*di persona*). **—place** *n.* luogo di nascita. **—rate** *n.* natalità. **—right** *n.* diritto di nascita, diritto ereditario; primogenitura.

biscuit (bĭs'kĭt) *n.* biscotto.

bishop (bĭsh'ŭp) *n.* vescovo.

bison (bī's'n; -z'n) *n.* bisonte.

bit (bĭt) (1) *n.* pezzetto, briciola, frammento; attimo: a — more, un po' di più; — by —, a poco a poco; not to care a —, infischiarsene.

bit (bĭt) (2) *n.* morso (*di cavallo*); punta di trapano.

bitch (bĭch) *n.* cagna; femmina (*di* lupo, *ecc.*); strega, donnaccia. *vi.* lagnarsi, brontolare.

bite (bīt) *n.* morso; presa; boccone; puntura (*d'insetto*). *vt.* (*pass.* bit, *pp.* bitten) mordere, rosicchiare; addentare; pungere, corrodere.

biting (bīt'ĭng) *agg.* mordente, mordace.

bitter (bĭt'ẽr) *agg.* amaro; accanito; pungente, aspro: to fight to the — end, lottare sino alla morte. **—ly** *avv.* amaramente, aspramente.

—ness *n.* amarezza. —sweet *agg.* agrodolce.

bitters *n. pl.* liquore amaro, stomatico.

blabber (blăb′ĕr) *vi.* chiacchierare.

black (blăk) *agg.* nero, scuro, cupo; iniquo; negro. *n.* nero; (*comm.*) attivo. *vt.* annerire; lustrare (*scarpe*). —**ball** *n.* palla nera; bocciatura. *vt.* bocciare. —**berry** *n.* mora. —**bird** *n.* merlo. —**board** *n.* lavagna. —**en** *vt.* annerire; scurire; denigrare. —**guard** (blăg′-)*n.* mascalzone. —**lead** *n.* grafite. —**leg** *n.* imbroglione. —**mail** *n.* ricatto. *vt.* ricattare. —**mailer** *n.* ricattatore. — **market**, mercato nero. —**marketeer** *n.* borsanerista. —**ness** *n.* nerezza, tenebra. —**out** *n.* oscuramento; ottenebramento; *vt.* oscurare; ottenebrare; censurare. —**smith** *n.* fabbro.

bladder (blăd′ĕr) *n.* vescica.

blade (blād) *n.* lama, parte tagliente (*di un utensile*); filo (*d'erba*); pala (*di remo o elica*)

blame (blām) *n.* biasimo, colpa. *vt.* biasimare, attribuire la colpa a, tenere responsabile. —**less** *agg.* innocente, irreprensibile.

blameworthy (blām′wûr′thĭ) *agg.* blasimevole.

blanch (blánch) *vt.* imbianchire, schiarire; mondare; scottare (*nell'acqua bollente*). *vi.* sbiancare, impallidire.

bland (blănd) *agg.* blando, soave, meliffuo. —**ishment** *n.* blandizie, lusinga

blank (blăngk) *n.* lacuna; spazio bianco; vuoto; centro (*del bersaglio*); pezzo semilavorato. *agg.* bianco, in bianco; (*fig.*) vuoto, sconcertato.— **form**, modulo in bianco; — **face**, volto inespressivo; — **countenance**, espressione sconcertata; — **verse**, verso sciolto; — **cartridge**, cartuccia a salve.

blanket (blăng′kĕt) *n.* coltre, coperta; **wet** —, guastafeste. *agg.* generale, complessivo, cumulativo.

blare (blâr) *n.* fragore; squillo (*di tromba*); nota sgargiante (*di colore*). *vi.* squillare (*di tromba, ecc.*); *vt.* proclamare a gran voce.

blaspheme (blăs-fēm′) *vt.*, *vi.* bestemmiare.

blasphemy (blăs′fē-mĭ) *n.* bestemmia.

blast (blåst) *n.* ventata, raffica di vento; squillo (*di strumento a fiato*); esplosione; bufera; maledizione. *vt.* distruggere; inaridire; far esplodere; far saltare, rovinare. — **furnace** *n.* alto forno. —**pipe** *n.* tubo di scappamento.

blatant (blā′tănt) *agg.* rumoroso; sguaiato; lampante, evidente.

blaze (blāz) *n.* fiamma, fuoco; luce viva, splendore. *vi.* risplendere, ardere, divampare. *vt.* far rifulgere, divulgare, proclamare.

blazer (blāz′ĕr) *n.* giubbetto a colori vivaci.

blazing (blāz′ĭng) *agg.* fiammante, fiammeggiante.

bleach (blēch) *n.* candeggio; decolorante. *vt.*, *vi.* imbiancare, scolorire, schiarire, candeggiare. —**er** *n.* decolorante; candeggiatore; *pl.* posti popolari (*di stadio sportivo*).

bleak (blēk) *agg.* pallido, smorto, squallido, freddo, deprimente.

blear (blēr) *vt.* annebbiare, offuscare (*la vista*).

bleary (blēr′ĭ) *agg.* annebbiato; infiammato; lagrimoso; cisposo.

bleat (blēt) *n.* belato. *vi.* belare.

bled (blĕd) *pass.*, *pp. di* to bleed.

bleed (blēd) *vi.* (*pass.*, *pp.* bled) sanguinare. *vt.* salassare, dissanguare; sfruttare.

blemish (blĕm′ĭsh) *n.* macchia, difetto. *vt.* macchiare, deturpare.

blench (blĕnch) *vi.* impallidire; indietreggiare; titubare. *vt.* imbiancare; far impallidire.

blend (blĕnd) *n.* miscuglio, fusione, miscela. *vt.* mescolare, miscelare, riunire, fondere. *vi.* fondersi, mescolarsi; armonizzare.

bless (blĕs) *vt.* benedire, consacrare; rendere felice. —**ed, blest** *agg.* benedetto, santo: to be — **with**, esser dotato di, aver la fortuna di possedere.

blessing (blĕs′ĭng) *n.* benedizione; felicità, fortuna.

blew (blōō) *pass. di* to blow.

blight (blīt) *n.* rovina; malocchio; calamità; carbonchio; golpe, ruggine (*delle piante*). *vt.* distruggere, rovinare, frustrare. —**er** *n.* (*gergo*) tizio: poor —, povero diavolo.

blimp (blĭmp) *n.* pallone frenato; **Colonel** —, nazionalista conservatore.

blind (blīnd) *agg.* cieco; chiuso; oscuro; alla cieca. *n.* tendaggio, tapparella, persiana; mascheratura; pretesto. *vt.* accecare, bendare gli occhi a; abbagliare, opacare; mascherare: —**man's buff**, mosca cieca.

blinder (blĭn′dĕr) *n.* paraocchio (*del cavallo*).

blindly *avv.* ciecamente, alla cieca.

blindness *n.* cecità; (*fig.*) ignoranza.

blindfold (blīnd′fōld) *vt.* bendare gli occhi a. — **benda** per gli occhi. *agg.* a occhi bendati; irriflessivo.

blink (blĭngk) *n.* strizzata d'occhio; occhiata; barlume. *vi.* ammiccare;

sogguardare, sbirciare; lampeggiare. to — at, chiudere un occhio su. *vt.* evadere, schivare. —er *n.* lampeggiatore; paraocchi.

bliss (blĭs) *n.* felicità, beatitudine.

blister (blĭs′tẽr) *n.* vescica, bolla. *vt.* applicare un vescicante. *vi.* coprirsi di vesciche.

blitz (blĭts) *n.* guerra lampo; bombardamento aereo.

blizzard (blĭz′ẽrd) *n.* tormenta.

bloat (blōt) *vt.* gonfiare, enfiare. *vi.* gonfiarsi.

block (blŏk) *n.* blocco, masso; ceppo; forma (*per cappelli*); manichino (*da parrucchieri*); carrucola, puleggia; (*tip.*) cliché; ostacolo; blocco di case, isolato urbano. *vt.* bloccare, ostacolare, opporsi a; ostruire.

blockade (blŏk-ād′) *n.* assedio, blocco navale: to run the —, rompere il blocco. *vt.* bloccare.

blockhead (blŏk′hĕd) *n.* imbecille.

blond (blŏnd) *n.*, *agg.* biondo.

blonde (blŏnd) *n.*, *agg.* bionda.

blood (blŭd) *n.* sangue; parentela; temperamento; razza: in cold —, a sangue freddo, spietatamente; — poisoning, avvelenamento del sangue.

bloodhound (blŭd′hound′) *n.* segugio.

bloodless *agg.* esangue; incruento.

bloodshed (-shĕd′) *n.* spargimento di sangue.

bloodshot (-shŏt′) *agg.* iniettato di sangue.

bloodthirsty (-thûrs′tĭ) *agg.* assetato di sangue, sanguinario.

bloody (blŭd′ĭ) *agg.* sanguinoso; insanguinato; maledetto.

bloom (blōōm) *n.* fiore, fioritura, freschezza. *vi.* fiorire, sbocciare. —ing, —y *agg.* fiorente, fiorito.

blossom (blŏs′ŭm) *n.* fiore, fioritura. *vi.* fiorire, essere in fiore, sbocciare.

blot (blŏt) *n.* macchia, chiazza. *vt.* macchiare, sporcare, scarabocchiare; cancellare; asciugare (*con carta assorbente*): to — out, cancellare; eliminare; celare alla vista. —ter *n.* carta assorbente; registro, brogliaccio. —ting-paper *n.* carta assorbente.

blotch (blŏch) *n.* pustola; macchia; scarabocchio. *vt.* macchiare.

blouse (blouz; blous) *n.* blusa.

blow (blō) *n.* colpo, ventata, folata; to come to blows, venire alle mani. *vt.*, *vi.* (*pass.* blew, *pp.* blown) soffiare, sbuffare, ansimare; suonare (*uno strumento a fiato*): to — away, spazzar via, dissipare; to — one's nose, soffiarsi il naso; to — out, soffiare, spegnere (*un lume*); to —

out one's brains, farsi saltar le cervella; to — over, dissiparsi, finire in niente; to — up, saltare in aria; (*fot.*) ingrandire. —er *n.* soffiatore; ventilatore, ventola; compressore; gradasso. —pipe *n.* tubo per soffiare il vetro; cerbottana.

blown (blōn) *pp.* di blow.

bludgeon (blŭj′ŭn) *n.* randello, sfollagente. *vt.* tramortire.

blue (blōō) *n.* blu: to have the blues, avere la malinconia. *agg.* blu, turchino, azzurro; triste, melanconico: to be in a — funk, essere atterrito. *vt.* tingere di blu; (*metal.*) brunire.

bluebell (blōō′bĕl′) *n.* giacinto.

bluebottle (blōō′bŏt′'l) *n.* fiordaliso.

blueprint (blōō′print) *n.* cianotipia; progetto; programma d'azione. *vt.* pianificare.

bluff (blŭf) *n.* contrafforte di roccia (*sul mare*); millanteria, vanteria; inganno. *agg.* cordiale; brusco; scosceso. *vt.* millantare, imbrogliare.

bluffer (blŭf′ẽr) *n.* millantatore.

bluish (blōō′ĭsh) *agg.* bluastro.

blunder (blŭn′dẽr) *n.* abbaglio, papera, errore, storditaggine. *vi.*, *vi.* commettere un errore, una papera.

blunt (blŭnt) *agg.* spuntato, ottuso; grossolano, brusco. *vt.* ottundere, spuntare. —ly *avv.* bruscamente, esplicitamente.

blur (blûr) *n.* macchia. *vt.* macchiare; confondere; offuscare.

blurt (blûrt) *vt.* parlare precipitosamente, rivelare (*un segreto, ecc.*) to — out, parlare storditamente, lasciarsi sfuggire.

blush (blŭsh) *n.* rossore. *vi.* arrossire.

bluster (blŭs′tẽr) *n.* frastuono, trambusto; fanfaronata; bufera; prepotenza. *vi.* infuriare (*degli elementi*); fare il gradasso; lanciar vane minacce. —ing *agg.* tempestoso, rumoroso, spavaldo.

boar (bōr) *n.* verro.

board (bōrd) *n.* tavola, asse; vitto, pensione; consiglio, consesso; scacchiera: above —, franco, a viso aperto; — and lodging, vitto e alloggio; — of directors, consiglio d'amministrazione; free on — (f.o.b.) franco bordo. *vt.* chiudere *o* coprire con tavole; prendere a pensione; (*naut.*) imbarcarsi su; salire su (*un treno, ecc.*); abbordare. *vi.* essere a pensione. —er *n.* pensionante. —ing-house *n.* pensione per famiglia.

boast (bōst) *vi.* vantarsi, gloriarsi. *vt.* vantare, decantare. *n.* vanteria. —er *n.* spaccone. —ful *agg.* vanaglorioso. —fulness *n.* vanagloria.

boat (bōt) *n.* barca, canotto, imbarcazione. —**house** *n.* darsena. —**swain** (bō's'n; bōt'swän') *n.* nostromo. —**ing** *n.* canottaggio.

bob (bŏb) *n.* cenno del capo; colpetto; piombino; pendente, orecchino; peso (*del pendolo*); romano (*peso mobile di stadera*); taglio (*di capelli*) alla bebè; parrucca a riccioli; coda mozza; esca (*da lenza*); beffa; imbroglio; dondolio, scossa: to wear a —, avere i capelli alla bebè. *vt.* dondolare (*il capo, ecc.*); battere. *vi.* oscillare; agitarsi, saltellare: to — up, venire a galla, apparire all'improvviso; to — up and down, oscillare in su e in giù.

bobbin (bŏb'ĭn) *n.* bobina.

bobby-soxer (bŏb'ĭ-sŏk'sĕr) *n.f.* adolescente, ragazzina.

bode (bōd) *pass., pp.* di to bide.

bodice (bŏd'ĭs) *n.* corpetto, busto.

bodily (bŏd'ĭ-lĭ) *agg.* corporeo, materiale. *avv.* materialmente; in massa; per intero; di peso.

body (bŏd'ĭ) *n.* corpo; gruppo; massa; raccolta; carrozzeria (*d'auto*); fusoliera (*d'aereo*): in a —, in massa.

bog (bŏg) *n.* palude, pantano. *vt.* impantanare.

boggle (bŏg''l) *vi.* esitare.

bogus (bō'gŭs) *agg.* finto, contraffatto.

bogy (bō'gĭ) *agg.* spauracchio, spettro.

Bohemian (bō.hē'mĭ-ăn) *n., agg.* boemo; bohemien.

boil (boil) *vi.* bollire, ribollire. *vt.* cuocere a lesso, bollire: to — down, condensare, ridursi. *n.* ebollizione; foruncolo. —**er** *n.* caldaia.

boisterous (bois'tĕr-ŭs) *agg.* violento, rumoroso, turbolento, vivace, allegro.

bold (bōld) *agg.* audace, temerario; impudente, sfacciato; chiaro, evidente: to make — to, prendersi la libertà di. —**faced** *agg.* impudente, sfrontato; (*tip.*) grassetto. —**ness** *n.* spavalderia, audacia; impudenza.

bolster (bōl'stĕr) *n.* cuscino, traversino, cuscinetto, supporto. *vt.* reggere, sorreggere, sostenere: to — up, dar manforte a.

bolt (bōlt) (1) *vt.* sprangare, scagliare. *vi.* scappare, spiccare un salto. *n.* catenaccio, chiavistello; fulmine; bullone; salto, balzo; (*naut.*) caviglia: — upright, diritto, irrigidito.

bolt (2) *vt.* setacciare, vagliare.

bomb (bŏm) *n.* bomba; bombola, spruzzatore. *vt., vi.* bombardare. —**er** *n.* bombardiere.

bombard (bŏm·bärd') *vt.* bombardare, cannoneggiare. —**ier** *n.* bombardiere. —**ment** *n.* bombardamento.

bombastic (bŏm·băs'tĭk) *agg.* tronfio, ampolloso.

bonanza (bō·năn'zà) *n.* fortuna, prosperità.

bond (bŏnd) *n.* vincolo, impegno, legame; (*comm.*) titolo, azione, obbligazione: goods in —, merci in sosta.

bondage (bŏn'dĭj) *n.* schiavitù.

bondholder (bŏnd'hōld'ĕr) *n.* azionista.

bondman (bŏnd'măn) *n.* servo, schiavo.

bone (bōn) *n.* osso; vertebra; lisca, stecca di balena; avorio; (*pl.*) ossatura; (*gergo*) dadi da gioco: — of contention, pomo della discordia; to make no bones about it, parlare esplicitamente, agire senza esitare, non farsi scrupoli; to have a — to pick with, avere un conto da regolare con. *vt.* disossare.

bonfire (bŏn'fīr') *n.* falò.

bonnet (bŏn'ĕt) *n.* berretto; (*naut.*) bonetta; (*autom.*) cofano.

bonus (bō'nŭs) *n.* gratifica, indennità, regalia, dividendo, premio.

bony (bōn'ĭ) *agg.* ossuto, scarno, pieno di lische.

boo (bōō) *vt.* disapprovare con urlacci.

booby (bōō'bĭ) *n.* tonto, sciocco; (*sport*) schiappa. —**trap** *n.* tranello; mina nascosta.

book (bōōk) *n.* libro, libretto, registro, quaderno. *vt.* registrare; iscrivere; prenotare (*un posto*); scritturare.

bookcase (bōōk'kās') *n.* scaffale.

bookkeeper (bōōk'kēp'ĕr) *n.* contabile.

bookkeeping (bōōk'kēp'ĭng) *n.* contabilità.

booklet (bōōk'lĕt) *n.* opuscolo, libriccino.

bookmaker (bōōk'māk'ĕr) *n.* allibratore.

bookmark (bōōk'märk) *n.* segnalibro.

bookseller (bōōk'sĕl'ĕr) *n.* libraio.

bookshelf (bōōk'shĕlf) *n.* scaffale.

bookshop (bōōk'shŏp), **bookstore** (-stōr) *n.* libreria.

bookstall (bōōk'stȯl') *n.* edicola.

boom (bōōm) (1) *n.* (*naut.*) boma.

boom (bōōm) (2) *n.* rimbombo; boato; rialzo in borsa, risveglio negli affari. *vt.* sviluppare; lanciare (*un prodotto*); *vi.* rimbombare.

boon (bōōn) *n.* beneficio, vantaggio; favore. *agg.* gaio, benigno.

boor (bōōr) *n.* zotico. —**ish** *agg.* grossolano.

boost (bōōst) *n.* spinta in su, aiuto. *vt.* dare una spinta in su; aumentare (*i prezzi*).

boot (bŏŏt) (1) *n.* stivale, scarpa; congedo, licenziamento; recluta della marina: **to give the —,** cacciar via.

boot (bŏŏt) (2) *n.* profitto, vantaggio: **to —,** per soprammercato. *vi.* servire, giovare.

bootblack (bŏŏt'blăk) *n.* lustrascarpe.

booth (bŏŏth) *n.* baracca, sgabuzzino; cabina telefonica *o* di proiezione.

bootlegger (bŏŏt'lĕg'ẽr) *n.* contrabbandiere di alcool.

boots (bŏŏts) *n.* facchino d'albergo.

booty (bŏŏ'tĭ) *n.* bottino.

booze (bŏŏz) *n.* (*gergo*) liquore spiritoso; orgia, sbornia.

border (bôr'dẽr) *n.* margine, orlo, ciglio; confine, frontiera; riva. *vt.* orlare; essere ai margini di, contiguo a; delimitare. *vi.*: **to — on, upon,** essere all'estremo limite di, confinare con, rasentare.

bore (bôr) (1) *vt.* bucare, forare, perforare. *n.* buco, calibro (*d'arma*).

bore (2) *vt.* annoiare, tediare; opprimere. *n.* noia, tedio; seccatore. **—dom** *n.* noia, stanchezza.

bore (3) *pass. di* to bear.

born (bôrn) *agg., pp. di* to bear, nato; innato: **to be —,** nascere, essere nato; **to be — again,** rinascere.

borne (bôrn) *pp. di* to bear.

borough (bûr'ŏ) *n.* borgo; capoluogo; comune.

borrow (bŏr'ŏ) *vt.* farsi prestare, chiedere *o* prendere a prestito.

borrower (bŏr'ŏ-ẽr) *n.* chi prende a prestito.

bosom (bŏŏz'ŭm; bŏŏ'zŭm) *n.* petto, seno: **— friend,** amico del cuore.

boss (bŏs) *n.* protuberanza; mozzo (*di ruota*); padrone; capo. *vt.* comandare, dominare.

bossy (bŏs'ĭ) *agg.* autoritario, dispotico.

botany (bŏt'd-nĭ) *n.* botanica.

both (bŏth) *agg., pron.* entrambi, l'uno e l'altro: **on — sides,** d'ambe le parti; **— of them,** tutti e due; **— this and that,** tanto questo quanto quello. *cong.* del pari. *avv.* ugualmente.

bother (bŏth'ẽr) *vt.* molestare, disturbare, irritare, infastidire, *vi.* preoccuparsi. *n.* seccatura, molestia, inconveniente. **—some** *agg.* seccante, molesto.

bottle (bŏt'l) *n.* bottiglia. *vt.* imbottigliare.

bottom (bŏt'ŭm) *n.* fondo, base: **to sink to the —,** sprofondare, andare a fondo. *agg.* ultimo, infimo.

boudoir (bŏŏ'dwär) *n.* stanza da letto di una signora.

bough (bou) *n.* ramo d'albero.

bought (bôt) *pass., pp. di* to buy.

boulder (bōl'dẽr) *n.* pietra, masso, roccia.

boulevard (bŏŏ'lĕ-värd; bŏŏl'ĕ-) *n.* viale; corso.

bounce (bouns) *n.* balzo, rimbalzo; vanteria. *vt.* far saltare, far rimbalzare. *vi.* saltare, balzare, rimbalzare; slanciarsi; vantarsi.

bound (bound) *n.* limite, confine; balzo, salto; rimbalzo. *vt.* limitare, contenere, cintare. *vi.* balzare, saltare. *agg.* rilegato, legato, tenuto (*a*), obbligato, impegnato; diretto (*a*); in partenza (*per*): **— up in,** assorto in; **— to happen,** destinato ad accadere; **I feel — to say,** sento il dovere di dire. *pp. di* to bind.

boundary (boun'dd-rĭ) *n.* limite, frontiera, confine.

boundless *agg.* sconfinato, illimitato.

bountiful (boun'tĭ-fŏŏl; f'l) *agg.* generoso.

bounty (boun'tĭ) *n.* generosità, liberalità; indennità, gratifica.

bouquet (bŏŏ-kā') *n.* mazzo di fiori; aroma (*di vini o liquori*).

bourgeois (bŏŏr-zhwä'; bŏŏr'zhwä) *n., agg.* borghese.

bout (bout) *n.* colpo; turno, volta; attacco, accesso.

bow (bou) *vt.* piegare, curvare, inclinare: **to — one's head,** chinare il capo. *vi.* piegarsi, curvarsi, inchinarsi, sottomettersi, rassegnarsi. *n.* inchino, riverenza; (bŏ) arco (*per frecce*); archetto (*di violino*); arcione, nodo, nastro, fiocco; (bou) (*naut.*) prora. **—legged** *agg.* (bŏ-)sbilenco, con le gambe arcuate. **—sprit** (bou-) *n.* bompresso.

bowels (bou'ĕlz) *n.pl.*in testini, budella, viscere.

bower (bou'ẽr) *n.* pergolato.

bowl (bŏl) *n.* vaso, coppa, ciotola; vaschetta; palla, boccia. *vt.* far rotolare. *vi.* giocare alle bocce: **to — over,** rovesciare, travolgere.

box (bŏks) (1) *n.* cassa, scatola, cassetta (*anche di vettura*); box (*di scuderia*), palco (*di teatro*); garritta, cabina, banco (*dei giurati o dei testimoni*). *vt.* incassare, mettere in cassa. **—office** *n.* botteghino (*di teatro*).

box (2) *n.* ceffone, pugno. *vi.* fare del pugilato, boxare. *vt.* schiaffeggiare, percuotere. **—er** *n.* pugile. **—ing** *n.* pugilato.

box (3) *n.* (*bot.*) bosso.

boy (boi) *n.* ragazzo, giovinetto; servitorello: **— Scout,** Giovane Esploratore.

boycott (boi'kŏt) *vt.* boicottare.

boyhood (boi'hŏŏd) *n.* infanzia.

boyish (boi'ĭsh) *n.* infantile, giovanile.

brace (brās) *n.* coppia (*al gioco dei dadi, ecc.*); paio; supporto, tirante; trapano; attacco; sospensione (*di un veicolo*); (*pl. in G.B.*) bretelle. *vt.* assicurare, agganciare, rafforzare: to — up, farsi forza.

bracelet (brās'lĕt) *n.* braccialetto; manetta.

bracket (brăk'ĕt) *n.* mensola; braccio (*supporto*); parentesi quadra. *vt.* munire di supporto; mettere tra parentesi quadre.

brag (brăg) *vi.* vantarsi, gloriarsi. *vt.* decantare. *n.* vanteria, fanfaronata. —gart *n.* fanfarone.

braid (brād) *n.* treccia (*di capelli*); spighetta. *vt.* intrecciare, rifinire, spighettare.

brain (brān) *n.* cervello; intelligenza: to puzzle (to rack) one's brains, lambiccarsi il cervello, — trust, consiglio di esperti. *vt.* far saltare le cervella a.

brake (brāk) *n.* freno; battitoio. *vt.* frenare. —man *n.* frenatore.

bramble (brăm'b'l), *n.* rovo.

bran (brăn) *n.* crusca.

branch (brănch) *n.* ramo, fronda; succursale, filiale; (*ferr.*) diramazione. *vi.* ramificare; biforcarsi, diramarsi.

brand (brănd) *n.* tizzone; marchio; stimmata; qualità. *vt.* marcare, marchiare, stigmatizzare. —new *agg.* nuovo di zecca.

brandish (brăn'dĭsh) *vt.* brandire.

brandy (brăn'dĭ) *n.* acquavite, cognac.

brash (brăsh) *agg.* avventato, impudente; friabile.

brass (brás) *n.* ottone; quattrini; alti ufficiali: as bold as —, con faccia tosta; to get down to — tacks, venire al sodo; —es, ottoni (*strumenti musicali*); — band, banda (*mus.*).

brassy (brás'ĭ) *agg.* d'ottone; impudente, sfrontato.

brassière (brá-zĕr') *n.* reggipetto.

brat (brăt) *n.* marmocchio.

bravado (brá-vä'dō) *n.* bravata; spavalderia.

brave (brāv) *agg.* coraggioso, ardito. *vt.* sfidare, affrontare. —ry *n.* ardimento.

brawl (brôl) *n.* zuffa, disputa, trambusto. *vi.* litigare.

brawn (brôn) *n.* muscolo, forza muscolare.

bray (brā) *n.* raglio. *vi.* ragliare.

brazen (brā'z'n) *agg.* di ottone; impudente, sfrontato.

breach (brēch) *n.* breccia; violazione, infrazione: — of promise, rottura di promessa; — of trust, abuso di fiducia. *vt.* far breccia in; infrangere.

bread (brĕd) *n.* pane: new —, pane fresco.

breadth (brĕdth) *n.* larghezza; ampiezza; (*tess.*) altezza.

break (brāk) *vt.* (*pass.* broke, *pp.* broken) rompere, frantumare; interrompere; domare; attutire; violare; rovinare; battere: to — news, comunicare notizie (*con delicatezza*); to — in, sfondare, irrompere; to — in upon, sorprendere; to — loose, liberarsi, scatenarsi to — up, sciogliere, disperdere. *vi.* rompere; rompersi, frantumarsi; (*comm.*) fallire; sorgere (*dell'alba*); scoppiare (*di conflitti, ecc.*); declinare, indebolirsi: to — away, svincolarsi; to — down, battersi; guastarsi (*di auto, ecc.*); classificare, analizzare; to — up, separarsi, sciogliersi. *n.* rottura; apertura; interruzione; pausa; possibilità: to give a — (*gergo*), concedere una possibilità.

breakdown (brāk'doun') *n.* crollo, collasso; incidente, guasto; insuccesso, catastrofe; classificazione, analisi: nervous —, esaurimento nervoso.

breaker (brāk'ẽr) *n.* violatore; domatore (*di cavalli*); maroso.

breakfast (brĕk'fást) *n.* prima colazione.

breakwater (brāk'wô'tẽr) *n.* tagliamare, diga.

breast (brĕst) *n.* petto, pettorale, seno; cuore, animo: to make a clean — of it, confessare tutto, vuotare il sacco. *vt.* affrontare.

breath (brĕth) *n.* respiro, soffio, fiato: short of —, ansimante; out of —, sfiatato, ansante.

breathe (brēth) *vi.*, *vt.*, respirare; prendere fiato; sbuffare; sussurrare.

bred (brĕd) *pass.*, *pp.* di to breed: well —, beneducato; ill —, maleducato.

breech (brēch) *n.* deretano, parte posteriore; culatta (*di cannone, ecc.*).

breeches (brĭch'ĕz) *n.pl.* brache, calzoni da cavallo.

breed (brēd) *vt.* (*pass.*, *pp.* bred) generare, mettere al mondo; allevare; causare. *vi.* moltiplicarsi; nascere; riprodursi. *n.* razza, covata; origine, schiatta. —er *n.* allevatore. —ing *n.* allevamento; educazione: good — compitezza.

breeze (brēz) *n.* brezza.

breezy (brēz'ĭ) *agg.* ventilato; vivace; loquace.

brethren (brĕth'rĕn) *n.pl.* frati; confratelli.

brevity (brĕv'ĭ·tĭ) *n.* brevità, concisione.

brew (brōō) *vt.*, *vi.* preparare (*il tè*); manipolare; fabbricare (*birra, ecc.*); tramare, complottare; fermentare, maturare: something is brewing, qualcosa bolle in pentola. —er *n.* birraio. —ery *n.* fabbrica di birra.

briar (brī'ĕr) *n.* radica; rosa selvatica, rovo; pipa di radica.

bribe (brīb) *n.* regalo (*per corrompere*), "bustarella"; allettamento. *vt.* corrompere, allettare.

bribery (brīb'ĕr·ĭ) *n.* corruzione, subornazione.

brick (brĭk) *n.* mattone. *vt.* mattonare.

bridal (brīd'ăl) *agg.* nuziale. *n.* nozze.

bride (brīd) *n.* sposa, sposina.

bridegroom (brīd'grōōm') *n.* sposo.

bridesmaid (brīdz'mād') *n.* damigella d'onore.

bridesman (brīdz'măn) *n.* testimone alle nozze.

bridge (brĭj) *n.* ponte, passerella; ponticello (*di strumento a corda*). *vt.* gettare un ponte; congiungere. —head *n.* testa di ponte.

bridle (brī'd'l) *n.* briglia, freno; (*naut.*) cavo d'ormeggio. *vt.* imbrigliare, metter la briglia a; frenare. *vi.* drizzare il capo; impennarsi. —path *n.* sentiero per cavalli.

brief (brēf) *agg.* breve, conciso, corto. *n.* breve papale; lettera; esposto, memoriale; riassunto; citazione; *vt.* dare le ultime istruzioni (*a un equipaggio militare prima di un'azione*); mettere al corrente. —case *n.* cartella, borsa da avvocato. —ing *n.* ultime istruzioni; ragguagli. —ly *avv.* brevemente.

brig (brĭg) *n.* brigantino; (*naut.*) prigione.

brigade (brĭ·gād') *n.* brigata: fire —, vigili del fuoco.

brigand (brĭg'ănd) *n.* brigante.

bright (brīt) *agg.* chiaro, luminoso; lucido, brillante, scintillante; allegro; bello; intelligente.

brighten (brīt'n) *vt.* rischiarare, illuminare, rallegrare, lucidare, abbellire. *vi.* rischiararsi, brillare; rallegrarsi: to — up, rasserenarsi.

brightness (brīt'nĕs) *n.* chiarità, chiarore; luminosità, scintillio; allegria.

brilliance (brĭl'yăns) brilliancy (brĭl'yăn·sĭ) *n.* intelligenza; splendore, scintillio.

brilliant (brĭl'yănt) *agg.* intelligente; brillante, splendente.

brim (brĭm) *n.* bordo, orlo (*di recipiente*), ala, tesa (*di cappello*). *vi.*: to — over, traboccare.

brine (brīn) *n.* acqua salata, acqua di mare, mare.

bring (brĭng) *vt.* (*pass., pp.* brought) portare, recare, condurre; indurre, provocare: to — forth, produrre, mettere alla luce; to — out, far uscire, far apparire, pubblicare; to — up, allevare, educare; to — up the rear, chiudere la marcia.

brink (brĭngk) *n.* orlo, limite estremo.

brisk (brĭsk) *agg.* vivace, svelto; sbrigativo; frizzante. —ly *avv.* vivacemente. —ness *n.* vivacità.

bristle (brĭs'l) *vi.* drizzare il pelo; irrigidirsi; mettersi sulla difensiva. *n.* setola.

bristly (brĭs'lĭ) bristling (brĭs'lĭng) *agg.* irto, irsuto.

British (brĭt'ĭsh) *agg.* britannico, inglese.

brittle (brĭt'l) *agg.* fragile, friabile.

broach (brōch) *n.* spiedo; trapano. *vt.* mettere allo spiedo; perforare; affrontare *o* svolgere (*un argomento*).

broad (brôd) *agg.* largo, ampio, vasto; grossolano, esplicito: — daylight, pieno giorno. —ly *avv.* esplicitamente, largamente. —minded *agg.* spregiudicato; indulgente; di larghe vedute.

broadcast (brôd'kàst') *n.* radiodiffusione, trasmissione, emissione; diffusione. *vt.* radiodiffondere, trasmettere; diffondere.

broadcloth (brôd'klôth') *n.* panno.

broaden (brôd'n) *vi.* allargarsi, estendersi. *vt.* allargare.

broadness *n.* larghezza; volgarità.

broadside (brôd'sīd') *n.* (*naut.*) bordo; bordata.

brocade (brō·kād') *n.* broccato.

broil (broil) *n.* tafferuglio, lite. *vt.* arrostire in graticola. *vi.* abbrustolirsi; fremere d'impazienza.

broke (brōk) *agg.* rovinato; al verde. *pass. di* to break.

broken (brō'kĕn) *agg.* rotto; sconnesso; incerto; interrotto; affranto: — English, inglese imperfetto. *pp. di* to break.

broker (brō'kĕr) *n.* mediatore, sensale; agente di cambio.

bronchitis (brŏn·kī'tĭs; brŏng-) *n.* bronchite.

bronco (brŏng'kō) *n.* cavallo selvaggio.

bronze (brŏnz) *n.* bronzo. *agg.* bronzeo. *vt.*, *vi.* bronzare, abbronzare.

brooch (brōch; brōōch) *n.* spilla, spillone.

brood (brōōd) *n.* covata. *vt.* covare; arzigogolare. *vi.* arrovellarsi: to — on (over), meditare su; ruminare.

brooder (brōōd′ĕr) *n.* incubatrice.

brook (brŏŏk) *n.* ruscello; *vt.* sopportare.

broom (brōōm) *n.* scopa, saggina. —stick *n.* manico di scopa.

broth (brŏth) *n.* brodo.

brothel (brŏth′ĕl; brŏth′-) *n.* postribolo, bordello.

brother (brŭth′ĕr) *n.* fratello.

brotherhood (brŭth′ĕr·hŏŏd) *n.* confraternità, fratellanza.

brother-in-law *n.* cognato.

brotherly (brŭth′ĕr ll) *agg.* fraterno.

brought (brŏt) *pass., pp. di* to bring.

brow (brou) *n.* ciglio, sopracciglio; fronte; sommità.

browbeat (brou′bēt′) *vt.* intimorire.

brown (broun) *agg.* bruno, marrone; scuro; castagno; abbronzato; rosolato. *vt., vi.* brunire; scurire; rosolare; rosolarsi.

browse (brouz) *vt., vi.* brucare, pascolare; leggiucchiare.

bruise (brōōz) *n.* contusione, ammaccatura. *vt.* ammaccare, percuotere, frantumare.

bruiser (brōōz′ĕr) *n.* pugile; gradasso.

brunette (brōō·nĕt′) *agg.* bruno. *n.f.* bruna, brunetta.

brunt (brŭnt) *n.* urto; furore.

brush (brŭsh) *n.* spazzola; pennello; coda (*di volpe*); scaramuccia, tafferuglio; colpo di spazzola; (*elett.*) scarica; conduttore volante. *vt.* spazzolare; sfiorare; rasentare: to — away, spazzar via; to — past, passare alla svelta, rasentare; to — up, ripulire; ripassare (*una materia*).

brusque (brŭsk; brōōsk) *agg.* brusco, ruvido.

brutal (brōō′tăl) *agg.* brutale, crudele. —ity *n.* brutalità, crudeltà.

brute (brōōt) *n.* bestia, animale, bruto. *agg.* bestiale, irragionevole, selvatico.

brutish (brōō′ĭsh) *agg.* brutale.

bubble (bŭb′l) *n.* bolla, bollicina; fantasticheria. *vi.* far bollicine: to — with, sprizzare.

buck (bŭk) *n.* daino, capriolo; maschio (*di lepre o coniglio*); (*gergo, S.U.*) dollaro: — private, recluta. to pass the —, scaricare la responsabilità (*addosso a qualcuno*). *vi.* sgroppare.

bucket (bŭk′ĕt) *n.* secchio: — seat, strapuntino.

buckle (bŭk′l) *n.* fibbia. *vt.* allacciare, agganciare; contorcere; accartocciare. to — down to, dedicarsi a, accingersi a.

buckram (bŭk′răm) *n.* tela da fusto, garza.

buckshot (buk′shŏt′) *n.* pallini da fucile (*per caccia grossa*).

buckwheat (buk′hwēt′) *n.* grano saraceno.

bud (bŭd) *n.* germoglio, bocciolo; (*gergo*) amico, compare. *vt.* innestare (*piante*). *vi.* germogliare.

buddy (bŭd′ĭ) *n.* amico, compare.

budge (bŭj) *vi.* muoversi. *vt.* far muovere, smuovere.

budget (bŭj′ĕt; -ĭt) *n.* sacco; bilancio, stanziamento. *vt., vi.* stanziare; fare un bilancio.

buff (bŭf) (1) *n.* pelle di bufalo; pelle nuda. *agg.* marrone chiaro. *vt.* lucidare, tingere color camoscio.

buff (2) *n.* colpo, buffetto: blindman's —, mosca cieca. —er *n.* respingente (*di vagone, ecc.*); cuscinetto.

buffet (bŏŏ·fā′; bŭ·fā′; bōō·fā′) *n.* buffet, ristorante; credenza; (bŭf′ĕt) pugno, ceffone.

buffoon (bŭ·fōōn′; bŭ-) *n.* buffone.

bug (bŭg) *n.* cimice; insetto; difetto: big — (*gergo*), pezzo grosso.

bugbear (bŭg′bâr′) *n.* spauracchio.

buggy (bŭg′ĭ) *n.* calesse; carrello, vagoncino.

bugle (bū′g′l) *n.* corno da caccia; tromba. *vi.* strombettare.

bugler (bū′glĕr) *n.* trombettiere.

build (bĭld) *vt.* (*pass., pp.* built) costruire; fondare, creare; basare: to — up one's health, rimettersi in salute. —er *n.* struttura; corporatura. —er *n.* costruttore. —ing *n.* fabbricato, edificio. buildup (bĭld′ŭp′) *n.* propaganda, soffietto.

bulb (bŭlb) *n.* bulbo, globo; lampadina.

bulge (bŭlj) *n.* protuberanza, gonfiore. *vi.* gonfiarsi, sporgere.

bulgy (bul′jĭ) *agg.* rigonfio.

bulk (bŭlk) *n.* massa, volume, quantità; (*naut.*) carico.

bulkhead (bŭlk′hĕd′) *n.* paratia.

bulky (bŭl′kĭ) *agg.* voluminoso, ingombrante.

bull (bŏŏl) (1) *n.* bolla (*papale*).

bull (2) *n.* toro; maschio (*di elefante, ecc.*); (*borsa*) rialzista. *vt.* (*borsa*) giocare al rialzo. —dog *n.* molosso. —fight *n.* corrida di tori. —fighter *n.* torero.

bull's-eye *n.* occhio di bue (*finestrino*); lente convessa; centro del bersaglio.

bulldozer (bŏŏl′dŏz′ĕr) *n.* gradasso, prepotente; (*mecc.*) livellatrice.

bullet (bŏŏl′ĕt) *n.* pallottola.

bulletin (bŏŏl′ĕ·tĭn) *n.* bollettino.

bullion (bŏŏl′yŭn) *n.* oro o argento in lingotti; frangia d'oro.

bullock (bŏŏl′ŭk) *n.* manzo (*animale*).

bully (bŏŏl′I) *n.* gradasso, prepotente; briccone. *agg.* magnifico, formidabile. *vt.* maltrattare; costringere con violenza.

bulwark (bŏŏl′wĕrk) *n.* contrafforte, parapetto; baluardo.

bum (bŭm) *n.* vagabondo, pelandrone; scroccone; orgia; gozzoviglia: to go on a —, fare gozzoviglia; to feel —, essere indisposto. *vi.* vivere di scrocco.

bumblebee (bŭm′b'l-bē′) *n.* calabrone.

bump (bŭmp) *n.* colpo; bernoccolo. *vt.* battere, urtare. *vi.* sbattere (*urtare contro qualcosa*). —er *n.* respingente, paraurti. *agg.* abbondante.

bumptious (bŭmp′shŭs) *agg.* tronfio, presuntuoso.

bun (bŭn) *n.* panino; pasticcino.

bunch (bŭnch) *n.* fascio, mazzo (*di fiori, chiavi, ecc.*), grappolo. *vt.* riunire in mazzo. *vi.* riunirsi, raggrupparsi, far massa.

bundle (bŭn′d'l) *n.* fagotto, involto, pacco, fascio, ammasso, mucchio (*di carte*). *vt.* impaccare, imballare. *vi.* : to — off (*out*), uscire frettolosamente; to — up, infagottarsi.

bung (bŭng) *n.* zaffo, zipolo, tappo; budello (*per salami*); bugia.

bungalow (bŭng′gá-lō) *n.* casetta a un piano.

bungle (bŭng′g'l) *n.* lavoro malfatto. *vt.* rovinare, guastare, eseguire malamente. *vi.* lavorare alla carlona.

bungler (bŭng′glĕr) *n.* incapace, pasticcione.

bunion (bŭn′yŭn) *n.* gonfiore, protuberanza.

bunk (bŭngk) *n.* cuccetta, letto; fuga; sciocchezza.

bunker (bŭngk′ĕr) *n.* (*naut.*) carbonile; (*mil.*) casamatta.

bunny (bŭn′I) *n.* coniglietto; scoiattolino.

buoy (bŏŏ′I; boi) *n.* boa: life —, salvagente. *vt.* mantenere a galla; delimitare con boe: to — up, rincuorare. —ancy *n.* leggerezza; galleggiabilità; gaiezza, esuberanza. —ant *agg.* galleggiante; allegro; esuberante.

burden (bûr′d'n) *n.* fardello, carico; peso; soma. *vt.* caricare, gravare. —some *agg.* greve, pesante; noioso.

bureau (bū′rō) *n.* ufficio, studio; comò: travel —, ufficio turistico; weather —, ufficio meteorologico.

bureaucracy (bū-rŏk′rá-sĭ; bū-rō′krá-sĭ) *n.* burocrazia.

burglar (bûr′glĕr) *n.* ladro, scassinatore.

burglary (bûr′glá-rĭ) *n.* furto con scasso.

burial (bĕr′ĭ-ăl) *n.* sepoltura, inumazione. — ground *n.* cimitero.

burlap (bûr′lăp) *n.* tela da sacco.

burlesque (bûr-lĕsk′) *n.* farsa, parodia, spettacolo comico. *agg.* burlesco.

burly (bûr′lĭ) *agg.* corpulento, ruvido, bonario.

burn (bûrn) *n.* bruciatura, ustione. *vt.* (*pass., pp.* burnt, burned) bruciare, incendiare; cauterizzare; cuocere (*mattoni, ecc.*). *vi.* bruciare, divampare; brillare; scottare. —er *n.* bruciatore; becco (*a gas, ecc.*). —ing *n.* bruciatura; combustione, incendio; infiammazione. *agg.* ardente, bruciante, rovente. —ing glass *n.* specchio ustorio.

burnish (bûr′nĭsh) *n.* brunitura; lucidatura. *vt.* brunire; lucidare.

burnt (bûrnt) *pass., pp. di* to burn.

burrow (bûr′ō) *n.* tana, buca. *vi.* rintanarsi, nascondersi.

burst (bûrst) *n.* scoppio, esplosione, impeto, accesso (*di collera, ecc.*). *vt., vi.* (*pass., pp.* burst) far scoppiare, fendere, sfondare, prorompere, traboccare, irrompere; scoppiare, esplodere, sfogarsi: to — open, forzare, sfondare, spalancare; to — into, irrompere in; to — into tears, scoppiare in lagrime.

bury (bĕr′ĭ) *vt.* (*pass., pp.* buried) seppellire, sotterrare; sprofondare; nascondere.

bus (bŭs) *n.* autobus. —man *n.* conducente d'autobus.

bush (bŏŏsh) *n.* cespuglio, macchia, boschetto; foresta: to beat about the —, menare il can per l'aia.

bushel (bŏŏsh′ĕl) *n.* staio.

busily (bĭz′ĭ-lĭ) *avv.* attivamente, energicamente; con aria affaccendata.

business (bĭz′nĕs) *n.* affare, affari, commercio; professione, occupazione; compito, missione: mind your own —, badate agli affari vostri; to make it one's —, provvedere, assumersi il compito. —like *agg.* pratico, sbrigativo, disinvolto; metodico, preciso.

bust (bŭst) *n.* busto. *vi.* andare in malora. *vt.* far saltare, mandare in rovina; (*gergo mil.*) degradare; domare (*un cavallo*).

bustle (bŭs′'l) *n.* movimento, trambusto, frastuono, attività, tramestio. *vi.* darsi attorno, affaccendarsi, affannarsi. *vt.* sollecitare, stimolare.

busy (bĭz'ĭ) *agg.* occupato; affannato; attivo; movimentato; affaccendato. *vt.* : to — oneself, occuparsi, affaccendarsi. —body *n.* ficcanaso.

but (bŭt) *cong.*, *prep.*, *avv.* ma, però, eccetto, salvo, a eccezione di; che non; soltanto, esclusivamente: no one — you, nessuno eccetto voi; — for, senza, in mancanza di; — for him, se non fosse (stato) per lui; the last — one, il penultimo; I can —, non posso a meno di; it is — a scratch, è soltanto un graffio; all —, quasi, pressochè; all — dead, pressochè morto.

butcher (bŏŏch'ẽr) *n.* macellaio. *vt.* macellare; massacrare; rovinare.

butchery (bŏŏch'ẽr.ĭ) *n.* macello; strage.

butler (bŭt'lẽr) *n.* maggiordomo.

butt (bŭt) *n.* estremità: mozzicone; bersaglio; meta, limite; cornata, testata; calcio (*di fucile*, *ecc.*): — end, estremità; impugnatura; calcio (*d'arma da fuoco*). *vt.*, *vi.* dar testate (*o* cornate) a; urtare; essere adiacente; congiungere testa a testa: to — out, sporgere, sbucare; to — in, intromettersi, interloquire.

butter (bŭt'ẽr) *n.* burro. *vt.* imburrare. —cup *n.* ranuncolo. —milk *n.* siero.

butterfly (bŭt'ẽr.flī') *n.* farfalla.

buttocks (bŭt'ŭks) *n.pl.* natiche, deretano.

button (bŭt'n) *n.* bottone; pulsante. *vt.* abbottonare.

buttonhole (bŭt'n.hōl') *n.* occhiello, asola. *vt.* fare gli occhielli a; trattenere; attaccare un bottone a.

buttonhook (bŭt'n.hŏŏk') *n.* allacciabottoni.

buttons *n.* inserviente in livrea.

buttress (bŭt'rĕs) *n.* contrafforte, sperone. *vt.* rinforzare; sostenere; avvalorare.

buxom (bŭk'sŭm) *agg.* gagliardo, allegro, esuberante; malleabile; procace.

buy (bī) *vt.* (*pass.*, *pp.* bought) comperare, acquistare; corrompere, subornare: to — off, comperare, corrompere; riscattare; to — out, liquidare (*un azionista*, *ecc.*); rilevare in blocco; to — over, corrompere; to — up, accaparrare.

buyer (bī'ẽr) *n.* compratore, acquirente.

buzz (bŭz) *n.* ronzio, brusio; (*gergo*) telefonata. *vi.* ronzare; (*aeron.*) volare a bassissima quota.

buzzard (bŭz'ẽrd) *n.* (*ornit.*) poiana.

by (bī) *prep.* per, di, a, su, presso, accanto, durante, per opera di: — night, di notte; — far, di gran lunga; — no means, per niente affatto; — dint of, a forza di; — the way, a proposito, tra parentesi; — tomorrow, domani; — one — one, a uno a uno. *avv.* presso, vicino; via, da parte: — and large, complessivamente, tutto, considerato; to stand —, esser presente, tenersi pronto a intervenire; — and —, fra poco, di lì a poco; days gone —, giorni lontani.

bye-bye (bī'bī) *int.* arrivederci, ciao.

bygone (bī'gŏn') *agg.* passato, andato: to let bygones be bygones, mettere una pietra sul passato.

bylaw (bī'lâ') *n.* legge locale, consuetudine, regolamento.

by-line *n.* occupazione secondaria; (*giorn.*) firma.

byname *n.* soprannome.

bypass *n.* circonvallazione esterna; via secondaria.

bypath (bī'pàth'), **byroad** (bī'rōd'), **byway** (bī'wā') *n.* strada privata, deviazione, scorciatoia.

by-product *n.* sottoprodotto.

bystander (bī'stăn'dẽr) *n.* astante, spettatore.

byword (bī'wûrd') *n.* proverbio, epiteto; oggetto di derisione.

C

cab (kăb) *n.* carrozza di piazza; autopubblica; cabina (*d'autocarro o di locomotiva*). —man, —driver *n.* vetturino; autista di piazza.

cabbage (kăb'ĭj) *n.* cavolo, verza.

cabin (kăb'ĭn) *n.* capanna, baracca; cabina: — class passenger, passeggero di classe cabina.

cabinet (kăb'ĭ.nĕt) *n.* armadietto; gabinetto, studio.

cable (kā'b'l) *n.* gomena; cablogramma; cavo. *vt.* ormeggiare; telegrafare: — address, indirizzo telegrafico. —gram *n.* cablogramma.

cackle (kăk''l) *n.* verso (*della gallina*, *ecc.*); cicaleccio, chiacchierio. *vi.* chiocciare, ciarlare, blaterare.

cad (kăd) *n.* furfante, buono a nulla.

cadaverous (kå.dăv'ẽr.ŭs) *agg.* cadaverico; scarno; pallidissimo.

caddie (kăd'ĭ) *n.* porta-mazze (*al golf*).

cadence (kā'dĕns) *n.* cadenza.

cadet (kå.dĕt') *n.* cadetto.

café (kå.fā') *n.* caffè (*ritrovo*), ristorante: — society, frequentatori dei ritrovi eleganti.

cafeteria (kăf'ê·tẽr'ĭ·á) *n.* (*S.U.*) mensa, bar-ristorante (*dove il cliente si serve da sè*); tavola calda.

cage (kāj) *n.* gabbia (*anche fig.*) *vt.* mettere in gabbia.

cagey (kāj'ĭ) *agg.* (*gergo*) astuto; cauto.

cake (kāk) *n.* focaccia, pasticcino; pezzo; crosta; grumo: a — of soap, una saponetta. *vi.* indurirsi, consolidarsi, incrostarsi; coagularsi.

calamity (ká·lăm'ĭ·tĭ) *n.* calamità.

calcium (kăl'sĭ·ŭm) *n.* calcio (*metallo*).

calculate (kăl'kû·lāt) *vt.* calcolare, valutare.

calculating machine *n.* macchina calcolatrice.

calculation (-lā'shŭn) *n.* calcolo.

calculus (kăl'kû·lŭs) *n.* calcolo.

calendar (kăl'ĕn·dẽr) *n.* calendario; programma: — month, mese solare.

calender (kăl'ĕn·dẽr) *n.* calandra. *vt.* calandrare.

calf (kàf) *n.* (*pl.* calves [kàvz]) vitello; (*anat.*) polpaccio.

caliber (kăl'ĭ·bẽr) *n.* calibro.

calico (kăl'ĭ·kō) *n.* calicò, cotone stampato.

calipers (kăl'ĭ·pẽrz) *n.pl.* compassi.

calisthenics (kăl'ĭs·thĕn'ĭks) *n. sing.* e *pl.* ginnastica a corpo libero.

call (kôl) *n.* chiamata, appello, grido, richiamo; visita; diritto; eccitamento sessuale, foia: to have no — to, non avere il diritto di. *vt.*, *vi.* chiamare, gridare; convocare, richiamare: to — upon somebody, far visita a qualcuno; to — at a port, fare scalo a un porto; to — for, richiedere; esigere; to — the roll, far l'appello; to — together, radunare; to — up, richiamare alla memoria; convocare; presentare (*un'istanza*, *un disegno di legge*, *ecc.*); telefonare a; chiamare alle armi. —er *n.* visitatore.

calling (kôl'ĭng) *n.* professione; vocazione.

callous (kăl'ŭs) *agg.* calloso; insensibile, spietato.

callow (kăl'ō) *agg.* imberbe, inesperto.

callus (kăl'ŭs) *n.* callo; callosità.

calm (käm) *agg.* calmo, quieto. *n.* calma, quiete. *vt.* calmare. *vi.* calmarsi. —ly *avv.* tranquillamente, quietamente. —ness *n.* placidità, calma.

calvary (kăl'vá·rĭ) *n.* calvario.

cam (kăm) *n.* (*mecc.*) camma, eccentrico.

camber (kăm'bẽr) *vt.* arcuare, curvare.

cambric (kăm'brĭk) *n.* batista.

came (kăm) *pass. di* to come.

camel (kăm'ĕl) *n.* cammello.

camelopard (ká·mĕl'ō·pård) *n.* giraffa.

camera (kăm'ẽr·á) *n.* macchina fotografica: motion picture —, macchina da presa; candid —, macchina fotografica in miniatura (*per scattare fotografie di nascosto*).

cameraman (-măn) *n.* operatore (*cinematografico*).

camouflage (kăm'ŏŏ·fläzh) *n.* mascheramento, mimetizzazione. *vt.* mascherare, mimetizzare.

camp (kămp) *n.* campo, accampamento. *vi.* accamparsi.

campaign (kăm·pān') *n.* (*mil.* e *pol.*) campagna. *vi.* fare una campagna; fare propaganda.

camphor (kăm'fẽr) *n.* canfora.

can (kăn) (1) *n.* barattolo, lattina, scatoletta, latta, bidone: — opener, apriscatole. *vt.* mettere in scatola: canned food, cibi in scatola.

can (kăn) (2) *v.* ausiliare difettivo (*negativo* cannot; *pass.* could; *non ha infinito nè pp.*) potere, essere in grado di; sapere, essere capace di: I — help you, io posso aiutarvi; I — speak Italian, so parlare l'italiano.

Canadian (ká·nā'd·ăn) *n.*, *agg.* canadese.

canal (ká·năl') *n.* canale.

canary (ká·nâr'ĭ) *n.* canarino.

cancel (kăn's'l) *vt.* annullare, disdire, cancellare, revocare. —ation (-ā'shŭn) *n.* cancellazione, annullamento, revoca.

cancer (kăn'sẽr) *n.* cancro.

candid (kăn'dĭd) *agg.* candido, franco, ingenuo: — camera, macchinetta fotografica (*per scattare fotografie di nascosto*).

candidacy (kăn'dĭ·dá·sĭ) *n.* candidatura.

candidate (kăn'dĭ·dāt) *n.* candidato.

candle (kăn'd'l) *n.* candela, lume. —stick *n.* candeliere, candelabro.

candor (kăn'dẽr) *n.* candore, ingenuità.

candy (kăn'dĭ) *n.* candito. *vt.* candire.

cane (kăn) *n.* canna, giunco, bastone: — chair, sedia di vimini; — sugar, zucchero di canna.

canine (kā'nĭn) *n.*, *agg.* canino.

canister (kăn'ĭs·tẽr) *n.* scatola di latta, barattolo; (*U.S.*) bidoncino per carburante.

canker (kăng'kẽr) *n.* canchero, cancrena delle piante; tara.

canned (kănd) *agg.* in barattoli: — food, scatolame, cibi in scatola.

cannibal (kăn'ĭ·băl) *n.* cannibale, antropofago.

canniness (kăn'ĭ·nĕs) *n.* astuzia.

cannon (kăn'ŭn) n. cannone; (biliardo) carambola. vt., vi. sparare il cannone; far carambola; urtare.

cannonade (kăn'ŭn·ād') n. cannonata. vt. bombardare, cannoneggiare.

canny (kăn'ĭ) agg. astuto, furbo.

canoe (kà·nōō') n. canoa, piroga.

canon (kăn'ŭn) n. canonico; canone (regola), norma, criterio.

canopy (kăn'ō·pǐ) n. baldacchino; volta; (aeron.) tetto (dell'abitacolo).

cant (kănt) (1) n. linguaggio ipocrita; affettazione; gergo; cantilena.

cant (2) (kănt) n. inclinazione. vi. inclinarsi, pendere.

cantaloupe (kăn'tà·lōp) n. melone.

cantankerous (kăn·tăng'kĕr·ŭs) agg. bisbetico.

canteen (kăn·tēn') n. spaccio; borraccia.

canter (kăn'tĕr) n. piccolo galoppo.

cantilever (kăn'tǐ·lē'vĕr) n. trave a sbalzo.

canton (kăn'tŏn) n. cantone, regione.

canvas (kăn'vàs) n. canovaccio, tela; vela: under — (naut.), a vele spiegate.

canvass (kăn'vàs) n. dibattito, discussione, vaglio; sollecitazione di suffragi; (comm.) raccolta di ordinazioni. vt. discutere, sollecitare. vi. sollecitare suffragi; (comm.) fare la piazza. —er n. agente elettorale; piazzista; propagandista.

canyon (kăn'yŭn) n. burrone.

caoutchouc (kōō'chŏŏk) n. caucciù; gomma.

cap (kăp) n. berretto, cuffia; (gergo) capsula; calotta. vt. coprire, incappucciare; superare, eccellere.

capability (kā'pà·bǐ'ǐ·tǐ) n. capacità, abilità.

capable (kā'pà·b'l) agg. capace, abile.

capacious (kà·pā'shŭs) agg. ampio, capace, vasto, spazioso.

capacity (kà·păs'ǐ·tǐ) n. capacità, veste: in the — of, in veste (in qualità) di.

cape (kāp) (1) n. cappa.

cape (kāp) (2) n. (geog.) capo.

caper (kā'pĕr) n. capriola: to cut capers, fare capriole.

capillary (kăp'ǐ·lĕr'ǐ) agg. capillare.

capital (kăp'ǐ·tăl) n. capitale, patrimonio; (città) capitale; (lettera) maiuscola; (arch.) capitello. agg. maiuscolo; capitale; eccellente, perfetto.

capitalism (kăp'ǐ·tăl·ǐz'm) n. capitalismo.

capitalist (-ǐst) n. capitalista.

capitalization (-ǐ·zā'shŭn) n. capitalizzazione.

capitalize (-ǐz) vt. capitalizzare; scrivere con la maiuscola.

capitol (kăp'ǐ·tŏl) n. campidoglio.

capitulate (kà·pǐt'ū·lāt) vi. capitolare.

capitulation n. capitolazione.

capon (kā'pŏn) n. cappone.

caprice (kà·prēs') n. capriccio.

capricious (kà·prǐsh'ŭs) agg. capriccioso, estroso.

capsizal (kăp·sǐz'ǎl) n. capovolgimento.

capsize (kăp·sǐz') vt. capovolgere. vi. capovolgersi.

capstan (kăp'stăn) n. argano.

capsule (kăp'sūl) n. capsula; riassunto, compendio; agg., riassuntivo, compendioso; in miniatura; aerodinamico; vt. delineare, riassumere.

captain (kăp'tǐn) n. capitano, comandante. vt. capitanare.

caption (kăp'shŭn) n. intestazione (di capitolo); didascalia.

captivate (kăp'tǐ·vāt) vt. conquistare; accattivarsi; sedurre; sottomettere.

captivating agg. seducente.

captive (kăp'tǐv) n., agg. prigioniero.

captivity (kăp'tǐv'ǐ·tǐ) n. prigionia.

captor (kăp'tĕr) n. chi esegue una cattura.

capture (kăp'tūr) n. cattura. vt. catturare.

car (kär) n. carro; automobile; navicella (di aerostato); carrozza, vettura, vagone.

caramel (kär'à·mĕl) n. caramella.

carat (kär'ăt) n. carato.

caravan (kär'à·văn) n. carovana; furgone; casa-rimorchio, roulotte.

carbide (kär'bǐd) n. carburo.

carbolic (kär·bŏl'ǐk) agg. fenico.

carbon (kär'bŏn) n. carbone; carbonio: — paper, cartacarbone.

carbuncle (kär'bŭng'k'l) n. carbonchio; foruncolo.

carburetor (kär'bū·rā'tĕr) n. carburatore.

carcass, carcase (kär'kàs) n. carcassa, carogna.

card (kärd) (1) n. biglietto; carta da gioco; partecipazione; tessera: in the cards, assai probabile; — index, schedario.

card (kärd) (2) n. carda. vt. cardare.

cardboard (kärd'bŏrd') n. cartone.

cardholder (kärd'hōl'dĕr) n. socio (di una biblioteca, ecc.); tesserato.

cardigan (kär'dǐ·găn) n. giubbetto di lana.

cardinal (kär'dǐ·năl) n. cardinale. agg. cardinale; principale, fondamentale.

cardsharper (kärd'shär'pĕr) n. baro.

care (kâr) n. cura, cautela; preoccupazione; sollecitudine; ansietà: to take — of, aver cura di, fare attenzione a. *vi.* interessarsi; voler bene; curarsi; provvedere; preoccuparsi: to — for, interessarsi, di apprezzare, avere simpatia per, voler bene a; I don't —, non me ne importa; I don't — for this, questo non mi piace.

careen (kà·rēn') *vt.* inclinare. *vi.* inclinarsi.

career (kà·rēr') *n.* carriera (*in tutte le accez.*) *vi.* correre.

careful (kâr'fŏŏl) *agg.* attento, accurato, prudente, economo; premuroso. —ly *avv.* accuratamente. —ness *n.* accuratezza, prudenza.

carefree (kâr'frē') *agg.* spensierato.

careless (kâr'lĕs) *agg.* noncurante, sbadato, negligente, indifferente. —ly *avv.* sbadatamente, imprudentemente. —ness *n.* sbadataggine, indifferenza, negligenza.

caress (kà·rĕs') *n.* carezza. *vt.* accarezzare.

caret (kâr'ĕt) *n.* segno d'omissione.

caretaker (kâr'tāk'ēr) *n.* custode, guardiano; *agg.* interinale, provvisorio, supplente.

careworn (-wôrn') *agg.* angosciato.

carfare (kâr'fâr) *n.* denari per il tram; spiccioli.

cargo (kär'gō) *n.* carico mercantile; nave da carico.

caricature (kàr'ĭ·kà·tūr) *n.* caricatura. *vt.* mettere in caricatura.

carmine (kär'mĭn) *n.* carminio.

carnage (kär'nĭj) *n.* carnaio, carneficina.

carnal (kär'năl) *agg.* carnale.

carnation (kär·nā'shŭn) *n.* incarnato; garofano.

carnival (kär'nĭ·văl) *n.* carnevale; festa, baldoria.

carnivorous (kär·nĭv'ō·rŭs) *agg.* carnivoro.

carob (kär'ŏb) *n.* carrubo, carruba.

carol (kär'ŭl) *n.* canto, canzone, nenia. *vi.* cantare.

carousal (kà·rouz'ăl) *n.* baldoria.

carouse (kà·rouz') *vi.* far baldoria, schiamazzare.

carousel (kär'ŏŏ·sĕl') *n.* giostra.

carpenter (kär'pĕn·tēr) *n.* carpentiere.

carpentry (-trĭ) *n.* carpenteria.

carpet (kär'pĕt; -pĭt) *n.* tappeto. —bag *n.* valigia di stoffa.

carport (kär'pōrt') *n.* tettola-autorimessa.

carriage (kär'ĭj) *n.* carrozza; (*ferr.*) vagone; (*comm.*) trasporto (*di merci*); spese di trasporto; (*fig.*) portamento, condotta.

carrier (kär'ĭ·ēr) *n.* trasportatore; portaerei: disease —, veicolo di malattie.

carrion (kär'ĭ·ŭn) *n.* carogna.

carrot (kär'ŭt) *n.* carota.

carrousel *vedi* carousel

carry (kär'ĭ) *vt., vi.* trasportare, portare; avere indosso; condurre; sopportare; conseguire; far votare o approvare; (*comm.*) avere in assortimento; fungere da latore o da guida; avere una portata di: to — on, continuare; to — out, compiere, portare a termine, effettuare; to — oneself, comportarsi, atteggiarsi; this gun carries a mile, questo fucile ha una portata di un miglio; his voice carries far, la sua voce porta lontano.

cart (kärt) *n.* carro, carretto, furgone, calesse: —horse cavallo da tiro. *vt.* trasportare col carro.

cartilage (kär'tĭ·lĭj) *n.* cartilagine.

carton (kär'tŏn) *n.* cartone; involucro, imballaggio, scatola; stecca (*di sigarette*).

cartoon (kär·tŏŏn') *n.* disegno, illustrazione, vignetta; cartone animato; caricatura.

cartoonist (kär·tŏŏn'ĭst) *n.*, caricaturista; disegnatore.

cartridge (kär'trĭj) *n.* cartuccia: blank —, cartuccia a salve. — belt *n.* cartuccera.

carve (kärv) *vt.* scolpire, intagliare, incidere; scalcare, trinciare.

carver (kärv'ēr) *n.* intagliatore, cesellatore; scalco; trinciante.

carving (kärv'ĭng) *n.* scultura, intaglio; scalcatura: — knife, trinciante.

cascade (kăs·kād') *n.* cascata. *vi.* riversarsi.

case (kās) (1) *n.* astuccio, involucro, cassa, cassetta.

case (2) *vt.* chiudere, imballare, rivestire, mettere in scatola; (*gergo*) osservare, ispezionare; occuparsi di.

case (kās) (3) *n.* caso, avvenimento, situazione; causa, processo; tesi (*d'accusa, ecc.*).

casement (kās'mĕnt) *n.* finestra, vetrata.

cash (kăsh) *n.* cassa; danaro contante. *vt.* pagare; incassare, scontare (*una cambiale*): to — in on, trarre profitto da. —box *n.* cassa. cashier (kăsh·ēr') *n.* cassiere. *vt.* espellere, silurare.

casing (kās'ĭng) *n.* involucro, rivestimento, cassa; budello (*per salami*); copertone (*per auto*).

cask (kàsk) *n.* barile, botte, fusto.

casket (kàs'kĕt) *n.* cofanetto; (*S.U.*) bara.

cassock (kăs′ŭk) *n.* (*eccles.*) tonaca.

cast (kȧst) *n.* lancio, getto; stampo, impronta; fusione; carattere; strabismo; (*teatr.*) complesso di attori; distribuzione delle parti. *vt., vi.* lanciare, gettare, scagliare; rivolgere (*lo sguardo*); spargere; fondere; plasmare; (*teatr.*) distribuire (*le parti*), reclutare (*attori*): to — about, andare in cerca; to be — down, essere abbattuto; to — off, scartare; respingere; mollare gli ormeggi; to — a ballot, votare.

cast iron *n.* ghisa.

castanets (kăs′tȧ·nĕts′) *n.* nacchere.

caste (kȧst) *n.* casta, classe: to lose —, disonorarsi, degradarsi.

caster *vedi* castor (2).

castigate (kăs′tĭ·gāt) *vt.* castigare, redarguire.

castle (kȧs′'l), *n.* castello; (*scacchi*) torre.

castor (kȧs′tẽr) (1) *n.* castoro.

castor (kȧs′tẽr) (2) *n.* rotella per mobili; pepaiuola.

castor oil *n.* olio di ricino.

castrate (kăs′trāt) *vt.* castrare.

casual (kăzh′ū·ȧl) *agg.* casuale, fortuito; distratto; indifferente; saltuario; (*di indumenti*) sciolto, comodo, sportivo, semplice.

casualty (-tĭ) *n.* incidente, sinistro; vittima. **casualties** *n.pl.* perdite (*morti, feriti, dispersi*).

cat (kăt) *n.* gatto, felino; (*fig.*) creatura perfida; staffile: to let the — out of the bag, scoprire gli altarini.

cataclysm (kăt′ȧ·klĭz′m) *n.* cataclisma.

catalogue (kăt′ȧ·lŏg) *n.* catalogo. *vt.* catalogare.

catapult (kăt′ȧ·pult) *n.* catapulta; (*aeron.*) catapulta di lancio. *vt.* catapultare.

cataract (kăt′ȧ·răkt) *n.* cateratta.

catarrh (kȧ·tär′) *n.* catarro.

catastrophe (kȧ·tăs′trṓ·fē̇) *n.* catastrofe.

catch (kăch) *n.* presa; cattura; trucco, tranello; pesca; bottino; guadagno; colpo; buon partito; gancio, catenaccio: — phrase, frase di richiamo. *vt.* (*pass., pp.* caught) prendere, afferrare; raggiungere; sorprendere sul fatto. *vi.* agganciarsi; impigliarsi; far presa; prender fuoco; dilagare (*di malattia, ecc.*): to — sight of, scorgere, intravedere; to — up with, mettersi alla pari con; raggiungere. —ing *agg.* attraente; (*med.*) contagioso; ricorrente.

catechism (kăt′ē̇·kĭz′m) *n.* catechismo.

category (kăt′ē̇·gṓ′rĭ) *n.* categoria.

cater (kā′tẽr) *vi.* provvedere, servire, procurare svaghi.

caterpillar (kăt′ẽr·pĭl′ẽr) *n.* bruco; cingolo: — tractor, trattrice a cingoli.

cathedral (kȧ·thē̇′drȧl) *n.* cattedrale.

cathode (kăth′ōd) *n.* catodo.

catholic (kăth′ṓ·lĭk; kăth′lĭk) *n., agg.* cattolico. —ism (kȧ·thŏl′ĭ·sĭz′m) *n.* cattolicesimo.

cattle (kăt′'l) *n.* bestiame (*spec. bovino*). —man *n.* bovaro.

catwalk (kăt′wŏk′) *n.* ballatoio, passerella, corsia.

caucus (kô′kŭs) *n.* comitato elettorale.

caught (kôt) *pass., pp. di* to catch.

cauliflower (kô′lĭ·flou′ẽr) *n.* cavolfiore.

caulk (kôk) *vt.* calafatare.

cause (kôz) *n.* causa, motivo; processo. *vt.* causare, provocare; indurre: to — anything to be done, far fare qualcosa.

causeway (kôz′wā′) *n.* strada in rialza in terreno poludoso.

caution (kô′shŭn), *n.* cautela, prudenza; ammonimento; avvertenza. *vt.* ammonire, mettere in guardia.

cautious (kô′shŭs) *agg.* prudente, circospetto.

cavalier (kăv′ȧ·lẽr′) *n.* cavaliere. *agg.* altezzoso, sdegnoso; sbrigativo.

cavalry (kăv′ȧl·rĭ) *n.* cavalleria.

cave (kāv) *n.* cava, caverna; antro; sotterraneo. *vt., vi.* scavare: to — in, far sprofondare; sprofondare; cedere; sottomettersi.

cavern (kăv′ẽrn) *n.* caverna. —ous *agg.* cavernoso.

caviar, caviare (kăv′ĭ·är′) *n.* caviale.

cavity (kăv′ĭ·tĭ) *n.* cavità.

cease (sēs) *vi.* cessare, smettere, interrompersi; decedere. *vt.* interrompere, far cessare. —less *agg.* incessante.

cedar (sē̇′dẽr) *n.* cedro (*albero*).

cede (sēd) *vt., vi.* cedere; piegarsi.

ceiling (sēl′ĭng) *n.* soffitto; prezzo massimo, calmiere.

celebrate (sĕl′ē̇·brāt) *vt.* celebrare.

celebrated (-brāt′ĕd) *agg.* celebrato, celebre.

celebration (-brā′shŭn) *n.* celebrazione.

celebrity (sē̇·lĕb′rĭ·tĭ) *n.* celebrità.

celery (sĕl′ẽr·ĭ) *n.* sedano.

celestial (sē̇·lĕs′chȧl) *n.* celestiale, celeste.

celibacy (sĕl′ĭ·bȧ·sĭ) *n.* celibato.

cell (sĕl) *n.* cellula; cella; alveolo; scompartimento.

cellar (sĕl′ẽr) *n.* cantina, sotterraneo, sottosuolo, scandinato.

cello (chĕl'ō) *n.* violoncello.
cellophane (sĕl'ō·fān) *n.* cellofane.
celluloid (sĕl'û·loid) *n.* celluloide.
cellulose (sĕl'û·lōs) *n.* cellulosa.
cement (sĕ·mĕnt') *n.* cemento: **reinforced —**, cemento armato. *vt.* cementare, consolidare, rafforzare.
cemetery (sĕm'ē·tĕr'ĭ) *n.* cimitero.
censor (sĕn'sĕr) *n.* censore. *vt.* censurare. **—ious** (sĕn·sō'rĭ·ŭs) *agg.* severo, aspro. **—ship** *n.* censura.
censure (sĕn'shĕr) *n.* censura, critica; biasimo. *vt.* censurare; criticare; biasimare.
census (sĕn'sŭs) *n.* censimento.
cent (sĕnt) *n.* centesimo (*di dollaro*): **ten per —**, dieci per cento.
centennial (sĕn·tĕn'ĭ·ăl) *n.* centenario. *agg.* centenario, secolare.
center (sĕn'tĕr) *n.* centro. *vt.*, *vi.* centrare, concentrare. **—bit** *n.* trapano.
centigrade (sĕn'tĭ·grăd) *agg.* centigrado.
centipede (sĕn'tĭ·pēd) *n.* scolopendra.
central (sĕn'trăl) *agg.* centrale.
centralize (sĕn'trăl·īz) *vt.* accentrare.
centre *vedi* center.
centrifugal (sĕn·trĭf'û·găl) *agg.* centrifugo.
century (sĕn'tŭ·rĭ) *n.* secolo; (*S.U.*) biglietto da cento dollari.
cereal (sēr'ē·ăl) *n.*, *agg.* cereale.
ceremonial (sĕr'ē·mō'nĭ·ăl) *n.*, *agg.* cerimoniale.
ceremonious *agg.* cerimonioso.
ceremony (sĕr'ē·mō'nĭ) *n.* cerimonia.
certain (sûr'tĭn) *agg.* certo, sicuro: **for —**, sicuramente. **—ly** *avv.* certamente. **—ty** *n.* certezza.
certificate (sĕr·tĭf'ĭ·kĭt) *n.* certificato. *vt.* certificare.
certify (sûr'tĭ·fī) *vt.* certificare, garantire.
certitude (sûr'tĭ·tūd) *n.* certezza, sicurezza.
cessation (sĕ·sā'shun) *n.* cessazione, sospensione.
cession (sĕsh'ŭn) *n.* cessione.
cesspool (sĕs'pōōl') *n.* pozzo nero.
cetacean (sĕ·tā'shăn) *n.*, *agg.* cetaceo.
chafe (chāf) *n.* irritazione; riscaldamento; sfregamento. *vt.* strofinare, logorare per attrito. *vi.* essere irritato, fremere; dolere; logorarsi.
chaff (cháf) *n.* burla, scherzo; paglia; rifiuto. *vt.*, *vi.* beffare, scherzare; sminuzzare.
chaffinch (chăf'ĭnch) *n.* fringuello.
chafing dish (chāf'ĭng) *n.* scaldavivande.
chagrin (shɑ·grĭn') *n.* angoscia, cruccio.

chain (chān) *n.* catena: **— stitch**, punto a catenella; **— reaction**, reazione a catena. *vt.* incatenare.
chair (châr) *n.* sedia, seggio; cattedra: **arm—**, **easy —**, poltrona; **bath —**, carrozzella per invalidi; **deck —**, sedia a sdraio; **rocking —**, poltrona a dondolo; **sedan —**, portantina; **— lift**, seggiovia.
chairman (châr'măn) *n.* presidente.
chairmanship *n.* presidenza.
chalice (chăl'ĭs) *n.* calice.
chalk (chôk) *n.* gesso. *vt.* segnare o scrivere col gesso; imbiancare: **to — out**, abbozzare.
chalk-talk *n.* conferenza illustrata (*con disegni o cartoni animati*).
chalky (chôk'ĭ) *agg.* gessoso.
challenge (chăl'ĕnj) *n.* sfida, provocazione; opposizione; (*mil.*) chi-va-là. *vt.*, *vi.* sfidare, provocare; impegnare; respingere; lanciare il chi-va-là.
chamber (chām'bĕr) *n.* camera, stanza, aula.
chambermaid (-mād') *n.* cameriera.
chamber pot (-pŏt) *n.* pitale.
chamois (shăm'ĭ) *n.* camoscio.
champ (chămp) *vt.* rosicchiare: **to — at the bit**, mordere il freno.
champion (chăm'pĭ·ŭn) *n.* campione; paladino. *vt.* difendere; farsi paladino di.
championship *n.* campionato.
chance (chans) *n.* caso, combinazione; sorte; imprevisto; probabilità; rischio: **by —**, per caso; **game of —**, gioco di azzardo. *vi.* accadere per caso. *vt.* arrischiare, tentare: **to — upon**, imbattersi in.
chancellor (chán'sĕ·lĕr) *n.* cancelliere.
chandelier (shăn'dĕ·lĕr') *n.* lampadario.
change (chānj) *n.* mutamento; muta (*di vestiario*); fase; cambio, moneta spicciola; variazione: **the — of life**, la menopausa. *vt.*, *vi.* cambiare; modificare; convertire in danaro spicciolo; modificarsi. **—able** *agg.* mutevole.
changer *n.* cambiavalute.
channel (chăn'ĕl) *n.* canale, stretto: **the English —**, la Manica.
chant (chánt) *n.* canto, cantilena. *vt.*, *vi.* cantare, salmodiare.
chaos (kā'ŏs) *n.* caos.
chaotic (kā·ŏt'ĭk) *agg.* caotico.
chap (chăp) (1) *n.* screpolatura. *vt.* screpolare. *vi.* screpolarsi.
chap (chăp) (2) *n.* individuo, tipo, tizio: **a fine —**, un brav'uomo o ragazzo.
chapel (chăp'ĕl) *n.* cappella.
chaperon (shăp'ĕr·ōn) *n.* scorta, accompagnatore o accompagnatrice. *vt.* scortare.

chaplain (chăp′lĭn) *n.* cappellano.

chapped (chăpt) *agg.* screpolato.

chapter (chăp′tĕr) *n.* capitolo.

char (chär) *vt.* carbonizzare. *vi.* carbonizzarsi.

character (kăr′ăk.tĕr) *n.* carattere; caratteristica; scrittura; benservito; personaggio, tipo caratteristico. —**istic** (-ĭs′tĭk) *agg.* caratteristico. *n.* peculiarità, caratteristica. —**ize** *vt.* caratterizzare.

charcoal (chär′kōl′)*n.*carbone di legna.

charge (chärj) *n.* carico; incarico; gravame, responsabilità; cura; accusa; carica; spesa, addebito: **to take — of**, incaricarsi di; **to be in — of**, essere incaricato di, dirigere; **under my —**, a mie spese; **free of —**, senza spese, gratis; **to give one in —**, consegnare uno alla polizia. *vt.* caricare; saturare; incaricare; accusare; addebitare.

charger (chär′jĕr) *n.* cavallo da battaglia; vassoio.

chariot (chär′ĭ.ŭt) *n.* cocchio.

charitable (chär′ĭ.tà.b'l) *agg.* caritatevole.

charity (chär′ĭ.tĭ) *n.* carità, elemosina, beneficenza: **out of —**, per beneficenza.

charlatan (shär′là.tăn) *n.* ciarlatano.

charm (chärm) *n.* fascino, incantesimo; talismano; ciondolo portafortuna. *vt.* affascinare; stregare; lusingare. —**ing** *agg.* affascinante, delizioso.

chart (chärt) *n.* carta nautica; grafico, statistica; cartella clinica. *vt.* tracciare, delineare.

charter (chär′tĕr) *n.* licenza, brevetto: **The Great —**, la Magna Carta: **— member**, socio fondatore. *vt.* concedere una licenza *o* un privilegio a; noleggiare. **— party** *n.* (*naut.*) contratto di noleggio.

chartered *agg.* munito di licenza: **— accountant** (*Ingh.*), ragioniere.

charwoman (chär′wŏŏm′ăn) *n.* domestica a ore.

chary (chär′ĭ) *agg.* prudente; parco.

chase (chās) *n.* caccia, inseguimento. *vt.* cacciare; inseguire; scacciare; cesellare, incidere.

chaser *n.* inseguitore; incisore; (*S.U.*) bicchiere d'acqua *o* selz (*da bersi dopo un liquore forte*), "ammazzaliquore."

chasm (kăz′m) *n.* voragine, crepaccio.

chaste (chāst) *agg.* casto; moderato; sobrio. —**ness** *n.* castità.

chastise (chăs-tīz′) *vt.* castigare, punire.

chastisement (chăs′tĭz-mĕnt) *n.* punizione.

chastity (chăs′tĭ.tĭ) *n.* castità.

chat (chăt) *n.* chiacchierata, conversazione. *vi.* chiacchierare.

chattel (chăt′'l) *n.* bene mobile.

chatter (chăt′ĕr) *n.* chiacchiera, chiacchierata; battito (*dei denti*); *vi.* chiacchierare, parlottare, cinguettare, battere i denti. —**box** *n.* chiacchierone.

chatty (chăt′ĭ) *agg.* vaniloquente, chiacchierone.

chauffeur (shō-fûr′; shō′fĕr) *n.*autista.

cheap (chēp) *agg.* economico, a buon mercato; di scarso valore; svalutato, deprezzato; spregevole: **dirt —**, a prezzo irrisorio; **to hold —**, disprezzare.

cheapen (chēp′ĕn) *vt.*, *vi.* svilire, deprezzare; mercanteggiare.

cheaply (-lĭ) *avv.* economicamente, a buon mercato.

cheapness (-nĕs) *n.* buon mercato, meschinità.

cheat (chēt) *n.* frode; imbroglione, truffatore; mistificatore. *vt.*, *vi.* ingannare, imbrogliare, barare.

check (chĕk) *n.* ostacolo, impedimento, freno; arresto brusco; verifica, controllo; contromarca, scontrino; assegno; quadretto (*nel disegno di tessuti, ecc.*); (*scacchi*) scacco: **blank —**, assegno in bianco; **crossed —**, assegno barrato. *vt.* fermare, bloccare, trattenere; moderare; verificare, controllare; dare scacco matto a, tenere in scacco. —**book** *n.* libretto d'assegni. —**mate** *n.* scacco matto. —**room** *n.* guardaroba.

checker (chĕk′ĕr) *n.* pedina (*per scacchi o dama*); scacchiera; scacco; ispettore, verificatore.

checkerboard (chĕk′ĕr·bōrd′) *n.* scacchiera.

checkered (chĕk′ĕrd) *agg.* quadrettato; variato: **a — career**, una carriera fortunosa.

checkers (chĕk′ĕrz) *n.* (gioco degli) scacchi.

cheek (chēk) *n.* guancia, gota; impudenza, faccia tosta.

cheekbone (chĕk′bōn′) *n.* zigomo.

cheeky (chĕk′ĭ) *agg.* insolente.

cheer (chĕr) *n.* allegria, animazione; acclamazione, applauso. *vt.* acclamare; rallegrare, incoraggiare. *vi.* rasserenarsi, rincuorarsi. —**ful** *agg.* allegro. —**fully** *avv.* allegramente. —**fulness** *n.* allegria. —**ily** *avv.* gaiamente. —**less** *agg.* triste, cupo. —**y** *agg.* gaio, allegro.

cheese (chēz) *n.* formaggio: **cottage —**, specie di ricotta.

cheesecake (chēz'kăk') *n.* torta a base di presame e uova; (*gergo*) fotografia di ragazza procace con le gambe in mostra.

chemical (kĕm'ĭ-kăl) *n.* prodotto chimico. *agg.* chimico.

chemist (kĕm'ĭst) *n.* chimico; farmacista.

chemistry (kĕm'ĭs-trĭ) *n.* chimica.

cheque (chĕk) *vedi* check.

cherish (chĕr'ĭsh) *vt.* custodire amorevolmente (*ricordi, ecc.*); curare con affetto; accarezzare, nutrire (*speranze, sentimenti*).

cherry (chĕr'ĭ) *n.* ciliegia. **— tree** *n.* ciliegio.

chess (chĕs) *n.* (gioco degli) scacchi. **—board** *n.* scacchiera. **—men** *n.* pezzi degli scacchi.

chest (chĕst) *n.* petto, torace, cassa, cofano: **— of drawers,** cassettone.

chestnut (chĕs'nŭt) *n.* castagna, castagno. *agg.* castagno, marrone, sauro.

chew (chōō, chū) *n.* masticazione; ciò che si mastica. *vt.* masticare.

chewing gum *n.* gomma da masticare.

chichi (shē'shē) *agg.* (*gergo*) elegante; ricercato; effemminato.

chick (chĭk) *n.* pulcino; bambino.

chicken (chĭk'ĕn) *n.* pollo, pollastra: **— -hearted,** vigliacco; **— -pox,** vaiolo, varicella.

chick-pea (chĭk'pē') *n.* cece.

chide (chīd) *vt.* (*pp.* chid) sgridare, biasimare, redarguire.

chief (chēf) *n.* capo, comandante. *agg.* principale, sommo, supremo. **—fy** *avv.* principalmente, soprattutto.

chiffon (shĭ-fon'; shĭf'on) *n.* velo.

chilblain (chĭl'blân) *n.* gelone.

child (chīld) *n.* (*pl.* children [chĭl'drĕn] bambino, figlio, figlia: **to be with —,** essere in stato interessante. **—bearing** *n.* gravidanza. **—birth** *n.* parto. **—hood** *n.* infanzia. **—ish** *agg.* infantile, puerile: **to grow —ish,** rimbambire. **—ishness** *n.* puerilità. **—less** *agg.* senza figli. **—like** *agg.* infantile, spontaneo.

chill (chĭl) *n.* freddo; raffreddamento; brivido; raffreddore. *vt.* raffreddare; raggelare. *vi.* raffreddarsi; raggelarsi.

chilly (chĭl'ĭ) *agg.* freddo, fresco.

chime (chīm) *n.* rintocco; scampanio; armonia. *vt.*, *vi.* scampanare; sonare armoniosamente; risonare; armonizzarsi; essere d'accordo: to **— in,** interloquire; to **— in with,** essere in armonia con, approvare.

chimney (chĭm'nĭ) *n.* camino; fumaiolo.

chin (chĭn) *n.* mento.

china (chī'nà) *n.* porcellana.

Chinese (chī'nēz') *n.*, *agg.* cinese: **— lantern,** lampioncino alla veneziana.

chink (chĭngk) *n.* fessura, crepa, screpolatura.

chip (chĭp) *n.* frammento, scheggia: **potato chips,** patatine fritte. *vt.* tagliuzzare, scheggiare, scorticare, affettare. *vi.* scheggiarsi, scrostarsi: to **— in,** contribuire, dare la propria offerta.

chirp (chûrp) *n.* cinguettio, trillo. *vi.* cinguettare.

chisel (chĭz'l) *n.* scalpello, cesello. *vt.* cesellare; (*gergo*) scroccare; imbrogliare.

chitchat (chĭt'chăt') *n.* chiacchierio.

chivalrous (shĭv'ăl-rŭs) *agg.* cavalleresco.

chivalry (shĭv'ăl-rĭ) *n.* cavalleria.

chloral (klō'răl) *n.* cloralio.

chloride (klō'rĭd) *n.* cloruro.

chlorine (klō'rēn) *n.* cloro.

chloroform (klō'rō-fôrm) *n.* cloroformio. *vt.* cloroformizzare.

chlorophyll (klō'rō-fĭl) *n.* clorofilla.

chock (chŏk) *n.* cuneo, bietta, supporto. **—full** *agg.* pieno, colmo.

chocolate (chŏk'ō-lĭt; chŏk'lĭt) *n.* cioccolata.

choice (chois) *n.* scelta; assortimento. *agg.* scelto; eccellente.

choir (kwīr) *n.* coro.

choke (chōk) *n.* strozzamento, strozzatura; soffocazione; (*mecc.*) regolatore (*d'aria, di carburante, ecc.*). *vt.* soffocare, strangolare; ostruire; colmare; (*mecc.*) togliere aria (*al carburatore*). *vi.* soffocare; ostruirsi.

choler (kŏl'ĕr) *n.* collera, bile.

cholera (kŏl'ĕr-à) *n.* colera.

choose (chōōz) *vt.* (*pass.* chose, *pp.* chosen) scegliere, decidere, volere: to **— to,** preferire: **I don't — to** do it, non mi va di farlo.

chop (chŏp) *n.* colpo di scure; trancio, costoletta. *vt.* tagliare. **—house** *n.* ristorante. **—py** *agg.* screpolato: **— sea,** mare agitato.

choral (kō'răl) *agg.* corale; *n.* (kō-răl'; -răl') corale.

chord (kôrd) *n.* corda; accordo.

chore (chōr) *n.* lavoro, faccenda; *pl.* lavori domestici.

choreography (kō'rē ŏg'rà fĭ) *n.* coreografia.

chorister (kŏr'ĭs-tĕr) *n.* corista.

chorus (kō'rŭs) *n.* coro, corpo di ballo (*nel varietà*); ritornello. **— girl** *n.* corista (*donna*); ballerina di varietà.

chose (chōz) *pass. di* to **choose.**

chosen (chō'z'n) *pp. di* to choose.

Christ (krĭst) *n.* Cristo.

christen (krĭs'n) *vt.* battezzare.

christening (krĭs'n·ĭng) *n.* battesimo.

Christian (krĭs'chăn) *n., agg.* cristiano: — name, nome di battesimo.

Christianity (krĭs'chĭ·ăn'ĭ·tĭ; -tĭ·ăn'ĭ·tĭ) *n.* cristianità; cristianesimo.

Christmas (krĭs'măs) *n.* Natale: Merry —! buon Natale! —tide *n.* periodo natalizio.

Christy (krĭs'tĭ) *n.* (*sci.*) cristiania.

chrome (krōm), chromium (krō'mĭ·ŭm) *n.* cromo.

chronic (krŏn'ĭk) *agg.* cronico.

chronicle (krŏn'ĭ·k'l) *n.* cronaca, cronistoria: *vt.* fare la cronaca di; raccontare.

chronicler (-klĕr) *n.* cronista.

chronological (krŏn'ô·lŏj'ĭ·kăl) *agg.* cronologico.

chronology (krô·nŏl'ô·jĭ) *n.* cronologia.

chronometer (krô·nŏm'ê·tĕr) *n.* cronometro.

chrysalis (krĭs'á·lĭs) *n.* crisalide.

chubby (chŭb'ĭ) *agg.* paffuto.

chuck (1) *n.* richiamo della chioccia. *vi.* chiocciare.

chuck (2) *n.* buffetto, colpetto sotto il mento. *vt.* dare un buffetto a; gettare, scaraventare: to — out, mettere alla porta, scacciare; to — (*a thing*) rinunciare a, abbandonare.

chuck (3) *n.* (*mecc.*) mandrino.

chuckle (chŭk''l) *n.* risatina. *vi.* ridacchiare; ridere sotto i baffi.

chum (chŭm) *n.* amico; compagno di stanza.

chump (chŭmp) *n.* ceppo, pezzo di legno; (*gergo*) testa; sciocco.

chunk (chŭngk) *n.* fettona; grosso pezzo.

church (chûrch) *n.* chiesa, tempio. —man *n.* ecclesiastico, uomo devoto. —yard *n.* cimitero.

churl (chûrl) *n.* zotico, villanzone.

churn (chûrn) *n.* zangola. *vt.,* sbattere il latte per fare il burro; spumeggiare (*dei flutti*); scuotere, agitare.

chute (shōōt) *n.* cascata; tromba, scarico; condotto; piano inclinato.

cider (sī'dĕr) *n.* sidro.

cigar (sĭ·gär') *n.* sigaro.

cigarette (sĭg'á·rĕt') *n.* sigaretta: — case, portasigarette; — holder, bocchino.

cinch (sĭnch) *n.* cinghia da sella; (*gergo*) certezza; impresa facile, giochetto. *vt.* legare strettamente, assicurare con cinghia; (*gergo*) agguantare, accaparrarsi.

cinder (sĭn'dĕr) *n.* tizzone; (*pl.*) ceneri.

Cinderella (sĭn'dĕr·ĕl'á) *n.* Cenerentola.

cinnamon (sĭn'á·mŭn) *n.* cannella.

cipher (sī'fĕr) *n.* cifra; zero; cifrario.

circle (sûr'k'l) *n.* circolo, cerchio, cerchia; (*astr.*) orbita. *vt.* circondare, accerchiare, aggirare. *vi.* rotare.

circuit (sûr'kĭt) *n.* rotazione, circuito; circonferenza, cinta; deviazione.

circuitous (sĕr·kū'ĭ·tŭs) *agg.* sinuoso, indiretto.

circular (sûr'kû·lĕr) *n., agg.* circolare: — staircase, scala a chiocciola.

circulate (sûr'kû·lāt) *vt.* diffondere, mettere in circolazione, distribuire; divulgare. *vi.* circolare.

circulation (-lā'shŭn) *n.* circolazione, diffusione.

circumcise (sûr'kŭm·sīz) *vt.* circoncidere.

circumcision (sûr·kŭm·sĭzh'ŭn) *n.* circoncisione.

circumference (sĕr·kŭm'fĕr·ĕns) *n.* circonferenza.

circumflex (sûr'kŭm·flĕks) *agg.* circonflesso.

circumlocution (sûr'kŭm·lō kū'shŭn) *n.* circonlocuzione.

circumscribe (sûr'kŭm·skrīb') *n.* circoscrivere.

circumspect (sûr'kŭm·spĕkt) *agg.* circospetto. —ion *n.* circospezione.

circumstance (sûr'kŭm·stăns) *n.* circostanza, condizione; cerimonia, solennità; (*pl.*) situazione economica, posizione.

circumstantial (sûr'kŭm·stăn'shăl) *agg.* particolareggiato; indiziario.

circumvent (sûr'kŭm·vĕnt') *vt.* circuire.

circus (sûr'kŭs) *n.* circo equestre; rotonda.

cistern (sĭs'tĕrn) *n.* cisterna, serbatoio.

citadel (sĭt'á·d'l) *n.* cittadella.

citation (sĭ·tā'shŭn) *n.* citazione.

cite (sīt) *vt.* citare.

citizen (sĭt'ĭ·zĕn) *n.* cittadino: fellow —, concittadino.

citizenship (-shĭp) *n.* cittadinanza.

citron (sĭt'rŭn) *n.* cedro (*frutto*).

citrous, citrus (sĭt'rŭs) *agg.* agrumario: — grove, agrumeto.

city (sĭt'ĭ) *n.* città; municipio; centro degli affari (*in grande città*). *agg.* urbano, municipale: — hall, municipio; — council, giunta comunale; — editor (*giorn.*), capocronaca.

civic (sĭv'ĭk) *agg.* civico.

civics (sĭv'ĭks) *n.* diritto politico.

civil (sĭv'ĭl) *agg.* civile; cortese, educato; municipale.

civilian (sĭ·vĭl'yăn) *n., agg.* borghese (*non militare*).

civility (sĭ·vĭl'ĭ·tĭ) n. urbanità, cortesia.

civilization (sĭv'ĭ·lĭ·zā'shŭn; -lĭ·zā'-) n. civiltà, civilizzazione.

civilize (sĭv'ĭ·līz) vt. civilizzare, incivilire.

civilized (-līzd) agg. civile, incivilito.

clad (klăd) pass., pp. di to clothe; agg. vestito, rivestito; placcato: armor—, agg, corazzato, blindato.

claim (klām) n. richiesta, pretesa, rivendicazione, diritto; (min.) concessione, zona concessa per lo sfruttamento o rivendicata: to lay — to, accampare diritti su. vt. reclamare, pretendere, rivendicare; asserire, affermare. —ant n. reclamante; pretendente.

clairvoyance (klâr·voi'ăns) n. chiaroveggenza.

clairvoyant (klâr·voi'ănt) n., agg. chiaroveggente.

clam (klăm) n. mollusco bivalve; (fig.) persona discreta.

clamber (klăm'bẽr) vi. arrampicarsi.

clammy (klăm'ĭ) agg. viscido, umidiccio.

clamor (klăm'ẽr) n. clamore, frastuono. vi. gridare, far clamori. —ous agg. clamoroso, rumoroso.

clamp (klămp) n. morsa; rampone. vt. stringere nella morsa; unire.

clan (klăn) n. tribù; fazione, cricca.

clandestine (klăn·dĕs'tĭn) agg. clandestino.

clang (klăng) n. clangore. vi. risonare. vt. far risonare.

clap (klăp) n. colpo; schiocco; battimani; scoppio (di tuono); manata. vt., vi. colpire; battere (le mani); sbattere (le ali, ecc.); applaudire; dar manate; schiaffare, scaraventare.

claret (klăr'ĕt) n. chiaretto (vino).

clarify (klăr'ĭ·fī) vt. chiarificare.

clarinet (klăr'ĭ·nĕt') n. clarinetto.

clash (klăsh) n. cozzo, scontro; frastuono; conflitto, contrasto. vi. urtarsi, cozzare; risonare; essere in conflitto; contrastare. vt. urtare; far risonare.

clasp (klăsp) n. gancio, fermaglio; presa; abbraccio; stretta. vt., vi. agganciare, allacciare; cingere; abbracciare; stringere (la mano): —knife, coltello a serramanico.

class (klăs) n. classe; categoria. vt. classificare.

classbook n. registro di classe.

classic (klăs'ĭk) n., agg. classico: —al scholar, umanista.

classification (klăs'ĭ·fĭ·kā'shŭn) n. classificazione.

classify (klăs'ĭ·fī) vt. classificare.

classmate n. compagno di scuola.

classroom n. aula scolastica.

clatter (klăt'ẽr) n. acciottolio, fracasso, vocio, schiamazzo. vi. far fracasso; risonare; blaterare.

clause (klôz) n. clausola; (gramm.) proposizione.

claw (klô) n. artiglio, grinfia; pinza (di crostaceo); taglio (di martello). vt. artigliare, lacerare con gli artigli, graffiare; afferrare; annaspare.

clay (klā) n. argilla, creta: baked —, terracotta.

clean (klēn) agg. pulito, puro, lustro; retto, onesto: to show a — pair of heels, darsela a gambe, sparire. avv. nettamente, completamente, chiaramente. vt. pulire, purificare; lucidare; smacchiare. —er n. pulitore, smacchiatore. —ing n. pulizia, lucidatura, smacchiatura. —liness (klĕn-) n. nettezza, purezza. —ly avv. pulitamente; nettamente. agg. lindo, ordinato. —ness n. pulizia, purezza, nitidezza.

cleanse (klĕnz) vt. lavare, pulire, detergere; purificare, purgare, depurare.

cleanser (klĕn'zẽr) n. detersivo.

clear (klēr) agg. chiaro, limpido; netto, evidente; innocente; immacolato: to keep — of, evitare; to steer — of, schivare, girar largo da; to be in the —, essere scagionato, essere fuori di sospetto. vt. chiarire, chiarificare; sgomberare; svincolare; guadagnare; discolpare, assolvere; superare (un ostacolo); scagionare, prosciogliere; passare (una barriera doganale, ecc.); (naut.) doppiare. vi. schiarirsi, rasserenarsi; sbarazzarsi. —ance n. liberazione; levata (delle lettere); svincolo; sgombero: —ance sale, liquidazione. —ing n. compensazione; liquidazione dei bilanci; radura. —inghouse n. camera di compensazione.

clearness (klēr'nĕs) n. chiarezza.

cleavage (klēv'ĭj) n. fenditura, scissione, sfaldamento.

cleave (klēv) vt. (pass. clove, cleft, pp. cloven, cleft) fendere, dividere, sfaldare. vi. fendersi, sfaldarsi.

clef (klĕf) n. (mus.) chiave.

cleft (klĕft) n. fessura. pp. di to cleave.

clemency (klĕm'ĕn·sĭ) n. clemenza.

clement (klĕm'ĕnt) agg. clemente.

clench (klĕnch) vt. ribadire; stringere (i denti, il pugno); afferrare.

clergy (klûr'jĭ) n. clero. —man n. (pl. —men) ecclesiastico; pastore evangelico.

clerical (klĕr'ĭ·kăl) agg. clericale; impiegatizio; sedentario.

clerk (klûrk) *n.* impiegato, commesso, contabile; cancelliere (*di tribunale*): chief —, capufficio.

clever (klĕv'ĕr) *agg.* abile, bravo; intelligente; astuto. —ly *avv.* abilmente; astutamente. —ness *n.* abilità; destrezza; disinvoltura.

clew (klōō) *n.* gomitolo; traccia, indizio.

click (klĭk) *n.* scatto, schiocco. *vi.*, *vt.* scattare, schioccare; far schioccare. —ing *n.* ticchettio.

client (klĭ'ĕnt) *n.* cliente. —ele (klĭ'-ĕn.tĕl') *n.* clientela.

cliff (klĭf) *n.* roccia, rupe, scarpata.

climate (klĭ'mĭt) *n.* clima.

climax (klī'măks) *n.* punto culminante, crescendo, apice, crisi risolutiva. *vt.* portare al punto culminante. *vi.* raggiungere il punto culminante.

climb (klīm) *vt.* scalare, dare la scalata a, salire. *vi.* -arrampicarsi; innalzarsi: to — down, ritirarsi, calar le arie. —er *n.* scalatore; pianta rampicante.

clime (klīm) *n.* clima; paese.

clinch (klĭnch) *n.* ribattitura; ribattino; (*pugilato*) corpo a corpo. *vt.* ribadire, stringere. *vi.* avvinghiarsi.

cling (klĭng) *vi.* (*pass.*, *pp.* clung) aggrapparsi, attaccarsi, appiccicarsi, aderire, avviticchiarsi.

clinic (klĭn'ĭk) *n.* clinica. —al *agg.* clinico.

clink (klĭngk) *n.* tintinnio.

clip (klĭp) *n.* taglio (*di capelli, ecc.*), tosatura; molletta; caricatore (*di arma da fuoco*): paper —, fermaglio, graffetta; to go at a good —, andare a passo rapido, avere un' andatura forte. *vt.* tagliare, tosare, abbreviare. —per *n.* tosatore, tosatrice (*macchinetta*); (*naut.*) veliero mercantile veloce; (*aeron.*) aeroplano transatlantico. —ping *n.* taglio, tosatura; ritaglio (*di giornale, ecc.*).

cloak (klōk) *n.* mantello, manto; maschera; pretesto. *vt.* ammantare, mascherare. —room *n.* guardaroba; (*ferr.*) deposito bagagli. — -and-dagger *agg.* (*di romanzi*) di cappa e spada.

clobber (klŏb'ĕr) *vt.* (*gergo*) bastonare; abbattere; tramortire.

clock (klŏk) *n.* orologio (*da muro*), pendola: alarm —, sveglia; it is two o'—, sono le due. —wise *agg.* destrorso. —work *n.* movimento di orologeria.

clod (klŏd) *n.* zolla, pezzo; tonto.

clodhopper (klŏd'hŏp'ĕr) *n.* aratore; *pl.*, scarponi.

clog (klŏg) *n.* pastoia; impedimento; ostruzione; zoccolo. *vt.* impastoiare; ostruire; ostacolare. *vi.* incagliarsi; ostruirsi.

cloister (klois'tĕr) *n.* chiostro.

close (klōz) *n.* fine, chiusura, conclusione; chiostro; recinto; corpo a corpo. *agg.* (klōs) chiuso, stretto; compatto; avaro; male arieggiato, soffocante; esatto; intimo; conciso; discreto; misterioso: questioning, interrogatorio serrato o minuzioso; — at hand, a portata di mano; — by, vicinissimo. *avv.* vicino, da vicino, strettamente, intimamente. *vt.* (-z) chiudere; terminare, concludere; stringere; serrare le file; togliere (*la seduta*). *vi.* chiudersi, concludere, finire; cicatrizzarsi (*di ferite*): to — in upon, accerchiare.

closely (klōs'lĭ) *avv.* da vicino; strettamente; intimamente; segretamente; attentamente.

closeness (klōs'nĕs) *n.* vicinanza; compattezza, pesantezza (*di atmosfera*).

closing (klōz'ĭng) *n.* chiusura, fine, conclusione.

closet (klŏz'ĕt) *n.* gabinetto; salottino; sgabuzzino; ripostiglio. *vt.* chiudere, rinchiudere; nascondere: to be —ed with, essere in conciliabolo con.

closure (klō'zhĕr) *n.*, chiusura, conclusione.

clot (klŏt) *n.* grumo, coagulo. *vi.* coagularsi, raggrumarsi.

cloth (klŏth) *n.* tela, stoffa, panno, drappo; tovaglia; clero.

clothe (klōth) *vt.* (*pass.*, *pp.* clad, clothed) vestire, rivestire, coprire, adornare.

clothes (klōthz; *fam.* klōz) *n.pl.* vestiti, indumenti; coltri: plain —, abiti borghesi; suit of —, (vestito) completo. —line, *n.* corda per bucato; cheria. —pin, *n.* molletta per biancheria.

clothier (klōth'yĕr) *n.* fabbricante di tessuti: ready-made —, negoziante d'abiti fatti.

clothing (klōth'ĭng) *n.* vestiario; coltri.

cloud (kloud) *n.* nuvola, nube; chiazza. *vt.* oscurare; confondere, rendere nebuloso. *vi.* rannuvolarsi, oscurarsi. —less *agg.* limpido, sereno, senza nubi.

cloudy (kloud'ĭ) *agg.* nuvoloso, nebuloso.

clout (klout) *n.* scapaccione; mazzata.

clove (klōv) *n.* chiodo di garofano; spicchio.

cloven (klōv''n) *pp. di* to cleave.

clover (klō'vĕr) n. trifoglio: to be in
—, vivere negli agi.

clown (kloun) n. buffone, pagliaccio.

cloy (kloi) vt. saziare, nauseare.

club (klŭb) n. mazza, bastone; circolo, associazione; fiore (nelle carte
da gioco). vt. bastonare, tramortire.
vi. quotarsi (versar danaro); associarsi.

cluck (klŭk) vi. chiocciare.

clue (klōō) vedi clew.

clump (klŭmp) n. massa, blocco;
cespuglio, boschetto. vt. ammonticchiare. vi. camminare con passo
pesante.

clumsiness (klŭm'zǐ-nĕs) n. goffaggine.

clumsy (klŭm'zǐ) agg. goffo, maldestro; sgraziato; mal fatto.

clung (klŭng) pass., pp. di to cling.

cluster (klŭs'tĕr) n. grappolo; mazzo
(di fiori); gruppo, sciame, folla. vi.
raggrupparsi, formare grappolo. vt.
raggruppare.

clutch (klŭch) n. stretta, presa; (pl.)
grinfie, artigli; (mecc.) manicotto
d'accoppiamento; (auto.) frizione.
vt., vi. afferrare, stringere, artigliare; aggrapparsi.

clutter (klŭt'ĕr) n. fracasso; trambusto; confusione, disordine. vt. gettare alla rinfusa; scompigliare. vi.
fare baccano; riversarsi in disordine.

coach (kōch) n. carrozza; diligenza;
ripetitore, istruttore; allenatore.
vt. istruire, preparare, allenare.
to — with, prendere lezione da.
—man n. cocchiere.

coagulate (kō-ăg'ū-lāt) vi. coagularsi. vt. coagulare.

coagulation (-lā'shŭn) n. coagulazione.

coal (kōl) n. carbone; tizzone. vt.
fornire o rifornire di carbone. vi.
(naut.) far carbone. —bin n. carbonile. — oil. petrolio. —tar n.
catrame.

coalesce (kō'á-les') vi. fondersi, unirsi.

coalition (kō'á-lĭsh'ŭn) n. coalizione.

coarse (kōrs) agg. grossolano, volgare; grezzo, ruvido.

coarseness (kōrs'nĕs; -nĭs) n. volgarità, grossolanità; ruvidezza.

coast (kōst) n. costa, litorale. vt., vi.
costeggiare, rasentare; scendere
(un pendio) in folle (detto di veicolo). —guard n. guardiacoste.
—line n. costa, litorale.

coat (kōt) n. giacca, abito; mantello
(anche di animale); copertura, rivestimento, strato, vernice; (S.U.)
soprabito: — of arms, stemma nobiliare. vt. vestire; rivestire; pitturare. —ing n. tessuto per abito;
rivestimento; strato (di vernice,
ecc.); patina.

coax (kōks) (1) vt., vi. blandire, adulare, circuire, persuadere.

coax (kō-ăks') (2) (abbr. di coaxial
cable) n. cavo coassiale.

cob (kŏb) n. cigno maschio; pannocchia di granoturco; cavallo da tiro.

cobble (kŏb''l) n. ciottolo. vt. acciottolare; accomodare, rattoppare.

cobbler (kŏb'lĕr) n. ciabattino.

cobweb (kŏb'wĕb') n. ragnatela.

cocaine (kō-kān') n. cocaina.

cock (kŏk) n. gallo; maschio (di
qualunque uccello); rubinetto; cane
(d'arma da fuoco): — -and-bull
story, panzana. vt., vi. drizzare,
raddrizzare; armare (un fucile,
ecc.). —ed hat, tricorno.

cockatoo (kŏk'á-tōō') n. cacatoa.

cockerel (kŏk'ĕr-ĕl) n. galletto.

cockeye (kŏk'wĕb') n. occhio strabico.
—d agg. strabico; (gergo) sbilenco;
sciocco, assurdo, scombinato.

cockle (kŏk''l) (1) n. loglio (erba parassita).

cockle (kŏk''l) (2) n. cardio (frutto di
mare bivalve).

cockpit (kŏk'pĭt') n. (naut.) castello
di poppa; (aeron.) abitacolo.

cockroach (kŏk'rōch') n. scarafaggio.

cocksure (kŏk'shōōr') agg. ostinato;
certissimo; presuntuoso.

cocktail (kŏk'tāl') n. miscuglio di
liquori; miscuglio di frutti di mare
in salsa serviti in coppa; cavallo
con coda mozza o bastardo.

cocky (kŏk'ĭ) agg. impudente, sfrontato.

coco (kō'kō) n. cocco. —nut n. noce di
cocoa (kō'kō) n. cacao. [cocco.

cocoon kō-kōōn') n. bozzolo.

cozolelle (kŏk'ō-zĕl'ĕ) n. zucchina.

cod (kŏd) (1) n. merluzzo. — -liver
oil, olio di fegato di merluzzo.

cod (kŏd) (2) n. guscio; (anat.) scroto.

coddle (kŏd''l) vt. curare, colmar di
premure; coccolare.

code (kōd) n. codice; cifrario. vt. codificare, tradurre in codice. agg.
cifrato.

codicil (kŏd'ĭ-sĭl) n. codicillo.

coeducational (school) (kō'ĕd-û-kā'-
shŭn-ál) n. scuola mista.

coefficient (kō'ĕ-fĭsh'ĕnt; kō'ĭ-) n.
coefficiente.

coerce (kō-ûrs') vt. costringere, forzare, reprimere.

coercion (kō-ûr'shŭn) n. coercizione.

coexist (kō'ĕg-zĭst') vi. coesistere.

coffee (kŏf'ĭ) n. caffè. — bean, —
berry n. chicco di caffè. — grounds
n.pl. fondi di caffè. —house ,—shop
n. caffè (ritrovo). —mill, — grinder
n. macinino da caffè. —pot n. caffettiera.

coffer (kŏf'ẽr) n. cofano, scrigno, forziere.

coffin (kŏf'ĭn) n. bara, cassa da morto.

cog (kŏg) n. dente (d'ingranaggio). —wheel n. ruota dentata, ingranaggio, cremagliera.

cogent (kō'jĕnt) agg. potente, persuasivo.

cognate (kŏg'nāt) agg., analogo, dello stesso ceppo.

cognition (kŏg·nĭsh'ŭn) n. cognizione, conoscenza, contezza.

cohere (kō·hẽr') vi. aderire.

coherence (kō·hẽr'ẽns) n. coerenza; aderenza.

coherent (-ĕnt) n. coerente; aderente.

coign (koin) n. (arch.) angolo, pietra angolare.

coil (koil) n. matassa, bobina, rotolo (di corda); spira (di un rettile); ciocca (di capelli); tumulto, affanno. vt. avvolgere, arrotolare. vi. arrotolarsi, aggomitolarsi.

coin (koin) n. moneta, danaro. vt. coniare, batter moneta: to — words, coniare vocaboli. —age n. conio, sistema monetario; invenzione.

coincide (kō'ĭn·sīd') vt. coincidere, concordare. coincidence (kō·ĭn'sĭdĕns) n. concidenza, concordanza.

coke (kōk) n. carbone coke; (gergo) cocaina; coca cola.

cold (kōld) agg. freddo: — cream, crema cosmetica; to be —, avere freddo; fare freddo. n. raffreddore; freddo, raffreddamento. — -blooded agg. a sangue freddo, insensibile. —ly avv. freddamente. —ness n. freddezza.

Coliseum (kŏl'ĭ·sē'ŭm) n. Colosseo.

collaborate (kŏ·lăb'ō·rāt) vi. collaborare.

collaboration (-rā'shŭn) n. collaborazione.

collaborator (-rā'tẽr) n. collaboratore.

collapse (kŏ·lăps') n. caduta; collasso; crollo, catastrofe; abbattimento; sgonfiamento. vi. crollare; afflosciarsi; scoraggiarsi. vt. far crollare, ribaltare.

collapsible (kŏ·lăp'sĭ·b'l) agg. sgonfiabile; pieghevole; ribaltabile.

collar (kŏl'ẽr) n. colletto, collo (di camicia), bavero, collare, collana. vt. agguantare, catturare, imporre il collare a. —bone n. clavicola.

collate (kŏ·lāt') vt. raffrontare.

collateral (kŏ·lăt'ẽr·ăl) n., agg. collaterale.

colleague (kŏl'ēg) n. collega.

collect (kŏl·ĕkt') vt. raccogliere, riunire, radunare; collezionare; esigere (incassare); fare la levata

(della posta): to — oneself, rimettersi, riprendersi. vi. adunarsi, raccogliersi; riprendere il dominio di sè. agg., avv. in porto assegnato, in assegno. —ed agg. raccolto; equilibrato, padrone di sè. —ion n. collezione, raccolta; esazione, incasso; assortimento; levata postale. —ive agg. collettivo. —ivism n. collettivismo. —ivist n. collettivista. —ivity n. collettività. —or n. collezionista; raccoglitore; esattore; (ferr.) controllore.

college (kŏl'ĕj) n. collegio (di professori, elettori, ecc.); scuola superiore; università: medical —, facoltà di medicina.

collide (kŏ·līd') vi. urtarsi, scontrarsi.

collier (kŏl'yẽr) n. minatore; carbonaio; (naut.) nave carboniera.

collision (kŏ·lĭzh'ŭn) n. collisione, urto, scontro; contrasto (d'interessi, ecc.).

collocate (kŏl'ō·kāt) vt. collocare.

colloquial (kŏ·lō'kwĭ·ăl) agg. familiare (di vocaboli). —ism n. vocabolo o espressione familiare.

collusion (kŏ·lū'zhŭn) n. collusione, connivenza.

colon (kō'lŏn) n. (gramm.) due punti; (anat.) colon.

colonel (kûr'nĕl) n. colonnello.

colonial (kŏ·lō'nĭ·ăl) agg. coloniale.

colonist (kŏl'ō·nĭst) n. colono, coloniale.

colonization (kŏl'ō·nĭ·zā'shŭn; -nĭ·zā'-) n. colonizzazione.

colonize (kŏl'ō·nīz) vt. colonizzare.

colony (kŏl'ō·nĭ) n. colonia.

color (kŭl'ẽr) n. colore, colorito; apparenza. pl. bandiera; colori (di squadra sport., ecc.): fast —, colore solido; high —, colorito acceso; — -blind, daltonico. vt. colorare, dipingere, tingere; (fig.) colorire (discorsi, ecc.) vi. arrossire, imporporarsi. —ation n. colorazione, colore. —ed agg. colorato, di colore: —ed person, persona di colore (non di razza bianca). —ful agg. multicolore; vivace; pittoresco. —ing. n. colorazione, coloritura: —ing matter, sostanza colorante. —less agg. incolore.

colossal (kŏ·lŏs'ăl) n. colossale.

colt (kōlt) n. puledro; novellino.

column (kŏl'ŭm) n. colonna; (giorn.) rubrica.

columnist (kŏl'ŭm·nĭst) n. (giorn.) titolare di una rubrica, giornalista.

coma (kō'mȧ) n. coma, torpore.

comb (kōm) n. pettine; striglia; cresta (del gallo, dell'onda); favo (di miele). vt. pettinare, strigliare;

rastrellare. *vi.* frangersi (*delle onde*).

combat (kŏm'băt; kŏm·băt') *n.* combattimento, lotta: — car, autoblindo. *vt.*, *vi.* combattere, lottare; avversare. —ant *n.*, *agg.* combattente.

combination (kŏm'bǐ·nă'shŭn) *n.* combinazione.

combine (kŏm·bīn') *n.* consorzio; combriccola. *vt.* combinare, riunire. *vi.* unirsi, accordarsi, coalizzarsi.

combustible (kŏm·bŭs'tǐ·b'l) *n.*, *agg.* combustibile.

combustion (kŏm·bŭs'chŭn) *n.* combustione.

come (kŭm) *vi.* (*pass.* came, *pp.* come) venire, arrivare, giungere; accadere, divenire, riuscire: — what may, avvenga che può; the time to —, l'avvenire; to — about, accadere; to — again, tornare; ripetere. to — against, urtare contro; to — asunder, separarsi, sfasciarsi; to — back, tornare; to — in, entrare; to — into, entrare in possesso di, ereditare; to — of age, diventare maggiorenne; to — off, staccarsi; riuscire, accadere; to — out, uscire; to — to, riprendere i sensi; to — to terms, accordarsi; to — undone, unsewed, disfarsi, scucirsi; to — up with, raggiungere.

comedian (kŏ·mē'dǐ·ǎn) *n.* commediante; (attore) comico, buffone.

comedy (kŏm'ě·dǐ) *n.* commedia; comica.

comeliness (kŭm'lǐ·něs) *n.* bellezza, grazia.

comely (kŭm'lǐ) *agg.* bello, aggraziato.

comet (kŏm'ět) *n.* cometa.

comfort (kŭm'fẽrt) *n.* conforto, consolazione; comodità, benessere, sollievo; coltre. *vt.* confortare, incoraggiare. —able *agg.* comodo, confortevole; rilassato. —ably *avv.* comodamente; agiatamente. —er *n.* consolatore; lo Spirito Santo-coltre; sciarpa di lana. —less *agg.* sconfortato, desolato, inconsolabile.

comic (kŏm'ĭk) *n.* comico; comica; (*pl.*) storiella *o* giornale a fumetti. *agg.* comico; a fumetti. —al *agg.* comico, ridicolo.

coming (kŭm'ĭng) *n.* arrivo, venuta, avvento: to be long in —, farsi aspettare; *agg.* veniente, prossimo; (*fam.*) promettente, sulla strada del successo.

comma (kŏm'ä) *n.* virgola.

command (kŏ·mánd') *n.* comando, ordine, autorità; padronanza. *vt.*

comandare, ǀdisporre di; incutere (*rispetto*); dominare (*un panorama, ecc.*); aver padronanza di.

commandeer (kŏm'ǎn·dẽr') *vt.* requisire.

commander (kŏ·mán'dẽr) *n.* comandante.

commanding (kŏ·mánd'ĭng) *agg.* imponente, autoritario: — officer, ufficiale superiore.

commandment (kŏ·mánd'měnt) *n.* comandamento.

commando (kŏ·mán'dō) *n.* formazione di guastatori, commando.

commemorate (kŏ·měm'ō·rāt) *vt.* celebrare, commemorare.

commence (kŏ·měns') *vt.*, *vi.* cominciare, esordire. —ment *n.* inizio, esordio, origine; cerimonia per la distribuzione di diplomi.

commend (kŏ·měnd') *vt.* raccomandare, approvare, lodare; affidare. —able *agg.* lodevole, raccomandabile. —ation *n.* elogio, raccomandazione.

comment (kŏm'ěnt) *n.* commento. *vt.*, *vi.* commentare, chiosare. —ary *n.* commentario. —ator *n.* commentatore.

commerce (kŏm'ûrs) *n.* commercio.

commercial (kŏ·mûr'shǎl) *agg.* commerciale. *n.* (*radio*, *T.V.*, *cinema*) pubblicità, annuncio.

commiserate (kŏ·mĭz'ẽr·āt) *vt.* commiserare, compiangere.

commiseration (-ā'shŭn) *n.* commiserazione.

commissary (kŏm'ĭ·sěr'ǐ) *n.* commissario; commissariato, ufficio approvvigionamenti; mensa.

commission (kŏ·mĭsh'ŭn) *n.* commissione; provvigione; ordine, incarico; comitato; (*mil.*) nomina (*a ufficiale*); perpetrazione: in — (*naut.*), in assetto di navigazione; out of —, fuori uso, guasto, in disarmo. *vt.* incaricare, autorizzare, affidare un comando a; armare (*una nave*). —ed officer *n.* ufficiale (*munito di nomina*).

commissioner *n.* commissario: — in bankruptcy, giudice delegato (*di fallimento*).

commit (kŏ·mĭt') *vt.* commettere, fare; affidare, consegnare; rinviare (*a giudizio*): to — oneself, compromettersi; impegnarsi: to — to memory, imparare a memoria; to — suicide, uccidersi.

committee (kŏ·mĭt'ǐ) *n.* comitato, commissione: — of one, delegato unico.

commode (kŏ·mōd') *n.* cassettone, comodino.

commodious (kŏ·mō′dĭ·ŭs) *agg.* comodo, spazioso.

commodity (kŏ·mŏd′ĭ·tĭ) *n.* merce, derrata.

common (kŏm′ŭn) *n.* comune. (*pl.*) plebe, (*la*) massa; refettorio. *agg.* comune; generale; pubblico; ordinario, volgare, corrente, triviale: — **sailor,** semplice marinaio; — **soldier,** soldato semplice. **—ly** *avv.* comunemente, solitamente, normalmente. **—ness** *n.* ordinarietà, volgarità.

commonplace (kŏm′ŭn·plās′) *n.* luogo comune, banalità. *agg.* banale, comune.

commonwealth (kŏm′ŭn·wĕlth′) *n.* stato, repubblica, collettività.

commotion (kŏ·mō′shŭn) *n.* commozione, agitazione, tumulto, disordine.

commune (kŏ·mūn′) *vi.* confabulare, conversare, scambiare idee, intrattenersi: to — with oneself, raccogliersi in meditazione, riflettere. *n.* (kŏm′ūn) comune (*divisione amministrativa di territori*).

communicate (kŏ·mū′nĭ·kāt) *vt.* comunicare, far conoscere, partecipare. *vi.* comunicarsi, comunicare.

communication (kŏ·mū′nĭ·kā′shŭn) *n.* comunicazione.

communicative (kŏ·mū′nĭ·kā′tĭv) *agg.* comunicativo.

communion (kŏ·mūn′yŭn) *n.* comunione.

communism (kŏm′û·nĭz′m) *n.* comunismo.

communist (-nĭst) *n.*, *agg.* comunista.

communistic (-nĭs′tĭk) *agg.* comunista.

community (kŏ·mū′nĭ·tĭ) *n.* comunità, collettività: — **chest,** fondo di beneficenza.

commutation (kŏm′û·tā′shŭn) *n.* commutazione: — **ticket** (*ferr.*), biglietto d'abbonamento tra città e suburbio.

commute (kŏ·mūt′) *vt.* commutare. *vi.* viaggiare con biglietto d'abbonamento, fare la spola.

compact (kŏm′păkt) *n.* patto, contratto, convenzione; portacipria. *agg.* (kŏm·păkt′) compatto, compresso, conciso, serrato. **—ness** *n.* compattezza; concisione.

companion (kŏm·păn′yŭn) *n.* compagno, amico, socio; dama di compagnia. **—able** *agg.* socievole. **—ship** *n.* amicizia, cameratismo.

companionway (-wā′) *n.* scaletta di piroscafo (*che scende sottocoperta*).

company (kŭm′pá·nĭ) *n.* compagnia; società; comitiva; equipaggio: to part —, dividersi, separarsi da.

comparable (kŏm′pá·ráb′l) *agg.* comparabile.

comparative (kŏm·păr′á·tĭv) *agg.*, *n.* comparativo.

compare (kŏm·pâr′) *vt.* comparare, confrontare, verificare: to — notes, avere uno scambio di idee; beyond —, senza uguali. *vi.* rivaleggiare, reggere al confronto.

comparison (kŏm·păr′ĭ·sŭn) *n.* confronto, paragone, raffronto: beyond —, incomparabile; in — with, in confronto a.

compartment (kŏm·pärt′mĕnt) *n.* compartimento, suddivisione; scompartimento.

compass (kŭm′pás) *n.* circonferenza, limite, area, àmbito, portata; (*naut.*) bussola. **—es** *pl.* compasso, compassi.

compassion (kŏm·păsh′ŭn) *n.* compassione, pietà. **—ate** (-ĭt) *agg.* compassionevole, caritatevole. *vt.* (-āt) compassionare.

compatible (kŏm·păt′ĭ·b′l) *agg.* compatibile.

compatriot (kŏm·pā′trĭ·ŭt) *n.* compatriota.

compel (kŏm·pĕl′) *vt.* costringere, obbligare, forzare, imporre.

compelling *agg.* imperioso; autorevole; imponente; impellente; irresistibile.

compendious (kŏm·pĕn′dĭ·ŭs) *agg.* succinto, compatto.

compensate (kŏm′pĕn·sāt) *vt.* compensare, ricompensare, risarcire.

compensation (-sā′shŭn) *n.* compensazione; risarcimento, indennità; assicurazione sul lavoro.

compete (kŏm·pēt′) *vi.* competere, rivaleggiare, concorrere.

competence (kŏm′pē·tĕns) *n.* competenza, capacità, attitudine; agiatezza.

competent (-tĕnt) *agg.* competente, abile, esperto.

competition (kŏm′pē·tĭsh′ŭn) *n.* competizione, gara, concorso; concorrenza.

competitive (kŏm·pĕt′ĭ·tĭv) *agg.* competitivo, di concorrenza.

competitor (kŏm·pĕt′ĭ·tĕr) *n.* concorrente, rivale.

compilation (kŏm′pĭ·lā′shŭn) *n.* compilazione.

compile (kŏm·pīl′) *vt.* compilare.

compiler (kŏm·pīl′ĕr) *n.* compilatore.

complacency (kŏm·plā′sĕn·sĭ) *n.* compiacenza, compiacimento, soddisfazione.

complacent (kŏm·plā′sĕnt) *agg.* compiacente, compiaciuto.

complain (kŏm-plān') vi. lagnarsi, dolersi. —ant n. querelante, attore (d'una causa).

complaint (kŏm-plānt') n. lagnanza, protesta, reclamo; malattia: to lodge a —, presentare un reclamo, sporgere querela.

complaisance (kŏm'plă-zăns) n. compiacenza.

complaisant (-zănt) agg. compiacente.

complement (kŏm'plĕ-mĕnt) n. complemento. vt. completare.

complete (kŏm-plēt') agg. completo. vt. completare, terminare. —ly avv. completamente. —ness n. completezza, perfezione.

completion (kŏm-plē'shŭn) n. completamento, perfezionamento; compimento.

complex (kŏm'plĕks) n. complesso; raccolta. agg. (kŏm-plĕks') complesso, complicato.

complexion (kŏm-plĕk'shŭn) n. complessione, temperamento; colorito, carnagione; aspetto.

complexity (kŏm-plĕk'sĭ tĭ) n. complessità.

compliance (kŏm-plī'ăns) n. acquiescenza, condiscendenza, obbedienza, osservanza: in — with, in conformità di.

complicate (kŏm'plĭ-kāt) vt. complicare.

complicated (-kāt'ĕd) agg. complicato.

complication (-kă'shŭn) n. complicazione.

compliment (kŏm'plĭ-mĕnt) n. complimento, omaggio, ossequio, cortesia, regalo: —s of the season, auguri. vt. complimentare, congratularsi con. —ary agg. lusinghiero; gratuito, in omaggio.

comply (kŏm-plī') vi. acconsentire, compiacere, ottemperare: to — with a request, accogliere una richiesta.

component (kŏm-pō'nĕnt) n., agg. componente.

compose (kŏm-pōz') vt., vi. comporre, scrivere, redigere: to — oneself, calmarsi, ricomporsi.

composed (-pōzd) agg. composto, calmo.

composer (-pōz'ĕr) n. compositore, paciere.

composite (kŏm-pōz'ĭt) n., agg. composto.

composition (kŏm'pŏ-zĭsh'ŭn) n. composizione; (comm.) compromesso, accordo.

compositor (kŏm-pōz'ĭ-tĕr) n. (tip.) compositore.

composure (kŏm-pō'zhĕr) n. calma, equilibrio, imperturbabilità.

compound (kŏm-pound') n., agg. composto. vt., vi. comporre; mescolare, combinare; transare; accordarsi: to — with one's creditors, ottenere un corcordato.

comprehend (kŏm'prĕ-hĕnd') vt. capire, concepire; abbracciare, includere.

comprehensible (-hĕn'sĭ-b'l) agg. comprensibile.

comprehension (-hĕn'shŭn) n. comprensione.

comprehensive (-hĕn'sĭv) agg. comprensivo, inclusivo; esauriente.

compress (kŏm-prĕs') n. compressa. vt. comprimere. —ion n. compressione.

comprise (kŏm-prīz') vt. contenere, comprendere, includere.

compromise (kŏm'prŏ-mīz) n. compromesso, accordo, transazione. vt., vi. compromettere; transare; transigere.

comptroller vedi controller.

compulsion (kŏm-pŭl'shŭn) n. costrizione, coercizione.

compulsory (-sŏ-rĭ) agg. obbligatorio; coercitivo; irresistibile.

compunction (kŏm-pŭngk'shŭn) n. compunzione, rimorso.

computation (kŏm'pū-tā'shŭn) n. computo, calcolo.

compute (kŏm-pūt') vt. computare, calcolare.

comrade (kŏm'răd; -rĭd) n. camerata, compagno. —ship n. cameratismo.

concave (kŏn'kāv; kŏn-kāv') agg. concavo, cavo.

conceal (kŏn-sēl') vt. nascondere, celare, dissimulare, occultare. —ment n. occultamento, nascondiglio.

concede (kŏn-sēd') vt. concedere; ammettere, riconoscere; accordare.

conceit (kŏn-sēt') n. presunzione; concetto, idea; immaginazione. —ed agg. presuntuoso, vanitoso.

conceivable (kŏn-sēv'ă-b'l) agg. concepibile.

conceive (kŏn-sēv') vt. concepire, immaginare, credere.

concentrate (kŏn'sĕn-trāt) vt. concentrare. vi. concentrarsi.

concentration (-trā'shŭn) n. concentrazione: — camp, campo di concentramento.

concept (kŏn'sĕpt) n. concetto.

conception (kŏn-sĕp'shŭn) n. concezione; concetto, idea.

concern (kŏn-sûrn') n. interesse, cura; preoccupazione, ansia; (comm.) impresa, azienda, ditta, affare: this is no — of mine, questo non mi riguarda. vt. concernere, interes-

sare, riguardare; preoccupare. **—ed**
agg. interessato (*a*); preoccupato,
in ansia. **—ing** *prep.* riguardo a.

concert (kŏn'sûrt) *n.* concerto. *vt.*
(kŏn·sûrt') concertare. *vi.* concertarsi, accordarsi.

concession (kŏn·sĕsh'ŭn) *n.* concessione.

conciliate (kŏn·sĭl'ĭ·āt) *vt.* conciliare.

conciliation (-ā'shŭn) *n.* conciliazione.

concise (kŏn·sīs') *agg.* conciso. **—ness**
n. concisione.

conclude (kŏn·klōōd') *vt.* concludere.
vi. concludersi, terminare.

conclusion (kŏn·klōō'zhŭn) *n.* conclusione, fine.

conclusive (-sĭv) *agg.* conclusivo,
persuasivo.

concoct (kŏn·kŏkt') *vt.* preparare;
tramare; architettare. **—ion** *n.*
mescolanza, intruglio; preparazione; macchinazione.

concord (kŏn'kôrd) *n.* concordia,
armonia; accordo; concordanza. *vi.*
concordare, accordarsi.

concourse (kŏn'kōrs) *n.* concorso,
affluenza; affollamento.

concrete (kŏn'krēt; kŏn·krēt') *n.*
cemento: reinforced **—**, cemento
armato. *agg.* concreto, solido. *vi.*
solidificarsi.

concur (kŏn·kûr') *vi.* concorrere, accordarsi, cooperare. **—rence** *n.*
concorso, consenso, cooperazione.
—rent *agg.* concorrente, simultaneo,
acquiescente.

concussion (kŏn·kŭsh'ŭn) *n.* trauma:
— of the brain, commozione
cerebrale.

condemn (kŏn·dĕm') *vt.* condannare,
biasimare; espropriare, confiscare.
—ation (-nā'shŭn) *n.* condanna.

condensation (kŏn·dĕn·sā'shŭn) *n.*
condensazione; riassunto.

condense (kŏn·dĕns') *vt.* condensare;
riassumere, compendiare. *vi.* condensarsi.

condenser (kŏn·dĕn'sĕr) *n.* condensatore.

condescend (kŏn·dē·sĕnd') *vi.* accondiscendere. **—ence** *n.* condiscendenza.

condescension (-sĕn'shŭn) *n.* degnazione, condiscendenza.

condiment (kŏn'dĭ·mĕnt) *n.* condimento.

condition (kŏn·dĭsh'ŭn) *n.* condizione,
stato; clausola. *vt.* sistemare a
dovere; determinare, limitare, condizionare; rimandare (*uno studente*).
—al *agg.* condizionale.

condole (kŏn·dōl') *vi.* condolersi,
rammaricarsi. **—nce** *n.* condoglianza.

condone (kŏn·dōn') *vt.* condonare,
perdonare.

conduce (kŏn·dūs') *vi.* condurre *o*
contribuire (*a un risultato*), tendere
(*verso*).

conducive (-dū'sĭv) *agg.* che contri-
buisce, tendente, apportatore: **—**
to slumber, che concilia il sonno.

conduct (kŏn'dŭkt) *n.* condotta;
direzione, guida. *vt.* (-dŭkt') condurre, dirigere, portare: to **—**
oneself, comportarsi. **—ive** *agg.*
conduttivo. **—ivity** *n.* conduttività.
—or *n.* conduttore, guida; capotreno; direttore d'orchestra.

conduit (kŏn'dĭt; -dŏŏ.ĭt) *n.* condotto.

cone (kōn) *n.* cono; (*bot.*) pigna.

confabulate (kŏn·făb'ū·lāt) *vi.* confabulare.

confection (kŏn·fĕk'shŭn) *n.* confezione; confettura, conserva. *vt.*
confezionare, preparare. **—er** *n.*
pasticcere. **—ery** *n.* pasticceria.

confederacy (kŏn·fĕd'ĕr·á·sĭ) *n.* confederazione; lega (*di cospiratori*);
associazione a delinquere.

confederate (kŏn·fĕd'ĕr·ĭt) *n.* confederato, alleato; complice, compare. *agg.* confederato, ausiliario.
vi. confederarsi, associarsi.

confederation (kŏn·fĕd'r·ā'shŭn) *n.*
confederazione.

confer (kŏn·fûr') *vt.* conferire, as-
segna e; accordare. *vi.* conferire
(*con*), consultarsi.

conference (kŏn'fĕr·ĕns) *n.* conferenza.

confess (kŏn·fĕs') *vt.* confessare, ammettere. *vi.* confessarsi. **—ion** *n.*
confessione. **—ional** *n.*, *agg.* confessionale. **—or** *n.* confessore.

confetti (kŏn·fĕt'ĭ) *n.pl.* coriandoli.

confidant *n.*, confidante *f.* (kŏn'fĭ·
dănt'; kŏn'fĭ·dănt) *n.* confidente.

confide (kŏn·fīd') *vt.* confidare; affidare. *vi.* confidarsi; fare affidamento (*su*).

confidence (kŏn'fĭ·dĕns) *n.* fiducia,
sicurezza, baldanza; confidenza: **—**
game (trick), truffa all'americana;
— ("con") man, truffatorea al-
l'americana.

confident (-dĕnt) *agg.* fiducioso,
sicuro; baldanzoso. **—ial** *agg.* confidenziale, riservato. **—ly** *avv.*
fiduciosamente, baldanzosamente.

confine (kŏn'fĭn) *n.* confine, limite.
vt. (-fīn') confinare, rinchiudere,
limitare; relegare; delimitare: to
— oneself, limitarsi e relegarsi. *vi.*
confinare (*con*): **—d** to bed, costretto
a letto. **—ment** *n.* confino, reclusione; isolamento; parto; degenza:
solitary **—ment**, segregazione cellulare.

confirm (kŏn·fûrm′) vt. confermare, convalidare; (relig.) cresimare. —ation n. conferma, ratifica; cresima. —ed agg. inveterato, convinto.

confiscate (kŏn′fĭs·kāt) vt. confiscare, requisire.

confiscation (-kā′shŭn) n. confisca.

conflagration (kŏn′flā·grā′shŭn) n. incendio, conflagrazione.

conflict (kŏn′flĭkt) n. conflitto, contrasto, lotta, guerra. vi. (-flĭkt′) lottare, contrastare, urtarsi. —ing agg. contrastante, contraddittorio.

conform (kŏn·fôrm′) vt. conformare. vi. conformarsi; ottemperare. —ity n. conformità: in — with, conformemente a.

confound (kŏn·found′) vt. confondere, scompigliare; devastare; turbare: mandare al diavolo: — you! va al diavolo!; — it! accidenti!

confront (kŏn·frŭnt′) vt. confrontare, raffrontare, paragonare, mettere a confronto, mettere di fronte.

confuse (kŏn·fūz′) vt. confondere, imbrogliare, arruffare, disorientare, sconcertare.

confused agg. confuso, sconcertato.

confusion (kŏn·fū′zhŭn) n. confusione, disordine; imbarazzo, vergogna.

congeal (kŏn·jēl′) vt. ghiacciare, congelare, gelare. vi. congelarsi.

congenial (kŏn·jēn′yăl) agg. affine; gradevole, simpatico; concorde (a).

congest (kŏn·jĕst′) vt. congestionare. vi. congestionarsi. —ion n. congestione; ammasso; ingombro.

conglomeration (kŏn·glŏm′ĕr·ā′shŭn) n. conglomerazione, conglomerato.

congratulate (kŏn·grăt′û·lāt) vt. felicitare, congratularsi con: to — oneself, rallegrarsi, compiacersi.

congratulation (-lā′shŭn) n. congratulazione.

congregate (kŏng′grē·gāt) vt. radunare. vi. radunarsi.

congregation (kŏng′grē·gā′shŭn) n. congregazione; riunione, assemblea; uditorio.

congress (kŏng′grĕs) n. congresso; (S.U.) Parlamento. —ional agg. di congresso. —man n. congressista; (S.U.) deputato al Parlamento.

conic (kŏn′ĭk), conical (-ĭ·kăl) agg. conico.

conjecture (kŏn·jĕk′tŭr) n. congettura. vt., vi. congetturare.

conjugate (kŏn′jōō·gāt) vt. coniugare.

conjugation (-gā′shŭn) n. coniugazione.

conjunction (kŏn·jŭngk′shŭn) n. congiunzione.

conjunctive (-tĭv) n., agg. congiuntivo.

conjure (kŭn′jĕr; kŏn′-) vt. invocare, evocare; fare giochi di prestigio; (kŏn·jōōr′) implorare, scongiurare.

conjurer (kŭn′jĕr·ĕr) n. mago; prestigiatore.

conk (kŏngk) vt. (gergo) colpire (alla testa), tramortire. vi. incepparsi, guastarsi.

connect (kŏ·nĕkt′) vt. collegare, associare, unire. vi. collegarsi; (ferr.) fare coincidenza. —ing rod n. biella. —ion n. connessione; attinenza; conoscenza; parentela: parente; setta religiosa; coincidenza (di treni, ecc.); clientela.

connivance (kŏ·nīv′ăns) n. connivenza.

connive (kŏ·nīv′) vi. essere connivente, farsi complice.

connoisseur (kŏn′ĭ·sûr′; -sūr′) n. competente, intenditore.

conquer (kŏng′kēr) vt. conquistare, vincere, domare, piegare. —or n. conquistatore; vincitore.

conquest (kŏng′kwĕst) n. conquista, vittoria.

conscience (kŏn′shĕns) n. coscienza.

conscientious (kŏn′shĭ·ĕn′shŭs) agg. coscienzioso: — objector, obiettore di coscienza.

conscious (kŏn′shŭs) agg. conscio, cosciente, edotto. —ly avv. consapevolmente, scientemente. —ness n. coscienza, percezione, conoscenza: to regain —, riprendere i sensi.

conscript (kŏn′skrĭpt) n., agg. coscritto. —ion n. coscrizione.

consecrate (kŏn′sē·krāt) vt. consacrare, benedire, santificare.

consecration (-krā′shŭn) n. consacrazione.

consecutive (kŏn·sĕk′û·tĭv) agg. consecutivo.

consensus (kŏn·sĕn′sŭs) n. accordo, concordanza; unanimità.

consent (kŏn·sĕnt′) n. consenso, accordo, adesione. vi. consentire, aderire.

consequence (kŏn′sē·kwĕns) n. conseguenza, risultato, effetto, importanza: it is of no —, non ha importanza.

consequent (-kwĕnt) n. conseguenza; (mat.) conseguente. agg. conseguente. —ly avv. conseguentemente, quindi, perciò.

conservation (kŏn′sẽr·vā′shŭn) n. conservazione.

conservative (kŏn·sûr′vá·tĭv) n. conservatore. agg. conservativo; prudente, cauto; tradizionale, tradizionalista.

conservatory (kŏn·sûr′vá·tō′rĭ) n. serra; conservatorio musicale.

conserve (kŏn·sûrv') *n.* conserva. *vt.* conservare, preservare, mettere in conserva.

consider (kŏn·sĭd'ẽr) *vt.* considerare, esaminare, valutare. *vi.* riflettere, pensare. **—able** *agg.* considerevole, notevole, importante. **—ableness** *n.* importanza. **—ably** *avv.* considerevolmente, assai.

considerate (kŏn·sĭd'ẽr·ĭt) *agg.* riguardoso, prudente, premuroso. **—ness** *n.* delicatezza; cautela, prudenza; discrezione.

consideration (kŏn·sĭd'ẽr·ā'shŭn) *n.* considerazione; esame; riguardo; giudizio, opinione; importanza; ricompensa.

considering *prep.*, *cong.* in vista di, tenendo conto (*che*, *di*), dato (*che*), tutto sommato, visto che.

consign (kŏn·sīn') *vt.* consegnare, affidare. **—ment** *n.* consegna, spedizione; fornitura *o* partita (*di merce*).

consist (kŏn·sĭst') *vi.* consistere, constare (*di*); sussistere; esser compatibile: to **—** in, of, essere compreso in; consistere di; **—ence**, **—ency** *n.* consistenza, coerenza, compatibilità, solidità. **—ent** *agg.* coerente, compatibile, costante.

consolation (kŏn·sŏl·ā'shŭn) *n.* consolazione.

console (kŏn·sōl') *vt.* consolare.

consolidate (kŏn·sŏl'ĭ·dāt) *vt.* consolidare. *vi.* consolidarsi.

consonant (kŏn'sō·nănt) *agg.* armonico, concorde, consono. *n.* (*gramm.*) consonante.

consort (kŏn'sôrt) *n.* consorte, coniuge, compagno. *vi.* (kŏn·sôrt'): to **—** with imbrancarsi con, frequentare, far lega con.

conspicuous (cŏn·spĭk'ū̇·ŭs) *agg.* cospicuo; evidente, vistoso: to make oneself **—**, farsi notare.

conspiracy (kŏn·spĭr'ȧsĭ) *n.* cospirazione, congiura.

conspirator (kŏn·spĭr'ȧ·tẽr) *n.* cospiratore, congiurato.

conspire (kŏn·spīr') *vi.* congiurare.

constable (kŭn·stȧ·b'l) *n.* conestabile; poliziotto, agente.

constancy (kŏn'stăn·sĭ) *n.* costanza.

constant (kŏn'stănt) *agg.* costante, scontinuo.

constellation (kŏn'stĕ·lā'shŭn) *n.* costellazione.

consternation (kŏn'stẽr·nā'shŭn) *n.* costernazione.

constipation (kŏn'stĭ·pā'shŭn) *n.* stitichezza, ingombro intestinale.

constituency (kŏn·stĭtụ̈·ĕn·sĭ) *n.* complesso degli elettori, circoscrizione.

constituent (-ĕnt) *n.* elemento costituente; elettore. *agg.* costituente.

constitute (kŏn'stĭ·tūt) *vt.* costituire, formare.

constitution (kŏn'stĭ·tū'shŭn) *n.* costituzione. **—al** *agg.* costituzionale. *n.* passeggiata igienica.

constrain (kŏn·strān') *vt.* costringere; comprimere; reprimere, trattenere; imprigionare.

constraint (kŏn·strānt') *n.* costrizione, repressione (*di sentimenti*); imbarazzo, riserbo.

constrict (kŏn·strĭkt') *vt.* comprimere; reprimere, **—or** *n.* costrittore (*muscolo*); (*zool.*) boa.

constriction (kŏn·strĭk'shŭn) *n.* costrizione, restrizione; restringimento.

construct (kŏn·strŭkt') *vt.* costruire; interpretare. **—ion** *n.* costruzione, interpretazione: to put a wrong **—** ion on, interpretare male. **—ive** *agg.* costruttivo.

construe (kŏn·strōō') *vt.* interpretare, spiegare, tradurre.

consul (kŏn'sŭl) *n.* console. **—ar** *agg.* consolare. **—ate** *n.* consolato.

consult (kŏn·sŭlt') *vt.* consultare. **—ation** *n.* consultazione, consulto.

consume (kŏn·sūm') *vt.* consumare, sprecare. *vi.* consumarsi; struggersi.

consumer (-sūm'ẽr) *n.* consumatore.

consummate (kŏn·sŭm'ĭt) *agg.* consumato, abile, raffinato. *vt.* (kŏn'sŭ·māt) compiere, consumare.

consumption (kŏn·sŭmp'shŭn) *n.* consumo; consunzione; tisi.

consumptive (kŏn·sŭmp'tĭv) *agg.* logorato; tisico.

contact (kŏn'tăkt) *n.* contatto; rapporto. *vt.* mettere in contatto; accostare, mettersi in comunicazione con. *vi.* prender contatto.

contagion (kŏn·tā'jŭn) *n.* contagio.

contagious (-jŭs) *agg.* contagioso.

contain (kŏn·tān') *vt.* contenere, includere; limitare, reprimere: to **—** oneself, dominarsi. **—er** *n.* recipiente, involucro, astuccio.

contaminate (kŏn·tăm'ĭ·nāt) *vt.* contaminare.

contamination (-nā'shŭn) *n.* contaminazione.

contango (kŏn·tăng'gō) *n.* (*ingl. borsa*) riporto.

contemplate (kŏn'tĕm·plāt; kŏn·tĕm'plāt) *vt.* contemplare, meditare, progettare, prevedere.

contemplation (kŏn'tĕm·plā'shŭn) *n.* contemplazione; progetto, proposito.

contemporaneous (kŏn·tĕm′pō·rā′nē-ŭs), **contemporary**) kŏn·tĕm′pō·rĕr′ĭ) *n.*, *agg.* contemporaneo; coetaneo.

contempt (kŏn·tĕmpt′) *n.* disprezzo, sdegno: — of court, offesa alla magistratura. —**ible** *agg.* spregevole. —**tuous** *agg.* sprezzante, sdegnoso.

contend (kŏn·tĕnd) *vt.*, *vi.* contendere; lottare; contestare, obiettare; sostenere, affermare.

content (kŏn′tĕnt′) (1) *n.* contentezza, soddisfazione: to one's heart's —, a sazietà. *agg.* contento, soddisfatto. *vt.* accontentare, soddisfare.

content (kŏn′tĕnt) (2) *n.* (*gen.pl.*) contenuto: table of —s, sommario, indice.

contented (kŏn·tĕn′tĕd) *agg.* soddisfatto.

contention (kŏn·tĕn′shŭn) *n.* contesa, disputa, dibattito; asserzione: bone of —, pomo della discordia.

contentious (-shŭs) *agg.* litigioso; controverso.

contest (kŏn′tĕst) *n.* contesa, controversia; gara. *vt.*, *vi.* (kŏn·tĕst′) contestare, disputare; lottare, competere.

context (kŏn′tĕkst) *n.* contesto.

contiguous (kŏn·tĭg′ū·ŭs) *agg.* contiguo.

continence (kŏn′tĭ·nĕns) *n.* continenza, moderazione, ritegno.

continent (kŏn′tĭ·nĕnt) (1) *agg.* moderato; morigerato.

continent (2) *n.* continente.

continental (-nĕn′t′l) *agg.* continentale; europeo.

contingency (kŏn·tĭn′jĕn·sĭ) *n.* contingenza, caso.

contingent (-jĕnt) *agg.* contingente.

continual (kŏn·tĭn′ū·ăl) *agg.* continuo. —**ly** *avv.* continuamente.

continuance (ăns) *n.* continuazione, continuità; permanenza.

continuation (kŏn·tĭn′ū·ā′shŭn) *n.* continuazione, seguito.

continue (kŏn·tĭn′ū) *vt.* continuare, perseverare; rimanere.

continuity (kŏn′tĭ·nū′ĭ·tĭ) *n.* continuità; (*cinema, radio, T.V.*) sceneggiatura.

continuous (kŏn·tĭn′ū·ŭs) *agg.* continuo.

contortion (kŏn·tòr′shŭn) *n.* contorsione, lussazione.

contour (kŏn′tōŏr) *n.* contorno, perimetro.

contraband (kŏn′trá·bănd) *n.* contrabbando.

contract (kŏn′trăkt) *n.* contratto, convenzione, appalto. *vt.* (kŏn′trăkt′) contrattare; contrarre; restringere. *vi.* contrarsi, restringersi; *comm.*) trattare, contrattare.

contraction (kŏn·trăk′shŭn) *n.* contrazione; scarsità.

contractor (kŏn·trăk′tĕr; kŏn′trăk-tĕr) *n.* contraente; imprenditore (*edile*); appaltatore; fornitore.

contradict (kŏn′trá·dĭkt′) *vt.* contraddire, smentire. —**ion** *n.* contraddizione, smentita. —**ory** *agg.* contraddittorio.

contrail (kŏn′trāl′) *n.* (*aeron.*) scia di vapore acqueo.

contrary (kŏn′trĕr·ĭ; -trá·rĭ) *n.* (*il*) contrario. *agg.* contrario, ostinato. *avv.* contrariamente, in senso contrario: on the —, al contrario.

contrast (kon′trăst) *n.* contrasto. *vt.* (kŏn·trăst′) mettere in contrasto, raffrontare. *vi.* contrastare, essere in contrasto.

contribute (kŏn·trĭb′ūt) *vt.*, *vi.* contribuire (*con*); collaborare.

contribution (kŏn′trĭ·bū′shŭn) *n.* contribuzione; collaborazione.

contributor (kŏn·trĭb′ū·tĕr) *n.* contributore; collaboratore.

contrite (kŏn·trīt′) *agg.* contrito.

contrition (kŏn·trĭsh′ŭn) *n.* contrizione.

contrivance (kŏn·trīv′ăns) *n.* meccanismo, invenzione, congegno, piano, artificio.

contrive (kŏn·trīv′) *vt.* escogitare, trovare il modo di; inventare, progettare; tramare (*a*). *vi.* adoperarsi, arrangiarsi, riuscire (*a*).

control (kŏn·trōl′) *n.* controllo, freno, autorità; (*pl.*) comandi: — panel, quadro di comando; (*aeron.*) cruscotto. *vt.* controllare, regolare; dirigere, dominare. —**ler** *n.* controllore; regolatore.

controversy (kŏn′trō·vûr′sĭ) *n.* controversia, polemica, disputa.

contumacious (kŏn′tū·mā′shŭs) *agg.* ostinato, perverso.

contusion (kŏn·tū′zhŭn) *n.* contusione, ammaccatura.

conundrum (kō·nŭn′drŭm) *n.* indovinello, enigma.

convalesce (kŏn′vá·lĕs′) *vi.* essere in convalescenza.

convalescence (kŏn′vá·lĕs′′ns) *n.* convalescenza.

convalescent (-ĕnt) *n.*, *agg.* convalescente: — home, convalescenziario.

convene (kŏn·vēn′) *vt.* riunire, convocare. *vi.* riunirsi.

convenience (kŏn·vēn′yĕns) *n.* convenienza; comodità, comodo.

convenient (-yĕnt) *agg.* comodo, conveniente. —**ly** *avv.* comodamente, acconciamente; opportunamente.

convent (kŏn′vĕnt) *n.* convento.

convention (kŏn·vĕn'shŭn) n. convenzione, patto; assemblea. —**al** agg. convenzionale; di convenzione; tradizionale; manierato.

converge (kŏn·vûrj') vi. convergere.

conversant (kŏn'vĕr·sănt) agg. versato, dotto, edotto: to be — with, essere ferrato in, intendersi di.

conversation (kŏn'vĕr·sā'shŭn) n. conversazione.

converse (kŏn·vûrs') (1) vi. chiacchierare, intrattenersi.

converse (kŏn'vûrs') (2) n., agg. converso, reciproco, contrario.

conversely avv. inversamente; viceversa, al contrario.

conversion (kŏn·vûr'zhŭn) n. conversione.

convert (kŏn'vûrt) n. convertito, neòfito. vt. (kŏn·vûrt') convertire, trasformare; adibire. vi. convertirsi, trasformarsi. —**ible** agg. trasformabile.

convex (kŏn'vĕks; kŏn·vĕks') agg. convesso.

convey (kŏn·vā') vt. trasportare, portare; esprimere, far capire; trasmettere (suoni, ecc.), riferire: to — thanks, porgere ringraziamenti.

conveyance (kŏn·vā'ăns) n. trasporto; trasmissione, comunicazione; veicolo; passaggio di proprietà.

convict (kŏn'vĭkt) n. condannato, galeotto. vt.(kŏn·vĭkt') condannare, dichiarare reo. —**ion** n. convinzione, persuasione; convinzione di reità, condanna.

convince (kŏn·vĭns') vt. convincere.

convincing (-vĭn'sĭng) agg. convincente.

convocation (kŏn'vô·kā'shŭn) n. convocazione.

convoke (kŏn·vōk') vt. convocare.

convoy (kŏn'voi) n. convoglio, scorta. vt. (kŏn·voi') convogliare; scortare.

convulsed (kŏn·vulst') agg. convulso, sconvolto; spasmodico.

convulsion (kŏn·vŭl'shŭn) n. convulsione; rivolgimento, convulso.

cony, coney (kō'nĭ) n. coniglio.

coo (kōō) vi. tubare.

cook (kŏŏk) n. cuoco, cuoca, cuciniere. vt., vi. cucinare, far cucina (la contabilità), cuocere, far cuocere; manipolare: to — up a plan, ordire un piano.

cookery (kŏŏk'ĕr·ĭ) n. culinaria, cucina.

cookie (kŏŏk'ĭ) n. pasticcino.

cooking (kŏŏk'ĭng) n. cucina, culinaria: — stove, cucina a gas o elettrica; — utensils, batteria di cucina.

cookout (kŏŏk'out') n. spuntino all'aperto, colazione sull'erba.

cool (kōōl) agg. fresco; calmo, freddo, impudente. n. freddezza, freschezza. vt. rinfrescare, raffreddare, calmare. vi. calmarsi; raffreddarsi: to — down, placarsi. —**er** n. ghiacciaia; (auto.) radiatore; (gergo) galera, cella. —**ness** n. freschezza, freddezza, indifferenza, sfacciataggine.

coop (kōōp) n. pollaio, stia. vt. rinchiudere, imprigionare.

cooper (kōōp'ĕr) n. bottaio.

co-operate (kô·ŏp'ĕr.āt) vi. cooperare, collaborare, concorrere.

co-operation (-ā'shŭn) n. cooperazione.

co-operative (kô·ŏp'ĕr·a'tĭv) n., agg. cooperativo.

co-ordinate (kô·ôr'dĭ·nāt) agg. coordinato. n. (mat.) coordinata. vt. (-nāt) coordinare.

co-ordination (-nā'shŭn) n. coordinazione.

coot (kōōt) n. fòlaga.

cop (kŏp) n. (gergo) poliziotto: **cops and robbers**, guardie e ladri.

copartner (kô·pärt'nĕr) n. socio, consocio.

cope (kōp) n. cappa, manto; volta. vt.: to — with, affrontare, lottare con, sostenere una lotta con, tener testa a: I can't — with this, non ce la faccio.

copious (kō'pĭ·ŭs) agg. copioso, abbondante.

copper (kŏp'ĕr) n. rame, paiolo; (gergo) poliziotto.

coppice (kŏp'ĭs), **copse** (kŏps) n. boschetto.

'copter (kŏp'tĕr) n. elicottero.

copy (kŏp'ĭ) n. copia; esemplare (di volume); imitazione; numero (di periodico, ecc.); materiale (letterario): rough —, minuta; true —, copia conforme. vt. copiare, imitare, trascrivere.

copybook (kŏp'ĭ·bŏŏk) n. quaderno.

copyright (kŏp'ĭ·rīt) n. diritto d'autore, proprietà letteraria.

coquetry (kō'kĕ·trĭ) n. civetteria.

coquette (kô·kĕt') n. civetta (ragazza provocante).

coquettish (kô·kĕt'ĭsh) agg. civettuolo, provocante.

coral (kŏr'ăl) n. corallo. agg. corallino.

cord (kôrd) n. cordone, corda, fune; (pl.) calzoni a coste: spinal —, spina dorsale.

cordial (kôr'jăl) n., agg. cordiale. —**ity** n. cordialità.

corduroy (kôr'dŭ·roi; -dŭ-) n. tessuto a coste: corduroys, calzoni di velluto a coste.

core (kōr) n. torsolo (di frutto), parte centrale; profondo dell'anima: rotten to the —, marcio fino al midollo. *vt.* togliere il torsolo a.

corespondent (kŏ'rē·spŏn'děnt) *n.* complice, coimputato, correo.

cork (kŏrk) *n.* sughero, turacciolo. *vt.* tappare, mettere il turacciolo a. —screw *n.* cavaturaccioli. — tree *n.* sughera quercia da sughero.

corn (kŏrn) (1) *n.* (*Ingl.*) cereale, grano, frumento; (*S.U.*) granoturco, mais: **Indian** —, granoturco; — meal, farina di mais.*vt.* salare (*carni, ecc.*); granulare: — beef, manzo salato.

corn (kŏrn) (2) *n.* callo.

corn (3) *n.* (*gergo*) banalità, cose risapute, vecchia trovata (*vedi corny*).

corner (kŏr'nĕr) *n.* angolo; (*comm.*) incetta, accaparramento. *vt.* mettere alle strette, accumulare, accaparrare. — cupboard, cantoniera. —stone *n.* pietra angolare.

cornet (kŏr·nĕt') *n.* cornetta; imbuto di carta; cono (*per gelato*).

cornice (kŏr'nĭs) *n.* cornicione.

corny (kŏr'nĭ) *agg.* banale, di maniera sentimentale, melodrammatico.

coronation (kŏr'ŏ·nā'shŭn) *n.* incoronazione.

coroner (kŏr'ŏ·nĕr) *n.* magistrato inquirente.

coronet (kŏr'ŏ·nĕt) *n.* diadema, corona.

corporal (kŏr'pŏ·răl) *n.* caporale. *agg.* corporale.

corporation (kŏr'pŏ·rā'shŭn) *n.* corporazione, società; (*gergo*) pinguedine, pancia.

corps (kŏr) *n.* corpo (*formazione mil.*): air —, aviazione.

corpse (kŏrps) *n.* cadavere.

corpulence (kŏr'pū·lĕns) *n.* corpulenza.

corpulent (-lĕnt) *agg.* corpulento.

corpuscle (kŏr'pŭs·'l) *n.* corpuscolo, cellula; elettrone; globulo (*sanguigno*).

corral (kŏ·răl') *n.* recinto (*per bestiame*).

correct (kŏ·rĕkt') *agg.* corretto, esatto; veritiero. *vt.* correggere, rettificare. —ion *n.* correzione, punizione. —ly *avv.* correttamente, giustamente. —ness *n.* correttezza, esattezza. —or *n.* correttore.

correlate (kŏr'ĕ·lāt) *vi.* essere in correlazione. *vt.* porre in correlazione.

correlation (-lā'shŭn) *n.* correlazione.

correspond (kŏr'ĕ·spŏnd') *vi.* corrispondere, accordarsi; essere in corrispondenza. —ence *n.* corrispondenza. —ent *n.*, *agg.* corrispondente. —ing *agg.* corrispondente.

corridor (kŏr'ĭ·dŏr' -dĕr) *n.* corridoio.

corroborate (kŏ·rŏb'ŏ·rāt) *vt.* corroborare, convalidare.

corroboration (-rā'shŭn) *n.* convalida, conferma.

corrode (kŏ·rōd') *vt.* corrodere. *vi.* corrodersi.

corrosion (kŏ·rō'zhŭn) *n.* corrosione.

corrosive (-rō'sĭv) *n.*, *agg.* corrosivo.

corrugate (kŏr'ū·gāt; kŏr'ŏŏ-) *vt.* corrugare, ondulare. *vi.* ondularsi: —d iron, lamiera ondulata.

corrupt (kŏ·rŭpt') *agg.* corrotto, marcio, infetto. *vt.* corrompere; guastare. *vi.* corrompersi, marcire. —ion *n.* corruzione, alterazione, decomposizione.

corset (kŏr'sĕt) *n.* busto (*da donna*).

cortisone (kŏr'tĭ·sŏn) *n.* cortisone.

corundum (kŏ·rŭn'dŭm) *n.* (*min.*) corindone.

cosmetic (kŏz·mĕt'ĭk) *n.*, *agg.* cosmetico: — surgery, chirurgia estetica.

cosmic (kŏz'mĭk) *agg.* cosmico.

cosmopolitan (kŏz'mŏ·pŏl'ĭ·tăn) *agg.* cosmopolita.

cost (kŏst) *n.* costo, prezzo, spesa. *vi.* (*pass., pp.* cost) costare.

costive (kŏs'tĭv) *agg.* stitico. —ness *n.* stitichezza.

costliness (kŏst'lĭ·nĕs) *n.* costosità.

costly (kŏst'lĭ) *agg.* costoso, dispendioso.

costume (kŏs'tūm) *n.* costume, vestiario.

cosy *vedi* cozy.

cot (kŏt) (1) *n.* capanna, casetta.

cot (kŏt) (2) *n.* branda, cuccetta.

cottage (kŏt'ĭj) *n.* villino, casetta: —cheese, specie di ricotta; —piano, pianoforte verticale.

cotton (kŏt'n) *n.* cotone.

couch (kouch) (1) *n.* divanetto, letto.

couch (2) *vi.* giacere. *vt.* esprimere: to — in difficult language, esprimere con parole difficili.

cough (kŏf) *n.* tosse: whooping —, tosse asinina. *vi.* tossire: to — up, espettorare; sputare quattrini.

could (kŏŏd) *pass. di* can.

council (koun'sĭl) *n.* consiglio, concilio: city —, giunta municipale; — board, consiglio d'amministrazione. —lor, —man *n.* consigliere, assessore.

counsel (koun'sĕl) *n.* consiglio, parere; discrezione; avvocato: — for the defense, avvocato difensore; to take — with, consultarsi con; to keep one's —, tacere, mantenere il segreto. *vt.* consigliare. —lor *n.* consigliere, avvocato.

count (kount) (1) *n.* conte.

count (kount) (2) *n.* conto, calcolo; conteggio, scrutinio; capo d'accusa. *vt.*, *vi.* contare, ritenere, tenere in conto, avere importanza, computare: **to — out**, escludere.

countenance (koun'tĕ·nảns) *n.* sembiante, espressione, volto, aria, contegno; approvazione, incoraggiamento: **out of —**, sconcertato; **to give —** to, approvare, incoraggiare; **to keep one's —**, mantenersi serio. *vt.* incoraggiare, approvare.

counter (koun'tĕr) (1) *n.* calcolatore; contatore.

counter (2) *n.* banco (*di negozio*); gettone (*da gioco*).

counter (3) *avv.* contro, contrariamente. *vi.* parare (*al pugilato, ecc.*); rispondere a un colpo. *vt.* ribattere; avversare.

counteract (koun'tĕr·ăkt') *vt.* frustrare, neutralizzare, controbilanciare.

counterbalance (koun'tĕr·băl'ảns) *n.* contrappeso. *vt.* controbilanciare.

counterfeit (koun'tĕr·fĭt) *n.* contraffazione, falsificazione. *agg.* contraffatto, falso, imitato. *vt.* contraffare, falsificare. **—er** *n.* falsario.

countermand (koun'tĕr·mánd) *n.* contrordine, disdetta. *vt.* contrordinare, disdire, revocare.

counterpane (koun'tĕr·pān') *n.* copriletto.

counterpart (-pärt') *n.* copia, complemento; sòsia.

counterpoint (-point') *n.* (*mus.*) contrappunto.

counterpoise (-poiz') *n.* contrappeso. *vt.* controbilanciare.

counterrevolution (-rĕv'ō·lū'shŭn) *n.* controrivoluzione.

countersink (-sĭngk) *n.* accecatoio, fresa. *vt.* fresare.

counterweight (-wāt') *n.* contrappeso.

countess (koun'tĕs) *n.* contessa.

countless (kount'lĕs) *agg.* innumerevole.

country (kŭn'trĭ) *n.* paese, nazione, patria; regione; campagna (*zona rurale*). **—man** *n.* contadino; compaesano: **fellow —man**, compatriota. **—woman** *n.* contadina; compaesana. **—side** *n.* campagna.

county (koun'tĭ) *n.* contea.

couple (kŭp''l) *n.* coppia, paio. *vt.* accoppiare; (*ferr.*) agganciare. *vi.* accoppiarsi.

coupling (kŭp'lĭng) *n.* accoppiamento.

coupon (kōō'pŏn) *n.* biglietto, tagliando, scontrino.

courage (kŭr'ĭj) *n.* coraggio. **—ous** (kŭ·rā'jŭs) *agg.* coraggioso.

courier (kŏōr'ĭ·ĕr) *n.* corriere, messaggero.

course (kōrs) *n.* corsa; corso (*di un fiume, di lezioni, dei cambi, ecc.*); serie; percorso, pista; portata (*a tavola*); rotta; punto (*della bussola*): **in due —**, a tempo debito; **of —**, naturalmente; **a matter of —**, una cosa ovvia; **— of conduct**, comportamento. *vi.* scorrere; dirigersi, seguire una rotta.

court (kōrt) *n.* corte, cortile; corte di giustizia; vicolo; autostello: **tennis —**, campo di tennis. *vt.* corteggiare, cercare: **to — danger**, andare in cerca di pericoli.

courteous (kûr'tĕ·ŭs) *agg.* cortese, educato, amabile.

courtesan (kôr'tĕ·zản) *n.* cortigiana, prostituta.

courthouse (kōrt'hous') *n.* palazzo di giustizia.

courtly (kōrt'lĭ) *agg.* raffinato, elegante, cortese.

court-martial (kōrt'mär'shăl) *n.* corte marziale. *vt.* processare davanti alla corte marziale.

courtship (kōrt'shĭp) *n.* corte, corteggiamento, periodo di fidanzamento.

courtyard (kōrt'yärd') *n.* cortile.

cousin (kŭz''n) *n.* cugino, cugina.

cove (kōv) *n.* baia, caverna; incàvo, nicchia; (*gergo*) tizio, individuo.

covenant (kŭv'ē·nảnt) *n.* convenzione, patto, contratto. *vt., vi.* pattuire, stipulare.

cover (kŭv'ĕr) *n.* coperchio; copertura; copertina, busta, riparo; tovaglia; pretesto, apparenza; cauzione: **under separate —**, in plico a parte. *vt.* coprire, celare; tenere a bada (*con un'arma*); percorrere; (*giorn.*) occuparsi di, fare un servizio su. **—ing** *n.* copertura. **—let** *n.* coperta, coltre.

covert (kŭv'ĕrt) *n.* rifugio, riparo. *agg.* (-ĕrt') coperto, nascosto, segreto, velato. **—ly** *avv.* di nascosto, in segreto.

covet (kŭv'ĕt) *vt.* agognare, desiderare. **—ous** *agg.* avido, bramoso.

cow (kou) *n.* mucca; femmina (*di altri mammiferi*).

coward (kou'ĕrd) *n.* codardo, vigliacco. **—ice**, **—liness** *n.* codardia, vigliaccheria. **—ly** *agg.* codardo, meschino. *avv.* vigliaccamente.

cowboy (kou'bol') *n.* bovaro, buttero.

cower (kou'ĕr) *vi.* rannicchiarsi (*per il terrore*); accasciarsi.

cowhide (kou'hīd') *n.* pelle di mucca; scudiscio.

cowl (koul) *n.* cappuccio (*da frate*); cappa (*del camino*).

coxswain (kŏk's'n; kŏk'swản) *n.* (*naut.*) timoniere.

coy (koi) *agg.* timido, riservato, modesto. **—ness** *n.* timidezza, riserbo.

coyote (kĭ'ŏt; kĭ·ō'tĕ) *n.* lupo della prateria.

cozy (kō'zĭ) *agg.* comodo; intimo.

crab (krăb) *n.* branchio; (*mecc.*) gru.

crack (krăk) *n.* spaccatura, screpolatura, crepa; detonazione; schianto, schiocco; spuntare (*dell'alba*); (*gergo*) frizzo, spiritosaggine, frottola; *vt.* incrinare, fendere, spaccare; far schioccare (*la frusta*): to — a joke, dire una spiritosaggine. *vi.* spaccarsi, screpolarsi; scricchiolare; schioccare.

crack-brained *agg.* pazzo.

cracker (krăk'ĕr) *n.* petardo; biscotto croccante, galletta.

crackle (krăk'l) *n.* crepitio, scricchiolio. *vi.* scricchiolare, crepitare.

crackling *n.* crepitio; ciccioli (*di maiale*).

crack-up (krăk'up') *n.* sfasciamento, caduta (*di un aereo*).

cradle (krā'd'l) *n.* culla; infanzia; (*naut.*) invasatura; (*min.*) setaccio per sabbie aurifere.

craft (kráft) *n.* mestiere, arte, abilità; astuzia, artificio; (*naut.*) imbarcazione, flottiglia di barche; aeroplano.

craftiness (kráft'ĭ-nĕs) *n.* astuzia, furberia.

craftsman (kráfts'măn) *n.* operaio, artigiano; artista.

crafty (kráf'tĭ) *agg.* astuto, abile; subdolo.

crag (krăg) *n.* picco, rocca scoscesa.

cram (krăm) *n.* folla, calca; preparazione affrettata (*in vista di esami*). *vt.* riempire eccessivamente, rimpinzare, affollare, preparare (*agli esami*). *vi.* rimpinzarsi; infarcire la propria mente di cognizioni.

crammer (krăm'ĕr) *n.* sgobbone; ripetitore.

cramp (krămp) *n.* crampo; (*tec.*) grappa; (*fig.*) intralcio, ostacolo. *vt.* stringere, serrare; ostacolare; assicurare con grappa. —ed *agg.* scomodo, stretto: —ed writing, scrittura scarabocchiata.

crane (krăn) *n.* gru (*uccello e macchina*). *vt.* allungare (*il collo*).

cranium (krā'nĭ-ŭm) *n.* cranio.

crank (krăngk) *n.* manovella; gomito (*di tubo, ecc.*); pedaliera (*di bicicletta*); (*fig.*) pazzoide, originale. *vt.* piegare, curvare; munire di manovella, girare la manovella; avviare (*un motore*) con la manovella; *vi.* serpeggiare.

crankcase (krăngk'kăs') *n.* copricatena (*di bicicletta*); carter (*di motori*).

crankshaft (krăngk'shăft') *n.* albero a gomito.

cranny (krăn'ĭ) *n.* crepaccio, fessura.

crape (krăp) *n.* crespo.

crash (krăsh) *n.* schianto, tonfo, colpo, crollo, rovinio, caduta; scoppio; (*comm.*) fallimento. *vt.* distruggere, abbattere. *vi.* crollare fragorosamente; cozzare, urtare (*contro*); (*aeron.*) precipitare, atterrare irregolarmente: to — the gate, intrufolarsi senza biglietto (*a teatro, ecc.*); partecipare a una festa senza esservi invitato.

crass (krăs) *agg.* crasso, grossolano, ottuso.

crate (krāt) *n.* gabbia d'imballaggio.

crater (krā'tĕr) *n.* cratere.

cravat (krá·văt') *n.* cravatta, sciarpa.

crave (krāv) *vt., vi.* bramare, desiderare ardentemente, abbisognare di, implorare.

craven (krā'vĕn) *n., agg.* vigliacco.

craving (krāv'ĭng) *n.* brama, desiderio impellente; sete.

craw (krô) *n.* gozzo (*di uccello*).

crawl (krôl) *n.* strisciamento; vivaio (*di pesci*); crawl (*stile di nuoto*). *vi.* strisciare; trascinarsi; insinuarsi; brulicare (*di*). —ing *agg.* strisciante; brulicante (*di*).

crayon (krā'ŏn) *n.* pastello per disegno. *vt.* disegnare a pastello.

craze (krăz) *n.* pazzia, mania, passione, entusiasmo; moda. *vt.* far impazzire; screpolare. *vi.* impazzire; screpolarsi.

crazy (krā'zĭ) *agg.* pazzo; instabile, precario: to go —, impazzire.

creak (krēk) *n.* scricchiolio, cigolio. *vi.* scricchiolare, cigolare. —ing *n.* cigolio. *agg.* cigolante, scricchiolante.

cream (krēm) *n.* crema, panna; (*il*) meglio, (*il*) fior fiore. —ery *n.* caseificio.

creamy (krēm'ĭ) *agg.* cremoso.

crease (krēs) *n.* piega, grinza. *vt.* raggrinzire, sgualcire. **creasy** *agg.* spiegazzato.

create (krē·āt') *vt.* creare.

creation (krē·ā'shŭn) *n.* creazione; (*il*) Creato.

creative (-tĭv) *agg.* creativo.

creator (-tĕr) *n.* creatore.

creature (krē'tŭr) *n.* creatura.

credence (krē'd'ns) *n.* fede, convinzione, credenza.

credentials (krē·dĕn'shălz) *n.pl.* credenziali.

credible (krĕd'ĭ·b'l) *agg.* credibile.

credit (krĕd'ĭt) *n.* credito, fiducia; (*fig.*) prestigio, merito; (*pl., cinema, T.V.*) titoli di testa: — and debit, dare e avere; that does him —, questo torna a suo onore. *vt.* credere;

accreditare: to — with, ascrivere, attribuire a.

creditable (-ȧ·b'l) *agg.* lodevole.

creditor (-ĭ·tẽr) *n.* creditore.

credulity (krė·dū′lĭ·tĭ) *n.* credulità.

credulous (krĕd′ū·lŭs) *agg.* credulo.

creed (krēd) *n.* credo, fede, culto.

creek (krēk) *n.* ansa, baia; (*S.U.*) fiumicello.

creep (krēp) *n.* strisciamento; pelle d'oca, (*fig.*) brivido: it gives me the —s, mi fa venire i brividi. *vi.* (*pass.*, *pp.* crept) trascinarsi, strisciare, arrampicarsi: to feel one's flesh —, sentirsi accapponare la pelle. —er *n.* rettile, verme; pianta rampicante.

crematory (krē′mȧ·tō′rĭ) *n.* forno crematorio.

creole (krē′ōl) *n.*, *agg.* creolo.

crept (krĕpt) *pass.*, *pp.* di to creep.

crescent (krĕs′ĕnt) *agg.* crescente: — moon, luna crescente. *n.* quarto di luna; (*fig.*) mezza luna.

cress (krĕs) *n.* crescione.

crest (krĕst) *n.* cresta, crinale, ciuffo di piume, criniera, cimiero, pennacchio; orgoglio.

crestfallen (krĕst′fôl′ĕn) *agg.* abbattuto, scoraggiato, sconcertato, deluso.

cretin (krē′tĭn) *n.* cretino.

crevasse (krė·vȧs′) *n.* crepaccio.

crevice (krĕv′ĭs) *n.* fessura, fenditura.

crew (krōō) (1) *pass.* di to crow.

crew (krōō) (2) *n.* ciurma, equipaggio; squadra; combriccola, masnada. — cut, capelli a spazzola. — neck, scollatura a barchetta.

crib (krĭb) *n.* letto da bambino; mangiatoia, rastrelliera; capanna, casetta; (*fam.*) furterello, plagio; (*gergo*) bigino (*trad. letterale di classici ad uso degli studenti*).

cricket (krĭk′ĕt) *n.* grillo; cricket (*sport*); sgabello. —er *n.* giocatore di cricket.

crime (krīm) *n.* delitto, reato.

criminal (krĭm′ĭ·nȧl) *n.* delinquente *agg.* criminale, colpevole, penale.

crimp (krĭmp) *vt.* arricciare, ondulare.

crimpy (krĭmp′ĭ) *agg.* arricciato.

crimson (krĭm′z'n) *n.*, *agg.* cremisi, rosso vivo.

cringe (krĭnj) *vi.* umiliarsi, sottomettersi, tremare; retrocedere.

cringing (krĭn′jĭng) *n.* servilismo. *agg.* servile; tremebondo, pauroso.

crinkle (krĭng′k'l) *n.* grinza, increspatura. *vt.*, *vi.* raggrinzire; frusciare; serpeggiare; raggrinzirsi.

cripple (krĭp′'l) *n.* storpio, zoppo, invalido. *vt.* storpiare, menomare, azzoppare; frustrare, avariare.

crisis (krī′sĭs) *n.* (*pl.* crises) crisi.

crisp (krĭsp) *agg.* crespo; ricciuto; croccante; friabile; frizzante (*dell'aria*); acuto; arzillo; efficiente. *vt.* arricciare (*chiome*, *ecc.*), increspare; *vi.* incresparsi.

criterion (krī·tē′rĭ·ŭn) *n.* (*pl.* criteria) criterio; valutazione; prova.

critic (krĭt′ĭk) *n.* critico. —al *agg.* critico, precario. —ism (sĭzm) *n.* critica; censura; recensione.

criticize (krĭt′ĭ·sīz) *vt.* criticare, censurare.

critique (krĭ·tēk′) *n.* critica (*la critica*); recensione.

croak (krōk) *n.* gracidìo (*della rana*), gracchio (*del corvo*). *vi.* gracidare, gracchiare; (*gergo*) crepare (*morire*).

crochet (krō·shā′) *n.* lavoro all'uncinetto. *vt.*, *vi.* lavorare all'uncinetto. — needle *n.* uncinetto.

crock (krŏk) *n.* vaso di terracotta, bacinella. —ery *n.* vasellame.

crocodile (krŏk′ō·dīl) *n.* coccodrillo.

Croesus (krē′sŭs) *n.* Creso.

crone (krōn) *n.* vecchia (*donna*).

crony (krō′nĭ) *n.* amico, compare.

crook (krŏŏk) *n.* curva, incavo, gomito (*di tubo*, *ecc.*); pastorale (*bastone del vescovo*); furfante, imbroglione: by hook or by —, con qualunque mezzo. *vt.* curvare. *vi.* curvarsi. —ed *agg.* curvo, ricurvo, storto, contorto, tortuoso, disonesto.

croon (krōōn) *n.* canto sommesso. *vt.*, *vi.* canticchiare, cantare in tono sentimentale. —er *n.* cantante sentimentale.

crop (krŏp) *n.* raccolto, messi; raccolta; gozzo (*di uccello*); frustino; pelle intera di animale (*conciata*); tosatura; chioma corta. *vt.*, *vi.* mietere, raccogliere, falciare; brucare; tosare; spuntare; seminare.

cropper (krŏp′ẽr) *n.* mietitore, coltivatore; (*fam.*) capitombolo: to come a —, fare un capitombolo.

croquet (krō·kā′) *n.* (*sport*) palamaglio.

cross (krŏs) *n.* croce; incrocio (*anche di razze*); crocevia; tormento, calamità. *agg.* trasversale, obliquo; adirato, imbronciato: — section, spaccato; gruppo rappresentativo (*di una totalità*); to be at — purposes, fraintendersi. *avv.* attraverso, trasversalmente. *vt.* attraversare; segnare con una croce; incrociare; cancellare; barrare (*un assegno*); ostacolare; contrariare; varcare· to — oneself, farsi il segno della croce. *vi.* incrociarsi (*incontrarsi*); accoppiarsi; compiere una traversata.

cross-armed (krŏs′ärmd) *agg.* a braccia conserte.

crosscut (krŏs'kŭt') *n.* scorciatoia.

cross-examination *n.* controinterrogatorio; (*fig.*) subisso di domande.

cross-examine *vt.* sottoporre a controinterrogatorio.

crossing (krŏs'ĭng) *n.* crocicchio, incrocio, passaggio pedonale; traversata (*per mare*): railroad —, passaggio a livello; river —, guado.

crossroad (krŏs'rōd') *n.* strada trasversale: to find oneself at the —s, essere a un bivio *o* a una svolta decisiva.

crosswise (krŏs'wīz') *avv.* di traverso.

crossword puzzle (krŏs'wûrd') *n.* cruciverba, parole incrociate.

crotchet (krŏch'ĕt) *n.* uncino; capriccio.

crouch (krouch) *vi.* chinarsi, accovacciarsi, inchinarsi, umiliarsi.

croup (krōōp) *n.* groppa, quarti posteriori (*di un animale*).

crow (krō) *n.* corvo, cornacchia; canto del gallo: —'s foot, zampe d'oca (*agli angoli degli occhi*). *vi.* (*pass.* crowed, crew, *pp.* crowed) cantare (*del gallo*); esultare, cantar vittoria.

crowbar (krō'bär') *n.* leva di ferro, piede di porco.

crowd (kroud) *n.* folla, massa. *vt.* pigiare, ingombrare: to —, affollarsi. —ed *agg.* affollato, stipato, pieno.

crown (kroun) *n.* corona; cima, sommità; cocuzzolo (*del cappello*). *vt.* coronare, incoronare, sormontare. —ing *n.* incoronazione. *agg.* supremo, ultimo, finale.

crucible (krōō'sĭ·b'l) *n.* crogiolo.

crucifix (krōō'sĭ fĭks) *n.* crocifisso. —ion *n.* crocifissione.

crucify (krōō'sĭ·fī) *vt.* crocifiggere; (*fig.*) angariare; stroncare.

crude (krōōd) *agg.* grezzo; acerbo, rozzo, esplicito. —ness, crudity *n.* crudezza, rozzezza.

cruel (krōō'ĕl) *agg.* crudele.

cruelty (krōō'ĕl·tĭ) *n.* crudeltà; sevizie.

cruet (krōō'ĕt) *n.* oliera, ampolla; ampolliera; calice.

cruise (krōōz) *n.* crociera. *vi.* andare in crociera; incrociare.

cruiser (krōō'zẽr) *n.* incrociatore; automobile della polizia munita di radiotelefono.

crumb (krŭm) *n.* briciola. *vt.* sbriciolare.

crumble (krŭm'b'l) *vt.* sbriciolare, sgretolare. *vi.* sbriciolarsi, frantumarsi: to — down, cadere in rovina, franare.

crumple (krŭm'p'l) *vt.* sgualcire. *vi.* sgualcirsi; accasciarsi.

crunch (krŭnch) *vt.* sgranocchiare; frantumare; calpestare rumorosamente.

crusade (krōō·sād') *n.* crociata. *vi.* combattere (*per*), essere paladino (*di*).

crusader (-sād'ẽr) *n.* Crociato.

crush (krŭsh) *n.* folla; pigiatura; schiacciamento; oppressione. *vt.* schiacciare, far scricchiolare, frantumare; gualcire; reprimere: to — in, sfondare. —er *n.* frantoio.

crust (krŭst) *n.* crosta, scorza; (*gergo*) sfacciataggine.

crustacean (krŭs·tā'shăn) *n.* crostaceo.

crutch (krŭch) *n.* gruccia, stampella.

crux (krŭks) *n.* (*pl.* cruxes *o* cruces [krōō'sēz]) difficoltà, perplessità; indovinello; crisi, punto cruciale.

cry (krī) *n.* grido, richiamo, pianto: a far — from, ben lontano da. *vt.*, *vi.* gridare, urlare, piangere: to — out, ritirarsi; to — down, biasimare; to — for, invocare.

crypt (krĭpt) *n.* cripta. —ic *agg.* occulto, oscuro, misterioso. —ogram *n.* crittogramma. —ography (krĭpt·ŏg'rá·fĭ) *n.* crittografia.

crystal (krĭs'tăl) *n.* cristallo. *agg.* cristallino. —line (-lĕn') *agg.* cristallino: crystalline lens, cristallino (*dell'occhio*).

crystallize (krĭs'tăl·īz) *vt.*, *vi.* cristallizzare.

cub (kŭb) *n.* cucciolo; (*aeron.*) piccolo velivolo da turismo: — reporter, giornalista principiante.

cubbyhole (kŭb'ĭ·hōl) *n.* sgabuzzino.

cube (kŭb) *n.* cubo: — root, radice cubica.

cubic (kū'bĭk) *agg.* cubico.

cubism (kūb'ĭz'm) *n.* cubismo.

cubist (kūb'ĭst) *n.* cubista.

cuckold (kŭk'ŭld) *n.* cornuto, becco.

cuckoo (kŏŏk'ōō) *n.* cuculo. *agg.* (*gergo*) matto.

cucumber (kū'kŭm·bẽr) *n.* cetriolo.

cud (kŭd) *n.* bolo alimentare: to chew the —, rimuginare.

cuddle (kŭd'l) *vt.* abbraccio. *vt.* abbracciare. *vi.* abbracciarsi; rannicchiarsi.

cudgel (kŭj'ĕl) *n.* randello, clava. *vt.* bastonare: to — one's brains, lambiccarsi il cervello.

cue (kū) (1) *n.* stecca da biliardo.

cue (kū) (2) *n.* spunto, indicazione, imbeccata, cenno. *vt.* dare lo spunto *o* l'imbeccata a.

cuff (kŭf) *n.* pugno, scapaccione; polsino (*di camicia*), paramano; risvolto (*dei calzoni*). *vt.* percuotere.

cull (kŭl) *vt.* cogliere, scegliere.

culpable (kŭl'pá·b'l) *agg.* colpevole.

culprit (kŭl'prĭt) *n.* imputato; colpevole.

cult (kŭlt) *n.* culto.

cultivate (kŭl'tĭ·vāt) *vt.* coltivare.

cultivation (-vā'shŭn) *n.* coltivazione, cultura.

cultivator (-vā'tẽr) *n.* coltivatore.

cultural (kŭl'tūr·ăl) *agg.* culturale.

culture (kŭl'tūr) *n.* cultura, istruzione.

cultured (-tūrd) *agg.* colto.

cumbersome (kŭm'bẽr·sŭm) **cumbrous** (kŭm'brŭs) *agg.* ingombrante, pesante, poco maneggevole.

cumulative (kū'mŭ·lā'tĭv) *agg.* cumulativo.

cuneiform (kū·nē'ĭ·fôrm) *agg.* cuneiforme.

cunning (kŭn'ĭng) *n.* astuzia. *agg* astuto.

cup (kŭp) *n.* tazza, coppa, cavità.

cupboard (kŭb'ẽrd) *n.* credenza, armadio: — love, amore interessato.

Cupid (kū'pĭd) *n.* Cupido.

cupidity (kū·pĭd'ĭ·tĭ) *n.* cupidigia.

cur (kûr) *n.* cane bastardo *o* randagio; (*gergo*) persona spregevole.

curare (kū·rä'rē) *n.* curaro.

curate (kū'rĭt) *n.* curato.

curb (kûrb) *n.* freno, barbazzale (*del cavallo*); cordone di marciapiede, ciglio di strada. *vt.* reprimere, frenare, dominare.

curd (kûrd) *n.* giuncata, latte rappreso.

curdle (kûr'd'l) *vt.* rapprendere. *vi.* rapprendersi.

cure (kūr) *n.* cura, rimedio. *vt.* guarire, sanare; rimediare; conservare sotto sale.

curfew (kûr'fū) *n.* coprifuoco.

curio (kū'rĭ·ō) *n.* oggetto raro, curiosità.

curiosity (kū'rĭ·ŏs'ĭ·tĭ) *n.* curiosità.

curious (kū'rĭ·ŭs) *agg.* curioso; strano.

curl (kûrl) *n.* ricciolo (*di capelli*), spirale, ondulazione; piega (*delle labbra*). *vt.* arricciare, arrotolare. *vi.* arricciarsi, arrotolarsi: to — up, accovacciarsi.

curly (kûr'lĭ) *agg.* ricciuto.

currant (kûr'ănt) *n.* sultanina (*uva*), ribes.

currency (kûr'ĕn·sĭ) *n.* circolante (*danaro*); corso legale; valutazione, moda; attualità.

current (kûr'ĕnt) *n.* corrente. *agg.* corrente, in corso, attuale, ammesso.

curry (kûr'ĭ) *vt.* conciare (*pelli*); strigliare (*un cavallo*); percuotere: to — favor, adulare per ottenere favori.

curse (kûrs) *n.* maledizione, imprecazione; calamità. *vt.* maledire, affliggere. *vi.* imprecare.

cursed (kûr'sĕd; kûrst) *agg.* maledetto; afflitto, malaugurato.

cursive (kûr's·v) *agg.* corsivo.

cursory (kûr'sō·rĭ) *agg.* rapido, superficiale.

curt (kûrt) *agg.* brusco, sbrigativo, sgarbato.

curtail (kûr·tāl') *vt.* accorciare, restringere.

curtain (kûr'tĭn) *n.* sipario, tendaggio, tendina; cortina.

curtsy (kûrt'sĭ) *n.* riverenza, inchino.

curve (kûrv) *n.* curva. *vt.* curvare.

curved (kûrvd) *agg.* curvo.

cushion (kŏŏsh'ŭn) *n.* cuscino, guanciale.

cuspidor (kŭs'pĭ·dôr) *n.* sputacchiera.

cuss (kŭs) *n.*, *vi.* (*gergo*) *vedi* curse.

custard (kŭs'tẽrd) *n.* crema di latte e uova.

custody (kŭs'tō·dĭ) *n.* custodia, guardia, arresto, detenzione: to take into —, trarre in arresto; to commit to someone's —, affidare a qualcuno.

custom (kŭs'tŭm) *n.* usanza, abitudine; clientela. — house, ufficio doganale: —house official, doganiere. —made, *agg.* fatto su ordinazione *o* su misura; (*autom.*) fuori serie.

customary (kŭs'tŭm·ẽr·ĭ) *agg.* consueto, abituale.

customs *n.pl.* dogana.

customer (kŭs'tŭm·ẽr) *n.* cliente, avventore; tipo, individuo.

cut (kŭt) *n.* taglio, linea; fetta, trancio; riduzione, scorciatoia. *vt.* (*pass.*, *pp.* cut) tagliare; troncare; affettare; ridurre; mettere al bando; togliere il saluto a: to — back, ridurre, diminuire; to — class, marinare la scuola. *vi.* tagliare (*esser tagliente*): to — a poor figure, fare una figura meschina.

cute (kūt) *agg.* astuto; carino, originale.

cuticle (kū'tĭ·k'l) *n.* cuticola, pellicola.

cutlass (kŭt'lås) *n.* scimitarra.

cutlery (kŭt'lẽr·ĭ) *n.* coltelleria.

cutlet (kŭt'lĕt) *n.* cotoletta.

cutter (kŭt'ẽr) *n.* tagliatore; (*naut.*) cutter (*canotto a vela*); (*tec.*) fresa.

cutthroat (kŭt'thrōt') *n.* assassino.

cutting (kŭt'ĭng) *n.* taglio, incisione; ritaglio, frammento. *agg.* tagliente, mordace.

cuttle (kŭt''l), **cuttlefish** *n.* seppia.

cutwater (kŭt'wô·tẽr) *n.* tagliamare.

cyanide (sī'á·nīd) *n.* cianuro.

cybernetics (sĭ'bĕr·nĕt'ĭks) *n.* cibernetica.

cyclamen (sĭk'lá·mĕn) *n.* ciclamino.

cycle (sī'k'l) *n.* ciclo; bicicletta. *vi.* andare a cicli; andare in bicicletta.

cyclist (sī'klĭst) *n.* ciclista.

cyclone (sī'klōn) *n.* ciclone, uragano.

cyclops (sī'klŏps) *n.* (*pl.* cyclopes [sĭklō'pēz]) ciclope.

cyclotron (sī'klō·trŏn) *n.* ciclotrone.

cylinder (sĭl'ĭn·dĕr) *n.* cilindro.

cylindrical (sĭl·ĭn'drĭ·kăl) *agg.* cilindrico.

cymbal (sĭm'băl) *n.* piatto (*da orchestra*).

cynic (sĭn'ĭk) *n.*, *agg.* cinico. —al *agg.* cinico. —ism (-sĭzm) *n.* cinismo.

cypress (sī'prĕs) *n.* cipresso.

cyst (sĭst) *n.* (*med.*) cisti.

D

dab (dăb) *n.* colpetto; chiazza. *vt.* sfiorare; cospargere.

dabble (dăb'l) *vi.* umettare, spruzzare, sguazzare; to— in (at) dilettarsi di.

dabbler (dăb'lĕr) *n.* dilettante, inesperto.

dad (dăd), daddy (dăd'ĭ) *n.* babbo, babbino.

daffodil (dăf'ŏ·dĭl) *n.* narciso selvatico.

daft (dăft) *agg.* sciocco, pazzoide.

dagger (dăg'ĕr) *n.* daga, pugnale; (*tip.*) croce: with —s drawn, ai ferri corti.

daily (dā'lĭ) *n.* quotidiano (*giorn.*). *agg.* quotidiano, giornaliero, diurno. *avv.* quotidianamente, di giorno in giorno.

dainty (dān'tĭ) *agg.* fine, delicato, prelibato, raffinato (*di gusti*).

dairy (dâr'ĭ) *n.* latteria, caseificio.

daisy (dā'zĭ) *n.* margherita.

dale (dāl) *n.* valle, valletta.

dally (dăl'ĭ) *vi.* oziare; amoreggiare; attardarsi: to — with danger, scherzare col pericolo.

dam (dăm) (1) *n.* sbarramento, diga, bacino artificiale. *vt.* arginare, bloccare, imbrigliare; munire di diga.

dam (2) *n.* madre (*in rif. ad animali*).

damage (dăm'ĭj) *n.* danno; torto; avaria. *vt.* danneggiare; avariare; nuocere; compromettere. *vi.* subire danni; avariarsi.

dame (dăm) *n.* dama; nobildonna; padrona di casa; direttrice di scuola; (*gergo S.U.*) donna.

damn (dăm) *n.* maledizione, imprecazione: I don't give a —! non me ne importa niente; *inter.* maledizione! accidenti! *vt.* maledire, condannare. —ation (nā'shŭn) *n.* dannazione, condanna. —ed (dămd) *agg.* dannato, maledetto, malaugurato.

damp (dămp) *n.* umidità, vapore; abbattimento, scoramento. *agg.* umido; abbattuto. *vt.* inumidire, umet-

tare; soffocare; demoralizzare. —en *vt.* inumidire. *vi.* inumidirsi. —er *n.* persona *o* cosa deprimente; regolatore (*di stufa, ecc.*); (*mus.*) sordina. —ness *n.* umidità.

damsel (dăm'zĕl) *n.* damigella.

dance (dáns) *n.* danza, ballo. *vi.*, *vt.* ballare.

dancer (dán'sĕr) *n.* ballerino, ballerina.

dandelion (dăn'dĕ·lĭ'ŭn) *n.* dente-dileone.

dander (dăn'dĕr) *n.* (*gergo*) collera.

dandruff (dăn'drŭf) *n.* forfora.

dandy (dăn'dĭ) *n.* damerino, elegantone; (*naut.*) jole a vela. *agg.* elegante; (*S.U.*) ottimo, di prim'ordine.

danger (dăn'jĕr) *n.* pericolo. —ous *agg.* pericoloso. —ously *avv.* pericolosamente.

dangle (dăng'g'l) *vt.* far penzolare. *vi.* penzolare; stare alle calcagna (*di qualcuno*).

dank (dăngk) *agg.* umido.

dapper (dăp'ĕr) *agg.* piccolo e attivo; inappuntabile; lindo.

dapple (dăp''l) *n.* chiazza. *agg.* chiazzato, pezzato. *vi.* macchiarsi. —gray *n.* grigio pomellato.

dare (dâr) *vt.* (*pass.* durst, dared, *pp.* dared) sfidare, affrontare. *vi.* osare. *n.* sfida; provocazione.

daredevil (dâr'dĕv''l) *n.*, *agg.* audace, temerario.

daring (dâr'ĭng) *n.* ardimento. *agg.* intrepido, audace.

dark (dărk) *n.* oscurità. *agg.* oscuro, cupo, scuro, buio, sinistro, bruno: — horse, cavallo sconosciuto (*che vince inaspettatamente la gara*); candidato politico che vince inaspettatamente le elezioni; — secret, segreto profondo, enigma. —ly *avv.* oscuramente, velatamente. —ness *n.* oscurità. — some *agg.* scuro, tetro.

darken (dăr'kĕn) *vt.* oscurare, scurire; turbare. *vi.* oscurarsi, rabbuiarsi.

darky (dăr'kĭ) *n.* (*S.U.*) negro (*sprezz.*).

darling (där'ling) n. prediletto, tesoro. agg. diletto, adorato: my —, mio caro, tesoro mio.

darn (därn) n. rammendo, rattoppo: —! acciderba! maledizione! vt. rammendare.

dart (därt) n. dardo, pungiglione, balzo. vt. dardeggiare, scagliare. vi. lanciarsi.

dash (dăsh) n. impeto; colpo, urto; spruzzo; pennellata (di colore); tratto di penna, lineetta. vt. scagliare, scaraventare, infrangere; spruzzare. vi. rompersi; piombare (al suolo, ecc.); slanciarsi: to — by, passare di corsa; to — off a letter, buttar giù una lettera. —board n. cruscotto. —ing agg. impetuoso; vistoso, appariscente.

dastard (dăs'tĕrd) n. vigliacco, furfante.

dastardly (-li) agg. vile, spregevole.

data (dā'tà) n.pl. dati, elementi.

date (dāt) (1) n. data; scadenza, termine; (S.U.) appuntamento: to bring up to —, aggiornare; up to —, aggiornato, moderno; out of —, antiquato; scaduto. vt., vi. datare; dare appuntamento a.

date (dāt) (2) n. dattero.

datum (dā'tŭm) n. dato.

daub (dôb) n. imbratto; crosta (quadro privo di valore). vt. imbrattare; pitturare malamente.

daughter (dô'tĕr) n. figlia. —in-law, nuora.

daunt (dônt) vt. intimidire; smorzare (gli entusiasmi). —less agg.intrepido.

davenport (dăv'ĕn-pôrt) n. (S.U.) divano; (Ingl.) scrivania.

davit (dăv'ĭt) n. (naut.) argano.

dawdle (dô'dl) vi. bighellonare; oziare.

dawdler (dô'dlēr) n. bighellone.

dawn (dôn) n. alba, aurora. vi. albeggiare; (fig.) balenare (nella mente).

day (dā) n. giorno, giornata: broad —, pieno giorno; (Ingl.) this — week, oggi otto; — after tomorrow, dopodomani; — before yesterday, avantieri; by —, di giorno; by the —, a giornata. to carry the —, riportare la vittoria.

daybook n. (comm.) libro-giornale.

daybreak n. alba.

daydream n. fantasticheria, sogno a occhi aperti. vi. fantasticare.

daylight n. giorno, luce del giorno.

dayroom n. (mil.) sala di lettura e di ricreazione.

daytime n. giorno: in the —, di giorno.

daze (dāz) n. stupore, intontimento. vt. sbalordire, inebetire.

dazzle (dăz''l) vt. abbagliare; stordire; confondere. n. bagliore.

deacon (dē'kŭn) n. diacono.

deactivate (dē·ăk'tĭ·vāt) vt. disattivare, fermare, interrompere; sciogliere (un ufficio, un reparto, ecc.); disinnescare.

dead (dĕd) agg. morto, estinto; spento (di fuoco); sordo (di suono); smorto (di colore): — body, cadavere; — sleep, sonno profondo; — stop, fermata improvvisa; — certainty, certezza matematica; — letter, lettera non reclamata; cosa antiquata; — loss, perdita assoluta; the — of night, il cuor della notte; the —, i morti. avv. completamente, assolutamente: — drunk, ubriaco fradicio; — sure, arcisicuro.

deaden (dĕd''n) vt. smorzare, attutire. vi. affievolirsi, smorzarsi.

deadlock n. punto morto, vicolo cieco.

deadly agg. mortale, micidiale.

deadpan (dĕd'păn') agg. detto con finta serietà, impassibile, staccato.

deaf (dĕf) agg. sordo.

deafen (dĕf'ĕn) vt. assordare.

deafening agg. assordante.

deafness n. sordità.

deal (dēl) n. quantità; affare; distribuzione; mano (al gioco); politica (amministrativa); asse o legno di abete o di pino: a good —, molto; a great —, moltissimo; it is my —, tocca a me; to give a square —, trattare con equanimità. vt. (pass., pp. dealt) distribuire, ripartire, assestare (un colpo). vi. agire, fare affari: to — in, occuparsi di, commerciare in; to — with, agire verso, avere a che fare con, vedersela con. —er n. commerciante; mazziere, croupier. —ing n. affare, trattativa, condotta.

dealt (dĕlt) pass., pp. di to deal.

dean (dēn) n. decano, prelato; (S.U.) preside di facoltà universitaria.

dear (dēr) agg. caro, amabile; costoso: — Sir, egregio signore. dear! dear!, dear me!, santo cielo!

dearly avv. caramente; a caro prezzo.

dearth (dûrth) n. carestia.

death (dĕth) n. morte, fine, trapasso: to beat to —, massacrare. — rate n. mortalità. — warrant n. ordine d'esecuzione capitale.

deb vedi debutante.

debase (dē·bās') vt. degradare, abbassare; adulterare, falsificare.

debasing agg. degradante.

debatable (dē·bāt'à·b'l) agg. discutibile, controverso.

debate (dē·bāt') n. dibattito, disputa. vt., vi. dibattere, discutere, deliberare.

debauch (dē·bôch') n. intemperanza.

debenture (dĕ·bĕn'tŭr) n. obbligazione.

debit (dĕb'ĭt) n. debito, addebito; (comm.) dare. vt. addebitare.

debonair (dĕb'ō·nâr') agg. amabile, bonario.

debris (dĕ·brē') n. detriti.

debt (dĕt) n. debito. —or n. debitore.

debut (dā'bū) n. esordio: to make a —, esordire, —ant n. esordiente (m.). —ante n. esordiente (f.).

decade (dĕk'ād) n. decennio.

decadence (dĕ·kā'dĕns) n. decadenza.

decadent n., agg. decadente.

decalogue (dĕk'á·lŏg) n. decalogo.

decanter (dē·kăn'tĕr) n. caraffa.

decay (dē·kā') n. decadenza, rovina; decomposizione; carie. vi. decadere, cadere in rovina; guastarsi; cariarsi.

decease (dē·sĕs') n. decesso. vi. decedere, morire.

deceased n., agg. defunto.

deceit (dē·sēt') n. inganno, frode. —ful agg. ingannevole, fraudolento.

deceive (dē·sēv') vt. ingannare.

deceiver n. ingannatore.

December (dē·sĕm'bĕr) n. dicembre.

decency (dē'sĕn·sĭ) n. correttezza, pudore.

decent (dē'sĕnt) agg. corretto, onesto; buono, cortese.

deception (dē·sĕp'shŭn) n. inganno, illusione.

decide (dē·sīd') vt. decidere. vi. decidersi; concludere.

decided agg. deciso, risoluto; chiaro.

decimal (dĕs'ĭ·măl) n., agg. decimale.

decipher (dē·sī'fĕr) vt. decifrare.

decision (dē·sĭzh'ŭn) n. decisione; risolutezza.

decisive (dē·sī'sĭv) agg. decisivo; deciso, risoluto.

deck (dĕk) (1) n. (naut.) ponte, tolda; mazzo di carte (da gioco).

deck (dĕk) (2) vt. adornare: to — oneself out, agghindarsi.

declaim (dē·klām') vt., vi. declamare.

declaration (dĕk'lá·rā'shŭn) n. dichiarazione.

declare (dē·klâr') vt. dichiarare, annunciare, asserire, proclamare. vi. dichiararsi, pronunciarsi.

decline (dē·klīn') n. declino, decadenza; deperimento; pendenza; diminuzione (dei prezzi). vt. declinare; rifiutare. vi. pendere, declinare; diminuire (dei prezzi).

declivity (dē·klĭv'ĭ·tĭ) n. declivio.

decode (dē·kōd') vt. decifrare, tradurre in chiaro (testi in codice).

decompose (dē'kŏm·pōz') vt. decomporre; scomporre. vi. decomporsi, marcire.

decorate (dĕk'ō·rāt) vt. decorare, abbellire, adornare; arredare.

decoration (dĕk'ō·rā'shŭn) n. decorazione; arredamento.

decorative (dĕk'ō·rā'tĭv) agg. decorativo, ornamentale.

decorator (dĕk'ō·rā'tĕr) n. decoratore; arredatore.

decorum (dē·kō'rŭm) n. decoro.

decoy (dē·koi') n. trappola, esca, uccello da richiamo. vt. adescare, intrappolare.

decrease (dē'krēs) n. diminuzione. (-krēs') vt., vi. diminuire.

decree (dē·krē') n. decreto, sentenza. vt. decretare.

decrepit (dē·krĕp'ĭt) agg. decrepito.

dedicate (dĕd'ĭ·kāt) vt. dedicare, consacrare.

dedicated agg. dedicato; ligio, scrupoloso; consacrato.

dedication (dĕd'ĭ·kā'shŭn) n. dedica, consacrazione; dedicazione.

deduce (dē·dūs') vt. dedurre, concludere.

deduct (dē·dŭkt') vt. dedurre; sottrarre; diffalcare. —ion n. deduzione; sottrazione; diffalco.

deed (dēd) n. azione, prodezza, impresa; titolo, contratto.

deem (dēm) vt., vi. ritenere, giudicare.

deep (dēp) n. profondità; mare. agg. profondo; scuro, cupo; astuto: — mourning, lutto stretto; to be in — waters, essere in difficoltà; — in debt, affogato nei debiti; — in thought, assorto.

deepen (dēp'ĕn) vt. approfondire, oscurire. vi. divenire più profondo, incupirsi.

deeply avv. profondamente; intensamente; astutamente.

deepness n. profondità; astuzia.

deer (dēr) n. cervo, daino, renna.

deface (dē·fās') vt. sfigurare, deturpare, mutilare, cancellare.

defame (dē·fām') vt. diffamare.

default (dē·fôlt') n. mancanza; insolvenza, morosità; contumacia. vi. essere insolvente; essere contumace; (sport) ritirarsi da una gara. —er n. persona contumace; debitore insolvente; malversatore; (sport) concorrente ritiratosi.

defeat (dē·fēt') n. sconfitta, disfatta. vt. sconfiggere, frustrare.

defect (dē·fĕkt') n. difetto, imperfezione.

defective (dē·fĕk'tĭv) agg. difettoso, insufficiente, difettivo.

defence vedi defense.

defend (dē·fĕnd') vt. difendere, proteggere.

defendant (dĕ·fĕn'dănt) n. imputato, convenuto.

defender (dĕ·fĕn'dẽr) n. difensore.

defense (dĕ·fĕns') n. difesa: self-—, legittima difesa. —less agg. indifeso.

defensive (de·fĕn'sĭv) n. difensiva. agg. difensivo.

defer (dĕ·fûr') vt. differire, rimandare; deferire. vi. temporeggiare: to — to, rimettersi al giudizio di.

deference (dĕf'ẽr·ẽns) n. deferenza, riguardo.

deferential (dĕf'ẽr·ĕn'shăl) agg. riguardoso.

defiance (dĕ·fī'ăns) n. sfida, provocazione; spavalderia: in — of, in dispregio a, a dispetto di.

defiant (dĕ·fī'ănt) agg. insolente, provocante; spavaldo.

deficiency (dĕ·fĭsh'ĕn·sĭ) n. deficienza, debolezza; (comm.) disavanzo.

deficient (dĕ·fĭsh'ănt) agg. insufficiente, deficiente.

deficit (dĕf'ĭ·sĭt) n. deficit.

defile (dĕ·fīl') (1) n. gola (di montagna).

defile (2) vi. sfilare, marciare in parata.

defile (3) vt. insudiciare; violare, profanare; corrompere.

define (dĕ·fīn') vt. definire, determinare.

definite (dĕf'ĭ·nĭt) agg. determinato, esatto, preciso, definito.

definitely (dĕf'ĭ·nĭt·lĭ) avv. definitivamente; assolutamente; senz'altro.

definition (dĕf'ĭ·nĭsh'ŭn) n. definizione.

definitive (dĕ·fĭn'ĭ·tĭv) agg. definitivo; determinativo.

deflate (dĕ·flāt') vt. sgonfiare.

deform (dĕ·fôrm') vt. deformare, sformare. —ation n. deformazione, alterazione. —ed agg. deforme, deformato. —ity n. deformità.

defraud (dĕ·frôd') vt. defraudare, privare.

defray (dĕ·frā') vt. risarcire, pagare.

defrost (dĕ·frôst') vt. decongelare; sbrinare (il frigorifero).

deft (dĕft) agg. abile, destro.

defy (dĕ·fī') vt. sfidare, mettere a dura prova; opporsi a; resistere a.

degeneracy (dĕ·jĕn'ẽr·ȧ·sĭ) n. degenerazione.

degenerate (dĕ·jĕn'ẽr·ĭt) n., agg. degenerato. (·āt) vi. degenerare.

degradation (dĕg'rȧ·dā'shŭn) n. degradazione, ignominia.

degrade (dĕ·grād') vt. degradare.

degree (dĕ·grē') n. grado, gradino, livello; diploma, laurea: to take one's —, conseguire una laurea. by —s, per gradi, a poco a poco.

dehydrate (dē·hī'drāt) vt. disidratare.

deign (dān) vt., vi. degnare, degnarsi.

deity (dē'ĭ·tĭ) n. divinità.

deject (dĕ·jĕkt') vt. scoraggiare.

dejected (dĕ·jĕk'tĕd) agg. scoraggiato, triste.

dejection (dĕ·jĕk'shŭn) n. abbattimento; (med.) defecazione.

delay (dĕ·lā') n. ritardo, indugio; rinvio, dilazione. vt. ritardare, rimandare. vi. indugiare.

delegate (dĕl'ĕ·gāt) n. delegato. vt. delegare.

delegation (-gā'shŭn) n. delegazione; delega.

delete (dĕ·lēt') vt. cancellare, cassare.

deletion (dĕ·lē'shŭn) n. cancellazione.

deliberate (dĕ·lĭb'ẽr·ĭt) agg. intenzionale; ponderato, misurato, cauto; lento. vt., vi. deliberare; ponderare, considerare, discutere. —ly avv. deliberatamente, intenzionalmente, apposta; lentamente. —ness n. ponderatezza, prudenza.

deliberation (-ā'shŭn) n. deliberazione; riflessione; lentezza.

delicacy (dĕl'ĭ·kȧ·sĭ) n. delicatezza, finezza; leccornia.

delicate (dĕl'ĭ·kĭt) agg. delicato.

delicateness (-nĕs) n. delicatezza.

delicatessen (dĕl'ĭ·kȧ·tĕs'ẽn) n. (S.U.) negozio di specialità alimentari.

delicious (dĕ·lĭsh'ŭs) agg. delizioso.

delight (dĕ·līt') n. gioia, diletto, entusiasmo. vt. deliziare, dilettare. vi. compiacersi, divertirsi, entusiasmarsi: to — in, compiacersi di, essere entusiasta di. —ed agg. contento, lieto, felice. —ful agg. delizioso, incantevole.

delineate (dĕ·lĭn'ē·āt) vt. delineare, abbozzare.

delinquency (dĕ·lĭng'kwĕn·sĭ) n. malefatta, colpa; negligenza, manchevolezza.

delinquent (-kwĕnt) n. colpevole, responsabile: tax —, evasore fiscale.

delirious (dĕ·lĭr'ĭ·us) agg. delirante: to be —, delirare, smaniare.

delirium (-ŭm) n. delirio.

deliver (dĕ·lĭv'ẽr) vt. liberare, salvare; consegnare; distribuire (posta), recapitare; pronunciare (un discorso); assestare (un colpo); partorire. —ance n. liberazione. —ed agg. recapito; parto; allocuzione. —er n. liberatore; latore.

delivery (dĕ·lĭv'ẽr·ĭ) n. consegna; distribuzione postale; liberazione; parto; eloquio.

dell (dĕl) n. valletta, conca.

delude (dĕ·lūd') vt. ingannare, illudere; deludere.

delusion (-lū'zhŭn) *n.* illusione, inganno, allucinazione.

delusive (-sĭv), **delusory** (-sŏ-rĭ) *agg.* illusorio, ingannevole.

deluge (dĕl'ūj) *n.* diluvio. *vt.* inondare.

delve (dĕlv) *vt.*, *vi.* frugare, scavare.

demand (dē-mȧnd') *n.* richiesta, domanda; esigenza: on —, a richiesta. *vt.* richiedere, domandare; esigere. —ing *agg.* esigente.

demeanor (dē-mēn'ẽr) *n.* condotta, comportamento, contegno.

demented (dē-mĕn'tĕd) *agg.* demente.

demerit (dē-mĕr'ĭt) *n.* demerito.

demigod (dĕm'ĭ-gŏd) *n.* semidio.

demijohn (-jŏn) *n.* damigiana.

demise (dē-mīz) *n.* decesso; trapasso di proprietà.

demobilization (dē-mō'bĭ-lĭ-zā'shŭn) *n.* smobilitazione.

demobilize (dē-mō'bĭ-līz) *vt.* smobilitare.

democracy (dē-mŏk'rȧ-sĭ) *n.* democrazia.

democrat (dĕm'ō-krȧt) *n.* democratico.

democratic (dĕm'ō-krȧt'ĭk) *agg.* democratico.

demolish (dē-mŏl'ĭsh) *vt.* demolire.

demolition (dē'mō-lĭsh'ŭn) *n.* demolizione.

demon (dē'mŭn) *n.* demonio.

demonstrate (dĕm'ŭn-strāt) *vt.* dimostrare.

demonstration (dĕm'ŭn-strā'shŭn) *n.* dimostrazione.

demonstrative (dē-mŏn'strȧ-tĭv) *agg.* dimostrativo; espansivo.

demote (dē-mōt') *vt.* retrocedere (*di grado*).

demur (dē-mûr') *n.* titubanza. *vi.* titubare, esitare; tergiversare, fare obiezioni.

demure (dē-mūr') *agg.* pudico, riservato, compassato.

den (dĕn) *n.* antro, tana, covo; stamberga; (*fam.*) studiolo personale.

denial (dē-nī'ȧl) *n.* diniego, rifiuto; rinnegazione: self—, altruismo, abnegazione.

denizen (dĕn'ĭ-zĕn) *n.* abitante; straniero naturalizzato.

denominate (dē-nŏm'ĭ-nāt) *vt.* denominare.

denomination (dē-nŏm'ĭ-nā'shŭn) *n.* denominazione; comunità, setta; taglio (*di banconota*).

denote (dē-nōt') *vt.* denotare, indicare.

denounce (dē-nouns') *vt.* denunciare, dichiarare, propalare.

dense (dĕns) *agg.* denso, compatto; folto, fitto; ottuso, stupido.

density (dĕn'sĭ-tĭ) *n.* densità.

dent (dĕnt) *n.* tacca, incavo; dente (*d'ingranaggio*). *vt.* dentellare, fare una tacca. *vi.* dentellarsi.

dental (dĕn'tȧl) *agg.* dentario, odontoiatrico. *n.*, *agg.* (*gramm.*) dentale.

dentist (dĕn'tĭst) *n.* dentista. —ry *n.* odontoiatria.

denunciation (dē-nŭn'sĭ-ā'shŭn) *n.* denuncia, aperta condanna, accusa.

deny (dē-nī', *vt.* negare; rinnegare, smentire, rifiutare: to — oneself, sacrificarsi; far dire che non si è in casa.

deodorize (dē-ō'dẽr-īz) *vt.* deodorare.

deodorizer (dē-ō'dẽr-īz'ẽr) *n.* deodorante.

depart (dē-pärt') *vi.* partire; dipartirsi; deviare, derogare. —ed *agg.* defunto: the departed, i defunti.

department (dē-pärt'mĕnt) *n.* dipartimento, reparto. — store *n.* (*S.U.*) grande emporio.

departure (dē-pär'tūr) *n.* partenza; dipartita, allontanamento; deviazione, deroga.

depend (dē-pĕnd') *vi.* dipendere: to — upon, fare affidamento su, credere a; — upon it, potete contarci, statene certo. —able *agg.* fidato, sicuro, attendibile. —ence *n.* dipendenza, subordinazione; fiducia. —ency *n.* dipendenza, edificio aggiunto, territorio annesso. —ent *n.* dipendente, familiare; *agg.* dipendente.

depict (dē-pĭkt') *vt.* dipingere, descrivere.

depilate (dĕp'ĭ-lāt) *vt.* depilare.

deplete (dē-plēt') *vt.* vuotare, svotare.

deplorable (dē-plōr'ȧ-b'l) *agg.* deplorevole.

deplore (dē-plōr') *vt.* deplorare.

deploy (dē-ploi') *vt.* schierare, spiegare. —ment *n.* schieramento, spiegamento.

depopulate (dē-pŏp'ū-lāt) *vt.* spopolare. *vi.* spopolarsi.

deport (dē-pōrt') *vt.* deportare: to — oneself, comportarsi. —ation *n.* deportazione. —ment *n.* condotta; portamento.

depose (dē-pōz') *vt.*, *vi.* deporre; destituire testimoniare.

deposit (dē-pŏz'ĭt) *n.* deposito. *vt.* depositare, deporre; versare.

deposition (dĕp'ō-zĭsh'ŭn) *n.* deposizione.

depositor (dē-pŏz'ĭ-tẽr) *n.* depositante, correntista.

depository (dē-pŏz'ĭ-tō'rĭ) *n.* deposito, ripostiglio, magazzino; depositario, fiduciario.

depot (dē'pō) *n.* magazzino, deposito; (*S.U.*) stazione ferroviaria.

depravity (dĕ·prăv′ĭ·tĭ) n. depravazione.

deprecate (dĕp′rĕ·kāt) vt. deprecare, deplorare, disapprovare.

deprecating agg. umile, supplichevole; disapprovante, di deplorazione.

depreciate (dĕ·prē′shĭ·āt) vt. deprezzare. vi. deprezzarsi, perdere di valore.

depreciation (dĕ·prē′shĭ·ā′shŭn) n. deprezzamento.

depress (dĕ·prĕs′) vt. deprimere; inclinare. —ed agg. depresso; abbassato. —ing agg. deprimente. —ion (dĕ·prĕsh′ŭn) n. depressione; avvallamento; crisi.

deprive (dĕ·prīv′) vt. privare; defraudare.

depth (dĕpth) n. profondità, spessore: the — of night, il cuor della notte; to be out of one's —, navigare in acque troppo profonde.

deputation (dĕp′ū·tā′shŭn) n. deputazione; delega.

depute (dĕ·pūt′) vt. deputare, delegare.

deputy (dĕp′ū·tĭ) n. deputato, delegato, sostituto; agente; vicesceriffo.

derail (dĕ·rāl′) vt. far deragliare. vi. deragliare.

derange (dĕ·rānj′) vt. scompigliare, sconvolgere, turbare.

deranged (dĕ·rānjd′) agg. scompigliato, disordinato; squilibrato, pazzo.

derby (där′bĭ) n. corsa inglese per puledri di tre anni; (dûr′bĭ) gran premio ippico; gara, partita; bombetta (cappello duro).

deride (dĕ·rīd′) vt. deridere, schernire.

derision (-rīzh′ŭn) n. derisione, scherno.

derisive (-rī′sĭv) agg. derisivo, beffardo; risibile.

derive (dĕ·rīv′) vt., vi. derivare; trarre, attingere; discendere (provenire).

derogation (dĕr′ō·gā′shŭn) n. calunnia, diffamazione, denigrazione.

derogatory (dĕ·rŏg′à·tō′rĭ) agg. calunnioso, diffamatorio; denigratorio.

derrick (dĕr′ĭk) n. gru meccanica; derrick, castello (di pozzo petrolifero).

descend (dĕ·sĕnd′) vt., vi. scendere, discendere, abbassarsi. —ant n. discendente.

descent (dĕ·sĕnt′) n. discesa, pendio; origine; calata.

describe (dĕ·skrīb′) vt. descrivere.

description (dĕ·skrĭp′shŭn) n. descrizione; specie; genere: of all —s, di tutti i generi.

descriptive (-tĭv) agg. descrittivo.

desecrate (dĕs′ĕ·krāt) n. profanare.

desecration (-krā′shŭn) n. profanazione.

desert (dĕ·zûrt′) (1) n. merito; giusta ricompensa; giusta punizione: to have one's —s, avere ciò che si merita.

desert (dĕz′ĕrt) (2) n., agg. deserto. vt. (dĕ·zûrt′) disertare, abbandonare. vi. (mil.) disertare. —er n. disertore. —ion n. diserzione; abbandono.

deserve (dĕ·zûrv′) vt. meritare.

deserving (-zûr′vĭng) agg. meritevole, degno.

desiccate (dĕs′ĭ·kāt) vt. essiccare. vi. essiccarsi.

design (dĕ·zīn′) n. disegno, progetto, mira. vt., vi. disegnare; ideare, progettare, proporsi; designare: industrial —, disegno industriale, estetica del prodotto.

designate (dĕz′ĭg·nāt) vt. designare.

designer (dĕ·zīn′ẽr) n. disegnatore; progettista; inventore; modellista.

designing (dĕ·zīn′ĭng) agg. astuto, subdolo.

desirability (dĕ·zīr′à·bĭl′ĭ·tĭ) n. opportunità, convenienza, utilità; desiderabilità.

desirable (dĕ·zīr′à·b′l) agg. desiderabile, auspicabile.

desire (dĕ·zīr′) n. desiderio; brama. vt. desiderare, bramare; augurare, auspicare.

desirous (dĕ·zīr′ŭs) agg. desideroso.

desist (dĕ·zĭst′) vi. desistere, cessare.

desk (dĕsk) n. scrivania; banco.

desolate (dĕs′ō·lĭt) agg. desolato, sconfortato; disabitato; squallido. vt. desolare, devastare; spopolare; affliggere.

desolation (dĕs′ō·lā′shŭn) n. desolazione; sconforto.

despair (dĕ·spâr′) n. disperazione. vi. disperare, disperarsi. —ing agg. disperato.

despatch (dĕs·păch′) vedi **dispatch**.

desperate (dĕs′pẽr·ĭt) agg. disperato; forsennato, accanito; terribile; gravissimo. —ly avv. disperatamente; perdutamente; gravemente.

desperation (dĕs′pẽr·ā′shŭn) n. disperazione, furore, accanimento.

despicable (dĕs′pĭ·kà·b′l) agg. spregevole, ignobile.

despise (dĕ·spīz′) vt. disprezzare, sdegnare.

despite (dĕ·spīt′) n. dispetto, astio, stizza. prep. nonostante, a dispetto di. vt. offendere, indispettire. —ful agg. dispettoso, maligno.

despoil (dĕ·spoil′) vt. spogliare.

despondency (dĕ·spŏn′dĕn·sĭ) n. abbattimento, sconforto.

despondent (-dĕnt) agg. scoraggiato, abbattuto.

despot (dĕs'pŏt) *n.* despota. —ic (-pŏt'ĭc) *agg.* dispotico. —ism (dĕs'-) *n.* dispotismo.

dessert (dĭ-zŭrt') *n.* dolce o frutta (*ultima portata a tavola*).

destination (dĕs't mȧ'shŭn) *n.* destinazione.

destine (dĕs'tĭn) *vt.* destinare.

destiny (dĕs'tĭ-nĭ) *n.* destino, fato.

destitute (dĕs'tĭ-tūt) *agg.* povero, diseredato; privo (*di*).

destitution (-tū'shŭn) *n.* povertà; abbandono.

destroy (dĕ-stroi') *vt.* distruggere.

destroyer (-ẽr) *n.* distruttore; (*naut.*) cacciatorpediniere; — **escort**, cacciasottomarini.

destruction (dĕ-strŭk'shŭn) *n.* distruzione, rovina.

destructive (-tĭv) *agg.* distruttivo, deleterio.

desultory (dĕs'ŭl-tō'rĭ) *agg.* saltuario, intermittente; sconnesso, irregolare.

detach (dĕ-tăch') *vt.* staccare, isolare. —**ment** *n.* distacco, separazione; indifferenza, imparzialità; (*mil.*) distaccamento.

detail (dĕ-tāl') *n.* particolare; rapporto particolareggiato; squadra, pattuglia: **to go into —**, entrare nei particolari. *vt.* specificare, riferire; distaccare (*una pattuglia, ecc.*).

detain (dĕ-tān') *vt.* trattenere; detenere; arrestare.

detect (dĕ-tĕkt') *vt.* scoprire, sorprendere; captare, avvertire, sentire. —**ion** *n.* scoperta, rivelazione. —**ive** *n.* investigatore, agente. —**or** *n.* (*radio*) rivelatore.

detention (dĕ-tĕn'shŭn) *n.* detenzione, arresto, fermo.

deter (dĕ-tûr') *vt.* trattenere, dissuadere, distogliere, frenare.

detergent (dĕ-tûr'jĕnt) *agg.*, *n.* detersivo.

deteriorate (dĕ-tẽr'ĭ-ō-rāt) *vi.* deteriorarsi.

deterioration (-rā'shŭn) *n.* deterioramento.

determination (dĕ-tûr'mĭ-nā'shŭn) *n.* determinazione, risolutezza, scadenza, conclusione.

determine (dĕ-tûr'mĭn) *vt.*, *vi.* determinare, stabilire, decidere, fissare.

determined (-mĭnd) *agg.* risoluto, deciso.

deterrent (dĕ-tûr'ĕnt) *n.* remora, freno.

detest (dĕ-tĕst') *vt.* detestare.

detour (dĕ-tōōr') *n.* deviazione, giravolta. *vi.* compiere una deviazione.

detract (dĕ-trăkt') *vt.*, *vi.* detrarre, sottrarre, diminuire; svilire, denigrare.

detriment (dĕt'rĭ-mĕnt) *n.* detrimento, danno.

detrimental (-mĕn'tăl) *agg.* dannoso.

deuce (dūs) *n.* sfortuna; diavolo; due (*a carte*); 40 pari (*al tennis*).

devastate (dĕv'ŭs-tāt) *vt.* devastare.

devastating *agg.* devastante; straziante; (*gergo S.U.*) sconvolgente; potentissimo.

develop (dĕ-vĕl'ŭp) *vt.* sviluppare. *vi.* svilupparsi; risultare. —**er** *n.* sviluppatore. —**ing**, —**ment** *n.* sviluppo; crescita; sfruttamento.

deviate (dĕ'vĭ-āt) *vi.* deviare; divagare. *vt.* sviare, far deviare.

deviation (-ȧ'shŭn) *n.* deviazione.

device (dĕ-vīs') *n.* meccanismo, dispositivo; accorgimento, disegno, espediente, mezzo; astuzia; divisa, motto.

devil (dĕv'l) *n.* diavolo, demonio: **the — to pay**, guai in vista. *vt.* tormentare; (*cucina*) arrostire e aromatizzare. —**ish** *agg.* diabolico.

devil-may-care *agg.* temerario.

deviltry (dĕv'l-rĭ) *n.* diavoleria.

devious (dĕ'vĭ-ŭs) *agg.* remoto, fuori di mano; errante; indiretto, tortuoso; stravagante, bizzarro; traviato.

devise (dĕ-vīz') *vt.* escogitare, inventare, tramare.

devoid (dĕ-void') *agg.* privo (*di*), sprovvisto (*di*), scevro (*di*).

devote (dĕ-vōt') *vt.* dedicare, consacrare.

devoted (-vōt'ĕd) *agg.* devoto, votato; predestin. to.

devotee (dĕv ȯ-tē')*n.* devoto, fanatico.

devotion (dĕ-vō'shŭn) *n.* devozione; preghiera.

devour (dĕ-vour') *vt.* divorare.

devout (dĕ-vout') *agg.* devoto, pio.

dew (dū) *n.* rugiada. *vt.* irrorare. —**drop** *n.* goccia di rugiada. —**worm** *n.* lombrico.

dewy (dū'ĭ) *agg.* rugiadoso.

dexterity (dĕks-tĕr'ĭ-tĭ) *n.* destrezza, abilità.

dexterous (dĕk'stẽr-ŭs) *agg.* destro, abile disinvolto. —**ness** *n.* destrezza abilità.

diabetes (dī ȧ-bē'tēs) *n.* diabete.

diabetic (-bĕt'ĭ agg. *n.* diabetico.

diabolic (dī ȧ-bŏl'ĭk) *agg.* diabolico.

diadem (dī'ȧ-dĕ n *n.* diadema.

diagnose (dī'ȧg-nōs') *vt.* diagnosticare.

diagnosis (-d sĭs) *n.* diagnosi.

diagonal (dī-ăg'ȯ-năl) *agg.*, *n.* diagonale.

diagram (dī'ȧ-grăm) *n.* diagramma, grafico.

dial (dī'ăl) *n.* quadrante (*dell'orologio*); meridiana; manometro; disco combinatore (*del telefono*). *vt.*, *vi.* misurare con un manometro; formare un numero telefonico, chiamare (*per telefono*).

dialect (dĭ·ă'lĕkt) *n.* dialetto.

dialectic (dĭ'ȧ·lĕk'tĭk) *n.* dialettica.

dialogue (dĭ'ȧ·lŏg) *n.* dialogo. *vt.*, *vi.* dialogare, conversare.

diameter (dĭ·ăm'ĕ·tẽr) *n.* diametro.

diamond (dĭ'ȧ·mŭnd) *n.* diamante; losanga, rombo; (*carte da gioco*) quadro.

diaper (dĭ'ȧ·pẽr) *n.* pannolino per neonati.

diarrhea (dĭ'ȧ·rē'ȧ) *n.* diarrea.

dice (dīs) *n.pl.* dadi (*da gioco*). *vi.* giocare ai dadi. *vt.* tagliare a cubetti, quadrettare.

dick (dĭk) *n.* (*gergo*) frustino; (*S.Ŭ.*) poliziotto.

dickens (dĭk'ĕnz) *inter.* diavolo, diamine!

dictate (dĭk'tāt) *n.* ordine, dettame, precetto. *vt.*, *vi.* dettare, ordinare.

dictation (dĭk·tā'shŭn) *n.* dettatura; ordine perentorio: **to take —,** scrivere sotto dettatura.

dictator (dĭk·tā'tẽr) *n.* dittatore. **—ship** *n.* dittatura.

diction (dĭk'shŭn) *n.* dizione

dictionary (dĭk'shŭn·ẽr'ĭ) *n.* dizionario.

did (dĭd) *pass. di* to do.

die (dī) (1) *n.* (*pl.* dies [dīz]) calco, stampo, marchio, conio; (*arch.*) dado.

die (dī) (2) *n.* (*pl.* diee [dīs]) dado da gioco; (*fig.*) sorte, alea: **the — is cast,** il dado è tratto: **no dice** (*gergo*), niente da fare.

die (dī) (3) *vi.* (*pass.* died, *ppr.* dying, *pp.* dead) morire, spegnersi; smorzarsi, affievolirsi; cessare.

diet (dī'ĕt) *n.* dieta, regime, alimentazione: **on a —,** a dieta. *vt.* mettere a dieta. *vi.* seguire una dieta. **—ary** *n.* regime dietetico. *agg.* dietetico. **—etics** *n.pl.* dietetica.

differ (dĭf'ẽr) *vi.* differire; dissentire. **—ence** *n.* differenza; divergenza, controversia. **—ent** *agg.* differente, divergente.

differentiate (dĭf'ẽr·ĕn'shĭ·āt) *vt.*, *vi.* differenziare; differenziarsi, discriminare.

difficult (dĭf'ĭ·kŭlt) *agg.* difficile.

difficulty (dĭf'ĭ·kŭl·tĭ) *n.* difficoltà, imbarazzo.

diffidence (dĭf'ĭ·dĕns) *n.* diffidenza, titubanza, timidezza.

diffident *agg.* diffidente, timido.

diffuse (dĭ·fūs') *agg.* diffuso, prolisso. *vt.* (-fūz') diffondere. *vi.* diffondersi, dilungarsi.

diffusion (-fū'zhŭn) *n.* diffusione, propagazione.

dig (dĭg) *n.* urto, gomitata; punzecchiatura, sarcasmo. *vt.*, *vi.* (*pass.*, *pp.* dug) scavare, frugare: **to —,** up, dissotterrare.

digest (dĭ'jĕst) *n.* digesto; compendio; *vt.*, *vi.* digerire; condensare, riassumere, redigere. **—ible** *agg.* digeribile, **—ion** *n.* digestione. **—ive** *n.*, *agg.* digestivo.

digger (dĭg'ẽr) *n.* scavatore, cercatore; (*mecc.*) scavatrice; (*gergo*) unghia; sgobbone.

diggings *n.pl.* scavi; (*fam.*) alloggio.

dignified (dĭg'nĭ·fīd) *agg.* dignitoso, solenne.

dignitary (dĭg'nĭ·tẽr'ĭ) *n.* dignitario.

dignity (dĭg'nĭ·tĭ) *n.* dignità.

digress (dĭ·grĕs'; dĭ-) *vi.* divagare. **—ion** (shŭn) *n.* digressione.

dike (dīk) *n.* diga, fossato; (*geol.*) basalto. *vt.* imbrigliare, arginare.

dilapidated (dĭ·lăp'ĭ·dāt'ĕd) *agg.* diroccato, dilapidato.

dilation (dĭ·lā'shŭn) *n.* dilatazione.

dilate (dĭ·lāt') *vt.* dilatare, estendere, ampliare. *vi.* dilatarsi, espandersi.

dilatory (dĭl'ȧ·tō'rĭ) *agg.* lento, dilatorio.

diligence (dĭl'ĭ·jĕns) *n.* diligenza, perseveranza; corriera.

diligent *agg.* diligente.

dilute (dĭ·lūt') *agg.* diluito. *vt.* diluire. *vi.* diluirsi.

dim (dĭm) *agg.* oscuro, vago; pallido, sbiadito; scettico; pessimistico: **—sighted** *agg.* corto di vista. *vt.* smorzare, offuscare, oscurare, annebbiare, confondere. *vi.* oscurarsi, offuscarsi, indebolirsi (*della luce, ecc.*).

dime (dīm) *n.* moneta da 10 centesimi di dollaro.

dimension (dĭ·mĕn'shŭn) *n.* dimensione.

diminish (dĭ·mĭn'ĭsh) *vt.*, *vi.* diminuire, abbassare, abbassarsi. **—ing** *agg.* decrescente.

diminution (dĭ·mĭ·nū'shŭn) *n.* diminuzione.

diminutive (dĭ·mĭn'ū·tĭv) *agg.* diminutivo; minuscolo, in miniatura.

dimly (dĭm'lĭ) *avv.* vagamente, oscuramente.

dimness (dĭm'nĕs) *n.* oscurità, debolezza (*di vista*), opacità; penombra.

dimple (dĭm'p'l) *n.* fossetta (*spec. del viso*).

din (dĭn) *n.* frastuono, clangore, clamore.

dine (dīn) *vi.* desinare. *vt.* offrire un desinare a.

diner (dīn'ẽr) *n.* chi desina; (*S.Ŭ.*) vagone ristorante.

dinghy (dĭng'gĭ) n. dingo, barchetta.
dinginess (dĭn'jĭ-nĕs) n. colore sbiadito; sporcizia; squallore.
dingy (dĭn'jĭ) agg. sbiadito; sporco; squallido.
dining ppr. di to dine: — car, vagone ristorante; — room, sala da pranzo.
dinner (dĭn'ĕr) n. pranzo, desinare: — jacket smoking (vestito da sera).
dint (dĭnt) n. forza, tacca: by — of, a forza di.
diocese (dī'ō-sēs) n. diocesi.
dip (dĭp) n. tuffo, immersione; inclinazione; candela di sego. vt. inclinare; intingere; inclinare; salutare (con la bandiera). vi. immergersi, tuffarsi; inclinarsi; abbassarsi.
diphtheria (dĭf-thēr'ĭ-á) n. difterite.
diphthong (dĭf'thŏng) n. dittongo.
diplomacy (dĭ-plō'má-sĭ) n. diplomazia.
diplomat (dĭp'lō-mǎt) n. diplomatico.
diplomatic (dĭp'lō-mǎt'ĭk) agg. diplomatico.
dipper (dĭp'ĕr) n. tuffatore; mestolo; uccello acquatico; escavatore; (fot.) vaschetta: the Big Dipper, l'Orsa Maggiore.
dipsomania (dĭp'sō-mā-nĭ-á) n. dipsomania, alcoolismo cronico.
dipsomaniac (-ǎk) n. dipsòmane; alcoolizzato.
dire (dīr) agg. terribile, tremendo, calamitoso; estremo.
direct (dĭ-rĕkt') agg. diretto; sincero, esplicito: — current, corrente continua; — object, accusativo, complemento oggetto. avv. direttamente, sùbito. vt. dirigere, ordinare, indirizzare; ragguagliare. vi. impartire ordini. —ion n. direzione, istruzione, ordine. —ive agg. direttivo. n. direttiva, ordine, comando. —ly avv. direttamente, immediatamente. —ness n. dirittura, sincerità, modo esplicito. —or n. direttore; (cinema) regista; (comm.) consigliere (di società). —ory n. direttorio; guida (dei telefoni, ecc.); indirizzario.
dirndl (dûrn'd'l) n. vestito alla tirolese (da donna).
dirge (dûrj) n. canto funebre.
dirigible (dĭr'ĭ-jĭ-b'l) n., agg. dirigibile.
dirt (dûrt) n. sudiciume, fango.
dirtiness (dûr'tĭ-nĕs) n. sporcizia, bassezza.
dirty (dûr'ĭ) agg. sudicio, immondo. vt. sporcare.
disability (dĭs'á-bĭl'ĭ-tĭ) n. incapacità, invalidità.

disable (dĭs-ā'b'l) vt. inabilitare, mettere fuori combattimento, interdire.
disadvantage (dĭs'ǎd-vǎn'tĭj) n. svantaggio, inconveniente.
disagree (dĭs'á-grē') vi. dissentire, differire, essere in disaccordo; nuocere: liquor disagrees with me, il liquore mi fa male.
disagreeable (-á-b'l) agg. sgradevole, dannoso.
disagreement (-grē'mĕnt) n. disaccordo, divergenza, contrasto.
disappear (dĭs'á-pēr') vi. sparire.
disappearance (-áns) n. sparizione.
disappoint (dĭs'á-point') vt. deludere. —ing agg. deludente. —ment n. delusione, disappunto.
disapprobation (dĭs'ǎp-rō-bā'shǔn) n. disapprovazione.
disapproval n. disapprovazione.
disapprove (dĭs'á-prōōv') vt., vi. disapprovare.
disarm (dĭs-ärm') vt., vi. disarmare.
disarmament (dĭs-är'má-mĕnt) n. disarmo.
disarming agg. disarmante, ingenuo.
disarrange (dĭs'á-rānj') vt. scompigliare mettere in disordine.
disarray (dĭs'á-rā') n. scompiglio, confusione. vt. scompigliare; spogliare.
disaster (dĭ-zǎs'tēr) n. disastro, catastrofe.
disastrous (-trǔs) agg. disastroso.
disavow (dĭs'á-vou') vt. rinnegare, sconfessare, disapprovare.
disband (dĭs-bǎnd') vt. sbandare, smobilitare disperdere. vi. sbandarsi.
disbelieve (dĭs'bē-lēv') vt., vi. non credere, essere scettico, mettere in dubbio.
disburden (dĭs-bûr'd'n) vt., vi. alleggerire, sgravare; liberarsi (di un fardello), sfogarsi.
disburse (dĭs-bûrs') vt. sborsare. —ment n. esborso.
disc vedi **disk**.
discard (dĭs-kärd') n. scarto. vt. scartare, eliminare.
discern (dĭ-zûrn') vt., vi. discernere, distinguere. —ing agg. accorto, avveduto. —ment n. discernimento.
discharge (dĭs-chärj') n. scarico, scarica (elett., d'arma, ecc.); scarcerazione, proscioglimento; (mil.) congedo; esecuzione (di un incarico); (comm.) quietanza; licenziamento; spurgo. vt. scaricare; licenziare, congedare; emettere; spurgare, eseguire (un incarico); compiere (un dovere); prosciogliere; scarcerare.
disciple (dĭ-sī'p'l) n. discepolo.
discipline (dĭs'ĭ-plĭn) n. disciplina. vt. disciplinare.

disclaim (dĭs·klām') vt. declinare (una responsabilità, ecc.); smentire; rinunciare (a un diritto).

disclose (dĭs·klōz') vt. svelare, rivelare.

disclosure (-klō'zhĕr) n. rivelazione.

discography (dĭs·kŏg'rȧ·fĭ) n. discografia.

discolor (dĭs·kŭl'ĕr) vt. macchiare. vi. macchiarsi, scolorirsi.

discomfiture (dĭs·kŭm'fĭ·tu̇r) n. sconfitta, confusione.

discomfort (dĭs·kŭm'fĕrt) n. disagio, scomodità. vt. incomodare, mettere a disagio.

disconcert (dĭs'kŏn·sûrt') vt. sconcertare.

disconnect (dĭs'kŏ·nĕkt') vt. dividere, staccare, interrompere, disinnestare. —ed agg. sconnesso; incoerente; interrotto.

disconsolate (dĭs·kŏn'sō·lĭt) agg. sconsolato.

discontent (dĭs'kŏn·tĕnt') n. malcontento, scontentezza. agg. scontento, malcontento. vt. scontentare. —ed agg. insoddisfatto.

discontinue (dĭs'kŏn·tĭn'ū) vt., vi. interrompere, far cessare, sospendere; disdire (un abbonamento); cessare, interrompersi, smettere.

discord (dĭs'kôrd) n. discordia, disarmonia.

discount (dĭs'kount) n. sconto, riduzione: — rate, (comm.) tasso di sconto. vt. scontare; ribassare, screditare. vi. effettuare uno sconto.

discountenance (dĭs·koun'tĕ·nȧns) vt. disapprovare; scoraggiare, mortificare.

discourage (dĭs·kûr'ĭj) vt. scoraggiare; dissuadere.

discouragement (-mĕnt) n. scoraggiamento.

discouraging agg. demoralizzante.

discourse (dĭs·kōrs') n. discorso, dissertazione. vi. discorrere, dissertare.

discourteous (dĭs·kûr'tē·u̇s) agg. scortese.

discourtesy (dĭs·kûr'tē·sĭ) n. scortesia.

discover (dĭs·kŭv'ĕr) vt. scoprire, rivelare.

discoverer (-ĕr·ĕr) n. scopritore.

discovery (-ĕr·ĭ) n. scoperta.

discredit (dĭs·krĕd'ĭt) n. discredito. vt. screditare, confutare.

discreet (dĭs·krēt') agg. discreto; prudente.

discrepancy (dĭs·krĕp'ȧn·sĭ) n. discrepanza, contraddizione.

discretion (dĭs·krĕsh'ŭn) n. discrezione, prudenza.

discriminate (dĭs·krĭm'ĭ·nāt) vt., vi. discriminare, distinguere: to — against, fare distinzioni a sfavore di.

discus (dĭs'kŭs) n. disco: — thrower, n. discobolo.

discuss (dĭs·kŭs') vt., vi. discutere.

discussion (-kŭsh'ŭn) n. discussione.

disdain (dĭs·dān') n. sdegno, disprezzo. vt. disdegnare, disprezzare. —ful agg. sdegnoso.

disease (dĭ·zēz') n. malanno, malattia.

diseased (dĭ·zēzd') agg. malato.

disembark (dĭs'ĕm·bärk') vt., vi. sbarcare.

disembowel (dĭs'ĕm·bou'ĕl) vt. sbudellare, sventrare.

disencumber (dĭs'ĕn·kŭm'bĕr) vt. sbarazzare, sgombrare.

disengage (dĭs'ĕn·gāj') vt. svincolare, sbarazzare; disincagliare; disinnestare.

disentangle (dĭs'ĕn·tăng'g'l) vt. liberare, districare.

disfavor (dĭs·fā'vĕr) n. sfavore.

disfigure (dĭs·fĭg'ūr) vt. sfigurare, deturpare.

disgorge (dĭs·gôrj') vt. emettere, riversare; vomitare; sborsare.

disgrace (dĭs·grās') n. disonore, sfavore, vergogna. vt. disonorare. —ful agg. vergognoso, disonorevole.

disgruntle (dĭs·grŭn't'l) vt. scontentare, mettere di cattivo umore, irritare.

disguise (dĭs·gīz') n. travestimento, inganno: in —, camuffato. vt. travestire, mascherare.

disgust (dĭs·gŭst') n. disgusto. vt. disgustare. —ful, —ing agg. disgustoso.

dish (dĭsh) n. piatto; vivanda. vt. scodellare, ammannire, servire.

dishearten (dĭs·här'z'n) vt. scoraggiare.

disheveled (dĭ·shĕv'ĕld) agg. scarmigliato.

dishonest (dĭs·ŏn'ĕst) agg. disonesto.

dishonesty (-ŏn'ĕs·tĭ) n. disonestà.

dishonor (dĭs·ŏn'ĕr) n. disonore. vt. disonorare; (comm.) non onorare (un assegno, una cambiale, ecc.). —able agg. disonorevole.

disillusion (dĭs'ĭ·lū'zhŭn) vt. disilludere.

disinclination (dĭs·ĭn'klĭ·nā'shŭn) n. avversione, contrarietà.

disinclined (dĭs'ĭn·klīnd') agg. contrario, restio, poco propenso (a).

disinfect (dĭs'ĭn·fĕkt') vt. disinfettare. —ant n. disinfettante. —ion (-fĕk'shŭn) n. disinfezione.

disintegrate (dĭs'ĭn·tē·grāt) vt. disgregare. vi. disgregarsi.

disinterested (dĭs·ĭn'tĕr·ĕs·tĕd) agg indifferente; disinteressato, imparziale.

disjoin (dĭs·join′) vt. disgiungere.

disjoint (dĭs·joint′) vt. dislogare, interrompere, guastare (un meccanismo, ecc.). vi. separarsi, slogarsi, guastarsi.

disk (dĭsk) n. disco: — jockey, n. presentatore radiofonico di dischi.

dislike (dĭs·lĭk′) n. antipatia, avversione. vt. detestare, esser contrario a, provare avversione per, avere in antipatia: I — it, non mi piace; I — him, mi è antipatico; to be —d, essere malvisto.

dislocate (dĭs′lō·kāt) vt. slogare, lussare; spostare, scompigliare.

dislocation (-kā′shŭn) n. slogatura, lussazione; spostamento.

dislodge (dĭs·lŏj′) vt. sloggiare, scacciare, spostare.

disloyal (dĭs·loi′ăl) agg. sleale, infedele.

dismal (dĭz′măl) agg. triste, tetro, squallido.

dismantle (dĭs·măn′t'l) vt. smantellare.

dismay (dĭs·mā′) n. sgomento, terrore. vt. sgomentare, spaventare.

dismiss (dĭs·mĭs′) vt. congedare, licenziare, respingere, scacciare: to — the meeting, togliere la seduta. —al n. congedo, licenziamento, rigetto.

dismount (dĭs·mount′) vt. disarcionare; appiedare; smontare (togliere dalla montatura, opp. disfare p. es. un meccanismo). vi. smontare (da cavallo, ecc.).

disobedience (dĭs′ō·bē′dĭ·ĕns) n. disobbedienza.

disobedient (-ĕnt) agg. disobbediente.

disobey (dĭs′ō·bā′) vt. disobbedire.

disoblige (dĭs′o·blĭj′) vt. offendere; essere scortese con; disturbare, importunare.

disobliging agg. scortese, scompiacente; importuno.

disorder (dĭs·ôr′dēr) n. disordine; (med.) disfunzione, malattia. vt. scompigliare. —ed agg. ammalato (spec. di mente). —ly agg. disordinato; sregolato; turbolento.

disorganization (dĭs·ôr′găn·ĭ·zā′shŭn) n. disorganizzazione.

disorganize (dĭs·ôr′găn·ĭz) vt. disorganizzare.

disown (dĭs·ōn′) vt. smentire, sconfessare, rinnegare, ripudiare.

disparage (dĭs·păr′ĭj) vt. disprezzare, denigrare.

disparaging agg. sprezzante, ingiurioso.

dispassionate (dĭs·păsh′ŭn·ĭt) agg. calmo, spassionato.

dispatch (dĭs·păch′) n. dispaccio; spedizione; diligenza, prontezza. vt.

spedire, sbrigare. — box n. portacarte, custodia.

dispel (dĭs·pĕl′) vt. dissipare, scacciare.

dispensable (dĭs·pĕn′sȧ·b'l) agg. superfluo.

dispensary (dĭs·pĕn′sȧ·rĭ) n. dispensario.

dispensation (dĭs′pĕn·sā′shŭn) n. distribuzione; dispensa, esenzione; provvidenza.

dispense (dĭs·pĕns′) vt. dispensare; distribuire somministrare. vi. concedere una dispensa: to — with, rinunciare a, fare a meno di.

dispenser (dĭs·pĕn′sēr) n. dispensatore; distributore.

dispersal (dĭs·pûr′săl) n. dispersione.

disperse (dĭs·pûrs′) vt. disperdere, spargere, spargliare. vi. sparpagliarsi, dissiparsi.

dispirit (dĭs·pĭr′ĭt) vt. scoraggiare.

displace (dĭs·plās′) vt. spostare; soppiantare, destituire; (naut.) dislocare, stazzare.

displaced agg. spostato: — person n. profugo.

displacement (dĭs·plās′mĕnt) n. spostamento, destituzione; cilindrata (di un motore); (naut.) stazza, tonnellaggio.

display (dĭs·plā′) n. esposizione, esibizione, ostentazione, spiegamento (di truppe). vt. esporre, esibire; ostentare rivelare.

displease (dĭs·plēz′) vt. contrariare, spiacere, offendere.

displeasure (dĭs·plĕzh′ēr) n. contrarietà, disapprovazione, displacere, sfavore.

disposal (dĭs·pōz′ăl) n. disposizione; vendita, realizzo.

dispose (dĭs·pōz′) vt., vi. disporre: to — of, disporre di, sbarazzarsi di, accudire a, eliminare.

disposition (dĭs′pō·zĭsh′ŭn) n. disposizione carattere, temperamento.

dispossess (dĭs′pō·zĕs′) vt. defraudare.

disproportion (dĭs′prō·pôr′shŭn) n. sproporzione. —ate (-ĭt) agg. sproporzionato.

disprove (dĭs·prōōv′) vt. confutare, invalidare.

dispute (dĭs·pūt′) n. disputa. vt., vi. disputare, discutere.

disqualify (dĭs·kwŏl′ĭ·fĭ) vt. squalificare.

disregard (dĭs′rē·gärd′) n. noncuranza; dispregio. vt. trascurare, tenere in dispregio, non curarsi (di).

disreputable (dĭs·rĕp′ū·tȧ·b'l) agg. indecoroso, screditato, losco, malfamato, disonorevole.

disrepute (dĭs′rē·pūt′) n. discredito, disonore.

disrespect (dĭs′rĕ·spĕkt′) *n.* irriverenza, insolenza. —**ful** *agg.* irriverente,
insolente.

disrupt (dĭs·rŭpt′) *vt.* spaccare; separare; distruggere. —**ion** *n.* scissione.

dissatisfied (dĭs·săt′ĭs·fīd) *agg.* malcontento.

dissatisfy (dĭs·săt′ĭs·fī) *vt.* scontentare,
deludere.

dissect (dĭ·sĕkt′) *vt.* sezionare; esaminare minuziosamente.

dissemble (dĭ·sĕm′b′l) *vt.*, *vi.* dissimulare, fingere, simulare, nascondere.

dissension (dĭ·sĕn′shŭn) *n.* dissenso

dissent (dĭ·sĕnt′) *n.* dissenso. *vi.* dissentire.

dissertation (dĭs′ĕr·tā′shŭn) *n.* dissertazione; tesi di laurea.

disservice (dĭs·sûr′vĭs) *n.* disservizio

dissimilar (dĭ(s)·sĭm′ĭ·lẽr) *agg.* dissimile, diverso. —**ity** (-lär′ĭ·tĭ) *n.* diversità.

dissimulate (dĭ·sĭm′ū·lāt) *vt.*, *vi.* dissimulare, fingere.

dissimulation (dĭ·sĭm′ū·lā′shŭn) *n.*
dissimulazione, finzione.

dissipate (dĭs′ĭ·pāt) *vt.* dissipare, sparpagliare. *vi.* dissiparsi, disperdersi,
traviarsi.

dissipated (-pāt″ĕd) *agg.* dissoluto.

dissipation (-pā′shŭn) *n.* dissipazione,
dissolutezza.

dissolute (dĭs′ō·lūt) *agg.* dissoluto.

dissolution (dĭs′ō·lū′shŭn) *n.* sfacelo,
dissoluzione; scioglimento.

dissolve (dĭ·zŏlv′) *vt.* dissolvere, sciogliere, separare; distruggere, risolvere, *vi.* sciogliersi; svanire.

dissuade (dĭ·swād′) *vt.* dissuadere.

distaff (dĭs′tȧf) *n.* conocchia.

distance (dĭs′tȧns) *n.* distanza. *vt.*
distanziare.

distant (dĭs′tȧnt) *agg.* lontano, distante; riservato.

distantly *avv.* lontanamente, vagamente; freddamente; in lontananza.

distaste (dĭs·tāst′) *n.* disgusto, avversione, ripugnanza. —**ful** *agg.* disgustoso, sgradevole, ostico.

distemper (dĭs·tĕm′pẽr) *n.* (*vet.*) stran-
guglione; (*pitt.*) tempera; malu-
more.

distend (dĭs·tĕnd′) *vt.* distendere, dilatare, gonfiare; allentare. *vi.* distendersi, gonfiarsi.

distil (dĭs·tĭl′) *vt.* distillare. —**lation**
(-ā′shŭn) *n.* distillazione. —**lery** *n.*
distilleria.

distinct (dĭs·tĭngkt′) *agg.* distinto,
diverso, singolo, netto. —**ion** *n.*
distinzione. —**ive** *agg.* distintivo,
caratteristico. —**ly** *avv.* distintamente, chiaramente.

distinguish (dĭs·tĭng′gwĭsh) *vt.*, *vi.* distinguere, discernere; far distin-
zione. —**ed** *agg.* distinto, illustre.
—**ing** *agg.* peculiare, caratteristico,
distintivo.

distort (dĭs·tòrt′) *vt.* deformare, alterare torcere, contrarre; falsare.

distract (dĭs·trăkt′) *vt.* distrarre; tormentare, sconvolgere. —**ed** *agg.*
sconvolto disperato. —**ion** *n.* disperazione confusione, pazzia; distrazione (*svago*): to love to —**ion**,
amare alla follia. —**ing** *agg.* straziante.

distress (dĭs·trĕs′) *n.* dolore, pena;
miseria, difficoltà; sequestro. *vt.*
affliggere addolorare; sequestrare:
— signal, segnale di soccorso. —**ed**
agg. afflitto, infelice, povero.

distribute (dĭs·trĭb′ūt) *vt.* distribuire.

distribution (dĭs′trĭ·bū′shŭn) *n.* distribuzione.

district (dĭs′trĭkt) *n.* distretto, regione,
zona quartiere (*di città*).

distrust (dĭs·trŭst′) *n.* sfiducia, diffidenza. *vt.* diffidare di. —**ful** *agg.*
diffidente, sospettoso.

disturb (dĭs·tûrb′) *vt.* disturbare, turbare mettere in disordine. —**ance**
n. perturbazione, trambusto, disordine alterazione mentale o
disuse (dĭs·ūs′) *n.* disuso. [psichica.

ditch (dĭch) *n.* fossato; canale: to
fight to the last —, resistere ad
oltranza. *vt.* *vi.* solcare; scavare
fossati gettare in un fossato; piantare in asso (*aeron.*) compiere un
ammaraggio forzato.

dither (dĭth′ẽr) *n.* (*fam.*) agitazione,
scombussolamento; tremito; *vi.*
essere in agitazione, essere scom-
bussolato tremare.

ditto (dĭt′ō) *n.* il suddetto, lo stesso.
avv. come sopra.

ditty (dĭt′ĭ) *n.* canzoncina, stornello.

divan (dĭ′văn) *n.* divano.

dive (dīv) *n.* tuffo, immersione; (*S.U.*)
taverna, bettola: — **bomber** (*aeron.*)
picchiatore. *vi.* tuffarsi, immergersi; (*aeron.*) scendere in picchiata.

diver (dīv′ẽr) *n.* tuffatore; palombaro sommozzatore.

diverge (dĭ·vûrj′) *vi.* divergere.

divergence (-vûr′jĕns) *n.* divergenza.

divers (dī′vẽrz) *agg.* vari, diversi.

diverse (dĭ·vûrs′) *agg.* diverso, differente variato.

diversion (dĭ·vûr′zhŭn) *n.* diversione,
deviazione, ricreazione, diversivo.

diversity (dĭ·vûr′sĭ·tĭ) *n.* diversità,
varietà.

divert (dĭ·vûrt′) *vt.* sviare, deviare;
divertire. —**ing** *agg.* divertente, che
distrae.

divide (dĭ·vīd') vt. dividere, separare. vi. dividersi, scindersi.

dividend (dĭv'ĭ·dĕnd) n. dividendo.

divination (dĭv'ĭ·nā'shŭn) n. divinazione.

divine (dĭ·vīn') agg. divino n. teologo. vt. divinare, predire.

diviner (dĭ·vīn'ĕr) n. indovino.

diving (dīv'ĭng) n. tuffo; immersione. — **bell** n. campana pneumatica. — **dress**, — **suit** n. scafandro.

divining rod n. bacchetta del rabdomante.

divinity (dĭ·vĭn'ĭ·tĭ) n. divinità; teologia.

division (dĭ·vĭzh'ŭn) n. divisione; scissione.

divorce (dĭ·vōrs') n. divorzio. vt. divorziare da, ripudiare.

divorcé m., **divorcée** fem. (dĭ·vor'sē') divorziato, divorziata.

divulge (dĭ·vŭlj') vt. divulgare.

dizziness (dĭz'ĭ·nĕs) n. vertigine, stordimento.

dizzy (dĭz'ĭ) agg. stordito, che ha le vertigini; vertiginoso.

do (dōō) vt. (1a pers.sing.pres.do; 2a dost; 3a does, pl. do; pass. did; pp. done; ppr. doing) fare, compiere, bastare; preparare, cucinare: to — into, tradurre (in) to — out of, defraudare, derubare; to — away with, eliminare, liquidare; to — in, rovinare, ammazzare, to — up, avvolgere, impacchettare, acconciare; riassettare pulire to — one's best, fare del proprio meglio; to — the dishes, lavare i piatti; to — one's hair, pettinarsi this will — me for today, questo mi basta per oggi. vi. agire essere in azione; stare (di salute) comportarsi, bastare: to — by, comportarsi verso; how — you —?, come state?; tanto piacere (di conoscervi); to make something —, far bastare, accontentarsi di qualcosa, to have to — with, avere a che fare con; to — without, fare a meno di; to — well in business, prosperare negli affari; do you like it? vi piace?; I — not know her, non la conosco; — come! suvvia, venite!; — you like this?, vi piace questo?; yes, I —, sì, mi piace.

docile (dŏs'ĭl) agg. docile.

dock (dŏk) (1) n. coda mozza. vt. mozzare; detrarre, ridurre: to — wages, abbassare la paga.

dock (dŏk) (2) n. bacino portuario, molo: dry —, bacino di carenaggio; wet —, darsena. vt., vi. portare o entrare in cantiere, attracca-

re. — **yard** n. arsenale, cantiere navale.

dock (dŏk) (3) n. banco degli accusati.

docket (dŏk'ĕt) n. etichetta; distinta di contenuto; (giur.) estratto, verbale; (S.U.) ordine del giorno, programma del lavori.

doctor (dŏk'tĕr) n. medico, dottore. vt. curare; accomodare, rimediare; adulterare: to — oneself, curarsi, prendere medicine.

doctrine (dŏk'trĭn) n. dottrina.

document (dŏk'ū·mĕnt) n. documento. vt. documentare.

documentary (dŏk'ū·mĕn'tà·rĭ) agg. documentario. n. film o, dramma o, libro documentario.

dodder (dŏd'ĕr) vi. tremare, vacillare.

dodge (dŏj) n. scarto (brusco movimento), balzo; espediente, trucco. vi. scartare; scantonare; temporeggiare. vt. schivare; eludere; (foto.) correggere.

doe (dō) n. daina; femmina (dell'antilope, del coniglio e altri animali).

does (dŭz) 1a pers.sing.pres. di to do.

doff (dŏf) vt. togliersi (un indumento, il cappello).

dog (dŏg) n. cane; (fig.) tipo, individuo: to go to the dogs, andare in malora; hot —, salsiccia calda. vt. braccare; spiare. avv. sommamente: —-tired, stanco morto. — **days** n.pl. canicola. —-**face** n. (S.U.) fante, marmittone. —-**fight** n. duello aereo. —-**hole** n. tana, tugurio. —-**house** n. canile: to be in the — (gergo S.U.) essere in disgrazia.

dogged (dŏg'ĕd) agg. ostinato, accanito. —-**ness** n. accanimento.

dogma (dŏg'mà) n. dogma. —-**tic** agg. dogmatico.

doily (dol'ĭ) n. tovagliolino, sottocoppa.

doings (dōō'ĭngz) n.pl. attività, azione; prodezze; sforzi: great —, gran daffare, gran festa.

dole (dōl) n. ripartizione, distribuzione, sussidio (per disoccupati). vt. (gen. seg. da out) distribuire (a poco a poco), distribuire per carità; lesinare.

doleful (dōl'fŏol) agg. dolente, afflitto.

doll (dŏl) n. bambola.

dollar (dŏl'ĕr) n. dollaro.

dolly (dŏl'ĭ) n. bambolina; (cinema) carrello.

dolor (dō'lĕr) n. dolore.

dolphin (dŏl'fĭn) n. delfino; (naut.) boa.

dolt (dōlt) n. stupido.

domain (dō·mān') n. regno, dominio; proprietà.

dome (dōm) *n.* cupola.
domestic (dŏ-mĕs'tĭk) *n., agg.* domestico.
domesticate (dŏ-mĕs'tĭ-kāt) *vt.* addomesticare, civilizzare, acclimatare.
domicile (dŏm'ĭ-sĭl) *n.* domicilio.
dominant (dŏm'ĭ-nănt) *agg.* dominante, predominante; autoritario.
dominate (dŏm'ĭ-nāt) *vt., vi.* dominare, prevalere, predominare.
domination (-nā'shŭn) *n.* dominazione.
domineer (dŏm'ĭ-nēr') *vt., vi.* tiranneggiare, far prepotenze. —**ing** *agg.* tirannico, prepotente, tracotante.
Dominican (dŏ-mĭn'ĭ-kăn) *agg., n.* domenicano.
dominion (dŏ-mĭn'yŭn) *n.* dominio, autorità, sovranità; possedimento, colonia autonoma.
don (dŏn) (1) *n.* don; signore; (*Ingl.*) docente *opp.* preside universitario.
don (dŏn) (2) *vt.* indossare; mettersi.
donate (dō-nāt) *vt., vi.* donare.
donation (dŏ-nā'shŭn) *n.* donazione, dono.
donator (dō'nā-tẽr) *n.* donatore.
done (dŭn) *pp. di* to do: fatto; compiuto; preparato; cucinato, cotto: —**in**, esausto.
donkey (dŏng'kĭ) *n.* asino.
donor (dō'nẽr) *n.* donatore.
don't (dōnt) = do not *vedi* to do.
doodle (dōō'd'l) *vt., vi.* (*S.U.*) imbrogliare; disegnare, scarabocchiare. *n.* babbeo; scarabocchio, disegnetto.
doom (dōōm) *n.* giudizio, condanna, sentenza; destino: the voice of —, la tromba del Giudizio Universale. *vt.* condannare, destinare. —**ed** *agg.* condannato; predestinato.
doomsday (dōōmz'dā') *n.* il giorno del giudizio: till —, fino all'eternità.
door (dōr) *n.* porta, sportello: out of —, fuori, all'aperto. —**mat** *n.* zerbino. —**nail** *n.* borchia. —**way** *n.* soglia, entrata.
dope (dōp) *n.* lubrificante, assorbente; (*aeron.*) vernice impermeabilizzante; (*gergo*) stupefacenti; informazione, ragguaglio; stupido, gonzo: — **fiend**, tossicomane. *vt.* somministrare stupefacenti, narcotizzare: to — **out**, capire l'antifona, escogitare, dedurre; to — **oneself up**, imbottirsi di medicine.
dormancy (dôr'măn-sĭ) *n.* letargo, torpore.
dormant (dôr'mănt) *agg.* dormiente, assopito, sopito; in letargo; latente, inattivo.
dormer (dôr'mẽr) *n.* abbaino, lucernario.
dormitory (dôr'mĭ-tō'rĭ) *n.* dormitorio.

dormouse (dôr'mous') *n.* (*pl.* dormice) (*zool.*) ghiro.
dory (dō'rĭ) *n.* barchetta a fondo piatto.
dose (dōs) *n.* dose. *vt.* dosare; somministrare una dose di medicina a.
dossier (dŏs'ĭ-ā) *n.* incartamento; curriculum vitae.
dot (dŏt) *n.* punto, chiazza, pallino: on the —, in punto. *vt.* punteggiare, mettere il punto su, costellare di puntini *o* pallini.
dotage (dōt'ĭj) *n.* rimbambimento: in one's —, rimbambito.
dotard (dō'tẽrd) *n.* rimbambito.
dote (dŏt) *vi.* rimbambire: to — **on**, upon, adorare, essere innamorato *o* cotto di.
double (dŭb''l) *agg.* doppio; falso, insincero: — **talk** *n.* frase senza senso, composta di parole astruse. *n.* doppio (*il doppio*), duplicato; ripiegamento, giravolta; sosia; (*teat.*) sostituto; (*cinema*) controfigura; (*tip-pica*) doppia; *pl.* (*tennis*) doppio. *avv.* doppiamente, al doppio. *vt.* raddoppiare, piegare in due, doppiare. *vi.* raddoppiare (*diventare il doppio*); piegarsi; (*cinema*) fare la controfigura di: to — **up**, piegarsi in due; to — **back**, ritornare sui propri passi.
double-breasted *agg.* a due petti.
double-cross *vt.* tradire. *n.* tradimento; imbroglio.
double-dealer *n.* imbroglione.
doubly (dŭb'lĭ) *avv.* doppiamente.
doubt (dout) *n.* dubbio, sospetto: no —, indubbiamente. *vt., vi.* dubitare (*di*), diffidare (*di*), temere; titubare —**ful** *agg.* dubbioso, incerto. —**less** *agg.* indubbio. —**lessly** *avv.* indubbiamente.
dough (dō) *n.* pasta; (*gergo*) danaro.
doughnut (dō'nŭt) *n.* frittella.
dour (dōr) *agg.* aspro; cocciuto.
dove (dŭv) *n.* colomba, piccione.
dovecot (dŭv'kŏt) *n.* colombaia.
dovetail (dŭv'tāl) *n.* (*carp.*) coda di rondine (*incastro*). *vt.* unire ad incastro, far combaciare. *vi.* incastrarsi, combaciare; concordare.
dowager (dou'à-jẽr) *n.* vedova usufruttuaria.
down (doun) (1) *n.* piuma, peluria, lanugine.
down (2) *n.* duna, collinetta.
down (3) *avv.* giù, in giù, in basso; in diminuzione, in declino: — **to**, sino a; — **East**, a oriente; — **the street**, in fondo alla strada, giù per la strada; to be — **with flu**, essere a letto con l'influenza; to be — **on one's luck**, attraversare un mo-

mento sfortunato; **to get — to work**, mettersi al lavoro; **to pay —**, pagare in contanti. *prep.* giù da, giù per. *agg.* discendente; depresso. *vt.* abbattere, dominare; tranguggiare.

downcast (doun'kåst') *agg.* abbattuto: **with — eyes**, a occhi bassi.

downgrade (doun'grād') *n.* declivio, discesa. *vt.*, retrocedere, degradare.

downhearted (-hår'tĕd) *agg.* scoraggiato, depresso.

downhill (-hĭl') *agg.* discendente, inclinato. *avv.* in discesa, in pendìo.

downpour (-pōr') *n.* scroscio di pioggia.

downright (-rīt') *agg.* netto, assoluto, vero; completo *avv.* completamente, assolutamente.

downstairs (doun'stårz') *avv.* da basso, al piano inferiore, al piano terreno. *n.* pianterreno.

downstream (doun'strēm') *avv.* verso valle, a valle, seguendo la corrente.

downtown (doun'toun') *n.* il centro (*di una città*). *agg.* centrale, del centro. *avv.* in centro, al centro (*di una città*).

downward (doun'wērd) *agg.* discendente, inclinato. *avv.* (*anche* **downwards**) in discesa; in declino; in giù, verso valle.

downy (doun'ĭ) *agg.* lanuginoso, soffice.

dowry (dou'rĭ) *n.* dote.

dowser (douz'ēr) *n.* rabdomante.

doze (dōz) *n.* assopimento. *vi.* assopirsi; sonnecchiare.

dozen (dŭz''n) *n.* dozzina.

drab (drăb) *n.* prostituta. *agg.* di colore morto, sbiadito; monotono.

draft (dråft) *n.* disegno, abbozzo, minuta; sorsata; corrente d'aria; tiraggio; (*naut.*) pescaggio; (*comm.*) tratta, prelevamento; (*med.*) pozione; (*mil.*) leva: **— beer**, birra spillata; **— horse**, cavallo da tiro. *vt.* disegnare, tracciare, redigere (*un progetto, ecc.*); (*mil.*) arruolare; requisire; aspirare (*liquidi*); tirare (*di fornace, ecc.*). **—sman** *n.* disegnatore.

drag (drăg) *n.* (*naut.*) draga (*rete*); (*agr.*) erpice; freno; carrozza a quattro cavalli (*giardiniera*); trazione; arpione; (*gergo*) influenza: **to have —**, essere influente. *vt.* trascinare, tirare; dragare, arare (*dell'ancora*). *vi.* trascinarsi, strisciare.

dragnet (drăg'nĕt') *n.* tramaglio; retata di polizia.

dragon (drăg'ŭn) *n.* drago; (*astr.*) Dragone.

dragonfly (-flī') *n.* libellula.

dragoon (drá·gōōn') *n.* dragone (*soldato*). *vt.* ridurre all'obbedienza: **to — into**, costringere a.

drain (drān) *n.* canale, scarico, tubazione; perdita, esborso continuo; (*chir.*) drenaggio. *vt.* prosciugare, filtrare, drenare. *vi.* defluire, prosciugarsi. **—age** *n.* scolo, drenaggio.

drake (drāk) *n.* maschio dell'anitra.

drama (drä'má) *n.* dramma; arte drammatica; teatro di prosa. **—tic** *agg.* drammatico. **—tist** *n.* drammaturgo.

dramatize (drăm'á·tĭz) *vt.* drammatizzare.

drank (drăngk) *pass. di* to drink.

drape (drāp) *n.* drappeggio, tendaggio. *vt.* drappeggiare.

draper (drāp'ēr) *n.* negoziante in tessuti.

drastic (drăs'tĭk) *agg.* drastico, violento.

draught (dråft) *vedi* draft.

draughts (dråfts) *n.pl.* dama (*gioco*).

draw (drò) *n.* trazione; attrazione; estrazione (*sorteggio*). *vt.* (*pass.* **drew**, *pp.* **drawn**) tirare, trascinare; disegnare, tracciare; percepire; estrarre; tendere; attingere; attrarre: **to — a sigh**, trarre un sospiro; **to — away**, trascinar via; **to — in**, trascinar dentro, raggirare; **to — lots**, tirare a sorte; **to — out**, indurre a parlare; **to — up**, issare, schierare, redigere. *vi.* esercitare attrazione, attrarre; contrarsi; muoversi; soffiare, tirare (*di canna fumaria, ecc.*): **to — back**, ritrarsi, retrocedere; **to — near**, avvicinarsi; **to — off**, allontanarsi; **to — oneself up**, raddrizzarsi; **to — up**, fermarsi.

drawback (drò'băk') *n.* inconveniente.

drawbridge (drò'brĭj') *n.* ponte levatoio.

drawer (drò'ēr) *n.* traente; cassetto (*di mobile*); (*pl.*) mutande.

drawing (drò'ĭng) *n.* tiraggio; sorteggio; disegno: **— room**, salotto; (*ferr. S.U.*) scompartimento riservato.

drawl (dròl) *vt.*, *vi.* parlare *o* dire lentamente, strascicare le parole.

drawn (dròn) *pp. di* to draw.

dread (drĕd) *n.* timore, terrore. *agg.* temuto, temibile. *vt.* temere. **—ful** *agg.* atroce, spaventevole.

dream (drēm) *n.* sogno. *vi.* (*pass., pp.* **dreamed, dreamt**) sognare; (*fig.*) fantasticare: **to — up**, inventare; escogitare; creare. **—er** *n.* sognatore, visionario.

dreamy (drēm'ĭ) *agg.* sognante, trasognato; chimerico.

dreary (drēr'ĭ) *agg.* squallido, desolato.

dredge (drĕj) *n.* draga. *vt.* dragare.

dregs (drĕgz) *n.pl.* feccia, sedimento, fondo.

drench (drĕnch) *vt.* inzuppare.

dress (drĕs) *n.* vestito, abito: full —, tenuta da cerimonia, alta tenuta; — coat, marsina; (*mil.*) tenuta di gala. — rehearsal, prova generale. *vt.* vestire; medicare (*una ferita*); pettinare; condire; (*mil.*) schierare. *vi.* vestirsi; (*mil.*) allinearsi: to — down, dare una lezione a; to — up, agghindarsi.

dresser (drĕs'ẽr) *n.* (*teat.*) guardarobiere guardarobiera (*degli attori*): a good —, una persona elegante.

dressing *n.* toletta, abbigliamento, medicazione; (*cucina*) salsa, condimento: — gown, veste da camera; — room, spogliatoio; (*teat.*) camerino; — table, tavolino da toletta.

dressmaker (drĕs'māk'ẽr) *n.* sarta.

drew (droō) *pass. di* to draw.

dribble (drĭb''l) *n.* goccia, spruzzo. *vt.*, *vi.* sgocciolare, sbavare.

dried (drĭd) *pass.*, *pp. di* to dry. *agg.* secco, appassito: — fig, fico secco.

drift (drĭft) *n.* corrente, deriva; direzione, corso; significato; rottami (*alla deriva*); monticello (*di neve o sabbia*): — ice, ghiaccio alla deriva. *vi.* andare alla deriva; esser trascinato (*dal vento*); accumularsi. —wood *n.* rottami di legno alla deriva; legna raccogliticcia.

drill (drĭl) *n.* trapano, perforatrice, solco; (*mil.*) esercitazione; seminatrice. *vt.* perforare, trapanare; seminare; istruire, alienare, addestrare.

drily (drī'lĭ) *avv.* seccamente.

drink (drĭngk) *n.* bevanda: to take to —, darsi all'alcool. *vt.*, *vi.* (*pass.* drank, *pp.* drunk) bere: to — in, assorbire, ascoltare attentamente; to — a toast, brindare (*a*); to — down, tranguglare. —able *agg.* bevibile, potabile. —ing water *n.* acqua potabile.

drip (drĭp) *n.* sgocciolio, stillicidio. *vi.* sgocciolare, grondare.

drive (drīv) *n.* corsa (*in veicolo*); viale, corso; spinta, impulso; tendenza; guida; energia; (*mecc.*) propulsione, trasmissione, trazione. *vt.* (*pass.* drove, *pp.* driven) spingere, azionare; piantare (*chiodi*, *ecc.*), introdurre; guidare; trasportare (*in auto*, *ecc.*); costringere: to — away, scacciare; to — back, respingere; to — mad, far impaz-

zire; to — a good bargain, concludere un buon affare. *vi.* andare, dirigersi, correre, guidare, andare in carrozza *o* in auto: what are you driving at? dove (a quale conclusione) volete arrivare?

drive-in *n.* cinema *o* ristorante *o* negozio per automobilisti.

drivel (drĭv''l) *n.* bava, saliva; vaniloquio; insulsaggine. *vi.* sbavare; vaneggiare.

driven (drĭv'ẽn) *pp. di* to drive.

driver (drīv'ẽr) *n.* guidatore.

driveway (drīv'wā') *n.* vialetto d'entrata.

driving *n.* guida (*il guidare*). *agg.* propulsore, di propulsione; impetuoso, dinamico: — power, forza motrice; — wheel, ruota motrice.

drizzle (drĭz''l) *n.* ploggerella. *vi.* piovigginare, sgocciolare.

droll (drōl) *agg.* comico, bizzarro.

drone (drōn) *n.* fuco (*maschio dell'ape*); ronzio; meccanismo telecomandato; (*fig.*) sfruttatore, fannullone. *vi.* ronzare, borbottare.

droop (droōp) *n.* portamento curvo; abbassamento. *vi.* curvarsi; penzolare, ricadere; afflosciarsi, indebolirsi, languire, deperire.

drop (drŏp) *n.* goccia; caduta, discesa; strapiombo, dislivello; ribasso; abbassamento (*della temperatura*); caramella; pastiglia: letter —, buca delle lettere. *vt.* far cadere; lasciar cadere, abbattere, scaricare; abbandonare (*un'impresa*): to — anchor, gettar l'ancora; to — a curtsey, fare una riverenza; to — a line, scrivere due righe. *vi.* cadere, precipitare, abbattersi; decadere, diminuire, aver termine; gocciolare: to — away, scomparire; to — asleep, addormentarsi; to — behind, restare indietro; to — in, entrare casualmente, fare una capatina; to — off, distaccarsi, allontanarsi, crollare (*di prezzi, ecc.*); to — out, ritirarsi; sparire.

dropsy (drŏp'sĭ) *n.* idropisia.

dross (drŏs) *n.* scoria, rifiuto.

drought (drout) *n.* siccità; arsura, sete.

drove (drōv) (1) *pass. di* to drive.

drove ( ) *n.* mandria, gregge, branco.

drover (drō'vẽr) *n.* mandriano.

drown (droun) *vt.*, *vi.* affogare, sommergere soffocare; annegare.

drowse (drouz) *n.* sopore. *vi.* sonnecchiare, assopirsi.

drowsiness (drou'zĭ-nĕs) *n.* sonnolenza.

drowsy (drou'zĭ) *agg.* sonnolento, sonnacchioso, assonnato.

drubbing (drŭb'ĭng) *n*. bastonatura.

drudge (drŭj) *n*. lavoratore, schiavo. *vi*. sfacchinare.

drug (drŭg) *n*. droga, rimedio, stupefacente, prodotto chimico, narcotico: to be a — on the market, essere invendibile. *vt*. narcotizzare; adulterare; drogare. —**gist** *n*. farmacista. —**store** *n*. farmacia.

drum (drŭm) *n*. tamburo; rullo; cassa; timpano (*dell'orecchio*). *vi*., *vt*. tamburellare, tambureggiare, ronzare; chiamare a raccolta (*a suon di tamburo*); (*fig*.) inculcare; to — out (*mil*.), espellere, degradare. —**mer** *n*. tamburino, batterista; (*S.U.*) piazzista, propagandista. —**stick** *n*. bacchetta del tamburo.

drunk (drŭngk) *agg*. ubriaco: to get —, ubriacarsi. —**ard** *n*. ubriacone. —**en** *agg*. ubriaco, alcoolizzato.

drunkenness (-nĕs) *n*. ubriachezza.

dry (drī) *agg*. asciutto, arido, secco (*di vino, ecc*.). — **dock**, bacino di carenaggio; — **goods**, tessili, tessuti. *vt*. (*pass., pp*. **dried**) seccare, disseccare, asciugare. *vi*. asciugarsi, seccarsi, inaridirsi: to — up, ammutolire.

dry-clean *vt*. lavare a secco. —**er** *n*. tintore, smacchiatore. —**ing** *n*. lavatura a secco.

dryness (drī'nĕs) *n*. siccità, aridità.

dub (dŭb) *vt*. nominare, qualificare; lisciare; (*cinema*) doppiare. —**bing**, *n*. doppiaggio.

dubious (dū'bĭ-ŭs) *agg*. dubbioso, dubbio, incerto.

duchess (dŭch'ĕs) *n*. duchessa.

duchy (dŭch'ĭ) *n*. ducato.

duck (dŭk) *n*. anitra; tuffo, immersione; tela grossolana; (*pl*.) calzoni di tela; camion anfibio. *vt*. immergere, tuffare; abbassare. *vi*. tuffarsi; abbassarsi; scantonare, schivare il colpo. —**ling** *n*. anatroccolo.

duct (dŭkt) *n*. condotto, canale; (*anat*.) vaso.

dude (dūd) *n*. damerino; cittadino: — ranch, ranch di villeggiatura.

due (dū) *n*. spettanza, debito; tributo, imposta; (*pl*.) quota: to give someone his —, render giustizia a qualcuno. *agg*. dovuto, debito, giusto; scaduto; previsto, voluto: in — time, a tempo debito; to fall —, scadere; to be —, essere in arrivo; essere previsto; scadere.

duel (dū'ĕl) *n*. duello, lotta, contesa.

duet (dū-ĕt') *n*. duetto.

dug (dŭg) *pass., pp. di* to dig.

dug *n*. capezzolo, mammella (*di animale*).

duke (dūk) *n*. duca. —**dom** (-dŭm) *n*. ducato.

dull (dŭl) *agg*. sciocco, tardo, ottuso; cupo, fosco; sordo, smorzato (*dei suoni*); triste, noioso: — season, stagione morta; — pain, dolore sordo. *vt*. smussare; rendere opaco, intorpidire, offuscare. *vi*. intorpidirsi; smussarsi. —**ard** *n*. imbecille. —**ness** *n*. ottusità, stupidità, lentezza; stasi, monotonia; opacità.

duly (dū'lĭ) *avv*. debitamente, puntualmente, regolarmente.

dumb (dŭm) *agg*. muto, taciturno; sciocco: — creature, animale; — show, pantomina. —**ness** *n*. mutismo, ottusità.

dumbfound, dumfound (dŭm'found') *vt*. sbalordire, far ammutolire.

dummy (dŭm'ĭ) *n*. muto, fantoccio; uomo di paglia; morto (*al gioco del bridge, ecc*.).

dump (dŭmp) *n*. magazzino; deposito di rifiuti. *vt*. scaricare, vuotare; ammassare; liquidare. —**ing** *n*. vendita a prezzi rovinosi.

dumps *n.pl*. umor nero: in the —, di umor nero.

dun (dŭn) *agg*. marrone grigiastro; cupo. *vt*., *vi*. importunare o perseguitare (*un debitore*).

dunce (dŭns) *n*. ignorante, sciocco.

dune (dūn) *n*. duna.

dung (dŭng) *n*. letame. *vt*. concimare. —**hill** *n*. concimaia.

dungeon (dŭn'jŭn) *n*. carcere sotterraneo, segreta.

dupe (dūp) *n*. gonzo. *vt*. gabbare.

duplicate (dū'plĭ-kåt) *agg.*, *n*. duplicato: in —, in doppia copia. *vt*. duplicare, copiare.

duplicity (dů-plĭs'ĭ-tĭ) *n*. duplicità, malafede.

durable (dū'rá-b'l) *agg*. durevole.

durance (dūr'åns) *n*. prigionia.

duration (dů-rā'shǔn) *n*. continuazione, durata; tempo; esistenza.

duress (dů-rĕs') *n*. coercizione, oppressione, prigionia.

during (dūr'ĭng) *prep*. durante.

dusk (dŭsk) *n*. imbrunire, crepuscolo; semi-oscurità.

dusky (dŭs'kĭ) *agg*. scuro, fosco, bruno.

dust (dŭst) *n*. polvere. *vt*. spolverare (*togliere la polvere opp. cospargere di polvere*).

dustbin (dŭst'bĭn') *n*. pattumiera.

duster (dŭs'tĕr) *n*. strofinaccio, spolverina: feather —, piumino.

dustman (dŭst'măn) *n*. spazzino.

dusty (dŭs'tĭ) *agg*. polveroso.

Dutch (dŭch) *agg.*, *n*. olandese: to go — treat, fare alla romana. —**man** *n*. olandese.

dutiful (dū'tĭ/fōŏl) *agg.* obbediente; rispettoso.

duty (dū'tĭ) *n.* dovere; tassa, imposta; obbligo; mansione: to do — for, fungere da; — free, esente da tasse.

dwarf (dwôrf) *n.*, *agg.* nano. *vt.* rimpicciolire; far sfigurare; impedire lo sviluppo di.

dwell (dwĕl) *vi.* (*pass.*, *pp.* dwelt) abitare; soffermarsi, dilungarsi. **—er** *n.* abitante. **—ing** *n.* abitazione. **—ing-place** *n.* residenza abituale.

dwelt (dwĕlt) *pass.*, *pp. di* to dwell.

dwindle (dwĭn'd'l) *vi.* diminuire, ridursi.

dye (dī) *n.* tintura, colorante. *vt.* tingere. *vi.* tingersi.

dyer (dī'ĕr) *n.* tintore: **—'s shop,** tintoria.

dying (dī'ĭng) *agg.* morente, supremo.

dyke (dīk) *vedi* dike.

dynamic (dī-năm'ĭk) *agg.* dinamico.

dynamics (dī-năm'ĭks) *n.pl.* dinamica.

dynamite (dī'nȧ-mīt) *n.* dinamite. *vt.* minare, far saltare.

dynamiter (dī'nȧ-mīt'ĕr) *n.* dinamitardo.

dynamo (dī'nȧ-mō) *n.* dinamo.

dynasty (dī'nȧs-tĭ) *n.* dinastia.

dysentery (dĭs'ĕn-tĕr'ĭ) *n.* dissenteria.

dyspepsia (dĭs-pĕp'shȧ) *n.* dispepsia.

dyspeptic (-tĭk) *agg.*, *n.* dispeptico.

E

each (ēch) *agg.*, *pron.* ciascuno, ogni, ognuno: — other, l'un l'altro, a vicenda.

eager (ē'gĕr) *agg.* bramoso, avido; impaziente; premuroso. **—ly** *avv.* avidamente, premurosamente. **—ness** *n.* brama, impazienza, premura, avidità.

eagle (ē'g'l) *n.* aquila.

ear (ēr) *n.* orecchio; (*bot.*) spiga: to prick up one's —s, drizzare le orecchie; to turn a deaf —, fare orecchio da mercante; — of corn, pannocchia; — of wheat, spiga; by —, a orecchio. **—drop** *n.* orecchino. **—drum** *n.* timpano. **—mark** *n.* marchio di riconoscimento. **—ring** *n.* orecchino (*ad anello*). **—shot** *n.* portata dell'udito. **— trumpet** *n.* cornetto acustico.

earl (ûrl) *n.* conte.

early (ûr'lĭ) *agg.* mattutino; mattiniero; primo; precedente; prematuro, precoce: **— riser,** persona mattiniera. *avv.* presto, di buonora, in anticipo.

earn (ûrn) *vt.* guadagnare, acquistare, meritare.

earnest (ûr'nĕst) *n.* caparra, anticipo. *agg.* serio, sincero, zelante: in —, sul serio; **— money,** caparra. **—ly** *avv.* seriamente, premurosamente. **—ness** *n.* serietà, zelo.

earnings (ûr'nĭngs) *n.pl.* guadagni, introiti.

earth (ûrth) *n.* terra.

earthquake (ûrth'kwāk') *n.* terremoto.

earthen (ûrth'n) *agg.* di terra.

earthenware (-wâr) *n.* vasellame di terracotta.

earthworm (-wûrm) *n.* bruco.

earthly (-lĭ) *agg.* terrestre, terreno; basso, meschino.

ease (ēz) *n.* comodità, agio, facilità; quiete; disinvoltura; sollievo: at —, a proprio agio; ill at —, a disagio. *vt.* sollevare, attenuare, calmare; allargare; (*naut.*) allentare, mollare.

easel (ē'z'l) *n.* cavalletto (*da pittore*).

easily (ēz'ĭ-lĭ) *avv.* facilmente; agevolmente; con disinvoltura.

easiness (- ĭěs) *n.* facilità, disinvoltura.

east (ēst) *n.* est, oriente. *agg.* dell'est, orientale the East, l'Oriente; the Far East, l'estremo Oriente.

Easter (ēs'tĕr) *n.* Pasqua: — Sunday, domenica di Pasqua.

eastern (ēs'tĕrn) *agg.* orientale.

eastward (ēst'wĕrd) *avv.* in direzione est.

easy (ēz'ĭ) *agg.* facile, comodo; bonario; accomodante; disinvolto; sciolto; scorrevole: — circumstances, agiatezza; — chair, poltrona; at an — pace, pian pianino, lemme lemme; by — stages, a piccole tappe; to take it —, prendersela con calma. *avv.* comodamente, con calma.

easygoing *agg.* indolente; accomodante, poco esigente; pacifico, pacioso.

eat (ēt) *vt.* (*pass.* ate, *pp.* eaten [ēt''n]) mangiare; corrodere: to — breakfast, fare colazione; to — dinner, pranzare; to — supper, cenare; to — one's heart out; rodersi il cuore, soffrire in silenzio; to — one's word, rimangiarsi la parola. *vi.* cibarsi. **—able** *agg.* commestibile. **—er** *n.* mangiatore.

eaves (ēvz) *n.pl.* grondaia.

eavesdrop (ēvz'drŏp') *vi.* origliare.

ebb (ĕb) *n.* marea, risucchio; decadenza. *vi.* defluire, abbassarsi, declinare. **—tide** *n.* bassa marea.

ebony (ĕb'ŭn·ĭ) *n.* ebano.

eccentric (ĕk·sĕn'trĭk) *agg., n.* eccentrico.

ecclesiastic (ĕ·klē'zĭ·ăs'tĭk) *agg., n.* ecclesiastico.

echelon (ĕsh'ĕ·lŏn) *n.* (*mil.*) scaglione; (*aeron.*) formazione; **in the higher —s,** nelle alte sfere.

echo (ĕk'ō) *n.* eco. *vt.* ripetere (*come l'eco*). *vi.* echeggiare, risuonare.

eclectic (ĕk·lĕk'tĭk), *agg.* eclettico.

eclipse (ē·klĭps') *n.* eclisse. *vt.* eclissare, superare.

economic (ē'kō·nŏm'ĭk) *agg.* economico.

economics (ē'kō·nŏm'ĭks) *n.pl.* economia, scienze economiche.

economist (ē·kŏn'ō·mĭst) *n.* economista.

economize (ē·kŏn'ō·mĭz) *vt., vi.* economizzare.

economy (ē·kŏn'ō·mĭ) *n.* economia, parsimonia.

ecstasy (ĕk'stà·sĭ) *n.* estasi.

ecstatic (ĕk·stăt'ĭk) *agg.* estatico, estasiante.

eddy (ĕd'ĭ) *n.* vortice, turbine. *vi.* turbinare.

Eden (ē'd'n) *n.* Paradiso Terrestre.

edge (ĕj) *n.* orlo, margine, filo (*di una lama*), limite estremo, taglio (*di un libro*); tensione: **to take off the —,** smussare, attenuare; **to be on —,** essere nervoso; **to have an —,** avere un piccolo vantaggio o superiorità. *vt.* affilare; orlare, rasentare; esasperare; spronare. *vi.* avanzare gradatamente, spostarsi lateralmente. **—ways, —wise** *avv.* di taglio; longitudinalmente; **a mala pena.**

edible (ĕd'ĭ·b'l) *agg.* commestibile.

edifice (ĕd'ĭ·fĭs) *n.* edificio.

edify (ĕd'ĭ·fī) *vt.* edificare.

edit (ĕd'ĭt) *vt.* pubblicare, redigere, curare (*un'edizione, ecc.*); (*cinema*) curare il montaggio. **—ing** *n.* (*cinema*) montaggio. **—ion** (ē·dĭsh'ŭn) *n.* edizione. **—or** *n.* redattore; direttore (*di giornale*); curatore (*di un'opera*)· **—orial** *agg.* editoriale; redazionale; *n.* articolo di fondo.

educate (ĕd̯ū·kāt) *vt.* educare, istruire.

education (ĕd̯ū·kā'shŭn) *n.* educazione; istruzione; pedagogia.

educational (-ăl) *agg.* educativo; pedagogico; della scuola.

educator (ĕd̯ū·kā'tẽr) *n.* educatore.

eel (ēl) *n.* anguilla.

eerie *opp.* **eery** (ẽr'ĭ) *agg.* irreale, strano, sovrannaturale.

efface (ĕ·fās') *vt.* cancellare: **to — oneself,** stare nell'ombra.

effect (ĕ·fĕkt') *n.* effetto; (*pl.*) effetti, masserizie. **to carry into —,** eseguire, mettere in pratica; **to take —,** entrare in vigore. *vt.* effettuare, compiere. **—ive** *agg.* efficace, effettivo. **—ual** *agg.* efficace, valido.

effeminate (ĕ·fĕm'ĭ·nĭt) *agg.* effeminato.

efficacious (ĕf'ĭ·kā'shŭs) *agg.* efficace.

efficacy (ĕf'ĭ·kà·sĭ) *n.* efficacia.

efficiency (ĕ·fĭsh'ĕn·sĭ) *n.* efficienza, rendimento.

efficient (ĕ·fĭsh'ĕnt) *agg.* efficiente, efficace.

effluvium (ĕ·flōō'vĭ·ŭm) *n.* esalazione.

effort (ĕf'ẽrt) *n.* sforzo. **—less** *agg.* agevole, senza sforzo, passivo.

effrontery (ĕ·frŭn'tẽr·ĭ) *n.* sfacciataggine.

effulgence (ĕ·fŭl'jĕns) *n.* splendore.

effulgent (ĕ·fŭl'jĕnt) *agg.* splendente.

effusion (ĕ·fū'zhŭn) *n.* effusione; emanazione, perdita.

effusive (-sĭv) *agg.* espansivo.

egg (ĕg) (1) *n.* uovo: **bad —** (*gergo*), cattivo soggetto; **boiled —,** uovo a la coque; **hard-boiled —,** uovo sodo.

egg (ĕg) (2) *vt.* spronare, esortare, incitare, indurre.

egghead *n.* (*gergo S.U.*) intellettuale, intellettualoide.

eggplant *n.* melanzana.

ego (ē'gō) *n.* l'io, spirito, personalità. **—ism** *n.* egoismo. **—ist** *n.* egoista. **—tism** *n.* egotismo. **—tist** *n.* egotista.

egress (ē'grĕs) *n.* uscita.

Egyptian (ē·jĭp'shăn) *agg., n.* egiziano.

eider (ī'dẽr) *n.* (*ornit.*) edrèdone: **—down,** piume di edrèdone; copriletto di piume.

eight (āt) *agg., n.* otto. **eighteen** *agg., n.* diciotto. **—eenth** *agg.* diciottesimo.

eighth (ātth) *agg.* ottavo. *n.* l'ottava parte.

eighty (ā'tĭ) *agg.* ottanta.

either (ē'thẽr) *pron.* l'uno o l'altro; uno dei due; ognuno dei due; entrambe: **I do not see — of them,** non vedo nè l'uno nè l'altro; **on — side,** d'ambe le parti; **in — case,** in entrambi i casi. *cong.:* **— you know him or you do not,** o lo conoscete o non lo conoscete. *avv.* nemmeno: **I do not see him —,** non lo vedo nemmeno io.

eject (ē·jĕkt') *vt.* espellere, emettere.

elaborate (ē·lăb'ō·rĭt) *agg.* accurato, elaborato. *vt.* (-āt) elaborare.

elapse (ē·lăps') *vi.* passare, trascorrere, intercorrere (*del tempo*).

elastic (ĕ·lăs'tĭk) agg. elastico.

elated (ĕ·lāt'ĕd) agg. fiero; esaltato; euforico.

elation (ĕ·lā'shŭn) n. esaltazione; euforia.

elbow (ĕl'bō) n. gomito: at one's —, molto vicino; out at —s, in cattivo arnese. vt., vi. prendere a gomitate; farsi largo a gomitate: to — one's way, aprirsi il varco a gomitate.

elder (ĕl'dĕr) agg. maggiore, più vecchio. —ly agg. anziano, vecchiotto.

eldest (ĕl'dĕst) agg. (il) più vecchio, (il) maggiore.

elect (ĕ·lĕkt') n., agg. scelto, designato, eletto. vt. eleggere designare, decidere. —ion n. elezione, scelta.

elector (ĕ·lĕk'tĕr) n. elettore.

electoral (-ăl) agg. elettorale.

electric (ĕ·lĕk'trĭk) agg elettrico: — meter, contatore elettrico.

electrician (ĕ·lĕk'trĭsh'ăn) n. elettrotecnico.

electricity (ĕ·lĕk'trĭs'ĭ·tĭ) n. elettricità.

electrify (ĕ·lĕk'trĭ·fĭ) vt. elettrificare; elettrizzare.

electrocute (ĕ·lĕk'trō·kūt) vt. giustiziare con elettrocuzione.

electrode (ĕ·lĕk'trōd) n. elèttrodo.

electrolier (ĕ·lek'trō·lĕr') n. lampadario.

electron (ĕ·lĕk'trŏn) n. elettròne. agg. elettrònico: — microscope, microscopio elettronico.

electronics (ĕ·lĕk'trŏn'ĭks) n. elettronica.

electrotype (ĕ·lĕk'trō·tĭp) n. (tip.) stereotipia.

elegance (ĕl'ĕ·găns) n. eleganza.

elegant (-gănt) agg. elegante.

element (ĕl'ĕ·mĕnt) n. elemento; fattore; (aeron.) squadriglia. —al agg. elementare. —ary agg. elementare, fondamentale.

elephant (ĕl'ĕ·fănt) n. elefante.

elevate (ĕl'ĕ·vāt) vt. elevare, innalzare, esaltare.

elevated n. (S.U.) ferrovia soprelevata. agg. elevato.

elevation (-vā'shŭn) n. elevazione.

elevator (ĕl'ĕ·vā'tĕr) n. elevatore; ascensore; (aeron.) timone di profondità.

eleven (ĕ·lĕv'ĕn) agg., n. undici. —th agg. undicesimo.

elicit (ĕ·lĭs'ĭt) vt. estrarre; suscitare; strappare; dedurre; appurare.

eligible (ĕl'ĭ·jĭ·b'l) agg. eleggibile; accettabile; conveniente.

eliminate (ĕ·lĭm'ĭ·nāt) vt. eliminare.

elimination (-nā'shŭn) n. eliminazione.

elk (ĕlk) n. (zool.) alce.

ellipse (ĕ·lĭps') n. (geom.) ellisse.

ellipsis (ĕ·lĭp'sĭs) n. (pl. ellipses) (gramm.) ellissi.

elm (ĕlm) n. (bot.) olmo.

elope (ĕ·lōp') vi. fuggire (spec. con l'amante). —ment n. fuga romantica.

eloquence (ĕl'ō·kwĕns) n. eloquenza.

eloquent (ĕl'ō·kwĕnt) agg. eloquente.

else (ĕls) avv. altrimenti, oppure. agg. altro (si aggiunge a pron.interr., opp. ai composti di some, any, no, every): anybody —, chiunque altro; nobody —, nessun altro; somebody —, qualcun altro; everything —, qualunque altra cosa; nothing —, nient'altro; anywhere —, da qualunque altra parte; nowhere —, da nessun'altra parte; what —?, che altro?; or —, altrimenti.

elsewhere (ĕls'hwâr) avv. altrove.

elucidate (ĕ·lū'sĭ·dāt) vt. spiegare, chiarire.

elucidation (-dā'shŭn) n. chiarificazione, delucidazione.

elude (ĕ·lūd') vt. eludere, schivare.

emaciated (ĕ·mā'shĭ·āt'ĕd) agg. emaciato, deperito.

emanate (ĕm'ā·nāt) vi. emanare.

emanation (-nā'shŭn) n. emanazione.

emancipate (ĕ·măn'sĭ·pāt) vt. emancipare.

emancipation (-pā'shŭn) n. emancipazione.

emasculation (ĕ·măs'kū·lā'shŭn) n. castrazione.

embalm (ĕm·bäm') vt. imbalsamare. —er n. imbalsamatore.

embankment (ĕm·băngk'mĕnt) n. diga, argine, terrapieno.

embargo (ĕm·bär'gō) n. embargo. vt. mettere l'embargo su.

embark (ĕm·bärk') vt., vi. imbarcare; imbarcarsi.

embarrass (ĕm·băr'ăs) vt. imbarazzare: financially —ed, a corto di fondi.

embarrassing agg. imbarazzante.

embarrassment n. imbarazzo, disagio.

embassy (ĕm'bá·sĭ) n. ambasciata.

embellish (ĕm·bĕl'ĭsh) vt. abbellire, adornare.

ember (ĕm'bĕr) n. bragia, tizzone.

embezzle (ĕm·bĕz'l) vt. appropriarsi fraudolentemente. —ment n. appropriazione indebita, malversazione.

embezzler (ĕm·bĕz'lĕr) n. malversatore.

embitter (ĕm·bĭt'ĕr) vt. amareggiare.

emblem (ĕm'blĕm) n. emblema.

embody (ĕm·bŏd'ĭ) vt. incorporare; incarnare, personificare; includere. vi. incorporarsi.

embolden (ĕm·bōl'dĕn) vt. imbaldanzire.

emboss (ĕm·bŏs') *vt.* dare rilievo, scolpire in rilievo.

embrace (ĕm·brās') *n.* abbraccio. *vt.*, *vi.* abbracciare; abbracciarsi.

embrasure (ĕm·brā'zhẽr) *n.* vano (*di porta, finestra, ecc.*); (*fort.*) feritoia.

embroider (ĕm·broi'dẽr) *vt.* ricamare. —**er** *n.* ricamatore, ricamatrice. —**y** *n.* ricamo.

embryo (ĕm'brĭ·ō) *n.* embrione.

emcee (ĕm'sē') *n.* (*radio, T.V.* = *m.c.*, *sigla di Master of Ceremonies*) presentatore (*di un programma*).

emerald (ĕm'ẽr·ăld) *n.* smeraldo.

emerge (ē·mûrj') *vi.* emergere.

emergence (ē·mûr'jĕns) *n.* emersione, apparizione imprevista.

emergency (ē·mûr'jĕn·sĭ) *n.* emergenza, crisi: — **exit**, uscita di sicurezza.

emery (ĕm'ẽr·ĭ) *n.* smeriglio.

emigrate (ĕm'ĭ·grāt) *vi.* emigrare.

eminence (ĕm'ĭ·nĕns) *n.* eminenza, altura.

eminent (-nĕnt) *agg.* eminente, illustre.

emission (ē·mĭsh'ŭn) *n.* emissione.

emit (ē·mĭt') *vt.* emettere, esalare.

emotion (ē·mō'shŭn) *n.* emozione; sentimento, moto dell'animo. —**al** *agg.* emotivo, ipersensibile; riguardante i sentimenti.

emperor (ĕm'pẽr·ẽr) *n.* imperatore.

emphasis (ĕm'fà·sĭs) *n.* enfasi; rilievo.

emphasize (-sīz) *vt.* ribadire, accentuare, mettere in rilievo.

emphatic (ĕm·făt'ĭk) *agg.* espressivo, deciso, efficace.

emphatically (-ĭ·kăl·ĭ) *agg.* energicamente, decisamente.

empire (ĕm'pīr) *n.* impero.

emplacement (ĕm·plās'mĕnt) *n.* collocazione; (*mil.*) piazzuola.

employ (ĕm·ploi') *n.* impiego: to be in somebody's —, essere impiegato presso o alle dipendenze di qualcuno. *vt.* impiegare, usare, utilizzare.

employee (ĕm·ploi'ē) *n.* impiegato.

employer (ĕm·ploi'ẽr) *n.* principale, datore di lavoro.

employment (-mĕnt) *n.* impiego, occupazione: out of —, disoccupato.

emporium (ĕm·pōr'ĭ·ŭm) *n.* emporio.

empower (ĕm·pou'ẽr) *vt.* autorizzare.

empress (ĕm'prĕs) *n.* imperatrice.

emptiness (ĕmp'tĭ·nĕs) *n.* il vuoto, vacuità.

empty (ĕmp'tĭ) *agg.* vuoto, vacuo, deserto, vano. *vt.* vuotare, scaricare. *vi.* vuotarsi, riversarsi.

emulate (ĕm'û·lāt) *vt.* emulare; uguagliare.

emulation (ĕm·û·lā'shŭn) *n.* emulazione.

enable (ĕn·ā'b'l) *vt.* consentire, mettere in grado (*di*).

enact (ĕn·ăkt') *vt.* decretare, ordinare; recitare (*una parte*).

enamel (ĕn·ăm'ĕl) *n.* smalto. *vt.* smaltare.

enamor (ĕn·ăm'ẽr) *vt.* innamorare.

encamp (ĕn·kămp') *vt.* accampare *vi.* accamparsi. —**ment** *n.* accampamento.

enchain (ĕn·chān') *vt.* incatenare.

enchant (ĕn·chànt') *vt.* incantare, affascinare. —**er** *n.* incantatore. —**ing** *agg.* incantevole. —**ment** *n.* incantesimo. —**ress** *n.* incantatrice.

encircle (ĕn·sûr'k'l) *vt.* cingere, aggirare.

enclose (ĕn·klōz') *vt.* rinchiudere, recingere; accludere.

enclosure (-klō'zhẽr) *n.* recinto, spazio cintato; allegato.

encompass (ĕn·kŭm'pás) *vt.* circondare, contenere; (*fam.*) superare in astuzia.

encore (äng·kōr') *int.* bis. *vt.* chiedere il bis (*di*).

encounter (ĕn·koun'tẽr) *n.* incontro; scontro (*combattimento*). *vt.* incontrare, affrontare.

encourage (ĕn·kûr'ĭj) *vt.* incoraggiare. —**ment** *n.* incoraggiamento.

encouraging *agg.* incoraggiante.

encroach (ĕn·krōch') *vi.* (*seg. da.* on, upon) insinuarsi; sconfinare, invadere; usurpare: to — rubare tempo (*a*).

encumber (ĕn·kŭm'bẽr) *vt.* ingombrare, gravare, imbarazzare.

encumbrance (-bráns) *n.* ingombro, impaccio, gravame; ipoteca.

encyclopaedia (ĕn·sĭ'klō·pē'dĭ·à) *n.* enciclopedia.

end (ĕnd) *n.* fine, termine; estremità; scopo, mira; decesso: to be at one's wit's —, non saper dove battere la testa; by the — of, prima della fine di; at the — of one's tether, al limite delle proprie risorse; to make both —s meet, sbarcare il lunario; to stand on —, drizzarsi; to put an — to, mettere fine a; no — of things, un'infinità di cose; odds and —s, cianfrusaglie. *vi.*, *vt.* finire: to — by, finire con o per.

endanger (ĕn·dān'jẽr) *vt.* mettere in pericolo, compromettere.

endear (ĕn·dēr') *vt.* rendere caro: to — oneself to, accattivarsi l'affetto di. —**ment** *n.* blandizie, tenerezza.

endeavor (ĕn·dĕv'ẽr) *n.* sforzo, tentativo, impresa. *vi.* sforzarsi, cercare.

ending (ĕn'dĭng) *n.* conclusione, fine; (*gramm.*) desinenza.

endless (ĕnd'lĕs) *agg.* interminabile.
endorse (ĕn·dôrs') *vt.* attergare; girare; avallare; sottoscrivere, approvare.
endorsee (ĕn'dôr·sē') *n.* giratario.
endorsement (ĕn·dôrs'mĕnt) *n.* girata; avallo; approvazione.
endorser (ĕn·dôr'sĕr) *n.* girante; avallante.
endow (ĕn·dou') *vt.* dotare, munire, corredare (*di*). —**ment** *n.* dotazione, dote, pregio.
endurance (ĕn·dūr'ᾰns) *n.* sopportazione, resistenza: beyond —, intollerabile.
endure (ĕn·dūr') *vt.*, *vi.* sopportare, tollerare. *vi.* durare, continuare.
endways (ĕnd'wāz'), **endwise** (-wīz') *avv.* in posizione eretta, con l'estremità in su o in fuori; testa a testa.
enema (ĕn'ē·mᾰ) *n.* clistere.
enemy (ĕn'ē·mῐ) *n.* nemico.
energetic (ĕn'ẽr·jĕt'ῐk) *agg.* energico, attivo, dinamico.
energy (ĕn'ẽr·jῐ) *n.* energia.
enervate (ĕn'ẽr·vāt) *vt.* snervare, scoraggiare.
enfeeble (ĕn·fē'b'l) *vt.* indebolire.
enfold (ĕn·fōld') *vt.* avvolgere, abbracciare.
enforce (ĕn·fôrs') *vt.* imporre; applicare (*leggi*, *ecc.*), render esecutivo. —**ment** *n.* coercizione; applicazione (*di un regolamento*, *ecc.*).
engage (ĕn·gāj') *vt.* ingaggiare, tener occupato; impegnare; prenotare (*un posto*); attirare. *vi.* impegnarsi; imbarcarsi (*in un'impresa*); (*mecc.*) ingranare.
engaged (ĕn·gājd') *agg.* impegnato, occupato; intento (*a*); fidanzato; ingranato.
engagement (-mĕnt) *n.* impegno, obbligo; fidanzamento; (*mil.*) scontro: to keep an —, andare a un appuntamento.
engaging (-ĭng) *agg.* impegnativo; attraente.
engender (ĕn·jĕn'dẽr) *vt.* generare; produrre; provocare.
engine (ĕn'jῐn) *n.* macchina; motore; locomotiva: fire —, pompa da incendio.
engineer (ĕn'jῐ·nēr') *n.* ingegnere; meccanico; macchinista; (*mil.*) geniere. *vt.* architettare. —**ing** *n.* ingegneria.
English (ῐng'glῐsh) *n.*, *agg.* inglese: the —, gli inglesi; in plain —, in parole povere, esplicitamente. —**man** *n.* (*pl.* —**men**) (*cittadino*) inglese. —**woman** *n.* (*pl.* —**women**) (*cittadina*) inglese.
engrave (ĕn·grāv') *vt.* incidere, scolpire, imprimere. —**r** *n.* incisore.

—**ing** *n.* incisione: wood —, silografia.
engross (ĕn·grōs') *vt.* assorbire (*l'attenzione*), occupare: to be —ed, essere assorto. —**ing** *agg.* interessante.
engulf (ĕn·gŭlf') *vt.* inghiottire, sommergere.
enhance (ĕn·hᾰns') *vt.* accentuare, intensificare, valorizzare.
enigma (ē·nῐg'mᾰ) *n.* enigma. —**tical** (-mᾰt'ῐ·kᾰl) *agg.* enigmatico.
enjoin (ĕn·join') *vt.* ingiungere: to — from, proibire di.
enjoy (ĕn·joi') *vt.* gustare, godere, apprezzare; compiacersi di: to — oneself, divertirsi; to — the use of, usufruire di. —**able** *agg.* gradevole, divertente. —**ment** *n.* godimento, divertimento.
enlarge (ĕn·lärj') *vt.* ampliare, dilatare. *vi.* dilungarsi; ampliarsi.
enlighten (ĕn·līt'n) *vt.* illuminare (*istruire*).
enlist (ĕn·lῐst') *vt.* arruolare, assicurarsi (*l'aiuto di qualcuno*). *vi.* arruolarsi: —ed man (*mil.*) gregario, soldato.
enlistment (-mĕnt) *n.* arruolamento; ferma.
enliven (ĕn·līv'ĕn) *vt.* ravvivare.
enmity (ĕn'mῐ·tῐ) *n.* inimicizia, ostilità.
ennoble (ĕ·nō'b'l) *vt.* nobilitare.
enormity (ē·nôr'mῐ·tῐ) *n.* enormità.
enormous (ē·nôr'mŭs) *agg.* enorme.
enough (ē·nŭf') *n.* sufficienza, quanto basta. *agg.* sufficiente. *avv.* sufficientemente, abbastanza: that is —, così basta; — of it! basta!
enquire (ĕn·kwīr') *vedi* inquire.
enrage (ĕn·rāj') *vt.* infuriare, esasperare.
enrapture (ĕn·răp'tūr) *vt.* estasiare.
enrich (ĕn·rῐch') *vt.* arricchire. —**ment** *n.* arricchimento.
enroll, **enrol** (ĕn·rōl') *vt.* arrotolare; registrare, iscrivere; arruolare. —**ment** *n.* iscrizione; arruolamento.
ensemble (än·sŏm'b'l) *n.* insieme; complesso.
ensign (ĕn'sῐn; ĕn'sῐn) *n.* insegna, bandiera; alfiere; (*marina S.U.*) (ĕn'sῐn) guardiamarina.
enslave (ĕn·slāv') *vt.* asservire, mettere in schiavitù.
ensnare (ĕn·snâr') *vt.* prendere in trappola; sedurre.
ensue (ĕn·sū') *vt.* succedere, verificarsi (*come conseguenza*).
ensure (ĕn·shŏŏr') *vt.* assicurare.
entail (ĕn·tāl') *vt.* comportare, imporre; vincolare (*un'eredità*).
entangle (ĕn·tăng'g'l) *vt.* arruffare, complicare, aggrovigliare, impego-

lare; coinvolgere. **—ment** *n.* complicazione; groviglio; legame.

enter (ĕn′tẽr) *vt., vi.* entrare, penetrare; iscrivere, registrare; abbracciare (*una professione*): **to — an application**, presentare una domanda, **to — upon a subject**, affrontare un argomento.

enterprise (ĕn′tẽr·prīz) *n.* impresa, prodezza; intraprendenza.

enterprising (-prīz′īng) *agg.* intraprendente.

entertain (ĕn′tẽr·tān′) *vt., vi.* intrattenere, ricevere; divertire, dare spettacolo; concepire (*una idea*), accarezzare (*speranze*); prendere in considerazione (*una proposta*). **—er** *n.* ospite (*chi ospita*). **—ing** *agg.* divertente. **—ment** *n.* ospitalità, festa, divertimento; spettacolo.

enthrall (ĕn·thrôl′) *vt.* asservire; incantare, ammaliare.

enthusiasm (ĕn·thū′zĭ·ăz′m) *n.* entusiasmo.

enthusiast (-ăst) *n.* entusiasta.

enthusiastic (-tĭk) *agg.* entusiastico.

entice (ĕn·tīs′) *vt.* adescare, sedurre. **—ment** *n.* seduzione, tentazione.

entire (ĕn·tīr′) *agg.* intero, completo. **—ly** *avv.* interamente, completamente. **—ty** (ĕn·tī′rĕ·tĭ) *n.* interezza, totalità.

entitle (ĕn·tī′t′l) *vt.* intitolare; dare diritto (*a*): **to be —d to**, aver diritto a o il diritto di.

entity (ĕn′tĭ·tĭ) *n.* entità.

entourage (än′tōō·räzh′) *n.* ambiente, cerchia.

entrails (ĕn′trĕlz) *n.pl.* interiora, viscere.

entrance (ĕn′trăns) (1) *n.* entrata, ingresso; esordio; iscrizione.

entrance (ĕn·träns′) (2) *vt.* incantare; rapire in estasi.

entrap (ĕn·trăp′) *vt.* intrappolare.

entreat (ĕn·trēt′) *vt.* supplicare.

entreaty (-ĭ) *n.* supplica.

entrench (ĕn·trĕnch′) *vt.* trincerare. *vi.* (*seg. da* on, upon) sconfinare, usurpare.

entry (ĕn′trĭ) *n.* entrata, ingresso; iscrizione, registrazione, annotazione: **double —**, partita doppia; **single —**, partita semplice.

enumerate (ē·nū′mẽr·āt) *vt.* enumerare.

enunciate (ē·nŭn′sĭ·āt) *vt.* enunciare.

enunciation (-sĭ·ā′shŭn) *n.* enunciazione.

envelop (ĕn·vĕl′ŭp) *vt.* avvolgere.

envelope (ĕn′vĕ·lōp) *n.* busta, rivestimento.

envenom (ĕn·vĕn′ŭm) *vt.* avvelenare.

enviable (ĕn′vĭ·á·b′l) *agg.* invidiabile.

envious (ĕn′vĭ·ŭs) *agg.* invidioso.

environment (ĕn·vī′rŭn·mĕnt) *n.* ambiente, contorno.

environs (ĕn·vī′rŭnz) *n.pl.* dintorni.

envoy (ĕn′voi) *n.* inviato.

envy (ĕn′vĭ) *n.* invidia. *vt.* invidiare.

epaulet (ĕp′ô·lĕt) *n.* spallina.

ephemeral (ĕ·fĕm′ẽr·ăl) *agg.* effimero, fuggevole.

epic (ĕp′īk) *n.* epica. *agg.* epico.

epicure (ĕp′ĭ·kūr) *n.* epicureo. **—an** (-kū·rē′ăn) *n., agg.* epicureo.

epidemic (ĕp′ĭ·dĕm′īk) *agg.* epidemico.

epidermis (ĕp′ĭ·dûr′mĭs) *n.* epidermide.

epigram (ĕp′ĭ·grăm) *n.* epigramma.

epigraph (ĕp′ĭ·gráf) *n.* epigrafe.

epilogue (ĕp′ĭ·lŏg) *n.* epilogo.

episode (ĕp′ĭ·sōd) *n.* episodio.

epistle (ĕ·pĭs′′l) *n.* epistola.

epistolary (ĕ·pĭs′tō·lĕr′ĭ) *agg.* epistolare.

epitaph (ĕp′ĭ·tàf) *n.* epitaffio.

epitome (ĕ·pĭt′ō·mē) *n.* epitome, compendio.

epoch (ĕp′ŏk) *n.* epoca.

epopee (ĕp′ō·pē′) *n.* epopea.

equable (ĕk′wá·b′l) *agg.* uniforme, calmo, equilibrato, equo.

equal (ē′kwǎl) *agg.* uguale, pari: **— to**, all'altezza di. *n.* uguale: **our —s**, i pari nostri. *vt.* eguagliare. **—ity** *n* eguaglianza.

equalize (ē′kwǎl·īz) *vt* uguagliare, pareggiare.

equally (ē′kwǎl·ĭ) *avv.* egualmente.

equanimity (ē′kwá·nĭm′ĭ·tĭ) *n.* equanimità.

equation (ē·kwā′zhŭn) *n.* equazione.

equator (ē·kwā′tẽr) *n.* equatore.

equilibrium (ē′kwĭ·lĭb′rĭ·ŭm) *n.* equilibrio.

equinox (ē′kwĭ·nŏks) *n.* equinozio.

uip (ē·kwĭp′) *vt.* equipaggiare. **—ment** *n.* equipaggiamento, utensileria.

equitable (ĕk′wĭ·tá·b′l) *agg.* equo, giusto.

equity (ĕk′wĭ·tĭ) *n.* equità, giustizia.

equivalent (ē·kwĭv′á·lĕnt) *n., agg.* equivalente.

equivocal (ē·kwĭv′ō·kǎl) *agg.* equivoco, ambiguo.

era (ē′rá) *n.* èra.

eradicate (ē·răd′ĭ·kāt) *vt.* sradicare.

erase (ē·rās′) *vt* cancellare, raschiare.

eraser (ē·rās′ẽr) *n.* raschietto; gomma da cancellare: **blackboard —**, cimosa.

erasure (ē·rā′shẽr) *n.* cancellatura.

ere (âr) *prep., cong.* prima, prima di, piuttosto che. **—long** *avv.* tra poco. **—now** *avv.* prima d'ora, finora, già. **—while** *avv.* poco fa, precedentemente.

erect (ĕr·ĕkt') *agg.* eretto, elevato. *vt.* erigere, drizzare, elevare.

ermine (ûr'mĭn) *n.* ermellino.

erode (ĕ·rōd') *vt.* corrodere.

erosion (ĕ·rō'zhŭn) *n.* erosione.

erosive (ĕ·rō'sĭv) *agg.* erosivo.

err (ûr) *vi.* errare, smarrirsi.

errand (ĕr'ănd) *n.* incarico, commissione: — boy, fattorino, galoppino.

errant (ĕr'ănt) *agg.* errante: knight —, cavaliere errante.

erratic (ĕ·răt'ĭk) *agg.* erratico; errante; irregolare, stravagante.

erroneous (ĕ·rō'nĕ·ŭs) *agg.* erroneo, scorretto.

error (ĕr'ẽr) *n.* errore, sbaglio; colpa.

ersatz (ĕr·zäts') *n.*, *agg.* surrogato: — coffee, surrogato di caffè.

erstwhile (ûrst'hwīl') *agg.*, *avv.* anticamente.

eruption (ĕ·rŭp'shŭn) *n.* eruzione.

erysipelas (ĕr'ĭ·sĭp'ĕ·lăs) *n.* risipola.

escalator (ĕs'kà·lā'tẽr) *n.* scala meccanica; scala mobile (*degli stipendi*).

escapade (ĕs'kà·pād') *n.* scappata, marachella.

escape (ĕs·kāp') *n.* evasione, fuga (*anche di gas, ecc.*): to have a narrow —, scamparla bella *o* per miracolo; fire —, scala di sicurezza; literature of — letteratura d'evasione. *vt.* sfuggire; evitare. *vi.* evadere; liberarsi. —ment *n.* via di scampo; scappamento.

escort (ĕs'kôrt) *n.* scorta: — carrier, portaerei ausiliaria. *vt.* scortare.

escutcheon (ĕs·kŭch'ŭn) *n.* scudo, blasone.

espalier (ĕs·păl'yẽr) *n.* spalliera (*di fiori, ecc.*).

esparto (ĕs·pär'tō) *n.* (*bot.*) sparto.

especial (ĕs·pĕsh'ăl) *agg.* speciale. —ly *avv.* specialmente, soprattutto.

espionage (ĕs'pĭ·ô·nĭj) *n.* spionaggio.

esplanade (ĕs'plà·nād') *n.* spianata, passeggiata.

esquire (ĕs·kwīr') *n.*: *posposto al nome corrisponde a*: egregio sig.: John Smith, Esq., egregio sig. J. S.

essay (ĕs'ā) *n.* saggio, prova. *vt.* (e·sā') provare.

essence (ĕs'ĕns) *n.* essenza.

essential (ĕ·sĕn'shăl) *agg.* essenziale.

establish (ĕs·tăb'lĭsh) *vt.* stabilire, costituire, consolidare, fondare. —ment *n.* fondazione; costituzione; sede, casa, stabilimento, istituto.

estate (ĕs·tāt') *n.* condizione; proprietà, tenuta: real —, beni immobili.

esteem (ĕs·tēm') *n.* stima, considerazione. *vt.* stimare, rispettare.

estimable (ĕs'tĭ·mà·b'l) *agg.* stimabile.

estimate (ĕs'tĭ·māt) *n.* valutazione, perizia, calcolo, giudizio. *vt.* valutare, calcolare, stimare.

estimation (-mā'shŭn) *n.* stima, valutazione.

estrange (ĕs·trānj') *vt.* alienare, estraniare, inimicarsi.

estuary (ĕs'tū·ĕr'ĭ) *n.* estuario.

etch (ĕch) *vt.* incidere all'acquaforte. —er *n.* incisore, acquafortista. —ing *n.* incisione, acquaforte.

eternal (ĕ·tûr'năl) *agg.* eterno.

eternity (ĕ·tûr'nĭ·tĭ) *n.* eternità.

ether (ē'thẽr) *n.* etere. —eal (ĕ·thẽr'ē·ăl) *agg.* etereo.

ethical (ĕth'ĭ·kăl) *agg.* etico.

ethics (ĕth'ĭks) *n.pl.* etica.

ethnology (ĕth·nŏl'ō·jĭ) *n.* etnologia.

ethyl (ĕth'ĭl) *n.* etile.

etiquette (ĕt'ĭ·kĕt) *n.* etichetta.

etymology (ĕt'ĭ·mŏl'ō·jĭ) *n.* etimologia.

Eucharist (ū'kà·rĭst) *n.* eucarestia.

eunuch (ū'nŭk) *n.* eunuco.

European (ū'rō·pē'ăn) *n.*, *agg.* europeo.

euthanasia (ū'thà·nā'zhĭ·à) *n.* eutanasia.

evacuate (ĕ·văk'ū·āt) *vt.* evacuare. *vi.* sfollare.

evacuee (ĕ·văk'ū·ē') *n.* sfollato.

evade (ĕ·vād') *vt.* eludere, schivare.

evaluate (ĕ·văl'ū·āt) *vt.* valutare.

evaluation (-ā'shŭn) *n.* valutazione.

evaporate (ĕ·văp'ō·rāt) *vt.* far evaporare, disidratare. *vi.* evaporare.

evaporation (-rā'shŭn) *n.* evaporazione.

evasion (ĕ·vā'zhŭn) *n.* evasione, scappatoia.

evasive (-sĭv) *agg.* evasivo.

eve (ēv) *n.* vigilia: New Year's —, l'ultimo dell'anno, San Silvestro; on the — of, alla vigilia di.

even (ē'vĕn) *agg.* pari; uguale; liscio; uniforme; equanime; allo stesso livello: — number, numero pari; — temper, carattere pacifico; to be — with someone, essere alla pari con qualcuno; to get — with, sdebitarsi con; rendere pan per focaccia. *avv.* persino, anche, proprio: — as, nel momento in cui; — so, eppure, ciò nonostante; — though, anche se, quantunque; not —, neppure, nemmeno. *vt.* uguagliare, livellare, levigare.

evening (ēv'nĭng) *n.* sera. *agg.* serale, da sera.

evenly (ē'vĕn·lĭ) *avv.* uniformemente; in parti uguali; pianamente; pacatamente.

evenness (ē'věn·něs) n. uniformità, pacatezza.

event (ė·věnt') n. evento, eventualità, caso; gara: in any —, in ogni caso, comunque; in the — of, in caso di. —ful agg. movimentato, pieno di avvenimenti, fortunoso.

eventual (ė·věn'tū·ăl) agg. eventuale, finale. —ity (—ăl'ĭ·tĭ) n. eventualità. —ly avv. finalmente; eventualmente.

ever (ěv'ēr) avv. sempre; continuamente; mai: for —, for — and —, per sempre; if —, se mai, se qualche volta; — after, — since, da allora in poi; — so, tanto, così; — so much, moltissimo; scarcely —, quasi mai; more than —, più che mai; the finest man I — met, il miglior uomo che io abbia mai visto.

evergreen (ěv'ēr·grēn) n., agg. sempreverde.

everlasting (ěv'ēr·lås'tĭng) n. eternità. agg. duraturo, eterno.

evermore (ěv'ēr·mōr') avv. sempre, per sempre.

every (ěv'ēr·ĭ) agg. ogni, ciascuno: — now and then, di tanto in tanto; — other, uno sì, uno no; — other day, a giorni alterni. —body pron. ognuno, tutti. —day agg. d'ogni giorno, comune, normale. —one pron. ognuno, tutti. —thing pron. ogni cosa, tutto. —where avv. dovunque.

evict (ė·vĭkt') vt. espellere, estromettere.

evidence (ěv'ĭ·děns) n. evidenza, prova, testimonianza: to give —, deporre. vt. manifestare, dimostrare.

evident (—děnt) agg. evidente.

evil (ē'v'l) n. male, danno. agg. cattivo, funesto, nocivo, maligno: — eye, malocchio; the — one, il maligno, il diavolo. avv. male, dannosamente.

evildoer (ē'v'l·dōō'ēr) n. malfattore.

evince (ė·vĭns') vt. manifestare.

evoke (ė·vōk') vt. evocare.

evolution (ěv'ȯ·lū'shŭn) n. evoluzione; (mat.) estrazione di radice.

evolve (ė·vŏlv') vt. sviluppare. vi. evolversi.

ewe (ū) n. pecora (femmina). — lamb n. agnella.

ewer (ū'ēr) n. brocca.

exact (ěg·zăkt') agg. esatto, preciso. vt. esigere, richiedere. —ing agg. esigente, gravoso, impegnativo. —itude. —ness n. esattezza. —ly avv. esattamente.

exaggerate (ěg·zăj'ēr·āt) vt., vi. esagerare.

exaggeration (—ā'shŭn) n. esagerazione.

exalt (ěg·zôlt') vt. esaltare, innalzare. —ation n. esaltazione. —ed agg. elevato; esaltato; sommo, altolocato.

examination (ěg·zăm'ĭ·nā'shŭn) n. esame: competitive —, esame di concorso; post-mortem —, autopsia; oral —, esame orale.

examine (ěg·zăm'ĭn) vt. esaminare, interrogare.

examiner (—ĭnēr) n. esaminatore.

example (ěg·zám'p'l) n. esempio.

exasperate (ěg·zăs'pēr·āt) vt. esasperare.

exasperation (—ā'shŭn) n. esasperazione.

excavate (ěks'kȧ·vāt) vt. scavare.

excavator (—vā'tēr) n. escavatore.

exceed (ěk·sēd') vt. superare. vi. eccedere; eccellere. —ing agg. eccessivo, straordinario. —ingly avv. estremamente, eccessivamente: — well, benissimo.

excel (ěk·sěl') vt. superare, battere. vi. eccellere. —lence (ěk'sě·lěns), —lency n. eccellenza; superiorità, perfezione. —lent agg. eccellente.

except (ěk·sěpt') prep. eccetto, a eccezione di, tranne, fuorché. cong. eccetto che. vt. eccettuare, escludere. vi. obiettare, sollevare obiezioni.

excepting prep. vedi except.

exception (ěk·sěp'shŭn) n. eccezione, obiezione: with the — of, eccetto, tranne; to take —, obiettare; offendersi. —al agg. eccezionale.

excess (ěk·sěs') n. eccesso; eccedenza: to —, eccessivamente, troppo; — baggage, eccedenza di bagaglio.

excessive (—sěs'ĭv) agg. eccessivo.

exchange (ěks·chănj') n. scambio; (telef.) centrale; borsa valori: bill of —, cambiale; rate of —, tasso di scambio; — broker, agente di cambio. vt. cambiare, scambiare: to — greetings, salutarsi.

excise (ěk'sīz) n. imposta indiretta, dazio: — duty, dazio.

excitable (ěk·sīt'ȧ·b'l) agg. eccitabile, impressionabile, irascibile.

excite (ěk·sīt') vt. eccitare, agitare, irritare, provocare.

excited (—sīt'ěd) agg. eccitato, sovreccitato, accalorato, concitato: to get —, accalorarsi; perdere la calma; entusiasmarsi.

excitedly (—lĭ) avv. concitatamente.

excitement (—měnt) n. eccitazione, sovreccitazione, emozione, agitazione; trambusto.

exciting (—ĭng) agg. emozionante, eccitante.

exclaim (ĕks·klām') vt., vi. esclamare.

exclamation (ĕks'klȧ·mā'shŭn) n. esclamazione: — point, punto esclamativo.

exclude (ĕks·klōōd') vt. escludere.

exclusion (-klōō'zhŭn) n. esclusione.

exclusive (ĕks·klōō'sĭv) agg. esclusivo, limitativo, rigoroso: — of, senza calcolare, eccettuato, escluso.

exclusiveness (-nĕs) n. esclusività.

excommunicate (ĕks'kŏ·mū'nĭ·kāt) vt. scomunicare.

excommunication (-kā'shŭn) n. scomunica.

excoriate (ĕks·kō'rĭ·āt) vt. escoriare, scorticare; criticare aspramente.

excoriation (-ā'shŭn) n. escoriazione.

excrement (ĕks'krē·mĕnt) n. escremento.

excrescence (ĕks·krĕs'ĕns) n. escrescenza.

excruciating (ĕks·krōō'shĭ·āt'ĭng) agg. tormentoso, straziante.

exculpate (ĕks'kŭl·pāt) vt. discolpare.

excursion (ĕks·kûr'zhŭn) n. escursione; digressione; (mecc.) corsa (di cilindro).

excusable (ĕks·kūz'ȧ·b'l) agg. scusabile, perdonabile.

excuse (ĕks·kūz') n. scusa, giustificazione. vt. scusare; dispensare; congedare: — me! scusami!, mi scusi!, scusatemi!

execrable (ĕk'sē·krȧ·b'l) agg. esecrabile, esecrando.

execrate (ĕk'sē·krāt) vt. esecrare.

execute (ĕk'sē·kūt) vt. eseguire, compiere; applicare (una sanzione, ecc.); giustiziare.

execution (ĕk'sē·kū'shŭn) n. esecuzione (anche capitale); sequestro; adempimento: to carry into —, mettere in atto.

executioner (-ēr) n. carnefice.

executive (ĕg·zĕk'ů·tĭv) n. funzionario, dirigente. agg. esecutivo.

executor (ĕg·zĕk'ů·tĕr) n. esecutore.

exemplar (ĕg·zĕm'plĕr) n. esemplare, modello.

exemplary (ĕg·zĕm'plȧ·rĭ) agg. esemplare.

exempt (ĕg·zĕmpt') agg. esente. vt. esentare. —ion n. esenzione.

exercise (ĕk'sẽr·sĭz) n. esercizio. vt. esercitare; preoccupare. vi. esercitarsi.

exert (ĕg·zûrt') vt. esercitare, compiere: to — oneself, compiere uno sforzo, adoperarsi. —ion n. sforzo.

exhalation (ĕks'hȧ·lā'shŭn) n. esalazione.

exhale (ĕks·hāl') vt., vi. esalare.

exhaust (ĕg·zôst') n. scarico, valvola, scappamento. vt. esaurire; vuotare;

fiaccare. vi. scaricarsi (di gas, ecc.). —ed agg. esaurito; esausto, sfinito. —ion n. esaurimento. —ive agg. esauriente; che esaurisce.

exhibit (ĕg·zĭb'ĭt) n. pezzo da esposizione, campione; (legge) reperto, documento agli atti. vt. esibire, esporre.

exhibition (ĕk's·ĭ·bĭsh'ŭn) n. esibizione; esposizione, mostra; spettacolo. —ism n. esebizionismo.

exhilarate (ĕg·zĭl'ȧ·rāt) vt. esilarare, rallegrare.

exhilaration (-rā'shŭn) n. ilarità.

exhort (ĕg·zôrt') vt. esortare, ammonire. —ation n. esortazione.

exigency (ĕk'sĭ·jĕn·sĭ) n. esigenza.

exigent (-jĕnt) agg. esigente.

exile (ĕk'sĭl) n. esilio; esule. vt. esiliare.

exist (ĕg·zĭst') vi. esistere. —ence n. esistenza: to be in —, esistere; to call into —, creare, far nascere. —ent, —ing agg. esistente, attuale.

existentialism n. esistenzialismo. existentialist n. esistenzialista.

exit (ĕk'sĭt) n. uscita; fine; morte; v. (teat.) esce. vi. uscire.

exodus (ĕk'sŏ·dŭs) n. esodo.

exonerate (ĕg·zŏn'ẽr·āt) vt. esonerare, dispensare, assolvere.

exorbitant (ĕg·zôr'bĭ·tȧnt) agg. esorbitante.

exorcise (ĕk'sôr·sĭz) vt. esorcizzare.

exotic (ĕks·ŏt'ĭk) agg. esotico; pittoresco; vistoso.

expand (ĕks·pănd') vt. espandere, dilatare, sviluppare. vi. espandersi, dilatarsi, svilupparsi.

expanse (-păns') n. distesa, estensione.

expansion (ĕks·păn'shŭn) n. espansione, estensione, dilatazione, sviluppo.

expansive (-sĭv) agg. espansivo, diffuso.

expatriate (ĕks·pā'trĭ·āt) vt. espatriare.

expect (ĕks·pĕkt') vt., vi. aspettare; prevedere; supporre; sperare; calcolare di: I — so, ritengo di sì, spero di sì. —ation n. attesa, speranza, prospettiva.

expectorate (ĕks·pĕk'tō·rāt) vt., vi. espettorare.

expedience (ĕks·pē'dĭ·ĕns), **expediency** (-ĕn·sĭ) n. convenienza, utilità; solerzia, fretta.

expedient (-ĕnt) n. espediente. agg. conveniente, utile.

expedition (ĕks'pē·dĭsh'ŭn) n. sveltezza, prontezza; spedizione. —ary agg. (mil.) di spedizione.

expel (ĕks·pĕl') vt. espellere.

expend (ĕks·pĕnd') *vt.* spendere; sborsare; profondere. —**able** *agg.* spendibile; (*mil.*) sacrificabile. —**lture** *n.* spesa, sborso.

expense (ĕks·pĕns') *n.* spesa, costo.

expensive (-pĕn'sĭv) *agg.* costoso, dispendioso.

experience (ĕks·pēr'ĭ·ĕns) *n.* esperienza. *vt.* provare, subire, patire.

experienced (-ĕnst) *agg.* esperto.

experiment (ĕks·pĕr'ĭ·mĕnt) *n.* esperimento. *vi.* (*seg. da* with) sperimentare. —**al** *agg.* sperimentale.

expert (ĕks'pûrt) *n.* perito, competente. *agg.* (ĕks·pûrt') esperto. —**ly** *avv.* espertamente, abilmente.

expiate (ĕks'pĭ·āt) *vt.* espiare.

expiation (-ā'shŭn) *n.* espiazione.

expiration (ĕks'spĭ·rā'shŭn) *n.* scadenza, termine, espirazione.

expire (ĕk·spīr') *vt.*, *vi.* espirare, spirare, scadere, emettere, esalare.

explain (ĕks·plān') *vt.*, *vi.* spiegare. —**able** *agg.* spiegabile.

explanation (ĕks'plá·nā'shŭn) *n.* spiegazione, schiarimento.

explanatory (ĕks·plăn'á·tō'rĭ) *agg.* esplicativo.

explicatory (ĕks'plĭ·ká·tō'rĭ) *agg.* esplicativo.

explicit (ĕks·plĭs'ĭt) *agg.* esplicito.

explode (ĕks·plōd') *vt.* far esplodere; svalutare, demolire (*una teoria*). *vi.* esplodere.

exploit (ĕks'ploit) (1) *n.* prodezza, impresa.

exploit (ĕks·ploit') (2) *vt.* sfruttare, utilizzare. —**ation** *n.* sfruttamento, utilizzazione.

exploration (ĕks'plō·rā'shŭn) *n.* esplorazione.

explore (ĕks·plōr') *vt.*, *vi.* esplorare.

explorer (ĕks·plōr'ĕr) *n.* esploratore.

explosion (ĕks·plō'zhŭn) *n.* esplosione.

explosive (-sĭv) *n.*, *agg.* esplosivo.

export (ĕks'pōrt) *n.* esportazione. *vt.* (ĕks·pōrt') esportare. —**ation** *n.* esportazione. —**er** *n.* esportatore.

expose (ĕks·pōz') *vt.* esporre, scoprire, svelare.

exposé (ĕks'pō·sā') *n.* (*giorn.*) denuncia, rivelazione (*di uno scandalo*).

exposer (-ĕr) *n.* espositore.

exposition (ĕks'pō·zĭsh'ŭn) *n.* esposizione.

expostulate (ĕks·pŏs'tū·lāt) *vi.* protestare, rimostrare.

expostulation (-lā'shŭn) *n.* rimostranza, protesta.

exposure (ĕks·pō'zhĕr) *n.* esposizione (*al sole, ecc.*); smascheramento, scandalo; (*fot.*) posa: — **meter** (*fot.*), esposimetro.

expound (ĕks·pound') *vt.* esporre, divulgare.

express (ĕks·prĕs') *n.* (*lettera*) espresso; (*treno*) rapido; messaggero: — **company**, società di trasporti. *agg.* apposito, espresso; rapido. *avv.* espressamente; per espresso. *vt.* esprimere; (*S.U.*) spedire per espresso. —**ion** *n.* éspressione. —**ive** *agg.* espressivo. —**way** *n.* superautostrada.

expropriate (ĕks·prō'prĭ·āt) *vt.* espropriare.

expulsion (ĕks·pŭl'shŭn) *n.* espulsione.

exquisite (ĕks'kwĭ·zĭt) *agg.* sublime, squisito, raffinato; acuto (*di dolore*).

extant (ĕks'tănt) *agg.* esistente, disponibile, attuale.

extend (ĕks·tĕnd') *vt.* estendere; prolungare; protrarre, prorogare; tendere; porgere. *vi.* estendersi, protrarsi: extended **play record**, disco a lunga durata.

extension (ĕks·tĕn'shŭn) *n.* estensione, prolungamento, proroga; (*telef.*) derivazione.

extensive (-sĭv) *agg.* vasto, ampio, diffuso. *avv.* ampiamente, diffusamente.

extent (ĕks·tĕnt') *n.* estensione; grado; punto; portata; limite: to a great —, in gran parte; to a certain —, sino a un certo punto.

extenuate (ĕks·tĕn'ū·āt) *vt.* attenuare, giustificare.

extenuating *agg.* attenuante.

extenuation (-ā'shŭn) *n.* attenuazione, attenuante.

exterior (ĕks·tēr'ĭ·ĕr) *agg.* esteriore, esterno.

exterminate (ĕks·tûr'mĭ·nāt) *vt.* sterminare.

extermination (-nā'shŭn) *n.* sterminio.

external (ĕks·tûr'năl) *n.*, *agg.* esterno, esteriore.

extinct (ĕks·tĭngkt') *agg.* estinto, scomparso. —**ion** *n.* estinzione, soppressione.

extinguish (ĕks·tĭng'gwĭsh) *vt.* estinguere, spegnere.

extirpate (ĕk'stĕr·pāt) *vt.* estirpare, sterminare.

extol (ĕks·tŏl') *vt.* esaltare, estollere.

extort (ĕks·tôrt') *vt.* estorcere. —**ion** *n.* estorsione; (*giur.*) concussione.

extra (ĕks'trá) *n.* supplemento; edizione straordinaria; avventizio; comparsa. *agg.* supplementare; straordinario; superiore. *avv.* straordinariamente; eccessivamente.

extract (ĕks·trăkt') *n.* estratto. *vt.* estrarre. —**ion** *n.* estrazione: of foreign —, di origine straniera.

extraneous (ĕks-trā'nĕ-ŭs) *agg.* estraneo.

extraordinary (ĕks-trôr'dĭ-nĕr'ĭ) *agg.* straordinario.

extravagance (ĕks-trăv'â-găns) *n.* prodigalità.

extravagant (-gănt) *agg.* prodigo; dispendioso; esorbitante (*di prezzo*); eccessivo.

extreme (ĕks-trēm') *n.*, *agg.* estremo. —ly *avv.* estremamente.

extremity (ĕks-trĕm'ĭ-tĭ) *n.* estremità; estremo; punto estremo; eccesso; estremo pericolo; dolore; bisogno.

extremities (-tĭz) *n.pl.* (le) estremità; estremi rimedi.

extricate (ĕks'trĭ-kāt) *vt.* districare, liberare.

extrude (ĕks-trōōd') *vt.* espellere. *vi.* sporgere.

exuberance (ĕg-zū'bĕr-ăns) *n.* esuberanza.

exuberant (-ănt) *agg.* esuberante.

exude (ĕks-ūd') *vt.*, *vi.* sudare, trasudare.

exult (ĕg-zŭlt') *vi.* esultare. —ance *n.* esultanza. —ant *agg.* esultante.

eye (ī) *n.* occhio; sguardo; mira; cruna (*d'ago*); direzione (*del vento*): in the twinkling of an —, in un batter d'occhio; to catch one's —, colpire l'occhio, destare l'attenzione; to have good eyes, avere buona vista; to keep an — on, tenere d'occhio; to see — to —, essere assolutamente d'accordo; to cry one's eyes out, sciogliersi in lacrime. *vt.* osservare, sbirciare. —ball *n.* bulbo oculare. — bank, banca degli occhi. —brow *n.* sopracciglio. —glass *n.* lente; (*pl.*) occhiali. —let *n.* occhiello. —lashes *n.pl.* ciglia. —lid *n.* palpebra. —shade *n.* visiera. —sight *n.* vista. —sore *n.* bruttura. —tooth *n.* dente canino. —witness *n.* testimone oculare.

F

fable (fā'b'l) *n.* favola.

fabric (făb'rĭk) *n.* tessuto, stoffa; struttura; grana.

fabricate (făb'rĭ-kāt) *vt.* fabbricare; inventare, falsificare.

fabrication *n.* fabbricazione; menzogna, invenzione.

fabulous (făb'û-lŭs) *agg.* favoloso.

face (fās) *n.* faccia; superficie; apparenza, aspetto, smorfia; facciata; faccetta; quadrante (*d'orologio*): — value, valore nominale; in the — of, davanti a; to lose —, perdere prestigio. to have the — to, aver l'impudenza di; to make faces, fare smorfiacce; to put a good — on a bad business, fare buon viso a cattiva sorte; on the — of it, giudicando dalle apparenze. *vt.* affrontare, sfidare; rivestire; volgere il viso verso, essere esposto a: to — about, fare dietro-front; to — a street, dare su una strada.

facer (fās'ẽr) *n.* sgrugno, pugno sul viso; difficoltà imprevista.

facet (fās'ĕt) *n.* faccetta. *vt.* sfaccettare.

facial (fā'shăl) *agg.* facciale. [tare.

facilitate (fâ-sĭl'ĭ-tāt) *vt.* facilitare, agevolare.

facility (fâ-sĭl'ĭ-tĭ) *n.* facilità; destrezza; (*pl.*) agevolazioni; installazioni, attrezzatura.

fact (făkt) *n.* fatto: in —, as a matter of —, effettivamente; to be matter-of-fact, essere positivo *o* sbrigativo.

faction (făk'shŭn) *n.* fazione, intrigo politico.

factious (făk'shŭs) *agg.* fazioso.

factor (făk'tẽr) *n.* fattore, agente.

factory (făk'tô-rĭ) *n.* fabbrica, azienda.

factual (făk'tū-ăl) *agg.* effettivo, reale, concreto.

faculty (făk'ŭl-tĭ) *n.* facoltà.

fad (făd) *n.* mania.

fade (fād) *vt.* sbiadire; affievolire. *vi.* sbiadire; affievolirsi, svanire. — in *n.* (*cinema*) dissolvenza (*in apertura*).

fag (făg) *n.* lavoro pesante; (*gergo*) sigaretta. —ged *agg.* sfinito, esausto.

fail (fāl) *n.* fallo; mancanza; insuccesso: without —, senza fallo. *vt.*, *vi.* mancare, fallire; indebolirsi; deludere; abbandonare: to — in an examination, essere bocciato a un esame; to — a student, bocciare uno studente; to — to do something, non fare una cosa; don't — to come, non mancare (di venire). —ing *n.* difetto, debolezza, fallimento. *agg.* declinante. *prep.* in mancanza di.

failure (fāl'ûr) *n.* mancanza, difetto, omissione; fallimento, insuccesso, indebolimento, fiasco.

faint (fānt) *agg.* debole, lieve, vago; abbattuto, scoraggiato: — - hearted, timido, codardo. *vi.* affievolirsi; svenire: to — away, perdere i sensi. —ing *n.* svenimento, indebolimento. —ly *avv.* debolmente, vagamente. —ness *n.* debolezza, languore; malore.

fair (fâr) (1) *n.* fiera, mercato, esposizione.

fair (fâr) (2) *agg.* bello, gradevole; favorevole; sereno; biondo; giusto; equo, leale, legittimo: — **chance of success,** buona probabilità; — **complexion,** carnagione chiara; — **name,** reputazione immacolata; — **play,** comportamento leale; — **sex,** sesso gentile, sesso debole; — **weather,** bel tempo. *avv.* onestamente, lealmente, favorevolmente. — **dealing** n. lealtà. — **-haired** *agg.* biondo di capelli. —**ing** n. (aeron.) carenatura. —**ly** *avv.* abbastanza; discretamente; onestamente, giustamente. —**ness** n. onestà, equità, giustezza; bellezza; purezza; biondezza.

fairy (fâr′ĭ) n. fata. *agg.* fatato. —**land** n. regno delle fate. — **tale,** racconto di fate.

faith (fāth) n. fede, credenza, fiducia; fedeltà: **breach of** —, mancanza di parola; **to keep** —, mantenere la parola; **to be in bad (good)** —, essere in mala (buona) fede. —**ful** n., *agg.* fedele. —**fully** *avv.* fedelmente, devotamente: — **yours,** vostro devotissimo. —**fulness** n. fedeltà. —**less** *agg.* infedele, miscredente, sleale.

fake (fāk) n. contraffazione, falso. *agg.* falso. *vt.*, *vi.* falsificare; fingere, simulare.

falcon (fôl′kŭn) n. falcone.

fall (fôl) n. caduta; decadenza; fine; declivio; cascata (d'acqua); ribasso; abbassamento; autunno. *vi.* (pass. **fell,** pp. **fallen**) cadere; decadere; abbattersi; diminuire; accadere: **to** — **away,** deperire; staccarsi; **to** — **asleep,** addormentarsi; **to** — **back,** retrocedere; **to** — **behind,** restare indietro; **to** — **due,** scadere; **to** — **foul of,** venire in collisione con; **to** — **in love with,** innamorarsi di; **to** — **off,** staccarsi; diminuire; **to** — **out,** litigare; **to** — **short,** essere insufficiente; **to** — **through,** andare a monte; **to** — **to blows,** venire alle mani.

fallen (fôl′ĕn) pp. di **to fall.** *agg.* caduto, degradato, disonorato.

fallible (făl′ĭ·b′l) *agg.* fallibile.

falling (fôl′ĭng) n. caduta, diminuzione, scadenza: — **in,** infossamento, crollo; — **off,** caduta; defezione; apostasia. *agg.* cadente: — **sickness,** epilessia.

false (fôls) *agg.* falso, sleale, finto, simulato. *avv.* falsamente: **to play** —, ingannare, tradire. —**hood** n. falsità, menzogna. —**ness** n. falsità.

falsies (fôl′sĭz) *n.pl.* (gergo) seno finto.

falsify (fôl′sĭ·fĭ) *vt.* falsificare.

falsity (-tĭ) n. falsità.

faltboat (fôlt′bŏt) n. sandolino (smontabile di tela impermeabilizzata).

falter (fôl′tĕr) n. titubanza, esitazione. *vt.*, *vi.* esitare; incespicare, barcollare; balbettare.

fame (fām) n. fama, gloria, nomea.

famed (fāmd) *agg.* famoso, rinomato.

familiar (fá·mĭl′yẽr) n., *agg.* familiare: **to be** — **with a subject,** conoscere bene un argomento, intendersene. —**ity** n. familiarità.

family (făm′ĭ·lĭ) n. famiglia: **to be in the** — **way,** essere incinta. — **name,** cognome. — **tree,** albero genealogico.

famine (făm′ĭn) n. carestia.

famish (făm′ĭsh) *vt.* affamare. *vi.* soffrire la fame. —**ed** *agg.* affamato.

famous (fā′mŭs) *agg.* famoso, celebre.

fan (făn) (1) n. ventaglio, ventilatore; mantice, pala (di mulino a vento). *vt.* sventolare, ventilare; (fig.) stimolare. *vi.*: **to** — **out,** aprirsi a ventaglio.

fan (2) n. ammiratore, appassionato, tifoso.

fanatic (fá·năt′ĭk) n., *agg.* fanatico. —**al** *agg.* fanatico. —**ism** (-ĭ·sĭz′m) n. fanatismo.

fancier (făn′sĭ·ẽr) n. amatore, appassionato; allevatore o coltivatore.

fanciful (făn′sĭ·fŏŏl) *agg.* fantasioso, capriccioso, originale; immaginario.

fancy (făn′sĭ) n. fantasia, capriccio, passione, desiderio: **to have a** — **for,** essere invaghito di; **to take a** — **to,** incapricciarsi di, affezionarsi a. *agg.* di fantasia, originale: decorativo: — **dress,** costume (carnevalesco, ecc.); — **dress ball,** ballo in costume. *vt.* immaginare, pensare; prediligere: **to** — **oneself,** stimarsi molto; **just** — **the idea!** ma guarda un po' che idea!, ma te lo immagini? — **goods,** tessuti fantasia; — **work,** ricamo decorativo.

fang (făng) n. zanna; dente velenoso (dei rettili); radice (dei denti).

fantastic (făn·tăs′tĭk) *agg.* antastico, bizzarro.

fantasy (făn′tá·sĭ) n. fantasia.

far (fär) *agg.* lontano, remoto: — **cry,** grande distanza. *avv.* lontano, a distanza; molto, assai: **as** — **as,** fino a; **as** — **as I know,** quanto ne so io; **by** —, di gran lunga; **how** —? sin dove? **so** —, sin qui; — **and wide,** da tutte le parti; — **better,** molto meglio; — **between,** a lunghi intervalli; — **off,** in lontananza;

thus —, sin qui. —away, agg. lontano, remoto; vacuo, assente. —
fetched agg. remoto, improbabile,
inverosimile, fittizio; —seeing, —
sighted agg. lungimirante, presbite.
farce (färs) n. farsa.
farcical (fär'sĭ-kăl) agg. burlesco.
fare (fâr) n. prezzo (di posto, viaggio,
ecc.), corsa (in tassì, ecc.), passeggero; cibo, nutrimento; bill of —,
lista delle vivande; car—, n. (costo
del) biglietto tranviario. vi. barcamenarsi, campare: to — badly, andar
male, essere in cattive condizioni;
to — well, andar bene, prosperare.
farewell (fâr'wĕl') n. addio, commiato. agg. d'addio. inter. addio!
farm (färm) n. fattoria. agg. agricolo.
vt. coltivare. vi. fare l'agricoltore.
—er n. agricoltore, fattore. —ing
n. agricoltura. —stead n. fattoria.
—yard n. aia.
farrow (fär'ō) vt., vi. figliare.
farther (fär'thĕr) agg. ulteriore, successivo, più lontano, estremo. avv.
oltre, inoltre, maggiormente, più
lontano, più a lungo.
farthest (fär'thĕst) agg. estremo, (il) più
lontano. avv. alla maggior distanza.
fascinate (făs'ĭ-nāt) vt. affascinare.
fascinating agg. affascinante, incantevole.
fascination (-nä'shŭn) n. fascino, attrazione.
fashion (făsh'ŭn) n. moda, foggia, stile,
maniera; consuetudine: — plate,
figurino; the latest —, l'ultima
moda; after a—, in qualche modo, alla
meglio; to come into —, diventare
di moda. vt. foggiare, adattare, modellare.—able agg. elegante, di moda.
fast (fäst) (1) n. digiuno. vi. digiunare.
fast (fäst) (2) agg. saldo, sicuro, fedele, costante; profondo (del sonno); solido (di colore); rapido; in
anticipo (di orologio); (fam.) dissoluto: — friend, amico fedele; to
make —, fissare, chiudere bene;
(naut.) ormeggiare. avv. saldamente,
fermamente; rapidamente: to hold
—, tener duro; to sleep —, dormire
profondamente.
fasten (fäs'n) vt. attaccare, fissare, assicurare; chiudere. vi. attaccarsi,
fissarsi. —er n. fibbia, fermaglio:
zip —, cerniera lampo.
fastidious (făs-tĭd'ĭ-ŭs) agg. schizzinoso, difficile (di gusti).
fat (făt) n. grasso. agg. grasso, pingue;
untuoso; ricco, fertile. vt., vi. ingrassare.
fatal (fā'tăl) agg. fatale, funesto,
mortale. —ity (fả-tăl'ĭ-tĭ) n. fatalità.
—ly avv. fatalmente.

fate (fāt) n. fato, sorte: The Fates, le
Parche.
fateful (fāt'fōōl) agg. fatale, decisivo.
father (fä'thĕr) n. padre: father-in-
law, suocero. vt. procreare; adottare, assumere la paternità di o la
responsabilità di. —hood n. paternità. —land n. patria. —ly agg.
paterno. avv. paternamente.
fathom (făth'ŭm) n. unità di lunghezza (circa m. 1,83). vt. sondare,
scandagliare.
fatigue (fả-tēg') n. stanchezza, fatica;
(mil.) corvè; tenuta da fatica; vt.
stancare, affaticare.
fatiguing (-tē'gĭng) agg. faticoso.
fatness (făt'nĕs) n. pinguedine; un-
tuosità; ricchezza, fertilità.
fatten (făt'n) vt. ingrassare, impinguare. vi. ingrassarsi, arricchirsi.
fatty (făt'ĭ) agg. grasso, untuoso.
fatuous (făt'ū-ŭs) agg. fatuo, sciocco.
faucet (fô'sĕt) n. rubinetto.
fault (fôlt) n. colpa, difetto, pecca:
to a —, eccessivamente, fin troppo;
to be at —, essere in colpa. to find
— with, trovar a ridire su. —finder
n. pignuolo, criticone. —less agg.
perfetto, innocente, impeccabile.
faulty (fôl'tĭ) agg. difettoso; colpevole,
biasimevole.
favor (fā'vĕr) n. favore; propensione;
lettera: to be in —, essere
nelle buone grazie di; to find —
with, trovar favore presso; I received your —, ricevetti la vostra
stimata lettera. vt. favorire, essere
favorevole a; assomigliare a. —able
agg. favorevole. —ed agg. favorito:
ill-favored, brutto (di persona).
—ite n., agg. preferito, favorito.
—itism n. favoritismo.
fawn (fôn) n. cerbiatto, capriolo.
agg. marrone-chiaro, giallastro.
fawn (2) n. adulazione, inchino servile. vi. far riverenze; far le feste
(di animali): to — upon, adulare.
fawning n. adulazione, servilismo.
agg. servile.
FBI (ĕf'bē'ī') n. Ufficio Federale Investigativo.
fear (fēr) n. paura, timore. vt. temere.
vi. aver paura: never fear! state
tranquillo! —ful agg. timoroso;
terribile. —less agg. intrepido.
—lessness n. intrepidezza. —some
agg. spaventoso.
feasible (fē'zĭ-b'l) agg. fattibile, probabile.
feast (fēst) n. festa, festino. vt. festeggiare. vi. far festa; banchettare;
bearsi.
feat (fēt) n. prodezza, impresa.

feather (fĕth'ẽr) *n.* piuma, penna, pennacchio: this is a — in his cap, questo va a onor suo; birds of a —, gente della stessa risma. *vt.* ornare o imbottire di piume; filare (*i remi*). *vi.* metter piume. **—less** *agg.* implume. **—y** *agg.* piumato, piumoso, leggerissimo.

feature (fē'tụr) *n.* lineamento; caratteristica; fisionomia, viso; manifestazione; (*S.U.*) film principale (*nel programma*); servizio, articolo speciale (*in giornali, ecc.*). *vt.* caratterizzare, delineare, mettere in risalto; (*fam.*) assomigliare a.

February (fĕb'rŏŏ·ĕr'ĭ) *n.* febbraio.

fecund (fē'kŭnd) *agg.* fecondo.

fed (fĕd) *pass.*, *pp. di* to feed: to be — up with, essere sazio o stufo di; (*fig.*) averne fin sopra i capelli.

federal (fĕd'ẽr·ăl) *n.* federalista; unionista. *agg.* federale.

federation (fĕd'ẽr·ā'shŭn) *n.* federazione.

fee (fē) *n.* onorario; ricompensa; proprietà ereditaria: admission —, prezzo d'entrata, quota, tassa d'iscrizione.

feeble (fē'bl) *agg.* debole, flebile. **—ness** *n.* debolezza.

feebly (-blĭ) *avv.* debolmente.

feed (fēd) *n.* nutrimento, alimentazione, rifornimento. *vt.* (*pass.*, *pp. fed*) nutrire, alimentare, rifornire; pascolare. *vi.* nutrirsi, cibarsi: to — upon, nutrirsi di. **—er** *n.* alimentatore; (*ferr.*) tronco secondario.

feel (fēl) *n.* tatto, sensazione tattile this cloth has a nice —, questo tessuto è gradevole al tatto. *vt.* (*pass.*, *pp. felt*) sentire, tastare; ritenere; sondare. *vi.* sentirsi, frugare; avere una convinzione (*seg. da* for, with) provar simpatia *o* compassione per: to — better, sentirsi meglio; to — one's way, procedere a tastoni; it feels soft, è morbido al tatto; it feels hot in here, fa caldo qua dentro. to — strongly on a subject, avere decise opinioni su un argomento. **—er** *n.* antenna (*di insetto*); tentacolo (*di mollusco*); sondaggio; approccio. **—ing** *n.* sensazione, sentimento, sensibilità: ill —, malanimo, rancore.

feet (fēt) *pl. di* foot.

feign (fān) *vt.*, *vi.* fingere, simulare.

felicitate (fē·lĭs'ĭ·tāt) *vt.* complimentare, congratularsi con.

felicitous (fē·lĭs'ĭ·tŭs) *agg.* acconcio, felice, opportuno.

felicity (fē·lĭs'ĭ·tĭ) *n.* felicità.

fell (fĕl) (1) *agg.* crudele, brutale. *vt.* abbattere, stroncare.

fell (fĕl) (2) *pass. di* to fall.

feller (fĕl'ẽr) *n.* boscaiolo; (*gergo*) vedi fellow.

fellow (fĕl'ō) *n.* compagno, collega; membro, socio; docente; ragazzo, tipo, individuo, tizio: a good —, un buon diavolo; poor —! poveraccio! *agg.* accompagnato, affine, analogo: — citizen, concittadino; — countryman, compatriota; — creature, simile (*il nostro simile*); — member, consocio; — student, condiscepolo; — sufferer, compagno di sventura; — traveler, compagno di viaggio; (*pol.*) simpatizzante (*spec. per il Comunismo*).

fellowship (fĕl'ō·shĭp) *n.* associazione; solidarietà; borsa di studio; (*univ.*) docenza.

felon (fĕl'ŭn) *n.* colpevole, criminale; (*med.*) patereccio.

felony (fĕl'ō·nĭ) *n.* reato grave, delitto.

felt (fĕlt) (1) *n.* feltro. *vt.* feltrare.

felt (fĕlt) (2) *pass.*, *pp. di* to feel.

female (fē'māl) *n.*, *agg.* femmina.

feminine (fĕm'ĭ·nĭn) *agg.* femminile.

femur (fē'mẽr) *n.* femore.

fence (fĕns) *n.* recinto, palizzata, barriera, scherma; (*fam.*) ricettatore: to be on the —, essere indeciso, non impegnarsi. *vt.* cintare, proteggere. *vi.* tirar di scherma.

fencing (fĕn'sĭng) *n.* recinto; scherma.

fend (fĕnd) *vt.* parare, schivare. *vi.* resistere: to — for oneself, ingegnarsi. **—er** *n.* parafuoco; paraurti.

fennel (fĕn'ĕl) *n.* finocchio.

ferment (fûr'mĕnt) *n.* fermento. *vi.* fermentare. **—ation** *n.* fermentazione.

fern (fûrn) *n.* felce.

ferocious (fē·rō'shŭs) *agg.* feroce. **—ness** *n.* ferocia.

ferocity (fē·rŏs'ĭ·tĭ) *n.* ferocia.

ferret (fĕr'ĕt) *n.* (*geol.*) furetto, puzzola. *vt.* stanare: to — out, snidare, scoprire.

ferroconcrete (fĕr'ō·kŏn'krēt) *n.* cemento armato.

ferrous (fĕr'ŭs) *agg.* ferroso, di ferro.

ferry (fĕr'ĭ) *vt.*, *vi.* traghettare. **—boat** *n.* nave-traghetto. **—man** *n.* traghettatore.

fertile (fûr'tĭl) *agg.* fertile, fecondo.

fertility (fẽr·tĭl'ĭ·tĭ) *n.* fertilità.

fertilize (fûr'tĭlĭz) *vt.* fertilizzare.

fertilizer (-lĭz'ẽr) *n.* fertilizzante, concime.

fervency (fûr'vĕn·sĭ) *n.* fervore.

fervent (fûr'vĕnt) *agg.* fervente. **—ly** *avv.* con fervore.

fervid (fûr'vĭd) *agg.* fervido, ardente.

fervor (fûr'vẽr) *n.* fervore, ardore.

fester (fĕs'tĕr) n. suppurazione, ulcera. vi. suppurare, marcire.

festival (fĕs'tĭ-vɑl) n. festa, festival. agg. festivo.

festive (fĕs'tĭv) agg. festivo, festoso.

festivity (fĕs-tĭv'ĭ-tĭ) n. festa, allegria.

fetch (fĕch) vt., vi. cercare; andare a prendere, andare a chiamare; assestare (un pugno, ecc.); cattivare; raggiungere, ottenere. —ing agg. attraente, piacevole.

fete (fāt) n. festa. vt. festeggiare.

fetish (fĕt'ĭsh) n. feticcio.

fetter (fĕt'ĕr) n. pastoia. vt. impastoiare, ostacolare.

feud (fūd) n. contesa; inimicizia; feudo: old —, vecchia ruggine. —al agg. feudale.

fever (fē'vĕr) n. febbre. —ish agg. febbrile, febbricitante. —ishly avv. febbrilmente. —ishness n. stato febbrile.

few (fū) n., agg. pochi: a —, alcuni, qualche; a good —, un discreto numero; not a —, non pochi. —er agg. in minor numero.

fiancé (fē'än-sā') n. fidanzato.

fiancée (fē'än-sā) n. fidanzata.

fib (fĭb) n. frottola. vi. mentire. —ber n. mentitore.

fiber (fī'bĕr) n. fibra.

fibrous (-brŭs) agg. fibroso.

fickle (fĭk'ʼl) agg. volubile, incerto, mobile.

fiction (fĭk'shŭn) n. finzione, invenzione; narrativa. —al agg. narrativo, immaginario.

fictitious (fĭk-tĭsh'ŭs) agg. fittizio, immaginario.

fiddle (fĭd'ʼl) n. violino: to play second — to, essere in sottordine a. vi. sonare il violino: to — around (gergo), gingillarsi.

fiddler (fĭd'lĕr) n. violinista.

fidelity (fĭ-dĕl'ĭ-tĭ) n. fedeltà.

fidget (fĭj'ĕt) vi. agitarsi, preoccuparsi, essere irrequieto.

fidgety (-tĭ) agg. inquieto, irrequieto.

field (fēld) n. campo; (min.) giacimento; gruppo (dei cavalli partecipanti a una corsa): to take the —, entrare in azione; — artillery, artiglieria da campagna; — glass, binocolo.

fiend (fēnd) n. demonio. —ish agg. demoniaco, perfido.

fierce (fērs) agg. accanito, feroce; ardente. —ness n. violenza; ardore.

fiery (fī'rĭ) agg. infiammato, ardente, focoso, infocato.

fifteen (fĭf'tēn') n., agg. quindici. —th n., agg. quindicesimo, (il) quindici (del mese).

fifth (fĭfth) n., agg. quinto; (il) cinque (del mese).

fifty (fĭf'tĭ) n., agg. cinquanta.

fig (fĭg) n. fico. —tree n. (albero di) fico.

fight (fĭt) n. battaglia, lotta, zuffa; combattività, forza, aggressività: to show —, reagire. vt., vi. (pass., pp. fought) avversare, combattere, lottare: to — it out, lottare sino in fondo, liquidare una disputa; to — one's way through, aprirsi un varco.

fighter (fĭt'ĕr) n. combattente, lottatore; (aeron.) caccia: prize —, pugile, campione di pugilato.

fighting (-ĭng) n. combattimento, lotta. agg. combattivo, combattente; da combattimento.

figment (fĭg'mĕnt) n. finzione; invenzione.

figurative (fĭg'ūr-á-tĭv) agg. figurato, metaforico, simbolico.

figure (fĭg'ūr) n. figura; volto; disegno; cifra; numero: — of speech, modo di dire; to be good at figures, essere forte in aritmetica, saper fare i conti bene; to cut a poor —, fare una magra figura. vt. figurare, raffigurare, immaginare. vi. calcolare; figurare, pensare, ritenere: to — on, far conto su, fidarsi di, avere intenzione di; to — out, decifrare, risolvere, capire.

filament (fĭl'á-mĕnt) n. filamento.

filch (fĭlch) vt. rubare, rubacchiare.

file (fĭl) (1) n. lima. vt. limare.

file (fĭl) (2) n. incartamento, schedario, raccolta; schieramento; fila, coda: — card, scheda; single —, fila indiana. vt. schedare, passare agli atti, presentare (un'istanza). vi. sfilare: (pol.) porre la propria candidatura.

filial (fĭl'ĭ-ɑl) agg. filiale.

filigree (fĭl'ĭ-grē) n. filigrana.

fill (fĭl) n. sufficienza, sazietà; riempitivo, carica. vt. riempire; gonfiare; rifornire, saziare; ricoprire (una carica); assolvere (un compito); otturare (un dente): to — up, completare. vi. riempirsi, gonfiarsi.

fillet (fĭl'ĕt) n. nastro per capelli, fregio; (cucina) filetto.

filling (fĭl'ĭng) n. riempimento; otturazione (di dente).

filly (fĭl'ĭ) n. puledra.

film (fĭlm) n. velatura; pellicola, velo, patina. vt. velare, coprire con pellicola; (cinema) filmare. vi. velarsi. — strip, proiezione, film illustrativo (per conferenze, ecc.).

filter (fĭl'tĕr) n. filtro. vt. filtrare.

filth (fĭlth) n. sudiciume. —iness n. sporcizia.

filthy (fĭl′thĭ) *agg.* sudicio, immondo.

fin (fĭn) *n.* pinna; (*gergo*) cinque dollari.

final (fī′nắl) *agg.* finale, ultimo, definitivo, decisivo. —ly *avv.* infine, finalmente, definitivamente.

finance (fĭ-năns′) *n.* finanza.

financial (fĭ-năn′shắl) *agg.* finanziario.

financier (fĭn-ắn-sḗr′) *n.* finanziere.

financing *n.* finanziamento.

finch (fĭnch) *n.* fringuello.

find (fīnd) *n.* scoperta, ritrovamento. *vt.* (*pass.*, *pp.* found) trovare, scoprire; ritenere, giudicare: to — out, scoprire, smascherare; to — fault with, trovar a ridire su. —er *n.* scopritore; (*fot.*) mirino. —ing *n.* scoperta, constatazione, sentenza; (*pl.*) utensili da artigiano.

fine (fīn) (1) *n.* multa, ammenda. *vt.* multare.

fine (fīn) (2) *agg.* bello; fine; delicato; lieve; bravo; perfetto, eccelente: a — boy, un bravo ragazzo, un ottimo figliolo; to have a — time, divertirsi; — arts, belle arti. *avv.* bene: to feel —, sentirsi bene o benone. —ly *avv.* finemente. —ness *n.* finezza. —ry (fīn′ẽr-ĭ) *n.* ornamenti, vestiario appariscente.

finesse (fĭ-nĕs′) *n.* finezza, sottigliezza, astuzia, stratagemma.

finger (fĭng′gẽr) *n.* dito: middle —, medio; ring —, anulare; little —; mignolo. *vt.* maneggiare, tastare. —board *n.* tastiera, manico (*di violino*). —nail *n.* unghia. —print *n.* impronta digitale.

finical (fĭn′ĭ-kắl) finicky (-kĭ) *agg.* minuzioso; affettato; pedante.

finish (fĭn′ĭsh) *n.* fine, conclusione; rifinitura, ornamento; educazione. *vt.* rifinire, terminare. *vi.* finire, aver termine. —ed *agg.* finito, rifinito.

fink (fĭngk) *n.* (*gergo*) spia; crumiro.

fir (fûr) *n.* abete.

fire (fīr) *n.* fuoco; incendio; ardore: to be on —, essere in fiamme; to set on —, incendiare. *vt.* bruciare, incendiare; sparare, far scoppiare; (*fam.*) licenziare. *vi.* incendiarsi; infiammarsi; far fuoco. —arms *n.pl.* armi da fuoco. — block, (*mil.*), sbarramento di fuoco. —brand *n.* tizzone. — department, corpo dei pompieri. — engine, pompa da incendio, carro dei pompieri; — escape, scala di sicurezza. —fly *n.* lucciola. — insurance, assicurazione incendi. —man *n.* pompiere, fochista. —place *n.* camino. —proof *agg.* incombustibile. —side *n.* focolare, focolare

domestico. —wood *n.* legna da ardere. —works *n.pl.* fuochi d'artificio.

firing (fīr′ĭng) *n.* accensione, sparatoria: — party, — squad, plotone d'esecuzione.

firm (fûrm) *n.* ditta, azienda. *agg.* saldo, fermo, forte, risoluto. *avv.* fermamente; risolutamente. —ly *avv.* fermamente; solidamente. —ness *n.* fermezza; solidità.

firmament (fûr′má-mĕnt) *n.* firmamento.

first (fûrst) *n.*, *agg.* primo: the very —, il primissimo. *avv.* prima, da principio, per primo, in primo luogo: at —, sulle prime; — and last, dal principio alla fine: —class *agg.* di prima classe. —rate *agg.* di prima categoria, di prim'ordine. —hand *agg.*, *avv.* di prima mano.

fisc (fĭsk) *n.* fisco. —al *agg.* fiscale.

fish (fĭsh) *n.* pesce: a queer —, un tipo ambiguo; neither — nor fowl, nè carne nè pesce: — story, storia incredibile. *vt.*, *vi.* pescare, frugare. —bone *n.* lisca di pesce. —hook *n.* amo. —monger *n.* pescivendolo. —er, —erman *n.* pescatore. —ery *n.* pesca, luogo pescoso. —ing *n.* pesca: — rod, canna da pesca; to go —, andare a pesca.

fishy (fĭsh′ĭ) *agg.* pescoso; ambiguo, losco; non convincente.

fission (fĭsh′un) *n.* fissione nucleare. —able *agg.* fissile.

fissure (fĭsh′ẽr) *n.* fessura, crepa.

fist (fĭst) *n.* pugno.

fit (fĭt) (1) *n.* accesso, attacco, crisi; capriccio: by fits and starts, saltuariamente, irregolarmente.

fit (fĭt) (2) *n.* l'adattarsi (*bene o male*): this coat is a good —, questa giacca sta a pennello. *agg.* adatto, conveniente, sano, in forma, idoneo: — to be tied, infuriato; to think —, ritenere opportuno. *vt.* adattare, rendere idoneo, calzare: to — out, equipaggiare. *vi.* convenire, adattarsi; attagliarsi, stare a pennello: to — in with, coincidere, concordare.

fitful (fĭt′fŏŏl) *agg.* saltuario, irregolare; capriccioso; intermittente.

fitness *n.* convenienza, idoneità, opportunità; (*sport, ecc.*) forma.

fitting (fĭt′ĭng) *n.* aggiustatura, adattamento, montaggio; prova (*di un vestito*); (*pl.*) arredamento; accessori. *agg.* conveniente, appropriato, opportuno.

five (fīv) *n.*, *agg.* cinque.

fiver (-ẽr) *n.* (*fam.*) banconota da cinque dollari.

fix (fĭks) *n.* difficoltà, imbarazzo; imbroglio, truffa: **in a bad —**, nei guai. *vt.* fissare, assicurare, sistemare, aggiustare, riparare. **—ed** *agg.* fisso, permanente, costante. **—ture** (fĭks'tŭr) *n.* infisso; persona (*o cosa*) installata stabilmente: **electric light fixtures**, impianto elettrico.

flabbiness (flăb'ĭ-nĕs) *n.* flaccidezza.

flabby (flăb'ĭ) *agg.* flaccido.

flag (flăg) (1) *n.* bandiera; bandiera ammiraglia: **— of truce**, bandiera bianca. *vt., vi.* imbandierare, pavesare; segnalare con bandierine. **— officer**, ammiraglio. **—ship** *n.* nave ammiraglia. **—staff** *n.* asta di bandiera. **—stone** *n.* lastra di pietra per pavimentazione.

flag (flăg) (2) *vi.* afflosciarsi, penzolare, indebolirsi, languire; rallentare.

flagellate (flăj'ě-lăt) *vt.* flagellare.

flagrant (flā'grănt) *agg.* flagrante, clamoroso.

flair (flâr) *n.* fiuto; istinto; acume; attitudine.

flak (flăk) *n.* artiglieria contraerea.

flake (flāk) *n.* fiocco, scaglia, falda: **corn flakes**, fiocchi di granturco. *vt.* sfioccare. *vi.* sfioccarsi.

flaky *agg.* fioccoso, sfaldato.

flamboyant (flăm-boi'ănt) *agg.* fiammeggiante; risplendente; appariscente, vistoso.

flame (flăm) *n.* fiamma, fuoco. *vi.* fiammeggiare, infiammarsi: **to — up** (*opp.* **out**), dare in escandescenze.

flaming (flăm'ĭng) *agg.* fiammeggiante, ardente: **— red**, rosso acceso, rosso fiamma.

flange (flănj) *n.* orlo, bordo, flangia.

flank (flăngk) *n.* fianco, lato. *vt.* fiancheggiare.

flannel (flăn'ĕl) *n.* flanella.

flap (flăp) *n.* colpo, battito; lembo, patta (*della tasca*); (*aeron.*) ipersostentatore; subbuglio, panico. *vt.* colpire, battere. *vi.* sbattere, penzolare.

flare (flâr) *n.* bagliore, fiammata; accesso (*di collera*); rifrazione; ampiezza, svasatura. *vt.* esibire, ostentare. *vi.* divampare; essere svasato, allargarsi: **to — up**, **to — out**, dare in escandescenze.

flaring (-ĭng) *agg.* fiammeggiante, accecante; svasato.

flash (flăsh) *n.* splendore, vampata, lampo; ostentazione: **— of hope**, raggio di speranza; **— of lightning**, lampo, saetta; **— of wit**, tratto di spirito; **in a —**, in un baleno. *vt.* trasmettere con segnalazioni lu-

minose, far lampeggiare; far esplodere; mostrare con ostentazione. *vi.* splendere, avvampare, balenare: **to — by**, passare come un lampo. **— bulb**, (*fot.*) lampada per fotolampo. **— gun**, (*fot.*) sincronizzatore del fotolampo. **—ing** *n.* vampata, splendore. *agg.* splendente. **—light** *n.* lampadina tascabile; (*fot.*) fotolampo.

flashy (flăsh'ĭ) *agg.* sgargiante, vistoso.

flask (flăsk) *n.* fiasco; borraccia.

flat (flăt) *n.* spianata, superficie piana: palmo (*della mano*); appartamento *agg.* piatto, piano; sgonfio; appiattito; pari disteso; uniforme; che ha perso l'effervescenza, insipido abbattuto; reciso, esplicito; (*mus.*) bemolle stonato: **— denial**, secco rifiuto con un bel no; **— rate**, cifra tonda; **to be — broke**, essere completamente al verde; **to fall —**, cadere disteso (*fig., di discorsi, ecc.*) cadere nel vuoto. **—foot** *n.* piede piatto (*gergo*) poliziotto. **—iron** *n.* ferro da stiro. **—ly** *avv.* fred da mente, recisamente perentoriamente. **—ness** *n.* uniformità, monotonia, banalità. **—top** *n.* portaerei.

flatten (flăt'n) *vt.* appiattire. *vi.* appiattirsi.

flatter (flăt'ĕr) *vt.* lusingare, adulare. **—er** *n.* adulatore. **—ing** *agg.* lusinghiero.

flattery (flăt'ĕr-ĭ) *n.* adulazione.

flaunt (flônt) *n.* ostentazione. *vt.* esibire, ostentare.

flavor (flā'vẽr) *n.* aroma, sapore, fragranza. *vt.* aromatizzare, profumare. **—less** *agg.* senza aroma.

flaw (flô) *n.* difetto pecca, fenditura. **—less** *agg.* perfetto, impeccabile.

flax (flăks) *n.* lino. **—en** *agg.* di lino; biondo-chiaro.

flay (flā) *vt.* scorticare.

flea (flē) *n.* pulce: **a — in one's ear**, un rabbuffo, un'umiliazione.

fled (flĕd) *pass., pp.* di **to flee**.

flee (flē) *vt* (*pass., pp.* **fled**) evitare, schivare. *vi.* fuggire.

fleece (flēs) *n.* vello. *vt.* tosare; defraudare, spogliare.

fleet (flēt) *n.* flotta; (*Ingl.*) braccio di mare, baia *agg.* rapido, lesto, agile. **—ing** *agg.* fuggevole.

Flemish (flĕm'ĭsh) *agg.* fiammingo.

flesh (flĕsh) *n.* carne, polpa (*di frutto*); **in the —**, in carne ed ossa; **— color**, incarnato. **—iness** *n.* carnosità; pinguedine. **—less** *agg.* scarno.

fleshy (flĕsh'ĭ) *agg.* carnoso, pingue.

flew (flōō) *pass.* di **to fly**.

flexibility (flĕk'sĭ-bĭl'ĭ-tĭ) *n.* flessibilità; duttilità.

flexible (flĕk'sĭ·b'l) agg. flessibile.
flicker (flĭk'ĕr) n. bagliore, barlume; tremolio, guizzo; vibrazione, battito. vt. far vacillare. vi. vacillare, vibrare, ondeggiare, svolazzare, guizzare. —ing n. tremolio. agg. tremolante, vacillante, svolazzante, guizzante.
flier (flī'ĕr) n. volatore, aviatore; (S.U.) volantino; veicolo veloce.
flight (flīt) n. fuga, volo; stormo (di uccelli); squadriglia. (di aerei); sciame (d'insetti); rampa (di scale): to put to —, mettere in fuga; to take —, prender la fuga.
flighty (flīt'ī) agg. leggero, volubile.
flimflam (flĭm'flăm') n. mistificazione, truffa. vt. imbrogliare, truffare.
flimsiness (-nĕs) n. leggerezza, inconsistenza, trasparenza, frivolezza.
flimsy (flĭm'zĭ) agg. sottile; trasparente; tenue, lieve; inconsistente, frivolo: — excuse, scusa magra. n. velina, copia in carta velina.
flinch (flĭnch) vi. ritrarsi, sottrarsi; rattrappirsi, contrarsi (per il dolore): without flinching, senza battere ciglio.
fling (flĭng) n. lancio, frecciata; tentativo: to have a — at, provare, tentare. vt. (pass., pp. flung) lanciare, spargere: to — away, respingere, buttar via; to — down, gettare in terra, abbattere; to — open, spalancare; to — shut, chiudere sbattendo; to — out, buttar fuori. vi. precipitarsi; dibattersi; imbizzarrirsi (di cavalli).
flint (flĭnt) n. selce, pietra focaia; pietrina (di accendisigari).
flip (flĭp) n. colpetto, buffetto, schiocco; sorta di zabaione. agg. impertinente. vt. spingere a ditate, dare un buffetto. vi. muoversi a scatti. —per n. pinna, natatoia.
flippancy (flĭp'ăn·sĭ) n. impertinenza, leggerezza.
flippant (flĭp'ănt) agg. impertinente, leggiero.
flirt (flûrt) n. civetta (donna); moto brusco. vt. sventolare; lanciare bruscamente. vi. civettare, "flirtare." —ation n. civetteria, amoretto.
flit (flĭt) n. fuggire; svolazzare, volteggiare, volar via.
float (flōt) n. guizzo. vt. galleggiante, salvagente. vt. far galleggiare, disincagliare; inondare, irrigare; varare. vi. fluttuare, galleggiare. —plane n. idrovolante.
flock (flŏk) n. gregge, branco; stormo (di uccelli); fiocco: — of people,

sciame di gente. vi. riunirsi o affluire in gruppo; sciamare.
floe (flō) n. banchisa.
flog (flŏg) vt. frustare, fustigare. —ging n. fustigazione.
flood (flŭd) n. diluvio, inondazione, alta marea. vt. inondare, sommergere: —tide n. alta marea.
floodgate (flŭd'gāt') n. chiusa.
flooding (flŭd'ĭng) n. inondazione; emorragia.
floodlight (flŭd'lĭt') n. riflettore, proiettore.
floor (flōr) n. pavimento; piano (di casa); tribuna (in Parlamento); limite minimo (di prezzi, ecc.): — show, numero di varietà (in un locale notturno); to have the —, aver la parola. vt. pavimentare; atterrare; ridurre al silenzio.
flop (flŏp) n. tonfo, caduta, insuccesso. vt. scaraventare. vi. stramazzare; sventolare; far fiasco.
florin (flŏr'ĭn) n. fiorino.
florist (flō'rĭst) n. fioraio, floricultore.
floss (flŏs) n. bavella; lanugine.
flounce (flouns) n. volante (di gonna).
flounder (floun'dĕr) vt. dibattersi; impappinarsi.
flour (flour) n. farina.
flourish (flûr'ĭsh) n. ostentazione; infiorazione; svolazzo (di scrittura); mulinello (col bastone, ecc.). vt. infiorare, fiorire; roteare (un bastone, ecc.), brandire. vi. fiorire, prosperare; fare svolazzi. —ing agg. fiorente.
floury (flour'ī) agg. farinoso.
flow (flō) n. flusso, corrente; facilità di parola. vi. scorrere; essere fluente; sgorgare, affluire.
flower (flou'ĕr) n. fiore. vt. infiorare. vi. fiorire: — bed, aiuola.
flowery (flou'ĕr·ĭ) agg. fiorito.
flowing (flō'ĭng) agg. fluente, scorrente, sciolto (di eloquio).
flown (flōn) pp. di to fly.
flu (flōō) n. influenza.
fluctuate (flŭk'tū̇·āt) vi. fluttuare.
fluctuation (-ā'shŭn) n. fluttuazione.
flue (flōō) n. gola (del camino).
fluency (flōō'ĕn·sĭ) n. facilità di parola.
fluent (flōō'ĕnt) agg. fluente, facile di parola. —ly avv. correntemente, speditamente.
fluff (flŭf) n. peluria, lanugine; (teat.) papera, stecca. vi. deventare lanuginoso; (teat.) impaperarsi, steccare.
fluffy (flŭf'ī) agg. lanuginoso; vaporoso.
fluid (flōō'ĭd) n., agg. fluido.
fluke (flōōk) n. marra (dell'ancora); (ittiol.) passera; (fam.) colpo di fortuna.

flung (flŭng) *pass.*, *pp. di* to fling.

flunk (flŭngk) *vi.* far fiasco. *vt.* espellere: to — out, abbandonare gli studi; ritirarsi.

flunky (flŭngk'ĭ) *n.* lacchè.

fluorescent (floŏ'ŏ·rĕs'ĕnt) *agg.* fluorescente. *n.* lampada fluorescente.

flush (flŭsh) *n.* rossore; impeto, vigore; (*poker*) colore; **straight** o **royal** —, scala reale. *agg.* pari, livellato; prosperoso, abbondante; imporporato; vigoroso: — **with**, allo stesso livello di, a fior di. *vt.* pareggiare, livellare; arrossare; risciacquare, innaffiare. *vi.* arrossire; crescer di livello; affluire; volar via.

fluster (flŭs'tĕr) *vt.* sconcertare.

flute (floŏt) *n.* flauto; scanalatura. *vt.* scanalare.

flutter (flŭt'ĕr) *n.* tremito, battito (*di ala*), agitazione, orgasmo; speculazione: **in a** —, in orgasmo. *vt.* agitare. *vi.* svolazzare, sbattere le ali, agitarsi, vibrare.

flux (flŭks) *n.* flusso; dissenteria.

fly (flī) (1) *n.* (*pl.* flies) mosca.

fly (flī) (2) *n.* volo; traiettoria; finta (*per nascondere i bottoni*); (*tip.*) levafoglio. *vt.* (*pass.* flew, *pp.* flown) sfuggire, evitare; far volare. *vi.* volare; scappare, slanciarsi: to — **asunder**, rompersi, scoppiare; to — **at**, lanciarsi su; to — **away**, scappare, volarsene via; to — **off the handle**, perdere le staffe. to — **into a passion**, andare in collera.

flyer *vedi* flier.

flying *agg.* volante: — **colors**, bandiere spiegate; — **ground**, aerodromo; — **bomb**, bomba volante, missile; — **saucer**, disco volante; — **wing** (*aeron.*), ala volante, tutt'ala.

flyleaf *n.* guardia (*foglio bianco al principio e alla fine di un libro*).

foal (fōl) *n.* puledro.

foam (fōm) *n.* schiuma. *vi.* spumeggiare, schiumare: — **rubber**, gommapiuma.

focal (fō'kăl) *agg.* focale.

focus (fō'kŭs) *n.* fuoco (*della lente*). *vt.* mettere a fuoco. —**ing** *n.* messa a fuoco.

fodder (fŏd'ĕr) *n.* foraggio. [fuoco.

foe (fō) *n.* nemico, avversario.

foetus (fē'tŭs) *n.* feto, embrione.

fog (fŏg) *n.* nebbia; confusione, oscurità. *vt.* annebbiare, offuscare, confondere. *vi.* annebbiarsi, confondersi: —**horn** *n.* sirena (acustica).

foggy (fŏg'ĭ) *agg.* nebbioso, oscuro.

fogy (fō'gĭ) *n.* barbogio, persona retrograda.

foil (foil) *n.* lamina metallica, amalgama (*degli specchi*); sconfitta,

scacco; risalto; (*scherma*) fioretto. *vt.* frustrare.

fold (fōld) (1) *n.* piega, ripiegatura. *vt.* piegare, avvolgere, stringere, abbracciare: to — **one's arms**, incrociare le braccia. *vi.* piegarsi; fallire, chiudere i battenti.

fold (fōld) (2) *n.* ovile, recinto.

-fold (3) *suff.*: **tenfold**, dieci volte, dieci volte tanto; **manifold**, molteplice, multiforme.

foldboat *vedi* faltboat.

folder (fōl'dĕr) *n.* pieghevole (*stampato*); cartella, raccoglitore; piegatrice.

folding *agg.* pieghevole: — **screen**, paravento.

foliage (fō'lĭ·ĭj) *n.* fogliame.

folio (fō'lĭ·ō) *n.* folio.

folk (fōk) *n.* gente; popolo; (*pl.*) persone di famiglia: — **dance**, danza popolare. —**lore** *n.* folclore; tradizioni popolari; colore locale.

follow (fŏl'ō) *vt.* seguire, inseguire; esercitare (*una professione*): to — **suit**, seguire l'esempio. *vi.* susseguirsi, derivare di conseguenza. —**er** *n.* seguace, imitatore; corteggiatore. —**ing** *n.* seguito. *agg.* seguente.

folly (fŏl'ĭ) *n.* pazzia, sciocchezza.

foment (fō·mĕnt') *vt.* fomentare.

fond (fŏnd) *agg.* appassionato, amante (*di*); affettuoso: —**of**, affezionato a.

fondle (fŏn'd'l) *vt.* vezzeggiare, accarezzare.

fondly *avv.* teneramente, appassionatamente.

fondness *n.* tenerezza; passione, propensione.

font (fŏnt) *n.* fonte battesimale, acquasantiera; (*tip.*) serie di caratteri.

food (foŏd) *n.* cibo, alimento.

foodstuff (foŏd'stŭf) *n.* commestibili, derrate.

fool (foŏl) *n.* sciocco, tonto; ingenuo; buffone: **All Fools' Day**, primo d'aprile; to **make a** — **of oneself**, fare una figura da sciocco; to **play the** —, fare lo sciocco; fare il tonto. *vt.* ingannare, mistificare: to — **away**, sperperare. *vi.* fare lo sciocco, scherzare. —**hardy** *agg.* temerario. —**ish** *agg.* sciocco, stolto. —**ishness** *n.* stoltezza. —**proof** *agg.* infallibile, a tutta prova.

foolscap (foŏlz'kăp') *n.* carta protocollo.

foot (foŏt) *n.* (*pl.* feet) piede; base (*di colonna*); falda (*di collina*); (*mil.*) fanteria: on — , a piedi; to **put one's** — **in it**, fare una papera. *vt.* pagare (*un conto*). *vi.* andare a piedi, ballare: to — up to, ammontare a. —ball, *n.* pallone, gioco del calcio. —board *n.* predellino. —fall *n.* passo, rumor di passi. —ing *n.* punto d'appoggio, rapporti, base: to miss one's —, mettere un piede in fallo; on an equal —, su piede di parità; to be on a good — with, essere in buoni rapporti con. —lights *n.pl.* (*teal.*) ribalta. —man *n.* domestico; (*mil.*) fantaccino. —note *n.* nota a piè di pagina. —path *n.* sentiero, passaggio pedonale, marciapiede. —print *n.* orma. —step *n.* passo, orma, vestigio. —stool *n.* sgabello. —way *n.* passaggio pedonale.

fop (fŏp) *n.* persona fatua. —pish *agg.* fatuo, affettato, ricercato.

for (fŏr) *prep.* per, a, di: as — him, in quanto a lui; but — him, se non fosse stato per lui; — all that, nonostante ciò; — the present, per adesso. *cong.* perchè, poichè.

forage (fŏr'ij) *n.* foraggio. *vt.* saccheggiare. *vi.* foraggiare.

foray (fŏr'ā) *n.* incursione, saccheggio, razzia. *vt.*, *vi.* predare.

forbad, forbade (fŏr-băd') *pass.* di to forbid.

forbear (fŏr-bâr') *vt.* (*pass.* forbore, *pp.* forborne) evitare, desistere da, trattenersi da, sopportare. *vi.* astenersi; esser paziente. —ance *n.* sopportazione, indulgenza.

forbid (fŏr-bĭd') *vt.* (*pass.* forbad, forbade, *pp.* forbidden) vietare, impedire, proibire. —den *agg.* vietato. —ding *n.* pauroso (*che fa paura*); severo, riservato; repellente.

forbore (fŏr'bōr') *pass.* di to forbear.

force (fōrs) *n.* forza, vigore; validità: in —, in vigore, vigente. *vt.* forzare, costringere: to — in, sfondare; to — something on, imporre qualcosa a; to — one's way into, entrare con la forza in; to — out, scacciare con la forza, far uscire di forza.

forced (fōrst) *agg.* forzato, sforzato.

forceful (fōrs'fŏŏl) *agg.* forte, possente; violento; energico; efficace.

forceps (fŏr'sĕps) *n.pl.* (*chir.*) forcipe.

forcible (fŏr'sĭ-b'l) *agg.* coercitivo; efficace, convincente.

forcibly (-blĭ) *avv.* con forza, per forza, efficacemente, in modo convincente.

ford (fōrd) *n.* guado. *vt.* guadare.

fore (fŏr) *n.* parte anteriore. *agg.* anteriore; (*naut.*) di prua. *avv.* a prua; avanti. *prep.*, *cong.* prima.

forearm *n.* (fŏr'ärm') avambraccio. *vt.* (-ärm') premunire.

forebear (fŏr'bâr) *n.* (*gen. al pl.*) antenato.

forebode (fŏr-bōd') *vt.* presagire, predire.

foreboding (-bōd'ĭng) *n.* presagio, presentimento.

forecast (fŏr'kàst) *n.* presagio, pronostico. *vt.* (kàst') prevedere, pronosticare.

forefather (fŏr'fä'thĕr) *n.* avo.

forefinger (fŏr'fĭng'ĕr) *n.* dito indice.

forefoot (fŏr'fŏŏt') *n.* piede anteriore (*di animale*).

forego (fŏr-gō') *vt.*, *vi.* (*pass.* forewent, *pp.* foregone) precedere.

foregoing (-gō'ĭng) *agg.* precedente.

foregone (fŏr-gŏn') *agg.* previsto, scontato: — conclusion, conclusione inevitabile, partito preso.

foreground (fŏr'ground') *n.* primo piano (*di una visuale*).

forehead (fŏr'ĕd) *n.* fronte.

foreign (fŏr'ĭn) *agg.* straniero, estero, forestiero; estraneo: Foreign Office, Ministero degli Esteri; — to one's nature, estraneo alla propria indole; — trade, commercio con l'estero; —born, nato all'estero. —er *n.* straniero.

foreleg (fŏr'lĕg') *n.* zampa anteriore.

forelock (fŏr'lŏk') *n.* ciuffo (*di capelli*): to take time by the —, cogliere il momento opportuno.

foreman (fŏr'măn) *n.* (*pl.* foremen) capo-operaio, caposquadra; capo dei giurati.

foremost (fŏr'mōst) *agg.* anteriore; primo, principale. *avv.* in avanti; innanzi tutto.

forename (fŏr'năm) *n.* nome di battesimo.

forenoon (fŏr'nōōn) *n.* mattino, mattinata.

forerun (fŏr-rŭn') *vt.* precedere, precorrere, presagire. —ner *n.* araldo, precursore, antenato; presagio.

foresaw *pass.* di to foresee.

foresee (fŏr-sē') *vt.* (*pass.* foresaw, *pp.* foreseen) prevedere.

foresight (fŏr'sĭt') *n.* previdenza; mirino (*d'arma*).

forest (fŏr'ĕst) *n.* foresta. —er *n.* guardaboschi; abitante della foresta. — ranger, guardia forestale. —ry *n.* silvicultura.

forestall (fŏr-stŏl') *vt.* prevenire; (*comm.*) accaparrare, incettare.

foretaste (fŏr'tàst) *n.* pregustazione; primo assaggio. *vt.* pregustare.

foretell (fŏr-tĕl') *vt.* predire.

forethought (fŏr'thŏt') *n.* previdenza.

foretold *pass.* e *pp.* di to foretell.

forever (fŏr-ĕv'ĕr) *avv.* per sempre; sempre, incessantemente.

forewarn (fŏr'wôrn') *vt.* preavvisare,

forfeit (fŏr'fĭt) *n.* multa, pena; perdita (*di un diritto*); confisca. *vt.* perdere (*un diritto*).

forgave *pass.* di to **forgive**.

forge (fôrj) *n.* fucina. *vt.* forgiare, inventare (*notizie*); alterare, contraffare.

forger (fŏr'jẽr) *n.* falsario. [fare.

forgery (fŏr'jẽr.ĭ) *n.* falso, contraffazione.

forget (fŏr.gĕt') *vt.*, *vi.* (*pass.* forgot, *pp.* forgot, forgotten) dimenticare: **to — oneself**, perdere il dominio di sè, mancare alla propria dignità.

forgetful (fŏr.gĕt'fŏŏl) *agg.* dimentico, smemorato. **—ness** *n.* oblio, smemorataggine.

forget-me-not *n.* miosòtide.

forgive (fŏr.gĭv') *vt.* (*pass.* forgave, *pp.* forgiven) perdonare. **—ness** *n.* perdono, indulgenza.

forgiven *pp.* di to **forgive**.

forgiving *agg.* clemente, misericordioso, indulgente.

forgo (fŏr.gō') *vt.* (*pass.* forwent, *pp.* forgone) astenersi da, rinunciare a.

forgot (fŏr.gŏt') *pass.* di to **forget**.

forgotten *pp.* di to **forget**.

fork (fôrk) *n.* forchetta; forca; biforcazione; forcella (*di ciclo*). *vt.* inforcare. *vi.* biforcarsi, diramarsi.

forlorn (fŏr.lôrn') *agg.* afflitto, desolato, sperduto.

form (fôrm) *n.* forma; figura; formalità; modulo; (*Ingl.*) banco di scuola, classe (*scolastica*): **blank —**, modulo da riempire *o* in bianco. *vt.* formare, costituire. *vi.* concretarsi, prender forma; disporsi.

formal (fôr'măl) *agg.* formale, formalista; di etichetta. **—ity** (-măl'ĭtĭ) *n.* formalità, affettazione: **to stand on —**, fare cerimonie. **—ly** *avv.* formalmente, con formalismo.

formation (fôr.mā'shŭn) *n.* formazione.

former (fôr'mẽr) *agg.*, *pron.* precedente, antico, ex, il primo (*di due*). **—ly** *avv.* precedentemente, in passato.

formidable (fôr'mĭ.dá.b'l) *agg.* formidabile, temibile.

formula (fôr'mû.lá) *n.* formula.

formulate (-lāt) *vt.* formulare.

forsake (fŏr.sāk') *vt.* (*pass.* forsook, *pp.* forsaken) abbandonare, disertare.

forsaken (fŏr.sāk'ĕn) *agg.* abbandonato, desolato. *pp.* di to **forsake**.

forsook *pass.* di to **forsake**.

fort (fôrt) *n.* forte, fortezza.

forth (fôrth) *avv.* avanti, in avanti, fuori; successivamente: **from this time —**, d'ora in poi; **to come —**,

venir fuori; **and so —**, e così via. **—coming** *agg.* prossimo, imminente. **—right** *agg.* retto, franco, esplicito. *avv.* immediatamente, esplicitamente. **—with** *avv.* sùbito, al più presto.

fortieth (fôr'tĭ.ĕth) *n.*, *agg.* quarantesimo.

fortification (fôr'tĭ.fĭ.kā'shŭn) *n.* fortificazione.

fortify (fôr'tĭ.fī) *vt.* fortificare, rafforzare.

fortifying *agg.* corroborante, fortificante.

fortitude (fôr'tĭ.tūd) *n.* coraggio, forza d'animo.

fortnight (fôrt'nīt; -nĭt) *n.* quattordici giorni: **a —** ago, due settimane or sono; **today —** (*Ingl.*), fra due settimane.

fortress (fôr'trĕs) *n.* fortezza.

fortuitous (fôr.tū'ĭ.tŭs) *agg.* fortuito. *avv.* fortuitamente.

fortunate (fôr'tû.nĭt) *agg.* fortunato, propizio. **—ly** *avv.* fortunatamente.

fortune (fôr'tûn) *n.* fortuna, sorte; patrimonio: **—hunter** *n.* cacciatore di dote; **—teller**, chiromante.

forty (fôr'tĭ) *n.*, *agg.* quaranta.

forum (fō'rŭm) *n.* fòro.

forward (fôr'wẽrd) *agg.* avanzato; ardente; precoce; impertinente, presuntuoso. *avv.* avanti, in avanti. *vt.* spedire, inviare, far proseguire, promuovere, agevolare. **—er** *n.* speditore, spedizioniere; promotore.

fossil (fŏs'ĭl) *n.*, *agg.* fossile.

foster (fŏs'tẽr) *vt.* allevare, nutrire; promuovere, favorire, incoraggiare, fomentare. **— brother**, fratello di latte. **— child**, **—ling** *n.* bimbo a balia *o* adottivo. **— father**, balio. **— mother**, balia. **— sister**, sorella di latte.

fought (fôt) *pass.* e *pp.* di to **fight**.

foul (foul) *agg.* sporco; immondo; torbido; fetido; fetido; brutto; osceno; (*sport*) irregolare, scorretto: **to fail — of**, scontrarsi con, aggredire; **— ball**, fallo, irregolarità; **— play**, dolo, condotta sleale *o* disonesta; (*sport*) fallo, gioco scorretto (*pugilato*), colpo proibito. *vt.* insudiciare; incrostare; speronare; aggrovigliare. **—mouthed** *agg.* triviale. **—ness** *n.* sporcizia, turpitudine.

found (found) (1) *pass.*, *pp.* di to **find**.

found (found) (2) *vt.* fondare, gettare le basi di; fondere; basare. **—ation** *n.* fondazione, fondamenta, fondamento; (*cosmetico*) base: **— garment**, bustino per donna; reggicalze.

founder (1) (foun'dẽr) *n.* fondatore; fonditore.

founder (2) *vt.* affondare, azzoppare (*un cavallo*). *vi.* sprofondare, naufragare; azzopparsi.

foundling (found'ling) *n.* trovatello.

foundry (foun'drī) *n.* fonderia.

fountain (foun'tĭn) *n.* fontana, sorgente; serbatoio: — pen, penna stilografica.

four (fōr) *n.*, *agg.* quattro: on all fours, carponi. —score *n.*, *agg.* ottanta.

fourteen (fōr'tēn') *n.*, *agg.* quattordici.

fourth (fōrth) *n.*, *agg.* quarto.

fowl (foul) *n.* pollo, pollame.

fox (fŏks) *n.* volpe. *vi.* dissimulare.

foxhole (fŏks'hōl) *n.* (*mil.*) buca da tiratore, buca-ricovero.

foxy (fŏk'sĭ) *agg.* astuto.

fraction (frăk'shŭn) *n.* frazione.

fracture (frăk'tǔr) *n.* frattura, rottura. *vt.* fratturare, rompere.

fragment (frăg'měnt) *n.* frammento.

fragrance (frā'grăns) *n.* fragranza.

fragrant (frā'grănt) *agg.* fragrante.

frail (frāl) *agg.* debole, fragile. —ness, —ty *n.* fragilità.

frame (frām) *n.* cornice, telaio; struttura; corporatura, scheletro; (*fot.*) fotogramma; (*cinema*) inquadratura: — of mind, stato d'animo; — of reference, teoria, opinione, punto di vista; — house, casa con incastellatura di legno. *vt.* costruire, montare, formare; incorniciare; predisporre fraudolentemente (*competizioni, ecc.*); incriminare con false accuse; riuscire. —work *n.* struttura, scheletro; (*edil.*) traliccio; (*mecc., naut.*) ossatura; teoria.

franchise (frăn'chĭz) *n.* franchigia; diritto di voto; esenzione.

frank (frăngk) *n.* franchigia (*postale*). *agg.* franco, sincero. *vt.* esentare, spedire in franchigia. —ly *avv.* francamente. —ness *n.* franchezza.

frankfurter (frăngk'fẽr·tẽr) *n.* salsiccia.

frantic (frăn'tĭk) *agg.* frenetico; pazzo (*di gioia o di dolore*). —ally *avv.* freneticamente.

fraternal (frȧ·tûr'năl) *agg.* fraterno.

fraternity (frȧ·tûr'nĭ·tĭ) *n.* fraternità, confraternita.

fraternize (frăt'ẽr·nĭz) *vi.* affratellarsi; fraternizzare.

fraud (frôd) *n.* frode, impostura; impostore. —ulent (frôd'ū·lĕnt) *agg.* fraudolento, doloso.

fraught (frôt) *agg.* carico (*di*): — with danger, pieno di pericoli.

fray (frā) (1) *n.* zuffa, lite, conflitto.

fray (frā) (2) *n.* logoratura. *vt.* logorare. *vi.* logorarsi. —ed *agg.* logoro.

freak (frēk) *n.* capriccio, bizzarria; scherzo di natura; striatura.

freckle (frĕk''l) *n.* lentiggine, efelide. *vi.* divenire lentigginoso.

freckled (frĕk''ld) freckly (frĕk'lĭ) *agg.* lentigginoso.

free (frē) *agg.* libero, indipendente; gratuito; esente; disinvolto; prodigo; esplicito; impudente: — on board (F.O.B.), franco a bordo; — of charge, gratis, gratuito; postage —, franco di porto; to give someone a — hand, lasciare a uno mano libera; to make — with, appropriarsi. *avv.* liberamente, gratuitamente. *vt.* (*pass., pp.* freed) liberare, emancipare, esimere; svincolare. —dom *n.* libertà, indipendenza; disinvoltura; esenzione. —ly *avv.* liberamente, apertamente; gratuitamente; generosamente. —mason *n.* massone; —masonry *n.* massoneria.

freeze (frēz) *vt.* (*pass.* froze, *pp.* frozen) gelare, congelare. *vi.* congelarsi, ghiacciarsi.

freezer (frēz'ẽr) *n.* congelante; frigorifero; cella frigorifera.

freezing (frēz'ĭng) *agg.* gelido, congelante: — point, punto di congelamento.

freight (frāt) *n.* carico mercantile; nolo marittimo, trasporto. *vt.* caricare, trasportare, noleggiare (*una nave*): — car, vagone merci; — train, treno merci. —er *n.* spedizioniere, noleggiatore; vapore mercantile.

French (frĕnch) *n.* il francese (*lingua*): the —, i francesi. *agg.* francese: to take — leave, svignarsela: — beans, fagiolini; — window, porta-finestra. —man *n.* francese (*maschio*).

frenzied (frĕn'zĭd) *agg.* frenetico, delirante.

frenzy (frĕn'zĭ) *n.* frenesia, delirio.

frequency (frē'kwĕn·sĭ) *n.* frequenza: — modulation (*radio*), modulazione di frequenza.

frequent (frē'kwĕnt) *agg.* frequente. *vt.* (frē·kwĕnt') frequentare. —ly *avv.* spesso, di frequente.

fresco (frĕs'kō) *n.* affresco. *vt.* affrescare.

fresh (frĕsh) *agg.* fresco, nuovo, recente; inesperto; insolente: — water, acqua dolce.

freshen (frĕsh'ĕn) *vt.* rinfrescare. *vi.* rinfrescarsi.

freshly (frĕsh'lĭ) *avv.* di fresco, recentemente, da poco tempo.

freshman (frĕsh'măn) *n.* novellino; studente del primo anno.

freshness *n.* freschezza; impudenza, insolenza.

fret (frĕt) *n.* erosione; agitazione, inquietudine; tasto (*di strumento a corde*); greca, fregio. *vt.* strofinare, logorare, agitare; infastidire; decorare con greca. *vi.* agitarsi. fremere, logorarsi, amareggiarsi. **—ful** *agg.* agitato, inquieto, impaziente.

friar (frī'ĕr) *n.* frate.

friction (frĭk'shŭn) *n.* attrito, frizione.

Friday (frī'dĭ) *n.* venerdì: **Good Friday**, Venerdì Santo.

fried (frīd) *pass. pp. di* to **fry.**

friend (frĕnd) *n.* amico, amica. **—less** *agg.* senza amici, abbandonato. **—liness** *n.* bonomia, cordialità. **—ly** *agg.* amichevole, affabile: **friendly society,** società di mutuo soccorso. **—ship** *n.* amicizia.

frigate (frĭg'ĭt) *n.* fregata (*nave*).

fright (frīt) *n.* spavento, orrore.

frighten (frīt'n) *vt.* spaventare. **—ed** *agg.* spaventato: **to become —,** spaventarsi.

frightful (frīt'fool) *agg.* spaventevole, straordinario. **—ly** *avv.* terribilmente; straordinariamente.

frigid (frĭj'ĭd) *agg.* freddo, frigido, glaciale.

fringe (frĭnj) *n.* frangia; orlo; periferia. *agg.* periferico; secondario. *vt.* orlare, ornare di frange.

frippery (frĭp'ĕr.ĭ) *n.* ostentazione; cianfrusaglie. fronzoli.

frisk (frĭsk) *n.* capriola, sgambetto. *vt.* (*gergo*) perquisire. *vi.* far capriole, sgambettare.

frisky (frĭs'kĭ) *agg.* vivace, allegro.

fritter (frĭt'ĕr) *n.* frittella; frammento, brandello. *vt.* sminuzzare: **to — away,** sperperare, sparpagliare.

frivolity (frĭ.vŏl'ĭ.tĭ) *n.* frivolezza.

frivolous (frĭv'ō.lŭs) *agg.* frivolo.

frizzle (frĭz'l) *vt.* arricciare, increspare.

fro (frō) *avv.* indietro: **to and —,** avanti e indietro.

frock (frŏk) *n.* vestito, tunica, saio. **— coat,** finanziera (*giacca*).

frog (frŏg) (1) *n.* rana, ranocchio: **— in the throat,** mal di gola, raucedine.

frog (frŏg) (2) *n.* alamaro. [cedine.

frogman (frŏg'măn') *n.* sommozzatore, uomo rana.

frolic (frŏl'ĭk) *n.* scherzo, farsa. *vi.* divertirsi, fare allegria. **—some** *agg.* allegro, giocoso.

from (frŏm) *prep.* da, sin da, per, a causa di: **to take something away —,** portare via qualcosa a.

front (frŭnt) *n.* fronte; faccia, facciata; sparato (*di camicia*); apparenza; prestanome, paravento. *agg.* frontale, di fronte, anteriore: **in — of,** davanti a. *vt.*, *vi.* affrontare; guardare su, essere di fronte a; essere esposto (*verso*).

frontier (frŭn'tẽr) *n.* frontiera. *agg.* di frontiera, confinario.

frost (frŏst) *n.* gelo, brina. *vt.* congelare, coprire di brina; smerigliare (*vetri*); candire. **—iness** *n.* gelo. **—ing** *n.* cappa per dolci.

frosty (frŏs'tĭ) *agg.* brinato, gelato.

froth (frŏth) *n.* schiuma, spuma. *vi.* spumeggiare, spumare, schiumare: **to — at the mouth,** schiumare di rabbia.

frown (froun) *n.* cipiglio, sguardo corrucciato. *vi.* aggrottare le sopracciglia, accigliarsi: **to — on, upon,** essere contrario a, disapprovare. **—ing** *agg.* accigliato, corrucciato.

froze (frōz) *pass. di* to **freeze.**

frozen (frō'z'n) *agg.* gelato; congelato; glaciale. *pp. di* to **freeze.**

frugal (froo'găl) *agg.* frugale, economo.

fruit (froot) *n.* frutto, frutta: **— tree,** albero da frutta. *vt.*, *vi.* fruttare, fruttificare. **—ful** *agg.*, fruttifero. **—less** *agg.* inutile, improduttivo.

frustrate (frŭs'trāt) *vt.* frustrare.

frustration (frŭs.trā'shŭn) *n.* frustramento, delusione, insuccesso.

fry (frī) *n.* fritto, frittura: **small —,** frittura minuta. *vt.*, *vi.* (*pass., pp.* fried) friggere. **—ing pan,** padella.

fuddle (fŭd''l) *vt.* ubriacare, stordire.

fuel (fū'ĕl) *n.* combustibile, carburante. *vt.*, *vi.* rifornire, rifornirsi di carburante.

fugitive (fū'jĭ.tĭv) *n.* fuggiasco. *agg.* fuggevole.

fulfill (fool·fĭl') *vt.* compiere, adempiere, realizzare, soddisfare. **—ment** *n.* adempimento, realizzazione.

full (fool) *agg.* pieno, completo, colmo, abbondante; ampio: **at — speed,** a gran velocità; **in —,** al completo, per intero; **to the —,** al massimo; **—-blooded,** di pura razza; **—-dress,** vestito da cerimonia; alta tenuta; **—-grown,** adulto, maturo; **—-fledged,** maturo, completo; **— stop,** punto, punto fermo. *avv.* molto, in pieno, perfettamente: **— in the face,** in pieno viso; **to know — well,** sapere benissimo.

fullness (-nĕs) *n.* pienezza, pieno.

fully (fool'ĭ) *avv.* pienamente, completamente.

fumble (fŭm'b'l) *vt.*, *vi.* maneggiare goffamente; annaspare.

fume (fūm) *n.* esalazione. *vt.* esalare. *vi.* evaporare; fremere (*per la collera*).

fumigate (fū'mĭ.gāt) *vt.* fumigare, disinfettare.

fun (fŭn) *n.* allegria, divertimento, scherzo: **to have —,** divertirsi; **to make — of,** farsi beffe di, mettere in ridicolo; in —, per scherzo; full of —, molto divertito.

function (fŭngk'shŭn) n. funzione, attribuzione; cerimonia. vi. funzionare.

fund (fŭnd) n. fondo, riserva: sinking —, fondo di ammortamento. vt. consolidare.

fundamental (fŭn'dá-měn'tăl) n. fondamento. agg. fondamentale.

funeral (fū'nĕr·ăl) n. funerale. agg. funebre, mortuario.

fungus (fŭng'gŭs) n. fungo.

funk (fŭngk) n. paura, panico: to be in a blue —, avere una paura del diavolo.

funnel (fŭn'ĕl) n. imbuto; ciminiera.

funny (fŭn'ĭ) agg. strano, buffo, faceto: the funnies (giorn.), i fumetti.

fur (fŭr) n. pelliccia, pelo; patina (della lingua). vt. impellicciare, ornare di pelliccia.

furious (fū'rĭ·ŭs) agg. furibondo, accanito.

furl (fŭrl) vt. ammainare, arrotolare. vi. arrotolarsi.

furlough (fŭr'lō) n. licenza: sick —, licenza di convalescenza. vt. (mil.) mandare in licenza.

furnace (fŭr'nĭs) n. fornace.

furnish (fŭr'nĭsh) vt. fornire; ammobiliare.

furniture (fŭr'nĭ·tŭr) n. mobilia: a piece of —, un mobile.

furrier (fŭr'ĭ·ĕr) n. pellicciaio.

furrow (fŭr'ō) n. solco, scia. vt. solcare, arare.

furry (fŭr'ĭ) agg. peloso; patinoso.

further (fŭr'thĕr) agg. ulteriore, successivo, più lontano; altro, nuovo: the — end, l'estremità. avv. inoltre, più avanti, ulteriormente, al di là. vt. favorire, assecondare. —more avv. per di più, d'altronde, inoltre.

furthest (fŭr'thĕst) agg. estremo, (il) più lontano. avv. alla massima distanza.

furtive (fŭr'tĭv) agg. furtivo, evasivo, subdolo.

fury (fū'rĭ) n. furore, frenesia, furia.

fuse (fūz) n. fusibile: spoletta: delayed action —, spoletta a tempo. vt., vi. fondere; far esplodere, fondersi.

fuselage (fū'zĕ·lĭj) n. fusoliera.

fuss (fŭs) n. agitazione inutile, trambusto; faccendone: to make a —, agitarsi sproporzionatamente. vi. inquietarsi, affannarsi; far confusione.

fussy (fŭs'ĭ) agg. meticoloso; inquieto, confusionario, concitato; vistoso.

fustian (fŭs'chăn) n. fustagno.

futile (fū'tĭl) agg. futile, insignificante.

future (fū'tŭr) n., agg. futuro, avvenire.

fuze (fūz) vedi fuse.

fuzz (fŭz) n. lanugine, pulviscolo.

fuzzy (fŭz'ĭ) agg. lanuginoso; confuso.

G

gab (găb) n. parlantina, chiacchiera. vi. ciarlare.

gabble (găb'l) n. borbottio, discorso confuso. vi. borbottare, affastellar parole.

gable (gā'b'l) n. (arch.) frontone: — roof, tetto a due spioventi.

gad (găd) vi. bighellonare.

gadfly (găd'flī') n. tafano.

gadget (găj'ĕt) n. aggeggio, meccanismo.

gag (găg) n. bavaglio; scherzo, trovata, improvvisazione; battuta o scenetta comica. vt., vi. far venire (o avere) i conati, dare (o avere) la nausea; imbavagliare; improvvisare battute; mistificare. —man n. comico, improvvisatore.

gage (gāj) n. scommessa, pegno. vt. scommettere, dare in pegno.

gaiety (gā'ĕ·tĭ) n. allegria, galezza.

gaily (gā'lĭ) avv. allegramente, vivacemente; vistosamente.

gain (gān) n. guadagno, vantaggio. vt. guadagnare, ottenere, vincere. vi. migliorare, fare progressi: to —

on, upon, guadagnar terreno su. —ings n.pl. utili, profitti.

gainsay (găn'sā') vt. contraddire.

gait (gāt) n. andatura.

galaxy (găl'ak·sĭ) n. galàssia, Via Lattea.

gale (gāl) n. vento, brezza, bufera.

gall (gôl) n. fiele, bile; rovello, stizza. vt., vi. irritare, infastidire: — bladder, vescica biliare.

gallant (găl'ănt) n. eroe; uomo galante, amante, seduttore. agg. ardito, nobile; galante. —ry n. ardimento, nobiltà; galanteria.

gallery (găl'ĕr·ĭ) n. galleria, pinacoteca; corridoio.

galley (găl'ĭ) n. galera; cucina di nave; (tip.) vantaggio: — proof, bozza in colonna; — slave, galeotto.

gallon (găl'ŭn) n. gallone (Inghil. = litro 4,546; S.U. = litro 3,785).

gallop (găl'ŭp) n. galoppo. vi. galoppare.

gallows (găl'ōz) n. forca: — bird, pendaglio da forca.

galore (gá·lōr') n. abbondanza; avv. in abbondanza, a volontà.

galosh (gȧ·lŏsh′) *n*. caloscia.

gamble (găm′b'l) *n*. gioco d'azzardo, rischio. *vt.*, *vi*. giocare d'azzardo, speculare, rischiare, puntare.

gambler (găm′blẽr) *n*. giocatore.

gambling (găm′blĭng) *n*. gioco d'azzardo.

gambol (găm′bŭl) *n*. piroetta, capriola *vi*. piroettare.

game (găm) *n*. gioco, partita; cacciagione, selvaggina: **to die —, resistere fino in fondo; to make a — of**, burlarsi di. *agg*. di caccia; coraggioso. *vi*. giocare d'azzardo. **— room**, sala di ricreazione, sala da gioco.

gamut (găm′ŭt) *n*. gamma.

gander (găn′dẽr) *n*. maschio dell'oca.

gandy dancer (găn′dĭ) *n*. (*ferr*.) manovale; lavoratore stagionale.

gang (găng) *n*. banda, associazione a delinquere; squadra (*di operai*); assortimento (*di utensili*). *vi*. raggrupparsi. **—ster** *n*. bandito.

gangplank (găng′plăngk′) *n*. (*naut*.) palanca; scalandrone; plancia di sbarco.

gangrene (găng′grēn) *n*. cancrena. *vt.*, *vi*. incancrenire.

gangway (găng′wā′) *n*. passaggio, corridoio; (*naut*.) passerella, barcarizzo.

gantlet (gŏnt′lĕt) *n*. bastonatura, fustigazione, tortura: **to run the —,** affrontare critiche severe.

gaol (jāl) *n*. carcere.

gap (găp) *n*. breccia, apertura, fessura, crepaccio; lacuna.

gape (găp; găp; găp) *n*. squarcio; apertura della bocca, stupore; sbadiglio. *vi*. aprirsi, essere aperto; aprire la bocca, restare a bocca aperta (*per la meraviglia, ecc*.): **to — at**, guardare a bocca aperta.

garage (gȧ·räzh′ [*S.U.*], găr′ĭj [*Ingl*.]) *n*. autorimessa.

garb (gärb) *n*. vestiario, tenuta. *vt*. vestire.

garbage (gär′bĭj)*n*. rifiuti, immondizia.

garden (gär′d'n) *n*. giardino. *vt.*, *vi*. coltivare a giardino, darsi al giardinaggio. **—er** *n*. giardiniere.

gargle (gär′g'l) *n*. gargarismo. *vt.*, *vi*. gargarizzare, gargarizzarsi.

gargoyle (gär′goil) *n*. garguglia (*mascherone da grondaia*); (*fig*.) mascherone.

garish (gãr′ĭsh) *agg*. sgargiante, vistoso.

garland (gär′lănd) *n*. ghirlanda.

garlic (gär′lĭk) *n*. aglio.

garment (gär′mĕnt) *n*. indumento.

garnish (gär′nĭsh) *n*. guarnizione, contorno. *vt*. guarnire, adornare.

garret (găr′ĕt) *n*. soffitta, abbaino.

garrison (găr′ĭ·sŭn) *n*. guarnigione, presidio: **— state**, stato militarista. *vt*. presidiare.

garter (gär′tẽr) *n*. giarrettiera.

gas (găs) *n*. gas; benzina: **— burner**, becco a gas; **— stove**, fornello a gas; **— tar**, catrame. **—eous** *agg*. gassoso.

gash (găsh) *n*. squarcio. *vt*. squarciare.

gasoline (găs′ō·lēn) *n*. benzina.

gasp (gȧsp) *n*. anelito, fiato sospeso, esclamazione soffocata. *vi*., boccheggiare, soffocare un'esclamazione: **to — for breath**, ansimare.

gate (gāt) *n*. porta, portone, cancello. **—way** *n*. andito, portone.

gather (găth′ẽr) *vt*. raccogliere, cogliere; concludere, dedurre: **to — dust**, impolverarsi. *vi*. riunirsi, venire a maturazione (*di ascesso*). **—ing** *n*. riunione, assemblea, raccolta; ascesso.

gaudy (gôd′ĭ) *agg*. vistoso, sgargiante.

gauge (gāj) *n*. portata, capacità, misura base; (*ferr*.) scartamento. *vt*. misurare, valutare.

gaunt (gônt; gänt) *agg*. magro, sparuto.

gauntlet (gônt′lĕt) *n*. manopola: **to take up the —,** raccogliere una sfida; **to throw down the —,** lanciare la sfida.

gauze (gôz) *n*. garza, velo.

gave (gāv) *pass*. di to give.

gawk (gôk) *n*. sciocco, persona goffa. *vi*. fissare con occhi imbambolati.

gawky (gôk′ĭ) *agg*. goffo, impacciato.

gay (gā) *agg*. gaio, allegro; vistoso, colorito. **—ety** *n*. gaiezza, allegria.

gaze (gāz) *n*. sguardo fisso. *vt*. guardare fissamente.

gazelle (gȧ·zĕl′) *n*. gazzella.

gazette (gȧ·zĕt′) *n*. gazzetta.

gazetteer (găz′ĕ·tẽr′) *n*. dizionario geografico; giornalista.

gear (gẽr) *n*. ingranaggio, congegno, meccanismo, innesto (*di ingranaggi*); (*auto*) marcia; attrezzatura; equipaggiamento, vestiario; moltiplica (*di bicicletta, ecc*.): **low —,** prima; **high —,** quarta, presa diretta; **—shift lever**, leva del cambio; **in —,** ingranato; **out of —,** disinnestato, guasto; **— box,** scatola del cambio; **— case,** copricatena. *vt*. innestare, ingranare; mettere in movimento; preparare, mettere a punto, organizzare, coordinare: **to — up,** accelerare, far accelerare. *vi*. combaciare, ingranarsi; organizzarsi; adattarsi.

gee (jē) *inter*. santo cielo!, caspita!, mamma mia!

geese (gēs) *pl. di* goose.

gelatin (jĕl′á.tĭn) *n.* gelatina.

geld (gĕld) *vt.* castrare.

gem (jĕm) *n.* gemma.

gender (jĕn′dẽr) *n.* (*gramm.*) genere.

general (jĕn′ẽr.ăl) *n., agg.* generale. **—ity** (-ăl′ĭ.tĭ) *n.* generalità, maggioranza.

generalize (jĕn′ẽr.ăl.ĭz) *vt., vi.* generalizzare.

generally (-lĭ) *avv.* generalmente; largamente, in genere.

generate (jĕn′ẽr.āt) *vt.* generare, produrre

generation (jĕn′ẽr.ā′shŭn) *n.* generazione.

generosity (jĕn′ẽr.ŏs′ĭ.tĭ) *n.* generosità.

generous (jĕn′ẽr.ŭs) *agg.* generoso.

genial (jĕn′yăl) *agg.* cordiale. **—ity** (-ăl′ĭ.tĭ) *n.* cordialità.

genius (jĕn′yŭs) *n.* genio, ingegno.

genocide (jĕn′ō.sīd) *n.* genocidio; genocida.

genteel (jĕn.tēl′) *agg.* raffinato, elegante, ricercato, distinto.

gentile (jĕn′tĭl) *agg., n.* gentile (*pagano, miscredente*).

gentility (jĕn.tĭl′ĭ.tĭ) *n.* raffinatezza, distinzione.

gentle (jĕn′t′l) *agg.* soave, delicato, docile, dolce, tranquillo; bennato. **—man** *n.* (*pl.* **—men**) signore, gentiluomo; uomo; **—manlike,** **—manly** *agg.* distinto, ben educato, da gentiluomo. **—woman** *n.* (*pl.* **—women**) gentildonna. **—ness** *n.* mitezza, bontà.

gently (jĕn′tlĭ) *avv.* dolcemente, delicatamente, cautamente.

gentry (jĕn′trĭ) *n.* alta borghesia; (*fam.*) gente.

genuine (jĕn′û.ĭn) *agg.* genuino, autentico; sincero.

geographer (jē.ŏg′rá.tẽr) *n.* geografo.

geographical (jē′ō-grăf′ĭ.kăl) *agg.* geografico.

geography (jē.ŏg′rá.fĭ) *n.* geografia.

geological (jē.ō.lŏj′ĭ.kăl) *agg.* geologico.

geologist (jē.ŏl′ō.jĭst) *n.* geologo.

geology (jē.ŏl′ō.jĭ) *n.* geologia.

geometrical (jē.ō-mĕt′rĭ.kăl) *agg.* geometrico.

geometry (jē.ŏm′ē.trĭ) *n.* geometria; configurazione; forma.

geopolitics (jē′ō-pŏl′ĭ.tĭks) *n.* geopolitica.

geranium (jē.rā′nĭ.ŭm) *n.* geranio.

geriatrics (jĕr′ĭ.ăt′rĭks) *n.* geriatria.

germ (jûrm) *n.* germe.

german (jûr′măn) (1) *agg.* germano, di primo grado.

German (jûr′măn) (2) *n., agg.* tedesco.

germinate (jûr′mĭ.nāt) *vt., vi.* produrre, germinare.

gesticulate (jĕs.tĭk′û.lāt) *vi.* gesticolare.

gesture (jĕs′tûr) *n.* gesto. *vi.* gestire, gesticolare.

get (gĕt) *vt., vi.* (*pass.* got, *pp.* got, gotten) ottenere, acquisire, acquistare, afferrare, procurare, catturare, indurre, generare; arrivare; divenire, farsi, riuscire: to **—** over, superare (*una crisi, ecc.*); to **—** married, sposarsi; to **—** somebody to, indurre qualcuno a; to **—** the better of, avere il sopravvento su; to **—** wind of, avere sentore di; to **—** ill, ammalarsi; to **—** old, invecchiare; to **—** tired, stancarsi; to **—** even with, pareggiare la partita con; to **—** off, sfuggire, cavarsela; partire; smontare (*da un veicolo*); to **—** away, andarsene, scappare; to **—** along, barcamenarsi, andar d'accordo; to **—** out, uscire, andarsene; trapelare (*di un segreto*); to **—** rid of, sbarazzarsi di; to **—** up, alzarsi, salire; to **—** through, passare; finire; I've got to do it, devo farlo, bisogna che lo faccia; I don't **—** it, non lo capisco, non ci arrivo; that's what gets me, è questo che mi lascia perplesso *o* che mi secca *o* che mi urta.

gewgaw (gū′gô) *n.* bagattella.

ghastly (gást′lĭ) *agg.* macabro, orrendo; livido, cadaverico.

gherkin (gûr′kĭn) *n.* cetriolino.

ghost (gōst) *n.* fantasma, apparizione: The Holy Ghost, lo Spirito Santo; **—** town (*S.U.*), città abbandonata; to give up the **—**, morire, spirare. **—like,** **—ly** *agg.* spettrale. **—writer** *n.* (*S.U.*) negro (*autore che lavora per un altro senza figurare*).

G.I. (jē′ī′) *n.* (*S.U.*) militare, soldato. *agg.* militare, soldatesco.

giant (jī′ănt) *n.* gigante. *agg.* gigantesco.

gibbet (jĭb′ĕt; jĭb′ĭt) *n.* forca. [sco.

gibbon (gĭb′ŭn) *n.* (*zool.*) gibbone.

gibe (jĭb) *n.* beffa, sarcasmo.

giddiness (gĭd′ĭ.nĕs) *n.* vertigine, stordimento; volubilità, frivolezza.

giddy (gĭd′ĭ) *agg.* stordito; vertiginoso, che dà il capogiro; volubile, frivolo: to feel **—**, avere le vertigini.

gift (gĭft) *n.* dono; dote (*morale o fisica*). **—ed** *agg.* dotato, valente.

gigantic (jī.gan′tĭk) *agg.* gigantesco.

giggle (gĭg′′l) *n.* riso convulso *o* sciocco. *vi.* ridere convulsamente *o* stoltamente.

gild (gĭld) *vt.* dorare.

gill (jĭl) *n.* gola, burrone; (*ittiol.*) (gĭl) branchia; (*ornit.*) bargigli.

gilt (gĭlt) *n.* doratura. *agg.* dorato. **—edged securities,** titoli solidi.

gimbals (gǐm'bălz) *n. pl.* sospensione cardanica: gimbal joint, giunto cardanico.

gimlet (gǐm'lĕt) *n.* succhiello.

gimmick (gǐm'ĭk) (*gergo*) *n.* trucco; espediente, stratagemma.

gin (jǐn) (1) *n.* liquore di ginepro, gin: — mill, bar, spaccio di liquori.

gin (jǐn) (2) *n.* trabocchetto; trappola; elevatore; sgranatrice.

ginger (jǐn'jĕr) *n.* zenzero; (*fig.*) vivacità. — ale (*Ingl.* — beer), sorta di gazzosa al zenzero.

gingerly (jǐn'jĕr·lǐ) *avv.* cautamente, delicatamente *agg.* cautissimo.

gingham (gǐng'ăm) *n.* rigatino.

gipsy (jǐp'sǐ) *n.* zingaro. *agg.* zingaresco.

giraffe (jǐ·ráf') *n.* giraffa.   [sco.

gird (gûrd) *vt.* (*pass.*, *pp.* girded, girt) cingere, circondare: to — oneself for, prepararsi a.

girder (gûr'dĕr) *n.* putrella.

girdle (gûr'd'l) *n.* cintura, cinturone; reggicalze. *vt.* cingere, recingere.

girl (gûrl) *n.* ragazza, ragazzina. —hood *n.* adolescenza, giovinezza (*di femmina*). —ish *agg.* fanciullesco (*di femmina*), da fanciulla.

girt (gûrt) *pass.*, *pp.* di to gird.

girth (gûrth) *n.* circonferenza; sottopancia. *vt.* cingere.

gist (jǐst) *n.* essenza, sostanza.

give (gǐv) *n.* cedevolezza, elasticità. *vt.*, *vi.* (*pass.* gave, *pp.* given) dare, consegnare, porgere, abbandonare; cedere, rilassarsi; retrocedere: to — away, regalare; rivelare (*un segreto*); tradire; to — back, restituire; to — birth to, generare, dare origine a; to — in, cedere; to — off, emanare, emettere; to — out, esaurirsi; distribuire, emettere; to — up, rinunciare, arrendersi, desistere; to — way, cedere.

given (gǐv'ĕn) *agg.* dato, specificato; dedito, proclive: — name, nome di battesimo; — time, data ora, ora prestabilita.

giver (gǐv'ĕr) *n.* datore, donatore.

gizzard (gǐz'ĕrd) *n.* ventriglio.

glacial (glā'shăl) *agg.* glaciale.

glacier (glā'shĕr) *n.* ghiacciaio.

glad (glăd) *agg.* lieto, contento; sgargiante: — rags (*gergo*), vestito della festa; to be only too —, non chieder di meglio.

gladden (glăd''n) *vt.* rallegrare.

glade (glād) *n.* radura.

gladiator (glăd'ǐ·à'tĕr) *n.* gladiatore.

gladly (glăd'lǐ) *avv.* volontieri.

gladness (glăd'nĕs) *n.* contentezza, piacere.

glamorize (glăm'ĕr·ǐz) *vt.* rendere affascinante; (*cinema*) valorizzare

la bellezza di, rendere affascinante.

glamorous (glăm'ĕr·ŭs) *agg.* affascinante.

glamour (glăm'ĕr) *n.* fascino; magia: — girl, maliarda, fatalona.

glance (glâns) *n.* sguardo; bagliore; rimbalzo. *vt.*, *vi.* guardare di sfuggita, dare un'occhiata; balenare; rimbalzare; intravedere.

gland (glănd) *n.* (*anat.*) glandola.

glare (glâr) *n.* bagliore, riverbero, barlume; sguardo intenso, occhiata malevola. *vi.* abbagliare, splendere: to — at, guardare con astio, dare un'occhiataccia a.

glaring (glâr'ǐng) *agg.* malevolo; abbagliante, splendente; sfrontato; lampante.

glass (glâs) *n.* vetro; bicchiere; (*pl.* glasses) occhiali, cannocchiale: — case, vetrinetta; looking —, specchio; weather —, barometro. *vt.* rispecchiare; mettere sotto vetro; confezionare in barattoli di vetro. —blower *n.* soffiatore di vetro. —ware *n.* vetrerie, cristalleria.

glassy (glâs'ǐ) *agg.* vitreo; vetroso.

glaze (glāz) *n.* smaltatura, vernice. *vt.* munire o coprire di vetro; smaltare; glassare (*dolci*, *ecc.*).

glazier (glā'zhĕr) *n.* vetraio.

gleam (glēm) *n.* raggio, barlume, sprazzo di luce. *vi.* brillare, splendere.

glean (glēn) *vt.*, *vi.* spigolare, raccogliere; racimolare.

glee (glē) *n.* gioia, gaiezza, ilarità.

glib (glǐb) *agg.* loquace; disinvolto: — excuse, scusa facile.

glide (glīd) *vi.* colare; scivolare, sdrucciolare; (*aeron.*) planare, volare a vela.

glider (glīd'ĕr) *n.* aliante; divanetto a dondolo *o* ad altalena.

gliding (glīd'ǐng) *n.* volo a vela.

glimmer (glǐm'ĕr) *n.* barlume; bagliore. *vi.* risplendere debolmente, balugínare.

glimpse (glǐmps) *n.* lampo; occhiata, colpo d'occhio: to catch a — of, intravedere. *vt.* intravedere.

glint (glǐnt) *n.* scintillio, bagliore. *vt.*, *vi.* rifrangere, brillare.

glisten (glǐs''n) *vi.* luccicare, risplendere.

glitter (glǐt'ĕr) *n.* lustro, scintillio. *vi.* brillare, scintillare, essere vistoso. —ing *agg.* scintillante.

gloat (glōt) *vi.* gongolare: to — over another's misfortune, godere delle altrui sventure.

globe (glōb) *n.* globo, sfera.

gloom (glōōm), gloominess (glōōm'ǐnĕs) *n.* oscurità, tenebre; tristezza, desolazione, umor nero.

gloomy (gloom'ĭ) *agg.* oscuro; triste, malinconico; nuvoloso.

glorify (glō'rĭ-fĭ) *vt.* glorificare.

glorious (glō'rĭ-ŭs) *agg.* glorioso, magnifico, radioso, splendido.

glory (glō'rĭ) *n.* gloria, aureola. *vi.* gloriarsi, esultare.

gloss (glŏs) *n.* lucentezza; chiosa, commento. *vt.* lustrare; commentare, chiosare: to — over, glissare, stare. **—ary** *n.* glossario. **—iness** *n.* lustro, splendore; levigatezza.

glossy (glŏs'ĭ) *agg.* liscio; lucido splendente. *n.* (*fot.*) foto su carta lucida.

glove (glŭv) *n.* guanto. *vt.* inguantare.

glover (glŭv'ẽr) *n.* guantaio.

glow (glō) *n.* calore, incandescenza, riflesso; ardore, splendore. *vi.* ardere, rosseggiare, brillare. **—ing** *agg.* brillante, rosseggiante, lucente, ardente, animato.

glower (glou'ẽr) *vi.* guardare torvamente o con occhi torvi.

glowworm (glō'wûrm) *n.* lucciola.

glucose (gloō'kōs) *n.* glucosio.

glue (gloō) *n.* colla. *vt.* incollare.

gluey (gloō'ĭ) *agg.* appiccicoso, colloso.

glum (glŭm) *agg.* arcigno, cupo. **—ly** *avv.* cupamente.

glut (glŭt) *vt.* saziare, colmare.

gluten (gloō'tĕn) *n.* glutine.

glutton (glŭt'n) *n.* ghiottone, mangione. **—ous** *agg.* ghiotto.

gluttony (glŭt'nĭ) *n.* ghiottoneria.

G-man (jē'măn') *n.* (*S.U.*) agente federale.

gnarled (närld) **gnarly** *agg.* nodoso, nocchieruto; perverso.

gnash (năsh) *vt.*, *vi.* stringere o digrignare i denti.

gnat (năt) *n.* zanzara, moscerino.

gnaw (nô) *vt.*, *vi.* (*pass.* gnawed, *pp.* gnawed, gnawn) rodere, rosicchiare.

go (gō) *n.* l'andare; vigore; moda; tentativo, successo: to have a — at, provarsi a fare; to make a — of, far andar bene; it's a —! affare fatto!; no —! niente da fare! *vi.* (*pass.* went, *pp.* gone) andare, partire, diventare, camminare, tendere, essere sul punto di, stare per. *vt.* sopportare, tollerare: to — astray, smarrirsi, traviarsi; to — away, andarsene; to — back, tornare; to — back on one's word, rimangiarsi la parola; to — between, interporsi; to — by, passare, scorrere (*del tempo*); regolarsi con; to — down, scendere, mettersi a letto, cadere, declinare; to — in, entrare; to — in for, dedi-

carsi a, intraprendere; to — into, entrare, partecipare, darsi a, addentrarsi (*in un argomento*); to — into mourning, prendere il lutto; to — off, partire, morire, spegnersi; to — on, proseguire; accadere, succedere; to — out, uscire, estinguersi; to — out of one's way to, sforzarsi di; to — over, attraversare, percorrere, esaminare, verificare; to — to sleep, addormentarsi; to — under, tramontare; affogare, affondare; soccombere, essere sopraffatto.

goad (gōd) *n.* pungolo, stimolo. *vt.* stimolare, spronare.

goal (gōl) *n.* meta, mira; (*sport*) porta. **—keeper**, portiere.

goat (gōt) *n.* capra.

goatee (gō'tē') *n.* barba caprina.

gobble (gŏb'l) *vt.* tranguiare.

gobbledygook (gŏb'l-dĭ-gŏŏk') (*gergo S.U.*) *n.* paroloni, discorso altisonante e astruso.

gobbler (gŏb'lẽr) *n.* mangione; tacchino.

go-between *n.* intermediario; ruffiano.

goblet (gŏb'lĕt) *n.* coppa.

goblin (gŏb'lĭn) *n.* folletto.

god (gŏd) *n.* dio. **—child** *n.* figlioccio. **—daughter** *n.* figlioccia. **—dess** *n.* dea. **—father** *n.* padrino. **—less** *agg.* ateo, empio. **—like** *agg.* divino. **—ly** *agg.* pio, devoto; divino. **—mother** *n.* madrina. **—send** *n.* fortuna inattesa. **—son** *n.* figlioccio.

goggle (gŏg'l) *vi.* stralunare gli occhi: to — at, sbirciare.

goggles (gŏg'lz) *n.pl.* (*fam.*) occhiali.

going (gō'ĭng) *n.* andamento, portamento, andatura; partenza: to be —, andare, andarsene; avere intenzione (*di*); I'm — to tell him, gli dirò. ., glielo dirò, *agg.* in movimento, funzionante: a — concern, una ditta avviata.

goiter (goi'tẽr) *n.* (*pat.*) gozzo.

gold (gōld) *n.* oro, danaro. **—bricker** *n.* scansafatiche. **—en** *agg.* d'oro, aureo.

goldfinch (gōld'fĭnch') *n.* (*ornit.*) cardellino.

goldfish (gōld'fĭsh') *n.* pesce dorato.

goldsmith (gōld'smĭth') *n.* orefice.

golf (gŏlf) *n.* (*sport*) golf: — course, — links, campo di golf.

golosh *vedi* galosh.

gondola (gŏn'dōlā) *n.* gondola; (*ferr.*) carro merci scoperto.

gone (gŏn) *agg.* andato, partito; fuggito; spacciato; aggiudicato (*all'asta*): far —, all'estremo; in days

—by, nei tempi passati; — under, rovinato, (*pp. di* to go).

goner (gŏn'ĕr) *n.* (*gergo S.U.*) uomo spacciato.

gong (gŏng) *n.* gong.

good (gŏŏd) *n.* bene; felicità; virtù; vantaggio, profitto: for —, per sempre, definitivamente. *agg.* buono; onesto; conveniente; valido, genuino; savio: **it is no —,** è inutile; — **breeding,** buona educazione, belle maniere; —**bye,** addio; **Good Friday,** Venerdì Santo; —**looking,** bello; —**natured,** bonario, affabile.

goodly (gŏŏd'lĭ) *agg.* bello, buono; considerevole, notevole.

goodness (gŏŏd'nĕs) *n.* bontà, nobiltà: — **knows!** sa Iddio!; **thank —!** grazie a Dio!

goody (gŏŏd'ĭ) *n.* dolciume.

gook (gŏŏk) *n.* (*gergo*) roba appiccicosa; robaccia, scarto; sciocchezze; indigeno del Sud Pacifico *o* del Nord Africa (*sprezz.*)

goose (gŏŏs) *n.* (*pl.* geese) oca; (*fig.*) imbecille, balordo: **wild— chase,** impresa vana; —**flesh** *n.* pelle d'oca.

gooseberry (gŏŏz'bĕr'ĭ; gŏŏs-) *n.* ribes.

gore (gōr) *n.* sangue, sangue coagulato; (*sartoria*) gherone. *vt.* trafiggere con le corna; mettere un gherone a.

gorge (gôrj) *n.* gola, fauci; forra. *vt.* trangugiare; ingozzare. *vi.* rimpinzarsi.

gorgeous (gôr'jŭs) *agg.* magnifico, sontuoso, fastoso.

gory (gōr'ĭ) *agg.* insanguinato, sanguinoso.

gospel (gŏs'pĕl) *n.* vangelo: — **truth,** verità sacrosanta.

gossamer (gŏs'á-mĕr) *n.* velo; ragnatela; filo di ragnatela. *agg.* sottile, velato; tenue; frivolo.

gossip (gŏs'ĭp) *n.* pettegolo, pettegola; pettegolezzo. *vi.* spettegolare. —**y** *agg.* pettegolo.

got (gŏt) *pass., pp. di* to get.

gotten (gŏt'n) *pp. di* to get.

Gothic (gŏth'ĭk) *agg.* gotico; barbarico.

gouge (gouj) *n.* cesello, sgorbia. *vt.* lavorare con la sgorbia, estirpare.

gourd (gōrd) *n.* zucca.

gout (gout) *n.* gotta, podagra.

govern (gŭv'ĕrn) *vt., vi.* governare; (*gramm.*) reggere: **to — oneself,** dominarsi. —**ess** *n.* istitutrice, governante. —**ment** *n.* governo, amministrazione, regime. —**mental** *agg.* governativo. —**or** *n.* governatore; (*mecc.*) regolatore; (*gergo*) padre, padrone, "capo."

gown (goun) *n.* veste, gonna, toga: **dressing —,** veste da camera; **night— —** *n.* camicia da notte.

grab (grăb) *n.* l'arraffare, presa, morsa. *vt.* afferrare, arraffare.

grace (grās) *n.* grazia, garbo; favore. *vt.* ornare, abbellire. —**ful** *agg.* grazioso, aggraziato, garbato. —**fully** *avv.* graziosamente, cortesemente. —**fulness** *n.* grazia. —**less** *agg.* sgraziato, perverso.

gracious (grā'shŭs) *agg.* clemente, cortese, favorevole.

gradation (grā-dā'shŭn) *n.* gradazione.

grade (grād) *n.* grado, rango; classe (*scolastica*); classificazione; pendenza, declivio: — **crossing,** passaggio a livello; **the grades,** la scuola elementare. *vt.* graduare; selezionare; pareggiare

gradual (grăd'ū̇.ăl) *agg.* graduale. —**ly** *avv.* gradatamente, a poco a poco.

graduate (grăd'ū̇.āt) *n.*, *agg.* laureato, diplomato; graduato. *vt.* graduare; conferire un diploma a. *vt.* graduare; conferire un diploma a. *vi.* diplomarsi, laurearsi.

graduation (grā'dū̇.ā'shŭn) *n.* graduazione; laurea.

graft (gráft) (1) *n.* innesto. *vt.* innestare. —**er** *n.* innestatore.

graft (gráft) (2) *n.* (*S.U.*) corruzione, mangeria, camorra. *vt., vi.* frodare, prevaricare. —**er** *n.* prevaricatore.

grain (grān) *n.* grano, chicco; grana, vena (*del marmo*), fibra (*del legno*) filo: **against the —,** contropelo; **di malavoglia.**

gram (grăm) *n.* grammo.

grammar (grăm'ĕr) *n.* grammatica: — **school,** scuola media (*dai 5° all' 8° anno*).

grammatical (grā-măt'ĭ-kăl) *agg.* grammaticale.

gramophone (grăm'ō-fōn) *n.* grammofono.

granary (grăn'á-rĭ) *n.* granaio.

grand (grănd) *n.* (*gergo, S.U.*) biglietto da mille. *agg.* grande, magnifico, illustre, maestoso, grandioso. —**dad** *n.* nonno. —**child** *n.* (*pl.* grandchildren) nipotino, nipotina. —**daughter** *n.* nipotina. —**eur** *n.* grandezza, lustro, splendore. —**father** *n.* nonno. —**ma,** —**mother** *n.* nonna. —**nephew** *n.* pronipote (*maschio*). —**ness** *n.* grandezza, magnificenza. —**niece** *n.* pronipote (*femmina*). —**son** *n.* nipote (*maschio*). —**stand** *n.* tribuna principale.

grange (grănj) *n.* fattoria, casa colonica; società fra agricoltori.

granite (grăn'ĭt) n. granito.

granny (grăn'ĭ) n. (fam.) nonna.

grant (grànt) n. concessione, assegnazione. vt., vi. accordare, assegnare, permettere, acconsentire, convenire, ammettere aggiudicare: **granted that**, ammesso che; **to take for granted**, ammettere come assodato, fare affidamento su.

granulate (grăn'ū·lāt) vt. granulare. vi. divenir granuloso.

grape (grāp) n. acino d'uva; (pl. **grapes**) uva: **a bunch of grapes**, un grappolo d'uva.

grapefruit (grāp'frōōt) n. pompelmo.

grapevine (grāp'vīn) n. vigna; diceria, voce; — **telegraph**, comunicazione a distanza (con tamburi, ecc.); diffusione di dicerie.

graph (grȧf) n. grafico; diagramma; (mat.) curva. vt. tracciare un grafico. —**ic** agg. grafico, descrittivo.

graphite (grăf'ĭt) n. grafite.

graphology (grȧf·ŏl'ō·jĭ) n. grafologia.

grapple (grăp'’l) n. rampone, lotta. vt. uncinare, afferrare. vi. avvinghiarsi, lottare; andare all'abbordaggio.

grasp (grȧsp) n. presa, stretta; percezione; conoscenza: **to be within one's —**, essere a portata di mano; **to have a good — of a subject**, essere padrone di una materia. vt. stringere, impugnare, afferrare.

grasping agg. avido taccagno.

grass (grȧs) n. erba: —**roots** n.pl. (fig.), radici, base; zone agricole. —**hopper** n. grillo, saltamartino. (aeron. mil.) apparecchio di collegamento.

grassy (grȧs'ĭ) agg. erboso, verdeggiante.

grate (grāt) n. grata, graticola, inferriata, focolare. vt. grattugiare, raschiare, munire di grata. vi. stridere; irritare, molestare.

grater (grāt'ẽr) n. grattugia; raspa.

grateful (grāt'fōōl) agg. grato; gradevole.

gratification (grăt'ĭ·fĭ·kā'shŭn) n. soddisfazione, piacere.

gratify (grăt'ĭ·fĭ) vt. accontentare, far piacere a, soddisfare; gratificare.

gratifying agg. gradevole, soddisfacente.

grating (grāt'ĭng) n. inferriata. agg. irritante, stridente.

gratis (grā'tĭs) avv. gratuitamente.

gratitude (grăt'ĭ·tūd) n. gratitudine.

gratuitous (grȧ·tū'ĭ·tŭs) agg. gratuito.

gratuity (grȧ·tū'ĭ·tĭ) n. mancia, gratifica.

grave (grāv) (1) n. tomba. —**digger** n. affossatore. —**stone** n. pietra tombale, lapide.

grave (grāv) (2) agg. grave, serio.

grave (grāv) (3) vt. incidere; (naut.) calafatare.

gravel (grăv'ĕl) n. ghiaia; (med.) calcolosi renale. vt. inghiaiare.

graver (grāv'ẽr) n. scultore, incisore; bulino.

graveyard (grāv'yärd') n. cimitero.

gravity (grăv'ĭ·tĭ) n. gravità.

gravy (grā'vĭ) n. sugo di carne.

gray (grā) agg. grigio; brizzolato. —**ish** agg. grigiastro, grigiognolo. —**ness** n. grigiore; color grigio; canizie.

graze (grāz) n. escoriazione, graffiatura. vt., vi. graffiare, scalfire, sfiorare; brucare, pascolare.

grease (grēs) n. unto, grasso. vt. dare il grasso a, ungere: **to — the palm**, ungere le ruote (fig.).

greasy (grēs'ĭ) agg. grasso, unto, sudicio.

great (grāt) agg. grande, considerevole, magnanimo, superiore: **a — deal**, un bel po', molto; **a — many**, moltissimi; **a — while**, un bel po' di tempo. —**er** agg. più grande. —**est** agg. (il) più grande. —**grandchild** n. pronipote. —**granddaughter** n. pronipote (femmina). —**grandfather** n. bisavolo. —**grandmother** n. bisavola. —**grandson** n. pronipote (maschio).

greatly avv. grandemente, molto, oltremodo, generosamente.

greatness n. grandezza.

Grecian (grē'shăn) agg., n. greco.

greed (grēd) n. avidità, cupidigia. —**ily** avv. avidamente. —**iness** n. cupidigia, avidità.

greedy (grēd'ĭ) agg. avido, ingordo.

Greek (grēk) agg., n. greco.

green (grēn) n. verde; prato; campo di golf; (pl.) frasche; verdura. agg. verde, verdeggiante; fresco, nuovo, novello, giovane; recente, inesperto: — **light**, segnale verde o di via libera; (fig.) benestare, autorizzazione. —**back** n. biglietto di banca (S.U.). —**grocer** n. erbivendolo, fruttivendolo. —**house** n. serra. —**ish** agg. verdastro. —**ness** n. verdezza; freschezza, acerbezza, ingenuità, inesperienza.

greet (grēt) vt., vi. salutare: **to — each other**, salutarsi. —**ing** n. saluto.

gregarious (grḗ·gâr'ĭ·ŭs) agg. socievole; (bot., zool.) gregario.

greige (grāzh) agg. greggio (di colore).

gremlin (grĕm'lĭn) n. (aeron. scherz.) folletto maligno degli aviatori.

grenade (grḗ·nād') n. granata: **hand —**, bomba a mano.

grenadier (grĕn'ȧ·dẽr') n. granatiere.

grew (grōō) *pass. di* to grow.

grey (grā) *vedi* gray.

greyhound (grā'hound') *n.* levriere.

greyish, greyness *vedi* gray.

grid (grĭd) *n.* griglia.

griddle (grĭd''l) *n.* teglia, piastra.

gridiron (grĭd'ī'ẽrn) *n.* graticola; impalcatura.

grief (grēf) *n.* dolore, calamità: to come to —, finire male.

grievance (grēv'ăns) *n.* afflizione, torto, pena, ingiustizia.

grieve (grēv) *vt.* affliggere, rattristare. *vi.* affliggersi, addolorarsi.

grievous (grēv'ŭs) *agg.* doloroso; grave; gravoso.

grill (grĭl) *n.* graticola. *vt.* cuocere in graticola, sottoporre a interrogatorio.

grim (grĭm) *agg.* arcigno, torvo; sinistro; implacabile; accanito.

grimace (grĭ-mās') *n.* smorfia, boccaccia. *vi.* fare smorfie *o* boccacce.

grime (grīm) *n.* sudiciume. *vt.* sporcare.

grimy (grīm'ĭ) *agg.* sudicio.

grin (grĭn) *n.* smorfia, sogghigno; sorriso. *vi.* sogghignare, sorridere.

grind (grīnd) *n.* macinazione, smerigliatura; lavoro arduo, preparazione a un esame; sgobbone: daily —, andazzo *o* tran-tran quotidiano. *vt.* (*pass., pp.* ground) macinare, smerigliare, rettificare; affilare; opprimere, tartassare, schiacciare; sonare (*l'organetto*). *vi.* digrignare (*i denti*); frantumarsi, sgobbare; raschiare. **—er** *n.* arrotino; mola, rettifica; macinino (*per caffè*); dente molare; sgobbone; banditore; (*radio*) scarica; tosto (*panino imbottito*). **—stone** *n.* mola.

grip (grĭp) *n.* presa, stretta; impugnatura; afflizione; valigetta: to come to grips, venire alle mani. *vt.* afferrare, stringere; impadronirsi di.

gripe (grīp) *n.* presa, grinfia; (*pl.*) crampi, coliche; (*gergo*) malumore, "buschere." *vt.* irritare, seccare. *vi.* borbottare, lagnarsi.

grisly (grĭz'lĭ) *agg.* orrendo, macabro.

grist (grĭst) *n.* grano da macinare; provvista; profitto: to bring the — to the mill, tirar l'acqua al proprio mulino.

grit (grĭt) *n.* sabbia; pietra arenaria; pulviscolo; pertinacia, coraggio. *vt., vi.* macinare; digrignare. **—ty** *agg.* sabbioso; pertinace.

grizzled (grĭz''ld) *agg.* grigio, brizzolato.

grizzly (grĭz'lĭ) *n.* orso grigio. *agg.* grigiastro.

groan (grōn) *n.* gemito, lamento. *vi.* gemere, lamentarsi.

grocer (grō'sẽr) *n.* droghiere.

grocery (grō'sẽr-ĭ) *n.* drogheria; (*pl.*) droghe e coloniali.

groin (groin) *n.* inguine.

groom (grōōm) *n.* palafreniere, stalliere; sposo. *vt.* agghindare; strigliare (*cavalli*); istruire: well-groomed, ben vestito, curato, in ordine. **—sman** *n.* compare d'anello.

groove (grōōv) *n.* scanalatura, solco. *vt.* scanalare.

grope (grōp) *vi.* brancolare, annaspare: to — for, cercare a tastoni.

gropingly (grōp'ĭng-lĭ) *avv.* a tastoni.

gross (grōs) *n.* grossa (*dodici dozzine*); massa. *agg.* grosso, grossolano; lordo: — weight, peso lordo; — ignorance, ignoranza crassa.

grot (grŏt) *n.* grotta.

grotesque (grō-tĕsk') *agg.* grottesco.

grotto (grŏt'ō) *n.* grotta.

grouch (grouch) *n.* malumore, broncio, rovello: to have a — against, avere rancore contro, avercela con. *vi.* essere di malumore, brontolare. **—y** *agg.* imbronciato, intrattabile.

ground (ground) (1) *pass., pp. di* to grind.

ground (ground) (2) *n.* terra, terreno, suolo; motivo, base, fondamento: to break —, arare, scavare; to give —, retrocedere, cedere terreno; to hold one's —, resistere (a piè fermo); — crew (*aeron.*) squadra di manutenzione a terra. *vt.* fondare, basare; far atterrare; far arenare; mettere a terra; atterrare. (*aeron.*) trattenere a terra, non autorizzare al volo. *vi.* basarsi; incagliarsi, arenarsi; (*aeron.*) atterrare: well-ed, benfondato. **—floor** *n.* piano terreno. **—less** *agg.* infondato.

grounds *n.pl.* parco; sedimento; sfondo.

groundwork *n.* base.

group (grōōp) *n.* gruppo. *vt., vi.* raggruppare, raggrupparsi. **—ing** *n.* raggruppamento.

grove (grōv) *n.* boschetto.

grovel (grŭv'l) *vi.* strisciare, umiliarsi. **—ling** *agg.* abbietto, strisciante.

grow (grō) *vt.* (*pass.* grew, *pp.* grown) allevare, coltivare. *vi.* crescere, progredire, aumentare; farsi, diventare; germogliare: to — better, migliorare; to — late, farsi tardi; to — worse, peggiorare; to — into, diventare; to — less, diminuire; to — out of a habit, perdere un'abitudine; to — up, crescere.

growl (groul) *n.* brontolio, ringhio. *vi.* ringhiare, brontolare. **—er** *n.*

brontolone; (gergo S.U.) barattolo (per birra).

grown (grōn) (pp. di to grow), agg. cresciuto, sviluppato, fatto: — man, adulto, uomo fatto; — with trees, coperto d'alberi. —up n., agg. adulto.

growth (grōth) n. crescita, sviluppo; raccolto; evoluzione; vegetazione; tumore, escrescenza.

grub (grŭb) n. larva, verme, baco; (fam.) cibo.

grudge (grŭj) n. rancore; invidia; livore, malevolenza. vt. invidiare; lesinare.

grudgingly (grŭj'ĭng.lĭ) avv. malvolontieri.

gruesome (grōo'sŭm) agg. macabro, lugubre, spaventoso.

gruff (grŭf) agg. burbero, brusco.

grumble (grŭm'b'l) n. brontolio. vi. brontolare, lagnarsi.

grumbler (grŭm'blĕr) n. brontolone.

grumpy (grŭm'pĭ) agg. bisbetico.

grunt (grŭnt) n. grugnito; brontolio. vt., vi. grugnire, borbottare.

G-suit (jē'sūt') n. (aeron.) tuta a pressione

guarantee (găr'ăn.tē') n. garanzia; garante. vt. garantire.

guarantor (găr'ăn.ôr) n. garante.

guaranty (găr'ăn.tĭ) n. garanzia.

guard   rd) n. guardia; difesa, protezione; (ferr.) capotreno: on —, in guardia; to be off one's —, essere impreparato (a un attacco); essere vt. sorvegliare, proteggere. vi. stare in guardia, difendersi, premunirsi.

guarded agg. prudente, circospetto.

guardian (găr'dĭ.ăn) n. guardiano, tutore: — angel, angelo custode. —ship n. tutela, difesa, protezione.

guerrilla (gĕ-rĭl'ă) n. guerriglia; franco tiratore, partigiano.

guess (gĕs) n. congettura, supposizione: at a rough —, a occhio e croce. vt., vi. ritenere, supporre, credere; indovinare. —work n. congettura.

guest (gĕst) n. ospite (invitato).

guffaw (gŭ.fô') n. risata sganherata. vi. sghignazzare.

guidance (gīd'ăns) n. guida, norma; direzione; regola.

guide (gīd) n. guida. vt. guidare: guided missile, missile telecomandato o radiocomandato.

guidebook (gīd'bŏŏk') n. guida (opuscolo): railroad —, orario ferroviario.

guild (gĭld) n. corporazione, associazione. —hall n. palazzo municipale.

guile (gīl) n. astuzia. —less agg. semplice, ingenuo, sincero, candido.

guilt (gĭlt) n. colpa, colpevolezza, misfatto. —less agg. innocente. —y agg. colpevole.

guinea (gĭn'ĭ) n. ghinea (moneta): — fowl, gallina faraona; — pig, cavia.

guise (gīz) n. guisa, maniera, apparenza: under the — of, camuffato da; col pretesto di.

guitar (gĭ.tär') n. chitarra.

gulf (gŭlf) n. golfo, baia; gorgo, abisso.

gull (gŭl) (1) n. gabbiano.

gull (gŭl) (2) n. gonzo.

gullet (gŭl'ĕt) n. gola, strozza.

gullible (gŭl'ĭ.b'l) agg. credulone.

gully (gŭl'ĭ) n. burrone.

gulp (gŭlp) n. sorsata, boccone. vt. inghiottire, ingoiare, trangugiare.

gum (gŭm) (1) n. gengiva.

gum (gŭm) (2) n. gomma: chewing —, gomma da masticare; vt. ingommare. —ming n. ingommatura. — tree, albero da gomma, eucaliptus.

gun (gŭn) n. fucile; cannone; pistola, rivoltella; arma da fuoco: big —, pezzo grosso, personaggio importante. vt., vi. prender di mira; dar la caccia (a); dare tutto gas (al motore): — license, porto d'armi; —boat n. cannoniera. —powder, n. polvere da sparo.

gunner (gŭn'ĕr) n. artigliere.

gunsmith (gŭn'smĭth') n. armaiolo.

gurgle (gûr'g'l) n. gorgoglio. vi. gorgogliare.

gush (gŭsh) n. zampillo; effusione, entusiasmo. vi. zampillare, scorrere; abbandonarsi a effusioni.

gust (gŭst) n. folata, raffica, accesso d'ira.

gusto (gŭs'tō) n. gusto, piacere; entusiasmo, foga.

gusty (gŭs'tĭ) agg. ventoso, impetuoso.

gut (gŭt) n. budello, intestino; (pl.) intestini, ventre; to have —s, (gergo S.U.) aver coraggio. vt. sventrare, vuotare.

gutter (gŭt'ĕr) n. grondaia; cunetta, rigagnolo, solco; (fig.) bassifondi.

guy (gī) n. individuo, tipo, soggetto; uomo, ragazzo; fantoccio; (naut.) tirante, catena di sostegno, cavo. vt. sostenere con tiranti o catene; burlarsi (di).

gymnasium (jĭm.nā'zĭ.ŭm) n. palestra.

gymnastics (jĭm.năs'tĭks) n. ginnastica.

gypsum (jĭp'sŭm) n. gesso.

gypsy (jĭp'sĭ) vedi gipsy.

gyrate (jī'rāt) vi. girare, turbinare.

gyration (jī.rā'shŭn) n. movimento rotatorio, vortice.

gyrene (jī.rēn') n. (gergo mil. S.U.) fante di marina, marine.

H

haberdasher (hăb'ĕr-dăsh'ĕr) *n.* merciaio. —**y** *n.* merceria.

habit (hăb'ĭt) *n.* abitudine, costume, usanza; abito: — **of body**, costituzione fisica; — **of mind**, abito mentale.

habitual (hă-bĭt'ū-ăl) *agg.* abituale.

hack (hăk) *n.* tosse secca; ronzino; carrozza da nolo; intaccatura; scrittore mercenario, scribacchino: —**work**, lavoro letterario mal retribuito. *vt.* tritare, sminuzzare, massacrare, scorticare. *vi.* tossire convulsamente; (*sport*) colpire un avversario (*spec. al polso*).

hackle (hăk''l) *n.* carda (*per fibre tessili*). *vt.* cardare.

hackneyed (hăk'nĭd) *agg.* banale, comune.

had (hăd) *pass. e pp. di* to have.

hag (hăg) *n.* megera, strega.

haggard (hăg'ĕrd) *agg.* sparuto, smunto, emaciato, spettrale; selvaggio, truce.

haggle (hăg''l) *vi.* mercanteggiare.

hail (hāl)(1) *n.* grandine. *vi.* grandinare.

hail (hāl) (2) *n.* saluto. *inter.* salve! *vt.* salutare, acclamare, chiamare: **to** — **from**, essere oriundo di.

hailstorm (-stôrm') *n.* grandinata.

hair (hâr) *n.* capello, capelli, pelo, peli, criniera, setole, peluria (*vegetale*): **to a** —, esattamente, con precisione; **not to turn a** —, non scomporsi; **to split hairs**, sottilizzare, cercare il pelo nell'uovo. —**breadth** *n.*: **to have a hairbreadth escape**, cavarsela per miracolo. —**brush** *n.* spazzola per capelli. —**cut** *n.* taglio di capelli. —**do** *n.* acconciatura, pettinatura. —**dresser** *n.* parrucchiere. —**less** *agg.* calvo, senza peli. —**pin** *n.* forcina per capelli. —**y** *agg.* capelluto, peloso.

hale (hāl) *agg.* robusto, sano, vigoroso. *vt.* trainare, trascinare a forza.

half (hăf) *n.* (*pl.* **halves** [hăvz]) metà, mezzo: — **as much as**, la metà di; — **an apple**, mezza mela. *agg.* mezzo, incompleto. *avv.* a metà, incompletamente. —**breed** *n.* meticcio. —**brother** *n.* fratellastro. —**done** *agg.* cotto a metà. —**hearted** *agg.* tepido, indifferente. —**mast** *agg.* a mezz'asta (*di bandiera*). —**open** *agg.* semiaperto. —**sister** *n.* sorellastra. —**way** *avv.* a metà (strada). —**witted** *agg.* tonto.

hall (hôl) *n.* sala, vestibolo; corridoio; palazzo; refettorio scolastico; aula

(*di palazzo di giustizia*). —**mark** *n.* marchio (*sull'oro o sull'argento*); impronta caratteristica.

hallo! (hă-lōō') *inter.* (*Ingl.*) ohè! (*telef.*) pronto.

hallow (hăl'ō) *vt.* santificare.

Halloween (hăl'ō-ēn') *n.* vigilia dell'Ognissanti.

hallucination (hă-lū'sĭ-nā'shŭn) *n.* allucinazione.

halo (hā'lō) *n.* alone, aureola.

halt (hôlt) *n.* fermata, sosta; zoppicamento. *agg.* zoppo. *vt.* fermare, trattenere. *vi.* fermarsi, trattenersi; zoppicare; esitare.

halter (hôl'tĕr) *n.* cavezza; capestro; bustino (*del prendisole*).

halting *agg.* esitante, vacillante.

halve (hăv) *vt.* dimezzare, spartire in due.

halves (hăvz) *pl. di* **half**: **to go** —, fare a mezzo.

halyard (hăl'yĕrd) *n.* (*naut.*) drizza.

ham (hăm) *n.* prosciutto; (*teat.*) gigione, istrione, radioamatore. *vi.* (*teat.*) caricare una parte, gigionare.

hamburger (hă·m'bûr·gĕr) *n.* polpetta di carne tra due fette di pane.

hamlet (hăm'lĕt) *n.* borgo, villaggio.

hammer (hăm'ĕr) *n.* martello; cane (*di fucile*). *vt.*, *vi.* martellare; tempestare inculcare.

hammock (hăm'ŭk) *n.* amaca.

hamper (hăm'pĕr) *n.* canestro, cesta; impedimento. *vt.* mettere in imbarazzo, impedire, ostacolare.

hand (hănd) *n.* mano; spanna (*misura*); scrittura; lancetta (*dell'orologio*); operaio; parte, lato: — **in** —, per mano, con la mano in mano; **at** —, a portata di mano; — **to** —, corpo a corpo; **on** —, pronto, disponibile; **on the other** —, d'altro canto, per contro; **second** —, d'occasione; **to be** — **and glove together**, essere come pane e cacio; **to get the upper** —, prendere il sopravvento; **to live from** — **to mouth**, vivere alla giornata; **to show one's** —, rivelare le proprie intenzioni. *vt.* porgere, dare, consegnare: **to** — **down**, aiutare a discendere; **to** — **over**, trasmettere, cedere. —**bag** *n.* valigetta, borsa. —**bill** *n.* manifesto, prospetto, volantino. —**book** *n.* manuale. —**cuff** *n.* manetta; *vt.* ammanettare. —**ful** *n.* manciata. —**made** *agg.* fatto a mano. —**out** *n.* (*gergo S.U.*) elemosina di cibo o vestiario; manifestino o pieghevole pubblicitario; (giorn.) comunicato stampa, dichiarazione ufficiale per la stampa. —shake n. stretta di mano. —writing n. scrittura.

handicap (hăn'dĭ-kăp) n. intralcio, svantaggio, ostacolo. vt. impedire, ostacolare.

handiwork (hăn'dĭ-wûrk') n. lavoro fatto a mano; opera.

handkerchief (hăng'kẽr-chĭf) n. fazzoletto.

handle (hăn'd'l) n. manico; impugnatura (di spada); maniglia (di porta); ansa (di brocca); manovella: to give a —, fornire il destro. vt. maneggiare; trattare; toccare; amministrare. —bar n. manubrio (di bicicletta).

handsome (hăn'sŭm) agg. bello, piacente; elegante; generoso.

handy (hăn'dĭ) agg. abile; comodo, maneggevole; a portata di mano: to come in —, tornare comodo, giungere opportuno.

hang (hăng) vt., vi. (pass., pp. hung, hanged [nel significato d'impiccare]) appendere, attaccare, tappezzare; pendere; abbassare (il capo): to — back, esitare, indugiare; to — on, tenersi avvinto a, dipendere da; penzolare da, essere appeso a; persistere; to — together, accordarsi, tenersi uniti; to — about, bighellonare, aggirarsi. n. modo di stare (di un indumento indosso); maneggio, manovra (di uno strumento); metodo (per risolvere un problema); significato: I don't give a—, non me ne importa un fico. —er n. uncino, gancio, gruccia (per vestiti): —on, seguace; parassita; paper—, tappezziere. —ing n. impiccagione; tappezzeria; tendaggio. agg. sospeso, appeso. —man n. boia. —over n. residuo, sopravvivenza; postumi di sbornia.

hanker (hăng'kẽr) vi.: to — after, bramare. —ing n. desiderio ardente.

haphazard (hăp'hăz'ẽrd) n. caso, agg. casuale. avv. casualmente, a casaccio.

hapless (hăp'lĕs) agg. sfortunato.

happen (hăp'ĕn) vi. avvenire, capitare: I happened to hear, udii per caso; if he happened to come, se per caso egli venisse; to — upon, imbattersi. —ing n. avvenimento.

happily (hăp'ĭ-lĭ) avv. fortunatamente, felicemente.

happiness (hăp'ĭ-nĕs) n. felicità.

happy (hăp'ĭ) agg. felice; contento. —go-lucky agg. spensierato.

harangue (há-răng') n. arringa. vt., vi. arringare, concionare.

harass (hăr'ás) vt. molestare, tormentare.

harbinger (här'bĭn-jẽr) n. precursore, pioniere; staffetta, messaggiero.

harbor (här'bẽr) n. porto; rifugio, asilo. vt. albergare, alloggiare, ospitare.

hard (härd) agg. duro, tenace; difficile, faticoso; rude, severo: — labor, lavori forzati; — liquor, liquore forte; — luck, sfortuna. — up, al verde, senza quattrini; in — cash, in moneta sonante. avv. duramente, faticosamente, fortemente: — by, accanto a, vicino. —hearted agg. insensibile, inumano. —working agg. laborioso. —of-hearing agg. duro d'orecchio.

harden (här'd'n) vt. indurire; (metal.) temperare. vi. indurirsi. —ing n. indurimento; (metal.) tempera.

hardihood (här'dĭ-hŏŏd) n. ardimento, audacia; resistenza.

hardly (härd'lĭ) avv. appena, a mala pena, stentatamente; duramente; difficilmente, probabilmente no: — ever, quasi mai.

hardness (härd'nĕs) n. durezza; fermezza; difficoltà; brutalità.

hardship (härd'shĭp) n. fatica; pena, privazione, avversità.

hardware (härd'wâr') n. utensileria, ferramenta.

hardy (här'dĭ) agg. ardito, coraggioso, duro, vigoroso, forte.

hare (hâr) n. lepre. —brained agg. scervellato.

hark (härk) vi. ascoltare: to — back, tornare a bomba.

harlot (här'lŏt) n. prostituta.

harm (härm) n. danno, male, torto: out of harm's way, in salvo. vt. nuocere a, danneggiare. —ful agg. dannoso, nocivo, malefico. —less ness n. innocuità.

harmonic (här-mŏn'ĭk) agg. armonico, armonioso.

harmonious (här-mō'nĭ-ŭs) agg. armonico, melodioso.

harmonize (här'mō-nīz) vt., vi. armonizzare, rendere armonioso; mettere d'accordo, andare d'accordo.

harmony (här'mō-nĭ) n. armonia.

harness (här'nĕs) n. bardatura, finimenti (di cavallo): to die in —, morire sul lavoro. vt. bardare; attaccare (a una carrozza).

harp (härp) n. arpa. vi. sonare l'arpa: to — on, upon, insistere su un argomento.

harpoon (här-pōōn') n. rampone, fiocina. vt. fiocinare.

harrow (här'ō) n. erpice. vt. erpicare; lacerare, straziare, torturare. —ing *n.* erpicamento, strazio. *agg.* straziante, doloroso.

harry (här'ǐ) *vt.* saccheggiare, devastare; tormentare.

harsh (härsh) *agg.* aspro, rude, agro, duro; roco; discordante. —ness *n.* asprezza, severità, discordanza.

hart (härt) *n.* cervo.

harvest (här'věst) *n.* messe, raccolto: — home, festa del raccolto. *vt.* mietere, raccogliere. —er *n.* mietitore; mietitrice (*macchina*).

hash (hash) *n.* carne trita; accozzaglia, mescolanza; manipolazione; confusione. *vt.* triturare.

hasp (hásp) *n.* fermaglio, lucchetto.

haste (hāst) *n.* fretta, precipitazione: to make —, affrettarsi, far presto. *vi.* affrettarsi: to — away, andarsene precipitosamente.

hasten (hās'n) *vt.* affrettare, accelerare. *vi.* affrettarsi.

hastily (hās'tǐ.lǐ) *avv.* affrettatamente, frettolosamente.

hasty (hās'tǐ) *agg.* frettoloso, rapido, precipitoso, impulsivo.

hat (hăt) *n.* cappello. to — band *n.* nastro per cappello.

hatch (hăch) *n.* covata, nidiata; botola, portello; boccaporto. *vt.* covare, incubare, far dischiudere; tramare; tratteggiare (*un disegno*). —er *n.* incubatrice.

hatchet (hăch'ĕt) *n.* scure, ascia, accetta: to bury the —, riconciliarsi; to take up the —, aprire le ostilità.

hatchway (hăch'wā') *n.* boccaporto.

hate (hāt) *n.* odio. *vt.* odiare, detestare. —ful *agg.* odioso, detestabile.

hatred (hā'trĕd) *n.* odio, avversione.

haughtily (hô'tǐ.lǐ) *avv.* altezzosamente, arrogantemente.

haughtiness (hô'tǐ.nĕs) *n.* orgoglio, alterigia.

haughty (hô'tǐ) *agg.* altezzoso, sprezzante, arrogante.

haul (hôl) *n.* rimorchio (*il rimorchiare*); trascinamento, retata (*di pesci*); bottino, guadagno. *vt.* tirare, trascinare, rimorchiare, trasportare: to — in (*naut.*); to — up, issare; to — down, ammainare.

haunt (hônt) *n.* ritrovo, luogo di convegno, rifugio. *vt.* frequentare, bazzicare; ossessionare, perseguitare: a haunted house, una casa abitata dagli spettri.

have (hăv) *vt. e aus.* (*pass., pp.* had) avere, possedere: had he known, se egli avesse saputo; I had to go there, dovetti andarci; I had better go away, è meglio che me ne vada; I will not — it, non lo permetterò; to — something done, far fare

qualche cosa; to — done with, finirla con, non aver più a che fare con; to — on, indossare; to — a look at, dare un'occhiata a.

haven (hā'věn) *n.* porto, rifugio.

havoc (hăv'ŭk) *n.* rovina, devastazione, strage: to play — with, devastare.

hawk (hôk) *n.* falco, sparviero. *vt.* portare attorno (*mercanzie*) per vendere.

hawthorn (hô'thôrn) *n.* biancospino.

hay (hā) *n.* fieno. —loft *n.* fienile. —rick, —stack *n.* mucchio di fieno.

hazard (hăz'ẽrd) *n.* azzardo, rischio. *vt.*, *vi.* arrischiare, osare, avventurarsi. —ous *agg.* azzardato, rischioso.

haze (hāz) *n.* nebbia, bruma; confusione. *vt.* annebbiare, angariare.

hazel (hā'z'l) *n.* nocciuolo. *agg.* di nocciuolo, color nocciuola: —nut, nocciuola.

hazy (hā'zǐ) *agg.* nebuloso, nebbioso, annebbiato, opaco, velato: — notions, idee poco chiare.

he (hē) (1) *pron.pers.m.* egli, colui: — who, colui che.

he (2) *pref.* maschio: he-elephant, elefante maschio; he-goat, caprone; a he-man, un vero uomo.

head (hĕd) *n.* testa, capo; prua; capezzale; sorgente (*di fiume*); punta (*di freccia*); pomo (*di bastone*); testata (*di pagina*): a —, per —, a testa, per persona; — over heels, perdutamente, a rotoli; — or tail, testa o croce; to come to a —, maturare; suppurare; risolversi; to keep one's —, controllarsi; to make — against, far fronte a. *agg.* primo, principale, in capo. *vt.* mettersi alla testa di, capeggiare, dirigere; intestare; affrontare. *vi.* dirigersi. —ache *n.* mal di capo, emicrania, (*fig.*) noia, grattacapo, rompicapo. —dress *n.* pettinatura, cappellino. —gear *n.* copricapo. —ing *n.* intestazione, titolo. —land *n.* promontorio. —light *n.* fanale anteriore. —line *n.* intestazione (*di articolo*), titolo (*di libro*). —long *avv.* a capofitto, a testa bassa, impetuosamente. —quarters *n.* quartier generale; direzione, sede centrale. —strong *agg.* testardo. —way *n.* progresso, avanzamento: to make —, avanzare, progredire. —wind, vento contrario.

heady (hĕd'ǐ) *agg.* inebriante.

heal (hēl) *vt.* guarire, cicatrizzare, sanare. —ing *n.* guarigione, cicatrizzazione.

health (hĕlth) *n.* salute. —**ful** *agg.* sano, salubre. —**fulness** *n.* salubrità, sanità.

healthy (hĕl'thĭ) *agg.* sano, salubre, salutare.

heap (hēp) *n.* mucchio, cumulo, quantità. *vt.* ammucchiare, accumulare.

hear (hēr) *vt., vi.* (*pass., pp.* heard) udire, ascoltare; apprendere: to — from, avere notizie da; to — of *o* about, avere notizie di. —**er** *n.* ascoltatore. —**ing** *n.* udito (senso); udienza; ascolto: **within** —, a portata di voce.

heard (hûrd) *pass* e *pp. di to* hear.

hearken (här'kĕn) *vt.* ascoltare.

hearsay (hēr'sā') *n.* diceria: by —, per sentito dire.

hearse (hûrs) *n.* carro funebre.

heart (härt) *n.* cuore, animo; centro; coraggio: at —, nell'intimo. in sostanza; by —, a memoria. in one's — of hearts, nel più profondo del cuore. *vt.* incoraggiare, rincuorare. —**ache** *n.* angoscia. —**break** *n.* crepacuore. —**breaking** *agg.* straziante. —**broken** *n.* angosciato, affranto.

hearten (här't'n) *vt.* incoraggiare, rincuorare.

heartfelt (härt'fĕlt') *agg.* cordiale, spontaneo.

hearth (härth) *n.* focolare; (*fig.*) famiglia.

heartily (här'tĭ-lĭ) *avv.* cordialmente; con slancio; di buon appetito.

heartiness (här'tĭ-nĕs) *n.* cordialità, vigore.

heartless (härt'lĕs) *agg.* spietato, vile.

heart-rending *agg.* straziante.

heartsease (härts'ēz) *n.* pace del cuore; (*bot.*) viola del pensiero.

hearty (här'tĭ) *agg.* sincero, cordiale; robusto, vigoroso; di buon appetito; nutriente; abbondante.

heat (hēt) *n.* calore, caldo; ardore. collera; (*S.U.*) applicazione severa delle leggi, persecuzione dei criminali; pressioni; tensione; (*sport*) prova: **the deciding** —, la prova finale. *vt., vi.* riscaldare, infiammare, riscaldarsi, infiammarsi. —**er** *n.* calorifero, apparecchio di riscaldamento. —**ing** *n.* riscaldamento.

heath (hēth) *n.* brughiera, erica.

heathen (hē'thĕn) *n., agg.* pagano.

heather (hĕth'ẽr) *n.* erica.

heave (hēv) *n.* sforzo, conato; scossa; sollevamento. *vt.* (*pass., pp.* heaved) alzare; sollevare, gettare, lanciare, emettere (*un sospiro*); (*naut.*) (*pass., pp.* hove) issare, virare. *vi.*

sollevarsi, gonfiarsi, palpitare; avere conati di vomito: to — in sight, apparire; to — to (*naut.*), mettere in panna.

heaven (hĕv'ĕn) *n.* paradiso, cielo. —**ly** *agg.* celeste, celestiale, divino.

heavily (hĕv'ĭ-lĭ) *avv.* pesantemente, penosamente, intensamente.

heaviness (hĕv'ĭ-nĕs) *n.* pesantezza; tristezza sonnolenza.

heavy (hĕv'ĭ) *agg.* pesante; gravoso; penoso, noioso; triste; difficile: — water, acqua pesante; — rain, pioggia fitta *o* scrosciante.

heckle (hĕk''l) *n.* carda. *vt.* cardare; tempestare di domande; schernire.

hectic (hĕk'tĭk) *agg.* tisico; febbrile.

hedge (hĕj) *n.* siepe. *vt.* cintare con siepe: to — a bet, agire in modo evasivo; to — in, rinchiudere, cintare. *vi.* nascondersi, sgattaiolare. —**hog** *n.* istrice. —**hop** *vi., vt.* volare *o* pilotare un apparecchio rasente al suolo.

heed (hēd) *n.* attenzione, diligenza. *vt., vi.* prestare attenzione, badare a. —**less** *agg.* sventato, disattento.

heel (hēl) *n.* tallone, calcagno, tacco; (*gergo*) farabutto vigliacco; sbandamento: **down at** —, in miseria; to go head over heels, andare a gambe all'aria to take to one's heels, darsela a gambe. *vt., vi.* seguire da vicino ballare sui tacchi; mettere il tacco (*a una scarpa*) *o* il calcagno (*a una calza*); (*naut.*) sbandare.

heifer (hĕf'ẽr) *n.* giovenca.

height (hīt) *n.* altezza, statura; altura culmine.

heighten (hīt'n) *vt.* innalzare, elevare, accrescere, intensificare. *vi.* innalzarsi, accentuarsi.

heinous (hā'nŭs) *agg.* atroce.

heir (âr) *n.* erede. —**ess** *n.* erede (*f.*), ereditiera.

held (hĕld) *pass., pp. di to* hold.

helicopter (hĕl'ĭ-kŏp'tẽr) *n.* elicòttero.

heliotrope (hē'lĭ-ō-trōp) *n.* (*bot.*) eliotropio.

heliport (hĕl'ĭ-pōrt) *n.* eliporto.

helix (hē'lĭks) *n.* (*pl.* helices) elice, spirale, voluta.

hell (hĕl) *n.* inferno; casa da gioco. —**cat** *n.* strega, bisbetica. —**ish** *agg.* infernale.

hello (hĕ-lō') *inter.* salve! pronto! (*al telefono*): — -girl, telefonista (*f.*).

helm (hĕlm) *n.* timone.

helmet (hĕl'mĕt) *n.* elmo; casco: casco coloniale.

helmsman (hĕlmz'măn) *n.* timoniere.

help (hĕlp) *n.* aiuto, assistenza, soccorso, rimedio; aiutante; domestico: **there's no — for it,** è inevitabile.

vt. aiutare, assistere, soccorrere, evitare, rimediare; servire *(cibo)*: **how can I — it?** che posso farci?; **I cannot — saying,** non posso fare a meno di dire; **to — down,** aiutare a discendere; **to — out,** aiutare ad uscire; **to — oneself,** aiutarsi; servirsi *(a tavola).* **—er** *n.* aiutante, soccorritore. **—ful** *agg.* utile, servizievole. **—ing** *n.* aiuto; porzione. **—less** *agg.* debole, impotente, disperato, incapace, smarrito, irreparabile. **—lessly** *avv.* debolmente, senza aiuto. **—lessness** *n.* debolezza, impotenza, irreparabilità.

helter-skelter (hĕl'tĕr-skĕl'tĕr) *avv.* confusamente, frettolosamente.

hem (hĕm) *n.* orlo, bordo. *vt.* orlare; tossicchiare. **to — in,** circondare, accerchiare.

hemisphere (hĕm'ĭ-sfĕr) *n.* emisfero.

hem·ck (hĕm'lŏk) *n.* cicuta.

hemorrhage (hĕm'ô-rĭj) *n.* emorragia.

hemp (hĕmp) *n.* canapa.

hemstitch (hĕm'stĭch') *n.* orlo a giorno. *vt.* orlare a giorno.

hen (hĕn) *n.* gallina; femmina *(degli uccelli):* **— party,** riunione di sole donne.

hence (hĕns) *avv.* di qui, donde, per questo motivo: **a week —,** tra una settimana. **—forth, —forward** *avv.* da oggi in poi, per l'avvenire.

her (hûr) *pron.pers.f.* lei, la, le. *agg. poss.f.* suo, sua, suoi, sue *(di lei).*

herald (hĕr'ăld) *n.* araldo, annunciatore; *(fig.)* precursore. *vt.* annunciare, proclamare.

herb (ûrb) *n.* erba.

herculean (hûr·kū'lĕ·ăn) *agg.* erculeo.

herd (hûrd) *n.* gregge, armento, mandra, branco, turba; mandriano: **the common —,** la plebaglia. *vt.* custodire, condurre una mandria, riunire in branco. *vi.* riunirsi in branco. **—sman** *n.* vaccaro, buttero; pastore.

here (hĕr) *avv.* qui, ecco: **that is neither — nor there,** questo non c'entra, questo è fuor di proposito; **here's to you!** alla vostra salute! **—about, —abouts** *avv.* qui vicino, nei dintorni. **—after** *n.* l'aldilà; *avv.* d'ora innanzi, in seguito, per l'avvenire. **—by** *avv.* con questo mezzo, con ciò, con la presente; qui vicino.

hereditary (hĕ·rĕd'ĭ·tĕr'ĭ) *agg.* ereditario.

heredity (hĕ·rĕd'ĭ·tĭ) *n.* ereditarietà.

herein (hĕr·ĭn') *avv.* qui dentro, in ciò; qui accluso.

heresy (hĕr'ĕ·sĭ) *n.* eresia.

heretic (hĕr'ĕ·tĭk) *n.* eretico.

hereto (hĕr'tŏŏ) *avv.* a tuttora, sin qui.

heretofore (hĕr'tŏŏ·fôr') *avv.* prima d'ora, sino ad ora, in passato.

hereupon (hĕr'ŭ·pŏn') *avv.* al che, dopo di che.

herewith (hĕr·wĭth') *avv.* con questo, unitamente, qui accluso.

heritage (hĕr'ĭ·tĭj) *n.* eredità, retaggio.

hermetic (hûr·mĕt'ĭk) *agg.* ermetico.

hermit (hûr'mĭt) *n.* eremita. **—age** *n.* eremitaggio, eremo.

hero (hĕr'ō) *n. (pl.* **heroes)** eroe, protagonista.

heroic (hē·rō'ĭk) *agg.* eroico.

heroine (hĕr'ō·ĭn) *n.* eroina, protagonista.

heroism (hĕr'ō·ĭz'm) *n.* eroismo.

heron (hĕr'ŭn) *n.* airone.

herring (hĕr'ĭng) *n.* aringa. **—bone** *n.* spina di pesce *(nei tessuti, ecc.).*

hers (hûrz) *pron.poss.f.* il suo, la sua, i suoi, le sue *(di lei).*

herself (hûr·sĕlf') *pron.rifl. f.* ella stessa, lei medesima: **she said it —,** lo disse lei stessa; **by —,** da sola.

hesitancy (hez'ĭ·tăn·sĭ) *n.* esitazione, indecisione.

hesitate (hĕz'ĭ·tāt) *vi.* esitare.

hesitation (hĕz'ĭ·tā'shŭn) *n.* esitazione.

heterogeneous (hĕt'ĕr·ô·jē'nĕ·ŭs) *agg.* eterogeneo.

hew (hū) *vt. (pass.* hewed, *pp.* hewn) tagliare, recidere, fendere: **to — down,** abbattere.

hewn (hūn) *pp. di* to hew.

hey (hā) *int.* ehi!, caspita!

heyday (hā'dā') *n.* rigoglio, freschezza; periodo felice.

hi (hī) *inter.* salve!, ehi!

hibernation (hī'bĕr·nā'shŭn) *n.* ibernazione.

hiccup (hĭk'ŭp) *n.* singhiozzo. *vi.* avere il singhiozzo.

hickory (hĭk'ô·rĭ) *n.* noce americano.

hid (hĭd) *pass. di* to hide.

hidden (hĭd''n) *pp. di* to hide. *agg.* nascosto, segreto, misterioso. **—most** *agg.* intimo, il più nascosto.

hide (hīd) (1) *vt. (pass.* hid, *pp.* hidden) nascondere. *vi.* nascondersi: **—and-seek,** rimpiattino.

hide (2) *n.* pelle d'animale, cuoio.

hideous (hĭd'ē·ŭs) *agg.* repellente, orribile.

hiding (hīd'ĭng) *n.* nascondiglio; *(fam.)* fustigazione.

hieroglyphic (hī'ĕr·ô·glĭf'ĭk) *n.* geroglifico.

hi-fi (hī'fī') *n.* alta fedeltà *(nella riproduzione dei suoni).*

high (hī) *agg.* alto, elevato; grande; importante; forte; violento; brillo;

acceso (*di colorito*); frollo (*di carne*):
— and low, dovunque; — fidelity,
alta fedeltà (*nella riproduzione
dei suoni*); — life, alta società; it's — time, è ormai tempo;
to act with a — hand, commettere soprusi. — altar *n.* altar maggiore. —ball *n.* (*S.U.*) liquore con
selz e ghiaccio; (*ferr.*) segnale di
via libera, treno direttissimo;
—born *agg.* di nobile nascita. —er
agg.comp. più alto, superiore: —
and —, sempre più in alto. —est
agg.superl. supremo, (il) più alto.
—handed *agg.* arbitrario, violento.
—land *n.* regione montagnosa,
altopiano. —lander *n.* montanaro.
—light *n.* (*disegno, pitt. e fot.*) luce,
zona più luminosa; (*fig.*) momento
di fulgore o di grande interesse. *vt.*
proiettare un fascio di luce su
(*fig.*) mettere in risalto. —ly *avv.*
altamente, sommamente, fortemente, molto. —most *agg.* altissimo, (il) più alto. —ness *n.* elevatezza, dignità; altezza (*titolo
regale*). —road *n.* strada maestra.
— school, scuola media. —sounding *agg.* pomposo, altisonante.
—strung *agg.* coraggioso, iper-
sensibile. —tail *vi.* (*gergo*) squagliarsela in fretta; correre a tutta
velocità. —water alta marea.
highway (hī'wā') *n.* strada maestra.
—man *n.* predone, rapinatore.
hijack (hī'jăk') *vt.* (*gergo*) rubare,
sottrarre; costringere con la prepotenza.
hike (hīk)*n.* passo pesante; gita o viaggio a piedi. *vt.* strappare, trascinare.
vi. camminare con passo pesante;
vagabondare; fare una gita o un
viaggio a piedi.
hill (hĭl) *n.* colle, collina, poggio: up
— and down dale, per monti e per
valli. —ock *n.* collinetta. —y *agg.*
collinoso, accidentato.
hilt (hĭlt) *n.* elsa, impugnatura.
him (hĭm) *pron.pers.m.* lui, lo, gli.
himself (hĭm-sĕlf') *pron.m.* egli stesso,
lui stesso, si: he came —, venne
lui stesso; he hurt —, si fece male;
by —, da solo.
hind (hīnd) (1) *n.* cerva.
hind (hīnd) (2) *agg.* posteriore. —most
· *agg.* l'ultimo, il più arretrato.
hinder (hīn'dĕr) (1) *agg.* posteriore.
hinder (hīn'dĕr) (2) *vt.* impedire,
ritardare, ostacolare.
hindrance (hīn'drăns) *n.* ostacolo,
impedimento, intralcio.
hindsight (hīnd'sīt) *n.* senno di poi.
hinge (hĭnj) *n.* cardine, ganghero,
cerniera, perno. *vt.* incardinare,

munire di cardini. *vi.* imperniarsi:
everything hinges on his decision,
tutto dipende dalla sua decisione.
hint (hĭnt) *n.* accenno, insinuazione,
allusione: to take the —, capire
l'antifona. *vt.*, *vi.* alludere, accennare, insinuare.
hip (hĭp) *n.* anca, fianco: to have one's
opponent on the —, trovarsi in vantaggio sull'avversario; to smite —
and thigh, distruggere, annientare.
hippodrome (hĭp'ŏ-drōm) *n.* ippodromo.
hippopotamus (hĭp'ŏ-pŏt'ă-mŭs) *n.*
ippopotamo.
hire (hīr) *n.* nolo, affitto; salario;
soldo. *vt.* noleggiare, prendere o
dare in affitto; prendere in prestito;
assoldare, assumere; corrompere.
hireling (hīr'lĭng) *n.* mercenario, servo
prezzolato.
hiring (hīr'ĭng) *n.* noleggio.
his (hĭz) *agg.*, *pron.poss.m.* suo, sua,
di lui, suoi, sue, il suo, la sua, i suoi,
le sue, il di lui: a friend of —, un
suo amico.
hiss (hĭs) *n.* fischio, sibilo. *vt.*, *vi.*
sibilare, fischiare. —ing *n.* sibilo.
agg. sibilante.
historian (hĭs-tō'rĭ-ăn) *n.* storico.
historic (hĭs-tŏr'ĭk) *agg.* storico.
history (hĭs'tō-rĭ) *n.* storia.
hit (hĭt) *n.* colpo; successo; idea, invenzione. *vt.* (*pass.*, *pp.* hit) colpire, urtare, raggiungere (*un bersaglio*), toccare: — or miss, o va o
spacca; to — it off well, andare
d'accordo; to — on, upon, imbattersi in, trovare, scoprire.
hitch (hĭch) *n.* strappo; uncino,
gancio, aggancio; difficoltà, ostacolo. *vt.*, *vi.* muoversi a strattoni;
impigliarsi; zoppicare; agganciare,
afferrare; trascinare; dare uno
strattone; attaccare (*un cavallo
alla carrozza*); andar d'accordo.
hitch-hike *vi.* viaggiare con l'autostop.
hither (hĭth'ĕr) *agg.* il più vicino. *avv.*
qui, qua: — and thither, qua e là.
—to *avv.* sin qui, sino a questo
momento.
hive (hīv) *n.* alveare, sciame (*anche di
persone*); (*pl.*) eruzione cutanea,
orticaria.
hoar (hōr) *n.* candore, vecchiaia.
—frost *n.* brina.
hoard (hōrd) *n.* mucchio, cumulo,
ammasso, tesoro. *vt.*, *vi.* ammassare, accumulare, tesaurizzare, accaparrare, accumularsi.
hoarse (hōrs) *agg.* roco, rauco; flebile: — throat, raucedine. —ness
n. raucedine, suono rauco.

hoary (hŏr'ĭ) agg. bianco, biancastro, canuto; vecchio, venerabile.

hoax (hŏks) n. mistificazione, trucco, scherzo, falsa notizia.

hobble (hŏb''l) n. zoppicamento, difficoltà, ostacolo, pastoia. vt. impastoiare, ostacolare. vi. zoppicare, incespicare.

hobby (hŏb'ĭ) n. passatempo favorito, mania: to ride one's —, trattare l'argomento favorito. —horse n. cavallino a dondolo.

hobo (hō'bō) n. (S.U.) vagabondo.

hock (hŏk) n. (1) garretto di cavallo.

hock (hŏk) (2) vt. (gergo) impegnare, dare in pegno.

hocus-pocus (hō'kŭs·pō'kŭs) n. gioco di prestigio, gherminella.

hodgepodge (hŏj'pŏj')n. guazzabuglio.

hoe (hō) n. zappa. vt., vi. zappare, scavare.

hog (hŏg) n. maiale, porco: to go whole —, andare sino fondo. vt., vi. arraffare. —wash n. beverone del porco.

hoist (hoist) n. paranco, montacarichi. vt., sollevare, issare.

hold (hōld) n. presa, appoggio, sostegno; custodia, prigione; autorità, influenza; fortificazione, dominio; (naut.) stiva; (aeron.) scompartimento merci: to get, to take — of, prendere, afferrare, aggrapparsi a. vt. (pass. pp. held) tenere; mantenere; sostenere; possedere, detenere; trattenere; contenere; occupare; avere; considerare: to — back, trattenere, frenare; to — forth, porgere, esporre, concionare; to — one's own, conservare quel che si ha; mantenere la propria opinione; to — off, tenere a distanza; to — up, sollevare, esibire, arrestare; rapinare. vi. tenersi, durare, sopportare, persistere, attaccarsi: to — back, esitare; to — on, perseverare; to — out, resistere. —er n. possessore, detentore, locatario; impugnatura; astuccio; serbatoio. —up n. aggressione, rapina.

hole (hōl) n. buco, buca; antro, tana, spelonca: to put in a —, mettere in una situazione difficile. vt. bucare, perforare. vi. rintanarsi.

holiday (hŏl'ĭ·dā) n. festa, vacanza.

holiness (hō'lĭ·nĕs) n. santità.

hollow (hŏl'ō) n. cavo, cavità, caverna. agg. cavo, scavato, vuoto, profondo, infossato; sordo (di suono), falso. vt., vi. scavare, incavare, incavarsi.

holly (hŏl'ĭ) n. agrifoglio.

holster (hŏl'stĕr) n. fondina di pistola.

holy (hō'lĭ) agg. santo, sacro, benedetto.

homage (hŏm'ĭj) n. omaggio: to do —, rendere omaggio.

home (hōm) n. casa, focolare domestico, dimora, patria, asilo: at —, in casa; to make oneself at —, mettersi a proprio agio. agg. domestico, casalingo, nazionale: — stretch (sport) dirittura d'arrivo; — rule, autogoverno, autonomia; — office, sede centrale, casa madre. avv. a o in casa, a segno, efficacemente: to strike —, colpire nel vivo, coglier nel segno. —land n. patria. —less agg. senza casa. —liness n. semplicità, domesticità, bruttezza. —ly agg. casalingo, semplice, brutto. —made agg. fatto in casa, di fabbricazione nazionale. —sick agg. nostalgico. —sickness n. nostalgia. —stead n. castello, fattoria. —ward avv. verso casa; verso la patria: — voyage, viaggio di ritorno. —work n. compiti di casa.

homicidal (hŏm'ĭ·sīd'ăl) agg. omicida.

homicide (hŏm'ĭ·sīd) n. omicidio, omicida.

homogeneous (hō'mō·jē'nē·ŭs) agg. omogeneo.

homologate (hō·mŏl'ō·gāt) vt. omologare.

hone (hōn) n. pietra da rasoio. vt. affilare.

honest (ŏn'ĕst) agg. onesto, sincero; genuino.

honesty (ŏn'ĕs·tĭ) n. onestà, sincerità.

honey (hŭn'ĭ) n. miele; dolcezza, tesoro, amore: — bee, ape. —comb n. favo. agg. a nido d'ape. —ed agg. melato. —moon n. luna di miele. —suckle n. caprifoglio.

honk (hŏngk) n. verso dell'oca; clacson. vi., vt. sonare il clacson.

honor (ŏn'ĕr) n. onore, rispetto, dignità. vt. onorare, far onore a. —able agg. onorevole, onorabile. —ableness n. onorabilità.

hood (hŏŏd) n. cappuccio, mantice (di veicolo); cofano (d'auto); (gergo) bandito, teppista, sicario. vt. incappucciare.

hoodlum (hŏŏd'lŭm) n. (S.U.) giovane delinquente, teppista.

hoodwink (hŏŏd'wĭngk) vt. bendare gli occhi a, imbrogliare.

hoof (hŏŏf) n. zoccolo (di quadrupede).

hook (hŏŏk) n. gancio, uncino, amo: by — or by crook, con ogni mezzo, a qualunque costo; on one's own —, per conto proprio. vt. agganciare, uncinare, prendere all'amo. vi. agganciarsi, incurvarsi; svignarsela.

hooked *agg.* uncinato, curvo, adunco; (*gergo*) dedito agli stupefacenti.

hooky (hōōk'ĭ): to play —, marinare la scuola.

hooligan (hōō'lĭ·găn) *n.* furfante; teppista.

hoop (hōōp) *n.* cerchio, cerchietto, cerchione. *vt.* cerchiare.

hoot (hōōt) *n.* grido, schiamazzo, gracchio, sirena (*di fabbrica*): not to give a —, infischiarsene. *vt.*, *vi.* urlare, schiamazzare, ululare.

hop (hŏp) *n.* salto, balzo; (*bot.*) luppolo. *vt.*, *vi.* saltare, saltellare, svignarsela; salire (*su un treno*, ecc.); (*aeron.*) decollare; trasvolare (*un oceano*): to — up (*gergo*), stimolare, eccitare (*spec. con stupefacenti*).

hope (hŏp) *n.* speranza. *vt.*, *vi.* sperare: to — against —, sperare l'impossibile. —ful *agg.* speranzoso; promettente. —fully *avv.* con speranza, con ottimismo. —less *agg.* disperato, inutile, irrimediabile. —lessness *n.* disperazione, inutilità, irrimediabilità.

horde (hŏrd) *n.* orda.

horizon (hō·rī'z'n) *n.* orizzonte.

horizontal (hŏr'ĭ·zŏn'tăl) *agg.* orizzontale.

horn (hŏrn) *n.* corno; antenna; cornetta; (*autom.*) tromba, segnale acustico: — of plenty, cornucopia. *vt.* dar cornate a, munire di corna. *vi.*: to — in, interloquire, intromettersi.

hornet (hŏr'nĕt) *n.* calabrone: hornets' nest, vespaio.

hornpipe (hŏrn'pīp') *n.* cornamusa.

horny (hŏr'nĭ) *agg.* calloso, corneo.

horoscope (hŏr'ō·skōp) *n.* oroscopo.

horrible (hŏr'ĭ·b'l) *agg.* orribile, atroce.

horribly (-blĭ) *avv.* orrendamente.

horrid (hŏr'ĭd) *agg.* orrido, odioso.

horrify (hŏr'ĭ·fī) *vt.* terrorizzare, far inorridire.

horror (hŏr'ĕr) *n.* orrore: to strike with —, orripilare; — book, romanzo nero.

horse (hŏrs) *n.* cavallo; cavalletto; (*mil.*) cavalleria, soldato di cavalleria: — chestnut, ippocastano; — opera (*cinema*), film western; — sense, fiuto, senso pratico; — trade, commercio di cavalli, (*fig.*) mercanteggiamento, compromesso. —back *n.* groppa: on —, in groppa, a cavallo. —fly *n.* mosca cavallina. —laugh, risata grassa. —man *n.* cavaliere, cavallerizzo. —manship *n.* abilità equestre. —power *n.* cavallo vapore. —shoe

n. ferro da cavallo. —woman *n.* amazzone, cavallerizza.

hose (hōz) *n.* calza; uosa; tubo; idrante: men's —, calze da uomo.

hosier (hō'zhĕr) *n.* calzettaio.

hosiery (hō'zhĕr·ĭ) *n.* calze; commercio delle calze; calzetteria.

hospitable (hŏs'pĭ·tà·b'l) *agg.* ospitale.

hospital (hŏs'pĭt·ăl) *n.* ospedale, clinica; ricovero per vecchi.

hospitality (hŏs'pĭ·tăl'ĭ·tĭ) *n.* ospitalità.

host (hōst) (1) *n.* ospite (*chi ospita*), albergatore.

host (2) *n.* turba, moltitudine, quantità.

Host (3) *n.* Ostia Consacrata.

hostage (hŏs'tĭj) *n.* ostaggio.

hostel (hŏs'tĕl) *n.* casa dello studente, albergo per la gioventù.

hostess (hŏs'tĕs) *n.* ospite (*donna che ospita*); ballerina stipendiata (*nei ritrovi*); (*aeron.*) hostess.

hostile (hŏs'tĭl) *agg.* ostile.

hostility (hŏs·tĭl'ĭ·tĭ) *n.* ostilità.

hot (hŏt) *agg.* caldo, rovente, bollente; accaldato; appassionato; violento; frenetico; piccante; recentissimo, fresco, alla moda; travolgente, entusiasmante; scottante, pericoloso: — from the press, fresco di stampa; — rod, automobile da corsa; — shot (*gergo*), persona dinamica, uomo in gamba; *agg.* dinamico, attivissimo, bravissimo; — war, conflitto armato. —bed *n.* vivaio; (*fig.*) focolaio. —blooded *agg.* ardente, sovreccitabile, focoso; (*di cavalli*) purosangue. —headed *agg.* violento, focoso. —house *n.* serra; postribolo.

hotel (hō·tĕl') *n.* albergo: — manager, direttore d'albergo. —keeper *n.* albergatore.

hotly (hŏt'lĭ) *avv.* caldamente, vivacemente, con veemenza.

hotness (hŏt'nĕs) *n.* calore, veemenza.

hound (hound) *n.* cane, segugio; mascalzone; tifoso. *vt.* braccare, inseguire.

hour (our) *n.* ora: an — ago, un'ora fa. —glass *n.* clessidra. — hand *n.* lancetta delle ore (*nell' orologio*). —ly *agg.* orario, frequente. *avv.* frequentemente, d'ora in ora.

house (hous) *n.* casa; famiglia, dinastia; albergo; teatro; aula (*parlamentare, ecc.*): full — (*teat.*), tutto esaurito. *vt.* alloggiare, ospitare, collocare. *vi.* abitare, ripararsi. —breaker *n.* ladro (*scassinatore*). —breaking *n.* furto con scasso. —coat *n.* vestaglia (*femminile*).

—hold *n.* famiglia, organizzazione domestica. *agg.* domestico, casalingo. —keeper *n.* governante di casa. —keeping *n.* governo della casa, faccende domestiche. —wife *n.* massaia. —wifery *n.* economia domestica. —work *n.* faccende domestiche.

housing (houz'ĭng) *n.* riparo, alloggio.

hove (hŏv) *pass.* e *pp. di* to heave.

hovel (hŏv'ĕl) *n.* capanna, tugurio.

hover (hŭv'ĕr) *vi.* librarsi, gravitare; attardarsi; gironzolare; esitare.

how (hou) *avv.* come, in che modo, quanto, perchè; — are you? come state? — far? sino a qual punto?, a quale distanza? — long? quanto tempo? — much? quanto? — many? quanti? — beautiful! che bello! how nice of you! molto gentile da parte vostra!; — early (late, soon)? quando, a che ora?; — old are you? quanti anni avete?; no matter — much, per quanto, non importa quanto.

however *cong.* ciononostante, eppure. *avv.* per quanto, in qualunque misura: — he may do it, in qualunque modo lo faccia; — important it may be, per quanto importante sia; — that may be, comunque sia; — did you manage to do it? come diamine ci siete riusciti?

howl (houl) *n.* grido, ululato, gemito. *vi.* ululare, gemere.

howsoever (hou'sŏ-ĕv'ĕr) *avv.* comunque, per quanto.

hub (hŭb) *n.* centro, fulcro, mozzo (*di ruota*).

hubbub (hŭb'ŭb) *n.* tumulto, baccano.

huckster (hŭk'stĕr) *n.* venditore ambulante; imbroglione; (*S.U.*) agente di pubblicità radiofonica.

huddle (hŭd''l) *n.* ammasso, confusione, folla; conciliabolo. *vt., vi.* ammassare, arruffare, raggomitolarsi, affollarsi.

hue (hū) (1) *n.* colore, sfumatura.

hue (hū) (2) *n.* clamore: — and cry, pandemonio, alzata di scudi.

huff (hŭf) *n.* collera; risentimento: to get into a —, andare in collera.

huffy (hŭf'ĭ) *agg.* arrogante, stizzito.

hug (hŭg) *n.* abbraccio *vt.* abbracciare, stringere: to — oneself, compiacersi (*con se stesso*); to — the shore, costeggiare.

huge (hūj) *agg.* enorme, gigantesco. —ly *avv.* enormemente. —ness *n.* enormità, mole imponente.

hulk (hŭlk) *n.* carcassa di nave; pontone ammasso. —ing *agg.* goffo, corpulento.

hull (hŭl) *n.* (*naut.*) scafo; (*aeron.*) fusoliera; (*bot.*) guscio, buccia. *vt.* squarciare (*uno scafo*), sgusciare, sbucciare.

hum (hŭm) *n.* mormorio, ronzio. *vt., vi.* canticchiare, mormorare, ronzare; darsi da fare.

human (hū'măn) *agg.* umano.

humane (hū-măn') *agg.* umanitario, umano.

humanitarian (hū-măn'ĭ-târ'ĭ-ăn) *n., agg.* umanitario.

humanity (hū-măn'ĭ-tĭ) *n.* umanità; (*pl.*), materie classiche.

humanly (hū'măn-lĭ) *avv.* umanamente.

humble (hŭm'b'l) *agg.* umile. *vt.* umiliare, mortificare. —ness *n.* umiltà.

humbly (hŭm'blĭ) *avv.* umilmente.

humbug (hŭm'bŭg') *n.* impostura, frode impostore: —! frottole!

humdrum (hŭm'drŭm') *agg.* monotono.

humiliate (hū-mĭl'ĭ-āt) *vt.* umiliare.

humiliating *agg.* umiliante.

humiliation (-ā'shŭn) *n.* umiliazione.

humility (hū-mĭl'ĭ-tĭ) *n.* umiltà.

humming (hŭm'ĭng) *n.* ronzio, mormorio. *agg.* ronzante; intenso, movimentato.

hummingbird (hŭm'ĭng-bûrd') *n.* colibrì.

humorist (hū'mĕr-ĭst) *n.* umorista.

humorous (-ŭs) *agg.* umoristico, comico.

humor (hū'mĕr) *n.* umore, umorismo, spirito, capriccio: out of —, di cattivo umore. *vt.* assecondare, blandire.

hump (hŭmp) *n.* gibbosità; malumore. *vt., vi.* far la gobba, ingobbire curvarsi. —back *n.* gobbo.

hunch (hŭnch) *n.* protuberanza, gibbosità; pezzo; (*S.U.*) sospetto, presentimento, intuizione. *vt.* curvare (*le spalle*). —back *n.* gobbo.

hundred (hŭn'drĕd) *n., agg.* cento, centinaio. —th *n.* la centesima parte. *agg.* centesimo.

hung (hŭng) *pass., pp.* di to hang.

hunger (hŭng'gĕr) *n.* fame, brama. *vt.* affamare. *vi.* aver fame: to — for, agognare, bramare.

hungrily (hŭng'grĭ-lĭ) *avv.* avidamente.

hungry (hŭng'grĭ) *agg.* affamato: to be —, aver fame.

hunk (hŭnk) *n.* grosso pezzo, blocco, massa.

hunt (hŭnt) *n.* caccia, inseguimento; muta di cani. *vt.* cacciare, inseguire, cercare accanitamente: to — down, perseguitare. *vi.* andare a caccia. —er *n.* cacciatore; cane da caccia. —sman *n.* cacciatore.

hurdle (hûr'd'l) *n.* ostacolo, siepe; (*pl.*) corsa a ostacoli.

hurl (hûrl) *vt.* lanciare, scagliare.

hurrah (hŏŏ-rä") *inter.* urrà, evviva. *vt., vi.* acclamare.

hurricane (hûr'ĭ-kăn) *n.* uragano, ciclone.

hurried (hûr'ĕd) *agg.* affrettato, frettoloso. **—ly** *avv.* frettolosamente, affrettatamente.

hurry (hûr'ĭ) *n.* fretta: to be in a —, aver fretta. *vt.* affrettare, precipitare, incalzare. *vi.* affrettarsi: to — away, allontanarsi in fretta; to — in (out); entrare (uscire) in fretta; to — up, far presto.

hurt (hûrt) *n.* male, danno, ferita. *vt.* (*pass., pp.* hurt) offendere, ferire, urtare, ledere; far male a: to — one's feelings, offendere, mortificare. *vi.* far male, nuocere, dolere. **—ful** *agg.* nocivo, doloroso.

hurtle (hûr't'l) *vt.* scaraventare. *vi.* cozzare; rovinare, precipitare.

hurtless (hûrt'lĕs) *agg.* innocuo; illeso.

husband (hŭz'bănd) *n.* marito, sposo.

hush (hŭsh) *n., inter.* silenzio. *vt.* far tacere, chetare; mettere in tacere: to — up a scandal, soffocare uno scandalo. *vi.* tacere, far silenzio.

husk (hŭsk) *n.* buccia, guscio, baccello, involucro. *vt.* sbucciare, sgusciare.

husky (hŭs'kĭ) *agg.* rauco; rude, vigoroso.

hussy (hŭz'ĭ) *n.* sgualdrina, insolente (*f.*).

hustle (hŭs''l) *n.* fretta; energia, spinta: — and bustle, andirivieni. *vt.* spingere. *vi.* affrettarsi.

hut (hŭt) *n.* capanna, tugurio, baracca.

hyacinth (hī'á-sĭnth) *n.* (*bot.*) giacinto.

hybrid (hī'brĭd) *n., agg.* ibrido.

hydraulic (hī-drô'lĭk) *agg.* idraulico.

hydrobomb (hī'drō-bŏm') *n.* siluro sganciato da un aerosilurante.

hydrofoil (boat) (hī'drō-foil') *n.* aliscafo idroscivolante.

hydrogen (hī'drō-jen) *n.* idrogeno: — bomb, bomba all'idrogeno.

hydroplane (hī'drō-plān) *n.* idroscivolante; idroplano.

hyena (hī-ē'ná) *n.* (*zool.*) iena.

hygiene (hī'jēn) *n.* igiene.

hygienic (hī'jĭ-ĕn'ĭk) *agg.* igienico.

hymn (hĭm) *n.* inno.

hypertension (hī'pĕr-tĕn'shŭn) *n.* ipertensione.

hypertensive (-sĭv) *agg., n.* iperteso.

hyphen (hī'fĕn) *n.* trattino, lineetta di congiunzione.

hypnosis (hĭp-nō'sĭs) *n.* ipnosi.

hypnotic (-nŏt' k) *n., agg.* ipnotico, narcotico.

hypnotist (hĭp'nō-tĭst) *n.* ipnotizzatore.

hypocrisy (hĭ-pŏk'rĭ-sĭ) *n.* ipocrisia.

hypocrite (hĭp'ō-krĭt) *n.* ipocrita.

hypocritical (-krĭt'ĭ-kăl) *agg.* ipocrito.

hypodermic (hī'pō-dûr'mĭk) *n.* iniezione sottocutanea. *agg.* ipodermico, sottocutaneo.

hypothesis (hī-pŏth'ē-sĭs) *n.* ipotesi.

hysteria (hĭs-tēr'ĭ-á) *n.* isterismo.

hysterical (-tēr'ĭ-kăl) *agg.* isterico.

I

I (ī) *pron. pers. nom.* Io.

Iberian (ī-bēr'ĭ-ăn) *n., agg.* iberico.

ice (īs) *n.* ghiaccio, gelo; gelato; zucchero cristallizzato. *vt., vi.* ghiacciare, gelare, glassare (*dolci*). **—berg** *n.* montagna di ghiaccio. **—box** *n.* ghiacciaia. **—breaker** *n.* nave rompighiaccio. **—cream** *n.* gelato; — parlor (*S.U.*) gelateria. **—man** *n.* venditore di ghiaccio.

Icelander (īs'lăn'dĕr) *n.* islandese.

icicle (ī'sĭk-'l) *n.* ghiacciolo.

icterus (ĭk'tĕr-ŭs) *n.* itterizia.

icy (ī'sĭ) *agg.* ghiacciato, gelido.

idea (ī-dē'á) *n.* idea, concetto.

ideal (ī-dē'ăl) *n., agg.* ideale. **—ism** *n.* idealismo. **—ist** *n.* idealista.

identical (ī-dĕn'tĭ-kăl) *agg.* identico, stesso, medesimo.

identification (ī-dĕn'tĭ-fĭ-kā'shŭn) *n.* identificazione.

identify (ī-dĕn'tĭ-fī) *vt.* identificare: to — oneself with, immedesimarsi con.

identity (ī-dĕn'tĭ-tĭ) *n.* identità.

ideological (ī'dĕ-ō-lŏj'ĭ-kăl) *agg.* ideologico.

ideology (ī'dĕ-ŏl'ō-jĭ) *n.* ideologia.

idiocy (ĭd'ĭ-ō-sĭ) *n.* idiozia.

idiom (ĭd'ĭ-ŭm) *n.* idioma, idiotismo.

idiosyncrasy (ĭd'ĭ-ō-sĭng'krá-sĭ) *n.* idiosincrasia, peculiarità.

idiot (ĭd'ĭ-ŭt) *n.* idiota. **—ic** (-ŏt'ĭc) *agg.* insensato, da idiota.

idle (ī'd'l) *n.* pigro, ozioso, inutile, inoperoso, morto (*di capitale*). *vt.* sprecare (*tempo*) in ozio. *vi.* oziare, impigrirsi; (*di motore*) andare al minimo, girare in folle. **—ness** *n.* pigrizia, ozio, inutilità.

idler (ī'dlĕr) *n.* pigro, sfaccendato.

idly (ī'dlĭ) *avv.* pigramente, oziosamente, vanamente.

idol (I'dŭl) *n.* idolo.—ater (I.dŏl'á·tĕr) *n.* idolatra.

idolize (I'dŭl·Iz) *vt.* idolatrare.

idyl, idyll (I'dĭl) *n.* idillio.

if (If) *cong.* se, qualora, sebbene, benchè: as —, come se; — anything, se mai; — so, in tal caso.

iffy (If'I) *agg.* (gergo) pieno di se e di ma, titubante.

ignite (Ig·nIt') *vt.* accendere, incendiare. *vi.* prender fuoco.

ignition (Ig·nish'ŭn) *n.* accensione.

ignoble (Ig·nŏ'b'l) *agg.* ignobile.

ignominy (Ig'nŏ·mĭn·I) *n.* ignominia.

ignoramus (Ig'nŏ·rā'mŭs) *n.* ignorante.

ignorance (Ig'nŏ·rȧns) *n.* ignoranza.

ignorant (-rȧnt) *agg.* ignorante.

ignore (Ig·nōr') *vt.* ignorare.

ill (Il) *n.* male, malanno, sfortuna. *agg.* cattivo, malvagio; ammalato. *avv.* male: —advised, sconsiderato, imprudente; — at ease, inquieto, a disagio; —bred, maleducato; —favored, brutto; —mannered, scortese; — nature, malvagità, malanimo; —natured, malvagio; —starred, sfortunato; —timed, intempestivo; —will, malevolenza, ostilità.

illegal (Il·lē'gȧl) *agg.* illegale.

illegible (Il·lĕj'I·b'l) *agg.* illeggibile.

illegitimacy (Il'lē·jIt'I·mȧ·sI) *n.* illegittimità.

illegitimate (Il'lē·jIt'I·mIt) *agg.* illegittimo, illegale.

illicit (Il·lĭs'It) *agg.* illecito.

illiteracy (Il·lĭt'ĕr·ȧ·sI) *n.* ignoranza; analfabetismo; errore.

illiterate (Il·lĭt'ĕr·It) *agg.* illetterato.

illness (Il'nĕs) *n.* malattia.

illogical (Il·lŏj'I·kȧl) *agg.* illogico.

illuminate (I·lū'mI·nāt) *vt.* illuminare, rischiarare; miniare, decorare.

illumination (-nā'shŭn) *n.* illuminazione; miniatura (*di un libro*).

illusion (I·lū'zhŭn) *n.* illusione.

illusive (-sĭv), illusory (-sŏ·rI) *agg.* illusorio, ingannevole, fallace.

illustrate (Il'ŭs·trāt) *vt.* illustrare.

illustration (Il'ŭs·trā'shŭn) *n.* illustrazione.

illustrator (Il'ŭs·trā'tĕr) *n.* illustratore.

illustrious (I·lŭs'trI·ŭs) *agg.* illustre.

I'm (Im) *contr. di* I am (*io sono*).

image (Im'Ij) *n.* immagine. —ry *n.* raffigurazione; fantasia; iconografia.

imaginary (I·măj'I·nĕr'I) *agg.* immaginario.

imagination (I·măj'I·nā'shŭn) *n.* immaginazione, fantasia; concezione.

imaginative (I·măj'I·nā'tĭv) *agg.* immaginativo; fantasioso.

imagine (I·măj'In) *vt.* immaginare, figurarsi.

imbecile (Im'bē·sĭl) *n.*, *agg.* imbecille.

imbed (Im·bĕd') *vedi* embed.

imbibe (Im·bIb') *vt.*, *vi.* assorbire, imbeversi, assimilare (*idee*).

imbue (Im·bū') *vt.* imbevere, inculcare.

imitate (Im'I·tāt) *vt.* imitare. *l*

imitation (Im'I·tā'shŭn) *n.* imitazione. *agg.* imitato, d'imitazione, finto.

imitator (Im'I·tā'tĕr) *n.* imitatore.

immaculate (I·măk'ū·lIt) *agg.* immacolato.

immaterial (Im'mȧ·tĕr'I·ȧl) *agg.* insignificante, indifferente; incorporeo.

immature (Im'ȧ·tūr') *agg.* immaturo, prematuro.

immeasurable (I·mĕzh'ẽr·ȧ·b'l) *agg.* incommensurabile, smisurato.

immediate (I·mē'dI·It) *agg.* immediato. —ly *avv.* immediatamente. *cong.* non appena.

immemorial (Im'mē·mō'rI·ȧl) *agg.* immemorabile.

immense (I·mĕns') *agg.* immenso.

immerse (I·mûrs') *vt.* immergere; battezzare. *vi.* sommergersi, immergersi.

immersion (I·mûr'shŭn) *n.* immersione.

immigrant (Im'I·grȧnt) *n.*, *agg.* immigrante.

immigrate (Im'I·grāt) *vi.* immigrare.

immigration (-grā'shŭn) *n.* immigrazione.

imminence (Im'I·nĕns) *n.* imminenza.

imminent (Im'I·nĕnt) *agg.* imminente.

immobility (Im'ō·bĭl'I·tI) *n.* immobilità.

immobilize (Im·mō'bI·lIz) *vt.* immobilizzare.

immoderate (Im·mŏd'ẽr·It) *agg.* immoderato, smodato.

immodest (Im·mŏd'ĕst) *agg.* immodesto, impudico.

immodesty (-ĕs·tI) *avv.* immodestia, impudicizia.

immoral (Im·mŏr'ȧl) *agg.* immorale. —ity (Im·mō·răl'I·tI) *n.* immoralità.

immortal (I·mŏr'tȧl) *agg.* immortale. —ity (Im'ŏr·tăl'I·tI) *n.* immortalità.

immortalize (I·mŏr'tȧl·Iz) *vt.* immortalare, perpetuare.

immovable (Im·mōōv'ȧ·b'l) *agg.* immobile, inamovibile; impassibile; irremovibile.

immune (I·mūn') *agg.* immune, esente.

immunity (I·mū'nI·tI) *n.* immunità.

imp (Imp) *n.* diavoletto.

impact (Im'păkt) *n.* urto, collisione.

impair (Im·pâr') *vt.* diminuire, svalutare, indebolire, danneggiare, pregiudicare. *vi.* deteriorarsi. —ment *n.* danno, diminuzione, deterioramento.

impalpable (Im·păl′pá·b'l) *agg.* impalpabile.

impart (Im·pärt′) *vt.* impartire, comunicare, riferire; concedere.

impartial (Im·pär′shăl) *agg.* imparziale. —**ity** (Im′pär·shĭ·ăl′ĭ·tĭ) *n.* imparzialità.

impassable (Im·pás′á.b'l) *agg.* impraticabile, insormontabile.

impassible (Im·păs′ĭ.b'l) *agg.* impassibile.

impassion (Im·păsh′ŭn) *vt.* appassionare, infiammare. —**ed** *agg.* appassionato, veemente, ardente.

impassive (Im·păs′ĭv) *agg.* impassibile.

impatience (Im·pā′shĕns) *n.* impazienza.

impatient (Im·pā′shĕnt) *agg.* impaziente; spazientito.

impeach (Im·pēch′) *vt.* incriminare, invalidare; mettere in stato d'accusa.

impecunious (Im′pē·kū′nĭ·ŭs) *agg.* povero.

impede (Im·pēd′) *vt.* impedire, ostacolare.

impediment (Im·pĕd′ĭ·mĕnt) *n.* impedimento, ostacolo.

impel (Im·pĕl′) *vt.* costringere, indurre.

impend (Im·pĕnd′) *vi.* minacciare, essere imminente, pendere (*sul capo*). —**ing** *agg.* imminente; minaccioso.

impenetrable (Im·pĕn′ē·trá·b'l) *n.* impenetrabile, inaccessibile.

imperative (Im·pĕr′á.tĭv) *agg.* imprescindibile; imperioso; urgente, impellente, necessario; imperativo.

imperceptible (Im′pĕr·sĕp′tĭ.b'l) *agg.* impercettibile.

imperfect (Im·pûr′fĕkt) *n.*, *agg.* imperfetto.

imperial (Im·pēr′ĭ.ăl) *n.* imperiale (*di veicolo*); mosca (*ciuffetto di barba*). *agg.* imperiale.

imperil (Im·pĕr′ĭl) *vt.* mettere in pericolo, compromettere.

imperious (Im·pēr′ĭ.ŭs) *agg.* imperioso; impellente.

imperishable (Im·pĕr′ĭsh·á.b'l) *agg.* duraturo, non deperibile.

impersonal (Im·pûr′sŭn·ăl) *agg.* impersonale.

impersonate (Im·pûr′sŭn.āt) *vt.* impersonare, personificare, rappresentare.

impertinence (Im·pûr′tĭ.nĕns) *n.* impertinenza; incongruità.

impertinent (Im·pûr′tĭ.nĕnt) *agg.* impertinente; incongruo, futile.

impervious (Im·pûr′vĭ·ŭs) *agg.* impervio; impermeabile; ostinato; — **to reason**, sordo alla ragione.

impetuous (Im·pĕt′û.ŭs) *agg.* impetuoso.

impetus (Im′pē.tŭs) *n.* impeto, impulso; (*fis.*) inerzia.

impinge (Im·pĭnj′) *vi.* sbattere: **to — upon**, urtare contro; interferire in.

impious (Im′pĭ.ŭs) *agg.* empio.

impish (Imp′ĭsh) *agg.* maligno, diabolico.

implacable (Im·plā′ká.b'l) *agg.* implacabile.

implant (Im·plánt′) *vt.* impiantare; inculcare.

implement (Im′plē.mĕnt) *n.* utensile. *vt.* compiere, eseguire; attuare.

implicate (Im′plĭ.kāt) *vt.* implicare, sottintendere; aggrovigliare.

implication (-kā′shŭn) *n.* implicazione; sottinteso; cosa implicita; groviglio: **by —**, implicitamente.

implicit (Im·plĭs′ĭt) *agg.* implicito, sottinteso; assoluto.

implied (Im·plīd′) *agg.* sottinteso, tacito.

implore (Im·plōr′) *vt.* implorare.

imply (Im·plī′) *vt.* comportare, implicare; sottintendere, significare; insinuare.

impolite (Im′pō.līt′) *agg.* scortese.

import (Im′pōrt) *n.* portata, significato, senso, importanza; importazione. *vt.* significare, indicare, comportare; importare.

importance (Im·pōr′tăns) *n.* importantanza.

important (Im·pōr′tănt) *agg.* importante. — **ly** *avv.* con importanza, con sussiego.

importation (Im′pōr·tā′shŭn) *n.* importazione.

importer (Im·pōr′tĕr) *n.* importatore.

importunate (Im·pōr′tū·nĭt) *agg.* importuno, insistente.

impose (Im·pōz′) *vt.*, *vi.* imporre; (*tip.*) impaginare: **to — upon**, approfittare di, raggirare.

imposing *n.* impaginazione. *agg.* imponente.

imposition (Im′pō·zĭsh′ŭn) *n.* imposizione, gravame; frode; impaginazione.

impossibility (Im·pŏs′ĭ.bĭl′ĭ·tĭ) *n.* impossibilità.

impossible (Im·pŏs′ĭ.b'l) *agg.* impossibile; insopportabile.

impostor (Im·pŏs′tĕr) *n.* impostore.

imposture (-tûr) *n.* impostura.

impotence (Im′pō.tĕns) *n.* impotenza.

impotent (Im′pō.tĕnt) *agg.* impotente.

impoverish (Im·pŏv′ĕr·ĭsh) *vt.* impoverire, depauperare.

impracticable (Im·prăk′tĭ.ká.b'l) *agg.* impraticabile, inapplicabile; intrattabile.

impregnable (Im·prĕg'nȧ·b'l) *agg.* inespugnabile, invincibile.

impregnate (Im·prĕg'nāt) *vt.* impregnare; fecondare.

impress (Im·prĕs') *n.* impressione, incisione, marchio. *vt.* imprimere; incidere; impressionare, far colpo. —**ion** *n.* impressione, impronta. —**ive** *agg.* impressionante, forte, convincente, suggestivo, imponente.

imprint (Im·print') *n.* impronta, impressione. *vt.* imprimere, stampare, incidere.

imprison (Im·prĭz''n) *vt.* imprigionare. —**ment** *n.* incarcerazione; false —, detenzione abusiva.

improbable (Im·prŏb'ȧ·b'l) *agg.* improbabile, inverosimile.

impromptu (Im·prŏmp'tū) *n.* improvvisazione. *agg.* improvvisato, e·stemporaneo. *avv.* estemporaneamente.

improper (Im·prŏp'ẽr) *agg.* sconveniente, scorretto; inadatto.

improve (Im·prōōv') *vt.* migliorare, perfezionare, far progredire: — one's time, risparmiare tempo. *vi.* migliorare, perfezionarsi, far progressi. —**ment** *n.* miglioramento, progresso, evoluzione.

improvident (Im·prŏv'ĭ·dĕnt) *agg.* imprevidente.

improvise (Im'prŏ·vīz) *vt.* improvvisare.

imprudence (Im·prōō'dĕns) *n.* imprudenza.

imprudent (Im·prōō'dĕnt) *agg.* imprudente.

impudence (Im'pū·dĕns)*n.* impudenza.

impudent (Im'pū·dĕnt) *agg.* impudente.

impulse (Im'pŭls), **impulsion** (Im·pŭl'shŭn) *n.* impulso, slancio, spinta: to act on —, agire d'impulso.

impulsive (Im·pŭl'sĭv) *agg.* impulsivo.

impunity (Im·pū'nĭ·tĭ) *n.* impunità.

impure (Im·pūr') *agg.* impuro.

impurity (·pū'rĭ·tĭ) *n.* impurità.

impute (Im·pūt') *vt.* imputare.

in (In) *agg.* interno. *avv.* dentro, in casa. *prep.* in, a; mentre; per; tra: — haste, in fretta, di premura; — writing, per iscritto; at two — the morning, alle due del mattino; come — a week, venite tra una settimana; come —, entrate, avanti; — spite of, nonostante, a dispetto di; to be —, essere in casa; to be the first —, arrivare per primo; to be all —, non poterne più, essere stanco morto; to have it — for someone, avercela con qualcuno; to put —, mettere; is the train —? è arrivato il treno?; to take —,

raggirare; to know all the ins and outs of, conoscere da cima a fondo, saperla lunga su.

inability (In'ȧ·bĭl'ĭ·tĭ) *n.* inabilità, incapacità.

inaccessible (In'ăk·sĕs'ĭ·b'l) *agg.* inaccessibile, inaccostabile.

inaccurate (In·ăk'ū·rĭt) *agg.* inesatto, impreciso.

inaction (In·ăk'shŭn) *n.* inerzia.

inactive (In·ăk'tĭv) *agg.* inattivo, inerte; in ozio.

inactivity (In'ăk·tĭv'ĭ·tĭ) *n.* inerzia.

inadequate (In·ăd'ē·kwĭt) *agg.* inadeguato, insufficiente.

inadmissible (In'ăd·mĭs'ĭ·b'l) *agg.* inammissibile.

inadvertent (-vûr'tĕnt) *agg.* disattento, sbadato; negligente; involontario. —**ly** *avv.* sbadatamente, inavvertitamente; involontariamente.

inanimate (In·ăn'ĭ·māt) *agg.* inanimato; esanime; inerte.

inapproachable (In'ȧ·prōch'ȧ·b'l) *agg.* inaccessibile, inaccostabile.

inappropriate (In'ȧ·prō'prĭ·ĭt) *agg.* inadatto, inadeguato; improprio.

inapt (In'ăpt) *agg.* inadatto, inetto.

inarticulate (In'är·tĭk'ū·lāt) *agg.* inarticolato; muto.

inasmuch (In'ȧz·mŭch') *avv.*: — as, visto che, in quanto, dato che.

inattentive (In'ȧ·tĕn'tĭv) *agg.* disattento, distratto.

inaugurate (In·ô'gū·rāt) *vt.* inaugurare.

inauguration (-rā'shŭn) *n.* inaugurazione.

inauspicious (In'ôs·pĭsh'ŭs) *agg.* infausto, malaugurato.

inborn (In'bôrn') *agg.* innato, congenito.

inbred (In'brĕd') *agg.* innato, connaturato.

incandescent (In'kăn·dĕs'ĕnt) *agg.* incandescente, rovente.

incapable (In·kā'pȧ·b'l) *agg.* incapace.

incautious (In·kô'shŭs) *agg.* incauto.

incense (In'sĕns) *n.* incenso. *vt.* (-sens') incensare; irritare, esasperare.

incentive (In·sĕn'tĭv) *n.* incentivo, stimolo. *agg.* stimolante.

inch (Inch) *n.* pollice (*misura=cm.* 2,54): by inches, — by —, gradatamente; every —, completamente, da cima a fondo; within an — of, a un pelo da. *vi.* spostarsi gradatamente.

incident (In'sĭ·dĕnt) *n.* incidente. *agg.* insito. —**al** *agg.* incidentale, fortuito, contingente. —**ally** *avv.* incidentalmente.

incinerator (ĭn-sĭn′ẽr-ā′tẽr) *n.* fornace per rifiuti.

incise (ĭn-sīz′) *vt.* incidere.

incite (ĭn-sīt′) *vt.* incitare, incoraggiare.

incivility (ĭn′sĭ-vĭl′ĭ-tĭ) *n.* scortesia.

inclination (ĭn′klĭ-nā′shŭn) *n.* inclinazione, pendio; propensione.

incline (ĭn-klīn′) *n.* pendio, piano inclinato. *vt.* inclinare. *vi.* propendere.

inclined (ĭn-klīnd′) *agg.* inclinato; incline, propenso.

inclose (ĭn-klōz′) *vedi* enclose.

include (ĭn-klōōd′) *vt.* includere, comprendere.

inclusive (ĭn-klōō′sĭv) *agg.* inclusivo, incluso, comprendente, compreso.

incoherent (ĭn′kō-hẽr′ĕnt) *agg.* incoerente.

income (ĭn′kŭm) *n.* reddito. — **tax,** imposta sul reddito.

incoming (ĭn′kŭm′ĭng) *agg.* subentrante; in arrivo; prossimo.

incommensurate (ĭn′kŏ-mĕn′shōō-rĭt) *agg.* sproporzionato; incommensurabile; inadeguato.

incommode (ĭn′kŏ-mōd′) *vt.* scomodare, disturbare.

incommodious (ĭn′kŏ-mō′dĭ-ŭs) *agg.* incomodo, scomodo; disadatto.

incommunicado (ĭn′kŏ-mū′nĭ kä′dō) *agg.* isolato, segregato.

incomparable (ĭn-kŏm′pá-rá-b′l) *agg.* incomparabile.

incompatible (ĭn′kŏm-păt′ĭ-b′l) *agg.* incompatibile.

incompetent (ĭn-kŏm′pē-tĕnt) *agg.* incompetente, incapace, inadeguato.

incomplete (ĭn′kŏm-plēt′) *agg.* incompleto, monco.

incomprehensible (ĭn′kŏm-prē-hĕn′sĭ-b′l) *agg.* incomprensibile.

incongruence (ĭn-kŏng′grōō-ĕns) *n.* incongruenza, discordanza; assurdità; sconvenienza.

incongruous (ĭn-kŏng′grōō-ŭs) *agg.* incongruo, discordante, incongruente; assurdo; sconveniente.

inconsequence (ĭn-kŏn′sē-kwĕns) *n.* incoerenza, mancanza di logica.

inconsequent (-kwĕnt) *agg.* incoerente; illogico; che non c'entra.

inconsiderate (ĭn′kŏn-sĭd′ẽr-ĭt) *agg.* inconsiderato; poco riguardoso.

inconsistency (ĭn′kŏn-sĭs′tĕn-sĭ) *n.* incoerenza, incompatibilità, disuguaglianza, contrasto.

inconsistent (ĭn′kŏn-sĭs′tĕnt) *agg.* incoerente, in contrasto (con).

inconspicuous (ĭn′kŏn-spĭk′ū-ŭs) *agg.* poco appariscente, sobrio, che non dà nell'occhio. —**ly** *avv.* discretamente, senza ostentazione.

inconstancy (ĭn-kŏn′stăn-sĭ) *n.* incostanza.

inconstant (ĭn-kŏn′stănt) *agg.* incostante, senza costanza.

inconvenience (ĭn′kŏn-vēn′yĕns) *n.* scomodità, disturbo; molestia, contrarietà. *vt.* incomodare, disturbare; molestare; ostacolare.

inconvenient (ĭn′kŏn-vēn′yĕnt) *agg.* inopportuno; scomodo, molesto.

incorporate (ĭn-kôr′pō-rāt) *agg.* consorziato; incorporato. *vt.* incorporare, consorziare. *vi.* incorporarsi, associarsi.

incorporated (ĭn-kôr′pō-rāt′ĕd) *agg.* incorporato; consorziato; (*di società*) anonima.

incorrect (ĭn′kŏ-rĕkt′) *agg.* inesatto.

incorrigible (ĭn-kŏr′ĭ-jĭ-b′l) *agg.* incorreggibile.

incorrupt (ĭn-kŏ-rŭpt′) *agg.* incorrotto, puro. —**ible** *agg.* incorruttibile.

increase (ĭn-krēs′) *n.* aumento, accrescimento. *vt.*, *vi.* accrescere, ingrandire; aumentare.

increasing *agg.* crescente. —**ly** *avv.* in modo crescente, sempre più.

incredible (ĭn-krĕd′ĭ-b′l) *agg.* incredibile; inverosimile.

incredulity (ĭn′krē-dū′lĭ-tĭ) *n.* incredulità.

incredulous (ĭn-krĕd′ū-lŭs) *agg.* incredulo.

increment (ĭn′krē-mĕnt) *n.* incremento. —**al** *agg.* che dà incremento, giovevole.

incriminate (ĭn-krĭm′ĭ-nāt) *vt.* incriminare; coinvolgere.

incriminating *agg.* incriminante; compromettente.

incubator (ĭn′kū-bā′tẽr) *n.* incubatrice.

inculcate (ĭn-kŭl′kāt) *vt.* inculcare.

incur (ĭn-kûr′) *vt.* incorrere in, esporsi a.

incurable (ĭn-kûr′á-b′l) *agg.* incurabile, inguaribile; irrimediabile.

indebted (ĭn-dĕt′ĕd) *agg.* indebitato; obbligato, grato. —**ness** *n.* debito.

indecency (ĭn-dē′sĕn-sĭ) *n.* indecenza, sconvenienza.

indecent (ĭn-dē′sĕnt) *agg.* indecente.

indecisive (ĭn′dē-sī′sĭv) *agg.* indeciso.

indecorous (ĭn-dē-kō′rŭs) *agg.* indecoroso, sconveniente, indecente.

indecorum (ĭn-dē-kō′rŭm) *n.* mancanza di decoro, indecenza.

indeed (ĭn-dēd′) *avv.* in verità, davvero, infatti, proprio, realmente, veramente; anzi.

indefatigable (ĭn′dē-făt′ĭ-gá-b′l) *agg.* instancabile. —**ness** *n.* instancabilità.

indefensible (ĭn'dĕ·fĕn's*ĭ*·b'l) *agg.* indifendibile, insostenibile.

indefinite (ĭn·dĕf'*ĭ*·nĭt) *agg.* indefinito, illimitato. **—ly** *avv.* vagamente, indefinitamente.

indelible (ĭn·dĕl'*ĭ*·b'l) *agg.* indelebile.

indelicate (ĭn·dĕl'*ĭ*·kĭt) *agg.* indelicato.

indemnification (ĭn·dĕm'nĭ·fĭ·kā'shŭn) *n.* indennizzo, indennità.

indemnify (ĭn·dĕm'nĭ·fĭ) *vt.* indennizzare, risarcire.

indemnity (ĭn·dĕm'nĭ·tĭ) *n.* garanzia, indennità.

indent (ĭn·dĕnt') *vt.*, *vi.* intaccare, dentellare; compiere una requisizione; stipulare un contratto; legare con un contratto; rientrare (*andare daccapo rientrando*). **—ation** *n.* dentellatura, tacca. **—ion** *n.* daccapo rientrato. **—ure** *n.* contratto, documento legalizzato.

independence (ĭn'dē·pĕn'dĕns) *n.* indipendenza.

independent (ĭn'dē·pĕn'dĕnt) *agg.* indipendente.

ndescribable (ĭn'dē·skrīb *á*·b'l) *agg* indescrivibile.

indestructible (ĭn'dē·strŭk'tĭ·b'l) *agg.* indistruttibile.

indeterminate (ĭn'dē·tûr'mĭ·nāt) *agg.* indeterminato, vago.

index (ĭn'dĕks) *n.* indice. *vt.* corredare d'indice, indicare; mettere in ordine alfabetico.

Indian (ĭn'dĭ·ăn) *n.*, *agg.* indiano: **—corn**, granoturco.

India rubber *n.* gomma elastica.

indicate (ĭn'dĭ·kāt) *vt.* indicare, designare; far capire, accenare (*a*).

indication (ĭn'dĭ·kā'shŭn) *n.* indicazione, indizio; accenno.

indicative (ĭn·dĭk'*á*·tĭv) *agg.* indicativo; sintomatico.

indict (ĭn·dīt') *vt.* accusare; perseguire; rinviare a giudizio. **—ment** *n.* accusa, atto d'accusa; rinvio a giudizio.

indifference (ĭn·dĭf'ẽr·ĕns) *n.* indifferenza, apatia.

indifferent (ĭn·dĭf'ẽr·ĕnt) *agg.* indifferente, apatico; mediocre.

indigenous (ĭn·dĭj'ē·nŭs) *agg.* indigeno.

indigestion (ĭn'dĭ·jĕs'chŭn) *n.* indigestione.

indignant (ĭn·dĭg'nănt) *agg.* indignato. **—ly** *avv.* sdegnosamente.

indignation (ĭn'dĭg·nā'shŭn) *n.* indignazione, sdegno.

indignity (ĭn·dĭg'nĭ·tĭ) *n.* oltraggio.

indigo (ĭn'dĭ·gō) *n.* indaco.

indirect (ĭn'dĭ·rĕkt') *agg.* indiretto; tortuoso.

ndiscreet (ĭn'dĭs·krēt') *agg.* indiscreto; imprudente.

indiscretion (ĭn'dĭs·krĕsh'ŭn) *n.* indiscrezione; imprudenza.

indiscriminate (ĭn'dĭs·krĭm'*ĭ*·nĭt) *agg.* indiscriminato; confuso.

indiscrimination (-nā'shŭn) *n.* mancanza di discernimento.

indispensable (ĭn'dĭs·pĕn'sá·b'l) *agg.* indispensabile.

indispose (ĭn'dĭs·pōz') *vt.* indisporre.

indisposed (ĭn'dĭs·pōzd') *agg.* indisposto, maldisposto.

indisposition (ĭn'dĭs·pō·zĭsh'ŭn) *n.* indisposizione; avversione.

indissoluble (ĭn·dĭs'ō·lû·b'l) *agg.* indissolubile.

indistinct (ĭn'dĭs·tĭngkt') *agg.* indistinto.

indistinguishable (ĭn'dĭs·tĭng'gwĭsh·á·b'l) *agg.* indistinguibile.

individual (ĭn'dĭ·vĭd'û·ăl) *n.* individuo. *agg.* individuale, singolo. **—ity** (-ăl'ĭ·tĭ) *n.* individualità.

individualize (-vĭd'û·ăl·īz) *vt.* individualizzare.

indivisible (ĭn'dĭ·vĭz'*ĭ*·b'l) *agg.* indivisibile.

indoctrinate (ĭn·dŏk'trĭ·nāt) *vt.* addottrinare, istruire; fanatizzare.

indolence (ĭn'dō·lĕns) *n.* indolenza, pigrizia.

indolent (ĭn'dō·lĕnt) *agg.* indolente.

indomitable (ĭn·dŏm'ĭ·tá·b'l) *agg.* indomabile; indomito.

indoor (ĭn'dōr) *agg.* domestico, interno, da casa.

indoors (ĭn·dōrz') *avv.* in casa: to go **—**, entrare (*in casa*).

indorse (ĭn·dôrs') *vedi* endorse.

induce (ĭn·dūs') *vt.* indurre. **—ment** *n.* incentivo, esortazione; movente; tentazione.

induct (ĭn·dŭkt') *vt.* introdurre; insediare; iniziare (*istruire*); (*mil.*) arruolare, mobilitare.

inductee (ĭn'dŭk·tē') *n.* (*mil.*) recluta, coscritto.

induction (ĭn·dŭk'shŭn) *n.* induzione; (*mil.*) coscrizione, leva. **— coil**, bobina d'induzione.

inductive (ĭn·dŭk'tĭv) *agg.* induttivo.

indulge (ĭn·dŭlj') *vt.*, *vi.* indulgere, tollerare; favorire, appagare, viziare; adulare: to **— in**, abbandonarsi a, permettersi il lusso di.

indulgence (ĭn·dŭl'jĕns) *n.* indulgenza, proroga; immoderatezza.

indulgent (ĭn·dŭl'jĕnt) *agg.* indulgente complacente.

industrial (ĭn·dŭs'trĭ·ăl) *agg.* industriale: **— design**, arte industriale, estetica del prodotto. **—ist** *n.* industriale.

industrialize (-īz) *vt.* industrializzare.

industrious (ĭn.dŭs′trĭ.ŭs) *agg.* industrioso, attivo, diligente.

industry (ĭn′dŭs.trĭ) *agg.* industria; laboriosità, diligenza.

inebriate (ĭn.ē′brĭ.āt) *n.*, *agg.* ubriaco, ebbro. *vt.* inebriare, ubriacare.

inebriation (-ā′shŭn) *n.* ubriachezza, ebbrezza.

ineffable (ĭn.ĕf′á.b'l) *agg.* ineffabile.

ineffective (ĭn′ĕ.fĕk′tĭv) *agg.* inefficace.

ineffectual (ĭn′ĕ.fĕk′tů.ăl) *agg.* inutile, inefficace.

inefficacious (ĭn′ĕf.ĭ.kā′shŭs) *agg.* inefficace.

inefficiency (ĭn′ĕ.fĭsh′ĕn.sĭ) *n.* incapacità, inefficacia.

inefficient (ĭn′ĕ.fĭsh′ĕnt) *agg.* inefficace, incapace.

ineligible (ĭn.ĕl′ĭ.jĭ.b'l) *agg.* ineleggibile; disadatto.

inept (ĭn.ĕpt′) *agg.* disadatto, incapace.

inequality (ĭn′ē.kwŏl′ĭ.tĭ) *n.* ineguaglianza, disparità; insufficienza; incompetenza.

inequitable (ĭn.ĕk′wĭ.tá.b'l) *agg.* ingiusto.

inert (ĭn.ûrt′) *agg.* inerte. —ia (ĭn.ûr′shá) *n.* inerzia.

inestimable (ĭn.ĕs′tĭ.má.b'l) *agg.* inestimabile, incalcolabile.

inevitable (ĭn.ĕv′ĭ.tá.b'l) *agg.* inevitabile; immancabile.

inexhaustible (ĭn′ĕg.zŏs′tĭ.b'l) *agg.* inesauribile.

inexistent (ĭn′ĕg.zĭs′tĕnt) *agg.* inesistente; (*S.U.*) insito, innato.

inexpedience (ĭn′ĕks.pē′dĭ.ĕns) *n.* inopportunità; inefficacia.

inexpedient (-ĕnt) *agg.* inopportuno, inefficace.

inexpensive (ĭn′ĕks.pĕn′sĭv) *agg.* economico, modico, poco costoso.

inexperience (ĭn′ĕks.pḗr′ĭ.ĕns) *n.* inesperienza.

inexperienced (-ĕnst) *agg.* inesperto.

inexplicable (ĭn.ĕks′plĭ.ká.b'l) *agg.* inesplicabile, incomprensibile.

inexpressible (ĭn′ĕks.prĕs′ĭ.b'l) *agg.* inesprimibile, indicibile.

inexpressibles *n.pl.* (*fam. scherz.*) calzoni.

inextinguishable (ĭn′ĕks.tĭng′gwĭsh.á.b'l) *agg.* inestinguibile.

infallible (ĭn.făl′ĭ.b'l) *agg.* infallibile.

infamous (ĭn′fá.mŭs) *agg.* infame, disonorato, infamante.

infamy (ĭn′fá.mĭ) *n.* infamia.

infancy (ĭn′făn.sĭ) *n.* infanzia.

infant (ĭn′fănt) *n.* infante; minorenne.

infantry (ĭn′făn.trĭ) *n.* fanteria. —man *n.* fante.

infect (ĭn.fĕkt′) *vt.* infettare, contaminare, contagiare. —ion *n.* infezione, contagio. —ious *agg.* infettivo, contagioso.

infer (ĭn.fûr′) *vt.*, *vi.* inferire, dedurre, arguire. —ence *n.* deduzione, illazione. —ential *agg.* deduttivo.

inferior (ĭn.fḗr′ĭ.ẽr) *n.*, *agg.* inferiore. —ity (-ĭ.ŏr′ĭ.tĭ) *n.* inferiorità.

infernal (ĭn.fûr′năl) *agg.* infernale.

infest (ĭn.fĕst′) *vt.* infestare. *vi.* incallire nel vizio.

infidel (ĭn′fĭ.dĕl) *n.*, *agg.* infedele, miscredente.

infiltrate (ĭn.fĭl′trāt) *vt.*, *vi.* infiltrare, infiltrarsi.

infinite (ĭn′fĭ.nĭt) *n.*, *agg.* infinito.

infinitive (ĭn.fĭn′ĭ.tĭv) *n.*, *agg.* (*gramm.*) infinito.

infinity (ĭn.fĭn′ĭ.tĭ) *n.* infinità, infinito.

infirm (ĭn.fûrm′) *agg.* infermo; malfermo, irresoluto; malsicuro. —ary *n.* infermeria, dispensario. —ity *n.* infermità, debolezza.

inflame (ĭn.flām′) *vt.* inflammare; infocare; infervorare. *vi.* infiammarsi; divampare.

inflammation (ĭn′flă.mā′shŭn) *n.* infiammazione.

inflate (ĭn.flāt′) *vt.* enfiare, gonfiare; (*fin.*) inflazionare.

inflation (ĭn.flā′shŭn) *n.* gonfiatura; vanità; inflazione.

inflection (ĭn.flĕk′shŭn) *n.* inflessione; flessione, curvatura.

inflict (ĭn.flĭkt′) *vt.* infliggere.

influence (ĭn′flŏŏ.ĕns) *n.* influenza, influsso. *vt.* influenzare, influire su.

influential (ĭn′flŏŏ.ĕn′shăl) *agg.* influente.

influx (ĭn′flŭks) *n.* influsso, affluenza, fiotto, afflusso.

infold (ĭn.fōld′) *vt.* abbracciare, avvolgere.

inform (ĭn.fôrm′) *vt.* informare, ispirare. *vi.* deporre: to — against, deporre contro.

informal (ĭn.fôr′măl) *agg.* senza cerimonie: — dinner, pranzo intimo *o* alla buona; — visit, visita di confidenza; — dress, vestito di tutti i giorni. —ity (-măl′ĭ.tĭ) *n.* irregolarità, difetto di forma; semplicità. —ly *avv.* senza cerimonie, alla buona.

informant (ĭn.fôr′mănt) *n.* informatore.

information (ĭn′fôr.mā′shŭn) *n.* informazione; deposizione; delazione.

informer (ĭn.fôr′mẽr) *n.* informatore, delatore.

infringe (ĭn.frĭnj′) *vt.*, *vi.* infrangere, violare, trasgredire: to — upon, usurpare, violare. —ment *n.* violazione, usurpazione.

infuriate (ĭn-fū'rĭ-āt) *vt.* infuriare.

infuse (ĭn-fūz') *vt.* infondere, ispirare.

infusible (ĭn-fū'zĭ-b'l) *agg.* inculcabile; non fusibile, infusibile.

infusion (ĭn-fū'zhŭn) *n.* infusione.

ingenious (ĭn-jēn'yŭs) *n.* ingegnoso.

ingenuity (ĭn-jĕ-nū'ĭ-tĭ) *n.* ingegnosità.

ingenuous (ĭn-jĕn'yū-ŭs) *agg.* ingenuo.

ingoing (ĭn'gō'ĭng) *n.* ingresso. *agg.* entrante, in arrivo.

ingot (ĭng'ŏt) *n.* lingotto.

ingrain (ĭn-grān') *vt.* incorporare; istillare, infondere, permeare. —ed *agg.* inveterato, radicato.

ingrate (ĭn'grāt) *n.* ingrateful (ĭn-grāt'fŏŏl) *agg.* ingrato.

ingratiate (ĭn-grā'shĭ-āt) *vt.* ingraziarsi.

ingratitude (ĭn-grăt'ĭ-tūd) *n.* ingratitudine.

ingredient (ĭn-grē'dĭ-ĕnt) *n.* ingrediente.

ingrowing (ĭn'grō'ĭng) *agg.*: — nail, unghia incarnata.

ingulf (ĭn-gŭlf') *vt.* inghiottire; sopraffare.

inhabit (ĭn-hăb'ĭt) *vt.*, *vi.* abitare, dimorare, occupare. —ant *n.* abitante.

inhale (ĭn-hāl') *vt.* inalare, aspirare.

inharmonious (ĭn'hār-mō'nĭ-ŭs) *agg.* disarmonico, stonato.

inherent (ĭn-hēr'ĕnt) *agg.* inerente, insito, intrinseco.

inherit (ĭn-hĕr'ĭt) *vt.*, *vi.* ereditare. —ance *n.* eredità.

inhibit (ĭn-hĭb'ĭt) *vt.* reprimere, inibire, impedire, proibire. —ion *n.* inibizione, proibizione.

inhospitable (ĭn-hŏs'pĭ-tȧ-b'l) *agg.* inospitale.

inhuman (ĭn-hū'mȧn) *agg.* inumano.

inimical (ĭn-ĭm'ĭ-kȧl) *agg.* ostile.

inimitable (ĭn-ĭm'ĭ-tȧ-b'l) *agg.* inimitabile.

iniquitous (ĭ-nĭk'wĭ-tŭs) *agg.* iniquo; ingiusto.

iniquity (ĭ-nĭk'wĭ-tĭ) *n.* iniquità; ingiustizia.

initial (ĭ-nĭsh'ȧl) *n.*, *agg.* iniziale. *vt.* mettere le iniziali, siglare. —ly *avv.* inizialmente, da principio.

initiate (ĭ-nĭsh'ĭ-āt) *vt.* cominciare; iniziare.

initiation (ĭ-nĭsh'ĭ-ā'shŭn) *n.* iniziazione.

initiative (ĭ-nĭsh'ĭ-ā'tĭv) *n.* iniziativa. *agg.* iniziale.

inject (ĭn-jĕkt') *vt.* iniettare. —ion *n.* iniezione, clistere. —or *n.* iniettore.

injunction (ĭn-jŭngk'shŭn) *n.* ingiunzione.

injure (ĭn'jĕr) *vt.* nuocere a, danneggiare, ferire.

injurious (ĭn-jŏŏr'ĭ-ŭs) *agg.* nocivo; ingiurioso.

injury (ĭn'jĕr-ĭ) *n.* torto; danno; ferita; avaria.

injustice (ĭn-jŭs'tĭs) *n.* ingiustizia.

ink (ĭngk) *n.* inchiostro. *vt.* imbrattare d'inchiostro; inchiostrare.

inkling (ĭngk'lĭng) *n.* indizio, sentore.

inkstand (ĭngk'stănd') *n.* calamaio.

inkwell (ĭngk'wĕl') *n.* calamaio.

inky (ĭngk'ĭ) *agg.* nero come l'inchiostro; sporco di inchiostro.

inland (ĭn'lănd) *n.* interno (*di un territorio*). *agg.* interno. *avv.* verso l'interno, all'interno.

inlay (ĭn-lā') *n.* intarsio. *vt.* (*pass.*, *pp.* inlaid) intarsiare, decorare.

inlaid (ĭn-lād') *pass.* e *pp. di* to inlay: — work, lavoro d'intarsio.

inlet (ĭn'lĕt) *n.* accesso, piccola baia.

inmate (ĭn'māt) *n.* abitante, inquilino.

inmost (ĭn'mōst) *agg.* (*il*) più interno, (*il*) più intimo, (*il*) più profondo, (*il*) più segreto.

inn (ĭn) *n.* albergo, locanda, taverna: —keeper, oste, albergatore.

innate (ĭn'nāt) *agg.* innato, istintivo.

inner (ĭn'ĕr) *agg.* interiore, più interno, più segreto, più profondo. —most *agg.superl.* intimo, (*il*) più interno.

inning (ĭn'ĭng) *n.* occasione; turno; raccolto, bonifica; (*baseball*) ripresa, tempo; turno (*del battitore*).

innocence (ĭn'ō-sĕns) *n.* innocenza, candore.

innocent (ĭn'ō-sĕnt) *n.* innocente. *agg.* innocente; innocuo; lecito; privo (*di*); ignaro (*di*); immacolato.

innocuous (ĭ-nŏk'ū-ŭs) *agg.* innocuo.

innovate (ĭn'ō-vāt) *vt.* innovare.

innovation (ĭn'ō-vā'shŭn) *n.* innovazione.

innuendo (ĭn'ū-ĕn'dō) *n.* insinuazione, allusione, sottinteso.

innumerable (ĭ-nū'mĕr-ȧ-b'l) *agg.* innumerabile, innumerevole.

inoculate (ĭn-ŏk'ū-lāt) *vt.* inoculare.

inoffensive (ĭn'ō-fĕn'sĭv) *agg.* innocuo.

inoperative (ĭn-ŏp'er-ȧ'tĭv) *agg.* inefficace; non in vigore, non vigente.

inopportune (ĭn-ŏp'ŏr-tūn') *agg.* inopportuno, intempestivo.

inordinate (ĭn-ôr'dĭ-nĭt) *agg.* smodato.

inquest (ĭn'kwĕst) *n.* inchiesta, indagine, istruttoria preliminare.

inquire (ĭn-kwīr') *vt.*, *vi.* domandare, interrogare, indagare, informarsi, esaminare: to — after, chiedere notizie di; to — into, indagare.

inquiry (ĭn-kwīr'ĭ) *n.* ricerca, interrogazione, indagine: — office, ufficio informazioni.

inquisition (ĭn'kwĭ-zĭsh'ŭn) *n.* inchiesta, indagine, inquisizione.

inquisitive (ĭn·kwĭz'ĭ·tĭv) *agg.* inquisitivo, curioso.

inroad (ĭn'rōd') *n.* invasione, irruzione, infiltrazione; defalco; sottrazione, perdita (*di tempo, denaro, ecc.*): to make inroads upon a supply, intaccare una scorta; to make inroads on one's time, rubare tempo a qualcuno.

insalubrious (ĭn'sȧ·lū'brĭ·ŭs) *agg.* insalubre.

insane (ĭn·sān') *agg.* pazzo: — asylum, manicomio.

insanity (ĭn·săn'ĭ·tĭ) *n.* pazzia.

insatiable (ĭn·sā'shĭ·ȧ·b'l) *agg.* insaziabile.

inscribe (ĭn·skrīb') *vt.* iscrivere; incidere; indirizzare.

inscription (ĭn·skrĭp'shŭn) *n.* iscrizione, dedica, titolo.

insect (ĭn'sĕkt) *n.* insetto.

insecure (ĭn'sē·kūr') *agg.* malsicuro, precario, incerto.

insecurity (ĭn'sē·kū'rĭ·tĭ) *n.* precarietà, incertezza.

insensate (ĭn·sĕn'sāt) *agg.* insensato; inconscio, inanimato; disumano, brutale.

insensible (ĭn·sĕn'sĭ·b'l) *agg.* insensibile; impercettibile; privo di sensi; inconsapevole; grossolano; insensato, stolto.

insensitive (ĭn·sĕn'sĭ·tĭv) *agg.* insensibile; impassibile, indifferente.

inseparable (ĭn·sĕp'ȧ·rȧ·b'l) *agg.* inseparabile.

insert (ĭn·sûrt') *n.* inserto, allegato. *vt.* inserire, introdurre. —**ion** *n.* inserzione, aggiunta.

inside (ĭn'sīd') *n.* interno, parte interna; (*pl.*) visceri. *agg.* interno. *avv.* internamente, dentro. *prep.* entro, dentro; nei limiti di: to turn — out, rovesciare, rivoltare.

insight (ĭn'sīt') *n.* conoscenza profonda, perspicacia, intuito.

insignia (ĭn·sĭg'nĭ·ȧ) *n.pl.* distintivi, emblemi: collar —, mostrine, fiamme; — of rank, distintivi di grado.

insignificance (ĭn'sĭg·nĭf'ĭ·kȧns) *n.* futilità, scarsa importanza.

insignificant (ĭn'sĭg·nĭf'ĭ·kȧnt) *agg.* insignificante.

insinuate (ĭn·sĭn'ū·āt) *vt.* insinuare; introdurre. *vi.* insinuarsi, penetrare.

insinuation (ĭn·sĭn'ū·ā'shŭn) *n.* insinuazione.

insipid (ĭn·sĭp'ĭd) *agg.* insipido.

insist (ĭn·sĭst') *vi.* insistere, persistere. —**ence** *n.* insistenza, persistenza. —**ent** *agg.* insistente, persistente.

insnare (ĭn·snâr') *vedi* ensnare.

insociable (ĭn·sō'shȧ·b'l) *agg.* insocievole.

insolation (ĭn'sō·lā'shŭn) *n.* esposizione al sole; elioterapia; insolazione.

insolence (ĭn'sō·lĕns) *n.* insolenza.

insolent (ĭn'sō·lĕnt) *agg.* insolente.

insolvency (ĭn·sŏl'vĕn·sĭ) *n.* insolvenza.

insolvent (ĭn·sŏl'vĕnt) *n.* debitore insolvente. *agg.* insolvente.

insomuch (ĭn'sō·mŭch') *avv.* al punto che; posto che.

inspect (ĭn·spĕkt') *vt.* ispezionare, esaminare, verificare. —**ion** *n.* ispezione, esame. —**or** *n.* ispettore.

inspiration (ĭn'spĭ·rā'shŭn) *n.* ispirazione.

inspire (ĭn·spīr') *vt., vi.* ispirare.

inspirit (ĭn·spĭr'ĭt) *vt.* animare.

install (ĭn·stôl') *vt.* installare. —**ation** *n.* installazione, insediamento.

installment (ĭn·stôl'mĕnt) *n.* installazione; rata; puntata (*di romanzo*).

instance (ĭn'stȧns) *n.* istanza; esempio, occasione, caso, circostanza: for —, ad esempio; in the first —, da principio, in primo luogo.

instant (ĭn'stȧnt) *n.* attimo, istante. *agg.* urgente, immediato; insistente; corrente: the 5th —, il 5 corrente. —**aneous** *agg.* istantaneo. —**ly** *avv.* istantaneamente, urgentemente.

instead (ĭn·stĕd') *avv.* invece, anziché.

instep (ĭn'stĕp) *n.* collo del piede.

instigate (ĭn'stĭ·gāt) *vt.* istigare.

instil (ĭn·stĭl') *vt.* istillare.

instinct (ĭn'stĭngkt) *n.* istinto, impulso. —**ive** *agg.* istintivo.

institute (ĭn'stĭ·tūt) *n.* istituto. *vt.* istituire, fondare.

institution (ĭn'stĭ·tū'shŭn) *n.* istituzione.

instruct (ĭn·strŭkt') *vt.* istruire, dare istruzioni a, incaricare. —**ion** *n.* istruzione, ordine. —**ive** *agg.* istruttivo. —**or** *n.* istruttore, insegnante.

instrument (ĭn'strŏŏ·mĕnt) *n.* strumento. —**al** *agg.* strumentale; utile, adatto (*allo scopo*). —**alist** *n.* orchestrale, sonatore. —**ality** *n.* cooperazione, utilità.

insufferable (ĭn·sŭf'ẽr·ȧ·b'l) *agg.* insopportabile, insoffribile.

insufficiency (ĭn'sŭ·fĭsh'ĕn·sĭ) *n.* insufficienza, deficienza; incapacità.

insufficient (ĭn'sŭ·fĭsh'ĕnt) *agg.* insufficiente; incapace.

insulate (ĭn'sū·lāt) *vt.* isolare.

insulation (ĭn'sū·lā'shŭn) *n.* isolamento.

insulator (ĭn'sū·lā'tẽr) *n.* isolatore, isolante.

insult (ĭn'sŭlt) *n.* insulto, affronto. *vt.* insultare.

insuppressible (ĭn'sŭ.prĕs'ĭ.b'l) *agg.* insopprimibile, irrefrenabile.

insurance (ĭn.shōōr'ăns) *n.* assicurazione: — broker, agente di assicurazione; life —, assicurazione sulla vita.

insure (ĭn.shōōr') *vt.* assicurare.

insurer (ĭn.shōōr'ĕr) *n.* assicuratore.

insurgence (ĭn.sûr.jĕns) *n.* insurrezione, rivolta.

insurgent (ĭn.sûr'jĕnt) *n.*, *agg.* insorto, ribelle, rivoltoso.

insurmountable (ĭn.sûr'moun'tà.b'l) *agg.* insuperabile, insormontabile.

insurrection (ĭn.sŭ.rĕk'shŭn) *n.* surrezione, sommossa, rivolta.

intact (ĭn.tăkt') *agg.* intatto.

intake (ĭn'tăk') *n.* immissione, aspirazione; strozzatura.

integral (ĭn'tĕ.grăl) *n.* parte integrante, totalità. *agg.* integrale, integrante; essenziale.

integration (ĭn'tĕ.grā'shŭn) *n.* integrazione.

integrity (ĭn.tĕg'rĭ.tĭ) *n.* integrità.

intellect (ĭn'tĕ.lĕkt) *n.* intelletto. —ual *n.*, *agg.* intellettuale.

intelligence (ĭn.tĕl'ĭ.jĕns) *n.* intelligenza; intesa, accordo; informazione, notizia; spionaggio

intelligent (ĭn.tĕl'ĭ.jĕnt) *agg.* intelligente.

intemperance (ĭn.tĕm'pĕr.ăns) *n.* intemperanza.

intemperate (ĭn.tĕm'pĕr.ĭt) *agg.* intemperante.

intend (ĭn.tĕnd') *vt.* intendere, destinare, significare. *vi.* avere intenzione di, pensare.

intense (ĭn.tĕns') *agg.* intenso.

intensify (ĭn.tĕn'sĭ.fĭ) *vt.* intensificare. *vi.* intensificarsi.

intensity (ĭn.tĕn'sĭ.tĭ) *n.* intensità.

intensive (ĭn.tĕn'sĭv) *agg.* intensivo, indefesso: — course, corso accelerato.

intent (ĭn.tĕnt') *n.* intenzione, intento. *agg.* intento, attento, assorto.

intention (ĭn.tĕn'shŭn) *n.* intenzione. —al *agg.* intenzionale. —ally *avv.* intenzionalmente, di proposito.

intentness (ĭn.tĕnt'nĕs) *n.* attenzione.

inter (ĭn.tûr') *vt.* sotterrare.

intercede (ĭn'tĕr.sēd') *vi.* intercedere.

intercept (ĭn'tĕr.sĕpt') *vt.* intercettare, bloccare. —ion intercettazione. —or *n.* intercettore; (*aeron.*) caccia intercettore.

intercession (ĭn'tĕr.sĕsh'ŭn) *n.* intercessione.

interchange (ĭn'tĕr.chānj') *n.* scambio, alternazione. *vt.*, *vi.* scambiare, scambiarsi; succedersi; alternarsi.

—**able** *agg.* intercambiabile, sostituibile.

intercom *vedi* **interphone.**

intercourse (ĭn'tĕr.kōrs) *n.* relazione, rapporto.

interdiction (ĭn'tĕr.dĭk'shŭn) *n.* divieto.

interest (ĭn'tĕr.ĕst) *n.* interesse; interessamento; profitto. *vt.* interessare, destare interesse in; cointeressare. —ed *agg.* interessato: to be (*o* become) — in, interessarsi di *o* a. —ing *agg.* interessante.

interfere (ĭn'tĕr.fēr') *vt.* interferire, intromettersi: to — with, contrastare, ostacolare, frustrare.

interference (-fēr'ĕns) *n.* intromissione, intralcio; interferenza.

interim (ĭn'tĕr.ĭm) *n.* intervallo, interim. *agg.* temporaneo, interinale.

interior (ĭn.tēr'ĭ.ĕr) *n.*, *agg.* interno, interiore.

interjection (ĭn'tĕr.jĕk'shŭn) *n.* interpolazione; interiezione.

interlace (ĭn'tĕr.lās') *vt.*, *vi.* intrecciare, intrecciarsi.

interline (ĭn'tĕr.līn') *vt.* interlineare.

interlock (ĭn'tĕr.lŏk') *vt.*, *vi.* collegare, coordinare; incastrarsi; essere in collegamento.

interloper (ĭn'tĕr.lōp'ĕr) *n.* intruso; esercente abusivo.

interlude (ĭn'tĕr.lūd) *n.* intermezzo.

intermediate (ĭn'tĕr.mē'dĭ.ĭt) *agg.* intermedio.

interment (ĭn.tûr'mĕnt) *n.* sepoltura.

interminable (ĭn.tûr'mĭ.nà.b'l) *agg.* interminabile.

intermingle (ĭn'tĕr.mĭng'g'l) *vt.*, *vi.* mescolare, mescolarsi.

intermission (ĭn'tĕr.mĭsh'ŭn) *n.* intervallo, pausa.

intermittent (ĭn'tĕr.mĭt'ĕnt) *agg.* intermittente.

intern (ĭn'tûrn) *n.* medico ospitaliero, assistente interino. *vt.* internare, confinare.

internal (ĭn.tûr'năl) *agg.* interno.

international (ĭn'tĕr.năsh'ŭn.ăl) *agg.* internazionale.

internationalize (ĭn'tĕr.năsh'ŭn.ăl.ĭz) *vt.* internazionalizzare.

interphone (ĭn'tĕr.fōn') *n.* citofono.

interpolate (ĭn.tûr'pō.lāt) *vt.* interpolare.

interpose (ĭn'tĕr.pōz') *vt.*, *vi.* interporre, interloquire, interporsi.

interpret (ĭn.tûr'prĕt) *vt.* interpretare. —ation *n.* interpretazione. —er *n.* interprete.

interrogate (ĭn.tĕr'ō.gāt) *vt.* interrogare.

interrogation (ĭn.tĕr'ō.gā'shŭn) *n.* interrogazione: note of —, punto interrogativo.

interrogative (In'tĕ·rŏg'á·tĭv) n., agg. interrogativo.

interrupt (In'tĕ·rŭpt') vt. interrompere. —ion n. interruzione.

intersect (In'tĕr·sĕkt') vt., vi. incrociare, incrociarsi, intersecare, intersecarsi. —ion n. intersezione; crocevia, incrocio.

intersperse (In'tĕr·spŭrs') vt. cospargere, disseminare.

intertwine (In'tĕr·twīn') vt. intrecciare. vi. intrecciarsi, confondersi.

interval (In'tĕr·văl) n. intervallo.

intervene (In'tĕr·vēn') vi. intervenire; sopravvenire; esser situato; intercorrere.

intervention (In'tĕr·vĕn'shŭn) n. intervento.

interview (In'tĕr·vū) n. colloquio, intervista. vt. interpellare, intervistare. —er n. intervistatore.

intestine (In·tĕs'tĭn) n., agg. intestino.

intimacy (In'tĭ·má·sĭ) n. intimità.

intimate (In'tĭ·mĭt) (1) n., agg. intimo.

intimate (In'tĭ·māt) (2) vt. annunciare, far sapere, notificare.

intimately (In'tĭ·mĭt·lĭ) avv. intimamente.

intimation (In'tĭ·mā'shŭn) n. annuncio, avvisaglia, sentore.

intimidate (In·tĭm'ĭ·dāt) vt. intimidire, minacciare.

intimidation (In·tĭm'ĭ·dā'shŭn) n. intimidazione, minaccia.

into (In'tŏŏ) prep. entro, dentro, in.

intolerable (In·tŏl'ĕr·á·b'l) agg. intollerabile.

intolerance (In·tŏl'ĕr·ăns) n. intolleranza.

intolerant (-ănt) agg. intollerante.

intonation (In'tŏ·nā'shŭn) n. intonazione, modulazione.

intone (In·tōn') vt., vi. intonare, intonarsi.

intoxicate (In·tŏk'sĭ·kāt) vt. ubriacare, esaltare, inebriare.

intoxicated agg. ubriaco, ebbro.

intoxicating agg. inebriante.

intoxication (In·tŏk'sĭ·kā'shŭn) n. ubriachezza, esaltazione.

intractability (In·trăk'tá·bĭl'ĭ·tĭ) n. intrattabilità.

intractable (In·trăk'tá·b'l) agg. intrattabile.

intransigence (In·trăn'sĭ·jĕns) n. intransigenza.

intransitive (In·trăn'sĭ·tĭv) agg. intransitivo.

intravenous (In'trá·vē'nŭs) agg. endovenoso.

intrench (In·trĕnch') vedi entrench.

intrepid (In·trĕp'ĭd) agg. intrepido.

intricacy (In'trĭ·ká·sĭ) n. intrico, groviglio; complessità.

intricate (In'trĭ·kĭt) agg. intricato complesso.

intrigue (In·trēg') n. intrigo. vt. incuriosire, rendere perplesso. vi. intrigare, tramare.

intriguer (In·trē'gĕr) n. intrigante.

introduce (In'trō·dūs') vt. introdurre; presentare.

introduction (In'trō·dŭk'shŭn) n. introduzione; presentazione.

intrude (In·trōōd') vt. intrudere, imporre. vi. intrufolarsi; disturbare: to — on o upon, importunare, usurpare; to — oneself, imporre la propria presenza.

intruder (In·trōōd'ĕr) n. intruso.

intrusion (In·trōō'zhŭn) n. intrusione.

intrusive (In·trōō'sĭv) agg. importuno.

intuition (In'tū·ĭsh'ŭn) n. intuizione.

inundate (In'ŭn·dāt) vt. inondare.

inundation (In'ŭn·dā'shŭn) n. inondazione.

inure (In·ūr') vt. assuefare; agguerrire.

invade (In·vād') vt. invadere.

invader (In·vād'ĕr) n. invasore.

invalid (In'vá·lĭd) n. infermo. agg. (In·văl'ĭd) invalido; non valido, nullo.

invalidate (In·văl'ĭ·dāt) vt. invalidare, anullare.

invaluable (In·văl'ū·á·b'l) agg. inestimabile, prezioso.

invariable (In·vâr'ĭ·á·b'l) agg. invariabile.

invariably (In·vâr'ĭ·á·blĭ) avv. invariabilmente.

invasion (In·vā'zhŭn) n. invasione.

inveigle (In·vē'g'l) vt. sedurre, indurre, coinvolgere, adescare. —ment n. adescamento, alliettamento.

invent (In·vĕnt') vt. inventare. —ion n. invenzione. —ive agg. inventivo. —iveness n. inventiva. —or n. inventore.

inventory (In'vĕn·tō'rĭ) n. inventario. vt. inventariare.

inverse (In·vûrs') n., agg. inverso, contrario.

invert (In·vûrt') vt. invertire; capovolgere.

invest (In·vĕst') (1) vt. investire (in ogni accezione); rivestire, adornare.

invest (2) vt. avvolgere, rivestire; investire. —ment n. investimento (di capitale).

investigate (In·vĕs'tĭ·gāt) vt. indagare, investigare, esaminare; ricercare.

investigation (In·vĕs'tĭ·gā'shŭn) n. investigazione, indagine; ricerca.

investigator (In·vĕs'tĭ·gā'tĕr) n. investigatore; ricercatore.

investor (In·vĕs'tĕr) n. chi investe danaro, capitalista.

inveterate (ĭn·vĕt'ĕr·ĭt) *agg.* inveterato, radicato.

invidious (ĭn·vĭd'ĭ·ŭs) *agg.* ingiusto.

invigorate (ĭn·vĭg'ĕr·āt) *vt.* invigorire.

invigorating *agg.* energetico.

invincible (ĭn·vĭn's'ĭ·b'l) *agg.* invincibile.

inviolable (ĭn·vī'ō·lȧ·b'l) *agg.* inviolabile.

invisible (ĭn·vĭz'ĭ·b'l) *agg.* invisibile.

invitation (ĭn'vĭ·tā'shŭn) *n.* invito.

invite (ĭn·vīt') *vt., vi.* invitare; provocare, indurre.

inviting *agg.* invitante, allettante, attraente.

invoice (ĭn'vois) *n.* fattura. *vt.* fatturare.

invoke (ĭn·vōk') *vt.* invocare.

involuntary (ĭn·vŏl'ŭn·tĕr'ĭ) *agg.* involontario.

involve (ĭn·vŏlv') *vt.* avvolgere; implicare, includere, complicare; coinvolgere: **to get —d,** impegolarsi.

invulnerable (ĭn·vŭl'nĕr·ȧ·b'l) *agg.* invulnerabile.

inward (ĭn'wĕrd) *agg.* interno, interiore, intimo. *avv.* (*anche* **inwards**) internamente, verso l'interno, nell'intimo.

inwrought (ĭn·rôt') *agg.* ornato, adorno, trapunto.

iodide (ī'ō·dīd) *n.* ioduro.

iodine (ī'ō·dĭn) *n.* iodio.

I.O.U. (ī'ō'ū') (*abbr. di* I owe you) cambiale.

I.Q. (ī'kū') *n.* (*abbr. di* intelligence quotient) (*grado di*) intelligenza.

irascible (ĭ·răs'ĭ·b'l) *agg.* irascibile.

irate (ī'rāt) *agg.* adirato, incollerito.

ire (īr) *n.* ira. **—ful** *agg.* iracondo.

iridescent (ĭr'ĭ·dĕs'ĕnt) *agg.* iridescente.

iris (ī'rĭs) *n.* arcobaleno; (*bot.*) giaggiolo; (*anat.*) iride.

Irish (ī'rĭsh) *n., agg.* irlandese.

irk (ûrk) *vt.* infastidire. **—some** *agg.* fastidioso.

iron (ī'ĕrn) *n.* ferro: **cast —,** ghisa; **— lung,** polmone d'acciaio. *agg.* ferreo, di ferro. *vt., vi.* stirare; rivestire di ferro: **to — out a difficulty,** appianare una difficoltà. **—clad** *n.* corazzata (*nave*). *agg.* corazzato. **—ing** *n.* stiratura. **—monger** *n.* commerciante in ferramenta. **—work** *n.* lavoro in ferro; (*pl.*) ferriera.

ironical (ī·rŏn'ĭ·kăl) *agg.* ironico.

irony (ī'rō·nĭ) *n.* ironia.

irrecognizable (ĭr·rĕk'ŏg·nīz'ȧ·b'l) *agg.* irriconoscibile.

irreconcilable (ĭr·rĕk'ŏn·sīl'ȧ·b'l) *agg.* irreconciliabile, incompatibile.

irrecoverable (ĭr'rĕ·kŭv'ĕr·ȧ·b'l) *agg.* irreparabile, irrecuperabile.

irredeemable (ĭr'rē·dēm'ȧ·b'l) *agg.* irredimibile, irrimediabile.

irreducible (ĭr'rē·dūs'ĭ·b'l) *agg.* irriducibile.

irrefutable (ĭr·rĕf'ū·tȧ·b'l) *agg.* irrefutabile.

irregular (ĭr·rĕg'ū·lĕr) *n., agg.* irregolare.

irrelevancy (ĭr·rĕl'ē·văn·sĭ) *n.* inconsistenza, scarsa importanza.

irrelevant (ĭr·rĕl'ē·vȧnt) *agg.* irrilevante; fuori luogo, estraneo all'argomento; inopportuno; non probatorio.

irreligious (ĭr'rē·lĭj'ŭs) *agg.* irreligioso, ateo.

irremediable (ĭr'rē·mē'dĭ·ȧ·b'l) *agg.* irrimediabile, irreparabile.

irremovable (ĭr'rē·mōōv'ȧ·b'l) *agg.* saldo, inamovibile.

irreparable (ĭ·rĕp'ȧ·rȧ·b'l) *agg.* irreparabile.

irreplaceable (ĭr'rē·plās'ȧ·b'l) *agg.* insostituibile.

irrepressible (ĭr·rē·prĕs'ĭ·b'l) *agg.* irrefrenabile; esuberante.

irreproachable (ĭr·rē·prōch'ȧ·b'l) *agg.* irreprensibile, impeccabile.

irresistible (ĭr'rē·zĭs'tĭ·b'l) *agg.* irresistibile.

irresolute (ĭ·rĕz'ō·lūt) *agg.* irresoluto.

irresponsible (ĭr'rē·spŏn's'ĭ·b'l) *n., agg.* irresponsabile.

irretrievable (ĭr'rē·trēv'ȧ·b'l) *agg.* irreparabile; irrecuperabile.

irreverence (ĭ·rĕv'ĕr·ĕns)*n.* irriverenza.

irreverent (-ĕnt) *agg.* irriverente.

irrigate (ĭr'ĭ·gāt) *vt.* irrigare.

irrigation (ĭr'ĭ·gā'shŭn) *n.* irrigazione.

irritability (ĭr'ĭ·tȧ·bĭl'ĭ·tĭ) *n.* irritabilità.

irritable (ĭr'ĭ·tȧ·b'l) *agg.* irritabile, irascibile.

irritate (ĭr'ĭ·tāt) *vt.* irritare.

irritation (ĭr'ĭ·tā'shŭn) *n.* irritazione.

irruption (ĭ·rŭp'shŭn) *n.* irruzione.

is (ĭz) 3a *pers.sing.pres. di* to be.

isinglass (ī'zĭng·glȧs') *n.* colla di pesce.

island (ī'lǎnd) *n.* isola. **—er** *n.* isolano.

isle (īl) *n.* isola.

islet (ī'lĕt) *n.* isoletta, isolotto.

isolate (ī'sō·lāt) *vt.* isolare, separare.

isolation (ī'sō·lā'shŭn) *n.* isolamento. **—ism** *n.* isolazionismo.

isotope (ī'sō·tōp) *n.* (*chim.*) isotopo.

Israeli (ĭz·rā'lĭ) *n., agg.* israeliano.

issue (ĭsh'ū) *n.* uscita; esito; passaggio; fascicolo, numero, edizione; sfogo; distribuzione, emissione, spedizione, rilascio; scolo(*di acque*); eredi, progenie; (*med.*) secrezione: **to take — with,** dissentire da. *vt.*

pubblicare; emettere, diffondere, rilasciare. *vi.* uscire, scaturire; originare; concludersi.

isthmus (ĭs′mŭs) *n.* istmo.

it (ĭt) *pron.neutro* lo, la (*accusativo*); (*introducibile in ital. se usato in forme impersonali*) esso, essa, ciò; (*col verbo in forma passiva*) si (*pron. indef.*): — snows, nevica; who is —? chi è?; — is I, sono io; — is said, si dice; how goes —? come va?; to foot —, andare a piedi.

Italian (ĭ·tăl′yăn) *n.*, *agg.* italiano.

Italic (ĭ·tăl′ĭk) *agg.* italico.

italics *n.pl.* corsivo.

italicize (ĭ·tăl′ĭ·sĭz) *vt.*, *vi.* comporre *o* stampare in corsivo, sottolineare.

itch (ĭch) *n.* scabbia, prurito; desiderio, voglia. *vi.* prudere, pizzicare; ardere dal desiderio. **—y** *agg.* scabbioso; pruriginoso: to feel —, avere prurito.

item (ī′tĕm) *n.* voce (*di fattura, catalogo, ecc.*); paragrafo, articolo.

itemize (ī′tĕm·ĭz) *vt.* specificare, enumerare, elencare.

iterate (ĭt′ĕr·āt) *vt.* reiterare.

itinerary (ĭ·tĭn′ĕr·ĕr′ĭ) *n.* itinerario.

its (ĭts) *agg.poss.neutro* di esso, suo, sua, di ciò.

itself (ĭt·sĕlf′) *pron.rifl.neutro* se stesso, esso stesso, se stessa, essa stessa, stesso, stessa: by —, da solo, isolato, in se stesso.

ivory (ī′vō·rĭ) *n.* avorio.

ivy (ī′vĭ) *n.* (*bot.*) edera.

J

jab (jăb) *n.* colpo, stoccata. *vt.*, *vi.* colpire, punzecchiare.

jabber (jăb′ĕr) *vt.* mormorare. *vi.* balbettare.

jack (jăk) *n.* individuo, tizio; brocca, otre; maschio (*di alcuni animali*); (*naut.*) marinaio; bandiera; (*ittiol.*) luccio; (*mecc.*) argano; verricello; (*auto.*) cric; (*carpent.*) cavalletto; (*carte da gioco*) fante; (*bocce*) pallino. *vt.* sollevare, issare: — of all trades, factotum; — pot, monte premi, premio massimo; successo; vincita.

jackknife (jăk′nĭf) *n.* coltello a serramanico.

jackal (jăk′ôl) *n.* (*zool.*) sciacallo.

jackass (jăk′ás′) *n.* asino.

jackdaw (jăk′dô′) *n.* cornacchia.

jacket (jăk′ĕt) *n.* giacca; involucro, buccia; sopraccoperta (*di libro*).

jade (jād) (1) *n.* (*min.*) giada.

jade (jād) (2) *n.* ronzino; megera, donnaccia. *vt.* affaticare, opprimere. *vi.* logorarsi.

jaded *agg.* esausto; sazio.

jag (jăg) *n.* frastaglio, dentellatura, protuberanza. *vt.* frastagliare. **—ged** *agg.* dentellato, frastagliato.

jaguar (jăg′wär) *n.* (*zool.*) giaguaro.

jail (jāl) *n.* carcere. *vt.* incarcerare. **—bird** *n.* delinquente. **—er** *n.* carceriere.

jalopy (já·lŏp′ĭ) *n.* (*gergo*) vecchia automobile, caffettiera (*fig.*); (*aeron.*) vecchio aereoplano, carcassone.

jam (jăm) (1) *n.* marmellata.

jam (jăm) (2) *n.* ammasso, compressione, accozzaglia; guaio; ingorgo: — session (*mus. jazz*) riunione di musicisti per suonare improv-visando; traffic —, ingorgo stradale. *vt.* comprimere, pigiare, ingombrare, stipare; inceppare; ingorgare: to — on the brakes, frenare di colpo; to — one's fingers, pestarsi le dita; *vi.* pigiarsi, ammassarsi; incepparsi. **—pack** *vt.* stipare; affollare.

jamb (jăm) *n.* stipite, pilastro.

jangle (jăng′g′l) *vt.*, *vi.* risuonare, far risuonare sgradevolmente.

janitor (jăn′ĭ·tĕr) *n.* portiere, custode.

January (jăn′ū·ĕr′ĭ) *n.* gennaio.

Japanese (jăp′á·nēs) *n.*, *agg.* giapponese.

jar (jär) (1) *n.* giara, brocca, boccale.

jar (jär) (2) *n.* vibrazione, dissonanza; urto; lite; spostamento: on the —, socchiuso. *vt.* far vibrare; contrariare; scuotere. *vi.* vibrare; stonare; urtare (*i nervi*); ferire (*l'orecchio*); urtarsi.

jargon (jär′gŏn) *n.* gergo, dialetto; (*min.*) zircone.

jasmine (jăs′mĭn) *n.* gelsomino.

jasper (jăs′pĕr) *n.* (*min.*) diaspro.

jaundice (jôn′dĭs) *n.* itterizia; prevenzione, pregiudizio.

jaunt (jônt) *n.* escursione, passeggiata. *vi.* fare una passeggiatina.

jaunty (jônt′ĭ) *agg.* gaio, vivace, sbarazzino; spavaldo; affettato, pretenzioso.

javelin (jăv′lĭn) *n.* giavellotto.

jaw (jô) *n.* mascella, mandibola; (*mecc.*) ganascia.

jawbone (jô′bōn′) *n.* osso mascellare, mandibola.

jay (jā) *n.* (*ornit.*) ghiandaia; (*fig.*) donna perduta; (*S.U.*) gonzo. **— walker** *n.* pedone indisciplinato *o* distratto.

jazz (jăz) *n.* musica sincopata. *vt.*, *vi.* sonare musica jazz, ballare musica jazz: to — up, sincopare; animare, rallegrare. — band n. orchestra jazz.

jealous (jĕl′ŭs) agg. geloso, invidioso.

jealousy n. gelosia, invidia.

jean (jēn) n. diagonale di cotone; (pl.) calzoni di tela, tuta.

jeep (jēp) n. camionetta, jeep.

jeer (jēr) n. scherno, beffa. vt. schernire, burlare. vi. farsi beffe (di).

jell (jĕl) vi. diventare gelatinoso; (fig.) cristallizzarsi, solidificarsi.

jelly (jĕl′Ĭ) n. gelatina. vt., vi. mettere in gelatina, diventare gelatinoso. —fish n. (ittiol.) medusa.

jenny (jĕn′Ĭ) n. filatolo.

jeopardize (jĕp′ĕr dĭz) vt. mettere a repentaglio, compromettere.

jeopardy (jĕp′ĕr dĬ) n. repentaglio.

jerk (jûrk) n. scossa, urto, spinta, strappo, scatto; carne in conserva; gelataio, venditore di bibite analcoliche; (gergo) poco di buono, puzzone, lazzarone. vt. lanciare, spingere, scaraventare, scuotere, gettare; conservare (carni). vi. scattare, muoversi a scatti; traballare. —y agg. convulso, irregolare, traballante.

jersey (jûr′zĬ) n. lana pettinata; maglione, giubbetto di lana.

jest (jĕst) n. scherzo, burla, arguzia, derisione. vt., vi. beffare, scherzare. —er n. burlone, buffone.

Jesuit (jĕz′û.Ĭt) n. gesuita.

jet (jĕt) n. getto, sbocco, zampillo; becco (a gas); ambra nera. agg. d'ambra nera, nero; a reazione: —black, nerissimo; — motor, motore a reazione; — propulsion, propulsione a reazione; — plane, velivolo a reazione, aviogetto. vt., vi. lanciare, scaturire.

jetty (jĕt′Ĭ) n. gettata, diga, argine.

Jew (jōō) n. ebreo, israelita. —ess n. ebrea. —ish n., agg. ebraico.

jewel (jōō′ĕl) n. gioiello, gemma. vt. ingioiellare, ingemmare. —er n. gioielliere. —ry n. gioielli, gioielleria (arte). — shop, gioielleria.

jib (jĬb) n. braccio di gru; (naut.) fiocco.

jiffy (jĬf′Ĭ) n. attimo, istante: in a —, in men che non si dica.

jig (jĬg) n. giga (danza); (mecc.) maschera: —saw, sega da intaglio: — puzzle, rompicapo.

jiggle (jĬg′l) vi. camminare a scatti, camminare come gli ubriachi.

jilt (jĬlt) vt., vi. piantare (un innamorato).

jingle (jĬng′g′l) n. tintinnio; tiritera. vt. far tintinnare. vi. tintinnare.

jingo (jĬng′gō) n. guerraiolo, naziona-

lista fanatico: by —! perdiana!

jink (jĬngk) n. giravolta, piroetta; (pl.) allegria, chiasso.

job (jŏb) n. lavoro, opera, compito; impresa; impiego; affare; speculazione; prevaricazione; (gergo) colpo ladresco; un esemplare di qualunque cosa o essere: a blonde —, una bionda; to work by the —, lavorare a cottimo. vt. noleggiare. vi. lavorare a cottimo. —ber n. operaio cottimista; agente di cambio; noleggiatore. —holder n. impiegato, impiegato statale. —work n. lavoro a cottimo; (tip.) lavoro miscellaneo.

jock (jŏk) n. fantino: — strap (gergo S.U.), sospensorio.

jockey (jŏk′Ĭ) n. fantino. vt., vi. montare (cavalli da corsa); ingannare, raggirare.

jocular (jŏk′û.lēr) agg. scherzoso.

jog (jŏg) n. scossa, urto; gomitata; asperità, sporgenza. vt. scuotere, spingere; dar di gomito. vi. procedere lentamente opp. ritmicamente: to — along, trotterellare; tirare avanti alla meglio, condurre vita monotona. — trot n. piccolo trotto; tran-tran.

John Doe (jŏn dō) n. (legge) persona fittizia.

join (join) vt., vi. unire, congiungere, allacciare; incrociare; raggiungere; unirsi, associarsi (a); partecipare; arruolarsi; essere contiguo, confinare (con): to — battle, iniziare la lotta, venire alle mani; to — issue, iniziare un dibattito.

joint (joint) n. congiunzione, giunto; grosso pezzo di carne; (anat.) articolazione; (bot.) nodo, connessura; (geol.) fessura: out of —, slogato, scompigliato; universal —, (mecc.) giunto cardanico. agg. aggiunto, unito, associato, collettivo: — action, azione collettiva; — committee, commissione mista; — session, seduta plenaria. vt. congiungere; tagliare alle giunture; unire; piallare. vi. unirsi. —ed agg. articolato, giuntato. —er o —ing plane n. pialla. —heir n. coerede. —ly avv. insieme, unitamente, di comune accordo. — stock n. capitale azionario. —stock company n. società anonima.

joke (jōk) n. arguzia, facezia, scherzo: a practical —, un tiro birbone; to crack a —, dire una spiritosaggine; vt. beffare, burlare. vi. celiare: no joking, scherzi a parte.

joker (jŏk′ēr) n. burlone; pagliaccio; (carte da poker, ecc.) 53a carta *(specie di "matta")* detta anche jolly joker.

jokingly (jŏk'ĭng∙lĭ) *avv.* per scherzo.

jolly (jŏl'ĭ) *agg.* allegro, spensierato, paffuto. *avv.* molto, grandemente.
—joker *vedi* joker.

jolt (jōlt) *n.* scossa, sobbalzo. *vt.* scuotere, far sobbalzare. *vi.* sobbalzare, traballare.

jostle (jŏs''l) *n.* urto; calca. *vt.* spingere, urtare. *vi.* spingersi, urtarsi; lottare.

jot (jŏt) *n.* jota, inezia. *vt.* (*gen.seg. da* down) annotare, scribacchiare.

journal (jûr'nəl) *n.* giornale, diario; (*naut.*) giornale di bordo; (*comm.*) libro giornale. —ese *n.* gergo giornalistico. —ism *n.* giornalismo. —ist *n.* giornalista.

journey (jûr'nĭ) *n.* viaggio (*spec. terrestre*), tragitto, tappa: by slow journeys, a piccole tappe. *vi.* viaggiare.

jovial (jō'vĭ∙əl) *agg.* gioviale, allegro.

jowl (joul) *n.* guancia, mascella (*spec.inf.*); pappagorgia; bargigli.

joy (joi) *n.* gioia, allegria, felicità.
—ful *agg.* gioioso, contento. —fully *avv.* gioiosamente, allegramente.
—less *agg.* afflitto, malinconico.
—ous *agg.* gioioso.

jubilant (jōō'bĭ∙lənt) *agg.* giubilante, trionfante.

jubilation (jōō'bĭ∙lā'shŭn) *n.* giubilo, tripudio.

jubilee (jōō'bĭ∙lē) *n.* giubileo, anniversario; (*fig.*) festa.

judge (jŭj) *n.* giudice, arbitro, intenditore: to be a — of, intendersi di. *vt., vi.* giudicare, credere, reputare; intendersene; distinguere sentenziare. —ment *opp.* judgment *n.* giudizio, sentenza; opinione: — day, giorno del giudizio.

judicial (jōō∙dĭsh'əl) *agg.* giudiziario, giuridico; sentenzioso.

judicious (jōō∙dĭsh'ŭs) *agg.* giudizioso.

jug (jŭg) *n.* brocca, boccale, anfora; (*gergo*) carcere.

juggle (jŭg''l) *n.* gioco di prestigio; imbroglio. *vt.* ingannare, gabbare; manipolare. *vi.* fare giochi di prestigio; imbrogliare.

juggler (jŭg'lẽr) *n.* giocoliere; impostore.

juice (jōōs) *n.* sugo, succo; (*bot.*) linfa.

juiciness (jōōs'ĭ∙nĕs) *n.* sugosità.

juicy (jōōs'ĭ) *agg.* sugoso, succoso; ricco di linfa; sostanzioso; piccante.

jujube (jōō'jōōb) *n.* (*bot.*) giuggiola.

jukebox (jook'bŏks) *n.* grammofono automatico *o* a gettone.

July (jōō∙lī'ĭ) *n.* luglio.

jumble (jŭm'b'l) *n.* confusione, guazzabuglio, mescolanza, congerie; ciambellina. *vt.* mescolare, confondere, gettare alla rinfusa. *vi.* confondersi, mescolarsi.

jump (jŭmp) *n.* salto, balzo; rialzo (*di prezzi*): to be always on the —, essere sempre in movimento *o* in agitazione. *vt., vi.* saltare; superare; arrischiare; slanciarsi; sobbalzare; cadere appropriarsi; accordarsi, coincidere: to — about, darsi d'attorno; to — at, balzare verso, affrettarsi ad accettare; to — over, scavalcare; to — up, sobbalzare, balzare in piedi; to — to conclusions, trarre conclusioni precipitose. —er *n.* saltatore; casacchina; camiciotto. —y *agg.* mal fermo; irrequieto, nervoso, teso.

junction (jŭngk'shŭn) *n.* congiunzione giuntura, unione, diramazione (*ferr.*) bivio.

juncture (jŭngk'tŭr) *n.* articolazione, congiunzione; congiuntura, situazione.

June (jōōn) *n.* giugno.

jungle (jŭng'g'l) *n.* giungla.

junior (jōōn'yẽr) *n., agg.* juniore, minore; cadetto; figlio: — college (*S.U.*) corso inferiore dell' università; — officer, ufficiale subalterno.

juniper (jōō'nĭ∙pẽr) *n.* (*bot.*) ginepro.

junk (jŭngk) *n.* giunca (*barca*); vecchio cordame; cianfrusaglie; carne salata.

jurisdiction (jōōr'ĭs∙dĭk'shŭn) *n.* giurisdizione.

jurisprudence (jōōr'ĭs∙prōō'dĕns) *n.* giurisprudenza.

juror (jōōr'ẽr) *n.* giurato.

jury (jōōr'ĭ) *n.* giuria, collegio di giurati: grand —, gran giurì. — box *n.* banco dei giurati.

just (jŭst) *agg.* giusto, retto, imparziale esatto, dovuto. *avv.* appunto, esattamente; solamente, solo, appena; quasi, un po'; or ora; giustamente: he has — gone out, è appena uscito; — now, ora, un momento fa; — as, nel momento in cui; — out, appena uscito, appena pubblicato; — a little boy, solo un bambino.

justice (jŭs'tĭs) *n.* giustizia; imparzialità, diritto; giudice.

justification (jŭs'tĭ∙fĭ∙kā'shŭn) *n.* giustificazione; assoluzione.

justify (jŭs'tĭ∙fī) *vt., vi.* giustificare, assolvere.

jut (jŭt) *n.* sporgenza; aggetto. *vi.* sporgere. —ting *n.* sporgenza. *agg.* sporgente.

jute (jōōt) *n.* iuta.

juvenile (jōō′vĕ·nĭl) *n.* giovane, attor giovane; libro per ragazzi. *agg.* giovanile.

juxtaposition (jŭks′td·pŏ·zĭsh′ŭn) *n.* contiguità; accostamento.

K

kale (kāl) cavolo arricciato.

kangaroo (kăng′gá·rōō′) *n.* (*zool.*) canguro.

kayak (kī′ăk) *n.* sandolino.

keck (kĕk) *vi.* avere conati di vomito, avere nausea.

keel (kēl) *n.* chiglia; nave. *vt.*, *vi.* capovolgere, capovolgersi.

keen (kēn) *agg.* acuto; acuminato, pungente; tagliente; perspicace; ansioso.

keep (kēp) *n.* custodia; mantenimento; condizione: for keeps, per sempre. *vt.*, *vi.* (*pass.*, *pp.* kept) tenere; custodire; trattenere; mantenere; allevare; sostenere; rispettare; garantire; continuare a, persistere; conservarsi: to — from, astenersi; to — away from, tenere *o* tenersi lontano da; to — back, nascondere, dissimulare; trattenere; to — bad hours, fare le ore piccole; to — going, andare avanti, non fermarsi; to — off, allontanare; tenersi in disparte; to — on, continuare; to — silent, tacere; to — to, attenersi a. —er *n.* custode; conservatore: jail —, carceriere, secondino. —ing *n.* custodia; mantenimento, manutenzione; armonia: in —ing with, consono a. —sake *n.* ricordo, pegno.

keg (kĕg) *n.* barilotto.

kennel (kĕn′ĕl) *n.* canile, tana.

kept (kĕpt) *pass.*, *pp. di* to keep.

kerb (kûrb) (*Ingl.* = *S.U.* curb) *n.* cordone del marciapiede.

kerchief (kûr′chĭf) *n.* fisciù; fazzoletto.

kernel (kûr′nĕl) *n.* gheriglio (*di noce*); seme, grano, chicco; mandorla (*del nocciolo di pesco, ecc.*); nucleo.

kerosene (kĕr′ō·sēn′) *n.* petrolio.

ketch (kĕch) *n.* (*naut.*) panfilio a due alberi, ketch.

ketchup (kĕch′ŭp) *n.* salsa di pomodoro aromatizzata.

kettle (kĕt′′l) *n.* pentolino; cuccuma; teiera. —drum *n.* (*mus.*) timpano.

key (kē) *n.* chiave, chiavetta; tasto (*di strumento musicale o di macchina per scrivere*); tono: in — (*mus.*), a tono, intonato; out of —, fuori tono, stonato. *vt.* intonare, accordare: to — up, stimolare, eccitare; elevare il tono di. —board *n.* tastiera. —hole *n.* toppa. —note *n.* nota tonica; idea *o* principio fondamentale. —ring *n.* portachia-

vi. —stone. *n.* chiave di volta, fondamento, nota dominante.

khaki (kăk′ĭ) *n.*, *agg.* cachi, kaki.

kibitz (kĭb′ĭts) *vi.* (*gergo*) intromettersi, dare consigli non richiesti. —er *n.* ficcanaso, consigliere non richiesto.

kick (kĭk) *n.* pedata, calcio; rinculo (*di arma*); forza; protesta; stimolo; interesse, spasso. *vt.* dare un calcio a, prendere · calci: to — out, scacciare a pedate; to — up a dust, sollevare polvere; to — up a row, fare una scenata; to — the bucket (*gergo*), morire. *vi.* scalciare, recalcitrare, rinculare: to — at, opporsi a. —back *n.* reazione violenta; rispostaccia, tassa clandestina pagata da un lavoratore per ottenere lavoro.

kid (kĭd) (1) *n.* tinozza.

kid (kĭd) (2) *n.* capretto; bimbo, ragazzo: — brother, fratellino, fratello minore. *vt.*, *vi.* (*gergo*) burlare, scherzare.

kidnap (kĭd′năp) *n.* ratto. *vt.* rapire. —per *n.* rapitore. —ping *n.* rapimento.

kidney (kĭd′nĭ) *n.* rene; rognone: — stones, calcoli renali; — bean, fagiolo.

kill (kĭl) *vt.* uccidere, ammazzare; distruggere; spegnere. *n.* preda, caccia. —er *n.* uccisore, assassino.

kiln (kĭln) *n.* forno, fornace.

kilogram (kĭl′ō·grăm) *n.* chilogrammo.

kilometer (kĭl′ō·mē′tēr) *n.* chilometro.

kilt (kĭlt) *n.* gonnellino degli scozzesi.

kin (kĭn) *n.* parentela, stirpe, famiglia, parente: next of —, parente più prossimo.

kind (kīnd) (1) *n.* genere, specie; natura; razza; maniera: to pay in —, pagare in natura; — of, alquanto.

kind (kīnd) (2) *agg.* gentile, benevolo, garbato: — regards, ossequi, distinti saluti. —hearted, *agg.* di buon cuore, buono.

kindergarten (kĭn′dĕr·gär′t′n) *n.* asilo infantile.

kindle (kĭn′d′l) *vt.* accendere, infiammare; eccitare; destare; incoraggiare. *vi.* infiammarsi, animarsi.

kindliness (kīnd′lĭ·nes) *n.* benevolenza, bontà.

kindly (kīnd′lĭ) *agg.* benevolo, bonario, buono. *avv.* amabilmente; favorevolmente; affettuosamente; di buon grado, volentieri.

kindness (kīnd′nĕs) *n.* gentilezza, bontà.

kindred (kīn′drĕd) *n.* parentela, parentado; affinità. *agg.* affine; imparentato.

kinetic (kĭ-nĕt′ĭk) *agg.* cinetico; (*fig.*) dinamico, energico, vivace.

king (kĭng) *n.* re. —**dom** *n.* regno. —**fisher** *n.* (*ornit.*) martin pescatore. —**ly** *agg.* regale; *avv.* regalmente. —**-size** *agg.* (*di sigaretta*) lunga; (*fig.*) grosso, enorme, straordinario.

kink (kĭngk) *n.* nodo, garbuglio; riccio. —**y** *agg.* ricciuto, crespo.

kinsfolk (kĭnz′fōk′) *n.* parenti, parentado.

kinsman (kĭnz′măn) *n.* parente.

kipper (kĭp′ĕr) *vt.* salare (*conservare sotto sale*). *n.* aringa salata.

kiss (kĭs) *n.* bacio. *vt.* baciare. *vi.* baciarsi.

kit (kĭt) *n.* equipaggiamento; armamentario, corredo, utensileria; astuccio; gattino: medicine —, cassetta dei medicinali; repair —, borsa *o* cassetta di attrezzi per riparazioni.

kitchen (kĭch′ĕn) *n.* cucina: — garden, orto; — range, cucina economica. —**ette** *n.* cucinino, stanza di cottura. —**ware** *n.* batteria di cucina.

kite (kīt) *n.* nibbio; aquilone (*cervo volante*); aliante; sfruttatore, imbroglione; (*comm.*) cambiale di favore.

kith (kĭth) *n.* cerchia di amici: — and kin, amici e parenti.

kitten (kĭt′′n) *n.* gattino, micetto.

knack (năk) *n.* abilità, facoltà; abitudine; trucco.

knapsack (năp′săk′) *n.* zàino.

knave (nāv) *n.* furfante; (*carte da giuoco*) fante.

knead (nēd) *vt.* impastare.

knee (nē) *n.* ginocchio: on one's knees, in ginocchio. —**cap** *n.* rotula; ginocchiera.

kneel (nēl) *vi.*, (*pass.*, *pp.* knelt) inginocchiarsi.

knell (nĕl) *n.* rintocco funebre. *vi.* sonare a morto.

knelt (nĕlt) *pass.* e *pp. di* to kneel.

knew (nū) *pass. di* to know.

knickknack (nĭk′năk′) *n.* gingillo; giocattolo; cianfrusaglia.

knife (nīf) *n.* (*pl.* knives) coltello, lama; bisturi: carving —, trinciante;

clasp —, coltello a serramanico; pen—, temperino. *vt.* accoltellare.

knight (nīt) *n.* cavaliere; paladino; (*scacchi*) cavallo. *vt.* creare cavaliere: —errant, cavaliere errante.

knighthood (nīt′hŏŏd) *n.* cavalleria.

knit (nīt) *vt.*, *vi.* lavorare a maglia, sferruzzare; unire, congiungere; aggrottare (*le sopracciglia*); aggrottarsi; saldarsi (*di ossa*); contrarsi. —**ting** *agg.* lavoro a maglia. —**ting** needle *n.* ferro da calza.

knob (nŏb) *n.* protuberanza, nodo, nodulo; maniglia.

knock (nŏk) *n.* colpo, bussata; battito. *vt.*, *vi.* bussare, battere, urtare, colpire: to — about, sballottare, malmenare; to — down, abbattere, rovesciare; smontare (*una macchina*); to — in, sfondare; to — off, smontare di servizio, smettere il lavoro; ribassare (*un prezzo*); far saltare via; to — out, far uscire a colpi; (*pugilato*) metter fuori combattimento; —**kneed**, sbilenco; che ha le ginocchia in dentro.

knocker (nŏk′ĕr) *n.* battaglio.

knockout (nŏk′out′) *n.* colpo che abbatte; successone; (*pugilato*) fuori combattimento.

knoll (nōl) (1) *n.* altura, collina.

knoll (nōl) (2) *vt.*, *vi.* sonare a morto.

knot (nŏt) *n.* nodo, nastro, vincolo, difficoltà, gruppo. *vt.*, *vi.* annodare, annodarsi. —**ty** *agg.* nodoso, annodato; complesso.

know (nō) *n.* conoscenza: —**how**, conoscenza *o* esperienza del mestiere; to be in the —, saperla lunga. *vt.*, *vi.* (*pass.* knew, *pp.* known) sapere; conoscere; riconoscere; capire: to — how to swim, saper nuotare; to — the ropes, saperla lunga; to — better than, guardarsi bene da, avere il buon senso di (*non fare una cosa*); he should — better, dovrebbe essere più saggio. —**ing** *agg.* perspicace, accorto. —**ingly** *avv.* accortamente; con l'aria di chi la sa lunga. —**ledge** *n.* conoscenza, cognizione.

known (nōn) *pp. di* to know.

knuckle (nŭk′′l) *n.* nocca; giuntura, giunto. *vt.* battere con le nocche. *vi.* fletter le dita: to — under, sottomettersi; — joint, giunto a cerniera.

kudos (kū′dŏs) *n.* gloria, fama.

L

lab (lăb) *n.* laboratorio.

label (lā′bĕl) *n.* etichetta, cartellino. *vt.* mettere l'etichetta a, classificare.

labor (lā′bĕr) *n.* lavoro, fatica, travaglio; mano d'opera, la classe operaia: — union, sindacato operaio;

to be in —, avere le doglie; hard —, lavori forzati. *vt.*, *vi.* lavorare, elaborare; arrancare; angosciarsi, soffrire; avere le doglie. —er *n.* lavoratore.

labyrinth (lăb′ĭ-rĭnth) *n.* labirinto.

lace (lās) *n.* pizzo; spighetta, stringa da scarpe. *vt.* ornare di pizzi; allacciare, intrecciare.

lack (lăk) *n.* mancanza, scarsità. *vt.* mancare di. *vi.* mancare, scarseggiare.

lackadaisical (lăk′d-dā′zĭ-kăl) *agg.* languido, sdolcinato.

lacking *agg.* mancante (*di*), scarso, insufficiente: — in, privo di.

lackluster (lăk′lŭs′tēr) *agg.* opaco.

lacquer (lăk′ēr) *n.* lacca. *vt.* laccare.

lad (lăd) *n.* ragazzo.

ladder (lăd′ēr) *n.* scala a pìuoli; (*Ingl.*) smagliatura (*delle calze*).

lade (lād) *vt.* (*pass.* laded, *pp.* laden) caricare, imbarcare.

lading (lād′ĭng) *n.* carico: bill of —, polizza di carico.

ladle (lād′′l) *n.* mestolo. *vt.* versare col mestolo: to — out, distribuire.

lady (lā′dĭ) *n.* (*pl.* ladies) signora, gentildonna, nobildonna, donna (*come titolo di cortesia premesso al nome*). —like *agg.* da vera signora. —love *n.* innamorata.

lag (lăg) *n.* ritardo, rallentamento; galeotto. *vi.* tardare; restare indietro, muoversi con lentezza.

laggard (lăg′ērd) *n.* infingardo, persona lenta.

lagoon (lă-gōōn′) *n.* laguna.

laid (lād) *pass.*, *pp.* di to lay.

lain (lān) *pp.* di to lie (2).

lair (lâr) *n.* tana, rifugio.

lake (lāk) *n.* lago.

lam (lăm) *n.* (*gergo*) fuga.

lamb (lăm) *n.* agnello.

lambkin (lăm′kĭn) *n.* agnellino.

lame (lām) *agg.* zoppo; debole. *vt.* azzoppare. —ly *avv.* zoppicando; debolmente, poco plausibilmente.

lament (lă-ment′) *n.* lamento. *vt.*, *vi.* lamentare, lamentarsi. —able (lăm′ēn-tă-b′l) *agg.* lamentevole, doloroso.

laminate (lăm′ĭ-nāt) *vt.* laminare; stratificare: laminated plastic, laminati plastici.

lamp (lămp) *n.* lampada, lanterna, fanale: street —, fanale, lampione; — shade, paralume. —black *n.* nerofumo. —post *n.* lampione.

lampoon (lăm-pōōn′) *n.* satira, libello.

lance (lăns) *n.* lancia, lanciere; (*chir.*) lancetta. *vt.* trafiggere con la lancia; incidere con la lancetta.

lancer (lăn′sēr) *n.* lanciere.

lancet (lăn′sĕt) *n.* (*chir.*) lancetta.

land (lănd) *n.* terra, suolo, terreno; nazione. *vt.* sbarcare, collocare, tirare a riva; prender possesso di, prendere, guadagnare. *vi.* sbarcare, approdare, metter piede al suolo; (*aeron.*) atterrare. —holder *n.* proprietario terriero.

landing *n.* approdo, sbarco; pianerottolo; (*aeron.*) atterraggio: — craft, mezzo da sbarco; — gear (*aeron.*), carrello d'atterraggio; — ground, campo d'atterraggio; — place, scatolo, pontile; — strip, pista di atterraggio.

landlady (lănd′lādĭ) *n.* albergatrice, affittacamere.

landlord (lănd′lôrd) *n.* albergatore, proprietario.

landmark (lănd′märk′) *n.* segno di confine, punto di riferimento; impronta, caratteristica.

landowner (lănd′ōn′ēr) *n.* proprietario di terre, proprietario terriero.

landscape (lănd′skāp) *n.* paesaggio, panorama.

landslide (lănd′slīd′) landslip (-slĭp′) *n.* frana.

lane (lān) *n.* sentiero, vicolo; corsia (*di autostrada*).

language (lăng′gwĭj) *n.* linguaggio, lingua: bad —, turpiloquio.

languid (lăng′gwĭd) *agg.* languido.

languish (lăng′gwĭsh) *vi.* languire.

languor (lăng′gēr) *n.* languore, stasi. —ous *agg.* languido.

lank (lăngk) *agg.* esile, allampanato.

lanky (lăngk′ĭ) *agg.* allampanato.

lantern (lăn′tērn) *n.* lanterna, faro.

lap (lăp) (1) *n.* grembo; lembo, falda (*di indumento, ecc.*), piega, sovrapposizione; giro di pista; riporto. *vt.* distendere, deporre; superare di un giro. *vi.* sovrapporsi.

lap (lăp) (2) *n.* sciacquio. *vt.*, *vi.* lambire; bere rumorosamente.

lapel (lă-pĕl′) *n.* risvolto (*di giacca*).

lapse (lăps) *n.* errore, dimenticanza; caduta; lasso (*di tempo*); lacuna; scadenza. *vi.* sbagliare; scorrere, trascorrere; cadere, decadere, scadere.

larboard (lär′bōrd) *n.* (*naut.*) sinistra.

larceny (lär′sĕ-nĭ) *n.* furto.

larch (lärch) *n.* (*bot.*) larice.

lard (lärd) *n.* strutto. *vt.* lardellare.

larder (lär′dēr) *n.* dispensa.

large (lärj) *n.* libertà, generalità: at —, in libertà, diffusamente; in generale; in —, su larga scala. *agg.* largo, ampio, spazioso, grande, grosso: as — as life, in bella vista.

—ly *avv.* ampiamente, prevalentemente.

largess (lär′jĕs) *n.* generosità, elargizione.

lark (lärk) *n.* allodola; (*fam.*) divertimento, beffa. *vi.* divertirsi, fare scherzi.

larynx (lär′ĭngks) *n.* (*pl.* larynges) laringe.

lash (lăsh) *n.* frusta, frustata; ciglio. *vt.* frustare; legare, ormeggiare; insultare; incitare.

lass (lăs) *n.* fanciulla, donna.

lassitude (lăs′ĭ-tūd) *n.* fiacchezza.

last (làst) *n.* ultimo; fine, conclusione; forma (*da scarpe*): at —, finalmente; to the —, fino alla fine. *agg.* ultimo, finale, scorso: — but one, penultimo; — night, ieri sera; — year, l'anno scorso. *avv.* ultimamente, da ultimo, l'ultima volta. *vi.* durare, resistere: to — out, sopravvivere, durare a lungo. —ing *agg.* durevole. —ly *avv.* in fine, in conclusione, da ultimo.

latch (lăch) *n.* saliscendi, serratura a scatto: on the —, chiuso con la sola maniglia (*di uscio*). *vt.* chiudere col saliscendi.

late (lāt) *agg.* tardo, in ritardo, ritardatario; ultimo, recente; defunto, ex: to be —, esser tardi, essere in ritardo; a — hour, un'ora avanzata; the — bishop, il defunto vescovo. *avv.* tardi, in ritardo, fino a tarda ora, tardivamente; recentemente; già (*un tempo*): — in the night, a notte tarda; — into the night, sino a notte tarda; — in the week, verso la fine della settimana; — of this firm, già appartenente a questa ditta; of —, recentemente; it is getting —, si fa tardi. —ly *avv.* ultimamente, recentemente.

later (lāt′ĕr) *agg.* posteriore, ulteriore. *avv.* più tardi: see you —! arrivederci!, a più tardi!

latest (lāt′est) *agg.* più recente, recentissimo, ultimo: at the —, al più tardi; — news, ultime notizie.

latent (lā′tĕnt) *agg.* latente, nascosto.

lateral (lăt′ĕr-ăl) *agg.* laterale.

lath (làth) *n.* corrente (*travicello per costruzione di tetti, ecc.*).

lathe (lāth) *n.* tornio.

lather (lăth′ĕr) *n.* schiuma, spuma. *vt.* insaponare, far spumeggiare. *vi.* spumeggiare, schiumare.

Latin (lăt′ĭn) *n.*, *agg.* latino.

latish (lāt′ĭsh) *agg.* alquanto tardivo.

latitude (lăt′ĭ-tūd) *n.* latitudine; ampiezza; larghezza di vedute; libertà.

latter (lăt′ĕr) *agg.* ultimo, posteriore, recente; secondo (*di due*): I prefer the — to the former, preferisco il secondo al primo.

lattice (lăt′ĭs) *n.* grata, inferriata, graticcio.

laud (lôd) *n.* inno, salmo. *vt.* esaltare, lodare. —able *agg.* lodevole.

laugh (làf) *n.* risata, riso. *vi.* ridere: to — at, farsi beffe di; to — up one's sleeve, ridere sotto i baffi. —able *agg.* ridicolo, risibile.

laughing (làf′ĭng) *n.* ilarità, risa. *agg.* ridente: — gas gas esilarante. —stock *n.* zimbello.

laughter (làf′tĕr) *n.* ilarità.

launch (lônch) *n.* lancio, varo; lancia (*imbarcazione*). *vt.* lanciare, varare. *vi.* slanciarsi, tuffarsi.

launder (lôn′dĕr) *vt.*, *vi.* lavare e stirare; fare il bucato. —er *n.* lavandaio.

laundress (lôn′drĕs) *n.* lavandaia.

laundry (lôn′drĭ) *n.* biancheria; lavanderia.

laurel (lô′rĕl) *n.* alloro.

lava (lä′và) *n.* lava.

lavatory (lăv′à-tō′rĭ) *n.* ritirata, latrina; lavatoio.

lavender (lăv′ĕn-dĕr) *n.* lavanda; agg. di lavanda; color lavanda.

lavish (lăv′ĭsh) *agg.* abbondante, sontuoso, prodigo, generoso. *vt.* elargire, sperperare: to — praise upon somebody, colmare qualcuno di lodi. —ly *avv.* abbondantemente, sontuosamente, prodigalmente.

law (lô) *n.* legge, diritto: criminal —, diritto penale; Law Courts, Palazzo di Giustizia: —abiding, ossequiente alle leggi. —breaker *n.* trasgressore. —ful *agg.* legale, legittimo. —less *agg.* illegale, sfrenato. —maker *n.* legislatore.

lawn (lôn) *n.* prato, tappeto erboso; rensa (*tessuto*): —mower *n.* falciatrice meccanica.

lawsuit (lô′sūt′) *n.* causa, processo.

lawyer (lô′yĕr) *n.* avvocato, notaio.

lax (lăks) *agg.* molle, lento, rilassato, noncurante. —ative *n.*, *agg.* lassativo. —ity, —ness *n.* rilassamento, fiacca, sbadataggine.

lay (lā) (1) *n.* situazione, posizione. *vt.* (*pass.*, *pp.* laid) porre, deporre, collocare; spegnere; abbattere; tendere (*un trabocchetto*); calmare: to — a wager, fare una scommessa; to — the blame on, attribuire la colpa a; to — claim to, accampare diritti su; to — aside, mettere da parte; to — bare, mettere a nudo, scoprire; to — down, adagiare; stabilire (*un principio*); tracciare: to — hold of, impossessarsi di; to — open, esporre, mettere a nudo; to — out, distendere, esporre, preparare; sborsare. *vi.* fare le uova, scommettere.

lay (là) (2) *pass. di* to lie.

lay (là) (3) *agg.* laico.

layer (là'ĕr) *n.* strato.

layman (là'măn) *n.* laico; profano, inesperto.

layout (là'out') *n.* disposizione; esposizione; situazione; piano, progetto; impaginazione, maestra (*facsimile*), menabò; armamentario.

lazily (là'zĭ-lĭ) *avv.* pigramente.

laziness (là'zĭ-něs) *n.* pigrizia.

lazy (là'zĭ) *agg.* pigro, indolente.

lead (lĕd) (1) *n.* piombo, scandaglio; mina per matita; pallottole; (*tip.*) interlinea: red —, minio; white —, biacca. *vt.* piombare, impiombare; (*tip.*) interlineare.

lead (lēd) (2) *n.* direzione, comando, guida, posizione di testa, vantaggio; esempio; guinzaglio; esordio; primo attore. *vt., vi.* (*pass., pp.* led) condurre, guidare, capeggiare, precedere, indurre, far da guida: to — an orchestra, dirigere un'orchestra; to — astray, sviare, traviare; to — the way, precedere, fare strada.

leaden (lĕd'n) *agg.* di piombo, plumbeo, greve.

leader (lēd'ĕr) *n.* condottiero, guida; articolo di fondo; cavallo di punta. —ship *n.* comando, guida (*il guidare*), direzione.

leading (lēd'ĭng) *agg.* principale, primo: — article, articolo di fondo; — man, primo attore; — strings, dande.

leaf (lēf) *n.* (*pl.* leaves) foglia; foglio, pagina; battente, ribalta (*di tavola*): to turn over a new —, cambiar vita. *vt.* sfogliare. *vi.* fogliare. —less *agg.* senza foglie, sfogliato. —let *n.* fogliolina; foglietto; volante.

leafy (lēf'ĭ) *agg.* frondoso.

league (lēg) (1) *n.* lega, società.

league (lēg) (2) *n.* lega (*misura di lunghezza*).

leak (lēk) *n.* falla, fessura, perdita (*di liquido*), il trapelare (*di notizie riservate, ecc.*): to spring a —, fare acqua. *vi.* perdere, colare, far acqua, trapelare. —age *n.* perdita (*di liquido*), fuga (*di gas*), falla.

lean (lēn) (1) *n.* inclinazione, pendenza. *vt.* (*pass., pp.* leaned, leant) appoggiare, inclinare. *vi.* appoggiarsi; inclinarsi; propendere; pendere.

lean (lēn) (2) *agg.* magro, esile.

leaning *n.* propensione. *agg.* pendente.

leant (lĕnt) *pass., pp. di* to lean.

leap (lēp) *n.* salto, balzo. *vt.* (*pass., pp.* leaped, leapt) saltare, scaval-

care. *vi.* balzare, slanciarsi. — year, anno bisestile.

leapt (lĕpt) *pass., pp. di* to leap.

learn (lûrn) *vt., vi.* (*pass., pp.* learned, learnt) imparare; venire a sapere; istruirsi. —ed (*gen.* lûrn'ĕd) *agg.* dotto. —er *n.* allievo, principiante. —ing *n.* erudizione, sapere.

learnt (lûrnt) *pass., pp. di* to learn.

lease (lēs) *n.* affittanza, contratto d'affitto. *vt.* dare o prendere in affitto.

leash (lēsh) *n.* guinzaglio. *vt.* tenere al guinzaglio, tenere a freno.

least (lēst) *n* quantità minima, minimo. *agg.* minimo, infimo, minore. *avv.* al minimo: at —, per lo meno; not in the —, nient'affatto; to say the —, a dir poco.

leather (lĕth'ĕr) *n.* pelle, cuoio: patent —, coppale. *vt.* rivestire di cuoio; staffilare.

leathern (lĕth'ĕrn) *agg.* di cuoio, coriaceo.

leathery (lĕth'ĕr-ĭ) *agg.* coriaceo; simile a cuoio.

leave (lēv) *n.* permesso, licenza, commiato: on —, in licenza; sick —, licenza di convalescenza; to take French —, filare all'inglese; to take — of, accomiatarsi da. *vt., vi.* (*pass., pp.* left) lasciare, abbandonare; andarsene, partire: I have nothing left, non mi resta nulla; to — alone, lasciare in pace; to — off, smettere.

leaven (lĕv'ĕn) *n.* lievito. *vt.* lievitare; impregnare.

leavings (lēv'ĭngz) *n.pl.* residui; rifiuti.

lecherous (lĕch'ĕr-ŭs) *agg.* libertino, osceno.

lection (lĕk'shŭn) *n.* lezione.

lecture (lĕk'tŭr) *n.* conferenza, lezione; ramanzina, predicozzo. *vt., vi.* tenere conferenze, istruire, rimproverare.

lecturer (lĕk'tŭr-ĕr) *n.* conferenziere, docente.

led (lĕd) *pass., pp. di* to lead (2).

ledge (lĕj) *n.* davanzale, ripiano, bordo, strato; (*min.*) vena.

ledger (lĕj'ĕr) *n.* libro mastro.

lee (lē) *n.* riparo; (*naut.*) sottovento.

leech (lēch) *n.* sanguisuga; medico.

leer (lēr) *n.* occhiata obliqua. *vi.* guardare di traverso, sbirciare.

lees (lēz) *n.pl.* feccia, sedimento.

leeway (lē'wā') *n.* deriva; agio, margine, (*aeron.*) angolo di deriva.

left (lĕft) (1) *pass., pp. di* to leave.

left (lĕft) (2) *n.* sinistra: at (on, to) the —, a sinistra. *agg.* sinistro. *avv.* a sinistra. —handed *agg.* mancino;

rotante da destra a sinistra; morganatico; ambiguo, goffo: — compliment, complimento ironico.

leftist (lĕft'ĭst) *n.* (pol.) persona di sinistra.

leftover (lĕft'ō'vẽr) *n.*, eccedenza. *agg.* eccedente.

leg (lĕg) *n.* gamba; piede (*di mobile*); zampa (*di animale*); asta (*di compasso*); tappa (*di viaggio o corsa*): to pull someone's —, prendere in giro qualcuno; to be on one's last —s, essere alle ultime risorse. *vi.* to — it (*gergo*), svignarsela.

legacy (lĕg'ȧ.sĭ) *n.* lascito, eredità.

legal (lē'gȧl) *agg.* legale, giuridico. —ity (lē.gȧl'ĭ.tĭ) *n.* legalità.

legalize (lē'gȧl.īz) *vt.* legalizzare, legittimare.

legate (lĕg'ĭt) *n.* legato, nunzio.

legatee (lĕg'ȧ.tē') *n.* legatario, erede.

legation (lē-gā'shŭn) *n.* legazione, ambasciata.

legend (lĕj'ẽnd) *n.* leggenda.

legendary (lĕj'ĕn.dẽr'ĭ) *agg.* leggendario.

legerdemain (lĕj'ẽr.dē.mān') *n.* gioco di prestigio, gherminella.

leggings (lĕg'gĭngz) *n.pl.* uose.

legible (lĕj'ĭ.b'l) *agg.* leggibile.

legion (lē'jŭn) *n.* legione; moltitudine.

legislate (lĕj'ĭs.lāt) *vi.* legiferare.

legislation (lĕj'ĭs.lā'shŭn) *n.* legislazione.

legislative (lĕj'ĭs.lā'tĭv) *agg.* legislativo.

legislature (lĕj'ĭs.lā'tūr) *n.* legislatura.

legitimate (lē-jĭt'ĭ.mĭt) *agg.* legittimo.

legman (lĕg'măn) *n.* cronista; galoppino.

leisure (lē'zhẽr;lĕzh'ẽr) *n.* riposo, agio, comodo: at —, con comodo; to be at —, essere in ozio, non aver niente da fare; — hours, ore libere, ore di riposo. —ly *agg.* calmo, deliberato. *avv.* con comodo, senza fretta.

lemon (lĕm'ŭn) *n.* limone; *agg.* color limone. —ade *n.* limonata.

lend (lĕnd) *vt., vi.* (*pass., pp.* lent) prestare, fornire; conferire.

lender *n.* prestatore.

lending *n.* prestito: — library, biblioteca circolante.

lend-lease *n.* affitti e prestiti.

length (lĕngth) *n.* lunghezza; estensione; durata, lasso; punto, grado: at —, diffusamente, per esteso; finalmente, infine; to go the whole —, andare fino in fondo.

lengthen (lĕng'thĕn) *vt.* allungare, prolungare, estendere. *vi.* allungarsi, prolungarsi, protrarsi.

lengthwise (lĕngth'wīz) *agg.* longitudinale. *avv.* longitudinalmente, per il lungo.

lengthy (lĕng'thĭ) *agg.* lungo, prolisso.

leniency (lē'nĭ.ĕn.sĭ) *n.* indulgenza, clemenza.

lenient (lē'nĭ.ĕnt) *agg.* clemente, indulgente.

lens (lĕnz) *n.* (ott.) lente; (anat.) cristallino.

lent (lĕnt) *pass., pp. di* to lend.

Lent (lĕnt) *n.* quaresima.

lentil (lĕn'tĭl) *n.* (bot.) lenticchia.

leopard (lĕp'ẽrd) *n.* leopardo.

leper (lĕp'ẽr) *n.* lebbroso.

leprosy (lĕp'rō.sĭ) *n.* lebbra.

leprous (lĕp'rŭs) *agg.* lebbroso.

less (lĕs) *n.* meno. *agg.* meno, minore, più piccolo, inferiore. *avv., prep.* meno: — and —, sempre meno.

lessee (lĕs.ē') *n.* affittuario.

lessen (lĕs''n) *vt., vi.* diminuire.

lesson (lĕs''n) *n.* lezione.

lest (lĕst) *cong.* per paura che, a scanso di: I feared — he might fall, temevo che egli cadesse.

let (lĕt) *vt., vi.* (*pass., pp.* let) lasciare, permettere; affittare; causare; ostacolare: — me alone, — me be, lasciatemi in pace; — us go, andiamocene; to — down, piantare in asso, deludere; to — in, far entrare, lasciar entrare; to — loose, allentare, sciogliere, scatenare; to — know, far sapere; to — off, rilasciare.

lethargy (lĕth'ẽr.jĭ) *n.* letargo.

letter (lĕt'ẽr) *n.* lettera: — of attorney, procura. *vt.* contrassegnare con lettere, iscrivere. — box, cassetta per lettere. —carrier *n.* portalettere. —head *n.* intestazione (*di una lettera*). —ing *n.* iscrizione.

lettuce (lĕt'ĭs) *n.* lattuga.

levee (lĕv'ē) *n.* diga, argine.

level (lĕv'ĕl) *n.* livello, piano; (tec.) livella: to be on the —, agire rettamente, essere in buona fede, avere intenzioni oneste. *agg.* orizzontale, piano, levigato, uguale, a livello (con), al livello (di): to do one's — best, fare del proprio meglio. *vt., vi.* livellare, spianare; dirigere, prendere di mira, puntare (un'arma); (aeron.) volare raso terra: to — with the dust, radere al suolo. —headed *agg.* equilibrato, assennato.

lever (lē'vẽr) *n.* leva: control —, asta di comando.

levy (lĕv'ĭ) *n.* coscrizione; esazione, requisizione. *vt.* mobilitare; esigere, requisire.

lewd (lūd) *agg.* osceno, spregevole. **—ness** *n.* oscenità, bassezza.

lexicon (lĕk'sĭ·kŏn) *n.* lessico, nomenclatura.

liability (lī'á·bĭl'ĭ·tĭ)*n.*obbligo, debito; pendenza, responsabilità; (*pl.*) passivo, passività.

liable (lī'á·b'l) *agg.* passibile, esposto (*a*), soggetto (*a*); proclive, suscettibile; profabile; impegnato, compromesso.

liar (lī'ẽr) *n.* buglardo.

libel (lī'bĕl) *n.* libello, diffamazione. *vi.* diffamare.

liberal (lĭb'ẽr·ắl) *n.* (*pol.*) liberale. *agg.* liberale, generoso, abbondante. **—ity** (-ăl'ĭ·tĭ) *n.* liberalità, larghezza di vedute.

liberate (lĭb'ẽr·āt) *vt.* liberare.

liberation(lĭb'ẽr·ā'shŭn) *n.*liberazione.

liberator (lĭb'ẽr·ā'tẽr) *n.* liberatore.

libertine (lĭb'ẽr·tēn) *n.* libertino. *agg.* licenzioso.

liberty (lĭb'ẽr·tĭ) *n.* libertà; facoltà: at **—**, in libertà; at **—** to, libero di, autorizzato a.

librarian (lī·brâr'ĭ·ắn) *n.* bibliotecario.

library (lī'brẽr'ĭ) *n.* biblioteca.

lice (līs) *n.* (*pl. di* louse) pidocchi.

license, licence (lī'sĕns) *n.* licenza, patente: gun **—**, porto d'armi; driver's **—**, patente di guida; **—** plate, targa di circolazione. *vt.* permettere, autorizzare.

licentious (lī-sĕn'shŭs) *agg.* licenzioso.

lick (lĭk) *n.* leccata. *vt.* leccare, lambire; malmenare, sopraffare, sconfiggere: to **—** someone's boots, leccare i piedi a qualcuno; to **—** the dust, mordere la polvere. **—ing** *n.* batosta.

licorice (lĭk'ō·rĭs) *n.* liquirizia.

lid (lĭd) *n.* coperchio; (*anat.*) palpebra.

lie (lī) (1) *n.* menzogna, smentita. *vi.* (*pass.*, *pp.* lied, *ppr.* lying) mentire.

lie (lī) (2) *n.* posizione, situazione. *vi.* (*pass.* lay, *pp.* lain, *ppr.* lying) giacere, coricarsi, trovarsi, riposare, stare; gravare; consistere: it **—**s in my power, dipende da me; to **—** down, coricarsi; to **—** low, star nascosto.

lief (lēf) *avv.* volontieri: I had as **—**, vorrei piuttosto, preferirei.

lieu (lū) *n.* luogo: in **—** of, invece di, a guisa di.

lieutenant (lū·tĕn'ắnt) *n.* tenente: first **—**, tenente; second **—**, sottotenente.

life (līf) *n.* vita, esistenza: from **—**, dal vero; to the **—**, al naturale; still **—**, natura morta; **—** imprisonment, ergastolo; **—** pension, pensione a vita; to come to **—**,

rianimarsi; to bring to **—**, rianimare, dar vita a. **—belt** *n.* cintura di salvataggio. **—boat** *n.* scialuppa. **—buoy** *n.* salvagente. **—guard** *n.* bagnino. **— insurance**, assicurazione sulla vita. **—less** *agg.* inanimato, prostrato. **—like** *agg.* al naturale. **—long** *agg.* perpetuo, che dura tutta la vita *o* una vita. **— preserver**, salvagente; sfollagente.

lifer (līf'ẽr) *n.* ergastolo, ergastolano.

life-size *agg.* in grandezza naturale.

lifetime *n.* esistenza.

lift (lĭft) *n.* sollevamento, rialzo; montacarichi, ascensore; ponte aereo: ski **—**, chair **—**, seggiovia. to give a **—**, dare un passaggio (*a qualcuno, su un veicolo*). *vt.* alzare, sollevare, soppesare; (*fam.*) rubare; (*S.U.*) estinguere (*un'ipoteca*): to **—** one's hat, scappellarsi. *vi.* alzarsi (*salire*); innalzarsi; dissiparsi (*delle nubi*).

light (līt) (1) *n.* luce, giorno; faro, fanale, semaforo. *agg.* chiaro, luminoso. *vt.* (*pass.*, *pp.* lighted, lit) illuminare, rischiarare, accendere. *vi.* accendersi, splendere, illuminarsi.

light (līt) (2) *agg.* leggiero, lieve, frivolo, gaio: to make **—** of, prendere alla leggiera. **—headed** *agg.* stordito; frivolo, incostante; squillibrato. **—hearted** *agg.* allegro, spensierato.

lighten (līt''n) (1) *vt.* illuminare. *vi.* schiarirsi, rischiararsi, balenare.

lighten (līt''n) (2) *vi.* alleggerire, alleviare.

lighthouse (līt'hous') *n.* faro.

lighting (līt'ĭng) *n.* illuminazione.

lightly (līt'lĭ) *avv.* leggermente, facilmente; allegramente.

lighter (līt'ẽr) *n.* (*naut.*) chiatta; accendino.

lightning (līt'nĭng) *n.* fulmine, lampo. **—conductor, —rod** *n.* parafulmine.

likable (līk'á·b'l) *agg.* piacevole, simpatico, gradevole.

like (līk) *n.* l'uguale; gusto, preferenza, simpatia; pariglia: our likes, i pari nostri; our likes and dislikes, le nostre simpatie e avversioni. *agg.* simile a, somigliante a, pari a, uguale a, caratteristico. *avv.* similmente; probabilmente: I feel **—** going, ho voglia di andare; to look **—**, somigliare a, aver l'aria di. *prep.* come, alla maniera di. *cong.* come se. *vt.*, *vi.* voler bene a, piacere (*rifl.*), aver simpatia per, gradire, convenire, garbare, volere: I **—**

this, questo mi piace; **to — better** o **best**, preferire.

likelihood (lĭk'lĭ-hŏŏd), **likeliness** (-nĕs) n. probabilità.

likely (lĭk'lĭ) agg. probabile, conveniente: **he is — to come**, è probabile che egli venga. avv. probabilmente.

liken (lĭk'ĕn) vt. paragonare, confrontare.

likeness (lĭk'nĕs) n. somiglianza, apparenza, ritratto, aspetto.

likewise (lĭk'wĭz') avv. ugualmente, similmente, così; anche; lo stesso.

liking (lĭk'ĭng) n. inclinazione, gusto, simpatia, amicizia: **to take a — to**, prendere in simpatia.

lilac (lī'lăk) n., agg. lilla.

lily (lĭl'ĭ) n. giglio. **—of-the-valley**, mughetto.

limb (lĭm) n. arto; ramo d'albero; alone; corolla; (pl.) membra.

limber (lĭm'bĕr) (1) n. avantreno.

limber (lĭm'bĕr) (2) agg. flessibile, agile. vt., vi. rendere o divenire flessibile.

lime (lĭm) n. calce; vischio; tiglio; limetta (agrume).

limelight (lĭm'lĭt') n. riflettore teatrale; notorietà: **to be in the —**, essere alla ribalta.

limestone (lĭm'stōn') n. pietra calcare.

limit (lĭm'ĭt) n. limite. vt. limitare. **—ation** n. limitazione; prescrizione. **—ed** agg. limitato, circoscritto: **— company**, società anonima.

limp (lĭmp) n. zoppicamento. agg. molle, fiacco, afflosciato. vi. zoppicare.

limpet (lĭm'pĕt) n. (ittiol.) patella.

limpid (lĭm'pĭd) agg. limpido.

linden (lĭn'dĕn) n. (bot.) tiglio.

line (lĭn) n. linea; corda, cordone; allineamento; contorno, limite; equatore; discendenza; campo (di attività), direzione; battuta (di commedia); assortimento (di merci); lenza: **to bring into —**, mettere in fila; **to get in —**, mettersi in fila. vt. bordare, foderare, rivestire; allineare. vi. allinearsi.

lineage (lĭn'ė-ĭj) n. lignaggio.

lined (lĭnd) agg. orlato (di); foderato (di).

linen (lĭn'ĕn) n. tela; biancheria. agg. di tela.

liner (lĭn'ĕr) n. piroscafo o velivolo di linea; opuscolo di accompagnamento (di un disco).

linger (lĭng'gĕr) vt. protrarre; passare (tempo) pigramente. vi. indugiare, soffermarsi, attardarsi; vagare; perdurare, prolungarsi.

lingo (lĭng'gō) n. gergo, frasario.

liniment (lĭn'ĭ-mĕnt) n. linimento.

lining (lĭn'ĭng) n. fodera, rivestimento interno.

link (lĭngk) n. vincolo, anello (di catena), collegamento; torcia, fiaccola: **cuff links**, gemelli per polsini. vt. collegare, unire, concatenare.

links (lĭngks) n. campo di golf.

linnet (lĭn'ĕt) n. (ornit.) fanello.

linseed (lĭn'sēd') n. seme di lino. **— oil**, olio di lino.

lint (lĭnt) n. filaccia per medicazioni.

lion (lī'ŭn) n. leone. **—ess** n. leonessa.

lip (lĭp) n. labbro; orlo; impertinenza: **— service**, fedeltà a parole; ipocrisia; conformismo.

lipstick (lĭp'stĭck') n. rossetto (per le labbra).

liquid (lĭk'wĭd) n., agg. liquido.

liquidate (lĭk'wĭ-dāt) vt. liquidare.

liquidation (lĭk'wĭ-dā'shŭn) n. liquidazione.

liquor (lĭk'ĕr) n. liquore.

lisp (lĭsp) n. pronuncia blesa. vt., vi. farfugliare, essere bleso.

list (lĭst) (1) n. lista, elenco. vt. elencare; arrolare. vi. arrolarsi.

list (lĭst) (2) n. orlo, vivagno, striscia, solco. vt. orlare, rigare, solcare.

list (lĭst) (3) n. inclinazione; (naut.) sbandamento. vi. inclinarsi, sbandare.

listen (lĭs''n) vt. ascoltare: **to — in**, ascoltare alla radio; orecchiare. **—er** n. ascoltatore.

listless (lĭst'lĕs) agg. disattento, svogliato, indifferente. **—ness** n. distrazione, indifferenza, svogliatezza.

lit (lĭt) pass., pp. di **to light** (1).

liter, litre (lē'tĕr) n. litro.

literal (lĭt'ĕr-ăl) agg. letterale. **—ly** avv. letteralmente.

literary (lĭt'ĕr-ĕr'ĭ) agg. letterario.

literature (lĭt'ĕr-á-tûr) n. letteratura.

lithograph (lĭth'ō-gráf) n. litografia (riproduzione).

lithography (lĭ-thŏg'rá-fĭ) n. litografia (arte).

litigant (lĭt'ĭ-gănt) n. contendente; parte in causa.

litigation (lĭt'ĭ-gā'shŭn) n. causa civile.

litter (lĭt'ĕr) n. lettiera, strame; lettiga; disordine; rifiuti. vt. sparpagliare, cospargere disordinatamente.

little (lĭt'l) n. poco, inezia. agg. piccolo, esiguo, poco: **Little Bear**, Orsa Minore; **a — sugar**, un po' di zucchero; **a — while**, un po' di tempo. avv. scarsamente, poco: **they — knew that**, non sapevano affatto che; **— by —**, a poco a poco.

live (lĭv) *agg.* vivo, ardente, acceso. (lĭv) *vt.*, *vi.* vivere, esistere; abitare; durare: to — from hand to mouth, vivere alla giornata; to — down, far dimenticare, cancellare (*il passato*). —lihood (lĭv'-) *n.* mezzi di sussistenza. —liness *n.* vivacità, animazione, vitalità. —ly *agg.* vivace, attivo, animato, brioso. *avv.* vivacemente, animatamente.

liver (lĭv'ēr) (1) *n.* chi vive, abitante.

liver (lĭv'ēr) (2) *n.* fegato.

livery (lĭv'ēr·ĭ) *n.* livrea; governo dei cavalli: high —, alta tenuta; undress —, bassa tenuta; — stable, rimessa che noleggia cavalli e veicoli.

lives (lĭvz) *pl. di* life.

livestock (lĭv'stŏk') *n.* bestiame, mandrie.

livid (lĭv'ĭd) *agg.* livido, smorto.

living (lĭv'ĭng) *n.* vita, mezzi di sussistenza, rendita. *agg.* vivo, vivente, parlante (*di ritratti*).

lizard (lĭz'ērd) *n.* (zool.) lucertola.

llama (lä'mä) *n.* (zool.) lama.

load (lōd) *n.* carico, soma, fardello: loads of, mucchi di, montagne di. *vt.* caricare, opprimere, appesantire: loaded dice, dadi truccati.

loaf (lōf) *n.* (*pl.* loaves) panino, pagnotta; porzione. *vt.*, *vi.* oziare, bighellonare, sprecare (*tempo, ecc.*). —er *n.* bighellone; (*pl.*) mocassini (*tipo di scarpe*).

loan (lōn) *n.* prestito. *vt.* prestare. — shark, strozzino.

loath (lōth) *agg.* restio, avverso: to be — to, essere avverso a.

loathe (lōth) *vt.* aborrire.

loathing *n.* avversione, ripugnanza.

loathsome (lōth'săm) *agg.* repulsivo, odioso.

lobby (lŏb'ĭ) *n.* vestibolo, corridoio.

lobster (lŏb'stēr) *n.* aragosta.

local (lō'kăl) *agg.* locale, regionale. —ity (lō·kăl'ĭ·tĭ) *n.* località.

localize (lō'kăl·īz) *vt.* localizzare.

locate (lō'kāt) *vt.* individuare, reperire, situare, collocare.

location (lō·kā'shŭn) *n.* posizione, collocamento, locazione; (*cinema*) esterni, luogo della ripresa.

lock (lŏk) *n.* serratura, lucchetto; chiusa (*di fiume, ecc.*); percussore, (*d'arma da fuoco*); fiocco (*di lana*); ciocca (*di capelli*). *vt.* chiudere a chiave, rinchiudere; abbracciare; bloccare; (*tip.*) chiudere (*una pagina*): to — up, rinchiudere, incarcerare. *vi.* chiudersi, unirsi saldamente: to — out, fare la serrata. —er *n.* ripostiglio. —et *n.*

medaglione. —out *n.* serrata (*di una fabbrica*). —smith *n.* fabbro.

locomotive (lō'kŏ·mō'tĭv) *n.* locomotiva: — engineer, macchinista.

locomotor (lō'kŏ·mō'tēr) *n.*, *agg.* locomotore: — ataxy, atassia locomotrice.

locust (lō'kŭst) *n.* (entom.) locusta; (bot.) robinia.

lode (lōd) *n.* (min.) filone, vena.

lodestar (lōd'stär) *n.* stella polare.

lodge (lŏj) *n.* padiglione, baracca, portineria (*di villa*), loggia. *vt.* collocare, fissare, alloggiare: to — a complaint, sporgere querela. *vi.* abitare, essere alloggiato, incastrarsi, essere collocato.

lodger (lŏj'ēr) *n.* inquilino.

lodging (lŏj'ĭng) *n.* alloggio.

loft (lŏft) *n.* granaio; soffitta; balconata.

lofty (lŏf'tĭ) *agg.* alto, elevato; altezzoso.

log (lŏg) *n.* ceppo, tronco; (naut.) solcometro; libro di bordo. *vt.*, *vi.* disboscare, tagliare alberi; (naut.) scrivere nel libro di bordo. —ger *n.* boscaiolo.

loggerhead (lŏg'ēr·hĕd) *n.* stupido; (zool.) tartaruga marina: to be at loggerheads, essere in disaccordo.

logic (lŏj'ĭk) *n.* logica. —al *agg.* logico.

loin (loin) *n.* lombo.

loiter (loi'tēr) *vt.* sprecare (*tempo*) in ozio. *vi.* oziare, attardarsi, bighellonare: to — behind, restare indietro. —er *n.* bighellone.

loll (lŏl) *vi.* penzolare, oscillare; sdraiarsi; afflosciarsi.

lone (lōn) *agg.* isolato, solitario, solo. —liness *n.* solitudine, desolazione. —ly *agg.* solitario, desolato, isolato. —some *agg.* solitario, solo, nostalgico.

long (lŏng) (1) *vi.* agognare, bramare: to — for, aspettare con impazienza.

long (lŏng) (2) *agg.* lungo, esteso, lento, noioso: — measure, misura di lunghezza; in the — run, alla lunga; all day —, tutto il santo giorno; two meters —, lungo due metri; to be — in coming, tardare a venire. *avv.* a lungo, lungamente, da (*o per*) molto tempo: before —, tra poco, in breve; — ago, molto tempo fa; so (*o as*) — as, fin tanto che; how —? quanto tempo?; so —! ciao!, arrivederci! —suffering *agg.* tollerante. —winded *agg.* prolisso, noioso. —playing *agg.* a lunga durata.

longer (lŏng'gēr) *agg.* più lungo, più esteso. *avv.* più a lungo, più ancora: no —, non più.

longest (lŏng′gĕst) *agg.* più lungo (*d'ogni altro*). *avv.* il più a lungo.

longevity (lŏn·jĕv′ĭ·tĭ) *n.* longevità.

longhair (lŏng′hâr′) (*gergo*) *n.* artista, musicista, appassionato di musica classica. *agg.* teorico; sognatore; intellettuale.

longing (lŏng′ĭng) *n.* brama, smania. —**ly** *avv.* bramosamente.

longitude (lŏn′jĭ·tūd) *n.* longitudine.

longshoreman (lŏng′shōr′măn) *n.* scaricatore del porto.

look (lŏŏk) *n.* sguardo; aspetto, apparenza: by the — of it, a quel che sembra; good looks, bell'aspetto. *vt., vi.* guardare; sembrare, aver l'aspetto, essere prospiciente: to — after, aver cura di, accudire a; to — alike, somigliare, sembrare uguali; to — down upon, guardare dall'alto in basso; to — for, cercare; to — forward to, non veder l'ora di, pregustare; to — into, esaminare; to — like, aver l'aria di, sembrare, somigliare a; to — out, cercare, stare in guardia; to — over, esaminare; to — up, alzare lo sguardo; cercare; to — up to, guardare a, guardare con ammirazione. —**er** *n.* chi guarda; persona bella: on looker, *n.* spettatore, astante. —**ing glass**, specchio.

lookout *n.* vigilanza; prospettiva; sentinella: that's my —, è affar mio; to be on the —, stare all'erta.

loom (lŏŏm) *n.* telaio (*per tessitura*); fusto del remo. *vt.* tessere al telaio. *vi.* apparire, delinearsi.

loony (lŏŏn′ĭ) *agg.* pazzo, pazzesco.

loop (lŏŏp) *n.* cappio, nodo scorsoio; occhiello, anello; circuito; (*aeron.*) cerchio della morte. *vt., vi.* annodare, allacciare; fare il cerchio della morte.

loophole (lŏŏp′hōl′) *n.* feritoia; scappatoia.

loose (lŏŏs) *agg.* sciolto, sfrenato, allentato; dissoluto; libero, sconnesso: to break —, scappare, liberarsi; to let —, lasciar andare; — change, spiccioli. *vt., vi.* sciogliere, slegare, allentare, allentarsi; liberare, scatenare; disormeggiare, levar l'ancora. —**ly** *avv.* liberamente; dissolutamente; negligentemente; non strettamente; impropriamente.

loosen (lŏŏs′'n) *vt.* slegare, allentare, smuovere. *vi.* allentarsi, sciogliersi.

looseness *n.* scioltezza, rilassatezza, trascuratezza, immoralità.

loot (lŏŏt) *n.* bottino, saccheggio. *vt., vi.* depredare, saccheggiare.

lop (lŏp) *vt., vi.* sfrondare, potare; penzolare.

loquacious (lō·kwā′shŭs) *agg.* loquace.

lord (lôrd) *n.* signore, padrone, sovrano, Pari d'Inghilterra: the Lord, Dio; Lord's Prayer, Padre Nostro. *vi.* signoreggiare. —**ly** *agg.* signorile, superbo, nobile, magnifico. *avv.* signorilmente, superbamente. —**ship** *n.* dominio, signoria, autorità.

lorry (lŏr′ĭ) *n.* (*Ingl.*) autocarro, carro matto; (*min.*) vagoncino.

lose (lŏŏz) *vt., vi.* (*pass., pp.* lost) perdere, smarrire, rimetterci: to — one's temper, andare in collera; to — sight of someone, perdere qualcuno di vista.

loser (lŏŏz′ẽr) *n.* perdente.

loss (lŏs) *n.* perdita, smarrimento: to be at a —, essere perplesso, non saper che pesci pigliare; to sell at a —, vendere in perdita; — leader, articolo venduto in perdita per scopi pubblicitari.

lost (lŏst) *agg.* (*e pass., pp. di* lose) perduto, smarrito, sprecato: — in thought, soprappensiero, assorto; to get —, smarrirsi.

lot (lŏt) *n.* destino, sorte; spettanza, lotto, quantità, porzione; (*comm.*) partita: a —, una gran quantità, molto; to cast (*opp.* draw) lots, tirare a sorte; to fall to one's —, toccare in sorte a uno.

lotion (lō′shŭn) *n.* lozione.

lottery (lŏt′ẽr·ĭ) *n.* lotteria.

loud (loud) *agg.* sonoro, rumoroso; forte, sgargiante. —**ly** *avv.* a gran voce, rumorosamente; vistosamente. —**speaker** *n.* altoparlante.

lounge (lounj) *n.* divano; atrio (*d'albergo, ecc.*). *vi.* oziare, bighellonare.

louse (lous) *n.* (*pl.* lice) pidocchio.

lousy (louz′ĭ) *agg.* pidocchioso; (*gergo*) spregevole, schifoso; pieno (*di*).

lout (lout) *n.* tanghero, villanzone.

lovable (lŭv′d·b'l) *agg.* amabile.

love (lŭv) *n.* amore, affetto, predilezione: to be in —, essere innamorato; to fall in — with, innamorarsi di; to make —, fare la corte a; give my — to X, salutatemi affettuosamente X; there is no — lost between those two, quel due si detestano; — affair, relazione (*amorosa*). *vt.* amare: I — it, mi piace molto.

loveliness (lŭv′lĭ·nĕs) *n.* grazia, bellezza, amabilità, incanto.

lovely (lŭv′lĭ) *agg.* incantevole, grazioso, meraviglioso.

lover (lŭv′ĕr) *n.* amante, innamorato, appassionato (*di*).

loving (lŭv′ĭng) *agg.* amorevole, affettuoso. —**ly** *avv.* affettuosamente, amorevolmente; con amore.

low (lō) (1) *agg.* basso, profondo; debole; volgare; depresso, abbattuto: — comedy, farsa; — gear (*auto.*), prima; — neck, scollatura profonda; in — spirits, abbattuto, demoralizzato; to be — on something, essere a corto di qualcosa. *avv.* in basso; a bassa voce; profondamente; a buon mercato; bassamente, vilmente.

low (lō) (2) *n.* muggito. *vi.* muggire.

lower (lō′ĕr) (1) *agg.* più basso, inferiore. *vt.* abbassare, diminuire; adagiare. *vi.* scemare, scendere.

lower (lou′ĕr) (2) *vi.* rannuvolarsi, accigliarsi.

lowest (lō′ĕst) *agg.* (*il*) più basso, (*il*) più profondo, infimo.

lowland (lō′lănd) *n.* bassa, bassopiano.

lowliness (lō′lĭ-nĕs) *n.* umiltà.

lowly (lō′lĭ) *agg.* basso, umile, inferiore. *avv.* umilmente.

loyal (loi′ăl) *agg.* leale, fedele. —**ty** *n.* lealtà, fedeltà.

lube (lūb) (*gergo*) *n.* olio lubrificante.

lubricant (lū′brĭ-kănt) *n.* lubrificante.

lubricate (lū′brĭ-kāt) *vt.* lubrificare.

lubrication (lū′brĭ-kā′shŭn) *n.* lubrificazione.

lucid (lū′sĭd) *agg.* lucido, lucente, limpido.

luck (lŭk) *n.* fortuna, sorte, caso: in —, fortunato; out of —, sfortunato. —**ily** *avv.* fortunatamente.

lucky (lŭk′ĭ) *agg.* fortunato; favorevole, propizio.

lucrative (lū′krȧ-tĭv) *agg.* lucrativo, profittevole.

ludicrous (lū′dĭ-krŭs) *agg.* ridicolo.

lug (lŭg) *vt.* trascinare, issare.

luggage (lŭg′ĭj) *n.* bagaglio.

lukewarm (lūk′wôrm′) *agg.* tiepido; indifferente.

lull (lŭl) *n.* tregua, pausa. *vt.* cullare, placare. *vi.* chetarsi, placarsi.

lullaby (lŭl′ȧ-bī′) *n.* ninnananna.

lumber (lŭm′bĕr) *n.* legname, cianfrusaglie. *vt.* ammassare, ingombrare. *vi.* fare un rumore sordo, far legna, trascinarsi. — room, ripostiglio (*Ingl.*). —yard, *n.* magazzino legnami.

luminous (lū′mĭ-nŭs) *agg.* luminoso.

lump (lŭmp) *n.* massa, pezzo, zolla, protuberanza. *vt.* ammucchiare, raggruppare, mettere insieme; *vi.* ammucchiarsi; raggrupparsi; formare una massa; ingigantirsi; avanzare pesantemente. *agg.* in blocco; a zolle.

lumpy (lŭmp′ĭ) *agg.* bernoccoluto; a blocchi.

lunar (lū′nĕr) *agg.* lunare, a forma di luna; d'argento.

lunatic (lū′nȧ-tĭk) *n.*, *agg.* pazzo. — asylum, manicomio.

lunch (lŭnch), **luncheon** (lŭn′shŭn) *n.* seconda colazione; (*S.U.*) spuntino: —room *n.* saletta da pranzo. *vi.* desinare, fare uno spuntino.

lung (lŭng) *n.* (*anat.*) polmone.

lurch (lûrch) *n.* scarto, scossa, barcollone: to leave in the —, lasciare nelle peste. *vi.* scartare (*deviare*), barcollare.

lure (lūr) *n.* allettamento, esca, attrazione. *vt.* allettare, adescare.

lurid (lū′rĭd) *agg.* pallido, livido, spettrale; sgargiante, acceso; impressionante; efferato; sensazionale.

lurk (lûrk) *vi.* nascondersi, stare in agguato, incombere.

luscious (lŭsh′ŭs) *agg.* delizioso, voluttuoso.

lust (lŭst) *n.* brama, concupiscenza, libidine. *vi.*: to — after, bramare.

luster (lŭs′tĕr) *n.* splendore, lucentezza; lampadario a gocce, goccia di lampadario.

lustiness (lŭst′ĭ-nĕs) *n.* vigore.

lustrous (lŭs′trŭs) *agg.* luccicante, splendente.

lusty (lŭs′tĭ) *agg.* vigoroso, gagliardo.

lute (lūt) *n.* liuto.

luxuriant (lŭks-ū′rĭ-ănt) *agg.* lussureggiante, rigoglioso, esuberante.

luxurious (lŭks-ū′rĭ-ŭs) *agg.* lussuoso, sontuoso, comodo.

luxury (lŭk′shŏŏ-rĭ) *n.* lusso, dovizia.

lyceum (lī-sē′ŭm) *n.* circolo culturale.

lye (lī) *n.* ranno, lisciva.

lying (lī′ĭng) (1) *ppr. di.* to lie (1). *agg.* bugiardo, ingannevole, mendace.

lying (2) *ppr. di.* to lie (2). *agg.* giacente, orizzontale. —in *n.* puerperio.

lymph (lĭmf) *n.* (*fisiol.*) linfa.

lynch (lĭnch) *vt.* linciare.

lynx (lĭngks) *n.* (*zool.*) lince.

lyre (līr) *n.* (*astr.*, *mus.*) lira.

lyric (lĭr′ĭk) *n.* lirica. —al *agg.* lirico.

M

macaroni (măk′ȧ-rō′nĭ) *n.* maccheroni.

macaroon (măk′ȧ-rōōn′) *n.* amaretto, spumiglia.

machine (mȧ-shēn') *n.* macchina, meccanismo: — gun, mitragliatrice.

machinery (mȧ-shēn'ēr-ĭ) *n.* meccanismo, macchinario.

machinist (mȧ-shēn'ĭst) *n.* macchinista, meccanico.

mackerel (măk'ēr-ĕl) *n.* sgombro (*pesce*).

mackintosh (măk'ĭn-tŏsh) *n.* impermeabile.

mad (măd) *agg.* pazzo, pazzesco, furioso; idrofobo; adirato: to drive —, far impazzire; to go —, impazzire; to get —, adirarsi.

madam (măd'ăm) *n.* signora.

madcap (măd'kăp') *n.* scervellato. *agg.* temerario, avventato.

madden (măd'n) *vt.* far impazzire, esasperare. —ing *agg.* esasperante.

made (măd) *pass., pp. di* to make. *agg.* fatto, riuscito: —up, artificioso, falso, truccato.

madhouse (măd'hous') *n.* manicomio.

madly (măd'lĭ) *avv.* pazzamente.

madman (măd'măn) *n.* pazzo.

madness (măd'nĕs) *n.* pazzia.

madwoman *n.f.* pazza.

magazine (măg'ȧ-zēn') *n.* magazzino; arsenale, polveriera; caricatore; serbatoio; rivista, pubblicazione periodica.

magenta (mȧ-jĕn'tȧ) *n., agg.* cremisi.

maggot (măg'ŏt) *n.* larva.

magic (măj'ĭk) *n.* magia. *agg.* magico.

magician (mȧ-jĭsh'ăn) *n.* mago.

magistrate (măj'ĭs-trāt) *n.* magistrato.

magnanimous (măg-năn'ĭ-mŭs) *agg.* magnanimo.

magnet (măg'nĕt) *n.* magnete, calamita. —ic, —ical (-nĕt'-) *agg.* magnetico: — recorder, magnetofono.

magnetize (măg'nė-tĭz) *vt.* magnetizzare.

magneto (măg-nē'tō) *n.* magnete.

magnificence (măg-nĭf'ĭ-sĕns) *n.* fasto, magnificenza.

magnificent (măg-nĭf'ĭ-sĕnt) *agg.* magnifico, splendido, generoso.

magnify (măg'nĭ-fī) *vt.* ingrandire, esagerare: **magnifying glass**, lente d'ingrandimento.

magnitude (măg'nĭ-tūd) *n.* grandezza, importanza, ampiezza.

magpie (măg'pī) *n.* gazza.

mahogany (mȧ-hŏg'ȧ-nĭ) *n.* mogano.

maid (măd) *n.* fanciulla; zitella; cameriera; old —, zitellona; — of honor, damigella d'onore.

maiden (măd'n) *n.* fanciulla, vergine. *agg.* di fanciulla, verginale, puro; inaugurale: — name, nome da ragazza; — voyage, viaggio inaugurale (*di una nave*).

mail (māl) (1) *n.* giaco (*armatura*).

mail (māl) (2) *n.* posta, corriere. *vt.* imbucare, spedire. —box *n.* cassetta delle lettere. —man *n.* portalettere. — train, treno postale.

maim (mām) *vt.* mutilare, storpiare, menomare.

main (mān) *n.* condotto principale (*d'acqua, gas, ecc.*); (la) maggior parte; forza; alto mare: **with might and** —, con tutta la forza. *agg.* principale, essenziale, primo; diretto.

mainland (mān'lănd') *n.* terraferma, continente.

mainly (mān'lĭ) *avv.* principalmente, essenzialmente, per lo più.

maintain (mān-tān') *vt.* mantenere, conservare; sostenere, asserire.

maintenance (mān't'n-ăns) *n.* mantenimento, manutenzione.

maize (māz) *n.* granturco.

majestic (mȧ-jĕs'tĭk) *agg.* maestoso.

majesty (măj'ĕs-tĭ) *n.* maestà.

major (mā'jēr) *n.* (*mil.*) maggiore; (*legge*) maggiorenne; corso universitario di specializzazione. *agg.* maggiore, grave, più grande, più importante. —ity (mȧ-jŏr'ĭ-tĭ) *n.* maggioranza; età maggiore; (*mil.*) grado di maggiore.

make (māk) *n.* foggia, forma; formazione; fabbricazione; marca; (*elett.*) contatto. *vt., vi.* (*pass., pp.* made) fare, creare, produrre, fabbricare, acquistare, raggiungere; riuscire; dirigersi: to — fast, ormeggiare; to — haste, affrettarsi: to — headway, progredire; to — light of, prendere alla leggera; to — much of, dare gran peso a; to — nothing of it, non capirci nulla; to — out, distinguere, capire, riuscire; to — over, cedere, trasferire; rifare, rimodernare; to — shift, arrangiarsi; to — up, completare; fare la pace; accomodare; inventare; impaginare; to — up for, supplire a; compensare di *o* per; rifarsi di; to — it up, riconciliarsi; to — up one's mind, decidersi; to — away with, sopprimere, alienare; to — for, dirigersi verso, contribuire a.

make-believe *n.* finzione.

maker (māk'ēr) *n.* fabbricante, artefice: **The Maker**, il Creatore.

makeshift (māk'shĭft') *n.* espediente. *agg.* di fortuna, improvvisato.

make-up *n.* formazione, costituzione, natura; truccatura; (*tip.*) impaginazione.

making *n.* formazione, creazione, fabbricazione; successo.

maladroit (măl'ȧ-droit') *agg.* goffo.

malady (măl'ȧ-dĭ) *n.* malattia.

malaria (mȧ-lâr'ĭ-ȧ) *n.* (*med.*) malaria.

male (māl) *n.* maschio. *agg.* maschio, maschile, mascolino.

malice (măl'ĭs) *n.* malizia, malevolenza, malignità; dolo: **to bear — towards**, avere del malanimo verso.

malicious (må-lĭsh'ŭs) *agg.* malevolo, maligno.

malign (må-līn') *n.* maligno, insidioso. *vt.* diffamare, malignare su.

malignant (må-lĭg'nånt) *agg.* maligno, nocivo, pernicioso.

mallet (măl'ĕt) *n.* martello di legno.

mallow (măl'ō) *n.* (*bot.*) malva.

malmsey (mäm'zĭ) *n.* malvasia.

malt (môlt) *n.* malto.

maltreat (măl·trēt') *vt.* maltrattare.

mamma, mama (mä'må; må·mä') (1) *n.* madre, mamma.

mamma (mä'må) (2) (*anat.*) mammella.

mammal (măm'ǎl) *n.* mammifero.

mammoth (măm'ŭth) *n.* mammut. *agg.* enorme.

man (măn) *n.* (*pl.* **men**) uomo, maschio; marito; servo, operaio, dipendente; soldato, (*scacchi*) pezzo, pedina: **— and wife**, marito e moglie; **enlisted —**, soldato, gregario. *vt.* fornire di uomini *o* di equipaggio, armare; fortificare.

manage (măn'ĭj) *vt.* dirigere, governare, amministrare, manipolare. *vi.* fare in modo (*di*), riuscire (*a*); cavarsela, destreggiarsi. **—able** *agg.* maneggevole, docile. **—ment** *n.* condotta, direzione, amministrazione.

manager (măn'ĭj·ẽr) *n.* amministratore, direttore.

mandate (măn'dāt) *n.* mandato.

mane (măn) *n.* criniera.

maneuver (må·nōō'vẽr) *n.* manovra. *vt.*, *vi.* manovrare.

manful (măn'fŏol) *agg.* virile, ardito, risoluto; da uomo.

mange (mănj) *n.* (*vet.*) rogna.

manger (măn'jẽr) *n.* mangiatoia.

mangle (măng'g'l) *n.* mangano, torchio. *vt.* maciullare, lacerare; manganare, torchiare; stirare.

mangy (măn'jĭ) *agg.* rognoso, spregevole.

manhole (măn'hōl) *n.* botola.

manhood (măn'hŏod) *n.* virilità, maturità; genere umano.

mania (mä'nĭ·å) *n.* mania, pazzia.

maniac (mä'nĭ·ăk) *n.*, *agg.* pazzo furioso.

manifest (măn'ĭ·fĕst) *n.* manifesto di carico. *agg.* manifesto, evidente. *vt.* manifestare. **—ation** *n.* manifestazione, dimostrazione.

manifesto (măn'ĭ·fĕs'tō) *n.* manifesto, proclama.

manifold (măn'ĭ·fōld) *agg.* molteplice, multiforme.

manikin (măn'ĭ·kĭn) *n.* nano, pigmeo; manichino, modello.

manila (må·nĭl'å) *n.* canapa di Manilla.

manipulate (må·nĭp'û·lāt) *vt.* manipolare, maneggiare, alterare.

manipulation (må·nĭp'û·lā'shŭn) *n.* manipolazione.

mankind (măn'kīnd') *n.* umanità (*genere umano*).

manliness (măn'lĭ·nĕs) *n.* virilità, coraggio.

manly (măn'lĭ) *agg.* virile, risoluto. *avv.* virilmente, risolutamente.

manner (măn'ẽr) *n.* modo, maniera, metodo; abitudine, stile; specie: **after the — of**, alla maniera di.

manners *n.pl.* modi, convenevoli, educazione: **to have no —**, essere maleducato.

mannish (măn'ĭsh) *agg.* mascolino.

manoeuvre (må·nōō'vẽr) (*Ingl.*) *vedi* **maneuver.**

man-of-war *n.* nave da guerra.

manor (măn'ẽr) *n.* maniero, castello, feudo.

mansion (măn'shŭn) *n.* palazzo, castello; dimora.

manslaughter (măn'slô'tẽr) *n.* omicidio colposo *opp.* non premeditato.

mantel (măn't'l) *n.* mensola del camino.

mantis (măn'tĭs) *n.* mantide: **praying —**, mantide religiosa.

mantle (măn't'l) *n.* mantello, copertura; reticella per gas.

manual (măn'û·ǎl) *n.*, *agg.* manuale.

manufactory (măn'û·făk'tō·rĭ) *n.* fabbrica.

manufacture (măn'û·făk'tûr) *n.* manifattura, industria, fabbricazione. *vt.* fabbricare, produrre, confezionare.

manufacturer *n.* fabbricante.

manufacturing *n.* fabbricazione. *agg.* industriale.

manumission (măn'û·mĭsh'ŭn) *n.* emancipazione (*di uno schiavo*).

manumit *vt.* emancipare.

manure (må·nūr') *n.* concime, letame. *vt.* concimare.

manuscript (măn'û·skrĭpt) *n.*, *agg.* manoscritto.

many (mĕn'ĭ) *n.* molti, moltitudine. *agg.pl.* molti, numerosi, parecchi, diversi: **as — again**, due volte tanto; **how —?** quanti? **as — as**, tanti quanti; **too —**, troppi; **one too —**, uno di troppo; **a great —**, moltissimi; **— a time**, molte volte.

map (măp) *n.* mappa, carta geografica. *vt.* tracciare, delineare, progettare; pianificare.

maple (mā'p'l) n. acero.

mar (mär) vt. guastare, sfigurare, mutilare.

marauder (má·rôd'ĕr) n. predone, rapinatore.

marble (mär'b'l) n. marmo, statua; biglia, pallina. agg. marmoreo.

March (märch) (1) n. marzo.

march (märch) (2) n. marcia, corso, progresso. vi. far marciare. vi. marciare: to — in, entrare marciando.

marchioness (mär'shŭn·ĕs) n. marchesa.

mare (mâr) n. cavalla, giumenta: —'s nest, parto della fantasia, mistificazione.

margin (mär'jǐn) n. margine; bordo. —al agg. marginale; periferico.

marigold (măr'ǐ·gōld) n. fiorrancio, calendula.

marine (má·rēn') n. marina; fante di marina: merchant —, marina mercantile. agg. marino, marittimo.

mariner (măr'ǐ·nĕr) n. marinaio.

maritime (măr'ǐ·tǐm) agg. marittimo.

mark (märk) n. marca, segno, impronta; voto (scolastico); bersaglio; marco: to make one's —, distinguersi; to hit the —, cogliere nel segno; question —, punto interrogativo; trade —, marchio di fabbrica. vt. marcare, segnare, notare: to — down, annotare; — my words! senti bene quel che ti dico! —er n. contrassegno; segnatore, segnapunti.

market (mär'kĕt) n. mercato: — place, mercato; meat —, macelleria; stock —, borsa. vt., vi. vendere e acquistare, commerciare: to go marketing, andare a far la spesa.

marking (märk'ǐng) n. marcatura, marchio.

marksman (märks'măn) n. tiratore esperto.

marmalade (mär'má·lād) n. composta (spec. di arance).

maroon (má·rōōn') (1) agg., n. marrone (colore).

maroon (má·rōōn') (2) vt. abbandonare su un'isola deserta; (fig.) isolare.

marquee (mär·kē') n. pensilina, tettoia.

marquis (mär'kwǐs), marquess (-kwĕs) n. marchese.

marquise (mär·kēz') n. marchesa.

marriage (măr'ǐj) n. matrimonio.

married (măr'ǐd) agg. sposato, coniugale: — couple, coniugi, due sposi; to get —, sposarsi.

marrow (măr'ō) n. midollo, parte essenziale.

marry (măr'ǐ) vt., vi. sposare.

marsh (märsh) n. palude, stagno: — gas metano.

marshmallow (märsh'măl'ō) n. (bot.) altea.

marshal (mär'shăl) n. maresciallo, prefetto, cerimoniere; sceriffo, cancelliere. vt. schierare, dirigere, scortare.

marshy (mär'shǐ) agg. paludoso, palustre.

marten (mär'tĕn) n. (zool.) martora.

martial (mär'shăl) agg. marziale.

martinet (mär'tǐ·nĕt') n. rigorista, castigamatti.

martyr (mär'tĕr) n. martire. vt. martirizzare. —dom n. martirio.

marvel (mär'vĕl) n. meraviglia. vi. stupirsi. —ous agg. meraviglioso.

mascot (măs'kŏt) n. portafortuna.

masculine (măs'kū·lǐn) agg. maschile, virile.

mash (măsh) vt. mescolare, ridurre in polpa, impastare: mashed potatoes, purea di patate.

mask (măsk) n. maschera. vt., vi. mascherare, mascherarsi: —ed ball, ballo in maschera.

mason (mā's'n) n. muratore: Free Mason, massone. —ry n. muratura, arte muraria: Free Masonry, massoneria.

masquerade (măs'kĕr·ād') n. mascherata. vi. camuffarsi.

mass (măs) (1) n. massa, ammasso: — meeting, riunione, adunata; — production, produzione in massa. vt. ammassare. vi. ammassarsi.

Mass (măs) (2) n. santa messa.

massacre (măs'á·kĕr) n. massacro. vt. massacrare.

massage (má·säzh') n. massaggio. vt. massaggiare.

massive (măs'ǐv) agg. massiccio; massivo; pesante; consistente; voluminoso.

mast (måst) n. (naut.) albero.

master (mås'tĕr) n. maestro, padrone, capo; signorino; (naut.) capitano: Master of Arts, laureato in lettere; band— n. direttore d'orchestra; — of ceremonies, gran cerimoniere; (radio) presentatore (di uno spettacolo). vt. dominare, soggiogare, impadronirsi di, imparare. —ful agg. autoritario. —ly agg. magistrale. avv. magistralmente. —piece n. capolavoro. —y n. maestria; predominio, vittoria.

mastiff (mås'tǐf) n. cane mastino.

mat (măt) (1) n. treccia, stuoia, stolno; sacco; cornice di cartone, passepartout; (tip.) matrice. vt. intrecciare, tessere (opp. coprire di) stuoie. vi. feltrarsi.

mat (măt) (2) agg. opaco, smerigliato.

match (măch) (1) n. fiammifero, miccia. —book n. bustina di fiammiferi.

match (măch) (2) n. eguale, compagno; oggetto gemello; coppia bene assortita; matrimonio; gara incontro, competizione; avversario di pari forza: to have no —, non aver l'uguale; to be a good —, accordarsi, intonarsi; essere un buon partito; to be a — for, tener testa a. vt., vi. uguagliare, accoppiare, far sposare; appaiarsi, intonarsi, corrispondere a. —less agg. incomparabile, senza pari.

mate (măt) n. compagno, amico; coniuge; (naut.) secondo; (scacchi) scaccomatto. vt., vi. unire, accoppiare, dare scaccomatto, accoppiarsi.

material (mǎ·tḗr'ĭ·ǎl) n. materiale, materia, stoffa: raw —, materia prima. agg. materiale, essenziale.

maternal (mǎ·tûr'nǎl) agg. materno.

maternity (mǎ·tûr'nǐ·tǐ) n. maternità.

mathematical (măth'ē·măt'ĭ·kǎl) agg. matematico.

mathematician (măth'ē·mǎ·tǐsh'ǎn) n. matematico.

mathematics (măth'ē·măt'ĭks) n. matematica.

matriculate (mǎ·trĭk'û·lāt) vt. matricolare. vi. iscriversi.

matriculation (mǎ·trĭk'û·lā'shǔn) n. immatricolazione, iscrizione.

matrimony (măt'rĭ·mō'nĭ) n.sposalizio.

matrix (mā'trĭks) n. (pl. matrices [māt'rĭ·sēz]) matrice.

matron (mā'trǔn) n. matrona; capoinfermiera; sorvegliante, vigilatrice (in collegi, carceri femminili, ecc.).

matter (măt'ēr) n. materia, sostanza, materiale, questione; pus: printed —, stampe; as a — of fact, effettivamente; as a — of course, come se niente fosse; no —, non importa; what is the — with you? che cosa vi prende?; what is the —? che cosa c'è? vi. importare, avere importanza.

matter-of-course agg. naturale.

matter-of-fact agg. pratico, positivo; banale; prosaico.

matting (măt'ĭng) n. stuoia.

mattress (măt'rĕs) n. materasso.

mature (mǎ·tūr') agg. maturo. vt., vi. maturare; scadere.

maturity (mǎ·tū'rĭ·tǐ) n. maturità; scadenza; maturazione.

maudlin (môd'lĭn) agg. sdolcinato, emotivo, piagnucoloso.

maul (môl) n. mazza, mazzuola. vt. martellare, malmenare.

mawkish (môk'ĭsh) agg. nauseante, sdolcinato.

maxim (măk'sĭm) n. massima, sentenza, norma, principio.

maximum (măk'sĭ·mǔm) n., agg. massimo.

may (mā) (1) v. ausiliario, difettivo (pass. might) potere, avere il permesso o la possibilità o la facoltà di: it — be true, può esser vero; be that as it —, comunque sia; — I go? posso andare? It — be that, può darsi che; he — be late, può darsi che arrivi in ritardo; I — go there, forse ci andrò.

May (mā) (2) n. maggio: — Day, primo maggio.

maybe (mā'bē) avv. forse.

mayhem (mā'hĕm) n. mutilazione, menomazione.

mayonnaise (mā'ô·nāz') n. maionese.

mayor (mā'ēr) n. sindaco.

maze (māz) n. labirinto; confusione, disorientamento: to be in a —, essere confuso.

me (mē) pron.pers. me, mi, io: give it to —, datelo a me; look at —, guardatemi; it is —, sono io.

meadow (mĕd'ō) n. prato.

meager (mē'gēr) n. magro, misero, scarso, povero.

meal (mēl) (1) n. pasto: —time n. l'ora del pasto.

meal (mēl) (2) n. farina.

mean (mēn) (1) n. punto intermedio, media; mezzo, strumento. agg. medio, intermedio: by all means, senza fallo, certamente; by no means, niente affatto; by means of, per mezzo di.

mean (mēn) (2) agg. basso, meschino, malvagio, losco.

mean (mēn) (3) vt., vi. (pass., pp. meant) significare, intendere, avere intenzione, destinare, predisporre: do you — it? dite sul serio? what does this —? che cosa significa ciò? to — well, avere buone intenzioni.

means n.pl. mezzi, rendite.

meaning (mēn'ĭng) n. significato; intenzione; importanza, valore. agg. significativo: well——agg. ben intenzionato. —less agg. senza senso, insignificante.

meanly (mēn'lĭ) avv. meschinamente, ignobilmente.

meanness (mēn'nĕs) n. bassezza, meschinità, malvagità.

meant (mĕnt) pass., pp. di to mean.

meantime (mēn'tīm') meanwhile (mĕn'hwīl') avv. nel frattempo, frattanto, intanto.

measles (mē'z'lz) n. (med.) rosolia, morbillo; (vet.) teniasi.

measly (mēz'lĭ) *agg.* insignificante, magro, spregevole.

measurable (mĕzh'ĕr.á.b'l) *agg.* misurabile, limitato.

measure (mĕzh'ẽr) *n.* misura; dimensione; moderazione; misurazione; tempo; ritmo, metro: beyond —, oltre misura. *vt., vi.* misurare, distribuire, adattare, delimitare.

measured *agg.* misurato, moderato, ritmico.

measurement *n.* misurazione, misura, dimensione.

meat (mēt) *n.* carne; polpa; alimento: — ball, polpetta; — market, macelleria.—y *agg.* carnoso; polposo; sostanzioso.

mechanic (mē·kăn'ĭk) *n., agg.* meccanico.

mechanical (mē·kăn'ĭ·kăl) *agg.* meccanico; macchinale.

mechanician (mĕk'á·nĭsh'ăn) *n.* meccanico.

mechanics (mē·kăn'ĭks) *n.* meccanica.

mechanism (mĕk'á·nĭz'm) *n.* meccanismo.

mechanize (mĕk'á·nīz) *vt.* motorizzare; meccanizzare.

medal (mĕd'l) *n.* medaglia.

meddle (mĕd'l) *vi.* impicciarsi, immischiarsi.

meddler (mĕd'lẽr) *n.* intrigante.

meddlesome (mĕd''l·sŭm) *agg.* inframmettente.

median (mē'dĭ·ăn) *n.* punto o linea o numero mediano. *agg.* mediano, di mezzo.

mediate (mē'dĭ·āt) *vt.* arbitrare, conciliare. *vi.* interporsi.

mediation (mē'dĭ·ā'shŭn) *n.* mediazione.

mediator (mē'dĭ·ā'tẽr) *n.* mediatore.

medical (mĕd'ĭ·kăl) *agg.* medico; medicinale: — jurisprudence, medicina legale.

medicinal (mē·dĭs'ĭ·năl) *agg.* medicinale.

medicine (mĕd'ĭ·sĭn) *n.* medicina; medicinale: to take one's —, rassegnarsi; — man, stregone.

medieval (mē'dĭ·ē'văl) *agg.* medievale.

mediocrity (mē'dĭ·ŏk'rĭ·tĭ) *n.* mediocrità.

meditate (mĕd'ĭ·tāt) *vt.* progettare. *vi.* meditare.

meditation (mĕd'ĭ·tā'shŭn) *n.* meditazione.

medium (mē'dĭ·ŭm) *n.* mezzo, strumento, tramite; elemento naturale; medium.

medlar (mĕd'lẽr) *n.* nespola, nespolo.

medley (mĕd'lĭ) *n.* mescolanza, miscuglio. *agg.* misto.

meek (mēk) *agg.* mite, mansueto. —ness *n.* mansuetudine, mitezza.

meerschaum (mẽr'shăm) *n.* schiuma di mare: — pipe, pipa di schiuma.

meet (mēt) *n.* riunione sportiva. *agg.* conveniente, adatto. *vt., vi.* (*pass., pp.* met) incontrare, andare incontro a: ar la conoscenza di; affrontare, rispondere a; soddisfare (*esigenze*): incontrarsi, riunirsi, far conoscenza: to — one's engagements far fronte ai propri impegni.

meeting (mēt'ĭng) *n.* incontro, riunione: to call a —, indire una riunione.

megaphone (mĕg'á·fōn) *n.* megafono.

melancholic (mĕl'ăn·kŏl'ĭk) *agg.* malinconico.

melancholy (mĕl'ăn·kŏl'ĭ) *n.* malinconia. *agg.* triste.

mellow (mĕl'ō) *agg.* maturo, polposo; morbido, bonario; friabile (*di terreno*): brillo. *vt.* far maturare, ammorbidire, ammansire. *vi.* maturare, addolcirsi, ammorbidirsi.

melodious (mē·lō'dĭ·ŭs) *agg.* melodioso.

melodrama (mĕl'ō·drä'má) *n.* melodramma.

melody (mĕl'ō·dĭ) *n.* melodia.

melon (mĕl'ŭn) *n.* melone: water —, anguria.

melt (mĕlt) *vt.* (*pp.* melted, molten) fondere, liquefare; intenerire. *vi.* fondersi, liquefarsi; commuoversi; svanire.

member (mĕm'bẽr) *n.* membro; elemento; arto. —ship *n.* appartenenza, associazione; qualità o qualifica di socio o di membro; numero dei soci.

membrane (mĕm'brān) *n.* membrana.

memento (mē·mĕn'tō) *n.* memento, ricordo.

memoir (mĕm'wär) *n.* memoria; relazione. memoriale; biografia.

memorable (mĕm'ō·rá·b'l) *agg.* memorabile.

memorandum (mĕm'ō·răn'dŭm) *n.* memorandum; scrittura privata; distinta: — book, taccuino d'appunti.

memorial (mē·mō'rĭ·ăl) *n.* monumento; memoriale. *agg.* commemorativo: Memorial Day, giorno delle rimembranze.

memorize (mĕm'ō·rīz) *vt.* imparare a memoria.

memory (mĕm'ō·rĭ) *n.* memoria, ricordo.

men (mĕn) *pl.* di man.

menace (mĕn'ĭs) *n.* minaccia. *vt.* minacciare.

menacing *agg.* minaccioso.

mend (mĕnd) *n.* riparazione, miglioramento: on the —, in via di miglioramento. *vt.* riparare, rammendare, correggere, migliorare. *vi.* migliorare, emendarsi: past —ing, senza rimedio.

mending *n.* riparazione.

menial (mē'nĭ-ăl) *n.* domestico. *agg.* domestico, servile.

menstruation (mĕn'strŏŏ-ā'shŭn) *n.* mestruazione.

mental (mĕn'tăl) *agg.* mentale. **—ity** (·ăl'·) *n.* mentalità.

mention (mĕn'shŭn) *n.* menzione, allusione. *vt.* menzionare, citare: don't — it, non c'è di che (*in risposta a "grazie"*).

mephitic (mē·fĭt'ĭk) *agg.* mefitico.

mercenary (mûr'sē·nĕr'ĭ) *n.*, *agg.* mercenario.

merchandise (mûr'chăn·dīz) *n.* mercanzia: piece of —, articolo commerciale. *vt.* propagandare (*una merce*).

merchant (mûr'chănt) *n.* mercante; (nave mercantile.) *agg.* commerciale, mercantile. **—man** *n.* nave mercantile.

merciful (mûr'sĭ·fŏŏl) *agg.* pietoso, misericordioso, provvidenziale.

merciless (mûr'sĭ·lĕs) *agg.* implacabile, spietato.

mercury (mûr'kū·rĭ) *n.* mercurio.

mercy (mûr'sĭ) *n.* misericordia, pietà, clemenza: to be at the — of, essere alla mercè di; — killing, eutanasia.

mere (mēr) *agg.* mero, semplice, autentico: a — formality, una pura formalità; a — trifle, un nonnulla. **—ly** *avv.* puramente, semplicemente, soltanto.

merge (mûrj) *vt.* incorporare, fondere, assorbire, amalgamare. *vi.* amalgamarsi, essere assorbito, sparire.

merger (mûr'jĕr) *n.* (*comm.*) fusione.

meridian (mē·rĭd'ĭ·ǎn) *n.*, *agg.* meridiano.

merit (mĕr'ĭt) *n.* merito, valore. *vt.* meritare. **—orious** (-tō'rĭ·ŭs) *agg.* meritorio, meritevole.

mermaid (mûr'mād') *n.* sirena.

merman (mûr'măn') *n.* tritone.

merrily (mĕr'ĭ·lĭ) *avv.* allegramente.

merry (mĕr'ĭ) *agg.* allegro, lieto, burlesco: Merry Christmas, buon Natale; to make —, divertirsi, fare baldoria. **—go-round** *n.* giostra. **—making** *n.* divertimento, festa. *agg.* allegro, festivo, festoso.

mesh (mĕsh) *n.* maglia, rete. *vt.* prendere nella rete; (*mecc.*) ingranare.

mess (mĕs) *n.* cibo, pasto; pasticcio, disordine; mensa: to be in a fine —, essere in un bell'imbroglio; to make a — of, rovinare, guastare, insudiciare, mettere in disordine. *vt.* dar da mangiare a; impasticciare, mettere in disordine. *vi.* far mensa comune; far confusione.

message (mĕs'ĭj) *n.* messaggio.

messenger (mĕs'ĕn·jĕr) *n.* messaggero.

Messrs. (mĕs''rz) *n.pl.* signori (*vale*: "Spett. Ditta").

messy (mĕs'ĭ) *agg.* sudicio, disordinato.

met (mĕt) *pass. e pp. di* to meet.

metal (mĕt'l) *n.* metallo; breccia, pietrisco (*per fondo stradale*); (*ferr.*) rotaia. *vt.* metallizzare; selciare. **—lic** (-ăl'ĭk) *agg.* metallico. **—lurgic** (-ûrj'ĭk) *agg.* metallurgico. **—lurgist** (mĕt'-) *n.* metallurgico (*lavoratore*). **—lurgy** *n.* metallurgia.

metamorphosis (mĕt'à·môr'fō·sĭs) *n.* metamorfosi.

metaphor (mĕt'à·fĕr) *n.* metafora.

metaphysics (mĕt'à·fĭz'ĭks) *n.* metafisica.

mete (mēt) *vt.* misurare: to — out, distribuire.

meteor (mē'tē·ĕr) *n.* meteora. **—ological** (-·ŏj'-) *agg.* meteorologico. **—ologist** (-ŏl'-) *n.* meteorologo. **—ology** *n.* meteorologia.

meter (mē'tĕr) *n.* metro; misuratore, contatore, tassametro.

method (mĕth'ŭd) *n.* metodo. **—ical** (-ŏd'ĭk·ăl) *agg.* metodico.

Methuselah (mē·thū'zē·là) *n.* Matusalemme.

metre *vedi* meter.

metrical (mĕt'rĭ·kăl) *agg.* metrico.

metropolis (mē·trŏp'ō·lĭs) *n.* metropoli.

metropolitan (mĕt'rō·pŏl'ĭ·tǎn) *n.* metropolita. *agg.* metropolitano.

mettle (mĕt'l) *n.* coraggio, pertinacia: to put someone on his —, metter qualcuno al puntiglio.

mew (mū) *n.* miagolio. *vi.* miagolare.

mews (mūz) *n.pl.* scuderie.

mice (mĭs) *pl. di* mouse.

microbe (mī'krōb) *n.* microbo.

microgroove (mī'krō·grōŏv') *n.*, *agg.* microsolco.

microphone (mī'krō·fōn) *n.* microfono.

microscope (mī'krō·skōp) *n.* microscopio.

microscopic (mī'krō·skŏp'ĭk) *agg.* microscopico.

mid (mĭd) *n.* mezzo, metà, centro. *agg.* medio, centrale, intermedio. *prep.* tra, in mezzo a: in —air, a mezz'aria.

midday (mĭd'dā') *n.* mezzodì. *agg.* meridiano, di mezzogiorno.

middle (mĭd''l) *n.* centro, mezzo, punto di mezzo. *agg.* medio, centrale, intermedio, mediano, mediocre: — age, mezza età; the Middle Ages, il Medioevo; — size, misura o statura media; in the — of, nel mezzo di, alla metà di. —aged *agg.* di mezza età. —man *n.* intermediario. —sized *agg.* di medie dimensioni.

middling (mĭd'lĭng) *agg.* medio, mediocre. *avv.* discretamente.

middy (mĭd'ĭ) *n.* (*fam.*) allievo guardiamarina:— blouse, camiciotto da marinaio.

midge (mĭj) *n.* moscerino.

midget (mĭj'ĕt) *n.* nano, pigmeo; piccola automobile da corsa.

midnight (mĭd'nĭt') *n.* mezzanotte. *agg.* di mezzanotte.

midriff (mĭd'rĭf) *n.* (*anat.*) diaframma; (*sartoria femminile*) bustino.

midshipman (mĭd'shĭp'măn) *n.* allievo guardiamarina.

midst (mĭdst) *n.* mezzo, centro: in the — of, nel mezzo di, tra; in our —, tra noi. *prep.* fra.

midsummer (mĭd'sŭm'ẽr) *n.* solstizio d'estate.

midtown (mĭd'toun') *n.* centro della città.

midway (mĭd'wā') *agg.* situato a metà strada, intermedio. *avv.* a metà strada.

midwife (mĭd'wĭf') *n.* levatrice.

mien (mēn) *n.* aspetto, cera.

might (mĭt) (1) *pass.* di may.

might (mĭt) (2) *n.* forza, potenza, potere: with — and main, con tutte le forze.

mighty (mĭt'ĭ) *agg.* forte, potente. *avv.* molto.

migrate (mĭ'grāt) *vi.* migrare.

migration (mĭ·grā'shŭn) *n.* migrazione, emigrazione.

mike (mīk) *n.* (*gergo*) microfono.

mild (mĭld) *agg.* mite, dolce, blando, moderato. —er *agg.* più dolce, più blando.

mildew (mĭl'dū) *n.* ruggine delle piante, muffa.

mildly (mĭld'lĭ) *avv.* dolcemente, blandamente, moderatamente.

mildness (mĭld'nĕs) *n.* dolcezza, mitezza, moderazione.

mile (mĭl) *n.* miglio (*misura* = m. 1609,31): nautical —, miglio marino (=m. 1853). —age *n.* lunghezza o distanza in miglia; autonomia; (*ferr.*) prezzo per miglio. —stone *n.* pietra miliare.

military (mĭl'ĭ·tĕr'ĭ) *n.*, *agg.* militare: the —, i militari, l'esercito.

militate (mĭl'ĭ·tāt) *vi.* (against o in favor of) militare (contro o a favore di), influire.

milk (mĭlk) *n.* latte. *vt.* mungere.

milkmaid (mĭlk'mād') *n.* lattaia.

milkman (mĭlk'măn) *n.* lattaio.

milky (mĭl'kĭ) *agg.* latteo, lattiginoso: the Milky Way, la Via Lattea.

mill (mĭl) (1) *n.* 1/1000 di dollaro.

mill (mĭl) (2) *n.* mulino; fabbrica: spinning —, filanda; sugar —, zuccherificio; textile —, fabbrica di tessuti. *vt.* macinare, polverizzare; sbattere; granire. —board *n.* cartone.

miller (mĭl'ẽr) *n.* mugnaio.

millet (mĭl'ĕt) *n.* (*bot.*) miglio.

milliner (mĭl'ĭ·nẽr) *n.* modista.

millinery (mĭl'ĭ·nẽr'ĭ) *n.* modisteria.

million (mĭl'yŭn) *n.* milione.

millionaire (mĭl'yŭn·âr') *n.* milionario.

millionth (mĭl'yŭnth) *n.*, *agg.* milionesimo.

millstone (mĭl'stōn') *n.* macina da mulino.

mime (mīm) *n.* mimo.

mimeograph (mĭm'ē·ō·grăf') *n.* duplicatore, ciclostile. *vt.* ciclostilare.

mimic (mĭm'ĭk) *agg.* mimico, imitativo. *n.* mimo; parodista. *vt.* imitare, parodiare. —ry *n.* imitazione, parodia.

mince (mĭns) *vt.* tritare, sminuzzare; attenuare. *vi.* muoversi o parlare con affettazione: not to — words, parlare in tutta franchezza. —meat *n.* ripieno, ammorsellato.

mind (mīnd) *n.* mente, pensiero; intenzione; desiderio; opinione; intelligenza: to have a — to, avere intenzione di; to be out of one's —, essere pazzo; to make up one's —, decidersi; to change one's —, cambiar parere; to speak one's —, dire quel che si pensa; to give a piece of one's —, cantarle chiare; to my —, a mio modo di vedere. *vt.*, *vi.* badare a, osservare, ascoltare, obbedire; preoccuparsi di; dispiacersi per; guardarsi da: I do not — , non mi preoccupo di, non m'importa di, non mi dà fastidio; — your own business, badate ai fatti vostri; never —, prego, non c'è di che; non disturbatevi; non fateci caso, lasciate perdere. —ful *agg.* circospetto, attento.

mine (mīn) (1) *pron.poss.* il mio, la mia, i miei, le mie: a friend of —, uno dei miei amici.

mine (mīn) (2) *n.* miniera, mina. *vt.* minare, scavare, estrarre (*minerali*). —layer *n.* posamine. —sweeper *n.* dragamine.

miner (mīn'ẽr) *n.* minatore.

mineral (mĭn'ẽr·ăl) *n.*, *agg.* minerale.

mingle (ming'g'l) *vt.* mischiare, confondere. *vi.* mischiarsi.

miniature (min'ĭ-á-t̯ụr) *n.* miniatura.
agg. in miniatura, in sedicesimo.

minimize (min'ĭ-mīz) *vt.* minimizzare;
svilire, svalutare, sminuire.

minimum (min'ĭ-mŭm) *n.* minimo.

mining (min'ing) *n.* lavoro minerario,
agg. minerario.

minister (min'ĭs-tĕr) *n.* ministro;
sacerdote. *vt.* somministrare, fornire. *vi.* dar aiuto, sopperire.

ministration (min'ĭs-trā'shŭn) *n.* somministrazione; soccorso; cura.

ministry (min'ĭs-trĭ) *n.* aiuto, soccorso;
ministero; clero.

miniver (min'ĭ-vẽr) *n.* (*zool.*) vaio.

mink (mingk) *n.* (*zool.*) visone.

minnow (min'ō) *n.* avannotto.

minor (mi'nẽr) *n.* minorenne. *agg.*
minore. —ity (mĭ-nŏr'ĭ-tĭ; mĭ-) *n.*
minoranza, minorità.

minstrel (min'strĕl) *n.* menestrello.

mint (mint) (1) *n.* menta.

mint (mint) (2) *n.* zecca, tesoro: to
have a — of money, avere un mucchio di danari. *vt.* coniare, fabbricare, inventare.

minus (mi'nŭs) *n.* meno (*segno di
sottrazione*); *prep.* meno, diminuito
di, privo di.

minute (mĭ-nūt') (1) *agg.* minuto,
piccolo, minuzioso.

minute (min'ĭt) (2) *n.* minuto (60*a
parte dell'ora*), istante; abbozzo,
minuta, verbale: — hand, lancetta
dei minuti (*dell'orologio*).

minx (mingks) *n.* smorfiosa, civetta.

miracle (mir'á-k'l) *n.* miracolo.

miraculous (mĭ-răk'û-lŭs) *agg.* miracoloso.

mirage (mĭ-räzh') *n.* miraggio.

mire (mir) *n.* fango, pantano. *vt.*
infangare; porre in difficoltà. *vi.*
infangarsi, impantanarsi.

mirror (mir'ẽr) *n.* specchio. *vt.* rispecchiare, riflettere.

mirth (mûrth) *n.* allegria, ilarità. —ful
agg. ilare.

miry (mir'ĭ) *agg.* fangoso, sudicio.

misadventure (mis'ăd-věn'tụr)*n.* disavventura.

misbehave (mis'bē-hāv') *vi.* comportarsi male.

misbehavior (mis'bē-hāv'yẽr) *n.* cattiva condotta.

misbelief (mis'bē-lēf') *n.* falsa credenza, incredulità.

misbelieve (mis'bē-lēv') *vt.* dubitare di,
non credere a. *vi.* avere una falsa
credenza.

miscalculate (mis-kăl'kû-lāt) *vt.*, *vi.*
calcolare male, sbagliare.

miscarriage (mis-kăr'ij) *n.* errore,
disguido; aborto: — of justice, errore giudiziario.

miscarry (mis-kăr'ĭ) *vi.* fallire, smarrirsi; abortire.

miscellaneous (mis'ĕ-lā'nĕ-ŭs) *agg.*
miscellaneo.

miscellany (mis'ĕ-lā'nĭ) *n.* miscellanea, zibaldone.

mischance (mis-chȧns') *n.* sfortuna,
disgrazia.

mischief (mis'chif) *n.* male, danno,
torto, cattiveria: out of —, per
cattiveria; — maker, seminatore di
discordia, malvagio.

mischievous (mis'chĭ-vŭs) *agg.* malizioso; maligno, nocivo.

misconduct (mis-kŏn'dŭkt) *n.* cattiva condotta, correttezza; cattiva gestione. *vt.* (-dŭkt')]dirigere *o*
gestire male: to — oneself, comportarsi male.

misconstruction (mis'kŏn-strŭk'shŭn)
n. falsa *o* errata interpretazione.

miscreant (mis'krē-ánt) *n.*, *agg.* scellerato.

misdeed (mis-dēd') *n.* misfatto.

misdemeanor (mis'dē-mēn'ẽr) *n.* colpa,
cattiva condotta, reato minore.

misdirect (mis'dĭ-rĕkt') *vt.* dirigere
male, informare male.

miser (mi'zẽr) *n.* avaro.

miserable (miz'ẽr-á-b'l) *agg.* infelice;
deplorevole, miserabile.

miserly (miz'ẽr-lĭ) *agg.* sordido,
avaro.

misery (miz'ẽr-ĭ) *n.* infelicità, miseria,
tormento.

misfire (mis'fir') *vi.* far cilecca (*di
motore o arma*).

misfortune (mis-fôr'tụn) *n.* sfortuna;
infortunio, disastro.

misgiving (mis-gĭv'ing) *n.* perplessità,
diffidenza, dubbio, sospetto.

mishap (mis-hăp') *n.* incidente, disavventura.

misinterpret (mis'in-tûr'prĕt) *vt.* fraintendere; interpretare erratamente.

misjudge (mis-jŭj') *vt.*, *vi.* giudicare
ingiustamente *o* erratamente.

mislay (mis-lā') *vt.* (*pass.*, *pp.* mislaid)
smarrire, metter fuori posto.

mislead (mis-lēd') *vt.* (*pass.*, *pp.*
misled) indurre in errore, sviare,
forviare, corrompere; ingannare.

misleading *agg.* ingannevole, fallace.

mismanagement *n.* cattiva amminí-
strazione.

mismatch *vt.* assortire male.

misplace (mis-plās') *vt.* collocar male,
metter fuori posto.

misplaced *agg.* fuori di posto, mal
riposto: — pride, orgoglio malinteso.

misprint (mĭs·prĭnt') *n.* refuso, errore di stampa.

mispronounce (mĭs'prŏ·nouns') *vt.* pronunziare scorrettamente.

misreckon (mĭs·rĕk'ŭn) *vt., vi.* calcolare erratamente.

misrepresent (mĭs'rĕp·rĕ·zĕnt') *vt., vi.* svisare, falsare, snaturare.

misrule (mĭs·rōōl') *n.* malgoverno.

miss (mĭs) (1) *n.* signorina, ragazza nubile: Miss Calvert, la signorina Calvert.

miss (mĭs) (2) *n.* omissione, errore; colpo mancato. *vt.* sbagliare, mancare, non raggiungere; dimenticare; sentire (*o* notare) la mancanza di, rimpiangere; perdere, lasciarsi sfuggire; schivare per un pelo: to — the bus *o* the boat, perdere l'autobus, (*fig.*), perdere un'occasione propizia. *vt.* mancare, non riuscire, essere assente; sbagliare il bersaglio.

misshapen (mĭs·shăp'ĕn) *agg.* deforme, malformato.

missile (mĭs'ĭl) *n.* proiettile, missile: guided —, missile telecomandato.

missing (mĭs'ĭng) *n.* mancante, scomparso, disperso: a cup is —, manca una tazza; a man is —, è scomparso un uomo.

mission (mĭsh'ŭn) *n.* missione. —ary *n., agg.* missionario.

missis (mĭs'ĭs), **missus** (mĭs'ŭs) *n.* (*fam.*) signora, padrona, moglie.

missive (mĭs'ĭv) *n.* missiva.

misspell (mĭs·spĕl') *vt., vi.* (*pass., pp.* misspelled *o* misspelt) scrivere (*o* pronunciare) erratamente, commettere errori d'ortografia.

misstate (mĭs·stāt') *vt.* esporre erratamente, svisare.

missus *vedi* missis.

mist (mĭst) *n.* nebbia, velo; pioggerella. *vi.* annebbiarsi, velarsi; piovigginare.

mistake (mĭs·tāk') *n.* errore, abbaglio. *vt.* (*pass.* mistook, *pp.* mistaken) sbagliare, confondere; capir male, fraintendere; scambiare (*una persona o una cosa per un'altra*). *vi.* errare.

mistaken (mĭs·tāk'ĕn) *agg.* erroneo, inesatto, frainteso: to be —, sbagliarsi, essere in errore. *pp. di* to mistake.

mister (mĭs'tĕr) *n.* signore, signor.

mistimed (mĭs·tīmd') *agg.* intempestivo.

mistletoe (mĭs''l·tō) *n.* (*bot.*) vischio.

mistook (mĭs·tŏŏk') *pass. di* to mistake.

mistreat (mĭs·trēt') *vt.* maltrattare.

mistress (mĭs'trĕs) *n.* signora, padrona, direttrice, istitutrice, mae-stra; amante: head— *n.* direttrice di scuola.

mistrust (mĭs·trŭst') *n.* diffidenza, sfiducia. *vt., vi.* diffidare di, sospettare. —ful *agg.* diffidente.

misty (mĭs'tĭ) *agg.* nebbioso, nebuloso, velato, vago.

misunderstand (mĭs'ŭn·dĕr·stănd')*vt., vi.* (*pass., pp.* misunderstood) fraintendere equivocare.

misunderstanding *n.* incomprensione, malinteso, screzio.

misunderstood *agg.* frainteso, incompreso, malinteso.

misuse (mĭs·ūs') *n.* abuso; cattivo uso; maltrattamento. *vt.* (-ūz') fare un cattivo uso (*opp.* abusare) di; maltrattare.

mite (mīt) *n.* soldino, inezia, piccolo contributo; acaro.

miter (mī'tĕr) *n.* mitra (*copricapo episcopale*); congiunzione ad angolo retto.

mitigate (mĭt'ĭ·gāt) *vt.* mitigare.

mitt (mĭt), **mitten** (mĭt''n) *n.* mezzo guanto, guanto a sacchetto; (*pugilato*) guantone.

mix (mĭks) *vt.* mischiare, unire, associare; confondere. *vi.* mischiarsi, associarsi. —age *n.* (*cinema*) missaggio. —ed (mĭkst) *agg.* misto, promiscuo, confuso. —ture *n.* miscuglio.

mizzen (mĭz''n) *n.* (*naut.*) vela di mezzana. —mast *n.* albero di mezzana.

moan (mōn) *n.* gemito, lamento. *vt., vi.* lamentare, lamentarsi, piangere, gemere.

moat (mōt) *n.* fosso, fossato.

mob (mŏb) *n.* folla, moltitudine, turba: — law, linciaggio. *vt.* assalire tumultuosamente *o* in massa.

mobile (mō'bĭl) *agg.* mobile, agile (*di mente*), versatile, incostante. *n.* parte mobile; macchina inutile (*tipo di soprammobile*).

mobilization (mō'bĭ·lĭ·zā'shŭn) *n.* mobilitazione.

mobilize (mō'bĭ·līz) *vt.* mobilitare.

mobster (mŏb'stĕr) *n.* tumultuante; gangster teppista.

moccasin (mŏk'd·sĭn) *n.* mocassino; (*zool.*) ancistrodonte.

mock (mŏk) *n.* canzonatura, parodia. *agg.* burlesco, ironico; falso, finto, fittizio, simulato. *vt.* beffare; parodiare; simulare, ingannare; frustrare: to — at, beffarsi di. —er *n.* burlone, impostore. —ery *n.* beffa, parodia, derisione.

mode (mōd) *n.* modo, forma, maniera, moda, metodo.

model (mŏd''l) *n.* modello, campione; modella; indossatrice. *agg.* esempiare. *vt.*, *vi.* modellare, plasmare; posare, fare la modella.

moderate (mŏd'ĕr.ĭt) *agg.* moderato, modico, modesto. *vt.* (-āt) moderare, temperare. *vi.* moderarsi.

moderation (mŏd'ĕr.ā'shŭn) *n.* moderazione.

modern (mŏd'ẽrn) *n.*, *agg.* moderno.

modernize (mŏd'ẽr.nīz) *vt.*, *vi.* modernizzare, modernizzarsi.

modest (mŏd'ĕst) *n.* modesto, moderato, castigato, pudico.

modesty (mŏd'ĕs.tĭ) *n.* modestia, moderazione; pudicizia.

modicum (mŏd'ĭ.kŭm) *n.* minima quantità, minimo.

modification (mŏd'ĭ.fĭ.kā'shŭn) *n.* modificazione.

modify (mŏd'ĭ.fĭ) *vt.* modificare. *vi.* modificarsi.

modish (mŏd'ĭsh) *agg.* elegante, di moda alla moda.

modulate (mŏd'ū.lāt) *vt.*, *vi.* modulare.

Mohammedan (mō.hăm'ĕ.dăn) *n.*, *agg.* maomettano.

moist (moist) *agg.* umido.

moisten (mois''n) *vt.* inumidire, umettare.

moisture (mois't̵ŭr) *n.* umidità.

molar (mō'lẽr) *n.*, *agg.* molare.

molasses (mō.lăs'ĕz) *n.* melassa.

mold (mōld) *n.* modello, stampo; modanatura; carattere; muffa; terriccio. *vt.* modellare, plasmare. **ammuffire. —er** *n.* modellatore. *vi.* sgretolarsi.

moldy *agg.* muffoso.

mole (mōl) (1) *n.* neo.

mole (mōl) (2) *n.* molo; mole.

mole (mōl) (3) *n.* (*zool.*) talpa.

molecule (mŏl'ē.kūl) *n.* molecola.

molehill (mōl'hĭl) *n.* talpaia: **to make a mountain out of a —,** drammatizzare, esagerare.

molest (mō.lĕst') *vt.* molestare.

mollify (mŏl'ĭ.fĭ) *vt.* mollificare, ammansire, attenuare. *vi.* ammansirsi, commuoversi.

molten (mōl'tĕn) *agg.* fuso, liquefatto.

moment (mō'mĕnt) *n.* momento, istante; importanza, significato; impulso: **of little —,** di scarsa importanza. **—ary** *agg.* momentaneo; imminente. **—ous** (-mĕnt'-) *agg.* grave, importante, critico, decisivo.

momentum (mō.mĕn'tŭm) *n.* (*fis.*) momento, impulso.

monarch (mŏn'ẽrk) *n.* monarca.

monarchy (mŏn'ẽr.kĭ) *n.* monarchia.

monastery (mŏn'ăs.tẽr'ĭ) *n.* monastero.

Monday (mŭn'dĭ) *n.* lunedì: **Black Monday,** lunedì di Pasqua.

monetary (mŏn'ē.tẽr'ĭ) *agg.* monetario.

money (mŭn'ĭ) *n.* danaro, moneta: **ready —,** danaro contante; **earnest —,** caparra; **paper —,** carta moneta; **— broker, —changer** *n.* cambiavalute; **—lender** *n.* usuraio; **— order,** vaglia; **—making** *agg.* lucrativo, redditizio.

mongoose (mŏng'gōōs) *n.* (*zool.*) mangusta.

mongrel (mŏng'grĕl) *n.*, *agg.* bastardo, ibrido.

monitor (mŏn'ĭ.tẽr) *n.* ammonitore; ammonimento; (*scol.*) capoclasse; (*radio e T.V.*) monitor; (*naut.*) monitore.

monk (mŭngk) *n.* monaco.

monkey (mŭng'kĭ) *n.* scimmia; buffone; babbeo: **— wrench,** chiave inglese. *vt.* scimmiottare. *vi.* gingillarsi: **to — with** (*gergo*) manomettere; intromettersi in.

monocle (mŏn'ō.k'l) *n.* monocolo (*lente*).

monogamist (mō.nŏg'á.mĭst) *n.* monogamo.

monogamy (mō.nŏg'á.mĭ) *n.* monogamia.

monogram (mŏn'ō.grăm) *n.* monogramma.

monologue (mŏn'ō.lŏg) *n.* monologo.

monopolize (mō.nŏp'ō.līz) *vt.* monopolizzare.

monopoly (mō.nŏp'ō.lĭ) *n.* monopolio.

monotonous (mō.nŏt'ō.nŭs) *agg.* monotono.

monotony (mō.nŏt'ō.nĭ) *n.* monotonia.

monotype (mŏn'ō.tĭp) *n.* monotipo (*f.*), monotype.

monotyper *n.* monotipista.

monster (mŏn'stẽr) *n.* mostro, prodigio. *agg.* mostruoso, enorme.

monstrosity (mŏn.strŏs'ĭ.tĭ) *n.* mostruosità.

monstrous (mŏn'strŭs) *agg.* mostruoso, prodigioso, enorme.

montage (mŏn.täzh') *n.* montaggio; fotomontaggio.

month (mŭnth) *n.* mese. **—ly** *n.* pubblicazione mensile. *agg.* mensile. *avv.* mensilmente.

monument (mŏn'ū.mĕnt) *n.* monumento. **—al** *agg.* monumentale.

moo (mōō) *n.* muggito. *vi.* muggire.

mood (mōōd) *n.* umore, stato d'animo; modo (*del verbo*): **to be in a good —,** essere di buon umore; **to be in the — to,** essere in vena di; **to be in no — for,** non essere in vena di; **— swing,** sbalzi d'umore. **—iness** *n.* malumore, tristezza, mutevolezza, scontrosità.

moody (mōōd'ĭ) *agg.* triste, imbronciato; lunatico, mutevole; scontroso.

moon (mōon) n. luna: once in a blue —, una volta ogni morte di vescovo. vi. vagare trasognato; incantarsi. —light n. chiaro di luna. —shine n. chiaro di luna; chimera; liquori di contrabbando. —struck agg. pazzo.

Moor (1) n. moro.

moor (mōor) (2) n. landa, brughiera.

moor (mōor) (3) vt., vi. ormeggiare, ormeggiarsi. —ing n. ormeggio.

Moorish (mōr'Ish) agg. moresco.

moose (mōos) n. alce americana.

moot (mōot) agg. discutibile, controverso.

mop (mŏp) n. strofinaccio; tampone; (naut.) radazza: — of hair, zazzera. vt. strofinare, tamponare: to — one's brow, asciugarsi la fronte.

mope (mōp) vt. deprimere. vi. essere triste o apatico.

moral (mŏr'ăl) n. morale (f.); (pl.) moralità, costumi. agg. morale.

morale (mŏ-răl') n. morale (f.); (m. = stato d'animo).

moralist (mŏr'ăl-Ist) n. moralista.

morality (mŏ-răl'I-tI) n. morale, moralità.

moralize (mŏr'ăl-Iz) vt. moralizzare. vi. trarre la morale, moraleggiare.

morass (mŏ-răs') n. palude.

morbid (mŏr'bId) agg. morboso; macabro, spaventoso. —ly avv. morbosamente; in modo macabro.

more (mōr) agg. più, maggiore: — courage than strength, più coraggio che forza; the — we have the — we want, più si ha più si desidera; some —, ancora un po'. avv. più, di più, maggiormente, ancora: — and —, sempre di più; once —, ancora una volta; — or less, più o meno, suppergiù.

moreover (mŏr-ō'vẽr) avv. inoltre, per giunta, anche.

morgue (mŏrg) n. obitorio; (giornalismo) archivio.

Mormon (mŏr'mŭn) n., agg. mormone.

morning (mŏr'nIng) n. mattino, mattina: tomorrow —, domattina; in the —, di mattina; good —! buon giorno! — star, stella del mattino. agg. mattutino.

morocco (mŏ·rŏk'ō) n. marocchino (pelle).

moron (mō'rŏn) n. deficiente mentale; scemo, imbecille.

morose (mŏ·rōs') agg. cupo, imbronciato, scontroso. —ness n. tristezza, scontrosità.

morphia (mŏr'fI·ă) morphine (mŏr'fēn) n. morfina.

morrow (mŏr'ō) n. (l')indomani: on the —, il giorno dopo.

morsel (mŏr'sĕl) n. frammento, boccone, pezzetto.

mortal (mŏr'tăl) n. mortale. agg. mortale, funesto; umano. —ity (-tăl'-I·tI) n. mortalità, natura umana. —ly avv. mortalmente, umanamente.

mortar (mŏr'tẽr) n. calcestruzzo; pestello; (art.) mortaio.

mortgage (mŏr'gIj) n. ipoteca. vt. ipotecare.

mortician (mŏr·tIsh'ăn) n. impresario di pompe funebri.

mortification (mŏr'tI·fI·kā'shŭn) n. mortificazione; (med.) necrosi.

mortify (mŏr'tI·fI) vt. mortificare; necrotizzare. vi. mortificarsi; andare in cancrena.

mortise (mŏr'tIs) n. incavo, incastro.

mosaic (mō·zā'Ik) n., agg. mosaico.

mosque (mŏsk) n. moschea.

mosquito (măs·kē'tō) n. zanzara: — net, zanzariera.

moss (mŏs) n. (bot.) musco: —grown, coperto di musco. —y agg. muscoso.

most (mōst) n. la maggior parte, il più: to make the — of, trarre il miglior partito da; the — you can do, il massimo che tu possa fare; at the —, tutt' al più. agg. moltissimo, più, più grande, maggiore, preponderante: — people, il più della gente; for the — part, nella maggior parte; the — votes, la maggioranza dei voti. avv. grandemente, estremamente, prevalentemente, il più; (gergo) quasi: — of all, soprattutto. —ly avv. per la maggior parte, per lo più, principalmente.

motel (mō·tĕl') n. autostello, motel.

moth (mŏth) n. tarma; falena: — ball, palla di naftalina. —eaten agg. tarmato.

mother (mŭth'ẽr) n. madre. agg. materno, di madre; naturale, innato; natio: — country, madrepatria; — tongue, madrelingua. vt. dar vita a, far da madre a, proteggere.

motherhood n. maternità.

mother-in-law n. suocera.

motherly agg. materno. avv. maternamente.

mother-of-pearl n. madreperla.

motif (mō·tēf') n. motivo, tema.

motion (mō'shŭn) n. movimento, moto, mozione; cenno, segnale. vt., vi. esortare col gesto, far cenno. —less agg. immobile. —picture n. film, agg. cinematografico.

motive (mō'tIv) n. motivo, movente. agg. motore, causale, motrice.

motley (mŏt'lI) n. accozzaglia. agg. variegato, eterogeneo, multicolore.

motor (mō'tĕr) *n.*, *agg.* motore. *vi.* andare in automobile.

motorboat (mō'tĕr-bōt') *n.* motoscafo.

motorbus (mō'tĕr-bŭs') *n.* autobus.

motorcar (mō'tĕr-kär) *n.* automobile.

motorcade (mō'tĕr-kād) *n.* autocorteo.

motorcoach (mō'tĕr-kōch) *n.* autocorriera, pullman, torpedone.

motorcycle (mō'tĕr-sī'k'l) *n.* motocicletta.

motorist (mō'tĕr-ĭst) *n.* automobilista.

motorize (mō'tĕr-īz) *vt.* motorizzare.

mottle (mŏt''l) *vt.* screziare, venare, variegare, maculare.

motto (mŏt'ō) *n.* motto, massima.

mould (mōld) *vedi* mold.

mound (mound) *n.* terrapieno, collinetta, tumulo.

mount (mount) *n.* monte; monta; montaggio; ascesa; cavalcatura; incastellatura, affusto; montatura (*di foto, ecc.*). *vt.*, *vi.* montare; ascendere, salire; aumentare.

mountain (moun'tĭn) *n.* montagna. *agg.* montano. —**eer** *n.* montanaro, alpinista. —**eering** (-ēr'ĭng) *n.* alpinismo. —**ous** *agg.* montuoso; enorme.

mourn (mōrn) *vt.* piangere (*qualcuno*); rimpiangere. *vi.* addolorarsi; essere in lutto. —**er** *n.* persona in lutto, dolente. —**ful** *agg.* triste, lugubre, funebre, lamentoso.

mourning *n.* lamentazione, lutto: deep —, lutto stretto; to go into —, prendere il lutto. *agg.* di (*o* da) lutto.

mouse (mous) *n.* (*pl.* mice) topo, sorcio.

moustache *vedi* mustache.

mouth (mouth) *n.* bocca. *vt.* (-th-) mettere in bocca, divorare; declamare; biascicare. —**ful** *n.* boccone. —**piece** *n.* bocchino, imboccatura (*di strumento mus.*), cornetto (*del telefono*); portavoce; (*gergo*) avvocato.

movable (mōōv'á-b'l) *n.* mobile: movables, *pl.* beni mobili. *agg.* movibile, mobile.

move (mōōv) *n.* mossa, movimento; trasloco. *vt.* muovere; commuovere; incitare, indurre; spostare, trasferire; proporre. *vi.* muoversi, mettersi in marcia; cambiare alloggio, traslocare; partire; fare una mossa: to — for, proporre; to — away, andarsene, spostarsi, appartarsi; to — forward, avanzare; to — on, avanzare, proseguire, camminare; to — out, andarsene, lasciare una casa, traslocare.

movement (mōōv'mĕnt) *n.* movimento.

mover (mōōv'ĕr) *n.* motore, movente.

movie (mōōv'ĭ) *n.* film, pellicola: the movies, il cinema.

moving (mōōv'ĭng) *agg.* commovente: — power, forza motrice.

mow (mō) *vt.*, *vi.* (*pass.* mowed, *pp.* mowed, mown) falciare, ammucchiare il fieno. —**er** *n.* falciatore; falciatrice (*macchina*).

Mr. (*abbr. di* mister) (mĭs'tĕr) signor, il signor. **Mrs.** (*vedi* missis) (mĭs'ĭz) signora, la signora.

much (mŭch) *n.*, *agg.*, *avv.* molto, tanto, assai, di gran lunga: as —, altrettanto; as — as, tanto quanto; — as, per quanto; how —? quanto? too —, troppo; so —, tanto, così, tutto questo; so — that, tanto che; so — the better (the worse), tanto meglio (peggio); very —, moltissimo; — the same, quasi lo stesso; not — of a book, non un gran che come libro; to make — of, dare molta importanza a.

muck (mŭk) *n.* letame, concime, sudiciume.

mucous (mū'kŭs) *agg.* mucoso: — membrane, mucosa.

mucus (mū'kŭs) *n.* muco.

mud (mŭd) *n.* fango.

muddle (mŭd''l) *n.* confusione, disordine, imbroglio. *vt.* confondere, abborracciare; intorbidare.

muddy (mŭd'ĭ) *agg.* torbido, fangoso, confuso, stordito. *vt.* oscurare, intorbidare, infangare; inebetire.

mudguard (mŭd'gärd') *n.* parafango.

muff (mŭf) *n.* manicotto (*di pelliccia*); sciocco. *vt.* impasticciare, lasciarsi sfuggire.

muffin (mŭf'ĭn) *n.* panino dolce.

muffle (mŭf''l) *n.* muffola. *vt.* imbacuccare; smorzare (*suoni*).

muffler (mŭf'lĕr) *n.* sciarpa; guantone (*da boxe*); silenziatore; (*mus.*) sordina.

mug (mŭg) *n.* boccale.

mulberry (mŭl'bĕr'ĭ) *n.* mora del gelso. — tree *n.* gelso.

mule (mūl) (1) *n.* mulo.

mule (mūl) (2) *n.* pantofola.

muleteer (mū'lĕ-tēr') *n.* mulattiere.

mull (mŭl) *vt.*, *vi.* macinare; faticare; rimuginare.

multiple (mŭl'tĭ-p'l) *n.*, *agg.* multiplo.

multiplication (mŭl'tĭ-plĭ-kā'shŏn) *n.* moltiplicazione: — table, tavola pitagorica.

multiplicity (mŭl'tĭ-plĭs'ĭ-tĭ) *n.* molteplicità.

multiply (mŭl'tĭ-plī) *vt.* moltiplicare. *vi.* moltiplicarsi.

multitude (mŭl'tĭ-tūd) *n.* moltitudine.

multitudinous (mŭl'tĭ·tū'dĭ·nŭs) *agg.* numeroso, sovrabbondante, affollato.

mum (mŭm) *agg.* silenzioso: to keep —, tenere acqua in bocca; —'s the word! acqua in bocca!

mumble (mŭm'b'l) *n.* borbottio. *vt., vi.* brontolare, borbottare.

mummy (mŭm'ĭ) *n.* mummia; poltiglia; cera per innesti.

mumps (mŭmps) *n.pl.* musoneria; (*med.*) orecchioni.

munch (mŭnch) *vt., vi.* biascicare, masticare rumorosamente.

municipality (mū·nĭs'ĭ·păl'ĭ·tĭ) *n.* municipio.

munificence (mū·nĭf'ĭ·sĕns) *n.* munificenza.

munificent (mū·nĭf'ĭ·sĕnt) *n.* munifico.

munitions (mū·nĭsh'ŭnz) *n.pl.* munizioni; equipaggiamento.

mural (mū'rǎl) *n.* pittura murale. *agg.* murale.

murder (mûr'dĕr) *n.* omicidio, assassinio. *vt.* assassinare. **—er** *n.* omicida, assassino. **—ess** *n.* assassina. **—ing**, **—ous** *agg.* omicida, feroce.

murk (mûrk) *n.* oscurità, tetraggine. **—y** *agg.* tenebroso, cupo, nebbioso.

murmur (mûr'mĕr) *n.* mormorio. *vt., vi.* mormorare.

muscle (mŭs'l) *n.* muscolo. *vi.* intrufolarsi.

muscular (mŭs'kû·lẽr) *agg.* muscolare.

Muse (mūz) (1) *n.* musa.

muse (mūz) (2) *n.* astrazione, meditazione. *vt., vi.* meditare, rimuginare.

museum (mū·zē'ŭm) *n.* museo.

mush (mŭsh) *n.* sorta di polenta, pappa; sentimentalismo.

mushroom (mŭsh'rŏŏm) *n.* fungo.

music (mū'zĭk) *n.* musica: to face the —, affrontare la situazione: — hall, caffè-concerto. — stand, leggio per musica, palco dell'orchestra.

musical *agg.* musicale *n.* (*anche* **musical comedy**) commedia musicale.

musician (mū·zĭsh'ăn) *n.* musicista.

musing (mūz'ĭng) *n.* meditazione. *agg.* meditabondo.

musk (mŭsk) *n.* muschio. **—rat** *n.* rat-misquè.

musket (mŭs'kĕt) *n.* moschetto. **—eer** (-tẽr') *n.* moschettiere.

musky (mŭs'kĭ) *agg.* muschiato.

muslin (mŭz'lĭn) *n.* mussolina.

muss (mŭs) *vt.* arruffare.

must (mŭst) (1) *vi.* difettivo ausil.

(*mancante dell'inf. e pp.; pass.* must) devo, devi, deve, dobbiamo, *ecc.*: it — be so, dev'essere così; something — be done, bisogna fare qualcosa. *agg.* da farsi assolutamente: a — book, un libro che si deve leggere.

must (mŭst) (2) *n.* mosto.

mustache (mŭs·tásh') *n.* baffo, baffi.

mustard (mŭs'tẽrd) *n.* senape: — plaster, senapismo.

muster (mŭs'tẽr) *n.* esposizione; assembramento, adunata: to pass —, superare l'esame, esser passabile. *vt., vi.* adunare, riunire, riunirsi: to — up courage, prendere il coraggio a due mani.

musty (mŭs'tĭ) *agg.* muffito, muffoso.

mute (mūt) *n.* muto; (*mus.*) sordina. *agg.* muto. *vt.* mettere la sordina a.

mutilate (mū'tĭ·lāt) *vt.* mutilare.

mutilation (mū'tĭ·lǎ'shŭn) *n.* mutilazione.

mutineer (mū'tĭ·nẽr') *n.* ammutinato.

mutinous (mū'tĭ·nŭs) *agg.* ribelle, turbolento, sedizioso.

mutiny (mū'tĭ·nĭ) *n.* ammutinamento. *vi.* ammutinarsi.

mutter (mŭt'ẽr) *n.* brontolio. *vt., vi.* brontolare, borbottare.

mutton (mŭt''n) *n.* montone: — chop, costoletta di montone.

mutual (mū'tû·ǎl) *agg.* mutuo, reciproco.

muzzle (mŭz''l) *n.* bocca (*d'arma da fuoco*); muso (*di animale*); museruola. *vt.* metter la museruola a, far tacere, imbavagliare.

my (mī) *agg.poss.* mio, mia, miei, mie.

myriad (mĭr'ĭ·ăd) *n.* miriade.

myrtle (mûr't'l) *n.* (*bot.*) mirto.

myself (mĭ·sĕlf') *pron.pers.* io stesso, me stesso, mi: I went there —, ci andai di persona; I broke it —, lo ruppi io stesso; I hurt —, mi feci male: I was by —, ero solo; I talked to —, parlavo fra me.

mysterious (mĭs·tẽr'ĭ·ŭs) *agg.* misterioso.

mystery (mĭs'tẽr·ĭ) *n.* mistero.

mystic (mĭs'tĭk) *n., agg.* mistico.

mystification (mĭs'tĭ·fĭ·kǎ'shŭn) *n.* mistificazione; perplessità, sconcerto.

mystify (mĭs'tĭ·fĭ) *vt.* mistificare; rendere perplesso, sconcertare, confondere.

myth (mĭth) *n.* mito. **—ology** (-ŏl'ŏ·jĭ) *n.* mitologia.

N

nab (năb) *vt.* afferrare, aguantare.

nabob (nă'bŏb) *n.* nababbo.

nacelle (nà·sĕl') *n.* navicella.

nacre (nă'kẽr) *n.* madreperla.

nag (năg) *n.* cavallino, ronzino. *vt.*, *vi.* tormentare, angariare; criticare.

naif (nă.ēf′) *agg.* ingenuo.

nail (nāl) *n.* chiodo; unghia, artiglio: on the —, seduta stante. *vt.* inchiodare; concludere (*un affare*); cogliere a volo; smascherare; ribadire. — file, lima da unghie.

naive (nă.ēv′) *n.*, *agg.*ingenuo.

naiveté (nă.ēv′tā′) *n.* ingenuità.

naked (nā′kĕd) *agg.* nudo; crudo (*della verità*); manifesto; indifeso; spoglio: stark —, tutto nudo. —ness *n.* nudità, crudezza.

name (nām) *n.* nome; reputazione: assumed —, pseudonimo; christian —, nome di battesimo; family —, cognome; to call someone names, insolentire qualcuno; to make a — for oneself, farsi una fama; *vt.* chiamare, nominare, menzionare; scegliere. *agg.* di gran nome, famoso. —less *agg.* anonimo, senza nome.

namely (nām′lĭ) *avv.* cioè, vale a dire.

namesake (nām-sāk′) *n.* omonimo.

nap (năp) peluria, lanuggine; pisolino: to take a —, schiacciare un pisolino. *vi.* sonnecchiare: to catch somebody napping, cogliere qualcuno alla sprovvista.

nape (năp) *n.* nuca.

naphtha (năf′thȧ) *n.* nafta.

napkin (năp′kĭn) *n.* tovagliolo; pannolino.

narcissus (när-sĭs′ŭs) *n.* (*bot.*) narciso.

narcotic (när-kŏt′ĭk) *n.*, *agg.*narcotico.

narrate (nă-rāt′) *vt.* narrare.

narration (nă-rā′shŭn) *n.* narrazione; trama, intreccio.

narrative (năr′ȧ-tĭv) *n.* resoconto; narrativa. *agg.* narrativo.

narrow (năr′ō) *n.* stretto, strettoia; (*pl.*) stretti. *agg.* stretto, limitato; di misura; meschino: — circumstances, ristrettezze; to have a — escape, scamparla bella. *vt.* restringere, limitare, ridurre al minimo. *vi.* restringersi. —ly *avv.* strettamente;minuziosamente;dappresso; di stretta misura: we — escaped falling, per poco non cademmo. —minded *agg.* gretto —ness *n.* strettezza; grettezza, ristrettezza.

nastiness (nàs′tĭ-nĕs) *n.* malvagità, volgarità, oscenità.

nasty (nàs′tĭ) *agg.* sudicio; osceno; malvagio; grossolano; ripugnante: to smell —, puzzare; — wound, ferita grave; — disposition, caratteraccio.

nation (nā′shŭn) *n.* nazione. —al

(năsh′-) *agg.* nazionale. —ality *n.* nazionalità.

nationalize (năsh′ŭn-ăl-īz) *vt.* nazionalizzare.

nationally (năsh′ŭn-ăl-ĭl) *avv.* su scala nazionale, in tutta la nazione.

native (nā′tĭv) *n.* indigeno. *agg.* nativo, indigeno, originario; naturale; innato to go —, insabbiarsi.

nativity (nȧ-tĭv′ĭ-tĭ) *n.* natività, nascita, oroscopo.

natty (năt′ĭ) *agg.* inappuntabile.

natural (năt′û-rȧl) *n.* idiota; natura, carattere; (*fam.*) successo; (*mus.*) bequadro. *agg.* naturale, istintivo, spontaneo: he is a — for that job, ha un'inclinazione naturale per quel lavoro, è nato per fare quel lavoro. —ism *n.* naturalismo, verismo. —ist *n.* naturalista, verista. —ization *n.* naturalizzazione.

naturalize (năt′û-rȧl-īz) *vt.* naturalizzare; acclimare; adottare (*espressioni straniere ecc.*).

naturally (năt′û-rȧl-ĭl) *avv.* naturalmente, spontaneamente.

naturalness (năt′û-rȧl-nĕs) *n.* naturalezza, spontaneità.

nature (nā′tûr) *n.* natura, indole: to copy from — copiare dal vero.

naught (nôt) *n.* nulla, zero: to set at —, disprezzare; to come to —, far fiasco. *agg.* nullo.

naughtiness (nô′tĭ-nĭs) *n.* perversità, cattiveria.

naughty (nô′tĭ) *agg.* cattivo.

nausea (nô′shē-ȧ) *n.* nausea.

nauseate (nô′shē-āt) *vt.* nauseare, disgustare.

nauseating *agg.* nauseabondo, stomachevole.

nautical (nô′tĭ-kȧl) *agg.* nautico, marittimo, marino.

naval (nā′vȧl) *agg.* navale: — officer, ufficiale di marina.

nave (nāv) *n.* mozzo (*di ruota*); (*arch.*) navata.

navel (nā′vĕl) *n.* ombelico; centro.

navigable (năv′ĭ-gȧ-b'l) *agg.* navigabile.

navigate (năv′ĭ-gāt) *vt.*, *vi.* navigare, governare; (*aeron.*) pilotare.

navigation (năv ĭ-gā′shŭn) *n.* navigazione: — laws, codice marittimo.

navigator (năv′ĭ-gā′tẽr) *n.* navigatore; ufficiale di rotta.

navy (nā′vĭ) *n.* marina; flotta: — blue, blu, turchino; — yard, arsenale.

nay (nā) *n.* diniego, voto negativo. *avv.* no, non solo, anzi.

Neapolitan *n.*, *agg.* napoletano: — ice, cassata.

near (nẽr) *agg.* vicino, prossimo, intimo; esatto: the — side of a car

il lato sinistro di un'automobile;
I had a — accident, per poco non
mi succede un incidente; — silk,
finta seta. *avv.* quasi, circa, vicino:
to draw —, avvicinarsi; I came —
forgetting to, per poco mi dimenti-
cavo di; — at hand, a portata di
mano; — by, vicinissimo. *prep.* accanto, presso: — the end of, verso
la fine di. *vt.*, *vi.* avvicinarsi (a).

nearly *avv.* quasi, pressappoco; da
vicino, strettamente: — related,
parente stretto; it is — five o'clock,
sono quasi le cinque; I — did it,
stavo per farlo, poco mancò che
non lo facessi.

nearness *n.* prossimità, vicinanza,
intimità, avarizia.

nearsighted *agg.* miope.

neat (nēt) *agg.* netto; elegante; abile,
accurato: puro. —**ly** *avv.* nettamente, abilmente, puramente, elegantemente. —**ness** *n.* lindezza,
precisione, chiarezza.

necessaries *n.pl.* (il) necessario.

necessarily (nĕs′ẽ·sĕr′ĭ·lĭ) *avv.* necessariamente.

necessary (nĕs′ẽ·sĕr′ĭ) *agg.* necessario.

necessitate (nĕ·sĕs′ĭ·tāt) *vt.* necessitare, rendere necessario.

necessity (nĕ·sĕs′ĭ·tĭ) *n.* necessità.

neck (nĕk) *n.* collo; scollatura;
manico (*di violino*); istmo, passo,
gola (*di montagna*): — and —, alla
pari; — or nothing, ad ogni costo.
—**lace** *n.* collana. —**length** *n.*
(*ippica*) incollatura.

necktie (nĕk′tĭ′) *n.* cravatta.

nectar (nĕk′tẽr) *n.* nettare.

need (nēd) *n.* bisogno; necessità;
povertà: for — of, in mancanza di;
if — be, se fosse necessario. *vt.*, *vi.*
abbisognare di, mancare di, occorrere: he — not go, non occorre
che egli vada. —**ful** *agg.* necessario,
indispensabile; bisognoso.

needle (nē′d'l) *n.* ago; puntina (*da
grammofono*); iniezione: the —,
nervosismo. *vt.* cucire; pungere,
punzecchiare; (*fig.*) dar colore, dar
brio.

needless (nēd′lĕs) *agg.* inutile, superfluo.

needlework (nē′d'l·wûrk′) *n.* lavoro di
cucito, ricamo.

needs (nēdz) *avv.* necessariamente,
assolutamente: I must —, devo
assolutamente.

needy (nē′dĭ′) *agg.* indigente, bisognoso.

ne'er (nâr) *avv.* (*contraz. di* never): —
-do-well, buono a nulla.

negation (nē·gā′shăn) *n.* diniego,
negazione.

negative (nĕg′á·tĭv) *n.* negazione;

negativa. *agg.* negativo. *vt.* smentire; respingere, votare contro.

neglect (nĕg·lĕkt′) *n.* negligenza,
trascuratezza, abbandono. *vt.* trascurare, tralasciare, omettere. —**ful**
agg. tra scurato, negligente.

negligence (nĕg′lĭ·jĕns) *n.* negligenza.

negligent (nĕg′lĭ·jĕnt) *n.* negligente.

negligible (nĕg′lĭ·jĭ·b'l) *agg.* trascurabile.

negotiate (nē·gō′shĭ.āt) *vt.*, *vi.* negoziare; superare (*un ostacolo, una
difficoltà, ecc.*).

negotiation (nē·gō′shĭ.ā′shăn) *n.* negoziato, trattativa.

Negress (nē′grĕs) *n.* negra.

Negro (nē′grō) *n.*, *agg.* negro.

neigh (nā) *n.* nitrito. *vi.* nitrire.

neighbor (nā′bẽr) *n.* vicino; coinqui-
lino: to love one's —, amare il
prossimo. *agg.* vicino, adiacente.
—**hood** *n.* vicinato, dintorni, vicinanza, quartiere. —**ing** *agg.* vicino, attiguo. —**ly** *agg.* di buon
vicino, amichevole. *avv.* da buon
vicino, socievolmente.

neither (nē′thẽr) *agg.*, *pron.* nè l'uno
nè l'altro: I saw — , non vidi nè
l'uno nè l'altro. *cong.* (*correlativo di
nor*) nè, neppure: — my father nor
my mother, nè mio padre nè mia
madre; — will I, e neppure io. *avv.*
in nessun caso.

nephew (nĕf′ū; nĕv′ū) *n.* nipote (*m.*).

nerve (nûrv) *n.* nervo; nervatura;
coraggio, energia; impudenza: (*pl.*)
nervi, nervoso: to get on one's —,
dare ai nervi; to lose one's —, perdere le staffe;. *vt.* dar forza o
coraggio.

nervous (nûr′vŭs) *agg.* nervoso;
nerboruto; timoroso, timido; inquieto. —**ness** *n.* nervosità; inquietudine; timidezza.

nervy (nûr′vĭ) *agg.* nervoso; audace.

nest (nĕst) *n.* nido; tana, rifugio:
wasp's —, vespaio. *vi.* nidificare,
rifugiarsi. —**egg** *n.* endice; gruzzolo.

nestle (nĕs′'l) *vt.* ospitare; coccolare.
vi. annidarsi, crogiolarsi.

net (nĕt) (1) *n.* rete, reticella. *vt.*
coprire con (*opp.* prendere nella)
rete.

net (nĕt) (2) *agg.* netto: — price,
prezzo netto. *vt.* introitare come
guadagno netto.

nether (nĕth′ẽr) *agg.* basso, inferiore.

netting (nĕt′ĭng) *n.* rete, reticolato.

nettle (nĕt′'l) *n.* (*bot.*) ortica. *vt.* pungere; irritare, indispettire.

network (nĕt′wûrk) *n.* rete, maglia:
radio —, rete radiofonica; railroad
—, rete ferroviaria.

neuralgia (nû.răl'já) n. nevralgia.

neurasthenia (nû'rǎs.thē'nǐ.á) n. nevrastenia.

neuritis (nû.rī'tǐs) n. (med.) nevrite.

neurosis (nû.rō'sǐs) n. nevrosi.

neurotic (nû.rŏt'ǐk) agg. nevrotico.

neuter (nū'těr) n., agg. neutro, neutrale.

neutral (nū'trǎl) agg. neutrale, neutro, acromatico. —ity n. neutralità.

neutralize (nū'trǎl.īz) vt. neutralizzare.

never (něv'ěr) avv. mai, giammai: — mind, non importa. —-ceasing agg. incessante. —-ending agg. perpetuo, eterno.

nevermore (něv'ěr.mōr') avv. mai più.

nevertheless (něv'ěr.thě.lěs') avv. ciononostante, tuttavia.

new (nū) agg. nuovo, recente, inesperto, fresco: as good as —, come nuovo; — look, linea nuova, nuovo corso. —born n. neonato. —comer n. nuovo venuto.

newel (nū'ěl) n. albero della scala a chiocciola; colonnina di ringhiera.

newfangled (nū'făng'g'ld) agg. di nuovo conio o genere, di nuova invenzione.

newly (nū'lǐ) avv. di recente, da poco, di fresco. —wed n. sposino, sposina; (pl.) sposini.

newness (nū'něs) n. freschezza, novità.

news (nūz) n. novità, notizia, annuncio: a piece of —, una notizia, — agency, agenzia d'informazioni; — agent, agente d'informazioni, giornalista; giornalaio; — dealer, giornalaio.

newsboy n. strillone.

newscast n. notiziario radio, radiogiornale; telegiornale. —er n. annunciatore; radiocommentatore; telecommentatore.

newsman n. giornalista; giornalaio, strillone.

newspaper n. giornale.

newsprint n. carta da giornale.

newsreel n. cinegiornale.

newsstand n. edicola.

newsworthy agg. (giorn.) meritevole di essere pubblicato.

next (někst) agg. vicino; prossimo; successivo, seguente; contiguo: — month, il mese venturo; — day, il giorno dopo; to be — in turn, essere (il prossimo) di turno; — best, il migliore subito dopo. avv. in seguito, subito dopo, quasi, accanto: — to impossible, quasi impossibile; what —? e poi?; — to me, accanto a me; — of kin, parente più prossimo.

nib (nǐb) n. becco (di uccello); punta (di penna), pennino.

nibble (nǐb''l) n. bocconcino, morso. vt., vi. rosicchiare, mordicchiare, sbocconcellare; brucare.

nice (nīs) agg. simpatico, buono, grazioso, piacevole, fine; preciso, accurato, scrupoloso. —ly avv. bene; amabilmente, piacevolmente, delicatamente; esattamente, scrupolosamente. —ty (nī'sě.tǐ) n. esattezza, raffinatezza, finezza, sfumatura; amabilità: to a —, esattamente, alla perfezione.

niche (nǐch) n. nicchia.

nick (nǐk) n. istante preciso; sbreccatura, tacca: in the — of time, al momento giusto, appena in tempo. vt. colpire giusto, cogliere, intaccare, sbreccare, troncare.

nickel (nǐk'ěl) n. nichelio; moneta da 5 cents. —plating agg. nichelatura.

nicknack vedi knickknack.

nickname (nǐk'nām') n. nomignolo. vt. soprannominare.

niece (nēs) n. nipote (f.).

niggard (nǐg'ěrd) n., agg. spilorcio. -liness n. spilorceria. -ly agg. spilorcio, misero. avv. avaramente.

nigh (nī) agg. vicino, affine, prossimo. avv. quasi. prep. presso, vicino.

night (nīt) n. notte, sera: good —! buona notte! tomorrow —, domani sera, domani notte; at —, di notte; to make a — of it, fare nottata. —cap n. berretta da notte; bevanda che si beve prima di coricarsi; ultima gara di una giornata sportiva. —dress, —gown n. camicia da notte. —fall n. crepuscolo, imbrunire, calar della notte.

nightingale (nīt'ǐn.gāl) n. usignolo.

nightly (nīt'lǐ) agg. notturno. avv. nottetempo; tutte le notti.

nightmare (nīt'mâr') n. incubo.

nihilism (nī'ǐ.lǐz'm) n. nichilismo.

nihilist n. nichilista.

nimble (nǐm'b'l) agg. agile, lesto, leggiero. —ness n. agilità, sveltezza.

nincompoop (nǐn'kǒm.pōōp) n. stupido, sciocco.

nine (nīn) n., agg. nove. —pins n. birilli. —teen n., agg. diciannove. —teenth n., agg. diciannovesimo. —tieth n., agg. novantesimo. —ty n., agg. novanta.

ninth (ninth) n., agg. nono.

nip (nǐp) n. pizzicotto, presa; morso; frizzo. vt., vi. pizzicare; mordere; strappare; frustrare; gelare; arraffare: to — away, svignarsela: to — in the bud, distruggere in germe.

—pers *n.pl.* pinza; tanaglie; manette.

nipple (nĭp′′l) *n.* capezzolo.

nit (nĭt) *n.* lendine.

nitrate (nī′trāt) *n.* (*chim.*) nitrato.

nitwit (nĭt′wĭt′) *n.* sciocco.

nix (nĭks) *n.* (*gergo*) niente. *avv.* no.

no (nō) *n.* no, negazione, voto contrario. *agg.* nessuno, non: have you — friends? non avete amici?; — doubt, senza dubbio; — one, nessuno; — matter, non importa; — matter how much I love you, per quanto io ti ami; I am — musician, non sono musicista; — smoking, vietato fumare; by — means, niente affatto; of — use, inutile. *avv.* no, no: — less, nientemeno; — more, non più; — longer, non più, non oltre.

nobility (nō-bĭl′l-tĭ) *n.* nobilità.

noble (nō′b′l) *n.*, *agg.* nobile —ness *n.* nobilità.

nobody (nō′bŏd.ĭ) *n.* nessuno: — else, nessun altro; to be —, essere un illustre sconosciuto.

nocturne (nŏk′tûrn) *n.* (*mus.*) notturno.

nod (nŏd) *n.* cenno del capo, cenno d'assenso; dondolio; pisolino. *vi.* fare un cenno col capo, assentire; assopirsi.

noddle (nŏd′′l) *n.* (*fam.*) testa.

node (nōd) *n.* nodo; nodulo.

nohow (nō′hou′) *avv.* (*gergo*) in nessun modo, niente affatto.

noise (noiz) *n.* rumore, chiasso. *vt.* divulgare, strombazzare: it is noised that, corre voce che. —less *agg.* silenzioso.

noisily (noiz′ĭ.lĭ) *avv.* rumorosamente.

noisome (noi′sŭm) *agg.* molesto, nocivo; puzzolente; disgustoso.

noisy (noiz′ĭ) *agg.* rumoroso, chiassoso.

nominal (nŏm′ĭ.năl) *agg.* nominale.

nominate (nŏm′ĭ.nāt) *vt.* nominare, designare.

nomination (nŏm′ĭ.nā′shŭn) *n.* nomina, designazione; designazione di un candidato.

nonagenarian (nŏn′á.jĕ.nâr′ĭ.ăn) *n.*, *agg.* novantenne.

nonce (nŏns) *n.* occasione presente, momento attuale: for the —, per il momento.

nonchalance (nŏn′shá.lăns) *n.* disinvoltura, indifferenza.

nonchalant (nŏn′shá.lănt) *agg.* disinvolto, indifferente.

noncommissioned officer (nŏn′kŏ-mĭsh′ŭnd) *n.* sottufficiale.

noncommittal (nŏn′kŏ-mĭt′ăl) *agg.* evasivo, vago, generico.

nondescript (nŏn′dĕ.skrĭpt) *agg.* indefinibile, indefinito, scialbo, insignificante.

none (nŭn) *pron.*, *agg.* nessuno, nessuna, niente: I have —, non ne ho; — of that, niente di tutto ciò; that is — of your business, non sono affari tuoi; to be — the happier for that, non essere cosa che renda più felice; — the less, nondimeno; — but, nessuno all'infuori di, soltanto. *avv.* nientaffatto, in nessun modo, tutt'altro che.

nonentity (nŏn-ĕn′tĭ-tĭ) *n.* inesistenza, nullità, fattore ipotetico.

nonplus (nŏn′plŭs) *vt.* disorientare, sbalordire.

nonsense (nŏn′sĕns) *n.* sciocchezza, assurdità.

nonsensical (nŏn-sĕn′sĭ-kăl) *agg.* assurdo, illogico, stupido.

noodles (nōō′d′lz) *n.pl.* tagliatelle all'uovo.

nook (nōōk) *n.* angolo, recesso.

noon (nōōn) *n.* mezzogiorno. —day *n.* mezzogiorno. *agg.* meridiano. —tide, —time *n.* mezzogiorno.

noose (nōōs) *n.* nodo scorsoio, cappio; tranello. *vt.* annodare a scorsoio; prendere al laccio.

nor (nôr) *cong.* nè, nemmeno: neither I — he, nè io nè lui.

norm (nôrm) *n.* norma.

normal (nôr′măl) *agg.* normale; perpendicolare. —cy *n.* normalità.

north (nôrth) *n.* nord. *agg.* del nord: — pole, polo nord; — American, nordamericano. *avv.* al nord. —east *n.* nord-est. —ern *agg.* settentrionale: northern lights, aurora boreale. —erner *n.* settentrionale. —ward *avv.* verso nord. —west *n.* nord-ovest.

Norwegian (nôr-wē′jăn) *n.*, *agg.* norvegese.

nose (nōz) *n.* naso, muso; fiuto; prua: — dive (*aeron.*) picchiata, tuffo. *vt.*, *vi.* fiutare; sporgere il naso o il muso; avanzarsi; insinuarsi; curiosare.

nosegay (nōz′gā′) *n.* mazzo di fiori.

nosewheel (nōz′hwēl′) *n.* (*aeron.*) ruota di prua (*del carrello triciclo*).

nosey (nōz′ĭ) *agg.* indiscreto, ficcanaso.

nostril (nŏs′trĭl) *n.* narice.

nosy (nōz′ĭ) *agg.* indiscreto.

not (nŏt) *avv.* non, no: — at all, niente affatto; non c'è di che (*risposta a* "thank you"); — even, neppure.

notable (nō′tá.b′l) *agg.* notevole.

notary (nō′tá.rĭ) *n.* notaio.

notation (nō-tā′shŭn) *n.* notazione.

notch (nŏch) *n.* tacca, intaccatura; gola (*di montagna*); grado. *vt.* intaccare.

note (nōt) *n.* nota, biglietto; punto, appunto; importanza: **bank —,** banconota; **— of exclamation,** punto esclamativo. *vt.* notare; annotare; denotare. **—book** *n.* taccuino, registro.

noted (nōt'ĕd) *n.* noto, cospicuo, famoso.

noteworthy (nōt'wûr'thĭ) *agg.* notevole, degno di nota.

nothing (nŭth'ĭng) *n.* niente, nulla; **next to —,** quasi niente; **to come to —,** finire in niente. *avv.* niente affatto, per nulla.

notice (nō'tĭs) *n.* notizia; notifica, disdetta; attenzione; avviso, preavviso; trafiletto; istruzione: **at short —,** a breve scadenza; **— to quit,** sfratto; **to come into —,** farsi conoscere; **to take — of,** fare caso a, badare a. *vt.* osservare; prendere nota di, badare a, notificare. **—able** *agg.* percettibile, notevole.

notify (nō'tĭ.fī) *vt.* notificare, avvertire, annunciare.

notion (nō'shŭn) *n.* nozione, idea, intenzione; (*S.U.*) aggeggio: **notions,** minuterie.

notorious (nō.tō'rĭ.ŭs) *agg.* notorio, famigerato.

notwithstanding (nŏt'wĭth.stăn'dĭng) *prep., cong., avv.* nonostante, sebbene, quantunque, benché, tuttavia.

nought (nôt) *vedi* **naught.**

noun (noun) *n.* nome, sostantivo.

nourish (nûr'ĭsh) *vt.* nutrire, alimentare. **—ing** *agg.* nutriente. **—ment** *n.* nutrimento, alimento.

novel (nŏv'ĕl) *n.* romanzo; racconto. *agg.* nuovo, novello. **—ette** *n.* romanzo breve. **—ist** *n.* romanziere.

novelty (nŏv'l.tĭ) *n.* novità.

November (nō.vĕm'bēr) *n.* novembre.

novice (nŏv'ĭs) *n.* novizio, principiante, novellino.

now (nou) *avv.* ora, attualmente; allora; ebbene, dunque. *cong.* ora che, poiché, dal momento che: **— and then,** di tanto in tanto; **from — on,** d'ora in poi; **by —,** ormai, a quest'ora; **just —,** or ora, poco fa.

nowadays (nou'á.dāz') *avv.* oggigiorno.

nowhere (nō'hwâr) *avv.* in nessun luogo: **to get —,** fare un buco nell'acqua, fallire.

nowise (nō'wīz) *avv.* in nessun modo.

noxious (nŏk'shŭs) *agg.* nocivo.

nozzle (nŏz''l) *n.* becco, boccaglio, ugello, iniettore; filiera.

nth (ĕnth) *agg.* ennesimo.

nuance (nû-äns') *n.* sfumatura.

nuclear (nū'klē.ēr) *agg.* nucleare.

nucleus (nū'klē.ŭs) *n.* nucleo.

nude (nūd) *n., agg.* nudo.

nudge (nŭj) *n.* gomitatina. *vt.* dare di gomito, toccare col gomito.

nugatory (nū'gá.tō'rĭ) *agg.* trascurabile, insignificante; vano, inefficace.

nugget (nŭg'ĕt) *n.* pepita.

nuisance (nū'sǎns) *n.* noia; molestia, seccatura; danno; seccatore.

null (nŭl) *agg.* nullo, non valido.

numb (nŭm) *agg.* torpido, tramortito: **to become —,** intorpidirsi. *vt.* intorpidire, tramortire.

number (nŭm'bēr) *n.* numero, cifra; compagine, complesso (*di persone, ecc.*); persona; articolo di vendita: **odd —,** numero dispari; **even —,** numero pari; **a — of people,** un certo numero di persone *o* molte persone; **times without —,** innumerevoli volte; **—s pool,** lotteria clandestina. *vt.* contare, numerare, annoverare. **—less** *agg.* innumerevole.

numbness (nŭm'nĕs) *n.* intorpidimento, torpore, tramortimento.

numeral (nū'mēr.ǎl) *n., agg.* numerale.

numerical (nû.mēr'ĭ.kǎl) *agg.* numerico.

numerous (nū'mēr.ŭs) *agg.* numeroso.

numskull (nŭm'skŭl') *n.* stupido.

nun (nŭn) *n.* monaca, suora.

nuncio (nŭn'shĭ.ō) *n.* nunzio, delegato apostolico.

nunnery (nŭn'ēr.ĭ) *n.* monastero.

nuptial (nŭp'shǎl) *agg.* nuziale. *n.pl.* nozze.

nurse (nûrs) *n.* nutrice, bambinaia; istitutrice; infermiera. *vt.* nutrire, allattare; allevare, curare, coltivare; covare (*rancori, ecc.*). **—maid** *n.* bambinaia.

nursery (nûr'sēr.ĭ) *n.* stanza dei bambini; (*bot.*) vivaio: **— school,** asilo infantile. **—man** *n.* coltivatore.

nursing home *n.* convalescenziario.

nurture (nûr'tūr) *n.* allevamento; nutrimento; educazione. *vt.* nutrire; educare; allevare.

nut (nŭt) *n.* noce, mandorla, nocciuola, seme; (*mecc.*) dado; (*fig.*) problema, situazione difficile; (*gergo*) testa, sciocco: **a hard — to crack,** un osso duro da rodere; **to be nuts about** (*gergo*), avere il pallino di; **nuts!** frottole!; sciocchezze.

nutcracker (nŭt'krăk'ēr) *n.* schiaccianoci; (*ornit.*) nucifraga.

nutmeg (nŭt'mĕg) *n.* noce moscata.

nutrition (nū.trĭsh'ŭn) *n.* nutrizione; nutrimento.

nutritious (nū-trĭsh'ŭs) *agg.* nutriente.
nutshell (nŭt'shĕl) *n.* guscio di noce: in a —, in poche parole.
nutty (nŭt'ĭ) *agg.* che abbonda di

noci; che ha sapore di noce; (*gergo*) pazzo; entusiasta.
nylon (nī'lon) *n.* nylon, nailon.
nymph (nĭmf) *n.* ninfa; crisalide.

O

oaf (ōf) *n.* scemo, stupido.
oak (ōk) *n.* quercia. —en *agg.* di quercia.
oakum (ō'kŭm) *n.* stoppa.   [cia.
oar (ōr) *n.* remo. *vt.*, *vi.* remare. —lock *n.* scalmiera.
oasis (ō.ā'sĭs) *n.* (*pl.* oases [ō.ā'sēz]) oasi.
oat (ōt) *n.* (*gen.pl.*) avena: to sow one's wild —s, darsi alla pazza gioia, correre la cavallina.
oath (ōth) *n.* giuramento; bestemmia.
obdurate (ŏb'dū.rāt) *agg.* impenitente, ostinato.
obedience (ō.bē'dĭ.ĕns) *n.* ubbidienza.
obedient (ō.bē'dĭ.ĕnt) *agg.* ubbidiente.
obeisance (ō.bā'sǎns) *n.* riverenza; ossequio.
obese (ō.bēs') *agg.* obeso.
obesity (ō.bēs'ĭ.tĭ) *n.* obesità.
obey (ō.bā') *vt.*, *vi.* ubbidire.
obituary (ō.bĭt'ū.ĕr'ĭ) *n.* necrologio, necrologia.
object (ŏb.'jĕkt) *n.* oggetto, scopo; (*gramm*). complemento oggetto. *vt.*, *vi.* (ŏb.jeckt') obiettare, opporsi, esser contrario.
objection (ŏb.jĕk'shŭn) *n* obiezione, contrarietà, disapprovazione.
objective (ŏb.jĕk'tĭv) *n.* oblettivo, scopo, mira. *agg.* oggettivo, oblettivo.
obligate (ŏb'lĭ.gāt) *vt.* obbligare.
obligation (ŏb'lĭ.gā'shŭn) *n.* obbligo, impegno, debito: to be under — to, avere un obbligo con.
obligatory (ŏb.lĭg'ā.tō'rĭ) *agg.* obbligatorio.
oblige (ō.blĭj') *vt.* obbligare, fare un piacere a, favorire: much obliged! mille grazie!, obbligatissimo!
obliging (ō.blĭj'ĭng) *agg.* complacente, gentile, cortese.
oblique (ŏb.lēk') *agg.* obliquo, tortuoso.
obliterate (ŏb.lĭt'ĕr.āt) *vt.* cancellare, distruggere.
oblivion (ŏb.lĭv'ĭ.ŭn) *n.* oblio: act of —, amnistia.
oblivious (ŏb.lĭv'ĭ.ŭs) *agg.* dimentico, ignaro.
oblong (ŏb'lŏng) *agg.* oblungo.
obnoxious (ŏb.nŏk'shŭs) *agg.* nocivo, molesto; odioso.
obscene (ŏb.sēn') *agg.* osceno, abominevole.
obscenity (ŏb.sĕn'ĭ.tĭ) *n.* oscenità.

obscure (ŏb.skūr') *agg.* oscuro. *vt.* oscurare, offuscare.
obscurity (ŏb.skū'rĭ.tĭ) *n.* oscurità.
obsequies (ŏb'sē.kwĭz) *n.* esequie.
obsequious (ŏb.sē'kwĭ.ŭs) *agg.* ossequioso.
observance (ŏb.zûr'vǎns) *n.* osservanza, rispetto; rito.
observant (ŏb.zûr'vǎnt) *n.* osservante, ligio; osservatore.
observation (ŏb'zēr.vā'shŭn) *n.* osservazione.
observatory (ŏb.zûr'vā.tō'rĭ) *n.* osservatorio.
observe (ŏb.zûrv') *vt.*, *vi.* osservare.
observer (ŏb.zûr'vēr) *n.* osservatore.
obsess (ŏb.sĕs') *vt.* ossessionare.
obsession (ŏb.sĕsh'ŭn) *n.* ossessione.
obsolete (ŏb'sō.lēt) *agg.* antiquato, in disuso.
obstacle (ŏb'stā.k'l) *n.* ostacolo.
obstetrics (ŏb.stĕt'rĭks) *n.* ostetricia.
obstinacy (ŏb'stĭ.nā.sĭ) *n.* ostinazione.
obstinate (ŏb'stĭ.nĭt) *agg.* ostinato.
obstruct (ŏb.strŭkt') *vt.* ostruire, ostacolare. —ion *n.* ostruzione, impedimento. —ionism *n.* ostruzionismo.
obtain (ŏb.tān') *vt.* ottenere, ricavare, procurarsi. *vi.* prevalere. —able *agg.* ottenibile.
obtuse (ŏb.tūs') *agg.* ottuso.
obviate (ŏb'vĭ.āt) *vt.* ovviare a.
obvious (ŏb'vĭ.ŭs) *agg.* ovvio, evidente.
occasion (ō.kā'zhŭn) *n.* occasione, caso; causa. *vt.* dar luogo a, causare. —ally *avv.* occasionalmente, sporadicamente, di quando in quando, a volte.
occident (ŏk'sĭ.dĕnt) *n.* occidente. —al *agg.*, *n.* occidentale.
occiput (ŏk'sĭ.pŭt) *n.* occipite.
occupant (ŏk'ŭ.pǎnt) *n.* occupante.
occupation (ŏk'ŭ.pā'shŭn) *n.* occupazione.
occupy (ŏk'ŭ.pī) *vt.* occupare, impiegare, usare.
occur (ō.kûr') *vi.* accadere; venire in mente. —rence *n.* contingenza, avvenimento.
ocean (ō'shŭn) *n.* oceano.
ochre (ō'kēr) *n.* ocra.
octane (ŏk'tān) *n.* (*chim.*) ottano.
October (ŏk.tō'bēr) *n.* ottobre.
octopus (ŏk'tō.pŭs) *n.* piovra.
ocular (ŏk'ū.lēr) *agg.* oculare.

oculist (ŏk'ū.lĭst) *n.* oculista.

odd (ŏd) *agg.* strano, singolare, bislacco; eccentrico; dispari; scompagnato; residuo; sporadico, avventizio: — **shoe,** scarpa scompagnata; — **man,** lavoratore avventizio; **at** — **moments,** a tempo perso; **ten** — **dollars,** dieci dollari e rotti. —**ity** *n.* stranezza. —**ly** *avv.* stranamente.

odds (ŏdz) *n.pl.* vantaggio concesso al più debole (*in una competizione*); disparità, differenza; probabilità; disputa: — **and ends,** cianfrusaglie; **at** —, in contrasto; **the** — **are against me,** la sorte mi è sfavorevole, non ho probabilità di vincere.

ode (ōd) *n.* ode.

odious (ō'dĭ.ŭs) *agg.* odioso.

odorous (ō'dēr.ŭs) *agg.* odoroso, fragrante.

odor (ō'dēr) *n.* odore; profumo. —**less** *agg.* inodoro.

oedipal (ĕd'ĭ.pǎl) *agg.* edipico.

o'er (ōr) *contraz. di* over.

of (ŏv) *prep.* di, del, della; a; in; da; per: **very kind** — **you,** molto gentile da parte vostra; — **late,** ultimamente; — **course,** naturalmente; **a quarter** — **five,** le cinque meno un quarto; **as** — **today,** a partire da oggi.

off (ŏf) *agg.* remoto, il più lontano; laterale, esterno; libero; destro (*di destra*): — **day,** giorno di libertà; — **side,** parte più lontana; **to have one's hat** —, essere a capo scoperto; **the electricity is** —, l'elettricità è interrotta; **to be** — **to war,** essere alla guerra. *avv.* via, fuori, a distanza, lontano; (*naut.*) al largo: **to go** —, spegnersi; **to be well** —, essere ricco; **to put** —, rimandare; **to take a day** —, prendersi un giorno di vacanza; **ten miles** —, a una distanza di dieci miglia; — **and on,** sporadicamente. *prep.* da; fuori di; giù da; davanti a; (*naut.*) al largo di.

offal (ŏf'ǎl) *n.* rifiuti.

offbeat (ŏf'bēt') *agg.* eterodosso, strano, originale.

offence *vedi* offense.

offend (ŏ.fĕnd') *vt.*, *vi.* offendere, molestare, displacere; violare; peccare. —**er** *n.* offensore, contravventore, peccatore, colpevole.

offense (ŏ.fĕns') *n.* offesa, oltraggio; colpa, reato.

offensive (ŏ.fĕn'sĭv) *n.* offensiva. *agg.* offensivo, sgradevole; aggressivo; criminoso.

offer (ŏf'ēr) *n.* offerta, proposta. *vt.* offrire, proporre, presentare: **to** —

violence, aggredire. *vi.* offrirsi, presentarsi. —**ing** *n.* offerta, sacrificio.

offhand (ŏf'hǎnd') *avv.* sul momento, impensatamente, senza indugio, estemporaneamente. *agg.* (*anche* —**ed**) impensato, improvviso, improvvisato, estemporaneo.

office (ŏf'ĭs) *n.* ufficio; filiale, sede; mansione, carica, funzione; ministero: — **building,** palazzo commerciale; — **post** —, ufficio postale; **our Rome** —, la nostra filiale (*o* sede) di Roma.

officer (ŏf'ĭ.sēr) *n.* ufficiale; poliziotto; funzionario. *vt.* fornire di ufficiali; comandare.

official (ŏ.fĭsh'ăl) *n.* funzionario. *agg.* ufficiale.

officiate (ŏ.fĭsh'ĭ.āt) *vi.* officiare.

officious (ŏ.fĭsh'ŭs) *agg.* ufficioso; inframmettente, importuno.

offing (ŏf'ĭng) *n.* (*naut.*) largo: **in the** —, poco distante, all'orizzonte, probabile, imminente.

offset (ŏf'sĕt') *n.* partenza; compensazione; germoglio; collaterale; deviazione; sperone (*di monte*); (*tip.*) controstampa, fotolito. *vt.* compensare, bilanciare. *vi.* sporgere; germogliare.

offspring (ŏf'sprĭng') *n.* risultato, conseguenza; progenie.

oft (ŏft) *vedi* often.

often (ŏf'ĕn) *avv.* spesso, frequentemente, in molti casi: **how** —? quante volte?

ogle (ō'g'l) *vt.*, *vi.* adocchiare; fare l'occhio di triglia.

ogre (ō'gēr) *n.* orco.

oil (oil) *n.* olio; petrolio: — **field,** giacimento *o* campo petrolifero; — **painting,** pittura a olio, dipinto a olio. — **well,** pozzo petrolifero. *vt.* oliare, lubrificare.

oilcloth *n.* tela incerata.

oilskin *n.* tela impermeabile; indumento di tela impermeabile.

oily (oil'ĭ) *n.* oleoso.

ointment (oint'mĕnt) *n.* unguento.

O.K., okay (ō'kā') *n.* approvazione, benestare. *avv.* bene, benissimo: **it's** —, sta bene. *vt.* approvare, sanzionare.

old (ōld) *agg.* vecchio; antiquato; usato: — **maid,** zitella; (*scherz.*) zitello; **one's** — **man,** il padre, il marito, il principale, il preside (*di una scuola*), il capitano (*di una nave*); **of** —, anticamente, una volta; **how** — **are you?** quanti anni avete? **I am twenty years** —, ho venti anni; **to be** — **enough to,**

essere in età di; **to be an — hand
at,** essere esperto in *o* di. **— age**
vecchiaia. **—clothesman** *n.* rigattiere. **—en** *agg.* antico. **—er** *agg.*
più vecchio, più anziano. **—est**
agg. il più vecchio. **—fashioned**
agg. antiquato; *n.* cocktail a base
di rye whisky e angostura. **—time**
agg. antico, vetusto, passato.
—timer *n.* veterano; persona al-
l'antica.

olive (ŏl'ĭv) *n.* ulivo, oliva: **— grove,**
oliveto; **— oil,** olio d'oliva; **— tree,**
olivo. *agg.* verde oliva.

omelette (ŏm'ĕ·lĕt) *n.* frittata.

omen (ō'mĕn) *n.* augurio, presagio.

ominous (ŏm'ĭ·nŭs) *agg.* sinistro, di
malaugurio, minaccioso.

omission (ō·mĭsh'ŭn) *n.* omissione.

omit (ō·mĭt') *vt.* omettere.

omnipotence (ŏm·nĭp'ō·tĕns) *n.* onnipotenza.

omnipotent (ŏm·nĭp'ō·tĕnt) *agg.* onnipotente.

on (ŏn) *prep.* su, sopra; in; vicino a;
verso; dopo, da: **— arriving,** al-
l'arrivo; **—board,** a bordo, sul treno;
— condition that, a patto che;
— credit, a credito; **— foot,** a piedi;
— horseback, a cavallo, in groppa;
— Monday, il lunedì; **— purpose,**
apposta; **— sale,** in vendita; **—
time,** a tempo, puntualmente. *avv.*
su, sopra; indosso; avanti: **and so
—,** e così via; **later —,** più tardi,
in seguito; **off and —,** saltuariamente. *agg.* in corso, in azione:
the light is —, la luce è accesa; **to
have one's hat —,** avere il cappello in testa.

once (wŭns) *n., avv.* una volta, un
tempo: **all at —,** tutt'a un tratto;
just this —, solo per questa volta;
— and for all, una volta per tutte;
in a while, di tanto in tanto; **—
upon a time,** una volta (*anticamente*); *cong.* una volta che, non
appena.

oncoming (ŏn'kŭm'ĭng) *n.* l'avvicinarsi. *agg.* che si avvicina, prossimo; audace; promettente.

one (wŭn) *n., agg.* uno, una, uno solo;
un certo: **— hundred,** cento; **—
thousand,** mille; **my — chance,** la
mia unica occasione; **his — and
only,** il suo solo e unico; **— John
Miller,** un certo J.M. *pron. indef.*
uno, uno solo; colui; quello; si
(*impers.*): **the blue pencil and the
red —,** la matita blu e quella
rossa; **the — who,** quello *o* colui che,
quella *o* colei che; **— another,** l'un
l'altro; **no —,** nessuno; **— by —,** a
uno a uno; **every—,** ciascuno;

this —, questo; **that —,** quello; **the
beloved —,** l'essere amato. **—
armed** *agg.* monco; **—eyed** *agg.*
guercio.

onerous (ŏn'ĕr·ŭs) *agg.* oneroso.

oneself (wŭn·sĕlf') *pron.rifl.* se stesso,
si: **by —,** da solo; **to wash —,** lavarsi; **to speak to —,** parlare tra sè,
ragionare con se stesso.

one-sided (wŭn'sĭd'ĕd) *agg.* avente un
solo lato, unilaterale; parziale.

onion (ŭn'yŭn) *n.* (*bot.*) cipolla.

onlooker (ŏn'lŏŏk'ĕr) *n.* spettatore.

only (ŏn'lĭ) *agg.* unico, solo. *avv.* solamente, unicamente. *cong.* solo che.

onrush (ŏn'rŭsh') *n.* impeto, assalto.

onset (ŏn'sĕt') *n.* attacco, assalto;
esordio.

onslaught (ŏn'slôt') *n.* aggressione,
assalto impetuoso.

onto (ŏn'tŏŏ) *prep.* in cima a, sopra,
su.

onward (ŏn'wĕrd) *agg.* avanzato,
avanzante. *avv.* avanti, in avanti.

ooze (ōŏz) *vi.* filtrare, fluire, colare;
trapelare.

opal (ō'pǎl) *n.* (*min.*) opale.

opaque (ō·pāk') *agg.* opaco.

open (ō'pĕn) *n.* luogo (*campo, mare*)
aperto, aria aperta. *agg.* aperto;
scoperto, libero; accessibile; manifesto; esposto (*a*): **— country,**
aperta campagna; **— library,** biblioteca aperta a tutti; **— question,**
argomento non ancora risoluto;
— teeth, denti radi; **— town** (*mil.*)
città aperta; (*S.U.*) città senza re-
strizioni sugli alcolici; **— to temptation,** esposto alle tentazioni;
— winter, inverno mite; **wide —,**
spalancato. *vt.* aprire; inaugurare,
iniziare. *vi.* aprirsi; esordire; confidarsi: **to — into,** dare in, affacciarsi in; **to — one's heart,** confidarsi; **to — out,** dischiudere, svelare; svolgere; allargare (*un foro*);
to — up, dischiudere, aprire, scoprire, svelare; presentarsi; parlare
apertamente. **—handed** *agg.* generoso. **—hearted** *agg.* buono, franco, spontaneo. **—minded** *agg.* di
larghe vedute. **—mouthed** *agg.* a
bocca aperta.

opening (ō'pĕn·ĭng) *n.* apertura; esordio, inaugurazione; radura; occasione; *agg.* primo, iniziale: **— night,**
serata d'inaugurazione, prima.

openly (ō'pĕn·lĭ) *avv.* apertamente.

opera (ŏp'ĕr·à) *n.* opera: **— glass,**
binocolo da teatro; **— house,** teatro dell'opera; **horse —,** film
western; **soap —** (*radio e T.V.*) programma diurno di commedie a
puntate dedicato alle massaie.

operate (ŏp′ẽr.ăt) *vt.*, *vi.* agire, operare, funzionare, manovrare, compiere.

operatic (ŏp′ẽr.ăt′ĭk) *agg.* d'opera, lirico.

operation (ŏp′ẽr.ā′shŭn) *n.* operazione, manipolazione, azione; funzionamento. —al *agg.* di lavoro, operativo; (*mil.*) da combattimento, strategico.

operative (ŏp′ẽr.ā′tĭv) *n.* agente; mezzo; operaio; artigiano; investigatore. *agg.* operativo, operante; efficace; operatorio; attivo.

operator (ŏp′ẽr.ā′tẽr) *n.* operatore; manovratore; speculatore: telegraph —, telegrafista; telephone —, centralinista.

opiate (ō′pĭ.ĭt) *n.* narcotico.

opinion (ō.pĭn′yŭn) *n.* opinione, parere: — poll, referendum. —ated *agg.* testardo; presuntuoso.

opium (ō′pĭ.ŭm) *n.* oppio.

opponent (ō.pō′nĕnt) *n.* oppositore, avversario.

opportune (ŏp′ŏr.tūn′) *agg.* opportuno.

opportunity (ŏp′ŏr.tū′nĭ.tĭ) *n.* occasione.

oppose (ō.pōz′) *vt.* avversare; opporre; combattere.

opposite (ŏp′ō.zĭt) *n.* (l′) opposto, (il) contrario. *agg.* opposto, contrario, dirimpetto. *prep.* di fronte a.

opposition (ŏp′ō.zĭsh′ŭn) *n.* opposizione, resistenza, ostacolo.

oppress (ō.prĕs′) *vt.* opprimere. —ion (-shŭn) *n.* oppressione. —ive *agg.* opprimente. —or *n.* oppressore.

opprobrious (ō.prō′brĭ.ŭs) *agg.* obbrobrioso.

opprobrium (ō.prō′brĭ.ŭm) *n.* obbrobrio.

optical (ŏp′tĭ.kăl) *agg.* ottico.

optician (ŏp.tĭsh′ăn) *n.* ottico.

optics (ŏp′tĭks) *n.* ottica.

optimism (ŏp′tĭ.mĭz′m) *n.* ottimismo.

optimist (ŏp′tĭ.mĭst) *agg.* ottimista. —ic *agg.* ottimistico.

option (ŏp′shŭn) *n.* opzione, scelta, preferenza. —al *agg.* facoltativo.

opulence (ŏp′ū.lĕns) *n.* opulenza.

opulent (ŏp′ū.lĕnt) *agg.* opulento.

or (ôr) *cong.* o, oppure: either this — that, o questo o quello; — else, altrimenti.

oracle (ŏr′ȧ.k′l) *n.* oracolo, profezia.

oral (ō′răl) *agg.* orale.

orange (ŏr′ĕnj) *n.* arancia: — grove, aranceto; — tree, arancio; — blossom, fiore d'arancio. *agg.* arancio, arancione; d'arancia. —ade *n.* aranciata.

oration (ō.rā′shŭn) *n.* discorso, orazione.

orator (ŏr′ȧ.tẽr) *n.* oratore.

oratory (ŏr′ȧ.tō′rĭ) *n.* oratoria; oratorio (*cappella*).

orb (ôrb) *n.* orbe, sfera, orbita.

orbit (ôr′bĭt) *n.* orbita.

orchard (ôr′chẽrd) *n.* frutteto.

orchestra (ôr′kĕs.trȧ) *n.* orchestra.

orchid (ôr′kĭd) *n.* (*bot.*) orchidea.

ordain (ôr.dān′) *vt.* ordinare (*conferire gli ordini*); decretare, designare.

ordeal (ôr.dēl′) *n.* prova, cimento.

order (ôr′dẽr) *n.* ordine, decreto: in — that, affinchè; in — to, per, allo scopo di; out of —, in cattivo stato, guasto (*di meccanismo*); made to —, fatto su commissione o su misura. *vt.*, *vi.* ordinare; ingiungere, comandare: to — away, scacciare, espellere. —liness *n.* ordine, metodicità, regolarità.

orderly (ôr′dẽr.lĭ) *n.* ordinanza, attendente (*soldato*); inserviente (*di ospedale*). *agg.* ordinato, metodico.

ordinance (ôr′dĭ.năns) *n.* ordinanza (*decreto*).

ordinarily (ôr′dĭ.nẽr′ĭ.lĭ) *avv.* ordinariamente, generalmente.

ordinary (ôr′dĭ.nẽr′ĭ) *n.* normalità; locanda; pasto a prezzo fisso; magistrato. *agg.* ordinario, comune, usuale.

ordnance (ôrd′năns) *n.* artiglieria.

ordure (ôr′dūr) *n.* sterco; luridume.

ore (ōr) *n.* minerale metallico.

organ (ôr′găn) *n.* organo: hand —, organetto.

organic (ôr.găn′ĭk) *agg.* organico.

organism (ôr′găn.ĭz′m) *n.* organismo.

organist (ôr′găn.ĭst) *n.* organista.

organization (ôr′găn.ĭ.zā′shŭn) *n.* organizzazione.

organize (ôr′găn.īz) *vt.* organizzare. *vi.* organizzarsi.

organizer (ôr′găn.īz′ẽr) *n.* organizzatore.

orgy (ôr′jĭ) *n.* orgia.

orient (ō′rĭ.ĕnt) *n.* oriente, levante. *agg.* orientale, sorgente; fulgido. *vt.* volgere a oriente, orientare, orientarsi. —al (-ĕn′-) *n.*, *agg.* orientale.

orifice (ŏr′ĭ.fĭs) *n.* orifizio, apertura.

origin (ŏr′ĭ.jĭn) *n.* origine. —al (ō.rĭj′ĭ.năl) *agg.* originale, originario. —ality (-ăl′ĭ.tĭ) *n.* originalità. —ally (-rĭj′-) *avv.* originariamente, originalmente.

originate (ō.rĭj′ĭ.nāt) *vt.* originare, provocare. *vi.* derivare, provenire.

oriole (ō′rĭ.ōl) *n.* (*ornit.*) rigogolo.

ornament (ôr′nȧ.mĕnt) *n.* ornamento. *vt.* ornare. —al (-mĕnt′ăl) *agg.* ornamentale, decorativo.

ornate (ôr·nāt') *agg.* ornato, sontuoso; fiorito (*di stile*).

ornithology (ôr'nĭ·thŏl'ō·jĭ) *n.* ornitologia.

orphan (ôr'fǎn) *n.*, *agg.* orfano. *vt.* rendere orfano. —age *n.* orfanotrofio.

orthodox (ôr'thō·dŏks) *agg.* ortodosso.

orthography (ôr·thŏg'rá·fĭ) *n.* ortografia.

oscillate (ŏs'ĭ·lāt) *vi.* oscillare; vacillare.

osier (ō'zhẽr) *n.* vimine.

ostentation (ŏs'tĕn·tā'shŭn) *n.* ostentazione.

ostentatious (ŏs'tĕn·tā'shŭs) *agg.* ostentatore.

ostrich (ŏs'trĭch) *n.* struzzo.

other (ŭth'ẽr) *agg.* altro, differente, ulteriore: every — day, a giorni alterni. *pron.* l'altro: any —, qualsiasi altro; each —, l'un l'altro; some day or —, un giorno o l'altro; some — time, un'altra volta; gifts — than flowers, regali che non siano fiori; natures — than ours, caratteri diversi dai nostri.

otherwise *avv.* altrimenti, diversamente, del resto. *cong.* se no.

otter (ŏt'ẽr) *n.* (*zool.*) lontra.

ought (ôt) *vi.irr.ausil.difett.* (indica condiz. pres., pass.prossimo) dovevo, dovevi, doveva, dovevamo, *ecc.*; dovrei, dovresti, dovrebbe, dovremmo, *ecc.*: we — to go, dovremmo andare; I — to have known it, avrei dovuto saperlo.

ounce (ouns) *n.* oncia.

our (our) *agg.poss.* nostro, nostri, nostra, nostre.

ours (ourz) *pron.poss.* il nostro, la nostra, i nostri, le nostre: a friend of —, un nostro amico.

ourselves (our·sĕlvz') *pron.rifl.pl.* noi stessi, ci: we will do it —, lo faremo noi stessi; by —, da soli.

oust (oust) *vt.* espellere; espropriare.

out (out) *n.* sporgenza; uscita, scappatoia; disaccordo. *agg.* spento; esterno, lontano; escluso; assente; errato; uscito, divulgato; terminato, disusato, fuori moda; spossato: — and — refusal, no chiaro e tondo; before the week is —, prima che termini la settimana; the book is just —, il libro è appena uscito; the secret is —, si è svelato il segreto. *avv.* fuori, al di fuori, via; completamente, esplicitamente: — of humor di malumore; — of money, senza soldi; — of touch with, isolato da; — of tune, stonato; to have it — with, farla fuori con; to speak —, parlare apertamente; to get —,

uscire; to find —, scoprire, smascherare; to be put —, essere malcontento.

out of *prep.* fuori di; privo di, senza; per, a causa di: — breath, senza respiro; — work, disoccupato; — charity, per carità; — print, esaurito (*di pubblicazione*); — date, antiquato.

outbalance (out·bǎl'áns) *vt.* superare.

outboard (out'bōrd') *agg.*, *avv.* (*naut.*) fuoribordo: — motor, motore fuoribordo.

outbreak (out'brāk') *n.* esplosione, scoppio; insurrezione, tumulto; epidemia.

outburst (out'bûrst') *n.* esplosione, scoppio; slancio, accesso.

outcast (out'kȧst') *n.*, *agg.* proscritto, reietto, abbandonato.

outcome (out'kŭm') *n.* risultato; conseguenza.

outcry (out'krĭ') *n.* grido, clamore.

outdo (out'dōō') *vt.* (*pass.* outdid, *pp.* outdone) superare.

outdoor (out'dōr') *agg.* esterno, all'aperto.

outdoors (out'dōrz') *avv.* all'aperto, fuori.

outer (out'ẽr) *agg.* esterno, esteriore.

outfit (out'fĭt) *n.* corredo, equipaggiamento; gruppo, unità. *vt.*, *vi.* equipaggiare, equipaggiarsi.

outgo (out'gō') *n.* uscita; spesa, esborso; risultato; prodotto. *vt.* (*pass.* outwent, *pp.* outgone) superare, sopravanzare. —er *n.* chi se ne va, l'uscente. —ing *agg.* che si allontana, uscente, in partenza; che spunta, sporgente; estrovertito, esuberante, espansivo. *n.* fuoriscita; emanazione.

outgrowth (out'grōth') *n.* escrescenza.

outing (out'ĭng) *n.* passeggiata.

outlaw (out'lô') *n.* fuorilegge. *vt.* proscrivere, vietare, metter fuori legge, bandire.

outlay (out'lā') *n.* esborso.

outlet (out'lĕt) *n.* uscita, sbocco, sfogo, scarico.

outline (out'lĭn') *n.* contorno, profilo, abbozzo. *vt.* delineare, disegnare, abbozzare.

outlive (out·lĭv') *vt.* sopravvivere a.

outlook (out'lŏŏk')*n.* vedetta; prospettiva, visuale.

outlying (out'lĭ'ĭng) *agg.* periferico, esterno, distante.

outnumber (out·nŭm'bẽr) *vt.* superare in numero.

out-of-date *agg.* fuori di moda.

outpost (out'pōst') *n.* avamposto.

output (out'pŏŏt') *n.* produzione.

outrage (out'rāj) *n.* oltraggio, reato. *vt.* oltraggiare: to be —ed, sentirsi offeso; essere scandalizzato. — ous *agg.* oltraggioso; atroce; vergognoso, scandaloso.

outran (out·rǎn') *pass. di* to outrun.

outright (out'rīt') *agg.* completo; immediato, diretto. *avv.* immediatamente; completamente.

outrun (out·rǔn') *vt.* (*pass.* outran, *pp.* outrun) sorpassare, superare; battere in velocità.

outset (out'sět') *n.* inizio, partenza.

outshine (out·shīn') *vt.* (*pass., pp.* outshone) eclissare, superare in splendore.

outside (out'sīd') *n.* esterno, parte esterna, margine: at the —, tutt'al più. *agg.* esterno, esteriore; superficiale. *avv.* esternamente; superficialmente, fuori. *prep.* fuori di, all'infuori di, oltre a.

outsider (out'sīd'ẽr) *n.* estraneo, forestiero; cavallo (*ecc.*) non favorito.

outsize (out'sīz') *n.* misura anormale. *agg.* fuori misura, sproporzionato.

outskirts (out'skŭrts') *n.pl.* margini; dintorni; sobborghi, periferia.

outsmart (out·smärt') *vt.* battere in astuzia.

outspoken (out·spō'kěn) *agg.* chiaro, esplicito.

outstanding (out·stǎn'dǐng) *agg.* insoluto (*non pagato*); sporgente; eminente: — bills, conti o fatture da pagare.

outstretch (out'strech') *vt.* protendere, tendere, allungare; stendere, tirare. —ed *agg.* teso, steso, proteso: with — arms, a braccia aperte.

outstrip (out·strip') *vt.* superare, lasciarsi alle spalle; eccellere (*su*), superare.

outward (out'wěrd) *agg.* esterno, esteriore. *avv.* verso l'esterno, esternamente, esteriormente.

outweigh (out·wā') *vt.* superare in peso o importanza.

outwit (out·wit') *vt.* battere in astuzia, mettere nel sacco.

oval (ō'vǎl) *agg.* ovale.

ovation (ō·vā'shǔn) *n.* ovazione.

oven (ǔv'ěn) *n.* forno.

over· (ō'vẽr) *agg.* finito; superiore; esterno; eccessivo. *prep.* su, sopra, al di sopra di oltre a, di là da; dalla parte opposta di; più di; a causa di: — the river, oltre il fiume; all — the country, per tutta la regione. *avv.* al di là; da una parte all'altra; da cima a fondo; d'avanzo; dalla parte opposta; al di sopra; troppo, attraverso; tutto, completamente:

all —, dappertutto, completamente; all — again, daccapo, di bel nuovo; — there, laggiù; — and —, ripetutamente; — again, di nuovo; to walk —, avvicinarsi.

overact (ō'vẽr·ǎkt') *vt., vi.* recitare (*una parte*) caricatamente, strafare.

over·all *agg.* totale, globale.

overall (ō'vẽr·ôl') *n.* spolverina; càmice.

overalls (ō'vẽr·ôlz') *n.* tuta.

overawe (ō'vẽr·ô') *vt.* intimidire, incutere rispetto a.

overbalance (ō'vẽr·bǎl'ǎns) *vt.* superare (*in peso o importanza*); far perdere l'equilibrio a.

overbearing (ō'vẽr·bâr'ǐng) *agg.* tirannico, autoritario, prepotente.

overboard (ō'vẽr·bôrd') *avv.* (*naut.*) fuori bordo, in acqua: to go —, andare agli estremi; entusiasmarsi eccessivamente. *agg.* eccessivo.

overburden (ō'vẽr·bûr'd'n) *vt.* sovraccaricare.

overcast (ō'vẽr·kǎst') *agg.* nuvoloso, cupo. *vt.* oscurare; rannuvolarsi; cucire a sopraggitto.

overcame (ō'vẽr·kǎm') *pass. di* to overcome.

overcharge (ō'vẽr·chärj') *vt.* sovraccaricare; chiedere un prezzo eccessivo a.

overcoat (ō'vẽr·kōt') *n.* soprabito.

overcome (ō'vẽr·kǔm') *vt., vi.* (*pass.* overcame, *pp.* overcome) superare, sopraffare, vincere.

overcrowd (ō'vẽr·kroud') *vt.* affollare eccessivamente, stipare.

overdo (ō'vẽr·dōō') *vt., vi.* (*pass.* overdid, *pp.* overdone) esagerare, affaticare, cuocere troppo, strafare.

overdone (ō'vẽr·dǔn') *agg.* troppo cotto, esagerato.

overdose (ō'vẽr·dōs') *n.* dose eccessiva.

overdraft (ō'vẽr·drǎft') *n.* (*banca*) prelevamento in scoperto; (*mil.*) leva esorbitante.

overdraw (ō'vẽr·drô') *vt.* (*pass.* overdrew, *pp.* overdrawn) tracciare attraverso; esagerare; (*banca*) prelevare allo scoperto.

overdue (ō'vẽr·dū') *agg.* scaduto, in ritardo.

overeat (ō'vẽr·ēt') *vt., vi.* mangiare troppo, rimpinzarsi.

overestimate (ō'vẽr·ěs'tǐ·māt) *vt.* sopravvalutare.

overexposure (ō'vẽr·ěks·pō'zhěr) *n.* (*fot.*) sovresposizione.

overflow (ō'vẽr·flō') *n.* inondazione; sovrabbondanza, eccedenza. *vt., vi.* inondare, riempire troppo; traboccare, straripare, rigurgitare.

overgrown (ŏ′vĕr·grōn′) agg. coperto (di vegatazione); troppo cresciuto: — boy, ragazzone.

overhang (ŏ′vĕr·hăng′) vt., vi. (pass., pp. overhung) incombere; esser sospeso su; adornare; strapiombare, sovrastare.

overhaul (ŏ′vĕr·hôl′) vt. ispezionare; guadagnar terreno su, raggiungere; (naut.) mollare; (mecc.) revisionare.

overhead (ŏ′vĕr·hĕd′) n. spese generali. agg. superiore, di sopra, aereo. avv. in alto, sopra la testa.

overhear (ŏ′vĕr·hēr′) vt. (pass., pp. overheard) udire per caso, sorprendere (una conversazione).

overlade (ŏ′vĕr·lād′) vt. (pp. overladen) sovraccaricare.

overland (ŏ′vĕr·lănd′) agg. terrestre. avv. per via di terra.

overlap (ŏ′vĕr·lăp′) vt., vi. sovrapporre, sovrapporsi.

overload (ŏ′vĕr·lōd′) n. sovraccarico. vt. sovraccaricare.

overlook (ŏ′vĕr·look′) vt. guardare (dall'alto); esaminare; sovrintendere; esser prospiciente a; passar sopra a, perdonare; omettere, trascurare.

overly (ŏ′vĕr·li) avv. eccessivamente.

overmaster (ŏ′vĕr·mås′tĕr) vt. sopraffare, dominare.

overmuch (ŏ′vĕr·mŭch′) n. sovrappiù. agg. eccessivo. avv. eccessivamente.

overnight (ŏ′vĕr·nīt′) agg. notturno, di una notte: — stop, pernottamento; — bag, valigetta per viaggi brevi. avv. durante la notte; dalla sera alla mattina; la sera precedente.

overpay (ŏ′vĕr·pā′) vt. pagare troppo.

overpower (ŏ′vĕr·pou′ĕr) vt. sopraffare. —ing agg. irresistibile; eccessivo.

overproduction (ŏ′vĕr·prō·dŭk′shŭn) n. superproduzione.

overrate (ŏ′vĕr·rāt′) vt. valutare troppo.

overreach (ŏ′vĕr·rēch′) vt., vi. raggiungere; superare, sorpassare; ingannare; eccedere: to — oneself, passare i limiti.

override (ŏ′vĕr·rīd′) vt. (pass. overrode, pp. overridden) affaticare (un cavallo, ecc.); trascurare; annullare; vincere (un'opposizione), superare (ostacoli).

overripe (ŏ′vĕr·rīp′) agg. troppo maturo, arcimaturo.

overrule (ŏ′vĕr·rool′) vt., vi. vincere, avere il sopravvento; respingere, invalidare, bocciare.

overrun (ŏ′vĕr·rŭn′) vt., vi. (pass. overran, pp. overrun) invadere, dilagare, infestare; sorpassare, superare, travolgere; eccedere; (tip.) trasportare.

oversea (ŏ′vĕr·sē′) agg. d'oltremare.

overseas (ŏ′vĕr·sēz′) avv. oltremare.

oversee (ŏ′vĕr·sē′) vt. ispezionare; sovrintendere.

overseer (ŏ′vĕr·sē′ĕr) n. sovrintendente; capofabbrica; critico.

overshadow (ŏ′vĕr·shăd′ō) vt. offuscare.

overshoe (ŏ′vĕr·shoo′) n. soprascarpa.

oversight (ŏ′vĕr·sīt′) n. sovrintendenza; svista, omissione, errore.

oversize (ŏ′vĕr·sīz′) n. misura o mole eccessiva.

oversleep (ŏ′vĕr·slēp′) vt., vi. (pass., pp. overslept) dormire oltre un'ora fissata opp. oltre il consueto.

overspread (ŏ′vĕr·sprĕd′) vt., vi (pass., pp. overspread) spandere, cospargere, spandersi.

overstate (ŏ′vĕr·stāt′) vt. esagerare. —ment n. esagerazione.

overstep (ŏ′vĕr·stĕp′) vt. oltrepassare: to — the bounds, superare i limiti.

overstock (ŏ′vĕr·stŏk′) n. sovrabbondanza.

overstrain (ŏ′vĕr·strān′) n. sforzo eccessivo, tensione eccessiva. vt., vi. tendere o sforzarsi troppo.

overt (ŏ′vûrt) agg. aperto, pubblico.

overtake (ŏ′vĕr·tāk′) vt. (pass. overtook, pp. overtaken) raggiungere.

overtax (ŏ′vĕr·tăks′) vt. tassare eccessivamente; mettere a troppo dura prova: to — one's strength, chiedere troppo alle proprie forze.

overthrow (ŏ′vĕr·thrō′) n. sconvolgimento; disfatta. vt. (pass. overthrew, pp. overthrown) rovesciare, sconvolgere, sconfiggere.

overtime (ŏ′vĕr·tīm′) n. ore straordinarie (di lavoro), straordinario.

overturn (ŏ′vĕr·tûrn′) vt. rovesciare, capovolgere, sovvertire.

overweigh (ŏ′vĕr·wā′) vt. superare nel peso; sopraffare, opprimere.

overweight (ŏ′vĕr·wāt′) n. sovraccarico.

overwhelm (ŏ′vĕr·hwĕlm′) vt. opprimere, sopraffare. —ing agg. opprimente, irresistibile.

overwork (ŏ′vĕr·wûrk′) n. lavoro eccessivo. vt., vi. lavorare o far lavorare troppo; elaborare o adornare all'eccesso.

overwrought (ŏ′vĕr·rôt′) agg. esausto; sovreccitato; troppo lavorato.

owe (ō) vt. dovere a, essere in debito con. vi. aver debiti.

owing (ō'ĭng) *agg.* dovuto, pendente (*non pagato*): — to, a causa di, in conseguenza di.

owl (oul) *n.* gufo, civetta, barbagianni.

own (ōn) *agg.* proprio, personale; caratteristico: of one's — accord, di propria iniziativa; on one's —, per conto proprio; a house of one's —, una casa propria; one's — people, la propria gente *o* famiglia; to come into one's —, entrare in possesso del proprio; to hold one's —, restare della propria opinione. *vt.* possedere, essere proprietario di; riconoscere, ammettere, confessare.

owner (ōn'ẽr) *n.* proprietario. **—ship** *n.* proprietà.

ox (ŏks) *n.* (*pl.* oxen) bue.

oxide (ŏk'sĭd) *n.* ossido.

oxygen (ŏk's*ĭ*·jĕn) *n.* ossigeno.

oyster (ois'tẽr) *n.* ostrica.

ozone (ō'zōn) *n.* (*chim.*) ozono.

P

pace (pās) *n.* passo, andatura, ritmo. *vt.* misurare a passi; addestrare (*cavalli, ecc.*). *vi.* camminare, marciare, passeggiare, andare al passo.

pachyderm (păk'ĭ·dûrm) *n.* pachiderma.

pacific (p*ȧ*·sĭf'ĭk) *agg.* pacifico.

pacify (păs'*ĭ*·fī) *vt.* pacificare, placare.

pack (păk) *n.* pacco, balla; mazzo (*di carte da gioco*); muta (*di cani*), turba; banchisa: — horse, cavallo da soma. *vt., vi.* imballare, impaccare, stipare; accalcarsi; fare i bagagli: to — off *o* away, andarsene a precipizio.

package (păk'ĭj) *n.* pacco, collo, balla.

packer (păk'ẽr) *n.* imballatore.

packet (păk'ĕt) *n.* pacchetto; vapore postale: — boat, piroscafo.

packing (păk'ĭng) *n.* imballaggio; (*mecc.*) guarnizione: — case, cassa d'imballaggio.

pact (păkt) *n.* patto, convenzione.

pad (păd) *n.* tampone, cuscinetto, imbottitura; blocco da annotazioni. *vt.* imbottire; ovattare. *vi.* camminare, andare a piedi. **—ding** *n.* imbottitura.

paddle (păd'*l*) *n.* pagaia, pala (*di remo o ruota idraulica*): — wheel, ruota a pale. *vt., vi.* remare, diguazzare, palpare, giocherellare.

paddock (păd'ŭk) *n.* prato annesso a una scuderia, recinto, paddock.

padlock (păd'lŏk') *n.* lucchetto. *vt.* chiudere col lucchetto.

pagan (pā'găn) *n., agg.* pagano. **—ism** *n.* paganesimo.

page (pāj) (1) *n.* pagina. *vt.* numerare le pagine di.

page (pāj) (2) *n.* paggio, valletto, inserviente d'albergo.

pageant (păj'ĕnt) *n.* corteo, carosello. **—ry** *n.* fasto, allegoria.

paid (pād) *pass., pp.* di to pay.

pail (pāl) *n.* secchio.

pain (pān) *n.* pena, sofferenza, dolore: to take —s to, prendersi il distur-

bo di. *vt.* affliggere, far soffrire. **—ful** *agg.* doloroso, penoso. **—less** *agg.* indolore; agevole.

painstaking (pānz'tāk'ĭng) *agg.* accurato, zelante, meticoloso.

paint (pānt) *n.* pittura, colore, vernice, belletto. *vt., vi.* dipingere, verniciare, truccare, imbellettarsi: to — the town red, farne di cotte e di crude. **—brush** *n.* pennello. **—er** *n.* pittore; (*naut.*) fune d'ormeggio. **—ing** *n.* pittura.

pair (pâr) *n.* paio, coppia. *vt.* accoppiare, appaiare. *vi.* appaiarsi, accoppiarsi.

pajamas (p*ȧ*·jä'm*ȧ*z) *n.pl.* pigiama.

pal (păl) *n.* amico, compagno.

palace (păl'ĭs) *n.* palazzo.

paladin (păl'*ȧ*·dĭn) *n.* paladino.

palatable (păl'ĭt·*ȧ*·b'l) *agg.* gustoso, gradevole; accettabile.

palate (păl'ĭt) *n.* palato; gusto.

palaver (p*ȧ*·läv'ẽr) *n.* conciliabolo, discussione. *vi.* confabulare.

pale (pāl) (1) *n.* palo, recinto; ambito. *vt.* cintare.

pale (pāl) (2) *agg.* pallido, scialbo, chiaro. *vi.* impallidire. **—ness** *n.* pallore.

palette (păl'ĕt) *n.* (*pitt.*) tavolozza.

paling (pāl'ĭng) *n.* palizzata.

palisade (păl'*ĭ*·sād') *n.* palizzata.

palisades *n. pl.* rupe, roccia.

pall (pôl) *n.* palio; drappo funebre. *vt., vi.* saziare, stancare, infastidire, disgustare, disgustarsi.

pallet (păl'ĕt) (1) *n.* tavolozza; paletta; ancora (*d'orologio*); (*mecc.*) dente d'arresto.

pallet (păl'ĕt) (2) *n.* pagliericcio.

palliate (păl'ĭ·āt) *vt.* attenuare, mitigare, alleviare.

pallid (păl'ĭd) *agg.* pallido, sbiadito.

palm (päm) *n.* palmo (*della mano*); palmizio; palma. *vt.* maneggiare; nascondere: to — something off on one, rifilare qualcosa a uno.

palmist (päm'ĭst) *n.* chiromante.

palmistry (päm'ĭs·trĭ) *n.* chiromanzia

palpable (pǎl'pȧ·b'l) *agg.* palpabile.

palpitate (pǎl'pĭ·tāt) *vi.* palpitare, pulsare.

palpitation (pǎl'pĭ·tā'shŭn) *n.* palpitazione.

palsied (pôl'sĭd) *agg.* intorpidito, paralizzato.

palsy (pôl'zĭ) *n.* paralisi.

paltry (pôl'trĭ) *agg.* meschino, esiguo.

pamper (pǎm'pẽr) *vt.* viziare, saziare.

pamphlet (pǎm'flĕt) *n.* opuscolo, libello.

pan (pǎn) *n.* padella; piatto (*di bilancia*); faccia; (*cinema*) panoramica. *vt.* cuocere in padella; ottenere, assicurarsi; vagliare; (*cinema*) muovere in panoramica. *vi.* riuscire, soddisfare; (*cinema*) carrellare.

pancake (pǎn'kāk') *n.* frittella.

pander (pǎn'dẽr) *n.* mezzano. *vt.*, *vi.* fare da mezzano (*a*).

pane (pǎn) *n.* riquadro di vetro, vetro di finestra, pannello.

panel (pǎn'ĕl) *n.* pannello, riquadro; lista dei giurati; (*radio e T.V.*) gruppo di concorrenti a un quiz: — heating, riscaldamento a pannelli. *vt.* munire di pannelli; incorniciare.

pang (pǎng) *n.* dolore, trafittura, angoscia.

panic (pǎn'ĭk) *n.*, *agg.* panico: —-stricken, atterrito. —ky *agg.* timoroso, atterrito.

pannikin (pǎn'ĭ·kĭn) *n.* pentolino.

pansy (pǎn'zĭ) *n.* viola del pensiero; (*gergo*) uomo effeminato; gagà; omosessuale.

pant (pǎnt) *n.* ansito, affanno. *vi.* ansare, palpitare.

panther (pǎn'thẽr) *n.* pantera; (*S.U.*) puma.

panties (pǎn'tĭz) *n. pl.* mutandine da donna o da bambino.

panting (pǎn'ĭng) *n.* ansito, affanno. *agg.* ansante, ansimante.

pantry (pǎn'trĭ) *n.* dispensa.

pants (pǎnts) *n.pl.* (*Ingl.*) mutande; (*S.U.*) calzoni.

papa (pä'pä) *n.* papà; vescovo.

papal (pā'pǎl) *agg.* papale.

paper (pā'pẽr) *n.* carta; documento; giornale; certificato; tema, saggio: — of pins, bustina di spilli; blotting —, carta assorbente; — knife, tagliacarte; — mill, cartiera; — money, carta moneta; — weight, fermacarte; on —, per iscritto. *agg.* di carta, cartaceo. *vt.* incartare, tappezzare con carta. —y *agg.* cartaceo.

papier-mâché (pà'pẽr·mȧ·shā') *n.* cartapesta.

par (pär) *n.* parità, livello normale; tasso di scambio; valore, quotazione: — value, valore alla pari; at —, alla pari; on a — with, alla pari con; to feel above —; sentirsi superiore alla media.

parable (pǎr'ȧ·b'l) *n.* parabola.

parachute (pǎr'ȧ·shōōt) *n.* paracadute. *vt.* paracadutare. *vi.* lanciarsi col paracadute.

parachutist (pǎr'ȧ·shōōt'ĭst) *n.* paracadutista.

parade (pȧ·rād') *n.* parata, esposizione, sfoggio, ostentazione. *vt.*, *vi.* disporre in parata; esporre; sfilare; aggirarsi; ostentare, pavoneggiarsi.

paradise (pǎr'ȧ·dĭs) *n.* paradiso.

paradox (pǎr'ȧ·dŏks) *n.* paradosso.

paraffin (pǎr'ȧ·fĭn) *n.* paraffina.

paragon (pǎr'ȧ·gŏn) *n.* paragone, modello, ideale.

paragraph (pǎr'ȧ·gráf) *n.* paragrafo, trafiletto.

parallel (pǎr'ǎ·lĕl) *n.* parallelo; (*geom.*) parallela. *agg.* parallelo. *vt.* porre parallelamente; uguagliare; confrontare.

paralyze (pǎr'ȧ·līz) *vt.* paralizzare.

paralysis (pȧ·rǎl'ĭ·sĭs) *n.* paralisi.

paramilitary (pǎr'ȧ·mĭl'ĭ·tẽr'ĭ) *agg.* paramilitare.

paramount (pǎr'ȧ·mount) *agg.* superiore, supremo, eminente, importantissimo.

paramour (pǎr'ȧ·mŏŏr) *n.* amante.

parapet (pǎr'ȧ·pĕt) *n.* parapetto.

parasite (pǎr'ȧ·sĭt) *n.* parassita.

parasol (pǎr'ȧ·sŏl) *n.* parasole.

paratroop (pǎr'ȧ·trōōp') *n.* corpo o scaglione di paracadutisti. —er *n.* (*mil.*) paracadutista.

parcel (pär'sĕl) *n.* parte, porzione; pacchetto; quantità: — post, servizio postale per pacchi. *vt.* spartire, dividere; involgere.

parch (pärch) *vt.*, *vi.* disseccare, riardere, inaridirsi: —ed lips, labbra riarse.

parchment (pärch'mĕnt) *n.* pergamena.

pardon (pär'd'n) *n.* perdono; grazia: I beg your —, scusatemi. *vt.* perdonare, graziare. —able *agg.* perdonabile.

pare (pâr) *vt.* sbucciare; tosare, pelare; rifinire: to — down, ridurre.

parent (pâr'ĕnt) *n.* genitore, genitrice, origine: my parents, i miei genitori. —age *n.* parentado, stirpe. —al (-ĕnt'ǎl) *agg.* dei genitori, paterno, materno.

parenthesis (pȧ·rĕn'thē·sĭs) *n.* (*pl.* parentheses) (-sēz) parentesi.

paring (pâr'ĭng) *n.* sbucciatura, scorza, buccia.

parish (păr'ĭsh) *n.* parrocchia, giurisdizione. —ioner (-ĭsh'-) *n.* parrocchiano.

Parisian (pȧ·rĭzh'ăn) *n.*, *agg.* parigino.

park (pärk) *n.* parco. *vt.* parcheggiare, posteggiare; collocare, depositare. —ing *n.* posteggio: — lot, posteggio per automobili, parcheggio; free —, posteggio gratuito; no —, vietato il posteggio, sosta vietata.

parlance (pär'lăns) *n.* linguaggio, terminologia, frasario.

parlay (pär'lā) *vt.*, *vi.* rigiocare la puntata con relativa vincita in altra partita *o* in corsa successiva; ingrandire, ampliare; convertire, trasformare; sfruttare (qualcosa *o* qualcuno) per avere successo.

parley (pär'lĭ) *n.* trattativa, conferenza (*spec. tra nemici*). *vi.* parlamentare.

parliament (pär'lĭ·mĕnt) *n.* parlamento. —ary (-mĕnt'-) *agg.* parlamentare.

parlor (pär'lēr) *n.* salotto: beauty —, salone di bellezza.

Parmesan (pär'mĕ·zăn') *n.*, *agg.* parmigiano.

parochial (pȧ·rō'kĭ·ăl) *agg.* parrocchiale.

parody (pär'ȯ·dĭ) *n.* parodia. *vt.* parodiare.

parole (pȧ·rōl') *n.* parola d'onore, parola d'ordine; libertà condizionata: to put on —, concedere la libertà condizionata a.

paroxysm (păr'ŏk·sĭz'm) *n.* parossismo, accesso.

parquet (pär·kā') *n.* pavimento di legno; (*S.U.*) platea.

parrot (păr'ŭt) *n.* pappagallo. *vt.* scimmiottare; ripetere pappagallescamente.

parry (păr'ĭ) *n.* (*sch.*) parata. *vt.*, *vi.* parare; eludere, evitare, sottrarsi.

parsley (pärs'lĭ) *n.* prezzemolo.

parsnip (pärs'nĭp) *n.* (*bot.*) pastinaca.

parson (pär's'n) *n.* parroco, curato.

parsonage (pär's'nĭj) *n.* canonica.

part (pärt) *n.* parte; divisione; scriminatura; (*pl.*) dote (*qualità*): in foreign —s, all'estero; spare —s, pezzi di ricambio; do your —, fai il tuo dovere; for my —, per quel che mi riguarda; on my —, da parte mia; — and parcel of, parte integrante di. *vt.* dividere, spartire, separare. *vi.* separarsi, dividersi, fendersi: to — with, rinunciare a, abbandonare; to — from, separarsi da, allontanarsi da; to — company, separarsi, lasciarsi.

partake (pär·tāk') *vt.*, *vi.* (*pass.* partook, *pp.* partaken) partecipare a,

comunicare, condividere, esser partecipe: to — of, prendere un po' di.

partial (pär'shăl) *agg.* parziale. —ity (ä-l'ĭ·tĭ) *n.* parzialità. —ly *avv.* parzialmente.

participant (pär·tĭs'ĭ·pănt) *n.*, *agg.* partecipante.

participate (pär·tĭs'ĭ·pāt) *vi.* spartire, partecipare (*a*).

participation (pär·tĭs'ĭ·pā'shŭn) *n.* partecipazione.

participle (pär'tĭ·sĭ·p'l) *n.* participio.

particle (pär'tĭ·k'l) *n.* particella.

particular (pĕr·tĭk'ū·lēr) *n.* particolare, minuzia. *agg.* particolare, speciale; individuale; minuzioso, esigente, ricercato. —ly *avv.* particolarmente, particolareggiatamente.

parting (pär'tĭng) *n.* separazione, addio; scriminatura. *agg.* di commiato; divisorio; ultimo.

partisan (pär'tĭ·zăn) *n.*, *agg.* partigiano.

partition (pär·tĭsh'ŭn) *n.* partizione, divisione, divisorio. *vt.* dividere, spartire, suddividere.

partly (pärt'lĭ) *avv.* in parte, parzialmente.

partner (pärt'nēr) *n.* socio, compagno; cavaliere (*ballerino*), dama (*ballerina*); coniuge. —ship *n.* società.

partridge (pär'trĭj) *n.* pernice.

party (pär'tĭ) *n.* comitiva, partito, riunione, ricevimento; parte in causa; (*mil.*) distaccamento; (*fam.*) persona: shooting —, partita di caccia; — line, linea del partito.

parvenu (pär'vĕ·nū) *n.* villano rifatto, nuovo ricco.

pas (pä) *n.* passo di danza.

pass (pȧs) *n.* passo, passaggio; apertura; botta; salvacondotto, permesso, biglietto gratuito; punto, situazione. *vt.* (*pass.*, *pp.* passed, past) attraversare, passare; trasmettere; approvare; promuovere (*un esaminando, ecc.*); tollerare. *vi.* passare; svenire; trascorrere; essere promosso: to come to —, accadere; to — away, svanire, sparire, morire; to — out, perdere conoscenza; distribuire; to — oneself off as, farsi passare per.

passable (pȧs'ȧ·b'l) *agg.* passabile; praticabile, navigabile, attraversabile.

passage (păs'ĭj) *n.* passaggio, traversata; corridoio, vestibolo; brano, passo.

passbook (pȧs'bŏŏk') *n.* libretto bancario.

passenger (păs'ĕn·jĕr) *n.* passeggiero, viaggiatore; — **pigeon,** piccione viaggiatore.

passer (pás'ĕr), **passer-by** *n.* (*pl.* passers-by) passante.

passion (păsh'ŭn) *n.* passione; collera: — **play,** sacra rappresentazione; **to fly into a —,** infuriarsi.

passionate (păsh'ŭn·ĭt) *agg.* appassionato.

passive (păs'ĭv) *n.*, *agg.* passivo.

passkey (păs'kē') *n.* chiave universale, comunella; grimaldello.

Passover (păs'ō'vĕr) *n.* Pasqua ebraica.

passport (păs'pōrt) *n.* passaporto.

password (păs'wûrd') *n.* parola d'ordine.

past (păst) *n.* passato. *agg.* passato, scorso, ultimo (*recente*): **a —** master, un intenditore, un maestro; — **tense,** passato remoto; **for some time —,** da un po' di tempo; **these — days,** in questi ultimi giorni. *prep.* dopo di; di là da; alla fine di; accanto a, davanti a: **half —** twelve, le dodici e mezza; **it is — ten,** sono le dieci passate; — **all** doubts, fuori di dubbio; — **cure,** incurabile; — **bearing,** insopportabile; **to be — forty,** aver superato la quarantina. *avv.* oltre, innanzi.

paste (păst) *n.* colla; pasta: **alimentary —,** pasta alimentare. *vt.* incollare, appicciccare.

pasteboard (păst'bōrd') *n.* cartone.

pasteurize (păs'tĕr·īz) *vt.* pastorizzare.

pastime (păs'tīm') *n.* passatempo.

pastor (păs'tĕr) *n.* pastore.

pastry (păs'trĭ) *n.* pasticceria: — **cook,** pasticciere; — **shop,** pasticceria.

pasturage (păs'tūr·ĭj) *n.* pascolo.

pasture (păs'tūr) *n.* pastura, pascolo. *vt.* pasturare. *vi.* pascolare.

pasty (păs'tĭ) *agg.* pastoso; flaccido, smorto.

P.A. system *vedi* Public-Address system.

pat (păt) *n.* colpetto, manata; panetto di burro. *agg.* pronto, adatto, opportuno: **to have a lesson —,** sapere una lezione a menadito; **to stand —,** restare immobile. *avv.* opportunamente. *vt.* dare un colpetto a, battere leggermente: **to — oneself on the back,** congratularsi da soli o con se stessi.

patch (păch) *n.* pezza, toppa; benda; neo artificiale; lembo di terra. *vt.* rattoppare, raffazzonare: **to — up a quarrel,** comporre una controversia.

patchwork (păch'wûrk') *n.* lavoro a toppe; raffazzonatura.

pate (păt) *n.* testa, zucca, cranio.

patent (păt'ĕnt) *n.* patente, brevetto, privilegio. *agg.* (pă'-) manifesto, patente; brevettato: — **leather** shoes, scarpe di vernice o di copale; — **medicine,** specialità medicinale. *vt.* brevettare.

paternal (pȧ·tûr'năl) *agg.* paterno.

paternity (pȧ·tûr'nĭ·tĭ) *n.* paternità.

path (păth) *n.* sentiero, percorso, via, traiettoria.

pathetic (pȧ·thĕt'ĭk) *agg.* commovente; patetico. *n.* espressione o gesto patetico.

pathos (pā'thŏs) *n.* patos.

pathway (păth'wā') *n.* sentiero.

patience (pā'shĕns) *n.* pazienza.

patient (pā'shĕnt) *n.*, *agg.* paziente.

patriarch (pā'trĭ·ärk) *n.* patriarca.

patrimony (păt'rĭ·mō'nĭ) *n.* patrimonio ereditario.

patriot (pā'trĭ·ŭt) *n.* patriota. **—ic** (-ŏt'ĭk) *agg.* patriottico. **—ism** *n.* patriottismo.

patrol (pȧ·trōl') *n.* pattuglia; agente. *vt.*, *vi.* perlustrare, pattugliare. **—man** *n.* poliziotto.

patron (pā'trŭn) *n.* patrono; sostenitore; cliente fedele: — **saint,** santo patrono. **—age** *n.* patronato, egida; protezione; clientela. **—ess** *n.* protettrice, patronessa.

patronize (pā'trŭn·īz) *vt.* proteggere, incoraggiare; trattare con condiscendenza; frequentare di preferenza (*un negozio, un ritrovo*), essere cliente abituale di.

patronizing *agg.* condiscendente, protettivo. **—ly** *avv.* con degnazione.

patter (păt'ĕr) *n.* chiacchiere, imbonimento; cantilena; crepitio, trepestio. *vt.*, *vi.* borbottare, recitare; picchiettare, camminare a passetti rapidi.

pattern (păt'ĕrn) *n.* modello, disegno, schema, motivo, campione, esempio: — **book,** campionario. *vt.* foggiare, decorare: **to — oneself after,** seguire l'esempio di, imitare; **to — something after,** modellare qualcosa a imitazione di. *vi.* comportarsi.

patty (păt'ĭ) *n.* pasticcino; polpetta.

paunch (pônch) *n.* pancia; rumine.

pauper (pô'pĕr) *n.* povero.

pause (pôz) *n.* pausa, interruzione, indugio. *vi.* fare una pausa, indugiare, sostare.

pave (pāv) *vt.* pavimentare, appianare: **to — the way,** appianare il terreno.

pavement (pāv'mĕnt) *n.* selciato; marciapiede.

pavilion (pȧ·vĭl'yŭn) *n.* padiglione, tenda.

paving (pāv'ĭng) *n.* pavimentazione.

paw (pô) *n.* zampa. *vt.* dare zampate a; raspare con le zampe; maneggiare goffamente. *vi.* zampettare, scalpitare.

pawn (pôn) *n.* pegno, garanzia, ostaggio; (*scacchi*) pedina. *vt.* impegnare, dare in pegno. **—broker** *n.* prestatore su pegno. **—shop** *n.* monte di pegni. **— ticket** polizza di pegno.

pay (pā) *n.* paga, salario, retribuzione. *vt.* (*pass., pp.* paid) pagare, rimunerare, tributare; (*naut.*) mollare: to **— attention**, fare attenzione; to **— back**, restituire, rifondere; to **— down**, pagare in contanti; to **— homage**, rendere omaggio; to **— one's respects**, presentare i saluti; to **— a visit**, fare visita. *vi.* rendere, essere redditizio, valer la pena, pagare; (*naut.*) portarsi sottovento: to **— off**, liquidare; vendicarsi; rendere, essere proficuo; to **— round**, virare di bordo; to **— the piper**, pagare lo scotto. **—able** *agg.* pagabile. **— day** giorno di paga. **—er** *n.* pagatore. **—master** *n.* ufficiale pagatore. **—ment** *n.* pagamento. **—off** *n.* pagamento, liquidazione; conseguenza; rendita, compenso; apice, acme, soluzione; fattore decisivo. *agg.* risolutivo, decisivo; proficuo. **—roll** *n.* libro paga.

pea (pē) *n.* pisello.

peace (pēs) *n.* pace, calma, silenzio: to hold one's **—**, tacere. **—able** *agg.* pacifico. **—ful** *agg.* pacifico, quieto. **—maker** *n.* paciere.

peach (pēch) *n.* pesca: **— tree**, pesco.

peacock (pē'kŏk') *n.* pavone.

peak (pēk) *n.* picco, cima; punta, punto massimo; visiera. **—ed** *agg.* appuntito; a visiera; deperito.

peal (pēl) *n.* squillo: **— of laughter**, risata squillante; **— of thunder**, tuono. *vt., vi.* sonare, risonare.

peanut (pē'nŭt') *n.* arachide.

pear (pâr) *n.* pera: **— tree**, pero.

pearl (pûrl) *n.* perla, granulo.

pearly (pûrl'ĭ) *agg.* perlaceo.

peasant (pĕz'ănt) *n.* contadino. *agg.* campagnuolo.

pease (pēz) *pl. di* pea.

peat (pēt) *n.* torba: **— bog**, torbiera.

pebble (pĕb''l) *n.* ciottolo; sassolino.

peccadillo (pĕk'ȧ-dĭl'ō) *n.* peccatuccio.

peck (pĕk) *n.* beccata; misura per cereali (*circa 9 litri*): **a — of trouble**, un mare di guai. *vt., vi.* beccare.

peculation (pĕk'ů-lā'shŭn) *n.* peculato, malversazione.

peculiar (pē-kūl'yĕr) *agg.* peculiare, particolare. **—ity** (-ăr'ĭ-tĭ) *n.* particolarità, peculiarità.

pedagogue (pĕd'ȧ-gŏg) *n.* pedagogo.

pedal (pĕd'ăl) *n.* pedale: **— pushers**, calzoni femminili alla pescatora. *vi.* pedalare, usare il pedale.

pedant (pĕd'ănt) *n.* pedante. **—ic** (-ănt'ĭk) *agg.* pedantesco.

peddle (pĕd''l) *vt.* vendere alla spicciolata. *vi.* fare il venditore ambulante.

peddler (pĕd'lĕr) *n.* venditore ambulante.

pedestal (pĕd'ĕs-tăl) *n.* piedestallo.

pedestrian (pē-dĕs'trĭ-ăn) *n.* pedone, podista. *agg.* pedestre. **—ism** *n.* podismo.

pedicab (pĕd'ĭ-kăb') *n.* ciclotassi.

pedigree (pĕd'ĭ-grē) *n.* genealogia, albero genealogico.

pediar (pĕd'lĕr) *vedi* peddler.

peek (pēk) *vedi* peep.

peel (pēl) *n.* buccia, scorza; pala, paletta. *vt.* pelare, sbucciare, mondare. *vi.* spellarsi, squamarsi: to keep one's eyes peeled, vigilare, stare con gli occhi aperti.

peep (pēp) *n.* occhiata, sguardo furtivo; fessura; pigolìo. *vi.* sbirciare; sbucare, apparire; pigolare. **—hole** *n.* spioncino.

peer (pēr) (1) *vi.* apparire, spuntare, sbucare; sbirciare; fissare.

peer (pēr) (2) *n.* pari; Pari (*d' Inghilterra*). **—less** *agg.* impareggiabile.

peeve (pēv) *vt.* irritare, seccare: to get peeved, seccarsi.

peevish (pē'vĭsh) *agg.* petulante; stizzoso; di malumore.

peg (pĕg) *n.* cavicchio, piuolo, zipolo; (*mus.*) bischero: to come down a **—**, abbassare le arie; to take someone down a **—**, far abbassare la cresta, umiliare. *vt.* incavicchiare, incavigliare: to **— away**, lavorare senza sosta; to **— out**, morire.

pellet (pĕl'ĕt) *n.* pallina, pallottola, pallino, pillola.

pell-mell (pĕl'mĕl') *agg.* disordinato. *avv.* alla rinfusa, disordinatamente.

pellucid (pĕ-lū'sĭd) *agg.* limpido, trasparente.

pelt (pĕlt) (1) *n.* scroscio, colpo, velocità. *vt.* tempestare, scagliare. *vi.* scrosciare: to **— with**, tempestare di.

pelt (pĕlt) (2) *n.* cuoio grezzo.

pen (pĕn) (1) *n.* recinto, ovile, pollaio; prigione. *vt.* (*pass., pp.* penned, pent) rinchiudere, imprigionare, reprimere.

pen (pĕn) (2) *n.* penna, piuma: **fountain-pen**, penna stilografica; **— name**, pseudonimo. *vt.* vergare, redigere. **—holder** *n.* portapenne; cannuccia.

penal (pē'năl) *agg.* penale: — servitude, lavori forzati. —ty *n.* punizione, multa, penalità; fio.

penance (pĕn'ăns) *n.* penitenza.

pence (pĕns) *vedi* penny.

penchant (păn'shän') *n.* propensione.

pencil (pĕn'sĭl) *n.* matita: — sharpener, temperamatite. *vt.* disegnare (*o* scrivere) a matita.

pendant (pĕn'dănt) *n.* ciondolo, pendaglio; cosa gemella; stendardo.

pendent (pĕn'dĕnt) *agg.* pendente, sospeso.

pending (pĕnd'ĭng) *agg.* pendente, indeciso, in corso, incombente. *prep.* durante, fino a, in attesa di.

pendulum (pĕn'ū·lŭm) *n.* pendolo, bilanciere.

penetrate (pĕn'ĕ·trāt) *vt.*, *vi.* penetrare, permeare, capire.

penetrating (pĕn'ĕ·trāt'ĭng) *agg.* penetrante, perspicace.

penetration (pĕn'ĕ·trā'shŭn) *n.* penetrazione, perspicacia.

penguin (pĕn'gwĭn) *n.* pinguino.

penicillin (pĕn'ĭ·sĭl'ĭn) *n.* penicillina.

peninsula (pĕn·ĭn'sŭ·lá) *n.* penisola.

penitence (pĕn'ĭ·tĕns) *n.* pentimento, penitenza.

penitent (pĕn'ĭ·tĕnt) *n.*, *agg.* penitente.

penitentiary (pĕn'ĭ·tĕn'shá·rĭ) *n.*, *agg.* penitenziario.

penknife (pĕn'nīf') *n.* temperino.

penman (pĕn'măn) *n.* scrivano, autore. —ship *n.* scrittura.

pennant (pĕn'ănt) *n.* pennone (*vessillo*), fiamma; (*naut.*) pennoncello.

penniless (pĕn'ĭ·lĕs) *agg.* povero, squattrinato.

penny (pĕn'ĭ) *n.* (*pl.* pennies *per indicare il numero di monete,* pence [*Ingl.*] *per indicare l'ammontare*) soldo (1/12 di scellino); (*S.U.*) un cent. di dollaro: a pretty —, una bella somma.

pension (pĕn'shŭn) *n.* pensione. *vt.* pensionare.

pensive (pĕn'sĭv) *agg.* pensieroso.

pent (pĕnt) *agg.* (*pass.*, *pp. di* to pen) chiuso, rinchiuso: —-up feelings, sentimenti repressi.

penthouse (pĕnt'hous') *n.* tettoia, riparo; sopralzo; appartamento di lusso costruito sul tetto.

penurious (pē·nū'rĭ·ŭs) *agg.* avaro, meschino.

peon (pē'ŏn) *n.* bracciante.

people (pē'p'l) *n.* popolo; massa, gente; famiglia, parentela. *vt.* popolare.

pep (pĕp) *n.* vigore, vivacità. *vt.* rinvigorire.

pepper (pĕp'ẽr) *n.* pepe; peperone: — box, — caster, pepaiuola. *vt.* im-

pepare; tempestare (*di colpi*), crivellare.

peppercorn (pĕp'ẽr·kôrn') *n.* grano di pepe; inezia.

peppermint (pĕp'ẽr·mĭnt) *n.* menta piperina.

peppery (pĕp'ẽr·ĭ) *agg.* pepato, pungente; collerico.

peppy (pĕp'ĭ) *agg.* energico, vivace.

per (pẽr) *prep.* per, per ogni: — annum, all'anno, annualmente; — capita, a testa; — cent, per cento; ten cents — dozen, dieci centesimi la dozzina.

perambulator (pẽr·ăm'bū·lā'tẽr) *n.* carrozzina per bambini.

perceive (pẽr·sēv') *vt.* percepire, scorgere, sentire, capire.

per cent (pẽr·sĕnt') per cento. —age *n.* percentuale, interesse, profitto.

perceptible (pẽr·sĕp'tĭ·b'l) *agg.* percettibile, sensibile.

perception (pẽr·sĕp'shŭn) *n.* percezione.

perch (pûrch) (1) *n.* pesce persico.

perch (pûrch) (2) *n.* trespolo, posatoio, palo, pertica. *vt.* mettere in bilico. *vi.* appollaiarsi, posarsi.

perchance (pẽr·cháns') *avv.* per caso, forse.

percolate (pûr'kō·lāt) *vt.*, *vi.* filtrare, colare.

percolator (pûr'kō·lā'tẽr) *n.* filtro.

percussion (pẽr·kŭsh'ŭn) *n.* percussione: — cap, percussore; — fuse, detonatore.

perdition (pẽr·dĭsh'ŭn) *n.* perdizione, rovina.

peremptory (pẽr·ĕmp'tō·rĭ) *agg.* perentorio.

perennial (pẽr·ĕn'ĭ·ăl) *n.* perenne.

perfect (pûr'fĕkt) *agg.* perfetto, completo. *n.* perfetto (*del verbo*). *vt.* perfezionare, completare. —ion (-fĕk'-) *n.* perfezione. —ly *avv.* perfettamente.

perfidious (pẽr·fĭd'ĭ·ŭs) *agg.* perfido, infido.

perfidy (pûr'fĭ·dĭ) *n.* perfidia.

perforate (pûr'fō·rāt) *vt.* perforare.

perforce (pẽr·fôrs') *avv.* necessariamente, per forza.

perform (pẽr·fôrm') *vt.* rappresentare, eseguire, compiere, adempire. *vi.* prodursi; funzionare. —ance *n.* esibizione, rappresentazione, esecuzione, prodezza; funzionamento, rendimento.

perfume (pûr'fūm) *n.* profumo. *vt.* profumare.

perfumery (pẽr·fūm'ẽr·ĭ) *n.* profumeria.

perfunctory (pẽr·fŭngk'tō·rĭ) *agg.* negligente, superficiale, macchinale.

perhaps (pĕr·hăps') *avv.* forse: — so, può darsi.

peril (pĕr'ĭl) *n.* pericolo. —ous *agg.* pericoloso.

perimeter (pĕ·rĭm'ē·tĕr) *n.* perimetro.

period (pē'rĭ·ŭd) *n.* periodo, durata, termine; (*gramm.*) punto fermo. —ic (-ŏd'ĭk) *agg.* periodico. —ical *n.* periodico (*pubblicazione*). *agg.* periodico.

periscope (pĕr'ĭs·skōp) *n.* periscopio.

perish (pĕr'ĭsh) *vi.* perire; sparire; deteriorarsi. —able *agg.* mortale; caduco; deteriorabile.

peritonitis (pĕr'ĭ·tŏ·nī'tĭs) *n.* peritonite.

periwig (pĕr'ĭ·wĭg) *n.* parrucca.

perjure (pûr'jẽr) *vt.*, *vi.* spergiurare: to — oneself, giurare il falso.

perjurer (pûr'jẽr·ẽr) *n.* spergiuro (*chi spergiura*).

perjury (pûr'jẽr·ĭ) *n.* spergiuro (*giuramento falso*); falsa testimonianza.

perk (pûrk) *agg.* spavaldo, impudente; azzimato; orgoglioso. *vt.* agghindare. *vi.* darsi delle arie; tener alta la testa.

permanence (pûr'má·nĕns) *n.* permanenza; durata.

permanent (pûr'má·nĕnt) *agg.* permanente, immutabile.

permeate (pûr'mē·āt) *vt.* permeare, penetrare, saturare. *vi.* permearsi, diffondersi.

permissible (pĕr·mĭs'ĭ·b'l) *agg.* lecito.

permission (pĕr·mĭsh'ŭn) *n.* permesso.

permit (pĕr·mĭt') *n.* permesso, autorizzazione, licenza. *vt.*, *vi.* permettere.

pernicious (pĕr·nĭsh'ŭs) *agg.* pernicioso.

peroxide (pĕr·ŏk'sĭd) *n.* acqua ossigenata.

perpendicular (pûr'pĕn·dĭk'û·lẽr) *n.*, *agg.* perpendicolare.

perpetrate (pûr'pē·trāt) *vt.* perpetrare.

perpetual (pĕr·pĕt'û·ăl) *agg.* perpetuo.

perpetuate (pĕr·pĕt'û·āt) *vt.* perpetuare.

perplex (pĕr·plĕks') *vt.* confondere, render perplesso. —ed *agg.* perplesso, imbarazzato. —ity *n.* perplessità, imbarazzo.

perquisite (pûr'kwĭ·zĭt) *n.* incerto, gratifica; introito, reddito.

persecute (pûr'sē·kūt) *vt.* perseguitare.

persecution (pûr'sē·kū'shŭn) *n.* persecuzione.

perseverance (pûr'sē·vēr'ăns) *n.* perseveranza.

persevere (pûr'sē·vēr') *vi.* perseverare.

persevering *agg.* perseverante.

persiflage (pûr'sĭ·fläzh) *n.* superficialità, frivolezza (*di tono*); ironia, canzonatura.

persist (pĕr·sĭst') *vi.* persistere, perseverare; ostinarsi. —ence *n.* persistenza, tenacia; ostinazione. —ent *agg.* tenace, persistente; ostinato.

person (pûr's'n) *n.* persona, personaggio. —able *agg.* bello, presentabile. —age *n.* personaggio. —al *agg.* personale. —ality (-ăl'ĭ·tĭ) *n.* personalità.

personate (pûr'sŭn·āt) *vt.* impersonare.

personnel (pûr'sŏ·nĕl') *n.* personale; equipaggio: — director, capo del personale.

perspective (pĕr·spĕk'tĭv) *n.* prospettiva, veduta. *agg.* prospettico.

perspicacious (pûr'spĭ·kā'shŭs) *agg.* perspicace, sagace.

perspicacity (pûr'spĭ·kăs'ĭ·tĭ) *n.* perspicacia.

perspiration (pûr'spĭ·rā'shŭn) *n.* traspirazione.

perspire (pĕr·spīr') *vt.*, *vi.* sudare, traspirare, trasudare.

persuade (pĕr·swād') *vt.* persuadere: to — into, indurre a; to — from, dissuadere.

persuasion (pĕr·swā'zhŭn) *n.* persuasione, persuasiva; fede.

persuasive (pĕr·swā'sĭv) *agg.* persuasivo.

pert (pûrt) *agg.* vivace; insolente; spavaldo.

pertain (pĕr·tān') *vi.* appartenere, riferirsi, avere attinenza (*con*).

pertinacity (pûr'tĭ·năs'ĭ·tĭ) *n.* pertinacia.

pertinent (pûr'tĭ·nĕnt) *agg.* adeguato, pertinente, attinente, opportuno.

pertly (pûrt'lĭ) *avv.* vivacemente; insolentemente, spavaldamente.

pertness (pûrt'nĕs) *n.* vivacità; insolenza, spavalderia.

perturb (pĕr·tûrb') *vt.* perturbare.

perusal (pē·rōōz'ăl) *n.* esame, lettura.

peruse (pē·rōōz') *vt.* leggere, esaminare attentamente.

pervade (pĕr·vād') *vt.* pervadere, invadere, permeare.

perverse (pĕr·vûrs') *agg.* perverso, bizzarro, ostinato.

pervert (pĕr·vûrt') *vt.* pervertire, deformare. *n.* (pûr'vûrt) pervertito.

pesky (pĕs'kĭ) *agg.* molesto.

pessimism (pĕs'ĭ·mĭz'm) *n.* pessimismo.

pessimist (pĕs'ĭ·mĭst) *n.* pessimista.

pest (pĕst) *n.* peste, flagello.

pester (pĕs'tẽr) *vt.* tormentare, perseguitare, assillare.

pestilence (pĕs'tĭ·lĕns) *n.* pestilenza.

pestle (pĕs''l) *n.* pestello.

pet (pĕt) (1) *n.* stizza.

pet (pĕt) (2) *n.* beniamino, preferito, prediletto, coccolo, animale domestico. *agg.* caro, prediletto: — aversion, bestia nera; — name, vezzeggiativo. *vt.* prediligere, coccolare.

petal (pĕt''l) *n.* petalo.

peter (pē'tēr) *vi.*: to — out (*gergo*) esaurirsi, affievolirsi; fare cilecca.

petition (pĕ·tĭsh'ŭn) *n.* petizione. *vt.* supplicare, presentare una petizione a. —er *n.* postulante, richiedente.

petrel (pĕt'rĕl) *n.* procellaria.

petrify (pĕt'rĭ·fī) *vt.* petrificare, pietrificare. *vi.* petrificarsi.

petrol (pĕt'rŏl) *n.* (*Ingl.*) benzina.

petroleum (pĕ·trō'lĕ·ŭm) *n.* petrolio naturale.

petticoat (pĕt'ĭkōt) *n.* gonnella, sottana.

pettifog (pĕt'ĭ·fŏg) *vi.* fare l'azzeccagarbugli; cavillare. —ger *n.* azzeccagarbugli, leguleio; novizio; incompetente, scagnozzo. —gery *n.* trucchi, cavilli. —ging *agg.* cavilloso, meschino; insignificante.

pettiness (pĕt'ĭ·nĕs) *n.* piccolezza, meschinità.

pettish (pĕt'ĭsh) *agg.* dispettoso, petulante.

petty (pĕt'ĭ) *agg.* piccolo, minimo; meschino, trascurabile; minore (*di reato*): — cash, piccola cassa; — officer, sottufficiale di marina.

petulance (pĕt'ū·lăns) *n.* petulanza.

petulant (pĕt'ū·lănt) *agg.* petulante.

pew (pū) *n.* banco di chiesa.

pewter (pū'tēr) *n.* peltro.

phalanx (fā'lăngks) *n.* falange.

phantom (făn'tŭm) *n.* fantasma.

Pharaoh (fâr'ō) *n.* faraone.

Pharisee (făr'ĭ·sē) *n.* fariseo.

pharmacist (fär'má·sĭst) *n.* farmacista.

pharmacy (fär'má·sĭ) *n.* farmacia.

pharynx (făr'ĭngks) *n.* faringe.

phase (fāz) *n.* fase.

pheasant (fĕz'ănt) *n.* fagiano.

phenomenon (fē·nŏm'ē·nŏn) *n.* (*pl.* phenomena) fenomeno.

phial (fī'ăl) *n.* fiala.

philanthropist (fĭ·lăn'thrŏ·pĭst) *n.* filantropo.

philanthropy (fĭ·lăn'thrŏ·pĭ) *n.* filantropia.

philharmonic (fĭl'här·mŏn'ĭk) *agg.* filarmonico.

Philistine (fĭ·lĭs'tĭn) *n.*, *agg.* filisteo.

philologist (fĭ·lŏl'ŏ·jĭst) *n.* filologo.

philology (fĭ·lŏl'ŏ·jĭ) *n.* filologia.

philosopher (fĭ·lŏs'ŏ·fēr) *n.* filosofo.

philosophical (fĭl'ŏ·sŏf'ĭ·kăl) *agg.* filosofico.

philosophize (fĭ·lŏs'ŏ·fīz) *vi.* filosofeggiare.

philosophy (fĭ·lŏs'ŏ·fĭ) *n.* filosofia.

philter, philtre (fĭl'tēr) *n.* filtro d'amore.

phlegm (flĕm) *n.* flemma; muco.

phlegmatic (flĕg·măt'ĭk) *agg.* flemmatico.

phone (fōn) *n.* telefono. *vt.*, *vi.* telefonare.

phoneme (fō'nēm) *n.* fonema.

phonemics (fō·nē'mĭks) *n.* fonematica, fonologia.

phonetic (fō·nĕt'ĭk) *agg.* fonetico.

phonetics *n.* fonetica.

phonogram (fō'nŏ·grăm) *n.* fonogramma.

phonograph (fō'nŏ·grăf) *n.* fonografo.

phonophile (fō'nŏ·fīl) *n.*, appassionato di dischi di alta fedeltà.

phony (fō'nĭ) (*gergo*) *n.* contraffazione, impostore. *agg.* contraffatto, fraudolento, falso, fasullo.

phosphorescence (fŏs'fŏ·rĕs'ĕns) *n.* fosforescenza.

phosphorescent (fŏs'fŏ·rĕs'ĕnt) *agg.* fosforescente.

phosphorus (fŏs'fŏ·rŭs) *n.* fosforo.

photo (fō'tō) *n.* foto, fotografia. *agg.* fotografico: — finish (*sport*), arrivo a fotografia.

photocell (fō'tō·sĕl') *n.* cellula fotoelettrica.

photofinishing *n.* (*fot.*) sviluppo e stampa.

photoflash lamp *n.* (*fot.*) lampada lampo.

photogenic (fō'tō·jĕn'ĭk) *agg.* fotogenico.

photograph (fō'tō·grăf) *n.* fotografia. *vt.* fotografare. —er (-ŏg'-) *n.* fotografo.

photography (fō·tŏg'rá·fĭ) *n.* fotografia (*arte*).

photomontage (fō'tō·mŏn·tăzh') *n.* fotomontaggio.

photomural (fō'tō·mū'răl) *n.* pannello fotografico.

photoplay (fō'tō·plā') *n.* film, pellicola; copione.

phrase (frāz) *n.* frase. *vt.* formulare, esprimere.

phrenology (frē·nŏl'ŏ·jĭ) *n.* frenologia.

physic (fĭz'ĭk) *n.* medicina, rimedio, purgante. *vt.* curare, purgare. —al *agg.* fisico.

physician (fĭ·zĭsh'ăn) *n.* medico.

physicist (fĭz'ĭ·sĭst) *n.* fisico.

physics (fĭz'ĭks) *n.* fisica.

physiological (fĭz'ĭ·ō·lŏj'ĭ·kăl) *agg.* fisiologico.

physiologist (fĭz'ĭ·ŏl'ŏ·jĭst) *n.* fisiologo.

physiology (fĭz'ĭ·ŏl'ŏ·jĭ) *n.* fisiologia.

physique (fĭ·zēk') *n*. costituzione fisica.

pianist (pē'a̅·nĭst) *n*. pianista.

piano (pĭ·ăn'ō) *n*. pianoforte: **grand —**, piano a coda.

piazza (pĭ·ăz'a̅) *n*. piazza; portico; veranda.

pick (pĭk) *n*. piccone; grimaldello; scelta, diritto di scelta; fior fiore; raccolto: **ice —**, scalpello per il ghiaccio. *vt., vi.* cogliere, spiccare; scegliere; pulire, spennare . forzare (*una serratura*); togliere, separare (*con le dita*); pungere; rubacchiare: **to — a hole in somebody's coat,** trovare a ridire su qualcuno; **to — flaws,** trovare difetti; **to — a quarrel with,** attaccar briga con; **to — up,** raccogliere; captare; imparare; rimettersi; **to — up speed,** accelerare, acquistare velocità.

pickax (pĭk'ăks') *n*. piccone.

picket (pĭk'ĕt) *n*. piuolo, palo; picchetto, pattuglia avanzata; scioperante in servizio di guardia: **— boat,** lancia addetta alla vigilanza portuale. *vt., vi.* picchettare, legare a un palo, far la guardia a, esser di picchetto.

pickle (pĭk''l) *n*. sottaceto; posizione spiacevole: **to be in a fine —,** essere in un bel pasticcio. *vt.* mettere sotto aceto.

picklock (pĭk'lŏk') *n*. grimaldello; scassinatore.

pickpocket (pĭk'pŏk'ĕt) *n*. borsaiuolo.

pickup (pĭk'ŭp') *n*. raccolta, radunamento; scelta; miglioramento; ripresa (*di attività*); affare colto al volo; pasto improvvisato; conoscenza casuale, donna conosciuta per la strada; passeggiero raccolto a bordo; oggetto trovato o rubato; (*auto.*) ripresa o accelerazione. camioncino scoperto; fonorivelatore, pickup; (*giorn.*) piombo pronto per la stampa.

picnic (pĭk'nĭk) *n*. merenda all'aperto.

pictograph (pĭk'tō·gráf') *n*. pittogramma; diagramma a figure, schema grafico.

picture (pĭk'tu̅r) *n*. quadro; illustrazione, immagine; pittura; ritratto; cinematografia: **— frame,** cornice; **— gallery,** pinacoteca; **— window,** finestrone panoramico. *vt.* dipingere, rappresentare, descrivere, immaginare.

pie (pī) *n*. timballo, pasticcio, torta ripiena: **to have a finger in the —,** avere le mani in pasta.

piece (pēs) *n*. pezzo; frammento: **— of advice,** consiglio; **— of money,** moneta; **— of news,** notizia; **— of**

nonsense, sciocchezza. *vt.* rappezzare, mettere insieme, unire. *vi.* mangiucchiare fuori dei pasti. **—meal** *agg., avv.* a pezzi, a poco a poco, gradatamente.

pier (pēr) *n*. gettata, molo, pontone, banchina; stipite, spalletta.

pierce (pērs) *vt., vi.* trafiggere, perforare, penetrare.

piercing (pēr'sĭng) *agg.* penetrante, pungente, lacerante (*di grido*).

piety (pī'ĕ·tĭ) *n*. pietà, devozione.

pig (pĭg) *n*. maiale; pane (*di metallo*): **guinea —,** cavia; **to buy a — in a poke,** comprare alla cieca.

pigeon (pĭj'ŭn) *n*. piccione: **carrier —,** piccione viaggiatore: **that's your —,** è affar vostro.

pigeonhole (pĭj'ŭn·hōl') *n*. nicchia di colombaia; casella. *vt.* archiviare, incasellare.

piggish (pĭg'ĭsh) *agg.* maialesco; cocciuto, ostinato.

pighead (pĭg'hĕd') *n*. ostinato, testa dura. **—ed** *agg.* testardo, cocciuto.

pigmy (pĭg'mĭ) *n*. pigmeo.

pigsty (pĭg'stī') *n*. porcile.

pigtail (pĭg'tāl') *n*. codino.

pike (pīk) *n*. picca, lancia, picco; (*ittiol.*) luccio.

pilchard (pĭl'chĕrd) *n*. (*ittiol.*) sardina.

pile (pīl) *n*. mucchio; rogo; catasta; edificio; pelo (*dei tessuti*); pila; gruzzolo, piuolo, palo: **— driver,** battipalo; **atomic —,** pila atomica. *vt., vi.* accumulare, ammonticchiare; ammassarsi, accumularsi.

piles (pīlz) *n*. emorroidi.

pilfer (pĭl'fẽr) *vt., vi.* rubacchiare. **—er** *n.* ladruncolo.

pilgrim (pĭl'grĭm) *n.* pellegrino.

pilgrimage (pĭl'grĭ·mĭj) *n.* pellegrinaggio.

pill (pĭl) *n.* pillola; (*gergo*) sigaretta; rompiscatole, persona assfissiante.

pillage (pĭl'ĭj) *n.* saccheggio, rapina. *vt., vi.* saccheggiare, depredare.

pillar (pĭl'ẽr) *n.* colonna, pilastro, sostegno: **from — to post,** da Erode a Pilato.

pillbox (pĭl'bŏks') *n.* scatoletta di pillole; carrozzella; (*mil.*) casamatta; cappellino a tamburello.

pillory (pĭl'ō·rĭ) *n.* gogna.

pillow (pĭl'ō) *n.* cuscino, guanciale, supporto: **—case, — slip,** federa.

pilot (pī'lŭt) *n.* pilota; timoniere; guida: **— plant,** cantiere pilota. *vt.* pilotare, guidare, condurre.

pimp (pĭmp) *n.* mezzano.

pimpernel (pĭm'pẽr·nĕl) *n.* primula.

pimple (pĭm'p'l) *n.* foruncolo, pustola.

pin (pĭn) *n.* spillo, spilla; zipolo (*di botte*); punzone; perno; catenaccio; bietta; bischero (*di strumento mus.*); birillo: **not to care a —,** infischiarsene; **— money,** spillatico; denaro per le piccole spese; **—wheel** *n.* girandola; mulinello. *vt.* agganciare, appuntare con gli spilli, immobilizzare: **to — on,** appioppare; **to — one's faith on,** fare affidamento su.

pinafore (pĭn'ȧ·fōr') *n.* grembiulino per bambini.

pincers (pĭn'sẽrz) *n.pl.* pinze, tenaglie; (*mil.*) manovra a tenaglia.

pinch (pĭnch) *n.* pizzico; pizzicotto; strettoia, difficoltà; furto: **in a —,** in caso di bisogno; **— hitter,** sostituto, supplente. *vt., vi.* pizzicare; stringere; affliggere; contrarre; rubare; arrestare.

pinchers *n. pl.* tenaglie.

pine (pīn) (1) *n.* pino: **— cone,** pigna; **— grove,** pineto; **— nut,** pinolo.

pine (pīn) (2) *n.* struggimento. *vt.* rimpiangere. *vi.* languire, deperire: **to — after,** spasimare per, agognare.

pineapple (pīn'ăp''l) *n.* ananasso; (*mil.*) bomba a mano.

pinhead (pĭn'hĕd') *n.* capocchia di spillo.

pinion (pĭn'yŭn) *n.* penna; (*mecc.*) pignone. *vt.* immobilizzare.

pink (pĭngk) (1) *n.* rosso chiaro, (color) rosa; garofano: **in the — of condition,** nelle migliori condizioni. *agg.* roseo, rosso, imporporato.

pink (2) *vt.* pungere; frastagliare.

pinnacle (pĭn'ȧ·k'l) *n.* pinnacolo; torretta; cima, apogeo.

pint (pīnt) *n.* pinta (*circa mezzo litro*).

pin-up (girl) (pĭn'ŭp') *n.* foto di ragazza procace da appendere al muro.

pin-up lamp *n.* lampada a muro.

pioneer (pī'ō·nẽr') *n.* pioniere; precursore. *vt.* scoprire, esplorare; guidare; essere il precursore di; aprire la strada a. *vi.* fare il pioniere.

pious (pī'ŭs) *agg.* pio, devoto.

pipe (pīp) *n.* pipa; tubo, condotto; voce; strumento a fiato; (*anat.*) faringe; (*bot.*) stelo; canna (*d'organo*). *vt.* convogliare con tubi, munire di tubature; eseguire con strumento a fiato. *vi.* sonare strumenti a fiato; fischiare; gridare, avere un suono acuto: **to — down,** abbassare la voce.

pipeline (pīp'līn') *n.* conduttura; oleodotto; (*fig.*) fonte di informazioni.

pipelines *n. pl.* zampogna.

piper (pīp'ẽr) *n.* zampognaro.

piping (pīp'ĭng) *n.* tubazione, tubatura; suono di strumento a fiato; cordoncino (*di seta, ecc.*). *agg.* stri-

dulo; morbido; tranquillo: **— hot,** caldissimo, scottante; recentissimo, caldo caldo.

pippin (pĭp'ĭn) *n.* specie di mela; seme.

piquant (pē'kȧnt) *agg.* piccante.

pique (pēk) *n.* puntiglio, picca. *vt.* offendere; provocare, piccare, stuzzicare; **to — oneself on,** piccarsi di.

piracy (pī'rȧ·sĭ) *n.* pirateria; (*fig.*) plagio.

pirate (pī'rĭt) *n.* pirata; plagiario. *vi.* pirateggiare; plagiare.

pirogue (pī·rōg') *n.* piroga.

pirouette (pĭr'ŏŏ·ĕt') *n.* piroetta. *vi.* piroettare.

pistol (pĭs't'l) *n.* pistola.

piston (pĭs'tŭn) *n.* pistone: **— rod,** biella.

pit (pĭt) *n.* buca, pozzo, cava; ascella; buttero (*del vaiolo*); (*teat.*) platea; nocciolo: **— of the stomach,** bocca dello stomaco. *vt., vi.* scavare, incavare; mettere alla prova; incavarsi.

pitch (pĭch) (1) *n.* punto; intensità; tonalità; lancio; pendenza; livello, immersione; distanza. *vt.* erigere; drizzare; scagliare, buttare, scaraventare; disporre, regolare: **to — into,** aggredire; rimproverare, strapazzare. *vi.* precipitarsi; immergersi; inclinarsi; allogarsi, posarsi; (*naut. e aeron.*) beccheggiare: **to — in,** mettersi al lavoro.

pitch (pĭch) (2) *n.* pece; resina: **—black** *agg.* nerissimo; **—dark** *agg.* scurissimo; buio pesto. *vt.* impeciare.

pitcher (pĭch'ẽr) (1) *n.* lanciatore.

pitcher (pĭch'ẽr) (2) *n.* brocca, boccale.

pitchfork (pĭch'fôrk') *n.* forca, forcone.

piteous (pĭt'ē·ŭs) *agg.* pietoso.

pitfall (pĭt'fôl') *n.* trappola, trabocchetto.

pith (pĭth) *n.* polpa; forza, vigore; parte essenziale.

pithy (pĭth'ĭ) *avv.* vigoroso, sostanzioso.

pitiable (pĭt'ĭ·ȧb'l) *agg.* pietoso.

pitiful (pĭt'ĭ·fŏŏl) *n.* pietoso, miserevole.

pitiless (pĭt'ĭ·lĕs) *agg.* spietato.

pittance (pĭt'ăns) *n.* alimenti; nonnulla.

pity (pĭt'ĭ) *n.* pietà, compassione, peccato: **what a —!** che peccato! **for —'s sake!** per l'amor dei cieli! *vt., vi.* compiangere, impietosirsi.

pivot (pĭv'ŭt) *n.* perno. *vt.* imperniare. *vi.* far perno, imperniarsi, rotare.

pix (pĭks) *n.pl.* fotografie; illustrazioni; films.

pixilated (pĭk'sĭ-lāt'ĕd) *agg.* (*gergo*) stravagante, picchiatello; farsesco.

placard (plă'kärd) *n.* manifesto, cartellone, affisso. *vt.* affiggere, annunciare con manifesti.

placate (plā'kāt) *vt.* placare.

place (plās) *n.* luogo; posto; locale; dimora; posizione; impiego; dovere: **in the first —**, in primo luogo; **in — of**, in vece di; **out of —**, fuori di luogo; disoccupato; **to take —**, aver luogo; **to take one's —**, mettersi al proprio posto, prendere posto; *vt.* collocare, porre, situare.

placid (plăs'ĭd) *agg.* placido.

plagiarism (plā'jĭ-à-rĭz'm) *n.* plagio.

plagiarist (plā'jĭ-à-rĭst) *n.* plagiario.

plagiarize (plā'jĭ-à-rĭz) *vt.*, *vi.* plagiare.

plague (plāg) *n.* piaga, flagello. *vt.* vessare, tormentare, appestare, assillare.

plaid (plăd) *n.* mantello scozzese, coperta da viaggio. *agg.* scozzese (*di tessuto a quadri*).

plain (plān) *n.* pianura. *agg.* semplice, puro, piano; brutto; esplicito; uniforme, a tinta unita; ordinario; evidente: **— fool**, perfetto cretino; **— woman**, donna brutta; **in — sight**, in piena vista; **—clothes man** *n.* agente in borghese; **—spoken**, *agg.* esplicito, franco. *avv.* (*anche* **—ly**) chiaramente, semplicemente; evidentemente; francamente.

plaint (plānt) *n.* lamento, lagnanza; istanza. **—iff** *n.* attore (*in causa*). **—ive** *agg.* lamentoso.

plait (plăt) *n.* piega, falda, treccia. *vt.* piegare, intrecciare.

plan (plăn) *n.* piano; progetto; metodo; pianta. *vt.*, *vi.* progettare, far progetti; pianificare: **planned economy**, economia pianificata. **—ner** *n.* progettista; pianificatore.

plane (plān) (1) *n.* piano, pianura, superficie piana; pialla; (*aeron.*) piano portante, aeroplano: **elevating —** (*aeron.*) timone di profondità. *agg.* piano. *vt.* piallare. *vi.* (*aeron.*) planare.

plane (2) **plane-tree** *n.* platano.

planer (plān'ĕr) *n.* (*mecc.*) piallatrice.

planet (plăn'ĕt) *n.* pianeta.

plank (plăngk) *n.* tavola, asse; piattaforma. *vt.* intavolare, coprire di assi; snocciolare (*danari*). **—ing** *n.* tavolato.

plant (plănt) *n.* (*bot.*) pianta; impianto; turlupinatura, tranello. *vt.* piantare, conficcare, fissare; stabilire; inculcare.

plantation (plăn-tā'shŭn) *n.* piantagione, colonia.

planter (plănt'ĕr) *n.* piantatore.

plaque (plăk) *n.* placca.

plasma (plăz'mà) *n.* plasma.

plaster (plàs'tĕr) *n.* intonaco, stucco, gesso; impiastro: **— cast**, modello in gesso; (*med.*) ingessatura. **— of Paris**, scagliuola, gesso; **court —**, cerotto. *agg.* falso. *vt.* ingessare, intonacare, cospargere; affiggere; mettere un impiastro a.

plastic (plăs'tĭk) *agg.* plastico. **—s** *n. sing.* plastica, materia plastica.

plat (plăt) *n.* appezzamento, progetto, mappa. *vt.* progettare, disegnare la pianta di.

plate (plāt) *n.* piatto; placca, piastra; targa; argenteria; incisione, lastra (*anche fot.*); illustrazione, tavola; catodo; (*sport*) trofeo, gara: **fashion —**, figurino; **license —**, targa di circolazione. *vt.* placcare, laminare, corazzare; patinare (*carta*); targare.

plateau (plă-tō') *n.* altipiano; piazza; vassoio; (*fig.*) periodo di stabilità.

platen (plăt'ʼn) *n.* (*tip.*) platina di pressione; rullo (*della macchina per scrivere*): **— press**, platina.

platform (plăt'fôrm') *n.* piattaforma; pianoro; (*ferr.*) banchina, marciapiede.

platinum (plăt'ĭ-nŭm) *n.* platino: **— blonde**, bionda platinata.

platitude (plăt'ĭ-tūd) *n.* banalità, luogo comune.

platoon (plă-tōōn') *n.* plotone.

platter (plăt'ĕr) *n.* piatto di portata.

plaudit (plô'dĭt) *n.* applauso.

plausible (plô'zĭ-b'l) *agg.* plausibile, persuasivo; specioso.

play (plā) *n.* gioco, scherzo, divertimento; dramma; libertà d'azione, esecuzione (*mus.*); commedia; manovra: **fair —**, condotta leale; **foul —**, dolo; (*sport*) fallo, scorrettezza; *vt.* giocare; far agire; sonare (*uno strumento*), eseguire (*mus.*); rappresentare. *vi.* divertirsi, scherzare; agire, comportarsi; funzionare; recitare: **to — cards**, giocare alle carte; **to — a joke**, combinare uno scherzo; **to — the fool**, far lo stupido; **to — truant**, marinare la scuola; **to — havoc with** devastare; **to — on words**, equivocare, giocare sulle parole; **—ed out**, esaurito. **—er** *n.* giocatore; esecutore; attore: **— piano**, pianola; **piano —**, pianista. **—ful** *agg.* giocoso, scherzoso. **—ground** *n.* luogo di ricreazione, parco di giochi. **—mate** *n.* compagno di giochi. **—pen**, *n.* recinto o box per poppanti. **—room** *n.* saletta da giuoco (*in una casa privata*). **—thing** *n.* trastullo. **—wright** *n.* commediografo, drammaturgo.

plea (plē) *n.* scusa, protesta; difesa, istanza, supplica.

plead (plēd) *vt.*, *vi.* addurre, difendere, perorare, dichiarare, invocare, argomentare, intercedere: to — guilty, dichiararsi colpevole.

pleasant (plĕz'ănt) *agg.* piacevole, gradevole, amabile, simpatico. —ry *n.* facezia; allegria.

please (plēz) *vt.*, *vi.* placere, essere gradito, compiacere, accontentare, soddisfare, degnarsi: if you —, per cortesia, vi prego; as you —, come preferite; — yourself, fate come vi pare; — do it, per favore, fatelo; abbiate la cortesia di farlo.

pleased *agg.* contento, soddisfatto: to be — to, essere lieto di; to be — with, essere soddisfatto di, compiacersi di; ill— *agg.* malcontento.

pleasing (plēz'ing) *agg.* piacevole.

pleasurable (plĕzh'ẽr·à·b'l) *agg.* dilettevole, piacevole.

pleasure (plĕzh'ẽr) *n.* placere; soddisfazione; piacimento: at —, a piacimento, a volontà; during your —, finchè vi piacerà; what is your —? che cosa desiderate?, che cosa preferite? — trip, viaggio di piacere.

pleat (plēt) *vedi* plait.

plebeian (plē·bē'(y)ăn) *n.*, *agg.* plebeo.

plebiscite (plĕb'ĭ·sĭt) *n.* plebiscito.

pledge (plĕj) *n.* garanzia, pegno, impegno, ostaggio: as a — of, in pegno di; to take the —, far voto di temperanza. *vt.* impegnare, depositare in garanzia, far giurare, garantire: to — one's word, dare la propria parola; to — to secrecy, impegnare al segreto.

plenipotentiary (plĕn'ĭ·pô·tĕn'shĭ·ĕr'ĭ) *n.*, *agg.* plenipotenziario.

plenteous (plĕn'tē·ŭs) *agg.* abbondante.

plentiful (plĕn'tĭ·fŏŏl) *agg.* abbondante, copioso.

plenty (plĕn'tĭ) *n.* abbondanza: — of time, tempo a volontà; that is —, ce n'è in abbondanza. *agg.* abbondante. *avv.* abbondantemente.

pleurisy (plŏŏr'ĭ·sĭ) *n.* pleurite.

plexus (plĕk'sŭs) *n.* (*anat.*) plesso.

pliable (plī'à·b'l) *agg.* pieghevole, adattabile, arrendevole.

pliant (plī'ănt) *agg.* flessibile, duttile; influenzabile, arrendevole.

pliers (plī'ẽrz) *n.pl.* pinze.

plight (plīt) *n.* stato, situazione critica; pegno; imbarazzo. *vt.* impegnare, promettere.

plod (plŏd) *vi.* camminare pesantemente; sgobbare.

plot (plŏt) *n.* mappa, appezzamento, macchia; complotto, piano; intreccio (*di romanzo, ecc.*). *vt.*, *vi.* trac-

ciare (il piano di); suddividere in lotti; complottare, tramare, macchinare. —ter *n.* cospiratore.

plough (plou) *vedi* plow.

plover (plŭv'ẽr) *n.* (*ornit.*) piviere.

plow (plou) *n.* aratro, spazzaneve. *vt.*, *vi.* arare, solcare, aprirsi un varco; (*gergo*) bocciare.

pluck (plŭk) *n.* strappo, strattone; frattaglie; coraggio. *vt.* cogliere, strappare, spennare; pizzicare (*le corde di uno strumento*); arraffare; bocciare: to — asunder, separarecon forza; to — up, svellere; raccogliere le forze (*o il coraggio*).

plucky (plŭk'ĭ) *agg.* coraggioso.

plug (plŭg) *n.* tappo, zaffo, tampone; spicchio; ronzino; libro che si vende poco; studente sgobbone; (*autom.*) candela; rubinetto; otturazione (*di un dente*); (*elett.*) spina; pubblicità insistente, pubblicità inserita in un programma radiofonico, pistolotto inserito in un discorso: fire —, idrante; — hat, cappello a cilindro. *vt.*, *vi.* tappare, tamponare; conficcare; colpire (*con un proiettile, in pugno, ecc.*); otturare (*un dente*); inserire (*una spina*); sgobbare; fare pubblicità intensa a.

plum (plŭm) *n.* susina; uva passa; il meglio: — cake, panfrutto; — tree, susino.

plumage (plŏŏm'ĭj) *n.* plumaggio.

plumb (plŭm) *n.* piombino, perpendicolo: — bob, piombino. *agg.* perpendicolare, verticale: — crazy (*gergo*) completamente pazzo. *avv.* a piombo, perpendicolarmente. *vt.* mettere a piombo, sondare, piombare.

plumber (plŭm'ẽr) *n.* idraulico.

plumbing (plŭm'ĭng) *n.* impianto idraulico; sondaggio.

plume (plŏŏm) *n.* penna, piuma, pennacchio. *vt.* impiumare: to — oneself on, vantarsi di, gloriarsi di.

plummet (plŭm'ĕt) *n.* piombino; scandaglio; (*fig.*) peso. *vt.* scandagliare. *vi.* cadere a piombo.

plump (plŭmp) (1) *n.* caduta, scroscio. *agg.* diretto, brusco. *avv.* pesantemente; improvvisamente; a perpendicolo. *vt.* far precipitare. *vi.* precipitare.

plump (plŭmp) (2) *agg.* grassoccio, paffuto. —ness *n.* grassezza, floridezza.

plunder (plŭn'dẽr) *n.* bottino, saccheggio. *vt.*, *vi.* saccheggiare, depredare. —er *n.* saccheggiatore.

plunge (plŭnj) *n.* tuffo, slancio: to take the —, rompere gli indugi. *vt.*

scaraventare, immergere. vi. tuffarsi, slanciarsi: to — headlong, buttarsi a capofitto.

plunger (plŭn'jẽr) n. tuffatore; (mecc.) pistone, stantuffo.

pluperfect (plōō'pûr'fĕkt) n., agg. piuccheperfetto.

plural (plōōr'ăl) n., agg. plurale.

plus (plŭs) n. più (+), sovrappiù. agg. più, addizionale, positivo. prep. più, più di, con: two — two, due più due.

plush (plŭsh) n. felpa. agg. felpato, di felpa; elegante all'eccesso; comodo; soffice.

plutocrat (plōō'tō-krăt) n. plutocrate.

ply (plī) n. piega; treccia. vt. piegare; usare, far buon uso di; percorrere, solcare; stimolare; assillare: to — a trade, esercitare un commercio; to — with questions, tempestare di domande; to — oneself with, riempirsi di. vi. affrettarsi; lavorare assiduamente; fare la spola.

plyers (plī'ẽrz) n.pl. pinze.

pneumatic (nŭ-măt'ĭk) n., agg. pneumatico.

pneumonia (nŭ-mō'nĭ-á) n. polmonite.

poach (pōch) vt., vi. cacciare di frodo; calpestare; trafiggere; impastare; intridersi; affogare (le uova). —er n. bracconiere.

pock (pŏk) n. pustola, buttero. vt. butterare.

pocket (pŏk'ĕt) n. tasca, taschino, cavità, sacca, buca (del biliardo). vt. intascare, sottrarre; sopportare (un affronto), rinfoderare (l'orgoglio): — battleship, corazzata tascabile. —book n. portafoglio, taccuino, libro tascabile. —knife n. coltello a serramanico.

pockmark (pŏk'märk') n. buttero (del vaiolo). —ed agg. butterato.

pod (pŏd) n. baccello, guscio.

poem (pō'ĕm) n. poesia, poema.

poesy (pō'ĕ-sĭ) n. poesia (arte).

poet (pō'ĕt) n. poeta. —ess n. poetessa. —ic (-ĕt'ĭk), —ical agg. poetico. —ics n. poetica. —ry n. poesia.

poignant (poin'yănt) agg. piccante, intenso; drammatico, straziante.

point (point) n. punto; grado; punta; scopo, mira; argomento; costrutto; posizione: it is not to the —, it is beside the —, non c'entra, è fuori dell'argomento; at all points, sotto tutti i riguardi; in —, adatto, calzante; in — of, per quanto riguarda; in — of fact, effettivamente; to come to the —, venire al fatto; to make a — to, farsi un dovere di; to stretch a — , fare uno strappo alla regola. vt., vi. appun-

tire, aguzzare; punteggiare; indicare, puntare: to — out, far notare. —-blank agg. diretto, esplicito. avv. direttamente, a bruciapelo.

pointed (poin'tĕd) agg. acuto, appuntito, diretto, mordente, efficace.

pointer (poin'tẽr) n. indice, indicatore, lancetta; suggerimento; cane da punta, pointer.

poise (poiz) n. peso, gravità; equilibrio; portamento; sospensione. vt. bilanciare, equilibrare. vi. bilanciarsi, librarsi.

poison (poi's'n) n. veleno. vt. avvelenare. —er n. avvelenatore.

poisonous (poi'z'n-ŭs) agg. velenoso.

poke (pōk) n. colpo, spinta, urto; sacco, tasca. vt., vi. spingere; urtare; smuovere; rovistare, attizzare (il fuoco); intrufolarsi; andare a tastoni: to — into, ficcare, conficcare; to — out, sbucare, spuntare; to — fun at, prendersi gioco di.

poker (pōk'ẽr) n. attizzatoio; poker (gioco di carte).

polar (pō'lẽr) agg. polare: — bear, orso bianco; — lights, aurora boreale.

polarize (pōl'ẽr-īz) vt. polarizzare.

pole (pōl) (1) n. palo, pertica; timone (di carro): greased —, albero della cuccagna; — vault, salto con l'asta.

pole (pōl) (2) n. polo.

Pole (pōl) (3) n. polacco.

polecat (pōl'kăt') n. puzzola.

polemic (pō-lĕm'ĭk) agg. polemico.

polemics n. arte polemica.

polestar (pōl'stär') n. stella polare.

police (pō-lēs') n. polizia: — state, stato poliziesco o totalitario; — station, commissariato di polizia. agg. poliziesco, piliziotto. vt. vigilare, mantenere l'ordine in.

policeman n. poliziotto, guardia.

policy (pŏl'ĭ-sĭ) n. politica; tattica, sistema; polizza assicurativa.

Polish (pōl'ĭsh) (1) agg. polacco.

polish (pŏl'ĭsh) (2) n. lucido, lucidatura, lucentezza; stile, buone maniere. vt. lucidare, levigare, ingentilire. vi. diventar lucido, raffinarsi.

polite (pō-līt') agg. cortese, garbato. —ness n. cortesia.

politic (pŏl'ĭ-tĭk) agg. sagace, diplomatico, prudente.

political (pō-lĭt'ĭ-kăl) agg. politico.

politician (pŏl'ĭ-tĭsh'ăn) n. uomo politico.

politics (pŏl'ĭ-tĭks) n. politica.

poll (pōl) n. testa, occipite; lista elettorale; scrutinio; referendum; urna elettorale. vt., vi. cimare; rapare; scrutinare, votare, raccogliere voti; consultare (in un referendum).

pollen (pŏl'ĕn) n. polline.

pollster (pōl'stēr) n. indagatore, scrutatore, addetto a un referendum.

pollute (pŏ·lūt') vt. corrompere, profanare, insudiciare, contaminare.

polo (pō'lō) n. (sport) polo: — coat, giacchettone di pelo di cammello; — shirt, camicia sportiva, camiciola, argentina.

polyclinic (pŏl'ĭ·klĭn'ĭk) n. policlinico.

polygamist (pŏ·lĭg'a·mĭst) n. poligamo.

polygamy (pŏ·lĭg'a·mĭ) n. poligamia.

polyglot (pŏl'ĭ·glŏt) n. poliglotta.

polyp (pŏl'ĭp) n. polipo.

pomade (pŏ·mād') n. pomata.

pomegranate (pŏm'grăn'ĭt) n. melagrana, melograno.

pomp (pŏmp) n. pompa, fasto.

pompous (pŏmp'ŭs) agg. pomposo.

pond (pŏnd) n. stagno, laghetto.

ponder (pŏn'dēr) vt., vi. ponderare.

ponderous (pŏn'dēr·ŭs) agg. ponderoso.

pontiff (pŏn'tĭf) n. pontefice.

pontoon (pŏn·tōōn') n. barcone, pontone; (aeron.) galleggiante: — bridge, ponte di barche.

pony (pō'nĭ) n. cavallo nano; bigino (vedi crib).

poodle (pōō'd'l) n. cane barbone.

pool (pōōl) n. stagno, pozza, sorgente; posta (di gioco); fusione, consorzio; fondo comune: swimming —, piscina. vt., vi. riunire in un fondo comune, contribuire a un fondo comune; consorziarsi.

poor (pōŏr) agg. povero, misero; scarso, magro; scadente; debole. — house n. ospizio di mendicità. —ly agg. misero, malaticcio. avv. miseramente, malamente.

pop (pŏp) n. scoppio; sparo; colpo sordo. vt., vi. spingere, buttare; impegnare; entrare (o uscire) di colpo; far esplodere; lanciarsi; sparare, detonare; saltare (di tappo).

pope (pŏp) n. papa.

popeyed (pŏp'īd') agg. con gli occhi sbarrati, stralunato.

popgun (pŏp'gŭn') n. fucile ad aria compressa.

poplar (pŏp'lēr) n. (bot.) pioppo.

poppy (pŏp'ĭ) n. papavero.

populace (pŏp'û·lĭs) n. popolino, plebe.

popular (pŏp'û·lēr) agg. popolare. —ity (-ăr'ĭ·tĭ) n. popolarità.

populate (pŏp'û·lāt) vt. popolare. vi. popolarsi.

population (pŏp'û·lā'shŭn) n. popolazione.

populous (pŏp'û·lŭs) agg. popoloso.

porcelain (pōr'sĕ·lĭn) n. porcellana.

porch (pōrch) n. portico, veranda.

porcupine (pōr'kû·pīn) n. porcospino.

pore (pōr) (1) n. (anat.) poro.

pore (pōr) (2) vi.: to — on, upon, over, esaminare, ponderare, leggere attentamente.

pork (pōrk) n. carne di porco: — pie, sformato di carne di maiale; cappello alla tirolese o a tronco di cono.

porpoise (pōr'pŭs) n. focena, delfino.

porridge (pōr'ĭj) n. pappa d'avena (o di altra farina).

port (pōrt) (1) n. porto, scalo; (naut.) sinistra (della nave); boccaporto.

port (pōrt) (2) n. porto (vino d'Oporto).

portable (pōr'ta·b'l) agg. portabile, portatile.

portend (pōr·tĕnd') vt. presagire, significare, denotare.

portent (pōr'tĕnt) n. presagio; portento. —ous (-tĕnt'ŭs) agg. sinistro; sintomatico; importante, prodigioso.

porter (pōr'tēr) n. facchino, portiere; birra forte; conduttore (di vagone letto).

portfolio (pōrt·fō'lĭ·ō) n. portafoglio (ministeriale e comm.), portacarte.

porthole (pōrt'hōl') n. feritoia; (naut.) portello, oblò.

portion (pōr'shŭn) n. porzione, parte. vt. dividere, distribuire.

portliness (pōrt'lĭ·nĕs) n. portamento maestoso, corpulenza.

portly (pōrt'lĭ) agg. maestoso, corpulento.

portrait (pōr'trāt) n. ritratto.

portray (pōr·trā') vt. ritrarre, fare il ritratto a, descrivere. —al n. ritratto, descrizione.

Portuguese (pōr'tû̇·gēs) n., agg. portoghese.

pose (pōz) n. posa, atteggiamento. vt. imbarazzare, confondere; mettere in posa; formulare. vi. posare: to — as, posare a, fingersi.

poser (pōz'ēr) n. rompicapo, domanda imbarazzante; posatore.

position (pŏ·zĭsh'ŭn) n. posizione, situazione, tesi.

positive (pŏz'ĭ·tĭv) n. positiva (fot.). agg. positivo, assoluto; sicuro, convinto. —ly avv. positivamente; sicuramente, decisamente.

posse (pŏs'ē) n. forza pubblica; pattuglia.

possess (pŏ·zĕs') vt. possedere; dominare.

possessed agg. invasato, pazzo.

possession (pŏ·zĕsh'ŭn) n. possesso, possedimento.

possessive (pŏ·zĕs'ĭv) n., agg. possessivo.

possibility (pŏs'ĭ·bĭl'ĭ·tĭ) n. possibilità, probabilita.

possible (pŏs′ĭ-b'l) n. probabile, possibile.

possibly (pŏs′ĭ-blĭ) avv. forse, probabilmente; in alcun modo.

possum (pŏs′ŭm) n. opossum: to play —, fare la marmotta.

post (pōst) n. palo, pilastro; posta, corrispondenza; posto, carica; (mil.) presidio: — free, franco di porto; — office, ufficio postale; —office box, casella postale; army —, guarnigione, distaccamento militare; — exchange (mil.), spaccio. vt. impostare, spedire; collocare; affiggere; ragguagliare; (comm.) riportare a mastro. vi. affrettarsi: to keep —ed, tenere o tenersi al corrente.

postage (pōs′tĭj) n. affrancatura: — stamp, francobollo.

postal (pŏs′tăl) agg. postale: — order, vaglia postale.

postcard n. cartolina postale.

poster (pōs′tĕr) n. cartellone, manifesto; attacchino.

poste restante (pōst′rĕs-tänt′) n. fermo-posta.

posterior (pŏs-tēr′ĭ-ĕr) agg. posteriore.

posterity (pŏs-tĕr′ĭ-tĭ) n. posterità.

posthaste (pōst′hāst′) avv. frettolosamente.

posthumous (pŏs′tŭ-mŭs) agg. postumo.

postman (pōst′măn) n. postino.

postmark (pōst′märk′) n. timbro postale.

postmaster (pōst′más′tĕr) n. ricevitore postale: — general n. ministro delle poste.

post-mortem (pōst′mŏr′tĕm) n. autopsia.

postpone (pōst-pōn′) vt. rimandare, posporre, differire. —ment n. rinvio, posposizione.

postscript (pōst′skrĭpt) n. poscritto.

posture (pŏs′tŭr) n. posa, atteggiamento, situazione. vt., vi. mettere (o mettersi) in posa.

posy (pō′zĭ) n. mazzo di fiori.

pot (pŏt) n. vaso, pentola, recipiente; premio.

potassium (pō-tăs′ĭ-ŭm) n. potassio.

potato (pō-tā′tō) n. patata: mashed potatoes, purè di patate; sweet —, patata dolce o americana.

potbellied (pŏt′bĕl′ĭd) agg. panciuto.

potency (pō′tĕn-sĭ) n. potenza, autorità; efficacia; capacità, potere.

potent (pō′tĕnt) agg. potente, efficace.

potential (pō-tĕn′shăl) n., agg. potenziale.

pothook (pŏt′hŏŏk′) n. catena del camino; scarabocchio.

potion (pō′shŭn) n. pozione, beveraggio.

potpourri (pō′pŏŏ′rē′) n. accozzaglia, miscela.

potter (pŏt′ĕr) n. vasaio: —'s field, cimitero dei poveri.

pottery (pŏt′ĕr-ĭ) n. vasellame, fabbrica di vasellame, ceramica (arte).

pouch (pouch) n. borsa, tasca.

poultice (pōl′tĭs) n. cataplasma.

poultry (pōl′trĭ) n. pollame.

pounce (pouns) n. artiglio. vt., vi. artigliare: to — upon, ghermire, balzare su; to — into a room, irrompere in una stanza.

pound (pound) (1) n. libbra; lira sterlina.

pound (pound) (2) vt. battere, tempestare; polverizzare; ammaccare. vi. camminare pesantemente.

pour (pōr) vt. versare, riversare. vi. fluire, traboccare, diluviare: to — in, affluire.

pout (pout) n. broncio. vi. fare il broncio, imbronciarsi.

poverty (pŏv′ĕr-tĭ) n. povertà.

POW (pē′ō′dŭb′ĭ-ŭ) n. (sigla di Prisoner Of War) prigioniero di guerra.

powder (pou′dĕr) n. polvere, polverina; cipria: — room, toilette per signore; to take a — (gergo) svignarsela. vt. polverizzare, cospargere, incipriare. vi. incipriarsi, andare in polvere.

power (pou′ĕr) n. potere, forza; potenza; facoltà, autorità; portata: — of attorney, procura (mandato); — plant, centrale elettrica; apparato motore; motive —, forza motrice. —ful agg. potente. —house n. centrale elettrica, (fig.) persona dinamica o attiva. —less agg. impotente.

practicable (prăk′tĭ-ká-b'l) agg. fattibile, praticabile.

practical (prăk′tĭ-kăl) agg. pratico: — joke, tiro birbone. —ly avv. praticamente, virtualmente.

practice (prăk′tĭs) n. pratica, prassi, procedura, abitudine, esercizio, uso; clientela o attività (di professionista). vt. praticare, studiare, esercitare. vi. esercitarsi.

practiced (prăk′tĭst) agg. addestrato, abile.

practise (prăk′tĭs) vedi practice.

practitioner (prăk-tĭsh′ŭn-ĕr) n. professionista, medico.

prairie (prâr′ĭ) n. prateria.

praise (prāz) n. lode, elogio. vt. lodare, elogiare, magnificare. —worthy agg. lodevole.

pram (prăm) n. (abbr. di perambulator) carrozzina per bambini.

prance (prăns) *vi.* caracollare; passeggiare con sussiego.

prank (prăngk) *n.* stravaganza, scherzo, burla, tiro birbone.

prate (prāt) *n.* vaniloquio. *vi.* cianciare.

pratfall (prăt'fôl') *n.* (*gergo*) capitombolo.

prattle (prăt''l) *n.* ciancia, chiacchiera, balbettio. *vi.* cianciare, balbettare.

pray (prā) *vt.*, *vi.* pregare, supplicare.

prayer (prâr) *n.* preghiera: Lord's —, Padre Nostro.

preach (prēch) *vt.*, *vi.* predicare. — *n.* predicatore. —ing *n.* predica, predicazione.

preamble (prē'ăm'b'l) *n.* preambolo.

prearrange (prē'ä·rānj') *vt.* predisporre.

precarious (prē·kâr'ĭ·ŭs) *agg.* precario.

precaution (prē·kô'shŭn) *n.* precauzione.

precede (prē·sēd') *vt.*, *vi.* precedere.

precedence (prē·sēd'ĕns) *n.* precedenza.

precedent (prĕs'ē·dĕnt) *n.*, *agg.* precedente.

preceding (prē·sēd'ĭng) *agg.* precedente, previo.

precept (prē'sĕpt) *n.* precetto.

precinct (prē'sĭngkt) *n.* limite; distretto; giurisdizione: *pl.* dintorni, vicinanze.

precious (prĕsh'ŭs) *agg.* prezioso; adorato; ricercato. *avv.* molto: — little, ben poco.

precipice (prĕs'ĭ·pĭs) *n.* precipizio.

precipitate (prē·sĭp'ĭ·tāt) *n.* (*chim.*) precipitato. *agg.* precipitoso, avventato, improvviso. *vt.*, *vi.* precipitare.

precipitation (prē·sĭp'ĭ·tā'shŭn) *n.* precipitazione.

precipitous (prē·sĭp'ĭ·tŭs) *agg.* precipitoso; scosceso, impervio.

precis (prā·sē') *n.* riassunto, compendio.

precise (prē·sīs') *agg.* preciso, esatto.

precisian (prē·sĭzh'ăn) *n.* formalista.

precision (prē·sĭzh'ŭn) *n.* precisione, accuratezza.

preclude (prē·klōōd') *vt.* precludere, escludere, impedire.

precocious (prē·kō'shŭs) *agg.* precoce.

preconceived (prē'kŏn·sēvd') *agg.* preconcetto.

preconception (prē'kŏn·sĕp'shŭn) *n.* preconcetto, pregiudizio.

predecessor (prĕd'ē·sĕs'ēr) *n.* predecessore.

predestine (prē·dĕs'tĭn) *vt.* predestinare.

predicament (prē·dĭk'á·mĕnt) *n.* situazione critica.

predicate (prĕd'ĭ·kāt) *n.* predicato.

predict (prē·dĭkt') *vt.* predire. —ion *n.* predizione.

predilection (prē'dĭ·lĕk'shŭn) *n.* predilezione.

predispose (prē'dĭs·pōz') *vt.* predisporre.

predominance (prē·dŏm'ĭ·náns) *n.* predominio, ascendente.

predominate (prē·dŏm'ĭ·nāt) *vt.*, *vi.* predominare, prevalere.

pre-empt (prē·ĕmpt') *vt.* acquistare la priorità su. —ion *n.* priorità, diritto di precedenza.

preen (prēn) *vt.* lisciarsi le penne; tirarsi a pomice; agghindarsi: to — oneself upon, gloriarsi di.

prefabricate (prē·făb'rĭ·kāt) *vt.* prefabbricare: prefabbricated smile, sorriso stereotipato.

preface (prĕf'ĭs) *n.* prefazione. *vt.* fare una (o servire da) prefazione a.

prefect (prē'fĕkt) *n.* prefetto.

prefer (prē·fûr') *vt.* preferire; presentare (*querela*, *ecc.*); promuovere. —able (prĕf'ēr·á·b'l) *agg.* preferibile. —ably *avv.* preferibilmente. —ence (prĕf'-) *n.* preferenza.

prefix (prē·fĭks') *n.* prefisso. *vt.* prefiggere, premettere, prestabilire.

pregnancy (prĕg'năn·sĭ) *n.* gravidanza.

pregnant (prĕg'nănt) *agg.* gravida; incinta, (*fig.*) gravido, significativo.

prehistoric (prē'hĭs·tŏr'ĭk) *agg.* preistorico.

prehistory (prē·hĭs'tō·rĭ) *n.* preistoria.

prejudge (prē·jŭj') *vt.* giudicare prematuramente o sommariamente.

prejudice (prĕj'ōō·dĭs) *n.* pregiudizio, detrimento. *vt.* pregiudicare, influenzare.

prejudicial (prĕj'ōō·dĭsh'ăl) *agg.* pregiudiziale.

prelate (prĕl'ĭt) *n.* prelato.

preliminary (prē·lĭm'ĭ·nĕr·ĭ) *n.*, *agg.* preliminare.

prelude (prĕl'ūd) *n.* preludio. *vt.*, *vi.* preludere a.

premature (prē'má·tūr') *agg.* prematuro, intempestivo.

premeditate (prē·mĕd'ĭ·tāt) *vt.* premeditare.

premier (prē'mĭ·ēr) *n.* capo, primo ministro. *agg.* primo, principale.

premise (prĕm'ĭs) *n.* supposizione, premessa: —s, *pl.* beni immobili, terreni; on the —s, sul luogo. *vt.* premettere.

premium (prē'mĭ·ŭm) *n.* premio, aggio: at a —, sopra il valore nominale.

preoccupy (prē·ŏk'ū·pī) *vt.* occupare prima; preoccupare.

preordain (prē'ôr·dān') *vt.* preordinare.

prepaid (prĕ·pād') agg. pagato anticipatamente: to send —, spedire franco di porto.

preparation (prĕp'd·rā'shŭn) n. preparazione, preparativo.

preparatory (prĕ·păr'd·tō'rĭ) agg. preparatorio, introduttivo.

prepare (prĕ·pâr') vt. preparare. vi. prepararsi.

preposition (prĕp'ō·zĭsh'ŭn) n. preposizione.

prepossess (prē'pŏ·zĕs') vt. influenzare, impressionare favorevolmente. —ing agg. simpatico, attraente.

preposterous (prē·pŏs'tēr·ŭs) agg. assurdo.

prerequisite (prē·rĕk'wĭ·zĭt) n. requisito, condizione necessaria. agg. indispensabile.

prerogative (prĕ·rŏg'd·tĭv) n. prerogativa.

presage (prĕ·sāj') n. presagio. vt. presagire.

prescribe (prĕ·skrīb') vt. prescrivere.

prescription (prĕ·skrĭp'shŭn) n. prescrizione.

presence (prĕz'ĕns) n. presenza: — of mind, prontezza di spirito.

present (prĕz'ĕnt) n. presente (il tempo attuale); dono, regalo: at —, ora, oggi; for the —, per ora, per il momento. agg. presente, attuale: — company excepted, esclusi i presenti. vt. (prĕ·zĕnt') presentare, esibire, regalare: to — someone with a pen, regalare una penna a qualcuno. —day agg. di oggi, odierno.

presentation (prĕz'ĕn·tā'shŭn) n. presentazione; dono, omaggio.

presentiment (prē·zĕn't ĭ·mĕnt) n. presentimento.

presently (prĕz'ĕnt·lĭ) avv. presentemente, ora; allora, in quel momento; immediatamente, tra poco, di lì a poco; direttamente; di conseguenza.

preservation (prĕz'ēr·vā'shŭn) n. preservazione, conservazione.

preserve (prĕ·zûrv') n. conserva; riserva (di caccia o pesca). vt. preservare, conservare, mettere in conserva, mantenere.

preside (prĕ·zīd') vt. presiedere: to — at (o over) a meeting, presiedere a un'assemblea.

presidency (prĕz'ĭ·dĕn·sĭ) n. presidenza.

president (prĕz'ĭ·dĕnt) n. presidente, preside, rettore.

press (prĕs) n. pressa; calca, folla; stampa, stamperia; calca, folla; fretta; armadio. vt., vi. pressare, premere, spremere; affrettare, incalzare, insistere; stirare; affrettarsi, accalcarsi: to —

one's point, insistere; to — through the crowd, aprirsi un varco tra la folla; hard-pressed by work, carico di lavoro; to be hard-pressed for money, avere bisogno impellente di soldi.

pressing agg. urgente, pressante.

pressure (prĕsh'ēr) n. pressione, oppressione, coercizione, urgenza: — gauge, manometro: — cooker, pentola a pressione.

pressurize (prĕsh'ēr·ĭz) vt. (aeron.) pressurizzare.

prestige (prĕs·tēzh') n. prestigio.

presto (prĕs'tō) avv. subito, all'improvviso.

presumable (prē·zūm'd·b'l) agg. presumibile, probabile.

presume (prē·zūm') vt., vi. presumere; agire con arroganza: to — to, permettersi di; to — on, upon, abusare di, fare eccessivo affidamento su.

presuming agg. presuntuoso.

presumption (prē·zŭmp'shŭn) n. presunzione; supposizione.

presumptuous (prē·zŭmp'tṵ·ŭs) agg. presuntuoso.

presuppose (prē'sŭ·pōz') vt. presupporre.

presupposition (prē'sŭp·ō·zĭsh'ŭn) n. presupposizione.

pretence vedi pretense.

pretend (prē·tĕnd') vt., vi. fingere, asserire, pretendere.

pretender (-dĕr) n. simulatore; pretendente.

pretense (prē·tĕns') n. finzione, pretesto; ostentazione; asserzione, pretesa: under — of, col pretesto di.

pretension (prē·tĕn'shŭn) n. pretesa, diritto, presunzione.

pretentious (prē·tĕn'shŭs) agg. pretenzioso.

pretext (prē'tĕkst) n. pretesto.

prettily (prĭt'ĭ·lĭ) avv. graziosamente.

prettiness (prĭt'ĭ·nĕs) n. grazia, leggiadria.

pretty (prĭt'ĭ) agg. grazioso, bello, gentile; (fam.) considerevole. avv. discretamente, un po', abbastanza.

prevail (prĕ·vāl') vi. prevalere, predominare, riuscire: to — on, upon, persuadere, vincere. —ing agg. prevalente, comune, generale.

prevalence (prĕv'd·lĕns) n. prevalenza.

prevalent (prĕv'd·lĕnt) agg. prevalente, generale, diffuso.

prevaricate (prē·văr'ĭ·kāt) vt. cavillare, giocare sull'equivoco; mentire.

prevent (prĕ·vĕnt') vt. prevenire, evitare, ostacolare, impedire. —ion n. prevenzione, precauzione, impedimento.

preview (pre'vū') *n.* visione privata, anteprima; il "prossimamente"; (*giorn.*) primizia; (*radio e T.V.*) prova generale.

previous (prē'vǐ·ǔs) *agg.* precedente, anteriore, previo. —ly *avv.* precedentemente.

prevision (prē·vǐzh'ǔn) *n.* previsione.

prey (prā) *n.* preda, bottino: birds of —, uccelli rapaci. *vi.* predare, saccheggiare; (*seg. da* on, upon) sfruttare, opprimere: to —on one's mind, angustiare, tormentare.

price (prīs) *n.* prezzo, valore, costo: at any —, a qualunque costo. *vt.* valutare, fissare il prezzo di.

priceless (prīs'lěs) *agg.* inestimabile, impareggiabile.

prick (prǐk) *n.* punta, puntura, pungolo; puntino. *vt.* punzecchiare, pungere; drizzare (*le orecchie*); rimordere (*della coscienza*); spronare. *vi.* ergersi, drizzarsi, sentirsi pungere.

prickle (prǐk''l) *n.* pungiglione, aculeo, puntura, spina.

prickly (prǐk'lǐ) *agg.* spinoso, pungente: — heat, sudamina; — pear, fico d'India.

pride (prīd) *n.* orgoglio, fierezza. *vt.* inorgoglire: to — oneself, inorgoglirsi; vantarsi di, essere fiero di.

priest (prēst) *n.* prete. —hood *n.* sacerdozio, clero. —ly *agg.* sacerdotale.

prig (prǐg) *n.* saputello, pedante.

priggish (prǐg'ǐsh) *agg.* affettato; sostenuto; pedante; cattedratico.

prim (prǐm) *agg.* compito; affettato, sostenuto; pieno di sussiego.

primacy (prī'mȧ·sǐ) *n.* primato, supremazia.

primarily (prī'měr·ǐ·lǐ) *avv.* primariamente, originariamente.

primary (prī'měr·ǐ) *n.* primario; originario; principale, fondamentale; elementare.

prime (prīm) *n.* origine, principio; primavera, giovinezza, rigoglio, fior fiore; numero primo: to be in one's —, essere nel fiore degli anni. *agg.* primo; originale, primitivo; fondamentale, principale: — cost, costo di produzione. *vt.*, *vi.* innescare, adescare; caricare; (*un'arma*); istruire tempestivamente.

primer (prīm'ēr) (1) *n.* sillabario.

primer (prīm'ēr) (2) *n.* detonatore.

primeval (prī·mē'văl) *agg.* primordiale.

priming (prīm'ǐng) *n.* esca, innesco.

primitive (prǐm'ǐ·tǐv) *n.*, *agg.* primitivo.

primness (prǐm'něs) *n.* affettazione.

primp (prǐmp) *vt.* agghindare. *vi.* agghindarsi.

primrose (prǐm'rōz') *n.* primula.

prince (prǐns) *n.* principe. —ly *agg.* principesco.

princess (prǐn'sěs) *n.* principessa.

principal (prǐn'sǐ·pȧl) *n.* principale; direttore; parte principale; mandante, responsabile; (*comm.*) capitale. *agg.* principale, essenziale.

principle (prǐn'sǐ·p'l) *n.* principio, regola, fondamento, base: on —, per principio; in —, in linea di massima.

prink (prǐngk) *vi.* agghindarsi.

print (prǐnt) *n.* stampa; giornale; impronta; stampo; tessuto stampato; incisione; (*fot.*) positiva: out of —, esaurito (*di libri*). *vt.*, *vi.* imprimere; stampare; scrivere in stampatello. —er *n.* stampatore.

printing (prǐnt'ǐng) *n.* stampa, tiratura; stamperia: — press, torchio tipografico; — works, stamperia di tessuti.

prior (prī'ēr) (1) *agg.* anteriore, precedente. *avv.* precedentemente: — to, prima di.

prior (prī'ēr) (2) *n.* priore.

prioress (prī'ēr·ĕs) *n.* madre superiora.

priority (prī·ŏr'ǐ·tǐ) *n.* priorità, precedenza.

priory (prī'ō·rǐ) *n.* convento.

prism (prǐz'm) *n.* prisma.

prison (prǐz''n) *n.* prigione, carcere. *vt.* imprigionare.

prisoner (prǐz''n·ēr) *n.* prigioniero; detenuto, imputato.

privacy (prī'vȧ·sǐ) *n.* solitudine, intimità; segreto, segretezza: to have no —, non aver luogo dove appartarsi.

private (prī'vǐt) *n.* soldato semplice. *agg.* privato, particolare, personale, confidenziale, intimo: — eye (*gergo*) investigatore privato.

privation (prī·vā'shŭn) *n.* privazione, perdita.

privet (prǐv'ĕt) *n.* (*bot.*) ligustro.

privilege (prǐv'ǐ·lǐj) *n.* privilegio.

privileged *agg.* privilegiato: to be — to, avere il privilegio o la fortuna di.

privy (prǐv'ǐ) *n.* gabinetto; (*legge*) parte in causa. *agg.* segreto: — chamber, camera del consiglio; to be — to, essere a conoscenza di.

prize (prīz) *n.* premio, ricompensa, preda, bottino, vincita; stima, valutazione: — fight, incontro di pugilato; — fighter, pugile. *vt.* tenere in gran conto, valutare; (*mecc.*) azionare con una leva.

probability (prŏb'ȧ·bǐl'ǐ·tǐ) *n.* probabilità.

probable (prŏb'á·b'l) *agg.* probabile.

probably (prŏb'á·blĭ) *avv.* probabilmente.

probate (prō'bāt) *n.* omologazione. *vt.* omologare.

probation (prō·bā'shŭn) *n.* prova, noviziato, esame, tirocinio; (*legge*) libertà vigilata. **—er** *n.* candidato novizio.

probe (prōb) *n.* sonda. *vt.* sondare; sviscerare, scrutare, esaminare a fondo.

problem (prŏb'lĕm) *n.* problema.

procedure (prō·sē'dûr) *n.* procedura.

proceed (prō·sēd') *n.* (*gen.pl.*) provento, ricavato. *vi.* procedere; disporsi (*a*); derivare, emanare; adire le vie legali.

proceeding (prō·sēd'ĭng) *n.* procedimento, azione; linea di condotta.

proceedings *pl.* resoconto, atti.

process (prŏs'ĕs) *n.* processo, procedimento, corso, ordine; citazione: **in the — of being made,** in via di preparazione; **in — of time,** col tempo; **to serve a —,** notificare una intimazione; **— printing,** tricromia, quadricromia; **—server,** ufficiale giudiziario. *vt.* lavorare (*un prodotto*), sottoporre a procedimento di lavorazione; addestrare (*attraverso un corso generale*).

procession (prō·sĕsh'ŭn) *n.* processione: **funeral —,** corteo fùnebre.

proclaim (prō·klām') *vt., vi.* proclamare, dichiarare, bandire.

proclamation (prŏk'lá·mā'shŭn) *n.* proclamazione, ordinanza.

procure (prō·kūr') *vt.* procurare, procacciare, causare.

prod (prŏd) *n.* pungolo, stimolo. *vt.* stimolare, incitare.

prodigal (prŏd'ĭ·gǎl) *n., agg.* prodigo.

prodigious (prō·dĭj'ŭs) *agg.* prodigioso.

prodigy (prŏd'ĭ·jĭ) *n.* prodigio.

produce (prō·dūs') *n.* prodotto. *vt., vi.* produrre.

producer (prō·dūs'ēr) *n.* produttore; (*teat.*) impresario; (*cinema*) produttore, direttore di produzione. **— gas,** gas povero.

product (prŏd'ŭkt) *n.* prodotto.

production (prō·dŭk'shŭn) *n.* produzione, opera.

productive (prō·dŭk'tĭv) *agg.* produttivo.

profanation (prŏf'á·nā'shŭn) *n.* profanazione.

profane (prō·fān') *agg.* profano. *vt.* profanare.

profanity (prō·făn'ĭ·tĭ) *n.* profanità, irriverenza, bestemmia.

profess (prō·fĕs') *vt.* professare, dichiarare.

profession (prō·fĕsh'ŭn) *n.* professione.

professional (prō·fĕsh'ŭn·ăl) *n.* professionista. *agg.* professionale.

professor (prō·fĕs'ēr) *n.* professore.

proffer (prŏf'ēr) *n.* offerta. *vt.* offrire.

proficiency (prō·fĭsh'ĕn·sĭ) *n.* abilità.

proficient (prō·fĭsh'ĕnt) *agg.* versato, abile, competente.

profile (prō'fĭl) *n.* profilo.

profit (prŏf'ĭt) *n.* profitto, guadagno, vantaggio: **— and loss,** perdite e profitti; **net —,** guadagno netto. *vi.* giovare. *vi.* profittare, avvantaggiarsi: **to — by,** trarre profitto da.

profitable (prŏf'ĭt·á·b'l) *agg.* lucroso, vantaggioso.

profiteer (prŏf'ĭ·tēr') *n.* profittatore, speculatore. *vi.* lucrare, speculare.

profligacy (prŏf'lĭ·gá·sĭ) *n.* dissolutezza.

profligate (prŏf'lĭ·gāt) *n., agg.* dissoluto.

profound (prō·found') *agg.* profondo.

profuse (prō·fūs') *agg.* eccessivo, sovrabbondante; prodigo; esuberante.

progeny (prŏj'ĕ·nĭ) *n.* progenie.

program, programme (prō'grăm) *n.* programma.

progress (prŏg'rĕs) *n.* progresso, sviluppo, corso, avanzamento. *vi.* (prō·grĕs') avanzarsi, progredire. **—ive** *n.* progressista. *agg.* progressivo.

prohibit (prō·hĭb'ĭt) *vt.* proibire.

prohibition (prō'ĭ·bĭsh'ŭn) *n.* proibizione.

project (prŏj'ĕkt) *n.* progetto, programma: **housing —,** piano edilizio, nuovo quartiere. *vt.* (prō·jĕkt') progettare; prolettare. *vi.* sporgere, proiettarsi. **—ile** (-jĕkt'ĭl) *n.* proiettile, proietto. **—ion** *n.* proiezione; sporgenza. **—ionist** *n.* (*cinema*) operatore di cabina. **—or** *n.* riflettore; proiettore: **flame —,** lanciafiamme; **gas —,** lanciagas.

proletarian (prō'lē·târ'ĭ·ǎn) *n., agg.* proletario.

proletariat (prō'lē·târ'ĭ·ǎt) *n.* proletariato.

prolix (prō·lĭks') *agg.* prolisso.

prologue (prō'lŏg) *n.* prologo.

prolong (prō·lŏng') *vt.* prolungare. **—ation** (-gā'shŭn) *n.* prolungamento, dilazione, propaggine.

promenade (prŏm'ē·nād') *n.* passeggiata. *vi.* passeggiare.

prominence (prŏm'ĭ·nĕns) *n.* prominenza, preminenza.

prominent (prŏm'ĭ·nĕnt) *agg.* prominente, saliente, preminente.

promiscuous (prō·mĭs'kū·ŭs) *agg.* promiscuo.

promise (prŏm'ĭs) n. promessa: **breach of** —, rottura di promessa (*matrimoniale*). vt., vi. promettere.

promising agg. promettente.

promissory (prŏm'ĭ·sŏ'rĭ) agg. promissorio: — **note**, cambiale.

promontory (prŏm'ŭn·tō'rĭ) n. promontorio.

promote (prō·mōt') vt. promuovere, favorire, sviluppare, incoraggiare.

promoter (prō·mōt'ẽr) n. promotore.

promotion (prō·mō'shŭn) n. promozione, avanzamento, incoraggiamento; incremento.

prompt (prŏmpt) n. termine di pagamento. agg. pronto, alacre, immediato. vt. suggerire, istigare, incitare. —**er** n. suggeritore, consigliere, istigatore. —**ing** n. incitamento, suggerimento, impulso. —**ly** avv. prontamente. —**ness** n. prontezza, alacrità.

promulgate (prō·mŭl'gāt) vt. promulgare.

prone (prōn) agg. prono, incline; propenso, soggetto (a).

prong (prŏng) n. rebbio, corno. —**ed** agg. dentato, a rebbi.

pronoun (prō'noun) n. pronome.

pronounce (prō·nouns') vt., vi. pronunziare; dichiarare, decretare.

pronounced (prō·nounst') agg. pronunziato: — **opinions**, opinioni precise.

pronto (prŏn'tō) avv. (S.U.) presto, fulmineamente.

pronunciation (prō·nŭn'sĭ·ā'shŭn) n. pronunzia.

proof (prōōf) n. prova, saggio; bozza di stampa; gradazione (*alcoolica*). agg. impenetrabile, impervio, resistente; probatorio: — **against**, a prova di; **bullet**—, a prova di proiettile; **galley** —, prima bozza, bozza in colonna; —**reader**, correttore di bozze; — **sheet**, bozza di stampa.

prop (prŏp) n. sostegno, appoggio; palo; (*teat. e cinema*) attrezzo scenico; (*aeron.*) elica. vt. puntellare, sostenere.

propagate (prŏp'à·gāt) vt. propagare, diffondere. vi. propagarsi.

propagation (prŏp'à·gā'shŭn) n. propagazione, trasmissione.

propel (prō·pĕl') vt. spingere avanti, azionare, lanciare. —**ler** n. propulsore, elica.

propensity (prō·pĕn'sĭ·tĭ) n. propensione.

proper (prŏp'ẽr) agg. proprio, vero e proprio; appropriato, adatto, giusto, conveniente, corretto: — **noun**, nome proprio; **the garden** —, il

giardino vero e proprio. —**ly** avv. propriamente, giustamente, correttamente, come si deve.

property (prŏp'ẽr·tĭ) n. proprietà, beni, possesso; (*teat.*) dotazione: **man of** —, possidente; — **man**, trovarobe.

prophecy (prŏf'ē·sĭ) n. profezia.

prophesy (prŏf'ē·sĭ) vt., vi. profetizzare.

prophet (prŏf'ĕt) n. profeta. —**ical** (-ĕt'ĭk·ăl) agg. profetico.

prophylactic (prō'fĭ·lăk'tĭk) agg. profilattico.

propitiate (prō·pĭsh'ĭ·āt) vt. propiziare.

propitious (prō·pĭsh'ŭs) agg. propizio, favorevole.

prop-jet (engine) n.(*aeron.*) turboelica.

proportion (prō·pōr'shŭn) n. proporzione: **out of** —, sproporzionato. vt. proporzionare.

proportionate (prō·pōr'shŭn·ĭt) agg. proporzionato.

proposal (prō·pōz'ăl) n. proposta.

propose (prō·pōz') vt. proporre. vi. fare una proposta di matrimonio; divisare, proporsi: **to** — **to do something**, ripromettersi di fare una cosa.

proposition (prŏp'ō·zĭsh'ŭn) n. proposta; proposizione.

propound (prō·pound') vt. sottoporre, proporre.

proprietary (prō·prī'ē·tĕr'ĭ) agg. padronale; esclusivo: — **classes**, classi abuienti; — **medicine**, specialità medicinale.

proprietor (prō·prī'ē·tẽr) n. proprietario. —**ial** (-tō'rĭ·ăl) agg. di padronanza.

propriety (prō·prī'ē·tĭ) n. proprietà, convenienza, correttezza, decoro.

prosaic (prō·zā'ĭk) agg. prosaico.

proscribe (prō·skrīb') vt. proscrivere, bandire.

prose (prōz) n. prosa. agg. di prosa; in prosa; prosaico.

prosecute (prŏs'ē·kūt) vt., vi. perseguire, proseguire, querelare; fungere da pubblico ministero.

prosecution (prŏs'ē·kū'shŭn) n. prosecuzione; azione legale; parte civile, accusa.

prosecutor (prŏs'ē·kū'tẽr) n. pubblico ministero; querelante.

prospect (prŏs'pĕkt) n. vista, prospettiva, prospetto, aspettativa, speranza; probabile cliente, candidato acquirente. vt., vi. esplorare (*in cerca di giacimenti*); fare ricerche (*spec. minerarie*). —**ive** n. prospettiva. agg. probabile, futuro.

prospector (prŏs'pĕk·tẽr) n. cercatore (*d'oro, ecc.*).

prosper (prŏs'pĕr) *vi.* prosperare. —**ity** (-pĕr'ĭ·tĭ) *n.* prosperità. —**ous** *agg.* prospero, prosperoso.

prostitute (prŏs'tĭ·tūt) *n.* prostituta. *vt.* prostituire.

prostitution (prŏs'tĭ·tū'shŭn) *n.* prostituzione.

prostrate (prŏs'trāt) *agg.* prosternato, prostrato, prono, supino. *vt.*, *vi.* prostrare, abbattere, coricare, rovinare; prosternarsi.

prosy (prōz'ĭ) *agg.* prosaico; tedioso.

protect (prŏ·tĕkt') *vt.* proteggere. —**ion** *n.* protezione, garanzia; passaporto, salvacondotto; protezionismo. —**ive** *agg.* protettivo. —**or** *n.* protettore. —**orate** *n.* protettorato.

protégé (prō'tě·zhā) *m.*, **protégée** *f.* *n.* protetto, protetta.

protein (prō'tē·ĭn) *n.* proteina.

protest (prŏ·tĕst') *n.* protesta; protesto. *vt.*, *vi.* protestare; mandare in protesto; disapprovare.

Protestant (prŏt'ěs·tănt) *n.*, *agg.* protestante.

Protestantism (prŏt'ěs·tănt·ĭz'm) *n.* protestantesimo.

protestation (prŏt'ěs·tā'shŭn) *n.* protesta.

protract (prŏ·trăkt') *vt.* protrarre.

protrude (prŏ·trōōd') *vt.*, *vi.* sporgere, proiettarsi.

protuberance (prŏ·tū'bĕr·ăns) *n.* protuberanza.

proud (proud) *agg.* orgoglioso, arrogante, superbo, grandioso.

prove (prōōv) *vt.* provare, dimostrare; verificare; omologare. *vi.* dimostrarsi, rivelarsi, risultare.

provender (prŏv'ĕn·dĕr) *n.* foraggio, vettovaglie.

proverb (prŏv'ûrb) *n.* proverbio.

provide (prŏ·vīd') *vt.*, *vi.* provvedere; fornire; prendere precauzioni; stipulare: to — for, prepararsi in previsione di; to — with, provvedere *o* fornire di.

provided (prŏ·vīd'ěd) *cong.* purchè, a condizione che, sempre che.

providence (prŏv'ĭ·děns) *n.* provvidenza, previdenza, economia.

provident (prŏv'ĭ·děnt) *agg.* previdente, provvido, economo. —**ial** (-děn'shăl) *agg.* provvidenziale.

provider (prŏ·vīd'ěr) *n.* fornitore: to be a good —, saper provvedere bene alla propria famiglia.

province (prŏv'ĭns) *n.* provincia; pertinenza, competenza: it is not within my —, non è di mia competenza.

provincial (prŏ·vĭn'shăl) *n.*, *agg.* provinciale.

provision (prŏ·vĭzh'ŭn) *n.* provvedimento; precauzione; preparativo; clausola: provisions, provviste. —**al**, —**ary** *agg.* provvisorio.

proviso (prŏ·vī'zō) *n.* condizione, clausola.

provocation (prŏv'ō·kā'shŭn) *n.* provocazione.

provoke (prŏ·vōk') *vt.* provocare, incitare; irritare.

provost (prŏv'ŭst) *n.* (*univ.*) rettore di facoltà: — marshal, capo della polizia militare.

prow (prou) *n.* prua.

prowess (prou'ĕs) *n.* prodezza, coraggio.

prowl (proul) *vt.*, *vi.* vagare in cerca di preda; aggirarsi furtivamente: — car, auto della polizia.

proximity (prŏks·ĭm'ĭ·tĭ) *n.* prossimità.

proxy (prŏk'sĭ) *n.* procuratore; procura: by —, per procura.

prude (prōōd) *n.* moralista.

prudence (prōō'děns) *n.* prudenza.

prudent (prōō'děnt) *agg.* prudente.

prudery (prōōd'ěr·ĭ) *n.* austerità affettata.

prudish (prōōd'ĭsh) *agg.* moraleggiante, austero.

prune (prōōn) (1) *n.* prugna secca.

prune (prōōn) (2) *vt.* potare, sfrondare, mondare.

prurient (prōōr'ĭ·ěnt) *agg.* smanioso, lascivo.

pry (prī) (1) *n.* indagatore; ficcanaso; curiosità indiscreta. *vt.*, *vi.* indagare; spiare; curiosare.

pry (prī) (2) *n.* leva, sbarra. *vt.* forzare (*con una leva, ecc.*): to — apart, separare con la forza; to — open, aprire con la forza; to — up, aprire con una leva; to — a secret out of, strappare un segreto a.

psalm (säm) *n.* salmo.

pseudonym (sū'dō·nĭm) *n.* pseudonimo.

psychiatrist (sī·kī'd·trĭst) *n.* psichiatra.

psychiatry (sī·kī'd·trĭ) *n.* psichiatria.

psychic (sī'kĭk) *agg.* psichico, telepatico.

psychoanalysis (sī'kō·d·năl'ĭ·sĭs) *n.* psicanalisi.

psychological (sī'kō·lŏj'ĭ·kăl) *agg.* psicologico.

psychologist (sī·kŏl'ō·jĭst) *n.* psicologo.

psychology (sī·kŏl'ō·jĭ) *n.* psicologia.

psychosis (sī·kō'sĭs) *n.* psicosi.

PT boat (pē'tē'bōt') *n.* (*naut.*) silurante.

ptomaine (tō'mān) *n.* ptomaina.

pub (pŭb) *n.* (*gergo Ingl.*, *abb. di* public-house) taverna, bar.

public (pŭb'lĭk) *n.*, *agg.* pubblico: — defender, difensore d'ufficio;

— prosecutor, pubblico ministero; — domain, dominio pubblico; (*S.U.*) terre demaniali; — house, taverna, bar, albergo; — relations, rapporti col pubblico, relazioni pubbliche; — utility, azienda di servizi pubblici. —-minded, —-spirited *agg.* dotato di civismo. —-mindedness, —-spiritedness *n.* civismo.

public-address system *n.* impianto di altoparlanti.

publication (pŭb'lĭ·kā'shŭn) *n.* pubblicazione.

publicist (pŭb'lĭ·sĭst) *n.* esperto di diritto internazionale; giornalista politico; agente pubblicitario.

publicity (pŭb·lĭs'ĭ·tĭ) *n.* pubblicità.

publicly (pŭb'lĭk·lĭ) *avv.* pubblicamente.

publish (pŭb'lĭsh) *vt.* pubblicare; divulgare. —er *n.* editore. —ing *agg.* editoriale: — house, casa editrice.

puck (pŭk) *n.* folletto; disco (*per hockey*).

pucker (pŭk'ĕr) *n.* piega, contrazione, grinza. *vt.* raggrinzare, contrarre. *vi.* raggrinzirsi, contrarsi.

pudding (pŏŏd'ĭng) *n.* torta, budino.

puddle (pŭd''l) *n.* pozzanghera.

pudgy (pŭj'ĭ) *agg.* tarchiato, grassoccio.

puff (pŭf) *n.* soffio, sbuffo; getto (*di vapore, ecc.*); protuberanza; piumino (*da cipria*); pistolotto, soffietto. *vt.* soffiar via; gonfiare; adulare. *vi.* soffiare, ansare; gonfiarsi; emetter fumo.

puffy (pŭf'ĭ) *agg.* gonfio, enfiato; tronfio; ventoso.

pug (pŭg) *n.* piccolo mastino; (*gergo*) pugile: — nose, naso camuso.

pugilism (pū'jĭ·lĭz'm) *n.* pugilato.

pugilist (pū'jĭ·lĭst) *n.* pugilista.

pugnacious (pŭg·nā'shŭs) *agg.* battagliero, combattivo.

puissance (pū'ĭ·săns) *n.* potenza, forza.

puissant (pū'ĭ·sănt) *agg.* potente, forte.

puke (pūk) *vi.* vomitare.

pull (pŏŏl) *n.* trazione; strappo, strattone; impulso; attrazione; prestigio, autorità; sorsata; sforzo; vantaggio: to have —, avere prestigio, essere influente. *vt., vi.* tirare, trascinare; strappare; arrancare; remare: to — a wry face, fare una smorfia; to — down, abbattere; tirar giù; to — up, trattenere; fermarsi; issare; to — oneself together, ricomporsi; to — somebody's leg, beffare qualcuno; to — through, riuscire, cavarsela, trarre d'impaccio; to — over to the right, portarsi alla destra; the

train —ed into the station, il treno si fermò in stazione.

pullet (pŏŏl'ĕt) *n.* pollastrella.

pulley (pŏŏl'ĭ) *n.* puleggia.

Pullman (car) (pŏŏl'mặn) *n.* vettura salone, vagone letto.

pulmotor (pŭl'mō'tĕr) *n.* polmone d'acciaio.

pulp (pŭlp) *n.* polpa; pasta, impasto; libro *o* rivista di carta scadente; libraccio, giornale scandalistico; letteratura *o* giornalismo deteriore.

pulpit (pŏŏl'pĭt) *n.* pulpito.

pulpy (pŭlp'ĭ) *agg.* polposo, molle.

pulsate (pŭl'sāt) *vi.* pulsare.

pulse (pŭls) *n.* polso, pulsazione.

pulverize (pŭl'vẽr·īz) *vt.* polverizzare. *vi.* andare in polvere.

pumice (pŭm'ĭs) *n.* pomice.

pump (pŭmp) *n.* pompa: gasoline —, distributore della benzina; hand —, pompa a mano; tire —, pompa per i pneumatici. *vt., vi.* pompare; gonfiare: to — someone, far cantare uno (*estorcergli un segreto*).

pumpkin (pŭmp'kĭn) *n.* (*bot.*) zucca.

pun (pŭn) *n.* gioco di parole. *vi.* fare giochi di parole.

punch (pŭnch) *n.* pugno; ponce; punzone; vigore, vitalità: — bowl, conca per ponce *o* liquori. *vt.* dare un pugno a; punzonare; forare; spronare: punching bag (*pugilato*), sacco.

puncheon (pŭn'chŭn) (1) *n.* grossa botte.

puncheon (2) *n.* punzone.

punctilious (pŭngk·tĭl'ĭ·ŭs) *agg.* preciso, formalista, scrupoloso, meticoloso.

punctual (pŭngk'tụ̄·ăl) *agg.* puntuale. —ity (-ăl'ĭ·tĭ) *n.* puntualità.

punctuate (pŭngk'tụ̄·āt) *vt.* punteggiare.

punctuation (pŭngk'tụ̄·ā'shŭn) *n.* punteggiatura.

puncture (pŭngk'tụ̄r) *n.* puntura; foratura (*di pneumatico*). *vt.* pungere; forare: to have a tire —, forare; to have a punctured tire, avere una gomma a terra.

punish (pŭn'ĭsh) *vt.* punire, castigare.

punishment (pŭn'ĭsh·mĕnt) *n.* punizione.

punt (pŭnt) *n.* chiatta.

puny (pū'nĭ) *agg.* debole, meschino, piccolo, insignificante.

pup (pŭp) *n.* cucciolo.

pupil (pū'p'l) (1) *n.* allievo, scolaro; pupillo, pupilla.

pupil (pū'p'l) (2) *n.* (*anat.*) pupilla.

puppet (pŭp'ĕt) *n.* bambola, marionetta: — show, spettacolo di marionette.

puppy (pŭp'ĭ) *n.* cucciolo.

purblind (pûr'blīnd') *agg.* debole di vista; ottuso.

purchase (pûr'chĭs) *n.* compera, acquisto; presa sicura, appiglio, appoggio; (*mecc.*) leva, paranco: to get a — on, far presa su, trovare un punto d'appoggio. *vt.* acquistare, comperare; sollevare (*con mezzi meccanici*).

purchaser (pûr'chĭs·ẽr) *n.* acquirente.

pure (pūr) *agg.* puro.

purely (pūr'lĭ) *avv.* puramente.

purgative (pûr'gà·tĭv) *agg.* purgativo.

purgatory (pûr'gà·tō'rĭ) *n.* purgatorio.

purge (pûrj) *n.* purga, epurazione. *vt.* purgare, espiare, purificare, epurare.

purify (pū'rĭ·fī) *vt.* purificare, depurare. *vi.* purificarsi.

purity (pū'rĭ·tĭ) *n.* purezza.

purloin (pûr·loin') *vt.*, *vi.* rubare.

purple (pûr'p'l) *n.* porpora. *agg.* purpureo; violetto; sgargiante.

purport (pûr·pōrt') *n.* senso, significato, portata, intenzione. *vt.* indicare, significare, implicare.

purpose (pûr'pŭs) *n.* scopo, proposito, mira, fine, funzione: to answer a —, servire a uno scopo; to no —, inutilmente; on —, a bella posta. *vt.*, *vi.* proporsi. —ful *agg.* deciso; intenzionale.

purr (pûr) *n.* fusa (*del gatto*); borbottio. *vi.* fare le fusa; borbottare.

purse (pûrs) *n.* borsa, borsetta, portamonete. *vt.* increspare, contrarre: to — one's lips, increspare le labbra.

purser (pûr'sẽr) *n.* (*naut.*) commissario di bordo.

pursuant (pẽr·sū'ănt) *agg.* conforme: — to, in conseguenza di, conformemente a.

pursue (pẽr·sū') *vt.*, *vi.* perseguire, proseguire, inseguire, perseguitare; dedicarsi a.

pursuer (pẽr·sū'ẽr) *n.* inseguitore.

pursuit (pẽr·sūt') *n.* inseguimento, caccia; continuazione; pratica; ricerca; occupazione, esercizio (*di una professione*): — plane, velivolo da caccia; in — of, alla caccia di, alla ricerca di.

purulent (pū'rŏŏ·lẽnt) *agg.* purulento.

purvey (pûr·vā') *vt.* procurare. *vi.* far provviste.

purveyor (pûr·vā'ẽr) *n.* fornitore.

pus (pŭs) *n.* (*med.*) pus.

push (pŏŏsh) *n.* urto, spinta, colpo; impulso, energia: — button, pulsante, bottone; (*agg.*) azionato a pulsante, automatico. *vt.*, *vi.* spingere, urtare, istigare: to be —ed for money, essere a corto di danaro; to — on, incalzare; to — through, aprirsi un varco a spintoni. —cart *n.* carretto a mano. —ing *agg.* intraprendente, energico.

pushmobile (pŏŏsh'mō·bĕl) *n.* automobilina a pedali.

pushover (pŏŏsh'ō'vẽr) *n.* avversario facile da battere; ingenuo, credulone; sinecura, pacchia, giochetto.

puss (pŏŏs) *n.* micio; (*gergo*) faccia.

put (pŏŏt) *n.* posa; lancio; colpo; spinta, opzione; tentativo. *vt.*, *vi.* (*pass.*, *pp.* put) mettere, porre, deporre, collocare; sottoporre; presentare; forzare; applicare; lanciare; dirigersi: to — aside, away, by, mettere da parte; risparmiare; to — about, virare di bordo; to — a question, fare una domanda; to — across condurre a termine; far capire; to — before, presentare, prospettare; to — down, sopprimere, reprimere; annotare; to — forth, produrre, proporre, pubblicare; to — in writing, metter per iscritto; to — off, togliersi; sviare; frustrare; rimandare; salpare; to — on, indossare; to — on airs, darsi arie; to — out, spegnere; turbare; estromettere, espellere; to — to shame, svergognare; to — up, innalzare, montare; ospitare; alloggiare; affiggere; to — up with, sopportare; to — up for sale, mettere in vendita.

putrefaction (pū'trẽ·făk'shŭn) *n.* putrefazione.

putrefy (pū'trẽ·fī) *vt.*, *vi.* putrefare, putrefarsi.

putrid (pū'trĭd) *agg.* putrido.

puttee (pŭt'ĭ) *n.* mollettiera.

putty (pŭt'ĭ) *n.* stucco, mastice. *vt.* stuccare.

puzzle (pŭz''l) *n.* perplessità; rompicapo, enigma: cross-word —, cruciverba. *vt.* confondere; rendere perplesso: to — out, sciogliere (*un enigma*). *vi.* arzigogolare.

puzzling (pŭz'lĭng) *agg.* sconcertante, enigmatico.

PX (pē'ĕks') *abbr. di.* post exchange.

pygmy (pĭg'mĭ) *n.*, *agg.* pigmeo.

pyjamas (pĭ·jà'màz) *n.pl.* pigiama.

pyramid (pĭr'à·mĭd) *n.* piramide.

pyre (pīr) *n.* pira.

pyrotechnics (pī'rŏ·tĕk'nĭks) *n.pl.* pirotecnica.

python (pī'thŏn) *n.* (*zool.*) pitone.

Q

quack (kwăk) *n.* gracidio (*dell'anatra*); ciarlatano, medicastro. *agg.* ciarlatanesco, empirico. *vi.* anatrare; fare il ciarlatano. —**ery** *n.* ciarlataneria; empirismo.

quadruped (kwŏd'rŏŏ.pĕd) *n.*, *agg.* quadrupede.

quadruple (kwŏd'rŏŏ-p'l) *n.*, *agg.* quadruplo. *vt.* (kwŏd-rŏŏ'p'l) quadruplicare.

quaff (kwàf) *vt.*, *vi.* tracannare.

quagmire (kwăg'mĭr') *n.* palude.

quail (kwāl) (1) *vi.* sgomentarsi, tremar di paura.

quail (kwāl) (2) *n.* quaglia.

quaint (kwānt) *agg.* strano, bislacco, originale; caratteristico; abile.

quake (kwāk) *n.* tremito, scossa. *vi.* tremare; oscillare.

quaker (kwāk'ẽr) *n.* quacquero.

qualification (kwŏl'ĭ.fĭ.kā'shŭn) *n.* requisito, dote, attitudine; condizione; modifica, restrizione.

qualify (kwŏl'ĭ-fĭ) *vt.* qualificare, abilitare, rendere idoneo; modificare, condizionare, fissare; addolcire. *vi.* qualificarsi, rendersi idoneo.

quality (kwŏl'ĭ-tĭ) *n.* qualità.

qualm (kwäm) *n.* nausea, malore; apprensione; dubbio, scrupolo.

quandary (kwŏn'dá.rĭ) *n.* imbarazzo, dilemma, difficoltà.

quantity (kwŏn'tĭ-tĭ) *n.* quantità.

quarantine (kwŏr'ăn-tēn) *n.* quarantena. *vt.* mettere in quarantena.

quarrel (kwŏr'ĕl) *n.* disputa, litigio: **to pick a —**, attaccar briga. *vi.* litigare.

quarrelsome (kwŏr'ĕl-sŭm) *agg.* litigioso.

quarry (kwŏr'ĭ) (1) *n.* preda, selvaggina.

quarry (kwŏr'ĭ) (2) *n.* cava (*di pietra*, *ecc.*). *vt.* estrarre da una cava; *vi.* lavorare in una cava.

quart (kwŏrt) *n.* quarto di gallone (*liquidi*: L. 0,9463; *aridi*: 1,1012).

quarter (kwŏr'tẽr) *n.* quarto; quarta parte; quarto d'ora; (*scuola*) bimestre; 25 centesimi di dollaro; parte, regione, distretto, quartiere; direzione; gruppo, cerchia, ambiente, sfera; (*pl.*) alloggio, caserma, quartiere: **at close —s**, a breve distanza, da vicino; **from all —s**, da tutte le parti; **to come to close —s**, venire alle mani; **to give no —**, non dar quartiere. *vt.* dividere in quarti; squartare; acquartierare, alloggiare. *vi.* acquartierarsi, alloggiarsi. *agg.* cor-

rispondente a un quarto: —**day**, quarto di giornata; —**moon**, quarto di luna; —**year**, trimestre.

quarterdeck *n* (*naut.*) cassero.

quarterly (kwŏr'tẽr-lĭ) *n.* pubblicazione trimestrale. *agg.* trimestrale. *avv.* trimestralmente.

quartermaster (kwŏr'tẽr-màs'tẽr) *n.* quartiermastro; ufficiale d'amministrazione, maresciallo d'alloggio: — **Corps**, intendenza Militare.

quartet (kwŏr-tĕt') *n.* quartetto.

quartz (kwŏrts) *n.* quarzo.

quash (kwŏsh) *vt.* schiacciare, annientare.

quaver (kwā'vẽr) *n.* tremolo, tremito. (*della voce*). *vi.* tremolare; cantare col tremolo.

quay (kē) *n.* molo, scalo.

queasy (kwē'zĭ) *agg.* nauseato; sconvolto, sconvolgente.

queen (kwēn) *n.* regina. —**ly** *agg.* da regina.

queer (kwẽr) *agg.* bizzarro, strano, singolare, ambiguo: **to feel —**, avere un malessere; **to be in — street** (*Ingl.*) essere nei guai. *n.* cosa o persona bislacca. *vt.* (*gergo*) rovinare, mandare a monte; mettere in ridicolo: **to — oneself with someone**, mettersi in disaccordo con qualcuno, attirarsi l'antipatia di qualcuno.

quell (kwĕl) *vt.* soffocare, stroncare, reprimere.

quench (kwĕnch) *vt.* estinguere (*sete*, *fuoco*, *ecc*); soggiogare, reprimere.

querulous (kwĕr'ū.lŭs) *agg.* querulo.

query (kwẽr'ĭ) *n.* domanda, punto interrogativo. *vt.* indagare, domandare, mettere in dubbio.

quest (kwĕst) *n.* inchiesta, ricerca, richiesta.

question (kwĕs'chŭn) *n.* domanda, dubbio, questione, discussione, problema — **mark**, punto interrogativo, **beyond all —**, fuor di dubbio, **out of the —**, da escludersi. *vt.*, *vi.* interrogare, esaminare, domandare, discutere, mettere in dubbio. —**able** *agg.* discutibile, dubbio. —**er** *n.* interrogatore. —**ing** *n.* interrogatorio, sospetto, interrogazione. —**naire** *n.* questionario.

queue (kū) *n.* codino (*di capelli*); coda (*di persone*). *vi.* formare una coda.

quibble (kwĭb''l) *n.* perifrasi; tergiversazione, scappatoia, cavillo. *vi.* tergiversare, cavillare.

quick (kwĭk) *n.* vivo, carne viva, parte vitale: **stung to the —**, punto sul vivo. *agg.* rapido, lesto, agile, vivo, pronto, veloce: — temper, temperamento infiammabile. irascibilità; — wit, spirito pronto. *avv. vedi* quickly.

quicken (kwĭk′ĕn) *vt.* animare, acuire, accelerare, affrettare, stimolare. *vi.* animarsi, affrettarsi.

quickly (kwĭk′lĭ) *avv.* rapidamente, presto; vivamente.

quickness (kwĭk′nĕs) *n.* rapidità, prontezza.

quicksand (kwĭk′sănd′) *n.* sabbia mobile.

quicksilver (kwĭk′sĭl′vĕr) *n.* mercurio.

quicky (kwĭk′ĭ) *n.* (*gergo*) cosa fatta in fretta e furia, cosa sbrigata alla svelta. *agg.* frettoloso, improvvisato, raffazzonato.

quid (kwĭd) *n.* cicca (*spec. di tabacco da masticare*).

quiet (kwī′ĕt) *n.* quiete, silenzio. *agg.* quieto, calmo; modesto, sobrio; silenzioso; immobile: be —I silenzio! on the —, clandestinamente. *vt.* chetare, calmare. *vi.* calmarsi, placarsi. —ly *avv.* quietamente, silenziosamente. —ness, —ude *n.* quiete, calma.

quill (kwĭl) *n.* penna; cannuccia; stuzzicadenti; aculeo (*di porcospino*); spola (*di telaio tessile*); (*mus.*) plettro.

quilt (kwĭlt) *n.* copripiedi, trapunta. *vt.* trapuntare, imbottire.

quince (kwĭns) *n.* cotogna.

quinine (kwĭ′nĭn) *n.* chinino.

quinsy (kwĭn′zĭ) *n.* tonsillite acuta.

quintet (kwĭn·tĕt′) *n.* quintetto.

quip (kwĭp) *n.* frizzo, sarcasmo.

quirk (kwûrk) *n.* peculiarità; cavillo; guizzo; svolazzo; scanalatura.

quit (kwĭt) *vt.* (*pass., pp.* quit, —ed) lasciare, cessare, interrompere, rinunciare a: — laughing! smettila di ridere! *vi.* interrompersi, andarsene.

quite (kwĭt) *avv.* completamente; notevolmente; realmente: — right, giustissimo; — so, proprio così; — a sight, una vista stupenda, un fior di panorama; to be — the fashion, essere l'ultimo grido della moda.

quits *agg.* pari: to be —, essere pari e patta.

quitter (kwĭt′ĕr) *n.* rinunziante, rinunciatario; vile; disertore.

quiver (kwĭv′ĕr) *n.* tremito, faretra. *vi.* tremare, fremere, vibrare.

quixotic (kwĭks·ŏt′ĭk) *agg.* donchisciottesco; idealistico.

quiz (kwĭz) *n.* enigma, indovinello; esame orale; occhialino; burlone, originale. *vt., vi.* burlare; esaminare, interrogare; mettere in imbarazzo. —zical *agg.* malizioso, beffardo.

quondam (kwŏn′dăm) *agg.* antico, ex, d'un tempo.

quorum (kwō′rŭm) *n.* numero legale (*che consente a un tribunale, ecc. di deliberare*), maggioranza.

quota (kwō′tă) *n.* quota.

quotation (kwŏ·tā′shŭn) *n.* citazione; quotazione: — marks, virgolette.

quote (kwōt) *vt.* citare; addurre; mettere tra virgolette; quotare: to — from, citare (da). *n.* citazione; (*pl.*) virgolette: in —s, tra virgolette.

quotient (kwō′shĕnt) *n.* quoziente.

R

rabbi (răb′ī) *n.* rabbino.

rabble (răb′′l) *n.* marmaglia, plebe, canaglia.

rabid (răb′ĭd) *agg.* furioso, fanatico, idrofobo, rabbioso.

rabies (rā′bĭ·ēz) *n.* idrofobia.

raccoon (ră·kōōn′) *n.* (*zool.*) procione.

race (rās) (1) *n.* razza, specie.

race (rās) (2) *n.* corsa, gara; corrente, canale: — course, — track, campo di corse, pista; boat —, regata. *vt.* far correre; imballare (*un motore*); accelerare; sfidare (*nella corsa*). *vi.* correre.

racer (rās′ĕr) *n.* corridore; cavallo (*o* veicolo, *o* scafo) da corsa.

racial (rā′shăl) *agg.* razziale.

racing (rās′ĭng) *n.* corsa, il correre. *agg.* da corsa: — form, schedina del racism (răs′ĭz′m) *n.* razzismo. [Totip.

rack (răk) *n.* rastrelliera; reticella (*portabagagli*); scaffale; tormento, ruota (*di tortura*); cremagliera: to go to — and ruin, finire in rovina assoluta. *vt.* affaticare, torturare; travasare: to — one's brain, lambiccarsi il cervello.

racket (răk′ĕt) *n.* fracasso, schiamazzo; racchetta (*da tennis*); (*gergo*) associazione a delinquere, attività criminosa; trucco, raggiro.

racketeer (răk′ĕ·tēr′) *n.* malfattore, imbroglione, bandito.

racy (rās′ĭ) *agg.* piccante, inebriante, aromatico, stimolante.

radar (rā′där) *n.* radiolocalizzatore, radar. —man *n.* radarista.

radial (rā′dĭ·ăl) *agg.* radiale.

radiance (rā′dĭ·ăns), radiancy *n.* splendore; irradiazione.

radiant (rā'dĭ·ǎnt) *agg.* raggiante, radioso.

radiate (rā'dĭ·āt) *vt.* irradiare. *vi.* raggiare, splendere.

radiator (rā'dĭ·ā'tẽr) *n.* radiatore.

radical (rǎd'ĭ·kǎl) *n.*, *agg.* radicale.

radio (rā'dĭ·ō) *n.* radio, radiofonia: by —, per radio, alla radio. —active *agg.* radioattivo. —activity *n.* radioattività. — beacon *n.* radiofaro. — broadcast *n.* radiotrasmissione. —graph *n.* radiografia. —graphy (-ŏg'rȧ·fĭ) *n.* radiologia. — link *n.* ponte radio. — listener *n.* radioascoltatore. —location *n.* radiolocalizzazione. —locator *n.* radiolocalizzatore, radar.

radish (rǎd'ĭsh) *n.* ravanello.

radium (rā'dĭ·ŭm) *n.* (*min.*) radio.

radius (rā'dĭ·ŭs) *n.* raggio.

radome (rā'dōm) *n.* abitacolo dell'antenna radar.

raffle (rǎf'l) *n.* riffa (*lotteria*); cianfrusaglia. *vt.* sorteggiare.

raft (rȧft) *n.* zattera.

rafter (rȧf'tẽr) *n.* trave.

rag (rǎg) *n.* brandello, cencio, straccio, collera: — doll, bambola di pezza.

ragamuffin (rǎg'ȧ·mŭf'ĭn) *n.* pezzente.

rage (rāj) *n.* furore, collera; mania, entusiasmo: to fly into a —, andare sulle furie. *vt.*, *vi.* infuriare, imperversare.

ragged (rǎg'ĕd) *agg.* aspro, scabro; cencioso; frastagliato: — edge, orlo frastagliato; on the — edge, sull'orlo dell'abisso; nervoso, agitato.

ragout (rȧ·gōō') *n.* ragù.

ragtime (rǎg'tĭm') *n.* musica sincopata.

raid (rād) *n.* razzia, incursione, irruzione: air —, incursione aerea. *vt.* compiere un'incursione su o in.

rail (rāl) *n.* sbarra; balaustra, cancellata; binario, rotaia: — fence, stecconata, recinto di paletti; by —, per ferrovia. *vt.* circondare con cancellata; spedire per ferrovia; redarguire; insolentire. —ing *n.* steccato, parapetto, rotaie; ingiurie.

raillery (rāl'ẽr·ĭ) *n.* beffa, scherzo.

railroad (rāl'rōd'), **railway** (rāl'wā') *n.* ferrovia, strada ferrata: — crossing, passaggio a livello.

raiment (rā'mĕnt) *n.* vestito, vestiario.

rain (rān) *n.* pioggia: — water, acqua piovana. *vt.* riversare (*come pioggia*). *vi.* piovere: it —s, piove; — or shine, che piova o faccia bel tempo; capiti quel che capiti.

rainbow (rān'bō') *n.* arcobaleno.

raincoat (rān'kōt') *n.* impermeabile.

raindrop (rān'drŏp') *n.* goccia di pioggia.

rainfall (rān'fôl') *n.* precipitazione, scroscio.

rainy (rān'ĭ) *agg.* piovoso.

raise (rāz) *n.* rialzo, aumento (*di paga*). *vt.* elevare, alzare, sollevare, aumentare; allevare, coltivare; erigere; levare (*l'assedio*); evocare; raccogliere (*danaro*): to — a question, fare una domanda, proporre una questione.

raisin (rā'z'n) *n.* uva passa.

rake (rāk) (1) *n.* rastrello; inclinazione; sporgenza. *vt.*, *vi.* rastrellare; raccogliere; cercare; raschiare; pulire; inclinare; far fuoco d'infilata: to — up, coprire con detriti; riesumare, rivangare.

rake (rāk) (2) *n.* libertino, dissoluto.

rake-off *n.* guadagno illecito, compenso illecito, "bustarella."

rally (rǎl'ĭ) (1) *n.* raccolta, adunata; ripresa (*delle forze*). *vt.* raccogliere; riorganizzare. *vi.* riorganizzarsi; adunarsi; rimettersi in forze.

rally (rǎl'ĭ) (2) *n.* burla. *vt.*, *vi.* burlare.

ram (rǎm) *n.* battipalo; ariete. *vt.* conficcare; stipare; battere, comprimere; urtare: to — it down one's throat, ingoiare la pillola.

ramble (rǎm'b'l) *n.* vagabondaggio; passeggiata. *vi.* vagare, serpeggiare; divagare.

ramp (rǎmp) *n.* rampa, balzo, pendìo.

rampart (rǎm'pȧrt) *n.* riparo, baluardo, bastione.

ramrod (rǎm'rŏd') *n.* calcatoio, scovolo.

ramshackle (rǎm'shǎk''l) *agg.* sconquassato.

ran (rǎn) *pass. di.* to run.

ranch (rǎnch) *n.* fattoria americana con grande allevamento di bestiame, ranch: — house, casa coloniaca, fattoria; villa o albergo di villeggiatura di modello rustico. —man *n.* proprietario di ranch; buttero.

rancid (rǎn'sĭd) *agg.* rancido.

rancor (rǎng'kẽr) *n.* animosità, rancore.

random (rǎn'dŭm) *agg.* a caso, casuale, irregolare; at —, a casaccio, a vanvera.

rang (rǎng) *pass. di.* to ring (2).

range (rānj) *n.* fila; gita, giro, scorribanda; catena montuosa; classe, ordine; gamma, varietà; distanza, portata (*di armi, della voce, ecc.*); àmbito, cerchia; recinto; fornello, cucina economica: gas —, cucina a gas; shooting —, campo di tiro; target —, poligono di tiro; —finder, telemetro; — of vision, campo visivo, capacità visiva; in — with, in linea con; out of —, fuori di portata; within —, a portata. *vt.* allineare; disporre; classificare; percorrere; avere la portata di. *vi.* allinearsi; estendersi.

ranger (rān'jĕr) *n.* guardia forestale; guastatore.

rangy (rān'jĭ) *agg.* snello e con le gambe lunghe, allampanato.

rank (rāngk) (1) *n.* ordine; schiera, fila; rango, classe; grado; dignità: — **and file** (*mil.*), truppa, bassa forza, ranghi. *vt.* schierare; classificare; (*S.U.*) essere superiore a. *vi.* schierarsi; essere classificato; to — **above**, essere superiore in grado a; to — **high with**, godere molta stima presso; to — **with**, essere alla pari con; to — **below**, essere inferiore di grado a.

rank (rāngk) (2) *agg.* vigoroso, forte (*di odore o sapore*); lussureggiante; rancido, violento, acre.

ranking *n.* classe, ordine. *agg.* (*il*) più anziano di grado; eminente, maggiore.

rankle (răng'k'l) *vt.* inasprire. *vi.* infiammarsi, esser fonte di rovello.

ransack (răn'săk) *vt.* frugare, perquisire, saccheggiare.

ransom (răn'sŭm) *n.* riscatto, prezzo del riscatto. *vt.* riscattare, redimere.

rant (rănt) *vi.* blaterare.

rap (răp) *n.* colpetto, colpo; (*gergo*) condanna, fio: **not worth a** —, privo d'ogni valore. *vt.* bussare.

rapacious (rá-pā'shŭs) *agg.* rapace.

rape (rāp) (1) *n.* ratto, violenza carnale. *vt.* rapire, violentare.

rape (2) *n.* vinaccia; (*bot.*) ravizzone.

rapid (răp'ĭd) *n.* (*gen.pl.*) rapida. *agg.* rapido.

rapier (rā'pĭ.ĕr) *n.* spada.

rapt (răpt) *agg.* rapito, estatico.

rapture (răp'tŭr) *n.* rapimento, estasi.

rare (râr) *agg.* raro, rado, straordinario; poco cotto (*di carni*).

rarefy (râr'ê.fĭ) *vt.* rarefare. *vi.* rarefarsi.

rarely (râr'lĭ) *avv.* raramente, eccezionalmente.

rareness (-nĕs) **rarity** (râr'ĭ.tĭ) *n.* rarità.

rascal (răs'kăl) *n.* briccone, farabutto.

rash (răsh) (1) *n.* eruzione cutanea.

rash (răsh) (2) *agg.* temerario, avventato, imprudente. —**ness** *n.* temerità, impulsività, imprudenza.

rasp (răsp) *n.* raspa. *vt.* raspare; (*fig.*) irritare.

raspberry (răz'bĕr'ĭ) *n.* (*bot.*) lampone; (*gergo S.U.*) pernacchia.

rasping (ràsp'ĭng) *agg.* stridente; esasperante.

raspy (ràsp'ĭ) *agg.* rauco; stridente; irascibile.

rat (răt) *n.* topo; (*fig.*) rinnegato, traditore; crumiro: —**race** (*fam.*), trambusto; circolo vizioso. *vi.* fare il crumiro, tradire.

rate (rāt) (1) *vt.* redarguire.

rate (rāt) (2) *n.* prezzo; tasso; (*Ingl.*) aliquota; grado; ritmo; velocità; qualità: — **of exchange**, cambio; **at the** — **of**, in ragione di; **at any** —, in ogni caso; **at this** —, stando così le cose; **first-** —, *agg.* di prim'ordine. *vt.* valutare; tassare; considerare; classificare. *vi.* essere classificato: **he** —**s as the best**, è considerato il migliore; **he** —**s high**, è molto stimato.

ratepayer (rāt'pā'ĕr) (*Ingl.*) *n.* contribuente.

rather (ràth'ĕr) *avv.* piuttosto; preferibilmente; alquanto: **or** —, o meglio; — **than**, piuttosto che; **I would** — **die than**, preferisco morire piuttosto che; **I would** — **not go**, preferirei non andare; **to have** —, preferire.

ratify (răt'ĭ.fĭ) *vt.* ratificare.

rating (rāt'ĭng) *n.* estimo, valutazione; classificazione.

ratio (rā'shŏ) *n.* proporzione, ragione, rapporto.

ration (rā'shŭn; răsh'ŭn) *n.* razione. *vt.* razionare.

rational (răsh'ŭn.ăl) *agg.* razionale, ragionevole.

rationing (rā'shŭn.ĭng; ră'-) *n.* razionamento: **gasoline** —, razionamento della benzina.

ratline (răt'lĭn) *n.* (*naut.*) grisella.

rattle (răt'l) *n.* strepito; crepitio; nacchere; sonaglio; cicaleccio; rantolo: **death** —, rantolo della morte. *vt.* far risonare, scrollare rumorosamente; dire velocemente; (*fam.*) sconcertare, confondere. *vi.* crepitare; tintinnare; risonare, strepitare, rumoreggiare; rantolare.

rattlesnake (răt'l·snāk') *n.* serpente a sonagli, crotalo.

raucous (rô'kŭs) *agg.* rauco.

ravage (răv'ĭj) *n.* devastazione, rovina; saccheggio. *vt.* devastare; saccheggiare.

rave (rāv) *vi.* delirare, farneticare; infuriare; agitarsi; entusiasmarsi, decantare, osannare. *n.* delirio, entusiasmo; infatuazione; lode sperticata. *agg.* laudatorio, osannante.

ravel (răv'ĕl) *n.* groviglio. *vt.* dipanare, sgrovigliare; chiarire.

raven (rā'vĕn) *n.* corvo. *agg.* corvino.

ravening (răv'ĕn·ĭng), **ravenous** (răv'-ĕn·ŭs) *agg.* rapace, vorace.

ravine (rà·vēn') *n.* burrone.

raving (răv'ĭng) *n.* delirio. *agg.* farneticante, delirante; straordinario.

ravish (răv'ĭsh) *vt.* rapire; violentare; estasiare. **—ing** *agg.* meraviglioso, incantevole.

raw (rô) *n.* vivo, carne viva. *agg.* crudo, grezzo; inesperto; brutale; liscio (*non diluito*); vivo, infiammato: **— material**, materia prima; **— recruit**, recluta, cappellone; **— silk**, seta cruda.

rawboned (rô'bŏnd') *agg.* scarno.

rawhide (rô'hīd') *n.* cuoio greggio; frustino di cuoio.

ray (rā) *n.* raggio; (*ittiol.*) razza.

rayon (rā'ŏn) *n.* raion, seta artificiale.

raze (rāz) *vt.* radere al suolo.

razor (rā'zĕr) *n.* rasoio: **— blade**, lametta per rasoio; **safety —**, rasoio di sicurezza.

reach (rēch) *n.* portata, distesa, limite: **beyond one's —**, fuori della portata di mano; **within one's —**, a portata di mano. *vt.* raggiungere; arrivare a; stendere, protendere, toccare, conseguire; mettersi in comunicazione con. *vi.* estendersi: **to — for**, allungare un braccio *o* la mano; **to — into**, infilare la mano; penetrare in.

react (rē·ăkt') *vi.* reagire.

reaction (rē·ăk'shŭn) *n.* reazione: **chain —**, reazione a catena.

reactionary (rē·ăk'shŭn·ĕr'ĭ) *n.*, *agg.* reazionario.

reactivate (rē·ăk'tĭ·vāt) *vt.* ripristinare, riattivare.

reactive (rē·ăk'tĭv) *agg.* reagente, reattivo.

reactor (rē·ăk'tĕr) *n.* reattore, reagente.

read (rēd) *vt.*, *vi.* (*pass.*, *pp.* read [rĕd]) leggere; studiare; decifrare; registrare, segnare (*di contatori, manometri, ecc.*); insegnare; interpretare: **to be well —**, essere colto; **to — for the bar**, studiare legge; **a novel that —s well**, un romanzo di facile lettura; **his letter —s as follows**, la sua lettera dice quanto segue.

reader (rēd'ĕr) *n.* lettore; correttore. **—ship** *n.* (*giorn.*) numero dei lettori, diffusione.

readily (rĕd'ĭ·lĭ) *avv.* prontamente; volentieri; facilmente.

readiness (rĕd'ĭ·nĕs) *n.* prontezza; facilità: **in —**, pronto.

reading (rēd'ĭng) *n.* lettura; interpretazione; cultura. *agg.* da leggere; che legge: **— room**, sala di lettura.

readjust (rē'ă·jŭst') *vt.* rassettare, rimettere in fase.

readmit (rē'ăd·mĭt') *vt.* riammettere. **—tance** *n.* riammissione.

ready (rĕd'ĭ) *agg.* pronto, preparato; svelto; volenteroso, facile: **to get —**, prepararsi; **—made clothes**, abiti fatti; **— money**, pronta cassa.

real (rē'ăl) *agg.* vero, effettivo, reale, genuino: **— estate**, proprietà immobiliare.

realism (rē'ăl·ĭz'm) *n.* realismo.

realist (rē'ăl·ĭst) *n.* realista.

realistic (rē'ăl·ĭs'tĭk) *agg.* realistico.

reality (rē·ăl'ĭ·tĭ) *n.* realtà.

realization (rē'ăl·ĭ·zā'shŭn) *n.* consapevolezza, comprensione (*il rendersi conto*); realizzazione.

realize (rē'ăl·īz) *vt.*, *vi.* rendersi conto di, capire, accorgersi di; realizzare.

really (rē'ăl·ĭ) *avv.* realmente, in realtà: **—? davvero?**

realm (rĕlm) *n.* reame, regno.

realtor (rē'ăl·tĕr) *n.* mediatore di immobili, agente immobiliare.

realty (rē'ăl·tĭ) *n.* beni immobili.

ream (rēm) (1) *n.* risma di carta.

ream (rēm) (2) *vt.* alesare.

reamer (rēm'ĕr) *n.* alesatrice.

reap (rēp) *vt.*, *vi.* mietere, raccogliere; guadagnare. **—er** *n.* mietitore.

reappear (rē'ă·pēr') *vi.* riapparire.

rear (rēr) (1) *n.* retro, parte posteriore, ultima fila; retroguardia. *agg.* posteriore, ultimo; **— admiral**, contrammiraglio; **—guard** *n.* retroguardia.

rear (rēr) (2) *vt.* alzare; allevare; innalzare, erigere. *vi.* impennarsi, inalberarsi, ergersi.

rearm (rē·ärm') *vt.* riarmare.

rearmament (rē·är'mà·mĕnt) *n.* riarmo.

rearrange (rē'ă·rānj') *vt.* riordinare.

reason (rē'z'n) *n.* ragione; causa, motivo: **by — of**, a causa di; **it stands to —**, è logico. *vt.*, *vi.* ragionare, arguire, argomentare, discutere: **to — someone into**, persuadere qualcuno a; **to — someone out of**, dissuadere qualcuno da; **to — out**, discorrere, ragionare.

reasonable (rē'z'n·à·b'l) *agg.* ragionevole, moderato.

reasonably (rē'z'n·à·blĭ) *avv.* ragionevolmente; abbastanza.

reasoning (rē'z'n·ĭng) *n.* ragionamento, argomentazione.

reassemble (rē'ă·sĕm'b'l) *vt.*, *vi.* radunare (*o* radunarsi) nuovamente; (*mecc.*) rimontare.

reassert (rē'ă·sûrt') vt. riaffermare, confermare.

reassurance (rē'ă·shŏŏr'ăns) n. rassicurazione; riassicurazione.

reassure (rē'ă·shŏŏr') vt. rassicurare; riassicurare.

rebate (rē'bāt) vt. diminuire, ribassare. n. diminuzione, ribasso. —ment n. diminuzione, ribasso.

rebel (rē·bĕl') vi. ribellarsi. n., agg. (rĕb'ĕl) ribelle. —lion n. ribellione, rivolta. —lious agg. ribelle.

rebirth (rē·bûrth') n. rinascita.

reborn (rē·bûrn') agg. rinato.

rebound (rē·bound') n. rimbalzo, contraccolpo: on the —, di rimbalzo. vi. rimbalzare, ripercuotersi.

rebuff (rē·bŭf') n. rabbuffo; smacco; rifiuto. vt. respingere, infliggere un rabbuffo (o uno smacco) a.

rebuild (rē·bĭld') vt. (pass., pp. rebuilt) ricostruire.

rebuke (rē·būk') n. rampogna, rimprovero. vt. rimproverare.

rebut (rē·bŭt') vt. confutare, respingere.

recall (rē·kôl') n. richiamo, revoca. vt. richiamare, revocare; ricordare, rievocare.

recant (rē·kănt') vt. ritrattare.

recap (rē'kăp) abbr. di recapitulate e recapitulation.

recapitulate (rē'kă·pĭt'û·lāt) vi. ricapitolare, riassumere.

recapitulation (-lā'shŭn) n. ricapitolazione, riassunto.

recede (rē·sēd') vi. recedere, ritirarsi, esser sfuggente.

receipt (rē·sēt') n. ricevuta, quietanza; ricevimento; ricetta; (pl.) entrate: on — of, dietro ricevuta di; we are in — of, siamo in possesso di. vt. quitanzare.

receive (rē·sēv') vt. ricevere.

receiver (rē·sēv'ẽr) n. ricevitore; ricettacolo; ricettatore; esattore; (radio) apparecchio ricevente; curatore, custode giudiziario.

recent (rē'sĕnt) agg. recente. —ly avv. recentemente: — married, sposato da poco o di fresco.

receptacle (rē·sĕp'tá·k'l) n. ricettacolo.

reception (rē·sĕp'shŭn) n. ricevimento; ricezione; accoglienza.

receptionist (-ĭst) n. impiegata che riceve (clienti, ecc.) in un ufficio, accoglitrice.

receptive (rē·sĕp'tĭv) agg. ricettivo.

recess (rē·sĕs') n. recesso; ripostiglio, nicchia, rientranza; intervallo, tregua; ricreazione. vt. sospendere (un lavoro, una seduta, ecc.); aprire una nicchia.

recession (rē·sĕsh'ŭn) n. recessione, regresso, ritrazione, posizione arretrata; crisi.

recidivist (rē·sĭd'ĭ·vĭst) n. recidivo.

recipe (rĕs'ĭ·pē) n. ricetta.

recipient (rē·sĭp'ĭ·ĕnt) n. ricevente; recipiente. agg. ricettivo.

reciprocal (rē·sĭp'rō·kăl) agg. reciproco, mutuo.

reciprocate (rē·sĭp'rō·kāt) vt. ricambiare, reciprocare. vi. contraccambiare; alternarsi, muoversi alternatamente.

reciprocity (rĕs'ĭ·prŏs'ĭ·tĭ) n. reciprocità.

recital (rē·sīt'ăl) n. enumerazione; recitazione; prova; resoconto, esposizione, descrizione; concerto.

recitation (rĕs'ĭ·tā'shŭn) n. recitazione.

recite (rē·sīt') vt., vi. recitare, enumerare, narrare.

reckless (rĕk'lĕs) agg. irriflessivo, temerario, avventato: — with one's money, spendaccione.

recklessness (-nĕs) n. temerità, imprudenza, irriflessività.

reckon (rĕk'ŭn) vt. contare, calcolare; reputare; valutare: to — up, addizionare. vi. far di conto: to — on, contare su; to — with, fare i conti con, tener conto di. —er n. calcolatore, contabile. —ing n. computo, calcolo, conto, regolamento (di conti): the day of —, il giorno del giudizio, la resa dei conti.

reclaim (rē·klām') vt. redimere, ricuperare; bonificare (terreni); (raro) reclamare.

reclamation (rĕk'lá·mā'shŭn) n. bonifica; redenzione, ricupero.

recline (rē·klīn') vt. reclinare, adagiare. vi. adagiarsi.

recluse (rĕk'lūs) n. eremita. agg. recluso, solitario.

recognition (rĕk'ŏg·nĭsh'ŭn) n. riconoscimento.

recognize (rĕk'ŏg·nīz) vt. riconoscere; ammettere.

recoil (rē·koil') n. il retrocedere, rimbalzo, rinculo; ripugnanza. vi. retrocedere, rinculare.

recollect (rĕk'ŏ·lĕkt') vt., vi. richiamare alla memoria, ricordare.

recollection (rĕk'ŏ·lĕk'shŭn) n. ricordo, reminiscenza.

recommence (rē'kŏ·mĕns') vt. ricominciare.

recommend (rĕk'ŏ·mĕnd) vt. raccomandare; consigliare. —ation n. raccomandazione; consiglio.

recompense (rĕk'ŏm·pĕns) n. ricompensa. vt. ricompensare.

reconcile (rĕk'ŏn·sĭl) vt. riconciliare,

armonizzare, mettere d'accordo: to — oneself to, adattarsi a.

reconciliation (rĕk'ŏn·sil'i·ā'shŭn) *n.* riconciliazione; armonizzazione; adattamento.

recondition (rē'kŏn·dish'ŭn) *vt.* riparare, rimettere in efficenza.

reconnaissance (rē·kŏn'i·sáns) *n.* ricognizione; esame.

reconnoiter (rĕk'ŏ·noi'tēr) *vt.* esplorare, ispezionare. *vi.* compiere una ricognizione.

reconsider (rē'kŏn·sĭd'ēr) *vt.* riesaminare. *vi.* ripensarci.

reconstruct (rē'kŏn·strŭkt') *vt.* ricostruire. —**ion** *n.* ricostruzione.

record (rĕk'ērd) *n.* documentazione, verbale, copia autentica; registro; storia; registrazione; incisione fonografica, disco (*fonografico*) precedenti personali; annale; (*sport*) primato, curriculum di un atleta: a man with a — (*legge*), un uomo con la fedina sporca; a man with no —, un uomo incensurato; this is off the —, è una cosa detta in confidenza; — player, giradischi. *vt.* (rē·kôrd') registrare, annotare; mettere a verbale; incidere (*dischi*).

recount (rē·kount') *vt.* raccontare, riferire; enumerare, elencare; ricontare. *n.* racconto; nuovo computo, nuovo conteggio.

recoup (rē·kōōp') *vi.* rifarsi (di una perdita).

recourse (rē·kōrs') *n.* ricorso; aiuto, fonte di aiuto; rifugio: to have — to, ricorrere a.

recover (rē·kŭv'ēr) *vt.* ricuperare; riprendere; ritrovare; riconquistare; vincere (*una malattia*); riparare (*una perdita*); ottenere (*un indennizzo*); guarire; salvare; restituire. *vi.* guarire, rimettersi; vincere una causa.

recovery (-i) *n.* ricupero, ritrovamento; guarigione: to be past —, essere inguaribile.

recreate (rĕk'rē·āt) *vt.* ricreare; rianimare; distrarre; ristorare. *vi.* ricrearsi; ristorarsi.

recreation (-ā'shŭn) *n.* ricreazione; divertimento: — room, saletta da giuoco (*in una casa privata*).

recruit (rē·krōōt') *n.* recluta; novellino, principiante; nuovo socio. *vt.* reclutare; rifornire, alimentare. *vi.* compiere un reclutamento; ristabilirsi. —**ing** *n.* reclutamento: — depot, centro di reclutamento.

rectangle (rĕk'tăng'g'l) *n.* rettàngolo.

rectification (rĕk'ti·fi·kā'shŭn) *n.* rettifica, correzione.

rectify (rĕk'ti·fī) *vt.* rettificare, correggere.

rectitude (rĕk'ti·tūd) *n.* rettitudine.

rector (rĕk'tēr) *n.* parroco; (*univ.*) rettore.

rectum (rĕk'tŭm) *n.* intestino retto.

recumbent (rē·kŭm'bĕnt) *agg.* sdraiato, inclinato; inerte.

recuperate (rē·kū'pēr·āt) *vt.* guarire, rimettere in salute. *vi.* guarire, rimettersi.

recuperation (rē·kū'pēr·ā'shŭn) *n.* ricupero; guarigione.

recur (rē·kûr') *vi.* ricorrere, ritornare periodicamente, ripetersi; tornare alla mente. —**rence** *n.* ricorrenza, ritorno, ricorso.

red (rĕd) *n.*, *agg.* rosso: Red Cross, Croce Rossa; — Cross nurse, crocerossina; — tape, burocrazia, pratiche burocratiche. —**blooded** *agg.* sanguigno; coraggioso; energico. —**breast** *n.* pettirosso. —**cap** *n.* (*S.U.*) facchino di stazione; (*Ingl.*) poliziotto militare; (*ornit.*) cardellino. —**coat** *n.* giubbarossa, soldato inglese. —**handed** *agg.* in flagrante, con le mani nel sacco. —**hot** *agg.* rovente, incandescente, ardente; irato, infuriato; vivissimo.

redden (rĕd''n) *vt.* arrossare. *vi.* arrossire, arrossarsi.

reddish (rĕd'ish) *agg.* rossiccio.

redeem (rē·dēm') *vt.* ricuperare, riscattare (*un pegno*); adempiere (*una promessa*); redimere, ripristinare. —**er** *n.* redentore, liberatore.

redemption (rē·dĕmp'shŭn) *n.* redenzione, riscatto, ricupero.

redness (rĕd'nĕs) *n.* rossezza, rossore.

redouble (rē·dŭb''l) *vt.*, *vi.* raddoppiare, intensificare.

redoubtable (rē·dout'á·b'l) *agg.* temibile.

redound (rē·dound') *vi.* ricadere, ripercuotersi, ridondare.

redress (rē·drĕs') *n.* riforma, emendamento, riparazione. *vt.* riformare, riparare, emendare.

redskin (rĕd'skin') *n.* pellerossa, indiano.

reduce (rē·dūs') *vt.* ridurre; costringere: to — to the ranks, degradare.

reduction (rē·dŭk'shŭn) *n.* riduzione.

redundancy (rē·dŭn'dăn·si) *n.* ridondanza, sovrabbondanza.

redundant (rē·dŭn'dănt) *agg.* ridondante.

redwood (rĕd'wŏŏd) *n.* sequoia, legno di sequoia.

reed (rēd) *n.* canna; zampogna; ancia (*di strumenti a fiato*).

reef (rēf) *n.* scogliera; (*min.*) vena;

(*naut.*) terzaruolo. *vt.* fare i terzaruoli.

reefer (rēf'ēr) *n.* giacchettone; carro *o* camion frigorifero, nave frigorifera; (*gergo*) sigaretta alla marijuana.

reek (rēk) *n.* puzza. *vi.* puzzare.

reel (rēl) *n.* rocchetto, bobina, aspo; oscillazione; (*fot.*) rotolo. *vt.* avvolgere: to — off, svolgere, srotolare; raccontare senza inciampi, snocciolare. *vi.* vacillare, ronzare, girare.

re-elect (rē'ē·lĕkt') *vt.* rieleggere.

re-election (rē'ē·lĕk'shŭn) *n.* rielezione.

re-enter (rē·ĕn'tēr) *vt.*, *vi.* registrare di nuovo; rientrare.

re-establish (rē'ĕs·tăb'lĭsh) *vt.* ristabilire, restaurare.

reface (rē·fās') *vt.* rinnovare (la facciata di).

refection (rē·fĕk'shŭn) *n.* refezione, pasto.

refectory (rē·fĕk'tō·rĭ) *n.* refettorio; tavolo da refettorio.

refer (rē·fûr') *vt.* riferire, indirizzare, rimandare, rimettere, attribuire. *vi.* riferirsi, alludere; rivolgersi, ricorrere.

referee (rĕf'ēr·ē') *n.* arbitro, giudice. *vt.*, *vi.* arbitrare.

reference (rĕf'ēr·ĕns) *n.* referenza, riferimento, rapporto, allusione; (*pl.*) referenze, note personali. book of —, libro di consultazione; — mark, richiamo, asterisco; letter of —, lettera di raccomandazione, benservito; with — to, per quanto riguarda, rispetto a.

referendum (rĕf'ēr·ĕn'dŭm) *n.* referendum.

refill (rē·fĭl') *vt.* riempire di nuovo, rifornire. *n.* ricambio.

refine (rē·fīn') *vt.* raffinare, purificare. *vi.* raffinarsi, purificarsi.

refined (rē·fīnd') *agg.* raffinato; ricercato; purificato.

refinement (rē·fīn'mĕnt) *n.* raffinatezza; raffinatura; ricercatezza.

refinery (rē·fīn'ēr·ĭ) *n.* raffineria.

refit (rē·fĭt') *vt.* riparare, rimettere in sesto; (*naut.*) riarmare.

reflect (rē·flĕkt') *vt.*, *vi.* riflettere, rifrangere; rifrangersi; meditare: to — on, upon, andare a discapito di, incidere su.

reflection (rē·flĕk'shŭn) *n.* riflessione, rifrazione; discapito; biasimo.

reflex (rē'flĕks) *n.* riflesso, azione riflessa. *agg.* riflesso: — camera (*fot.*), macchina reflex.

reflexive (rē·flĕk'sĭv) *agg.* riflessivo.

reform (rē·fôrm') *n.* riforma. *vt.*, *vi.* riformare, migliorare; emendarsi.

—ation (rĕf'ŏr·mā'shŭn) *n.* riforma, emendamento. —atory (rē·fôr'mȧ·tō'rĭ) *n.* riformatorio. —er *n.* riformatore.

refract (rē·frăkt') *vt.* rifrangere. —ion *n.* rifrazione.

refractory (rē·frăk'tō·rĭ) *agg.* indocile, refrattario, ostinato.

refrain (rē·frān') (1) *vt.* reprimere, frenare. *vi.* trattenersi, astenersi (*da*).

refrain (rē·frān') (2) *n.* ritornello.

refresh (rē·frĕsh') *vt.* rinfrescare, ristorare. *vi.* ristorarsi, rianimarsi. —er *n.* cosa *o* persona che rianima, rinfresco, bibita; promemoria; corso di aggiornamento. —ing *agg.* rinfrescante; ristoratore; gradevole; consolante, rincuorante. —ment *n.* rinfresco, ristoro.

refrigerate (rē·frĭj'ēr·āt) *vt.* refrigerare.

refrigeration (rē·frĭj'ēr·ā'shŭn) *n.* refrigerazione.

refrigerator (rē·frĭj'ēr·ā'tēr) *n.* frigorifero.

refuge (rĕf'ūj) *n.* ricovero, rifugio, asilo.

refugee (rĕf'ū·jē') *n.* rifugiato, profugo.

refund (rē·fŭnd') *vt.* rifondere, rimborsare. *n.* rimborso.

refusal (rē·fūz'ăl) *n.* rifiuto; diritto di opzione.

refuse (rĕf'ūs) *n.* rifiuti, scorie, detriti. *vt.* (rē·fūz') rifiutare, respingere. *vi.* rifiutarsi, non volere.

refute (rē·fūt') *vt.* confutare.

regain (rē·gān') *vt.* riguadagnare, riacquistare.

regal (rē'găl) *agg.* regale.

regale (rē·gāl') *vt.*, *vi.* intrattenere, festeggiare, banchettare.

regalia (rē·gā'lĭ·ȧ) *n.pl.* insegne *o* prerogative regali; insegne di un ordine; pompa; alta tenuta.

regard (rē·gärd') *n.* sguardo, attenzione; riguardo, considerazione; riferimento: in, with — to, rispetto a, per quanto riguarda; —s, complimenti, auguri; *vt.* guardare, considerare, valutare; riguardare, concernere: as —s this, quanto a questo.

regarding *prep.* riguardo a.

regardless *agg.* noncurante, negligente: — of, nonostante, a dispetto di.

regatta (rē·găt'ȧ) *n.* regata.

regency (rē'jĕn·sĭ) *n.* reggenza.

regenerate (rē·jĕn'ēr·āt) *agg.* rigenerato. *vt.* rigenerare; emendare. *vi.* rigenerarsi; emendarsi.

regeneration (-ȧ'·shŭn) *n.* rigenerazione; emendamento.

regent (rē'jĕnt) *n.* reggente.

regimen (rĕj'ĭ-mĕn) *n.* regime.

regiment (rĕj'ĭ-mĕnt) *n.* reggimento.

regimental (rĕj'ĭ-mĕn'tăl) *agg.* reggimentale. *n.pl.* uniforme militare.

region (rē'jŭn) *n.* regione.

register (rĕj'ĭs-tēr) *n.* registro; protocollo, archivio, registrazione; (*mecc.*) regolatore. *vt.* registrare, iscrivere; raccomandare (*una lettera*). *vi.* iscriversi.

registered *agg.* registrato; raccomandato (*di posta*).

registrar (rĕj'ĭs-trär) *n.* cancelliere, archivista.

registration (rĕj'ĭs-trā'shŭn) *n.* registrazione; raccomandazione (*di lettere*).

registry (rĕj'ĭs-trĭ) *n.* registrazione, cancelleria, archivio.

regret (rē-grĕt') *n.* rammarico, rimpianto, dispiacere: to send one's —s, inviare le proprie scuse. *vt.* rammaricarsi di, rimpiangere, deplorare.

regretful ('-fool) *agg.* dolente.

regrettable (-á-b'l) *agg.* doloroso, deplorevole.

regular (rĕg'û-lēr) *agg.* regolare, metodico, ordinato; autentico; completo: a — fool, un autentico cretino; — price, prezzo corrente. —ity (-ăr'ĭ-tĭ) *n.* regolarità.

regulate (rĕg'û-lāt) *vt.* regolare.

regulation (rĕg'û-lā'shŭn) regolamento; (*pl.*) regolamento, norme: — uniform, divisa d'ordinanza. *agg.* regolamentare.

regulator (rĕg'û-lā'tēr) *n.* regolatore.

rehabilitate (rē'há-bĭl'ĭ-tāt) *vt.* riabilitare; ricostruire.

rehabilitation (rē-'há-bĭl'ĭ-tā'shŭn) *n.* riabilitazione; ricostruzione.

rehearsal (rē-hûr'săl) *n.* recitazione, narrazione; (*teat.*) prova: dress —, prova generale.

rehearse (rē-hûrs') *vt., vi.* ripetere, recitare, provare.

reign (rān) *n.* regno. *vi.* regnare.

reimburse (rē'ĭm-bûrs') *vt.* rimborsare.

reimbursement *n.* rimborso.

rein (rān) *n.* redine. *vt.* guidare con le redini; tenere a freno.

reincarnate (rē'ĭn-kär'nāt) *vt.* reincarnare.

reindeer (rān'dēr') *n.* renna.

reinforce (rē'ĭn-fōrs') *vt.* rinforzare, rafforzare: —d concrete, cemento armato.

reinforcement (rē'ĭn-fōrs'mĕnt) *n.* rafforzamento, rinforzo.

reinstate (rē'ĭn-stāt') *vt.* reintegrare.

reinsurance (rē'ĭn-shoō'răns) *n.* riassicurazione.

reiterate (rē-ĭt'ēr-āt) *vt.* reiterare.

reiteration (rē-ĭt'ēr-á'shŭn) *n.* ripetizione.

reject (rē-jĕkt') *vt.* rifiutare, scartare, respingere.

rejoice (rē-jois') *vt.* rallegrare. *vi.* esultare, gioire.

rejoicing (rē-jois'ĭng) *n.* giubilo, esultanza.

rejoin (rē-join') *vt., vi.* raggiungere, ricongiungere; riunirsi; rispondere.

rejoinder (rē-join'dēr) *n.* replica, risposta.

rejuvenate (rē-joō'vē-nāt) *vt.* ringiovanire.

rekindle (rē-kĭn'd'l) *vt.* riaccendere.

relapse (rē-lăps') *n.* ricaduta. *vi.* ricadere.

relapser *n.* recidivo.

relate (rē-lāt') *vt.* raccontare, riferire; mettere in relazione. *vi.* riferirsi.

related (rē-lāt'ĕd) *agg.* connesso; imparentato: to become —, imparentarsi.

relation (rē-lā'shŭn) *n.* relazione, rapporto; parente. —ship *n.* parentela; rapporto, attinenza.

relative (rĕl'á-tĭv) *n.* parente, congiunto. *agg.* relativo.

relativity (rĕl'á-tĭv'ĭ-tĭ) *n.* relatività.

relax (rē-lăks') *vt.* rilassare, allentare, mitigare. *vi.* rilassarsi, afflosciarsi; distendere i nervi, abbandonarsi. —ation (='á'shŭn) *n.* rilassamento, distensione, attenuazione.

relay (rē-lā') *n.* cambio; (*tecn.*) relais, relè: — race, corsa a staffetta. *vt.* dare il cambio a; trasmettere, ritrasmettere.

release (rē-lēs') *n.* liberazione, svincolo; sollievo, scarico. *vt.* liberare, rilasciare, svincolare; cedere; esonerare, alleviare; concedere: to — a piece of news, divulgare una notizia, comunicare una notizia alla stampa.

relegate (rĕl'ē-gāt) *vt.* relegare; assegnare, collocare; demandare, attribuire.

relent (rē-lĕnt') *vi.* impietosirsi, ammansirsi, cedere. —less *agg.* inflessibile, implacabile. —lessly *avv.* implacabilmente. —lessness *n.* inflessibilità, implacabilità.

relevance (rĕl'ē-văns), **relevancy** (-văn-sĭ) *n.* pertinenza, attinenza.

relevant (rĕl'ē-vănt) *agg.* pertinente, attinente.

reliability (rē-lī'á-bĭl'ĭ-tĭ)🔲*n.* attendibilità, fondatezza, integrità.

reliable (rē-lī'á-b'l) *agg.* attendibile; leale; sicuro, degno di fiducia.

reliance (rē-lī'ăns) *n.* fiducia: self—, fiducia in sè.

relic (rĕl'ĭk) *n.* reliquia, ricordo.

relict (rĕl'ĭkt) *n.* vedova.

relief (rĕ·lēf') *n.* sollievo, soccorso, sussidio; cambio (*della guardia, ecc.*); rilievo: to be on —, vivere di sussidi.

relieve (rĕ·lēv') *vt.* alleviare, soccorrere, liberare; dare il cambio a; mettere in rilievo.

religion (rĕ·lĭj'ŭn) *n.* religione.

religious (rĕ·lĭj'ŭs) *agg.* religioso.

relinquish (rĕ·lĭng'kwĭsh) *vt.* abbandonare, rinunziare a.

relish (rĕl'ĭsh) *n.* gusto, fragranza; voluttà; condimento. *vt.* gustare, insaporire, godere. *vi.* aver sapore (*di*).

reload (rē·lōd') *vt.* ricaricare.

reluctance (rē·lŭk'tăns) *n.* riluttanza, ripugnanza.

reluctant (rē·lŭk'tănt) *agg.* rilluttante, restio. —ly *avv.* di malavoglia, con riluttanza, a malincuore.

rely (rē·lī') *vi.*: to — on, upon, fare affidamento su, fidarsi di.

remain (rē·mān') *vi.* restare, rimanere; spettare. —der *n.* rimanenza, residuo.

remains *n. pl.* resti; spoglie; scorie.

remake (rē·māk') *n.* rifacimento. *vt.* (*pass., pp.* remade) rifare.

remark (rē·märk') *n.* osservazione, commento, frase. *vt.* commentare, osservare: to — on, fare commenti su.

remarkable (rē·mär'kȧ·b'l) *agg.* notevole, considerevole.

remarkably (rē·mär'kȧ·blĭ) *avv.* notevolmente, spiccatamente.

remarry (rē·măr'ĭ) *vt., vi.* risposare.

remedial (rē·mē'dĭ·ăl) *agg.* riparatore.

remedy (rĕm'ĕ·dĭ) *n.* rimedio, cura past —, irrimediabile. *vt.* rimediare

remember (rē·mĕm'bēr) *vt., vi.* ricordare, ricordarsi: — me to him, salutatelo da parte mia.

remembrance (rē·mĕm'brăns) *n.* ricordo, memoria.

remind (rē·mīnd') *vt.* ricordare a.

reminder (rē·mīn'dēr) *n.* avvertimento, memorandum, memento, promemoria.

reminiscence (rĕm'ĭ·nĭs'ĕns) *n.* reminiscenza.

remiss (rē·mĭs') *agg.* negligente.

remission (rē·mĭsh'ŭn) *n.* remissione, perdono.

remit (rē·mĭt') *vt.* rimettere, condonare; trasmettere; rinunziare (*a*). —tal *n.* remissione, condono. —tance *n.* rimessa (*di danaro*). —tent *agg.* intermittente.

remnant (rĕm'nănt) *n.* rimanenza, avanzo, residuo, scampolo.

remodel (rē·mŏd''l) *vt.* rimodellare, rifare, rimodernare.

remonstrance (rē·mŏn'străns) *n.* rimostranza.

remonstrate (rē·mŏn'strāt) *vi.* rimostrare, protestare.

remorse (rē·môrs') *n.* rimorso. —ful *agg.* pentito. —less *agg.* spietato, senza rimorso.

remote (rē·mōt') *agg.* remoto, lontano, estraneo.

removal (rē·mōōv'ăl) *n.* rimozione; trasporto destituzione; trasloco; eliminazione; estrazione.

remove (rē·mōōv') *vt.* rimuovere; sfrattare; destituire; togliere, eliminare, estirpare. *vi.* allontanarsi, trasferirsi

removed *agg.* distante, separato.

remunerate (rē·mū'nēr·āt) *vt.* rimunerare.

renaissance (rĕn'ȧ·săns') *n.* rinascimento.

rename (rē·nām') *vt.* ribattezzare.

rend (rĕnd) *vt.* (*pass., pp.* rent) squarciare, spaccare, lacerare. *vi.* spaccarsi, lacerarsi.

render (rĕn'dēr) *vt.* rendere; rimborsare; tradurre; interpretare; purificare.

rendering (-ĭng) *n.* traduzione, interpretazione, versione.

rendez-vous (rän'dȧ·vōō) *n.* appuntamento. riunione.

rendition (rĕn·dĭsh'ŭn) *n.* resa, rendimento.

renegade (rĕn'ē·gād) *n.* rinnegato.

renew (rē·nū') *vt.* rinnovare, ripristinare. —al *n.* ripresa, rinnovamento; rinnovo, proroga.

rennet (rĕn'ĕt) *n.* caglio.

renounce (rē·nouns') *vt.* rinunziare a.

renovate (rĕn'ō·vāt) *vt.* rinnovare, ravvivare rimettere a nuovo.

renown (rē·noun') *n.* rinomanza, fama.

renowned (rē·nound') *agg.* rinomato, famoso.

rent (rĕnt) (1) *n.* (*pass., pp di* to rend) squarcio, strappo, spaccatura.

rent (rĕnt) (2) *n.* rendita, affitto, pigione: for —, da affittare. *vt.* prendere (*o* dare) in affitto, affittare.

rental (rĕn'tăl) *n.* rendita, affitto.

renunciation (rē·nŭn'sĭ·ȧ'shŭn) *n.* rinunzia.

reopen (rē·ō'pĕn) *vt.* riaprire. *vi.* riaprirsi.

reorganization (rē·ôr'găn·ĭ·zā'shŭn) *n.* riorganizzazione.

reorganize (rē·ôr'găn·īz) *vt.* riorganizzare.

repair (rē·pâr') *n.* riparazione, condizione, rifugio: in good —, in buono stato. *vt.* riparare, rimediare a, restaurare. *vi.* andare spesso; recarsi (*a*); ritornare (*in salute*).

reparation (rĕp'á·rā'shŭn) *n.* riparazione.

repartee (rĕp'ēr·tē') *n.* risposta pronta; frizzo.

repast (rĕ·pást') *n.* pasto.

repatriate (rē·pā'trĭ·āt) *vt.* rimpatriare.

repatriation (-ā'shŭn) *n.* rimpatrio.

repay (rē·pā') *vt.* (*pass.*, *pp.* repaid) ripagare; rimborsare; contraccambiare. —ment *n.* rimborso; contraccambio.

repeal (rē·pēl') *n.* revoca, abrogazione. *vt.* revocare, abrogare.

repeat (rē·pēt') *vt.*, *vi.* ripetere. *n.* ripetizione. —ed *agg.* ripetuto, reiterato. —edly *avv.* ripetutamente.

repel (rē·pĕl') *vt.*, *vi.* respingere; ripugnare: it —s me, mi ripugna. —lent *agg.* repellente.

repent (rē·pĕnt') *vt.* pentirsi di, rimpiangere. *vi.* pentirsi. —ance *n.* pentimento. —ant *n.*, *agg.* penitente.

repercussion (rē'pēr·kŭsh'ŭn) *n.* ripercussione.

repertoire (rĕp'ēr·twär) *n.* (*teat.*) repertorio.

repertory (rĕp'ēr·tō'rĭ) *n.* magazzino, deposito; (*teat.*) repertorio: — company, compagnia stabile.

repetition (rĕp'ē·tĭsh'ŭn) *n.* ripetizione.

repine (rē·pīn') *vi.* (*gen.seg.da* at, against) dolersi.

replace (rē·plās') *vt.* ricollocare, reintegrare; sostituire. —able *agg.* ricollocabile; sostituibile. —ment *n.* ricollocamento; sostituzione.

replenish (rē·plĕn'ĭsh) *vt.* riempire, colmare, rifornire.

replete (rē·plēt') *agg.* pieno; sazio.

replica (rĕp'lĭ·ká) *n.* copia, riproduzione, replica.

reply (rē·plī') *n.* risposta. *vt.*, *vi.* rispondere.

report (rē·pōrt') *n.* rapporto, resoconto; diceria; detonazione, fragore: news —, notizia, notiziario. *vt.* riportare; riferire; denunziare: it is —ed that, si dice che. *vi.* fare un rapporto, fare il cronista; presentarsi, andare a rapporto.

reporter (rē·pōr'tēr) *n.* cronista, giornalista; relatore.

repose (rē·pōz') *n.* riposo. *vt.*, *vi.* riposare; posare: to — one's confidence in, fidarsi di, confidare in.

repository (rē·pŏz'ĭ·tō'rĭ) *n.* deposito; depositario.

reprehend (rĕp're·hĕnd') *vt.* biasimare, rimproverare, riprendere.

reprehensible (rĕp're·hĕn'sĭ·b'l) *agg.* reprensibile, riprovevole.

reprehension (rĕp're·hĕn'shŭn) *n.* riprovazione, biasimo.

represent (rĕp're·zĕnt') *vt.* esprimere, simboleggiare, rappresentare.

representation (rĕp're·zĕn·tā'shŭn) *n.* rappresentazione; rappresentanza; asserzione, istanza; protesta.

representative (rĕp're·zĕn'tá·tĭv) *n.* rappresentante, deputato. *agg.* rappresentativo.

repress (rē·prĕs') *vt.* reprimere.

repression (rē·prĕsh'ŭn) *n.* repressione.

reprieve (rē·prēv') *n.* tregua, sospensione. *vt.* accordare una proroga a; sospendere l'esecuzione capitale di.

reprimand (rĕp'rĭ·mánd) *n.* rimprovero. *vt.* rimproverare.

reprint (rē·prĭnt') *n.* ristampa. *vt.* ristampare.

reprisal (rē·prīz'ál) *n.* rappresaglia.

reproach (rē·prōch') *n.* rimprovero; vergogna, vituperio. *vt.* rimproverare, biasimare. —ful *agg.* di rimprovero, severo.

reprobate (rĕp'rō·bāt) *n.* reprobo, depravato.

reprobation (rĕp'rō·bā'shŭn) *n.* biasimo, riprovazione.

reproduce (rē'prō·dūs') *vt.* riprodurre.

reproduction (rē'prō·dŭk'shŭn) *n.* riproduzione.

reproof (rē·prōōf') *n.* rimprovero, biasimo.

reprove (rē·prōōv') *vt.* rimproverare, riprovare, biasimare.

reptile (rĕp'tĭl) *n.* rettile.

republic (rē·pŭb'lĭk) *n.* repubblica.

republican (rē·pŭb'lĭ·kán) *n.*, *agg.* repubblicano.

republish (rē·pŭb'lĭsh) *vt.* ripubblicare.

repudiate (rē·pū'dĭ·āt) *vt.* ripudiare.

repugnance (rē·pŭg'náns) *n.* ripugnanza, avversione.

repugnant (rē·pŭg'nánt) *agg.* ripugnante, incompatibile.

repulse (rē·pŭls') *n.* ripulsa, rifiuto. *vt.* respingere.

repulsion (rē·pŭl'shŭn) *n.* repulsione; ripulsa.

repulsive (rē·pŭl'sĭv) *agg.* repulsivo.

reputable (rĕp'ū·tá·b'l) *agg.* rispettabile, stimato.

reputation (rĕp'ū·tā'shŭn) *n.* riputazione, fama.

repute (rē·pūt') *n.* fama, notorietà: of ill —, malfamato. *vt.* reputare, giudicare, ritenere.

reputed (rē·pūt'ĕd) *agg.* presunto.

request (rē·kwĕst') *n.* richiesta, istanza: at the — of, per richiesta di. *vt.* richiedere, esigere, pregare.

require (rĕ·kwīr') vt. richiedere, esigere, chiedere. —ment n. esigenza, richiesta, necessità, requisito.

requisite (rĕk'wĭ·zĭt) n. requisito. agg. richiesto, necessario.

requisition (rĕk'wĭ·zĭsh'ŭn) n. requisizione, richiesta. vt. requisire, mobilitare; richiedere.

requital (rĕ·kwĭt'ăl) n. ricompensa, contraccambio; rappresaglia.

requite (rĕ·kwĭt') vt. ricompensare, ripagare.

resale (rē·sāl') n. rivendita.

rescind (rĕ·sĭnd') vt. rescindere, annullare.

rescue (rĕs'kū) n. soccorso, salvamento, salvataggio: to go to the — of, andare in soccorso di, andare a salvare. vt. salvare, soccorrere.

research (rĕ·sûrch') n. ricerca, indagine. vi. fare ricerche.

resell (rē·sĕl') vt. (pass., pp. resold) rivendere.

resemblance (rĕ·zĕm'blǎns) n. rassomiglianza.

resemble (rĕ·zĕm'b'l) vt. rassomigliare a.

resent (rĕ·zĕnt') vt. risentirsi di, infastidirsi per. —ful agg. sdegnato, offeso; permaloso, suscettibile. —ment n. risentimento, offesa.

reservation (rĕz'ẽr·vā'shŭn) n. riserva; riserbo; prenotazione: — of a room, prenotazione di una camera.

reserve (rĕ·zûrv') n. riserva; riservatezza, moderazione. vt. riservare.

reserved (rĕ·zûrvd') agg. riservato, circospetto, reticente.

reservoir (rĕz'ẽr·vwôr) n. serbatoio, cisterna, deposito.

reset (rĕ·sĕt') vt. (pass., pp. reset) rimontare (gemme, ecc.); (tip.) ricomporre.

reside (rĕ·zīd') vi. risiedere.

residence (rĕz'ĭ·dĕns) n. residenza.

resident (rĕz'ĭ·dĕnt) n., agg. residente.

residual (rĕ·zĭd'ū·ǎl) n., agg. residuo, rimanente.

residuary (rĕ·zĭd'ū·ẽr'ĭ) agg. residuale, rimanente.

residue (rĕz'ĭ·dū) n. residuo, resto.

resign (rĕ·zīn') vt. rinunziare a, abbandonare: to — oneself, rassegnarsi. vi. dare le dimissioni; cedere.

resignation (rĕz'ĭg·nā'shŭn) n. rassegnazione; dimissione; rinunzia.

resilience (rĕ·zĭl'ĭ·ĕns), resiliency (rĕ·zĭl'ĭ·ĕn·sĭ) n. elasticità, duttilità.

resilient (rĕ·zĭl'ĭ·ĕnt) agg. elastico, duttile, facile a riprendersi.

resin (rĕz'ĭn) n. resina.

resist (rĕ·zĭst') vt. resistere a, av-

versare. vi. resistere. —ance n. resistenza. —ant agg. resistente.

resolute (rĕz'ō·lūt) agg. risoluto.

resolution (rĕz'ō·lū'shŭn) n. risoluzione.

resolve (rĕ·zŏlv') n. risoluzione. vt. risolvere; sciogliere; indurre. vi. decidere, stabilire, risolversi: to — into, risolversi in; ridursi a; trasformarsi in; to — to, proporsi, risolversi a.

resonance (rĕz'ō·nǎns) n. risonanza.

resonant (rĕz'ō·nǎnt) agg. risonante.

resort (rĕ·zôrt') n. risorsa; affluenza; stazione climatica: summer —, luogo di villeggiatura; vice —, casa di malaffare; to have — to, ricorrere a; as a last —, come ultima risorsa. vi.: to — to, ricorrere a; affluire a. —er n. frequentatore; summer —, villeggiante.

resound (rĕ·zound') vi. risonare, ripercuotersi, rimbombare.

resource (rĕ·sôrs') n. risorsa; ingegnosità prontezza: natural —s, ricchezze naturali. —ful agg. pieno di risorse, ingegnoso.

respect (rĕ·spĕkt') n. rispetto, considerazione, aspetto: in — of, with — to, riguardo a. vt. rispettare.

respectable (rĕ·spĕk'tà·b'l) agg. rispettabile, perbene.

respectful (rĕ·spĕkt'fŏŏl) agg. rispettoso.

respecting prep. riguardo a.

respective (rĕ·spĕk'tĭv) agg. rispettivo.

respiration (rĕs'pĭ·rā'shŭn) n. respirazione.

respirator (rĕs'pĭ·rā'tẽr) n. respiratore; maschera anti-gas.

respite (rĕs'pĭt) n. dilazione, tregua.

resplendent (rĕ·splĕn'dĕnt) agg. risplendente.

respond (rĕ·spŏnd') vt., vi. rispondere, reagire a. corrispondere.

response (rĕ·spŏns') n. risposta; responso; reazione, riflesso; rispondenza.

responsibility (rĕ·spŏn'sĭ·bĭl'ĭ·tĭ) n. responsabilità.

responsible (rĕ·spŏn'sĭ·b'l) agg. responsabile; di responsabilità, di fiducia.

rest (rĕst) (1) n. riposo, pausa; appoggio, sostegno; quiete: at —, in riposo, in pace, tranquillo. vt. dar riposo a; posare; basare. vi. riposare, stare, adagiarsi; poggiare (su); fondarsi (su).

rest (rĕst) (2) n. resto, residuo: the —, il resto, tutto l'altro.

restaurant (rĕs'tō·rǎnt) n. ristorante; trattoria.

restful agg. quieto, riposante.

restitution (rĕs'tĭ·tū'shŭn) n. restituzione.

restive (rĕs'tĭv) agg. irrequieto, impaziente.

restless (rĕst'lĕs) agg. irrequieto, agitato, inquieto, turbolento.—ness n. inquietudine, nervosismo, agitazione, turbolenza.

restoration (rĕs'tō·rā'shŭn) n. restaurazione; restauro, restituzione.

restore (rĕ·stōr') vt. ristabilire; restituire; restaurare; risanare.

restrain (rĕ·strān') vt. trattenere, reprimere; imprigionare.

restraint (rĕ·strānt') n. freno, ritegno, limitazione, moderazione; detenzione.

restrict (rĕ·strĭkt') vt. restringere, limitare.—ion n. restrizione.

result (rĕ·zŭlt') n. risultato, conseguenza: as a — of, come conseguenza di, in séguito a. vi. risultare, risolversi (in), finire (in).

resume (rĕ·zūm') vt. riprendere, continuare, ricominciare.

resumé (rā'zū·mā') n. riassunto.

resurrect (rĕz'ŭ·rĕkt') vt., vi. risuscitare.—ion n. risurrezione.

resuscitate (rĕ·sŭs'ĭ·tāt) vt., vi. risuscitare.

retail (rē'tāl) n. vendita al minuto. agg. al minuto: — dealer, commerciante al minuto;— price, prezzo al minuto. vt. vendere al minuto; raccontare minuziosamente; ripetere, propalare.

retailer n. rivenditore, commerciante al minuto.

retain (rĕ·tān') vt. ritenere, servare; assicurarsi i servigi di; trattenere.

retainer (rĕ·tān'ẽr) n. seguace; domestico; caparra, anticipo (spec. a un avvocato).

retake (rĕ·tāk') n. (cine) seconda ripresa. vt. (pass. retook, pp. retaken) riprendere, riportare.

retaliate (rĕ·tăl'ĭ·āt) vt., vi. fare rappresaglie, vendicarsi.

retaliation (rĕ·tăl'ĭ·ā'shŭn) n. rappresaglia, vendetta, ripicco.

retard (rĕ·tärd') vt., vi. ritardare, rallentare.

retch (rĕch) vi. avere conati di vomito.

retention (rĕ·tĕn'shŭn) n. memoria; ritenzione, mantenimento.

retina (rĕt'ĭ·nà) n. (anat.) retina.

retinue (rĕt'ĭ·nū) n. seguito (persone al seguito).

retire (rĕ·tīr') vt. ritirare; mettere a riposo. vi. ritirarsi.

retired (rĕ·tīrd') agg. ritirato, appartato; a riposo, in ritiro.

retirement (rĕ·tīr'mĕnt) n. ritiro, isolamento; collocamento a riposo.

retiring (rĕ·tīr'ĭng) agg. riservato, timido.

retort (rĕ·tôrt') n. replica, risposta arguta; (chim.) storta. vt. ritorcere, ribattere; (chim.) distillare.

retouch (rĕ·tŭch') vt. ritoccare. n. ritocco.

retrace (rĕ·trās') vt. riandare; ricalcare: to — one's steps, ritornare sui propri passi.

retract (rĕ·trăkt') vt. ritirare, ritrattare, revocare. vi. ritirarsi, ritrattarsi. —ion n. ritrazione, ritrattazione.

retread (rĕ·trĕd') vt. (autom.) rinnovare il battistrada. n. (rē'trĕd) battistrada nuovo, gomma con battistrada nuovo.

retreat (rĕ·trēt') n. ritirata; eremo, ritiro. vi. ritirarsi, retrocedere.

retrench (rĕ·trĕnch') vt. ridurre, diminuire. vi. risparmiare.

retribution (rĕt'rĭ·bū'shŭn) n. ricompensa; punizione.

retrieval (rĕ·trēv'ǎl) n. ricupero; riparazione.

retrieve (rĕ·trēv') vt. ricuperare, riparare.

retriever (-ẽr) n. cane da riporto.

retrospect (rĕt'rō·spĕkt) n. sguardo retrospettivo: in —, in retrospettiva.

return (rĕ·tûrn') n. ritorno; restituzione; guadagno, profitto; contraccambio; ricorrenza; elezione; rendiconto, rapporto; biglietto di ritorno: in — for, in cambio di; by — mail, a giro di posta; — game, — màtch (sport), rivincita; — ticket, biglietto di andata e ritorno; income tax —, dichiarazione dei redditi, modulo delle tasse; many happy —s! cento di questi giorni! vt. restituire; ricambiare; produrre; eleggere: to — a favor, ricambiare un favore. vi. ritornare; rispondere.

reunion (rē·ūn'yŭn) n. riunione; riconciliazione.

reunite (rē'ū·nīt') vt. riunire; riconciliare. vi. riunirsi, riconciliarsi.

rev (rĕv) vt. (fam.): to — up a motor, mandar su di giri un motore.

revamp (rē·vămp') vt. rimontare (scarpe); (fam.) rimettere a nuovo, rispolverare.

reveal (rĕ·vēl') vt. rivelare, svelare.

reveille (rĕv'ĕ·lĭ) n. sveglia, diana.

revel (rĕv'ĕl) n. festa, baldoria. vi. gozzovigliare, far festa: to — in, bearsi di.

revelation (rĕv'ĕ·lā'shŭn) n. rivelazione.

revelry (rĕv'ĕl·rĭ) n. baldoria, gozzoviglia, festa rumorosa.

revenge (rĕ·vĕnj') *n.* vendetta, rivincita. *vt.* vendicare. *vi.* vendicarsi. —**ful** *agg.* vendicativo.

revenue (rĕv'ĕ·nū) *n.* fisco; rendita, reddito:— cutter, guardacoste della finanza; — officer, funzionario delle imposte; — stamp, marca da bollo.

reverberate (rĕ·vûr'bĕr·āt) *vt.* ripercuotere. *vi.* ripercuotersi.

revere (rĕ·vēr') *vt.* venerare.

reverence (rĕv'ĕr·ĕns) *n.* venerazione; riverenza; rispetto. *vt.* venerare; rispettare.

reverend (rĕv'ĕr·ĕnd) *n.*, *agg.* reverendo.

reverent (rĕv'ĕr·ĕnt) *agg.* riverente.

reverie (rĕv'ĕr·ĭ) *n.* sogno (a occhi aperti), fantasticheria.

reversal (rĕ·vûr'săl) *n.* revoca; capovolgimento; riforma (*di sentenza*).

reverse (rĕ·vûrs') *n.* inversione tergo dorso; rovescio, opposto, contrario; contrattempo. *agg.* inverso, invertito, contrario: — gear, retromarcia. *vt.* rovesciare, invertire; revocare; rivoltare.

reversion (rĕ·vûr'zhŭn) *n.* ritorno, reversione.

revert (rĕ·vûrt') *vi.* ritornare (*a una condizione precedente opp. su un argomento*); ricadere.

review (rĕ·vū') *n.* rivista; revisione recensione, critica. *vt.* rivedere riesaminare; recensire, criticare.

reviewer (-ĕr) *n.* revisore; recensore, critico: film —, critico cinematografico.

revile (rĕ·vīl') *vt.*, *vi.* insultare.

revise (rĕ·vīz') *vt.* rivedere, modificare.

revision (rĕ·vĭzh'ŭn) *n.* revisione.

revival (rĕ·vīv'ăl) *n.* ravvivamento, ripristino, riesumazione. ritorno. risveglio: religious —, risveglio religioso; — of a play, riesumazione di un lavoro teatrale · — of a film, ripresa o ritorno di un film.

revive (rĕ·vīv') *vt.* ravvivare, rinnovare; risuscitare, riesumare. *vi.* rivivere, rianimarsi.

revoke (rĕ·vōk') *vt.* revocare, annullare.

revolt (rĕ·vōlt') *n.* rivolta, insurrezione. *vt.* rivoltare, disgustare. *vi.* rivoltarsi; provar disgusto. —**ing** *agg.* rivoltante.

revolution (rĕv'ō·lū'shŭn) *n.* rivoluzione. —**ary** *n.*, *agg.* rivoluzionario. —**ist** *n.* rivoluzionario.

revolve (rĕ·vŏlv') *vt.* ponderare; far rotare: to — in one's mind, rivolgere nella mente, riflettere (*su*). *vi.* rotare, girarsi.

revolver (rĕ·vŏl'vĕr) *n.* rivoltella.

revolving *agg.* rotante, girevole.

revue (rĕ·vū') *n.* (*teat.*) rivista.

revulsion (rĕ·vŭl'shŭn) *n.* evoluzione improvvisa. revulsione.

reward (rĕ·wôrd') *n.* ricompensa; taglia. *vt.* ricompensare.

rewrite (rĕ·rīt') *vt.* (*pass.* rewrote, *pp.* rewritten) riscrivere.

rhapsody (răp'sō·dĭ) *n.* rapsodia.

rheostat (rē'ō·stăt) *n.* reostato.

rhetoric (rĕt'ō·rĭk) *n.* retorica, eloquenza.

rhetorical (rĕ·tŏr'ĭ·kăl) *agg.* retorico.

rheum (rōōm) *n.* catarro, muco.

rheumatism (rōō'mă·tĭz'm) *n.* reumatismo.

rheumy (rōōm'ĭ) *agg.* catarroso.

rhinoceros (rī·nŏs'ĕr·ŏs) *n.* rinoceronte.

rhubarb (rōō'bärb) *n.* rabarbaro; (*gergo*) tafferuglio, gazzarra.

rhyme (rīm) *n.* rima. *vt.*, *vi.* rimare.

rhythm (rĭth'm) *n.* ritmo.

rib (rĭb) *n.* costa (*di maglia*); costola, nervatura; stecca (*d'ombrello*), sostegno. (*aeron.*) centina. *vt.* munire di costole o stecche; (*fam.*) canzonare. *sfottere.*

ribald (rĭb'ăld) *agg.* scurrile, volgare.

riband (rĭb'ănd) *vedi* ribbon.

ribbon (rĭb'ŭn) *n.* nastro; brandello.

rice (rīs) *n.* riso: — field, risaia.

ricer (rīs'ĕr) *n.* schiacciapatate.

rich (rĭch) *agg.* ricco, fecondo; saporoso; ornato. costoso; abbondante; succulento, intenso: — color, colore vivo · intenso; — food, alimento sostanzioso.

riches (rĭch'ĕz) *n.pl.* ricchezza.

rick (rĭk) *n* covone.

rickets (rĭk'ĕts) *n.* rachitismo.

rickety (rĭk'ĕ·tĭ) *agg.* rachitico; sgan?gherato traballante.

ricochet (rĭk'ō·shā') *n.* rimbalzo (*di proiettile*). *vi.* (*pass.*, *pp.* ricocheted (-shād' rimbalzare.

rid (rĭd) *vt* (*pass.*, *pp.* rid) sbarazzare, liberare eliminare: to get — of, sbarazzarsi di.

ridden (rĭd' n) *pp.* di to ride.

riddle (rĭd' l) (1) *n.* crivello. *vt.* crivellare, vagliare: — d with bullets, crivellato di proiettili.

riddle (rĭd' l) (2) *n.* enigma, indovinello, problema.

ride (rīd) *n.* cavalcata; scorrazzata, corsa (*su qualunque veicolo*); percorso, pista. *vt.* (*pass.* rode, *pp.* ridden) montare, cavalcare, percorrere (*a cavallo, ecc.*); spronare, angariare: to — a bicycle, andare in bicicletta; to — a horse, andare a cavallo; to — someone, dominare una persona; prendersi gioco di una persona. *vi.* viaggiare; andare a cavallo (*in carrozza, in bicicletta, ecc.*); galleggiare, fluttuare; essere all'ancora: to — over a country, attraversare un paese (*in auto, in ferrovia, a cavallo, ecc.*).

rider (rīd'ĕr) *n.* cavaliere, fantino; ciclista; appendice (*a un documento*), codicillo.

ridge (rĭj) *n.* catena o cresta (*di montagna*), dorso, cima, costura; (*agric.*) porca.

ridgepole (rĭj'pōl') *n.* trave maestra.

ridicule (rĭd'ĭ·kūl) *n.* ridicolo, derisione. *vt.* deridere, beffare.

ridiculous (rĭ·dĭk'û·lŭs) *agg.* ridicolo; assurdo.

rife (rīf) *agg.* prevalente, diffuso, abbondante.

riffraff (rĭf'răf') *n.* rifiuti; marmaglia, canaglia.

rifle (rī'f'l) *n.* carabina, fucile. *vt.* svaligiare.

rift (rĭft) *n.* crepa, squarcio.

rig (rĭg) *vt.* equipaggiare, armare (*navi*): to — oneself up, azzimarsi.

rigging (rĭg'ĭng) *n.* (*naut.*) sartiame, attrezzatura.

right (rīt) *n.* diritto; giusto, bene; destra (*lato destro, mano destra*): — of way, diritto di precedenza; by —, di diritto; from — to left, da destra a sinistra; to the —, a destra. *agg.* dìritto, dritto, diretto; destro; giusto, retto: — angle, angolo retto; — side, lato destro; dritto (*di un tessuto, ecc.*); all —, va bene! to be all —, essere ineccepibile (*opp. illeso*); andare bene, star benissimo; to be —, aver ragione; that is —, è vero che; to be in one's — mind, essere sano di mente. *avv.* direttamente; in linea retta; giustamente, giusto; a destra; proprio: — away, — off, immediatamente: — now, proprio adesso; — there, proprio lì; to be — hungry, avere una fame da lupo; go — home! va direttamente a casa! it is — where you left it, è esattamente dove lo hai lasciato. *vt.* raddrizzare, correggere. *vi.* raddrizzarsi.

righteous (rī'chŭs) *agg.* giusto, virtuoso. —**ness** *n.* dirittura, virtù.

rightful (rīt'fŏōl) *agg.* legittimo, giusto.

right-hand *agg.* destro, di destra: he is my — man, egli è il mio braccio destro.

rightist (rīt'ĭst) *n.* (*pol.*) uomo di destra, conservatore.

rightly (rīt'lĭ) *avv.* rettamente, giustamente, esattamente.

rigid (rĭj'ĭd) *agg.* rigido.

rigidity (rĭ·jĭd'ĭ·tĭ) *n.* rigidezza.

rigmarole (rĭg'ma·rōl) *n.* tiritera; frottole.

rigor (rĭg'ĕr) *n.* rigore, severità.

rigor mortis (rī'-) rigidità cadaverica.

rigorous (rĭg'ĕr·ŭs) *agg.* rigoroso.

rile (rīl) *vt.* (*gergo*) irritare.

rill (rĭl) *n.* ruscello.

rim (rĭm) *n.* orlo, margine; cerchio (*di ruota*).

rime (rīm) (1) *n.* brina.

rime (rīm) (2) *n.* rima.

rind (rīnd) *n.* crosta, scorza, buccia.

ring (rĭng) (1) *n.* anello, cerchio; cricca; (*sport*) quadrato, pugilato: — wedding, fede nuziale. *vt.* cerchiare; accerchiare. —**shaped** *agg.* a forma di anello.

ring (rĭng) (2) *n.* suono, squillo; tono; tintinnio; telefonata: — of defiance, accento di sfida; — of shouts, urlìo; — of a telephone, squillo di un telefono. *vt.* (*pass.* rang, *pp.* rung) sonare; far sonare; telefonare. *vi.* sonare; echeggiare; telefonare: to — up, telefonare a; to — off (*telef.*), troncare la comunicazione; to — for something, sonare il campanello per farsi portare qualcosa.

rink (rĭngk) *n.* pista per pattinaggio.

rinse (rĭns) *vt.* (ri)sciacquare. *n.* (ri)sciacquo.

riot (rī'ŭt) *n.* tumulto, rivolta, gazzarra: — of colors, orgia di colori; to run —, scatenarsi. *vi.* tumultuare; ammutinarsi; far gazzarra.

riotous (rī'ŭt·ŭs) *agg.* tumultuoso.

rip (rĭp) *n.* scucitura, strappo, squarcio. *vt.* scucire, stracciare, strappare, squarciare. *vi.* stracciarsi, aprirsi.

ripe (rīp) *agg.* maturo: — for, maturo per, pronto per.

ripen (rīp'ĕn) *vt., vi.* maturare.

ripeness (rīp'nĕs) *n.* maturità.

ripper (rĭp'ĕr) *n.* sventratore.

ripple (rĭp'l) *n.* increspatura (*del l'acqua*). *vt.* increspare (*l'acqua*). *vi.* incresparsi.

rise (rīz) *n.* il sorgere (*del sole, ecc.*), levata; ascesa; salita, aumento; altura; miglioramento; origine, fonte: to give — to, dare origine a. *vi.* (*pass.* rose, *pp.* risen) sorgere, alzarsi, sollevarsi; salire; lievitare, gonfiarsi; aumentare; nascere, provenire; ribellarsi, insorgere.

risen (rĭz''n) *pp.* di rise.

riser (rīz'ĕr) *n.*: to be an early —, essere mattiniero.

rising (rīz'ĭng) *n.* (il) sorgere; erta; lievitatura; ascesa, resurrezione; insurrezione; gonfiore. *agg.* crescente, nascente; promettente.

risk (rĭsk) *n.* rischio. *vt.* arrischiare.

risky (rĭs'kĭ) agg. rischioso.

rite (rĭt) n. rito.

ritual (rĭt'ū.ăl) n., agg. rituale.

rival (rī'văl) n., agg. rivale, avversario. vt. compet erecon. vi. rivaleggiare. —ry n. rivalità, emulazione.

rive (rīv) vt. (pass. rived, pp. rived, riven) fendere. vi. fendersi.

river (rĭv'ēr) n. fiume, (tip.) sentiero, verme: —head n. sorgente. —side n. sponda di fiume. agg. ripario.

rivet (rĭv'ĕt) n. (mecc.) ribattino. vt. unire con ribattini; ribadire, fissare saldamente, consolidare.

rivulet (rĭv'ū.lĕt) n. rivoletto, ruscello.

roach (rōch) n. scarafaggio; (ittiol.) carpa; baffo d'acqua (provocato da idrovolante in corsa).

road (rōd) n. strada, stradone; itinerario; (naut., pl.) ancoraggio: — map, carta stradale; — police, polizia stradale; on the —, lungo la strada, in cammino, in viaggio di affari. —ability n. (autom.) tenuta di strada. —bed n. fondo stradale, massicciata. — block blocco stradale, posto di blocco. —house n. autostello. —man n. cantoniere; commerciante girovago; commesso viaggiatore. —side n. ciglio della strada. —stead n. (naut.) ancoraggio. —ster n. cavallo da tiro; (autom.) due-posti. —way n. strada, carreggiata, parte (di strada) riservata ai veicoli.

roam (rōm) vi. vagare, aggirarsi.

roar (rōr) n. ruggito, mugghio; scroscio (di risa); urlo; rombo. vi. urlare; ruggire, mugghiare; tuonare; rombare; to — with laughter, sbellicarsi dalle risa.

roast (rōst) n. arrosto. agg. arrostito: — beef, rosbif, manzo arrosto. vt. arrostire; torrefare (caffè); abbrustolire; beffare, criticare.

rob (rŏb) vt. derubare, defraudare: to — someone of something, rubare qualcosa a qualcuno.

robber (rŏb'ēr) n. ladro.

robbery (rŏb'ēr·ĭ) n. furto, rapina.

robe (rōb) n. veste, tunica, manto; toga; abito talare.

robin (rŏb'ĭn) n. pettirosso.

robot (rō'bŏt) n. automa: — bomb, bomba volante, missile.

robust (rō·bŭst') agg. robusto.

rock (rŏk) (1) n. roccia, rupe, baluardo; (gergo) gemma: — alum, allume di rocca; — salt, salgemma, sale. to go on the —s, finire in rovina. — crystal, cristallo di rocca.

rock (rŏk) (2) n. dondolio. vt. cullare, dondolare, scuotere: to — to sleep,

cullare fino ad addormentare. vi. dondolarsi.

rocker (rŏk'ēr) n. dondolo; sedia a dondolo.

rocket (rŏk'ĕt) n. razzo: — launcher, lanciarazzi. —ry n. studio o uso dei razzi; missilistica.

rocking (rŏk'ĭng) n. oscillazione, dondolio. agg. oscillante: — chair, sedia a dondolo; — horse, cavallo a dondolo.

rocky (rŏk'ĭ) agg. roccioso; instabile.

rod (rŏd) n. bacchetta, verga, canna; pertica (misura di lunghezza = 5 metri circa); (mecc.) albero, biella; (gergo) pistola: fishing —, canna da pesca; hot — (gergo), automobile col motore supercompresso.

rode (rōd) pass. di to ride.

roe deer (rō) n. capriolo.

Roger (rŏj'ēr) n.pr. Ruggero. inter. (radio) ricevuto.

rogue (rōg) n. furfante.

roguish (rō'gĭsh) agg. bricconesco, malizioso.

roister (rois'tēr) n. bontempone; gradasso. vi. fare il gradasso; far gazzarra.

role (rōl) n. parte (di attore, ecc.).

roll (rōl) n. rotolo, rullo; cilindro; panino; ruolo, lista; (naut.) rollio: to call the —, fare l'appello: — call, appello. vt. rotolare, arrotolare; avvolgere; roteare; spianare: to — up one's sleeves, arrotolarsi le maniche. vi. rotolare, ruzzolare, arrotolarsi, rotolarsi; rullare; rollare: to — over in the snow, rotolarsi nella neve.

roller (rōl'ēr) n. rullo, cilindro rotante, laminatoio; ondata, maroso; rotolo (di garza, ecc.): — bearing, cuscinetto a sfere; — coaster, otto volante. — skates pattini a rotelle.

Roman (rō'măn) n., agg. romano: — nose, naso aquilino.

romance (rō·măns') n. racconto di cappa e spada, racconto fantastico; esagerazione, romanticheria; amore, idillio; (mus.) romanza. vi. raccontare storie fantasiose; fantasticare; fare il romantico.

romantic (rō·măn'tĭk) agg. romantico; romanzesco. —ism (—tĭ·sĭz'm) n. romanticismo. —ist n. romantico.

romp (rŏmp) n. monello, maschiaccio. vi. ruzzare.

rompers (rŏmp'ērz) n. tuta da bambino.

rood (rōōd) n. crocifisso, croce; ¼ di acro.

roof (rōōf) n. tetto, volta; imperiale (di veicoli); (anat.) palato: — garden, giardino pensile. vt. coprire con tetto, ricoverare.

rook (rŏŏk) *n.* cornacchia; (*scacchi*) torre; (*gergo*) baro.

room (rōōm) *n.* camera, stanza, sala; spazio, posto; possibilità: to give —, fare posto; ritirarsi; there is no — for, non c'è posto per. *vi.* alloggiare. —er *n.* pensionante. —mate *n.* compagno di stanza.

roominess (rōōm′ĭ-nĕs) *n.* spaziosità.

roomy (rōōm′ĭ) *agg.* vasto, spazioso.

roost (rōōst) *n.* pollaio, posatoio (*dei polli*). *vi.* appollaiarsi; riposare, pernottare.

rooster (rōōs′tẽr) *n.* gallo domestico.

root (rōōt) *n.* radice; origine. *vt.* piantare: to — up, out, sradicare. *vi.* radicarsi, attecchire; grufolare: to — for (*sport e fig.*) fare il tifo per.

rooted *agg.* radicato; inveterato.

rope (rōp) *n.* corda, fune: to be at the end of one's —, non saper più a che santo voltarsi; to give one —, lasciare che uno faccia; to know the —s, conoscere il mestiere, sapere il fatto proprio; — of sand, legame effimero, amicizia instabile. *vt.* legare (o delimitare) con una corda: to — in, adescare, coinvolgere; to — off, cintare o isolare con funi.

rosary (rō′zȧ-rĭ) *n.* rosario.

rose (rōz) (1) *pass.* di to rise.

rose (rōz) (2) *n.* rosa (*fiore e colore*). —bud *n.* bocciuolo di rosa. —bush *n.* roseto. —mary *n.* rosmarino.

rosin (rŏz′ĭn) *n.* resina.

roster (rŏs′tẽr) *n.* ruolo, lista.

rostrum (rŏs′trŭm) *n.* rostro; tribuna.

rosy (rōz′ĭ) *agg.* roseo, rosato: — future, roseo avvenire.

rot (rŏt) *n.* putrefazione, marciume; (*gergo*) sciocchezza. *vt.* far imputridire, macerare. *vi.* imputridire: to — away, off, andare in rovina.

rotary (rō′tȧ-rĭ) *agg.* rotatorio, rotante: — press, rotativa. *n.* (*traffico stradale*) rotonda.

rotate (rō′tāt) *vt.* rotare. *vi.* roteare, girare; voltarsi; procedere a rotazione.

rotation (rō-tā′shŭn) *n.* rotazione.

rote (rōt) *n.* trantran; ripetizione macchinale: by —, macchinalmente.

rotor (rō′tẽr) *n.* rotore.

rotten (rŏt′'n) *agg.* putrido, corrotto cariato, malsicuro; ignobile.

rotter (rŏt′ẽr) *n.* farabutto; (*un*) poco di buono; scansafatiche.

rouge (rōōzh) *n.* rossetto, belletto. *vt.* imbellettare. *vi.* imbellettarsi, darsi il rossetto.

rough (rŭf) *n.* parte ruvida, terreno ineguale; gradasso; violento. *agg.*

rude, rozzo, ruvido; ispido; aspro; ineguale; crudele, violento; approssimativo, grezzo; tempestoso: — diamond, diamante grezzo; — draft, brutta copia, minuta; — estimate, calcolo approssimato; — going, strada accidentata; corsa a sobbalzi. (*fig.*) difficoltà, ostacoli; — ground, terreno accidentato; — idea, idea approssimativa; — sea, mare grosso o agitato; — weather, tempaccio. *vi.*: to — it, adattarsi a tutto, vivere alla meglio.

roughen (rŭf′ẽn) *vt.*, *vi.* irruvidire, irruvidirsi.

roughhew (rŭf′hū′) *vt.* potare; abbozzare.

roughly (rŭf′lĭ) *avv.* duramente; rozzamente, ruvidamente; approssimativamente.

roughness (-nĕs) *n.* durezza, asprezza, ruvidezza; violenza.

round (round) *n.* tondo, cerchio, rotonda giro; ciclo; turno; circonvallazione; distribuzione; piuolo (*di scala*); carica (*di cartucce*); ronda; (*pugilato*) ripresa: — of applause, scroscio di applausi; to go the —s, fare la ronda. *agg.* rotondo, circolare; completo; pingue: — trip, viaggio completo, viaggio di andata e ritorno; — numbers, cifre tonde. *avv.* intorno, all'intorno all'incirca: all the year —, tutto l'anno; to come — again, tornare di nuovo, ritornare; — about (tutt') intorno a; dalla parte opposta, indirettamente; all'incirca in girotondo; to look —, voltarsi a guardare. *prep.* attorno a, ai margini di: — the corner, oltre la cantonata; — the clock, per ventiquattr'ore di seguito. *vt.*, *vi.* arrotondare, circondare; svoltare; fare il giro di; completare; arrotondarsi (*naut.*) doppiare: to — off, arrotondare (*un orlo*); rifinire completare; to — on, rivoltarsi contro. to — out, completare mettersi in salute; to — to, rimettersi in salute; tornare alle condizioni normali, riprendersi; to — up, radunare.

roundabout (round′ȧ-bout′) *n.* giro vizioso perifrasi; giostra. *agg.* indiretto, tortuoso.

roundness (round′nĕs) *n.* rotondità.

roundup (round′ŭp′) *n.* raccolta (*del bestiame, ecc.*); retata.

rouse (rouz) *vt.* svegliare, destare; far alzare, infuriare. *vi.* alzarsi, svegliarsi, scuotersi.

roustabout (roust′ȧ-bout′) *n.* scaricatore.

rout (rout) *n.* folla, plebaglia; (*mil.*) rotta. *vt.* sbaragliare, mettere in fuga: **to — out**, scacciare, mettere in fuga.

route (rōōt) *n.* via, percorso, itinerario. *vt.* instradare; smistare.

routine (rōō·tēn') *n.* trantran, andazzo; abitudine.

rove (rōv) *vi.* vagare, vagabondare.

rover (rōv'ẽr) *n.* vagabondo; pirata.

row (rou) (1) *n.* rissa, lite, tumulto. *vi.* litigare.

row (rō) (2) *n.* fila, filare.

row (rō) (3) *n.* remata, gita in barca. *vt.* spingere a remi; trasportare in barca. *vi.* vogare.

rowboat (rō'bōt') *n.* barca a remi.

rowdy (rou'dl) *n.* briccone.

rower (rō'ẽr) *n.* rematore.

rowlock (rō'lŏk') *n.* scalmiera.

royal (roi'ăl) *agg.* reale, regio, regale.

royalist (roi'ăl·ĭst) *n.* realista, legittimista.

royalty (roi'ăl·tǐ) *n.* regalità, maestà, tributo; (*comm., gen.pl.* **royalties**) compartecipazione agli utili, diritti d'autore.

rub (rŭb) *n.* sfregamento, frizione; ostacolo, difficoltà; sarcasmo: **there is the —!** questo è il guaio! *vt.* strofinare, frizionare spalmare: **to — off, out,** eliminare strofinando, cancellare; **to — someone the wrong way,** prendere uno di contropelo. *vi.* sfregarsi, fare attrito irritare; logorarsi: **to — along,** tirare avanti.

rubber (rŭb'ẽr) *n.* strofinaccio; pulitore; gomma, caucciù gomma da cancellare; soprascarpa (*bridge*) partita, *agg.* di gomma elastico: **— band,** elastico; **— plantation,** piantagione di caucciù; **— tree,** albero della gomma.

rubbish (rŭb'ĭsh) *n.* rifiuti; cianfrusaglie; sciocchezze.

rubble (rŭb''l) *n.* ciottoli, calcinacci, breccia; macerie; pietra grezza.

ruby (rōō'bĭ) *n.* rubino.

rucksack (rŭk'săk') *n.* sacco da montagna.

rudder (rŭd'ẽr) *n.* timone.

ruddy (rŭd'ĭ) *agg.* rubicondo, florido.

rude (rōōd) *agg.* rude, scortese; villano rozzo, aspro. **—ness** *n.* villania, rudezza, scortesia.

rudimentary (rōō'dǐ·mĕn'tá·rǐ) *agg.* rudimentale, primitivo.

rue (rōō) (1) *n.* (*bot.*) ruta.

rue (rōō) (2) *n.* pentimento, rimpianto. *vt.* pentirsi di, rammaricarsi di.

rueful (rōō'fŏŏl) *agg.* triste; doloroso; compassionevole.

ruffian (rŭf'ĭ·ăn) *n.* ribaldo, scellerato.

ruffle (rŭf''l) *n.* increspatura; balza pieghettata; turbamento. *vt.* spiegazzare; increspare; turbare, scompigliare. *vi.* incresparsi, spiegazzarsi; turbarsi.

rug (rŭg) *n.* tappeto, coperta.

rugged (rŭg'ĕd) *agg.* ruvido, scabro; rozzo; roccioso; solcato; severo; vigoroso; inclemente: **a — sport,** uno sport arduo; **a — individualist,** un individualista accanito.

ruin (rōō'ĭn) *n.* rovina: **to go to —,** finire in rovina. *vt.* rovinare. *vi.* andare in rovina.

ruinous (rōō'ĭ·nŭs) *agg.* rovinoso.

rule (rōōl) *n.* regola, regolamento; governo; metodo; legge; regolo, riga: **as a —,** generalmente. *vt.* regolare; governare; decretare; rigare: **to — out,** espellere, radiare. *vi.* regnare: **to — over,** governare, reggere.

ruler (rōōl'ẽr) *n.* governante, sovrano; regolo, riga.

ruling (-ĭng) *n.* regola, regolamento; decisione, governo; rigatura. *agg.* prevalente, dominante.

rum (rŭm) *n.* rum (*liquore*).

rumble (rŭm'b'l) *n.* rombo, brontolio: **— seat** (*autom.*) sedile posteriore scoperto (*delle spider*). *vi.* rombare, brontolare.

ruminate (rōō'mǐ·nāt) *vt., vi.* ruminare; meditare, rimuginare.

rummage (rŭm'ĭj) *n.* ricerca, rovistio; cianfrusaglie. **— sale** *n.* vendita di oggetti smarriti; fiera di beneficenza; liquidazione. *vt., vi.* rovistare, frugare.

rummy (rŭm'ĭ) *n.* ramino (*giuoco*).

rumor (rōō'mẽr) *n.* diceria. *vt.* propalare, divulgare: **it is —ed that,** si vocifera che.

rump (rŭmp) *n.* parte posteriore (*di animale*), deretano.

rumple (rŭm'p'l) *n.* grinza, piega. *vt.* sgualcire, arruffare.

rumpus (rŭm'pŭs) *n.* strepito, tumulto: **— room,** saletta da giuoco (*in una casa privata*).

run (rŭn) *n.* corsa; corso, andamento; classe, categoria; durata; direzione, gestione; recinto; conduttura; smagliatura (*di calza*): **a — for one's money,** compenso (*per uno sforzo fatto*); **a — of luck,** un periodo di fortuna; **the common —,** la gente comune; **in the long —,** alla lunga, col tempo; **on the —,** indaffarato, in trambusto; in fretta e furia, in corsa; in fuga; **to get the — of,** impadronirsi di (*un mestiere*), imparare il funzionamento di (*un meccanismo*); **to have a long —**

(*teat.*), tenere il cartellone a lungo. *vt.* (*pass.* ran, *pp.* run) correre (*un rischio*); far correre, condurre; gestire, dirigere; introdurre; forzare (*un blocco*). *vi.* correre; accorrere; scorrere; fuggire; passare; estendersi; fondersi o stingere (*di colori*); funzionare; essere in corso; diventare; suppurare; liquefarsi, grondare, colare: to — a fever, avere la febbre; to — across, imbattersi, incontrare; to — after, inseguire; to — against, imbattersi; ostacolare, opporsi a; to — away, fuggire; sfuggire al controllo di; to — down, dare la caccia a; rintracciare, trovare; urtare, investire, travolgere; calunniare; scaricarsi (*di orologi, ecc.*); perdere salute; guastarsi; finire in rovina; scorrere, dare una scorsa a; to — dry, asciugarsi, seccarsi; to — errands, fare commissioni; to — for, durare; essere candidato a; (*teat.*) tenere il cartellone per; to — in, rodare (*un motore*); arrestare; fare una scappata da; to — into, entrare di corsa; cozzare contro; trasformare; imbattersi in; ammontare a; fare (*debiti*); to — mad, impazzire; to — off, far fluire; fluire, scaricarsi; fuggire; pubblicare; preparare o fare in fretta; esaurirsi; to — on, parlare ininterrottamente; to — out, finire, esaurirsi; sperperare; scorrere; scacciare; protendersi; diffondersi; to — out of, restare senza; to — out on, abbandonare, piantare; to — over, traboccare; dare un'occhiata a, scorrere; travolgere, investire; eccedere, superare; to — risks, correre rischi; to — short, scarseggiare (*di*); to — through, trafiggere; scorrere, dare una scorsa a; sperperare; correre per, pervadere; to — to, assommare a; to — to earth, scovare, stanare; to — up, innalzare; aumentare; costruire in fretta; far crescere; to — wild, crescere come un selvaggio; to — with, frequentare, associarsi a; andare d'accordo con, coincidere.

runabout (rŭn′ȧ-bout′) *n.* (*autom.*) vetturetta.

runaround (rŭn′ȧ-round′) *n.*: to give someone the —, far fare a una persona (*in cerca di informazioni, ecc.*) il giro di tutti gli uffici.

runaway (rŭn′ȧ-wā′) *n.* fuggiasco; fuga; cavallo imbizzarrito. *agg.* fuggitivo; rapido; imbizzarrito.

rung (rŭng) (1) *pass., pp.* di to ring.

rung (rŭng) (2) *n.* piuolo, bastone.

runner (rŭn′ẽr) *n.* corridore; messaggiero; piazzista; spianatoio, cursore; contrabbandiere; passatoia; lama (*di pattino*); pattino (*di slitta*); smagliatura (*di calza*); (*bot.*) viticcio.

running (rŭn′ĭng) *n.* corso, corsa; flusso; secrezione; gestione: to be out of the —, essere fuori della battaglia. *agg.* corrente; in corso; dilagante; fluido; scorrente; continuo; purulento; — board, predellino, montatoio; — expenses, spese giornaliere; — knot, nodo scorsoio; — fire, fuoco di fila; — water, acqua corrente; in — condition, in buono stato; for ten days —, per dieci giorni di séguito.

runt (rŭnt) *n.* nanerottolo, omiciattolo.

runway (rŭn′wā′) *n.* pista (*anche di aeroporto*); sentiero; canale.

rupture (rŭp′tửr) *n.* rottura; scoppio; disaccordo; (*med.*) ernia. *vt., vi.* rompere; scoppiare (*di ascesso, ecc.*); rompersi.

rural (rōōr′ăl) *agg.* rurale, rustico.

rurban (rûr′băn) *agg.* posto ai confini tra città e campagna, periferico.

rush (rŭsh) (1) *n.* giunco: — chair, sedia di vimini.

rush (rŭsh) (2) *n.* impeto, foga, furia, urgenza; afflusso, affluenza: — of business, forte movimento commerciale; — of people, afflusso o ondata di gente. *agg.* urgente: — hours, ore di punta; — order, ordine urgente. *vt.* spingere (o trascinare) con foga; trasportare d'urgenza; prendere d'assalto; affrettare; sbrigare in fretta. *vi.* precipitarsi, slanciarsi; affluire: to — out, precipitarsi fuori; to — past, passare accanto (*a uno*) di corsa.

russet (rŭs′ĕt) *n.* color ruggine; mela ruggine.

Russian (rŭsh′ăn) *n.*, *agg.* russo.

rust (rŭst) *n.* ruggine. *vt., vi.* arrugginire.

rustic (rŭs′tĭk) *n.*, *agg.* rustico.

rustle (rŭs′'l) *n.* fruscio; bisbiglio. *vi.* stormire, frusciare: to — cattle, rubare bestiame.

rustler (rŭs′lẽr) *n.* ladro di bestiame.

rusty (rŭst′ĭ) *agg.* rugginoso, arrugginito; color ruggine; logoro; irrequieto, indocile.

rut (rŭt) *n.* solco; andazzo, tran-tran. *vt.* solcare: to be in a —, seguire il solito tran-tran.

ruthless (rōōth′lĕs) *agg.* spietato, crudele. —**ness** *n.* crudeltà.

rutty (rŭt′ĭ) *agg.* solcato.

rye (rī) *n.* (*bot.*) segala: **spurred** —, segala cornuta.

S

Sabbath (săb′ăth) n. giorno del riposo; sabato ebraico.

saber (sā′bĕr) n. sciabola.

sable (sā′b′l) n. zibellino; (pl.) gramaglie, abito da lutto.

sabotage (săb′ō·tăzh′) n. sabotaggio.

saboteur (săb′ō·tûr′) n. sabotatore.

sabre vedi saber.

saccharine (săk′ȧ·rĭn) n. saccarina. agg. zuccherino.

sachem (sā′chĕm) n. capo pellirossa.

sack (săk) n. sacco, sacchetto; saccheggio; (gergo) licenziamento; (fam.) letto: to hit the —, andare a dormire; a sad —, un povero gonzo. vt. saccheggiare; insaccare; licenziare. —cloth, tela di sacco, cilicio.

sacrament (săk′rȧ·mĕnt) n. sacramento.

sacred (sā′krĕd) agg. sacro, consacrato. —ness n. santità, inviolabilità.

sacrifice (săk′rĭ·fīs) n. sacrificio. vt. sacrificare.

sacrilege (săk′rĭ·lĕj) n. sacrilegio.

sacrilegious (săk′rĭ·lē′jŭs) agg. sacrilego.

sacrum (să′krŭm) n. osso sacro.

sad (săd) agg. triste, pietoso, deplorabile.

sadden (săd′′n) vt. rattristare. vi. rattristarsi.

saddle (săd′′l) n. sella. vt. sellare: to —one with responsibilities, accollare responsabilità a uno.

sadiron (săd′ī′ĕrn) n. ferro da stiro.

sadism (săd′ĭz′m) n. sadismo.

sadist (săd′ĭst) n. sadico.

sadistic (sȧ·dĭs′tĭk) agg. sadico.

sadness (săd′nĕs) n. tristezza.

safe (sāf) n. cassaforte. agg. salvo, sicuro, sano, fuori pericolo, certo, fidato: — and sound, sano e salvo. —conduct n. salvacondotto.

safeguard (sāf′gärd′) n. salvaguardia. vt. salvaguardare.

safely (sāf′lĭ) avv. sicuramente; felicemente, senza incidenti (o pericoli).

safety (sāf′tĭ) n. sicurezza, salvezza, garanzia, sicura (di arma): — pin, spilla di sicurezza; — belt, cintura di sicurezza; in —, con sicurezza, senza pericolo.

saffron (săf′rŭn) n. (bot.) zafferano. agg. giallo-zafferano.

sag (săg) n. incavo, depressione, cedimento, flessione. vi. piegarsi, abbassarsi, avvallarsi, cedere, afflosciarsi: his shoulders —, ha le spalle spioventi.

sagacious (sȧ·gā′shŭs) agg. sagace.

sagacity (sȧ·găs′ĭ·tĭ) n. sagacia.

sage (sāj) (1) n. (bot.) salvia.

sage (sāj) (2) n., agg. saggio, savio.

said (sĕd) pass., pp. di to say.

sail (sāl) n. vela, velame; viaggio o gita in barca a vela; veliero: to set —, salpare; at full —, a vele spiegate. vi. veleggiare, far vela, navigare, salpare: to — a kite, far volare un aquilone.

sailor (sāl′ĕr) n. marinaio: to be a bad —, soffrire il mal di mare.

saint (sānt) n. santo. agg. santo, san, sacro. vt. canonizzare, santificare.

sake (sāk) n. ragione, causa, scopo, fine, amore, riguardo: for God's —, per l'amor di Dio; for her (his) —, per amor suo; for the — of appearances, per salvare le apparenze; for love's —, per amore; for the — of argument, per amor di discussione.

salable (sāl′ȧ·b′l) agg. vendibile.

salad (săl′ăd) n. insalata: — dressing, condimento per insalata.

salamander (săl′ȧ·măn′dĕr) n. salamandra.

salaried (săl′ȧ·rĭd) agg. salariato, stipendiato.

salary (săl′ȧ·rĭ) n. salario, stipendio.

sale (sāl) n. vendita: goods on — or return, merce in deposito; — by auction, vendita all'asta; for (on) —, in vendita, da vendere.

saleable (sāl′ȧ·b′l) vedi salable.

salesman (sālz′măn) n. venditore, commesso viaggiatore, piazzista.

saleswoman (sālz′wŏŏm′ăn) n. venditrice, commessa viaggiatrice.

salient (sā′lĭ·ĕnt) n., agg. saliente.

saline (sā′lĭn) agg. salino, salso.

saliva (sȧ·lī′vȧ) n. saliva.

sallow (săl′ō) (1) agg. giallastro, olivastro, smorto.

sallow (2) n. salice.

sally (săl′ĭ) n. slancio, irruzione; capriccio; tratto di spirito, frecciata; (mil.) sortita. vi. sortire, fare una sortita.

salmon (săm′ŭn) n. salmone.

saloon (sȧ·lōōn′) n. salone: cabina di lusso; bar, taverna: dining —, salone da pranzo.

salt (sôlt) n. sale; spirito, acume: — mine, salina; the — of the earth, il fior fiore dell'umanità; smelling —s, sali da fiutare. agg. salato salino: — water, acqua salata, acqua di mare. vt. salare: to — away, down, conservare sotto sale; accumulare (ricchezze).

saltpeter (sòlt'pē'tẽr) *n.* (*chim.*) salnitro.

salty (sòlt'ĭ) *agg.* salato, salmastro; caustico, pungente.

salubrious (sd·lū'brĭ·ŭs) *agg.* salubre.

salutary (săl'ū·tẽr'ĭ) *agg.* salutare.

salutation (săl'ū·tā'shŭn) *n.* saluto.

salute (sd·lūt') *n.* saluto; salva (*di artigl.*). *vt.* salutare.

salvage (săl'vĭj) *n.* salvataggio, ricupero, merci ricuperate (*da naufragio, incendio, ecc.*).

salvation (săl·vā'shŭn) *n.* salvezza, salvamento: Salvation Army, Esercito della Salvezza.

salve (săv) *n.* unguento, balsamo. *vt.* lenire, preservare.

salver (săl'vẽr) *n.* vassoio.

salvo (săl'vō) *n.* salva (*d'artiglieria*); scroscio (*d'applausi*), ovazione. *vt.*, *vi.* salutare con una salva.

samba (săm'bà) *n.* samba. *vi.* ballare la samba.

same (sām) *pron.* la stessa cosa (*o persona*), lo stesso: all the —, ciononostante; just the —, tuttavia; at the — time, nello stesso tempo, d'altronde; it's all the — to me, per me è la stessa cosa. *agg.* stesso, medesimo, uguale, anzidetto.

sample (săm'p'l) *n.* campione, esempio: book of —s, campionario. *vt.* prelevare un campione di, giudicare dal campione, assaggiare.

sampler (săm'plẽr) *n.* saggio (*spec. di ricamo*).

sanatorium (săn'à·tō'rĭ·ŭm) *vedi* sanitarium.

sanctify (săngk'tĭ·fī) *vt.* santificare.

sanctimonious (săngk'tĭ·mō'nĭ·ŭs) *agg.* bigotto, ipocrita.

sanction (săngk'shŭn) *n.* sanzione. *vt.* sanzionare, sancire.

sanctity (săngk'tĭ·tĭ) *n.* santità.

sanctuary (săngk'tū·ĕr'ĭ) *n.* santuario, asilo.

sanctum (săngk'tŭm) *n.* luogo sacro *o* privato; studio, ufficio personale.

sand (sănd) *n.* sabbia, rena. *vt.* coprire di sabbia; mescolare con sabbia; strofinare con la sabbia; smerigliare.

sandal (săn'dàl) *n.* sandalo. —wood *n.* legno di sandalo.

sandpaper (sănd'pā'pẽr) *n.* carta smerigliata.

sandstone (sănd'stōn') *n.* pietra arenaria.

sandwich (sănd'wĭch) *n.* panino imbottito. *vt.* mettere fra (*due cose*).

sandy (săn'dĭ) *agg.* sabbioso; — hair, capelli biondi.

sane (sān) *agg.* sano di mente, ragionevole, savio.

sang (săng) *pass. di* to sing.

sanguine (săng'gwĭn) *agg.* sanguigno; ardente; ottimista, fiducioso: — hopes, rosee speranze.

sanitarium (săn'ĭ·târ'ĭ·ŭm) *n.* casa di cura, convalescenziario.

sanitary (săn'ĭ·tĕr'ĭ) *agg.* sanitario, igienico.

sanitation (săn'ĭ·tā'shŭn) *n.* igiene.

sanity (săn'ĭ·tĭ) *n.* sanità mentale.

sank (săngk) *pass. di* to sink.

Santa Claus (săn'tà klòz) *n.* Babbo Natale.

sap (săp) *n.* succo, linfa, sangue; (*gergo*) stupido. *vt.* indebolire, fiaccare.

sapling (săp'lĭng) *n.* arboscello; giovanetto.

sapphire (săf'īr) *n.* zaffiro.

sarcasm (săr'kăz'm) *n.* sarcasmo.

sarcastic (săr·kăs'tĭk) *agg.* sarcastico.

sarcophagus (săr·kŏf'à·gŭs) *n.* sarcofago.

sardine (săr·dēn') *n.* sardina.

Sardinian (săr·dĭn'ĭ·ăn) *n.*, *agg.* sardo.

sarsaparilla (săr'sà·pà·rĭl'à) *n.* (*bot.*) salsapariglia.

sash (săsh) *n.* cintura, sciarpa; intelaiatura di finestra: — window, finestra a ghigliottina.

sat (săt) *pass.*, *pp. di* to sit.

Satan (sā'tăn) *n.* Satana, demonio.

satchel (săch'ĕl) *n.* cartella da scolaro, borsa da viaggio.

sate (sāt) *vt.* saziare, soddisfare.

sateen (să·tēn') *n.* satin (*tessuto*).

satellite (săt'ĕ·līt) *n.* satellite; stato satellite.

satiate (sā'shĭ·āt) *vt.*, *vi.* saziare; rimpinzare, rimpinzarsi.

satiety (sà·tī'ĕ·tĭ) *n.* sazietà.

satin (săt'ĭn) *n.* raso.

satire (săt'īr) *n.* satira.

satirical (sà·tĭr'ĭ·kàl) *agg.* satirico.

satirize (săt'ĭ·rīz) *vt.* satireggiare.

satisfaction (săt'ĭs·făk'shŭn) *n.* sodisfazione.

satisfactory (săt'ĭs·făk'tō·rĭ) *agg.* sodisfacente; convincente; esauriente.

satisfied (săt'ĭs·fīd) *agg.* sodisfatto; convinto.

satisfy (săt'ĭs·fī) *vt.*, *vi.* sodisfare; convincere: to — oneself, sincerarsi, convincersi. —ing *agg.* sodisfacente; convincente.

saturate (săt'ū·rāt) *agg.* saturo. *vt.* saturare.

saturation (săt'ūrā'shŭn) *n.* saturazione.

Saturday (săt'ẽr·dĭ) *n.* sabato.

saturnine (săt'ẽr·nĭn) *agg.* cupo, taciturno.

satyr (săt'ẽr; sā'tẽr) *n.* satiro.

sauce (sòs) *n.* salsa; impudenza; (*S.U.*) frutta cotta. *vt.* insaporire, condire; dire impertinenze a. —boat n. salsiera. —pan n. casseruola.

saucer (sô'sĕr) n. piattino.

saucily (sô'sĭ-lĭ) avv. sfacciatamente, insolentemente; pepatamente.

sauciness (sô'sĭ-nĕs) n. sfacciataggine, impertinenza; vivacità.

saucy (sô'sĭ) agg. insolente, impertinente; piccante, pepato.

saunter (sôn'tĕr) n. passeggiata, andatura calma. vi. bighellonare, passeggiare.

sausage (sô'sĭj) n. salame, salsiccia.

savage (să'vĭj) n. selvaggio. agg. selvaggio, selvatico, feroce, violento, crudele. —ly avv. selvaggiamente, ferocemente, villanamente, irosamente. —ness, —ry n. ferocia, villania, brutalità, barbarie.

savant (să-vän') n. dotto.

save (săv) prep. salvo, eccetto, tranne. vt. salvare, risparmiare, conservare, tenere in serbo. vi. fare economia.

saver (săv'ĕr) n. salvatore, liberatore; risparmiatore.

saving (săv'ĭng) n. risparmio, economia: —s, risparmi; —s bank, cassa di risparmio. agg. economo, economico, protettivo. prep. eccetto, salvo.

savior (săv'yĕr), **saviour** n. salvatore, redentore.

savor (să'vĕr) n. sapore, gusto. vt. assaporare, gustare; insaporire. vi. sapere (di).

savory (să'vĕr-ĭ) agg. saporito.

saw (sô) 1 pass. di to see.

saw (sô) 2 n. proverbio, massima.

saw (sô) 3 n. sega: vt. (pass. sawed, pp. sawn) segare. —dust n. segatura. —horse n. cavallo di frisia; cavalletto. —mill n. segheria.

Saxon (săk'sŭn) n., agg. sassone.

saxophone (săk'sō-fōn) n. sassofono.

say (sā) n. discorso, diritto di parola, turno (per parlare): to have one's —, dire la propria opinione; to have a — in a matter, avere voce in una questione; the final —, l'ultima parola. vt., vi. (pass., pp. said) dire, affermare: it is said, si dice; you don't — I che dite mai! that is to —, vale a dire; I dare —, immagino; to the least, a dir poco. —ing n. detto, proverbio, massima: as the —ing goes, come dice il proverbio; it goes without —ing, è ovvio, non occorre dire (che).

scab (skăb) n. crosta (di ferita); scabbia; crumiro. vi. formare la crosta, coprirsi di croste.

scabbard (skăb'ĕrd) n. guaina, fodero di spada.

scabby (skăb'ĭ) agg. coperto di croste, scabbioso.

scabrous (skā'brŭs) agg. scabro, scabroso; salace, osceno.

scaffold (skăf'ōld) n. palco, impalcatura, patibolo. —ing n. impalcatura.

scald (skôld) n. bruciatura, scottatura. vt. scottare, ustionare, scaldare sino all'ebollizione. —ing agg. scottante.

scale (skăl) 1 n. scaglia, squama. vt. scrostare, togliere le scaglie a. vi. sfaldarsi, squamarsi.

scale (skăl) 2 n. bilancia, piatto di bilancia; gradazione, proporzione, scala: a pair of —s, una bilancia; platform —, bascula; sliding —, scala mobile. vt., vi. pesare, misurare, graduare; scalare, arrampicarsi: to — down, abbassare gradatamente.

scallop (skŏl'ŭp) n. conchiglia, mollusco bivalve; dentellatura, smerlo. vt. dentellare, smerlare; cucinare al gratin.

scalp (skălp) n. cuoio capelluto, capigliatura. vt. scotennare; rivendere (biglietti di teatro, ecc.) a prezzo maggiorato.

scalpel (skăl'pĕl) n. (chir.) scalpello.

scalper (skăl'pĕr) n. scotennatore; bagarino.

scaly (skăl'ĭ) agg. squamoso.

scamp (skămp) n. furfante, scioperato.

scamper (skăm'pĕr) n. fuga frettolosa. vi. correre, darsela a gambe.

scan (skăn) vt. scandire; scorrere frettolosamente, scrutare; (T.V.) esplorare.

scandal (skăn'dăl) n. scandalo, maldicenza, vergogna.

scandalize (skăn'dăl-ĭz) vt. scandalizzare, calunniare.

scandalmonger (skăn'dăl-mŭng'gĕr) n. pettegolo, seminatore di scandali.

scandalous (skăn'dăl-ŭs) n. scandaloso, diffamatorio.

scant (skănt) agg. scarso, insufficiente, esiguo. vt., vi. limitare, lesinare, scarseggiare. —iness n. meschinità, scarsezza.

scanty (skăn'tĭ) agg. scarso, meschino, debole, insufficiente. **scanties** n. pl. mutandine (da donna).

scapegoat (skāp'gōt') n. capro espiatorio.

scapegrace (skāp'grās') n. monello, scapestrato.

scar (skăr) n. sfregio, cicatrice. vt. sfregiare. vi. cicatrizzarsi.

scarab (skăr'ăb) n. scarabeo.

scarce (skărs) agg. scarso, raro: to make oneself —, eclissarsi. —ly avv. a malapena, difficilmente, raramente: — ever, quasi mai.

scarcity (skăr'sĭ·tĭ) *n.* scarsità, rarità, penuria.

scare (skâr) *n.* allarme, paura, panico. *vt.*, *vi.* spaventare, spaventarsi, allarmare, sgomentarsi: to — up, racimolare; to — away, mettere in fuga; to — easily, spaventarsi per ogni nonnulla.

scarecrow (skâr'krō') *n.* spauracchio, spaventapasseri.

scarehead (skâr'hĕd') *n.* (*S.U.*) titolo cubitale (*su quotidiano*).

scaremonger (skâr'mŭng'gĕr) *n.* allarmista.

scarf (skärf) *n.* sciarpa, fascia, cravatta; tappeto da tavola.

scarlet (skär'lĕt) *n.*, *agg.* rosso scarlatto: — fever, scarlattina.

scarred (skärd), **scarry** (skär'ĭ) *agg.* sfregiato, cosparso di cicatrici.

scary (skâr'ĭ) *agg.* allarmistico; timoroso.

scathing (skāth'ĭng) *agg.* caustico, aspro.

scatter (skăt'ĕr) *vt.* disperdere, disseminare, dissipare. *vi.* disperdersi, sparpagliarsi. —brain *n.* scervellato. —brained *agg.* scervellato.

scavenger (skăv'ĕn·jĕr) *n.* spazzino.

scene (sēn) *n.* scena, spettacolo, panorama: to make a —, fare una scenata; — painter, scenografo.

scenery (sēn'ĕr·ĭ) *n.* scenario, panorama.

scent (sĕnt) *n.* odore, profumo; olfatto, odorato; pista, traccia: to put off the —, sviare; to be on the — of, essere sulle tracce di. *vt.* odorare, fiutare, profumare. *vi.* odorare (*di*).

scepter (sĕp'tĕr) *n.* scettro.

sceptic *vedi* skeptic.

schedule (skĕd'ūl) *n.* lista, tabella; orario; programma: on —, in orario. *vt.* registrare, programmare, predisporre; assegnare un incarico (*da compiere in un determinato momento*).

scheme (skēm) *n.* schema, progetto, piano; ordine; disegno; macchinazione: color —, combinazione di colori. *vt.*, *vi.* progettare, complottare, macchinare.

schemer (skēm'ĕr) *n.* progettista; macchinatore, intrigante.

scheming (skēm'ĭng) *n.* macchinazioni. *agg.* intrigante, subdolo.

schism (sĭz'm) *n.* scisma.

schizophrenic (skĭz'ō·frĕn'ĭk) *n.*, *agg.* schizofrenico.

scholar (skŏl'ĕr) *n.* discepolo; erudito. —ly *agg.*, *avv.* da erudito. —ship *n.* erudizione, scienza; (*univ.*) borsa di studio: to get a —, guadagnare una borsa di studio.

scholastic (skŏ·lăs'tĭk) *n.*, *agg.* scolastico, pedante.

school (skōōl) *n.* scuola, scolaresca; collegio, convitto; branco (*di pesci*). *vt.* istruire, ammaestrare, disciplinare. —boy *n.* scolaro. —girl *n.* scolara. —house *n.* scuola, edificio scolastico. —ing *n.* istruzione insegnamento, addestramento. —master *n.* maestro di scuola. —mate *n.* condiscepolo. —mistress *n.* maestra (o direttrice) di scuola. —room *n.* aula, classe. —teacher *n.* insegnante.

schooner (skōōn'ĕr) *n.* (*naut.*) goletta; (*gergo*) bicchierone: prairie —, carriaggio.

science (sī'ĕns) *n.* scienza, sapere.

scientific (sī'ĕn·tĭf'ĭk) *agg.* scientifico. —ally *avv.* scientificamente.

scientist (sī'ĕn·tĭst) *n.* scienziato.

scintilla (sĭn·tĭl'ă) *n.* scintilla, particella.

scion (sī'ŭn) *n.* rampollo, discendente; (*bot.*) germoglio.

scissors (sĭz'ĕrz) *n.pl.* forbici.

scoff (skŏf) *n.* beffa, derisione. *vt.* deridere. *vi.*: to — at, ridersi di, farsi beffe di.

scold (skōld) *n.* brontolone, brontolona. *vt.*, *vi.* sgridare, rimproverare, brontolare.

scolding *n.* sgridata. *agg.* brontolone.

scone (skōn) *n.* focaccina.

scoop (skōōp) *n.* ramaiuolo, paletta, palettata; (*naut.*) gottazza; (*giornalismo*) notizia sensazionale, colpo giornalistico; (*comm.*) grosso colpo. *vt.* scavare, vuotare; arraffare; (*giornalismo*) accaparrarsi una notizia prima degli altri.

scoot (skōōt) *vi.* (*fam.*) filare, svignarsela.

scooter (skōōt'ĕr) *n.* monopattino; (*S.U.*) barca a vela anfibia.

scope (skōp) *n.* veduta, campo, portata, raggio d'azione.

scorch (skôrch) *vt.* bruciacchiare, strinare, scottare; devastare, mettere a ferro e a fuoco. *vi.* scottarsi, bruciacchiarsi: —ed earth, terra bruciata o devastata.

score (skōr) *n.* tocco, traccia, linea; ventina; scotto, debito; punteggio; segnatura; causa, ragione; (*mus.*) partitura; (*gergo*) (*la*) realtà dei fatti, (*la*) situazione reale: on that —, a quel riguardo; on the — of, a causa di; to keep —, segnare il punteggio; to pay off old scores, liquidare un vecchio conto; to know what the — is, sapere come stanno le cose. *vt.*, *vi.* intaccare, segnare, notare, addebitare; tracciare, rigare; (*mus.*)

orchestrare; segnare (*punti*); riportare (*un successo*).

scorer *n.* segnapunti.

scoring *n.* punteggio, tacca, solco.

scorn (skôrn) *n.* scorno, disprezzo. *vt.* disprezzare, solegnare.

scornful (skôrn'fŏŏl) *agg.* sprezzante.

scorpion (skôr'pĭ-ŭn) *n.* scorpione.

scot (skŏt) (1) *n.* scotto, tributo: to go — free, passarla liscia.

Scot (skŏt) (2) *n.* scozzese.

scotch (skŏch) *n.* whisky scozzese.

Scots (skŏts) Scottish (skŏt'ĭsh) *n.* lingua scozzese. *agg.* scozzese.

scoundrel (skoun'drĕl) *n.* mascalzone.

scour (skour) (1) *vt.* pulire, sgrassare, detergere, lustrare.

scour (skour) (2) *vt.* perlustrare.

scourge (skûrj) *n.* sferza, punizione. *vt.* sferzare, punire.

scout (skout) (1) *n.* esploratore; (*aeron.*) ricognitore: — car (*mil.*), camionetta da ricognizione. *vt.*, *vi.* esplorare, perlustrare: to — for, andare in cerca di.

scout (skout) (2) *vt.* respingere con sdegno, beffare.

scowl (skoul) *n.* sguardo torvo, cipiglio. *vi.* acciglarsi, aggrottare le sopracciglia.

scrabble (skrăb'l) *n.* strisciamento, l'arrancare; scarabocchio. *vi.* arrancare, grattare, strisciare; scarabocchiare.

scraggy (skrăg'ĭ) *agg.* scarno, irregolare.

scram (skrăm) *vi.* (*gergo S.U.*) togliersi di mezzo, svignarsela: —! fila via!, filate via!

scramble (skrăm'b'l) *n.* scalata, arrampicata, corsa (*alla conquista di qualcosa*); mischia. *vt.* raccogliere alla rinfusa, arraffare; mischiare; strapazzare (*uova*). *vi.* arrampicarsi; gareggiare, lottare (*per il possesso di qualcosa*); affannarsi.

scrap (skrăp) (1) *n.* pezzetto, frammento, brano, ritaglio; *pl.* rimasugli: — iron, rottami di ferro. *vt.* scartare, gettar via.

scrap (2) *n.* zuffa. *vi.* azzuffarsi.

scrapbook *n.* album.

scrape (skrăp) *n.* raschiatura; difficoltà, perplessità: to get into a —, cacciarsi in un gualo. *vt.*, *vi.* raschiare; cancellare; raggrannellare; razzolare, grufolare: to — acquaintance with, insinuarsi presso; to — along, tirare avanti.

scraper (skrăp'ĕr) *n.* raschiatolo, raschietto; avaro.

scratch (skrăch) *n.* graffio, scarabocchio; linea di partenza (*in una gara*); (*gergo*) baruffa: from —,

dal principio, dal niente; — paper, carta da minuta. *vt.*, *vi.* grattare, graffiare, scalfire, strofinare; scribacchiare; cancellare; grattarsi.

scrawl (skrôl) *n.* scarabocchio. *vt.*, *vi.* scarabocchiare.

scrawny (skrôn'ĭ) *agg.* scarno, ossuto.

screak (skrēk) *n.* grido, cigolio. *vi.* gridare, cigolare.

scream (skrēm) *n.* grido, strillo; (*gergo*) "asso," "cennone"; "cannonata"; spasso; cosa assurda. *vt.*, *vi.* strillare, urlare. — ing *agg.* urlante, lacerante; scargiante; esilarante.

screech (skrēch) *n.* strido, stridore; *vi.* stridere. — owl *n.* allocco, gufo.

screen (skrēn) *n.* schermo; paravento, parafuoco; divisorio, riparo; vaglio, crivello. *vt.* riparare, coprire; schermare; vagliare; (*cinema*) proiettare, ridurre per lo schermo: — door, porta di rete metallica; wire —, rete metallica; — writer, scrittore cinematografico, sceneggiatore. — ing *u.* schermatura; vagliatura.

screw (skrōō) *n.* vite, elica: to put the — s to somebody, mettere qualcuno alle strette; — bolt, bullone a vite; — nut, dado; — propeller, propulsore a elica; — wrench, chiave inglese. *vt.*, *vi.* avvitare, torcere, torcersi, avvitarsi: to — a lid on, avvitare un coperchio su. to — up one's courage, prendere il coraggio a due mani; to — up one's face, fare una smorfia.

screwball (skrōō'bôl) (*gergo*) *n.*, *agg.* mattoide, "suonato."

screwdriver (skrōō'drīv''ĕr) *n.* cacciavite.

screwy (skrōō'ĭ) *agg.* prepotente; avaro; (*gergo*) brillo, alticcio; mattoide, "suonato": — horse, ronzino.

scribble (skrĭb''l) *n.* scarabocchio. *vi.*, *vi.* scribacchiare, scarabocchiare.

scrimmage (skrĭm'ĭj) *n.* mischia.

scrimp (skrĭmp) *vt.*, *vi.* restringere; lesinare, economizzare.

scrimpy (skrĭmp'ĭ) *agg.* esiguo; avaro.

script (skrĭpt) *n.* scrittura; (*tip.*) corsivo; (*teat.*, *cinema*, *radio*, *T.V.*) copione, sceneggiatura.

Scriptures (skrĭp'tūrz) *n. pl.* Sacre Scritture.

scroll (skrōl) *n.* rotolo di carta (*o pergamena*); ruolo, lista; cartiglio.

scrub (skrŭb) *n.* cespuglio, boscaglia. *agg.* di fortuna, improvvisato; stentato, inferiore. *vt.* strofinare energicamente, detergere. *vi.* sgobbare: — woman *n.* donna delle pulizie.

scruff (skrŭf) *n.* nuca, cervice.

scruple (skrōō'p'l) *n.* scrupolo. *vi.* aver scrupoli, esitare.

scrupulous (skrōō'pû·lŭs) *agg.* scrupoloso.

scrutinize (skrōō'tĭ·nīz) *vt.* scrutare, esaminare a fondo.

scrutiny (skrōō'tĭ·nĭ) *n.* esame scrupoloso, indagine.

scud (skŭd) *n.* nube. *vi.* correre velocemente.

scuffle (skŭf''l) *n.* zuffa, tafferuglio. *vi.* azzuffarsi, accapigliarsi; strascicare i piedi.

scull (skŭl) *n.* remo. *vt.*, *vi.* vogare con un remo, gondolare.

scullery (skŭl'ẽr·ĭ) *n.* retrocucina, acquaio.

sculptor (skŭlp'tẽr) *n.* scultore.

sculptress (skŭlp'trĕs) *n.* scultrice.

sculpture (skŭlp'tûr) *n.* scultura. *vt.* scolpire.

scum (skŭm) *n.* schiuma, scoria, rifiuto, feccia. *vt.*, *vi.* schiumare.

scupper (skŭp'ẽr) *n.* (*naut.*) ombrinale.

scurf (skûrf) *n.* squama, forfora.

scurrilous (skûr'ĭ·lŭs) *agg.* scurrile.

scurry (skûr'ĭ) *vi.* correre, affrettarsi.

scurvy (skûr'vĭ) *n.* scorbuto. *agg.* vile, spregevole.

scutcheon (skŭch'ŭn) *n.* scudo, blasone.

scuttle (skut''l) *n.* cesto; botola; passo rapido, corsa; (*naut.*) boccaporto. *vt.* aprire falle in (*uno scafo*), affondare (*uno scafo*). *vi.* correre, affrettarsi: to — away, fuggire; —butt *n.* (*gergo*) diceria, voce: — has it that, si vocifera che.

scythe (sīth) *n.* falce.

sea (sē) *n.* mare, onda, cavallone: to be at —, essere in alto mare *opp.* disorientato; to put to —, salpare; — biscuit, galletta; — gull, gabbiano; — level, livello del mare; — lion, otaria.

seaboard (sē'bōrd') *n.* costa, litorale. *agg.* costiero, litoraneo.

seafarer (sē·fâr'ẽr) *n.* navigatore, marinaio.

seal (sēl) (1) *n.* vitello marino, foca.

seal (sēl) (2) *n.* sigillo, suggello. *vt.* suggellare, sigillare, chiudere, stabilire.

sealing *n.* suggello: — wax, ceralacca.

seam (sēm) *n.* cucitura, giuntura, costura, solco, sutura; (*min.*) filone, vena. *vt.* cucire, suturare.

seaman (sē'măn) *n.* marinaio.

seamstress (sēm'strĕs) *n.* cucitrice.

seaplane (sē'plān') *n.* idrovolante.

seaport (sē'pōrt') *n.* porto di mare: — town, città marittima.

sear (sēr) *agg.* secco, avvizzito. *vt.* bruciacchiare, cauterizzare, inaridire.

search (sûrch) *n.* ricerca, perquisizione, investigazione: in — of, in cerca di, alla ricerca di. — warrant, mandato di perquisizione. *vt.*, *vi.* cercare; perquisire; ispezionare; sondare, scandagliare.

searchlight (sûrch'līt') *n.* faro.

seashore (sē'shōr') *n.* spiaggia.

seasick (sē'sĭk') *agg.* affetto da mal di mare: I got —, mi è venuto il mal di mare.

seasickness *n.* mal di mare.

seaside (sē'sīd') *n.* spiaggia, mare: to go to the —, andare al mare.

season (sē'z'n) *n.* stagione; epoca, tempo, momento opportuno: in good —, tempestivamente; out of —, a sproposito; opera —, stagione operistica *o* lirica. *vt.* maturare; assuefare; aromatizzare, condire; stagionare, salare; allenare, agguerrire.

seasoning (sē'z'n·ĭng) *n.* condimento; stagionatura.

seat (sēt) *n.* sedile, sedia; posto; sede; base, posizione; fondo dei calzoni, sedere: — of learning, centro di cultura. *vt.* insediare; collocare; far sedere, fornire di sedili: to — oneself, insediarsi; mettersi a sedere.

seaward (sē'wẽrd) *agg.*, *avv.* verso il mare *o* il largo.

seaweed (sē'wēd') *n.* alga marina.

seaworthy (sē'wûr'thĭ) *agg.* atto a navigare.

sebaceous (sē·bā'shŭs) *agg.* sebaceo.

secede (sē·sēd') *vi.* compiere una scissione, scindersi, staccarsi.

seclude (sē·klōōd') *vt.* separare, isolare, rinchiudere: to — oneself, isolarsi.

secluded *agg.* ritirato, appartato, solitario.

seclusion (sē·klōō'shŭn) *n.* ritiro, solitudine, isolamento.

second (sĕk'ŭnd) *n.* minuto secondo; secondo (*in duello o incontro sportivo*); secondo arrivato; (*pl.comm.*) merci di seconda scelta. *agg.* secondo, inferiore; favorevole: every — day, ogni due giorni; on — thought, dopo averci ripensato. *vt.* assecondare, aiutare. —ary *agg.* secondario. ——best *agg.* secondo (*in qualità*); mediocre: to come off ——best, riuscire secondo (*in classifica*), essere sconfitto. — hand lancetta dei secondi (*nell'orologio*). —hand *agg.* d'occasione, di seconda mano. —ly *avv.* in secondo luogo. —rate *agg.* inferiore, di second'ordine.

secrecy (sē'krē·sǐ) *n.* segretezza, discrezione, reticenza.

secret (sē'krĕt) *n.* segreto. *agg.* segreto, occulto, riservato.

secretariat (sĕk'rē·tār'ĭ·ăt) *n.* segretariato, segreteria.

secretary (sĕk'rē·tĕr'ĭ) *n.* segretario; ministro, funzionario; scrivania.

secrete (sē·krēt') *vt.* celare, nascondere; (*fisiol.*) secernere.

secretion (sē·krē'shŭn) *n.* secrezione.

secretive (sē·krē'tǐv) *agg.* segreto, riservato; secretivo: — gland, ghiandola secretiva.

secretly (sē'krĕt·lǐ) *avv.* segretamente, privatamente, intimamente.

sect (sĕkt) *n.* setta. —arian (sĕk·târ'ĭ·ăn) *n.*, *agg.* settario.

section (sĕk'shŭn) *n.* sezione; suddivisione, parte, pezzo; spaccato; settore, tratto, regione. *vt.* suddividere, sezionare, fare lo spaccato di.

secular (sĕk'ū·lĕr) *n.* laico. *agg.* secolare, laico.

secure (sē·kūr') *agg.* sicuro, saldo, fiducioso: — from, al riparo da. *vt.* assicurare, mettere al sicuro, impadronirsi di, procurarsi. —ly *avv.* sicuramente, al sicuro, saldamente.

security (sē·kū'rǐ·tǐ) *n.* sicurezza, salvezza, protezione; garanzia, cauzione, pegno; securities *n. pl.* titoli, certificati azionari: Security Council, Consiglio di Sicurezza.

sedan (sē·dăn') *n.* guida-interna (*auto*).

sedate (sē·dāt') *agg.* calmo, tranquillo, sereno, equilibrato. —ly *avv.* posatamente, serenamente, con calma.

sedative (sĕd'ȧ·tǐv) *n.*, *agg.* sedativo.

sedentary (sĕd'ĕn·tĕr'ĭ) *agg.* sedentario, inerte, stabile.

sediment (sĕd'ĭ·mĕnt) *n.* sedimento.

sedition (sē·dǐsh'ŭn) *n.* sedizione.

seditious (sē·dǐsh'ŭs) *agg.* sedizioso.

seduce (sē·dūs') *vt.* sedurre, allettare.

seducer (-ẽr) *n.* seduttore.

seduction (sē·dŭk'shŭn) *n.* seduzione.

seductive (sē·dŭk'tǐv) *agg.* seducente.

sedulous (sĕd'ū·lŭs) *agg.* diligente.

see (sē) (1) *n.* seggio (o giurisdizione) episcopale: the Holy See, la Santa Sede.

see (sē) (2) *vt.*, *vi.* (*pass.* saw, *pp.* seen) vedere, scorgere; accompagnare; consultare; capire: to — somebody home, accompagnare qualcuno a casa; to — a person off, accompagnare alla stazione una persona; to — somebody through a difficulty, aiutare uno a superare una difficoltà; to — through a

person, indovinare le intenzioni di una persona; to — to, provvedere a, occuparsi di; — that you do it, ti raccomando di farlo.

seed (sēd) *n.* seme, semenza, granello, germe: to run to —, tallire, andare in decadenza. *vt.* seminare, disseminare, mondare dai semi. *vi.* produrre semi. —ling *n.* pianta nata da un seme, pianticella.

seedy (sēd'ǐ) *agg.* pieno di semi; logoro, male in arnese, malaticcio.

seeing (sē'ǐng) *cong.* visto che, dato che, tenuto conto di.

seek (sēk) *vt.*, *vi.* (*pass.*, *pp.* sought) cercare; perseguire; chiedere; indagare: to be sought after, essere cercato (*desiderato*).

seem (sēm) *vi.* sembrare, avere l'aria (*di*), apparire, aver l'impressione: I — to, mi par di; it —s to me that, mi sembra che. —ing *agg.* apparente. —ingly *avv.* apparentemente. —ly *agg.* decoroso, conveniente.

seen (sēn) *pp.* di to see.

seep (sēp) *vi.* filtrare, penetrare.

seer (sēr) *n.* veggente, indovino.

seesaw (sē'sô') *n.* altalena. *vi.* dondolare, altalenare.

seethe (sēth) *vt.*, *vi.* bollire, schlumare; fremere (*di collera, ecc.*).

seething *agg.* bollente, fremente.

segment (sĕg'mĕnt) *n.* segmento.

segregate (sĕg'rē·gāt) *vt.* isolare. *vi.* isolarsi.

segregation (sĕg'rē·gā'shŭn) *n.* segregazione, isolamento.

seismic (sīz'mǐk) *agg.* sismico.

seize (sēz) *vt.* afferrare, catturare, impossessarsi di, sequestrare.

seizure (sē'zhẽr) *n.* confisca, cattura, presa di possesso; attacco, accesso.

seldom (sĕl'dŭm) *avv.* raramente.

select (sē·lĕkt') *agg.* scelto, speciale. *vt.* scegliere, preferire.

selectivity (sē·lĕk'tǐv'ǐ·tǐ) *n.* selettività.

self (sĕlf) *n.* la propria persona, l'io, personalità, egoismo: for one's own —, per se stesso; one's better —, il lato migliore del proprio io; beside one's —, fuori di sè; to be one's —, essere in piena coscienza. *agg.* proprio, personale, stesso. *pron.* (*pl.* selves) me stesso, se stesso: payable to —, pagabile all'ordine proprio.

self-acting *agg.* automatico.

self-addressed *agg.*: — envelope, busta già munita di indirizzo.

self-assurance *n.* sicumera.

self-centered *agg.* egocentrico.

self-command *n.* dominio di sè, sangue freddo.

self-complacent agg. tronfio, vanitoso.
self-conscious agg. imbarazzato, iper-sensibile, schivo.
self-control n. padronanza di sè.
self-defense n. legittima difesa.
self-denial n. abnegazione.
self-educated agg. autodidatta.
self-esteem n. rispetto di se stesso, amor proprio.
self-evident agg. lampante.
self-explanatory agg. ovvio.
self-government n. autogoverno, autonomia.
self-importance n. presunzione, boria.
self-important agg. tronfio, borioso.
self-interest n. interesse personale, egoismo.
selfish (sĕl'fĭsh) agg. egoista. **—ly** avv. egoisticamente. **—ness** n. egoismo.
selfless (self'lĕs) agg. altruista.
self-love n. amore di sè.
self-made agg. che si è fatto da sè.
self-mailer n. modulo da spedire senza bisogno di busta.
self-possessed agg. equilibrato, padrone di sè.
self-reliant agg. autonomo; sicuro di sè.
self-respect n. rispetto di sè, dignità.
self-restraint n. dominio di sè.
self-sacrifice n. abnegazione.
selfsame (sĕlf'sām') agg. stesso, identico.
self-satisfied agg. soddisfatto di sè, vanitoso.
self-starter n. (mecc.) avviamento automatico.
self-styled agg. sedicente.
self-sufficient agg. autosufficiente, presuntuoso.
self-willed agg. ostinato.
sell (sĕl) vt., vi. (pass., pp. sold) vendere, smerciare; vendersi (trovare smercio): it **—s** well, si vende bene; to **—** out, vendere tutto, esaurire, liquidare. **—er** n. venditore: best **—er,** libro di grande vendita.
selvage, selvedge (sĕl'vĭj) n. vivagno, cimosa.
selves (sĕlvz) pl. di self.
semblance (sĕm'blăns) n. sembiante, apparenza; simulacro, parvenza.
semicircle (sĕm'ĭ·sûr'k'l) n. semicerchio.
semicolon (sĕm'ĭ·kō'lŏn) n. punto e virgola.
semimonthly (sĕm'ĭ·mŭnth'lĭ) n., agg. quindicinale.
seminary (sĕm'ĭ·nĕr'ĭ) n. seminario.
semiweekly agg. bisettimanale.
sempstress (sĕm(p)'strĕs) n. cucitrice.
senate (sĕn'ĭt) n. senato.
senator (sĕn'à·tĕr) n. senatore.

send (sĕnd) vt. (pass., pp. sent) mandare; spedire; inviare; lanciare; trasmettere; diffondere; (gergo) mandare in estasi, entusiasmare: to **—** for, mandar a chiamare; to **—** forth, spedire, inviare, emettere; esalare, emanare; to **—** word, mandare a dire; to **—** about one's business, mandare a quel paese. **—er** n. speditore, mittente; trasmettitore.
senility (sē·nĭl'ĭ·tĭ) n. senilità.
senior (sēn'yĕr) n. anziano, decano; studente dell'ultimo anno. agg. maggiore (di età), più anziano; (mil.) superiore: Mr. Brown, **—,** il signor Brown padre; he is my **—** by three years, è maggiore di me di tre anni. **—ity** (sēn·yŏr'ĭ·tĭ) n. anzianità, decanato: **—** in rank, anzianità in grado.
sensation (sĕn·sā'shŭn) n. sensazione, fatto sensazionale, scalpore.
sensational (sĕn·sā'shŭn·ăl) agg. sensazionale.
sense (sĕns) n. senso, significato, senso comune, sentimento, discernimento, ragione: common **—,** buon senso; to make **—,** avere senso, essere logico; senses, facoltà mentali; to be out of one's **—s,** sragionare. vt. sentire, avere la sensazione di, intuire, capire. **—less** agg. tramortito, svenuto; privo di significato, insensato, assurdo.
sensibility (sĕn'sĭ·bĭl'ĭ·tĭ) n. sensibilità, assennatezza.
sensible (sĕn'sĭ·b'l) agg. sensibile: ragionevole, assennato, conscio; percettibile.
sensibly (sĕn'sĭ·bĭl) avv. sensibilmente; ragionevolmente, assennatamente.
sensitive (sĕn'sĭ·tĭv) agg. sensibile, sensitivo, suscettibile, impressionabile. **—ness, sensitivity** n. sensitività, suscettibilità.
sensual (sĕn'shŏŏ·ăl) agg. sensuale.
sensuality (sĕn'shŏŏ·ăl'ĭ·tĭ) n. sensualità.
sent (sĕnt) pass., pp. di to send.
sentence (sĕn'tĕns) n. sentenza; frase; (gramm.) proposizione: death **—,** condanna a morte. vt. condannare.
sentiment (sĕn'tĭ·mĕnt) n. sentimento, opinione. **—al** (sĕn'tĭ·mĕn'tăl) agg. sentimentale. **—alist** n. sentimentale. **—ality** (ăl'ĭ·tĭ) n. sentimentalità, sentimentalismo.
sentinel (sĕn'tĭ·nĕl) sentry (sĕn'trĭ) n. sentinella.
sentry-box n. garitta.
separate (sĕp'à·rĭt) agg. separato, disgiunto, diviso, singolo, a parte: under **—** cover, in plico a parte.

vt. (-rāt) separare, disgiungere, dividere. *vi.* separarsi, dividersi.—ly *avv.* separatamente.

separation (sĕp′ȧ-rā′shŭn) *n.* separazione (*anche legale*).

September (sĕp·tĕm′bĕr) *n.* settembre.

septic (sĕp′tĭk) *agg.* settico.

septicemia (sĕp′tĭ·sē′mĭ·ȧ) *n.* setticemia.

sepulchral (sē·pŭl′krȧl) *agg.* sepolcrale.

sepulcher (sĕp′ŭl·kĕr) *n.* sepolcro.

sepulture (sĕp′ŭl·tūr) *n.* sepoltura.

sequel (sē′kwĕl) *n.* sequela, seguito, conseguenza, continuazione.

sequence (sē′kwĕns) *n.* sequenza, serie, ordine, successione, conseguenza.

sequin (sē′kwĭn) *n.* zecchino.

seraphic (sē·răf′ĭk) *agg.* serafico, angelico.

serenade (sĕr′ĕ·nād′) *n.* serenata. *vt., vi.* fare la serenata (*a*).

serene (sē·rēn′) *agg.* sereno, calmo.

serenity (sē·rĕn′ĭ·tĭ) *n.* serenità.

serge (sûrj) *n.* sala (*tessuto*).

sergeant (sär′jĕnt) *n.* sergente.

serial (sēr′ĭ·ȧl) *n.* periodico, pubblicazione a dispense (*o* puntate). *agg.* periodico; a dispense (*o* puntate): — **novel**, romanzo a puntate.

serialize (sēr′ĭ·ȧl·īz) *vt.* pubblicare a puntate.

series (sēr′ēz) *n. sing., pl.* serie, sequenza, successione.

serious (sēr′ĭ·ŭs) *agg.* serio; grave.—ly *avv.* seriamente; gravemente.—ness *n.* serietà; gravità.

sermon (sûr′mŭn) *n.* sermone, predica.

serpent (sûr′pĕnt) *n.* serpente.

serrate (sĕr′āt) *agg.* dentellato.

serried (sĕr′ĭd) *agg.* serrato, compatto.

serum (sēr′ŭm) *n.* siero.

servant (sûr′vȧnt) *n.* servitore, domestico, schiavo: **public** —, pubblico funzionario; —**girl**, —**maid**, domestica, cameriera.

serve (sûrv) *n.* (*tennis*) servizio. *vt., vi.* servire, fungere (*da*); scontare (*una pena*): **to** — **as**, servire da; **to** — **one's purpose**, fare al caso proprio; **to** — **time**, scontare un periodo di reclusione; **to** — **a writ**, notificare una citazione; **it** —**s him right!** gli sta bene!

server (sûrv′ĕr) *n.* chi serve (*anche la messa*); vassoio; piatto —, ufficiale giudiziario.

service (sûr′vĭs) *n.* servizio: **at your** —, a vostra disposizione; **to be of** —, rendersi utile; **funeral** —, esequie; **mail** —, servizio postale; **table** —, servizio da tavola, vasellame; — **station**, stazione di ser-

vizio. *vt.* provvedere alla manutenzione di; fornire assistenza tecnica a; rivedere, revisionare, ripassare.

serviceable (sûr′vĭs·ȧ·b′l) *agg.* utile, vantaggioso, pratico.

serviceman *n.* militare.

servicing (sûr′vĭs·ĭng) *n.* manutenzione; assistenza tecnica; revisione.

servile (sûr′vĭl) *agg.* servile.

servitude (sûr′vĭ·tūd) *n.* schiavitù: **penal** —, lavori forzati.

session (sĕsh′ŭn) *n.* sessione.

set (sĕt) *n.* assortimento, collezione, serie, complesso, servizio; accolita, gruppo; tendenza, posizione; (*teat., cinema*) scena; (*naut.*) direzione (*del vento*); partita (*di tennis*); (*radio*) apparecchio ricevente: — **of teeth**, dentiera. *agg.* fisso, stabile, determinato, rigido, ostinato; pronto (*a*): **deep**— **eyes, occhi infossati** *vt.* (*pass., pp.* set) posare, mettere, deporre; fissare, stabilire; regolare; apparecchiare; montare, incastonare; irrigidire; orientare; (*tip.*) comporre. *vi* tramontare, declinare; consolidarsi; covare; accingersi; tendere: **to** — **aside**, mettere da parte, annullare; **to** — **forth**, esporre, manifestare, mettere in valore, dar risalto a, partire, avviarsi; **to** — **in**, sopravvenire, calare; **to** — **off**, mettere in risalto; partire; far esplodere; **to** — **on fire**, incendiare; **to** — **out**, disporre; esporre, descrivere; assegnare, stabilire; progettare; avviarsi, partire; adornare; equipaggiare; **to** — **right**, rettificare; **to** — **sail**, spiegare le vele, salpare; **to** — **up**, fondare, avviare, rivendicare; (*tip.*) comporre; montare (*una macchina*).

setback (sĕt′băk′) *n.* riflusso; scacco, ostacolo.

settee (sĕ·tē′) *n.* divanetto.

setter (sĕt′ĕr) *n.* cane da ferma, setter; montatore.

setting (sĕt′ĭng) *n.* posa, adattamento, disposizione; incastonatura, montatura; scenario, ambiente; tramonto, declino; solidificazione; (*tip.*) composizione. *agg.:* — **sun**, sole al tramonto.

settle (sĕt′′l) *n.* panca. *vt.* fissare, stabilire, assegnare; colonizzare; regolare, accomodare, risolvere; saldare (*un conto*); comporre (*una vertenza*); intestare (*beni*). *vi.* stabilirsi, fissarsi; consolidarsi; decidersi; posarsi, calmarsi; depositare; rimettersi al bello (*del tempo*): **to** — **a pension on**, assegnare una pensione a; **to** — **down**, accasarsi, stabilirsi, darsi a una vita regolare; to — down to, applicarsi a.

settlement (sĕt'l·mĕnt) n. accordo; pagamento; saldo, liquidazione; assegnazione o trapasso (di proprietà); colonia, colonizzazione; dote; sedimento; sistemazione; stabilimento; rendita, pensione: marriage —, dote; — day, giorno di liquidazione.

settler (sĕt'lẽr) n. colono, colonizzatore, pioniere; liquidatore: — of disputes, arbitro; paciere.

settling (sĕt'lĭng) n. accomodamento, regolamento (di conti, ecc.); sistemazione; deposito, sedimento.

setup (sĕt'ŭp') n. portamento; situazione; organizzazione; (gergo S.U.) imbroglio (in competizioni sportive).

seven (sĕv'ĕn) n., agg. sette.

seventeen (sĕv'ĕn·tēn') n., agg. diciassette.

seventeenth (sĕv'ĕn·tēnth') n., agg. diciassettesimo.

seventh (sĕv'ĕnth) n., agg. settimo.

seventieth (sĕv'ĕn·tĭ·ĕth) n., agg. settantesimo.

seventy (sĕv'ĕn·tĭ) n., agg. settanta.

sever (sĕv'ẽr) vt. dividere, recidere, troncare. vi. dividersi, scindersi.

several (sĕv'ẽr·ăl) agg. vari, parecchi, svariati, distinti.

severe (sē·vẽr') agg. severo, rigoroso, grave, austero; violento, aspro, acuto (di dolore).

severity (sē·vĕr'ĭ·tĭ) n. severità, austerità, asprezza, gravità.

sew (sō) vt., vi. (pass. sewed, pp. sewed, sewn) cucire.

sewage (sū'ĭj) n. scolo di fogna.

sewer (sō'ẽr) (1) n. cucitore, cucitrice.

sewer (sū'ẽr) (2) n. cloaca, fogna.

sewerage (sū'ẽr·ĭj) n. fognatura.

sewing (sō'ĭng) n. cucitura, il cucire: — machine, macchina per cucire.

sewn (sōn) pp. di to sew.

sex (sĕks) n. sesso: — appeal, attrazione sessuale, fascino carnale.

sextant (sĕks'tănt) n. sestante.

sextette (sĕks·tĕt') n. (mus.) sestetto.

sexton (sĕks'tŭn) n. sagrestano.

sexual (sĕk'shŏŏ·ăl) agg. sessuale.

shabbily (shăb'ĭ·lĭ) avv. sciattamente, meschinamente; ignobilmente.

shabbiness (shăb'ĭ·nĕs) n. meschinità, sciatteria; grettezza.

shabby (shăb'ĭ) agg. cencioso, logoro, ignobile, gretto, vile, spregevole.

shack (shăk) n. capanna, baracca.

shackle (shăk''l) n. ostacolo, anello del lucchetto, staffa; (naut.) maniglia: shackles, pastoie, ceppi, ferri. vt. mettere le pastoie a, ostacolare.

shade (shād) n. ombra; ombreggiatura, sfumatura; paralume,

schermo, riparo; gradazione (di colore); tendaggio: a — longer, un tantino più lungo; — of meaning, sfumatura di significato; —s of the schoolroom, ricordi di scuola; in the — of, all'ombra di. vt. ombreggiare, oscurare, riparare; adombrare.

shading (shăd'ĭng) n. ombreggiatura, chiaroscuro, sfumatura.

shadow (shăd'ō) n. ombra; (S.U.) pedinatore: under the — of, all'ombra di, col favore di. vt. ombreggiare, adombrare, oscurare; spiare, pedinare.

shadowy (shăd'ō·ĭ) agg. ombroso, oscuro, vago.

shady (shād'ĭ) agg. ombreggiato, ombroso; (fam.) losco, ambiguo: — character, individuo losco, poco di buono.

shaft (shȧft) n. dardo; asta; fusto (di colonna), gambo; stanga; biella; manico; palo; tromba (d'ascensore); pozzo (di miniera).

shaggy (shăg'ĭ) agg. peloso, irsuto, villoso, ispido: —dog story, racconto insipido, barzelletta fiacca.

shagreen (shȧ·grēn') n. zigrino; pelle di squalo.

shake (shāk) n. scossa; stretta (di mano); tremito; scrollata. vt. (pass. shook, pp. shaken) scuotere, scrollare, sconvolgere; (gergo) sbarazzarsi di. vi. tremare, agitarsi, tentennare, barcollare: to — hands with, stringere la mano a; to — one's head, tentennare il capo; to — with cold, tremare di freddo.

shaky (shāk'ĭ) agg. tremante, vacillante, malfermo.

shale (shāl) n. (geol.) schisto.

shall (shăl) v.aus.difettivo (pass. should; mancano: inf., ppr., pp.) esprime il concetto di: dovere. Il presente è l'ausiliare con cui si forma il futuro (predicente: 1a pers. sing. e pl.; volitivo: 2a e 3a sing. e pl.): I — go, io andrò; we — work, noi lavoreremo; you — sing, voi canterete (o dovete cantare); they — obey, essi obbediranno (o devono obbedire). Il passato ha valore di condizionale opp. di imperfetto soggiuntivo ed è l'ausiliare con cui si forma il cond. degli altri verbi: I — be glad, sarei lieto; you — have more sense, dovreste avere maggior prudenza; — you go to London, se voi andaste a Londra; in case they — be unable to come, qualora essi fossero nell'impossibilità di venire.

shallop (shăl'ŭp) n. barchetta.

shallow (shăl'ō) *n.* bassofondo. *agg.* poco profondo; superficiale; futile. —**ness** *n.* scarsa profondità; superficialità, frivolezza.

sham (shăm) *n.* finta, imitazione, impostura, finzione. *agg.* finto, contraffatto. *vt., vi.* fingere, simulare.

shamble (shăm'b'l) *n.* andatura goffa. *vi.* camminare goffamente, trascinarsi.

shambles (shăm'b'lz) *n.pl.* macello, mattatoio; carnaio, carneficina.

shame (shăm) *n.* vergogna, disonore, ignominia; pudore: to put to —, far vergognare; for —! vergogna! it's a —, è una vergogna; è un peccato. *vt.* svergognare, far arrossire, disonorare.

shamefaced (shăm'făst') *agg.* vergognoso (*che si vergogna*), pudico; confuso; mortificato.

shameful (shăm'fŏŏl) *n.* infame, vergognoso.

shameless (shăm'lĕs) *agg.* spudorato, sfrontato.

shamelessness (-nĕs) *n.* sfrontatezza, spudoratezza.

shampoo (shăm-pŏŏ') *n.* lavaggio dei capelli. *vt.* lavare (*la testa*).

shamrock (shăm'rŏk) *n.* trifoglio.

shanghai (shăng-hī') *vt.* (*gergo*) attirare con l'inganno; (*naut.*) imbarcare (*un marinaio*) con l'inganno.

shank (shăngk) *n.* gamba, tibia, stinco; gambo, fusto.

shan't (shănt) *contr. di* shall not.

shanty (shăn'tĭ) *n.* capanna, tugurio.

shape (shăp) *n.* forma, figura, sagoma: to be in bad —, stare male; to put into —, mettere in ordine, aggiustare. *vt.* formare, foggiare, adattare, regolare. *vi.* prendere forma, adattarsi: things are —ing well, le cose prendono una buona piega.

shapeless (-lĕs) *agg.* informe.

shapeliness (shăp'lĭ-nĕs) *n.* armonia di linee, bellezza.

shapely (shăp'lĭ) *agg.* bello, ben fatto.

share (shăr) *n.* parte, porzione, spartizione; (*comm.*) azione (*titolo*) dividendo, caratura; vomero (*d'aratro*): to go —s, dividere in parti uguali. *vt., vi.* dividere, spartire, avere in comune, condividere: to — in, essere cointeressato in, condividere. —**cropper** *n.* mezzadro.

shark (shärk) *n.* squalo; furfante, speculatore: loan —, usuraio, strozzino.

sharp (shärp) *n.* parte aguzza; (*gergo*) truffatore, esperto; (*mus.*) diesis.

agg. acuto, aguzzo, affilato, tagliente, pungente; marcato; penetrante; perspicace; aspro; furbo; acre; squillante: — turn, svolta improvvisa, curva stretta; — ear, udito fine; — temper, carattere aspro. *avv.* in punto (*dell'ora*); puntualmente; bruscamente; (*mus.*) in tono maggiore.

sharpen (shär'pĕn) *vt.* affilare, aguzzare, arrotare; temperare (*una matita*); acuire, stimolare. *vi.* acuirsi, divenire aguzzo (*o* tagliente).

sharper (shär'pĕr) *n.* truffatore; baro.

sharply (shärp'lĭ) *avv.* acutamente; bruscamente; nettamente; puntualmente.

sharpness (shärp'nĕs) *n.* acume, acutezza; asprezza; intensità; filo (*del rasoio*).

shatter (shăt'ĕr) *n.* frammento: shatters, frantumi: to break into —s, mandare (*o* andare) in frantumi. *vt.* frantumare, sconquassare, devastare; distruggere. *vi.* frantumarsi.

shave (shăv) *n.* rasatura; pialla; scheggia, truciolo: to have a close —, scamparla bella. *vt.* (*pass.* shaved *pp.* shaved *o* shaven) radere; tosare; piallare; raschiare; sfiorare. *vi.* radersi, farsi la barba.

shaving (shăv'ĭng) *n.* rasatura; tosatura; scheggia; truciolo: — brush, pennello da barba; — soap, sapone da barba; wood —s, trucioli.

shawl (shôl) *n.* scialle.

she (shē) *pron.f.* ella, essa, colei: a —cat *n.* una gatta.

sheaf (shēf) *n.* (*pl.* sheaves) covone, fascio. *vt., vi.* legare in covoni, riunire in fascio.

shear (shēr) *vt.* (*pass.* sheared, shore, *pp.* sheared, shorn) tosare, tranciare; spogliare, potare; falciare.

shears (shērz) *n.pl.* cesole.

sheath (shēth) *n.* guaina, fodero; membrana.

sheathe (shēth) *vt.* rivestire, inguainare.

sheave (shēv) *n.* ruota di puleggia.

sheaves *pl.* di sheaf.

shed (shĕd) (1) *n.* tettoia, riparo, capannone, baracca.

shed (shĕd) (2) *vt.* (*pass., pp.* shed) spandere; versare; emettere (*suono, luce, ecc.*); lasciar cadere, perdere (*capelli, ecc.*); spogliarsi di: to — leaves, sfogliarsi, perdere le foglie.

sheen (shēn) *n.* splendore. *vi.* risplendere, luccicare.

sheep (shēp) *n.* sing., *pl.* pecora, ovini: — dog, cane da pastore. —**fold** *n.* ovile, gregge. —**skin** *n.*

pelle di pecora, pergamena; (S.U.) diploma, laurea.

sheepish (shēp'ĭsh) *agg.* timido, smarrito; impacciato; melenso.

sheer (shēr) (1) *agg.* puro; semplice; fine, trasparente, diafano; ininterrotto; perpendicolare: — silk, seta trasparente o impalpabile; — stockings, calze velate.

sheer (shēr) (2) *vt.*, *vi.* (*naut.*) deviare dalla rotta, virare.

sheet (shēt) *n.* lenzuolo; foglio, lastra, distesa; giornale; (*naut.*) scotta; teglia (*per cibi*): — anchor, ancora di salvezza; — lightning, lampo diffuso.

shelf (shĕlf) *n.* (*pl.* shelves) scaffale, mensola; strato di roccia, banco di sabbia.

shell (shĕl) *n.* guscio, conchiglia, involucro; tartaruga; barchetta; padiglione (*dell'orecchio*); mollusco; proiettile, pallottola, bossolo. *vt.* sgusciare, sgranare; bombardare.

shellac (shĕ-lăk') *n.* gommalacca, lacca. *vt.* laccare.

shellacking (shĕ-lăk'ĭng) *n.* (*gergo*) bastonatura, batosta.

shellfish (shĕl'fĭsh') *n.* mollusco, crostaceo.

shelter (shĕl'tẽr) *n.* riparo, ricovero, protezione, rifugio. *vt.* riparare, difendere, nascondere, proteggere. *vi.* ripararsi, ricoverarsi.

shelve (shĕlv) *vt.* scaffalare, mettere in disparte, archiviare. *vi.* digradare.

shelves *pl.* *di* shelf.

shepherd (shĕp'ẽrd) *n.* pastore: — dog, cane da pastore. *vt.* scortare, guidare, vigilare su.

shepherdess (shĕp'ẽr-dĕs) *n.* pastora, pastorella.

sherbet (shûr'bĕt) *n.* sorbetto.

sherry (shĕr'ĭ) *n.* vino di Xeres.

shield (shēld) *n.* scudo, difesa, protezione, riparo. *vt.*, *vi.* difendere, riparare.

shift (shĭft) *n.* cambio, mutamento; espediente; sostituzione, spostamento; squadra (*di operai*, *ecc.*), turno; camicia (*da donna*): to make —, arrangiarsi, riuscire. *vt.* mutare, spostare, trasferire; (*auto*) cambiare (*marcia*): to — the blame on, addossare la colpa a. *vi.* trasferirsi, spostarsi; cambiarsi d'abito; ricorrere a espedienti, ingegnarsi.

shiftless (shĭft'lĕs) *agg.* indolente, inetto.

shifty (shĭft'ĭ) *n.* furbo, subdolo, evasivo.

shilling (shĭl'ĭng) *n.* scellino.

shimmer (shĭm'ẽr) *vi.* luccicare.

shin (shĭn) *n.* tibia, stinco, garretto. *vi.* arrampicarsi.

shine (shĭn) *n.* splendore, lucentezza, lucidatura. *vt.* far risplendere; lucidare. *vi.* sfolgorare, brillare.

shingle (shĭng'g'l) *n.* ghiaia, embrice di legno, targhetta; capelli corti. *vt.* coprire di embrici di legno; tagliare (*i capelli*) corti.

shining (shĭn'ĭng) *n.* splendore. *agg.* brillante, splendente, luminoso.

shiny (shĭn'ĭ) *agg.* lucente, luccicanta, splendente, lucido.

ship (shĭp) *n.* nave, bastimento; aeronave, velivolo: on —board, a bordo. *vt.* imbarcare, caricare, trasportare su una nave. *vi.* imbarcarsi. —builder *n.* armatore navale. —master *n.* capitano di una nave. —mate *n.* compagno di bordo.

shipment (-mĕnt) *n.* imbarco, carico.

shipper (shĭp'ẽr) *n.* spedizioniere marittimo.

shipping (shĭp'ĭng) *n.* flotta; tonnellaggio; spedizione; caricamento, imbarco.

shipshape (shĭp'shāp) *agg.*, *avv.* in perfetto ordine.

shipwreck (shĭp'rĕk') *n.* naufragio. *vt.* far naufragare. *vi.* naufragare.

shipyard (shĭp'yärd') *n.* cantiere navale.

shire (shĭr; come suffisso: shĭr) *n.* contea.

shirk (shûrk) *vt.* schivare, evitare: —er *n.* scansafatiche; (*mil.*) renitente.

shirt (shûrt) *n.* camicia (*da uomo*): in — sleeves, in maniche di camicia; to keep one's — on, (*gergo*) reprimere la collera; —waist *n.* camicetta.

shiver (shĭv'ẽr) *n.* brivido, fremito; scheggia, frammento. *vi.* frantumare. *vi.* frantumarsi, tremare, rabbrividire.

shoal (shōl) *n.* branco di pesci; banco di sabbia, bassofondo; moltitudine.

shock (shŏk) *n.* colpo, scossa, urto, trauma, emozione; — of hair, ciuffo di capelli; — absorber, ammortizzatore; — troops, truppe d'assalto o d'urto; *vt.*, *vi.* urtare, disgustare, spaventare, scandalizzare, colpire, cozzare.

shocking (shŏk'ĭng) *agg.* offensivo, repulsivo, sconveniente, scandaloso.

shod (shŏd) *pass.*, *pp.* *di* shoe.

shoe (shōō) *n.* scarpa, calzatura; ferro (*da cavallo*), zoccolo; copertone (*d'auto*); pattino (*del freno*): — polish, lucido da scarpe. *vt.* (*pass.*, *pp.* shod) calzare; ferrare.

shoeblack *n.* lustrascarpe.

shoehorn *n.* calzascarpe.

shoelace *n.* stringa da scarpe.

shoemaker *n.* calzolaio.

shoestring *n.* stringa da scarpe; (*gergo*) somma esigua, capitale insufficiente.

shone (shōn) *pass., pp. di* to shine.

shook (shŏŏk) *pass. di* to shake.

shoot (shōōt) *n.* colpo, lancio, tiro; germoglio; cascata. *vt., vi.* (*pass., pp.* shot) sparare; fucilare; lanciare; emettere, cacciare; far brillare (*mine*); variegare; germogliare; dolorare; fotografare, riprendere *o* girare (*una scena*): to — forth, germogliare, scaturire; to — ahead, slanciarsi in avanti; to — by, passare rapidamente; to — the breeze (*gergo*), fare quattro chiacchiere.

shooter *n.* sparatore, cacciatore.

shooting *n.* sparatoria; caccia; il germogliare: — range, poligono, tiro al bersaglio. *agg.*: — pain, dolore acuto; — star, stella filante.

shop (shŏp) *n.* bottega, negozio; officina, laboratorio: to talk —, parlare di lavoro. *vi.* fare le compere.

shopkeeper *n.* negoziante.

shoplifter *n.* taccheggiatore, taccheggiatrice.

shopman *n.* commesso.

shopper (shŏp'ẽr) *n.* compratore, persona in giro per i negozi.

shopping (shŏp'ĭng) *n.* spesa, compere: to go —, andare in giro per i negozi; andare a far compere.

shop window *n.* vetrina.

shore (shōr) *n.* riva, spiaggia, costa, lido; puntello: on shore, sbarcare; Shore Patrol (*mil.*), Polizia della Marina. *vt.* arenare; puntellare.

shorn (shōrn) *pp. di* to shear.

short (shōrt) *n.* sommario, compendio; la parte corta (*di uno cosa*); (*cinema*) cortometraggio; *pl.* calzoncini; deficienze: —cut, scorciatoia; the long and — of, la conclusione di; in —, in breve. *agg.* corto, breve, scarso, piccolo, basso; a corto (*di*); brusco, conciso: to make — work of, liquidare per le spicce; in a — time, in poco tempo, tra poco. *avv.* bruscamente, di botto, laconicamente: to fall —, essere inadeguato; to fall — of, non riuscire a raggiungere; to be — of, essere a corto di; to run — of, restare a corto di; to cut —, accorciare, interrompere bruscamente; to stop —, fermarsi di botto.

shortage (shōr'tĭj) *n.* scarsità, carestia, ammanco.

shortcoming (shōrt'kŭm'ĭng) *n.* deficienza, inconveniente.

shorten (shōr't'n) *vt.* accorciare, abbreviare, contrarre. *vi.* accorciarsi.

shortening (shōr't'n·ĭng) *n.* accorciamento, abbreviazione; (*pasticceria*) grasso.

shorthand (shōrt'hănd') *n.* stenografia.

shortly (shōrt'lĭ) *avv.* brevemente, bruscamente, fra poco, subito, di lì a poco.

shortness (shōrt'nĕs) *n.* brevità, piccolezza (*di statura*); irascibilità.

shot (shŏt) (1) *agg.* variegato.

shot (shŏt) (2) *pass., pp. di* to shoot. *n.* sparo; lancio; mira; proiettile; pallini da fucile; tiratore; portata (*d'arma*); tentativo; fotografia; (*gergo*) iniezione, sorso: a dead —, un tiratore infallibile; not by a long —, niente affatto, per nulla; a big— (*gergo*) un pezzo grosso.

shotgun (shŏt'gŭn') *n.* fucile da caccia.

should (shŏŏd) *pass. di* shall.

shoulder (shōl'dẽr) *n.* spalla, prominenza, sostegno: — belt, bandoliera; — blade, scapola; to give the cold —, trattare freddamente; straight from the —, con tutta franchezza. *vt.* caricarsi sulle spalle, assumersi, addossarsi.

shout (shout) *n.* grido. *vt., vi.* gridare, acclamare.

shouting (shout'ĭng) *n.* urlio.

shove (shŭv) *n.* colpo, spinta, urto. *vt., vi.* sospingere, spingere, ficcare: to — off, spinger via una barca, portarsi al largo.

shovel (shŭv''l) *n.* pala, paletta. *vt.* spalare, scavare. —er *n.* spalatore.

show (shō) *n.* mostra, esposizione, spettacolo; indicazione, traccia; esibizione, ostentazione, pompa; dumb —, pantomima. *vt.* (*pass.* showed, *pp.* shown) mostrare, mettere in mostra, dimostrare, denotare, accompagnare. *vi.* apparire, esibirsi; affacciarsi, vedersi; (*gergo sport.*) arrivare piazzato: to — in, introdurre; to — out, condurre alla porta; to — off, mettere (*o* mettersi) in mostra; to — up, condurre di sopra; smascherare; comparire.

showcase (shō'kās') *n.* vetrinetta, teca.

shower (shou'ẽr) *n.* scroscio, gragnuola; doccia; abbondanza. *vi.* bagnare, inondare, riversare, elargire. *vi.* piovere a rovesci; fare la doccia. —bath *n.* doccia. —y *agg.* piovoso.

showman (shō'măn) *n.* presentatore, imbonitore, espositore.

shown (shōn) *pp. di* to show.

showy (shō′I) *agg.* ostentato, sfarzoso, vistoso, appariscente.

shrank (shrăngk) *pass. di* to shrink.

shrapnel (shrăp′něl) *n.* (*art.*) granata.

shred (shrĕd) *n.* brandello, frammento, pezzetto: to tear to —s, fare a pezzetti *o* brandelli. *vt.* (*pass. pp.* shred, shredded) sminuzzare; sbrindellare.

shrew (shrōō) *n.* megera; (*zool.*) toporagno.

shrewd (shrōōd) *agg.* sagace, scaltro.

shriek (shrēk) *n.* strillo, sibilo, stridio. *vt., vi.* strillare, sibilare, stridere.

shrill (shrĭl) *agg.* acuto, penetrante, stridulo. *vi.* strillare.

shrimp (shrĭmp) *n.* gamberetto di mare; (*fig.*) omiciattolo.

shrine (shrīn) *n.* reliquiario, altare.

shrink (shrĭngk) *vt.* (*pass.* shrank, shrunk, *pp.* shrunk, shrunken) accorciare, contrarre, restringere. *vi.* ritrarsi, accorciarsi, restringersi, contrarsi. —age *n.* contrazione, accorciamento, calo.

shrivel (shrĭv′l) *vt.* contrarre, raggrinzire, far avvizzire. *vi.* raggrinzirsi, avvizzire.

shroud (shroud) *n.* sudario; *pl.* (*naut.*) sartie. *vt.* avvolgere in un sudario; coprire, riparare.

shrub (shrŭb) *n.* arbusto, cespuglio. —bery *n.* macchia d'arbusti.

shrug (shrŭg) *n.* alzata di spalle. *vt., vi.* scrollare (*le spalle*); stringersi nelle spalle.

shrunk (shrŭngk) *pass., pp. di* to shrink.

shrunken (shrŭngk′ěn) *pp. di* to shrink.

shudder (shŭd′ěr) *n.* brivido, fremito. *vi.* tremare, rabbrividire, fremere.

shuffle (shŭf′l) *n.* andatura strascicata; mescolata; inganno, sotterfugio. *vt., vi.* strascicare; arruffare, mischiare (*le carte*); tergiversare; ciabattare: to — along, camminare con passo strascicato; to — in, intrufolarsi; to — out, sgattaiolare fuori.

shun (shŭn) *vt.* evitare, schivare, scansare, sfuggire.

shunt (shŭnt) *n.* (*ferr.*) diramazione, scambio. *vt.* smistare. *vi.* far manovra.

shut (shŭt) *vt., vi.* (*pass., pp.* shut) chiudere, rinchiudere; chiudersi: to — up, confinare; tacere, far tacere; to — out, impedire l'accesso a; to — off the light, spegnere la luce; to — off from, isolare da, escludere da; — up! silenzio!

shutter (shŭt′ěr) *n.* chiusura, sportello, persiana di finestra; (*fot.*)

otturatore. — bug *n.* (*gergo*) fotoamatore.

shuttle (shŭt′′l) *n.* navetta, spoletta; (*S.U.*) treno locale. *vi.* andare avanti e indietro, fare la spola.

shy (shī) *agg.* timido; riservato; restio (*a*): to be — on, essere scarso di. *vi.* adombrarsi, fare uno scarto, imbizzarrirsi, ritrarsi (*da*).

shyly (shī′lI) *avv.* timidamente, timorosamente.

shyness *n.* timidezza, ritrosia, diffidenza.

shyster (shī′stěr) *n.* imbroglione; avvocato equivoco, azzeccagarbugli.

Siamese (sī′*à*-mēs′) *n.*, *agg.* siamese: — cat, gatto siamese; — twins, fratelli siamesi; the —, i siamesi.

sibyl (sĭb′Il) *n.* sibilla.

sibylline *agg.* sibillino.

sick (sĭk) *agg.* ammalato; nauseato, stufo, disgustato: to be —, avere la nausea, vomitare (*Ingl.*); to be — at heart, essere demoralizzato; to grow —, stufarsi; to be — of, essere stufo di; — bay, infermeria di bordo; — leave, licenza di convalescenza.

sicken (sĭk′ěn) *vt.* far ammalare; disgustare, nauseare. *vi.* ammalarsi; disgustarsi, essere disgustoso.

sickening *agg.* disgustoso, stomachevole; di nausea *o* malessere.

sickle (sĭk′l) *n.* falcetto: — and hammer, falce e martello.

sickly (sĭk′lI) *agg.* malaticcio, malsano.

sickness (sĭk′něs) *n.* malattia, indebolimento nausea.

side (sīd) *n.* lato, estremità; fianco, versante, pendio; campo, partito: the wrong —, il rovescio; to take —s with, schierarsi con, parteggiare per; — by —, fianco a fianco; to put on — (*gergo*), darsi delle arie; — glance, occhiata in tralice; — issue, questione secondaria; — light, luce laterale, ragguaglio incidentale. *agg.* laterale, indiretto. *vi.*: to — with, parteggiare per, schierarsi con.

sideboard (sīd′bōrd′) *n.* credenza.

sidecar (sīd′kär′) *n.* carrozzino di motociclo.

sideline (sīd′līn′) *n.* attività secondaria, diramazione stradale, strada secondaria; (*sport.*) linea laterale.

sidetrack (sīd′trăk′) *vt.* (*ferr.*) smistare su un binario morto; (*fig.*) sviare; mettere da parte.

sidewalk (sīd′wŏk′) *n.* marciapiedi.

sideways (sīd′wāz′) **sidewise** (sīd′wīz′) *avv.* obliquamente; lateralmente; di traverso; di fianco. *agg.* obliquo; laterale.

siding (sĭd'ĭng) *n.* binario morto; binario di manovra.

sidle (sĭd'l) *vi.* spostarsi lateralmente, sgattaiolare.

siege (sēj) *n.* assedio: to lay — to, assediare.

sieve (sĭv) *n.* staccio, vaglio. *vt.* vagliare.

sift (sĭft) *vt.* stacciare, vagliare, esaminare.

sigh (sī) *n.* sospiro. *vi.* sospirare.

sight (sīt) *n.* vista; visione, veduta; spettacolo; sguardo; mirino (*di arma da fuoco*): at —, a vista; by —, di vista; to buy — unseen, comprare alla cieca; to catch — of, avvistare, intravedere, adocchiare; to lose — of somebody, perdere di vista qualcuno; to see the —s, visitare i luoghi interessanti (*di una città*). *vt.* avvistare, prendere di mira. *vi.* mirare.

sightseeing (sīt'sē'ĭng) *n.* turismo: — tour, giro turistico, passeggiata turistica.

sightseer (sīt'sē'ẽr) *n.* turista, curioso.

sign (sīn) *n.* segno, cenno; insegna; indizio. *vt.*, *vi.* firmare, segnare; scritturare; indicare: to — up for a job, firmare un contratto di assunzione.

signal (sĭg'nǎl) *n.* segnale, contrassegno, segnalazione. *agg.* segnalato, notevole, eminente. *vt.*, *vi.* segnalare, far segnalazioni.

signature (sĭg'nȧ·tûr) *n.* firma; (*tip.*) segnatura; (*radio*) sigla.

signboard (sīn'bōrd') *n.* insegna.

signer (sīn'ẽr) *n.* firmatario.

signet (sĭg'nĕt) *n.* sigillo: — ring, anello con sigillo.

significance (sĭg·nĭf'ĭ·kȧns) *n.* significato, senso, importanza.

significant (sĭg·nĭf'ĭ·kȧnt) *agg.* sintomatico, significativo.

signify (sĭg'nĭ·fī) *vt.*, *vi.* significare.

signpost (sīn'pōst') *n.* cartello indicatore.

silence (sī'lĕns) *n.* silenzio. *vt.* far tacere, chetare, ridurre al silenzio.

silencer (sī'lĕn·sẽr) *n.* silenziatore.

silent (sī'lĕnt) *agg.* silenzioso, tacito; (*gramm.*) muto: — partner, socio che non figura, finanziatore; — butler, scatola raccoglirifiuti (*cenere, mozziconi, ecc.*).

silhouette (sĭl'ōȯ·ĕt') *n.* profilo, sagoma. *vt.*, proiettare, delineare. *vi.* profilarsi, delinearsi, stagliarsi (*contro*).

silk (sĭlk) *n.* seta: raw —, seta greggia; sheer —, seta trasparente *o* impalpabile. *agg.* di seta, serico.

silken (sĭl'kĕn) *agg.* serico, morbido.

silkworm (sĭlk'wûrm) *n.* baco da seta.

silky *agg.* setaceo, morbido.

sill (sĭl) *n.* basamento, soglia: window —, davanzale.

silly (sĭl'ĭ) *agg.* stupido, assurdo, insulso, sciocco.

silver (sĭl'vẽr) *n.* argento, argenteria. *agg.* d'argento, argenteo, argentino: — plate, —ware, argenteria; — wedding, nozze d'argento. *vt.* inargentare. *vi.* inargentarsi.

silversmith *n.* argentiere.

silvery *agg.* argenteo, inargentato, argentino.

similar (sĭm'ĭ·lẽr) *agg.* similare, analogo, simile. —ity (–ăr'ĭ·tĭ) *n.* somiglianza, analogia. —ly *avv.* similmente, analogamente.

simile (sĭm'ĭ·lē) *n.* paragone, similitudine.

similitude (sĭ·mĭl'ĭ·tūd) *n.* somiglianza.

simmer (sĭm'ẽr) *vi.* bollire a fuoco lento; schiumare (*di rabbia*).

simper (sĭm'pẽr) *n.* smorfietta, sorriso affettato. *vi.* sorridere affettatamente.

simple (sĭm'p'l) *n.* sciocco; erba medicinale. *agg.* semplice, puro; ignorante, ottuso: —minded *agg.* semplice, ingenuo, spontaneo.

simpleton (sĭm'p'l·tŭn) *n.* sempliciotto.

simplicity (sĭm·plĭs'ĭ·tĭ) *n.* semplicità.

simplify (sĭm'plĭ·fī) *vt.* semplificare.

simply (sĭm'plĭ) *avv.* semplicemente, puramente, soltanto.

simulate (sĭm'ū·lāt) *vt.* simulare.

simulation (sĭm'ū·lā'shŭn) *n.* simulazione.

simulcast (sī'mŭl·kȧst) *vt.*, *vi.* trasmettere simultaneamente per radio e per televisione, radioteletrasmettere.

simultaneous (sī'mŭl·tā'nē·ŭs) *agg.* simultaneo.

simultaneity (sī'mŭl·tȧ·nē'ĭ·tĭ) *n.* simultaneità.

sin (sĭn) *n.* peccato. *vi.* peccare.

since (sĭns) *avv.* in seguito, dopo d'allora, prima d'ora, fa: ever —, da quell'epoca; long —, da molto tempo *prep.* da, dopo: we have been here — four, siamo qui dalle quattro. *cong.* dopo di, dacché, in seguito a, poiché, dal momento che, visto che.

sincere (sĭn·sēr') *agg.* sincero. —ly *avv.* sinceramente: yours —, vostro devotissimo (*nella corrispondenza*).

sincerity (sĭn·sĕr'ĭ·tĭ) *n.* sincerità.

sinecure (sī'nē·kūr) *n.* sinecura.

sinew (sĭn'ū) *n.* tendine, nervo, vigore.

sinewy (sĭn'ū·ĭ) agg. nervoso; vigoroso.

sinful (sĭn'fŏol) agg. peccaminoso.

sing (sĭng) vt., vi. (pass. sang, pp. sung) cantare: to — a child to sleep, addormentare un bimbo cantando; to — small, assumere un tono umile; to — out of tune, stonare.

singe (sĭnj) n. strinatura, scottatura. vt. strinare, bruciacchiare.

single (sĭng'g'l) agg. singolo, solo, unico, semplice, individuale; celibe (m.), nubile (f.): — blessedness, — life, celibato. vt. (gen. seg. da out) scegliere, prescegliere, isolare; esemplare.

singlehanded agg. con le proprie forze. avv. senza aiuto; con una sola mano.

singly (sĭng'glĭ) avv. a uno a uno, separatamente.

singsong (sĭng'sŏng') n. cantilena.

singular (sĭng'gū·lẽr) agg. singolare, unico, individuale. —ity (-ãr'ĭ·tĭ) n. singolarità.

sinister (sĭn'ĭs·tẽr) agg. sinistro.

sink (sĭngk) n. acquaio. vt. (pass. sank, pp. sunk) affondare, sommergere; diminuire, abbassare (spec. la voce); scavare; investire (danaro) in speculazioni: to — into one's mind, entrare in mente. vi. andare a fondo, sprofondare; decrescere; penetrare; affievolirsi. —er n. peso, piombino; (min.) sonda, escavatrice.—hole n. scarico. —ing n. depressione; escavazione: — fund, fondo d'ammortamento.

sinner (sĭn'ẽr) n. peccatore.

sinuous (sĭn'ū·ŭs) agg. sinuoso, tortuoso, indiretto.

sinus (sī'nŭs) n. insenatura; (anat.) seno (cavità).

sip (sĭp) n. sorso. vt., vi. sorseggiare, centellinare.

siphon (sī'fŏn) n. sifone. vt., vi. travasare con sifone, passare attraverso un sifone.

sir (sûr) n. signore.

sire (sīr) n. padre, genitore; sire, maestà.

siren (sī'rĕn) n. sirena.

sirloin (sûr'loin') n. lombo (di bue).

sirup (sĭr'ŭp) vedi syrup.

sis (sĭs) n. fam. sorella.

sissy (sĭs'ĭ) n., agg. effeminato.

sister (sĭs'tẽr) n. sorella; suora; infermiera. agg. analogo: — ship, nave gemella.

sister-in-law n. cognata.

sit (sĭt) vt. (pass., pp. sat) far sedere. vi. sedersi, sedere; appollaiarsi; stare; riunirsi; posare (per un ritratto); covare (degli ovipari); adattarsi (d'indumenti): to — tight,

aggrapparsi al sedile, tener duro; to — up, drizzarsi a sedere; vegliare; to — down, sedersi.

sit-down strike n. sciopero bianco.

site (sīt) n. posto, posizione, area.

sitting (sĭt'ĭng) n. seduta, sessione; posto da sedere; cova. agg. seduto; in cova: — room, salotto.

situate (sĭt'ū·āt) vt. collocare, situare; sistemare.

situation (sĭt'ū·ā'shŭn) n. situazione, posizione, impiego.

six (sĭks) n., agg. sei.

sixteen (sĭks'tēn') n., agg. sedici.

sixteenth (sĭks'tēnth') n., agg. sedicesimo; (il) sedici del mese.

sixth (sĭksth) n., agg. sesto; (il) sei del mese.

sixtieth (sĭks'tĭ·ĕth) n., agg. sessantesimo.

sixty (sĭks'tĭ) n., agg. sessanta.

sizable (sīz'á·b'l) agg. cospicuo, considerevole, voluminoso.

size (sīz) (1) n. glutine, appretto. vt. apprettare.

size (sīz) (2) n. grandezza, taglia, dimensioni, misura: full —, grandezza naturale. vt. misurare, proporzionare: to — up, giudicare, valutare.

sizeable vedi sizable.

sizzle (sĭz'l) n. sfrigolio. vi. sfrigolare.

skate (skāt) n. pattino; (ittiol.) razza: roller —s, pattini a rotelle. vi. pattinare.

skater (skāt'ẽr) n. pattinatore.

skedaddle (skĕ·dăd'l) vi. (gergo) svignarsela, sparpagliarsi nella fuga.

skein (skān) n. matassa, groviglio.

skeleton (skĕl'ē·tŭn) n. scheletro; intelaiatura, carcassa: — key, grimaldello, chiave universale.

skeptic (skĕp'tĭk) n., agg. scettico. —al agg. scettico. —ism n. (-tĭ-sĭz'm) scetticismo.

sketch (skĕch) n. schizzo, abbozzo; (teat.) scenetta, numero. vt. schizzare, abbozzare. —ily avv. approssimativamente, affrettatamente.

sketchy agg. abbozzato, approssimativo.

skewer (skū'ẽr) n. spiedo.

ski (skē) n. sci.: — lift, seggiovia; — suit, costume da sciatore. vi. sciare.

skid (skĭd) n. slittata; sbandamento; freno a scarpa; piano inclinato; (aeron.) pattino di coda: — row, — road, via dei bassifondi; bassifondi. vt., vi. frenare; scivolare; slittare, sbandare.

skiff (skĭf) n. schifo (barca).

skill (skĭl) n. abilità, capacità, intelligenza, destrezza. —ed *agg.* abile, esperto; specializzato.

skillful (skĭl'fŏŏl) *agg.* abile, esperto.

skillet (skĭl'ĕt) *n.* casseruola.

skim (skĭm) *n.* schiuma, crema. *vt., vi.* schiumare, scremare; sfiorare; leggere superficialmente, scorrere: to — over, guardare di sfuggita.

skimp (skĭmp) *vt., vi.* lesinare, abborracciare, fare il taccagno, economizzare. —y *agg.* meschino, tirchio.

skin (skĭn) *n.* pelle; scorza, buccia; pergamena: to save one's —, salvare la pelle; by the — of one's teeth, per un pelo. *vt.* scorticare, pelare. —-deep *agg.* a fior di pelle, epidermico, superficiale.

skinflint (skĭn'flĭnt') *n.* spilorcio.

skinny (skĭn'ĭ) *agg.* magro, scarno.

skip (skĭp) *n.* salto, balzo, omissione. *vt., vi.* saltare, sorvolare, omettere, sfuggire a, saltellare, rimbalzare: — it! sorvola!, lascia perdere!

skipper (skĭp'ĕr) (1) *n.* saltatore.

skipper (skĭp'ĕr) (2) *n.* (*naut.*) padron marittimo, capitano.

skirmish (skûr'mĭsh) *n.* scaramuccia.

skirt (skûrt) *n.* margine; falda; gonna. *vt., vi.* costeggiare, circondare, orlare, rasentare.

skit (skĭt) *n.* scherzo, burla, satira.

skulk (skŭlk) *vi.* appiattarsi, sgattaiolare.

skull (skŭl) *n.* cranio, teschio.

skunk (skŭngk) *n.* (*zool.*) moffetta.

sky (skī) *n.* (*pl.* skies) cielo: — blue, azzurro-cielo; — train, aereo per traino di alianti; — truck, aereo da trasporto, vagone volante.

skylark (skī'lärk') *n.* allodola.

skylight (skī'līt') *n.* lucernario.

skyscraper (skī'skrāp'ĕr) *n.* grattacielo.

slab (slăb) *n.* lastra, lastrone, fetta.

slack (slăk) *n.* polvere di carbone; inerzia, stasi; *pl.* calzoni sportivi. *agg.* allentato, lento, molle, pigro, fiacco, negligente, inerte: — season, stagione morta. *vt., vi.* (*anche* slacken) allentare, rilassare, diminuire, moderare; allentarsi, infiacchirsi, rilassarsi, rallentare. —ness (-nĕs) *n.* rilassatezza, lentezza, trascuratezza.

slag (slăg) *n.* scoria.

slain (slān) *pp. di* to slay.

slake (slāk) *vt.* saziare, placare, rallentare; allentare, spegnere (*la calce viva*). *vi.* placarsi, spegnersi.

slam (slăm) *n.* sbatacchiata; slam (*al bridge*). *vt.* sbatacchiare; scaraventare: to — the door, sbattere la porta.

slander (slăn'dĕr) *n.* calunnia, diffamazione. *vt.* calunniare, diffamare. —er *n.* calunniatore. —ous *agg.* calunnioso, diffamatorio.

slang (slăng) *n.* gergo. —y *agg.* di gergo, in gergo.

slant (slănt) *n.* declivio, inclinazione; punto di vista. *agg.* inclinato, obliquo. *vt.* inclinare; dare un particolare indirizzo a (*un giornale, uno spettacolo, ecc.*); addomesticare (*una notizia, ecc.*). *vi.* essere inclinato, inclinarsi, pendere.

slap (slăp) *n.* manata; ceffone; rabbuffo, umiliazione. *avv.* violentemente, di colpo. *vt.* schiaffeggiare; gettare con violenza; dare una manata a.

slash (slăsh) *n.* sfregio; squarcio, spacco. *vt.* tagliare; sfregiare, squarciare; sferzare; ridurre, falcidiare.

slat (slăt) *n.* striscia, stecca; lastra.

slate (slāt) *n.* ardesia, tegola d'ardesia; (*pol. S.U.*) lista dei candidati.

slattern (slăt'ẽrn) *n.* sciamannona. —ly *agg.* sciamannato.

slaughter (slô'tẽr) *n.* strage, carneficina, macellazione. *vt.* far strage di, trucidare, macellare. —er *n.* massacratore.

slave (slāv) *n.* schiavo; sgobbone: — driver, negriero, aguzzino. *vi.* lavorare come uno schiavo, sgobbare.

slaver (slāv'ĕr) (1) *n.* nave negriera; negriero.

slaver (slăv'ĕr) (2) *n.* bava, saliva. *vi.* sbavare, essere servile.

slavery (slāv'ĕr·ĭ) *n.* schiavitù.

slavish (slāv'ĭsh) *agg.* servile.

slay (slā) *vt.* (*pass.* slew, *pp.* slain) uccidere.

sleazy (slē'zĭ) *agg.* sottile, tenue.

sled (slĕd) *n.* slitta. *vt., vi.* trasportare (*o andare*) in slitta.

sledge (slĕj) (1) *n.* slitta, traino.

sledge (slĕj) (2) *n.* (*anche* — hammer) martello, mazza.

sleek (slēk) *agg.* liscio, lucente, levigato; ben pasciuto; inappuntabile; mellifluo. *vt.* lisciare, levigare.

sleep (slēp) *n.* sonno, letargo: to go to —, addormentarsi; to put to —, (far) addormentare. *vt., vi.* (*pass., pp.* slept) dormire, sopirsi: to — on it, dormirci sopra (*detto di preoccupazioni, ecc.*). —er *n.* dormiente; (*ferr.*) traversina; vettura letto. —ily *avv.* sonnacchiosamente. —iness *n.* sonnolenza.

sleeping *n.* sonno. *agg.* dormiente, sopito: — car, vagone letto; — draught, sonnifero; — sickness, malattia del sonno, encefalite letargica.

sleepless *agg.* insonne.

sleeplessness *n.* insonnia.

sleepwalker *n.* sonnambulo.

sleepwalking *n.* sonnambulismo.

sleepy (slēp'ĭ) *agg.* assonnato; inattivo: to be —, aver sonno.

sleet (slēt) *n.* nevischio, neve mista a pioggia. *vi.* cadere neve mista a pioggia.

sleeve (slēv) *n.* manica; (*mecc.*) manicotto: to laugh up one's —, ridere sotto i baffi. **—less** *agg.* senza maniche; (*fig.*) futile.

sleigh (slā) *n.* slitta. *vi.* andare in slitta.

sleight (slīt) *n.* destrezza: — of hand, gioco di prestigio.

slender (slĕn'dĕr) *agg.* snello, sottile; tenue, vago, scarso.

slept (slĕpt) *pass.*, *pp. di* to sleep.

sleuth (slōōth) *n.* segugio, investigatore.

slew (slōō) *pass. di* to slay.

slice (slīs) *n.* fetta, porzione, spicchio; spatola. *vt.* affettare.

slick (slĭk) *agg.* liscio, disinvolto, astuto; viscido; (*gergo*) di prim'ordine: — paper, rivista raffinata, rivista di lusso. *vt.* lisciare, abbellire: to — up, agghindarsi, farsi bello. **—er** *n.* (*S.U.*) impermeabile; imbroglione.

slid (slĭd) *pass.*, *pp. di* to slide.

slide (slīd) *n.* slittamento, frana; piano inclinato, declivio; diapositiva; vetrino (*da microscopio*); (*mus.*) modulazione; — fastener, cerniera lampo; — knot, nodo scorsoio; — rule, regolo calcolatore; — cover, persiana avvolgibile, chiusura a serranda; color —, diapositiva a colori. *vt.* (*pass.* slid, *pp.* slid) far scorrere, far scivolare. *vi.* scivolare, sdrucciolare, slittare, scorrere: to — in, out, away, sgusciare dentro, fuori, via.

slight (slīt) *n.* indifferenza, insulto. *agg.* tenue, leggiero, insignificante. *vt.* denigrare, trascurare, disprezzare. **—ing** *agg.* offensivo, sprezzante. **—ly** *avv.* lievemente, scarsamente.

slim (slĭm) *agg.* snello, magro, scarso, misero.

slime (slīm) *n.* mucillagine, melma, bava.

slimy (slīm'ĭ) *agg.* viscoso, melmoso.

sling (slĭng) *n.* fionda; catena del verricello; cinghia; fascia (*per mettere il braccio al collo*); (*naut.*) braca. *vt.* (*pass.*, *pp.* slung) lanciare; sospendere; appendere; legare: to — a rifle over one's shoulder, mettere il fucile a tracolla. **—shot** *n.* fionda, tirasassi.

slink (slĭngk) *vt.*, *vi.* (*pass.*, *pp.* slunk) sgattaiolare: to — in, sgusciar dentro.

slip (slĭp) *n.* scivolata; passo falso; fuga; foglietto, tagliando; germoglio; errore; indiscrezione; sottoveste, federa, mutandina; (*naut.*) calata: to give the —, piantare in asso; to make a —, fare una papera. *vt.*, *vi.* far scorrere; infilare; rifilare; sbagliare; lasciarsi sfuggire; omettere; liberarsi di; eludere; sfuggire (*di mente*); scivolare; scorrere; sgattaiolare.

slipknot (slĭp'nŏt') *n.* nodo scorsoio.

slipper (slĭp'ĕr) *n.* pantofola.

slippery (slĭp'ĕr'ĭ) *agg.* sdrucciolevole, viscido; infido.

slipshod (slĭp'shŏd) *agg.* scalcagnato; scalcinato, trasandato.

slit (slĭt) *n.* fenditura, screpolatura, fessura. *vt.* (*pass.*, *pp.* slit) fendere, stracciare, squarciare: to — into strips, tagliare a fette *o* strisce.

slither (slĭth'ĕr) *vt.* scivolare, strisciare.

sliver (slĭv'ĕr) *n.* scheggia.

slobber (slŏb'ĕr) *n.* bava. *vi.* sbavare; fare il sentimentale. **—ing** *agg.* bavoso; sentimentale.

sloe (slō) *n.* prugnola, prugnolo.

slogan (slō'găn) *n.* motto pubblicitario; parola d'ordine.

sloop (slōōp) *n.* specie di cutter, imbarcazione leggiera.

slop (slŏp) *n.* pozzanghera, risciacquatura di stoviglie, acqua sporca, brodaglia. *vt.*, *vi.* versare, spandere, sbrodolare.

slope (slōp) *n.* pendio, inclinazione; versante. *vt.* inclinare. *vi.* pendere, inclinarsi, digradare.

sloping (slōp'ĭng) *agg.* in discesa, inclinato.

sloppy (slŏp'ĭ) *agg.* umido, melmoso, viscido; disgustoso, sciatto.

slot (slŏt) *n.* sbarra, catenaccio; scanalatura, fessura; buca (*per le lettere*): — machine, lotteria automatica; distributore automatico. *vt.* praticare una fessura in.

sloth (slŏth; slōth) *n.* indolenza. **—ful** *agg.* pigro, indolente.

slouch (slouch) *n.* andatura (*o persona*) goffa; scompostezza, portamento curvo: — hat, cappello a cencio. *vi.* camminare goffamente *o* curvo, pencolare.

slough (slou) (1) *n.* pozzanghera, pantano.

slough (slŭf) (2) *n.* spoglia (*di rettile*), squama. *vt.* spogliarsi di. *vi.* cadere, sfaldarsi, squamarsi.

sloven (slŭv'ĕn) *n.* sudicione, sciattone.

slovenliness n. sciatteria.

slovenly (slŭv'ĕn·lǐ) agg. sciatto, trasandato.

slow (slō) agg. lento, tardo, in ritardo, tardivo, indolente, ottuso, che ritarda (di orologio), tedioso. avv. lentamente. vt., vi. rallentare, indugiare, ritardare. —ly avv. lentamente, adagio, piano. —ness n. lentezza, indolenza; ottusità.

sludge (slŭj) n. fango, neve fangosa.

slug (slŭg) (1) n. (gergo) pallottola; pugno; sorso (di liquore). vt. percuotere, colpire.

slug (slŭg) (2) n. limaccia (specie di lumaca).

sluggard (slŭg'ẽrd) n. infingardo.

sluggish (slŭg'ĭsh) agg. pigro, lento.

sluice (slōōs) n. cateratta, scarico, canale, chiavica, chiusa: — gate, porta di chiusa. vt. far defluire, inondare. vi. defluire.

slum (slŭm) n. quartiere miserabile. vi. visitare i quartieri miserabili.

slumber (slŭm'bẽr) n. torpore, sonno. vi. sonnecchiare, dormire.

slump (slŭmp) n. caduta improvvisa, sprofondamento, crisi, tracollo, ribasso (dei prezzi). vi. stramazzare, sprofondare; ribassare, subire un tracollo.

slunk (slŭngk) pass., pp. di to slink.

slur (slûr) n. onta, sfregio, calunnia; (mus.) legatura.

slush (slŭsh) n. neve fangosa, fanghiglia; morcia; sentimentalismo.

slut (slŭt) n. sciattona, sgualdrina.

sly (slī) agg. scaltro, sornione, insidioso: on the sly, di nascosto. sly-ness n. scaltrezza.

smack (smăk) n. schiocco, schiaffo; bacio schioccante; sapore. avv. di botto, in pieno. vt. far schioccare, sbattere violentemente; schiaffeggiare; baciare rumorosamente. vi. schioccar le labbra: to — of, sapere di. —ing agg. schioccante, sonoro.

small (smôl) agg. piccolo; basso; sottile; minuto; meschino: — change, spiccioli; — letter, lettera minuscola; — talk, chiacchiere; to feel —, sentirsi piccolo.

smallpox (smôl'pŏks') n. (med.) varicella.

smalltime (smôl'tīm') n. teatro di second' ordine. agg. scadente, di mezza tacca, misero, da poco.

smart (smärt) n. dolore, bruciore. agg. elegante; furbo; abile, intelligente; acuto; doloroso: — remark, osservazione acuta; the — set, il bel mondo, gli elegantoni. vi. dolere, soffrire.

smash (smăsh) n. fracasso, sconquasso, rovina; scontro, urto. vt. fracassare, sfondare, rovinare; vi. frantumarsi: to — against, into, andare a sbattere contro, cozzare contro.

smattering (smăt'ẽr·ǐng) n. infarinatura.

smear (smẽr) n. macchia; vt. macchiare, impiastricciare; spalmare; (gergo) rovinare, mandare a monte; calunniare, diffamare: — campaign, campagna diffamatoria.

smell (smĕl) n. odore, profumo; odorato, fiuto. vt. (pass., pp. smelled o smelt) fiutare; (gergo) appestare. vi. odorare (di), puzzare: to — a rat, insospettirsi.

smelly agg. puzzolente.

smelt (smĕlt) (1) pass., pp. di to smell.

smelt (smĕlt) (2) vt. (metal.) fondere.

smile (smīl) n. sorriso. vi. sorridere.

smiling agg. sorridente. —ly avv. sorridendo, col sorriso sulle labbra.

smirch (smûrch) vt. insudiciare.

smirk (smûrk) n. sorriso affettato. vi. sorridere affettatamente.

smite (smīt) vt., vi. (pass. smote, pp. smitten) colpire, percuotere; angariare; rimordere; ferire.

smith (smǐth) n. fabbro, artigiano.

smithereens (smǐth'ẽr·ēnz') n.pl. frantumi. to smash to —, mandare in frantumi.

smithy (smǐth'ǐ) n. fucina.

smitten (smǐt'n) pp. di to smite.

smock (smŏk) n. camicia da donna; camiciotto, spolverina, camice.

smog (smŏg) n. caligine.

smoke (smōk) n. fumo, vapore. vt., vi. affumicare; fumare.

smoker (smōk'ẽr) n. fumatore; vagone per fumatori.

smoking (smōk'ǐng) agg. fumante: — carriage, scompartimento per fumatori; — room, sala per fumatori, fumoir (fr.).

smoky (smōk'ǐ) agg. fumoso, fumante.

smolder (smōl'dẽr) vi. ardere lentamente, covare sotto la cenere; fremere (di collera).

smooth (smōōth) agg. liscio, levigato; morbido; facile, regolare; blando, calmo. vt. lisciare, appianare; calmare; levigare; accarezzare. —en vt. levigare. —ly avv. pianamente, dolcemente; agevolmente. —ness n. dolcezza, levigatezza; agevolezza, scorrevolezza.

smote (smōt) pass. di to smite.

smother (smŭth'ẽr) vt., vi. soffocare.

smoulder (smōl'dẽr) vedi smolder.

smudge (smŭj) n. macchia, imbrattamento; fumo. vt., vi. affumicare;

imbrattare, macchiare, macchiarsi.

smug (smŭg) *agg.* tronfio.

smuggle (smŭg''l) *vt.* contrabbandare.

smuggler (smŭg'lĕr) *n.* contrabbandiere.

smut (smŭt) *n.* fuliggine, baffo (*di carbone*); carbone (*malattia dei cereali*); oscenità. *vt.* sporcare, annerire.

smutty (smŭt'I) *agg.* sporco, annerito; osceno; (*bot.*) affetto dal carbone.

snack (snăk) *n.* spuntino, porzione, assaggio.

snaffle (snăf''l) *n.* morso semplice (*del cavallo*).

snafu (snă-fōō') (*gergo*) *n.* guazzabuglio, confusione. *vt.* ingarbugliare, scompigliare. *agg.* ingarbugliato, in uno stato di confusione.

snag (snăg) *n.* nodo; ramo conficcato sott'acqua; ostacolo; moncone. *vt.* ostruire, ostacolare.

snail (snāl) *n.* lumaca, chiocciola.

snake (snăk) *n.* serpente: — charmer, incantatore di serpenti. *vi.* serpeggiare.

snap (snăp) *n.* rottura, schianto; chiusura a scatto, scatto, schiocco; morso; vivacità, energia: not to care a —, infischiarsene. *vt.*, *vi.* addentare, tentare di mordere; scattare, chiudere con un colpo secco; spezzare, spezzarsi; schioccare (*le dita*); ribattere, redarguire: to — one's fingers at, ridersi di.

snapdragon (snăp'drăg'ŭn) *n.* (*bot.*) bocca di leone.

snappish (snăp'Ish) *agg.* brusco, secco, irascibile.

snappy (snăp'I) *agg.* crepitante; mordace; rapido; vivace: make it —! sbrigati!

snapshot (snap'shŏt) *n.* (*fot.*) istantanea.

snare (snâr) *n.* trappola, agguato, insidia. *vt.* prendere in trappola, insidiare.

snarl (snärl) (1) *n.* groviglio; nodo (*del legno*); complicazione. *vt.* aggrovigliare, ingarbugliare. *vi.* aggrovigliarsi.

snarl (snärl) (2) *n.* ringhio. *vi.* ringhiare, brontolare.

snarling *agg.* ringhioso.

snatch (snăch) *n.* presa, strattone; brano, frammento; attimo. *vt.*, *vi.* afferrare, agguantare, ghermire; aggrapparsi a.

sneak (snēk) *n.* ladruncolo; spia; persona abietta. *vi.* strisciare, intrufolarsi, sgattaiolare; far la spia.

sneaker *n.* persona subdola.

sneakers *n. pl.* scarpe da ginnastica.

sneaky *agg.* subdolo, furtivo.

sneer (snēr) *n.* sogghigno, risata di scherno, sarcasmo. *vt.*, *vi.* irridere, deridere, sogghignare.

sneering *agg.* beffardo.

sneeze (snēz) *n.* starnuto. *vi.* starnutire.

snicker (snĭk'ĕr) *vedi* snigger.

sniff (snĭf) *n.* fiutata, zaffata (*di profumo, ecc.*). *vt.*, *vi.* aspirare rumorosamente, fiutare, tirare su col naso; piagnucolare: to — at, annusare; disprezzare.

sniffle (snĭf''l) *vi.* moccicare; piagnucolare; tirar su col naso.

snigger (snĭg'ĕr) *n.* risatina soffocata. *vi.* ridacchiare.

snip (snĭp) *n.* taglio, forbiciata; pezzetto, ritaglio; persona insignificante. *vt.*, *vi.* tagliare, tagliuzzare.

snipe (snĭp) *n.* beccaccino. *vi.* sparare in appostamento.

snitch (snĭch) (*gergo*) *n.* spia, traditore. *vt.* rubare. *vi.* fare la spia.

snivel (snĭv''l) *n.* moccio; singhiozzo. *vi.* moccicare; piagnucolare; tirar su col naso.

snob (snŏb) *n.* snob, villano rifatto. —bish *agg.* da snob, pretenzioso. —bery, —bishness *n.* snobismo.

snoop (snōōp) *n.* spia, ficcanaso. *vi.* spiare, curiosare.

snoot (snōōt) *n.* (*gergo*) naso.

snooze (snōōz) *n.* sonnellino: to take a —, fare un pisolino. *vi.* sonnecchiare.

snore (snōr) *n.* (il) russare. *vi.* russare.

snort (snōrt) *n.* sbuffata. *vi.* sbuffare.

snout (snout) *n.* muso, proboscide; naso; beccuccio (*di recipiente*).

snow (snō) *n.* neve. *vi.* nevicare: it is snowing, nevica; to be snowed under, essere sommerso dalla neve.

snowball (snō'bôl') *n.* palla di neve. *vt.* colpire con palle di neve. *vi.* fare alle palle di neve; (*S.U.*) aumentare a ritmo accelerato.

snowdrift (snō'drift') *n.* bufera (o cumulo) di neve.

snowfall (snō'fôl') *n.* nevicata.

snowflake (snō'flāk') *n.* fiocco di neve.

snowplow (snō'plou') *n.* spazzaneve.

snowstorm (snō'stôrm') *n.* bufera di neve.

snowy (snō'I) *agg.* nevoso; candido, niveo.

snub (snŭb) *n.* affronto, rimprovero, rabbuffo. *agg.* camuso; all'insù: — nose, naso camuso. *vt.* rimproverare, umiliare, mortificare; frenare.

snuff (snŭf) *n.* tabacco da naso, fiutata; presa (*di tabacco*); zaffata; smoccolatura (*di candela*). *vt.*, *vi.* smoccolare (*la candela*); fiutare.

snuffbox (snŭf'bŏks') n. tabacchiera.

snuffle (snŭf''l) n. fiutata. vt., vi. respirare (o fiutare) rumorosamente; naseggiare.

snug (snŭg) agg. comodo; nascosto; compatto; riparato. vi. rannicchiarsi, accomodarsi.

snuggle (snŭg''l) vi. rannicchiarsi.

snugly (snŭg'lI) avv. comodamente, a proprio agio.

snugness (snŭg'nIs) n. comodità, agio.

so (sō) avv., cong. così, quindi, di modo che, perciò; talmente, tanto: — and — on (opp. forth), e così via; — as to, in modo da; — much, tanto; — many, tanti; — far, sin qui, sinora; —— , così così, passabilmente; Mr. — and —, il signor Tal-dei-Tali; — much the better, tanto meglio; — that, di modo che; an hour or —, un'ora circa; I think —, credo di sì; is that —? ah, sì?, ma davvero?

soak (sōk) n. imbibizione, bagnata, immersione; (gergo) pugno; beone, bevuta; pegno; costo eccessivo. vt. inzuppare, assorbire, immergere; (gergo) ubriacare, bere all'eccesso; percuotere; far pagare; impregnare. vi. inzupparsi, filtrare: to be soaked through, essere bagnato sino al midollo.

soap (sōp) n. sapone: — bubble, bolla di sapone; — dish, portasapone; — opera, (radio, TV) commedia a puntate (offerta da una ditta commerciale). vt. insaponare.

soapbark (sōp'bärk') n. saponaria.

soapstone (sōp'stōn') n. steatite.

soapsuds (sōp'sŭdz') n. pl. saponata.

soapy (sōp'I) agg. saponoso.

soar (sōr) vi. prendere lo slancio; librarsi; salire, prender quota.

sob (sŏb) n. singhiozzo, singulto: —-stuff, scritto (o film) lacrimogeno; vi. singhiozzare.

sober (sō'bĕr) agg. sobrio, moderato; lucido; serio, calmo; non ubriaco: to be —, avere la mente lucida, non essere ubriaco. vt. far passare l'ubriachezza a; calmare, placare; disilludere. vi. rinsavire, calmarsi; divenir serio o lucido; smaltire la sbornia. —ly avv. sobriamente, seriamente, con calma.

sobriety (sō-brī'ĕ-tĬ) n. sobrietà, calma, moderazione, serietà, lucidità.

sobriquet (sō'brĬ-kā) n. soprannome.

so-called agg. cosiddetto.

soccer (sŏk'ĕr) n. (giuoco del) calcio.

sociable (sō'shá-b'l) n. riunione. agg. socievole, cordiale.

social (sō'shál) n. riunione. agg. sociale, di società; socievole.

socialism (sō'shál-Ĭzm) n. socialismo.

socialist (-Ĭst) n. socialista.

socialite (-Ĭt) n. (S.U.) persona del bel mondo.

society (sō-sī'ĕ-tĬ) n. società.

sociology (sō'sĬ-ŏl'ō-jĬ) n. sociologia.

sock (sŏk) (1) n. calzino, calzettone.

sock (sŏk) (2) n. (gergo) pugno. vt. dare un pugno a.

socket (sŏk'ĕt) n. alveolo, cavità; portalampada; orbita (dell'occhio).

sod (sŏd) n. zolla, tappeto erboso. vt. coprire di zolle.

soda (sō'dá) n. soda: — fountain, spaccio di bibite; — water, acqua gasata; baking —, bicarbonato di soda; — jerk (gergo). gelataio, venditore di bibite analcooliche.

sodden (sŏd''n) agg. inzuppato, impregnato; ubriaco, tumefatto; ebete, ottuso.

sodium (sō'dĬ-ŭm) n. (chim.) sodio.

sofa (sō'fá) n. sofà, divano: — bed, divano-letto.

soft (sŏft) agg. molle, morbido, tenero; debole, dolce, sommesso: — drink, bibita analcoolica; — water, acqua dolce; —-boiled egg, uovo à la coque. avv. vedi softly.

soften (sŏf'ĕn) vt. addolcire, ammorbidire, lenire, ammansire; fiaccare, indebolire. vi. ammorbidirsi, rammollirsi, addolcirsi, placarsi, intenerirsi.

softening n. ammorbidimento, indebolimento, intenerimento: — of the brain, rammollimento cerebrale.

softly (sŏft'lĬ) avv. mollemente, dolcemente, sommessamente; adagio.

softness (sŏf'nĕs) n. morbidezza, delicatezza, dolcezza; facilità.

soft-pedal n. pedale del piano, sordina. vt., vi. attenuare, moderare; abbassare il tono.

soft-soap n. adulazione. vt. adulare.

soft-spoken agg. blando, persuasivo.

soggy (sŏg'Ĭ) agg. inzuppato.

soil (soil) n. macchia, sudiciume; fango; letame; terra, suolo, terreno. vt. sporcare, infangare, profanare; concimare.

sojourn (sō'jûrn) n. soggiorno. vi. soggiornare.

solace (sŏl'Ĭs) n. consolazione, sollievo. vt. consolare, confortare.

solar (sō'lĕr) agg. solare.

sold (sōld) pass., pp. di sell: to be — on, essere convinto di.

solder (sŏd'ĕr) n. saldatura. vt., vi. saldare, saldarsi.

soldier (sōl'jĕr) n. soldato.

sole (sōl) (1) *agg.* solo, unico, singolo; esclusivo; non coniugato.

sole (sōl) (2) *n.* sogliola.

sole (sōl) (3) *n.* pianta (*del piede*), suola (*di scarpa*); fondo, base. *vt.* solare, risolare.

solely (sōl′li) *avv.* solamente, esclusivamente, puramente.

solemn (sŏl′ĕm) *agg.* solenne, serio. —ity (sō·lĕm′nĭ·tĭ) *n.* solennità; ricorrenza.

solicit (sō·lĭs′ĭt) *vt.*, *vi.* sollecitare, importunare; far la piazza.

solicitor (sō·lĭs′ĭ·tẽr) *n.* propagandista; (*ingl.*) procuratore, avvocato.

solicitous (sō·lĭs′ĭ·tŭs) *agg.* sollecito; desideroso, ansioso.

solicitude (sō·lĭs′ĭ·tūd) *n.* sollecitudine; ansia.

solid (sŏl′ĭd) *n.* solido. *agg.* solido, intiero; massiccio, compatto, concreto; unanime; serio; solvibile: — red, rosso unito; — gold, oro massiccio; for one — hour, per un'ora intiera.

solidarity (sŏl′ĭ·dăr′ĭ·tĭ) *n.* solidarietà.

solidify (sō·lĭd′ĭ·fĭ) *vt.* solidificare. *vi.* solidificarsi.

solidity (sō·lĭd′ĭ·tĭ) *n.* solidità.

soliloquy (sō·lĭl′ō·kwĭ) *n.* soliloquio.

solitaire (sŏl′ĭ·târ′) *n.* solitario (*brillante e giuoco di carte*).

solitary (sŏl′ĭ·tẽr′ĭ) *agg.* solitario, isolato; unico, solo: — confinement, segregazione cellulare.

solitude (sŏl′ĭ·tūd) *n.* solitudine.

solo (sō′lō) *n.* (*mus.*) assolo.

soloist (sō′lō·ĭst) *n.* (*mus.*) solista.

Solomonic (sŏl′ō·mŏn′ĭk) *agg.* salomonico.

solstice (sŏl′stĭs) *n.* solstizio.

soluble (sŏl′ū·b′l) *agg.* solubile.

solution (sō·lū′shŭn) *n.* soluzione.

solvable (sŏl′vȧ·b′l) *agg.* solubile.

solve (sŏlv) *vt.* risolvere, spiegare; sciogliere.

solvency (sŏl′vĕn·sĭ) *n.* solvibilità.

solvent (sŏl′vĕnt) *n.* (*chim.*) solvente; *agg.* solvente; (*comm.*) solvibile.

somber, sombre (sŏm′bẽr) *agg.* fosco, scuro, tenebroso, cupo.

some (sŭm) *agg.*, *pron.* partitivo qualche, qualcuno, alcuni; ne, un po' di, del, della, delle, dei: — thirty years ago, circa trent'anni fa. *avv.* circa, all'incirca.

somebody (sŭm′bŏd′ĭ) *n.*, *pron.* qualcuno: — else, qualcun altro.

somehow (sŭm′hou) *avv.* chissà come, in qualche modo, in certo qual modo: — or other, in un modo o nell'altro, per questo o quel motivo.

someone (sŭm′wŭn) *n.*, *pron.* qualcuno.

somersault (sŭm′ẽr·sôlt) *n.* capriola, salto mortale: to turn somersaults, far salti mortali.

something (sŭm′thĭng) *n.* qualche cosa, qualcosa: — else, qualcos'altro; *avv.* alquanto, piuttosto, un po'.

sometime (sŭm′tĭm′) *agg.* passato, già, ex, d'altri tempi: my — general, il mio ex generale. *avv.* un tempo, una volta o l'altra, a qualche ora, uno di questi giorni.

sometimes (sŭm′tĭmz′) *avv.* a volte, qualche volta, di quando in quando.

somewhat (sŭm′hwŏt′) *n.* qualche cosa. *avv.* alquanto, un poco.

somewhere (sŭm′hwâr′) *avv.* da qualche parte, in qualche luogo: — else, altrove; — about, all'incirca.

somnolence (sŏm′nō·lĕns) *n.* sonnolenza.

somnolent (sŏm′nō·lĕnt) *agg.* sonnolente.

son (sŭn) *n.* figlio.

son-in-law *n.* genero.

song (sŏng) *n.* canto, canzone: to buy something for a —, comprare qualcosa a prezzo irrisorio.

sonnet (sŏn′ĕt) *n.* sonetto.

sonorous (sō·nō′rŭs) *agg.* sonoro.

soon (sōōn) *avv.* presto, ben presto, subito: as — as, non appena; as — as possible, il più presto possibile; how —? quando?; — after, subito dopo.

sooner *avv.* più presto: — or later, presto o tardi; — than, piuttosto che.

soot (sōōt) *n.* fuliggine.

soothe (sōōth) *vt.* placare, alleviare, blandire.

soothing (sōōth′ĭng) *agg.* calmante, dolce, consolante; adulatore.

soothsayer (sōōth′sā′ẽr) *n.* profeta, indovino.

sooty (sōōt′ĭ) *agg.* fuligginoso, nero.

sop (sŏp) *n.* pezzo di pane (*ecc.*) inzuppato; dono (*per placare o corrompere*). *vt.* inzuppare, assorbire; *vi.* inzupparsi: sopping wet, bagnato sino alle ossa.

sophomore (sŏf′ō·mōr) *n.* (*univ.*) studente di secondo anno.

soporific (sŏp′ō·rĭf′ĭk) *agg.* soporifero.

sopping (sŏp′ĭng) *agg.* inzuppato.

soprano (sō·prä′nō) *n.* soprano; parte per soprano; voce da soprano.

sorcerer (sôr′sẽr·ẽr) *n.* stregone, mago.

sorceress (sôr′sẽr·ĕs) *n.* strega; maga.

sorcery (sôr′sẽr·ĭ) *n.* sortilegio, magia.

sordid (sôr′dĭd) *agg.* sordido, abietto.

sore (sōr) *n.* piaga, ulcera; male, dolore. *agg.* infiammato, doloroso, dolente, indolenzito; offeso, sdegnato, imbronciato; grave, violento: — eyes, male agli occhi; — throat, mal di gola; to be — at, essere risentito con; to make —, irritare; a sight for — eyes, una vista rincuorante. —ly avv. dolorosamente, gravemente; fortemente: you are sorely mistaken, vi sbagliate di grosso. —ness n. indolenzimento, dolore; amarezza, rancore.

sorrel (sŏr'ĕl) n. cavallo sauro; agg. sauro.

sorrow (sŏr'ō) n. angoscia, pena, tristezza, rincrescimento. vi. affliggersi, affannarsi, addolorarsi. —ful agg. triste, afflitto, doloroso. —fully avv. penosamente, tristemente, dolorosamente.

sorry (sŏr'ĭ) agg. dolente, triste, meschino, doloroso; miserabile, deplorevole: I am —, scusatemi, mi dispiace; I am — for him, mi rincresce per lui, mi fa pena.

sort (sŏrt) n. sorta, specie, genere, classe: of sorts, mediocre, di genere imprecisato; out of sorts, indisposto; di malumore; all sorts of people, gente di ogni genere. vt. scegliere, classificare, selezionare, riordinare.

sot (sŏt) n. ubriacone.

sought (sŏt) pass., pp. di to seek.

soul (sōl) n. anima: All Soul's Day, il giorno dei morti; not a —, neppure un'anima.

soulful (sōl'fŏŏl) agg. ascetico, spirituale.

sound (sound) (1) n. stretto, braccio di mare; (med.) sonda. vt., vi. sondare, scandagliare, indagare.

sound (sound) (2) n. suono, rumore: — track (cinema), colonna sonora; — wave (radio), onda sonora; — barrier (aeron.), muro del suono. vt., vi. sonare; proclamare; risonare; sembrare; avere il tono di.

sound (sound) (3) agg. solido, sano, saldo; saggio, logico, fondato: safe and —, sano e salvo; — sleep, sonno profondo.

soundless agg. silenzioso, muto.

soundness n. saldezza, solidità; rettitudine, giustezza, saggezza; salute.

soundproof (sound'prōōf') agg. antisonoro.

soup (sōōp) n. minestra, zuppa.

sour (sour) agg. agro, acido, acerbo, aspro; arcigno: to turn —, inacidire. vt. rendere agro, far inacidire, inasprire, irritare. vi. inacidire; inasprirsi, irritarsi.

source (sŏrs) n. fonte, origine.

sourness (sour'nĕs) n. acidità; acrimonia.

souse (sous) n. salamoia, viveri in salamoia. vt. marinare, immergere, inzuppare.

south (south) n. sud, mezzogiorno. agg. del sud, meridionale, australe: the South Sea, l'Oceano Pacifico; the — pole, il polo sud.

southeast (south''ĕst') n. sud-est. agg. di sud-est.

southeastern (south'ĕs'tĕrn) agg. sud-orientale.

southern (sŭth'ĕrn) agg. meridionale, del sud: the Southern Cross, la Croce del Sud.

southward (south'wĕrd) avv. a sud, verso sud.

southwest (south'wĕst') n., agg. sud-ovest. di sud-ovest.

southwestern (south'wĕs'tĕrn) agg. sud-occidentale.

souvenir (sōō'vĕ-nēr') n. pegno, ricordo.

sovereign (sŏv'ĕr-ĭn) n., agg. sovrano.

sovereignty (sŏv'ĕr-ĭn-tĭ) n. sovranità.

soviet (sō'vĭ-ĕt) agg. sovietico: the Soviet, la Repubblica Sovietica.

sow (sou) (1) n. scrofa.

sow (sō) (2) vt., vi. (pass. sowed, pp. sowed o sown) seminare, disseminare, sparpagliare.

soy (soi) n. (bot.) soia.

spa (spä) n. sorgente minerale.

space (spās) n. spazio, intervallo. vt. spazieggiare, spaziare. agg. spaziale, interspaziale: — station, stazione spaziale; — ship, astronave.

spacious (spā'shŭs) agg. spazioso, vasto.

spade (spād) n. vanga, pala; spades, spade o picche (nelle carte di giuoco); to call a — a —, dir pane al pane; vt. vangare.

span (spän) n. spanna, palmo; portata; apertura (di un arco); apertura d'ala; luce (di ponte); lasso di tempo; pariglia: life —, durata della vita. vt. misurare a spanne, abbracciare, attraversare.

spangle (spăng'g'l) n. pagliuzza, lustrino. vt. ornare di lustrini; vi. luccicare: the Star-Spangled Banner, la Bandiera Stellata, la Bandiera degli S.U.

Spaniard (spän'yĕrd) n. spagnuolo.

spaniel (spän'yĕl) n. spaniel (cane da caccia).

Spanish (spän'ĭsh) n., agg. spagnuolo.

spank (spăngk) n. sculacciata; vt. sculacciare.

spanker n. (naut.) vela di randa.

spanking n. sculacciatura. agg. vigoroso; straordinario; sferzante.

spanner (spăn'ĕr) *n.* chiave inglese.
spar (spär) *n.* palo, stanga; (*naut.*) albero, pennone; (*aeron.*) longarone. *vi.* fare la box, battersi; discutere.
spare (spār) *n.* pezzo di ricambio. *agg.* disponibile, superfluo, di avanzo; scarso; frugale; magro; economo: di ricambio: — time, ritagli di tempo; — parts, pezzi di ricambio. *vt.* risparmiare; tralasciare; tenere in serbo; esentare; riservare: I cannot — another dollar, non posso spendere un altro dollaro; I cannot — my car today, oggi non posso restare senza la macchina; to — no expense, non badare a spese; *vi.* fare economia: to have no time to —, non aver tempo da perdere; enough and to —, più che a sufficienza.
sparing (spār'ing) *agg.* economo, frugale.
spark (spärk) *n.* scintilla, favilla; luccichìo: — plug (*auto.*), candela. *vi.* scintillare, mandar faville.
sparkle (spär'k'l) *n.* scintilla, scintillio; vivacità; effervescenza. *vi.* scintillare; essere effervescente; luccicare.
sparkling *agg.* scintillante; spumeggiante; vivace: — wine, vino spumante.
sparrow (spăr'ō) *n.* passero, passerotto.
sparse (spärs) *agg.* raro, rado; scarso; sparpagliato.
spasm (spăz'm) *n.* contrazione, accesso, spasmo spasimo.
spat (spăt) (1) *pass., pp.* di to spit.
spat (spăt) (2) *n.* uova di mollusco.
spat (spăt) (3) *n.* battibecco; colpo; schiaffetto, scappellotto. *vt., vi.* scappellottare, bisticciare.
spat (spăt) (4) *n.* ghetta.
spatial (spā'shăl) *agg.* spaziale.
spatter (spăt'ĕr) *n.* spruzzo, schizzo; picchiettio. *vt.* spruzzare, aspergere; picchiettare.
spatula (spăt'û.lá) *n.* spatola.
spawn (spôn) *n.* uova di pesce; progenie.
speak (spēk) *vt., vi.* (*pass.* spoke, *pp.* spoken) dire, denotare, parlare: to — one's mind, dire il proprio parere; so to —, per così dire; to — up (*o* out), parlare ad alta voce, parlare francamente; to — up for, parlare in favore di; to — for, parlare a nome di.
speaker *n.* chi parla; interlocutore; oratore; (*radio*) annunziatore.
spear (spēr) (1) *n.* germoglio, stelo.
spear (spēr) (2) *n.* lancia, giavellotto;

fiocina. *vt.* trafiggere; arpionare, fiocinare.
spearfish (spēr'fĭsh') *vi.* fare pesca subacquea. —ing *n.* pesca subacquea.
speargun *n.* fucile subacqueo.
spearhead (spēr'hĕd') *n.* punta di lancia; (*fig.*) araldo. *vt.* mettersi all' avanguardia di.
spearmint (spēr'mĭnt') *n.* (*bot.*) menta.
special (spĕsh'ăl) *n.* cosa (*o* persona, *o* treno) speciale; edizione straordinaria. *agg.* speciale, particolare, straordinario.
specialist (spĕsh'ăl.ĭst) *n.* specialista.
speciality (spĕsh'ĭ.ăl'ĭ.tĭ) *n.* specialità, particolarità; (*pl.*) particolari.
specialize (spĕsh'ăl.īz) *vi.* specializzarsi.
specially (spĕsh'ăl.lĭ) *avv.* specialmente, particolarmente, soprattutto.
specialty (spĕsh'ăl.tĭ) *n.* specialità; carattere distintivo, particolarità.
specie (spē'shĭ) *n.* valuta metallica.
species (spē'shĭz) *n.* (*pl.* species) specie, sorta, classe, genere.
specific (spĕ.sĭf'ĭk) *n.* specifico, rimedio. *agg.* specifico, particolare, preciso, caratteristico: — gravity, peso specifico. —ally *avv.* specificamente, particolarmente.
specify (spĕs'ĭ.fī) *vt., vi.* specificare.
specimen (spĕs'ĭ.mĕn) *n.* campione, esemplare, saggio, modello.
speck (spĕk) *n.* macchiolina, puntino, bruscolo. *vt. vedi* speckle.
speckle (spĕk''l) *n.* chiazza, segno, macchiolina. *vt.* chiazzare, macchiettare.
speckled *agg.* chiazzato, macchiettato: — with freckles, lentigginoso.
spectacle (spĕk'tà.k'l) *n.* spettacolo; vista: spectacled, occhialuto; spectacles, occhiali.
spectacular (spĕk.tăk'û.lĕr) *agg.* spettacoloso; teatrale; sensazionale.
spectator (spĕk.tā'tĕr) *n.* spettatore.
spectral (spĕk'trăl) *agg.* spettrale.
spectre (spĕk'tĕr) *n.* spettro.
spectrum (spĕk'trŭm) *n.* (*fis.*) spettro.
speculate (spĕk'û.lāt) *vi.* speculare; meditare.
speculation (spĕk'û.lā'shŭn) *n.* speculazione, meditazione.
speculative (spĕk'û.lā'tĭv) *agg.* speculativo; meditativo; teorico.
speculator (spĕk'û.lā'tĕr) *n.* speculatore.
sped (spĕd) *pass., pp.* di to speed.
speech (spēch) *n.* discorso; linguaggio, eloquio, parlata.

speechless *n.* ammutolito, muto. **—ly** *avv.* senza parola, mutamente.

speed (spĕd) *n.* velocità, rapidità; fretta, prontezza: **at full —**, a tutta velocità; **— limit**, velocità massima. *vt., vi. (pass., pp.* **sped**) affrettare, accelerare; incrementare; affrettarsi, passare in fretta, correre; eccedere in velocità.

speedily (spĕd'ĭ-lĭ) *avv.* velocemente, alacremente, prontamente.

speeding (spĕd'ĭng) *n.* eccesso di velocità.

speedometer (spĕd·ŏm'ĕ·tĕr) *n.* tachimetro.

speedway (spĕd'wā) *n.* autostrada.

speedy (spĕd'ĭ) *agg.* rapido, svelto; spiccio.

spell (spĕl) *n.* incantesimo, magia, incanto; periodo; accesso; intervallo, turno di lavoro. *vt., vi. (pass., pp.* spelled *o* spelt) rimpiazzare, dare il cambio a; compitare, sillabare; significare; preannunziare: **how do you — it?** come si scrive? **— it, please**, ditemi come si scrive, per favore; **to — out**, spiegare chiaramente.

spellbinder (spĕl'bĭn'dĕr) *n. (S.U.)* affascinatore.

spellbound (spĕl'bound') *agg.* incantato, affascinato; ammutolito.

speller (spĕlĕr) *n.* chi compita; sillabario.

spelling *n.* compitazione, ortografia: **— book**, sillabario; **the — of this word is . . .**, questa parola si scrive così . . .

spelunker (spĕ·lŭngk'ĕr) *n. (fam.)* speleologo.

spend (spĕnd) *vt., vi. (pass., pp.* spent) spendere, sprecare; esaurire; consumare; trascorrere, impiegare; consumarsi, esaurirsi.

spendthrift (spĕnd'thrĭft') *n.* prodigo, scialacquatore.

spent (spĕnt) *pass., pp. di* to spend; *agg.* esaurito, esausto.

spew (spū) *vt., vi.* vomitare.

sphere (sfēr) *n.* sfera; àmbito.

spherical (sfĕr'ĭ·k* al*) *agg.* sferico.

sphinx (sfĭngks) *n.* sfinge.

spice (spīs) *n.* spezie, droga, aroma. *vt.* condire con spezie, aromatizzare.

spick-and-span (spĭk'ănd·spăn') *agg.* nuovo di zecca; in perfetto ordine; lustro e ordinato.

spicy (spīs'ĭ) *agg.* pepato, aromatico, piccante.

spider (spī'dĕr) *n.* ragno. **—web** *n.* ragnatela.

spigot (spĭg'ŭt) *n.* zipolo, rubinetto.

spike (spīk) *n.* punta, aculeo, chiodo;

spiga. *vt.* inchiodare, chiodare; trafiggere; frustrare, stroncare.

spill (spĭl) *n.* versamento, zampillo, spruzzo; sfioratore *(di diga, ecc.)*; caduta; zipolo. *vt. (pass., pp.* spilled *o* spilt) versare, spandere; disarcionare, buttar giù; *(gergo)* confessare, rivelare. *vi.* rovesciarsi, riversarsi; confessare, "cantare."

spin (spĭn) *n.* rotazione, corsa; *(aeron.)* vite. *vt., vi. (pass.* spun, *pp.* spun) filare; far la tela *(dei ragni)*; arrotolare, attorcigliare; far girare, girare, torcersi, roteare; passare velocemente: **to — a yarn**, farla lunga.

spinach (spĭn'ĭch) *n.* spinaci.

spinal (spī'nal) *agg.* spinale: **— column**, colonna vertebrale; **— cord**, midollo spinale.

spindle (spĭn'd'l) *n.* fuso, perno.

spine (spĭn) *n.* spina, aculeo; spina dorsale.

spinet (spĭn'ĕt) *n. (mus.)* spinetta.

spinner (spĭn'ĕr) *n.* filatore, filatrice *(macchina)*.

spinning (spĭn'ĭng) *n.* filatura: **— jenny**, filatoio; **— mill**, filanda; **— top**, trottola; **— wheel**, filatoio.

spinster (spĭn'stĕr) *n.* zitella.

spinstress (spĭn'strĕs) *n.* filatrice.

spiral (spī'ral) *n.* spirale. *agg.* a spirale: **— staircase**, scala a chiocciola.

spire (spīr) *n.* cima, cuspide; guglia; campanile; stelo.

spirit (spĭr'ĭt) *n.* spirito, forza, vigore, coraggio; alcool; vivacità: **low spirits**, malumore, abbattimento; **good spirits**, buon umore; **to be out of spirits**, essere di malumore. *vt.*: **to — off** *(o away)*, portar via, rapire.

spirited (spĭr'ĭ·tĕd) *agg.* coraggioso; brioso.

spiritless (spĭr'ĭt·lĕs) *agg.* scoraggiato, abbattuto.

spiritual (spĭr'ĭ·tŭ·al) *n.* canto mistico *(spec. dei negri am.)*. *agg.* spirituale.

spiritualism (spĭr'ĭ·tŭ·al·ĭz'm) *n.* spiritismo.

spirituous (spĭr'ĭ·tŭ·ŭs) *agg.* alcoolico.

spit (spĭt) (1) *n.* penisoletta, capo; spiedo. *vt.* infilzare sullo spiedo, trafiggere.

spit (spĭt) (2) *n.* sputo, saliva, spruzzo di pioggia, breve nevicata. *vt., vi. (pass.* spat, *pp.* spit) sputare, sputacchiare; piovigginare.

spite (spīt) *n.* dispetto, rancore, astio: **in — of**, a dispetto di, nonostante; **out of —**, per dispetto. *vt.* indispettire, vessare, contrariare.

spiteful (spīt'fŏŏl) agg. astioso, dispettoso, ostile.

spittoon (spĭ·tōōn') n. sputacchiera.

splash (splǎsh) n. chiazza, pillacchera,
spruzzo; tonfo. vt. schizzare, chiazzare, inzaccherare. vi. diguazzare,
spruzzare.

splay (splā) agg. sguancio; sbilenco.
vt. sguanciare; slogare.

spleen (splĕn) n. (anat.) milza; malinconia, umor nero.

splendid (splĕn'dĭd) agg. splendido.

splendor (splĕn'dĕr) n. splendore.

splice (splīs) n. (naut.) implombatura;
(carp.) calettatura. vt. implombare;
calettare.

splint (splĭnt) n. stecca, asticciola. vt.
steccare.

splinter (splĭn'tĕr) n. scheggia, stecca.
vt. scheggiare, ridurre in schegge.
vi. scheggiarsi, frantumarsi.

split (splĭt) n. fessura, fenditura;
scissione, separazione; splits, spac-
cata (movimento coreografico). agg.
diviso, spaccato; sdoppiato. vt.
(pass., pp. split) fendere, dividere;
sdoppiare, scindere; staccare; distribuire. vi. spaccarsi, fendersi,
separarsi: to — hairs, sottilizzare;
to — asunder, spaccare in due; to
— the difference, dividere il male a
metà; to — one's sides with laughter, sbellicarsi dalle risa; —ting agg.
lacerante, violento.

splotch (splŏch) n. chiazza.

splurge (splûrj) n. (gergo) ostentazione, sfarzo.

splutter (splŭt'ĕr) vedi sputter.

spoil (spoil) n. bottino, preda. vt.
(pass., pp. spoiled o spoilt) spogliare, rovinare, guastare, viziare;
vi. deperire, guastarsi, sciuparsi.

spoke (spōk) (1) pp. di to speak.

spoke (spōk) (2) n. razza (o raggio) di
ruota; piuolo.

spoken (spō'kĕn) pp. di to speak; agg.
orale, parlato: English is — here,
(qui) si parla l'inglese.

spokesman (spōks'mǎn) n. oratore,
portavoce, relatore.

spoliation (spō'lĭ·ā·shǔn) n. spogliazione, saccheggio.

sponge (spǔnj) n. spugna, spugnatura: — cake, torta Margherita.
vt., vi. assorbire (o lavare) con la
spugna; scroccare, vivere a scrocco.

sponger (spǔn'jĕr) n. beone; parassita, scroccone.

spongy (spǔn'jĭ) agg. spugnoso, poroso.

sponsor (spǒn'sĕr) n. padrino, madrina; garante; patrocinatore, promotore; cliente abituale; (S.U.)
ditta che offre trasmissioni radio-
foniche (per pubblicità). vt. patro-

cinare, promuovere; garantire per;
essere cliente assiduo di.

spontaneity (spŏn'tá·nē'ĭ·tĭ) n. spontaneità.

spontaneous (spŏn·tā'nē·ŭs) agg. spontaneo.

spoof (spōōf) vt. (gergo) imbrogliare.

spook (spōōk) n. fantasma.

spool (spōōl) n. rocchetto, bobina.
vt. incannare (filati).

spoon (spōōn) n. cucchiaio, cucchiaino. vt., vi. raccogliere col cucchiaio;
pescare col cucchiaino.

spoonful (spōōn'fŏŏl) n. cucchiaiata.

sporadic (spŏ·rǎd'ĭk) agg. sporadico.

sport (spōrt) n. sport, giuoco; svago,
piacere, passatempo; scherzo;
(fam.) bontempone; amico; (biol.)
anomalia: to be a good —, essere
condiscendente, prenderla con spirito; to make — of, prendersi
giuoco di; to be the — of, essere lo
zimbello di. vt., vi. divertire; ostentare, sfoggiare; divertirsi, scherzare, dedicarsi allo sport: to — a
new hat, sfoggiare un cappello
nuovo; to — a roll of money, ostentare ricchezza.

sports agg. sportivo: — clothes, abiti
sportivi, abbigliamento sportivo.

sportsman (spōrts'mǎn) n. sportivo;
buon giocatore; vero signore.

sportswoman (spōrts'wŏŏm'ǎn) n.f.
sportiva.

sporty (spōr'tĭ) agg. sportivo, da sportivo; spendaccione; volgare, appariscente, ricercato.

spot (spŏt) n. macchia, punto, puntino, chiazza; luogo; goccia, sorso:
on the —, immediatamente; sul
luogo. vt. macchiare, chiazzare;
scoprire, individuare, scorgere.

spotless agg. immacolato.

spotted agg. macchiato, chiazzato.

spouse (spous) n. sposo, sposa.

spout (spout) n. condotto, tubo di
scarico, fontana, grondaia; becco
(di brocca, ecc.). vt., vi. versare, far
scaturire; declamare, concionare;
sgorgare, zampillare.

sprain (sprān) n. storta, distorsione.
vt. storcere, slogare: to — one's
ankle, slogarsi una caviglia.

sprang (sprǎng) pass. di to spring.

sprawl (sprôl) n. scarabocchio; posa
scomposta. vi. sdraiarsi (o sedersi)
scompostamente; scarabocchiare:
to send someone sprawling, mandare qualcuno lungo disteso.

spray (sprā) n. frasca, ramoscello;
spruzzo (dei marosi), spuma (di
mare); raffica (di proiettili); spruzzatore. vt., vi. spruzzare, annaffiare; vaporizzare.

spread (sprĕd) *n.* distesa, estensione; festa, festino; coperta da letto, tappeto da tavola; diffusione; sostanza da spalmare; sfoggio; (*aeron.*) apertura d'ale. *vt.*, *vi.* (*pass., pp.* spread) estendere, spandere; spalmare; divulgare, diffondere; stendere, spiegare (*una vela*), allargare; estendersi; spalmarsi; diffondersi: to — apart, aprirsi, divaricarsi; to — butter, spalmare burro; to — out the tablecloth, stendere la tovaglia; to — with, spalmare di, ungere di.

spree (sprē) *n.* orgia, scappata, baldoria: to go on a —, andare in bagordi.

sprig (sprĭg) *n.* ramoscello.

sprightly (sprīt'lĭ) *agg.* vivace, animato, allegro, brioso.

spring (sprĭng) *n.* primavera; fonte, sorgente; elasticità; slancio, salto; causa, origine; molla. *vt.*, *vi.* (*pass.* sprang *o* sprung, *pp.* sprung) far sorgere; far esplodere; saltare, far saltare; molleggiare; scavalcare; far scattare; germogliare, scaturire; scagliarsi, balzare; provenire (*da*), sorgere; aprirsi, fendersi: to — at, slanciarsi contro; to — a leak, avere una falla; to — a piece of news, dare una notizia di sorpresa; to — to one's feet, balzare in piedi.

springboard (sprĭng'bôrd') *n.* trampolino.

springtide (sprĭng'tīd'), **springtime** (sprĭng'tīm') *n.* primavera.

springy (sprĭng'ĭ) *agg.* elastico.

sprinkle (sprĭng'k'l) *n.* aspersorio; spruzzata; pioggerella. *vt.* spruzzare, aspergere, cospargere. *vi.* piovigginare.

sprint (sprĭnt) *n.* scatto, slancio; gara di velocità su breve percorso. *vi.* correre a tutta velocità.

sprinter *n.* velocista.

sprite (sprīt) *n.* spirito.

sprout (sprout) *n.* germoglio, gemma: Brussels sprouts, cavolini di Brusselle; *vi.* germogliare.

spruce (sproos) (1) *n.* (*bot.*) abete.

spruce (sproos) (2) *agg.* lindo, inappuntabile, affettato. *vt.*, *vi.*: to — up, mettere (*o* mettersi) in ghingheri.

sprung (sprŭng) *pp. di* to spring.

spry (sprī) *agg.* agile, vivace.

spud (spŭd) *n.* zappetta; (*fam.*) patata.

spume (spūm) *n.* spuma, schiuma.

spun (spŭn) *pass.*, *pp. di* to spin. *agg.* filato, ritorto.

spunk (spŭngk) *n.* coraggio, foga.

spunky (spŭngk'ĭ) *agg.* coraggioso.

spur (spûr) *n.* sperone, sprone; artiglio; puntello: on the — of the moment, d'acchito, impulsivamente; to win one's spurs, far buona prova. *vt.* spronare, incitare.

spurious (spū'rĭ-ŭs) *agg.* spurio, falso.

spurn (spûrn) *vt.* respingere con sdegno, disprezzare, ripudiare.

spurt (spûrt) *n.* getto; vampata; schizzo; impeto momentaneo; scatto, volata. *vt.*, *vi.* schizzare, scaturire; compiere uno sforzo; fare una volata.

sputter (spŭt'ẽr) *n.* spruzzo; scoppiettio; balbettamento; *vt.*, *vi.* sbavare, spruzzare; balbettare, farfugliare.

sputum (spū'tŭm) *n.* sputo.

spy (spī) *n.* spia, delatore. *vt.*, *vi.* spiare, scrutare; scorgere. —**glass** *n.* cannocchiale.

squab (skwŏb) *n.* piccioncino.

squabble (skwŏb'l) *n.* bisticcio, disputa. *vi.* bisticciare.

squad (skwŏd) *n.* squadra; plotone: — car *n.* auto radio-comandata (*della polizia*).

squadron (skwŏd'rŭn) *n.* squadrone; squadra navale; (*aeron.*) stormo.

squalid (skwŏl'ĭd) *agg.* squallido.

squall (skwôl) *n.* raffica, scroscio. *vi.* soffiare a raffiche.

squalor (skwŏl'ẽr) *n.* squallore.

squander (skwŏn'dẽr) *vt.* profondere, scialacquare.

square (skwâr) *n.* quadrato, piazza; squadra da disegno; (*gergo*) gonzo, minchione, sempliciotto: on the —, in buona fede, onestamente. *agg.* quadrato, ad angolo retto; giusto, leale, esatto; saldato (*di un conto*): to get —, pareggiare i conti; — root, radice quadrata; a — refusal, un no chiaro e tondo; a — deal, un trattamento onesto, un comportamento leale; a — meal, un pasto sostanzioso. *avv. vedi* squarely. *vt.* squadrare, quadrare, regolare, pareggiare; corrompere; (*mat.*) elevare al quadrato. *vi.* quadrare, concordare; to — one's shoulders, raddrizzare le spalle. —**ly** *avv.* equamente, onestamente; precisamente, in pieno; direttamente.

squash (skwŏsh) *n.* polpa, poltiglia; urto (*di corpi molli*); caduta; (*bot.*) zucca. *vt.* schiacciare, ridurre in polpa; *vi.* spiaccicarsi.

squat (skwŏt) *agg.* tozzo, tarchiato; allargato; accoccolato. *vi.* accoccolarsi, accucciarsi, sedersi alla turca; (*S.U.*) installarsi senza diritto su un terreno. —**ter** *n.* pioniere.

squaw (skwô) *n.* donna (*o* sposa) del pellirossa.

squawk (skwôk) *n.* gracchio, gracidio. *vi.* gracchiare.

squeak (skwēk) *n.* grido rauco, stridore, gracchio. *vi.* gridare raucamente, stridere, gracchiare.

squeal (skwēl) *n.* strillo; delazione. *vt.*, *vi.* strillare; rivelare, farsi delatore.

squeamish (skwēm'ĭsh) *agg.* delicato, schizzinoso.

squeeze (skwēz) *n.* spremitura; strizzata, abbraccio; (*gergo*) estorsione. *vt.* strizzare, stringere, spremere; abbracciare strettamente; introdurre a forza. *vi.* incunearsi, insinuarsi: to — through, aprirsi faticosamente un varco.

squelch (skwĕlch) *vt.* sfracellare, annientare; tacitare: to — a revolt, soffocare una rivolta. *vi.* diguazzare.

squint (skwĭnt) *n.* occhiata obliqua, sbirciata; inclinazione; strabismo. *agg.* obliquo; strabico. *vt.*, *vi.* guardare con gli occhi socchiusi, guardare in cagnesco, sbirciare; essere strabico.

squint-eyed *agg.* strabico.

squire (skwîr) *n.* scudiero, signorotto. *vt.* scortare.

squirm (skwûrm) *vi.* contorcersi.

squirrel (skwûr'ĕl) *n.* scoiattolo.

squirt (skwûrt) *n.* spruzzo; siringa; (*fam.*) omiciattolo. *vt.*, *vi.* siringare; schizzare, zampillare.

stab (stăb) *n.* pugnalata, coltellata, stoccata. *vt.* pugnalare, accoltellare, trafiggere; punzecchiare.

stability (stă·bĭl'ĭ·tĭ) *n.* stabilità.

stabilize (stă'bĭ·līz) *vt.* stabilizzare.

stabilizer (stă'bĭ·lĭz'ĕr) *n.* stabilizzatore.

stable (stā'b'l) (1) *n.* stalla, scuderia; *vt.* mettere (o tenere) nella stalla.

stable (stā'b'l) (2) *agg.* stabile.

stack (stăk) *n.* fascio ⸱ catasta, covone, mucchio; camino, ciminiera. *vt.* affastellare ammucchiare; preparare (*le carte*) per barare.

staff (stăf) *n.* (*pl.* staffs *o* staves) bastone, asta; puntello, palo; manico; (*mus.*) pentagramma ⸱ personale (*di ufficio, ecc.*), corpo (*diplomatico*); (*mil.*) stato maggiore: editorial —, corpo redazionale; teaching —, corpo insegnante; — college, scuola militare; — officer, ufficiale di stato maggiore; — of life, sostegno della vita.

stag (stăg) *n.* cervo maschio; (*S.U.*) uomo solo. *agg.* per uomini soli.

stage (stāj) *n.* palco, palcoscenico, teatro, scena; stadio (*grado*); tappa: to go on the —, darsi alle scene;

by easy stages, a piccole tappe, con calma; landing —, pontile d'approdo; — box, palco di proscenio; —coach, diligenza, corriera; — director, regista teatrale; — door, entrata al palcoscenico; — hand (*teat.*) attrezzista; — manager, direttore di scena. *vt.* inscenare.

stagger (stăg'ĕr) *n.* barcollamento, vacillamento. *vt.* far vacillare, scuotere, sconcertare, sbalordire. *vi.* barcollare, esitare, vacillare.

stagnant (stăg'nănt) *agg.* stagnante: to become —, stagnare.

stagnate (stăg'nāt) *vi.* stagnare, ristagnare.

staid (stād) *agg.* posato, serio.

stain (stān) *n.* macchia, chiazza; tintura, sostanza colorante, tinta. *vt* macchiare; colorire; tingere. *vi.* macchiarsi: stained glass, vetro colorato (o istoriato).

stainless *agg.* immacolato; inossidabile.

stair (stâr) *n.* gradino; *pl.* scala, scale, gradinata.

staircase (stâr'kās') *n.* scala.

stairway (stâr'wā') *n.* scalinata.

stake (stāk) *n.* palo, steccato; rogo; premio, posta (*di scommessa*): at —, in ⸱giuoco *o* a repentaglio. *vt.* rischiare, scommettere; palettare, puntellare.

stale (stāl) *agg.* stantio, raffermo; inacidito, vecchio, ritrito; caduto in prescrizione. *vt.* rendere stantio; *vi.* invecchiare, inacidire.

stalk (stôk) *n.* stelo; sostegno; ciminiera; inseguimento; pedinamento. *vt.* braccare, pedinare. *vi.* camminare rigidamente; appostarsi.

stall (stôl) (1) *n.* palo (*complice di un ladro*), trucco, finzione. *vt.*, *vi.* ingannare; tergiversare: quit stalling! smettila di tergiversare!

stall (stôl) (2) *n.* stallo, scanno, palchetto; edicola, chiosco. *vt.* chiudere in uno stallo; rallentare, bloccare. *vi.* fermarsi, perdere velocità: to be stalled in the mud, essere bloccato dal fango.

stallion (stăl'yŭn) *n.* stallone.

stalwart (stôl'wẽrt) *agg.* robusto, aitante; risoluto.

stamina (stăm'ĭ·nà) *n.* resistenza fisica.

stammer (stăm'ẽr) *n.* balbettamento, balbuzie. *vt.*, *vi.* balbettare, essere balbuziente.

stammerer *n.* balbuziente.

stammering *n.* balbettamento. *agg.* balbettante, balbuziente.

stamp (stămp) *n.* stampo, marchio; francobollo, timbro; punzone, sigillo; trancia: postage —, francobollo; revenue —, marca da bollo; — collector, filatelico. *vt.* stampare, marcare, timbrare; punzonare; affrancare; calpestare, battere (*il piede*); caratterizzare. *vi.* pestare i piedi, scalpitare.

stampede (stăm-pēd') *n.* fuga precipitosa e disordinata, fuggifuggi. *vt.* mettere in fuga disordinata. *vi.* fuggire in disordine.

stanch (stänch) *agg.* forte, resistente, solido; fido, costante; stagno. *vt.* stagnare (*il sangue*, *ecc.*).

stanchion (stän'shŭn) *n.* puntello.

stand (ständ) *n.* fermata, sosta; luogo; tribuna; piedestallo, leggio, appoggio, sostegno; posteggio, banco, edicola; posizione; resistenza: to make a —, opporre resistenza; to take one's —, prendere posizione. *vt.* (*pass.*, *pp.* **stood**) posare, collocare; sopportare, subire, resistere a. *vi.* trovarsi; stare in piedi, rizzarsi; fermarsi; resistere, sussistere; esitare: to — one's ground, mantenere le proprie posizioni; to — a chance of, avere la probabilità di; it stands to reason, è ovvio; to — an expense, sostenere una spesa; to — aside, appartarsi, tirarsi da parte; to — by, assistere, difendere; stare all'erta; to — for, prendere le parti di, sostituirsi a; significare; to — in the way, ostacolare; to — off, tenersi al largo; to — out, sporgere, spiccare; to — up, alzarsi; to — up for, prendere le difese di; to — six feet in one's stockings, essere alto un metro e ottanta.

standard (stän'dĕrd) *n.* palo, asta, sostegno; stendardo, insegna; modello, misura; base monetaria; norma, criterio, tipo uniforme; livello: — of life, tenore di vita; to be up to —, essere soddisfacente, rispondere ai criteri. *agg.* classico, tipico, regolamentare, usuale, basilare, uniformato; di serie, standardizzato, uniformato.

standardization(stăn'dĕr-dĭ-zā'shŭn)*n.* standardizzazione, uniformazione.

standardize (stän'dĕr-dĭz) *vt.* standardizzare, uniformare.

stand-in *n.* (*cinema, teat.*) controfigura; (*fam.*) sostituto.

standing (stän'dĭng) *n.* posizione, situazione; durata, anzianità: twenty years' —, vent'anni di servizio; of long —, di antica data. *agg.* in piedi, eretto; fisso, fermo: — account, conto corrente; — pool, stagno (*acqua stagnante*); — room, posto in piedi.

standpoint (ständ'point') *n.* punto di vista.

standstill (ständ'stil') *n.* fermata, sosta, punto morto, vicolo cieco.

stank (stängk) *pass.* di to stink.

stanza (stän'zå) *n.* strofa.

staple (stā'p'l) (1) *n.* prodotto principale; merce di consumo; fibra tessile; mercato; materia prima; *pl.* articoli di prima necessità. *agg.* principale, indispensabile; corrente, di normale produzione (*o* consumo).

staple (stā'p'l) (2) *n.* chiodo ricurvo a due punte; anello (*o* bocchetta) di chiavistello; punto metallico (*per quaderni*, *ecc.*). *vt.* cucire a punto metallico.

stapler (stā'plĕr) *n.* cucitrice a punto metallico.

star (stär) *n.* stella, astro; asterisco; primo attore, prima attrice: — -spangled, stellato. *vt.* ornare di stelle, costellare; segnare con asterisco; avere come protagonista (*detto di film*, *ecc.*). *vi.* brillare, splendere; essere il primo attore.

starboard (stär'bŏrd) *n.* dritta. *agg.* destro; *avv.* a dritta.

starch (stärch) *n.* amido, fecola. *vt.* inamidare.

starchy (stär'chĭ) *agg.* amidaceo; rigido, inamidato.

stare (stär) *n.* sguardo fisso. *vi.* sbarrare gli occhi; restare attonito: to — at, guardare fissamente.

starfish (stär'fĭsh') *n.* stella di mare.

stark (stärk) *agg.* rigido, stecchito; vero e proprio; desolato; assoluto. *avv.* assolutamente, completamente: — naked, completamente nudo; — raving mad, pazzo da legare.

starlet (stär'lĕt) *n.* stellina (*anche di cinema*).

starlight (stär'lit') *n.* luce stellare.

starry (stär'ĭ) *agg.* stellare; stellato; lucente come le stelle; a forma di stella; stellante.

start (stärt) *n.* sobbalzo; impulso; partenza, avviamento, principio, punto di partenza; vantaggio: by fits and starts, saltuariamente; to wake with a —, svegliarsi di soprassalto. *vt.* far trasalire; far partire, mettere in moto, avviare, iniziare. *vi.* trasalire, riscuotersi; cominciare, avviarsi, partire: to — out on a trip, mettersi in viaggio. —er *n.* iniziatore; (*mecc.*) messa in moto; (*sport*) mossiere.

startle (stär't'l) *vt.* far trasalire, allarmare. *vi.* trasalire, allarmarsi.

startling (stär'tlĭng) *agg.* sconcertante, allarmante, sensazionale.

starvation (stär·vā'shŭn) *n.* inedia, fame.

starve (stärv) *vt.* far morire di fame, affamare. *vi.* morire di fame.

state (stāt) *n.* stato; condizione, rango. *agg.* statale, di stato; solenne. *vt.* dichiarare, stabilire, formulare.

stateliness (stāt'lĭ-nĕs) *n.* pompa, solennità.

stately (stāt'lĭ) *agg.* imponente, grandioso, solenne.

statement (stāt'mĕnt) *n.* dichiarazione; rapporto; affermazione, testimonianza: — **of account**, estratto conto.

stateroom (stāt'rōōm') *n.* cabina riservata (*su navi, treni, ecc.*).

Stateside (stāt'sīd') *agg.* diretto a o proveniente da o caratteristico degli Stati Uniti. *avv.* dagli, negli, verso gli Stati Uniti.

statesman (stāts'măn) *n.* statista, uomo politico.

static (stāt'ĭk) *agg.* statico *n.* (*radio*) scarica, disturbo.

statics *n.* (*fis.*) statica.

station (stā'shŭn) *n.* stazione; posto, posteggio; posizione, condizione, rango; commissariato; (*mil.*) presidio: **broadcasting —**, stazione trasmittente; **police —**, commissariato di polizia; **service —**, stazione di servizio; **— wagon**, giardinetta; **weather —**, osservatorio meteorologico. *vt.* mettere (di stanza), dislocare; collocare. *vi.* essere di stanza.

stationary (stā'shŭn-ĕr-ĭ) *agg.* stazionario; fisso, fermo, immobile.

stationer (stā'shŭn-ĕr) *n.* cartolaio.

stationery (stā'shŭn-ĕr'ĭ) *n.* cancelleria, articoli di cartoleria.

statistics (stà·tĭs'tĭks) *n.* statistica.

statuary (stăt'ū·ĕr'ĭ) *n.* collezione di sculture, statuaria.

statue (stăt'ū) *n.* statua.

status (stā'tŭs) *n.* stato, condizione, rango, figura giuridica.

statute (stăt'ūt) *n.* statuto, decreto, legge, regolamento.

statutory (stăt'ū·tō'rĭ) *agg.* statutario.

staunch (stônch) *vedi* **stanch**.

stave (stāv) *n.* doga (*di botte*); piuolo, stecca; (*mus.*) pentagramma, strofa. *vt.* sfondare, fendere, fracassare: **to — off**, tenere a distanza, evitare, respingere.

stay (stā) (1) *n.* fermata, sosta, permanenza, soggiorno; proroga; ostacolo, freno; sostegno; *pl.* busto (*da donna*). *vt.* (*pass., pp.* stayed) fermare, sospendere, trattenere; sostenere. *vi.* stare, sostare, rimanere, soggiornare, abitare, fer-

marsi; resistere: **to — up**, restare alzato, vegliare.

stay (stā) (2) *n.* (*naut.*) straglio.

stead (stĕd) *n.* luogo, servizio, vece: **in his —**, in sua vece; **to stand in good — to**, essere molto utile a.

steadfast (stĕd'fàst) *agg.* saldo, costante, fisso, fermo; risoluto; fedele.

steadily (stĕd'ĭ-lĭ) *avv.* fermamente, saldamente; regolarmente, ininterrottamente.

steadiness (stĕd'ĭ-nĕs) *n.* fermezza, costanza, saldezza; uniformità, regolarità, solidità.

steady (stĕd'ĭ) *agg.* fermo, saldo; coerente, uniforme, regolare; fisso, continuo; sicuro. *vt.* appoggiare; mettere in equilibrio; sorreggere, rinfrancare. *vi.* rimettersi in equilibrio, rinfrancarsi, calmarsi.

steak (stāk) *n.* braciuola, bistecca.

steal (stēl) *vt., vi.* (*pass.* stole, *pp.* stolen) rubare, derubare, carpire: **to — in** (out), sgusciare dentro (fuori); **to — a glance**, lanciare un'occhiata furtiva; **to — away**, svignarsela.

stealth (stĕlth) *n.* segretezza; azione subdola: **by —**, in segreto, furtivamente. **—ily** *avv.* di nascosto, furtivamente, subdolamente.

stealthy (stĕl'thĭ) *agg.* segreto, furtivo, subdolo, clandestino.

steam (stēm) *n.* vapore. *agg.* di vapore; a vapore: **— boiler**, caldaia a vapore; **— engine**, macchina a vapore; **— roller**, rullo compressore. *vt.* esporre al vapore, vaporizzare; cuocere a vapore. *vi.* fumare, emettere vapore: **to — in**, entrare in porto; **to — off**, dileguarsi.

steamboat (stēm'bōt') *n.* battello a vapore.

steamer (stēm'ĕr) *n.* piroscafo.

steamship (stēm'shĭp') *n.* bastimento a vapore.

steamy (stēm'ĭ) *agg.* fumante, pieno di vapore.

steed (stēd) *n.* destriero, corsiero.

steel (stēl) *n.* acciaio, lama. *agg.* d'acciaio: **— works**, acciaieria. *vt.* rivestire d'acciaio; rendere inflessibile, indurire: **to — one's heart**, fare il cuore duro; **to — oneself**, prepararsi l'animo, prepararsi a combattere, corazzarsi. **—y** *agg.* d'acciaio; duro, inflessibile.

steelyard (stēl'yärd) *n.* stadera.

steep (stēp) (1) *vt.* immergere, imbevere, saturare. *vi.* imbeversi.

steep (stēp) (2) *n.* precipizio, pendio, scarpata. *agg.* ripido, inclinato; arduo, impraticabile; eccessivo, esorbitante.

steeple (stē'p'l) *n.* campanile, torre, guglia.

steeplechase (stē'p'l·chăs') *n.* corsa a ostacoli; corsa campestre.

steepness (stēp'nĕs) *n.* ripidezza.

steer (stēr) (1) *n.* manzo.

steer (stēr) (2) *n.* (gergo) suggerimento. *vt., vi.* guidare, pilotare, sterzare, orientare, dirigersi: to — clear of, girar largo da; this car —s easily, questa macchina ha un buono sterzo.

steerage (stēr'ĭj) *n.* governo (di nave, ecc.), guida; terza classe (sulle navi).

steering wheel *n.* ruota del timone; (auto.) volante, sterzo.

stem (stĕm) *n.* gambo, stelo; cannello o bocchino (di pipa); ceppo (di famiglia); prua; (gramm.) radice: from — to stern, da poppa a prua; da cima a fondo. *vt.* risalire (una corrente); resistere a; arginare, stagnare (un'emorragia); tappare. *vi.* provenire (da).

stench (stĕnch) *n.* puzzo, fetore.

stencil (stĕn'sĭl) *n.* stampino.

stenographer (stĕ·nŏg'rȧ·fẽr) *n.* stenografo.

stenography (stĕ·nŏg'rȧ·fĭ) *n.* stenografia.

stentorian (stĕn·tō'rĭ·ȧn) *agg.* stentoreo.

step (stĕp) *n.* passo, orma; gradino, scalino, piuolo, predellino; andatura: — by —, passo passo, gradualmente; to be in — with, marciare di pari passo con; essere consono a; to take —s, prendere provvedimenti. *vi.* fare un passo, camminare, andare, salire, scendere: to — aside, tirarsi da parte; to — back, retrocedere; to — in, entrare, intervenire; to — out, uscire; to — on, calpestare, salire su; to — on the gas (auto.), premere l'acceleratore, dare gas; to — over, attraversare.

stepbrother *n.* fratellastro.

stepchild *n.* figliastro.

stepdaughter *n.* figliastra.

stepfather *n.* patrigno.

stepladder *n.* scala a piuoli.

stepmother *n.* matrigna.

steppe (stĕp) *n.* steppa.

stepsister *n.* sorellastra.

stepson *n.* figliastro.

stereoscope (stĕr'ē·ō·skōp') *n.* stereoscopio.

stereotype (stĕr'ē·ō·tĭp') *n.* stereotipia.

sterile (stĕr'ĭl) *agg.* sterile.

sterility (stĕ·rĭl'ĭ·tĭ) *n.* sterilità.

sterilize (stĕr'ĭ·līz) *vt.* sterilizzare.

sterling (stûr'lĭng) *n.* (metall.) titolo. *agg.* puro, genuino, di buona lega: — qualities, doti preclare: pound —, lira sterlina.

stern (stûrn) (1) *agg.* rigido, severo, duro, austero.

stern (stûrn) (2) *n.* poppa.

sternness (stûrn'nĕs) *n.* severità, durezza, austerità.

stethoscope (stĕth'ō·skōp) *n.* stetoscopio.

stevedore (stē'vĕ·dōr') *n.* stivatore.

stew (stū) *n.* stufato, umido: to be in a —, essere sossopra, essere preoccupato. *vt.* cuocere a fuoco lento. *vi.* cuocersi lentamente; (gergo) agitarsi, preoccuparsi.

steward (stū'ẽrd) *n.* dispensiere, fattore, economo, amministratore; (sport) commissario; cameriere di bordo, inserviente. —ess *n.* cameriera di bordo.

stick (stĭk) *n.* bastone, randello, bacchetta; bastoncino; dynamite —, tubo di dinamite; control — (aeron.), barra di comando; walking —, bastone da passeggio. *vt.* (pass., pp. stuck) ficcare, conficcare; appiccicare; ferire, trafiggere; appuntare; appioppare; affiggere; (fam.) sopportare. *vi.* appiccicarsi; incepparsi; essere conficcato, restare; attenersi, ostinarsi; radicarsi (nella mente); restar fedele; sporgere, spuntar fuori; persistere: to — at, arretrare davanti a; to — close, tenersi vicino; to — up, alzarsi; assaltare, rapinare; to — up for, difendere, proteggere; to — out, sporgere, essere evidente; to — to a job, perseverare in un lavoro; — to it! tieni duro!, continua così! —er *n.* persona pertinace; attacchino; scioperante; etichetta (cartellino); (fam.) problema.

stickler (stĭk'lẽr) *n.* formalista, intransigente; ostinato.

stick-up *n.* rapinatore; rapina a mano armata: — man, rapinatore; — collar, colletto duro, colletto troppo alto.

sticky (stĭk'ĭ) *agg.* appiccicoso.

stiff (stĭf) *n.* (gergo) cadavere. *agg.* rigido, duro; intirizzito; faticoso, difficile; impacciato; elevato (di prezzi): scared —, paralizzato dalla paura; — neck, torcicollo; ostinazione, cocciutaggine.

stiffen (stĭf'ĕn) *vt.* indurire, irrigidire. *vi.* indurirsi, irrigidirsi.

stiffly (stĭf'lĭ) *avv.* rigidamente, ostinatamente; con sussiego.

stiffness (stĭf'nĕs) *n.* rigidezza, inflessibilità, irrigidimento; sussiego.

stifle (stī'f'l) *vt.*, *vi.* soffocare, estinguere, reprimere: to — a yawn, soffocare uno sbadiglio; to — a revolt, reprimere una rivolta.

stifling (stī'fling) *agg.* soffocante.

stigma (stig'mà) *n.* marchio d'infamia; *pl.* stigmata, stimmate, stimma.

stile (stīl) *n.* gradino, gradinata; arganello (*cancelletto a ruota*).

still (stīl) (1) *n.* alambicco.

still (stīl) (2) *avv.* ancora, tuttora; tuttavia: — less, ancor meno; — more, ancor più; *cong.* nondimeno.

still (stīl) (3) *n.* quiete, silenzio; (*fot.*) fotografia a posa; (*cine*) foto di lavorazione. *agg.* immobile, tranquillo, silenzioso, calmo: — life, natura morta. *vt.* calmare, sedare, far tacere. *vi.* calmarsi.

stillborn (stīl'bôrn') *agg.* nato morto.

stillness (stīl'nĕs) *n.* tranquillità, silenzio, immobilità.

stilt (stīlt) *n.* trampolo; palafitta.

stilted (stīl'tĕd) *agg.* ricercato, sostenuto, pomposo.

stimulant (stīm'û-lănt) *n.*, *agg.* stimolante.

stimulate (stīm'û-lāt) *vt.* stimolare.

stimulating *agg.* stimolante.

stimulation (stīm'û-lā'shŭn) *n.* stimolo.

stimulus (stīm'û-lŭs) *n.* (*pl.* stimuli) stimolo.

sting (sting) *n.* aculeo, pungiglione; pungolo; puntura, dolore; bruciore; asprezza; ironia. *vt.*, *vi.* (*pass.*, *pp.* stung) pungere, dolere, bruciare; punzecchiare, irritare: stung to the quick, punto sul vivo.

stinginess (stīn'jī-nĕs) *n.* meschinità, avarizia.

stingy (stīn'jī) *agg.* avaro, meschino.

stink (stīngk) *n.* puzza, fetore. *vt.*, *vi.* (*pass.* stank *o* stunk, *pp.* stunk) puzzare, appestare; avere cattiva reputazione.

stint (stīnt) *n.* restrizione, limite. *vt.* limitare, lesinare. *vi.* limitarsi, economizzare: to — oneself, lesinarsi il necessario. —er *n.* avaro.

stipulate (stīp'û-lāt) *vt.*, *vi.* stipulare, pattuire.

stipulation (stīp'û-lā'shŭn) *n.* stipulazione; condizione, clausola.

stir (stûr) (1) *n.* (*gergo*) carcere.

stir (stûr) (2) *n.* movimento, trambusto, fermento. *vt.* (*spesso seg. da* up) muovere, scuotere, rimescolare; destare, risvegliare, commuovere, istigare, agitare, fomentare. *vi.* muoversi, affaccendarsi, scuotersi, agitarsi, stormire.

stirring (stûr'ing) *agg.* emozionante, eccitante, commovente.

stirrup (stir'ŭp) *n.* staffa.

stitch (stich) *n.* punto; maglia, puntura, trafittura. *vt.*, *vi.* cucire, suturare.

stoat (stōt) *n.* ermellino d'estate.

stock (stŏk) *n.* blocco, tronco; palo, manico; ceppo; stirpe; fusto (*dell'ancora*); calcio (*d'arma da fuoco*); materia prima; provviste, assortimento, riserve; (*teat.*) repertorio: live—, bestiame; — company, società anonima; (*teat.*) compagnia di repertorio; — exchange, borsa valori; — in trade, assortimento di merci; armamentario; repertorio; — market, mercato finanziario; —room *n.* magazzino; sala di esposizione. to take — of, fare l'inventario di, stimare. *vt.* fornire, provvedere, riempire; fornire di bestiame; immanicare; immagazzinare; mettere in ceppi.

stocks *n.pl.* (*naut.*) tacchi; (*finanza*) titoli azionari, capitale (*di società*).

stockade (stŏk-ād') *n.* palizzata; *vt.* munire di palizzata.

stockbroker (stŏk'brō'kĕr) *n.* agente di cambio.

stockholder (stŏk'hōl'dĕr) *n.* azionista.

stocking (stŏk'ing) *n.* calza.

stockjobber (stŏk'jŏb'ĕr) *n.* speculatore; agente di cambio.

stock-still *agg.* immobile.

stocky (stŏk'ī) *agg.* tarchiato, massiccio.

stockyard (stŏk'yärd') *n.* parco per il bestiame.

stodgy (stŏj'ī) *agg.* pesante, noioso.

stoic ((stō'ĭk) *n.*, *agg.* stoico.

stoke (stōk) *vt.* attizzare; alimentare (*una fornace*).

stoker (stōk'ĕr) *n.* fochista.

stole (stōl) (1) *n.* stola.

stole (stōl) (2) *pass. di* to steal.

stolen (stō'lĕn) *pp. di* to steal.

stolid (stŏl'ĭd) *agg.* stolido, impassibile.

stomach (stŭm'ăk) *n.* stomaco; *vt.* digerire, tollerare.

stone (stōn) *n.* sasso, pietra, lapide; nocciolo (*di frutto*); (*med.*) calcolo, calcolosi; within a stone's throw, a due passi, vicinissimo. *agg.* di pietra, di sasso: Stone Age, età della pietra; — blind, completamente cieco; — dead, morto stecchito; — deaf, sordo come una talpa. *vt.* lapidare; acciottolare; levare il nocciolo a.

stony (stōn'ī) *agg.* di pietra; duro, insensibile, impassibile.

stood (stŏod) *pass.*, *pp. di* to stand.

stooge (stōōj) *n.* (*teat.*) spalla; (*fig.*) fantoccio, tirapiedi, sicario.

stool (stōōl) *n.* sgabello; posatoio (*per uccelli*); gabinetto di decenza; evacuazione (*di escrementi*): — **pigeon**, piccione da richiamo (*anche fig.*); (*gergo S.U.*) spia, confidente (*della polizia*).

stoop (stōōp) *n.* inclinazione, portamento curvo; sostegno; gradinata, porticato; condiscendenza; to walk with a —, camminare ricurvo. *vi.* chinarsi, abbassarsi, curvarsi, essere curvo; umiliarsi; accondiscendere. —**shouldered** *agg.* con le spalle curve o spioventi.

stop (stŏp) *n.* fermata, sosta, scalo; interruzione, impedimento; tappo, zipolo; fermo; (*mus.*) tasto registro (*d'organo*); punto (*segno d'interpunzione*): —**watch**, cronometro. *vt.* fermare, impedire, ostacolare; turare, otturare; sospendere; sopprimere; interrompere; (*sport*) bloccare, parare. *vi.* fermarsi, sostare, desistere, cessare, smettere: to — short, fermarsi di colpo; to — at nothing, non avere scrupoli, essere capace di tutto; to — over at, fare tappa a; to — somebody from, impedire a qualcuno di.

stoppage (stŏp'ĭj) *n.* interruzione, fermata, arresto; ostruzione, occlusione.

stopover (stŏp'ō'vĕr) *n.* tappa, fermata, scalo.

stopper (stŏp'ĕr) *n.* chiusura, tappo.

storage (stōr'ĭj) *n.* deposito, magazzino; magazzinaggio: to keep in —, immagazzinare, conservare; in cold —, in refrigerante; — battery, accumulatore.

store (stōr) *n.* magazzino, deposito, negozio; riserva; assortimento, provvista: department —, grandi magazzini, emporio; grocery —, drogheria; shoe —, calzoleria; in —, in serbo; to set little (great) by, tenere in scarsa (grande) considerazione. *vt.* fornire, rifornire, immagazzinare, far provvista di: to — up, accumulare; to — away, mettere in serbo.

storehouse (stōr'hous') *n.* magazzino.

storekeeper (stōr'kēp'ĕr) *n.* magazziniere; negoziante.

storeroom (stōr'rōōm') *n.* magazzino; dispensa.

stork (stôrk) *n.* cicogna.

storm (stôrm) *n.* uragano, bufera, tempesta, gragniuola; assalto, tumulto; scroscio (*d'applausi*): hail —, grandinata; snow —, tormenta (*di neve*); wind —, tempesta di vento; — troops, reparti d'assalto, truppe d'urto; to take by —, prendere d'assalto. *vt.* assaltare. *vi.* scatenarsi, infuriare, imperversare; riversarsi.

stormy (stôr'mĭ) *agg.* burrascoso, tempestoso.

story (stō'rĭ) (1) *n.* piano (*di un edificio*).

story (stō'rĭ) (2) *n.* storia, racconto; favola; articolo, resoconto; (*cinema*) trama, soggetto, vicenda; versione; frottola; diceria.

storyteller (stō'rĭ-tĕl'ĕr) *n.* narratore.

stout (stout) *n.* birra forte (*nera*). *agg.* forte, robusto; grasso, tarchiato; energico. —**ly** *avv.* risolutamente. —**ness** *n.* risolutezza; corpulenza.

stove (stōv) (1) *pass.*, *pp.* di to stave.

stove (stōv) (2) *n.* stufa, fornello da cucina, cucina (*a gas o elettrica*).

stow (stō) *vt.* colmare; riporre; (*naut.*) stivare.

stowaway (stō'á-wā') *n.* passeggiero clandestino.

straddle (străd''l) *vt.* inforcare; mettersi a cavalcioni su. *vi.* divaricare le gambe; tenere il piede in due staffe.

straggle (străg''l) *vi.* staccarsi (*da un gruppo*), sparpagliarsi, scompigliarsi; vagare; smarrirsi.

straggler (străg'lĕr) *n.* disperso, sbandato, vagabondo.

straight (strāt) *n.* dirittura; linea retta; (*poker*) scala. *agg.* dritto, diretto; onesto; puro, liscio (*non diluito*); attendibile: to let someone have it —, dire a qualcuno il fatto suo: — flush, scala reale; — face, faccia seria; — hair, capelli lisci; *avv.* dritto, direttamente; immediatamente; francamente, onestamente; in linea retta: — from the shoulder, esplicitamente; for two hours —, per due ore di fila.

straightaway (strāt'á-wā') *n.* dirittura. *agg.* dritto, rettilineo. *avv.* immediatamente.

straighten (strāt'n) *vt.* raddrizzare; appianare, accomodare, riordinare. *vi.* raddrizzarsi.

straightforward (strāt'fôr'wĕrd) *agg.* dritto, diretto; rettilineo; esplicito; onesto, franco. *avv.* in linea retta, direttamente; schiettamente.

straightness (strāt'nĕs) *n.* dirittura, rettitudine.

straightway (strāt'wā') *avv.* direttamente, immediatamente.

strain (strān) *n.* sforzo; tensione; strappo (*muscolare*); suono, tono, motivo (*mus.*); razza, ramo. *vt.*

tendere (*anche l'orecchio*); stiracchiare, forzare, tirare; spremere,
filtrare; costringere; aguzzare (*gli
occhi*). *vi.* sforzarsi, tendere i mu-
scoli: to — one's wrist, storcersi un
polso; to — a point, fare un'eccezione, fare l'impossibile. —ed *agg.*
forzato, non spontaneo. —er *n.*
colatoio, filtro; tirante.

strait (strāt) *n.* (*spesso pl.*) stretto (*di
mare*); difficoltà, imbarazzo, ristrettezze finanziarie; strettoia. *agg.*
stretto, disagevole: — jacket,
camicia di forza.

straiten (strāt'n) *vt.* stringere, restringere; mettere in difficoltà.

strand (strănd) (1) *n.* riva, spiaggia.
vt. arrenare; abbandonare, lasciare
nelle peste. *vi.* arrenarsi: to be
stranded, essere arrenato.

strand (strănd) (2) *n.* fibra, filaccia,
corda; filo (*di perle*); treccia (*di
capelli*). *vt.* attorcigliare, intrecciare; sfilacciare; rammendare.

strange (strānj) *agg.* strano, bizzarro;
spaesato; straniero, sconosciuto;
inusitato.

strangeness (strānj'něs) *n.* stranezza.

stranger (strān'jěr) *n.* straniero, forestiero, estraneo, sconosciuto.

strangle (străng'g'l) *vt.*,*vi.* strangolare,
soffocare.

strangler (străng'glěr) *n.* strangolatore.

strap (străp) *n.* cinghia, correggia;
cinturino; maniglia; coramella (*da
rasoio*); spallina; metal —, cinturino di metallo. *vt.* assicurare con
cinghie; staffilare; cingere; affilare.

strapping (străp'ing) *agg.*bello, aitante.

stratagem (străt'ă·jěm) *n.* stratagemma.

strategic (stră·tē'jĭk) *agg.* strategico.

strategist (străt'ē·jĭst) *n.* stratega.

strategy (străt'ē·jĭ) *n.* strategia.

stratosphere (străt'ō·sfēr) *n.* stratosfera.

stratovision (străt'ō·vĭzh'ŭn) *n.* ritrasmissione televisa da aerei in
volo nella stratosfera, stratovisione.

straw (strô) *n.* paglia, pagliuzza, fuscello; inezia: not to be worth a —,
non valere nulla; not to care a —,
infischiarsene; — color, giallo paglierino.

strawberry (strô'běr'ĭ) *n.* fragola.

stray (strā) *n.* animale sperduto;
vagabondo. *agg.* sperduto, smarrito; sviato; sporadico; *vi.* smarrirsi, girovagare; divagare; sviarsi.

streak (strēk) *n.* striscia, striatura,
linea, traccia; vena. *vt.* rigare,
striare.

stream (strēm) *n.* corrente; flusso,
corso d'acqua, fiume; fiotto; getto
(*di vapore*); fascio (*di luce*): against
the —, controcorrente. *vt.* inondare;
vi. scorrere, riversarsi; filtrare, irradiarsi; sfilare (*di processione,ecc.*);
fluire; sventolare: to — out of,
sgorgare da, fluire da.

streamer (strēm'ěr) *n.* nastro svolazzante, banderuola; testata (*di
giornale*).

streamline (strēm'līn') *n.* linea aerodinamica. *vt.* dare una linea aerodinamica a.

streamlined *agg.* aerodinamico.

street (strēt) *n.* via, strada: in queer
—, nell'imbarazzo; in poverty —,
in ristrettezze.

streetcar (strēt'kär') *n.* (*S.U.*) tram.

strength (strĕngth) *n.* forza, potenza,
resistenza: on the — of, in base a.

strengthen (strĕng'thěn) *vt.* rafforzare,
fortificare, rinfrancare. *vi.* raf-
forzarsi, rinfrancarsi.

strenuous (strĕn'û·ŭs) *agg.* energico;
strenuo, accanito.

stress (strĕs) *n.* forza, risalto; pressione; urgenza; importanza; (*mecc.*)
sforzo; accento: to lay — upon,
dare grande rilievo a. *vt.* accentare;
accentuare, mettere in risalto;
ribadire, sottoporre a uno sforzo.

stretch (strĕch) *n.* stiramento; estensione; tensione, sforzo; periodo,
portata; rettifilo: at a —, difilato;
home —, dirittura d'arrivo. *vt.*
tendere, estendere; spiegare, stendere; sforzare; (*naut.*) tesare. *vi.*
stendersi; estendersi, allungarsi;
allargarsi; sforzarsi: to — oneself,
stiracchiarsi; to — out one's hand,
porgere la mano.

stretcher (strĕch'ěr) *n.* telaio; barella; tenditore, tenditoio: — bearer,
portaferiti.

strew (strō̄) *vt.* (*pass.* strewed, *pp.*
strewed *o* strewn) sparpagliare,
spargere, disseminare.

strewn (strō̄n) *pp. di* to strew: —
with, cosparso di.

stricken (strĭk'ěn) *pp. di* to strike.

strict (strĭkt) *agg.* stretto, ristretto;
rigido, scrupoloso, severo. —ness *n.*
strettezza, esattezza, rigorosità.
—ure *n.* critica, censura, stroncatura; (*med.*) strozzatura, restringimento.

stridden (strĭd''n) *pp. di* to stride.

stride (strĭd) *n.* passo lungo, andatura,
lunghezza del passo: to take in
one's —, affrontare con disinvoltura. *vi.* (*pass.* strode, *pp.* stridden) camminare a gran passi.

strife (strīf) *n.* lotta, contesa.

strike (strīk) *n.* sciopero; scoperta di un giacimento: —breaker *n.* crumiro; air —, attacco aereo. *vt.* (*pass.* struck, pp. stricken *o* struck) colpire, percuotere, battere; sonare (*delle ore*); imprimere; strofinare (*un fiammifero*); sembrare, coniare; assumere (*un atteggiamento*); scoprire (*giacimenti*); (*naut.*) ammainare: to — off, out, tagliar via, cancellare; diffalcare; far uscire, eliminare; to — down, abbattere; to — one's attention, richiamare l'attenzione di; to — one's fancy, colpire la fantasia di; to — up a friendship, stringere un'amicizia; to — with terror, terrorizzare; how does the boy — you? che impressione ti fa quel ragazzo?. *vi.* urtare, battere, cozzare; bussare; prendere una direzione; scioperare; attecchire: to — on, upon, colpire, rifrangersi in, ripercuotersi su; imbattersi in, scoprire; to — at, assalire, colpire; to — home, colpire nel segno; to — a light, accendere un fiammifero; to — a bargain, concludere un affare; to — dumb, far ammutolire; to — oil, scoprire un giacimento di petrolio; far fortuna.

striker *n.* battitore; percussore; scioperante.

striking *agg.* notevole, impressionante; netto.

string (strĭng) *n.* fettuccia, funicella, fibra, laccio, cordoncino; fila, filza; (*mus.*) corda: strings, strumenti a corda, archi. *vt.* (*pass.*, *pp.* strung) fornire di corde; infilare (*perle, ecc.*); tendere; rinforzare; adornare di festoni; mondare dei fili (*p.es.i fagiuolini*); impiccare; (*mus.*) accordare: to — out, allungarsi, dipanarsi; to — up, innervosire; impiccare.

stringbean *n.* fagiuolino.

stringy (strĭng'ĭ) *agg.* fibroso, elastico.

strip (strĭp) *n.* striscia, fascia; lembo (*di terra*); (*aeron.*) pista (di decollo *o* di atterraggio): comic strips, fumetti. *vt.* privare, spogliare, denudare, mondare; spanare (*una vite*). *vi.* spogliarsi, svestirsi: to — off, strappare. —tease *n.* (*teat.*), spogliarello.

stripe (strĭp) *n.* sferzata, staffilata; striscia, riga; tipo; *pl.* galloni. *vt.* rigare, listare, variegare.

striped (strĭpt) *agg.* rigato, a strisce.

strive (strīv) *vi.* (*pass.* strove, *pp.* striven) sforzarsi, gareggiare, lottare; mirare.

strode (strōd) *pass. di* to stride.

stroke (strōk) (1) *n.* colpo, percossa; tratto; accesso (*attacco*); bracciata (*al nuoto*); lampo (*di genio*); tocco; corsa (*di stantuffo*); (*naut.*) vogata, capovoga: — of a bell, tocco di campana; brush —, spazzolata; pennellata; — of the pen, tratto di penna; on the — of two, allo scoccar delle due. *vt.* segnare; cancellare (*con un tratto di penna, ecc.*); essere capovoga in.

stroke (2) *n.* carezza, lisciata. *vt.* accarezzare, lisciare, sfiorare.

stroll (strōl) *n.* passeggiata. *vi.* passeggiare, gironzolare.

strong (strŏng) *agg.* forte, solido, resistente; energico, risoluto; impetuoso: *avv.* fortemente, intensamente.

strongbox *n.* forziere.

stronghold *n.* fortilizio, roccaforte.

strongly *avv.* fortemente, intensamente.

strong room *n.* camera blindata (*di banca, ecc.*)

strop (strŏp) *n.* coramella (*per rasoio*). *vt.* affilare sulla coramella.

strove (strōv) *pass. di* to strive.

struck (strŭk) *pass.*, *pp. di* to strike: — with a disease, colpito da una malattia.

structural (strŭk'tŭr-ăl) *agg.* strutturale.

structure (strŭk'tŭr) *n.* struttura, edificio.

struggle (strŭg''l) *n.* lotta, sforzo. *vi.* lottare, dibattersi; affaticarsi.

strum (strŭm) *vt.*, *vi.* strimpellare.

strumpet (strŭm'pĕt) *n.* prostituta.

strung (strŭng) *pass.*, *pp. di* to string.

strut (strŭt) *n.* andatura pettoruta. *vi.* camminare pettoruto, pavoneggiarsi.

strychnine (strĭk'nĭn) *n.* stricnina.

stub (stŭb) *n.* ceppo, moncone; mozzicone; matrice (*di ricevuta, ecc.*). *vt.* sbattere.

stubble (stŭb''l) *n.* stoppia; pelame ispido, barba ispida.

stubborn (stŭb'ĕrn) *agg.* ostinato, testardo, inflessibile, caparbio.

stubbornness *n.* caparbietà, ostinazione; inflessibilità.

stucco (stŭk'ō) *n.* stucco, lavoro a stucco. *vt.* ornare con stucco.

stuck (stŭk) *pass.*, *pp. di* to stick.

stud (stŭd) (1) *n.* borchia, chiodo; bozza; bottone per polsino. *vt.* costellare; fissare con borchie; disseminare.

stud (stŭd) (2) *n.* scuderia, allevamento di cavalli da corsa; stallone: — horse, stallone.

student (stū'dĕnt) *n.* studente; studioso.

studied (stŭd′ĭd) *agg.* studiato.

studio (stū′dĭ·ō) *n.* studio (*d'artista*); (*radio*) auditorium; (*cinema*) teatro di posa.

studious (stū′dĭ·ŭs) *agg.* studioso; studiato, elaborato.

study (stŭd′ĭ) *n.* studio; cura, attenzione, diligenza; ufficio, gabinetto di lavoro. *vt.*, *vi.* studiare.

stuff (stŭf) *n.* stoffa, tessuto; roba, materia, sostanza: that liquor was good —, quel liquore era roba buona; sob —, roba lagrimogena; — and nonsense! tutte sciocchezze! *vt.* riempire, imbottire, rimpinzare; ammucchiare; tappare; impagliare. *vi.* rimpinzarsi. —ing *n.* borra, imbottitura, ripieno.

stuffy (stŭf′ĭ) *agg.* afoso, soffocante; noioso; retrogrado, codino; compassato.

stultify (stŭl′tĭ·fī) *vt.* mettere in ridicolo; infirmare.

stumble (stŭm′b'l) *n.* inciampata, passo falso, errore. *vt.* far incespicare, rendere perplesso. *vi.* inciampare, incespicare; impappinarsi; esitare: to — on, upon, across, imbattersi in, trovare per caso.

stumbling (stŭm′blĭng) *n.* inciampo: — block, ostacolo, scoglio.

stump (stŭmp) *n.* ceppo, moncone; torsolo; radice (*di dente*); moncherino; mozzicone. *vt.* troncare; confondere, disorientare. *vi.* camminare pesantemente; concionare.

stumpy *agg.* tozzo.

stun (stŭn) *vt.* stordire, sbalordire; assordare; tramortire.

stung (stŭng) *pass.*, *pp.* di to sting.

stunk (stŭngk) *pass.*, *pp.* di to stink.

stunning (stŭn′ĭng) *agg.* sbalorditivo, meraviglioso; che tramortisce.

stunt (stŭnt) (1) *n.* (*gergo*) esibizione, prodezza. *vi.* esibirsi.

stunt (stŭnt) (2) *vt.* impedire la crescita di, far intristire; ostacolare.

stunted *agg.* nano, mal sviluppato.

stupefy (stū′pē·fī) *vt.* intorpidire; stupire; intontire, abbrutire.

stupendous (stū·pĕn′dŭs) *agg.* prodigioso.

stupid (stū′pĭd) *agg.* stupido. —ity (-ĭd′ĭ·tĭ) *n.* stupidità.

stupor (stū′pēr) *n.* stordimento, abbrutimento: in a —, stordito.

sturdy (stûr′dĭ) *agg.* vigoroso, forte.

sturgeon (stûr′jŭn) *n.* storione.

stutter (stŭt′ēr) *n.* balbuzie, balbettamento. *vt.*, *vi.* balbettare, essere balbuziente. —er *n.* balbuziente. —ing *n.* balbettamento. *agg.* balbuziente.

sty (stī) (1) *n.* (*med.*) orzaiuolo.

sty (stī) (2) *n.* porcile.

style (stīl) *n.* stile, maniera; stilo, gnomone (*di meridiana*); (*comm.*) ragione sociale. *vt.*, *vi.* denominare; decorare; foggiare (*secondo lo stile di moda*).

stylish (stīl′ĭsh) *agg.* elegante, ricercato.

stymie (stī′mĭ) *vt.* ostacolare, bloccare.

suave (swäv) *agg.* blando, mellifluo.

subaltern (sŭb·ôl′tẽrn) *n.*, *agg.* subalterno.

subcommittee (sŭb′kŏ·mĭt′ĭ) *n.* sottocomitato.

subconscious (sub·kŏn′shŭs) *n.* subcosciente. *agg.* del subcosciente, inconscio: the — self, il subcosciente.

subcutaneous (sŭb′kū·tā′nē·ŭs) *agg.* sottocutaneo.

subdivide (sŭb′dĭ·vīd′) *vt.* suddividere.

subdivision (sŭb′dĭ·vĭzh′ŭn) *n.* suddivisione.

subdue (săb·dū′) *vt.* reprimere; attenuare; soggiogare, sottomettere, ammansire; abbassare (*la voce*).

subdued (săb·dūd′) *agg.* ammansito, attenuato; sommesso; docile, moderato: — light, luce attenuata, luce tenue.

subeditor (sub·ĕd′ĭ·tēr) *n.* vice-redattore.

subject (sŭb′jĕkt) *n.* argomento, materia, tema; suddito; (*gramm.*) soggetto. *agg.* soggetto, esposto (*a*); suscettibile (*di*); sottomesso: — matter, sostanza, essenza; argomento (*di una discussione, ecc.*); dati essenziali (*di un argomento, ecc.*). *vt.* (săb·jĕkt′) assoggettare, soggiogare; sottoporre (*a*); esporre (*a*).

subjection (săb·jĕk′shŭn) *n.* sottomissione.

subjective (sŭb·jĕk′tĭv) *agg.* soggettivo.

subjugate (sŭb′jŏŏ·gāt) *vt.* soggiogare.

subjunctive (săb·jŭngk′tĭv) *agg.* soggiuntivo.

sublease (sŭb′lēs′) *n.* subaffitto. *vt.* subaffittare (*prendere o dare in subaffitto*).

sublet (sŭb·lĕt′) *vt.* (*pass.*, *pp.* sublet) subaffittare (*a*).

sublime (săb·līm′) *agg.* sublime.

submachine gun (sŭb′mȧ·shēn′) *n.* fucile mitragliatore, mitra.

submarine (sŭb′mȧ·rēn′) *n.* sottomarino, sommergibile.

submerge (săb·mûrj′) *vt.* sommergere. *vi.* inabissarsi, tuffarsi.

submission (săb·mĭsh′ŭn) *n.* sottomissione, umiltà; rassegnazione.

submissive (săb·mĭs′ĭv) *agg.* sottomesso, umile; rassegnato.

submit (sŭb·mǐt') vt. sottomettere, sottoporre; presentare. vi. sottomettersi, assoggettarsi.

subordinate (sŭ·bôr'dĭ·nĭt) n., agg. subordinato, inferiore, subalterno. vt. (-āt) subordinare.

suborn (sŭb·ôrn') vt. subornare.

subpoena (sŭb·pē'nd) n. citazione di testimone. vt. citare a testimone.

subscribe (sŭb·skrīb') vt., vi. sottoscrivere; firmare; abbonarsi; impegnarsi, aderire (a).

subscriber (sŭb·skrīb'ẽr) n. sottoscrittore, abbonato.

subscription (sŭb·skrĭp'shŭn) n. sottoscrizione, abbonamento.

subsequent (sŭb'sē·kwĕnt) agg. susseguente. —ly avv. successivamente, conseguentemente.

subservient (sŭb·sûr'vĭ·ĕnt) agg. subordinato, sussidiario; servile.

subside (sŭb·sīd') vi. decrescere, attenuarsi; calar di livello; calmarsi; smetter di parlare; cessare.

subsidiary (sŭb·sĭd'ĭ·ĕr'ĭ) n., agg. ausiliario, sussidiario, accessorio; tributario (di corso d'acqua).

subsidize (sŭb'sĭ·dīz) vt. sovvenzionare, sussidiare.

subsidy (sŭb'sĭ·dĭ) n. sovvenzione, sussidio.

subsist (sŭb·sĭst') vt. mantenere. vi. sussistere, esistere; consistere; sopravvivere, vivere (di). —ence n. sussistenza; esistenza, sopravvivenza; mezzi di sussistenza. —ent agg. sussistente, esistente, inerente.

subsoil (sŭb'soil') n. sottosuolo.

substance (sŭb'stǎns) n. sostanza, essenza.

substantial (sŭb·stǎn'shǎl) agg. sostanziale, cospicuo; solido, concreto: to be in — agreement, essere d'accordo in linea di massima.

substantiate (sŭb·stǎn'shǐ·āt) vt. comprovare, suffragare.

substantive (sŭb'stǎn·tǐv) n. sostantivo.

substitute (sŭb'stǐ·tūt) n. sostituto; surrogato; ripiego; supplente. vt. sostituire.

substitution (sŭb'stǐ·tū'shŭn) n. sostituzione.

subterfuge (sŭb'tẽr·fūj) n. sotterfugio.

subterranean (sŭb'tẽ·rā'nē·ăn) agg. sotterraneo; subdolo, segreto.

subtitle (sŭb'tī'tl) n. sottotitolo.

subtle (sŭt''l) agg. scaltro, sottile. —ness, —ty n. sottigliezza, astuzia.

subtract (sŭb·trăkt') vt. sottrarre.

subtraction (sŭb·trăk'shŭn) n. sottrazione.

suburb (sŭb'ûrb) n. suburbio, sobborgo.

suburban (sŭb·ûr'bǎn) agg. suburbano, periferico.

subversive (sŭb·vûr'sĭv) agg. sovversivo, sovvertitore.

subvert (sŭb·vûrt') vt. sovvertire.

subway (sŭb'wǎ') n. sottopassaggio; (S.U.) ferrovia sotterranea.

succeed (sŭk'sēd') vt. succedere a, seguire; subentrare a. vi. succedere, seguire; riuscire, aver successo.

success (sŭk·sĕs') n. successo, riuscita; a man of —, un uomo affermato. —ful agg. fortunato, riuscito, felice: to be a —, avere successo, riuscire, avere esito felice. —fully avv. vittoriosamente, felicemente, con successo.

succession (sŭk·sĕsh'ŭn) n. successione.

successive (sŭk·sĕs'ĭv) agg. successivo.

successor (sŭk·sĕs'ẽr) n. successore.

succor (sŭk'ẽr) n. soccorso; vt. soccorrere.

succulent (sŭk'ū·lĕnt) agg. succulento.

succumb (sŭ·kŭm') vi. soccombere.

such (sŭch) agg. tale, simile: — a good man, un uomo tanto buono; — a, quale, quali; chi, coloro; at — an hour, a un'ora simile; at — and — a place, nel tal posto; and —like, e altre cose del genere; pron. colui, colei, quello, quelli, quelle, coloro, tale, tali.

suck (sŭk) n. succhiata, poppata, sorsata; risucchio; gorgo. vt., vi. succhiare, poppare; aspirare.

sucker (sŭk'ẽr) n. poppante; parassita; ventosa; (mecc.) pistone di pompa aspirante; (S.U.) credulone, stupido, gonzo, "fesso."

suckle (sŭk''l) vt., vi. allattare.

suckling (sŭk'ling) n. lattante.

suction (sŭk'shŭn) n. aspirazione, assorbimento, succhiamento: agg. aspirante: — pump, pompa aspirante.

sudden (sŭd''n) agg. improvviso, inatteso; precipitoso: all of a —, tutt'a un tratto.

suddenly avv. improvvisamente, repentinamente.

suddenness n. subitaneità.

suds (sŭdz) n.pl. saponata.

sue (sū) vt., vi. richiedere; corteggiare; citare, perseguire: to — for damages, citare per danni.

suède (swād) n. pelle scamosciata.

suet (sū'ĕt) n. grasso, sugna.

suffer (sŭf'ẽr) vt., vi. tollerare; soffrire, subire; permettere: he was suffered to go, lo lasciarono andare. —er n. vittima; paziente. —ing n.

sofferenza, dolore. *agg.* sofferente; ammalato (*di*).

suffice (sŭ·fīs') *vt.*, *vi.* bastare, soddisfare.

sufficiency (sŭ·fīsh'ĕn·sĭ)*n.* sufficienza.

sufficient (sŭ·fīsh'ĕnt) *agg.* sufficiente, bastante. —**ly** *avv.* abbastanza, sufficientemente.

suffix (sŭf'ĭks) *n.* (*gramm.*) suffisso.

suffocate (sŭf'ō·kāt) *vt.*, *vi.* soffocare, asfissiare.

suffocation (sŭf'ō·kā'shŭn) *n.* soffocazione, asfissia.

suffrage (sŭf'rĭj) *n.* suffragio.

suffragette (sŭf'rā·jĕt') *n.* suffragetta.

sugar (shŏŏg'ẽr) *n.* zucchero: lump —, zucchero in zollette; — bowl, zuccheriera. *agg.* di zucchero, zuccherino: — beet, barbabietola da zucchero; — cane, canna da zucchero. *vt.* inzuccherare. *vi.* cristallizzarsi. —**y** *agg.* zuccherino, zuccheroso.

suggest (sŭg·jĕst') *vt.* proporre, suggerire, ispirare, indicare.

suggestion (sŭg·jĕs'chŭn) *n.* proposta, suggerimento; traccia.

suggestive (sŭg·jĕs'tĭv) *agg.* suggestivo; indicativo; allusivo.

suicidal (sū'ĭ·sīd'ăl) *agg.* suicida.

suicide (sū'ĭ·sīd) *n.* suicidio; suicida: to commit —, togliersi la vita.

suit (sūt) *n.* assortimento; vestito (*da uomo*); petizione; corteggiamento; (*legge*) causa, azione; seme (*di carte da gioco*), colore (*al poker*): to bring a — against, intentare causa a; to follow —, seguire l'esempio. *vi.* adattare; convenire a, piacere a, far comodo a: it suits me, mi conviene; — yourself, fate come vi pare.

suitable (sūt'ă·b'l) *agg.* conveniente, adatto, opportuno.

suitably (sūt'ă·bĭl) *avv.* acconciamente, opportunamente, convenientemente.

suitcase (sūt'kās) *n.* valigia.

suite (swēt) *n.* serie, collezione; infilata; seguito (*codazzo*); appartamento: — of furniture, ammobiliamento; — of rooms, appartamento.

suitor (sūt'ẽr) *n.* richiedente; corteggiatore, pretendente; querelante.

sulfa, sulpha (sŭl'fā) *agg.* sulfamidico: — drugs, sulfamidici.

sulk (sŭlk) *n.* malumore, broncio. *vi.* tenere il broncio, essere di malumore.

sulkiness (sŭlk'ĭ·nĕs) *n.* scontrosità, malumore.

sulky (sŭl'kĭ) *agg.* arcigno, imbronciato, scontroso.

sullen (sŭl'ĕn) *agg.* tetro, scontroso, torvo, imbronciato, taciturno.

sully (sŭl'ĭ) *vt.* sporcare. *vi.* sporcarsi.

sulphate (sŭl'fāt) *n.* solfato.

sulphide (sŭl'fīd) *n.* solfuro.

sulphite (sŭl'fīt) *n.* solfito.

sulphur (sŭl'fẽr) *n.* zolfo.

sulphuric (sŭl·fū'rĭk) *agg.* solforico.

sultan (sŭl'tăn) *n.* sultano.

sultriness (sŭl'trĭ·nĕs) *n.* afa, umidità.

sultry (sŭl'trĭ) *agg.* afoso, soffocante, opprimente; umido.

sum (sŭm) *n.* somma, cifra; sommario; quantità, essenza, sostanza; addizione, problema. *vt.* (*spesso seg. da* up) sommare; riassumere, ricapitolare.

summarize (sŭm'ā·rīz) *vt.* riassumere, compendiare.

summary (sŭm'ā·rĭ) *n.* sommario, compendio, riassunto. *agg.* sommario, sbrigativo, conciso.

summer (sŭm'ẽr) *n.* estate. *agg.* estivo: — resort, stazione estiva, luogo di villeggiatura. *vi.* passare l'estate.

summit (sŭm'ĭt) *n.* cima, sommità, apice, vetta.

summon (sŭm'ŭn) *vt.* citare, convocare, adunare, chiamare, raccogliere.

summons (sŭm'ŭnz) *n.* chiamata, convocazione, citazione.

sumptuous (sŭmp'tụ̄·ŭs) *agg.* suntuoso.

sun (sŭn) *n.* sole: — porch, — parlor, solario. *vt.* esporre al sole. *vi.* esporsi al sole: to — oneself, crogiolarsi al sole.

sunbeam (sŭn'bēm) *n.* raggio di sole.

sunburn (sŭn'bûrn') *n.* scottatura da sole; abbronzatura. *vt.*, *vi.* bruciare esponendo al sole; abbronzare, abbronzarsi, crogiolarsi al sole.

sunburnt (sŭn'bûrnt') *agg.* scottato dal sole; abbronzato.

sundae (sŭn'dĭ) *n.* cassata.

Sunday (sŭn'dĭ) *n.* domenica.

sunder (sŭn'dẽr) *vt.* separare; *vi.* separarsi, scindersi.

sundial (sŭn'dī'ăl) *n.* meridiana.

sundown (sŭn'doun') *n.* tramonto del sole.

sundries (sŭn'drĭz) *n.pl.* miscellanea, oggetti diversi.

sundry (sŭn'drĭ) *agg.* separati, diversi, parecchi.

sunflower (sŭn'flou'ẽr) *n.* girasole.

sung (sŭng) *pp. di* to sing.

sunk (sŭngk) *pass.*, *pp. di* to sink. *agg.* affondato; incavato, sprofondato; sommerso; infossato.

sunlamp (sŭn'lămp') *n.* lampada solare.

sunlight (sŭn'līt') *n.* luce solare, sole.

sunlit (sŭn'lĭt') *agg.* soleggiato.

sunny (sŭn'ĭ) *agg.* soleggiato, assolato; solatio; radioso, felice: — day, giornata di sole; — disposition, carattere allegro.

sunrise (sŭn'rīz') *n.* levar del sole, alba.

sunset (sŭn'sĕt') *n.* tramonto del sole.

sunshade (sŭn'shād') *n.* parasole.

sunshine (sŭn'shīn') *n.* luce del sole, sereno.

sunstroke (sŭn'strōk') *n.* colpo di sole.

sup (sŭp) *vt.* centellinare. *vi.* cenare.

superabundant (sū'pĕr·å·bŭn'dănt) *agg.* sovrabbondante.

superannuate (sūp'ĕr·ăn'û·āt) *vt.* mandare in pensione.

superb (sū·pûrb') *agg.* superbo; eccellente, splendido.

supercargo (sū'pĕr·kär'gō) *n.* (*naut.*) sovraccarico (*sovrintendente al carico*).

supercharger (sū'pĕr·chär'jĕr) *n.* (*mecc.*) turbocompressore.

supercilious (sū'pĕr·sĭl'ĭ·ŭs) *agg.* altezzoso, sprezzante, arrogante.

superficial (sū'pĕr·fĭsh'ăl) *agg.* superficiale.

superficies (sū'pĕr·fĭsh'ĭ·ēz) *n.* superficie.

superfine (sū'pĕr·fīn') *agg.* sopraffino. *n.pl.* merci sopraffine.

superfluous (sū·pûr'flōō·ŭs) *agg.* superfluo.

superhighway (sū'pĕr·hī'wā') *n.* superautostrada.

superhuman (sū'pĕr·hū'măn) *agg.* sovrumano.

superimpose (sū'pĕr·ĭm·pōz') *vt.* sovrapporre.

superintend (sū'pĕr·ĭn·tĕnd') *vt.* sovrintendere a, dirigere.

superintendent (sū'pĕr·ĭn·tĕn'dĕnt) *n.* sovrintendente; direttore; ispettore.

superior (sū·pēr'ĭ·ĕr) *n.*, *agg.* superiore: a — air, un'aria di superiorità.

superiority (sū·pēr'ĭ·ŏr'ĭ·tĭ) *n.* superiorità.

superlative (sū·pûr'lă·tĭv) *n.*, *agg.* superlativo.

superman (sū'pĕr·măn') *n.* superuomo.

supermarket (sū'pĕr·mär'kĕt) *n.* supermercato.

supernatural (sūp'ĕr·năt'û·răl) *n.*, *agg.* soprannaturale.

supernumerary (sū'pĕr·nū'mĕr·ĕr'ĭ) *n.* impiegato in soprannumero; (*teat.*) comparsa. *agg.* soprannumerario.

supersede (sū'pĕr·sēd') *vt.* soppiantare, sostituire.

supersonic (sū'pĕr·sŏn'ĭk) *agg.* ultrasonoro; (*aeron.*) supersonico.

superstition (sū'pĕr·stĭsh'ŭn) *n.* superstizione.

superstitious (sū'pĕr·stĭsh'ŭs) *agg.* superstizioso.

supervise (sū'pĕr·vīz) *vt.* sovrintendere a, sorvegliare, dirigere.

supervision (sū'pĕr·vĭzh'ŭn) *n.* controllo, direzione, sovrintendenza.

supervisor (sū'pĕr·vī'zĕr) *n.* sovrintendente.

supine (sû·pīn') *agg.* supino, inerte, indifferente.

supper (sŭp'ĕr) *n.* cena.

supplant (sŭp·lánt') *vt.* soppiantare.

supple (sŭp'l) *agg.* flessibile, elastico, duttile, docile, cedevole.

supplement (sŭp'lĕ·mĕnt) *n.* supplemento; *vt.* completare, integrare; aggiungere a.

suppliant (sŭp'lĭ·ănt), **supplicant** (sŭp'-lĭ·kánt) *n.*, *agg.* postulante.

supplicate (sŭp'lĭ·kāt) *vt.* supplicare.

supplication (sŭp'lĭ·kā'shŭn) *n.* supplica.

supplier (sŭ·plī'ĕr) *n.* fornitore.

supply (sŭp'lĭ) (1) *avv.* elasticamente, docilmente, cedevolmente.

supply (sŭ·plī') (2) *n.* (*spesso usato al pl.*: supplies) provvista; fornitura, rifornimento; viveri. *agg.* di rifornimento. *vt.*, *vi.* (*gen.seg. da* with) fornire, rifornire, provvedere, soddisfare; sostituire.

support (sŭ·pōrt') *n.* sostegno, appoggio, puntello; mantenimento, sostentamento; (*teat.*) attore secondario. *vt.* reggere, sostenere; difendere; mantenere; appoggiare.

supporter *n.* sostenitore, difensore, fautore; fascia elastica, giarrettiera.

suppose (sŭ·pōz') *v.* supporre, immaginare: it is supposed, si presume.

supposed (sŭ·pōzd') *agg.* presunto, ipotetico. —ly (-ĕd·lĭ) *avv.* presumibilmente, ipoteticamente.

supposition (sŭp'ō·zĭsh'ŭn) *n.* supposizione, ipotesi.

suppress (sŭ·prĕs') *vt.* sopprimere; reprimere, soffocare; nascondere. —ed *agg.* soppresso; represso, soffocato. —ion *n.* soppressione; repressione.

suppurate (sŭp'û·rāt) *vi.* suppurare.

supremacy (sû·prĕm'å·sĭ) *n.* supremazia.

supreme (sû·prēm') *agg.* supremo.

surcharge (sûr·chärj') *n.* sovraccarico; stampigliatura.

sure (shōōr) *agg.* sicuro, certo, stabile: to make —, assicurare, assicurarsi; to be —! certo!; *avv.* (*anche* —ly) sicuramente, indubbiamente. —ness *n.* sicurezza, certezza.

surety (shōōr'tĭ) *n.* sicurezza; pegno, garanzia; garante: to stand — for, farsi garante di.

surf (sûrf) *n.* risacca, spuma.

surface (sûr′fĭs) *n.* superficie. *agg.* di superficie; superficiale. *vt.* lisciare, spianare, rifinire; far emergere. *vi.* emergere, affiorare.

surfeit (sûr′fĭt) *n.* eccesso, sazietà, disgusto. *vt.* saziare, disgustare.

surge (sûrj) *n.* maroso, ondata; tumulto. *vi.* gonfiarsi, sollevarsi, tumultuare.

surgeon (sûr′jŭn) *n.* chirurgo.

surgery (sûr′jẽr·ĭ) *n.* chirurgia; ambulatorio; sala-operatoria.

surly (sûr′lĭ) *agg.* sgarbato, burbero, arcigno.

surmise (sûr·mīz′) *n.* supposizione, congettura. *vt.*, *vi.* arguire, intuire, dedurre.

surmount (sûr·mount′) *vt.* sormontare, superare, valicare.

surname (sûr′nām′) *n.* cognome.

surpass (sẽr·pàs′) *vt.* superare, sorpassare. **—ing** *agg.* eccellente, superiore, straordinario.

surplice (sûr′plĭs) *n.* (*eccles.*) cotta.

surplus (sûr′plŭs) *n.* soprappiù, eccedenza; residuo (*attivo*), maggior utile. *agg.* in soprappiù, eccedente.

surprisal (sẽr·prīz′ăl) *n.* sorpresa.

surprise (sẽr·prīz′) *n.* sorpresa, stupore. *vt.* cogliere alla sprovvista, meravigliare, stupire.

surprising (sẽr·prīz′ĭng) *agg.* sorprendente.

surrender (sŭ·rĕn′dẽr) *n.* resa, capitolazione; consegna; rinunzia. *vt.*, *vi.* consegnare; abbandonare; arrendersi; rinunziare (*a*); sottomettersi, costituirsi.

surreptitious (sûr′ĕp·tĭsh′ŭs) *agg.* fraudolento, clandestino, furtivo.

surrogate (sûr′ō·gât) *n.* sostituto, interino, supplente; surrogato.

surround (sŭ·round′) *vt.* circondare, cingere, attorniare.

surrounding *n.* accerchiamento. *agg.* circostante.

surroundings *n.pl.* dintorni; ambiente; circostanze.

surtout (sûr·tōōt′) *n.* finanziera, soprabito.

surveillance (sûr·vāl′ăns) *n.* vigilanza.

survey (sẽr·vā′) *n.* veduta generale; esame, ispezione, estimo, perizia; planimetria. *vt.* osservare, ispezionare; stimare (*terreni*, *ecc.*); esaminare, contemplare.

surveyor (sẽr·vā′ẽr) *n.* ispettore (*della dogana*, *ecc.*); agrimensore.

survival (sẽr·vīv′ăl) *n.* sopravvivenza; residuo (*o* superstite) di tempi passati.

survive (sẽr·vīv′) *vt.* sopravvivere a. *vi.* sopravvivere.

survivor (sẽr·vī′vẽr) *n.* superstite.

susceptibility (sŭ·sĕp′tĭ·bĭl′ĭ·tĭ) *n.* suscettibilità.

susceptible (sŭ·sĕp′tĭ·b′l) *agg.* suscettibile, sensibile, ricettivo.

suspect (sŭs′pĕkt) *n.* sospetto; persona sospetta, indiziato. (*sŭs·pĕkt′*) *vt.* sospettare, diffidare di. *vi.* avere dei sospetti.

suspend (sŭs·pĕnd′) *vt.* appendere; sospendere: suspended animation, morte apparente.

suspenders (sŭs·pĕn′dẽrz) *n.pl.* bretelle; giarrettiere.

suspense (sŭs·pĕns′) *n.* incertezza, ansia, dubbio; sospensione: to keep in —, tenere con l'animo sospeso.

suspension (sŭs·pĕn′shŭn) *n.* sospensione: — bridge, ponte sospeso.

suspicion (sŭs·pĭsh′ŭn) *n.* sospetto, diffidenza; traccia.

suspicious (sŭs·pĭsh′ŭs) *agg.* sospettoso; sospetto, losco.

sustain (sŭs·tān′) *vt.* sostenere, sorreggere; sopportare, subire; sostentare; prolungare.

sustenance (sŭs′tĕ·năns) *n.* alimento; mantenimento, mezzi di sussistenza.

swab (swŏb) *n.* straccio per pavimenti; scovolo da cannone; (*med.*) tampone; (*naut.*) radazza.

swaddle (swŏd′'l) *vt.* fasciare.

swaddling (swŏd′lĭng) *n.* fasciatura: — clothes, fasce per neonato.

swag (swăg) *n.* fardello; (*gergo*) bottino, refurtiva.

swage (swāj) *n.* (*mecc.*) punzone.

swagger (swăg′ẽr) *n.* bravata, fanfaronata; andatura spavalda. *vi.* fare il rodomonte, pavoneggiarsi.

swain (swān) *n.* innamorato (*spec. campagnuolo*); giovanotto.

swallow (swŏl′ō) (1) *vt.* inghiottire, trangugiare. *vi.* deglutire.

swallow (swŏl′ō) (2) *n.* rondine.

swam (swăm) *pass.* di to swim.

swamp (swŏmp) *n.* palude, marcita. *vt.*, *vi.* inondare, impantanare; (*naut.*) riempire d'acqua; affondare; imbarcare acqua: swamped with work, sommerso dal lavoro. *agg.* paludoso.

swan (swŏn) *n.* cigno.

swank (swăngk) *n.* (*gergo*) vanteria, esagerazione; *agg.* (*anche* swanky) pretenzioso, vistoso, ricercato; snello, flessibile.

swap (swŏp) *n.* baratto. *vt.* barattare.

swarm (swôrm) *n.* sciame, moltitudine. *vt.*, *vi.* invadere, affollare, sciamare, pullulare, accalcarsi, brulicare.

swarthy (swòr'thǐ) *agg.* scuro (*di pelle*), olivastro.

swash (swòsh) *n.* canale, sciacquio. *vt.*, *vi.* diguazzare, guazzare; turbinare, sferzare; far roteare.

swat (swòt) *n.* colpo violento.

swath (swòth) *n.* falciata; solco.

swathe (swāth) *vt.* fasciare, bendare.

sway (swā) *n.* ondeggiamento; potere, potenza, preponderanza. *vt.* sballottare, dominare, far dondolare, influenzare. *vi.* ondeggiare, bilanciarsi, barcollare; propendere; predominare.

swear (swâr) *vt.*, *vi.* (*pass.* swore, *pp.* sworn) giurare, far giurare, testimoniare; imprecare, bestemmiare; to — at, imprecare contro.

sweat (swĕt) *n.* sudore, traspirazione. *vt.* (*pass.*, *pp.* sweat *o* sweated) far sudare; trasudare; far sgobbare. *vi.* sudare; sfacchinare.

sweater (swĕt'ĕr) *n.* sudatore; maglione; aguzzino.

sweaty (swĕt'ĭ) *agg.* sudato; faticoso.

Swede (swēd) *n.*, *agg.* svedese.

Swedish (swēd'ĭsh) *n.* lingua svedese: the —, gli svedesi. *agg.* svedese.

sweep (swēp) *n.* spazzata; spazzatura; colpo; curva; gesto (*o* moto) circolare; strascico; spazzacamino; (*pl.*) remi: to make a clean —, fare un repulisti. *vt.*, *vi.* (*pass.*, *pp.* swept) scopare, spazzar via; strisciare; sfiorare; dragare; passare rapidamente; camminare con portamento eretto; sfilare; estendersi: to — down on, piombare su.

sweeper *n.* spazzino; spazzola.

sweeping *n.* spazzata; sweepings, immondizia. *agg.* rapido; ampio; generale, completo: — victory, vittoria assoluta.

sweet (swĕt) *n.* dolce, dolcezza; *agg.* dolce, zuccherino, fragrante, piacevole, fresco: to be — on, essere innamorato di: to have a — tooth, essere ghiotto di dolciumi; — bay, alloro, magnolia virginiana; — pea, pisello odoroso; — potato, patata americana.

sweetbread (swĕt'brĕd') *n.* animella.

sweeten (swĕt'n) *vt.* addolcire, inzuccherare, ammansire.

sweetheart (swĕt'härt') *n.* innamorato, innamorata.

sweetish (swĕt'ĭsh) *agg.* dolciastro.

sweetly (swĕt'lĭ) *avv.* dolcemente, soavemente; melodiosamente.

sweetmeat (swĕt'mĕt') *n.* dolciume.

sweetness (swĕt'nĕs) *n.* dolcezza, soavità.

swell (swĕl) *n.* protuberanza, gonfiore; aumento; monticello; caval-lone (*onda*); crescendo. *agg.* grandioso; elegante magnifico. *vt.* (*pass.* swelled, welled *o* swollen) enfiare, gonfiare accrescere; insuperbire. *vi.* gonfiarsi, aumentare; espandersi; sollevarsi; intensificarsi; insuperbirsi.

swelling *n.* protuberanza, gonfiore; piena (*di fiume*). *agg.* gonfio, tronfio, crescente.

swelter (swĕl'tĕr) *n.* afa. *vt.*, *vi.* opprimere; soffocare dal caldo.

swept (swĕpt) *pass.*, *pp. di* to sweep.

swerve (swûrv) *n.* scarto, svolta, deviazione. *vt.* sviare. *vi.* deviare, svoltare; fare uno scarto.

swift (swĭft) *n.* rapida (*di fiume*); mulinello; rondone. *agg.* rapido, svelto, leggiero, pronto. —ly *avv.* velocemente, prontamente. —ness *n.* rapidità, prontezza.

swig (swĭg) *n.* lunga sorsata. *vt.* tracannare.

swill (swĭl) *n.* lunga sorsata (*di liquore*); beverone del maiale; rifiuti. *vt.* tracannare avidamente; lavare, risciacquare.

swim (swĭm) *n.* nuotata. — suit, costume da bagno. *vt.* (*pass.* swam, *pp.* swum) far galleggiare. *vi.* nuotare, galleggiare; essere inondato (*o* inzuppato), girare (*della testa*), avere le vertigini.

swimmer *n.* nuotatore.

swindle (swĭn'd'l) *n.* truffa, frode. *vt.*, *vi.* truffare, abbindolare.

swindler (swĭn'dlĕr) *n.* truffatore.

swine (swĭn) *n.* maiale, porco; maiali, porci.

swing (swĭng) *n.* oscillazione, dondolamento; altalena; impulso, propulsione, slancio: in full —, in piena attività, al colmo; — door, porta a molle. *vt.* (*pass.*, *pp.* swung) dondolare, far oscillare; appendere; brandire, far rotare. *vi.* oscillare, rotare; girare (*sui cardini*); voltarsi; ondeggiare, bilanciarsi; svoltare; penzolare, morire impiccato.

swipe (swĭp) *n.* (*gergo*) manata, colpo violento; *vt.* colpire violentemente; (*gergo*) rubacchiare, rubare.

swirl (swûrl) *n.* turbine, gorgo; ricciolo; guizzo. *vt.* prillare, far turbinare; *vi.* turbinare, guizzare.

swish (swĭsh) *n.* fruscio.

Swiss (swĭs) *n.*, *agg.* svizzero.

switch (swĭch) *n.* bacchetta, verga; cambiamento; treccia posticcia; (*ferr.*) scambio; (*elett.*) interruttore, commutatore; *vt.*, *vi.* sviare, sferzare; deviare, mutare: to — on, accendere (*la luce*); to — off, spegnere, interrompere.

switchboard (swĭch'bōrd') *n.* quadro elettrico, centralino telefonico.

switchblade knife (swĭch'blād') *n.* coltello a serramanico.

swivel (swĭv''l) *n.* perno, gancio girevole. *vt.* far rotare. *vi.* rotare, girare.

swollen (swōl'ĕn) *pp. di* to swell. *agg.* gonfio, tronfio, turgido.

swoon (swōōn) *n.* svenimento. *vi.* svenire.

swoop (swōōp) *n.* calata (*del rapace*); assalto. *vt.* ghermire. *vi.* piombare sulla preda: **to — down upon,** piombare addosso a.

sword (sōrd) *n.* spada: **— cane,** bastone animato.

swordsman (sōrdz'măn) *n.* schermidore, spadaccino; soldato.

swore (swōr) *pass. di* to swear.

sworn (swōrn) *pp. di* to swear.

swum (swŭm) *pp. di* to swim.

swung (swŭng) *pass., pp. di* to swing.

sycophant (sĭk'ō-fănt) *n.* adulatore.

syllable (sĭl'á-b'l) *n.* sillaba.

syllabus (sĭl'á-bŭs) *n.* sommario.

sylph (sĭlf) *n.* silfo, silfide.

symbol (sĭm'bŭl) *n.* simbolo; sigla. **—ic, —ical** (-bŏl'ĭk-ăl) *agg.* simbolico. **—ism** *n.* simbolismo.

symmetrical (sĭ-mĕt'rĭ-kăl) *agg.* simmetrico.

symmetry (sĭm'ê-trĭ) *n.* simmetria.

sympathetic (sĭm'pá-thĕt'ĭk) *agg.* comprensivo, compassionevole, solidale.

sympathize (sĭm'pá-thīz) *vi.* provare (*o* esprimere) comprensione: **to —** **with,** compiangere, fare le condoglianze a; approvare, condividere l'opinione di; comprendere.

sympathy (sĭm'pá-thĭ) *n.* comprensione, compassione, solidarietà; condoglianze.

symphonic (sĭm-fŏn'ĭk) *agg.* sinfonico.

symphony (sĭm'fō-nĭ) *n.* sinfonia: **— orchestra,** orchestra sinfonica.

symptom (sĭmp'tŭm) *n.* sintomo, indizio. **—atic** (-măt'ĭk) *agg.* sintomatico.

synagogue (sĭn'á-gŏg) *n.* sinagoga.

synchronism (sĭng'krō-nĭz'm) *n.* sincronismo.

synchronize (sĭng'krō-nīz) *vt.* sincronizzare. *vt.* coincidere; essere sincrono.

synchronous (sĭng'krō-nŭs) *agg.* sincrono.

syncopate (sĭng'kō-pāt) *vt.* sincopare.

syncopation (sĭng'kō-pā'shŭn) *n.* sincopatura.

syndicalism (sĭn'dĭ-kăl-ĭz'm) *n.* sindacalismo.

syndicate (sĭn'dĭ-kăt) *n.* sindacato, consiglio, società, consorzio. *vt.* consorziare; pubblicare simultaneamente in vari periodici; *vi.* consorziarsi.

synonym (sĭn'ō-nĭm) *n.* sinonimo. **—ous** (-ŏn'ĭ-mŭs) *agg.* sinonimo, equivalente.

synopsis (sĭ-nŏp'sĭs) *n.* sintesi, sunto.

syntax (sĭn'tăks) *n.* sintassi.

synthesis (sĭn'thê-sĭs) *n.* sintesi.

synthetic (sĭn-thĕt'ĭk) *agg.* sintetico.

syntony (sĭn'tō-nĭ) *n.* sintonia.

syphilis (sĭf'ĭ-lĭs) *n.* (*med.*) sifilide.

syphon *vedi* siphon.

syringe (sĭr'ĭnj) *n.* siringa. *vt.* siringare, iniettare.

syrup (sĭr'ŭp) *n.* sciroppo.

syrupy (sĭr'ŭp-ĭ) *agg.* sciropposo.

system (sĭs'tĕm) *n.* sistema; (*gergo*) organismo; (*ferr.*) rete. **—atic** (-ăt'ĭk) *agg.* sistematico.

systematize (sĭs'tĕm-á-tīz) *vt.* metodizzare, ridurre a sistema.

T

tab (tăb) *n.* linguetta, aletta; etichetta, talloncino: **to keep tabs on,** vigilare; tenersi al corrente di.

tabby (tăb'ĭ) *n.* gatto; (*tess.*) moire.

tabernacle (tăb'ẽr-năk''l) *n.* tenda, tabernacolo; (*naut.*) pozzo dell'albero.

table (tāb''l) *n.* tavola; tabella, lapide; indice: **multiplication —,** tavola pitagorica; **— cover,** tappeto da tavola. *vi.* ordinare in tabella; porre sulla tavola; rinviare (*una discussione, ecc.*)

tableau (tăb-lō') *n.* quadro.

tablecloth (tā'b'l-clŏth') *n.* tovaglia.

tableland (tā'b'l-lănd') *n.* altipiano.

tablespoon (tā'b'l-spōōn') *n.* cucchiaio da minestra. **—ful** *n.* cucchiaiata.

tableware (tā'b'l-wâr') *n.* vasellame, servizio da tavola.

tablet (tăb'lĕt) *n.* tavoletta; pastiglia, compressa; blocco per annotazioni, taccuino.

tabloid (tăb'loid) *n.* pasticca; giornale a formato ridotto.

tabulate (tăb'ů-lāt) *vt.* ridurre a sinossi, catalogare.

tachometer (tá-kŏm'ê-tẽr) *n.* tachimetro.

tacit (tăs'ĭt) *agg.* tacito, implicito. [tro.

taciturn (tăs'ĭ-tûrn) *agg.* taciturno.

tack (tăk) *n.* chiodo, bulletta, puntina da disegno; (*naut.*) mura (*fune che* *fissa l'angolo di una vela*), bordata, virata, rotta, bordeggio: to be on the right —, essere sulla buona via; to change —, cambiar rotta. *vt.*, *vi.* inchiodare, attaccare, imbastire; (*naut.*) andar di bolina, bordeggiare, virare.

tackle (tak''l) *n.* carrucola; armamentario; (*naut.*) paranco; sartiame; attrezzatura; (*calcio*) carica, attaccante: **fishing** —, attrezzi per la pesca. *vt.* impugnare, afferrare; affrontare; avvighiarsi a; bardare; (*calcio*) ostacolare, attaccare.

tact (tăkt) *n.* tatto, diplomazia.

tactful (tăkt'fŏŏl) *agg.* accorto, diplomatico: — **man**, uomo di tatto.

tactics (tăk'tĭks) *n.sing.* tattica.

tactile (tăk't'l) *agg.* tattile.

tactless (tăkt'lĕs) *agg.* privo di tatto, indelicato.

tadpole (tăd'pōl') *n.* (*zool.*) girino.

taffrail (tăf'rāl) *n.* (*naut.*) parapetto di poppa.

taffy (tăf'ĭ) *n.* caramella.

tag (tăg) *n.* pendaglio, appiccagnolo; punta ferrata (*di stringa, ecc.*); etichetta (*da appendere al bagaglio, ecc.*); estremità; (*teat.*) battuta: to play —, giocare a rincorrersi. *vt.* mettere l'etichetta a; attaccare, appendere; (*fam.*) pedinare.

tail (tāl) *n.* coda; estremità; seguito; rovescio (*di moneta*); (*fam.*) pedinatore; *pl.* narsina. *vt.* metter la coda a; mettere in fila; (*gergo*) pedinare. *vi.* formare una coda: to — off (out, away, down), diminuire, affievolirsi, disperdersi —**light** *n.* fanale di coda. —**spin** *n.* (*aeron.*) caduta in vite.

tailor (tā'lēr) *n.* sarto. —**ing** *n.* sartoria (*arte*).

tailpiece (tāl'pēs') *n.* aggiunta; trave.

taint (tānt) *n.* infezione; magagna, macchia; discredito. *vt.* contaminare, insozzare, guastare. *vi.* guastarsi.

take (tāk) *n.* presa; pesca; (*cinema*) ripresa; (*gergo*) incasso, introito. *vt.*, *vi.* (*pass.* took, *pp.* taken) prendere; i mpadronirsi di; condurre, guidare, portare; credere; attrarre; contenere; subire; chiedere (*un prezzo*); attecchire; riuscire bene (*in fotografia*): to — **aback**, cogliere ii sorpresa; to — **after**, somigliare a; to — **amiss**, prendere in mala parte; to — **apart**, smontare, scomporre; to — **away**, togliere, privare, sottrarre, portare via; to — **back**, riprendere, ritirare; to — **back one's word**, rimangiarsi la parola; to — **down**, annotare; de-

molire; smontare; mandare giù, inghiottire; umiliare; to — **for**, prendere per, scambiare per; to — **for granted**, avere la certezza che; to — **from**, prendere a, prendere da, portare via a; to — **in**, comprendere; includere; accogliere; contenere; ingannare, imbrogliare; stringere (*un vestito*); to — **off**, togliere, togliersi; distogliere; dedurre; cessare; partire; (*aeron.*) decollare; parodiare; to — (**oneself**) **off**, andarsene; to — **on**, prendere; assumere; accogliere; addossarsi (*una responsabilità*); accettare (*un avversario*); agitarsi, eccitarsi; to — **out**, togliere, portare via; asportare; separare; sottrarre; omettere; portare a, condurre a; to — **over**, subentrare a, prendere la direzione di; to — **to**, darsi a; affezionarsi a; correre a, buttarsi a; to — **up**, occupare, portare via (*tempo*); raccogliere (*passeggieri*); assorbire; interrompere, correggere (*uno che parla*); darsi a, intraprendere; riprendere (*un discorso*); adottare; accollarsi; fare onore a (*un impegno*); to — **to one's heels**, darsela a gambe; to — **to heart**, prendersi a cuore; to — **to pieces**, fare a pezzi; to — **to task**, richiamare all'ordine; to — **a chance**, correre un rischio; to — **a fancy to**, incapricciarsi di, innamorarsi di; to — **a jump**, spiccare un salto; to — **a look at**, dare un'occhiata a; to — **a notion to**, mettersi in testa di; to — **an oath**, prestare un giuramento; to — **a trip**, fare un viaggio; to — **advantage of**, approfittare di; to — **care**, stare attento; to — **care of**, aver cura di; to — **charge of**, incaricarsi di, assumere la direzione di; to — **effect**, avere effetto, fare effetto; to — **exercise**, fare esercizio; to — **leave**, congedarsi, salutare; to — **offense**, offendersi; to — **place**, aver luogo, avverarsi, capitare; to — **stock in**, avere stima di, avere fiducia in; to — **stock of**, fare l' inventario di; prendere visione di; to — **the floor**, prendere la parola; to — **one's time**, fare con comodo o con calma; — **it easy!** calmal, non agitatevil, non prendetevela!, andateci piano!

taken (tāk'ĕn) *pp. di* to take: to be — **ill**, cadere ammalato, ammalarsi.

takeoff (tāk'ôf') *n.* caricatura, parodia; (*aeron.*) decollo, involo.

talc, talcum (tăl'kŭm) *n.* talco.

tale (tāl) *n.* racconto, favola, storiella; bugia; pettegolezzo; resoconto:

the — of years, la somma degli anni.

talebearer (tāl′bâr′ĕr) *n.* propalatore, malalingua.

talent (tăl′ĕnt) *n.* ingegno, propensione, abilità, talento. **—ed** *agg.* abile, intelligente, di ingegno.

talk (tôk) *n.* conversazione, discorso, colloquio; eloquio; diceria: small —, chiacchiere insulse; the — of the town, l'argomento di cui tutti parlano. *vt.* parlare di, dire. *vi.* parlare, chiacchierare: to — nonsense, dire sciocchezze; to — someone out of, dissuadere qualcuno da; to — someone into, persuadere qualcuno a; to — over, discutere. **—ative** (-á·tĭv) *agg.* loquace, ciarliero. **—er** *n.* parlatore; chiacchierone. **—ing** *agg.* parlante: — picture, film sonoro *o* parlato.

tall (tôl) *agg.* alto, grande: a — order, un compito arduo, una richiesta eccessiva; a — story, una storia incredibile.

tallow (tăl′ō) *n.* sego.

tally (tăl′ĭ) *n.* tacca; conto; spunta; etichetta, talloncino; duplicato. *vt.* spuntare; registrare; calcolare; munire d'etichetta. *vi.* fare la spunta; corrispondere, collimare.

talon (tăl′ŭn) *n.* artiglio.

tame (tām) *agg.* domestico, addomesticato, mansueto, docile; insulso, fiacco. *vt.* domare, addomesticare.

tamely *avv.* docilmente, passivamente.

tamer (tām′ĕr) *n.* domatore.

tamper (tăm′pĕr) *vi.* immischiarsi; armeggiare: to — with, adulterare; manomettere; tentar di forzare.

tan (tăn) *n.* tannino, concia; abbronzatura; marrone (colore). *vt.* conciare; abbronzare; (fam.) malmenare. *vi.* abbronzarsi.

tang (tăng) *n.* sapore violento, aroma; codolo (di lama).

tangent (tăn′jĕnt) *n., agg.* tangente: to go off on a —, partire per la tangente.

tangerine (tăn′jĕ·rēn′) *n.* mandarino.

tangible (tăn′jĭ·b'l) *agg.* tangibile.

tangle (tăng′g'l) *n.* groviglio, complicazione, imbroglio. *vt.* aggrovigliare, ingarbugliare, complicare. *vi.* ingarbugliarsi.

tangly (tăng′glĭ) *agg.* aggrovigliato.

tank (tăngk) *n.* serbatoio, cisterna; carro armato.

tankard (tăngk′ĕrd) *n.* boccale.

tanker (tăngk′ĕr) *n.* nave cisterna.

tanner (tăn′ĕr) *n.* conciatore.

tannery (tăn′ĕr·ĭ) *n.* conceria.

tannin (tăn′ĭn) *n.* (chim.) tannino.

tanning (tăn′ĭng) *n.* concia; abbronzatura; (fam.) bastonatura.

tantalization (tăn′tá·lĭ·zā′shŭn) *n.* supplizio di Tantalo, tormento.

tantalize (tăn′tá·lĭz) *vt.* sottoporre al supplizio di Tantalo, tormentare.

tantamount (tăn′tá·mount′) *agg.* equivalente.

tantrum (tăn′trŭm) *n.* accesso di collera; bizze, capricci.

tap (tăp) *n.* colpetto, segnale; rubinetto, zipolo, spina; banco di mescita, bar; (elett.) presa, inserimento: (pl., mil.) silenzio: — dance, tip-tap; beer on —, birra spillata. *vt., vi.* battere, bussare; spillare; forare; inserirsi (su una linea elett. o telef.).

tape (tăp) *n.* fettuccia, nastro, striscia; nastro magnetico: — line, — measure, metro a nastro; — recorder, magnetofono. *vt.* misurare (o legare) con nastro; incidere su nastro.

taper (tā′pĕr) *n.* assottigliamento; candela, cero. *vt., vi.* assottigliare, assottigliarsi, diminuire, affusolare, affusolarsi, rastremare.

tapering *agg.* affusolato; rastremato.

tapestry (tăp′ĕs·trĭ) *n.* arazzo, tappezzeria.

tapeworm (tāp′wûrm′) *n.* tenia.

taproom (tăp′rōōm′) *n.* sala di taverna.

tapster (tăp′stĕr) *n.* barista.

tar (tär) *n.* pece; catrame. *vt.* impeciare; incatramare.

tardy (tär′dĭ) *agg.* lento, tardivo: to be —, arrivare in ritardo.

tare (tär) *n.* (comm.) tara.

target (tär′gĕt) *n.* bersaglio; obiettivo.

tariff (tăr′ĭf) *n.* tariffa.

tarn (tärn) *n.* lago di montagna.

tarnish (tär′nĭsh) *vt.* macchiare; opacare; annerire; ossidare; inquinare. *vi.* annerirsi, ossidarsi. *n.* opacità; annerimento; ossidazione; macchia.

tarpaulin (tär′pô′lĭn) *n.* tela incerata (o catramata).

tarry (tăr′ĭ) (1) *agg.* incatramato.

tarry (tăr′ĭ) (2) *vi.* sostare, indugiare, attardarsi.

tart (tärt) (1) *n.* crostata, pasticcio; (gergo) sgualdrina.

tart (tärt) (2) *agg.* agro, aspro. **—ly** *avv.* aspramente.

task (tăsk) *n.* mansione, compito, fatica; (mil.) missione: to take to —, redarguire; — force, contingente destinato a una missione. *vt.* assegnare (un compito) a; caricare (di); mettere alla prova; accusare (di).

tassel (tăs′'l) *n.* fiocco, nappa.

taste (tāst) *n.* gusto, sapore, assaggio, buon gusto. *vt.* assaggiare, gustare. *vi.* sapere (di). **—ful** *agg.* elegante, di buon gusto. **—less** *agg.* insipido, insapore; privo di buon gusto.

tasty *agg.* saporito; elegante, di buon gusto.

tatter (tăt'ĕr) *n.* brandello, straccio.

tatterdemalion (tăt'ĕr·dē·māl'yŭn) *n.* straccione.

tattered (tăt'ĕrd) *agg.* lacero, cencioso.

tattle (tăt''l) *n.* chiacchierio. *vi.* cicalare, chiacchierare.

tattoo (tă'tōō') (1) *n.* tatuaggio. *vt.* tatuare.

tattoo (2) *n.* rullo di tamburo, stamburamento; (*mil.*) segnale di ritirata; battito ritmato.

taught (tòt) *pass., pp. di* to teach.

taunt (tònt) *n.* punzecchiatura, sarcasmo; sfida. *vt.* beffare, punzecchiare; sfidare.

taut (tòt) *agg.* rigido, teso; lindo.

tauten (tòt''n) *vt.* tendere, irrigidire. *vi.* tendersi, irrigidirsi.

tavern (tăv'ĕrn) *n.* taverna, locanda.

taw (tò) *n.* biglia, pallina.

tawdry (tò'drĭ) *agg.* pacchiano, vistoso.

tawny (tò'nĭ) *agg.* bruno, bronzeo, fulvo.

tax (tăks) *n.* tassa, imposta; compito, gravame: income **—**, tassa sul reddito. *vt.* tassare, imporre; mettere a dura prova; tacciare, accusare.

taxi (tăk'sĭ), **taxicab** (tăk'sĭ·kăb') *n.* tassì, autopubblica. *vi.* andare in tassì; (*aeron.*) rullare.

taxidermist (tăk'sĭ·dûr'mĭst) *n.* imbalsamatore.

taximeter (tăk'sĭ·mē'tēr) *n.* tassametro.

taxpayer (tăks'pā'ēr) *n.* contribuente.

tea (tē) *n.* tè: beef **—**, brodo di carne; **— kettle**, cuccuma per tè. **—cup**, *n.* tazza da tè. **—pot** *n.* teiera. **—spoon** *n.* cucchiaino da tè.

teach (tēch) *vt., vi. (pass. pp.* taught) insegnare, istruire. **—er** *n.* insegnante. **—ing** *n.* insegnamento.

team (tēm) *n.* tiro (a due, a quattro, ecc.); coppia; gruppo, squadra (anche sport.). *vt.* aggiogare; raggruppare; accoppiare.

teamster (tēm'stēr) *n.* guidatore.

teamwork (tēm'wûrk') *n.* lavoro di squadra.

tear (tēr) (1) *n.* lagrima, pianto.

tear (târ) (2) *n.* strappo, lacerazione; impeto: wear and **—**, logorio. *vt.* strappare, stracciare, lacerare. *vi.* stracciarsi, lacerarsi; andare a precipizio; infuriare: to **— apart**, smontare; separare, staccare; dilaniare; strappare; to **— down**,

abbattere, demolire; smontare; to **— into**, entrare precipitosamente; to **— oneself away**, andarsene a malincuore.

tearful (tēr'fŏŏl) *agg.* lagrimoso, piangente.

tease (tēz) *n.* tormentatore, tormento. *vt.* stuzzicare, importunare, tormentare.

teasel (tē'z'l) *n.* (bot.) cardo; (mecc.) cardatrice.

teat (tēt) *n.* capezzolo.

technical (tĕk'nĭ·kăl) *agg.* tecnico.

technicality (tĕk'nĭ·kăl'ĭ·tĭ) *n.* particolare tecnico.

technician (tĕk·nĭsh'ăn) *n.* tecnico.

technic (tĕk'nĭk) *n.* tecnica.

technique (tĕk·nēk') *n.* tecnica, metodo.

technology (tĕk·nŏl'ō·jĭ) *n.* tecnologia.

tedious (tē'dĭ·ŭs) *agg.* tedioso. **—ness** *n.* tediosità.

tedium (tē'dĭ·ŭm) *n.* tedio.

teem (tēm) *vi.* essere fecondo, abbondare: to **— with**, abbondare di.

teen (tēn) *agg.* dell' adolescenza: **— age**, età dell'adolescenza, età dai 13 al 19 anni.

teen-age *agg.* caratteristico dell'adolescenza; da adolescente.

teen-ager *n.* adolescente; giovanetto; fanciulla.

teens (tēnz) *n.pl.* età dai 13 ai 19 anni: to be in one's **—**, avere fra i 13 e i 19 anni, essere adolescente.

teeny (tēn'ĭ) *agg.* minuscolo.

teeth (tēth) *pl. di* tooth: by the skin of one's **—**, per il rotto della cuffia; in the **— of**, a dispetto di.

teethe (tēth) *vi.* mettere i denti.

teething *n.* dentizione.

teetotal (tē·tō't'l) *agg.* astemio.

teevee (tē'vē') *n.* televisione, TV.

telecast (tĕl'ē·kàst') *n.* trasmissione televisiva. *vt.* teletrasmettere, trasmettere per televisione.

telegenic (tĕl'ē·jĕn'ĭk) *agg.* telegenico.

telegram (tĕl'ē·grăm) *n.* telegramma.

telegraph (tĕl'ē·gràf) *n.* telegrafo. *vt., vi.* telegrafare.

telegraphic *agg.* telegrafico.

telegraphy (tē·lĕg'rá·fĭ) *n.* telegrafia.

telemeter (tē·lĕm'ē·tēr) *n.* telemetro.

telepathy (tē·lĕp'á·thĭ) *n.* telepatia.

telephone (tĕl'ē·fōn) *n.* telefono: **— booth**, cabina telefonica; **— directory**, guida telefonica; **— exchange**, centralino telefonico; **— operator**, telefonista. *vt., vi.* telefonare.

teleprinter (tĕl'ē·prĭn'tēr) *n.* telescrivente.

telescope (tĕl'ē·skōp) *n.* telescopio; cannocchiale. *vi.* (di oggetti) infilarsi uno nell'altro.

teletype (tĕl'ē·tip) n. telescrivente.

teleview (tĕl'ē·vū') vt. vedere al televisore. —er n. telespettatore.

television (tĕl'ē·vĭzh'ŭn) n. televisione: — set, televisore.

tell (tĕl) vt. (pass., pp. told) dire, raccontare; indicare, denotare, rivelare; distinguere, giudicare. vi. parlare; essere efficace; fare effetto: the hard work told on him, lo strenuo lavoro lo ha logorato; to — one from the other, distinguere l'uno dall'altro; to — somebody|off, cantarle chiare a qualcuno.

teller (tĕl'ẽr) n. narratore; computista, cassiere; (pol.) scrutatore.

telling (tĕl'ĭng) agg. efficace.

telltale (tĕl'tāl) n. informatore. agg. significativo, rivelatore.

telpher (tĕl'fẽr) n. teleferica.

temerity (tē·mĕr'ĭ·tĭ) n. temerità.

temper (tĕm'pẽr) n. umore, indole; malumore, collera; tempera; tempra (di metallo): in a good —, di buon umore; out of —, fuori dei gangheri; to keep one's —, dominarsi; to lose one's —, perdere la pazienza. vt. temperare, temprare, attenuare.

temperament (tĕm'pẽr·à·mĕnt) n. temperamento, personalità. —al agg. eccitabile, emotivo; collerico.

temperance (tĕm'pẽr·ăns) n. temperanza.

temperate (tĕm'pẽr·ĭt) agg. temperato; temperante, moderato.

temperature (tĕm'pẽr·à·tūr) n. temperatura; febbre.

tempest (tĕm'pĕst) n. tempesta, uragano.

tempestuous (tĕm·pĕs'tū·ŭs) agg. tempestoso; turbolento.

temple (tĕm'p'l) (1) n. tempio.

temple (tĕm'p'l) (2) n. (anat.) tempia.

temporal (tĕm'pō·rǎl) agg. temporale.

temporarily (tĕm'pō·rẽr'ĭ·lĭ) avv. temporaneamente, provvisoriamente.

temporary (tĕm'pō·rẽr'ĭ) agg. provvisorio, temporaneo, momentaneo.

tempt (tĕmpt) vt. allettare, tentare, provocare, indurre. —ation (-ā'shŭn) n. tentazione. —er n. tentatore. —ing agg. allettante. —ress n. tentatrice.

ten (tĕn) n., agg. dieci.

tenable (tĕn'à·b'l) agg. sostenibile, resistente.

tenacious (tē·nā'shŭs) agg. tenace; adesivo.

tenacity (tē·nǎs'ĭ·tĭ) n. tenacia; adesività.

tenancy (tĕn'ăn·sĭ) n. locazione.

tenant (tĕn'ănt) n. locatario, inquilino.

tench (tĕnch) n. (ittiol.) tinca.

tend (tĕnd) vt. curare, vegliare su, badare a, servire; custodire. vi. tendere (avere tendenza).

tendency (tĕn'dĕn·sĭ) n. tendenza.

tendentious (tĕn·dĕn'shŭs) agg. tendenzioso, capzioso, interessato: — writings, scritti tendenziosi, interessati, partigiani.

tender (tĕn'dẽr) (1) n. offerta, proposta. vt. offrire, porgere.

tender (tĕn'dẽr) (2) n. custode, servitore; (naut.) nave ausiliaria; scialuppa a rimorchio; (ferr.) tender, carro scorta.

tender (tĕn'dẽr) (3) agg. tenero, sensibile, delicato, debole, immaturo, affettuoso: —hearted agg. sensibile, di cuore tenero.

tenderloin (tĕn'dẽr·loin') n. filetto.

tenderness (tĕn'dẽr·nĕs) n. tenerezza, delicatezza, morbidezza.

tendon (tĕn'dŭn) n. (anat.) tendine.

tendril (tĕn'drĭl) n. (bot.) viticcio.

tenement (tĕn'ē·mĕnt) n. abitazione, possesso, casa d'affitto: — house, casa popolare.

tenet (tĕn'ĕt) n. principio, precetto, canone, dogma.

tenfold (tĕn'fōld') agg. decuplo. avv. dieci volte tanto.

tennis (tĕn'ĭs) n. tennis: — court, campo da tennis.

tenon (tĕn'ŭn) n. incastro.

tenor (tĕn'ẽr) n. tenore; tono, livello.

tenpins (tĕn'pĭnz') n. giuoco dei birilli.

tense (tĕns) n. tempo (del verbo). agg. teso, contrario, rigido.

tension (tĕn'shŭn) n. tensione.

tent (tĕnt) n. tenda. vt. (chir.) sondare. vi. attendarsi.

tentacle (tĕn'tà·k'l) n. tentacolo.

tentative (tĕn'tà·tĭv) agg. di prova, di sondaggio, sperimentale. —ly avv. sperimentalmente, a titolo di indagine, per tastare il terreno.

tenter (tĕn'tẽr) n. tenditoio.

tenterhook (-hōŏk') n. uncino di tenditoio: on tenterhooks, sulle spine.

tenth (tĕnth) n., agg. decimo.

tenuous (tĕn'ū·ŭs) agg. tenue.

tenure (tĕn'ūr) n. gestione, occupazione; periodo (di carica, ecc.).

tepid (tĕp'ĭd) agg. tiepido.

term (tûrm) n. termine, durata, limite (di tempo), periodo, sessione; pl. trattative, condizioni, prezzi: on good terms, in buoni rapporti; to come to terms, venire a patti. vt. definire, nominare.

termagant (tûr'mà·gănt) n. megera.

terminal (tûr'mĭ·nǎl) n. estremità, limite; (elett.) collegamento, innesto; stazione di testa, capolinea. agg. terminale, finale, confinario.

terminate (tûr′mĭ·nāt) vt., vi. terminare, delimitare, concludere.

termination (tur′mĭ·nā′shŭn) n. termine, conclusione; desinenza.

terminology (tûr′mĭ·nŏl′ō·jĭ) n. terminologia.

terminus (tûr′mĭ·nŭs) n. limite, confine; scalo, stazione di testa, capolinea.

terrace (tĕr′ĭs) n. terrazza, altura, terrapieno. vt. terrazzare.

terrapin (tĕr′á·pĭn) n. tartaruga ac-
quatica.

terrestrial (tĕr·ĕs′trĭ·ăl) agg. terrestre,
terragno.

terrible (tĕr′ĭ·b′l) agg. terribile, atroce; formidabile.

terribly (tĕr′ĭ·blĭ) avv. terribilmente;
estremamente, straordinariamente.

terrier (tĕr′ĭ·ĕr) n. cane terrier.

terrific (tĕ·rĭf′ĭk) agg. terribile; fenomenale, sbalorditivo, vertiginoso.

terrify (tĕr′ĭ·fī) vt. atterrire.

territory (tĕr′ĭ·tō′rĭ) n. territorio.

terror (tĕr′ĕr) n. terrore.

terrorism (tĕr′ĕr·ĭz′m) n. intimidazione, terrorismo.

terrorist (tĕr′ĕr·ĭst) n. terrorista.

terrorize (tĕr′ĕr·īz) vt. terrorizzare.

terse (tûrs) agg. terso, chiaro; conciso, elegante.

tessellate (tĕs′ĕ·lāt) vt. lavorare a mosaico, tessellare.

test (tĕst) n. prova, saggio, collaudo,
esperimento, esame, test: — tube,
provetta; to undergo a —, essere
sottoposto a una prova; — pilot, pilota collaudatore. vt. esaminare, collaudare, mettere alla prova, analizzare.

testament (tĕs′tá·mĕnt) n. testamento.

testator (tĕs·tā′tĕr) n. testatore.

tester (tĕs′tĕr) (1) n. sperimentatore,
collaudatore.

tester (tĕs′tĕr) (2) n. baldacchino.

testify (tĕs′tĭ·fī) vt., vi. testimoniare.
attestare.

testimonial (tĕs′tĭ·mō′nĭ·ăl) n. attestato.

testimony (tĕs′tĭ·mō·nĭ) n. testimonianza.

testiness (nĕs) n. petulanza.

testy (tĕs′tĭ) agg. petulante, stizzoso.

tetanus (tĕt′á·nŭs) n. (med.) tetano.

tether (tĕth′ĕr) n. catena, cavezza,
limite, risorse: the end of one's —,
allo stremo delle proprie risorse.
vt. legare con la cavezza.

text (tĕkst) n. testo: — edition, edizione nuova o corrente.

textbook (tĕkst′bŏŏk′) n. libro di testo.

textile (tĕks′tĭl) n. tessuto, fibra tessile. agg. tessile: — mill, fabbrica
di tessuti.

texture (tĕks′tûr) n. tessitura; struttura, trama, grana.

than (thăn) cong. che, di, che non,
di quello che, di quanto: older — I
am, più vecchio di me; less — a
hundred, meno di cento; rather —,
piuttosto di: more — once, più
d'una volta; more — he knows,
più di quanto egli non sappia.

thank (thăngk) vt. ringraziare: —
God, grazie a Dio; I will — you to
explain, abbiate la compiacenza di
spiegare; thanks, grazie, ringraziamenti; — you! grazie!

thankful agg. riconoscente. —ly avv.
con riconoscenza. —ness n. riconoscenza.

thankless agg. ingrato; non apprez-
zato. —ness n. ingratitudine.

thanksgiving (thăngks′gĭv·ĭng) n. ringraziamento, preghiera di ringraziamento: — Day, giorno del ringraziamento (S.U., l'ultimo giovedì di novembre).

that (thăt) agg., pron. dimostrativo (pl.
those) quello, quella; ciò; lo: —'s
right, è giusto, proprio così; —
one, quello, quella, quella. pron.rel. che,
il quale, la quale, le quali, i quali.
cong. che, se. avv. così, a tal segno,
in tal modo (o misura), tanto: — is,
cioè, ossia; — much, così, tanto;
— far, così lontano, sino a quel
punto; he was — weak he could
not stand, era così debole da non
potersi reggere; so —, sicchè, in
modo da, affinchè.

thatch (thăch) n. paglia (per tetti);
stoppie. vt. coprire di paglia:
thatched roof, tetto di paglia o di
stoppie.

thaw (thô) n. disgelo. vt., vi. disgelare;
ammansire, ammansirsi.

the (thē) art.determ. il, lo, gli, i, la,
le: of —, del, della, dei, delle; to —,
al, allo, agli, alle; from —, dal,
dallo, dalla, dagli, dalle. avv. tanto:
— more so, tanto più; — more I
see it, — less I like it, quanto più lo
vedo, tanto meno mi piace.

theater, theatre (thē′á·tĕr) n. teatro:
— of war, teatro di guerra; arena
—, teatro a pista centrale.

theatrical (thē·ăt′rĭ·kăl) agg. teatrale;
istrionico; esagerato; melodrammatico.

theatricals n.pl. rappresentazione di
prosa (spec. di filodrammatici);
pose teatrali.

thee (thē) pron.pers. te, ti.

theft (thĕft) n. furto.

their (thâr) agg. il loro, la loro, i loro,
le loro.

theirs (thârz) pron.poss. il loro, la loro,

i loro, le loro: **a friend of** —, un loro amico.

them (thĕm) *pron.pers.* essi, esse, loro, li, quelli, quelle, coloro: **give me** — **books** (*forma dialett.*), datemi quel libri.

theme (thēm) *n.* tema, argomento; (*radio*, *TV*) sigla.

themselves (thĕm-sĕlvz′) *pron.rifl.pl.* essi stessi, esse stesse, se stessi, se stesse, sì, se, sè: **they wash** —, essi si lavano; **by** —, da se stessi, da soli.

then (thĕn) *avv.* pol, in seguito, indi; allora, in quell'epoca, in tal caso: **now and** —, di tanto in tanto; — **and there**, seduta stante; **since** —, dopo di allora, da quel tempo; **by** —, a quell'ora, ormai; **now** — dunque, allora!; **well** —! bene, allora! *cong.* dunque, perciò, cosicchè. *agg.* di allora, di quell'epoca: **the** — **president**, il presidente di allora.

thence (thĕns) *avv.* dopo d'allora, successivamente, da quel luogo, di là, donde, perciò.

thenceforth (thĕns′fôrth′), **thenceforward** (thĕns′fôr′wĕrd) *avv.* d'allora in pol, in seguito.

theologian (thē′ō-lō′jl-ăn) *n.* teologo.

theological (thē′ō-lŏj′ĭ-kăl) *agg.* teologico.

theology (thē-ŏl′ō-jĭ) *n.* teologia.

theorem (thē′ō-rĕm), *n.* teorema.

theoretical (thē′ō-rĕt′ĭ-kăl) *agg.* teorico, ipotetico.

theory (thē′ō-rĭ) *n.* ipotesi, teoria.

therapeutic (thĕr′ă-pū′tĭk) *agg.* terapeutico.

therapeutics (thĕr′ă-pū′tĭks) *n.* terapeutica.

therapy (thĕr′ă-pĭ) *n.* terapia.

there (thâr) *avv.* là, colà, vi, ci; ecco: — **is, c'è** — **are**, ci sono; **down** —, laggiú; **here and** —, qua e là; — **and then**, immediatamente; — **he is**, eccolo là; — **you are!** eccol, ecco qua!; qui ti volevo, visto?; — **are many people**, c'è molta gente.

thereabouts (thâr′ă-bouts′) *avv.* là intorno, nei dintorni; all'incirca.

thereafter (thâr-ăf′tĕr) *avv.* dopo di che, in seguito, da allora in pol.

thereat (thâr-ăt′) *avv.* al che, in quel luogo, dopo di che.

thereby (thâr-bī′) *avv.* con ciò; all'incirca; in conseguenza di ciò; con tale mezzo.

therefor (thâr-fôr′) *avv.* in cambio, a causa di ciò, per cui.

therefore (thâr′fôr) *avv.* di conseguenza, quindi, per questo (*o* quello), perciò.

therein (thâr-ĭn′) *avv.* in questo (*o* quel) luogo, entro quel lasso di tempo, là dentro.

thereof (thâr-ŏv′) *avv.* di quello, di ciò, da ciò.

thereon (thâr-ŏn′) *avv.* su quello, su ciò, al che, successivamente.

thereupon (thâr′ă-pŏn′) *avv.* al che, dopo di che, in seguito.

therewith (thâr-wĭth′) *avv.* con ciò, oltre a ciò.

therewithal (thâr′wĭth-ôl′) *avv.* per soprammercato, per giunta.

thermal (thûr′măl) *agg.* termale.

thermometer (thĕr-mŏm′ē-tĕr) *n.* termometro.

thermonuclear (thûr′mō-nū′klē-ĕr) *agg.* termonucleare.

Thermos (*marca*) **bottle** (thûr′mŏs) *n.* termos.

thermostat (thûr′mō-stăt) *n.* termostato.

thesaurus (thē-sô′rŭs) *n.* lessico, raccolta, compendio.

these (thēz) *pron.dimostrativo*, *agg.* (*pl. di* this) questi, queste.

thesis (thē′sĭs) *n.* (*pl. theses*) tesi.

Thespian (thĕs′pĭ-ăn) *n.* attore drammatico *agg.* di Tespi, drammatico.

they (thā) *pron.pers.* essi, esse, coloro: — **say**, si dice, dicono.

thick (thĭk) *n.* fitto, folto: **through** — **and thin**, a dispetto di tutto; **in the** — **of the fight**, nel folto della mischia. *agg.* denso, spesso, folto, fitto; grosso, massiccio; stupido; confuso; (*fam.*) stretto, intimo: **as** — **as thieves**, amici inseparabili. —**headed** *agg.* stupido. —**skinned** *agg.* coriaceo, insensibile. —**witted** *agg.* tardo, ottuso; *avv.* *vedi* **thickly**.

thicken (thĭk′ĕn) *vt.*, *vi.* inspessire, aumentare, infittire; inspessirsi; complicarsi.

thicket (thĭk′ĕt) *n.* boschetto, macchia.

thickly (thĭk′lĭ) *avv.* fittamente, densamente; confusamente; strettamente.

thickness (thĭk′nĕs) *n.* spessore, densità, consistenza; difficoltà (*di pronunzia*); torbidezza.

thickset (thĭk′sĕt′) *agg.* massiccio, tarchiato.

thief (thēf) *n.* (*pl. thieves*) ladro.

thieve (thēv) *vt.*, *vi.* rubare.

thigh (thī) *n.* (*anat.*) coscia: — **bone**, femore.

thimble (thĭm′b'l) *n.* ditale.

thin (thĭn) *agg.* magro, sottile; rado; leggiero, inconsistente; smilzo, scarso; debole, rarefatto; trasparente: — **broth**, brodo leggiero, brodino; — **hair**, capelli radi. *vt.* assottigliare, dimagrare, ridurre; diradare, rarefare. *vi.* dimagrire, assottigliarsi, diradarsi, rarefarsi.

thine (thīn) *pron.poss.* il tuo, la tua, i tuoi, le tue.

thing (thǐng) *n.* cosa; faccenda: not a — to eat, niente da mangiare; the things of the mind, le qualità spirituali *o* morali; the —s of the body, le necessità del corpo; of all —s! incredibile!, inaudito! poor —! povera creatura! taking one — with another, tutto considerato; for one —, innanzi tutto; the very — for me, proprio quel che mi ci vuole; to be quite the —, essere molto di moda; to feel quite the —, sentirsi bene.

think (thǐngk) *vt.*, *vi.* (*pass.*, *pp.* thought) pensare; credere; immaginare; giudicare; supporre: to — better of it, cambiar parere; to — nothing of, non dar peso a; to — of, pensare a, pensare di; to — up an excuse, inventare *o* trovare una scusa; to my way of thinking, a mio modo di vedere, secondo me.

thinker *n.* pensatore.

thinking *n.* pensiero: to my —, secondo me. *agg.* pensante, ragionante.

thinly (thǐn'lǐ) *avv.* scarsamente, radamente; leggermente.

thinness (thǐn'nĕs) *n.* sottigliezza, magrezza; trasparenza, inconsistenza.

third (thûrd) *n.*, *agg.* terzo: —-rate *agg.* di terz'ordine.

thirst (thûrst) *n.* sete, brama. *vi.* aver sete: to — for, after, bramare.

thirsty (thûrs'tǐ) *agg.* assetato: to be —, aver sete.

thirteen (thûr'tēn') *n.*, *agg.* tredici.

thirteenth (thûr'tēnth') *agg.* tredicesimo.

thirtieth (thûr'tǐ-ěth) *agg.* trentesimo.

thirty (thûr'tǐ) *n.*, *agg.* trenta.

this (thǐs) *agg.*, *pron.* (*pl.* these) questo, questa: like —, così; by — time, a quest'ora, ormai.

thistle (thǐs'l) *n.* (*bot.*) cardo.

thither (thǐth'ēr) *avv.* là, da quella parte, a quella volta.

tho *vedi* though.

thole (thōl) *n.* (*naut.*) scalmo.

thong (thǒng) *n.* correggia, striscia di cuoio.

thorax (thō'răks) *n.* (*anat.*) torace.

thorn (thôrn) *n.* spina, pruno; tormento.

thorny (thôr'nǐ) *agg.* spinoso.

thorough (thûr'ō) *agg.* intero, completo, perfetto, approfondito; meticoloso; radicale.

thoroughbred (thûr'ō-brĕd') *n.* purosangue. *agg.* di pura razza, ben nato.

thoroughfare (thûr'ō-fâr') *n.* arteria stradale: no —, passaggio vietato.

thoroughly (thûr'ō-lǐ) *avv.* completamente, fino in fondo; radicalmente, minuziosamente.

those (thōz) *agg.*, *pron.* (*pl. di* that) quei, quegli, quelli, coloro, quelle: — who, — which, quelli che, quelle che.

thou (thou) *pron.pers.* tu.

though (thō) *cong.* benchè, anche se, quantunque, però, nonostante. *avv.* tuttavia, ciononostante: as —, come se; even —, ancorchè, quand'anche, anche se.

thought (thôt) (1) *pass.*, *pp. di* to think.

thought (thôt) (2) *n.* pensiero, idea, ispirazione, opinione, concetto, intenzione: on second —, ripensandoci; lost in —, assorto, soprappensiero.

thoughtful *agg.* pensieroso; riflessivo; premuroso; previdente. —ly *avv.* pensosamente; premurosamente, previdentemente. —ness *n.* attenzione, sollecitudine, previdenza; raccoglimento.

thoughtless *agg.* irriflessivo, sbadato, trascurato. —ly *avv.* sbadatamente; spensieratamente; trascuratamente. —ness *n.* spensieratezza; sbadataggine, trascuratezza, negligenza.

thousand (thou'zănd) *n.*, *agg.* mille: by the —, al mille; by thousands, a migliaia.

thrall (thrô) *n.* schiavo; schiavitù.

thrash (thrăsh) *vt.*, *vi.* trebbiare (*grano, ecc.*); bastonare, malmenare: to — out, dibattere, sceverare. —er *n.* trebbiatore.

thread (thrĕd) *n.* filo, filetto (*anche di vite*); filamento, vena. *vt.*, *vi.* infilare; filettare; aprirsi un varco, procedere a fatica, serpeggiare; (*cucina*) filare.

threadbare (thrĕd'bâr') *agg.* spelato, logoro, liso; misero.

threat (thrĕt) *n.* minaccia.

threaten (thrĕt''n) *vt.*, *vi.* minacciare.

threatening *agg.* minaccioso, incombente.

three (thrē) *n.*, *agg.* tre.

three-dimensional *agg.* tridimensionale.

thresh (thrĕsh) *vedi* to thrash.

threshold (thrĕsh'ōld) *n.* soglia, limitare.

threw (thrōō) *pass. di* to throw.

thrice (thrīs) *avv.* tre volte.

thrift (thrĭft) *n.* risparmio; frugalità.

thrifty *agg.* economo, frugale; prosperoso.

thrill (thrĭl) *n.* fremito, brivido, emozione. *vt.* far fremere, elettrizzare,
procurare un'emozione a. *vi.* fremere, emozionarsi, commuoversi,
eccitarsi.

thriller (thrĭl'ĕr) *n.* racconto *o* romanzo *o* dramma del brivido.

thrilling (thrĭl'ĭng) *agg.* emozionante,
elettrizzante, eccitante.

thrive (thrĭv) *vi.* (*pass.* throve, *pp.*
thriven) prosperare.

thriving *agg.* fiorente, prosperoso.

throat (thrōt) *n.* gola: to have a sore
—, avere il mal di gola.

throaty *agg.* gutturale.

throb (thrŏb) *n.* battito, palpito,
pulsazione. *vi.* battere, pulsare,
palpitare; —bing *agg.* pulsante.

throe (thrō) *n.* angoscia; travaglio,
doglie; agonia.

throne (thrōn) *n.* trono.

throng (thrŏng) *n.* moltitudine, folla.
vt. affollare, stipare. *vi.* affollarsi.

throttle (thrŏt''l) *n.* trachea, gola;
(*mecc.*) valvola a farfalla, acceleratore. *vt.* strangolare, soffocare; (*mecc.*) strozzare: to —
down, rallentare, diminuire la
velocità.

through (thrōō) *agg.* completo; diretto, continuo; finito: — train, treno
diretto, direttissimo; — ticket,
biglietto per treno diretto. *prep.*
durante, attraverso, per, fra, in
mezzo a; per mezzo di, mediante;
a causa di. *avv.* da parte a parte;
fino in fondo, dal principio alla
fine; a buon fine; completamente:
to be — with, non aver più nulla
a che fare con; wet —, bagnato
fradicio; to carry —, attuare,
eseguire, portare a compimento;
to fall —, far fiasco, andare a monte.

throughout (thrōō-out') *prep.* in ogni
punto di; durante; dal principio
alla fine di. *avv.* da ogni parte;
a ogni momento; completamente.

throve (thrōv) *pass.* di to thrive.

throw (thrō) *n.* lancio, colpo, tiro;
portata. *vt.*, *vi.* (*pass.* threw, *pp.*
thrown) gettare, scagliare; ritorcere (*filati*); disarcionare; far
girare; abbattere, travolgere: to —
off, disfarsi di, rinunciare a; to —
open, spalancare; to — about, disseminare, sparpagliare; sperperare;
agitare (*le braccia*); to — away,
buttar via; sprecare; to — down,
buttare a terra, abbattere, rovesciare; to — in, dare in aggiunta;
buttare lì (*una frase*); arrendersi;
to — in gear, ingranare (*una*

marcia); to — off, sbarazzarsi di,
liberarsi di; rinunciare a; to —
out, emettere, buttar fuori; respingere; aggiungere (*un'ala a un
edificio*); distrarre, far perdere il
filo; to — over, abbandonare; to —
overboard, buttare a mare; to —
up, issare, rinunziare a; vomitare.

throwaway (thrō'á-wā') *n.* (*S.U.*)
volantino pubblicitario.

thrown (thrōn) *pp.* di to throw.

thrum (thrŭm) *vt.*, *vi.* strimpellare.

thrush (thrŭsh) *n.* tordo.

thrust (thrŭst) *n.* colpo, urto, pressione; botta, stoccata; (*mecc.*)
forza di propulsione. *vt.*, *vi.* (*pass.*,
pp. thrust) spingere, sospingere,
ficcare; imporre; trafiggere, colpi re;
insinuarsi; dare una botta: to —
away, respingere; to — in, inserire,
cacciar dentro, introdurre di forza;
to — something upon, imporre
qualcosa a.

thud (thŭd) *n.* tonfo, colpo sordo. *vt.*
colpire. *vi.* risonare sordamente.

thug (thŭg) *n.* brigante, furfante.

thumb (thŭm) *n.* dito pollice: under
the — of, dominato da. *vt.* sporcare;
sfogliare (*un libro*) alla svelta;
chiedere un passaggio con l'autostop. *vi.* viaggiare con l'autostop.

thumbtack (thŭm'tăk') *n.* puntina da
disegno.

thump (thŭmp) *n.* colpo, tonfo. *vt.*
colpire (*o* cadere) con un tonfo;
percuotere; bussare. *vi.* palpitare;
camminare pesantemente.

thunder (thŭn'dĕr) *n.* tuono, uragano.
vt., *vi.* tuonare, minacciare: it
thunders, tuona. —bolt *n.* fulmine.
—clap *n.* colpo di tuono. —ing *agg.*
tonante; (*fam.*) straordinario, enorme. —ous *agg.* tonante, burrascoso. —storm *n.* temporale,
uragano.

Thursday (thûrz'dĭ) *n.* giovedì.

thus (thŭs) *avv.* così, come segue, nel
modo seguente, in questo (*o* quel)
modo: — far, fin qui (*o* là); a tal
segno; fino ad ora.

thwart (thwôrt) *vt.* attraversare;
ostacolare, sventare, frustrare.

thy (thī) *agg.poss.* tuo, tua, tuoi, tue.

thyme (tīm) *n.* (*bot.*) timo.

thymus (thī'mŭs) *n.* (*anat.*) timo.

thyroid (thī'roid) *n.* (*anat.*) tiroide.

thyself (thī-sĕlf') *pron.rifl.* te stesso (*o*
stessa), tu stesso (*o* stessa).

tick (tĭk) *n.* ticchettio, tocco leggiero; traliccio; puntino; segno
della spunta; attimo; (*entom.*) zecca, acaro. *vt.*, *vi.* ticchettare, fare
tictac, battere: to — off, spuntare,
fare la spunta.

ticket (tĭk'ĕt) *n.* biglietto, tagliando; bolletta, scheda, cartellino; lista elettorale: return —, biglietto di andata e ritorno; **season** —, abbonamento; **mileage** —, biglietto circolare; **single** (*opp.* one-way) —, biglietto di corsa semplice; — **office**, biglietteria.

tickle (tĭk''l) *n.* solletico, titillamento. *vt.* solleticare, stuzzicare; lusingare; divertire. *vi.* sentire solletico: **to be** —**d to death**, essere lusingatissimo; divertirsi un mondo.

ticklish (tĭk'lĭsh) *agg.* sensibile al solletico; delicato, precario, difficile.

tidbit (tĭd'bĭt) *vedi* titbit.

tide (tīd) *n.* marea, flusso, corrente; tempo, stagione, epoca, periodo; corso, andamento; occasione, festa. *vt.:* **to** — **someone over a crisis**, aiutare qualcuno a superare una crisi.

tidings (tī'dĭngz) *n.pl.* novità, notizie.

tidy (tī'dĭ) *agg.* ordinato, lindo: **a** — **sum**, una buona sommetta. *vt.*, *vi.* riordinare, pulire, riassettare, riassettarsi.

tie (tī) *n.* nodo, vincolo, legame; cravatta; pareggio (*in gare, ecc.*); (*pol.*) parità di voti; (*ferr.*) traversina. *vt.*, *vi.* legare, allacciare, vincolare, annodare; pareggiare: **to** — **up**, avvolgere in pacco e legare; vincolare; bloccare, ostruire.

tier (tēr) *n.* ordine (*di posti a teatro*); fila, filare.

tiff (tĭf) *n.* stizza; bisticcio.

tiger (tī'gēr) *n.* tigre: **American** —, giaguaro; **red** —, puma; — **cat**, gattopardo.

tight (tīt) *agg.* stretto; attillato; scarso; tirchio; difficile; teso; chiuso, ermetico, stagno; (*gergo*) alticcio: **to be in a** — **spot**, essere in grande imbarazzo. *avv.* strettamente; ermeticamente: **to sit** —, tener duro.

tighten (tīt''n) *vt.* stringere, restringere, serrare; tendere, tirare. *vi.* stringersi; tendersi.

tightness (tīt'nĕs) *n.* tensione, strettezza, aderenza; tirchieria.

tights (tīts) *n.pl.* maglia da palcoscenico, calzamaglia.

tigress (tī'grĕs) *n.* tigre (*femmina*).

tile (tīl) *n.* tegola, embrice; piastrella; *vt.* coprire di tegole, piastrellare.

till (tĭl) (1) *prep.* fino a. *cong.* finchè.

till (tĭl) (2) *n.* cassetto del danaro, cassa (*di negozio*).

till (tĭl) (3) *vt.*, *vi.* arare, coltivare.

tillage (tĭl'ĭj) *n.* coltivazione, aratura.

tiller (tĭl'ēr) *n.* agricoltore; (*naut.*) barra del timone.

tilt (tĭlt) *n.* inclinazione, pendio; contesa, disputa. *vt.* inclinare, far pendere. *vi.* pendere, inclinarsi; capovolgersi.

timber (tĭm'bēr) *n.* legname da costruzione; bosco; trave, tronco; (*naut.*) costola.

time (tīm) *n.* tempo; orario; ora, momento; epoca; ritmo; volta (*occasione*): **at most** —**s**, generalmente; **as** —**s go**, coi tempi che corrono; **to have a wonderful** —, spassarsela; **against** —, a ritmo accelerato; **at** —**s**, ogni tanto, certe volte; **behind** —, in ritardo; **from** — **to** —, di tanto in tanto; **in no** —, in quattro e quatt'rotto, all'istante; **in** —, in tempo; **coi tempo, a suo tempo; a tempo** (*mus.*); **on** —, puntualmente, in orario; **al momento giusto; out of** —, troppo presto; troppo tardi; **for the** — **being, per il momento; — and again, ripetutamente; what** — **is it?** che ora è? *vt.* regolare, far coincidere; cronometrare, fissare l'ora (*o* la durata) di; scegliere il momento per; sincronizzare.

timeliness (tīm'lĭ-nĕs) *n.* opportunità, tempestività.

timely (tīm'lĭ) *agg.* opportuno, tempestivo. *avv.* opportunamente, tempestivamente.

timepiece (tīm'pēs') *n.* orologio.

timetable (tīm'tā'b'l) *n.* orario.

timid (tĭm'ĭd) *agg.* timido, timoroso.

timidity (tĭ-mĭd'ĭ-tĭ) *n.* timidezza.

timing (tīm'ĭng) *n.* sincronizzazione, calcolo dei tempi; ritmo.

timorous (tĭm'ēr-ŭs) *agg.* timoroso.

tin (tĭn) *n.* stagno (*metallo*); latta, barattolo di latta; *agg.* di stagno, di latta: — **foil**, foglio di stagno (*o* latta); — **plate**, latta stagnata. *vt.* stagnare; mettere in scatola (*conserve*).

tincture (tĭngk'tŭr) *n.* tintura; tinta; traccia. *vt.* tingere; mescolare.

tinder (tĭn'dēr) *n.* acciarino, esca.

tinge (tĭnj) *n.* tinteggiatura; sapore; parvenza; pizzico. *vt.* tinteggiare: **to** — **with**, dare una sfumatura di.

tingle (tĭng'g'l) *n.* formicolio; puntura. *vt.* punzecchiare. *vi.* fremere, formicolare.

tinker (tĭngk'ēr) *vt.*, *vi.* rattoppare; abborracciare.

tinkle (tĭng'k'l) *n.* tintinnio. *vi.* tintinnare.

tinsel (tĭn'sĕl) *n.* orpello. *agg.* falso; vistoso.

tinsmith (tĭn'smĭth') *n.* lattonaio.

tint (tĭnt) *n.* tinta; sfumatura, tratteggio. *vt.* colorire; sfumare, tratteggiare.

tiny (tī′nĭ) *agg.* minuscolo.

tip (tĭp) *n.* punta, cima, apice; puntale; (*fam.*) mancia; informazione confidenziale, consiglio. *vt.*, *vi.* appuntire; dare la mancia a; dare un consiglio (*o* un'informazione) a; inclinare. *vi.* inclinarsi; ribaltarsi, capovolgersi: to — off, mettere al corrente, avvertire: to — one's hat, toccarsi il cappello.

tipple (tĭp′'l) *vt.*, *vi.* bere all'eccesso; sorseggiare.

tipsy (tĭp′sĭ) *agg.* ubriaco; instabile.

tiptoe (tĭp′tō′) *n.* punta dei piedi: on —, in punta di piedi. *vi.* camminare in punta di piedi.

tire (tīr) (1) *n.* pneumatico (*di ruota*); cerchione. *vt.* munire di pneumatici (*o* cerchioni).

tire (tīr) (2) *vt.* stancare, annolare. *vi.* stancarsi, annoiarsi.

tired (tīrd) *agg.* stanco; annoiato: — out, esausto, sfinito.

tiredness (tīrd′nĕs) *n.* stanchezza.

tireless (tīr′lĕs) *agg.* instancabile.

tiresome (tīr′săm) *agg.* faticoso; noloso.

tissue (tĭsh′ū) *n.* tessuto: — paper, carta velina, tovagliolino di carta (*per cosmesi*)

titbit (tĭt′bĭt′) *n.* bocconcino prelibato, leccornia; notiziola prelibata.

tithe (tĭth) *n.* decima.

title (tī′t'l) *n.* titolo: — page, frontespizio. *vt.* intitolare.

titmouse (tĭt′mous′) *n.* cincia.

titter (tĭt′ĕr) *n.* risolino. *vi.* ridacchiare.

tittle (tĭt′'l) *n.* particella, iota.

tittle-tattle (tĭt′'l·tăt′'l) *n.* pettegolezzi, chiacchiere.

to (tōō; tŏŏ) *prep.* a, al, alla, alle, agli; per, al fine di; verso, in, nel, nello, nella, negli, nelle; fino a; a paragone di: a quarter — four, le quattro meno un quarto; — my surprise, con mio stupore; ten — one, con dieci probabilità contro una; — this day, fino ad oggi, ancor oggi; from house — house, di casa in casa; you have — go, devi andare. *avv.* accosto, addosso: to come —, rinvenire (*riprendere i sensi*); to push the door —, accostare la porta; — and fro, avanti e indietro.

toad (tōd) *n.* (*zool.*) rospo.

toadstool (tōd′stōōl′) *n.* fungo velenoso.

toady (tōd′ĭ) *n.* parassita; piaggiatore, adulatore. *agg.* orribile, repellente.

toast (tōst) *n.* crostino, pane abbrustolito; brindisi. *vt.* abbrustolire; brindare a. *vi.* abbrustolirsi. —er *n.* chi brinda; tostatore, tostino.

tobacco (tŏ·băk′ō) *n.* (*bot.*) tabacco.

tobacconist (tŏ·băk′ŏ·nĭst) *n.* tabaccaio.

toboggan (tŏ·bŏg′ăn) *n.* toboga.

tocsin (tŏk′sĭn) *n.* segnale d'allarme; campana a martello.

today (tōŏ·dā′) *avv.* oggi, oggigiorno.

toddle (tŏd′'l) *vi.* vacilare.

to-do (tŏŏ·dōō) *n.* trambusto, tumulto.

toe (tō) *n.* dito del piede; punta (*di piede, calza o scarpa*). *vt.* toccare (*o* smuovere) con la punta del piede: to — in, camminare con i piedi in dentro.

toenail (tō′nāl′) *n.* unghia del piede.

together (tŏŏ·gĕth′ĕr) *avv.* insieme, unitamente; a raccolta; contemporaneamente: — with, insieme con; all —, tutti insieme; to bring —, mettere a contatto, riunire.

togs (tŏgz) *n.pl.* indumenti.

toil (toil) *n.* fatica, lavoro; pena, travaglio, lotta. *vi.* faticare, affannarsi.

toilet (toi′lĕt) *n.* toletta, gabinetto di decenza: — paper, carta igienica.

toilsome (toil′săm) *agg.* penoso, faticoso, gravoso.

token (tō′kĕn) *n.* segno, pegno; indizio; ricordo; gettone, contrassegno. *agg.* simbolico, nominale: — payment, pagamento simbolico.

told (tōld) *pass.*, *pp. di* to tell.

tolerance (tŏl′ĕr·ăns) *n.* tolleranza.

tolerant (tŏl′ĕr·ănt) *agg.* tollerante.

tolerate (tŏl′ĕr·āt) *vt.* tollerare, sopportare.

toleration (tŏl′ĕr·ā′shŭn) *n.* tolleranza.

toll (tōl) (1) *n.* rintocco. *vt.* sonare (*le campane*). *vi.* rintoccare.

toll (tōl) (2) *n.* tributo, pedaggio: — bridge, ponte a pedaggio; — call (*S.U.*), telefonata interurbana; — gate, barriera di pedaggio; — line, linea interurbana; — road, strada a pedaggio.

tomato (tŏ·mā′tō) *n.* (*bot.*) pomodoro.

tomb (tōōm) *n.* tomba.

tomboy (tŏm′boi′) *n.* maschietta, sbarazzina, maschiaccio (*detto di bambina*).

tombstone (tōōm′stōn′) *n.* lapide sepolcrale.

tomcat (tŏm′kăt′) *n.* gatto (*maschio*).

tome (tōm) *n.* tomo, volume.

tommy (tŏm′ĭ) *n.* pagnotta; soldato inglese: — gun, fucile mitragliatore, mitra.

tomorrow (tŏŏ·mŏr′ō) *n.*, *avv.* domani: — morning, domani mattina; —

night, domani sera *o* notte; **the day after** —, dopodomani; — **week** (*Ingl.*) domani a otto.

ton (tŭn) *n.* tonnellata.

tone (tōn) *n.* tono, accento, timbro. *vt.* intonare; colorire; modificare il tono di. *vi.* intonarsi, armonizzare; (*fot.*) sottoporre a viraggio: **to — down,** smorzare, attenuare; **to — up,** accentuare, rinforzarsi.

tongs (tŏngz) *n.pl.* pinze, molle.

tongue (tŭng) *n.* lingua, linguaggio; linguetta; ardiglione (*di fibbia*); timone (*di carro*); ancia (*di strumento a fiato*); ago (*di scambio ferr.*): **—tied** *agg.* impacciato (*nell'eloquio*), ammutolito.

tonic (tŏn'ĭk) *n.* tonico; acqua gasata. *agg.* tonico.

tonight (tŏŏ·nīt') *avv.* questa sera; questa notte.

tonnage (tŭn'ĭj) *n.* tonnellaggio.

tonneau (tŭn·ō') *n.* (*auto*) compartimento posteriore con sedile.

tonsil (tŏn'sĭl) *n.* tonsilla.

too (tōō) *avv.* anche, inoltre, per giunta; troppo, di troppo: **he will come —,** verrà anche lui; **— much,** troppo; **— many,** troppi; **one — many,** uno di troppo; **you were none —** early, sei arrivato appena appena in tempo; **you are really — kind!** molto gentile da parte vostra! **I shall be only — glad to,** sarò lietissimo di; **that's — bad!** che peccato!, mi rincresce tanto! **to go — far,** esagerare, eccedere.

took (tŏŏk) *pass. di* to take.

tool (tōōl) *n.* utensile, attrezzo, strumento.

toot (tōōt) *n.* squillo; fischio; suono di tromba; urlo (*di sirena*). *vt.*, *vi.* sonare, strombettare.

tooth (tōōth) *n.* (*pl.* teeth) dente: **to fight — and nail,** lottare con tutte le proprie forze; **to have a sweet —,** essere goloso di cose dolci. **—ache** *n.* odontalgia, mal di denti. **—brush** *n.* spazzolino da denti. **—less** *agg.* sdentato. **—paste** *n.* dentifricio. **—pick** *n.* stuzzicadenti. **—some** *agg.* gustoso, buono, saporito, appetitoso.

top (tŏp) *n.* cima, sommità; estremità; coperchio; colmo, apice, cocuzzolo; testa; trottola; superficie; imperiale (*di autobus*); (*naut.*) coffa: **to be at the — of,** essere il primo di; **at the — of one's voice,** a squarciagola; **filled up to the —,** pieno sino all'orlo; **from — to bottom,** da cima a fondo; **from — to toe,** da capo a piedi. *agg.* superiore, primo; massimo; sommo; princi-

pale; estremo: **— hat,** cappello a cilindro; **— speed,** velocità massima; **— secret,** segreto assoluto. *vt.* sovrastare; coprire; coronare; sormontare; sorpassare; completare; cimare. *vi.* elevarsi, eccellere.

topcoat (tŏp'kōt') *n.* soprabito.

topflight (tŏp'flīt') *agg.* di altissimo grado; eminente; massimo.

topmast (tŏp'mȧst') *n.* (*naut.*) albero di gabbia.

topmost (tŏp'mōst) *agg.* (*il*) più in alto.

topee (tō·pē') *n.* casco coloniale.

toper (tōp'ẽr) *n.* ubriacone.

topic (tŏp'ĭk) *n.* argomento, tema.

topical (tŏp'ĭ·kȧl) *agg.* attuale, di attualità; pertinente.

topography (tō·pŏg'rȧ·fĭ) *n.* topografia.

topper (tŏp'ẽr) *n.* cimatore (*di piante*); smoccolatoio; baro (*ai dadi*); casacchino da donna; (*gergo*) coperchio, strato superiore, cappa; campione, fuoriclasse.

topping (tŏp'ĭng) *agg.* (*gergo*) superiore, eccellente.

topple (tŏp'l) *vt.*, *vi.* ribaltare.

topsail (tŏp'sāl') *n.* vela di gabbia.

topsy-turvy (tŏp'sĭ·tûr'vĭ) *n.* scompiglio. *agg.* capovolto, sovvertito. *avv.* sottosopra.

torch (tôrch) *n.* torcia, fiaccola.

tore (tōr) *pass. di* to tear.

torment (tôr'měnt) *n.* tormento, supplizio. *vt.* (tŏr·měnt') tormentare.

tormentor (tôr·měn'tẽr) *n.* tormentatore; (*teat.*) quinta.

torn (tôrn) *pp. di* to tear.

tornado (tôr·nā'dō) *n.* uragano, ciclone.

torpedo (tôr·pē'dō) *n.* siluro, torpedine: **— boat,** torpediniera; **— boat destroyer,** cacciatorpediniere. *vt.* silurare.

torpid (tôr'pĭd) *agg.* torpido, inerte.

torpor (tôr'pẽr) *n.* torpore, inerzia.

torrent (tôr'ěnt) *n.* torrente. *agg.* torrenziale, impetuoso.

torrid (tôr'ĭd) *agg.* torrido.

torsion (tôr'shŭn) *n.* torsione.

tortoise (tôr'tŭs) *n.* tartaruga.

tortuous (tôr'tṳ·ŭs) *agg.* tortuoso.

torture (tôr'tûr) *n.* tortura, tormento. *vt.* torturare, tormentare.

toss (tŏs) *n.* lancio, colpo, scossa, moto brusco; beccheggio. *vt.* gettare, lanciare, sballottare, scuotere; alzare bruscamente; esaminare. *vi.* agitarsi, rivoltolarsi, slanciarsi, dimenarsi; beccheggiare: **to — off,** tracannare; **to — up,** giocare a testa o croce.

tot (tŏt) *n.* bimbo; bicchierino.

total (tō'tăl) *n.*, *agg.* totale.

totalitarian (tō·tăl'ĭ·târ'ĭ·ăn) *agg.* totalitario. **—ism** *n.* totalitarismo.

tote (tōt) *vt.* (*S.U.*) portare, trasportare.

totter (tŏt'ẽr) *vi.* vacillare, traballare, barcollare.

touch (tŭch) *n.* tocco, tatto; contatto; leggiero attacco; sfumatura, pizzico; **to keep in —** with, mantenersi in comunicazione con; **a —** of fever, un po' di febbre; **a —** of the sun, una lieve insolazione. *vt.* toccare, sfiorare, raggiungere; concernere; commuovere; maneggiare. *vi.* combaciare, toccarsi, essere a contatto: **to — at**, fare scalo a; **to — on**, upon, accennare a, fare allusione a; **to — off**, accendere la miccia di (*un cannone*); (*fig.*) far esplodere.

touch-and-go *n.* situazione precaria *o* delicata. *agg.* precario, rischioso; incerto.

touchiness (tŭch'ĭ-nĕs) *n.* suscettibilità.

touching (tŭch'ĭng) *agg.* commovente. *prep.* riguardo a.

touchstone (tŭch'stōn') *n.* pietra di paragone.

touchwood (tŭch'wŏŏd') *n.* esca; persona irascibile.

touchy (tŭch'ĭ) *agg.* permaloso, suscettibile.

tough (tŭf) *n.* (*gergo*) furfante; violento. *agg.* duro, coriaceo, resistente, tenace, inflessibile, ostinato; violento; coercitivo, minaccioso; difficile: **a — customer**, un tipaccio; **— policy**, politica di forza.

toughen (tŭf'ĕn) *vt.* indurire. *vi.* indurirsi.

toughness (tŭf'nĕs) *n.* durezza, tenacia; difficoltà; ostinazione; violenza.

tour (tŏŏr) *n.* giro (*turistico o artistico*), escursione, viaggio. *vt.*, *vi.* visitare (*una regione, ecc.*); compiere un giro (*turistico o artistico*).

tourism (tŏŏr'ĭz'm) *n.* turismo.

tourist (tŏŏr'ĭst) *n.* turista. *agg.* turistico: **— class**, classe turistica.

tournament (tŏŏr'ná-mĕnt) *n.* torneo, concorso, competizione.

tousle (tou'z'l) *vt.* scompigliare, arruffare.

tow (tō) (1) *n.* filaccia, stoppa.

tow (tō) (2) *n.* rimorchio: **in —**, a rimorchio. *vt.* rimorchiare.

toward (tō'ẽrd), **towards** (tō'ẽrdz) *prep.* verso; alla volta di; nei confronti di; a favore di; in previsione di: **— midnight**, verso la mezzanotte.

towboat (tō'bōt') *n.* rimorchiatore.

towel (tou'ĕl) *n.* asciugamano.

tower (tou'ẽr) *n.* torre; rocca. *vi.* torreggiare, innalzarsi. **—ing** *agg.* torreggiante, elevato.

towline (tō'līn') *n.* cavo di rimorchio.

town (toun) *n.* città, cittadina, borgata; cittadinanza (*popolazione*): **— hall**, municipio.

township (toun'shĭp) *n.* comune; unità primaria di governo; area demaniale di sei miglia quadrate.

towpath (tō'páth') *n.* alzaia.

toxic (tŏk'sĭk) *agg.* tossico.

toxicology (tŏk'sĭ-kŏl'ō-jĭ) *n.* tossicologia.

toxin (tŏk'sĭn) *n.* tossina.

toy (toi) *n.* giocattolo. *agg.* che ha forma di giocattolo; minuscolo: **— dog**, cane giocattolo, cagnolino. *vi.* giocare, giocherellare, gingillarsi.

trace (trās) (1) *n.* tirella (*di carrozza*).

trace (trās) (2) *n.* traccia, indizio; pizzico, parvenza; grafico. *vt.* tracciare; rintracciare, risalire alle origini di; ricalcare, delineare; attribuire.

tracing (trās'ĭng) *n.* tracciato; ricalco, copia a lucido.

track (trăk) *n.* traccia, orma, solco; scia; cammino, carreggiata; pista; (*ferr.*) linea, binario: **race —**, pista da corsa; **cinder —**, pista di cenere; **to be on the — of**, essere sulla pista di; **to follow in somebody's —**, seguire le orme di; **the beaten —**, il sistema invalso, il solito trantran; **to keep — of**, tenersi al corrente di; **to go off the —s**, sviarsi; divagare. *vt.* tracciare; braccare, seguire la pista di: **to — down**, catturare.

tract (trăkt) (1) *n.* tratto; spazio: **digestive —**, apparato digerente.

tract (trăkt) (2) *n.* opuscolo (*spec. religioso*).

traction (trăk'shŭn) *n.* trazione; attrito; forza motrice.

tractor (trăk'tẽr) *n.* trattore, trattrice; (*aeron.*) elica traente.

trade (trād) *n.* commercio, traffico, scambio; arte, mestiere, occupazione, professione; clientela. *agg.* commerciale; sindacale; di categoria: **— agent**, agente di commercio; **— agreement**, accordo sindacale; **— association**, associazione di categoria; **— goods**, merci; **— paper**, giornale *o* organo di categoria; **— name**, nome commerciale; **— school**, scuola d'arti e mestieri; **— edition**, edizione di lusso. *vt.*, *vi.* commerciare, barattare, negoziare: **to — upon**, speculare su.

trademark (trăd'märk') *n.* marchio di fabbrica, marca.

trader (trād'ĕr) *n.* mercante; nave mercantile.

tradesman (trādz'măn) *n.* negoziante.

trade union (trād'ūn'yŭn), **trades union** (*Ingl.*) (trādz'ūn'yŭn), sindacato, camera del lavoro.

trade unionism (trād'ūn'yŭn·ĭz'm) sindacalismo.

trade winds venti alisei.

tradition (trá·dĭsh'ŭn) *n.* tradizione.

traditional (trá·dĭsh'ŭn·ăl) *agg.* tradizionale.

traduce (trá·dūs') *vt.* diffamare, calunniare.

traffic (trăf'ĭk) *n.* traffico, commercio; circolazione stradale, movimento. *vt., vi.* (*pass., pp.* trafficked, *ppr.* trafficking) commerciare, barattare, trafficare.

tragedian (trá·jē'dĭ·ăn) *n.* autore (*o* attore) drammatico.

tragedienne (trá·jē'dĭ·ĕn') *n.f.* attrice drammatica.

tragedy (trăj'ẻ·dĭ) *n.* tragedia.

tragic (trăj'ĭk) *agg.* tragico.

trail (trāl) *n.* solco, traccia, pista, sentiero; strascico; seguito. *vt., vi.* strascinare, seguire la pista di; trascinarsi: **to — off,** affievolirsi, disperdersi.

trailer (trāl'ĕr) *n.* rimorchio; roulotte (*fr.*).

train (trān) *n.* treno, convoglio; seguito, corteo; serie, andamento; strascico (*di vestito*); (*mecc.*) trasmissione. *vt.* istruire, allenare, addestrare; puntare (*un'arma, ecc.*). *vi.* esercitarsi, allenarsi.

trainee (trăn·ē') *n.* allievo, novizio; (*mil.*) recluta.

trainer *n.* istruttore, allenatore.

training *n.* addestramento, allenamento: **— ship,** nave scuola.

trait (trāt) *n.* tratto, caratteristica.

traitor (trā'tĕr) *n.* traditore.

traitorous (trā'tĕr·ŭs) *agg.* insidioso, infido, sleale.

trajectory (trá·jĕk'tō·rĭ) *n.* traiettoria.

tram (trăm) *n.* tram, carrello; (*mecc.*) messa a punto.

trammel (trăm'ĕl) *n.* tramaglio; ellissografo; *pl.* pastoie, ostacolo. *vt.* ostacolare, impastoiare.

tramp (trămp) *n.* vagabondaggio, viaggio a piedi; rumor di passi; vagabondo; (*fam.*) prostituta; (*naut.*) mercantile. *vt., vi.* percorrere a piedi; calpestare; vagabondare; camminare pesantemente.

trample (trăm'p'l) *n.* calpestio. *vt.* calpestare. *vi.* camminare pesantemente: **to — on, upon,** opprimere, inferire su.

tramway (trăm'wā') *n.* tram; teleferica.

trance (tráns) *n.* ipnosi, estasi: **to be in a —,** essere in stato di ipnosi, essere come ipnotizzato.

tranquil (trăng'kwĭl) *agg.* tranquillo.

tranquillity (trăn·kwĭl'ĭ·tĭ) *n.* tranquillità.

transact (trăns·ăkt') *vt., vi.* negoziare, trattare, portare a termine. **—ion** *n.* trattativa, affare; operazione (*bancaria*); accordo.

transatlantic (trăns'ăt·lăn'tĭk) *agg.* transatlantico.

transcend (trăn·sĕnd') *vt.* trascendere, superare. *vi.* eccellere.

transcontinental (trăns'kŏn·tĭ·nĕn'tăl) *agg.* transcontinentale.

transcribe (trăn·skrīb') *vt.* trascrivere.

transcript (trăn'skrĭpt) *n.* trascrizione, copia.

transfer (trăns'fûr) *n.* trasporto, trasferimento; cessione, trapasso; trasbordo; (*S.U.*) biglietto cumulativo (*tramviario, ecc.*). *vt., vi.* trasportare; trasferire; cedere; riprodurre (*un disegno*); trasferirsi; trasbordare.

transfigure (trăns·fĭg'ûr) *vt.* trasfigurare.

transform (trăns·fôrm') *vt.* trasformare. *vi.* trasformarsi.

transformation (trăns'fôr·mā'shŭn) *n.* trasformazione, metamorfosi.

transformer (trăns·fôr'mĕr) *n.* trasformatore.

transfuse (trăns·fūz') *vt.* trasfondere, infondere; iniettare, fare una trasfusione di.

transfusion (trăns·fū'zhŭn) *n.* trasfusione.

transgress (trăns·grĕs') *vt., vi.* trasgredire; oltrepassare; violare; peccare.

transgression (trăns·grĕsh'ŭn) *n.* trasgressione, abuso, violazione.

transgressor (trăns·grĕs'ĕr) *n.* trasgressore.

transistor (trăn·zĭs'tĕr) *n.* transistor.

transient (trăn'shĕnt) *n.* ospite di passaggio. *agg.* transitorio, provvisorio, di passaggio.

transit (trăn'sĭt) *n.* transito: **in —,** in transito, di passaggio.

transition (trăn·zĭsh'ŭn) *n.* transizione.

transitive (tran'sĭ·tĭv) *n.* verbo transitivo. *agg.* transitivo.

transitory (trăn'sĭ·tō'rĭ) *agg.* transitorio.

translate (trăns·lāt') vt. tradurre; trasferire; (teleg.) ritrasmettere.
translation (trans·lā'shŭn) n. traduzione; (teleg.) ritrasmissione.
translator (trăns·lā'tĕr) n. traduttore.
translucent (trăns·lū'sĕnt) agg. traslucido, diafano.
transmission (trăns·mĭsh'ŭn) n. trasmissione.
transmit (trăns·mĭt') vt. trasmettere.
transmitter (trăns·mĭt'ĕr) n. trasmettitore.
transom (trăn'sŭm) n. lunetta (di porta); (naut.) traversa di poppa.
transparence (trăns·pâr'ĕns) n. trasparenza.
transparency (trăns·pâr'ĕn·sĭ) n. trasparenza; effigie su lastra trasparente, vetrino; diapositiva.
transparent (trăns·pâr'ĕnt) agg. trasparente.
transpire (trăn·spīr') vt., vi. traspirare, trasudare; trapelare.
transplant (trăns·plănt') vt. trapiantare.
transport (trăns·pōrt') n. trasporto, impeto; nave (o aereo) da trasporto. vt. trasportare, deportare; rapire in estasi; mandare in collera: to be transported with, essere trasportato da.
transportation (trăns'pŏr·tā'shŭn) n. trasporto; mezzi di trasporto; biglietto di viaggio; deportazione.
transpose (trăns·pōz') vt. trasporre, invertire.
transship (trăns·shĭp') vt., vi. trasbordare.
transverse (trăns·vûrs') agg. traversale.
trap (trăp) n. trappola, insidia; sifone; calesse; (S.U.) bocca: — door, botola. vedi traps. vt. intrappolare.
trapeze (tră·pēz') n. trapezio.
trapper (trăp'ĕr) n. trappolatore.
trappings (trăp'ĭngz) n.pl. ornamenti, fronzoli; vestiario; gualdrappa.
traps (trăps) n.pl. bagaglio, effetti personali; (mus.) batteria.
trash (trăsh) n. rimasugli, scorie; cianfrusaglie, robaccia; stupidaggini; marmaglia.
travail (trăv'āl) n. travaglio, fatica; doglie del parto.
travel (trăv'ĕl) n. viaggio; (mecc.) corsa. vt., vi. percorrere; viaggiare, muoversi.
traveler n. viaggiatore: —'s check, assegno turistico, assegno per viaggiatori.
traveling n. il viaggiare. agg. viaggiante: — salesman, commesso viaggiatore.
traverse (trăv'ĕrs) n. traversa. agg. obliquo, trasversale: — rod (opp.

track), rotaia per tendaggi, riloga. vt. attraversare; pattugliare; ostacolare.
travesty (trăv'ĕs·tĭ) n. farsa, parodia. vt. parodiare.
trawl (trôl) n. strascino (rete).
tray (trā) n. vassoio.
treacherous (trĕch'ĕr·ŭs) agg. infido, proditorio, sleale; precario.
treachery (trĕch'ĕr·ĭ) n. tradimento.
treacle (trē'k'l) n. melassa.
tread (trĕd) n. passo, andatura; suola; pianta (del piede e del gradino); battistrada (del pneumatico). vt. (pass. trod, pp. trodden) percorrere, calpestare. vi. camminare: to — on, upon, calpestare.
treadle (trĕd'l) n. pedale.
treason (trēz'n) n. tradimento.
treasonable (trēz'n·ȧ·b'l) agg. proditorio, sleale.
treasure (trĕzh'ĕr) n. tesoro. vt. accantonare; far tesoro di, custodire gelosamente, tesaurizzare.
treasurer (trĕzh'ĕr·ĕr) n. tesoriere.
treasury (trĕzh'ĕr·ĭ) n. erario, tesoro, tesoreria.
treat (trēt) n. festa, trattenimento, piacere. vt. trattare, curare; offrire.
treatise (trē'tĭs) n. trattato (libro).
treatment (trēt'mĕnt) n. trattamento; cura; (lett.) adattamento.
treaty (trē'tĭ) n. trattato, patto.
treble (trĕb'l) n. (mus.) soprano; suono acuto; squillo; vocetta, voce sottile. agg. triplice; di soprano, acuto. vt., vi. triplicare, triplicarsi.
tree (trē) n. albero; palo, asta; forma da scarpe: to be up a —, essere nei guai.
treeless agg. senz'alberi.
trefoil (trē'foil) n. trifoglio.
trellis (trĕl'ĭs) n. graticcio.
tremble (trĕm'b'l) n. tremito; trepidazione, timore. vi. tremare, fremere.
trembling (trĕm'blĭng) n. tremito. agg. tremante.
tremendous (trē·mĕn'dŭs) agg. terribile; straordinario, fenomenale.
tremor (trĕm'ĕr) n. tremito.
tremulous (trĕm'û·lŭs) agg. tremulo, tremolante.
trench (trĕnch) n. fossato, solco, trincea.
trend (trĕnd) n. direzione, andamento, tendenza.
trepan (trē·păn') n. (chir.) trapano. vt. trapanare (spec. il cranio).
trephine (trē·fīn') n. (chir.) trapano. vt. trapanare.
trepidation (trĕp'ĭ·dā'shŭn) n. trepidazione.
trespass (trĕs'pȧs) n. sconfinamento; trasgressione; peccato. vi. scon-

finare; trasgredire; abusare; peccare: no —ing, vietato l'accesso.

tress (trĕs) *n.* treccia; ricciolo.

trestle (trĕs''l) *n.* cavalletto.

trial (trī'ăl) *n.* prova, collaudo; avversità; tentativo; processo: on —, in prova; — **flight**, volo di prova.

triangle (trī'ăng'g'l) *n.* triangolo.

triangular (trī-ăng'gû-lĕr) *agg.* triangolare.

tribe (trīb) *n.* tribù, famiglia.

tribulation (trĭb'û-lā'shŭn) *n.* tribolazione.

tribunal (trī-bū'năl) *n.* tribunale.

tributary (trĭb'û-tĕr'ĭ) *n.* affluente; *agg.* tributario.

tribute (trĭb'ūt) *n.* tributo; omaggio.

trice (trīs) *n.* attimo, istante.

trick (trĭk) *n.* trucco, artificio, frode, gherminella; ticchio, vezzo; abitudine; malizia; (*gergo*) ragazzina: a dirty —, uno scherzo di cattivo genere; to do the —, risolvere il problema. *vt.* burlare, gabbare, ingannare: to — somebody into doing something indurre con un trucco qualcuno a fare qualcosa.

trickery (trĭk'ĕr-ĭ) *n.* astuzia, disonestà.

trickle (trĭk''l) *n.* sgocciolio, stillicidio. *vi.* colare, sgocciolare.

tricky (trĭk'ĭ) *agg.* furbo, disonesto; malsicuro; difficile.

tricot (trē'kō) *n.* tessuto a maglia, lavoro a maglia; maglia; calzamaglia nera (*per ballerini*).

tricycle (trī'sĭk.'l) *n.* triciclo.

tried (trīd) *pass., pp. di* to try. *agg.* provato, sperimentato.

triennial (trī-ĕn'ĭ-ăl) *agg.* triennale.

trifle (trī'f'l) *n.* bagattella, frivolezza, gingillo, inezia. *vi.* scherzare, gingillarsi: to — with, prendere alla leggiera; amoreggiare con; to — away, sprecare.

trifling (trī'flĭng) *agg.* insignificante, frivolo.

trig (trĭg) *agg.* lindo, ordinato.

trigger (trĭg'ĕr) *n.* grilletto. *vt.*: to — off, far scattare.

trigonometry (trĭg'ō-nŏm'ĕ-trĭ) *n.* trigonometria.

trill (trĭl) *n.* trillo. *vt., vi.* trillare; canticchiare: to — one's r, parlare con la erre moscia.

trillion (trĭl'yŭn) *n.* trilione (*Ingl.*: un milione alla terza potenza; *S.U.*: un milione di milioni).

trilogy (trĭl'ō-jĭ) *n.* trilogia.

trim (trĭm) *n.* stato, assetto, condizione, ordine; ornamento; equilibrio; rifinitura; to be in — form, essere in forma per. *agg.* lindo,

ordinato, curato, elegante; attrezzato. *vt.* attrezzare; mettere in ordine, decorare; potare, sfrondare; rifinire; (*naut., aeron.*) equilibrare il carico di, stabilizzare; (*fam.*) sconfiggere. *vi.* barcamenarsi, orientarsi.

trimming *n.* allestimento, fronzolo, guarnizione, rifinitura; lezione, sconfitta; *pl.* ritagli; contorno (*di vivande*); cascami; fronzoli; guadagni disonesti: the truth without —, la verità senza fronzoli *opp.* nuda e cruda.

Trinity (trĭn'ĭ-tĭ) *n.* Trinità.

trinket (trĭng'kĕt) *n.* bagattella, gingillo, aggeggio.

trip (trĭp) *n.* viaggio, viaggetto; sgambetto, inciampo. *vt.* fare lo sgambetto a; urtare; cogliere in fallo; (*mecc.*) sganciare, mettere in moto. *vi.* inciampare, mettere il piede in fallo; sbagliare, commettere una indiscrezione; saltellare.

tripe (trĭp) *n.* trippa; (*gergo*) sciocchezze.

triple (trĭp''l) *agg.* triplo, triplice. *vt.* triplicare.

triplicate (trĭp'lĭ-kāt) *agg.* triplicato, triplice. *vt.* triplicare.

tripod (trī'pŏd) *n.* tripode, treppiede.

triptych (trĭp'tĭk) *n.* trittico.

trite (trīt) *agg.* trito, banale, comune.

triumph (trī'ŭmf) *n.* trionfo. *vi.* trionfare, esultare. —**al** (-ŭm'făl) *agg.* fale.

triumphant (trī-ŭm'fănt) *agg.* trionfante, esultante. —**ly** *avv.* con esultanza, trionfalmente.

trivet (trĭv'ĕt) *n.* treppiede.

trivial (trĭv'ĭ-ăl) *agg.* insignificante, trascurabile, banale; triviale.

trod (trŏd) *pass., pp. di* to tread.

trodden (trŏd''n) *pp. di* to tread.

trolley (trŏl'ĭ) *n.* carrello; asta di presa (*del tram*), pantografo (*del treno elettrico*); rotella scanalata: — **bus**, filovia, filobus.

trollop (trŏl'ŭp) *n.* sudiciona, prostituta.

troop (trōōp) *n.* truppa; branco, frotta; (*teat.*) compagnia. *vt.* raggruppare. *vi.* intrupparsi; affluire; sfilare. —**er** *n.* soldato di cavalleria; poliziotto a cavallo.

trophy (trō'fĭ) *n.* trofeo.

tropic (trŏp'ĭk) *n.* tropico.

tropical (trŏp'ĭ-kăl) *agg.* tropicale.

trot (trŏt) *n.* trotto. *vt.* far trottare. *vi.* trottare.

trouble (trŭb''l) *n.* disturbo, briga; afflizione, malanno; preoccupazione; turbolenza; guaio; guasto, avaria: heart —, disturbo di cuore;

it is not worth the —, non ne vale la pena; to get into —, mettersi nei pasticci. *vt.* disturbare, turbare, importunare, affliggere. *vi.* turbarsi; prendersi la briga (*di*): may I — you to? posso pregarvi di?

troubled (trŭb'l'd) *agg.* turbato, inquieto; torbido.

troublemaker (trŭb'l·māk'ĕr) *n.* agitatore, facinoroso, provocatore, indisciplinato.

troublesome (trŭb''l·sŭm) *agg.* noioso, molesto; turbolento; penoso; complicato, faticoso.

troublous (trŭb'lŭs) *agg.* irrequieto, sconvolto; torbido; molesto.

trough (trôf) *n.* truogolo; condotto; solco, avvallamento.

troupe (trōōp) *n.* (*teat.*) compagnia.

trousers (trou'zĕrz) *n.pl.* calzoni.

trousseau (trōō'sō') *n.* corredo (*da sposa*).

trout (trout) *n.* (*ittiol.*) trota.

trowel (trou'ĕl) *n.* cazzuola, appianatoia.

troy weight (troi-) *n.* peso troy.

truant (trōō'ănt) *n.* infingardo; chi marina la scuola. *agg.* svogliato, ozioso, trascurato: to play —, marinare la scuola.

truce (trōōs) *n.* tregua, armistizio.

truck (trŭk) (1) *n.* carro; carrello, piattaforma di carico; autocarro: (*ferr.*) carrello (*di vagone*): — trailer, rimorchio di autocarro. *vt.*, *vi.* trasportare (*o* caricare) su autocarro.

truck (trŭk) (2) *n.* baratto; commercio; rapporti; mercanzia: to have no — with, non aver nulla da spartire con; garden —, frutta e verdura; — garden, orto. *vt.*, *vi.* barattare, commerciare.

trucker (trŭk'ĕr) *n.* autotrasportatore; camionista.

truckle (trŭk''l) *n.* puleggia. *vi.* sottomettesi.

trudge (trŭj) *vi.* camminare faticosamente, arrancare. *n.* camminata, maratona.

true (trōō) *agg.* vero, onesto, fedele, genuino, fidato; conforme (*a*), esatto. *vt.* rendere conforme (*a*), rettificare.

truffle (trŭf''l) *n.* (*bot.*) tartufo.

truism (trōō'ĭz'm) *n.* assioma.

truly (trōō'lĭ) *avv.* veramente, onestamente, esattamente, fedelmente: yours — (*nella corrispondenza*), vostro devotissimo.

trump (trŭmp) *n.* (*carte da giuoco*) trionfo, briscola. *vt.*, *vi.* battere con la briscola, giocar di briscola: to — up, inventare, falsificare.

trumpet (trŭm'pĕt) *n.* registro d'organo, tromba; cornetto acustico; barrito. *vt.* strombazzare, proclamare. *vi.* sonare la tromba; barrire.

truncheon (trŭn'chŭn) *n.* randello, sfollagente.

trundle (trŭn'd'l) *vt.* far rotolare. *vi.* rotolare.

trunk (trŭngk) *n.* tronco, fusto; condotto, tubo; proboscide; baule; (*telef.*) linea interurbana; *pl.* mutandine (*da bagno, atletica, ecc.*); — line, linea principale.

truss (trŭs) *n.* balla, fascio; cinto erniario; bendaggio; armatura (*costruzione*). *vt.* legare; imballare; immobilizzare.

trust (trŭst) *n.* fiducia, fede; custodia; credito; monopolio; consorzio; cura: breach of —, abuso di fiducia. *vt.* fidarsi di, affidarsi a, far affidamento su, far credito a. *vi.* fidare, confidare: to — somebody with, affidare a qualcuno.

trustee (trŭs·tē') *n.* depositario, curatore, fidecommissario.

trustful (trŭst'fŏŏl) *agg.* fiducioso.

trustworthy (trŭst'wûr'thĭ) *agg.* fidato, attendibile.

trusty (trŭs'tĭ) *agg.* sicuro, fidato, leale. *n.* prigioniero cui si concedono certi privilegi per buona condotta.

truth (trōōth) *n.* verità, realtà; sincerità, fedeltà, rettitudine. —ful *agg.* veritiero. —fulness *n.* veracità.

try (trī) *n.* prova, tentativo. *vt.*, *vi.* provare, tentare; mettere alla prova, stancare; sforzarsi, sperimentare; verificare, saggiare; processare, giudicare: to — to, cercare *o* tentare di; to — on a suit, provarsi un vestito; to — one's luck, tentare la fortuna; to — somebody's patience, mettere alla prova la pazienza di qualcuno.

trying (trī'ĭng) *agg.* difficile, penoso, faticoso, critico.

T-shirt (tē'shûrt') *n.* maglietta estiva (*senza collo e con le maniche corte*).

tub (tŭb) *n.* tino, tinozza, vasca, bagno; (*fam.*) barca.

tube (tūb) *n.* tubo; galleria (*o* ferrovia) sotterranea; (*anat.*) tromba, canale; (*S.U., radio*) valvola: inner —, camera d'aria; test —, provetta.

tuber (tū'bĕr) *n.* (*bot.*) tubero.

tubercular (tû·bûr'kû·lĕr) *agg.* tubercolare.

tuberculosis (tû·bûr'kû·lō'sĭs) *n.* (*med.*) tubercolosi.

tuberculous (tû·bûr'kû·lŭs) *agg.* tubercoloso.

tubing (tūb'ĭng) *n.* tubatura, tubi.

tubular (tū'bū-lĕr) *agg.* tubolare.

tuck (tŭk) *n.* piega, basta (*d'indumento*); (*S.U.*) energia, vita. *vt.* piegare, ripiegare; ficcare; rimboccare: to — away, mangiare con gusto; to — in the bedclothes, rimboccare le coltri.

Tuesday (tūz'dĭ) *n.* martedì.

tuft (tŭft) *n.* ciocca, ciuffo, nappa, batuffolo; cespuglio.

tug (tŭg) *n.* sforzo, strattone, strappo; (*naut.*) rimorchiatore: — of war, tiro della fune. *vt.*, *vi.* tirare con forza, trascinare, rimorchiare; faticare.

tugboat (tŭg'bōt) *n.* rimorchiatore.

tuition (tū·ĭsh'ŭn) *n.* insegnamento; tassa scolastica.

tulip (tū'lĭp) *n.* tulipano.

tumble (tŭm'b'l) *n.* ruzzolone, capitombolo; disordine, ammasso. *vt.* rovesciare, scompigliare: — far capitombolare. *vi.* rotolare, capitombolare, far capriole *o* acrobazie: to — to (*gergo*), intuire; to — into someone, incontrare qualcuno per caso.

tumbledown (tŭm'b'l-doun') *agg.* diroccato, in rovina.

tumbler (tŭm'blĕr) *n.* acrobata; bicchiere cilindrico; nasello (*di serratura*), cane.

tumor (tū'mĕr) *n.* tumore.

tumult (tū'mŭlt) *n.* tumulto.

tumultuous (tū-mŭl'tū·ŭs) *agg.* tumultuoso, agitato.

tun (tŭn) *n.* botte, tino.

tuna (tōō'nà) *n.* tonno; (*bot.*) fico d'India.

tune (tūn) *n.* tono; melodia, motivo, aria; (*radio*) sintonia: in —, d'accordo; out of —, in contrasto. *vt.*, *vi.* accordare, intonare, sincronizzare: to — in (*radio*), sintonizzare, sintonizzarsi; to — up a motor, mettere a punto un motore.

tungsten (tŭng'stĕn) *n.* tungsteno.

tunic (tū'nĭk) *n.* tunica; (*mil.*) giubba.

tuning (tūn'ĭng) *n.* accordo, accordatura: — fork, diapason.

tunnel (tŭn'ĕl) *n.* galleria sotterranea, traforo; (*fam.*) ciminiera. *vt.*, *vi.* perforare, scavare una galleria.

tunny (tŭn'ĭ) *n.* tonno.

turban (tûr'bǎn) *n.* turbante.

turbine (tûr'bĭn) *n.* (*mecc.*) turbina.

turbojet (tûr'bō-jĕt') *n.* turbogetto.

turbopropeller (tûr'bō-prō-pĕl'ĕr), turboprop *n.* turboelica.

turbulent (tûr'bū-lĕnt) *agg.* turbolento.

tureen (tū·rēn') *n.* zuppiera.

turf (tûrf) *n.* prato, piota; ippica, ippodromo.

turgid (tûr'jĭd) *agg.* turgido.

Turk (tûrk) *n.* turco, turca.

Turkey (tûr'kĭ) (1) *n.* Turchia.

turkey (tûr'kĭ) (2) *n.* tacchino; (*gergo teatr.*) fiasco.

turmoil (tûr'moil) *n.* tumulto, agitazione.

turn (tûrn) *n.* giro, turno; svolta, curva; rotazione; piega; servigio; direzione; (*fam.*) sussulto, sgomento, smarrimento: to a —, alla perfezione; by turns, a rotazione, a intervalli; a bad —, un brutto tiro; a good —, un buon servigio. *vt.* voltare, girare, rivoltare; cambiare, tramutare, tradurre; tornire; rivolgersi; voltarsi, deviare; trasformarsi; dirigersi, accingersi: to — adrift, mandare alla deriva; to — aside, deviare; distogliere il viso; to — back, mandare (*o* tornare) indietro; to — down, respingere; to — in, entrare, coricarsi; to — into, trasformarsi (*o* trasformare) in; to — off, chiudere (*il gas, l'acqua*), spegnere (*la luce*); to — out, espellere; porre in vendita; rivelarsi; to — over, sfogliare; rigirare; esaminare; consegnare; to — round, volgersi; to — sour, inacidire; to — up, comparire; to — upside down, capovolgere, rivoltare, capovolgersi.

turnaround (tûrn'à·round') *n.* spiazzo per girare (*con l'automobile, ecc.*); voltafaccia; tempo totale di un viaggio di andata e ritorno (*di una nave, un aereo, ecc.*).

turncoat (tûrn'kōt') *n.* voltagabbana.

turner (tûr'nĕr) *n.* tornitore.

turning (tûr'nĭng) *n.* giro, rotazione, svolta; tornitura: — point, svolta decisiva, fulcro; — lathe, tornio.

turnkey (tûrn'kē') *n.* carceriere.

turnout (tûrn'out') *n.* tenuta, vestiario; utile netto; riunione; produzione; (*ferr.*) raccordo.

turnover (tûrn'ō'vĕr) *n.* movimento di danaro (*o* d'affari); rovesciamento; labor —, rotazione di personale operaio; apple —, torta di mele. *agg.* rovesciabile, rivoltato.

turnpike (tûrn'pĭk') *n.* cancello a ruota di strada a pedaggio; (*S.U.*) strada a pedaggio; autostrada.

turnscrew (tûrn'skrōō') *n.* cacciavite.

turnstile (tûrn'stĭl') *n.* arganello (*cancelletto a ruota*).

turntable (tûrn'tā'b'l) *n.* piatto girevole (*del grammofono*), giradischi; piattaforma girevole.

turnip (tûr'nĭp) *n.* (*bot.*) rapa.

turpentine (tûr′pĕn·tĭn) *n.* trementina.

turpitude (tûr′pĭ·tūd) *n.* turpitudine.

turquoise (tûr′koiz) *n.* turchese.

turret (tûr′ĕt) *n.* torretta.

turtle (tûr′t'l) *n.* tartaruga: **to turn —**, capovolgersi.

turtledove (tûr′t'l·dŭv′) *n.* tortora.

tusk (tŭsk) *n.* zanna; (*mecc.*) dente.

tussle (tŭs′'l) *n.* zuffa, rissa. *vi.* rissare, azzuffarsi.

tutor (tū′tẽr) *n.* istitutore, precettore; tutore. *vt.*, *vi.* istruire, educare, fare il precettore.

tutu (tōō′tōō) *n.* tutù, gonnellino da ballerina.

tuxedo (tŭk·sē′dō) *n.* (*S.U.*) smoking, abito nero.

tuyère (twẽr) *n.* (*metall.*) ugello.

twaddle (twŏd′'l) *vi.* cianciare.

twang (twăng) *n.* suono vibrato, tono nasale; sapore violento. *vt.* far vibrare. *vi.* emettere un suono vibrato; parlare con voce nasale.

tweak (twēk) *n.* tirata, strattone. *vt.* pizzicare, tirare (*le orecchie*), torcere.

tweed (twēd) *n.* panno di lana, tweed: **— suit,** abito di tweed.

tweezers (twēz′ẽrz) *n.pl.* pinzette.

twelfth (twĕlfth) *n.*, *agg.* dodicesimo.

twelve (twĕlv) *n.*, *agg.* dodici.

twelve-tone *agg.* (*mus.*) dodecafonico: **— system,** dodecafonia.

twentieth (twĕn′tǐ·ĕth) *n.*, *agg.* ventesimo.

twenty (twĕn′tǐ) *n.*, *agg.* venti.

twerp (twûrp) *n.* (*gergo*) persona insignificante *o* spregevole, balordo, gonzo, povero stupido, babbeo.

twice (twīs) *avv.* due volte: **— as much,** due volte tanto; **— as big,** grosso il doppio.

twiddle (twĭd′'l) *vt.* rigirare oziosamente, giocherellare con. *vi.* roteare, piroettare; oziare: **to — one's thumbs,** figurarsi i pollici.

twig (twĭg) *n.* rametto, ramoscello.

twilight (twī′līt) *n.* crepuscolo, semioscurità.

twill (twĭl) *n.* diagonale (*tess.*)

twin (twĭn) *n.*, *agg.* gemello. *vt.* accoppiare. *vi.* accoppiarsi; avere un parto gemellare.

twine (twīn) *n.* attorcigliamento, groviglio; funicella, spago. *vt.* intrecciare, attorcigliare, avvolgere, legare. *vi.* attorcigliarsi, avviticchiarsi, aggrovigliarsi, serpeggiare.

twinge (twĭnj) *n.* spasimo, fitta. *vt.* pungere, trafiggere.

twinkle (twĭng′k'l) *n.* scintillio, ammicco, balenio, attimo; *vi.* ammiccare, scintillare, tremolare.

twinkling (twĭng′klĭng) *n.* balenio; ammicco: **in the — of an eye,** in un batter d'occhio.

twirl (twûrl) *n.* rotazione, evoluzione, voluta, spira; piroetta. *vt.*, *vi.* roteare, rigirare, avvolgere; piroettare.

twist (twĭst) *n.* torcitura, attorcigliamento, torsione; propensione; contorsione; corda, cordoncino, treccia; capriccio; curva, tortuosità; **to give a —,** torcere; attorcigliare; **to give a humorous — to a novel,** dare a un romanzo un piglio umoristico. *vt.* torcere, attorcigliare, ritorcere, avvolgere; deformare, pervertire, snaturare. *vi.* attorcigliarsi, contorcersi; serpeggiare; voltarsi; intrecciarsi.

twisted *agg.* attorcigliato, contorto, ritorto; pervertito, snaturato.

twister (twĭs′tẽr) *n.* torcitore; bugiardo; bugia; piroetta; turbine.

twitch (twĭch) *n.* fitta, contrazione, spasimo, guizzo; strattone. *vt.* tirare bruscamente, muovere di scatto, pizzicare. *vi.* contrarsi spasmodicamente, guizzare.

twitter (twĭt′ẽr) *n.* cinguettio; risatina; orgasmo. *vt.*, *vi.* cinguettare; ridacchiare; essere in orgasmo.

two (tōō) *n.*, *agg.* due.

twofold (tōō′fōld′) *agg.* doppio, duplice.

two-master *n.* (*naut.*) due-alberi.

two-time (tōō′tīm′) *vt.* (*gergo*) tradire, ingannare, fregare; fare le corna a.

two-timing *agg.* falso, traditore, ipocrita, infedele.

two-seater *n.* automobile a due posti.

tycoon (tī·kōōn′) *n.* (*S.U.*) magnate.

tympanum (tĭm′pȧ·nŭm) *n.* (*anat.*, *zool.*, *arch.*) timpano; (*elett.*) diaframma.

type (tīp) *n.* tipo, modello; (*tip.*) carattere: **in —,** composto. *vt.*, *vi.* simboleggiare; scrivere a stampatello; dattilografare.

typesetter (tīp′sĕt′ẽr) *n.* (*tip.*) compositore.

typewrite (tīp′rīt′) *vt.*, *vi.* dattilografare.

typewriter (tīp′rīt′ẽr) *n.* macchina per scrivere; dattilografo.

typewriting (tīp′rīt′ĭng) *n.* dattilografia.

typewritten (tīp′rīt′'n) *pp. di* to typewrite, dattiloscritto, scritto a macchina.

typhoid (tī′foid) *n.* tifoidea. *agg.* tifoide.

typhoon (tī′fōōn) *n.* tifone, ciclone.

typhus (tī′fŭs) *n.* (*med.*) tifo.

typical (tĭp′ĭ·kȧl) *agg.* tipico.

typist (tīp′ĭst) *n.* dattilografo, dattilografa.

typography (tī-pŏg′rá-fĭ) *n.* arte grafica.

tyrannical (tī-răn′ĭ-kăl) *agg.* tirannico.

tyrannize (tĭr′á-nīz) *vt.*, *vi.* tiranneggiare.

tyrannous (tĭr′á-nŭs) *agg.* dispotico.

tyranny (tĭr′á-nĭ) *n.* tirannia.

tyrant (tī′rănt) *n.* tiranno, despota.

tyre (tīr) (*Ingl.*) *n.* pneumatico (*di ruota*).

tyro (tī′rō) *n.* novizio, principiante.

Tyrolean (tĭ-rō′lē-ăn) *agg.* tirolese.

Tyrrhenian (tĭ-rē′nĭ-ăn) *n.*, *agg.* etrusco: the — Sea, il Mar Tirreno.

U

ubiquitous (ū-bĭk′wĭ-tŭs) *agg.* onnipresente.

udder (ŭd′ĕr) *n.* (*zool.*) ghiandola mammaria.

ugliness (ŭg′lĭ-nĕs) *n.* bruttezza, bassezza, viltà; caparbietà; gravità, pericolosità.

ugly (ŭg′lĭ) *agg.* brutto, odioso; preoccupante, pericoloso; caparbio.

ukulele (ū′kŭ-lā′lĕ) *n.* chitarra hawaiana.

ulcer (ŭl′sĕr) *n.* ulcera.

ulterior (ŭl-tēr′ĭ-ĕr) *agg.* ulteriore, recondito.

ultimate (ŭl′tĭ-mĭt) *agg.* ultimo, estremo; definitivo, finale. **—ly** *avv.* finalmente, definitivamente.

ultimo (ŭl′tĭ-mō) *agg.* scorso. *avv.* nel mese scorso.

ultra (ŭl′trá) *agg.* estremo, eccessivo.

ultramarine (ŭl′trá-má-rēn′) *n.* oltremare (*colore*). *agg.* d'oltremare, oltremarino.

ultramontane (ŭl′trá-mŏn′tān) *n.*, *agg.* oltremontano.

ultramundane (ŭl′trá-mŭn′dān) *agg.* oltremondano.

ululate (ŭl′ū-lāt) *vi.* ululare.

umber (ŭm′bĕr) *n.* terra d'ombra.

umbrage (ŭm′brĭj) *n.* ombra; fogliame; accenno; offesa: **to take —**, adombrarsi.

umbrella (ŭm′brĕl′á) *n.* ombrello, parapioggia.

umpire (ŭm′pīr) *n.* arbitro. *vt.*, *vi.* arbitrare.

un- (ŭn) *pref. negativo* non, senza, in-, dis-.

unabashed (ŭn′á-băsht′) *agg.* imperterrito, disinvolto, spavaldo.

unable (ŭn-ā′b'l) *agg.* incapace, impossibilitato, impotente, inetto: **I am — to do it,** non so farlo, non posso farlo, non riesco a farlo.

unabridged (ŭn′á-brĭjd′) *agg.* integrale, completo.

unaccountable (ŭn′á-koun′tá-b'l) *agg.* inesplicabile; non responsabile.

unaccounted-for *agg.* inspiegato; ingiustificato.

unaccustomed (ŭn′á-kŭs′tŭmd) *agg.* non abituato, inusitato, insolito.

unacquainted (ŭn′á-kwān′tĕd) *agg.* ignaro, estraneo, insolito.

unadorned (ŭn′á-dôrnd′) *agg.* disadorno.

unadvised (ŭn′ăd-vīzd′) *agg.* sconsiderato, imprudente, inopportuno.

unaffected (ŭn′á-fĕk′tĕd) *agg.* non influenzato; indifferente, imperterrito; naturale, spontaneo.

unafraid (ŭn′á-frād′) *agg.* intrepido.

unaided (ŭn-ād′ĕd) *agg.* senza aiuto.

unalloyed (ŭn′á-loid′) *agg.* puro, non mescolato.

unalterable (ŭn-ôl′tĕr-á-b'l) *agg.* inalterabile.

un-American (ŭn′á-mĕr′ĭ-kăn) *agg.* (*S.U.*) antiamericano.

unanimity (ū′ná-nĭm′ĭ-tĭ) *n.* unanimità.

unanimous (ū-năn′ĭ-mŭs) *agg.* unanime.

unannealed (ŭn′á-nēld′) *agg.* (*metal.*) dolce.

unannounced (ŭn′á-nounst′) *agg.* inaspettato, non annunziato, inopinato.

unanswerable (ŭn-án′sĕr-á-b'l) *agg.* inconfutabile; inesplicabile.

unanswered (ŭn-án′sĕrd) *agg.* inconfutato; inevaso; insoluto; non ricambiato.

unapproachable (ŭn′á-prōch′á-b'l) *agg.* impareggiabile; inavvicinabile, inaccessibile.

unarm (ŭn-ärm′) *vt.* disarmare, rendere innocuo.

unarmed (ŭn-ärmd′) *agg.* inerme, disarmato.

unashamed (ŭn′á-shāmd′) *agg.* spudorato, imperterrito.

unasked (ŭn-áskt′) *agg.* spontaneo, non richiesto; non invitato.

unassuming (ŭn′á-sūm′ĭng) *agg.* modesto, senza pretese.

unattached (ŭn′á-tacht′) *agg.* separato, indipendente; esterno (*di studente univ.*).

unattainable (ŭn′á-tān′á-b'l) *agg.* inaccessibile; irraggiungibile.

unattended (ŭn′á-tĕn′dĕd) *agg.* solo, senza scorta (*o* cure); privo di uditorio.

unattractive (ŭn′ă·trăk′tĭv) *agg.* brutto, sgradevole.

unauthorized (ŭn·ô′thĕr·īzd) *agg.* abusivo, arbitrario, illegale.

unavailing (ŭn′ă·vāl′ĭng) *agg.* inefficace, inutile.

unavoidable (ŭn′ă·void′ă·b'l) *agg.* inevitabile.

unaware (ŭn′ă·wâr′) *agg.* inconscio, ignaro. *avv.* (*anche* **unawares**) alla sprovvista, inopinatamente, inavvertitamente.

unbalanced (ŭn·băl′ănst) *agg.* sbilanciato, instabile; squilibrato; precario: — **account**, conto scoperto.

unbearable (ŭn·bâr′ă·b'l) *agg.* insopportabile.

unbeaten (ŭn·bēt′'n) *agg.* imbattuto, indenne; non frequentato (*di strada, ecc.*).

unbecoming (ŭn′bē·kŭm′ĭng) *agg.* disadatto, indecoroso: **an — dress**, un vestito che sta male.

unbelief (ŭn′bē·lēf′) *n.* incredulità, scetticismo.

unbelievable (ŭn′bē·lēv′ă·b'l) *agg.* incredibile.

unbeliever (ŭn′bē·lēv′ĕr) *n.* miscredente, scettico.

unbelieving *agg.* incredulo.

unbend (ŭn·bĕnd′) *vt.* (*pass., pp.* **unbent**) allentare; raddrizzare; mettere a proprio agio; (*naut.*) mollare. *vi.* allentarsi; raddrizzarsi; ammansarsi.

unbending *agg.* inflessibile, risoluto, rigido.

unbiased, unbiassed (ŭn′bī′ăst) *agg.* imparziale, senza prevenzioni.

unbind (ŭn·bīnd′) *vt.* (*pass., pp.* unbound) slegare, sciogliere, liberare.

unblemished (ŭn·blĕm′ĭsht) *agg.* immacolato senza macchia; perfetto.

unblushing (ŭn·blŭsh′ĭng) *agg.* impudente sfrontato.

unborn (ŭn·bôrn.) *agg.* non ancora nato, inesistente, futuro, increato.

unbosom (ŭn·bŏŏz′ŭm) *vt.* confidare, rivelare: **to — oneself**, sfogarsi, confidarsi.

unbound (ŭn·bound) *pass., pp. di* to **unbind**, *agg.* slegato, sciolto, libero, non rilegato.

unbreakable (ŭn·brăk′ă·b'l) *agg.* infrangibile.

unbridled (ŭn·brī′d′ld) *agg.* sfrenato, sbrigliato.

unbroken (ŭn·brō′kĕn) *agg.* ininterrotto, continuo; intiero, intatto; indomo; uniforme.

unburnt (ŭn·bûrnt′) *agg.* incombusto, senza bruciature, crudo.

unbusinesslike (ŭn·bĭz′nĕs·līk′) *agg.* malpratico, anticommerciale.

unbutton (ŭn·bŭt′'n) *vt.* sbottonare.

uncalled (ŭn·kôld′) *agg.* non chiamato, non invitato: **— for**, inopportuno; inutile: ineducato, impertinente.

uncanny (ŭn·kăn′ĭ) *agg.* magico, fantastico, soprannaturale.

unceasing (ŭn·sēs′ĭng) *agg.* incessante. **—ly** *avv.* incessantemente.

uncertain (ŭn·sûr′tĭn) *agg.* incerto, malsicuro, vago.

uncertainty (ŭn·sûr′tĭn·tĭ) *n.* incertezza.

unchallenged (ŭn·chăl′ĕnjd) *agg.* incontestato, indisturbato, non sfidato.

unchangeable (ŭn·chān′jă·b'l) *agg.* immutabile, invariabile.

unchanged (ŭn·chānjd′) *agg.* immutato.

unchanging (ŭn·chān′jĭng) *agg.* invariabile, costante.

uncharitable (ŭn·chăr′ĭ·tà·b'l) *agg.* severo, poco caritatevole.

uncivil (ŭn·sĭv′ĭl) *agg.* scortese, sgarbato, villano.

uncivilized (ŭn·sĭv′ĭ·līzd) *agg.* incivile, barbaro.

unclasp (ŭn·klåsp′) *vt.* lasciare la presa di; slacciare; sgrovigliare, sciogliere.

uncle (ŭng′k'l) *n.* zio; (*gergo*) prestatore su pegno: **— Sam**, gli (*S.U.*); **to talk like a Dutch —**, catechizzare.

unclean (ŭn·klēn′) *agg.* sudicio, peccaminoso, losco. **—ness** *n.* sporcizia; impudicizia.

unclouded (ŭn·kloud′ĕd) *agg.* senza nubi.

uncoil (ŭn·koil′) *vt.* svolgere, srotolare, dipanare.

uncomely (ŭn·kŭm′lĭ) *agg.* brutto, sgraziato sconveniente.

uncomfortable (ŭn·kŭm′fĕrt·à·b'l) *agg.* scomodo, nolesto, inquietante, spiacevole, imbarazzante.

uncomfortably (ŭn·kŭ′n′fĕrt·à·bĭl) *avv.* a disagio, scomodamente, inquietamente, nolestamente.

uncommon (ŭn·kŏm′ŭn) *agg.* poco comune, insolito, raro. **—ly** *avv.* insolitamente, eccezionalmente.

uncommunicative (ŭn′kŏ·mū′nĭ·kā′tĭv) *agg.* non communicativo, taciturno.

uncomplaining (ŭn′kŏm·plān′ĭng) *agg* rassegnato, paziente.

uncomplimentary (ŭn′kŏm·plĭ′mĕn′tà·rĭ) *agg.* non lusinghiero, offensivo.

uncompromising (ŭn·kŏm′prō·mīz′ĭng) *agg.* inflessibile, ostinato.

unconcern (ŭn′kŏn·sûrn′) *n.* disinteresse, indifferenza.

unconcerned (ŭn′kŏn·sûrnd′) *agg.* indifferente, imperterrito.

unconditional (ŭn'kŏn·dĭsh'ŭn·ăl) *agg.* incondizionato, assoluto.

unconformable (ŭn'kŏn·fôr'mả·b'l) *agg.* incompatibile.

uncongenial (ŭn'kŏn·jēn'yăl) *agg.* incompatibile; sgradevole, antipatico.

unconnected (ŭn'kŏ·nĕk'tĕd) *agg.* staccato; estraneo (*a*), senza rapporti, non imparentato, indipendente (*da*); vago, slegato.

unconquerable (ŭn·kŏng'kĕr·ả·b'l) *agg.* invincibile, indomabile, insormontabile.

unconquered (ŭn·kŏng'kĕrd) *agg.* invitto, indomito, inespugnato.

unconscionable (ŭn·kŏn'shŭn·ả·b'l) *agg.* irragionevole, eccessivo; non coscienzioso; smisurato.

unconscious (ŭn·kŏn'shŭs) *n.* (*psic.*) inconscio. *agg.* inconscio, ignaro, inconsapevole; svenuto; involontario.—*ness n.* stato di incoscienza; automatismo.

unconstrained (ŭn'kŏn·strānd') *agg.* spontaneo, libero, disinvolto.

unconstraint (ŭn'kŏn·strānt') *n.* disinvoltura, spontaneità, libertà.

uncontrollable (ŭn'kŏn·trōl'ả·b'l) *agg.* incontrollabile, irresistibile.

unconventional (ŭn'kŏn·vĕn'shŭn·ăl) *agg.* non convenzionale, semplice, schietto, alla buona.

unconvinced (ŭn'kŏn·vĭnst') *agg.* incredulo, scettico.

uncork (ŭn·kôrk') *vt.* sturare, stappare.

uncorrupted (ŭn·kŏ·rŭp'tĕd) *agg.* incorrotto; genuino; non putrefatto.

uncounted (ŭn·koun'tĕd) *agg.* innumerevole, incalcolabile.

uncouple (ŭn·kŭp''l) *vt.* disgiungere, sganciare; spaiare; disinnestare.

uncouth (ŭn·kōōth') *agg.* goffo, rozzo, sgraziato, grottesco, strano.

uncover (ŭn·kŭv'ĕr) *vt.* scoprire, scoperchiare; rivelare; esporre. *vi.* scoprirsi (*il capo*).

unction (ŭngk'shŭn) *n.* unzione, santità, grazia divina, fervore; balsamo.

unctuous (ŭngk'tů·ŭs) *agg.* untuoso, oleoso; insinuante, mellifluo.

uncultivated (ŭn·kŭl'tĭ·vāt'ĕd) *agg.* incolto (*di terreno*).

uncultured (ŭn·kŭl'tůrd) *agg.* incolto (*ignorante*).

uncurl (ŭn·kûrl') *vt.* raddrizzare, svolgere, spianare. *vi.* raddrizzarsi (*spec. da una posa raggomitolata*).

uncut (ŭn·kŭt') *agg.* non tagliato, intero, intonso, grezzo (*di diamante*).

undamaged (ŭn·dăm'ĭjd) *agg.* indenne, intatto, in buono stato.

undaunted (ŭn·dôn'tĕd) *agg.* imperturbato, intrepido, pertinace.

undeceive (ŭn'dē·sēv') *vt.* disingannare, aprire gli occhi a.

undecided (ŭn'dē·sīd'ĕd) *agg.* indeciso, incerto.

undelivered (ŭn'dē·lĭ'vĕrd) *agg.* non recapitato, giacente.

undeniable (ŭn'dē·nī'ả·b'l) *agg.* innegabile.

under (ŭn'dĕr) *agg.* inferiore, subordinato. *prep.* sotto, al di sotto di, meno di, dipendente da: — **sail**, in navigazione; — **way**, in corso, in viaggio; — **age**, minore di età; — **cover of**, col favore di, al riparo di; — **pretense of**, col pretesto di; **to be** — **obligation to**, essere in debito con.—*avv.* sotto, al di sotto, in grado inferiore, in soggezione: **to go** —, fallire, far fiasco.

underact (ŭn'dĕr·ăkt') *vt.*, *vi.* recitare in maniera fiacca; recitare in maniera sobria o scarna (*per dar maggior vigore alla parte*).

underbred (ŭn'dĕr·brĕd') *agg.* maleducato; bastardo.

underbrush (ŭn'dĕr·brŭsh') *n.* sottobosco.

undercarriage (ŭn'dĕr·kăr'ĭj) *n.* (*auto*) telaio; (*aeron.*) carrello d'atterraggio.

undercharge (ŭn'dĕr·chärj') *vt.* fare un prezzo di favore a; applicare un prezzo ridotto a.

underclothes (ŭn'dĕr·klōthz) *n.pl.* biancheria personale.

undercurrent (ŭn'dĕr·kûr'ĕnt) *n.* corrente subacquea; influenza (*o* tendenza) segreta.

undercut (ŭn'dĕr·kŭt') *vt.*, *vi.* vendere (*o* lavorare) a prezzo minore.

underdog (ŭn'dĕr·dŏg') *n.* (*fam.*) diseredato; chi ha la peggio, vinto, perdente.

underdone (ŭn'dĕr·dŭn) *agg.* poco cotto.

underdose (ŭn'dĕr·dōs') *n.* dose scarsa.

underestimate (ŭn'dĕr·ĕs'tĭ·māt) *vt.* sottovalutare.

underexposed (ŭn'dĕr·ĕks·pōzd') *agg.* (*fot.*) sottesposto.

underfed (ŭn'dĕr·fĕd') *agg.* malnutrito.

underfoot (ŭn'dĕr·fŏŏt') *avv.* sotto i piedi; sul terreno.

undergarment (ŭn'dĕr·gär'mĕnt) *n.* indumento intimo.

undergo (ŭn'dĕr·gō') *vt.* (*pass.* underwent, *pp.* undergone) subire, sottostare a, sopportare.

undergraduate (ŭn'dĕr·grăd'ů·åt) *agg.* laureando.

underground (ŭn'dĕr.ground') *n.* sottosuolo; passaggio sotterraneo; metropolitana (*ferrovia*); (*pol.*) resistenza partigiana. *agg.* sotterraneo, clandestino. *avv.* sotterra; clandestinamente.

underhand (ŭn'dĕr.hǎnd') **underhanded** *agg.* segreto, tortuoso, subdolo.

underlie (ŭn'dĕr.lī') *vt.* (*pass.* underlay, *pp.* underlain) sottostare a, essere passibile di; essere sotto a; essere alla base di; formare il substrato di.

underline (ŭn'dĕr.līn') *vt.* sottolineare.

underling (ŭn'dĕr.lĭng) *n.* subalterno.

underlying (ŭn'dĕr.lī'ing) *agg.* fondamentale, sottostante, inferiore.

undermine (ŭn'dĕr.mīn') *vt.* minare alle fondamenta; pregiudicare, insidiare.

undermost (ŭn'dĕr.mōst) *agg.sup.* imo, infimo, più basso.

underneath (ŭn'dĕr.nēth') *prep.* sotto a, al di sotto di. *avv.* sotto, di sotto.

undernourished (ŭn'dĕr.nûr'ĭsht) *agg.* denutrito.

undernourishment (ŭn'dĕr.nûr'ĭshmĕnt) *n.* denutrizione.

underpaid (ŭn'dĕr.pād') *agg.* mal pagato.

underpay (ŭn'dĕr.pā') *vt.* pagare inadeguatamente.

underproof (ŭn'dĕr.proof') *agg.* a bassa gradazione alcoolica.

underrate (un'dĕr.rāt') *vt.* sottovalutare.

underscore (un'dĕr.skōr') *vt.* sottolineare.

under secretary (ŭn'dĕr sĕk'rĕ.tĕr.ĭ) vicesegretario; sottosegretario.

undersell (ŭn'dĕr.sĕl') *vt.* (*pass., pp.* undersold) svendere; vendere più a buon mercato di.

undershirt (ŭn'dĕr.shûrt') *n.* maglietta; camicetta.

underside (ŭn'dĕr.sīd') *n.* parte inferiore.

undersign (ŭn'dĕr.sīn') *vt.* sottoscrivere.

undersigned (un'dĕr.sīnd') *n., agg.* sottoscritto.

undersized (ŭn'dĕr.sīzd') *agg.* in miniatura, di misura minima.

underskirt (ŭn'dĕr.skûrt') *n.* sottana, sottoveste.

understand (ŭn'dĕr.stǎnd') *vt., vi.* (*pass., pp.* understood) capire, afferrare; rendersi conto di; sentir dire, essere informato di; sottintendere: I — that he is coming, mi risulta che egli verrà; it is understood that, resta inteso che; to make oneself understood, farsi capire.

understandable (ŭn'dĕr.stǎn'dá.b'l) *agg.* comprensibile.

understanding *n.* intelligenza, comprensione; intesa; competenza, discernimento; *agg.* competente, comprensivo.

understate (ŭn'dĕr.stāt') *vt.* esporre inefficacemente, sminuire.

understatement (ŭn'dĕr.stāt'mĕnt) *n.* esposizione inadeguata, attenuazione.

understood (ŭn'der.stŏŏd') *pass., pp. di* to understand. *agg.* inteso, convenuto, stabilito, sottinteso.

understudy (ŭn'dĕr.stŭd'ĭ) *n.* attore sostituto. *vt., vi.* studiare una parte per sostituire un attore.

undertake (ŭn'dĕr.tāk') *vt., vi.* (*pass.* undertook, *pp.* undertaken) intraprendere, tentare; assumersi, impegnarsi (*a*); prendere in appalto.

undertaker (ŭn'dĕr.tāk'ĕr) *n.* impresario di pompe funebri.

undertaking (ŭn'dĕr.tāk'ĭng) *n.* impresa, compito, impegno.

undertone (ŭn'dĕr.tōn') *n.* tono sommesso, susurro, sfumatura.

undertook (ŭn'dĕr.tŏŏk') *pass. di* undertake.

undervalue (ŭn'dĕr.vǎl'ū) *vt.* sottovalutare, sminuire, deprezzare.

underwear (ŭn'dĕr.wâr') *n.* biancheria personale.

underwent (ŭn'dĕr.wĕnt') *pass. di* to undergo.

underwood (ŭn'dĕr.wŏŏd') *n.* sottobosco.

underworld (ŭn'dĕr.wûrld') *n.* malavita, bassifondi, delinquenza; inferno; antipodi.

underwrite (ŭn'dĕr.rīt') *vt.* (*pass.* underwrote, *pp.* underwritten), sottoscrivere, assicurarsi (*contrarre un'assicurazione*). *vi.* fare l'assicuratore.

undeserved (ŭn'dĕ.zûrvd') *agg.* immeritato, ingiusto.

undeserving *agg.* immeritevole.

undesirable (ŭn'dĕ.zīr'á.b'l) *n., agg.* indesiderabile, inauspicabile.

undetected (ŭn'dĕ.tĕkt'ĭd) *agg.* inavvertito, inosservato, non scoperto.

undeveloped (ŭn'dĕ.vĕl'ŭpt) *agg.* non sviluppato.

undignified (ŭn.dĭg'nĭ.fīd) *agg.* non dignitoso, incomposto, indecoroso.

undiluted (ŭn'dĭ.lūt'ĭd) *agg.* puro, non diluito.

undiminished (ŭn'dĭ.mĭn'ĭsht) *agg.* costante, non diminuito, implacato.

undine (ŭn.dēn') *n.* ondina, ninfa.

undisciplined (ŭn.dĭs'ĭ.plĭnd) *agg.* indisciplinato.

undiscovered (ŭn'dĭs·kŭv'ĕrd) *agg.* non scoperto, nascosto, sconosciuto.

undisguised (ŭn'dĭs·gīzd') *agg.* senza travestimento; aperto, sincero, genuino, esplicito.

undismayed (ŭn'dĭs·mād') *agg.* imperterrito.

undisputed (ŭn'dĭs·pūt'ĕd) *agg.* incontestato.

undistinguishable (ŭn'dĭs·tĭng'gwĭsh·á·b'l) *agg.* indistinguibile, confuso, irriconoscibile.

undistinguished (ŭn'dĭs·tĭng'gwĭsht) *agg.* indistinto, oscuro; privo di distinzione.

undisturbed (ŭn'dĭs·tûrbd') *agg.* indisturbato, imperturbato.

undivided (ŭn'dĭ·vīd'ĕd) *agg.* indiviso.

undo (ŭn·dōō') *vt.* (*pass.* undid, *pp.* undone) disfare, sciogliere, snodare; annullare; distruggere, rovinare: **to — one's hair**, sciogliersi i capelli.

undoing (ŭn·dōō'ĭng) *n.* rovina; annullamento; distruzione.

undone (ŭn·dŭn') *pp. di* to undo, *agg.* disfatto, distrutto; incompiuto; omesso; annullato: **it is still —**, è ancora da farsi; **to come —**, disfarsi, sciogliersi.

undoubted (ŭn·dout'ĕd) *agg.* indubitato, certo.

undress (ŭn·drĕs') *n.* (*mil.*) bassa tenuta. *vt.* svestire, sbendare. *vi.* svestirsi.

undue (ŭn·dū') *agg.* superfluo, eccessivo, abusivo, indebito.

undulate (ŭn'dū̇·lāt) *vt.* ondulare, far ondeggiare. *vi.* ondeggiare, vibrare.

undulation (ŭn'dū̇·lā'shŭn) *n.* ondulazione, ondeggiamento.

undulatory (ŭn'dū̇·lá·tō'rĭ) *agg.* ondulatorio.

unduly (ŭn·dū'lĭ) *avv.* indebitamente, abusivamente; eccessivamente.

undying (ŭn·dī'ĭng) *agg.* immortale.

unearned (ŭn·ûrnd') *agg.* immeritato.

unearth (ŭn·ûrth') *vt.* dissotterrare; stanare, rintracciare.

uneasily (ŭn·ēz'ĭ·lĭ) *avv.* a disagio, penosamente, inquietamente.

uneasiness (ŭn·ēz'ĭ·nĕs) *n.* disagio, ansia, inquietudine, imbarazzo.

uneasy (ŭn·ēz'ĭ) *agg.* gravoso, molesto, imbarazzante; imbarazzato, preoccupato, inquieto: **to feel —**, sentirsi a disagio.

uneatable (ŭn·ēt'á·b'l) *agg.* immangiabile.

uneducated (ŭn·ĕd'û·kāt'ĕd) *agg.* ignorante.

unembarrassed (ŭn'ĕm·băr'ăst) *agg.* libero da impacci; imperturbato, disinvolto.

unemotional (ŭn'ē·mō'shŭn·ăl) *agg.* non emozionante; non emotivo; calmo, imperturbabile.

unemployed (ŭn'ĕm·ploid') *agg.* inutilizzato; disoccupato.

unemployment (ŭn'ĕm·ploi'mĕnt) *n.* disoccupazione.

unending (ŭn·ĕn'dĭng) *agg.* interminabile, infinito.

unendurable (ŭn'ĕn·dūr'á·b'l) *agg.* insopportabile.

unequal (ŭn·ē'kwăl) *agg.* ineguale; sproporzionato; inferiore (*non all'altezza di*), impari: **to be — to one's task**, non essere all'altezza del proprio compito.

unequivocal (ŭn'ē·kwĭv'ō·kăl) *agg.* palese, chiaro, schietto.

unerring (ŭn·ûr'ĭng) *agg.* infallibile.

unessential (ŭn'ē·sĕn'shăl) *agg.* superfluo.

uneven (ŭn·ē'vĕn) *agg.* ineguale; scabroso; dispari (*di numero*).

uneventful (ŭn'ē·vĕnt'fŏŏl) *agg.* quieto, monotono, senza incidenti.

unexceptionable (ŭn'ĕk·sĕp'shŭn·á·b'l) *agg.* ineccepibile, irreprensibile.

unexpected (ŭn'ĕks·pĕk'tĕd) *agg.* inatteso, imprevisto. **—ly** *avv.* inaspettatamente, improvvisamente.

unexpensive (ŭn'ĕks·pĕn'sĭv) *agg.* economico, a buon mercato.

unexperienced (ŭn'ĕks·pēr'ĭ·ĕnst) *agg.* inesperto.

unexplained (ŭn'ĕks·plānd') *agg.* inesplicato.

unexplored (ŭn'ĕks·plōrd') *agg.* inesplorato.

unexpressed (ŭn'ĕks·prĕst') *agg.* inespresso, sottinteso.

unexpurgated (ŭn·ĕks'pĕr·gāt'ĕd) *agg.* integrale, non espurgato.

unextinguished (ŭn'ĕks·tĭng'gwĭsht) *agg.* inestinto.

unfailing (ŭn·fāl'ĭng) *agg.* infallibile, immancabile.

unfair (ŭn·fâr') *agg.* ingiusto, sleale, disonesto. **—ly** *avv.* ingiustamente, slealmente.

unfaithful (ŭn·fāth'fŏŏl) *agg.* infedele.

unfaltering (ŭn·fôl'tĕr·ĭng) *agg.* fermo, impassibile; risoluto; immutabile.

unfamiliar (ŭn'fá·mĭl'yĕr) *agg.* non familiare, inusitato, nuovo, sconosciuto: **to be — with**, non intendersi di, non sapere.

unfashionable (ŭn·făsh'ŭn·á·b'l) *agg.* inelegante, fuori moda: **to be —**, non essere di moda.

unfasten (ŭn·fàs''n) *vt.* slegare, slacciare, sganciare, aprire. *vi.* sganciarsi, slegarsi.

unfathomable (ŭn·făth'ŭm·á·b'l) *agg.* insondabile.

unfathomed (ŭn·făth̆'ŭmd) *agg.* insondato.

unfavorable (ŭn·fā'vēr·á·b'l) *agg.* sfavorevole, contrario.

unfeeling (ŭn·fēl'ĭng) *agg.* insensibile, crudele.

unfeigned (ŭn·fānd') *agg.* genuino, sincero.

unfetter (ŭn·fĕt'ēr) *vt.* liberare dalle pastoie.

unfinished (ŭn·fĭn'ĭsht) *agg.* incompleto, incompiuto, mal rifinito.

unfit (ŭn·fĭt') *agg.* disadatto, inidoneo, indegno (*di*). *vt.* rendere disadatto, inabilitare, squalificare.

unfledged (ŭn·flĕjd') *agg.* implume, inesperto.

unflinching (ŭn·flĭn'chĭng) *agg.* risouto, imperterrito.

unfold (ŭn·fōld') *vt.* aprire, spiegare, esporre, sviluppare, rivelare. *vi.* espandersi, displegarsi, aprirsi.

unforced (ŭn·fōrst') *agg.* non forzato, spontaneo, naturale.

unforeseen (ŭn·fōr·sēn') *agg.* imprevisto.

unforgettable (ŭn'fŏr·gĕt'á·b'l) *agg.* indimenticabile.

unforgivable (ŭn'fŏr·gĭv'á·b'l) *agg.* imperdonabile.

unformed (ŭn·fôrmd') *agg.* informe, embrionale.

unfortunate (ŭn·fôr'tû̄·nĭt) *n.* sventurato; donna perduta. *agg.* sfortunato, deplorevole. **—ly** *avv.* sfortunatamente; deplorevolmente; purtroppo.

unfounded (ŭn·foun'dĕd) *agg.* non fondato, infondato.

unfrequented (ŭn'frē·kwĕn'tĕd) *agg.* poco frequentato, solitario.

unfriendly (ŭn·frĕnd'lĭ) *agg.* scontroso; malevolo, ostile.

unfruitful (ŭn·frōōt'fōōl) *agg.* improduttivo, vano, sterile.

unfulfilled (ŭn'fōōl·fĭld') *agg.* non adempluto, incompiuto.

unfurl (ŭn·fûrl') *vt.* srotolare, svolgere; (*naut.*) spiegare. *vi.* distendersi.

unfurnished (ŭn·fûr'nĭsht) *agg.* smobiliato, sprovvisto.

ungainly (ŭn·gān'lĭ) *agg.* rozzo, goffo.

ungenerous (ŭn·jĕn'ēr·ŭs) *agg.* ingeneroso; taccagno.

ungentle (ŭn·jĕn't'l) *agg.* aspro, scortese, sgarbato.

ungentlemanly (ŭn·jĕn't'l·măn·lĭ)*agg.* indegno di un gentiluomo, riprovevole.

unglazed (ŭn·glāzd') *agg.* senza vetri.

ungodly (ŭn·gŏd'lĭ) *agg.* empio, irreligioso.

ungovernable (ŭn·gŭv'ēr·ná·b'l) *agg.* ingovernabile, sfrenato, sregolato.

ungraceful (ŭn·grās'fōōl) *agg.* goffo, sgraziato.

ungracious (ŭn·grā'shŭs) *agg.* scortese, scompiacente; spiacevole.

ungrateful (ŭn·grāt'fōōl) *agg.* ingrato.

unguarded (ŭn·gär'dĕd) *agg.* improtetto; disattento, incauto.

unhallowed (ŭn·hăl'ōd) *agg.* profano, empio.

unhappiness (ŭn·hăp'ĭ·nĕs) *n.* infelicità.

unhappy (ŭn·hăp'ĭ) *agg.* infelice, sfortunato, inopportuno.

unharmed (ŭn·härmd') *agg.* illeso, intatto, incolume.

unhealthful (ŭn·hĕlth'fōōl) *agg.* insalubre, malsano, cagionevole.

unhealthy (ŭn·hĕl'thĭ) *agg.* malsano, insalubre, pernicioso.

unheard (ŭn·hûrd') *agg.* non udito, inascoltato, inesaudito: **— of,** inaudito, sconosciuto.

unheeded (ŭn·hēd'ĕd) *agg.* negletto, ignorato, inascoltato.

unhesitating (ŭn·hĕz'ĭ·tāt'ĭng) *agg.* risoluto. **—ly** *avv.* risolutamente.

unhinge (ŭn·hĭnj') *vt.* togliere dai cardini, sganherare, sbilanciare, sconvolgere, staccare.

unhitch (ŭn·hĭch) *vt.* disincagliare, sganciare, distaccare.

unholy (ŭn·hō'lĭ) *agg.* empio, profano.

unhook (ŭn·hōōk') *vt.* sganciare, sfibbiare.

unhorse (ŭn·hôrs') *vt.* disarcionare, far smontare da cavallo.

unhurried (ŭn·hûr'ĭd) *agg.* calmo, comodo, senza fretta. **—ly** *avv.* con calma, con comodo, senza fretta.

unhurt (ŭn·hûrt') *agg.* incolume.

unhygienic (ŭn'hī·jĭ·ĕn'ĭk) *agg.* antiigienico.

unification (ū'nĭ·fĭ·kā'shŭn) *n.* unificazione.

uniform (ū'nĭ·fôrm) *n.* uniforme, divisa. *agg.* uniforme, regolare. *vt.* uniformare.

uniformity (ū'nĭ·fôr'mĭ·tĭ) *n.* uniformità.

unify (ū'nĭ·fī) *vt.* unificare.

unimaginative (ŭn'ĭ·măj'ĭ·nā'tĭv) *agg.* prosaico; privo di fantasia.

unimpaired (ŭn'ĭm·pârd') *agg.* inalterato, intatto, in pieno vigore.

unimpeachable (ŭn'ĭm·pēch'á·b'l) *agg.* irreprensibile; incontestabile, inattaccabile; inaccusabile.

unimportant (ŭn'ĭm·pôr'tănt) *agg.* trascurabile, insignificante.

uninformed (ŭn'ĭn·fôrmd') *agg.* non informato, ignaro, ignorante.

uninhabitable (ŭn'ĭn·hăb'ĭ·tā·b'l) *agg.* inabitabile.

uninhabited (ŭn'ĭn·hăb'ĭ·tĕd) *agg.* disabitato.

uninjured (ŭn·ĭn'jĕrd) *agg.* incolume, intatto.

unintelligent (ŭn'ĭn·tĕl'ĭ·jĕnt) *agg.* ottuso, stupido.

unintelligible (ŭn'ĭn·tĕl'ĭ·jĭ·b'l) *agg.* inintelligibile, incomprensibile.

unintentional (ŭn'ĭn·tĕn'shŭn·ăl) *agg.* involontario.

uninterested (ŭn·ĭn'tĕr·ĕs·tĕd) *agg.* indifferente.

uninteresting (ŭn·ĭn'tĕr·ĕs·tĭng) *agg.* privo di interesse, insulso, tedioso.

uninterrupted (ŭn'ĭn·tĕ·rŭp'tĕd) *agg.* ininterrotto.

uninvited (ŭn'ĭn·vīt'ĕd) *agg.* non invitato, indesiderato; inopinato.

union (ūn'yŭn) *n.* unione; matrimonio, combinazione; sindacato; confederazione; tessuto misto; *(mecc.)* giunto: trade —, sindacato di categoria; — leader, capo di sindacato, sindacalista.

unique (û·nēk') *agg.* unico.

unison (ū'nĭ·sŭn) *n.* unisono: in —, all'unisono.

unit (ū'nĭt) *n.* unità, quantità fissa.

unite (û·nīt') *vt.* unire, riunire. *vi.* unirsi, riunirsi.

unity (ū'nĭ·tĭ) *n.* unità, concordia.

universal (ū'nĭ·vûr'săl) *agg.* universale.

universe (ū'nĭ·vûrs) *n.* universo.

university (ū'nĭ·vûr'sĭ·tĭ) *n.* università.

unjust (ŭn·jŭst') *agg.* ingiusto.

unkempt (ŭn·kĕmpt') *agg.* arruffato; trasandato; spettinato.

unkind (ŭn·kīnd') *agg.* scortese; malvagio, crudele. **—liness** *n.* scortesia; malvagità. **—ly** *agg.* sgarbato, malvagio; inclemente *(del tempo). avv.* sgarbatamente, crudelmente: **to take something** —, prendere qualcosa in mala parte. **—ness** *n.* scortesia, durezza, crudeltà.

unknowing (ŭn·nō'ĭng) *agg.* ignaro; ignorante.

unknown (ŭn·nōn') *agg.* sconosciuto, ignoto: — **quantity,** incognita.

unlace (ŭn·lās') *vt.* slacciare.

unlade (ŭn·lād') *vt.* scaricare.

unlatch (ŭn·lăch') *vt.* aprire la serratura di.

unlawful (ŭn·lô'fŏŏl) *agg.* illegale, illecito, illegittimo.

unlearn (ŭn·lûrn') *vt.* disimparare.

unlearned (ŭn·lûrnd') *agg.* ignorante; uon imparato, intuito, istintivo.

unleash (ŭn·lēsh') *vt.* sguinzagliare.

unleavened (ŭn·lĕv'ĕnd) *agg.* non lievitato, azzimo.

unless (ŭn·lĕs') *cong.* a meno che, se non, fuorchè, eccetto che. *prep.* eccetto.

unlike (ŭn·līk') *agg.* dissimile, diverso, non somigliante. *prep.* diversamente da, a differenza di.

unlikelihood (ŭn·līk'lĭ·hŏŏd), **unlikeliness** (ŭn·līk'lĭ·nĕs) *n.* inverosimiglianza, improbabilità.

unlikely (ŭn·līk'lĭ) *agg.* improbabile, inverosimile. *avv.* improbabilmente.

unlimited (ŭn·lĭm'ĭ·tĕd) *agg.* illimitato.

unlit (ŭn·lĭt') *agg.* spento.

unload (ŭn·lōd') *vt., vi.* scaricare; *(S.U.)* smaltire, liquidare.

unlock (ŭn·lŏk') *vt.* aprire *(una porta chiusa a chiave, ecc.).*

unlooked-for (ŭn·lŏŏkt·fôr') *agg.* inatteso, imprevisto.

unloose (ŭn·lōōs') *vt.* sciogliere, slegare, allentare *(un nodo),* liberare, mollare.

unlucky (ŭn·lŭk'ĭ) *agg.* sfortunato; sinistro, malaugurato, funesto.

unman (ŭn·măn') *vt.* abbattere, scoraggiare, snervare; rammollire; evirare; *(naut.)* disarmare.

unmanageable (ŭn·măn'ĭj·d·b'l) *agg.* ingovernabile, indomabile, intrattabile, ribelle.

unmanly (ŭn·măn'lĭ) *agg.* molle, effeminato, debole, vile, infantile.

unmannerly (ŭn·măn'ĕr·lĭ) *agg.* maleducato, sgarbato, grossolano. *avv.* villanamente, sgarbatamente.

unmarked (ŭn·märkt') *agg.* non marcato *(o* contrassegnato); illeso; inosservato.

unmarried (ŭn·măr'ĭd) *agg.* celibe; nubile; non sposato.

unmask (ŭn·másk') *vt.* smascherare. *vi.* gettare la maschera.

unmatched (ŭn·măcht') *agg.* incomparabile, senza pari; scompagnato.

unmeaning (ŭn·mēn'ĭng) *agg.* privo di significato; insignificante.

unmeasured (ŭn·mĕzh'ĕrd) *agg.* incommensurato, illimitato; irregolare.

unmentionable (ŭn·mĕn'shŭn·d·b'l) *agg.* innominabile, indegno di menzione. *n. pl. (scherz.)* calzoni.

unmerciful (ŭn·mûr'sĭ·fŏŏl) *agg.* inesorabile, crudele.

unmindful (ŭn·mīnd'fŏŏl) *agg.* immemore, noncurante.

unmistakable (ŭn'mĭs·tāk'd·b'l) *agg.* inconfondibile, evidente.

unmitigated (ŭn·mĭt'ĭ·gāt'ĕd) *agg.* non mitigato, implacato: — **impu-**

dence, sfrontatezza senza pari; — liar, bugiardo fatto e finito; — ass, asino calzato e vestito; — fraud, truffa bella e buona.

unmolested (ŭn'mō-lĕs'tĕd) *agg.* indisturbato.

unmoor (ŭn-mōōr') *vt.* (*naut.*)disormeggiare. *vi.* levare l'ancora.

unmovable (ŭn-mōōv'ȧ-b'l) *agg.* saldo, inamovibile, inflessibile.

unmoved (ŭn-mōōvd') *agg.* immoto, freddo, indifferente.

unmusical (ŭn-mū'zĭ-kȧl) *agg.* disarmonico, stridente.

unnamed (ŭn-nāmd') *agg.* anonimo, innominato.

unnatural (ŭn-năt'û-rȧl) *agg.* innaturale, anormale, snaturato, artificioso, eccessivo: — mother, madre snaturata.

unnecessary (ŭn-nĕs'ĕ-sĕr'ĭ) *agg.*superfluo, inutile.

unnerve (ŭn-nûrv') *vt.* togliere forza a, togliere fermezza a, togliere coraggio a.

unnerved (ŭn-nûrvd') *agg.* privato di forza o di fermezza o di coraggio.

unnoticed (ŭn-nō'tĭst) *agg.* inosservato, inavvertito.

unnumbered (ŭn-nŭm'bĕrd) *agg.* non numerato; innumerevole.

unobliging (ŭn'ō-blīj'ĭng) *agg.* scompiacente.

unobserved (ŭn'ŏb-zûrvd') *agg.* inosservato.

unobstructed (ŭn'ŏb-strŭk'tĕd) *agg.* libero, non ostruito, non ostacolato.

unobtainable (ŭn'ŏb-tān'ȧ-b'l) *agg.* introvabile; non ottenibile.

unobtrusive (ŭn'ŏb-trōō'sĭv) *agg.* modesto, timido, discreto.

unoccupied (ŭn-ŏk'û-pĭd) *agg.* disoccupato, ozioso; disabitato, vacante, libero.

unoffending (ŭn'ŏ-fĕn'dĭng) *agg.* innocuo, innocente.

unofficial (ŭn'ŏ-fĭsh'ȧl) *agg.* non ufficiale.

unopened (ŭn-ō'pĕnd) *agg.* chiuso, sigillato, non aperto.

unorganized (ŭn-ôr'gȧn-īzd) *agg.* non organizzato, inorganico.

unorthodox (ŭn-ôr'thō-dŏks) *agg.* eterodosso.

unostentatious (ŭn'ŏs-tĕn-tā'shŭs) *agg.* sobrio, semplice, privo d'ostentazione.

unpack (ŭn-păk') *vt.* disimballare, scaricare, disfare (*valigie, ecc.*). *vi.* disfare i bagagli.

unpaid (ŭn-pād') *agg.* non pagato, insoluto: — bills, conti da pagare.

unpalatable (ŭn-păl'ĭt-ȧ-b'l) *agg.* sgradevole al gusto; (*fig.*) ostico.

unparalleled (ŭn-păr'ȧ-lĕld) *agg.* senza pari, ineguagliabile, unico.

unpardonable (ŭn-păr'd'n-ȧ-b'l) *agg.* imperdonabile.

unpaved (ŭn-pāvd') *agg.* non pavimentato.

unperceived (ŭn'pĕr-sēvd') *agg.* inosservato, inavvertito.

unperturbed (ŭn'pĕr-tûrbd') *agg.* imperturbato.

unpleasant (ŭn-plĕz'ȧnt) *agg.* sgradevole, villano. —**ly** *avv.* sgradevolmente villanamente. —**ness** *n.* spiacevolezza; villania; disaccordo; complicazione, incidente, dissapore.

unpolished (ŭn-pŏl'ĭsht) *agg.* rozzo, grezzo, non rifinito.

unpopular (ŭn-pŏp'û-lĕr) *agg.* impopolare.

unpracticed (ŭn-prăk'tĭst) *agg.* inesperto.

unprecedented (ŭn-prĕs'ē-dĕn'tĕd)*agg.* senza precedenti, nuovo.

unpredictable (ŭn'prē-dĭk'tȧ-b'l) *agg.* imprevedibile; (*fam.*) capriccioso, balzano.

unprejudiced (ŭn-prej'ŏŏ-dĭst) *agg.* imparziale, senza pregiudizi.

unpremeditated (ŭn'prē-mĕd'ĭ-tāt'ĕd) *agg.* impremeditato.

unprepared (ŭn'prē-pârd') *agg.* impreparato.

unprepossessing (ŭn'prē-pŏ-zĕs'ĭng) *agg.* sgradevole, antipatico.

unpretentious (ŭn'prē-tĕn'shŭs) *agg.* sobrio, non pretenzioso.

unpreventable (ŭn'prē-vĕn'tȧ-b'l) *agg.* inevitabile.

unprincipled (ŭn-prĭn'sĭ-p'ld) *agg.*amorale.

unprintable (ŭn-prĭn'tȧ-b'l) *agg.* non stampabile.

unprofitable (ŭn-prŏf'ĭt-ȧ-b'l) *agg.* non redditizio, poco proficuo, inutile.

unpromising (ŭn-prŏm'ĭs-ĭng) *agg.* poco promettente.

unpronounceable (ŭn'prō-noun'sȧ-b'l) *agg.* impronunziabile.

unprotected (ŭn'prō-tĕk'tĕd) *agg.* non protetto.

unprovided (ŭn'prō-vĭd'ĕd) *agg.* sprovvisto; impreparato.

unprovoked (ŭn'prō-vōkt') *agg.* non provocato, gratuito.

unpublished (ŭn-pŭb'lĭsht) *agg.* inedito, segreto.

unpunished (ŭn-pŭn'ĭsht) *agg.* impunito.

unqualified (ŭn-kwŏl'ĭ-fĭd) *agg.* inidoneo; incondizionato, assoluto.

unquenchable (ŭn-kwĕn'chȧ-b'l) *agg.* inestinguibile.

unquestionable (ŭn-kwĕs'chŭn-ȧ-b'l) *agg.* incontestabile.

unquote (ŭn'kwŏt') *vt.* (*S.U.*) chiudere una citazione, chiudere le virgolette.

unravel (ŭn·răv'ĕl) *vt.* districare, sbrogliare, sciogliere, dipanare, chiarire, risolvere. *vi.* sciogliersi, districarsi.

unread (ŭn·rĕd') *agg.* non letto; illetterato, ignorante, incolto. .

unreal (ŭn·rē'ăl) *agg.* irreale, fantastico.

unreasonable (ŭn·rē'z'n·ȧ·b'l) *agg.* irragionevole, eccessivo, assurdo.

unrecognizable (ŭn·rĕk'ŏg·nīz'ȧ·b'l) *agg.* irriconoscibile.

unreconcilable (ŭn·rĕk'ŏn·sīl'ȧ·b'l) *agg.* irreconciliabile, incompatibile.

unrecorded (ŭn'rĕ·kôr'dĕd) *agg.* non registrato; dimenticato, ignorato.

unreel (ŭn·rēl') *vt.* svolgere (*dalla bobina*).

unrefined (ŭn'rē·fīnd') *agg.* non raffinato, grezzo, grossolano.

unregretful (ŭn'rē·grĕt'fŏŏl) *agg.* senza rimpianti, rassegnato.

unregretted (ŭn'rē·grĕt'ĭd) *agg.* non rimpianto.

unrehearsed (ŭn'rē·hûrsd') *agg.* (*teat.*) senza prove; improvvisato.

unrelated (ŭn'rē·lāt'ĕd) *agg.* senza rapporto (*con*), non imparentato, non attinente (*a*), indipendente.

unrelenting (ŭn'rē·lĕn'tĭng) *agg.* inesorabile.

unreliable (ŭn'rē·lī'ȧ·b'l) *agg.* che non dà affidamento, inattendibile, dubbio; insolvibile; precario.

unremitting (ŭn'rē·mĭt'ĭng) *agg.* pertinace, incessante.

unrequested (ŭn'rē·kwĕst'ĭd) *agg.* non richiesto, spontaneo.

unrequited (ŭn'rē·kwīt'ĕd) *agg.* non ripagato, non ricambiato, inulto.

unreserved (ŭn'rē·zurvd') *agg.* non riservato; assoluto, completo; comunicativo, franco.

unresisting (ŭn'rē·zĭs'tĭng) *agg.* acquiescente, sottomesso.

unrest (ŭn·rĕst') *n.* inquietudine, agitazione.

unresting *agg.* perseverante, indefesso.

unrestrained (ŭn'rē·strānd') *agg.* sfrenato, scatenato.

unrestraint (ŭn'rē·strānt') *n.* sfrenatezza, abbandono.

unrestricted (ŭn'rē·strĭk'tĕd) *agg.* non limitato.

unrig (ŭn·rĭg') *vt.* disarmare (*un veliero*); (*fam.*) spogliare, svestire.

unripe (ŭn·rīp') *agg.* immaturo, acerbo.

unrivaled (ŭn·rī'vǎld) *agg.* unico, senza pari.

unroll (ŭn·rōl') *vt.* srotolare, svolgere. *vi.* srotolarsi, svolgersi.

unruffled (ŭn·rŭf'l'd) *agg.* tranquillo, calmo, liscio, imperturbato.

unruly (ŭn·rōōl'ĭ) *agg.* indisciplinato, turbolento, ribelle.

unsaddle (ŭn·săd''l) *vt.* dissellare, disarcionare.

unsafe (ŭn·sāf') *agg.* malsicuro, pericoloso.

unsaid (ŭn·sĕd') *agg.* non detto: **to leave —**, sottacere.

unsalable, **unsaleable** (ŭn·sāl'ȧ·b'l) *agg.* invendibile. **—ness** *n.* invendibilità.

unsatisfactory (ŭn'săt·ĭs·făk'tō·rĭ) *agg.* non soddisfacente, insufficiente.

unsavory (ŭn·sā'vẽr·ĭ) *agg.* insipido; disgustoso, rivoltante.

unscathed (ŭn·skāthd') *agg.* incolume, illeso.

unscientific (ŭn'sī·ĕn·tĭf'ĭk) *agg.* non scientifico, empirico.

unscrew (ŭn·skrōō') *vt.* svitare.

unscrupulous (ŭn·skrōō'pū·lŭs) *agg.* disonesto, senza scrupoli.

unseal (ŭn·sēl') *vt.* dissigillare, aprire.

unseasonable (ŭn·sē'z'n·ȧ·b'l) *agg.* intempestivo, fuori stagione.

unseat (ŭn·sēt') *vt.* sloggiare, disarcionare, destituire.

unseeing (ŭn·sē'ĭng) *agg.* che non vede, cieco.

unseemly (ŭn·sēm'lĭ) *agg.* sconveniente, deplorevole, disdicevole. *avv.* sconvenientemente, deplorevolmente.

unseen (ŭn·sēn') *agg.* invisibile, non visto, inosservato.

unselfish (ŭn·sĕl'fĭsh) *agg.* disinteressato, altruista. **—ness** *n.* disinteresse, altruismo.

unsettle (ŭn·sĕt''l) *vt.* scompigliare, scuotere, smuovere, rendere precario.

unsettled *agg.* non stabilito; sconvolto; pendente (*di conto*); precario, squilibrato: **— weather**, tempo instabile; **— liquid**, liquido torbido.

unshakable (ŭn·shāk'ȧ·b'l) *agg.* incrollabile.

unshaken (ŭn·shāk'ĕn) *agg.* fermo, imperturbato, inconcusso, saldo.

unshaven (ŭn·shāv'ĕn) *agg.* non rasato.

unsheathe (ŭn·shēth') *vt.* sguainare.

unsheltered (ŭn·shĕl'tẽrd) *agg.* senza riparo, scoperto.

unshorn (ŭn·shōrn') *agg.* non tosato, non tagliato.

unshrinkable (ŭn·shrĭngk'ȧ·b'l) *agg.* irrestringibile.

unsightly (ŭn·sīt'lĭ) *agg.* brutto, spiacevole a vedersi.

unsigned (ŭn·sīnd') *agg.* non firmato.

unsinkable (ŭn·sĭngk'á·b'l) *agg.* inaffondabile.

unskillful (ŭn·skĭl'fŏŏl) *agg.* inabile, goffo.

unskilled (ŭn·skĭld') *agg.* inesperto, non specializzato.

unslaked (ŭn·slākt') *agg.* insaziato, inestinto: — lime, calce viva.

unsociable (ŭn·sō'shá·b'l) *agg.* scontroso, riservato, rustico.

unsold (ŭn·sōld') *agg.* invenduto.

unsought (ŭn·sôt') *agg.* non richiesto.

unsound (ŭn·sound') *agg.* malfermo; squilibrato; disonesto; difettoso, guasto; precario, fallace; insolvibile.

unsparing (ŭn·spâr'ĭng) *agg.* generoso, prodigo.

unspeakable (ŭn·spēk'á·b'l) *agg.* indicibile, inesprimibile; inqualificabile.

unspoiled (ŭn·spoild') *agg.* non rovinato, non sciupato; incorrotto, non viziato; intatto; puro.

unstable (ŭn·stā'b'l) *agg.* instabile, precario.

unstained (ŭn·stānd') *agg.* non macchiato, non colorato, non tinto.

unsteadily (ŭn·stĕd'ĭ·lĭ) *avv.* precariamente, irresolutamente; con passo malfermo; irregolarmente.

unsteadiness (ŭn·stĕd'ĭ·nĕs) *n.* precarietà, irresolutezza, irregolarità, scarsa solidità, incertezza.

unsteady (ŭn·stĕd'ĭ) *agg.* precario, malfermo, irresoluto, incerto; irregolare, vacillante.

unsubdued (ŭn'sŭb·dūd') *agg.* indomato, indomito.

unsuccessful (ŭn'sŭk·sĕs'fŏŏl) *agg.* vano, mancato, infruttuoso: to be —, non avere successo, andare male. —ly *avv.* senza successo, infruttuosamente, vanamente.

unsuitable (ŭn·sūt'á·b'l) *agg.* disadatto, sconveniente, inopportuno.

unsuited (ŭn·sūt'ĕd) *agg.* disdicevole, disadatto.

unsullied (ŭn·sŭl'ĭd) *agg.* incontaminato, immacolato, puro.

unsupported (ŭn·sŭ·pōr'tĕd) *agg.* non sostenuto, non aiutato, non suffragato.

unsure (ŭn·shŏŏr') *agg.* incerto, malsicuro.

unsurpassed (ŭn'sẽr·pàst') *agg.* insuperato, non sorpassato.

unsuspected (ŭn'sŭs·pĕk'tĕd) *agg.* insospettato, ignorato.

unsuspecting (ŭn'sŭs·pĕk'tĭng) *agg.* non sospettoso, impreparato.

untainted (ŭn·tān'tĕd) *agg.* incorrotto, immacolato, puro.

untalented (ŭn·tăl'ĕn·tĕd) *agg.* inetto, privo di doti (o d'ingegno).

untamed (ŭn·tāmd') *agg.* indomato.

untarnished (ŭn·tär'nĭsht) *agg.* non appannato, pulito, lucente; puro; non denigrato; non annerito, non ossidato.

untenable (ŭn·tĕn'á·b'l) *agg.* indifendibile, insostenibile.

unthankful (ŭn·thăngk'fŏŏl) *agg.* ingrato.

unthinkable (ŭn·thĭngk'á·b'l) *agg.* inconcepibile, impensabile.

unthinking (ŭn·thĭngk'ĭng) *agg.* irriflessivo, stordito.

untidy (ŭn·tī'dĭ) *agg.* disordinato, sudicio, trasandato, sciatto.

untie (ŭn·tī') *vt.* slegare, sciogliere (*un nodo*).

until (ŭn·tĭl') *prep.* sino (*a*). *cong.* finchè, fintantochè, non prima di: — now, — this day, fino a oggi, finora; — then, fino allora.

untimely (ŭn·tīm'lĭ) *agg.* intempestivo, inopportuno, prematuro. *avv.* intempestivamente, prematuramente.

untiring (ŭn·tīr'ĭng) *agg.* costante, pertinace; infaticabile.

unto (ŭn·tŏŏ) *prep.* a, verso, nei confronti di, sino a.

untold (ŭn·tōld') *agg.* non detto, non raccontato, inespresso, sottaciuto, sottinteso; innumerevole, immenso, incalcolabile.

untouched (ŭn·tŭcht') *agg.* intatto; non menzionato; non commosso: to leave —, non toccare, lasciare intatto.

untoward (ŭn·tō'ẽrd) *agg.* sfavorevole, malaugurato; indocile, goffo, perverso.

untrained (ŭn·trānd') *agg.* non addestrato, inesperto, indisciplinato.

untrammeled (ŭn·trăm'ĕld) *agg.* senza intralci.

untried (ŭn·trīd') *agg.* intentato; inesperto; non provato; non processato.

untrod (ŭn·trŏd'), **untrodden** (ŭn·trŏd''n) *agg.* deserto, non battuto, non calpestato.

untroubled (ŭn·trŭb''ld) *agg.* imperturbato, calmo, limpido.

untrue (ŭn·trŏŏ') *agg.* falso, inesatto; insincero, sleale.

untruth (ŭn·trŏŏth') *n.* menzogna, falsità.

unturned (ŭn·tûrnd') *agg.* non voltato: to leave no stone —, non lasciar nulla di intentato.

untutored (ŭn·tū'tẽrd) *agg.* non istruito, ignorante.

untwine (ŭn·twīn'), **untwist** (ŭn·twĭst')

vt. disfare (*ciò che è ritorto*), districare. *vi.* disfarsi (*detto di fune, ecc.*).

unused (ŭn·ūzd′) *agg.* non usato, nuovo; non abituato.

unusual (ŭn·ū′zhŏŏ·ăl) *agg.* insolito, eccezionale, raro, straordinario.

unutterable (ŭn·ŭt′ẽr·á·b′l) *agg.* inesprimibile, indicibile.

unvalued (ŭn·văl′ūd) *agg.* non valutato, inestimabile.

unvarnished (ŭn·vär′nĭsht) *agg.* non verniciato; (*fig.*) non artefatto, semplice, naturale, puro, schietto.

unvarying (ŭn·vâr′ĭ·ĭng) *agg.* invariabile, costante, invariato.

unveil (un·vāl′) *vt.* svelare, scoprire.

unverified (ŭn·vĕr′ĭ·fĭd) *agg.* non verificato.

unwanted (ŭn·wŏn′tĕd) *agg.* indesiderato; superfluo.

unwarranted (ŭn·wŏr′ăn·tĕd) *agg.* abusivo; ingiustificato; non garantito.

unwary (ŭn·wâr′ĭ) *agg.* incauto.

unwashed (ŭn·wŏsht′) *agg.* non lavato, sporco.

unwavering (ŭn·wā′vẽr·ĭng) *agg.* saldo, risoluto, pertinace.

unwearied (ŭn·wẽr′ĭd) *agg.* inesausto, infaticabile.

unwelcome (ŭn·wĕl′kŭm) *agg.* sgradito, inopportuno, malaugurato.

unwell (ŭn·wĕl′) *agg.* malato, indisposto.

unwholesome (ŭn·hōl′sŭm) *agg.* malsano, insalubre, nocivo, repulsivo.

unwieldy (ŭn·wēl′dĭ) *agg.* difficile a maneggiarsi, pesante, ingombrante, voluminoso.

unwilling (ŭn·wĭl′ĭng) *agg.* maldisposto, restio, riluttante: **to be — to,** non avere disposto a, non avere voglia di. **—ly** *avv.* malvolentieri, a malincuore. **—ness** *n.* riluttanza, avversione.

unwind (ŭn·wĭnd′) *vt.* (*pass., pp.* **unwound**) sbrogliare, svolgere, dipanare. *vi.* svolgersi, disfarsi.

unwise (ŭn·wĭz′) *agg.* insensato, incauto, malaccorto.

unwitting (ŭn·wĭt′ĭng) *agg.* ignaro, inconsapevole, avventato. **—ly** *avv.* inconsapevolmente, avventatamente, involontariamente.

unwonted (ŭn·wŏn′tĕd) *agg.* insolito, straordinario.

unworthy (ŭn·wûr′t͟hĭ) *agg.* indegno, immeritevole; sconveniente.

unwrap (ŭn·răp′) *vt.* svolgere, disfare (*un involto*).

unwritten (ŭn·rĭt′'n) *agg.* non scritto, orale, tradizionale: **— law,** legge naturale, tradizione.

unyielding (ŭn·yēl′dĭng) *agg.* non cedevole, inflessibile, duro, ostinato.

unyoke (ŭn·yōk′) *vt.* sciogliere dal giogo, liberare.

up (ŭp) *n.*: **the ups and downs of life,** gli alti e bassi della vita. *agg.* ascendente; alto; ritto, eretto; inferiore; informato; terminato, scaduto; in vantaggio: **to be one point —,** essere in vantaggio di un punto. *avv.* su, sopra, in alto, in aria, in piedi, in posizione eretta, in rivolta, alla fine, in rialzo: **to be —,** essere in piedi; essere alzato; essere intento a, essere pronto a, essere capace di; **time is —,** è ora, è venuto il momento, è scaduto il termine; **— to date,** alla moda; sino al momento attuale; aggiornato; **to be — against,** dover affrontare; **— to,** all'altezza di, fino a; **to be — to,** essere intento a, essere pronto a, essere capace di; **it is — to him,** dipende da lui, spetta a lui decidere (*o* agire); **what's —?** che cosa succede? *prep.* su per, al disopra di, in cima a: **to go — the stairs,** salire le scale. *vt.* (*fam.*) aumentare, elevare; issare. *vi.* saltar su; salire, alzarsi.

up-and-down *agg.* completo. *avv.* verticalmente; su e giù; qua e là.

upbraid (ŭp·brād′) *vt., vi.* sgridare, redarguire, rimproverare.

upbringing (ŭp′brĭng′ĭng) *n.* allevamento, educazione.

update (ŭp·dāt′) *vt.* aggiornare; ammodernare, modernizzare.

upgrade (ŭp·grād′) *vt.* migliorare; promuovere, portare a un grado superiore.

upheaval (ŭp·hēv′ăl) *n.* sollevamento.

upheld (ŭp·hĕld′) *pass., pp. di* to uphold.

uphill (ŭp′hĭl′) *agg.* erto, ripido; difficile, improbo. *avv.* in salita, in su.

uphold (ŭp·hōld′) *vt.* (*pass., pp.* **upheld**) sostenere; sollevare.

upholster (ŭp·hōl′stẽr) *vt.* tappezzare, imbottire. **—er** *n.* tappezziere. **—y** *n.* tappezzeria, tendaggi.

upkeep (ŭp′kēp) *n.* mantenimento; manutenzione.

upland (ŭp′lănd′) *n.* altipiano, altura. *agg.* alto, elevato, montuoso.

uplift (ŭp·lĭft′) *n.* sollevamento, innalzamento, incoraggiamento. *vt.* sollevare, innalzare, incoraggiare, esaltare.

upon (*ă*·pŏn′) *prep.* su, sopra, al disopra di, nell'atto di: **to take oneself,** assumersi, accollarsi; **to call —,** far visita (*o* rivolgersi) a; **depend — it,** contateci, statene certo; — his arrival, al momento del suo arrivo.

upper (ŭp′ĕr) *n.* tomaia; cuccetta superiore; *pl.* ghette; tomaia: on one's —s, al verde, a terra. *agg.* superiore, più elevato, più alto: to have the — hand, avere il sopravvento.

uppercut (ŭp′ĕr·kŭt) *n.* pugno dal basso all'alto, montante.

uppermost (ŭp′ĕr·mōst) *agg.* sommo, il più elevato, il più alto, il primo.

upraise (ŭp·rāz′) *vt.* sollevare, elevare.

upright (ŭp′rīt′) *n.* pianoforte verticale; pilastro, montante. *agg.* dritto, perpendicolare, eretto; giusto, leale, onesto. *avv.* (*anche* —ly) verticalmente; lealmente, rettamente. **—ness** *n.* perpendicolarità; rettitudine.

uprising (ŭp·rīz′ĭng) *n.* levata, ascesa; sollevazione, rivolta.

uproar (ŭp′rōr′) *n.* tumulto, gazzarra, strepito, clamore.

uproarious (ŭp·rōr′ĭ·ŭs) *agg.* chiassoso, tumultuoso.

uproot (ŭp·rōōt′) *vt.* sradicare, estirpare.

upset (ŭp·sĕt′) *n.* rovesciamento, sconvolgimento; disordine; indisposizione. *agg.* rovesciato, capovolto; sconvolto; preoccupato: — price, prezzo iniziale. *vt.* (*pass.*, *pp.* upset) rovesciare, sconvolgere, scompigliare, turbare. *vi.* capovolgersi, rovesciarsi.

upsetting *n.* capovolgimento, sconvolgimento. *agg.* sconvolgente.

upshot (ŭp′shŏt′) *n.* risultato, conclusione, esito, sostanza.

upside (ŭp′sĭd′) *n.* parte superiore. *avv.* sopra; — down, sottosopra; to turn — down, capovolgere.

upstairs (ŭp′stārz′) *n.* piano superiore. *agg.* del piano superiore. *avv.* di sopra, al piano superiore; (*aeron.*) ad alta quota.

upstanding (ŭp·stăn′dĭng) *agg.* eretto; onesto.

upstart (ŭp′stärt′) *n.* nuovo ricco, villano rifatto.

upstream (ŭp′strēm′) *avv.* a monte, contro corrente: to go —, risalire il fiume.

uptake (ŭp′tāke′) *n.*: to be quick on the —, capire al volo.

up-to-date *agg.* aggiornato; moderno.

uptown (ŭp′toun′) *avv.* nella parte alta di una città, alla periferia.

uptrend (ŭp′trĕnd′) *n.* tendenza (*spec.* dell'economia) verso una situazione migliore, sintomi di miglioramento.

upturn (ŭp·tûrn′) *n.* rialzo, ripresa. *vt.* voltare all'insù, rivoltare.

upward (ŭp′wĕrd) *agg.* rivolto verso l'alto, ascendente. *avv.* (*anche* upwards) verso l'alto, all'insù, oltre: upwards of, più di, al disopra di.

uranium (û·rā′nĭ·ŭm) *n.* (*min.*) uranio.

urban (ûr′băn) *agg.* urbano, cittadino.

urbane (ûr·bān′) *agg.* urbano, cortese.

urchin (ûr′chĭn) *n.* monello: sea —, riccio di mare.

urge (ûrj) *n.* impulso, brama, stimolo. *vt.*, *vi.* addurre, sostenere, spingere, urgere, sollecitare, incitare, stimolare, incalzare, caldeggiare; affrettarsi.

urgency (ûr′jĕn·sĭ) *n.* urgenza, insistenza, pressione.

urgent (ûr′jĕnt) *agg.* urgente, incalzante, insistente, imperioso.

urine (û′rĭn) *n.* orina.

urn (ûrn) *n.* urna; bricco, cuccuma: coffee —, caffettiera, macchina per il caffè (*nei bar*).

us (ŭs) *pron.pers.* noi; ci.

usable (ūz′à·b'l) *agg.* servibile.

usage (ūz′ĭj) *n.* uso, usanza, consuetudine; trattamento: to meet with hard —, essere maltrattato.

use (ūs) *n.* uso, impiego; utilità, vantaggio; trattamento; abitudine; servizio; scopo: it is no —, è inutile, non c'è rimedio; to have no — for, non aver bisogno di, non saper che farsene di; what is the —? a che serve? *vt.* (ūz) usare, adoperare; abituare, servirsi di, fare uso di. *vi.* solere: to — up, consumare, logorare.

used (ūst) *agg.* usato, abituato, abituale: to get — to, abituarsi; to be — to, essere abituato a, aver fatto l'abitudine a; he — to do it, era solito farlo, lo faceva sempre.

useful (ūs′fŏŏl) *agg.* utile. —ly *avv.* utilmente, proficuamente. **—ness** *n.* utilità.

useless (ūs′lĕs) *agg.* inutile. —ly *avv.* inutilmente. **—ness** *n.* inutilità.

user (ūz′ĕr) *n.* utente, consumatore.

usher (ŭsh′ĕr) *n.* usciere; maschera (*inserviente di teatro, ecc.*). *vt.* introdurre, annunziare: to — in, into, far entrare; to — out, far uscire, accompagnare alla porta.

usherette (ŭsh′ĕr·ĕt′) *n.f.* maschera, mascherina (*inserviente di teatro, ecc.*).

usual (û′zhŏŏ·ăl) *agg.* abituale, solito, frequente: as —, come al solito. —ly *avv.* solitamente, abitualmente.

usurer (û′zhŏŏ·rĕr) *n.* usuraio.

usurious (û·zhŏr′ĭ·ŭs) *agg.* esoso, esorbitante.

usurp (û·zûrp′) *vt.* usurpare.

usurper (û·zûr′pĕr) *n.* usurpatore.

usury (ū′zhŏŏ·rĭ) *n.* usura, strozzinaggio.

utensil (û·těn′sĭl) *n.* utensile, arnese.

uterus (ū′těr·ŭs) *n.* utero.

utility (û·tĭl′ĭ·tĭ) *n.* utilità, servizio, profitto: public —, servizio di pubblica utilità; — man, uomo a tutto fare; (*teat.*) generico; — room, lavanderia, stanzino della caldaia, ripostiglio.

utilize (ū′tĭ·lĭz) *vt.* utilizzare.

utmost (ŭt′mōst) *n.* estremo, (*il*) meglio, massimo grado, massimo: at the —, tutt'al più; to the —, sino a non poterne più; to do one's —, fare del proprio meglio. *agg.* estre-

mo, (il) più lontano; ultimo; massimo, sommo.

utter (ŭt′ẽr) (1) *agg.* estremo, completo, totale, assoluto, massimo, perfetto.

utter (ŭt′ẽr) (2) *vt.* esprimere, proferire, dire, emettere.

utterance (ŭt′ẽr·ǎns) *n.* espressione, pronunzia, suono vocale, emissione; to give — to, manifestare.

utterly (ŭt′ẽr·lĭ) *avv.* completamente.

uttermost (ŭt′ẽr·mōst) *n.* massimo, limite estremo, sommo grado. *agg.* estremo, ultimo, (il) più remoto, (il) più lontano: to the —, all'estremo.

uvula (ū′vû·lǎ) *n.* ugola.

V

V (vē), Vittoria (*nella 2a guerra mondiale*): V-sign, segno della vittoria (*anulare e medio divaricati*); V-E Day, Giorno della Vittoria in Europa (8 *maggio* 1945); V-J Day, Giorno della Vittoria sul Giappone (14 *agosto* 1945).

vacancy (vā′kǎn·sǐ) *n.* vacanza (*l'esser vacante*), disponibilità; posto vacante; lacuna, vuoto.

vacant (vā′kǎnt) *agg.* vacante, vuoto, libero, disponibile; vacuo, distratto, ebete.

vacate (vā′kāt) *vt.* lasciar libero, abbandonare, sgomberare; annullare.

vacation (vǎ·kā′shǔn) *n.* vacanza (*ferie*); sgombero, sospensione.

vaccinate (văk′sǐ·nāt) *vt.* vaccinare.

vaccination (văk′sǐ·nā′shǔn) *n.* vaccinazione.

vaccine (văk′sēn) *n.* vaccino.

vacillate (văs′ǐ·lāt) *vi.* vacillare.

vacuous (văk′û·ǔs) *agg.* vacuo, ebete.

vacuum (văk′û·ǔm) *n.* vuoto, vuoto pneumatico. *agg.* vuoto, a vuoto, nel vuoto; pneumatico: — bottle, termos; — cleaner, aspirapolvere; — tube, valvola termoionica.

vagabond (văg′ǎ·bŏnd) *n.*, *agg.* vagabondo, nomade.

vagary (vǎ·gâr′ĭ) *n.* stravaganza.

vagrancy (vā′grǎn·sǐ) *n.* vagabondaggio.

vagrant (vā′grǎnt) *n.*, *agg.* vagabondo.

vague (văg) *agg.* vago, incerto, impreciso. —ly *avv.* vagamente.

vain (vān) *agg.* vano, infruttuoso; vanitoso: in —, invano.

vainglorious (vān′glō′rǐ·ǔs) *agg.* vanaglorioso.

vainglory (vān′glō′rǐ) *n.* vanagloria.

vale (vāl) *n.* valle, valletta.

valedictory (văl′ê·dǐk′tō·rǐ) *agg.* d'addio, di commiato.

valence (vā′lěns) *n.* (*chim.*) valenza.

valentine (văl′ěn·tǐn) *n.* dono *opp.* cartoncino decorato e contenente una dichiarazione, che le giorno di S. Valentino si invia alla persona amata; innamorata o innamorato (*scelto il giorno di S. Valentino*): to my —, al mio amore.

valet (văl′ět) *n.* cameriere, domestico. *vt.*, *vi.* servire.

valetudinarian (văl′ê·tû′dǐ·nâr′ǐ·ǎn) *n.*, *agg.* infermo.

valiant (văl′yǎnt) *agg.* valoroso, coraggioso.

valid (văl′ǐd) *agg.* valido, valevole.

validity (vǎ·lǐd′ǐ·tǐ) *n.* validità.

valise (vǎ·lēs′) *n.* valigia.

valley (văl′ǐ) *n.* valle, vallata.

valor (văl′ẽr) *n.* valore, ardimento.

valorous (văl′ẽr·ǔs) *agg.* valoroso.

valuable (văl′û· à·b′l) *agg.* prezioso, costoso, valutabile; *pl.* preziosi, oggetti di valore.

valuation (văl′û·à′shǔn) *n.* valutazione.

value (văl′û) *n.* valore, pregio, significato. *vt.* stimare, valutare, apprezzare.

valued (văl′ûd) *agg.* valutato, stimato, pregiato.

valueless (văl′û·lěs) *agg.* privo di valore; da poco insignificante.

valve (vălv) *n.* valva; valvola: safety —, valvola di sicurezza.

vamoose (vǎ·mōōs′) *vi.* (*gergo*) svignarsela, sparire.

vamp (vămp) (1) *n.* tomaia, rimonta. *vt.* rimontare (*scarpe*), rimettere a nuovo.

vamp (vămp) (2) *n.* (*gergo*) donna fatale. *vt.* irretire. *vi.* far la donna fatale.

vampire (văm′pǐr) *n.* vampiro.'

van (văn) *n.* furgone; (*mil.*) avanguardia.

vandal (văn'dᾰl) *n.* vandalo.

vane (văn) *n.* banderuola, ventaruola; pala (*d'elica o mulino*).

vanguard (văn'gärd') *n.* avanguardia.

vanilla (vᾰ·nĭl'ᾰ) *n.* (*bot.*) vaniglia.

vanish (văn'ĭsh) *vi.* svanire, sparire.

vanity (văn'ĭ·tĭ) *n.* vanità: — case, portacipria, trousse (*fr.*); — table, pettiniera, toilette (*fr.*).

vanquish (văng'kwĭsh) *vt.* vincere, sopraffare, soggiogare.

vantage (văn'tĭj) *n.* vantaggio: — point, posizione di vantaggio; punto d'osservazione.

vapid (văp'ĭd) *agg.* insipido, insulso.

vaporizer (vā'pĕr·ĭz·ĕr) *n.* vaporizzatore, atomizzatore.

vapor (vā'pĕr) *n.* vapore, esalazione.

variable (vâr'ĭ·ᾰ·b'l) *n.*, *agg.* variabile.

variance (vâr'ĭ·ᾰns) *n.* discrepanza, divergenza, disaccordo: at —, in contrasto.

variation (vâr'ĭ·ā'shᾰn) *n.* variazione.

varied (vâr'ĭd) *agg.* vario, variato.

variety (vᾰ·rī'ĕ·tĭ) *n.* varietà.

various (vâr'ĭ·ᾰs) *agg.* vario, diverso, variabile, molteplice; vari, parecchi, diversi.

varnish (vär'nĭsh) *n.* vernice. *vt.* verniciare.

varsity (vär'sĭ·tĭ) *n.* (*fam.*) università.

vary (vâr'ĭ) *vt.*, *vi.* variare, modificare, trasformare; differire. —ing *agg.* mutevole.

vase (vās; văz) *n.* vaso.

vassal (văs'ᾰl) *n.* vassallo.

vast (văst) *agg.* vasto, esteso, abbondante. —ly *avv.* vastamente; molto; immensamente; in gran parte. —ness *n.* vastità, immensità.

vat (văt) *n.* serbatoio, tino.

vaudeville (vōd'vĭl) *n.* commedia musicale; (*spettacolo di*) varietà.

vault (vôlt) *n.* volta; sotterraneo; camera di sicurezza (*di banca*); cripta, tomba; salto, volteggio: pole —, salto con l'asta. *vt.* coprire con una volta, costruire a volta; scavalcare con un volteggio. *vi.* volteggiare; saltare l'ostacolo, saltare con l'asta.

vaulted *agg.* a volta, arcuato.

vaunt (vônt) *n.* vanto, vanteria. *vt.* millantare, ostentare. *vi.* gloriarsi.

veal (vēl) *n.* carne di vitello.

veep (vēp) *n.* (*fam.*) vicepresidente.

veer (vēr) *n.* virata. *vt.*, *vi.* voltare, orientare; (*naut.*) poggiare, mollare; cambiare direzione.

vegetable (vĕj'ĕ·tᾰ·b'l) *n.*, *agg.* vegetale; *pl.* verdura, ortaggi; — garden, orto.

vegetate (vĕj'ĕ·tāt) *vi.* vegetare.

vegetation (vĕj'ĕ·tā'shᾰn) *n.* vegetazione.

vehemence (vē'ĕ·mĕns) *n.* veemenza, ardore, impeto.

vehement (vē'ĕ·mĕnt) *agg.* veemente, impetuoso.

vehicle (vē'ĭ·k'l) *n.* veicolo.

veil (văl) *n.* velo. *vt.* velare.

vein (văn) *n.* vena; nervatura; filone; umore. *vt.* venare. —ed *agg.* venato.

vellum (vĕl'ᾰm) *n.* pergamena.

velocity (vĕ·lŏs'ĭ·tĭ) *n.* velocità.

velvet (vĕl'vĕt) *n.* velluto. *agg.* vellutato, di velluto.

velveteen (vĕl'vĕ·tēn') *n.* velluto di cotone; *pl.* calzoni di velluto.

velvety (vĕl'vĕ·tĭ) *agg.* vellutato.

vendor (vĕn'dŏr) *n.* venditore.

veneer (vĕ·nēr') *n.* impiallacciatura, rivestimento; apparenza superficiale. *vt.* impiallacciare, rivestire.

venerable (vĕn'ĕr·ᾰ·b'l) *n.*, *agg.* venerabile; venerando.

venerate (vĕn'ĕr·āt) *vt.* venerare.

veneration (vĕn'ĕr·ā'shᾰn) *n.* venerazione.

venereal (vĕ·nēr'ĕ·ᾰl) *agg.* venereo; carnale.

Venetian (vĕ·nē'shᾰn) *n.*, *agg.* veneziano: — blind, (persiana alla) veneziana.

vengeance (vĕn'jᾰns) *n.* vendetta: with a —, violentemente; all'eccesso.

vengeful (vĕnj'fŏŏl) *agg.* vendicativo.

venison (vĕn'ĭ·z'n) *n.* cacciagione, selvaggina (*spec. carne di cervo*).

venom (vĕn'ᾰm) *n.* veleno; astio.

venomous (vĕn'ᾰm·ᾰs) *agg.* velenoso; astioso.

venous (vē'nᾰs) *agg.* venoso.

vent (vĕnt) *n.* apertura, sfiatatolo, condotto, sbocco, sfogo; focone (*d'arma da fuoco*): to give — to, dar libero corso a. *vt.* manifestare, sfogare, dar sfogo a.

ventilate (vĕn'tĭ·lāt) *vt.* ventilare.

ventilation (vĕn'tĭ·lā'shᾰn) *n.* ventilazione.

ventilator (vĕn'tĭ·lā'tĕr) *n.* ventilatore.

ventriloquism (vĕn·trĭl'ŏ·kwĭz'm) *n.* ventriloquio.

ventriloquist (vĕn·trĭl'ŏ·kwĭst) *n.* ventriloquo.

venture (vĕn'tŭr) *n.* ventura, impresa, rischio; posta: business —, speculazione, impresa rischiosa. *vt.*, *vi.* tentare, arrischiare, osare, avventurarsi.

venturesome (vĕn'tŭr·sᾰm), venturous (vĕn'tŭr·ᾰs) *agg.* avventuroso; rischioso; audace.

Venus (vē'nŭs) n. Venere.

veracious (vḗ-rā'shŭs) agg. verace, autentico.

veracity (vḗ-răs'ĭ-tĭ) n. veracità.

veranda (vḗ-răn'dȧ) n. veranda.

verb (vûrb) n. verbo.

verbal (vûr'băl) agg. verbale.

verbatim (vûr-bā'tĭm) avv. testualmente.

verbiage (vûr'bĭ-ĭj) n. verbosità.

verbose (vûr-bōs') agg. verboso.

verdant (vûr'dănt) agg. verdeggiante; (fam.) ingenuo, inesperto.

verdict (vûr'dĭkt) n. sentenza, verdetto: — of not guilty, assoluzione.

verdigris (vûr'dĭ-grēs) n. verderame.

verdure (vûr'ḍūr) n. verzura, freschezza, rigoglio.

verge (vûrj) n. bordo, limite, margine, orlo; verga: on the — of, sul punto di. vi. tendere, propendere: to — on, upon, rasentare, costeggiare.

verify (vĕr'ĭ-fĭ) vt. verificare, attestare, comprovare, confermare.

verily (vĕr'ĭ-lĭ) avv. veramente, sinceramente.

verisimilitude (vĕr'ĭ-sĭ-mĭl'ĭ-tūd) n. verosimiglianza.

veritable (vĕr'ĭ-tȧ-b'l) agg. vero, autentico.

verity (vĕr'ĭ-tĭ) n. verità.

vermifuge (vûr'mĭ-fūj) n., agg. vermifugo.

vermilion (vẽr-mĭl'yŭn) agg. vermiglio.

vermin (vûr'mĭn) n. sing., pl. parassita; gentaglia, feccia.

vermouth (vẽr-mōōth') n. vermut.

verse (vûrs) n. verso, strofa.

versed (vûrst) agg. versato, dotto.

version (vûr'shŭn) n. versione.

verso (vûr'sō) n. tergo, rovescio; (tip.) pagina pari.

versus (vûr'sŭs) prep. contro.

vertex (vûr'tĕks) n. vertice, apice.

vertical (vûr'tĭ.kăl) n., agg. verticale.

vertigo (vûr'tĭ-gō) n. (med.) vertigine.

very (vĕr'ĭ) agg. stesso, vero, reale; solo: this — day, oggi stesso; the — man who ..., proprio l'uomo che, lo stessissimo uomo che; the — thought of ..., il semplice pensiero di ... avv. molto, grandemente, estremamente: — many, moltissimi; — much, moltissimo; — good, buonissimo; benissimo; — cold, freddissimo, molto freddo.

Vesper (vĕs'pẽr) n. vespro.

vessel (vĕs''l) n. nave, bastimento; velivolo; recipiente; (anat., bot.) condotto, vaso.

vest (vĕst) n. panciotto; maglia. vt. conferire, devolvere. vi. vestirsi; essere devoluto: to — an estate in,

assegnare una proprietà a; to — with powers, investire di poteri.

vesta (vĕs'tȧ) n. cerino, fiammifero.

vestibule (vĕs'tĭ-būl) n. vestibolo; piattaforma (di vagone).

vestige (vĕs'tĭj) n. vestigio, traccia.

vestment (vĕst'mĕnt) n. vestito, abito sacerdotale, paramento.

vestry (vĕs'trĭ) n. sagrestia, consiglio parrocchiale, fabbriceria.

veteran (vĕt'ẽr.ăn) n., agg. veterano, reduce: Veterans Day (S.U.), Anniversario dei Veterani (11 novembre).

veterinarian (vĕt'ẽr.ĭ-nâr'ĭ-ăn) n. veterinario.

veterinary (vĕt'ẽr.ĭ-nĕr'ĭ) n., agg. veterinario.

veto (vē'tō) n. veto, divieto. vt. porre il veto a, proibire.

vex (vĕks) vt. vessare, infastidire, preoccupare, affliggere.

vexation (vĕks.ā'shŭn) n. vessazione; irritazione; contrarietà.

via (vī'ȧ) prep. via, per, attraverso: — air mail, per via (o posta) aerea.

viable (vī'ȧ-b'l) agg. vitale.

viaduct (vī'ȧ-dŭkt) n. viadotto.

vial (vī'ăl) n. fiala.

viand (vī'ănd) n. commestibili, vivande.

vibrate (vī'brāt) vt. far vibrare; scagliare, misurare, scandire. vi. vibrare, oscillare.

vibration (vī-brā'shŭn) n. vibrazione, oscillazione.

vicar (vĭk'ẽr) n. delegato; vicario.

vicarage (vĭk'ẽr-ĭj) n. vicariato, presbiterio.

vicarious (vī-kâr'ĭ-ŭs) agg. sostitutivo, indiretto.

vice (vīs) (1) n. vizio; imperfezione.

vice (vīs) (2) prep. in luogo di. pref. vice.

viceroy (vīs'roi) n. vicerè.

vice versa (vī'sḗ-vûr-sȧ) avv. viceversa.

vicinity (vĭ-sĭn'ĭ-tĭ) n. vicinanza, dintorni, vicinato.

vicious (vĭsh'ŭs) agg. vizioso; malvagio, nocivo; maligno; violento; fallace.

vicissitude (vĭ-sĭs'ĭ-tūd) n. vicissitudine.

victim (vĭk'tĭm) n. vittima.

victor (vĭk'tẽr) n. vincitore.

victorious (vĭk-tō'rĭ-ŭs) agg. vittorioso.

victory (vĭk'tō-rĭ) n. vittoria.

victrola (vĭk-trō'lȧ) n. (S.U.) grammofono.

victuals (vĭt''lz) n.pl. viveri, vettovaglie.

vicuña (vĭ·kōōn′yä) *n.* vigogna (*animale e tessuto*).

video (vĭd′ē·ō) *n.* televisione; video (*parte visiva della TV*). *agg.* video: — **channel**, canale video.

videogenic (vĭd′ē·ō·jĕn′ĭk) *agg.* telegenico.

vie (vī) *vi.* (*pass.* vied, *ppr.* vying) competere, gareggiare.

view (vū) *n.* vista, veduta, panorama; ispezione; prospettiva, aspetto; opinione, intenzione, proposito: **field of —**, campo visivo; **in — of**, in vista di; **on —**, esposto al pubblico; **with a — to**, allo scopo di; **— finder** (*fot.*), mirino. *vt.* considerare, esaminare, contemplare.

viewpoint (vū′point′) *n.* punto di vista.

vigil (vĭj′ĭl) *n.* veglia, vigilia; vigilanza: **to keep —**, vigilare.

vigilance (vĭj′ĭ·lăns) *n.* vigilanza, cautela.

vigilant (vĭj′ĭ·lănt) *agg.* vigile, cauto.

vigor (vĭg′ĕr) *n.* vigore.

vigorous (vĭg′ĕr·ŭs) *agg.* vigoroso.

vile (vīl) *agg.* spregevole, ignominioso, pessimo, odioso.

vilify (vĭl′ĭ·fī) *vt.* vilipendere, diffamare.

village (vĭl′ĭj) *n.* paese, villaggio.

villager (vĭl′ĭj·ĕr) *n.* villico, paesano.

villain (vĭl′ĭn) *n.* furfante, colpevole, malvagio.

villainous (vĭl′ĭn·ŭs) *agg.* infame, scellerato.

villainy (vĭl′ĭn·ĭ) *n.* infamia, misfatto, scelleratezza.

vim (vĭm) *n.* vigore, energia.

vindicate (vĭn′dĭ·kāt) *vt.* giustificare, difendere, sostenere; riscattare, rivendicare.

vindication (vĭn′dĭ·kā′shŭn) *n.* rivincita, difesa, rivendicazione.

vindictive (vĭn·dĭk′tĭv) *agg.* vendicativo.

vine (vīn) *n.* vigna, vite.

vinegar (vĭn′ĕ·gĕr) *n.* aceto.

vinegarish (vĭn′ĕ·gĕr·ĭsh) *agg.* acetoso, che sa di aceto; (*fig.*) aspro, acido, caustico, sarcastico.

vineyard (vĭn′yĕrd) *n.* vigna.

vintage (vĭn′tĭj) *n.* vendemmia; annata (*vinicola*).

violate (vī′ō·lāt) *vt.* violare.

violation (vī′ō·lā′shŭn) *n.* violazione.

violence (vī′ō·lĕns) *n.* violenza.

violent (vī′ō·lĕnt) *agg.* violento.

violet (vī′ō·lĕt) *n.* viola mammola, violetta; color viola. *agg.* violetto.

violin (vī′ō·lĭn′) *n.* violino.

violinist (vī′ō·lĭn′ĭst) *n.* violinista.

VIP (vĭp, vē′ī′pē′) *n.* (*gergo*) pezzo grosso, alto papavero (*sigla di very important person*).

viper (vī′pĕr) *n.* vipera.

virgin (vûr′jĭn) *n.* vergine. *agg.* vergine, virginale.

virginal *agg.* virgineo.

virosis (vī·rō′sĭs) *n.* virosi.

virtu (vûr·tōō′) *n.* amore per l'arte: **articles of —**, soggetti d'arte.

virtual (vûr′tụ·ăl) *agg.* virtuale, potenziale.

virtue (vûr′tụ) *n.* virtù; rettitudine; pregio, dote, valore, merito; castità; efficacia.

virtuoso (vûr′tụ·ō′sō) *n.* collezionista di opere d'arte.

virtuous (vûr′tụ·ŭs) *agg.* virtuoso.

virulence (vĭr′ụ·lĕns), **virulency** (vĭr′ụ·lĕn·sĭ) *n.* virulenza, acrimonia.

virus (vī′rŭs) *n.* virus.

visa (vē′zä) *n.* visto, vidimazione. *vt.* vidimare.

visage (vĭz′ĭj) *n.* faccia, aspetto.

vis-à-vis (vē·zä·vē′) *n.* dirimpettaio. *avv.* a faccia a faccia.

viscose (vĭs′kōs) *n.* viscosa.

viscosity (vĭs·kŏs′ĭ·tĭ) *n.* viscosità.

viscous (vĭs′kŭs) *agg.* viscoso, tenace.

visé (vē′zā) *vedi* visa.

visible (vĭz′ĭ·b'l) *agg.* visibile.

visibly (vĭz′ĭ·blĭ) *avv.* visibilmente.

vision (vĭzh′ŭn) *n.* vista, visione, visuale, campo visivo.

visionary (vĭzh′ŭn·ĕr′ĭ) *n.*, *agg.* visionario.

visit (vĭz′ĭt) *n.* visita, soggiorno: **to pay a —**, fare una visita. *vt.* visitare, andare a trovare, ispezionare: **to — punishment upon**, infliggere un castigo a.

visitation (vĭz′ĭ·tā′shŭn) *n.* visitazione, visita; castigo divino.

visitor (vĭz′ĭ·tĕr) *n.* visitatore, ospite.

visor (vī′zĕr) *n.* visiera.

vista (vĭs′tä) *n.* panorama, prospettiva, visuale.

visual (vĭzh′ụ·ăl) *agg.* visivo, ottico.

visualize (vĭzh′ụ·ăl·īz) *vt.* prospettare; figurarsi.

vital (vī′tăl) *agg.* vitale, essenziale.

vitals *n.pl.* parti vitali, organi vitali.

vitamin (vī′tá·mĭn) *n.* vitamina.

vitriol (vĭt′rĭ·ăl) *n.* vetriolo.

vivacious (vī·vā′shŭs) *agg.* vivace, animato.

vivacity (vī·văs′ĭ·tĭ) *n.* vivacità.

vivid (vĭv′ĭd) *agg.* vivido, intenso.

vivisection (vĭv′ĭ·sĕk′shŭn) *n.* vivisezione.

vixen (vĭk′s'n) *n.* volpe femmina; megera.

vocabulary (vō·kăb′ụ·lĕr′ĭ) *n.* vocabolario.

vocal (vō′kăl) *n.* vocale; *agg.* vocale; parlante; eloquente; sonoro.

vocalist (vō′kăl·ĭst) *n.* cantante.

vocation (vṓ·kā′shŭn) *n.* vocazione, professione, occupazione. —**al** *agg.* professionale: —**al school,** scuola d'arti e mestieri.

vocative (vŏk′à·tĭv) *n.*, *agg.* vocativo.

vociferous (vṓ·sĭf′ĕr·ŭs) *agg.* clamoroso, vociferante.

vogue (vōg) *n.* voga, moda.

voice (vois) *n.* voce, suono, voto: **with one —,** all'unanimità. *vt.* esprimere, manifestare; intonare (*strumenti*).

voiceless (vois′lĕs) *agg.* afono, muto; — **consonant,** consonante sorda.

void (void) *n.* lacuna, vuoto. *agg.* vuoto; privo (*di*); inconsistente, nullo. *vt.* vuotare, annullare.

volatile (vŏl′à·tĭl) *agg.* volatile; incostante.

volcanic (vŏl·kăn′ĭk) *agg.* vulcanico.

volcano (vŏl·kā′nō) *n.* vulcano.

volition (vṓ·lĭsh′ŭn) *n.* volizione, volontà.

volley (vŏl′ĭ) *n.* raffica, scarica; (*tennis*) volata. *vt.*, *vi.* sparare a raffica; (*tennis*) ribattere: —**ball** *n.* palla a volo.

volplane (vŏl′plān′) *n.* volo planato. *vi.* librarsi, planare.

volt (vōlt) *n.* (*elett.*) volta.

voltage (vōl′tĭj) *n.* voltaggio.

voltameter (vŏl·tăm′ê·tẽr) *n.* voltametro.

voltammeter (vōlt′ăm′mê·tẽr) *n.* voltamperometro.

voltmeter (vōlt′mê′tẽr) *n.* voltmetro.

voluble (vŏl′ū·b′l) *agg.* sciolto, loquace.

volume (vŏl′ûm) *n.* volume; massa; libro; quantità.

voluminous (vṓ·lū′mĭ·nŭs) *agg.* voluminoso.

voluntary (vŏl′ŭn·tẽr′ĭ) *agg.* volontario, spontaneo, intenzionale.

volunteer (vŏl′ŭn·tẽr′) *n.*, *agg.* volontario. *vt.*, *vi.* offrire, offrirsi spontaneamente, offrire i propri servigi; arruolarsi volontario.

voluptuous (vṓ·lŭp′tū·ŭs) *agg.* voluttuoso.

vomit (vŏm′ĭt) *n.* vomito. *vt.*, *vi.* vomitare.

voracious (vṓ·rā′shŭs) *agg.* vorace, ingordo.

vortex (vôr′tĕks) *n.* turbine, vortice.

votary (vō′tà·rĭ) *n.* devoto, seguace.

vote (vōt) *n.* voto, suffragio. *vt.*, *vi.* votare.

voter (vōt′ẽr) *n.* votante, elettore.

vouch (vouch) *vt.*, *vi.*: **to — for,** convalidare; garantire per, rispondere di.

voucher (vouch′ẽr) *n.* garante; garanzia, pezza giustificativa, ricevuta.

vouchsafe (vouch·sāf′) *vt.* concedere, sancire.

vow (vou) *n.* voto, promessa solenne. *vt.* votare, consacrare, promettere solennemente. *vi.* fare un voto.

vowel (vou′ĕl) *n.* vocale.

voyage (voi′ĭj) *n.* viaggio (*per mare o in aereo*), traversata. *vi.* viaggiare, navigare.

vulcanization (vŭl′kăn·ĭ·zā′shŭn) *n.* vulcanizzazione.

vulcanize (vŭl′kăn·īz) *vt.* vulcanizzare.

vulgar (vŭl′gẽr) *agg.* volgare, comune.

vulgarian (vŭl·gâr′ĭ·ăn) *n.* zoticone.

vulgarity (vŭl·gâr′ĭ·tĭ) *n.* volgarità.

vulgarization (vŭl′gẽr·ĭ·zā′shŭn) *n.* volgarizzazione.

vulnerable (vŭl′nẽr·à·b′l) *agg.* vulnerabile.

vulture (vŭl′tūr) *n.* avvoltoio.

W

wabble (wŏb′l) *n.* vacillamento, oscillazione. *vi.* vacillare, traballare, tentennare, oscillare.

WAC (wăk) *n.* Ausiliaria dell' Esercito Americano.

wacky (wăk′ĭ) *agg.* (*gergo*) pazzo, tocco, svanito, suonato.

wad (wŏd) *n.* stoppaccio, batuffolo, tampone, imbottitura; rotolo (*di banconote*); (*gergo*) gruzzolo. *vt.* imbottire, tamponare, appallare, ovattare. —**ding** *n.* imbottitura, ovatta.

waddle (wŏd′′l) *n.* andatura ciondolante. *vi.* camminare a passetti ciondolando.

wade (wād) *vt.*, *vi.* guadare, fendere; avanzare penosamente: **to — into** (*gergo*), attaccare vigorosamente.

WAF (wăf) *n.* Ausiliaria dell' Aviazione Americana.

wafer (wā′fẽr) *n.* ostia, cialda; sigillo (*di carta gommata, ecc.*).

waffle (wŏf′′l) *n.* galletta.

waft (wăft) *n.* zaffata, folata, segnalazione. *vt.* trasportare sui flutti (*o attraverso l'aria*), sospingere. *vi.* fluttuare.

wag (wăg) *n.* burlone; dimenamento, scotimento. *vt.* dimenare, scuotere. *vi.* dimenarsi: **to have a wagging tongue,** avere la lingua troppo lunga; **to — the tail,** scodinzolare.

wage (wāj) *n.* (*anche pl.*)salario, paga: —**earner** *n.* salariato. *vt.*, *vi.* intraprendere (*una guerra*), impegnarsi in (*una competizione*).

wager (wā'jĕr) *n.* scommessa. *vt.*, *vi.* scommettere.

waggish (wăg'ĭsh) *agg.* scherzoso.

waggle (wăg''l) *vt.* dimenare.

wagon (wăg'ŭn) *n.* furgone, carro.

wagoner (wăg'ŭn.ĕr) *n.* carrettiere.

wagonette (wăg'ŭn.ĕt') *n.* giardiniera (carrozza).

wail (wāl) *n.* gemito, lamento. *vt.* deplorare, rimpiangere. *vi.* gemere, lamentarsi.

wain (wān) *n.* carro.

wainscot (wān'skŭt), **wainscoting** *n.* rivestimento in legno; zoccolo (*di parete*).

waist (wāst) *n.* cintola, cinta, vita, parte centrale; corpetto, blusa: —band *n.* cintura.

waistcoat (wās(t)'kōt') *n.* panciotto.

wait (wāt) *n.* attesa; imboscata. *vt.*, *vi.* aspettare: to — for somebody, aspettare qualcuno; to lie in — for someone, appostare qualcuno; to — at table, servire a tavola; to — on, upon, assistere, servire.

waiter (wāt'ĕr) *n.* cameriere; vassoio.

waiting (wāt'ĭng) *n.* attesa; servizio: — room, sala d'aspetto.

waitress (wāt'rĕs) *n.* cameriera (*di ristorante*).

waive (wāv) *vt.* abbandonare, rinunziare a.

waiver (wāv'ĕr) *n.* rinunzia.

wake (wāk) (1) *n.* scia, solco: in the — of, nel solco di.

wake (wāk) (2) *n.* veglia (*anche funebre*). *vt.*, *vi.* svegliare, destare, vegliare; svegliarsi.

wakeful (wāk'fŏŏl) *agg.* sveglio, vigilante, insonne.

waken (wāk'ĕn) *vt.* svegliare, risvegliare. *vi.* svegliarsi.

wale (wāl) *n.* riga, striscia, costa.

walk (wôk) *n.* passeggiata; andatura; percorso, cammino; passo; sentiero: a ten-minute —, una passeggiatina di dieci minuti; — of life, sfera di azione, carriera. *vt.* far camminare, percorrere. *vi.* camminare, passeggiare, andare a piedi: to — back home, tornare a casa a piedi; to — down, scendere; to — in, entrare; to — off, svignarsela; to — out, uscire, andarsene; far sciopero; to — the streets, girare per le strade, andare in giro.

walkie-talkie (wôk'ĭ-tôk'ĭ) *n.* (*radio*) trasmittente-ricevente portatile.

walking (wôk'ĭng) *n.* marcia, andatura. *agg.*: at — pace, al passo; — stick, bastone da passeggio.

walkout (wôk'out') *n.* sciopero.

walkover (wôk'ō'vĕr) *n.* facile vittoria.

walk-up (wôk'ŭp) *n.* (*S.U.*) casa senza ascensore.

wall (wôl) *n.* muro, muraglia, parete: to go to the —, soccombere; to drive to the —, mettere con le spalle al muro. *vt.* cingere con muro, fortificare; murare.

wallet (wôl'ĕt) *n.* borsa; portafoglio.

walleyed (wôl'īd') *agg.* dagli occhi scialbi; strabico; sbieco (*di sguardo*).

wallflower (wôl'flou'ĕr) *n.* violacciocca; persona che fa tappezzeria (*a un ballo*).

wallop (wôl'ŭp) *n.* (*gergo*) pugno, sgrugnone. *vt.* colpire con violenza.

wallow (wôl'ō) *vi.* diguazzare, rotolarsi (*nel fango*); crogiolarsi.

wallpaper (wôl'pā'pĕr) *n.* tappezzeria.

walnut (wôl'nŭt) *n.* noce.

walrus (wôl'rŭs) *n.* tricheco.

waltz (wôlts) *n.* valzer. *vi.* ballare il valzer.

wan (wŏn) *agg.* pallido, scialbo, languido, malaticcio.

wand (wŏnd) *n.* verga, bacchetta magica, bastone di comando.

wander (wŏn'dĕr) *vi.* vagare; sviarsi; divagare; deviare; distrarsi; vaneggiare. — *vt.* vagabondo. —ing *n.* peregrinazione; vaneggiamento. *agg.* errante, nomade; vaneggiante.

wane (wān) *n.* declino, diminuzione: on the —, in decadenza. *vi.* diminuire.

want (wŏnt) *n.* bisogno, necessità, mancanza, deficienza, indigenza: to stand in — of, aver bisogno di; — ad, offerta di lavoro o impiego (*sul giornale*). *vt.*, *vi.* aver bisogno di, desiderare, scarseggiare di; difettare, mancare, essere bisognoso.

wanting *agg.* mancante, assente, insufficiente. *prep.* in mancanza di, senza, meno.

wanton (wŏn'tŭn) *n.* libertino, persona lasciva, donnaccia. *agg.* sregolato; ingiustificato; spietato; licenzioso, lascivo; folle.

war (wôr) *n.* guerra: to be at —, essere in guerra; War Office, Ministero della Guerra: — of nerves, guerra dei nervi, guerra psicologica; cold —, guerra fredda. *vi.* guerreggiare, combattere.

warble (wôr'b'l) *n.* gorgheggio. *vt.*, *vi.* cantare, gorgheggiare.

warbler (wôr'blĕr) *n.* gorgheggiatore, uccello canoro.

ward (wôrd) *n.* guardia, custodia, tutela; pupillo, pupilla; rione, quartiere; reparto (*d'ospedale*); raggio (*di carcere*). *vt.*, *vi.* custodire, proteggere, parare, stare in guardia:

to — off, respingere, parare, schivare.

warden (wòr'd'n) n. custode; guardiano; governatore (di carcere, ecc.); direttore (di collegio).

warder (wòr'dĕr) n. custode, carceriere.

wardrobe (wòrd'rōb') n. guardaroba.

ware (wâr) n. (gen.pl.) merce; mercanzia, articolo.

warehouse (wâr'hous') n. magazzino, deposito.

warfare (wòr'fâr') n. guerra, lotta.

warlike (wòr'lìk') agg. bellicoso, guerriero, guerresco, militare.

warm (wòrm) agg. caldo, caloroso, animato, violento, accalorato; cordiale; recente, scottante: —hearted agg. di buon cuore, imbarazzante; to be —, avere caldo; it is —, fa caldo. vt., vi. scaldare, scaldarsi: to — over, riscaldare; to — up, scaldare, scaldarsi, accalorare, accalorarsi, entusiasmarsi. —ly avv. caldamente, calorosamente, cordialmente, concitatamente. —ness n. tepore, calore.

warmth (wòrmth) n. calore, ardore.

warn (wòrn) vt. avvertire, ammonire, mettere in guardia, prevenire: to — off, diffidare; allontanare.

warning n. avvertimento, ammonimento, diffida; preavviso; licenziamento.

warp (wòrp) n. ordito; torsione, incurvatura, deformazione; prevenzione (preconcetto), fissazione; (naut.) gherlino. vt. ordire; falsare, deformare, snaturare; (naut.) tonneggiare. vi. torcersi, incurvarsi, deformarsi.

warrant (wòr'ănt) n. autorizzazione, garanzia, mandato, citazione, ordine; brevetto: — officer, sottufficiale. vt. garantire, giustificare, sanzionare, certificare, autorizzare.

warren (wòr'ĕn) n. conigliera; tana; casa popolare.

warrior (wòr'ĭ-ĕr) n. guerriero.

warship (wòr'shĭp') n. nave da guerra.

wart (wòrt) n. porro, verruca.

wary (wâr'ĭ) agg. circospetto, cauto: to be — of, diffidare di.

was (wŏz) 1a e 3a pers.sing. pass. di to be.

wash (wŏsh) n. lavatura, bucato; sciacquio; corrente; risucchio; scoria; pantano; beverone, brodaglia; placcatura: mouth —, sciacquo per la bocca, dentifricio liquido. vt. lavare, purificare, bagnare; placcare. vi. lavarsi, fare il bucato, scorrere, essere lavabile, frangersi: to — away, off, eliminare lavando,

scomparire; to — out, mondare, pulire, togliere (lavando); sfinire, stremare; escludere, scartare, espellere, eliminare; bocciare; scolorirsi.

washable (wŏsh'á·b'l) agg. lavabile.

washed-out (wŏsht'out') agg. mondo, lavato; sbiadito; esausto, sfinito; escluso, scartato, eliminato; bocciato.

washer (wŏsh'ĕr) n. lavatore, macchina per lavare; (mecc.) ranella, guarnizione. —woman n. lavandaia.

washing (wŏsh'ĭng) n. lavaggio, bucato, lavatura: — machine, macchina per lavare.

washout (wŏsh'out') n. erosione prodotta dall'acqua; stasatura; (gergo) fallito; fallimento, fiasco; bocciato; bocciatura.

washy (wŏsh'ĭ) agg. acquoso, fiacco.

wasp (wŏsp) n. vespa.

Wasp (wŏsp) n. Ausiliaria Aviatrice dell' Aviazione Americana.

waspish (wŏsp'ĭsh) agg. irascibile, pungente.

wastage (wās'tĭj) n. logorio, consumo.

waste (wāst) n. perdita, sciupìo; rovina, devastazione; deperimento; regione incolta, deserto, distesa; rifiuti: to run to —, andare in rovina. agg. devastato, sterile, incolto; sprecato, inutile, di scarto: — land, distesa; deserto; regione incolta. vt. sprecare, sciupare, devastare, deteriorare, consumare. vi. sciuparsi, deperire, logorarsi.

wastebasket n. cestino dei rifiuti.

wasteful (wāst'fŏŏl) agg. prodigo, dispendioso, rovinoso, devastatore.

wastepaper n. carta straccia.

wastrel (wās'trĕl) n. rifiuto; buono a nulla.

watch (wŏch) n. orologio; veglia, vigilanza; guardia, sentinella, pattuglia: on the —, all'erta, di guardia. vt., vi. osservare, sorvegliare, aspettare, vegliare, vigilare: to — out for, stare attento a; — out! attento!, attenti!

watchdog (wŏch'dŏg') n. cane da guardia.

watcher (wŏch'ĕr) n. sorvegliante, osservatore.

watchful (wŏch'fŏŏl) agg. vigilante, attento, circospetto.

watchmaker (wŏch'māk'ĕr) n. orologiaio.

watchman (wŏch'măn) n. guardiano.

watchtower (wŏch'tou'ĕr) n. torre di vedetta.

watchword (wŏch'wûrd') n. parola d'ordine.

water (wŏ'tĕr) n. acqua. agg. d'acqua, da acqua, ad acqua, acquatico, idraulico: — color, acquerello; — power, forza idraulica; — sports, sport acquatici. vt. inumidire, irrigare, irrorare. abbeverare, annacquare; marezzare (tessuti). vi. fare acqua, rifornirsi d'acqua, abbeverarsi, secernere: to make one's mouth —, far venire l'acquolina in bocca; my eyes —, mi piangono gli occhi.

waterfall (wô′tĕr·fôl′) n. cascata.

watering (wô′tĕr·ĭng) n. anaffiamento, irrigazione; marezzatura; abbeveramento, rifornimento d'acqua: — place, stazione balneare o termale.

watermark (wô′tĕr·märk′) n. livello delle acque; filigrana.

watermelon (wô′tĕr·mĕl′ŭn) n. anguria.

waterproof (wô′tĕr·prōōf′) n., agg. impermeabile. vt. impermeabilizzare.

watershed (wô′tĕr·shĕd′) n. spartiacque, versante.

waterside (wô′tĕr·sīd′) n. riva. agg. rivierasco.

waterspout (wô′tĕr·spout′) n. tromba d'acqua, grondaia.

watertight (wô′tĕr·tīt′) agg. stagno, ermetico.

waterway (wô′tĕr·wā′) n. idrovia, canale navigabile.

waterworks (wô′tĕr·wûrks′) n.pl. impianto idrico; fontana ornamentale.

watery (wô′tĕr·ĭ) agg. acqueo, acquatico, acquoso, bagnato.

watt (wŏt) n. (elett.) watt.

wattle (wŏt′l) n. ramoscello, cannicciata, vimine; (zool.) bargiglio.

wave (wāv) n. onda, ondata; ondulazione; ondeggiamento; cenno (della mano): permanent —, ondulazione permanente. vt. far ondeggiare, sventolare, agitare, ondulare. vi. ondeggiare, fluttuare; far cenno con la mano: to — away, allontanare con un cenno; to — one's hand, agitare la mano; to — hair, ondulare capelli.

WAVE (wāv) n. Ausiliaria della Marina Americana.

waver (wā′vĕr) vi. ondeggiare; vacillare; titubare. n. ondeggiamento; vacillamento; titubanza.

wavy (wāv′ĭ) agg. ondulato, ondoso, ondeggiante.

wax (wăks) (1) vi. svilupparsi, aumentare, trasformarsi; essere in fase crescente (della luna).

wax (wăks) (2) n. cera, cerume, pece, ceralacca. vt. incerare: — paper, carta cerata.

waxen (wăk′sĕn) agg. cereo, di cera.

waxy (wăk′sĭ) agg. cereo; molle; adesivo.

way (wā) n. via, cammino, passaggio; direzione; mezzo, metodo; stato, condizione, modo; (naut.) rotta: a long — off, molto lontano; by the —, a proposito; by — of, a guisa di, a titolo di; to be in the —, ingombrare; to make one's —, avanzarsi; to be in the family —, essere incinta; to have one's own —, fare a modo proprio; out of the —, fuori mano, fuori del comune; this —, da questa parte; to be in a bad —, essere in una brutta situazione; to get into the — of, prendere l'abitudine di; the — in, l'ingresso; the — out, l'uscita; a — through, un passaggio; under —, in corso, in rotta.

wayfarer (wā′fâr′ĕr) n. viandante.

waylay (wā′lā′) vt. tendere un agguato a, aggredire; sequestrare (una persona).

wayside (wā′sīd′) n. ciglio della strada.

wayward (wā′wĕrd) agg. capriccioso; ostinato; perverso; irregolare, zigzagante.

we (wē) pron.pers. noi.

weak (wēk) agg. debole; leggiero (di tè, brodo, liquore, ecc.); fiacco, malaticcio: —headed agg. tardo, ottuso; —sighted agg. debole di vista.

weaken (wēk′ĕn) vt. indebolire, affievolire, diluire. vi. indebolirsi, attenuarsi.

weakling (wēk′lĭng) n., agg. debole, inetto.

weakly (wēk′lĭ) agg. debole, malaticcio. avv. debolmente.

weakness (wēk′nĕs) n. debolezza.

weal (wēl) n. lividura.

wealth (wĕlth) n. ricchezza, prosperità, abbondanza.

wealthy (wĕl′thĭ) agg. ricco, opulento.

wean (wēn) vt. svezzare, slattare, disabituare.

weapon (wĕp′ŭn) n. arma.

wear (wâr) n. uso, logorio; durevolezza; vestiario, moda: — and tear, usura, logorio; to be the worse for —, essere in pessime condizioni; men's —, abbigliamento maschile. vt. (pass. wore, pp. worn) portare, indossare, logorare, corrodere, consumare, stancare. vi. consumarsi, logorarsi; resistere, durare; passare (del tempo): to — out, esaurire, consumare; to — away, logorare, logorarsi; to — off, cancellare, sparire; to — well, resistere, conservarsi bene; as the day wore on, col passare della giornata.

wearied (wēr′ĭd) agg. stanco, annoiato.

wearily (wēr′ĭ·lĭ) avv. stancamente, tediosamente, fiaccamente.

weariness (wẽr'ĭ-nĕs) *n.* stanchezza, tedio.

wearing (wâr'ĭng) *agg.* logorante, faticoso: — apparel, indumenti.

wearisome (wẽr'ĭ-sŭm) *agg.* faticosi, gravoso, monotono, tedioso.

weary (wẽr'ĭ) *agg.* annoiato, stanco; tedioso, gravoso. *vt.* affaticare, annoiare. *vi.* stancarsi.

weasel (wē'z'l) *n.* donnola.

weather (wĕth'ẽr) *n.* tempo (*atmosferico*): — bureau, ufficio meteorologico; — conditions, condizioni atmosferiche; it is fine —, c'è bel tempo, fa bel tempo; under the —, indisposto, ubriaco. *agg.* (*naut.*) di sopravvento. *vt.* resistere a (*una burrasca, ecc.*); esporre alle intemperie; stagionare (*o far seccare*) all'aria; (*naut.*) passare sopravvento, doppiare. *vi.* superare una burrasca; stagionarsi.

weather-beaten *agg.* battuto dalle intemperie, logoro, agguerrito.

weathercock (wĕth'ẽr-kŏk') *n.* girotta.

weatherglass (wĕth'ẽr-glàs') *n.* barometro.

weatherproof (wĕth'ẽr-prōōf') *agg.* resistente alle intemperie.

weave (wēv) *n.* tessitura. *vt.*, *vi.* (*pass.* wove, *pp.* woven) intrecciare, tessere, intessere.

weaving *n.* tessitura.

web (wĕb) *n.* tessuto, tela, rete, ragnatela, trama; membrana interdigitale (*dei palmipedi*).

wed (wĕd) *vt.* (*pass.* wedded, *pp.* wedded, wed) sposare, unire, legare. *vi.* sposarsi.

wedded (wĕd'ĕd) *agg.* sposato; coniugale; legato.

wedding (wĕd'ĭng) *n.* matrimonio: — card, partecipazione di nozze; — day, giorno di nozze, anniversario del matrimonio; — ring, fede nuziale.

wedge (wĕj) *n.* cuneo, bietta. *vt.* incuneare, spaccare (*o allargare*) con un cuneo. *vi.* incunearsi.

wedlock (wĕd'lŏk) *n.* matrimonio.

Wednesday (wĕnz'dĭ) *n.* mercoledì.

wee (wē) *agg.* piccolo, minuscolo.

weed (wēd) (1) *n.* fascia di lutto; *pl.* gramaglie.

weed (wēd) (2) *n.* erbaccia, zizzania; (*fam.*) tabacco, sigaro. *vt.* sarchiare, ripulire, epurare; —y *agg.* pieno di erbacce.

week (wēk) *n.* settimana: this day —, oggi a otto; a — of Sundays, un'eternità: — day, giorno feriale; — end, fine-settimana.

weekly (wēk'lĭ) *n.* pubblicazione set-timanale. *agg.* settimanale. *avv.* settimanalmente.

weep (wēp) *vt.*, *vi.* (*pass.*, *pp.* wept) piangere; secernere: to — one's eyes out, piangere disperatamente.

weeping *agg.* piangente: — willow, salice piangente. *n.* pianto, lagrime.

weevil (wē'v'l) *n.* gorgoglione.

weft (wĕft) *n.* trama (*di tessuto*).

weigh (wā) *vt.*, *vi.* pesare; soppesare, ponderare; levare (*l'ancora*); aver peso (*o importanza*); gravare: to — down, opprimere.

weight (wāt) *n.* peso, gravità; importanza. *vt.* appesantire, gravare; valutare.

weighty (wāt'ĭ) *agg.* pesante, gravoso; efficace, importante.

weir (wẽr) *n.* chiusa, cateratta, diga.

weird (wẽrd) *agg.* magico, soprannaturale, sconcertante, fatale.

welcome (wĕl'kŭm) *n.* benvenuto, accoglienza. *agg.* benvenuto, gradito, opportuno, tempestivo: — home! bentornato! to be — to, esser libero di; you are —, (in risposta a "thank you") non c'è di che, prego. *vt.* dare il benvenuto a, accogliere bene, gradire.

weld (wĕld) *n.* saldatura, sutura. *vt.* saldare, unire. *vi.* saldarsi.

welder (wĕl'dẽr) *n.* saldatore.

welfare (wĕl'fâr') *n.* benessere, bene, prosperità.

well (wĕl) (1) *n.* pozzo, serbatoio, sorgente, fonte, tromba (*di scala, ecc.*); (*naut.*) sentina. *vi.* scaturire, sgorgare: tears welled up in her eyes, le sgorgarono le lagrime.

well (wĕl) (2) *agg.* in buona salute; fortunato; in buone condizioni: to be —, star bene; to get —, ristabilirsi. *avv.* bene; giustamente; molto; pienamente: everything is going — with me, sto bene, vado bene, tutto mi sta andando bene; to do oneself —, vivere bene, vivere negli agi; to stand — with, godere la simpatia di; he ought to be — beaten, meriterebbe proprio una lezione coi fiocchi; he must be — over fifty, deve avere cinquant'anni sonati da un pezzo; you may — be surprised, hai ben ragione di meravigliarti; we may as — begin at once, ci conviene cominciare subito; you might just as — throw away your money, tanto vale che tu butti il denaro dalla finestra; he gave me advice and money as —, non solo mi ha dato consigli, ma anche denaro. *int.* dunque, ebbene bene. —-behaved *agg.* cortese, corretto. —-being *n.* benessere. —-

born agg. bennato. —**bred** agg. di buona razza, beneducato. —**meaning** agg. benintenzionato. —**meant** agg. a fin di bene. —**nigh** avv. quasi. —**off** agg. benestante, in buone condizioni. —**read** agg. colto. — **to-do** agg. agiato.

welsh (wĕlsh) (1) vt., vi. (gergo) truffare, svignarsela senza pagare.

Welsh (wĕlsh) (2) n., agg. gallese.

welt (wĕlt) n. orlo, guàrdolo (di scarpa). vt. orlare, munir di guàrdolo.

welter (wĕl'tĕr) n. tumulto, confusione. vi. tumultuare, sguazzare, avvoltolarsi (nel fango, ecc.).

welterweight (wĕl'tĕr-wāt') n. medioleggiero (pugile).

wen (wĕn) n. natta.

wench (wĕnch) n. ragazza, cameriera.

went (wĕnt) pass. di to go.

wept (wĕpt) pass., pp. di to weep.

were (wûr) pass. (nel pl. e nella 2a pers. sing.dell'indic.), cong.imperfetto di to be: if I — you, se fossi al posto tuo.

werewolf, werwolf (wēr'wŏŏlf') n. lupo. mannaro, licantropo.

west (wĕst) n. ovest, ponente, occidente. agg. occidentale, dell'ovest. avv. all'ovest: to go —, (gergo) andare al Creatore.

westerly (wĕs'tĕr.lĭ) agg. occidentale.

western (wĕs'tẽrn) n. (S.U.) racconto (o film) sull'ovest degli U.S.A.. agg. occidentale.

westerner (wĕs'tĕr.nẽr) n. occidentale (degli S.U.).

Westwall (wĕst'wŏl') n. Linea Sigfrido (2a guerra mondiale.)

westward (wĕst'wẽrd) agg. diretto (o rivolto) a ovest. avv. verso ovest.

wet (wĕt) n. umidità, pioggia; (S.U.) antiproibizionista. agg. umido, bagnato, piovoso: — **blanket**, guastafeste; — **dock** (naut.), bacino; — **nurse**, nutrice. vt. (pass., pp. wet, —ted) inumidire, umettare, bagnare. vi. bagnarsi.

wether (wĕth'ẽr) n. montone castrato.

wetness (wĕt'nĕs) n. umidità.

whack (hwăk) n. pacca, colpo; (gergo) tentativo. vt., vi. battere, menar pacche; (gergo) spartire.

whale (hwāl) n. (zool.) balena. vt. (gergo) malmenare, percuotere. vi. andare alla pesca della balena.

whalebone (hwāl'bōn') n. stecca di balena.

whaler (hwāl'ẽr) n. baleniera, baleniere.

wharf (hwôrf) n. molo, banchina. vt. attraccare, ormeggiare.

what (hwŏt) agg.interr. di quale specie?, quanto?, quale? pron.rel.

ciò che, quello che. pron.interr. che?, che cosa?, quale? avv. come?, perchè? cong. che, tanto che: **and** — not, eccetera; — **for**? perchè?, a che scopo? — **of** that? che importa? **to know** —'s —, saperla lunga; —'s **up**? che succede? —'s **the matter with you**? che avete?; — **a car**! che automobile!

whatever (hwŏt.ĕv'ẽr) agg., pron. tutto ciò che, qualunque, qualsiasi cosa, quel poco di. agg. di nessuna specie: **of no use** —, assolutamente inutile; — **happens**, accada quel che accada.

whatnot (hwŏt'nŏt') n. scaffale; (fam.) qualunque cosa.

whatsoever (hwŏt'sŏ.ĕv'ẽr) vedi **whatever**.

wheat (hwēt) n. frumento, grano.

wheedle (hwē'd'l) vt., vi. carpire; adulare, adescare: **to** — **somebody into**, persuadere qualcuno a.

wheel (hwēl) n. ruota; volante; ciclo; girandola; cerchio; rotazione, conversione; (fam.) bicicletta: **driving** —, ruota motrice; **cog** —, ruota dentata; **steering** —, volante di guida; ruota del timone; — **chair**, poltrona a rotelle o ruote. vt. far girare, trasportare su ruote. vi. rotare, girare; cambiare direzione, voltarsi; andare in bicicletta: **to** — **around**, voltarsi, fare un voltafaccia.

wheelbarrow (hwēl'băr'ō) n. carriola.

wheeze (hwēz) n. respiro affannoso, sibilo; artificio, dispositivo; (gergo) luogo comune, banalità. vi. ansimare.

wheezy (hwēz'ĭ) agg. asmatico.

whelp (hwĕlp) n. cucciolo.

when (hwĕn) avv., cong. quando, mentre, allorchè; qualora; benchè: **since** —? da quando in qua?

whence (hwĕns) avv., cong. donde, dal che, per cui.

whenever (hwĕn.ĕv'ẽr) cong. ogni volta che, quando, in qualunque momento.

where (hwâr) avv., cong. dove; a quale punto; in quale situazione; in che senso.

whereabout (hwâr'á.bout'); **whereabouts** n. luogo, posto, località in cui qualcuno si trova, ubicazione: **I don't know her whereabouts**, non so dove ella si trovi. avv., cong. ove, in qual luogo, in quali paraggi.

whereas (hwâr.ăz') cong. mentre, invece, in considerazione di, stante che, poichè.

whereat (hwâr.ăt') avv., cong. al che.

whereby (hwâr.bī') avv., cong. per il

quale, per cui; per mezzo del quale;
attraverso cui; secondo cui.

wherefore (hwâr'fōr) n. causa, motivo.
avv., cong. ragione per cui, perciò;
(interr.) perchè?

wherefrom (hwâr·frŏm') avv. donde,
da cui.

wherein (hwâr·ĭn') avv. in cui, nel
quale, nei quali; (interr.) in che
cosa?, dove?

whereof (hwâr·ŏv') avv., cong. del
quale, di cui; (interr.) di che?

whereon (hwâr·ŏn') avv. su cui;
(interr.) su che cosa?

wheresoever (hwâr'sō·ĕv'ẽr) avv., cong.
dovunque.

whereupon (hwâr'ŭ·pŏn') avv. (interr.)
su che cosa?. cong. al che, dopo
di che.

wherever (hwâr·ĕv'ẽr) avv. (interr.)
dove?, dove mai? cong. dovunque,
in qualunque luogo; in ogni caso.

wherewith (hwâr·wĭth') avv., cong
con cui, col quale, per mezzo del
quale: —? con che cosa?

wherewithal (hwâr'wĭth·ôl') n. mezzi,
fondi, soldi.

whet (hwĕt) vt. aguzzare, affilare,
stimolare.

whether (hwĕth'ẽr) cong. se; sia; sia
che: — ... or, se ... oppure; we
do not know — he will pay (or not),
non sappiamo se egli pagherà (o no);
— we stay or — we go, sia che
restiamo, sia che ce ne andiamo;
I doubt —, dubito che.

whetstone (hwĕt'stōn') n. cote.

whey (hwā) n. siero del latte.

which (hwĭch) agg. qualunque; (interr.)
quale? pron.rel. che, il quale, la
quale, i quali, le quali, il che: I
cannot tell — is —, non so dis-
tinguerli l'uno dall'altro; — way?
da quale parte?, da che parte?

whichever (hwĭch·ĕv'ẽr) agg., pron.
chiunque, qualunque; quello che,
quella che: —? quale?, quali?;
take — road you like, prendete la
strada che volete.

whiff (hwĭf) n. zaffata, ondata, soffio,
scatto. vt., vi. sbuffare, aspirare,
fumare.

while (hwīl) n. momento, tempo, lasso: in a little —, in breve, tra poco;
for a short —, per un po', per poco,
poco tempo; a short — ago, poco
fa, da poco. once in a —, una volta
tanto; to be worth —, valere la
pena. cong. mentre, intanto che,
nello stesso tempo che. vt. trascorrere (il tempo): to — away
time, ammazzare il tempo.

whilst (hwīlst) vedi while.

whim (hwĭm) n. capriccio, ubbia.

whimper (hwĭm'pẽr) n. piagnisteo,
lamento. vi. lamentarsi, piagnucolare.

whimsical (hwĭm'zĭ·kǎl) agg. fantastico, capriccioso, comico.

whine (hwīn) n. piagnisteo, lamento,
gemito. vi. piagnucolare, lagnarsi
piagnucolando.

whiner n. piagnone.

whinny (hwĭn'ĭ) n. nitrito. vi. nitrire.

whip (hwĭp) n. frusta, sferza, scudiscio, staffile; sferzata; (naut.)
paranco. vt. frustare; criticare,
stimolare; sbattere, frullare (uova,
panna, ecc.); (fam.) sopraffare,
vincere. vi. guizzare, slanciarsi: to
— out, tirar fuori fulmineamente.

whippet (hwĭp'ĕt) n. levriere inglese.

whipping (hwĭp'ĭng) n. frustata,
flagellazione.

whir (hwûr) n. ronzio, fruscio. vi.
ronzare, frusciare.

whirl (hwûrl) n. turbine, rotazione,
vortice; voluta, spirale (di fumo);
confusione. vt., vi. far turbinare,
roteare; turbinare, girare: my head
whirls, mi gira la testa.

whirligig (hwûr'lĭ·gĭg') n. giostra;
trottola.

whirlpool (hwûrl'pōōl') n. gorgo.

whirlwind (hwûrl'wĭnd') n. tromba
d'aria, bufera.

whish (hwĭsh) vi. sibilare.

whisk (hwĭsk) n. spazzolata; movimento rapido; spazzola, scopa, frullino. vt. spazzar via, portar via,
arraffare; sbattere, frullare (uova,
ecc.). vi. fuggire rapidamente, guizzare: to — away, far sparire, trascinar via.

whisker (hwĭs'kẽr) n. pelo di barba,
baffo pl. basette; barba.

whisky, whiskey (hwĭs'kĭ) n. whisky,
uischi (acquavite di cereali).

whisper (hwĭs'pẽr) n. mormorio,
susurro; ronzio; diceria. vt., vi.
bisbigliare, mormorare; confabulare; insinuare; ronzare, stormire:
it is whispered that ..., si mor-
mora che.

whispering n. bisbiglio, mormorio,
diceria. agg. mormorante, frus-
ciante.

whistle (hwĭs'l) n. fischietto, fischio,
sibilo; (fam.) gola: paesucolo. vt.,
vi. fischiare, zufolare, sibilare.

whit (hwĭt) n. inezia, iota.

white (hwīt) n., agg. bianco; puro,
innocente, onesto, leale: to show
the — feather, mostrarsi vigliacco;
— hot, rovente; — lie, bugia
perdonabile (o pietosa); —-livered,
agg. codardo, vigliacco.

whiten (hwīt'n) vt., vi. imbiancare.

whiteness (hwĭt′nĕs) n. bianchezza, candore; pallore; purezza.

whitewash (hwĭt′wŏsh′) n. calce da imbianchino, pittura bianca. vt. imbiancare a calce; passare la spugna su (errori, colpe); scagionare (senza giustizia), mandare impunito.

whither (hwĭth′ĕr) avv. dove, nella quale direzione; (interr.) dove?, in quale direzione?

whitish (hwĭt′ĭsh) agg. biancastro.

whitlow (hwĭt′lō) n. patereccio.

Whitsunday (hwĭt′sŭn′dĭ) n. Domenica della Pentecoste.

Whitsuntide (hwĭt′sŭn·tĭd′) n. Pentecoste.

whittle (hwĭt′′l) vt., vi. temperare, truciolara; far la punta a (un lapis); assottigliare; ridurre (spese, ecc.).

whiz (hwĭz) n. sibilo; passaggio rapido; (gergo) affare; persona (o cosa) straordinaria. vt. centrifugare. vi. fischiare, sibilare; vi. sfrecciare.

whizzer n. centrifuga.

who (hōō) pron.rel. chi, il quale, la quale, i quali, le quali, che; (interr.) chi?: he —, colui che; — is it? chi è?

whodunit (hōō′dŭn′ĭt) n. (gergo) racconto poliziesco.

whoever (hōō·ĕv′ĕr) pron.rel. chiunque; (interr.) chi mai?

whole (hōl) n. totalità, tutto, totale: on the —, in complesso, tutto considerato; as a —, come una cosa unica, nel complesso; the — of us, tutti noi. agg. tutto, intero, completo, integrale, sano, intatto: the — day, tutto il giorno; —-hearted agg. cordiale, sincero, leale; —-heartedly avv. cordialmente, lealmente.

wholesale (hōl′sāl′) n. vendita all'ingrosso. agg., avv. all'ingrosso, in grande quantità: — dealer, grossista; — slaughter, carneficina, ecatombe.

wholesaler n. grossista.

wholesome (hōl′sŭm) agg. sano, salutare.

wholly (hōl′lĭ) avv. interamente, completamente.

whom (hōōm) pron.rel. e interr. che, chi, il quale, la quale, i quali, le quali: to —, cui, a chi; — did you give it to? a chi lo hai dato?

whoop (hōōp) n. urlo; ululato (della tosse canina). vt., vi. gridare, ululare; esultare (o protestare) clamorosamente.

whooping cough (hōōp′ĭng) n. tosse canina.

whore (hōr) n. prostituta.

whorl (hwôrl) n. spirale, spira.

whose (hōōz) pron.rel. di cui, del quale, della quale, dei quali, delle quali; (interr.) di chi?: — book is this?, di chi è questo libro?

why (hwī) (1) n. (il) perchè, causa, motivo. avv. (anche interr.) perchè, per quale ragione, per cui: the reason —, la ragione per cui.

why! (2) inter. diamine!, suvvia!, ma guarda!, ma come!, oh bella!, perbacco!, caspita!: —, of course! ma naturale!

wick (wĭk) n. lucignolo, stoppino (di candela, ecc.).

wicked (wĭk′ĕd) agg. malvagio, tristo; molesto; indocile.

wickedness n. malvagità; indocilità.

wicker (wĭk′ĕr) n. vimine. agg. di vimini.

wicket (wĭk′ĕt) n. sportello; usciolo; cancelletto; porta (del cricket); archetto (del croquet); cateratta (di chiusa).

wide (wĭd) agg. ampio, largo, aperto, esteso, lontano: —-open, spalancato; — of the mark, lontano dal segno. avv. largamente, lontano, a distanza: far and —, in lungo e in largo; — apart, distanziati.

wide-awake (wĭd′á·wāk′) n. cappello floscio. agg. completamente sveglio, pronto, vigile.

widely (wĭd′lĭ) avv. largamente, ampiamente; prevalentemente.

widen (wĭd′′n) vt. allargare, ampliare, estendere, dilatare. vi. aprirsi, allargarsi, estendersi, dilatarsi.

widespread (wĭd′sprĕd′) agg. diffuso.

widow (wĭd′ō) n. vedova.

widower (wĭd′ō·ĕr) n. vedovo.

widowhood (wĭd′ō·hŏŏd) n. vedovanza.

width (wĭdth) n. larghezza, ampiezza; (tess.) altezza.

wield (wēld) vt. esercitare (autorità); maneggiare; brandire.

wife (wīf) n. (pl. wives) moglie, sposa.

wig (wĭg) n. parrucca.

wiggle (wĭg′′l) vedi wriggle.

wigwag (wĭg′wăg′) n. (naut.) segnalazione con bandierine.

wigwam (wĭg′wŏm) n. capanna del pellirosse; (gergo) sala da comizi.

wild (wĭld) n. deserto, selva, luogo selvaggio, solitudine. agg. selvaggio; silvestre; violento, feroce, incontrollato, selvatico, irruento, ribelle, indomato, irragionevole, stravagante, incauto, pazzo, furioso; (fam.) entusiasta: a — goose chase, un'impresa vana, l'impossibile. avv. vedi wildly.

wildcat (wĭld′kăt′) n. gatto selvatico;

(*S.U.*) locomotiva di manovra; impresa sballata.

wilderness (wïl'dĕr·nĕs) *n.* selva, deserto.

wildly (wïld'lĬ) *avv.* selvaggiamente, impetuosamente, disordinatamente, furiosamente, a vanvera.

wildness (wïld'nĕs) *n.* selvatichezza, ferocia, sregolatezza, furore, irruenza.

wile (wïl) *n.* astuzia, raggiro. *vt.* raggirare; adescare.

wilful (wïl'fŏŏl) *vedi* willful.

will (wïl) (1) *verbo aus. difettivo* (*pass.* would); *esprime il concetto di* volere: *il pres.* (will) voglio, *ecc.*; vogliamo, *ecc.*, è l'aus. con cui si forma il *futuro* (*predicente*: 2a e 3a *pers. sing.* e *pl.*); *volitivo*: 1a *pers. sing.* e *pl.*): I — go, io andrò (*voglio andare*); we — work, noi lavoreremo (*vogliamo lavorare*); you — sing, voi canterete; they — obey, essi obbediranno. *Il pass.* (would) *ha valore di condizionale*: vorrei, *ecc.*; vorremmo, *ecc.*; *opp. d'imperfetto soggiuntivo*: (io) volessi, *ecc.*; volessimo, *ecc.*; *indica spesso azione abituale, ed è un aus. con cui si forma il condizionale degli altri verbi*: I would refuse if, rifiuterei se; he would work from morning to night, lavorava giorno e notte.

will (wïl) (2) *n.* volontà, volere, arbitrio; testamento: at —, a volontà, a discrezione; free —, libero arbitrio; ill——, malavoglia, malevolenza; to have one's —, spuntarla; with a —, con entusiasmo, di lena. *vt.*, *vi.* ordinare, ingiungere, deliberare, imporre; lasciare per testamento, disporre; costringere a: the king willed that, il re dispose che; to — oneself to, imporsi di.

willful (wïl'fŏŏl) *agg.* intenzionale, doloso; ostinato, caparbio.

willing (wïl'Ĭng) *agg.* disposto, compiacente, volenteroso, spontaneo, volontario.

willingly *avv.* volontariamente, spontaneamente, volontieri.

willingness *n.* spontaneità, compiacenza, propensione, buon volere.

willow (wïl'o) *n.* salice; (*tess.*) cardatrice meccanica.

willy-nilly (wïl'Ĭ·nïl'Ĭ) *avv.* volente o nolente.

wilt (wïlt) *vt.* far avvizzire. *vi.* avvizzire, languire, deprimersi.

wily (wïl'Ĭ) *agg.* astuto.

wimble (wïm'b'l) *n.* succhiello.

wimple (wïm'p'l) *n.* soggolo.

win (wïn) *vt.*, *vi.* (*pass.*, *pp.* won) vin-

cere, trionfare; ottenere, conquistare; sedurre; accattivarsi; persuadere, indurre: to — back, riguadagnare; to — out, vincere, trionfare; to — over, persuadere; conquistare.

wince (wïns) *vi.* ritrarsi, trasalire, fare una smorfia dolorosa; imbizzarrirsi (*di cavallo*).

winch (wïnch) *n.* manovella, arganello.

wind (wïnd) (1) *n.* svolta, curva; (*elett.*) avvolgimento. *vt.* (*pass.*, *pp.* wound) avvolgere; caricare (*orologi, ecc.*); issare. *vi.* serpeggiare, mutare direzione, avvolgersi, attorcigliarsi, arrotolarsi; caricarsi; insinuarsi: to — up, caricare; concludere, terminare.

wind (wïnd) (2) *n.* vento, soffio, respiro, respirazione; flatulenza; sentore, notizia; vaniloquio: to get — of, venire a sapere; to get the — up, agitarsi, montarsi. *vt.* (*pass.*, *pp.* winded) esporre al vento, arleggiare; sfiatare; fiutare; far riprender fiato.

windbag (wïnd'băg') *n.* (*gergo*) parolaio, chiacchierone.

wind cone (*o* sleeve *o* sock), manica a vento.

windfall (wïnd'fôl') *n.* vento improvviso; frutta abbattuta dal vento; colpo di fortuna; eredità insperata.

winding (wïn'dĬng) *n.* svolta, curva, sinuosità, avvolgimento. *agg.* sinuoso, serpeggiante, a chiocciola: — engine, argano; — sheet, sudario.

windlass (wïnd'lăs) *n.* argano.

windmill (wïnd'mïl') *n.* mulino a vento.

window (wïn'dō) *n.* finestra; finestrino (*di auto, ecc.*); sportello (*di banca, ecc.*); vetrina: show —, vetrina; — dresser, vetrinista; — sash, telaio di finestra; — sill, davanzale. — pane *n.* vetro di finestra.

windpipe (wïnd'pïp') *n.* trachea.

wind-screen, **windshield** *n.* (*auto*) parabrezza: — wiper, tergicristallo.

windup (wïnd'ŭp') *n.* conclusione.

windy (wïn'dĬ) *agg.* ventoso, tempestoso, battuto dal vento; vaniloquente: it is —, tira vento.

wine (wïn) *n.* vino: — cellar, cantina; — stone, tartaro.

wing (wïng) *n.* ala; volo; (*teat.*) quinta; *pl.* distintivo di pilota militare, distintivo di una specializzazione nell'aviazione militare: on the —, in volo; to take —, spiccare il volo, fuggire; under the — of, sotto la protezione di. *vt.* munire di ali, sorvolare; colpire in un'ala, ferire in un braccio. *vi.* volare.

winged (wǐngd) *agg.* alato.

wingspread (wǐng'sprěd') *n.* apertura d'ala.

wink (wǐngk) *n.* strizzata d'occhio, ammicco; istante: not to sleep a —, non chiudere occhio. *vt., vi.* battere (*gli occhi, le palpebre*), ammiccare; vacillare; brillare a intermittenza; lampeggiare: to — at, chiudere un occhio su, fingere di non vedere; strizzare l'occhio a.

winner (wǐn'ĕr) *n.* vincitore.

winning (wǐn'ǐng) *n.* vittoria; *pl.* guadagni, vincita. *agg.* vincitore, vincente, cattivante: — post, palo d'arrivo.

winsome (wǐn'sŭm) *agg.* incantevole, affascinante.

winter (wǐn'tĕr) *n.* inverno. *agg.* da inverno, invernale. *vt.* riparare per l'inverno. *vi.* svernare.

wintry (wǐn'trǐ) *agg.* invernale, freddo, triste.

wipe (wǐp) *vt.* asciugare, pulire: to — away, off, out, cancellare; spazzare via; eliminare; annientare, distruggere; asciugare.

wiper (wǐp'ĕr) *n.* pulitore; strofinaccio; (*gergo*) fazzoletto; (*elett.*) spazzola; (*auto*) tergicristallo.

wire (wǐr) *n.* filo metallico; reticolato; cavo (*telegrafico, ecc.*); (*fam.*) telegrafo, telegramma: barbed —, filo spinato; — recorder, magnetofono; to pull wires, esercitare influenze. *vt., vi.* legare con (*o munire di, o infilare su*) filo metallico; fare un impianto elettrico; telegrafare.

wiredraw (wǐr'drô') *vt.* (*pass., pp.* wiredrawn) trafilare.

wire-glass *n.* vetro armato.

wireless (wǐr'lĕs) *n.* radiotelegrafia (*o* telefonia); apparecchio radio; radiotelegramma. *agg.* senza fili, radiotelegrafico, radiofonico.

wirephoto (wǐr'fō'tō) *n.* radiofoto.

wiry (wǐr'ǐ) *agg.* di (*o simile a*) filo metallico; robusto, segaligno; agile.

wisdom (wǐz'dŭm) *n.* saggezza, prudenza: — tooth, dente del giudizio.

wise (wǐz) *n.* maniera, modo. *agg.* saggio, prudente, giudizioso; edotto: to be — to, essere informato di.

wiseacre (wǐz'ā'kĕr) *n.* sapientone.

wisecrack (wǐz'krăk') *n.* (*S.U.*) spiritosaggine, battuta.

wisely (wǐz'lǐ) *avv.* saggiamente, prudentemente.

wish (wǐsh) *n.* augurio, desiderio, richiesta. *vt., vi.* desiderare, augurare, augurarsi: I — I could go, vorrei poter andare; I — it were true! magari fosse vero! I — I had not struck him, rimpiango di averlo

colpito; to — for, desiderare. —ful *agg.* desideroso: — thinking, pio desiderio, illusione.

wisp (wǐsp) *n.* ciuffo.

wistful (wǐst'fŏŏl) *agg.* nostalgico; pensoso; malinconico, mesto.

wit (wǐt) *n.* (*spesso pl.*) acume, ingegno; arguzia; sagacia; lucidità; persona sagace: to be at one's —'s end, non saper più dove battere la testa; out of one's —s, fuor di senno; to live by one's —s, vivere di espedienti; to —, cioè, vale a dire.

witch (wǐch) *n.* maga, strega: — doctor, stregone.

witchcraft (wǐch'krăft') *n.* stregoneria, magia.

with (wǐth) *prep.* con; per mezzo di; insieme con; presso; alle dipendenze di: what do you want — her? che volete da lei?; — a view to, con l'intenzione di; to begin —, innanzi tutto; filled —, pieno di; ill —, malato di.

withdraw (wǐth-drô') *vt.* (*pass.* withdrew, *pp.* withdrawn) ritirare, ritrarre, ritrattare. *vi.* ritirarsi, arretrare, andarsene.

withdrawal (wǐth-drô'ăl) *n.* ritirata, ritiro, ritrattazione.

withdrawn (wǐth-drôn') *pp. di* to withdraw. *agg.* ritirato, appartato; (*di carattere*) chiuso, schivo.

withdrew (wǐth-drōō') *pass. di* to withdraw.

wither (wǐth'ĕr) *vt.* disseccare, far avvizzire; (*fig.*) annientare (*con lo sguardo*). *vi.* avvizzire, disseccarsi, deperire.

withers (wǐth'ĕrz) *n.pl.* garrese (*del cavallo*).

withhold (wǐth-hōld') *vt.* (*pass., pp.* withheld) trattenere, frenare; negare, rifiutare. *vi.* astenersi.

within (wǐth-ǐn') *prep.* entro, fra nell'ambito di, in, nel: — a year of my arrival, entro un anno dal mio arrivo; nemmeno un anno dopo il mio arrivo; — five miles, entro un raggio di cinque miglia; it is not — my power, non ne ho la facoltà, non ho la facoltà *o* possibilità di; — an ace of, a un pelo da. *avv.* dentro, in casa; from —, dall'interno.

without (wǐth-out') *prep.* senza; fuori di, all'esterno di; oltre. *avv.* fuori, all'esterno, esteriormente.

withstand (wǐth-stănd') *vt.* (*pass., pp.* withstood) subire, sopportare, affrontare. *vi.* opporsi, resistere.

witless (wǐt'lĕs) *agg.* stupido, insulso.

witness (wǐt'nĕs) *n.* testimonio, testimonianza. *vt.* testimoniare; assistere a; convalidare; firmare come testimone.

witticism (wĭt′ĭ-sĭz′m) *n.* arguzia, spiritosaggine, freddura.

witty (wĭt′ĭ) *agg.* intelligente, arguto.

wives (wīvz) *pl. di* wife.

wizard (wĭz′ẽrd) *n.* mago, stregone.

wizardry (wĭz′ẽrd-rĭ) *n.* stregoneria, magia.

wizened (wĭz′′nd) *agg.* disseccato, raggrinzito, avvizzito.

wobble (wŏb′′l) *vedi* wabble.

woe (wō) *n.* dolore, pena; sventura. *int.* guai (*a*), sventura!: — is me! oh, me infelice!

woebegone (wō′bē-gŏn′) *agg.* afflitto, sconsolato.

woke (wōk) *pass. di* to wake.

wolf (wo͝olf) *n.* (*pl.* wolves) lupo; (*fam.*) donnaiolo, gallo, "pappagallo"; *vt.* (*fam.*) divorare. —'s bane *n.* (*bot.*) aconito.

wolfram (wo͝ol′frăm) *n.* tungsteno.

woman (wo͝om′ăn) *n.* (*pl.* women) donna: — writer, scrittrice.

womanhood (wo͝om′ăn-ho͝od) *n.* femminilità; il sesso femminile, le donne.

womanish (wo͝om′ăn-ĭsh) *agg.* femminile; effeminato.

womankind (wo͝om′ăn-kīnd′) *n.* il sesso femminile, le donne.

womanly (wo͝om′ăn-lĭ) *agg.* femminile. *avv.* femminilmente.

womb (wo͝om) *n.* utero, matrice; ventre, cavità.

women (wĭm′ĕn) *pl. di* woman.

won (wŭn) *pass., pp. di* to win.

wonder (wŭn′dẽr) *n.* meraviglia, miracolo, stupore, ammirazione, prodigio: to work —s, fare prodigi; no — that, non c'è da meravigliarsi che. *vt., vi.* meravigliarsi; domandarsi; meditare: I — at you, mi meraviglio di voi; I — what happened, mi domando che cosa è successo; I should not — if, non mi stupirei se.

wonderful (wŭn′dẽr-fo͝ol) *agg.* meraviglioso, prodigioso. —ly *avv.* meravigliosamente, prodigiosamente.

wondering (wŭn′dẽr-ĭng) *agg.* stupito, perplesso.

wondrous (wŭn′drŭs) *agg.* mirabile, prodigioso, incredibile.

wont (wŏnt) *n.* usanza, abitudine. *agg.* abituato, avvezzo: to be — to, essere solito, solere.

wonted (wŏn′tĕd) *agg.* abituato, abituale.

woo (wo͝o) *vt.* corteggiare, circuire; chiedere in matrimonio; sollecitare, cercare.

wood (wo͝od) *n.* bosco, foresta; elgno,

legname; *pl.* bosco, foresta, selva: — engraving, incisione in legno. *vt.* piantare ad alberi; fornire di legna. *vi.* far legna.

woodcut (wo͝od′kŭt′) *n.* incisione su legno.

woodcutter (wo͝od′kŭt′ẽr) *n.* legnaiuolo, taglialegna; incisore in legno.

wooded (wo͝od′ĕd) *agg.* boscoso, alberato.

wooden (wo͝od′′n) *agg.* di legno, legnoso; rigido, impassibile.

woodland (wo͝od′lănd′) *n.* terreno boscoso, foresta.

woodman (wo͝od′măn) *n.* (*pl.* —men) boscaiuolo; guardia forestale.

woodpecker (wo͝od′pĕk′ẽr) *n.* (*ornit.*) picchio.

woodshed (wo͝od′shĕd′) *n.* baracca della legna.

woodsman (wo͝odz′măn) *n.* uomo dei boschi.

woodwork (wo͝od′wûrk′) *n.* lavoro in legno; rivestimento in legno.

woody (wo͝od′ĭ) *agg.* boscoso, legnoso.

wooer (wo͝o′ẽr) *n.* corteggiatore, pretendente.

woof (wo͝of) *n.* (*tess.*) trama.

wool (wo͝ol) *n.* lana, fibra, lanugine. *agg.* di lana, capelli crespi.

woolen, woollen (wo͝ol′ĕn) *n.* tessuto di lana. *agg.* di lana: — mill, fabbrica di tessuti di lana.

woolly (wo͝ol′ĭ) *agg.* lanoso; arruffato.

word (wûrd) *n.* parola, vocabolo; promessa; notizia, ambasciata, messaggio: by — of mouth, a viva voce; to be as good as one's —, essere di parola. *vt.* formulare, esprimere.

wore (wōr) *pass. di* to wear.

work (wûrk) *n.* lavoro, opera, fatica; impiego; azione, effetto, funzionamento; movimento; *pl.* fabbrica, officina; meccanismo; fortificazioni: to make short — of, sbrigare alla svelta; to give the —s to (*gergo*) dare il fatto suo a. *vt., vi.* (*pass., pp.* worked o wrought) lavorare, elaborare, produrre, ottenere, far lavorare, far funzionare, manovrare, maneggiare, manipolare; causare; operare, funzionare, agire; riuscire: to — out, sfruttare; risolvere, escogitare, calcolare; to — one's way, procedere a fatica, aprirsi un varco; it didn't —, non ha funzionato, non è riuscita, non è andata bene; it —ed well, è andata bene, è riuscita.

workbook (wûrk′bo͝ok′) *n.* manuale; diario di lavoro; libro di esercizi.

workday (wûrk′dā′) *n.* giorno lavorativo, giorno feriale.

worker (wûr′kẽr) *n.* lavoratore.

working (wûr'kĭng) *n.* lavoro, funzionamento, lavorazione, elaborazione; fermentazione. *agg.* operaio; lavorativo; operoso; da lavoro; in vigore: in — order, in perfetto stato di funzionamento; — class, classe lavoratrice; — hours, orario di lavoro.

workman (wúrk'măn) *n.* operaio, artigiano.

workmanship (wûrk'măn∙shĭp) *n.* lavoro, abilità manuale, fattura, esecuzione.

workshop (wúrk'shŏp) *n.* officina, bottega; corso di specializzazione (*basato su metodi pratici*).

workwoman (wûrk'wŏŏm'ăn) *n.* operaia.

world (wûrld) *n.* mondo: all over the —, in tutto il mondo; World War I (II), la prima (seconda) guerra mondiale.

worldly (wûrld'lĭ) *agg.* mondano, terreno, umano, materialistico.

worm (wûrm) *n.* verme; baco, lombrico; filetto (*di vite*). *vt.* ottenere tortuosamente, strappare (*un segreto, ecc.*). *vi.* strisciare, serpeggiare: to — one's way, insinuarsi; to — oneself out, sgattaiolare fuori; to — oneself into, insinuarsi; to — a secret out of somebody, strappare un segreto a qualcuno.

wormeaten *agg.* tarlato; decrepito.

worn (wŏrn) *pp. di* to wear. *agg.* logoro, consumato: —out *agg.* molto logoro, esausto.

worried (wûr'ĭd) *agg.* ansioso, preoccupato, tormentato.

worry (wûr'ĭ) *n.* preoccupazione, ansietà, tormento. *vt.* tormentare, preoccupare; straziare. *vi.* preoccuparsi, tormentarsi: don't —! non preoccupatevi!, non abbiate paura!

worrying (wû'rĭ'ĭng) *agg.* tormentoso, preoccupante.

worrywart (wûr'ĭ∙wôrt') *n.* (*gergo*) pessimista; cacadubbi.

worse (wûrs) *n.* (*il*) peggio (*di*): to change for the —, cambiare in peggio. *agg.* peggiore, meno buono, più cattivo. *avv.* peggio: — and —, di male in peggio; to get —, peggiorare; so much the —, tanto peggio.

worsen (wûr's'n) *vt.*, *vi.* peggiorare.

worship (wûr'shĭp) *n.* venerazione, adorazione, culto: his —, sua signoria, sua eccellenza. *vt.*, *vi.* adorare, venerare.

worshiper *n.* adoratore, fedele.

worst (wûrst) *n.* (*il*) peggio (*in senso assoluto*). *agg.* pessimo, (*il*) peggiore (*di tutti*). *avv.* nel peggior modo possibile, peggio: at the —, alla peggio. *vt.* sopraffare, sconfiggere. *vi.* peggiorare.

worsted (wŏŏs'tĕd) *n.* tessuto (*di lana*) pettinato.

worth (wûrth) *n.* valore, prezzo, pregio, merito, importanza: two cents — of, due soldi di; to get one's money's —, ricevere una cosa pari alla spesa, spendere bene il proprio denaro. *agg.* del valore di, degno di: to be — ten millions, possedere dieci milioni; it is not — while, non ne vale la pena.

worthless (wûrth'lĕs) *agg.* privo di valore, indegno, spregevole, inutile.

worthy (wûr'thĭ) *n.* valentuomo; personaggio illustre. *agg.* meritevole, degno, stimabile, conveniente.

would (wŏŏd) *pass., cong. di* will: we — go if it weren't raining, noi andremmo se non piovesse; they said they — come, dissero che sarebbero venuti; — you do it? lo faresti? that's just what you — say, è proprio quel che avresti detto; è proprio quel che prevedevo di sentirti dire; he —n't help me, non voleva *opp.* non volle aiutarmi; he — say that, diceva sempre che, era solito dire che; I — rather go, preferirei andarmene; — to God I had not gone, mai ci fossi andato!

wound (wound) (1) *pass., pp. di* to wind.

wound (wŏŏnd) (2) *n.* ferita, lesione. *vt.* ferire.

wove (wŏv) *pass. di* to weave.

woven (wŏ'vĕn) *pp. di* to weave.

wow (wou) *n.* deformazione della voce o dei suoni riprodotti da un grammofono, magnetofono, ecc., dovuta a imperfetto funzionamento dell'apparecchio. *inter.* accipicchia!, caspita! *vt.* entusiasmare, mandare in visibilio.

wraith (rāth) *n.* fantasma.

wrangle (răng'g'l) *n.* disputa, rissa. *vt.*, *vi.* disputare, discutere, litigare; (*S.U.*) imbrancare (*il bestiame*).

wrap (răp) *n.* sciarpa; coperta; involucro; mantello; (*pl.*) segreto, censura: under military —s, protetto da segreto militare. *vt.* avvolgere, avviluppare, nascondere: to — up, involtare, avvolgere, avvolgersi: to be —ped up in, essere avvolto in (*o* assorto in).

wrapper (răp'ĕr) *n.* spolverina, ve staglia; sopraccoperta (*di libro*) foglia esterna del sigaro.

wrapping (răp'ĭng) *n.* involucro, confezione, imballaggio, copertura: — paper, carta da pacchi.

wrath (ràth)*n.*ira, indignazione,furore.

wrathful (ràth'fŏŏl) *agg.* adirato, furibondo.

wreak (rēk) *vt.* sfogare (*collera*) su: to — vengeance on, vendicarsi su.

wreath (rēth) *n.* ghirlanda, corona, anello: — of smoke, spirale di fumo.

wreathe (rēth) *vt.* intrecciare, inghirlandare, cingere.

wreck (rĕk) *n.* naufragio; relitto, rudere, rottame; distruzione, rovina, devastazione. *vt.* far naufragare; distruggere, rovinare: to — a train, far deragliare un treno. *vi.* naufragare, andare in rovina.

wreckage (rĕk'ĭj) *n.* distruzione; relitto.

wrecker (rĕk'ẽr) *n.* demolitore; ricuperatore di relitti; carro attrezzi *o* di soccorso.

wren (rĕn) *n.* (*ornit.*) scricciolo.

WREN (rĕn) *n.* Ausiliaria della Marina Britannica.

wrench (rĕnch) *n.* torsione violenta, slogatura, storta; (*mecc.*) chiave fissa: monkey —, chiave inglese. *vt.* torcere, strappare torcendo, slogare.

wrest (rĕst) *n.* torsione, strappo. *vt.* torcere, strappare, forzare, falsare.

wrestle (rĕs''l) *n.* lotta; colluttazione. *vi.* lottare, far la lotta, colluttarsi, arrabattarsi.

wrestler (rĕs'lẽr) *n.* lottatore.

wrestling (rĕs'lĭng) *n.* (*sport.*) lotta.

wretch (rĕch) *n.* sciagurato, sventurato, scellerato, miserabile.

wretched (rĕch'ĕd) *agg.* pietoso, sfortunato, infelice; doloroso; ignobile, abominevole, disgraziato: this aching tooth makes me feel —, questo mal di denti mi riduce a uno straccio; a — life, una vita miseranda; — weather, tempaccio; his — stupidity, la sua colossale stupidaggine.

wriggle (rĭg''l) *vt.* torcere, contorcere. *vi.* torcersi, contorcersi, dimenarsi, strisciare: to — in, intrufolarsi; to — out, scapolarsela, cavarsela, sgusciar fuori.

wring (rĭng) *n.* torsione, strizzatura. *vt.* torcere; stringere, spremere, strizzare; estorcere, *vi.* torcersi: to — the truth out of, estorcere la verità a; to — somebody's hand, stringere la mano a qualcuno; to — linen, strizzare la biancheria; to — anything from, estorcere qualcosa a.

wrinkle (rĭng'k'l) (1) *n.* trovata, novità; congegno; suggerimento; bernoccolo, tendenza.

wrinkle (rĭng'k'l) (2) *n.* ruga, grinza, increspatura, sgualcitura. *vt.* contrarre; corrugare, raggrinzire, increspare, spigazzare. *vi.* spiegazzarsi, incresparsi, raggrinzirsi.

wrinkly (rĭng'klĭ) *agg.* rugoso, grinzoso, facile a sgualcirsi.

wrist (rĭst) *n.* polso: — band, polsino; — watch, orologio da polso.

writ (rĭt) *n.* decreto, mandato, ordinanza: Holy —, Sacra Scrittura.

write (rĭt) *vt.*, *vi.* (*pass.* wrote, *pp.* written) scrivere: to — down, registrare, annotare; to — off, scrivere speditamente; cancellare (*un addebito*), annullare; to — out, scrivere per esteso; to — up, scrivere il resoconto di, descrivere, redigere, aggiornare.

writer (rĭt'ẽr) *n.* scrittore, autore; scrivente: woman —, scrittrice.

writhe (rĭth) *vt.* torcere. *vi.* contorcersi, divincolarsi.

writing (rĭt'ĭng) *n.* scrittura, scritto; produzione letteraria; stile, forma: — desk, scrivania; — paper, carta per scrivere; to put in —, mettere per iscritto.

written (rĭt'n) *pp. di* to write.

wrong (rŏng) *n.* torto, ingiustizia, male, danno, reato, sopruso: to be in the —, avere torto, essere dalla parte del torto; to do —, fare torto a, offendere. *agg.* falso, sbagliato, erroneo; disadatto; in errore, scorretto; spostato; ingiusto; illegittimo; rovescio; (*mecc.*) guasto: to be —, aver torto; essere guasto; something is — with this dress, questo vestito ha qualcosa che non va; what's — with you? che hai?, che c'è?, qualcosa che non va?; to take the — train, sbagliare treno; to go the — way, andare di traverso; the — side, il rovescio. *avv.* male, a torto, ingiustamente, erroneamente; a rovescio; al contrario: to go —, andar male, sbagliare, traviarsi. *vt.* far torto a, danneggiare, ledere, offendere, accusare ingiustamente.

wrongdoer (rŏng'dōō'ẽr) *n.* malfattore, peccatore.

wrongful (rŏng'fŏŏl) *agg.* ingiusto, illegittimo, illegale; nocivo; iniquo.

wrongly (rŏng'lĭ) *avv.* male, ingiustamente, a torto, erroneamente.

wrote (rōt) *pass. di* to write.

wroth (rôth) *agg.* adirato, iracondo.

wrought (rŏt) *pass.*, *pp. di* to work. *agg.* lavorato, operato, elaborato: — iron, ferro battuto.

wrung (rŭng) *pass.*, *pp. di* to wring.
wry (rĭ) *agg.* storto, di traverso, obliquo, contorto; snaturato, falso: to make a — face, fare una smorfia.

wryneck (rĭ'něk') *n.* torcicollo.

X

xanthous (zăn'thŭs) *agg.* giallo.
xebec (zē'běk) *n.* (*naut.*) sciabecco.
xenogenesis (zĕn'ō·jĕn'ē·sĭs) *n.* (*biol.*) eterogenesi.
xenomania (zĕn'ō·mā'nĭ·á) *n.* esterofilia.
xenophobia (zĕn'ō·fō'bĭ·á) *n.* xenofobia.

xylograph (zĭ'lō·gràf) *n.* silografia (*opera*). —er (-ŏg'-) silografo.
xylography (zĭ·lŏg'rá·fĭ) *n.* silografia (*arte*).
xyloid (zĭ'loid) *agg.* xiloide, ligneo.
xylophone (zĭ'lō·fōn) *n.* (*mus.*) silo-
xylophonist (-ĭst) *n.* silofonista. [fono.
xyster (zĭs'tĕr) *n.* (*chir.*) raschiatoio.

Y

yacht (yŏt) *n.* (*naut.*) panfilio. *vi.* navigare su un panfilio.
yank (yăngk) (1) *n.* (*fam.*) strattone. *vt.*, *vi.* strappare, tirare violentemente, dare uno strattone.
Yank (yăngk) (2) (*gergo*) vedi Yankee.
Yankee (yăng'kē) *n.*, *agg.* americano del nord degli S.U.; (*fam.*) statunitense, americano.
yap (yăp) *n.* latrato; (*gergo*) chiacchiera rumorosa. *vi.* abbaiare; blaterare.
yard (yärd) *n.* corte, cortile; cantiere; iarda (*misura di lunghezza*); (*ferr.*) parco di smistamento; (*naut.*) pennone: navy —, cantiere navale.
yardstick (yärd'stĭk') *n.* asta di una iarda (*per misurare*); misura, norma, metro.
yarn (yärn) *n.* filo, fibra tessile, filato; storia, racconto.
yaw (yô) *vi.* (*naut.*) straorzare; (*aeron.*) deviare dalla rotta.
yawl (yôl) *n.* (*naut.*) iole, scialuppa.
yawn (yôn) *n.* sbadiglio; apertura, voragine. *vi.* sbadigliare; aprirsi.
yea (yā) *n.* assenso, voto affermativo. *avv.* sì, già,
year (yĕr) *n.* anno, annata: leap —, anno bisestile; by the —, per anno, annualmente. —book *n.* annuario.
yearly (yĕr'lĭ) *agg.* annuale. *avv.* annualmente, ogni anno.
yearn (yúrn) *vi.* intenerirsi; anelare: to — for, agognare, sospirare per, avere la nostalgia di.
yearning (yûr'nĭng) *n.* brama; nostalgia. *agg.* bramoso, nostalgico.
yeast (yĕst) *n.* lievito, fermento; schiuma. *vi.* fermentare, lievitare.
yell (yĕl) *n.* urlo. *vt.*, *vi.* urlare, strillare.
yellow (yĕl'ō) *n.* giallo; tuorlo d'uovo. *agg.* giallo; vile, vigliacco; infido; sensazionale, scandalistico: the —

press, la stampa scandalistica; — jack, febbre gialla; (*naut.*) bandiera gialla. *vt.*, *vi.* ingiallire, ingiallirsi.
yellowish (yĕl'ō·ĭsh) *agg.* giallastro.
yelp (yĕlp) *n.* guaito, latrato, grido. *vi.* guaire, latrare, gridare.
yen (yĕn) *n.* (*gergo*) passione, desiderio, nostalgia.
yes (yĕs) *n.*, *avv.* sì: — man, persona ossequiosa, tirapiedi, servo.
yesterday (yĕs'tĕr·dĭ) *n.*, *avv.* ieri: the day before —, l'altro ieri.
yet (yĕt) *avv.*, *cong.* ancora, di più, finora, eppure, però; prima o poi, in ogni caso; tuttora, ma, d'altronde: as —, finora; not —, non ancora.
yew (yōō) *n.* (*bot.*) tasso.
yield (yēld) *n.* prodotto, produzione, rendimento, reddito. *vt.*, *vi.* produrre, rendere, fruttare, cedere, concedere, emettere, rassegnare, rinunciare: to — oneself up, costituirsi, arrendersi.
yoke (yōk) *n.* giogo; basto; coppia (*di animali aggiogati*). *vt.* aggiogare, appaiare.
yolk (yōk) *n.* tuorlo d'uovo; lanolina.
yonder (yŏn'dĕr) *agg.* di laggiù, il più lontano, quello, quelli, quella, quelle. *avv.* laggiù.
yore (yōr) *n.* (il) passato: of —, di un tempo; passato (*agg.*).
you (yōō) *pron. pers.* voi, a voi, vi, tu, te, ti, lei, le: I gave it to —, l'ho dato a voi; as I said to you, come vi dissi.
young (yŭng) *n.* piccolo; piccoli *o* cuccioli (*di animali*); (*i*) giovani. *agg.* giovane, immaturo, fresco, inesperto: — lady, signorina; — man, giovane, giovanotto; — people, *i* giovani.
younger (-gĕr) *agg.* più giovane (*di*), cadetto.

youngest (-gĕst) *agg.* il più giovane.

youngster (yŭng'stĕr) *n.* bambino, giovanetto, giovinotto.

your (yŏŏr) *agg.poss.* vostro, vostra, vostri, vostre, tuo, tua, tuoi, tue.

yours (yŏŏrz) *pron.poss.* il vostro, la vostra, i vostri, le vostre, il tuo, ecc. a friend of —, un vostro amico; — truly, vostro devotissimo.

yourself (yŏŏr-sĕlf') *pron.* (*pl.* yourselves) voi stesso, voi stessa, vi, tu stesso, te stesso, ti.

youth (yŏŏth) *n.* giovinezza, gioventù; adolescenza; adolescente, giovane.

youthful (yŏŏth'fŏŏl) *agg.* giovane, giovanile.

youthfulness *n.* gioventù, aspetto giovanile, freschezza.

yowl (youl) *n.* ululato, gemito. *vi.* ululare, gemere.

yule (yŏŏl) *n.* Natale.

yuletide (yŏŏl'tīd') *n.* periodo natalizio.

Z

zany (zā'nĭ) *n.* buffone,

zeal (zēl) *n.* zelo, entusiasmo, fervore.

zealot (zĕl'ŭt) *n.* fanatico.

zealous (zĕl'ŭs) *agg.* zelante, fervente.

zenith (zē'nĭth) *n.* zenit; apogeo, apice.

zephyr (zĕf'ĕr) *n.* zefiro, brezza; (*tess.*) zefir.

zero (zē'rō) *n.* zero, nulla.

zest (zĕst) *n.* gusto, sapore, aroma, interesse, ardore.

zigzag (zĭg'zăg') *n.* zigzag, serpeggiamento. *agg., avv.* a zigzag. *vi.* andare a zigzag, serpeggiare.

zinc (zĭngk) *n.* zinco: — white, ossido di zinco, biacca. *vt.* zincare.

Zionism (zī'ăn-ĭz'm) *n.* Sionismo.

zip (zĭp) *n.* sibilo (*di proiettile*); (*fam.*) forza, energia.

zipper (zĭp'ĕr) *n.* chiusura lampo.

zodiac (zō'dĭ-ăk) *n.* zodiaco.

zone (zōn) *n.* zona, area, fascia: time —, fuso orario. *vt.* cingere, dividere in zone.

zoo (zŏŏ) *n.* giardino zoologico.

zoological (zō'ō-lŏj'ĭ-kăl) *n.* zoologico.

zoologist (zō-ŏl'ō-jĭst) *n.* zoologo.

zoology (zō-ŏl'ō-jĭ) *n.* zoologia.

zoophilist (zō-ŏf'ĭ-lĭst) *n.* zoofilo.

zoophily (zo-ŏf'ĭ-lĭ) *n.* zoofilia.

zoophyte (zō'ō-fīt) *n.* (*zool.*) zoofito.

zooplasty (zō'ō-plăs'tĭ) *n.* trapianto di tessuto animale.

Phrases for Travelers

Prepared by Robert T. Giuffrida, M.A., Ph.D.
Department of Foreign Languages, The University of Rochester

BASIC PHRASES

Good morning.	Buon giorno.
Good afternoon.	Buon giorno.
Good evening.	Buona sera.
Good night.	Buona notte.
How are you?	Come sta?
I'm well, thanks, and how are you?	Sto bene, grazie, e lei?
Until we meet again.	Arrivederla.
So long.	Ciao; arrivederci.
Thanks.	Grazie.
Please.	Per favore; per piacere.
You're welcome.	Non c'è di che; prego.
How much is, how much are . . . ?	Quanto è, quanto sono . . . ?
Where is, where are . . . ?	Dov'è, dove sono . . . ?
When?	Quando?
Excuse me.	Mi scusi.
I wish . . .	Desidero . . .
Give me . . .	Mi dia . . .
Please wait a moment.	Aspetti un momento, per favore.

SOCIAL CONVERSATIONS

My name is . . .	Mi chiamo . . .
May I introduce you to (Mister, Mrs., Miss) . . .	Permetta che le presenti (il Signor, la Signora, la Signorina) . . .
This is my wife, husband, son, daughter, mother, father, friend (m.), friend (f.) . . .	Quest'è mia moglie, mio marito, mio figlio, mia figlia, mia madre, mio padre, il mio amico, la mia amica . . .
This is my (our) first trip to Italy.	Questo è il mio (nostro) primo viaggio in Italia.
I am (we are) having a wonderful time.	Mi sto (ci stiamo) divertendo moltissimo.
Italy is very beautiful.	L'Italia è molto bella.

299

Have you ever been to the United States?	Lei è mai stato negli Stati Uniti?
Yes, America is beautiful, too.	Sì, anche l'America è bella.
I live in New York State.	Io abito nello Stato di New York.
It's a pleasure to meet you.	Piacere di fare la sua conoscenza.
Sit down.	Si accomodi.
You have been most kind.	Lei è stato molto gentile.

LANGUAGE DIFFICULTIES

I speak English.	Parlo inglese.
Do you speak English?	Lei parla inglese?
I understand Italian a little.	Capisco un poco l'italiano.
I don't understand Italian at all.	Non capisco affatto l'italiano.
How do you say in Italian . . . ?	Come si dice in italiano . . . ?
What does this word mean?	Che vuol dire questa parola?
I need an interpreter, a guide.	Ho bisogno d'un interprete, d'un cicerone.
I am looking for someone who speaks English.	Cerco qualcuno che parli inglese.
Excuse me, I'm American and do not speak Italian.	Scusi, sono americano e non parlo italiano.
Please speak more slowly.	Parli più adagio, per favore.
Would you be kind enough to repeat . . .	Per cortesia, vuole ripetere . . .
Italian is very beautiful but also difficult.	L'italiano è molto bello ma anche difficile.

ASKING DIRECTIONS

Where is . . . Street?	Da che parte è Via . . . ?
Where is the Hotel Continental?	Dove si trova l'Albergo Continentale?
Where is the police station, the train station, the airport, the center of the city, a church, a travel agency . . . ?	Dove si trova la questura, la stazione ferroviaria, l'aeroporto, il centro della città, una chiesa, un'agenzia di viaggi . . . ?
I would like to go to the American Consul.	Vorrei andare dal console americano.
Where is the nearest bank?	Dov'è la banca più vicina?
Do I have to take a taxi?	Bisogna prendere un tassì?
I would like to make a telephone call.	Vorrei fare una telefonata.

I would like to send a telegram, a cablegram.

Vorrei mandare un telegramma, un cablogramma.

Where are we going now?

Dove andiamo adesso?

EMERGENCIES

I don't feel well. Please send for a doctor.

Non mi sento bene. Per favore, vorrei un medico.

Where can I find a drugstore, a pharmacy?

Dove posso trovare una farmacia?

Police! Help! I've been robbed!

Polizia! Aiuto! Sono stato derubato!

Don't bother me or I'll call the police.

Non mi disturbi o chiamo una guardia.

Where is the lost properties office?

Dove si trova l'ufficio oggetti smarriti?

TELLING TIME

What time is it?

Che ora è?

It's two in the morning.

Sono le due del mattino.

It's five P.M.

Sono le cinque del pomeriggio.

It's four-thirty.

Sono le quattro e mezzo.

It's six-forty-five.

Sono le sette meno un quarto.

It's eleven-twenty.

Sono le undici e venti.

ABOARD SHIP

I'm looking for my ship.

Cerco il mio piroscafo.

Is it time to go aboard?

È ora di salire a bordo?

When is the next departure?

Quando sarà la prossima partenza?

Excuse me, please tell me which way to go.

Scusi, mi indichi, per favore, da che parte andare.

Where is the steward, the captain?

Dov'è il cameriere, il capitano?

Where is the upper deck, the lower deck?

Dov'è il ponte superiore, il ponte inferiore?

Will you bring our luggage to Deck C?

Vuol portare il nostro bagaglio sul Ponte C?

Where is the purser's office?

Dov'è l'ufficio del commissario?

I'm seasick.

Ho mal di mare.

At what time is lunch (dinner) served?

A che ora si serve la colazione (il pranzo)?

Please show me the lifeboat.	Mi mostri la barca di salvataggio, per favore.

TRAVELING BY PLANE

I would like to go to the airport.	Vorrei andare all'aeroporto.
How long does it take to get to . . . ?	Quanto tempo ci si mette per andare a . . . ?
Is there a plane for . . . ?	C'è un aereo per . . . ?
What time does it leave?	A che ora parte?
How much does the ticket cost?	Quanto costa il biglietto?
I want to reserve a seat.	Voglio prenotare un posto.
Please give me a round-trip ticket.	Mi dia, per favore, un biglietto di andata e ritorno.

TRAVELING BY TRAIN

Where is the railroad station?	Dov'è la stazione ferroviaria?
A ticket to Rome, please.	Un biglietto per Roma, per favore.
First (second) class.	Di prima (seconda) classe.
Where does one get the train to Milan?	Dove si prende il treno per Milano?
Is this seat taken?	È occupato questo posto?
Where is the washroom?	Da che parte è la toilette?
Is the dining car open now?	È aperto adesso il vagone ristorante?
Where is the baggage room, the sleeping car, the smoking car?	Dov'è il bagagliaio, il vagone letto, lo scompartimento per fumatori?

CUSTOMS

Where is the customs office?	Dove si trova la dogana?
Here is my luggage.	Ecco il mio bagaglio.
Is it necessary to open my suitcases?	Bisogna aprire le valigie?
There are only personal things here.	Ci sono soltanto degli effetti personali.
This is my identity card.	Questa è la mia carta d'identità.
Here is my passport.	Ecco il mio passaporto.
These are toilet articles.	Questi sono oggetti da toilette.

This is my camera, my movie camera.

Questa è la mia macchina fotografica, la mia cinepresa.

I brought one carton (two cartons) of cigarettes.

Ho portato una stecca (due stecche) di sigarette.

Please call a porter for me.

Mi chiami un facchino, per favore.

I would like to take a taxi and go directly into town.

Vorrei prendere un tassì e andare direttamente in città.

THE HOTEL

May I speak to the manager?

Si può parlare col direttore?

Do you accept personal checks?

Si accettano assegni personali?

I made a reservation by telegram.

Ho fatto una prenotazione telegrafica.

I want a room with one bed, with twin beds, with a double bed.

Desidero una camera a un letto, a due letti, con letto matrimoniale.

I want an air-conditioned room.

Desidero una camera con aria condizionata.

Yes, I want a room with bath, without bath.

Sì, desidero una camera con bagno, senza bagno.

I would like to see the room.

Vorrei vedere la camera.

What is the price of this room?

Qual è il prezzo di questa camera?

I shall remain probably three days.

Rimarrò probabilmente tre giorni.

Would it be possible to deposit my valuables?

Sarebbe possibile depositare i miei valori?

May I have the key to my room?

Mi favorisce la chiave della mia camera?

Are there any letters or messages for me?

Ci sono delle lettere o dei messaggi per me?

Where is the elevator?

Dov'è l'ascensore?

Please call me at seven.

Mi svegli alle sette, per favore.

May I have another blanket?

Desidererei un'altra coperta.

I need some hangers, a glass, some soap, some towels. . . .

Ho bisogno di alcuni appendiabiti, di un bicchiere, di una saponetta, degli asciugamani. . . .

THE RESTAURANT

Where is there a good restaurant?	Dove si trova un buon ristorante?
May I please have the menu.	Mi favorisce la lista?
Can you recommend something to me?	Mi può suggerire qualche piatto?
Something simpler and less expensive.	Qualche cosa di più semplice e meno caro.
A little cold water, please.	Un po' d'acqua fresca, per piacere.
Waiter, you forgot to give me a napkin.	Cameriere, ha dimenticato di darmi il tovagliolo.

SHOPPING

I would like to find the largest department stores.	Vorrei andare ai grandi magazzini più importanti.
Can I get there by walking?	È possibile andarci a piedi?
Good morning, I would like to look at the merchandise, please.	Buon giorno, vorrei dare una occhiata alle merce, per favore.
My size in the United States is . . .	La mia misura negli Stati Uniti è . . .
This is too small, too big.	Questo è troppo piccolo, troppo grande.
This is too narrow, too wide.	Questo è troppo stretto, troppo largo.
Do you have this in a lighter (darker) color?	Questo si trova in colore più chiaro, più scuro?
Do you have something better?	Ha qualcosa di meglio?
How much is it?	Quanto costa?
It seems expensive.	Mi sembra caro.
Fine.	Va bene.
Would you be kind enough to send it to the hotel?	Per cortesia, me lo manda in albergo?
Now I would like to buy a gift for my husband, for my wife.	Adesso vorrei comprare un regalo per mio marito, per mia moglie.

CHURCH

I wish to go to church.	Voglio andare in chiesa.
Where is the nearest church?	Dove si trova la chiesa più vicina?
Where is the cathedral?	Dov'è la cattedrale, il duomo?

Where is the synagogue?	Dov'è la sinagoga?
Is this a Catholic (Protestant) church?	Questa è una chiesa cattolica (protestante)?
I would like to meet the minister, the priest, the rabbi.	Vorrei fare la conoscenza del ministro, del sacerdote, del rabbino.

CAR TROUBLES

I hate to bother you, but my car has broken down.	Mi dispiace disturbare, ma la mia automobile ha un guasto.
Is it possible to tow (push) it?	È possibile rimorchiarla, spingerla?
It's necessary to change a tube, a tire.	Bisogna cambiare una camera d'aria, un copertone.
I need a jack.	Ho bisogno di un cricco.
Perhaps it would be better to take it to a garage.	Forse sarebbe meglio portarla a un' autorimessa.

SIGNS

Caution! Danger!	Attenzione! Pericolo!
Caution! Trains!	Attenzione ai treni!
Work in progress!	Lavori in corso!
One-way traffic.	(Circolazione a) Senso unico.
Two-way traffic ahead.	Circolazione in senso opposto.
Dangerous curve.	Curva pericolosa.
No U-turns.	Vietato invertire direzione.
No parking.	Divieto di sosta.
Reserved parking.	Parcheggio riservato.
Crossroads, intersection.	Incrocio.
Railroad crossing.	Passaggio a livello.
Speed limit.	Limitazione di velocità.
Slow down.	Rallentare.
Gas station.	Stazione di rifornimento.
Savings bank.	Cassa di rispiarmo.
Post office.	Poste e telegrafi, P.T.
Post office box.	Cassetta postale.
Telephone directory.	Elenco telefonico.
Streetcar (bus) stop.	Fermata tranviaria (autobus).
Spitting forbidden.	Vietato sputare.
No jaywalking.	Proibito attraversare.
Pedestrians only.	Passaggio pedonale.
Traffic policeman.	Vigile urbano.